DATE DUE

			PRINTED IN U.S.A.

Literature Criticism from 1400 to 1800

Guide to Gale Literary Criticism Series

For criticism on	Consult these Gale series
Authors now living or who died after December 31, 1959	*CONTEMPORARY LITERARY CRITICISM (CLC)*
Authors who died between 1900 and 1959	*TWENTIETH-CENTURY LITERARY CRITICISM (TCLC)*
Authors who died between 1800 and 1899	*NINETEENTH-CENTURY LITERATURE CRITICISM (NCLC)*
Authors who died between 1400 and 1799	*LITERATURE CRITICISM FROM 1400 TO 1800 (LC)* *SHAKESPEAREAN CRITICISM (SC)*
Authors who died before 1400	*CLASSICAL AND MEDIEVAL LITERATURE CRITICISM (CMLC)*
Black writers of the past two hundred years	*BLACK LITERATURE CRITICISM (BLC)*
Authors of books for children and young adults	*CHILDREN'S LITERATURE REVIEW (CLR)*
Dramatists	*DRAMA CRITICISM (DC)*
Hispanic writers of the late nineteenth and twentieth centuries	*HISPANIC LITERATURE CRITICISM (HLC)*
Poets	*POETRY CRITICISM (PC)*
Short story writers	*SHORT STORY CRITICISM (SSC)*
Major authors from the Renaissance to the present	*WORLD LITERATURE CRITICISM, 1500 TO THE PRESENT (WLC)*

Volume 25

Literature Criticism from 1400 to 1800

Excerpts from Criticism of the Works
of Fifteenth-, Sixteenth-, Seventeenth-, and
Eighteenth-Century Novelists, Poets, Playwrights,
Philosophers, and Other Creative Writers,
from the First Published Critical Appraisals
to Current Evaluations

James E. Person, Jr.
Editor

Judith Galens
Alan Hedblad
Michael W. Jones
Michael Magoulias
Zoran Minderović
Anna J. Sheets
Associate Editors

 **Gale Research Inc.** · DETROIT · WASHINGTON, D.C. · LONDON

STAFF

James E. Person, Jr., *Editor*

Michael W. Jones, Judith Galens, Alan Hedblad, Michael Magoulias, Zoran Minderović, Anna J. Sheets, *Associate Editors*

Deron Albright, George H. Blair, Thomas Carson, Sean McCready, Paul Sassalos, Debra A. Wells, *Assistant Editors*

Jeanne A. Gough, *Permissions & Production Manager*
Linda M. Pugliese, *Production Supervisor*
Donna Craft, Paul Lewon, Maureen Puhl, Camille P. Robinson, Sheila Walencewicz, *Editorial Associates*

Sandra C. Davis, *Permissions Supervisor (Text)*
Maria L. Franklin, Josephine M. Keene, Michele M. Lonoconus, Shalice Shah, Kimberly F. Smilay,
Permissions Associates
Jennifer A. Arnold, Brandy C. Merritt, *Permissions Assistants*

Margaret A. Chamberlain, *Permissions Supervisor (Pictures)*
Pamela A. Hayes, Arlene Johnson, Keith Reed, Barbara A. Wallace, *Permissions Associates*
Susan Brohman, *Permissions Assistant*

Victoria B. Cariappa, *Research Manager*
Maureen Richards, *Research Supervisor*
Robert S. Lazich, Mary Beth McElmeel, Donna Melnychenko, Tamara C. Nott, *Editorial Associates*
Julie A. Kriebel, Jaema Paradowski, Stefanie Scarlett, *Editorial Assistants*

Mary Beth Trimper, *Production Director*
Catherine Kemp, *Production Assistant*

Cynthia Baldwin, *Product Design Manager*
Sherrell Hobbs, *Desktop Publisher*
Willie Mathis, *Camera Operator*

Library of Congress Catalog Card Number 84-643008
ISBN 0-8103-8463-9
ISSN 0732-1864

Printed in the United States of America
Published simultaneously in the United Kingdom
by Gale Research International Limited
(An affiliated company of Gale Research Inc.)
10 9 8 7 6 5 4 3 2 1

I(T)P™

The trademark **ITP** is used under license.

Contents

Preface   vii

Acknowledgments   xi

Preface

*L*iterature Criticism from 1400 to 1800 (LC) presents criticism of world authors of the fifteenth through eighteenth centuries. The literature of this period reflects a turbulent time of radical change that saw the rise of drama equal in stature to that of classical Greece, the birth of the novel and personal essay forms, the emergence of newspapers and periodicals, and major achievements in poetry and philosophy. Much of modern literature reflects the influence of these centuries. Thus the literature treated in *LC* provides insight into the universal nature of human experience, as well as into the life and thought of the past.

Scope of the Series

LC is designed to serve as an introduction to authors of the fifteenth through eighteenth centuries and to the most significant interpretations of these authors' works. The great poets, dramatists, novelists, essayists, and philosophers of this period are considered classics in every secondary school and college or university curriculum. Because criticism of this literature spans nearly six hundred years, an overwhelming amount of critical material confronts the student. *LC* therefore organizes and reprints the most noteworthy published criticism of authors of these centuries. Readers should note that there is a separate Gale reference series devoted to Shakespearean studies. For though belonging properly to the period covered in *LC*, William Shakespeare has inspired such a tremendous and ever-growing corpus of secondary material that the editors have deemed it best to give his works extensive coverage in a separate series, *Shakespearean Criticism*.

Each author entry in *LC* attempts to present a historical survey of critical response to the author's works. Early criticism is offered to indicate initial responses, later selections document any rise or decline in literary reputations, and retrospective analyses provide students with modern views. The size of each author entry is intended to reflect the author's critical reception in English or foreign criticism in translation. Articles and books that have not been translated into English are therefore excluded. Every attempt has been made to identify and include the seminal essays on each author's work and to include recent commentary providing modern perspectives.

The need for *LC* among students and teachers of literature was suggested by the proven usefulness of Gale's *Contemporary Literary Criticism (CLC)*, *Twentieth-Century Literary Criticism (TCLC)*, and *Nineteenth-Century Literature Criticism (NCLC)*, which excerpt criticism of works by nineteenth- and twentieth-century authors. Because of the different time periods covered, there is no duplication of authors or critical material in any of these literary criticism series. An author may appear more than once in the series because of the great quantity of critical material available and because of the aesthetic demands of the series's *thematic organization*.

Thematic Approach

Beginning with Volume 12, all the authors in each volume of *LC* are organized in a thematic scheme. Such themes include literary movements, literary reaction to political and historical events, significant eras in literary history, and the literature of cultures often overlooked by English-speaking readers.

Organization of the Book

Each entry consists of the following elements: author or thematic heading, introduction, list of principal works (in author entries only), annotated works of criticism (each followed by a bibliographical citation), and a bibliography o further reading. Also, most author entries contain author portraits and others illustrations.

- The **Author Heading** consists of the author's full name, followed by birth and death dates. If an author wrote consistently under a pseudonym, the pseudonym is used in the author heading, with the real name given in parentheses on the first line of the biographical and critical introduction. Also located here are any name variations under which an author wrote, including transliterated forms for authors whose native languages use nonroman alphabets. Uncertain birth or death dates are indicated by question marks. The **Thematic Heading** simply states the subject of the entry.

- The **Biographical and Critical Introduction** contains background information designed to introduce the reader to an author and to critical discussion of his or her work. Parenthetical material following many of the introductions provides references to biographical and critical reference series published by Gale in which additional material about the author may be found. The **Thematic Introduction** briefly defines the subject of the entry and provides social and historical background important to understanding the criticism.

- Most *LC* author entries include **Portraits** of the author. Many entries also contain illustrations of materials pertinent to an author's career, including author holographs, title pages, letters, or representations of important people, places, and events in an author's life.

- The **List of Principal Works** is chronological by date of first book publication and identifies the genre of each work. In the case of foreign authors whose works have been translated in to English, the title and date of the first English-language edition are given in brackets beneath the foreign-language listing. Unless otherwise indicated, drama are dated by first performance, not first publication.

- **Criticism** is arranged chronologically in each author entry to provide a useful perspective on changes in critical evaluation over the years. For the purpose of easy identification, the critic's name and the composition or publication date or the critical work are given at the beginning of each piece of criticism. Unsigned criticism is preceded by the title of the source in which it appeared. All titles by the author featured in the critical entry are printed in boldface type. Publication information (such as publisher names and book prices) and parenthetical numerical references (such as footnotes or page and line references to specific editions of works) have been deleted at the editors' discretion to provide smoother reading of the text.

- Critical essays are prefaced by **Annotations** as an additional aid to students using *LC*. These explanatory notes may provide several types of useful information, including: the reputation of a critic, the importance of a work of criticism, the commentator's individual approach to literary criticism, the intent of the criticism, and the growth of critical controversy or changes in critical trends regarding an author's work. In some cases, these notes cross-reference the work of critics within the entry who agree or disagree with each other.

- A complete **Bibliographical Citation** of the original essay or book follows each piece of criticism.

- An annotated bibliography of **Further Reading** appears at the end of each entry and suggests resources for additional study of authors and themes. It also includes essays for which the editors could not obtain reprint rights.

Cumulative Indexes

Each volume of *LC* includes a cumulative **Author Index** listing all the authors that have appeared in *Contemporary Literary Criticism, Twentieth-Century Literary Criticism, Nineteenth-Century Literature Criticism, Literature Criticism from 1400 to 1800,* and *Classical and Medieval Literature Criticism,* along with cross-references to the Gale series *Short Story Criticism, Poetry Criticism, Children's Literature Review, Authors in the News, Contemporary Authors, Contemporary Authors Autobiography Series, Contemporary Authors Bibliographical Series, Dictionary of Literary Biography, Concise Dictionary of Literary Biography, Something about the Author, Something about the Author Autobiography Series,* and *Yesterday's Authors of Books for Children.* Readers will welcome this cumulative author index as a useful tool for locating an author within the various series. The index, which includes authors' birth and death dates, is particularly valuable for those authors who are identified with a certain period but whose death dates cause them to be placed in another, or for those authors whose careers span two periods. For example, F. Scott Fitzgerald is found in *TCLC,* yet a writer often associated with him, Ernest Hemingway, is found in *CLC.*

Beginning with Volume 12, *LC* includes a cumulative **Topic Index** that lists all literary themes and topics treated in *LC, NCLC* Topics volumes, *TCLC* Topics volumes, and the *CLC* Yearbook. Each volume of *LC* also includes a cumulative **Nationality Index** in which authors' names are arranged alphabetically under their respective nationalities and followed by the numbers of the volumes in which they appear.

Each volume of *LC* also includes a cumulative **Title Index,** an alphabetical listing of the literary works discussed in the series since its inception. Each title listing includes the corresponding volume and page numbers where criticism may be located. Foreign-language titles that have been translated followed by the tiles of the translation—for example, *El ingenioso hidalgo Don Quixote de la Mancha (Don Quixote).* Page numbers following these translated titles refers to all pages on which any form of the titles, either foreign-language or translated, appear. Title of novels, dramas, nonfiction books, and poetry, short story, or essays collections are printed in italics, while individual poems, short stories, and essays are printed in roman type within quotation marks.

A Note to the Reader

When writing papers, students who quote directly from any volume in the Literary Criticism Series may use the following general forms to footnote reprinted criticism. The first example pertains to material drawn from periodicals, the second to material reprinted from books.

T. S. Eliot, "John Donne," *The Nation and the Athenaeum,* 33 (9 June 1923), 321-32; excerpted and reprinted in *Literature Criticism from 1400 to 1800,* Vol. 10, ed. James E. Person, Jr. (Detroit: Gale Research, 1989), pp. 28-9.

Clara G. Stillman, *Samuel Butler: A Mid-Victorian Modern* (Viking Press, 1932); excerpted and reprinted in *Twentieth-Century Literary Criticism,* Vol. 33, ed. Paula Kepos (Detroit: Gale Research, 1989), pp. 43-5.

Suggestions Are Welcome

In response to various suggestions features have been added to *LC* since the series began, including a nationality index, a Literary Criticism Series topic index, thematic entries, a descriptive table of contents, and more extensive illustrations.

Readers who wish to suggest new features, themes or authors to appear in future volumes, or who have other suggestions, are cordially invited to write to the editor.

Acknowledgments

The editors wish to thank the copyright holders of the excerpted criticism included in this volume, the permissions managers of many book and magazine publishing companies for assisting us in securing reprint rights, and Anthony Bogucki for assistance with copyright research. We are also grateful to the staffs of the Detroit Public Library, the Library of Congress, the University of Detroit Mercy Library, Wayne State University Purdy/Kresge Library Complex, and the University of Michigan Libraries for making their resources available to us. Following is a list of the copyright holders who have granted us permission to reprint material in this volume of *LC*. Every effort has been made to trace copyright, but if omissions have been made, please let us know.

COPYRIGHTED EXCERPTS IN *LC*, VOLUME 25, WERE REPRINTED FROM THE FOLLOWING PERIODICALS:

Church History, v. 48, June, 1979 for "William Penn, Model of Protestant Liberalism" by Hugh Barbour. © 1979, The American Society of Church History. Reprinted by permission of the publisher and the author.—*The Hudson Review,* v. XXXII, Summer, 1979. Copyright © 1979 by The Hudson Review, Inc. Reprinted by permission of the publisher.—*IMPRIMIS,* 1975. Copyright 1975. Reprinted by permission from *IMPRIMIS,* the monthly journal of Hillsdale College.—*The Occasional Review,* n. 4, Winter, 1976 for "Visions of Disorder: Patrick Henry and the American Founding" by J. Michael Bordelon.—*The Pennsylvania Magazine of History and Biography,* v. XCIV, April, 1970. Copyright 1970, by The Historical Society of Pennsylvania. Reprinted by permission of the publisher.—*The Quarterly Journal of Speech,* v. LXIII, October, 1972 for "The Textual and Cultural Authenticity of Patrick Henry's 'Liberty or Death' Speech" by Judy Hample. Copyright 1972 by the Speech Communication Association. Reprinted by permission of the publisher and the author.—*The Southern Speech Communication Journal,* v. XLVI, Summer, 1981. Both reprinted by permission of the publisher.—*Texas Studies in Literature and Language,* v. IV, Winter, 1963 for "The Worldly Franklin and the Provincial Critics" by Robert Freeman Sayre. Copyright © 1963, renewed 1991 by the University of Texas Press. Reprinted by permission of the publisher and the author.—*The Virginia Magazine of History and Biography,* v. 95, July, 1987 for "The Democratic Faith of Patrick Henry" by Richard R. Beeman. Reprinted by permission of the publisher and the author.—*The William and Mary Quarterly,* third series, v. XVII, October, 1960. Copyright, 1960, renewed 1988, by the Institute of Early American History and Culture. Reprinted by permission of the Institute./Third series, v. XXXVIII, October, 1981 for "The 'Liberty or Death' Speech: A Note on Religion and Revolutionary Rhetoric" by Charles L. Cohen. Copyright, 1981, by the Institute of Early American History and Culture. Reprinted by permission of the Institute and the author.—*The Yale Review,* v. LIII, Winter, 1964. Copyright 1963, renewed 1992, by Yale University. Reprinted by permission of the editors.

COPYRIGHTED EXCERPTS IN *LC*, VOLUME 25, WERE REPRINTED FROM THE FOLLOWING BOOKS:

Albanese, Catherine L. From *Sons of the Fathers: The Civil Religion of the American Revolution.* Temple University Press, 1976. © 1976 by Temple University. All rights reserved. Reprinted by permission of Temple University Press.—Aldridge, Alfred Owen. From *Benjamin Franklin and Nature's God.* Duke University Press, 1967. Copyright © 1967 by Duke University Press, Durham, NC. Reprinted with permission of the publisher.—Amacher, Richard E. From *Benjamin Franklin.* Twayne, 1962. Copyright © 1962 by Twayne Publishers, Inc. Renewed 1990 by Richard E. Amacher. Reprinted by permission of the author.—Andrew, William D. From "Philip Freneau and Francis Hopkinson," in *American Literature, 1764-1789: The Revolutionary Years.* Edited by Everett Emerson. University of Wisconsin Press, 1977. Copyright © 1977 The Regents of the University of Wisconsin System. All rights reserved. Reprinted by permission of the publisher.—Bailyn, Bernard. From *The*

Ideological Origins of the American Revolution. The Belknap Press of Harvard University Press, 1967. Copyright © 1967 by the President and Fellows of Harvard College. All rights reserved. Excerpted by permission of the publisher and the author.—Boorstin, Daniel J. From *The Genius of American Politics.* The University of Chicago Press, 1953. Copyright 1953 by The University of Chicago. Renewed 1981 by Daniel J. Boorstin. All rights reserved. Reprinted by permission of the publisher and the author.—Canby, Henry Seidel. From *Classic Americans: A Study of Eminent American Writers from Irving to Whitman, with an Introductory Survey of Our National Literature.* Harcourt, Brace & Company, 1931. Copyright 1931, renewed 1958 by Henry Seidel Canby.—Charles, Joseph. From *The Origins of the American Party System: Three Essays.* The Institute of Early American History and Culture, 1956. Copyright by the Institute of Early American History and Culture, Williamsburg, Virginia, 1956, renewed 1983. Reprinted by permission of the publisher.—Chase, Gilbert. From *America's Music: From the Pilgrims to the Present.* McGraw-Hill Book Company, Inc., 1955. Copyright, 1955, renewed 1983 by Gilbert Chase. All rights reserved. Reproduced with permission.—Comfort, William Wistar. From *William Penn, 1644-1718: A Tercentenary Estimate.* University of Pennsylvania Press, 1944. Copyright 1944 University of Pennsylvania Press. Reprinted by permission of the publisher.—Crane, Verne W. From an introduction to *Benjamin Franklin's Letters to the Press, 1758-1775.* Edited by Verne W. Crane. University of North Carolina Press, 1950. Copyright, 1950, by The University of North Carolina Press. Renewed 1978 by Margaret Vining Crane. Reprinted by permission of the publisher.—Dauber, Kenneth. From *The Idea of Authorship in America: Democratic Poetics from Franklin to Melville.* The University of Wisconsin Press, 1990. Copyright © 1990 The Board of Regents of the University of Wisconsin System. All rights reserved. Reprinted by permission of the publisher.—Dobrée, Bonamy. From *William Penn: Quaker and Pioneer.* Houghton Mifflin Company, 1932. Copyright, 1932, renewed 1960 by Bonamy Dobrée. All rights reserved. Reprinted by permission of the Literary Estate of Bonamy Dobrée.—Dunn, Mary Maples. From "The Personality of William," in *The World of William Penn.* Edited by Richard S. Dunn and Mary Maples Dunn. University of Pennsylvania Press, 1986. Copyright © 1986 by the University of Pennsylvania Press. All rights reserved. Reprinted by permission of Mary Maples Dunn.—Farrand, Max. From an introduction to *The Autobiography of Benjamin Franklin: A Restoration of a "Fair Copy."* Edited by Max Farrand. University of California Press, 1949. Copyright, 1949, renewed 1977 by The Regents of the University of California. Reprinted by permission of the publisher.—Furtwangler, Albert. From *American Silhouettes: Rhetorical Identities of the Founders.* Yale University Press, 1987. Copyright © 1987 by Yale University. All rights reserved. Reprinted by permission of the publisher.—Granger, Bruce Ingham. From *Benjamin Franklin: An American Man of Letters.* University of Oklahoma Press, 1976. New edition copyright 1976 by the University of Oklahoma Press. Reprinted by permission of the University of Oklahoma Press.—Hastings, George Everett. From *The Life and Works of Francis Hopkinson.* The University of Chicago Press, 1926. Copyright 1926 by The University of Chicago. Renewed 1954 by Mildred B. Rudolph. Reprinted by permission of the publisher.—Hughes, Jonathan. From *The Vital Few: American Economic Progress and Its Protagonist.* Houghton Mifflin Company, 1965. Copyright © 1965 by Jonathan R. T. Hughes. All rights reserved. Reprinted by permission of the Literary Estate of Jonathan Hughes.—Jackson, Donald. From an introduction to *The Diaries of George Washington, 1748-65, Vol. I.* Edited by Donald Jackson and Dorothy Twohig. University Press of Virginia, 1976. Copyright © 1976 by the Rector and Visitors of the University of Virginia. Reprinted by permission of the publisher.—Jensen, Merrill. From *The New Nation: A History of the United States During the Confederation, 1781-1789.* Knopf, 1950. Copyright 1950 by Alfred A. Knopf, Inc. Renewed 1977 by Merrill M. Jensen. All rights reserved. Reprinted by permission of the publisher.—Lawrence, D. H. From *Studies in Classic American Literature.* Thomas Seltzer, 1923, The Viking Press, 1964. Copyright 1923 by Thomas Seltzer, Inc. Renewed 1950 by Frieda Lawrence. Copyright © 1961 by the Estate of the Late Mrs. Frieda Lawrence. All rights reserved. Reprinted by permission of Viking Penguin, a division of Penguin Books USA Inc.—Leder, Lawrence. From *Liberty and Authority: Early American Political Ideology, 1689-1763.* Quadrangle Books, 1968. Copyright © 1968 by Lawrence H. Leder. All rights reserved. Reprinted by permission of Random House, Inc.—Malone, Dumas. From *Jefferson, the Virginian.* Little, Brown and Company, 1948. Copyright 1948, renewed 1976 by Dumas Malone. All rights reserved. Reprinted by permission of Little, Brown and Company.—McCants, David A. From *Patrick Henry, The Orator.* Greenwood Press, 1990. Copyright © 1990 by David A. McCants. All rights reserved. Reprinted by permission of Greenwood Publishing Group, Inc., Westport, CT.—Meyer, Donald H. From "Franklin's Religion," in *Critical Essays on Benjamin Franklin.* Edited by Melvin H. Buxbaum. G. K. Hall &

PHOTOGRAPHS AND ILLUSTRATIONS APPEARING IN *LC*, VOLUME 25, WERE RECEIVED FROM THE FOLLOWING SOURCES:

Colonial America: The Intellectual Background

INTRODUCTION

What is called the great American experiment has its origins in the European Renaissance at the time of the Protestant Revolt, and later in the scientific and philosophical program of the Enlightenment. During the age of exploration and discovery, many religious groups outside the mainstream of English society—Quakers, Puritans, and Roman Catholics—left for America, where they pursued their own social, political, and religious agendas under British rule. After the signing of the Treaty of Paris in 1763, which ended French power in North America, the original thirteen British colonies began a struggle for political and economic autonomy, while recognizing the advantages of maintaining some connection with Britain. At the same time, the British Crown attempted to strengthen its political and economic control over its American possessions, setting the stage for a confrontation between the colonies and Britain. In response to this political crisis, American statesmen forged a unique democratic ideology whose aims were disseminated through various kinds of writings and orations.

The emergence of an American form of self-government may be traced to religious persecution in England during the seventeenth and eighteenth centuries. Religious refugees arrived in America firmly convinced that they had an ideal opportunity to live according to their own tenets. In William Penn's Pennsylvania, for example, the Quaker religion influenced both political and social life. Though distinguished by tolerance and brotherhood, Quaker laws prohibited war, theatrical productions, and other morally questionable activities. Puritan colonials, on the other hand, combined their ascetic Calvinism with a strong work ethic, which ultimately produced an affluent and worldly Puritan gentry. Religious leaders, such as Cotton Mather in his *Magnalia Christi Americana,* vigorously defended the necessity of maintaining a strong Puritan ethic. Nevertheless, the opportunities provided by the colonial economy ultimately superseded the Puritan vision of establishing God's kingdom in the American wilderness.

The increasing importance of the colonial mercantile economy, together with a burgeoning population, reinforced the desire of the colonies to administer their own affairs. To achieve that autonomy, American colonials relied heavily on the code of English common law, which ensured that the governed, as represented in parliament, would help govern in concert with the monarch. When during the 1760s King George III moved to give his colonial governors greater authority to impose a new series of taxes on business and trade, Americans saw an increasing contradiction between their rights as upheld by English common law and the threat of arbitrary royal power. Contemporary philosophical ideas also supported the American demand for self-government; Edmund Burke's and John Locke's theories concerning natural law, for example, maintained that each person, guided by specific principles derived from nature, could perfect himself and society. In France, François -Marie Arouet Voltaire and Jean-Jacques Rousseau upheld similar views concerning the citizen's right to certain inalienable political liberties. Thus, by the time America formally declared its independence from England on 4 July 1776, colonial statesmen had formulated a democratic ideology reflecting eighteenth-century European thought.

American politicians, statesmen, and writers expressed their views through a variety of mediums, including pamphlets, jeremiads, speeches, sermons, songs, and poetry. Apart from Benjamin Franklin's unique *Autobiography of Benjamin Franklin* and his *Poor Richard's Almanac,* the pamphlet was the most popular literary form: it was brief and could be quickly printed and disseminated. Pamphlets were very influential during the Revolutionary period. They were the principal forum for political thought and criticism, as evidenced by Thomas Jefferson's *A Summary of the Rights of British America* and Thomas Paine's *Common Sense.* At the same time, the jeremiad, a prolonged lamentation or complaint derived from the biblical book of the prophet Jeremiah, gained prominence as a literary form. It was primarily used to promote religious and spiritual values in a colonial society increasingly preoccupied with the pursuit of economic advantage. Poetry, as well, became a vehicle for political and religious agitation, as exemplified by Francis Hopkinson's *The Battle of the Kegs,* a satirical attack on the British navy based on a minor incident during the Revolutionary War. Speeches and sermons were also popular vehicles for the presentation of political and religious views. Some eighteenth-century political speeches have been preserved in collections of colonial state papers or in personal memoirs, such as Virginia representative Edmund Randolph's record of Patrick Henry's famous 1775 *Liberty or Death* speech. Colonial sermons were also written down, collected, and later published, thus preserving the words of such influential preachers as Cotton and Increase Mather, and Jonathan Edwards. Many of these sermons, written during the Revolution, were openly confrontational. It was not uncommon to find preachers such as Jonathan Mayhew portraying the American Revolution as a holy war against King George III. Songs, too, became a popular forum for political expression. For example, the famous tune "Yankee Doodle Dandy" became the musical signature of the Revolution and the American nation.

As Daniel J. Boorstin has suggested in his three-volume work *The Americans,* the great American experiment, if not particularly original in its philosophical foundation or its political structure, was, nonetheless, innovative and energetic in applying European models to national conditions. Consequently, the 1787 Constitution reflects a pluralistic vision, based on the principles of English common law, the republican models of antiquity, and the French Enlightenment.

REPRESENTATIVE WORKS

Franklin, Benjamin
  *Autobiography of Benjamin Franklin (autobiography) 1868
  †Poor Richard's Almanac (nonfiction) 1733-58
Henry, Patrick
  Liberty or Death (speech) 1775
Hopkinson, Francis
  The Pretty Story (allegory) 1774
  The Battle of the Kegs (poem) 1778
Jefferson, Thomas
  A Summary of the Rights of British America (essay) 1774
  In Congress, July 4, 1776: A Declaration by the Representatives of the United States of America, in General Congress Assembled (state paper) 1776
Mather, Cotton
  Magnalia Christi Americana (essay) 1702
Paine, Thomas
  Common Sense (essay) 1776
  Rights of Man (essay) 1791
Penn, William
  The Frame of the Government of the Province of Pennsylvania (prose) 1662
  No Cross, No Crown (essay) 1669
Washington, George
  Farewell Address (speech) 1796

*Originally written in four separate parts between 1771 and 1790, the autobiography was published in its entirety in 1868.

†Published yearly.

OVERVIEWS

Carl Becker

[*In the excerpt below, Becker discusses the notions of God, nature, and reason found in eighteenth-century natural rights philosophy, demonstrating how these elements influenced the values and attitudes of pre-revolutionary Colonial American society.*]

Whether the political philosophy of the Declaration of Independence is "true" or "false" has been much discussed. In the late eighteenth century it was widely accepted as a commonplace. At a later time, in 1822, John Adams made this a ground for detracting from the significance of Jefferson's share in the authorship of the famous document. He was perhaps a little irritated by the laudation which Fourth of July orators were lavishing on his friend, and wished to remind his countrymen that others had had a hand in the affair. "There is not an idea in it," he wrote to Pickering, "but what had been hackneyed in Congress for two years before" [*Works of John Adams,* II]. This is substantially true; but as a criticism, if it was intended as such, it is wholly irrelevant, since the strength of the Declaration was precisely that it said what everyone was thinking. Nothing could have been more futile than an attempt to justify a revolution on principles which no one had ever heard of before.

In replying to Adams' strictures, Jefferson had only to state this simple fact.

> Pickering's observations, and Mr. Adams' in addition, that it contained no new ideas, that it is a commonplace compilation, its sentiments hacknied in Congress for two years before . . . may all be true. Of that I am not to be the judge. Richard H. Lee charged it as copied from Locke's treatise on Government. . . . I know only that I turned to neither book nor pamphlet while writing it. I did not consider it as any part of my charge to invent new ideas altogether and to offer no sentiment which had ever been expressed before. [*The Writings of Thomas Jefferson,* 1869]

In writing to Lee, in 1825, Jefferson said again that he only attempted to express the ideas of the Whigs, who all thought alike on the subject. The essential thing was

> Not to find out new principles, or new arguments, never before thought of, not merely to say things which had never been said before; but to place before mankind the common sense of the subject, in terms so plain and firm as to command their assent. . . . Neither aiming at originality of principles or sentiments, nor yet copied from any particular and previous writing, it was intended to be an expression of the American mind. . . . All its authority rests then on the harmonizing sentiments of the day, whether expressed in conversation, in letters, printed essays, or the elementary books of public right, as Aristotle, Cicero, Locke, Sidney, etc.

Not all Americans, it is true, would have accepted the philosophy of the Declaration, just as Jefferson phrased it, without qualification, as the 'common sense of the subject'; but one may say that the premises of this philosophy, the underlying preconceptions from which it is derived, were commonly taken for granted. That there is a 'natural order' of things in the world, cleverly and expertly designed by God for the guidance of mankind; that the 'laws' of this natural order may be discovered by human reason; that these laws so discovered furnish a reliable and immutable standard for testing the ideas, the conduct, and the institutions of men—these were the accepted premises, the preconceptions, of most eighteenth century thinking, not only in America but also in England and France. They were, as Jefferson says, the 'sentiments of the day, whether expressed in conversation, in letters, printed essays, or the

The Pennsylvania State House, now called Independence Hall, as it looked at the time of the signing of the Declaration of Independence.

speaking, men are influenced by books which clarify their own thought, which express their own notions well, or which suggest to them ideas which their minds are already predisposed to accept. If Jefferson had read Rousseau's *Social Contract* we may be sure he would have been strongly impressed by it. What has to be explained is why the best minds of the eighteenth century were so ready to be impressed by Locke's treatise on civil government and by Rousseau's *Social Contract.* What we have to seek is the origin of those common underlying preconceptions that made the minds of many men, in different countries, run along the same track in their political thinking.

It is well known that Locke's treatise, written in reply to Filmer's *Patriarcha,* was an apology for the Revolution of 1688. "Kings," said Filmer, "are as absolute as Adam over the creatures"; and in general the Stuart partisans had taken their stand, as Sir Frederick Pollock [in his *History of the Science of Politics*] says, "on a supposed indefeasible right of kings, derived from a supposed divine institution of monarchy. . . . The Whigs needed an antidote, and Locke found one in his modified version of the original compact." This means that political circumstances had brought the Whigs to the point of overturning the existing government, that they were human enough to wish to feel that this was a decent and right thing to do, and that, accordingly, their minds were disposed to welcome a reasoned theory of politics which would make their revolution, as a particular example under the general rule, respectable and meritorious. The Whigs needed a theory of politics that would make their revolution of 1688 a 'glorious revolution.' Locke said himself that he had made all his discoveries by "steadily intending his mind in a given direction." Inevitably the Whigs steadily 'intended their minds' away from the idea of a divine right in kings, since no glorious revolution was to be found there, and towards a new idea—in fact, towards Locke's modified version of the compact theory.

It is significant that English writers were formulating a new version of the compact theory in the seventeenth century, while French and American writers made little use of it until the late eighteenth century. This does not necessarily mean that British writers were more intelligent and up-to-date, but is probably due to the fact that in British history the seventeenth century was the time of storm and stress for kings, whereas this time fell later in France and America. Jefferson used the compact theory to justify revolution just as Locke did: the theory came with the revolution in both cases. Rousseau was indeed not justifying an actual revolution; but, as Chateaubriand said, the Revolution in France "was accomplished before it occurred." It was accomplished in men's minds before they made it the work of their hands; and Rousseau spoke for all those who were 'intending their minds' away from an actual, irrational, and oppressive political order which rested in theory upon the divine right of kings and priests to rule—and misrule. In all three countries this common influence—the widespread desire to limit the power of kings and priests—was one source of those underlying presuppositions which determined the character of political speculation in the eighteenth century; a strong antipathy to kings and priests predisposed Jefferson and Rousseau, as it predisposed

elementary books of public right.' Where Jefferson got his ideas is hardly so much a question as where he could have got away from them.

Since these sentiments of the day were common in France, and were most copiously, and perhaps most logically, expressed there, it has sometimes been thought that Jefferson and his American contemporaries must have borrowed their ideas from French writers, must have been 'influenced' by them, for example by Rousseau. But it does not appear that Jefferson, or any American, read many French books. So far as the 'Fathers' were, before 1776, directly influenced by particular writers, the writers were English, and notably Locke. Most Americans had absorbed Locke's works as a kind of political gospel; and the Declaration, in its form, in its phraseology, follows closely certain sentences in Locke's second treatise on government. This is interesting, but it does not tell us why Jefferson, having read Locke's treatise, was so taken with it that he read it again, and still again, so that afterwards its very phrases reappear in his own writing. Jefferson doubtless read Filmer as well as Locke; but the phrases of Filmer, happily, do not appear in the Declaration. Generally

Locke, to 'intend their minds' towards some new sanction for political authority.

The idea that secular political authority rested upon compact was not new—far from it; and it had often enough been used to limit the authority of princes. It could scarcely have been otherwise indeed in that feudal age in which the mutual obligations of vassal and overlord were contractually conceived and defined. Vassals were often kings and kings often vassals; but all were manifestly vassals of God who was the Lord of lords and the King of kings. Thus mediaeval philosophers had conceived of the authority of princes as resting upon a compact with their subjects, a compact on their part to rule righteously, failing which their subjects were absolved from allegiance; but this absolution was commonly thought to become operative only through the intervention of the Pope, who, as the Vicegerent of God on earth, possessed by divine right authority over princes as well as over other men. Thus princes ruled by divine right after all, only their right was a second hand right, deriving from God through the Pope. Afterwards the princes, when they had become kings and as kings had got the upper hand, jostled the Pope out of his special seat and became coequals with him in God's favor; so that in the seventeenth century the right of kings to rule was commonly thought to come directly from God, and the Pope lost his power of intervening to absolve subjects from allegiance to a bad king. Charles II of England and Louis XIV of France both thought this a reasonable doctrine, nor did either of them lack learned men to back them up; Bossuet proved that it was obviously good religious doctrine—*Politique tirée de l' Écriture Sainte;* while Cambridge University assured Charles II that "Kings derive not their authority from the people but from God; . . . To Him only they are accountable."

This clearly closed the door to relief in case there should be any bad kings. In the sixteenth and seventeenth centuries there were a number of bad kings; and so some people were always to be found seeking a method of bringing bad kings to book. Popular resistance to kings was commonly taught both by the Jesuits and the Protestant dissenters: by the Jesuits (by Catholic monarchists called "dissenters") on the ground that only the Pope has Divine authority; by Protestant Dissenters (by Protestant monarchists called "Jesuits") on the ground that it was possible for subjects themselves to claim as intimate relations with God as either king or Pope. Calvin was one of the writers who opened up this latter inviting prospect to succeeding generations.

> The first duty of subjects towards their rulers is to entertain the most honorable views of their office, recognizing it [the office not the king] as a delegated jurisdiction from God, and on that account receiving and reverencing them as the ministers and ambassadors of God.

This is admitted; but then the ambassador must clearly abide by his instructions; and therefore,

> In that obedience which we hold to be due to the commands of rulers we must . . . be particularly careful that it is not incompatible with obedience to Him to whose will the wishes of all kings

should be subject. . . . The Lord, therefore, is King of Kings. . . . We are subject to men who rule over us, but subject only in the Lord. If they command anything against Him, let us not pay the least heed to it. [John Calvin, in his *Institutes of Christianity,* Bk. IV, Ch. 20, sec. 22]

What God had commanded, subjects might plainly read in holy writ—the scriptures as interpreted by those ministers whose business it was to understand them; for which reason, no doubt, Calvin would have ministers and magistrates walk together in close communion.

In 1579, another Frenchman, Hubert Languet, or whoever it was that wrote the *Vindiciae contra tyrannos,* gave greater precision to this idea. Subjects are obviously not bound to obey a king who commands what is contrary to the will of God. But are they bound to resist such a king? According to the *Vindiciae* they are. When kings were set up, two compacts were entered into: in the first, God on the one side, and people and king on the other, engaged to maintain the ancient covenant which God had formerly made with his chosen people of Israel; in the second, the king contracted with his subjects to rule justly, and they with him to be obedient. Thus kings are under binding contract to rule justly, while subjects have a covenant with God to see that they do so. In the seventeenth century English sectaries not only preached but practiced resistance to kings and magistrates, finding their justification, not so much in an explicit compact with God, as in natural law, which was that right reason or inner light of conscience which God had given to men for their guidance. The Levellers were complained of because, be the "Lawes and customes of a Kingdom never so plain and cleer against their wayes, yet they will not submit, but cry out for natural rights derived from Adam and right reason." Milton [in "Tenure of Kings and Magistrates"; *Works of John Milton,* IV, 1851] spoke for the refractory dissenters of that age when he said,

> There is no power but of God (Paul, *Rom.* 13), as much as to say, God put it in man's heart to find out that way at first for common peace and preservation, approving the exercise thereof. . . . For if it needs must be a sin in them to depose, it may as likely be a sin to have elected. And contrary, if the people's act in election be pleaded by a king, as the act of God and the most just title to enthrone him, why may not the people's act of rejection be as well pleaded by the people as the act of God, and the most just reason to depose him?

Here was a 'version of the original compact' which Locke might have used to justify the Revolution of 1688. He might have said, with any amount of elaboration, that the people had a compact with God which reserved to them the right to rebel when kings ruled unrighteously. Why was Locke not satisfied with this version? Certainly no one had less desire than Locke to deny that God was the maker and ruler of all. He could quote scripture too, as well as Milton or Filmer. We see, he says, that in the dispute between Jephthah and the Ammonites, "he [Jephthah] was forced to appeal to Heaven: "The Lord the Judge (says he) be judge this day." Well, of course, says Locke, "everyone knows what Jephthah here tells us, that the Lord the Judge shall judge" ["Of Civil Government," Bk. II, sec. 21; *Works of John Locke,* V, 1812]. But the trouble is the Lord does not do it now; he reserves his decision till the Day of Judgment. Jephthah appealed to the Lord, but the Lord did not speak, did not decide the dispute between Jephthah and the Ammonites; the result of which was that Jephthah had to decide it himself by leading out his armies. So it always is in the affairs of men: whether I shall appeal to Heaven, "I myself can only be the judge in my own conscience, as I will answer it, at the great day, to the supreme judge of all men." If we resist kings, God will no doubt judge us for it in the last day; but men will judge us now. Let us, therefore, ask whether there is not happily a compact between men and kings, God not interfering, on which we can stand to be judged by men when we resist kings.

The truth is that Locke, and the English Whigs, and Jefferson and Rousseau even more so, had lost that sense of intimate intercourse and familiar conversation with God which religious men of the sixteenth and seventeenth centuries enjoyed. Since the later seventeenth century, God had been withdrawing from immediate contact with men, and had become, in proportion as he receded into the dim distance, no more than the Final Cause, or Great Contriver, or Prime Mover of the universe; and as such was conceived as exerting his power and revealing his will indirectly through his creation rather than directly by miraculous manifestation or through inspired books. In the eighteenth century as never before, 'Nature' had stepped in between man and God; so that there was no longer any way to know God's will except by discovering the 'laws' of Nature, which would doubtless be the laws of 'nature's god' as Jefferson said. "Why should I go in search of Moses to find out what God has said to Jean Jacques Rousseau?" Why indeed, when the true revelation was all about him in Nature, with sermons in stones, books in the running brooks, and God in everything. The eighteenth century, seeking a modified version of the original compact, had to find it in nature or forever abandon the hope of finding it.

The concept of Nature was of course nothing new either, any more than the theory of compact. Stoic philosophers and Roman jurists had made much of Nature and Natural Law. Thomas Aquinas, in the thirteenth century, noted three distinct meanings of the word natural as applied to man. The third of these meanings, which mediaeval writers had taken over from the classical world, Aquinas defines as "an inclination in man to the good, according to the *rational* nature which is proper to him; as, for example, man has a natural inclination to know the truth about God, and to live in society." Natural law was accordingly that part of law discoverable by right reason, and as such occupied a strictly subordinate place in the mediaeval hierarchy of laws. According to Aquinas, the highest of all laws, comprehending all others, was the Eternal Law, which was nothing less than the full mind of God. Something, but not all, of the mind of God could be known to man: part of it had been revealed in the Bible or might be communicated through the Church (Positive Divine Law); and part of it could be discovered by human reason (Natural Law); lowest of all in the hierarchy came Human Law, or the positive laws of particular states. Thus Natu-

ral Law obviously took precedence over Human Law, but must always be subordinate to that part of the Eternal Law which God had revealed in the Bible or through the Church. Natural Law was in fact not the law of nature, but a natural method of learning about the law of God. Above all, what could be learned by this method was strictly limited: Natural Law was that part of the mind of God which man could discover by using his reason, but God had provided beforehand, through the Bible and the Church, a sure means of letting man know when his reason was not right reason but unreason.

The concept of Nature which held the field in the eighteenth century seems at first sight very different from this; but the difference is after all mainly on the surface. The eighteenth century did not abandon the old effort to share in the mind of God; it only went about it with greater confidence, and had at last the presumption to think that the infinite mind of God and the finite mind of man were one and the same thing. This complacent view of the matter came about partly through the Protestant Reformation, which did much to diminish the authority of the Church as the official interpreter of God's will; but it came about still more through the progress of scientific investigation which had been creating, since the time of Copernicus, a strong presumption that the mind of God could be made out with greater precision by studying the mechanism of his created universe than by meditating on the words of his inspired prophets. Some of the 'laws' of this curious mechanism had already been formulated by Kepler and Galileo. Well, what if all the 'laws' of God's universe could be discovered by the human reason? In that case would not the infinite mind of God be fully revealed, and the Natural Law be identical with the Eternal Law? Descartes was bold enough to suggest this wonderful possibility. "I think, therefore, I am." Whatever is, is rational; hence there is an exact correspondence between human reason and the objective world. I think, therefore I am; and if I can think straight enough and far enough, I can identify myself with all that is. This 'all that is' the eighteenth century understood as Nature; and to effect a rational explanation of the relation and operation of all that is, was what it meant by discovering the 'laws' of Nature. No doubt Natural Law was still, as in the time of Aquinas, that part of the mind of God which a rational creature could comprehend; but if a rational creature could comprehend all that God had done, it would, for all practical purposes, share completely the mind of God, and the Natural Law would be, in the last analysis, identical with the Eternal Law. Having deified Nature, the eighteenth century could conveniently dismiss the Bible and drop the concept of Eternal Law altogether.

In this deification of Nature, a decisive influence must be ascribed to Isaac Newton, whose great work, the *Principia,* was first published in 1686. Newton probably had no intention of deifying Nature. He was engaged in more commonplace occupations: noting the effect which an ordinary glass prism had upon rays of light which passed through it; determining whether the deflection of the moon's orbit, in any minute of the moon's progress, was the same as the distance which a body at that height would move in the first minute of its fall towards the earth. But

Newton struck the imagination of his time, as Darwin did of his time, just because his important conclusions were arrived at by such commonplace methods. If the character of so intangible a thing as light could be discovered by playing with a prism, if, by looking through a telescope and doing a sum in mathematics, the force which held the planets could be identified with the force that made an apple fall to the ground, there seemed to be no end to what might be definitely known about the universe. Perhaps after all God moved in these clear ways to perform his wonders; and it must be that he had given man a mind ingeniously fitted to discover these ways. Newton, more than any man before him, so it seemed to the eighteenth century, banished mystery from the world. In his hands 'Philosophy' came to be no more than a matter of observation and mathematics, an occupation which any intelligent person might in some measure pursue, instead of the manipulation of a subtle dialectic which only the adept could follow and which created more difficulties than it solved.

The interest of the scientific world in Newton's work is indicated by the appearance, prior to 1789, of some eighteen editions or reprintings of the *Principia.* British universities were teaching the new doctrine before the end of the seventeenth century; and when Newton, crowned with honors and offices, died in 1727, his funeral was a national event, observed with forms usually accorded only to royalty. At that time Descartes was still in the ascendant in France. Newton was not indeed unknown there, having been admitted, as early as 1699, to the small number of foreign associates of the Academy of Sciences; but it was not until after his death that his doctrines were much attended to in France. In 1734, the annual prize of the Academy was shared by John Bernoulli, who had submitted a Cartesian memoir, and his son Daniel, who had defended the Newtonian theories. The last prize granted for a Cartesian paper was in 1740. Voltaire, who was in England at the time of Newton's death, came home and devoted himself to convincing his countrymen that they were behind the times in still holding to Descartes, for that purpose preparing the very influential book of exposition, *Elemens de la philosophie de Neuton,* which was published in 1738. Fontenelle, the most distinguished defender of Cartesianism in France, died in 1756; and by 1759, when the *Principia* appeared in a French translation, it may be said that French scientists had generally accepted the Newtonian philosophy.

But the fame of Newton was not confined to the scientific fraternity. It was not necessary to read the *Principia* in order to be a good Newtonian, any more than it is necessary to read the *Origin of Species* in order to be a good Darwinian. Relatively few people read the *Principia,* which contains much difficult mathematics. No less a person than Dr. Richard Bentley wrote to Newton for a list of books on mathematics by the aid of which he could study the *Principia* intelligently; and John Locke, himself no mean philosopher, had to take the word of Huygens that the mathematical parts of the book were sound. "Very few people read Newton," said Voltaire, 'because it is necessary to be learned to understand him. But everybody talks about him" ["Lettres philosophiques," XIV,

XXII, 1879]. These people could subscribe to the Newtonian philosophy without ever having to open the formidable *Principia;* and they were well aware that the great scientist had uncovered the secrets of Nature, and of Nature's God, in a way that, to an earlier generation, might have seemed almost indiscreet. They were indoctrinated into the new philosophy through conversation, and through popular lectures and books which humanely omitted the mathematics of the *Principia,* devoting the space thus gained to a confident and edifying amplification of its cautious conclusions which might have astonished Sir Isaac himself, but which made the new philosophy interesting and important to the average man. (pp. 24-44)

This generalized conception of the universe, through which the work of Newton so powerfully affected the social and political thought of the eighteenth century, is very clearly formulated by M. Leon Bloch, a competent modern student, in his recent book, *La philosophie de Newton.*

> What the human spirit owes to Newton . . . is the *rapprochement* effected by this great man between God and nature. Henceforth it will be possible for natural science, that is to say physics, not only to struggle against theology, but to supplant it. The contradictory Gods of the revealed religions will be replaced by a new idea, that of a being who is known to us through his works, and to whom we can attain only through science. The universal order, symbolized henceforth by the law of gravitation, takes on a clear and positive meaning. This order is accessible to the mind, it is not preestablished mysteriously, it is the most evident of all facts. From this it follows that the sole reality which can be accessible to our means of knowledge, matter, nature, appears to us as a tissue of properties, precisely ordered, and of which the connection can be expressed in terms of mathematics.
>
> (pp. 47-8)

The eighteenth century, obviously, did not cease to bow down and worship; it only gave another form and a new name to the object of worship: it deified Nature and denatured God. Since Nature was now the new God, source of all wisdom and righteousness, it was to Nature that the eighteenth century looked for guidance, from Nature that it expected to receive the tablets of the law; and it was just as necessary now as ever for the mind of the rational creature to share in the mind of this new God, in order that his conduct, including the 'positive laws of particular states,' might conform to the universal purpose. The Philosopher, as Maclaurin says, 'while he contemplates and admires so excellent a System, *cannot but be himself excited and animated to correspond with the general harmony of Nature.*' The words may be taken as a just expression of the eighteenth century state of mind: on its knees, with uplifted eyes contemplating and admiring the Universal Order, it was excited and animated to correspond with the general harmony.

This was no doubt an inspiring idea, but certainly not a new one. Great and good men in all ages had endeavored to correspond with the general harmony. Formerly this was conceived as an endeavor to become one with God; and for some centuries the approved method, in Europe, was thought to be fasting and prayer, the denial of the flesh, the renunciation of the natural man. "Who shall deliver me from the body of this death!" cried the saint. The physical and material world was thought to be a disharmony, a prison house, a muddy vesture of decay, closing in and blinding the spirit so that it could not enter into the harmony that was God. But the eighteenth century, conceiving of God as known only through his work, conceived of his work as itself a universal harmony, of which the material and the spiritual were but different aspects.

In breaking down the barriers between the material and the spiritual world, between man and nature, John Locke played a great rôle. His *Essay Concerning the Human Understanding,* published in 1690, was an enquiry into "the original, certainty, and extent of human knowledge," an enquiry which the author thought of the highest use "since it is the understanding that sets man above the rest of sensible beings, and gives him all the advantage and dominion which he has over them." (pp. 51-3)

Locke's 'sensational' philosophy became, with some modifications in detail, the psychological gospel of the eighteenth century. A trained philosopher might think that the conception of 'innate ideas' which Locke destroyed was no more than a man of straw, a "theory of innate ideas," as Mr. Webb [in his *Studies in the History of Natural Theology*] says, "so crude that it is difficult to suppose any serious thinker ever held it." That may be. Yet it is certain that Locke's book had a great influence on the common thought of his age, which may be due to the fact that serious thinkers are few, while crude theories, generally speaking, rule the world. Put in the form in which it entered into the common thought of the eighteenth century, Locke's theory may be stated as follows: God has not revealed the truth that is necessary for man's guidance, once for all, in holy writ, or stamped upon the minds of all men certain intuitively perceived intellectual and moral ideas which correspond to the truth so revealed; on the contrary, all the ideas we can have come from experience, are the result of the sensations that flow in upon us from the natural and social world without, and of the operations of the reflecting mind upon these sensations; from which it follows that man, as a thinking and an acting creature, is part and parcel of the world in which he lives, intimately and irrevocably allied to that Universal Order which is at once the work and the will of God. (pp. 55-6)

It went without saying that kings and ministers and priests, as well as philosophers, ought to be 'excited and animated to correspond with the general harmony of Nature'; and if, once fully enlightened on that point, they would not do so, they must unquestionably be pronounced no better than rebels against the Great Contriver, the Author and Governor of the Universe. But how, after all, could you tell for sure whether kings and ministers and priests were, or were not, in accord with Nature? The presumption was no doubt against them, but how be sure? In appealing from custom and positive law to the over-ruling law of God, the eighteenth century followed well established precedent; but a practical difficulty arose when the will of God was thought to be revealed, neither in papal command nor in the words of scripture, but in the endless,

half-deciphered Book of Nature. Nature was doubtless an open book, yet difficult to read, and likely to convey many meanings, so various a language did it speak. George III, as well as Sam Adams, was presumably God's work; and if God's will was revealed in his work, how were you to know that the acts of George III, whose nature it was to be tyrannical, were not in accord with Natural Law, while the acts of Sam Adams, whose nature it was to be fond of Liberty, were in accord with Natural Law? Everything in the physical world was certainly part of God's universe, and therefore according to nature; why was not everything in the world of human relations part of God's universe also, and equally according to nature?

It was easy enough to read the Book of Nature in this sense, and even to make verse out of it, as Pope did.

> All are but parts of one stupendous whole,
> Whose body Nature is, and God the soul; . . .
> All Nature is but art, unknown to thee;
> All chance, direction, which thou canst not see;
> All discord, harmony not understood;
> All partial evil, universal good:
> And, spite of pride, in erring reason's spite,
> One truth is clear, whatever is, is right.

According to this reading it seemed that Nature, having devoured God, was on the point of incontinently swallowing Man also—a monstrous conclusion for those who were convinced that all was *not* right. That all was not right was a belief that became widespread and profoundly held in the latter eighteenth century; and those who were thus 'steadily intending their minds' away from the actual political and social order in search of a better, had at all hazards to make out that certain aspects of actual human relations were not in harmony with Nature, while other aspects were. Convinced that the torture of Calas, for example, or the Stamp Act, or George III, was something less than 'harmony not understood,' they had to demonstrate that 'life, liberty, and the pursuit of happiness' were according to Nature and the will of God, whereas tyranny and cruelty and the taking of property without consent were not.

This is only another way of saying that in order to find a fulcrum in Nature for moving the existing order, the eighteenth century had to fall back upon the commonplace distinction between good and bad; unless the will of God, as revealed in the nature of man, was to be thought of as morally indifferent, some part of this nature of man had to be thought of as good and some part as bad. The eighteenth century had to appeal, as it were, from nature drunk to nature sober. Now the test or standard by which this appeal could be validly made was found in nature itself—in reason and conscience; for reason and conscience were parts of man's nature too, and God had manifestly given man reason and conscience, as natural guides, precisely in order that he might distinguish that part of his own thought and conduct which was naturally good from that which was naturally bad. Natural law, as a basis for good government, could never be found in the undifferentiated nature of man, but only in human reason applying the test of good and bad to human conduct. Thus the eighteenth century, having apparently ventured so far afield, is nevertheless to be found within hailing distance of the thirteenth; for its conception of natural law in the world of human relations was essentially identical, as Thomas Aquinas' conception had been, with right reason.

It is true that right reason had a much freer field in the eighteenth century than in the thirteenth; it was not limited either by a special revelation or by an established Church; and above all it could appeal for support to history, to the experience of mankind. From the record of human activities in all times and in all places, as well as from the established laws of the material universe, it would be easily possible to verify and to substantiate the verdict of right reason. Whatever the Bible might say, right reason could reject miracles because they were contrary to common sense and the observed procedure of the physical world. Whatever the Church might command, right reason could denounce cruelty and intolerance because the common conscience of mankind revolted at cruelty and intolerance. Whatever the dogmas of particular religions might be, right reason could prefer the precepts of natural Religion which were to be found as Voltaire said, in the "principles of morality common to the human race." Whatever customs and positive laws might prevail in particular states, right reason could estimate their value in the light of the customs and laws common to all states. What I have searched for, said Montaigne, is "la connaissance de l'homme en général"—the knowledge of man in general. This is precisely what the eighteenth century did: with the lantern of enlightenment it went up and down the field of human history looking for man in general, the universal man, man stripped of the accidents of time and place; it wished immensely to meet Humanity and to become intimate with the Human Race. If it could find Humanity it would have found man in general, the natural man; and so it would have some chance of knowing what were the rights and laws which, being suited to man in general, were most likely to be suited to particular men, everywhere and always.

We have now got a long way from the Declaration of Independence and Thomas Jefferson, and even from John Locke, in whose book Jefferson found so well expressed the ideas which he put into the Declaration. Let us then return to John Locke, whom we have too long left to his own devices, seeking a 'modified form of the original compact,' being unable to make use of the older version. The older version, which was a compact between the people and God in person, Locke could not use because, as we saw, nature had stepped in between God and man. Locke, like every one else, had therefore to make his way, guided by reason and conscience, through Nature to find the will of God; and the only version of the original compact from which he could derive governmental authority, was such a compact as men, acting according to their nature, would enter into among themselves. Since the will of God was revealed in Nature, you could find out what God had willed governments to be and do only by consulting Nature—the nature of man. The question which Locke had to answer was therefore this: What kind of political compact would men enter into, if they acted according to the nature which God had given them?

To answer this question, Locke says, we must consider

> What state all men are naturally in, and that is, a state of perfect freedom to order their actions and dispose of their possessions and persons, as they think fit, within the bounds of the law of nature, without asking leave, or depending upon the leave of any other man. A state also of equality, wherein all power and jurisdiction is reciprocal, no one having more than another. ["Of Civil Government," Bk. II, sec. 4; *Works* (ed. 1812)]

This state which all men are 'naturally in,' this state of nature, is not a state of licence; it is a state of perfect freedom and equality, but of freedom and equality only *'within the bounds of the law of nature.'* What is this law of nature?

> The state of nature has a law to govern it, which obliges every one: and *reason, which is that law,* teaches all mankind, who will but consult it, that being all equal and independent, no one ought to harm another in his life, health, liberty, or possessions. . . .
>
> In transgressing the law of nature, the offender declares himself to live by another rule than that of *reason and common equity, which is that measure God has set to the actions of men.* . . .
>
> A criminal, who having renounced *reason, the common rule and measure God hath given to mankind,* hath, by the unjust violence and slaughter he hath committed on one, declared war against all mankind.

In Locke's state of nature all men are thus free and all are bound. Is not this a paradox? No, because the state of nature, in which Locke seeks the origin of government, is not the actual pre-social state of history, but an imaginative state rationally constructed. Locke, like the political writers of the eighteenth century, was not concerned to know how governments had come to be what they were; what he wanted to know was whether there was any justification for their being what they were. "Man is born free, and is everywhere in chains," exclaimed Rousseau [in his *Du contract social, ou principes du droit politique,* 1762]. "How was this change made? I do not know. What can make it legitimate? I believe I can answer that question." This is the question Locke seeks to answer—what can justify governments in binding men by positive laws? In order to answer it he first asks what law would bind men if government, positive law, and custom were, conceivably, nonexistent? His answer is that in that case no law would bind them except the law of reason. Reason would bind them, because reason is the 'common rule and measure God hath given to mankind'; reason would at once bind and make free; it would, as Locke says, *oblige* every one: but it would oblige them precisely in this, that it would teach them that all are perfectly free and equal and that no one 'ought to harm another in his life, health, liberty, or possessions.' Locke's natural law is the law of reason, its only compulsion is an intellectual compulsion, the relations which it prescribes such as would exist if men should follow reason alone. (pp. 57-66)

The sum and substance of Locke's elaborate enquiry into the origin and character of government is this: since reason is the only sure guide which God has given to men, reason is the only foundation of just government; and so

I ask, not what authority any government has in fact, but what authority it ought in reason to have; and I answer that it ought to have the authority which reasonable men, living together in a community, considering the rational interests of each and all, might be disposed to submit to willingly; and I say further that unless it is to be assumed that any existing government has of right whatever authority it exercises in fact, then there is no way of determining whether the authority which it exercises in fact is an authority which it exercises of right, except by determining what authority it ought in reason to have. Stripped of its decorative phrases, of its philosophy of 'Nature' and 'Nature's God' and the 'Universal Order,' the question which Locke asked was a simple one: 'I desire to know what kind of government that is . . . where one man . . . may do to all his subjects whatever he pleases, without the least liberty to any one to question or control those who execute his pleasure?' This, generally speaking, was what the eighteenth century desired to know. The answer which it gave to that question seemed self-evident: Such a government is a bad government; since governments exist for men, not men for governments, all governments derive their just powers from the consent of the governed.

If the philosophy of Locke seemed to Jefferson and his compatriots just 'the common sense of the matter,' it was not because Locke's argument was so lucid and cogent that it could be neither misunderstood nor refuted. Locke's argument is not particularly cogent unless you accept his assumptions as proved, nor lucid until you restate it to suit yourself; on the contrary, it is lumbering, involved, obscured by innumerable and conflicting qualifications—a dreary devil of an argument staggering from assumption posited as premise to conclusion implicit in the assumption. It was Locke's conclusion that seemed to the colonists sheer common sense, needing no argument at all. Locke did not need to convince the colonists because they were already convinced; and they were already convinced because they had long been living under governments which did, in a rough and ready way, conform to the kind of government for which Locke furnished a reasoned foundation. The colonists had never in fact lived under a government where 'one man . . . may do to all his subjects whatever he pleases.' They were accustomed to living under governments which proceeded, year by year, on a tacitly assumed compact between rulers and ruled, and which were in fact very largely dependent upon 'the consent of the governed.' How should the colonists not accept a philosophy, however clumsily argued, which assured them that their own governments, with which they were well content, were just the kind that God had designed men by nature to have!

The general philosophy which lifted this common sense conclusion to the level of a cosmic law, the colonists therefore accepted, during the course of the eighteenth century, without difficulty, almost unconsciously. That human conduct and institutions should conform to the will of God was an old story, scarcely to be questioned by people whose ancestors were celebrated, in so many instances, for having left Europe precisely in order to live by God's law. Living by God's law, as it turned out, was much the same as living according to "the strong bent of their spirits."

The strong bent of their spirits, and therefore God's law, had varied a good deal according to the locality, in respect to religion more especially; but so far as one could judge at this late enlightened date, God had showered his blessings indifferently upon all alike—Anglicans and Puritans, Congregationalists and Presbyterians, Catholics, Baptists, Shakers and Mennonites, New Lights and Old Lights. Even Quakers, once thought necessary to be hanged as pestilent blasphemers and deniers of God's will, now possessed a rich province in peace and content. Many chosen peoples had so long followed God's law by relying upon their own wits, without thereby running into destruction, that experience seemed to confirm the assertion that nature was the most reliable revelation of God's will, and human reason the surest interpreter of nature.

The channels through which the philosophy of Nature and Natural Law made its way in the colonies in the eighteenth century were many. A good number of Americans were educated at British universities, where the doctrines of Newton and Locke were commonplaces; while those who were educated at Princeton, Yale, or Harvard could read, if they would, these authors in the original, or become familiar with their ideas through books of exposition. The complete works of both Locke and Newton were in the Harvard library at least as early as 1773. Locke's works were listed in the Princeton catalogue of 1760. As early as 1755 the Yale library contained Newton's *Principia* and Locke's *Essay;* and before 1776 it contained the works of Locke, Newton, and Descartes, besides two popular expositions of the Newtonian philosophy. The revolutionary leaders do not often refer to the scientific or philosophical writings of either Newton or Locke, although an occasional reference to Locke's *Essay* is to be found; but the political writings of Locke, Sidney, and Milton are frequently mentioned with respect and reverence. Many men might have echoed the sentiment expressed by Jonathan Mayhew [in *The Patriot Preachers of the American Revolution*] in 1766:

> Having been initiated, in youth, in the doctrines of civil liberty, as they were taught by such men as Plato, Demosthenes, Cicero and other renowned persons among the ancients; and such as Sidney and Milton, Locke and Hoadley, among the moderns, I liked them; they seemed rational.

And Josiah Quincy expressed the common idea of his compatriots when, in 1774, he wrote into his will these words:

> I give to my son, when he shall arrive at the age of 15 years, Algernon Sidney's Works, John Locke's Works, Lord Bacon's Works, Gordon's Tacitus, and Cato's Letters. May the spirit of Liberty rest upon him! [Rosenthal, "Rousseau at Philadelphia"; *Magazine of American History,* XII]

For the general reader, the political philosophy of the eighteenth century was expounded from an early date in pamphlet and newspaper by many a Brutus, Cato, or Popliocola. An important, but less noticed, channel through which the fundamental ideas of that philosophy—God, Nature, Reason—were made familiar to the average man, was the church. Both in England and America preachers and theologians laid firm hold of the Newtonian conception of the universe as an effective weapon against infidelity. Dr. Richard Bentley studied Newton in order to preach a 'Confusion of Atheism,' deriving a proof of Divine Providence from the physical construction of the universe as demonstrated by that 'divine theorist,' Sir Isaac Newton. What a powerful support to Revelation (and to Revolution) was that famous argument from design! The sermons of the century are filled with it—proving the existence and the goodness of God from the intelligence which the delicately adjusted mechanism of Nature everywhere exhibited.

In 1750 there was published at Boston a book of Twenty Sermons, delivered in the Parish Church at Charleston, South Carolina, by the Reverend Samuel Quincy. In these sermons we find the Nature philosophy fully elaborated.

> For a right knowledge of God by the Light of Nature, displays his several amiable Perfections; acquaints us with the Relation he stands in to us, and the Obligations we owe to him. . . . It teaches us that our greatest Interest and Happiness consists in loving and fearing God, and in doing his Will; that to imitate his moral Perfections in our whole Behaviour, is acting up to the Dignity of our Natures, and that he has endowed us with Reason and Understanding (Faculties which the Brutes have not) on purpose to contemplate his Beauty and Glory, and to keep our inferior Appetites in due Subjection to his Laws, written in our Hearts.

In his famous election sermon of 1754, Jonathan Mayhew uses this philosophy, without the formulae, for deriving the authority of government. Government, he says,

> is both the ordinance of God, and the ordinance of man: of God, in respect to his original plan, and universal Providence; of man, as it is more immediately the result of human prudence, wisdom and concert. [in his *A Sermon Preached in the Audience of His Excellency William Shirley, Esq., May 29, 1754*]

In later Massachusetts election sermons, from 1768 to 1773, we find both the philosophy and the formulae; the three concepts of God, Nature, and Reason, which Samuel Quincy made the foundation of religion, are there made the foundation of politics and government as well. And so there crept into the mind of the average man this conception of Natural Law to confirm his faith in the majesty of God while destroying his faith in the majesty of Kings.

English writers in the nineteenth century, perhaps somewhat blinded by British prejudice against the French Revolution and all its works, complacently took it for granted that the political philosophy of Nature and natural rights upon which the Revolution was founded, being particularly vicious must be peculiarly French; from which it followed, doubtless as the night the day, that the Americans, having also embraced this philosophy, must have been corrupted by French influence. The truth is that the philosophy of Nature, in its broader aspects and in its particular applications, was thoroughly English. English literature of the seventeenth and eighteenth centuries is steeped

in this philosophy. The Americans did not borrow it, they inherited it. The lineage is direct: Jefferson copied Locke and Locke quoted Hooker. In political theory and in political practice the American Revolution drew its inspiration from the parliamentary struggle of the seventeenth century. The philosophy of the Declaration was not taken from the French. It was not even new; but good old English doctrine newly formulated to meet a present emergency. In 1776 it was commonplace doctrine, everywhere to be met with, as Jefferson said, "whether expressed in conversation, in letters, printed essays, or the elementary books of public right." And in sermons also, he might have added. But it may be that Jefferson was not very familiar with sermons. (pp. 71-9)

> *Carl Becker, "Historical Antecedents of the Declaration: The Natural Rights Philosophy," in his* The Declaration of Independence: A Study in the History of Political Ideas, *1922. Reprint by Alfred A. Knopf, 1942, pp. 24-79.*

An excerpt from Lord Byron's "The Age of Bronze":

> But lo! a Congress! What! that hallowed name
> Which freed the Atlantic! May we hope the same
> For outworn Europe? With the sound arise,
> Like Samuel's shade to Saul's monarchic eyes,
> The prophets of young Freedom, summoned far
> From climes of Washington and Bolivar;
> Henry, the forest-born Demosthenes,
> Whose thunder shook the Philip of the seas;
> And stoic Franklin's energetic shade,
> Robed in the lightnings which his hand allayed;
> And Washington, the tyrant-tamer, wake,
> To bid us blush for these old chains, or break.
> But *who* compose this Senate of the few
> That should redeem the many? *Who* renew
> This consecrated name, till now assigned
> To councils held to benefit mankind?
> Who now assemble at the holy call?
> The blest Alliance, which says three are all!
> An earthly Trinity! which wears the shape
> Of Heaven's, as man is mimicked by the ape.
> A pious Unity! in purpose one—
> To melt three fools to a Napoleon.

> *Lord Byron, in his* The Works of Lord Byron: Poetry, *Vol. V, edited by Ernest Hartley Coleridge, 1966.*

Clinton Rossiter

[In the following excerpt, Rossiter discusses the social, economic, and political aspects of American society on the eve of the 1787 Constitutional Convention.]

The United States in 1787 was a good country in which to live, work, and aspire—if not for men with the tastes of English dukes, the appetites of French tax collectors, or the memories of Italian bishops, certainly for men with a modest desire to be free, prosperous, and respectable. "Europe with all its pomp," the French-American Crèvecoeur wrote [in his *Letters from an American Farmer,*

1782], "is not to be compared to this continent, for men of middle station, or laborers"—so long, he would have been the first to admit, as their skins were white.

In the opinion of half the philosophers of Europe and all citizens of the United States itself, there was no better country on the face of the earth. It had extent, resources, and opportunities unbounded; it harbored a "numerous, brave, and hardy people"; it had dreams of glory that summoned this people to be up and doing. It had problems, too, as would any country still licking the wounds of a quarter-century of disruption, invasion, and civil war, but the problems were unfelt by many Americans and unseen by many others, and were by no means thought to be insoluble by those who could both feel and see.

The largest problem of all was the momentous question whether America was a country like England and France or a "country" like Germany and Italy, whether the Union formed under the pressures of Boston, Valley Forge, and Saratoga was to be the groundwork of a true nation or a polite title for a league of petty sovereignties. The hardheaded men in the courts of Europe were fairly certain that the American experiment in nationhood, complicated as it was by simultaneous experiments in independence, republicanism, and expansion, would never succeed. Although some hardheaded men in the assemblies, law offices, and countinghouses of America were disposed to agree, others were hopeful that, given a forceful political and emotional shove, the United States would move into the fullness of nationhood. It was just such a group of men, with a few unhappy exceptions, who came together in Philadelphia in May of 1787 to "revise" the confederate, congressional form of common government under which the United States had muddled through the first years of its existence—informally but in the main successfully from 1774 to 1781, formally but ever more ineffectively under the Articles of Confederation ratified at last on March 1 of that year. In order to understand the intentions and assess the performance of the men of Philadelphia, we must first look at the society out of which they came. The conditions and prospects of this society gave direction, and at the same time set limits, to their gropings for a political solution to their overriding problems.

The very size of the United States was enough to set alarmists to shivering, dreamers to dreaming, and realists to gambling. From the Atlantic to the Mississippi, from the Great Lakes to just short of the Gulf of Mexico stretched a land as vast as France, Italy, Spain, Germany, Britain, and Ireland combined, a land that, give a few parcels of forest to Spanish greed in the far south and take a few from British obstinacy in the far north, counted some 890,000 square miles. No man knew, except in a casual way, that rich stores of coal, iron, copper, and other minerals waited below the surface for the pick and shovel of industry; every man knew that the surface itself was a profligate treasure-house of the one thing for which all men of that age hungered: deep, well-watered, fertile soil, which commanded toil beyond our imagining yet often paid off in rewards beyond theirs.

Less than one-half of this expanse of land had come under effective control of the new Republic, whether the control

was designed by state authorities or Congress, whether it was exercised by officers of a government, agents of a land company, or impatient pursuers of their own happiness. Most Americans lived where their colonial fathers had lived—between the Appalachians and the sea—and even in this territory, larger than all France, they seemed hardly to have begun the task of subduing the wilderness. Except in the eastern parts of the Middle States and the southern part of New England, the forest, not the clearing, was the dominant feature of the landscape. "Compared with such a country as France," a tart-voiced stranger noted in 1796, the United States "may justly be denominated one vast forest." [in C. F. Volney, *A View of the Soil and Climate of the United States of America,* 1804]

Travel through this forest, or even through the most settled parts of the country, was not lightly to be undertaken. Roads were bad, bridges few, ferries leaky, rivers whimsical, stagecoaches cranky, and inns ill-kept. Yet a determined man—a peddler bound from Boston to Richmond, a settler bound from Pittsfield to Pittsburgh, a delegate bound from Charleston to Philadelphia—could always make his way even in the worst season. What is intriguing about transportation in early America is not so much its primitive state as the startling mobility of a "determined man" like Washington the surveyor, warrior, and statesman.

No one knew—although several inquiring minds had tried to guess (almost always too modestly)—how many persons the United States could count as citizens and chattels. The census of 1790, a handsome exercise in demography for so new and inexperienced a nation, turned up a population of 3,929,214, of whom 681,834 were Negro slaves. (Most of the thousands of Indians lived uncounted and unloved beyond the advancing frontier.) Since Spain had a population of around ten million, the German states twenty million, France twenty-five million, and the British Isles fifteen million (Ireland alone counting five million), the Americans were not yet a people of more than trifling consequence in a world that took its orders from London, Paris, Madrid, and Rome. Most Americans lived on the land, many in towns and settlements but just as many in isolation. Only twenty-four places had more than 2,500 inhabitants, only five cities had more than 10,000: Philadelphia (45,000), New York (33,000), Boston (18,000), Charleston (16,000), and Baltimore (13,500). However proud the leading men of these busy ports might be of their shops, libraries, and paved squares, enough of them had been to industrious Amsterdam (200,000), arrogant Paris (600,000), or teeming London (950,000) to realize that theirs was the pride of provincials. Some of them, it might be added, had looked hard enough behind the glitter of Paris and London to wish a kinder fate than mere tumescence for New York and Philadelphia.

The most attractive and exciting city in the new Republic was Philadelphia, which, thanks to the imaginative energy of Benjamin Franklin and several dozen exponents of one or another aspect of his many-sided genius, was a center of commerce, finance, politics, science, art, architecture, learning, philanthropy, and good living. The wharves of Philadelphia were piled high with everything for which

American housewives might yearn, from the cutlery of Sheffield to the teas of Canton; the presses of Philadelphia groaned without rest to produce ten newspapers for the edification of its citizens, especially those interested in disasters, funerals, furniture sales, or political name-calling; the academies, streetlamps, fire companies, mansions, museums, and prisons of Philadelphia were models for civic-minded men all over America. "The cleanliness, evenness, and length of the streets," an admiring visitor from South America wrote, "their illumination at nightime, and the vigilance of the guards, posted at each corner to maintain security and good order, make Philadelphia one of the most pleasant and well-ordered cities in the world" [Francisco de Miranda, *The New Democracy in America,* 1783]. A city in which Franklin lived out his last days, Robert Morris stirred a hundred financial pots, Benjamin Rush dispensed medical lore to eager youths, Charles Willson Peale painted portraits and collected old bones, and David Rittenhouse divided his time between inventing telescopes and surveying disputed boundaries was a place in which to think big thoughts about the American future. When the same visitor complained that "the men are almost always immersed in their business affairs and in political intrigue," little did he realize that this bustling city was setting a pattern for Americans for generations to come.

For most citizens of the new Republic the pleasures and opportunities of civilized Philadelphia, Salem, and Savannah, even of half-civilized Pittsburgh and Boonesboro, were unreachable, unpurchasable, and almost unimaginable. Although life for the American down on the farm was more rewarding than it had been for him or for his ancestors in the Old World, it was certainly no easier. Most men, women, and children of that simple age spent most of their waking hours in the backbreaking toil of plow and hoe; and for those who pushed beyond the settled regions of New England, the valleys of the Middle States, and the coastal plains of the South, the hours of rest and recreation brought contact with only a scatter of neighbors. Cut off from the centers of commerce and culture, forced to rely on his own wits for survival in a hard game with a half-smiling, half-fierce nature, farming largely and often wholly for subsistence, the pioneering yeoman developed a self-respecting dependence on those around him and a headstrong independence of those remote from him—qualities that boded well for democracy yet ill for nationhood. There were, as we shall see, many lines dividing the Americans of 1787 into groups or classes, but none so sharp as that between the involved and the isolated, the necessarily concerned and the fortuitously indifferent, the men who lived in cities and along lines of communication and therefore were in society and the men who lived by themselves and therefore were not. It took an extra measure of effort to dwell in the backwoods and stay in touch with the issues of civilization. For many Americans the gains to be expected were not worth the effort to be expended. Isolation, of a kind and to a degree we cannot imagine, was the dominating fact in the lives of perhaps a half-million Americans.

One thing was certain about the people of the United States: they were growing in numbers every year, and it was not just audacious patriotism that moved learned men to foretell a day when this newest nation in the world would also be the largest. The growth of population in this period was largely natural, and was a monument to the unexampled fertility of American mothers. Although the Republic was already being celebrated as "the Asylum of the Oppressed," and although boatloads of Germans, Irish, Scots, and others who had been oppressed (or simply bored) in the Old World docked from time to time in New York and Philadelphia, migration from Europe to America was light all through the troubled years from 1775 to 1815. For every new citizen gained by immigration in this period, twelve new citizens were born in America.

The Union of 1787, like the Union of today, was made up of a number of demographic, social, and political components. Nature and the responses of men to it were chiefly responsible for the five large sections into which the entire country was loosely but visibly divided.

Three of these were settled areas, although thousands of square miles in each were still wilderness: New England, a region of small farms, busy docks, far-ranging fisheries, democratic manners, proud memories, and ingrained habits of self-reliance and frugality; the Middle States, a region boasting the best-balanced economy, most diverse origins and faiths, and largest cities in America; and the South, then as now a nation within a nation pursuing its own version of the American way of life. The line between any two of these historic sections was no sharper than that, let us say, between England and Scotland. Sizable parts of New York—for example, the area east of Albany as well as most of Long Island—were culturally if not politically related to New England, while Maryland faced with open eyes in two directions. According to the census of 1790 the population of the settled areas was: New England, just over 1,000,000; the Middle States (including Maryland), more than 1,300,000; the South, just over 1,500,000.

Two other sections were only beginning to open up to permanent settlement: the wilderness north of the Ohio, which promised to be an extension of New England and the Middle States, and the wilderness south of the Ohio, much of which was already marked out for an economy and society based on chattel slavery. The census takers of 1790 found in the old Northwest only about 5,000 forerunners of the swarm to come, in the old Southwest something over 100,000. The first three sections were therefore the ones that counted politically in 1787; the pioneer areas, especially the country between the Ohio and the Great Lakes, were shadows gradually taking on substance in the minds of leading men, captivating some and disturbing others. Although the thirteen states that had fought the Revolution were still in command of the political situation—to the extent that it was subject to command at all—no decisions could be taken that ignored the three new states that were at the gates (Vermont, Kentucky, and Tennessee) and the eight or ten others that were no farther down the road than the eye of Thomas Jefferson of Virginia or Rev. Manasseh Cutler of the Ohio Company could see. The decisions of 1787 were taken by men who represented the communities long ago marked out, in casual style but with enduring consequence, by gentleman adventurers and their patrons in London.

Yet these men, many of whom had their own plans for the West, could see for themselves that the country was on the move. Not immigration from abroad but migration within the land was the dynamic of American demography in the 1780's. By boat, wagon, horse, and foot the men of the old states were moving on in an ever-rising flood. "A rage for emigrating to the western country prevails," the Secretary of Foreign Affairs wrote in wonder to an American in Paris in 1785, "and thousands have already fixed their habitations in that wilderness. . . . The seeds of a great people are daily planting beyond the mountains" [John Jay to William Bingham, May 31, 1785; *Correspondence of Jay,* III]. Kentucky, still a part of Virginia, counted almost 75,000 persons in 1790 where 150 woodsmen had roamed in 1776; Maine, still a part of Massachusetts, had grown almost overnight to one-fourth the size of its parent; New Yorkers, long confined to the southwest part of colony and state, now pushed in startling numbers up the Mohawk; and as many as 100,000 people gave up scratching for a living in New England in the years just after the Revolution and set off for greener, less rock-strewn fields. The "course of empire," as never before in American history, pressed relentlessly westward even as the Convention was sitting.

However jumbled the social order might be on the banks of the Cumberland and Muskingum, it had long since shaken down into a pattern of classes and distinctions on the banks of the Merrimac, Hudson, Delaware, Potomac, and Santee. Each of the thirteen states, even intensely republican Connecticut, had a more visible class structure than that of modern America. The Old World tradition of social stratification, which had been challenged but not demolished in the Revolution, and an ever more versatile economy, which offered large profits to the adventurous and well-being to the industrious, provided solid underpinning for a social system less rigid than that of England yet clear-cut enough to work a decisive influence on culture, education, religion, and above all politics. From the bottom of society to the top was a short step; from top to bottom was not much longer a slide. Top and bottom nevertheless existed, and none knew better than the sturdy farmers, shopkeepers, and independent artisans in between—the "middling sort," as they were still known in parts of post-Revolutionary America—of the enviable prestige of the rich merchants, large landholders, and successful lawyers who made up the "better sort," or of the latent power of the laborers, servants, and hardscrabble

The Old Senate Chamber of the Maryland State House, Annapolis, where the Continental Congress convened in 1783 and 1784.

farmers who crowded the ranks of the "meaner sort." While men from Europe were constantly exclaiming about the absence both of "great lords who possess everything" and of "a herd of people who have nothing," and reporting the sight of large areas in New Jersey and Connecticut in which no person was "ill clothed, hungry, sick, or idle," Americans were not so sure that "a pleasing uniformity of decent competence" was the mark of their society.

These visitors from the old, privilege-ridden countries of Europe who found no peers and few peasants in their journeys from Savannah to Portsmouth were also constantly exclaiming about the "spirit of republicanism" and bewailing or applauding (depending on the prejudices they had brought with them) the general lack of deference in American manners. Yet anyone who had dined with a Rutledge in Charleston, ridden out with a Blair in Virginia, exchanged bows with a Mifflin in Philadelphia, or heard the opinions of a Schuyler in New York would have agreed with the French chargé d'affaires that although there were "no nobles in America," there were "gentlemen" who enjoyed a kind of "pre-eminence" because of "their wealth, their talents, their education, their families, or the offices they hold" [Louis Otto to the Comte de Vergennes, October 10, 1786]. Some enjoyed a good deal more pre-eminence than others because they had helped to launch, guide, fight, and finance the Revolution. The Tory gentry who had fled from the wrath of rebellious America left room at the top in places like Boston and Philadelphia which patriots—some well-born, others self-made, and still others so "upwardly mobile" as to invite envy rather than respect—were quick to fill and determined to defend.

Although all thirteen states had some kind of property-owning or taxpaying qualification for political participation, most Americans who cared could meet these qualifications with something to spare—which means that most Americans had the vote, even though many were too preoccupied or isolated to use it. Then as now poverty was more a psychological than a legal bar to entrance into the political arena, and the bar was too formidable for the "meaner sort" to assault. As a result, the Republic for which the Constitution of 1787 was written had two classes that counted politically: the "rich and well-born" and the "body of sober and steady people" [in a letter of Madison to Jefferson, December 9, 1787; *Writings of Madison*, V]. Men divided politically, as they still do in America, on the basis of personal allegiances and sectional jealousies as well as along class lines. Although organized political parties had not yet sprung to life, except perhaps in the struggle of Constitutionalists and Republicans in Pennsylvania, semipermanent factions flourished in every state, and the most powerful of these factions depended on gentlemen for leadership and yeomen for votes. The line between the thinly populated top and the numerous middle in American society was therefore kept healthily fuzzy; the line between the middle and the bottom was more clearly seen, and was perhaps more politically meaningful. Despite the efforts of some historians to cram almost all Americans of the new Republic into one big, happy middle class, at least three per cent of the people had risen upward to form an American-style aristocracy; perhaps 20 per cent were mired in a swamp of much poverty and little hope, and thus were victims of a depressing political apathy.

Below the bottom of the class system of the new Republic, in legal status if not always in economic condition, was that vast group of "strangers in the land," the Negro slaves, who were an important component of the American economy, a presence if not a power in American politics, and a challenge to the American conscience. That the challenge had never been taken up, that only a handful of Negroes had been set free (and only a handful of white men had accepted such Negroes as even second-class citizens) in a country proclaiming the natural rights and equality of "all men," has been attributed to many causes. Four of these bear particular mention because they are so often and easily overlooked: inertia, by which I mean that slavery flourished in the new Republic primarily because it had flourished in the old empire, and that to legislate it out of existence in any state south of Pennsylvania would have called for an economic, political, and cultural revolution far greater than that of 1776; apprehension, by which I mean the suspicions voiced by even the most decent men that American society could not absorb so numerous and culturally alien a people without changing its own ways for the worse; lack of imagination, by which I mean both the ability of ordinary Americans to look right through the Negroes around them and the inability of leading ones to devise even small-scale schemes to give emancipated slaves the substance as well as the appearance of freedom; and ideology, by which I mean the rising American commitment to the principle of equality. If whites in the new Republic were to think of blacks as men at all, they were bound by the articles of their republican faith to think of them as equals, which was an impossible thought for all but a handful of eccentrics to entertain about persons who did not seem to be even potentially Americans. An America less dedicated to the principles of liberty and equality might, like the more status-conscious and caste-bound societies of Latin America, have had less trouble taking the first step toward emancipation of slaves and their incorporation as citizens of a free society. Since the first step seemed to command every other step to the end, few Americans could bring themselves to take it. Negroes were Africans, and that was that. The fact that they had not come to America of their own will and could never leave it was one with which few white men were willing to grapple courageously.

Whatever the causes of this unhappy situation, the facts are clear: at the time of the Convention there were perhaps 650,000 Negro slaves in the United States; well over nine-tenths of them lived in the five southernmost states, and in those states they made up more than one-third of the total population; in one northern state (Massachusetts) emancipation had taken place, in four (New Hampshire, Connecticut, Rhode Island, and Pennsylvania) it had begun, in two it was being pushed (New York and New Jersey), and in all except Negro-hungry Georgia the slave trade had been halted or at least heavily discouraged by law. Although men of good will in many parts of America professed to be sure in their hearts that slavery was on the way to extinction, their minds held no timetable for this vast revolution.

The American economy, although it lagged well behind that of England on the road to industrialization, was one about which farsighted men had every right to be "bullish." It displayed, as it had from the first planting, an essentially agrarian character: perhaps eight in ten Americans dug for their living in the dirt; one in ten worked in a closely allied extractive industry such as fishing or lumbering; one in ten had a place, whether as merchant, lawyer, sailor, clerk, or cartman, in the scheme of commerce. Small wonder that the possession of land—what Crèvecoeur saluted as the "precious soil," the "riches of the freeholder"—was still the widest door to well-being, profit, independence, status, and political power.

Although much of American farming was for subsistence or barter, much was for shipment to people in other lands. The prosperity of many families in the United States depended on the export of produce—wheat, corn, tobacco, rice, and indigo, as well as meat, fish, furs, naval stores, hides, lumber, whale oil, potash, and horses—to the West Indies and Europe. The American economy was a trading economy, and few parts of the Atlantic world could do for long without its products. American commerce, in turn, depended on the soil for its articles of trade. Although farmed in a generally primitive and wasteful way, this soil was able to produce a large enough surplus to permit America to be a factor in the world economy.

No part of America, on the other hand, was willing to do for long without the manufactured goods of Europe, which the new Republic was not yet ready to produce for itself in more than trifling quantities. Here and there in the rural landscape were tiny shops for converting wood, iron ore, skins, sugar, fibers, and wheat into finished articles, but most of what we would call manufacturing was carried on in households, and most members of these households did their share of digging in off hours. The fact that only three of the fifty-five delegates to the Philadelphia Convention had invested in manufacturing enterprises is evidence enough that the sway of agriculture went as yet unchallenged.

Although not yet officially dedicated to the glories and hazards of free enterprise, America was a country of free-enterprisers. Private ownership of the land and all other means of production was virtually universal; the profit motive sent men up over the mountains in search of new lands or down to the sea in ships; the use of credit and the wage system were fixed parts of the pattern of commerce. Mercantilism was dying, and feudalism had never had more than a marginal existence. Commercial capitalism was already preparing the way for America's surge to industrial might.

If the state of manufacturing was primitive, the state of learning was a cause for self-congratulation, a fashion in which many articulate Americans were not slow to indulge. Although reliable statistics do not exist, a long look through official records, deeds, petitions, letters, diaries, and other documents of the period leaves an impression of a remarkably literate people. This high state of literacy had not been easily won. Primary schools and academies were few and crude, and almost non-existent in rural areas; the family was therefore counted on, as we would never count on it today, to shoulder most of the burden for teaching young Americans to read, write, and cipher, as well as to understand their duties to God and their fellow men. The strongly knit family system, to its eternal credit, responded with an effectiveness that surprised many European observers. The new Republic was full of men who had never seen the inside of a schoolhouse and yet were extremely well educated for the responsibilities of their stations in life.

The fifteen-odd colleges (one can never be certain in egalitarian America whether a "college" is really a college, a self-inflated academy, or simply a board of trustees) were the special pride of the new Republic. Nine of them—Harvard, William and Mary, Yale, Princeton, Pennsylvania, Columbia, Brown, Rutgers, and Dartmouth—had been founded before 1776, and were now well established despite some economic, ideological, and political troubles stemming from the Revolution and its aftermath. At least six others—among them Dickinson, Hampden-Sydney, St. John's (Annapolis), Franklin and Marshall, the College of Charleston, and Washington College—were added in the 1780's; and even as the Convention sat, the first state universities were struggling to be born. It is easy to smile at the crabbed, often dogmatic methods of instruction that prevailed in these colleges, yet if we judge them by their fruits, they appear to have been rich fields of learning, reason, and the love of liberty. The overall performance of the college graduates in the Convention of 1787 speaks forcefully for the proposition that Latin, rhetoric, philosophy, and mathematics can be a healthy fare for political heroes.

Equally deserving of notice as servants in the cause of republican liberty and learning were the newspapers of America, of which there were a full eighty (most of them weeklies) scattered from Portland to Savannah, and from Bennington in Vermont to Lexington in Kentucky, at the time of the Convention. The eagerness with which editors published the full text of the proposed constitution and the amount of precious space they then made available to both the proponents and opponents of ratification reveal the useful role of the press in the politics of the young Republic. Then as now the dutiful citizen had to wade through pages of advertising in order to find the news; then as now he could be fairly certain that the news he read was uncensored and, so far as it ever can be, unperjured.

Although the secular culture of the new nation was still in a thinly productive state—with Noah Webster, David Rittenhouse, Francis Hopkinson, Philip Freneau, Charles Willson Peale, Jedidiah Morse, David Ramsay, Joel Barlow, Thomas Jefferson, and John Trumbull the "hopeful proofs of genius"—its religion was moving into new ways of believing and behaving. The Old World pattern of state-church relations had been hurried toward its doom by the Revolution, the most splendid milestone being Virginia's (that is to say Jefferson's) Statute of Religious Liberty of 1786; the New World pattern of multiplicity, democracy, private judgment, mutual respect, and widespread indifference was well on its way to maturity. Although America was still largely a nation of believers in 1787, many of the believers—and almost all of them in high political station—were thoroughly tolerant of the beliefs of others.

Neither upper-class ritualism nor lower-class enthusiasm had much appeal for the solid citizens of the United States, and men who still claimed to enjoy a monopoly of religious truth were no longer in a position to impose their dogmas on dissenting neighbors. As the perceptive Crèvecoeur wrote for the instruction of the Old World:

> Persecution, religious pride, the love of contradiction, are the food of what the world commonly calls religion. These motives have ceased here; zeal in Europe is confined; here it evaporates in the great distance it has to travel; there it is a grain of powder inclosed, here it burns away in the open air, and consumes without effect. [*Letters from an American Farmer*, 1782]

Live-and-let-live, worship-and-let-worship was the essence of religion in this land of vast distances and a hundred religions, of which the most important in terms of politics was the vaguely Christian rationalism that governed the tolerant minds of men like Jefferson, Franklin, Hamilton, and Washington. (The last and least skeptical of these rationalists loaded his First Inaugural Address with appeals to the "Great Author," "Almighty Being," "invisible hand," and "benign parent of the human race," but apparently could not bring himself to speak the word "God.") Although it was still far more comfortable for Americans to be Congregationalists, Presbyterians, Episcopalians, Methodists, Quakers, Lutherans, or Baptists than to be Catholics, the ever milder climate encouraged the feared and harried "Papists" to come out in the open, especially in Baltimore and Philadelphia. Even in old-fashioned parts of Connecticut and Massachusetts, the new orthodoxy of America was a many-voiced unorthodoxy.

One of the strongest forces in American society in 1787 was the fresh memory of the Revolution. For some men the tortuous course of events from 1765 to 1783 had been primarily a war against imperialism, for others a savagely fought civil war, for still others an upheaval that had sent them careening upward or downward in the social order. For all it had been an experience that had given new directions to their lives. Although these directions had been anticipated in the development of colonial America, the winning of independence had made them fixed conditions of the American way of life, conditions that would-be givers of a new fundamental law to the people would ignore at their peril.

The first of these was independence itself, which encouraged Americans to turn their backs on the old world of "corruption and decay," to pursue a self-reliant foreign policy, to dream of a continental "empire" from which every last Briton and Spaniard had been driven, and to consider themselves, like the children of Israel, a "peculiar treasure" singled out for a destiny higher than their own well-being. The second was republicanism, which was both a system of political, religious, and social institutions that had been cleansed of any taint of hereditary privilege and a spirit of self-respect that forbade the tugging of forelocks to even the grandest merchant in Boston or planter in Prince George County. And the third was dynamism, a wholesale quickening of ambition and aspiration, which stirred Americans of every class and calling to reach out

for prosperity as persons and for glory as citizens. The pace of American life had picked up sharply during the Revolution; progress had become a favorite topic of preachers, poets, and politicians.

Yet another solid legacy of the Revolution was the existence of thirteen near-sovereign states, every one of which, with the possible exceptions of Delaware and New Jersey, had a vision of the American future in which it was a proud, permanent, respected, and largely self-contained unit. The British colonies in North America had developed over the generations as separate entities; the course of events from resistance in 1765 to victory in 1783 first turned these colonies into states and then stiffened them in the sense of their own importance. Each state, even doubting Delaware and New Jersey, was or wanted to be a self-directing republic, a discrete social and economic community, and an object of loyalty to its inhabitants. Whether any state, even lordly Virginia or ambitious New York, was a rising nation was a question that few Americans were able to answer with a convincing "yes," and it was exactly this widespread assumption—that the states, however indestructible, were nothing more than states—which opened the way to the building of the American nation.

This assumption was both effect and cause of another legacy of the Revolution, itself the consequence of generations of unplanned yet hardy growth: the fact of incipient nationhood hinted at by the Stamp Act Congress, affirmed in the Declaration of Independence, nourished by the blood shed at Bunker Hill and Cowpens, reaffirmed in the Articles of Confederation, and left in the bones by almost every alert, active, literate man in the new Republic. Most of the ingredients of American nationalism were in the pot by 1787: common language, common origin and outlook, common legal and political institutions, common culture, common enemies, and common memories of a successful drive toward independence. There lacked, indeed, only that condition of political unity and sense of emotional unity which would follow on the creation of a central government with dignity and authority.

Here, then, were both the problem and the opportunity of the forward-looking leaders of the 1780's: that while many of their fellow countrymen everywhere in America feared *the fact of a national government,* few men anywhere opposed *the idea of a nation.* While men like George Clinton, Patrick Henry, and Richard Henry Lee were ready to be Americans, they were not ready to submit to the commands of an American government, which could not, they were convinced, extend its sway over half a continent without destroying the states and turning away from republican principles. It was up to men like Washington, Madison, and James Wilson to persuade those who thought like Clinton, Henry, and Lee that such a government, if prudently constructed out of the soundest materials, would respect and indeed confirm the existence and legitimate interests of the states and would be a support rather than a menace to American republicanism. Although handicapped in many ways in the battles of rhetoric and political maneuver with the fearful republicans, the nationalists had one advantage that, in the long run and therefore in the end, would prove decisive: they knew, as did many of their opponents, that the prescriptive course of nation-building in America had run beyond the capacity of the Articles of Confederation to serve national needs. By 1787, . . . the constitutional lag had become too exaggerated for men like Washington and Madison to bear patiently.

Whether possibly or probably or actually a nation, the United States of 1787, like the United States of every year of its existence, was a society trying to have the best of the two worlds of unity and diversity. Common forces and principles worked powerfully to hold it together; a jumbled array of antagonisms tended just as powerfully to pull it apart. Although the Framers of the Constitution would never even have assembled at Philadelphia if the elements of a "more perfect Union" had not existed in abundance, they were well aware of the countervailing elements of disruption in the society they had come to rescue from the defects of its virtues.

To James Madison, in particular, as the keenest student then living of the causes and consequences of "faction," the crosscutting tensions of American society were a source of wonder and worry. Everywhere one looked the lines of suspicion were drawn: between states and nation, and between one state and its neighbors; between New England and the Middle States, between North and South, and between one part of the South and the other; between over-represented seaboard, under-represented piedmont, and unrepresented frontier; between city, village, and countryside; between merchant, farmer, and artisan, and between the successful and less successful in each calling; between rich, substantial, struggling, and poor; between the holders of various kinds and amounts of property, and between all those who held property and all those who did not; between better sort, middling sort, and meaner sort, between all white men and all Negroes, and between free Negroes and slaves; between one kind of Protestant and another, and between all Protestants and the rest; between zealous Revolutionists, reluctant Revolutionists, indifferents, and former loyalists; between, I repeat, the involved and the isolated; and, wherever Madison and his friends were finally able to force the issue, between those who wanted a new government and those who preferred to drift indefinitely with the old one. How to prevent these lines of suspicion from hardening into lines of battle, how to convince all these private interests of the necessary existence of a public interest, how to reinforce politically all the elements in the emerging American consensus—these were the principal tasks of statemanship ordained by the twin facts of unity and diversity in the new Republic.

The United States in 1787 was a society in which the means for accomplishing these tasks were abundant if not prodigal. Let us go. . . to the three "large aspects" of the Philadelphia Convention. . . . The Convention is a classic case-study in the political process of constitutional democracy because the Republic abounded in public skills, because it was full of capable men who had had years of experience in issue-posing, information-gathering, interest-adjusting, and decision-making. It is a classic case-study in nation-making because the Republic had already

moved so far toward nationhood in its institutions and emotions. And it is a classic case-study in the attempt of men to take control of their own destiny because the emerging nation was, or at least appeared to be, the product of a conscious effort to lay a hand on history.

If we will put these three realities together and view them as one massive fact, the fact was the existence throughout the new Republic of an extraordinary political elite, most members of which, having already made their share of history, had a mind to make a little more before going to rest. The fifty-five men who got to Philadelphia and the hundreds who were ready to support them throughout the thirteen states were, in a more than symbolic sense, the United States in 1787. (pp. 23-40)

> *Clinton Rossiter, "The United States in 1787,"
> in his* 1787: The Grand Convention, *The Macmillan Company, 1966, pp. 23-40.*

PHILOSOPHY AND POLITICS

Dumas Malone

[*Malone is an historian and author of the notable biography* Jefferson and His Time *(1948). In the following essay, Malone examines the political philosophy of Jefferson's pamphlet* A Summary of the Rights of British America *(1774), contending that his conception of a union of self-governing colonies with loose connections to England was both idealistic and radical.*]

Jefferson's chief literary contribution to the patriotic cause before the Declaration of Independence was made in the summer of 1774, somewhat by accident and under circumstances that were disappointing to him at the time. For quite different reasons the situation was discouraging to Lord Dunmore. Having dissolved one Assembly because of the solemn mischief which Jefferson and his little group of zealots had started, the Governor hopefully ordered the election of another one. He soon learned, however, that he was going to be confronted with the same determined faces, and hastened to prorogue the new body before all the returns were in. He did not permit the Assembly to convene, actually, until nearly a year had passed.

There was another meeting which he could not stop—a convention which was called for August in Williamsburg and consisted of the selfsame burgesses. He had no troops wherewith to disperse these resourceful gentlemen; they were unable to assemble officially with his consent but were quite able to do so unofficially without it. That is, most of them were; but unluckily Jefferson could not get there.

The freeholders of Albemarle, meeting in Charlottesville toward the end of July, 1774, conformed with the general pattern of procedure. They left their delegation exactly as it had been before by re-electing Jefferson and John Walker as their representatives. Also, they adopted resolutions which the former had drawn. He elaborated these ideas, expecting to present them to the convention, but after he had set out for Williamsburg he was stricken with dysentery on the hot road and forced to turn back. Besides being unheroic in itself, this necessary retreat occurred at a most unfortunate time, for the crisis had incited him to put his thoughts in order and had emboldened him to essay a more conspicuous public role.

Perhaps he would not have moved any faster toward a position of commanding leadership if he had continued his journey to the provincial capital. He might have received more votes for delegate to the general Congress in Philadelphia if he had been present at the convention, but the seven who were actually chosen would probably have been elected in any case. All the members of the delegation, which was headed inevitably by Peyton Randolph, were Jefferson's seniors in public life and better known than he; and they were generally regarded as "glowing patriots." George Washington stood third on the list, and Patrick Henry was fourth. Later in Virginia, Jefferson was described as the penman of the Revolution, as Washington was its sword and Henry its tongue; but no one of the three was pre-eminent as yet, and Jefferson least of all.

He foreshadowed his fame, however, by now appearing, not as a soldier or speaker, but as a writer. He had presented his ideas in the form of resolutions, which were to be moved as instructions to the Virginia delegates to Congress and then be embodied by Congress, he hoped, in an address to the King. Unable to be the bearer of his own paper, he sent it on in two copies, one of these he addressed to Peyton Randolph, whom he expected to preside, and the other to Patrick Henry. He never knew what happened to Henry's copy; probably that careless orator mislaid it somewhere. The other one was laid on the table for inspection and was read in the presence of a large number at Randolph's house, where it was applauded though not wholly approved. It was never acted on officially, but, without his knowledge, it was printed in Williamsburg as *A Summary View of the Rights of British America.* He did not supply the title and did not appear by name. Before the year was out it was reprinted in Philadelphia and appeared twice in England. This accidental pamphlet of twenty-three pages gained wider currency than any other writing of his that was published during the Revolution except the Declaration, and it clearly anticipated that more famous and more polished document. It contributed to his contemporary reputation, and until this day it has commanded the deeply respectful attention of historians.

Jefferson had not had time to perfect his paper and realized that there were inaccuracies in it. The pamphlet reveals very considerable learning and contains glowing sentences, but it is more noteworthy for boldness and fervor than for historical precision or literary grace. Written in the white heat of indignation against the coercive acts of the British government, the *Summary View* has a distinct place in the controversial literature of the period. But it was more than a tract for the times; it embodied a reasoned theory of imperial relations which, actually, was better adapted to a later era. As a contemporary indictment of British policy it bordered on recklessness, but it

was distinctive in its emphasis on philosophical fundamentals and its prophetic quality. When the circumstances of its writing are remembered, "a range of inquiry not then very frequent, and marching far beyond the politics of the day" will surely be granted it, as Edmund Randolph said [in the *Virginia Magazine* XLIII].

The intemperance of Jefferson's language would have made his resolutions unacceptable as the official statement of a responsible group desiring to accommodate a dispute, and he himself recognized that his paper was too strong for the Virginia convention. He was modest about it after his passions had cooled. When twice as old as when he wrote it he said: "If it had any merit, it was that of first taking our true ground, and that which was afterwards assumed and maintained" [*The Writings of Thomas Jefferson,* edited by Paul Leicester Ford, 1892-99]. One thing he meant by the expression "true ground" was the complete denial of the authority of Parliament over the colonies. Inseparable from his position was a theory of imperial organization which he afterwards claimed that he had held from the beginning of the controversy. This was that the relation between the colonies and the Mother Country was the same as that between Scotland and England from the accession of James I to the Act of Union, and between Hanover and England in his own time, "having the same executive chief but no other necessary political connection." In Virginia up to August, 1774, nobody but George Wythe had agreed with him in these matters, as he remembered. Edmund Randolph, also relying on memory, afterwards said that the principle of bowing to external taxation by Parliament, "as resulting from our migration, and a necessary dependence on the mother country," was generally conceded in Virginia until Jefferson shook it [Ford, I]. But ideas like his had occurred to some other American minds.

The logic of the situation was quite clear to Benjamin Franklin, for one, before Jefferson had even entered the House of Burgesses. As early as 1768 that sage observer had concluded that, in logic, there was really no middle ground between the power of Parliament to make all laws for the colonies and that of making none; and he had drawn an analogy between the colonies and Scotland that was practically identical with the one Jefferson afterwards employed. In earlier stages of the growing controversy, colonial opposition had unquestionably been directed against particular measures which could be termed unconstitutional; but the readiness of certain Americans to take the next step and repudiate Parliament altogether, while avowing loyalty to the King, had been observed by Lord North four years before Jefferson put himself definitely on record. Jefferson's concept was essentially that of "imperial partnership" or a "commonwealth of nations," and he was one of the Americans who anticipated the British empire of self-governing states, even if he was not the only one.

Undoubtedly, he put himself in the vanguard of the Patriots in Virginia and in the colonies as a whole by publicly advocating the repudiation of Parliament at this juncture. Events were moving rapidly and ideas were crystallizing with them, but not even at the Continental Congress, which met in the early fall, was it possible to go as far as he desired. Congress then claimed for the provincial assemblies the exclusive power of legislation in all matters of taxation and internal policy, subject only to the negative of the King, but they cheerfully consented to the operation of parliamentary acts that were limited to the regulation of external commerce. Throughout his paper Jefferson's emphasis was on what Parliament could *not* do. He minimized necessary concessions and practical limitations, and proclaimed colonial "rights" in a sweeping and dogmatic way. "The young ascended with Mr. Jefferson to the source of those rights," said a later commentator [Randolph]; "the old required time for consideration, before they could tread this lofty ground, which, if it had not been abandoned, at least had not been fully occupied throughout America."

At the moment it did not seem the part of political wisdom to assume such a lofty position, and Jefferson would have been lonely in it if the controversy with the Mother Country had been soon resolved. By attempting to ascend to the source of authority in a time of crisis he laid himself open to the charge of being an impractical theorist. Nevertheless, he located ultimate authority in precisely the same place that he did two years later when he was drafting a much more important document. Fortunately for him, general opinion had caught up with him by then. Or, to be more precise, the uncompromising Patriots were then in control of Congress, and they were ready to square action with theory.

Jefferson gave no general statement of the doctrine of natural rights in his *Summary View,* but he based his whole argument on it. Even on practical grounds he might have come to the same conclusion about Parliament. He might have contented himself with saying that the British Americans had once been essentially self-governing, and that because of their present stature and circumstances they *ought* to be. But he grounded his argument on the nature of things—as they were in the beginning and evermore should be. His presuppositions may be questioned, and there were flaws in his historical presentation, but morally his case was strong.

He took the position that originally, in England, the ancestors of these British Americans had been free, just as their more remote Saxon forefathers had been in their native wilds; and that they had a natural right to emigrate and establish laws and regulations of their own, just as the Saxons did. His cousin Richard Bland had said much the same thing a decade earlier. In his own studies, however, Jefferson had given particular attention to the Saxons, especially in connection with land tenure, and he believed that they exemplified English liberty in its purest form. The important consideration is not that he idealized them, though he did; it is that his mind craved historical as well as philosophical authority, and that he could not be content without finding precedent somewhere for the freedom he was so sure was right.

He also followed Bland in asserting dogmatically that the conquest and settlement of the American wilds had been made wholly at the expense of individual colonists: "for themselves they fought, for themselves they conquered,

and for themselves alone they have right to hold" [Ford, I]. No aid from the British treasury was given them until after they had become valuable for commercial purposes, he said. In his opinion, this later help gave no title to the authority of Parliament; it was wholly a commercial matter and could be repaid by trade privileges. He greatly overstated the case for the individual settlers, who could not have survived without British protection prior to the time that he himself became grown. But he was not writing history; he was trying to play a part in making it by passionately pleading what seemed to him a sacred cause.

These settlers, having emigrated by right and established themselves by their own exertions, "thought proper to adopt that system of laws under which they had hitherto lived in the mother country, and to continue their union with her by submitting themselves to the same common Sovereign, who was thereby made the central link connecting the several parts of the empire thus newly multiplied" [Ford, I]. He claimed that there was a compact between the colonists and the King which was embodied, partly at least, in the early charters. He by no means regarded these charters as royal gifts; on the contrary, he emphasized the restrictions that they imposed on royal power. For example, he perceived tyranny in the Stuart practice of parceling out lands to favorites and in erecting new governments. To his mind, this family of princes had no more right to dismember the province of Virginia when once established by charter than they had to divide England itself. The Stuarts had met their deserved reward, however, and he found more pertinent examples of arbitrary power in later acts of Parliament.

By the time that he drafted this paper Jefferson had arrived at a conclusion which would have caused any English mercantilist to raise his eyebrows; namely, that the exercise of free trade with all parts of the world was a natural right of the colonists. No law of their own had taken away or abridged this right. Indeed, he found confirmation of it in the "solemn treaty" of March 12, 1651, between the Commonwealth and the House of Burgesses. Some of the later acts for the regulation of commerce seemed to him indefensible on practical grounds, but his most important assertion was this: "The true ground on which we declare these acts void is, that the British parliament has no right to exercise its authority over us" [Ford, I].

His historical arguments were one-sided, and in the scholar's sense they are no more than half-truths. His grounds were not historical after all; they were moral. He lived in an age when philosophers as well as statesmen quoted history for their purposes; and it is from his purposes, primarily, that he must be judged. These were clear and, as human hearts go, they were pure. His chief aim was to overthrow parliamentary authority which had been unwise in practice and was wrong in principle, and at the same time to safeguard self-government.

Like other patriotic pamphleteers he was most disturbed, not by restrictions on trade, but by parliamentary meddling with the internal affairs of the colonies. Violations of right were less alarming during the reigns immediately before that of George III, he said, "because repeated at more distant intervals than that rapid and bold succession of injuries which is likely to distinguish the present from all other periods of American story." He continued:

> Scarcely have our minds been able to emerge from the astonishment into which one stroke of parliamentary thunder had involved us, before another more heavy, and more alarming, is fallen on us. Single acts of tyranny may be ascribed to the accidental opinion of a day; but a series of oppressions, begun at a distinguished period, and pursued, unalterably through every change of ministers, too plainly prove a deliberate and systematical plan of reducing us to slavery. [Ford, I]

He used strikingly similar language two years later, then laying the onus not on Parliament but on the King and thus becoming an open secessionist.

He cited the specific acts prior to 1774 which formed a "connected chain of parliamentary usurpation," speaking at considerable length and with great emotion about the suspension of the legislature of New York which had occurred even before he became a burgess. "One free and independent legislature hereby takes upon itself to suspend the powers of another, free and independent as itself; this exhibiting a phenomenon unknown in nature," he said [Ford, I]. The measures against Boston, which had precipitated the present conflict and provided the occasion for his own pamphlet, he regarded as "acts of power, assumed by a body of men, foreign to our constitutions, and unacknowledged by our laws" [Ford, I]. He admitted that the actions of the exasperated participants in the Boston Tea Party were not strictly regular, that these men did wrong in destroying the "obnoxious commodity," and that they were properly amenable to the laws of the land, that is, to the laws of Massachusetts Bay. But the coercive acts of Parliament which followed this famous event were wholly intolerable to him. He entered solemn and determined protest against them, addressing this to the King, "as yet the only mediatory power between the several states of the British empire." At the same time he boldly pointed out the King's own deviations from the line of duty.

Several of these charges reappeared in his draft of the Declaration of Independence, and one of them was too strong for the stomachs of the patriots even when they were ready to renounce allegiance to the King. Jefferson erred on the side of optimism when he asserted in his *Summary View* that the abolition of domestic slavery was the great object of desire in the colonies. Speaking for Virginia, he was correct in saying that previous attempts to prevent importations of slaves from Africa had been defeated by the royal negative. No doubt he caused his more temperate colleagues to shake their heads, however, when he termed this a shameful abuse of royal power, which showed that His Majesty preferred the immediate advantage of a few British corsairs to "the lasting interests of the American states, and to the rights of human nature" [Ford, I].

He really need not have bothered to address the King at this time, for his language was so unconciliatory as to doom his appeal to failure. One of his more positive proposals would have aroused the fears of the English Whigs

immediately, if they had been disposed to pay any attention to this rash young man. He suggested that the King resume the exercise of his negative upon parliamentary legislation, in order to prevent the passage of laws injurious to other parts of the empire. This was one way of saying that the colonies had just the same rights as England, and he hedged the King about with restrictions, but it would have seemed to many that he was advocating an increase of royal power. He said that fortune had placed the King in a post where he held the balance in an empire; and that this empire would be great if it were well-poised. The latter reflection was prophetic.

More important than his specific appeal to the King was the philosophy which underlay it. This left no place for royal tyranny, or for tyranny of any sort. He regarded himself as the spokesman of a free people who had derived their rights from God and the laws. "Let those flatter who fear," he said, "it is not an American art. To give praise which is not due . . . would ill beseem those who are asserting the rights of human nature. They know, and will therefore say, that kings are the servants, not the proprietors of the people. Open your breast, sire, to liberal and expanded thought. Let not the name of George the third be a blot in the page of history" [Ford, I]. He revealed his own moral emphasis but underrated the practical difficulties when he said: "The whole art of government consists in the art of being honest." It is doubtful if his chiding admonition ever reached the royal ear, but some of his own countrymen remembered that he had subordinated the King himself to natural law and had boldly charged him with specific offenses, and within two years they gave him opportunity to base on this philosophy a convincing justification of revolution.

He talked little of colonial concessions, but at the moment he claimed that he did not seek independence of the Mother Country:

> . . . It is neither our wish nor our interest to separate from her. We are willing, on our part, to sacrifice everything which reason can ask to the restoration of that tranquillity for which all must wish. On their part, let them be ready to establish union on a generous plan. Let them name their terms, but let them be just. Accept of every commercial preference it is in our power to give for such things as we can raise for their use, or they make for ours. But let them not think to exclude us from going to other markets to dispose of those commodities which they cannot use, or to supply those wants which they cannot supply. Still less let it be proposed that our properties within our own territories shall be taxed or regulated by any power on earth but our own.

Then he uttered a saying which of itself entitles this bold pamphlet to immortality. It belongs, not to the American colonies, but to mankind; not to the year 1774 merely, but to all the years thereafter.

> . . . The God who gave us life gave us liberty at the same time; the hand of force may destroy, but cannot disjoin them.

From the beginnings of his conspicuous public career the

blessings of liberty were much dearer to Jefferson than those of empire. He may be properly charged with failure to appreciate the practical problems which the generally incompetent British officials of his time were facing, and with insistence upon a degree of local self-rule which not even the English friends of American liberties could have been expected to concede in theory. The sort of empire he advocated, and the only sort he would have been content with, was one composed of self-governing units, bound together only by mutual benefits. In recognizing the King as the formal tie he had no thought of substituting an omnipotent monarch for an omnipotent Parliament. To his mind, ultimate authority lay in the laws of nature and the human beings whom God had made free; day-to-day authority lay in the various local legislatures, those of America and England itself. The King was the mediator but he was subject to natural law. The ability of such a loose-jointed empire to survive any serious crisis might have been gravely doubted on both sides of the Atlantic.

Never in his life did Jefferson value political organization or governmental power for their own sakes; his major concern was for the ends they served. The net result might have been much the same if the legislative authority of Parliament in external matters had been conceded by the colonists, and that body in turn had sharply restricted itself in practice. Even if the alternative had been clearly presented, however, Jefferson would have thought that this would be to start at the wrong end. He placed his faith supremely in individuals and in local units of a manageable size, and he believed that the power to grant necessary practical concessions should be left with them.

There is no evidence that this pamphlet led to the threat of the author's proscription in England, as he believed, or that it was utilized by the opponents of the ministry. If it had any immediate effect there it was to play into the hands of the ministry, who were seeking to justify their repressive policy by claiming that the Americans were going to extremes. It was no service to the opposition for Jefferson to press his theoretical claims, and he had definitely parted company with the handful of English leaders who were still championing colonial liberties. Edmund Burke had a liberal concept of empire and regarded the American love of freedom as an inescapable fact, but that eminent conciliator begged the philosophical question and sought a solution based on common sense. He avoided a "refined policy," eschewed abstract ideas of right, and in this crisis regarded the resort to "mere general theories of government" as "arrant trifling" [*Parliamentary History,* XVIII, March 22, 1775]. Jefferson's line of argument would not have appealed to him. And certainly the young Virginian did not at this time see eye to eye with Chatham, though in many ways he admired him, for that great imperialist viewed the distinction between external and internal control as sacred. He conceded to the colonies the right of taxation, but the supreme power of Parliament to regulate commerce he would yield to the insistence of no man. [Jan. 20, 1775, *Parliamentary History,* XVIII]

Jefferson's first important political paper caused him to appear as a champion of freedom and self-government who would yield little or nothing to the exigencies of the moment. That is, he would yield practically nothing to the far-distant Mother Country. To his brethren on the American continent, on the other hand, he was quite prepared to make concessions. Individual rights and local self-government came first in his thinking, but he fully realized the necessity for concerted action on a continental scale and had a clear vision of colonial union. In this sphere he was no impractical theorist, nor merely a long-range prophet, but a realistic statesman.

He had played an important part in the creation of the Virginia Committee of Correspondence, and at successive stages of the imperial controversy he had consistently made common cause with the Patriots of other provinces. It would be improper to employ the term "nationalist" this early, but he was a strong unionist from the start. No saying of his is as vivid as Patrick Henry's at the first Continental Congress: "I am not a Virginian, but an American." Neither he nor the fervid orator had any real thought of ceasing to be a Virginian. But if his interests were not imperial they were far more than provincial; they had assumed a continental scope.

In the year 1774 he gave a sign of this which could not have been expected from Patrick Henry. Not long after the adjournment of the Virginia convention, he received from another province a printed proposal for a complete collection of American state papers. The man who sent it, Ebenezer Hazard, then living in New York, became a pioneer editor of historical records; while the patriotic gentleman who received it in Albemarle County afterwards performed distinctive service as a collector of Americana. The episode was prophetic. Jefferson proceeded to get an impressive list of subscribers from his friends and neighbors and left Hazard in no possible doubt of his enthusiastic patronage.

These actions had to do with the past—with "curious monuments of the infancy of our country," as he afterwards described them. They illustrate at this early date the lifelong Americanism which accompanied his loyalty to Virginia and which, to his mind, conflicted with it in no way. Of more immediate importance, as reflecting his unionism, was a private comment which he made on the limited sovereignty of the Continental Congress. A score of years later, when he sought to limit the centralizing tendencies which Alexander Hamilton personified, his undiscriminating political foes might have found this early observation of his surprising.

> We are to conform to such resolutions only of the Congress as our deputies assent to: which totally destroys that union of conduct in the several colonies which was the very purpose of calling a Congress. [Ford, I]

This illuminating comment on the dangerous limitations of congressional power was coupled with others of a critical nature on the Association which Congress adopted in October. He did not wholly approve of that famous nonimportation, nonconsumption agreement—not because it went too far, though he disliked certain of its details, but because it did not go far enough. He duly signed his printed copy, notwithstanding, and he had others attach their names to it. Among these were his young brother Randolph, who was now nineteen, his brother-in-law Francis Eppes, and his violin teacher Francis Alberti.

He intended to be "a conscientious observer of the measures generally thought requisite for a preservation of our independent rights," he said; and he was much embarrassed in December by one of his own orders which turned out to be in violation of them. The restrictions came at an unfortunate time for him, since he was engaged in building operations. Some months earlier he had ordered for use at Monticello fourteen pairs of sash windows, and these were now *en route* despite his countermand. He fully expected his glazed windows to be condemned when they reached the Virginia shore, however, and he acquiesced in this infringement on his liberty as an individual.

He bowed to virtual necessity beyond a doubt, for in Virginia the provisions for the enforcement of the Association were rigorously carried out. Congress had enjoined that every county, town, and city should choose a committee to observe the conduct of all persons respecting the agreement, to publish the names of offenders, and thus to cause the "enemies of American liberty" to be condemned and outlawed [*Journals of the Continental Congress,* I]. This was high-handed action which a theoretical advocate of personal freedom might have been expected to condemn. But there is no indication that Jefferson questioned its essential wisdom, and there is evidence that he played a patriotic part in carrying the restrictions into effect. The Albemarle committee was not among the first to be elected; the earliest work of organization in Virginia was done in the eastern counties. When a committee was selected, however, his name was the first upon the list, followed by that of his friend and fellow burgess John Walker. In late 1774 and early 1775, he was not only the first citizen of his County but its first Patriot as well. Meanwhile, in the neighboring County of Orange, young James Madison had been elected as a member of a similar committee, and service on it constituted his introduction to public life.

No less a person than Lord Dunmore [in a letter to Dartmouth, Dec. 24, 1774] is authority for the statement that the county committees now constituted virtually the only government in the Province. "There is not a Justice of the Peace in Virginia that acts, except as a committee-man," he said [given at Dartmouth, Dec. 24, 1774, and printed in the Dixon and Hunter, *Virginia Gazette*]. Thus he testified to the suspension of the county courts, as he also did to the great unwillingness of lawyers to attend the General Court, which was now largely restricted to criminal cases. This was what Jefferson meant when he said that the Revolution shut up the courts of justice and ended his own career as a practising lawyer. The last case that he listed in his formal record was dated Nov. 9, 1774, and was numbered 939. This referred only to an opinion on a will, anyway; so to all practical purposes his legal career ended before that. He turned over his unfinished cases to young Edmund Randolph, son of the Attorney General, apparently expecting to abandon practice for good. He would have been fully warranted in doing so even if times had been more peaceful, for the Wayles inheritance had greatly increased his burdens as a man of business, while relieving him of any need to supplement his income.

There is no reason to suppose, however, that he welcomed the closing of the courts in order to escape his own debts to British merchants, as Dunmore and some of his partisans asserted that many of the planters did. He had provided for his debts, or so at least he thought. Nor did he have the desire or occasion to apply tar and feathers as a local committeeman. There was little violence or disorder among these people who were so accustomed to self-government.

In the middle of March, 1775, Jefferson set out for Richmond to attend a provincial convention as the first delegate from his County. He had no reason whatever to suppose that his appeal to the King, or any other, had been heeded. His knowledge of occurrences in England was at least two months behind the events themselves; but, by the month of February, he could have read in the *Virginia Gazette* a speech of George III at the opening of Parliament and the addresses of the Lords and Commons which strongly supported it. He undoubtedly knew that the opposition to the policy of coercion had been ruthlessly beaten down. The King had complained bitterly of "violences of a very criminal nature" in Massachusetts and of "unwarrantable attempts" to obstruct commerce, and had assured Parliament of his determination to withstand every attempt to weaken or impair its "supreme authority." Such attitudes were irreconcilable with the views Jefferson had expressed, and thus he must have reflected as he took the Richmond road.

Before the convention assembled, however, a later item appeared in the *Virginia Gazette.* This reported that the petition of Congress to the King had been received in London the day before Christmas and had been duly communicated to Lord Dartmouth. The petition led to no change in policy but the Virginians did not know that yet. Some of them seized upon what appeared to be a fresh hope of conciliation, as Patrick Henry and Thomas Jefferson soon found out.

The Virginia convention of March, 1775, amounted to a meeting of the burgesses without the authorization of the Governor, and it was held at a place where they were wholly free from his control. Richmond was a central point, though by no means a city, and the sessions were held in the structure known to history as Old Saint John's Church. It was a simple white building, and its atmosphere befitted the solemnity of the occasion. Here Patrick Henry uttered his most famous words: "Give me liberty, or give me death." The clash of resounding arms had not yet been heard at Lexington and Concord, but he believed war inevitable unless the colonists should become abject. He said, "let it come." So far as is known, Jefferson did not say that, but he strongly supported Henry's resolutions, even going so far as to make a speech.

The just fame of Patrick Henry as a Revolutionary statesman is attributable to his insistence upon decisive action in successive crises. No one else did so much as he to give impetus to the ball of Revolution in the Province. Jefferson said that several times but, unlike Henry's biographers, he did not magnify the importance of this particular occasion; he did not regard it as the beginning of the Revolution. Henry's audacity in urging defense measures at this time, and Jefferson's in backing him, should not be exaggerated. There had already been considerable military preparation in Virginia and the citizens generally were in a resolute state of mind. Three months before this, Lord Dunmore had reported that independent companies of militia were being formed in the counties—to protect the committees, he said. Dissatisfied with the colorless resolutions which had been presented to the convention, Henry introduced more vigorous ones. He moved that steps be taken by the Colony as a whole and that a committee be chosen to prepare a plan for embodying, arming, and disciplining a sufficient number of men. Since such action gave promise of greater unity and effectiveness it was naturally favored by a realist like George Washington. The support of this man of solid worth was invaluable but he was characteristically silent. The more philosophical Jefferson was not. "He argued closely, profoundly and warmly" on the side of the redoubtable Patrick Henry and eloquent Richard Henry Lee (otherwise designated as Demosthenes and Cicero), his post in the debate being "that at which the theories of republicanism were deposited" [Edmund Randolph, in *Virginia Magazine,* XLIII]. They managed to carry the resolutions—but the vote was dangerously close.

The opposing "conservatives" could hardly have been against arming the Colony at a time when the citizens were already arming themselves; and most if not all of these delegates were active in connection with the county committees. Ostensibly, they objected to the timing of the action. Men like Robert Carter Nicholas, Edmund Pendleton, Benjamin Harrison, and Richard Bland still had hopes of conciliation and clung to the properties. Beneath the surface of the resolutions, furthermore, they suspected deeper designs on the part of Henry. Apparently he purposed that the committee should assume the full powers of government, many of which had already slipped from the Governor's hands. However, his scheme was scotched, and thus it came about that this was not a revolutionary gathering, after all.

Jefferson was a member of the committee of twelve that was set up to prepare a plan for the militia, though his name was next to the last while Henry's was first. The plan which was adopted was innocuous enough. In general the convention regularized and provided for the enlargement of the county organizations which had already sprung up independently. More picturesquely, it recognized the tomahawk as standard equipment along with the rifle, and prescribed as uniform the hunting shirt. The militiamen were already good shots, and some of them afterwards printed "Liberty or Death" on their hunting shirts, but they did not become an effective military body under centralized control because an orator made an immortal speech.

Jefferson may have wanted the Patriots to assume the full form of governmental authority at this time, since they had already assumed so much of the substance. Yet, despite his radicalism on the imperial question and the uncompromising spirit he had manifested in his pamphlet of the previous summer, the presumption is that he did not. His later silence about the meeting suggests that there was

something about it that he did not like; and, even if he had favored taking this revolutionary step in advance of actual bloodshed, he was willing to modify his natural pace in the interest of unity.

A motion of his own in the convention reveals his continuing concern for unity in the colonies. This merely called upon the Committee of Correspondence to inquire about the state of sentiment in the Province of New York, where, as the newspapers reported, there had been a defection of the House of Representatives from the Association. It is the language not the substance of Jefferson's resolution that is significant. To his mind, a defection from the compact of Association was an atrocious perfidy, a desertion of "the Union with the other American Colonies formed in General congress for the preservation of their just rights." He was unwilling to condemn the New Yorkers on the basis of hearsay, but he left no possible doubt of his own determination that the Union should be preserved.

One late action at this meeting turned out to be important to him, personally. The convention re-elected its delegation to Congress, leaving Peyton Randolph at its head. Next after the perennial presiding officer came Washington and Henry, but until the last day of the session the name of Jefferson was still absent from the list. Then he was appointed a deputy to serve in case of Randolph's nonattendance. If he had cared to be mathematical, he might have regarded himself as one of the first eight or ten leaders of Virginia. Despite his abilities and zeal he could hardly have expected to stand higher than that as yet, for he was only thirty-two. He went to Philadelphia in the summer after Peyton Randolph was called home, and by that time the appeal to reason had given place to the appeal to arms. (pp. 180-96)

Dumas Malone, "Championing Colonial Rights: 1774-75," in his Jefferson, the Virginian, *Little, Brown and Company, 1948, pp. 180-96.*

Lawrence H. Leder

[*In the essay below, Leder examines the changing philosophy of colonial American government, contending that during the eighteenth century, colonial statesmen moved away from a religious view of government as an extension of the God's will towards a secular concept which held government responsible to the people.*]

Basic to an understanding of the theory of government is man's view of what existed before the creation of society. Upon this foundation rest his ideas as to why government was established and as to what, consequently, its nature, purpose, and function should be. In eighteenth-century America two main ideas, two basic approaches, contended with each other. Thomas Hobbes's views reflected the ideas of the English Civil War era, while John Locke's concepts codified English thought at the time of the Glorious Revolution a generation later.

Hobbes offered a pessimistic view of man's condition in the state of nature, which he considered to have a philosophical rather than an historical existence. This distinction allowed him to argue that the social contract was an arrangement between subject and subject rather than subject and ruler. Such reasoning readily led to a concept of the state in which the subject is powerless and can exert no control over his destiny. In simple terms, Hobbes advocated unlimited obedience to the sovereign.

Locke, on the other hand, took a more optimistic view of man in a state of nature which to him had been a real, not imaginary, period of existence. At that time man lived under rules and regulations, not jungle-like conditions, and that framework was the law of nature. This seemingly idyllic condition was abandoned for society and government, which he viewed as two separate entities, because each person was unable to avail himself of the full protection of natural law for his person and property. Society and government thus came into being as supplements to rather than replacements for natural law or right reason, and therefore they must abide by it. When they depart from natural law, they collapse. The Lockean interpretation of the state of nature includes of necessity the right of revolution whenever government fails to fulfill the function for which it was created—an unsettling thought which Thomas Hobbes would have rejected.

With both ideas in circulation in eighteenth-century America, it is somewhat surprising at first glance that few adhered to the more pessimistic Hobbes thesis. But an examination of the Americans' experience leads one quickly to the conclusion that Locke's appeal was bound to be greater. The Americans had entered a new world with no guidelines but those of their own past experience. They set up governments in the wilderness, but they certainly believed they established them on "right reason." There was little in what they were doing to suggest that they were living through the Hobbesian jungle. Moreover, in the garrison century from 1603 to 1689 they had been forced to adjust and modify government according to their immediate local needs, without waiting for directions from the Crown and often in contradiction to Crown policy. Thus the ideas expressed by Locke were indeed meaningful; they were a rationalization of the Americans' own experience.

Few writers in eighteenth-century America gave more than cursory attention to the theories of Hobbes. His view of the state of nature was described by the redoubtable Cotton Mather as this "detestable Hobbianism" according to which "men are as the fishes of the sea, to one another; where the greater still devour the lesser" [*Lex Mercatoria: or, The Just Rules of Commerce Declared,* 1705]. Although Mather rejected his ideas outright, Hobbes did have a few advocates. The Reverend Samuel Cheever warned that government was God's ordinance "that men might not live as beasts. . . . Licentious nature doth not love to be controlled, and would have no lord over it; but sound reason will tell every man that there is no living where every man may do what he will without control" [*God's Sovereign Government Among the Nations,* 1712]. When Archibald Cummings delivered the funeral sermon for Lieutenant Governor Patrick Gordon of Pennsylvania, he warned the quarrelsome inhabitants of the colony that without government men would turn "into beasts of prey"

because they would be freed of all legal restraints. This denied Locke's basic point that the law of nature antedated government's establishment. Later, in 1755, the Reverend Moses Dickinson returned to the same theme when he declared that men were mutually dependent upon one another, and that without the restraints of civil society "we should be in a state of confusion; like an herd of wild beasts; the strongest, and most mischievous, would domineer over and oppress others. There would be no peace, to him that should go out, or to him that should come in; our lives, and properties . . . would . . . depend upon the ungoverned lusts of the sons of fraud and violence. . . . To suppose (as some have done) that mankind were ever in such a mere state of nature as to have no laws, no regulations, no sort of government, is to suppose a contradiction; for such a wild and savage state could not with any propriety be called a state of nature; for it would be a very unnatural state" [*A Sermon Preached Before the General Assembly of the Colony of Connecticut,* 1755].

These were not the views of the majority of those Americans who expressed themselves in print. The Lockean concepts dominated men's imaginations from the beginning and soon became a crescendo overwhelming the ideas of Cheever, Cummings, and Dickinson. One cannot even claim that Hobbes's theory was advocated by any particular group or class in American society because, even though a few Congregationalist clergymen embraced Hobbesian concepts, most spokesmen for this denomination stood at the very forefront of Lockean ideas, not only advocating them but refining and making them more precisely applicable to the American scene.

Perhaps the first Congregational minister to declaim the ideas of John Locke was Thomas Maule. "In the beginning," he wrote in 1712, "when men grew numerous they contracted themselves into societies, for preservation of concord and good discipline, and began to think on foundations to set their structures upon. . . . First, the civil society united that they might live safely and enjoy their liberties without opposition" [*Tribute to Caesar, How Paid by the Best Christians,* 1712?]. His concern was with the separation of civil and ecclesiastical societies, but his use of the word "preservation" implies acceptance of the Lockean approach. When men multiplied to the point that conflict became inevitable and prior existing liberties were challenged, society came into being to facilitate man's enjoyment of what he already possessed.

This same theme was developed by the Reverend John Wise in greater detail five years later. Man in a state of "natural being," he observed in his famous *Vindication,* was a "freeborn subject under the crown of heaven, and owing homage to none but God himself." Man's "prime immunity" was that "he is most properly the subject of the law of nature. . . . Reason is cognate with his nature, wherein by a law immutable, stamped upon his frame, God has provided a rule for men in all their actions . . . which is nothing but the dictate of right reason founded in the soul of man. . . . That which is to be drawn from man's reason . . . when unperverted, may be said to be the law of nature. . . . When we acknowledge the law of nature to be the dictate of right reason, we must mean that the understanding of man is endowed with such a power as to be able from the contemplation of humane condition to discover a necessity of living agreeably with this law." These principles of natural law, Wise continued, could be discovered "by a narrow watch, and accurate contemplation of our natural condition, and propensions."

For John Wise, natural law contained three principles: self-love and self-preservation, sociable disposition, and an affection to mankind in general. While self-love and self-preservation were basic, man was often incapable of securing his safety and maintenance alone, and thus the need for the second principle—sociability. "Every man as far as in him lies, do maintain a sociableness with others, agreeable with the main end and disposition of humane nature in general" [*A Vindication of the Government of the New England Churches,* 1717]. The third principle emerged from the fact that man was not so wedded to self-interest that he was blinded to the advantages of the common good, and it is this which encouraged him to enter society.

Maule and Wise were theologically oriented commentators. A secular interpretation of the same problem came from John Webbe, who wrote a series of newspaper essays in 1736 under the pseudonym "Z." He began with the statement that men were born equal and subject to no superior. Thus when men relinquished liberty, they did so for "a more valuable consideration, as protection from injuries, security of property, mutual defense, etc."

To Webbe, Hobbes's idea that people confer all of their power permanently upon a ruler was merely a "specious pretext." If the state of nature "is a state of war, which implies a natural equality, I presume I have as much right to repel wrongs as another has to impose them. Yet, say the Hobbists, it is our interest to submit to be governed by the will of one man. I would feign ask . . . how they [rulers] came by such a social affection? Whence, all this tenderness for their fellow creatures? It cannot be hypocrisy, as they have openly declared themselves to be villains in grain. It must therefore proceed from a natural irresistible impulse" [*Pennsylvania Gazette,* April 8-15 and 15-22, 1736].

Still another secular explanation of Lockean theory appeared in the speech of Chief Justice Samuel Chew to the Newcastle County grand jury in 1741. Life and liberty, he stated, "were common to all men," and each had a natural title to their full enjoyment and a right to preserve and defend them. "If, indeed, all men, from the beginning, had acted up to the genuine law of nature, and had done what was perfectly right, all other provisions or laws would have been useless." But rapaciousness and corruption entered the world, and "it is more than probable that men in a state of nature . . . must have suffered much." Their desire for happiness and the instinct of self-preservation led them into compacts. The difference, Chew continued, between men in a state of nature and in political societies was the absence in the former of a common judge, with every man having the right to judge and punish for himself. Such judgments were based on "the law of reason, or . . . a rule for the doing what is fit and proper for rational creatures to do as they are capable of discovering by

the right use of the natural faculties, unassisted by supernatural revelation" [*The Speech of Samuel Chew, Esq., Chief Justice of the Government of New Castle, Kent, and Sussex Upon Delaware,* 1741].

The general enthusiasm for Lockean theory had to overcome certain criticisms of technical aspects of the state of nature. One of the serious ones was the lack of historical evidence of such a state. Hobbes had avoided this problem by posing his state of nature as a philosophical concept, but Locke had argued that it had actually existed in the beginning of all things. Jared Eliot, in his Hartford election sermon of 1738, answered those who criticized on this point. The fact that no records of such a state existed proved nothing, said Eliot, since government itself antedated record-keeping.

A further criticism of Locke was the anomaly of the status of children. It was all well and good to talk of man's liberty either in the state of nature or society, but who would insist upon the same liberty for a young child? These critics argued that if man was born into a state of nature, and if that situation was governed by natural law or right reason, and if man must use his rational faculties to control his situation, how then did one explain the subservient position of the child to his parent and the child's utter inability to use right reason?

This contrast between the theoretical equality of men and

Christ Church in Philadelphia, which numbered many colonial notables among its congregation.

the practical problem of parental rule was tackled by Elisha Williams in 1744. Children were "not born in this full state of equality, yet they are born to it," he announced. Parental jurisdiction was temporary until reason matured in the child. "When he comes to such a state of reason as made the father free, the same must make the son free too." Freedom was grounded on reason, and therefore it "is not a liberty for everyone to do what he pleases . . . but it consists in a freedom from any superior power on earth . . . and having only the law of nature (or in other words, of its maker) for his rule" [*The Essential Rights and Liberties of Protestants,* 1744].

Williams also expounded on the role of property in the state of nature. The earth was granted by God in common to all men, and since each man's principal property was his own person, the labor of his body is his own. When he "removes anything out of the state that nature has provided and left it in, he has mixed his labor with it and joined something to it that is his own, and thereby makes it his property." If each person had a right to his person, he had a right to the property created by his bodily efforts, and concomitantly the right to punish all insults to either. This led to the question of providing protection, and Williams then quoted Locke on the three factors lacking in the state of nature to render the individual and his property safe: an established law to distinguish right from wrong, an indifferent judge, and a power to execute sentence against wrongdoers. Reason, Williams believed, taught men to remedy these defects by uniting in society.

A panegyric in the Boston *Independent Advertiser* in 1749 reaffirmed this concept of the state of nature. "The perfection of liberty, therefore, in a state of nature, is for every man to be free from any external force and to perform such actions as in his own mind and conscience he judges to be rightest. . . . This is liberty in a state of nature; which as no man ought to be abridged of, so no man has a right to give up, or even to part with any portion of it, but in order to secure the rest and place it upon a more solid foundation. . . . And had mankind continued in that innocent and happy state . . . it is probable that this liberty would have been enjoyed in such perfection as to have rendered the embodying into civil society and the security of human laws altogether needless" [*Independent Advertiser,* April 10, 1749].

William Livingston, in one issue of his *Independent Reflector,* dwelt on the idea of the state of nature. "Men of true principles would rather return to a state of primitive freedom," he declared, "in which every man has a right to be his own carver, than be the slaves of the greatest monarch or even suffer under the most unlimited democracy in the universe. It is true that society is the most eligible state in which man can exist; nor can it also be denied that government is absolutely necessary for the happiness of society. But still, it will appear . . . to be the height of madness to purchase the advantages of society by giving up all our title to liberty. . . . Had man been wise from his creation, he would always have been free. We might have enjoyed the gifts of liberal nature unmolested, unrestrained."

Livingston's statement incorporated the Lockean assumption that the state of nature involved absolute equality. A sharp criticism appeared in 1753 in the *New York Mercury:* Livingston "must appear very absurd, and very far from acting rationally himself, when he would pawn upon his readers an old contract of very great importance to them, of which he produces no record, nor any footsteps, but from his own notions of absurdity, and suppositions that mankind in a state of nature must needs have acted rationally."

The same critic declared that mankind seemed to have been under some government from the very beginning of his existence, and that "no man was ever so independent as that he might do whatever was right in his own eyes. If Adam and Cain, the first of mankind, were accountable for their actions, when could any others claim the liberty of Mr. Reflector's state of nature and his original native power in man?" [*New York Mercury,* September 10 and 17, 1753]. Power emanated from God, and it was His will, without compacts, that was imposed on men from the beginning.

But such carping was swept aside by a flurry of support for the Lockean theory in the 1750's and early 1760's. "Rusticus" in Boston discussed the qualities of the state of nature by quoting Locke. "Plebeian" in the *Pennsylvania Journal,* followed by the "Watchman" in the same paper, reiterated similar interpretations. The Reverend Abraham Williams summed up the argument most effectively in his 1762 election sermon in Boston. Indeed, one can almost claim unanimity of viewpoint when he envisions a Congregational minister delivering an election sermon to the Massachusetts General Court and completely paraphrasing John Locke!

Although Americans in the eighteenth century seemed to agree upon their definition of the state of nature, their concept of the origin of government and its nature and purpose was much more controversial. They could and did acquiesce in the myth of man's original purity and his early apostasy, but the question of government itself hit close to home, and the colonists' reactions to it depended more immediately on their attitude toward local, everyday problems.

Perhaps the earliest discussion of the origin of government was in the Reverend Samuel Willard's 1694 election sermon. He chose for his topic "The Character of a Good Ruler." He acknowledged the controversy over the origin of government—whether it was a law of nature invoked as mankind increased in number, or a positive right introduced upon man's apostasy—and concluded that God, even in a state of nature, had ordained orders of superiority and inferiority, and since man's unhappy fall from grace, "necessity requires and the political happiness of a people is concerned in the establishment of civil government."

To Willard [in his *The Character of a Good Ruler,* 1694] the purpose of government was "to prevent and cure the disorders that are apt to break forth among the societies of men; and to promote the civil peace and prosperity of such a people, as well as to suppress impiety and to nourish religion." Civil rulers, he continued, "are God's

Viceregents here upon earth; hence they are sometimes honored with the title of Gods. . . . Government is God's ordinance; and those that are vested with it, however mediately introduced into it, have their rightful authority from Him." Willard's absolutist notion of government was later weakened when he admitted that "people are not made for rulers, but rulers for a people. It is indeed an honor which God puts upon some above others . . . but it is for the people's sake. . . . And, however they are seated in authority by men, yet God, who rules over all, hath put them in only *Durante Bene Placito*. . . . They are stewards, and whensoever God pleaseth, He will call for a reckoning and put them out." Civil authority was not given to certain persons or families by natural right, nor did God determine the form of government. Sometimes He pointed to persons or families, sometimes He "judicially delivers a people up to the will of their enemies," and sometimes He permitted a voluntary arrangement by the free consent of the people. But regardless of the method, His hand was always evident.

The ultimate consequence of this God-oriented political philosophy was simply expressed by the Reverend Ebenezer Pemberton in 1710: "Rebellion and disobedience against God's Viceregents in the lawful execution of their office is rebellion against God himself" [*The Divine Original of Government Asserted*, 1710]. But this left several important questions unanswered. How did one determine whom God had chosen? How did one know whether the ruler was following God's dictates or his own? What marked off the bounds of "lawful execution"? If the answer to these questions was the ruler himself, then the circle was complete, and so was the absolutism. If the answer was the clergy, the circle had simply been enlarged slightly, and the concept had progressed from autocracy to theocracy.

As long as the Congregational clergy of New England remained the most vocal exponents of political thought, the idea that government was God's blessing to mankind remained dominant. The first significant dissent came from Thomas Maule in 1712, who said that when men "grew numerous they contracted themselves into societies. . . . First, the civil society united, that they might live safely and enjoy their liberty without opposition, and [then] they were united into churches to live religiously" [*Tribute to Caesar*, 1712]. But the more traditional theme was restated by John Woodward's Hartford election sermon in the same year. Civil rulers, he announced, were "ministers of the great God, to whom obedience is undoubtedly due." He acknowledged that all forms of government were not divinely ordained, but power itself was. This was seconded by the Boston election sermon of Samuel Cheever that same year.

The first major break in the united approach of the Congregational ministers came with the Hartford election sermon of the Reverend Joseph Moss in 1715. "All just government, whether it be monarchy or popular, or a mixture of both, or of any differing form, is originally founded in either compact or conquest." If created by compact, the authority of government was limited. "None can make a just claim to any natural original right to rule over

others . . . so mankind never did nor will submit themselves voluntarily to the government of others their fellowmen, but upon some agreement of what rules the ruler or rulers should observe" [*An Election Sermon Preached Before the General Assembly of the Colony of Connecticut*, 1715]. For the first time, new answers had been offered to some of the basic questions.

Moss' position was non-absolutist, and another theologian—the Reverend John Wise in 1717—adopted a similar stance. "The formal reason of government is the will of a community, yielded up and surrendered to some other subject." The method used to accomplish this came straight from Locke: first, men covenanted with one another to join in society; next, a government was established by the majority; and, finally, a new covenant was created between the society and the rulers. Wise's definition of a civil government was simply: "a compound moral person, whose will (united by those covenants before passed) is the will of all; to the end it may use and apply the strength and riches of private persons towards maintaining the common peace, security, and well-being of all" [*A Vindication*, 1717].

Yet there were not many in the early eighteenth century who adopted such advanced thought. The ideas of Wise and Moss seem to be departures from the generally accepted tendency to view government in an absolutist sense. That view was not limited to theologians, for an admiralty judge, in sentencing two culprits for contempt of the Crown, declared in 1721: "If we consult the law of God, that will tell us that the powers which be are ordained of God: If we will hear the voice of Reason, that will convince us that . . . our own preservation requires us to pay a dutiful obedience to the prince."

> Curse not the king,
> no not in thy thoughts;
> For the birds of the air
> will reveal the secret,
> And that which hath wings
> will utter the voice
> [*American Weekly Mercury*, March 16-23,
> 1721]

But this authoritarianism contained within itself the seeds of self-destruction. Or, to put it another way, there was inherent in these statements a way out of the dilemma. If government was ordained by God, and if the powers of government were given to certain individuals by God, and if the purpose of these arrangements was the protection and happiness of men, some method must be available to remedy a ruler's perversion of God's intent. One of the first to explore this path was the Congregationalist minister William Burnham in 1722: "Civil rulers are to be obeyed in that which is lawful, otherwise we must obey God rather than man" [*God's Providence in Placing Men in Their Respective Stations and Conditions Asserted and Shewed*, 1722].

Burnham's theme was picked up in a letter in the *New England Courant* in 1722:

> Civil government (when . . . regulated by the
> Divine Standard) is the strength, glory, and safe-
> ty of nations and commonwealths. . . . The

great design of God in the institution of government among men, was . . . the weal and happiness of those who are governed. . . . The power of civil rulers is derivative and limited, and therefore they must not arrogate to themselves an absolute uncontrollable empire, which appertains to God alone. . . . When men in high places assume despotic power . . . they rebel against heaven. . . . The power of civil rulers is but a ministry under God, derived from Him and designed by Him for the good of man. . . . Princes and judges of the earth are gods by office, and they act like such when justice and truth are the steady basis of their thrones. . . . When they act contrary hereto, there belongs another name to them, too horrible to be mentioned . . . and consequently [they] expose themselves to divine resentments and the heavy curses of their people." [*New England Covnant,* May 21-28, 1722]

Now there were potentially effective limits prescribed for government. If "men in high places" rebelled against God, they lost His protection. All that was lacking was the definition of what constituted their rebellion. The *Courant* letter was still vague on this point: the revolt occurred when the rulers assumed "despotic power," when they abandoned "justice and truth." Once those terms could be given more precision, the next logical step would be the right of the ruled to determine the existence of rebellion by their rulers.

Although no one had yet had the temerity to define the limits of the ruler's power, a more secular, more non-absolutist approach which would eventually demand such a definition was beginning to permeate colonial thought. Sir William Keith, speaking to the corporation of Newcastle in 1724, announced: "Government of any society is only the voluntary establishment of an artificial but just force, upon every individual person, to discharge such obligations as he has received from the public or his neighbor, with justice and gratitude" [*New England Courant,*]. There was no longer even a hint of the role of God in government.

Five years later the *Pennsylvania Gazette* elaborated on this theme. "The original of all power is in the people"; government was created as "a bulwark against the depredations of an open enemy, or the designing craft of a hypocrite"; if men observed the law of nature, government would be unnecessary, but by experience it was known that men differed. All could not legislate, and therefore trust was reposed in a few who had the time and inclination to do so efficaciously. "Hence government arises with all its beauties when that trust is discharged with honor; but as power is of an increasing nature thro' the weakness and imperfections of human kind, what was designed to support us in our rightful liberties sometimes springs up into unlimited prerogative." Absolute government, the *Gazette* concluded, "implies a renouncing [of] their reasoning." This new attitude toward government was reinforced by "Philo-Patriae" in John Peter Zenger's newspaper: "Civil government was first introduced to guard the safety of mankind . . . and every man in his wits will confess, that 'tis a sin of a very heinous kind to oppose a lawful ruler, whilst acting within the limits of his authority" [*The Universal Instructor in All Arts and Sciences: and the Pennsylvania Gazette,* April 3, 1729, *New York Weekly Journal,* November 26, 1733].

What was perhaps most significant about such essays was their acceptance of the fact that absolutism was wrong, that government was a trust, and that the ruler operated within limits prescribed to his authority. Even the clergy were beginning to imbibe this new wine, and they began viewing the divine role more as a limiting factor than as one transferring all authority directly from God to the ruler. According to Jeremiah Wise in 1729, God gave rulers their powers, but He did it mediately not immediately, and "according to the divers constitutions of kingdoms and states." Moreover, as He granted power, He limited it "by His word and providence." Governors operated under "fixed rules, even the rules of God's word, and humane laws agreeable thereto." The Reverend Nathaniel Chauncey's 1734 election sermon went so far as to describe the origin of government without once mentioning God. Civil government, he stated, was man's invention to replace God's rule after the apostasy. It was created when "mankind have generally consented, to leave that state of natural freedom to judge for themselves, and so resign it into the hands of a public ruler" [*The Faithful Ruler Described and Excited,* 1734].

This is not to suggest that all Boston clergymen shared Chauncey's opinion. John Barnard firmly declared in the same year that government arose from God, "who is the God of order and not of confusion." The existence of government was not left to man's option, it was not "a matter of liberty and freedom." Rather, it "comes to us with a thus saith the Lord." Since divine power formed and fitted man for society, it was obvious that omnipotent reason had also fitted society to man's needs. Government then simply became man's subjection to laws concerning his conduct with his Maker and his fellow creatures. Barnard went so far as to suggest that government was necessary even in Eden, because man was a fallible creature needing rules to guide his actions, although the form of government in a state of innocence was far different from that necessary in a state of apostasy.

Barnard did not, however, connect the divine necessity of government with any divine preference as to its form. He openly declared that "it remains with any civil society to alter and change the form of their government when they see just reason for it and all parties are consenting." He went even further by denying the "Adamitical" or patriarchal concept of the divine right of rulers, doing so in a statement that a Thomas Paine might have found acceptable: "After all is said, the right to rule takes its rise from the consent and agreement, that is the choice and election, of the community, state, or kingdom" [*The Throne Established by Righteousness,* 1734].

The earlier rigidity of the theologians appeared to be softening. Ideas which had been dominant in the seventeenth century, and which in their strength had spilled over into the eighteenth, were now being significantly modified. Jared Eliot's 1738 election sermon in Hartford suggested the growing secularism that had invaded the political thought of the clergy. "Civil government is set up by force, fraud, or by compact," he declared. It is created by the necessity of resolving hostilities among people. "Whether this union be from a principle of fear or love of society, or from both, has been a matter of dispute. But that some kind of government is for the good of mankind is beyond all dispute" [*Give Caesar His Due*, 1738].

When Chief Justice Samuel Chew addressed the Newcastle County grand jury in 1741, there was little evidence of theology in his description of government. "The natural desire then of happiness and that principle of self-preservation, common to all men, must first have inspired them, for their common protection and safety, with notions of compacts, of laws, and of governments, as absolutely necessary, and without which it was impossible for them to be happy in any degree." The Governor of Virginia, addressing the House of Burgesses, spoke in a similar vein: "The expectation of faring better under such civil combinations than when living separately is the origin of all communities, the great purpose for which government was created." And Chief Justice Chew, a year later, reiterated his position: "The end of all civil government being happiness, that happiness consists in the security and protection of the lives, liberties, and properties of the people who form or constitute the community" [*American Weekly Mercury*, June 24-July 1, 1742].

These highly secular approaches to the origin and purpose of government effectively eliminated concepts of divine right and ensconced Lockean theory firmly in the American mind. Elisha Williams proclaimed in 1744:

> The fountain and original of all civil power is from the people, and is certainly instituted for their sakes; or in other words . . . the great end of civil government is the preservation of their persons, their liberties and estates, or their property.

It was by this means that men filled the voids that existed in the state of nature—the lack of established law, an indifferent judge, and a power to carry out sentence against wrongdoers. "It is they who thus unite together, viz., the people, who make and alone have a right to make the laws that are to take place among them; which comes to the same thing, appoint those who shall make them, and who shall see them executed" [*The Essential Rights and Liberties of Protestants*, 1744].

There were still echoes of the older theological approach abroad in the land. The Reverend James Allen delivered an election sermon in 1744 and challenged the secular interpretation of government's origin. "An ungoverned society of men would be no better than a herd of savage beasts, worrying and devouring one another. . . . To prevent this confusion, God has instituted civil government to be a guard upon our persons and lives." But Allen admitted certain limits. The fact that government was "an institution of Christ" did not mean that "any particular form of it is so," for the Apostle expressly stated that the form "is an human ordinance." He also admitted the absurdity of stating that kings and governors "are sent down immediately from Heaven, with their commissions in their hands." The power of rulers, Allen acknowledged, flowed

from the constitutions they were under, and they were limited by those constitutions to doing that "which is just and right to all under that constitution."

Allen thus accepted the divine origin of government but not of governors. He went further by agreeing that rulers who exercised illegal authority need not be obeyed. When a ruler extended his authority beyond its proper limits, man had a "duty to disobey. . . . God must be obeyed rather than man." Unfortunately, Allen failed to provide the necessary guidelines for determining the bounds of lawful authority, and he also neglected to spell out the recourses available to the subject in the event a ruler acted illegally [*Magistracy an Institution of Christ Upon The Throne*, 1744].

Allen's sermon provided a concession by the clergy to the growing tide of secularism. He could not admit that God played no role whatsoever in the establishment of so basic an institution as government, but he had agreed that the forms, powers, and authorities of government were all human devices. In a 1746 election sermon, Samuel Hall repeated much of Allen's position. "And among the various forms," Hall declared, "one is calculated for a people under such and such circumstances; another for people under different circumstances." This meant that monarchies, aristocracies, and even democracies could be justified, although Hall preferred tyranny to democracy because the only danger came from "the enormities of a few" rather than a situation in which "everyone is a tyrant" [*The Legislatures Right, Charge, and Duty in Respect of Religion*, 1746].

An essay by "Layman" in 1747 challenged these clerical concessions to secularism. Written as a gloss on the first seven verses of the thirteenth chapter of St. Paul to the Romans, the argument was rather obvious. "All temporal government that is established in any country is of God, tho' it's done and acted by man, yet it's by God's permission and appointment." As a consequence, man had no right to dispute how the "supreme magistrate" came by his power, or whether it was lawful. "Whoever has got the government in their hands, it immediately becomes our duty to become subject." The only limitation, and a weak one at that, was that men should not act "contrary to our duty to God" [*New York Evening Post*, August 3, 1747].

An anonymous correspondent quickly responded in the same journal. Government was ordained and instituted by God, the essayist admitted, but He limited it "to be exercised according to the laws of nature." Governors were designed by God to act for the "safety, welfare, and prosperity of those over whom they are established." And the same reasons that obliged men to submit to be ruled in accord with laws and constitutions equally obliged them to oppose rulers who designed their ruin or destruction.

The theme of divine intervention in the establishment of government and in the institution of rulers found fewer advocates as time elapsed. The volume and strength of argument mounted instead on behalf of the Lockean interpretation. An essay in the Boston *Independent Advertiser* in 1748 elaborated on the theme that civil government was instituted by God "for the happiness and security of all."

All men were by nature on a level, endowed with an equal share of freedom and with capacities "nearly alike," but each had a strong propensity to dominion. That, plus self-interest, made political society necessary. However, "there is no positive law either in nature or revelation, for any particular form." And the purpose of government was to protect the people and promote their prosperity, and any government contradicting that aim immediately left the people "discharged from all obedience" to it. A few issues later, the same paper carried an essay which summed up the matter: "What is government but a trust committed by all or most to one or a few, who are to attend upon the affairs of all, that every one may with the most security attend upon his own?" Another journal almost simultaneously announced: "It is an undeniable maxim that the first end and design of all government was for the benefit of the whole people" [*Independent Advertiser,* January 11, 1748; February 29, 1748 (#9); *Pennsylvania Gazette,* May 27, 1750].

The pressure for a completely secular concept of government, and even a democratization of its purpose, found some clergy still unconvinced. The Reverend Samuel Philips [in his *Political Rulers Authorized and Influenced By God Our Savior, To Decree and Execute Justice*] announced in 1750, in an unequivocal statement, that civil government was "not barely a permission of providence, no, but an appointment of Heaven: The distinction of rulers and ruled is not the contrivance of crafty and ambitious men, no, but of divine ordination." From this followed the "unquestionable duty" of submission to rulers unless they "pervert their authority" or violated their oath and appeared as enemies to the civil and religious constitution. But Philips failed to provide any hint as to who would determine such perversions or violations.

When Noah Hobart offered the election sermon in 1751, he took a similar approach, but without even the minor qualifications suggested by Philips. Civil government, he argued, was a consequence of God's permissiveness, and its nature required that there be men of different orders, some with authority to command and others with a duty to obey. The variety of governmental forms was perfectly proper because it was the result of differing "conditions and circumstances." The "original design and great end" of government was "public happiness," and therefore a man "must certainly have very absurd notions of the divine being, if he can persuade himself that God, in appointing civil government, aimed at nothing higher than aggrandizing rulers" [*Civil Government The Foundation of Social Happiness,* 1751]. But Hobart did not suggest that rulers could be evil, let alone that a solution might be needed to that problem.

Some of the clergy by 1751 had begun to accept, at least partially, the more liberal conclusions of the non-theologians. A case in point was the Reverend William Welsteed. Although he could declare "that some bear rule over others, is certainly of God," and that "it comes to us with the most evident stamp of divinity upon it," he accepted the basic limitation of John Locke. While the authority and right of government extended from God, "the best right and title to power and rule over men . . . must

finally be resolved into compact, consent, and agreement" [*The Dignity and Duty of The Civil Magistrate,* 1751].

By the early 1750's the secular viewpoint was frequently being expressed in public prints. A letter in the *Boston Weekly Newsletter* declared that as the "people are the source of all that power which is vested in governors for the public weal, they have an undoubted right to judge for themselves whether that power is improved to good purposes or not." This shift of the locus of power over rulers from God to man found further support in William Livingston's *Independent Reflector.* Communities, Livingston announced, "were formed not for the advantage of one man, but for the good of the whole body." Government "at best is a burden, tho' a necessary one. Had man been wise from his creation, he would always have been free. We might have enjoyed the gifts of liberal nature, unmolested, unrestrained. It is the depravity of mankind that has necessarily introduced government" [*Independent Reflector,* July 12, 1753]. Livingston did not attempt to balance man's depravity with God's benevolence in the formation of government.

A counterthrust to this secularism appeared in the form of some "farther animadversions" on the sentiments of the *Independent Reflector.* "Some government, it seems then, mankind was under from the beginning of his existence, and no man was ever so independent as that he might do whatever was right in his own eyes. . . . Almighty God, the fountain of all beings, is the fountain of all power, too. . . . And this will of the creator is a law obligatory upon the creature without any compact of his own" [*New York Mercury,* September 17, 1753]. To this commentator, government was a divinely ordained institution, governors were similarly created, and man's only response was unconditional submission to those designated by God to rule over him.

Despite such occasional reverberations of the old theological view, the newer secular attitudes dominated the public press. In 1754 "Rusticus" ventured the simple statement that the "only true state of liberty" was the state of nature, but that mankind thought it best to form societies by first creating a constitution through a majority of voices. This was the origin of government. A theological liberal, the Reverend Jonathan Mayhew, repeated in 1754 that civil power originated with God, but he added that "it is to be remembered that this power is derived from God not immediately, but mediately as other talents and blessings are." No one form has His blessing more than any other—such ideas "are not drawn from the Holy Scriptures, but from a far less pure and sacred fountain."

Mayhew had made two significant concessions: power was derived from God mediately, and government was a "talent and blessing" rather than a penalty imposed upon mankind. And, he continued, as all governments were immediately man's creation, "so from men, from common consent, it is that lawful rulers immediately receive their power." We were bound to obey our rulers because government was an "appointment of heaven," but "it is not to be forgotten, that . . . law, and not will, is the measure of the executive magistrate's power; so it is the measure of the subject's obedience and submission" [*A Sermon*

Preached in the Audience of His Excellency William Shirley, 1754]. Mayhew's capitulation to the ideas of Locke was complete, for he had agreed that the rulers were bound by law and that the ruled had the right to measure the rulers' actions against that law.

Perhaps the clearest exposition of the secular attitude toward the origin, nature, and purpose of government is found in Daniel Fowle's 1756 [*An Appendix to the Late Total Eclipse of Liberty*]. He completely removed God from any active role in the establishment or processes of government. Political institutions, he declared, began as a means of resolving disputes among men, not as divine institutions. Governors were neither "the natural parents [n]or progenitors" of their people nor were they nominated by God, nor was their power limited by Him, nor had He described any plan for civil polity. Rather, a civil state was formed by three acts: a contract by each person for all to enter into a society, a decree of the people providing a plan of government for that society, and finally a contract between the people and those whom they had designated to rule them. Fowle dismissed divine right as "a mere dream of court flatterers," for if anything were divine it was the people's rights which were constituted by God and nature. The power of rulers was a simple delegation by the people.

By the mid-1750's even the most rigid theologians were being forced to make concessions to these ideas. Moses Dickinson's 1755 election sermon is typical. Although he reaffirmed the divine origin of government, he had to admit, albeit reluctantly, the right of popular control—political societies "were not formed for the sake of the rulers, but rulers were made for the sake of the societies." A further admission was made by Thomas Frink in his election sermon [*A King Reigning in Righteousness, and Princes Ruling in Judgement*] in 1758. He distinguished between God's direct role in instituting civil government over Israel and His failure to prescribe for any other nation. "Nor has Jesus Christ," he declared, "left any designed plan or model for the political government of Christian nations—nor doth God himself name and appoint the person who shall hold the sceptre." Rather, authority was conveyed to individuals or families "by compact, consent, or choice of the persons governed." And, once the people's right to choose their governors was conceded, the means whereby they could call their rulers to account was admitted—the exercise time and again of that same right.

Although the Reverend James Lockwood could reiterate as late as 1759 that "the source and original of civil government, in general, is divine and from God," there were few clergymen who now took a similar view. The role of God in the political affairs of men was, on the contrary, being denied by the clergy. The Reverend Benjamin Stevens, using as his source Burlamaqui rather than Scripture, defined civil liberty as "natural liberty itself, divested of that part which constitutes the independence of individuals by the authority it confers on sovereigns, attended with a right of insisting on his making a good use of his authority" [*A Sermon Preached at Boston* . . . , 1761]. Thus the subject who entered civil society retained the

right to judge his ruler and to act as the occasion required. The magistrate must be secure in the allegiance of his subject, Stevens wrote, but the subject must also be secure in the protection of the magistrate.

In 1762 the Reverend Abraham Williams went even further by denying God's responsibility for civil institutions and their operation. "The nature of civil society or government is a temporal worldly constitution, formed upon worldly motives, to answer valuable worldly purposes. The constitution, laws, and sanctions of civil society respect this world and are therefore essentially distinct and different from the Kingdom of Christ, which is not of this world" [in *A Sermon Preached at Boston* . . . , 1762]. When Williams washed his hands of the whole matter, he fully capitulated to the theory of John Locke.

Perhaps the best summation of the views of eighteenth-century Americans on this problem is in James Otis' famous [*A Vindication of the Conduct of the House of Representatives of the Province of Massachusetts-Bay,* 1762]. Certainly his statement is the pithiest:

> 1. God made all men naturally equal. 2. The ideas of earthly superiority, pre-eminence, and grandeur are educational, at least acquired, not innate. 3. Kings were . . . made for the good of the people, and not the people for them. 4. No government has a right to make hobby horses, asses, and slaves of the subject, nature having made sufficient of the two former, for all the lawful purposes of man . . . but none of the last, which infallibly proves they are unnecessary. 5. Tho' most governments are de facto arbitrary . . . yet none are de jure arbitrary.
>
> (pp. 37-60)

> *Lawrence H. Leder, "The State of Nature and the Origin of Government," in his* Liberty and Authority: Early American Political Ideology, 1689-1763, *Quadrangle Books, 1968, pp. 37-60.*

EARLY RELIGIOUS INFLUENCES IN COLONIAL AMERICA

Thomas Jefferson Wertenbaker

[In the excerpt below, Wertenbaker considers the influence of the Quaker religion on Colonial American life.]

In planning his colony on the bank of the Delaware William Penn was actuated by a desire not only to establish a refuge for his oppressed fellow Quakers, but to make a hitherto untried experiment in government. Believing that great harm had resulted from the tendency of governments to make expediency rather than right their guiding star, he based the political structure of his colony on truth, justice and righteousness. There must be no compromise with wrong. If war is wrong, then there must be no war whatever the cost; if intolerance is unjust, there must be religious freedom even though it should ultimately overthrow the Quaker principles themselves.

Penn and his followers reserved to themselves, however, the all-important privilege of deciding what was right and what was wrong, and so founded the government of Pennsylvania on Quaker principles. Fortunately these principles were in the main enlightened and liberal, although some were perhaps impractical, and some actually reactionary. When once the government had been established and the Quaker code enacted into law, it remained to be seen whether the experiment would be successful. Penn himself had his moments of doubt. If another government committed a wrong against his province, could it reply always with right; if it became the object of aggression, could it defend itself only with protestations of friendship; could it answer injustice with justice?

The Quakers lay down as a main fundamental in religion that God gives every man a "light within," or "manifestation" to inform him of his duty and to enable him to do it. By this "they understand something that is divine, and though in man, yet not of man but of God; and that it came from him, and leads to him all those that will be led by it" [William Penn, *Primitive Christianity Revived*, 1783]. Since God speaks directly to the individual, and not indirectly through the Church, salvation may be attained without the intervention of an ordained priesthood. Baptism, the Lord's Supper and other sacraments, and all forms and ceremonies are unnecessary.

From these views the advocacy of religious freedom followed as a matter of course. Penn promised that no person in his colony who believed in God should be molested for his "persuasion or practice," not only because of his own sufferings for conscience sake, but because the Quakers could not consistently establish a State Church. The Puritans in migrating to Massachusetts Bay had as one of their main purposes the setting up of a Church which could be defended from heresy by the stern hand of the law. Persecution was the logical consequence of their belief that salvation was possible only through this Church and the observance of its ordinances. The Quakers, on the contrary, averring that religion was a matter between the individual and his Maker, could not interfere with this holy relationship by prescribing for it rules and regulations. So Pennsylvania was thrown open to Christians of all denominations, and Anglicans, Presbyterians, Lutherans, Mennonites, Moravians, Reformed rushed in.

But though the Quakers made no effort to enforce their own tenets by law, they had emphatic views as to morality, and enacted them into laws backed by severe penalties. The theatre was prohibited. "How many plays did Jesus Christ and his apostles recreate themselves at? What poems, romances, comedies and the like did the apostles and saints make or use to pass away their time withal?" wrote the youthful William Penn from his cell in the Tower ["No Cross, No Crown," *Friends Library,* Vol. I]. "Plays, parks, balls, treats, romances, musics, lovesonnets, and the like, will be a very invalid plea . . . at the revelation of the righteous judgment of God." The Quakers objected to plays, not only as tending to immorality, but because of the simulating of passions, joys and grief by the actors. Christianity requires simplicity and truth, they said, and it is contrary to its spirit to create imaginary scenes and episodes.

Gambling in any form was severely condemned, the Great Law of Pennsylvania prescribing a fine or imprisonment for "playing cards, dice, lotteries, or such like enticing, vain and evil sports and games." The practice of duelling the Quakers made punishable with hard labor in the house of correction. Profanity was considered so serious an offense that those guilty of it were often given an opportunity to cleanse their vocabulary in prison on a diet of bread and water. Drunkenness was punishable with fine or imprisonment.

But the Quakers were even more concerned with preventing legislation inconsistent with their principles than with these positive prohibitions. There must be no law requiring the taking of oaths, no prohibition of wearing hats in court or in the presence of the governor, no infringement of religious liberty, and above all no policy of belligerency towards the Indians or foreign powers and no participation in war. We "believe that war ought to cease," said William Penn. Jesus taught his disciples to forgive and to love their enemies, not to war against them and kill them, therefore Christians should substitute love and persuasion for weapons and war. Since the very worst of men will not hurt those who really love them, peace must in the end have the victory. (pp. 188-90)

So the Pennsylvania Quakers had no desire to have the government of the province fall into the hands of other denominations. Were the Anglicans to gain control they might, with the aid of the British government, attempt to rescind or at least to weaken the guarantees of religious freedom. Should a coalition of Anglicans, Lutherans, Presbyterians and Reformed fill the Assembly, many of the precepts dear to the hearts of the Quakers would be endangered, the province might be forced into war and Quakers punished for refusing to bear arms. In other words the Friends dared not weaken their grip on the government lest they suffer in their own refuge the same persecutions and abuses as in Europe, lest they find themselves balked in carrying out their basic principles and policies.

For the safety of many of their customs and beliefs which involved them in no serious conflict with law or with the interests or principles of others, the Friends had no apprehension from the government. Their neighbors might smile or even openly deride their prejudice against music, ornamental furniture, novels, dancing, elaborate dress, holy days, titles; their taciturnity; their quiet, sedate manner; their discarding of the "pagan" names of the months and the days of the week, but these things were unlikely to call forth hostile legislation. Their continuance depended upon something even more fundamental than the control of the government, they depended upon the supremacy in the colony of the Quaker spirit. If the policy of religious freedom together with the open door to immigrants made the overthrow of this supremacy inevitable even in Philadelphia itself, the Friends could do little more than foster and protect their ideals within their own Society.

Yet the struggle for Quaker control, both legislative and moral, continued throughout the colonial period.

In the eyes of Fox and Penn dancing was a sin of grievous consequences. They agreed with Saint Augustine that the steps of the dancer were just so many "leaps to hell," that the good man who enters a ballroom "cometh forth a corrupt and wicked man" [William Penn, "No Cross, No Crown"]. The young Friend who so forgot himself as to attend a dance was certain to receive a visit from a committee of overseers, and if he persisted, to be "disowned" or expelled from the Society.

Music was viewed with suspicion. Fox warned the pious against its insidious, sensuous, frivolous influence, while Penn thought it almost as sinful as dancing itself. To bewitch the heart with temporal delight by playing upon instruments and singing, was to forget God. Moreover, to sacrifice the time necessary to acquire efficiency in either vocal or instrumental music was inconsistent with the Quaker pattern of life, in which each moment must be devoted to some useful task or to good thoughts. It was right that the individual "saint" should sing the praises of God, but not a "mixed multitude" in which there might be some unregenerate [A. C. Applegarth, "Quakers in Pennsylvania," Thos. Clarkson, *A Portraiture of Quakerism*].

Plainness in dress was at first not considered essential by the Friends, for some contended that it was "no vanity to use what the country naturally produced." Some of the early Quaker men wore wigs, while the women sometimes arrayed themselves in white satin petticoats embroidered with flowers, pearl satin gowns and peach-colored cloaks. Nonetheless, vanity of this kind was bitterly condemned by Penn. "How many pieces of riband and what feathers, lacebands and the like did Adam and Eve wear in paradise, or out of it?" he asked. "What rich embroideries, silks, points, etc., had Abel, Enoch, Noah, and good old Abraham? Did Eve, Sarah, Suzannah, Elizabeth and the Virgin Mary use to curl, powder, patch, paint, wear false locks of strange colors, rich points, trimmings, laced gowns, embroidered petticoats?"

Unable to resist this reasoning, the Quaker gentlemen discarded their handsome attire for broad-brimmed hats, coats with straight collars, drab stockings and shoes fastened with leather straps, while the women contented themselves with caps or hoods, plain gowns of a drab, gray or buff color, and green aprons. In time the man who appeared at meeting with silver buckles, metal buttons or ruffled collar, or the woman who wore satin or lace at once became objects of suspicion. "O that our young women would cease from all unseemly and immodest appearance in their apparel," said the Philadelphia Meeting, "certainly both males and females who take such undue liberties flee from the cross of Christ" [*Christian Advices*, by the Yearly Meeting of Friends, 1808].

The good Friend was supposed to avoid excess in food and drink as in other things, and George Fox warned all "God's freemen and women" to beware of "feastings and revellings, banquetings and wakes" ["Institution of Discipline," *The Friends' Library*, Vol. I]. The Quaker's home should be plain and unostentatious, devoid of costly silver and gold utensils and of richly carved furniture. In his conversation he must be reserved, even taciturn, free of all idle gossip or vain boastings; in his bearing quiet, sedate and dignified. The good people of Burlington were deeply concerned when some of the young men came to meeting "galloping and riding after an airy flurting manner" inconsistent with the "moderation and gravity" becoming the Friends.

With tenets and principles so different from those of other sects the Friends were determined to retain their ascendancy both political and moral. After all the colony had been founded by a Quaker, in part as a refuge for members of the Society, in part as a proving ground for Quaker concepts. Penn had wished to demonstrate to the world that it was practical to live under a government based on religious freedom, democratic principles, good will and conciliation in foreign relations; to establish a social life dominated by piety, simplicity, sincerity, moderation and strict adherence to moral law. It was not only entirely right and just, but absolutely necessary, so his followers reasoned, for the control of the colony to remain in their own hands.

The first serious threat to the Holy Experiment came not from the non-Quaker elements, however, but from within the body of the Society itself. The man who challenged the leadership of Fox and Penn, denied some of their fundamental tenets and drew off hundreds in Pennsylvania and New Jersey was George Keith. Born in Scotland, graduated from Aberdeen University, a man of deep learning, Keith deserted the Presbyterian Church for the Society of Friends as a young man of twenty-five or twenty-six. Coming to American in 1684, he attracted wide attention by a series of able discourses and sermons and gradually drew around him a group of devoted followers. Had he not strayed from the accepted doctrines and practices of the Friends, he would no doubt rank second only to Penn in the history of the Society in America. But his restless mind, his love of controversy and his unrestrained temper got him into trouble. Charging the visiting Quaker ministers with placing all their emphasis upon the "inner light" to the neglect of the historic Christ and the Scriptures, he gave way to bitter and intemperate language. There were "more damnable heresies and doctrines of devils among the Quakers than among any profession of Protestants," he said [quoted in R. M. Jones, *The Quakers in the American Colonies*].

Had Pennsylvania been a Puritan colony the remedy would have been simple; for the Church would have tried Keith, and left it to the civil authorities to drive him into banishment. But this would have been inconsistent with Quaker ideals. Knowing this, Keith dared them to do their worst, declaring that "his back had long itched to be whipped." Some of the Quaker magistrates took him at his word so far as to arrest and convict him on a charge of disturbing the peace, but they soon saw their mistake and refused to enforce the penalty.

There was no reason why the Society as a religious body should not take action against him, however, so the Yearly Meeting, after condemning "that spirit of reviling, railing, lying, slandering and falsely accusing which hath risen . . . in George Keith and his adherents," disowned them as Friends. Although Keith was now the leader of a new sect and set up Meetings in Philadelphia, Burlington and Bucks County, he still had hopes of winning the seal of orthodoxy from the parent Society in England. But the English Yearly Meeting condemned him as a deserter from the "holy fellowship," and soon after he made another major shift by joining the Anglican Church. Upon receipt of this news some of his bewildered followers in America returned to the Quaker fold, some became Baptists, many united with the Episcopalians.

The Keith schism seems to have awakened the Friends to the necessity of solidarity. Should they split up permanently into two or more factions, if Meetings should be divided and old friends turned into enemies, the Holy Experiment would be doomed. They must stand shoulder to shoulder to combat any encroachments of the British government, the Anglican Church or the Presbyterian Church; they must bring the threat of expulsion against Friends who showed an inclination to laxness, and social ostracism against non-Quakers whose conduct they considered scandalous or a reproach to the colony.

The so-called *Discipline* of the Friends grew out of the letters of George Fox and the official epistles of the London Yearly Meeting giving advice on matters of doctrine, morals and organization. There were admonitions as to dress, language, the treatment of the poor, bearing arms, salutations, amusements, etc. To the American Friends they had a sanctity second only to the Bible, so that in time they were codified into the *Discipline* which became obligatory upon all the Meetings. It was the duty of the overseers to inquire into cases of "drinking to excess, swearing, cursing, lying," of "superfluity of apparel and furniture," of "calling the days and months contrary to Scripture," of "smoking tobacco in streets, roads and public-houses," of "tale-bearing," of "keeping vain and loose company," of not using "the plain Scripture language of *thee* and *thou*," and other infringements of the *Discipline*. Offending members were admonished and, in cases of obstinacy, expelled by the Monthly Meeting.

The Quaker youth who cast an eye upon a maid of another sect was inviting trouble, for mixed marriages were forbidden. "Let our dear youth avoid the too frequent and familiar converse with those from whom may arise a danger of entanglement, by their alluring passions and drawing the affections after them," said a book of *Advices,* for "marriage implies union as well in spiritual as temporal concerns." No doubt the pleadings of parents or the warnings of the overseers broke up many a budding love affair, but if the erring Quaker youth or maid persisted, expulsion from the Society was the penalty. This exclusiveness tended ultimately to stagnation and isolation, but for the moment it seemed to bring compactness and unity and so to enhance the influence of the Society.

Strength came also from the fact that the Quaker organization was benevolent as well as religious. Penn's admonition to the Monthly Meetings "to supply the wants of the poor," and to care for "widows and orphans and such as are helpless," was so well heeded that need among the Friends was practically eliminated. George Keith says in his *Journal* that great sums were collected, not only for the Quaker poor, but as a means of winning converts from the indigent of other sects.

Money was contributed with a liberal hand to pay the expenses of travelling ministers, many of them pious and learned men from England, who exercised a powerful influence in solidifying the Society and inspiring the members. Since the Friends would have no "paid priests," as they called the ministers of other denominations, these visitors, who were always listened to with reverent attention, played a vital rôle in interpreting and defending Quaker tenets, answering criticisms and linking Meeting with Meeting, and province with province.

The Meetings kept a strict eye upon the reading of the members, not only discouraging "the reading of plays, romances, novels and other pernicious books," but importing from England the works of eminent Quaker writers. Penn's *No Cross, No Crown,* Fox's *Journal,* Robert Barclay's *Apology* and similar writings served to fortify the faith of the Quakers themselves and to make new converts. If an Episcopalian or a Presbyterian had Quaker friends or relatives, he was apt to be plied with the *Apology,* which one critic termed the "glory and Alcoran" of the Friends.

Thus were the ranks of the Quakers solidified into a well-disciplined phalanx. The strength imparted to some denominations by the hierarchy, or by a close alliance of Church and State, the Friends attained by other means, by a compact organization which extended its control over the thoughts, the lives, the education of the members. And in the hearts of all was constantly the thought that upon them depended the success of the Holy Experiment, the experiment which eventually was to transform the world.

No doubt many of the more thoughtful Quakers realized that not all the solidarity of their Society, not all their pride of accomplishment, not even their simple faith were enough to overcome the difficulties which lay ahead. With the control of a great and growing province entrusted to their hands, could the Quaker magistrates retain the old humility; with wealth increasing rapidly could the Quaker merchant refrain from luxury and ostentation; with broad frontiers open to the attacks of French and Indians and a broad river leading into the heart of the colony inviting hostile fleets, could the Assembly hold to its resolution not to arm the people?

Penn's colony had been in existence but a few decades when its rich soil and splendid facilities for trade began to expose the Society to the dangers of rapidly increasing wealth. Penn himself could only guess at the potentialities of the vast domain to which his charter entitled him. And even though only the eastern fringe of the colony was settled in his day, he lived to see it surpass some of the older colonies in population and wealth. In the four years from 1681 to 1685 the population grew from 2000 to 7200; by 1700 it had doubled again; by 1740 it was exceeded only by that of Virginia, Massachusetts and Maryland.

The settlers spread out over the agricultural lands of Chester, Bucks and Philadelphia Counties along the west bank of the Delaware River and up the Schuylkill and Brandywine, and in the "lower counties" comprising the present State of Delaware. With incredible swiftness trees were felled, crops laid out, houses, barns and fences built, and the wilderness converted into thriving farms. The soil was found to be excellent, not only for Indian corn but for wheat and other English grain, and for various kinds of fruits and vegetables. The reports of the settlers were enthusiastic. "Our lands have been grateful to us and have begun to reward our labors with abounding crops of corn," wrote one; "If God continues his blessing to us this province will be certainly the granery of the world," said another; it would gladden Penn's heart to see how the country was "becoming a fruitful field and a pleasant garden," said a third. (pp. 191-98)

This rich land poured its bounty into Philadelphia. In late summer and early fall the river and bay were dotted with picturesque sails as the little wherries plied back and forth with their cargoes of farm products or European manufactured goods. Even the New Jersey trade, despite all efforts to develop Burlington into a great port, was in large part diverted to Philadelphia. The riverfront must have presented a busy scene indeed: here a 200-ton ship from London tied up at the Chestnut Street wharf while busy sailors unload boxes of cloth, hardware, and farm implements; here a brig just coming in from the West Indies with sugar, molasses and wine; here a swarm of wherries waiting to dispose of their barrels of wheat, flour or pork; there a Philadelphia-owned ship taking on staves, bread and beef for Jamaica or Barbados. In October, 1753, there were no less than 117 seagoing vessels in the harbor at one time. The vessels of overseas and inland commerce almost touched noses, for while the prows of brigs and ships came up within a few feet of the storehouses of Samuel Carpenter or William Fishbourn, Conestoga wagons in long lines were discharging the products of the German farms at the door.

By far the most important export was flour, but Indian corn, bread, staves, and iron were also shipped out in considerable quantities. "They send great quantities of corn (wheat) to Portugal and Spain, frequently selling their ships as well as cargo, and the produce of both is sent thence to England where it is laid out in goods and sent home to Pennsylvania," it was stated in 1731. "They trade to our provinces of New England, Virginia, Maryland, Carolina, and to all the islands of the West Indies (excepting the Spanish ones) as also to the Canaries, Madeira and the Azores Isles; likewise to Newfoundland for fish which they carry to Spain, Portugal and the Mediterranean. . . . Lastly, the Pennsylvanians build about 2000 tons of shipping a year for sale, over and above what they employ in their own trade, which may be about 6000 tons more" [*The Importance of the British Plantations in America*]. One has only to select at random an issue of *The Gazette* to realize the extent of Philadelphia's trade. The number of March 16, 1758, shows incoming vessels from Barbados, Antigua, Jamaica, Liverpool, North Carolina, South Carolina, London, Boston, New York and Saint Christopher.

The quiet, simple Quakers, most of them from the humbler walks of life, suddenly found wealth dumped in their laps. The former Somerset yeoman now became a landed proprietor; the London clerk became a great merchant

with a large storehouse on Front Street and perhaps a brig or two engaged in the West India trade. Men who had lived in frame cabins and had been content with pewter utensils and the plainest furniture now erected "stately piles of brick" and surrounded themselves with costly silver and Chippendale chairs and highboys.

The insidious effects of wealth in undermining the old Quaker spirit, if not Quaker principles, is interestingly described by John Smith, of Marlborough, writing in 1760. The Friends were originally "a plain lowly-minded people," he said, whose meetings were marked by "much tenderness and contrition." By 1720, however, "the Society increasing in wealth and in some degree conforming to the fashions of the world, true humility was less apparent, and their meetings in general were not so lively and edifying." In twenty more years "many of them were grown very rich, and many made a specious appearance in the world," so that "marks of outward wealth and greatness appeared in some in our meetings of ministers and elders." In fact "there had been a continual increase of such ways of life" until "weakness" and "barrenness overspread the Society."

The Friends seem to have been fully aware of the danger, and tried to meet it by stiffening their warnings against pride and ostentation. "Our forefathers were drawn out of the vain fashions and customs of the world," they said. "If our youth and others should make light of that plainness of speech, apparel and furniture . . . they will find that so far as they embrace such vanities they weaken themselves in the practice of religious duties." Yet many a good Quaker, despite an almost ostentatiously plain exterior, lived in a style which to visitors seemed luxurious. "This plain Friend and his plain though pretty wife, with her Thees and Thous had provided us the most costly entertainment," a guest of Miers Fisher tells us, "ducks, hams, chickens, beef, pig, tarts, creams, custards, jellies, fools, trifles, floating islands, beer, porter, punch, wine, and a long etc." We know that many Quakers entered fully into the gayety and enjoyment of life in Philadelphia. "Hiltzheimer's horse-racing, fox-hunting, punch-drinking and city-governing friends were three fourths of them Quakers; all of them were substantial citizens" [G. Fisher, *Pennsylvania Colony and Commonwealth*]. So early as 1724 Christopher Sauer noted the change. "According to appearances plainness is vanishing pretty much," he said. "The dear old folks, most of whom are dead by this time, may have spoken to their children a good deal about plainness. It is still noticeable in the clothes except that the material is very costly, or is even velvet" [*Pennsylvania Magazine,* Vol. XLV].

In the quarter of a century from 1750 to 1775, Philadelphia assumed an air of elegance which excited the admiration of visitors from other colonies and even from Europe and was the despair of old-line Quakers. Stately buildings arose in the public square, handsome homes of brick set off by marble appeared on the residential streets, and charming country seats in the suburbs. The traveller Burnaby as he approached the city found the whole country "covered with villas, gardens and luxuriant orchards." Music and dancing were indulged in without qualms, while the city became famous for the sumptuousness of its dinners. Chastellux, who spent some time in Philadelphia during the Revolution, describes one of the assemblies or subscription balls. "At Philadelphia, as at London, Bath Spa, etc. there are places appropriated for the young people to dance in," or to "play at different games of cards. . . . A master of ceremonies presides at these methodical amusements." He presents to each dancer a billet which "decides the male or female partner for the whole evening. . . . These dances, like the toasts we drink at table, have some relation to politics: one is called the success of the campaign, another the defeat of Burgoyne" [Marquis de Chastellux, *Travels in North America,* 1827]. (pp. 199-201)

The line drawn by the Quakers between practices to be forbidden by law and those to be opposed only by moral pressure was drawn arbitrarily. A theatrical play was a matter for the police; dancing and fencing only for admonition or reproach. When Thomas Kinnett advertised in 1746 that he was prepared "to teach the noble art of defense with small swords, and also dancing," the Friends were horrified. Yet they contented themselves with expressing their surprise at "his audacity and brazen impudence in giving these detestable vices those high encomiums." Despite all their efforts both seem to have gained in popularity. In January 1758 George Abington, "late from London," gave notice of his intention to open a dancing school, while a few months later John Egerton, "master of arms" started "a school for the practice of the small sword" at Thomas Riche's store, on Water Street. When Ludewig Kuhn opened a music school at the "sign of the Golden Rose," Third and Arch Streets, to teach the German flute and guitar, he too was probably regarded by the Quakers as an evil influence.

Against the theatre the Quakers waged unrelenting war. It was enacted as a part of the Great Law of the colony in 1682 that "whoever shall introduce into this province or frequent such rude and riotous sports and practices as prizes, stage-plays, masques," shall suffer "imprisonment at hard labor" or "forfeit twenty shillings." Although this law was vetoed by William and Mary it was re-enacted in 1696. In the end, however, after repeated efforts by Penn and the Assembly to ban the theatre, the British government made it clear that they would not tolerate this restriction upon "healthy and innocent diversions" [William S. Dye, "Pennsylvania versus the Theatre," *Pennsylvania Magazine,* Vol. 55]. Nonetheless, within the bounds of the borough of Philadelphia plays were prohibited by the Quaker magistrates. When, in 1749, it was reported to the Common Council "that certain persons had lately taken upon them to act plays," the shocked city fathers "unanimously requested the magistrates to take the most effectual measures for the suppressing of this disorder" [Scharf and Wescott, *History of Philadelphia,* Vol. II]. (pp. 203-04)

Thus not only did the growth of "worldliness" defile the Quaker city and corrupt many of the Quakers themselves, but it placed the Society of Friends in a defensive position which restricted its influence and curtailed its growth. It forced upon them the adoption and strict observance of rules of conduct which tended to mere formalism. It caused them to draw a sharp line between their own members and the unregenerate of the world, to insist more firmly upon Quaker dress, language, customs, to repudiate those who married outside the fold. The Pilgrim fathers left Holland for America in part to avoid contamination from the religious beliefs of the surrounding population; the Friends now found themselves in the midst of worldly influences in the community which they themselves had founded.

The adoption of this defensive policy against worldly contamination caused the Society to sacrifice aggressiveness and growth for purity. With the political control of Pennsylvania largely in their hands, with a wealthy membership and overflowing treasury, the Society might have opened a missionary campaign especially on the frontiers which would have expanded their influence indefinitely. But efforts of this kind came almost to a complete stop; the energies of the Society were spent in warning and encouraging the members to be faithful; the ministers from England confined their visits chiefly to the old congregations.

Their growth was retarded also by their educational policies. The New England Puritans, the Anglicans of Virginia, the Presbyterians, the Dutch Reformed all recognized the need of institutions of higher learning where young men could be educated for the ministry or for other forms of leadership. But the Friends, who had no established ministry, placed the emphasis upon secondary rather than higher education. As for their visiting ministers, it was a widely accepted view that their spiritual insight and power would be diminished rather than heightened by scholarship. It was more than two centuries after the founding of Harvard and a century and a half after the founding of William and Mary, that the first Quaker college in America opened its doors.

George Fox seems to have understood the value of higher learning and urged the founding of institutions for the teaching of "everything civil and useful in creation." But he failed to press the point, his followers were convinced that colleges were unnecessary and so the Quaker youths found themselves cut off from cultural opportunities. In time the Society had good reason to regret this narrow policy, for it weakened their leadership and placed them at a disadvantage with other groups.

On the other hand, the Friends always placed great emphasis upon secondary education. One of the first laws of the province required parents to provide instruction for their children in reading and writing "so that they may be able to read the Scriptures," and at the age of twelve to begin their preparation for "some useful trade or skill" [Isaac Sharpless, *A Quaker Experiment in Government*]. Hardly had the first foundations been laid in Philadelphia when Governor and Council erected a large schoolhouse and employed Enoch Flower as teacher, allowing him "for boarding a scholar, that is to say, dyet, washing, lodging and schooling, ten pounds for one whole year" [*Colonial Records,* Vol. I]. Such immediate success attended the venture that three years later children were enrolled, not only from several neighboring provinces, but from far-off Barbados. (pp. 206-07)

At last, during the Revolution, when there was an awakening to the situation, the opportunity for the Society to win its rightful place in the civilization of America had passed. And even at that late date conservatism was not lightly to be overcome. No one seemed capable of breaking away from the ideal of a "guarded education," with its plan for handing on "safe ideas" at the expense of constructive thought and intellectual curiosity. It was the kind of conservatism which Rufus M. Jones illustrates by an incident in a Philadelphia Quaker meeting. A liberal spirit tried to introduce a slight innovation. As he pleaded with eloquence and with vivid illustrations not a face changed; all was peace, patience and resignation. And when he had concluded the clerk arose and said: "The interruption having ceased, we will now proceed with the business." For a group such as this the founding of a liberal college was a radical step indeed, so radical that a full half-century more was to elapse before the first real steps were taken. (pp. 208-09)

It must not be assumed that the Quakers as individuals had no share in the intellectual movement which brought . . . distinction to Philadelphia. John Bartram, the botanist, Thomas Godfrey, the inventor of the quadrant, John Dickinson, famous for his *Farmer's Letters,* Benjamin West, the painter, were Quakers. But the inspiration came from other groups. Long before the Quakers had relinquished their political control in Pennsylvania, the intellectual leadership in the city of Penn itself had fallen into the hands of rival sects, especially of the Episcopalians. While Franklin and his circle were attracting wide attention by their achievements in science, art, education, architecture and the artistic crafts, the Quakers as a body retired more and more within themselves as a "peculiar people," whose purpose it was to avoid contamination and to preserve the truth in the midst of a wicked and perverse world.

But they retained a firm control in political matters throughout the colonial period, despite the vigorous attempts of other groups to loosen it. The Friends always remembered that Pennsylvania had been founded by their great leader as a Quaker Utopia, where their ideals in both religion and government were to be maintained forever. But they had to battle unceasingly against the attacks of other groups, for some of their beliefs made them especially vulnerable. Was it right that a sect which refused to protect the province from foreign enemies should dominate the government, their opponents asked? Should they be entrusted to administer important offices or act as judges, when they refused to take oaths? (pp. 212-13)

The Quakers met the menace of the newcomers who were filling up the "west" by the simple expedient of withholding from them their proportionate share of representation in the Assembly. There was an obvious reluctance to admit new counties even in the German districts, and the number of representatives from each was narrowly limited. By 1752 Lancaster, York, Cumberland, Berks and Northampton had been admitted with a total of ten seats as compared with twenty-four for Chester, Bucks and

Philadelphia, the Quaker counties, and two for Philadelphia city. We need no further explanation of the fact that in 1755 twenty-eight of the thirty-six members were Quakers. The injustice of this "rotten borough" system is revealed by the fact that in 1760 the five new counties, with more than half the taxables in the colony, had less than a third of the representatives.

The situation was made the more acute by religious, racial and economic differences. Much of the new region was inhabited by Scotch-Irish Presbyterians who regarded the Quakers as dangerous fanatics, and were in turn heartily disliked as Calvinists who were of the same stamp as the New England Puritans who had whipped and hanged Quakers in the seventeenth century. Moreover, the trade connections of the Susquehanna valley with Maryland tended to weaken the economic tie with eastern Pennsylvania and so to render political bondage all the more galling. The troubles of the French and Indian War, when the frontier counties complained bitterly of Quaker pacifism and unfitness to govern, was but one phase of a political struggle which lasted half a century. "Why should we be taxed for many thousands of pounds by the Assembly," the westerners complained, "to be spent at the dictation of a Quaker minority maintained in power through unjust means?" "What lies at the bottom of all their grievances, and must be complained of as the source of all their suffering, is their not being fairly represented in the Assembly," stated a petition in 1764 from "upwards of twelve hundred inhabitants" of Cumberland County. But their pleadings were in vain. It is true the Assembly admitted three more counties in 1771, 1772 and 1773, but with a total of only five representatives, so that when the old charter government fell, the members from the Quaker districts outnumbered those from the non-Quaker counties by twenty-six to fifteen. (pp. 217-18)

The most vulnerable point in the Quaker armor was their opposition to war. It was one thing for a religious society to forbid its members to bear arms, it was a far more serious matter when that society was the ruling power in a great province and tried to shape its policies in conformity with their views. How could they keep Pennsylvania in peace when the British government declared war? How could they refuse to take measures of defense with French and Spanish privateers making captures in the Delaware Bay? How could they withhold appropriations for troops, arms, ammunition and forts, with the Indian warwhoop resounding along the frontiers? The Friends in the Assembly found these questions hard to answer, so hard that it led them into evasions or to compromising with their convictions. On one occasion they caused a number to withdraw from public life.

The great bugbear of requests from the Crown for subsidies for war purposes recurred as often as England became embroiled with other nations. So early as 1693 Governor Fletcher suggested the way out. "If there be any amongst you that scruple the giving of money to support war," he told the Assembly, "there are a great many other charges in that government . . . your money shall be converted to these uses and shall not be dipped in blood." It was not long after this that the Assembly solemnly voted £300 "for the relief of the distressed Indians" of the Six Nations, although they were fully aware that "relief" was to take the form of bullets and other war supplies. (p. 219)

With the advent of the war with Spain in 1739 the old question of aid once more came up. The Quakers made their position clear. We "do not (as the world is now circumstanced) condemn the use of arms in others, yet are principled against it" ourselves. Those who wish to fight have "an equal right to liberty of conscience with others." Therefore they would not consent to a compulsory militia law, but did not oppose those who wished to organize voluntary companies. Five years later, when France had joined Spain against England, Franklin actually recruited 1200 men with the tacit approval of the Assembly. "These all furnished themselves as soon as they could with arms, formed themselves into companies and regiments, chose their own officers and met every week to be instructed in the manual exercise" [John Bigelow, editor, *Works of Benjamin Franklin,* Vol. I]. In this matter the Assembly was much in the position of the Quaker boat captain who, when he was being crowded out from a place at the wharf, called to his mate in despair, "Thee will have to come here and use some of thy language."

But the crucial test came with the French and Indian War. The Quakers prided themselves upon their Indian policy. While other colonies had cheated the Indians, robbed them of their lands, debauched them with rum, made treaties only to break them, waged wars of extermination, the Friends had shown fairness and kindness. Penn's famous treaty, supposed to have been signed under the great elm at Philadelphia, was adhered to faithfully both in letter and in spirit. "This was the only treaty between these people and the Christians that was not ratified by an oath and that was never broken," wrote Voltaire. On their part the Indians loved and revered Penn, carried out their obligations, and looked upon the Quakers as their allies and protectors. It seemed a conclusive answer to those who said that the Quaker policy of amity and peace was impractical.

But matters assumed a different aspect when some of the immigrants, tempted by the fertility of the soil, began clearing land and erecting their cabins on tracts belonging to the Indians. The proprietors tried to buy the land as fast as it was settled, but the complaints of the Indians grew louder and louder. The situation was aggravated when, in 1737, by the fraudulent Walking Purchase the proprietors got title to a vast tract in the Minisink region north of the Lehigh River. When the Delawares who lived there refused to leave, the Six Nations were bribed with a present of £300 to drive them off. This they did with threats and insults which sank deep into the hearts of the Delawares, and brought them back later, tomahawk in hand, to seek revenge upon both the Six Nations and the whites. When this was followed by a purchase at the Albany Conference of 1754 of vast areas west of the Susquehanna, in which the tribes concerned were not even consulted, the situation reached the breaking point.

This favorable moment was selected by the French to occupy the Ohio valley and to incite the Indians against the English. George Crogham, the Indian trader, urged the

Assembly to build a fort at the forks of the Ohio, but the Quakers not only refused, but would do nothing to aid Washington when Virginia undertook the work. Aroused at last to the gravity of the situation, they would have voted funds to aid Braddock's expedition, had not an inopportune controversy with Governor Morris over constitutional rights interfered. Franklin was sent out to procure wagons and pack-horses which proved invaluable, but in the battle which opened the Pennsylvania frontier to the Indian terror there were no Pennsylvania troops to fight beside the British and the Virginians. It is true that had Colonel Dunbar, who succeeded Braddock, not fallen back to Philadelphia leaving the frontiers exposed, disaster might still have been averted. But the Scotch-Irish frontiersmen, who were exposed to the fury of the Indian raids, laid the blame upon the Quaker Assembly. (pp. 220-22)

The time was not far distant when the Scotch-Irish, in concert with the Philadelphia populace and other discontented elements, were to overthrow forever the Quaker ascendency. No one in Pennsylvania suspected when the Sugar Act and the Stamp Act were passed, that these measures were the prelude, not only to independence but to a political revolution within the colony itself. The Quaker merchants, their trade with the foreign West Indies crippled, were among the first to protest and fifty of them signed the non-importation agreement. Taxation of the colonies by Parliament threatened to undermine all the rights and liberties won by the Quaker Assembly during eight decades of political strife, and so long as resistance was confined to protests and peaceful coercion, they were foremost in the American cause.

But when matters took a more serious turn they began to draw back. The Quaker merchants of Philadelphia, like the merchants of other ports, shrank from a war which would drive their ships from the ocean and bring desolation to their wharves and warehouses. The Society as a whole now as always opposed armed resistance and pleaded for patience and compromise. Moreover, when they realized that independence would entail the overthrow of the provincial charter, and with it their own traditional ascendency, they became thoroughly alarmed. After all the rule of the British government, however reactionary, was better than handing over the province to Scotch-Irish Presbyterians and the Philadelphia populace.

The turn affairs were taking became apparent when Paul Revere arrived in Philadelphia in May, 1774, to plead with the Pennsylvanians to join in measures of resistance to the Boston Port Bill. The popular party wished to give assurances of full sympathy to the Bostonians, the Quakers and other conservatives were for proceeding cautiously. A public meeting at the City Tavern expressed its sympathy with the people of Boston who were "suffering in the general cause," but a committee of the Assembly wrote somewhat coolly advising them to seek redress only through constitutional means. This in turn was offset by a spontaneous demonstration on the day the Port Bill went into effect. "If we except the Friends, I believe nine-tenths of the citizens shut up their houses," wrote one observer. "The bells were rang muffled all day, and the ships in the port had their colors half hoisted." A few days later 8000 persons gathered in the State House yard, and passed resolutions declaring the Port Bill unconstitutional and calling for a Continental Congress. (pp. 225-26)

Arouse themselves the Pennsylvanians did, but not until Congress itself had given them the cue. On May 15, 1776, a resolution was passed aimed especially at the Pennsylvania Assembly, recommending the overthrow of the royal and charter governments and the setting up of state constitutions under the authority of the people. The news of this important step spread like wildfire throughout the city and the province and at once became the subject of excited discussion in every coffee-house and tavern. The conservatives were dismayed. "I think the Assembly of this province will not consent to change their constitution," said James Allen, "and then heigh for a convention. A convention chosen by the people will consist of the most fiery Independents; they will have the whole executive and legislative authority in their hands." (p. 227)

On June 18, a Provincial Conference, representing the city and county committees, met in Carpenters Hall to prepare for the constitutional convention. With one brief resolution it swept the old rotten borough system into the discard, declaring that in "any question which may come before them the city and counties respectively have one vote" [*Pennsylvania Archives,* Vol. III]. With the franchise they were equally thorough. It was resolved that every As-

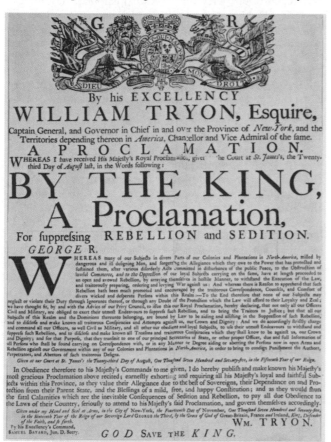

King George III's proclamation calling colonists to put down the rebellion in the Province of New York.

sociator who paid either provincial or county taxes "should be admitted to vote for members of the convention." Having thus increased their own strength by many thousands of votes, they proceeded to weaken the conservatives by imposing a severe test oath or affirmation repudiating allegiance to George III. It remained only for the convention, which opened its sessions in the West Room of the State House on July 15, to crown the work thus started and Quaker ascendency in Pennsylvania was at an end. (p. 228)

> *Thomas Jefferson Wertenbaker, "Penn's Holy Experiment," in his* The Founding of American Civilization: The Middle Colonies, *Charles Scribner's Sons, 1938, pp. 188-230.*

Daniel J. Boorstin

[*Boorstin, a renowned historian, is best known for his* The History of the American People *(1958-73),* The Discoverers *(1983), and* The Creators *(1992), which explore the origins of the ideas and inventions that have had a major impact on the twentieth century. In the excerpt below, Boorstin examines Puritanism and its influence on the early social structures and values of Colonial America, focusing on such leaders as Cotton and Increase Mather, John Adams, and Thomas Jefferson.*]

The forces which have led us to seek our values in our land rather than in our philosophy have been numerous and can be traced back to the earliest period of settlement. The experience of the New England Puritans, despite its remoteness, is among the most instructive episodes of our history for helping us understand the place of theory in American political life. For the Puritans were the first, and perhaps the last, sizable community in American history to import from Europe a fully developed and explicit social dogma, and to try to live by it on this continent. The fate of Puritanism in America thus gives us our unique opportunity to see what kind of success and what kind of failure a self-conscious and comprehensive theory has actually met here.

If ever there was a dogma fit to arm a weak settlement on a savage frontier, it was Puritanism. And yet the very success of the Puritan community on that frontier was to be the undoing of their philosophy. Their success induced them gradually to seek their standards in their own experience, to make what they had accomplished the yardstick of what they might have, or ought to have, accomplished. We shall see how the pragmatic spirit, the belief in "givenness," seeped into the interstices of the Puritan dogma and was gradually to dissolve it into a more general faith in the magical definition of American purpose out of the American success.

It is doubtful if there has ever anywhere been a more subtle, a more comprehensive, or more beautifully put-together theory of society than that which the Pilgrims and Puritans brought with them in the early seventeenth century. One of its marvels was that it was equally capable of communication in heavy treatises like William Ames's *Marrow of Sacred Divinity* and in five-minute talks like John Winthrop's speech to the General Court. It was a miracle of logic, with its own way of asking and of answering any question you might put. Of all people in modern history, these early Puritans could be least accused of confusion about their ends or of that inarticulateness which I have described as a characteristic of American political thought. These people were eager to tell why they were here, what their community was about, and where they were going. The Pilgrims came to the New World, William Bradford explains in his *History,* "not out of any newfangledness, or other such like giddie humor, by which men are oftentimes transported to their great hurt and danger, but for sundrie weightie and solid reasons."

Not only did the early settlers come to New England with an explicit philosophy, but their philosophy, as I shall try to show, had characteristics which fitted it admirably to be a prop for people struggling in the wilderness. In the very beginning, at least, the American experience, far from corroding Puritan dogma, actually seemed its strongest possible proof. For a while, New England would give a dazzling vividness to their dogma. But only in the beginning. For, as the Puritans threw themselves into the struggle against nature, developed their equipment for that struggle, and finally succeeded in building Zion in the wilderness, they were increasingly subject to those influences which were to persist in American history. We can see the growing sense of "givenness," the growing tendency to make the "is" the guide to the "ought," to make America as it was (or as they had now made it) a criterion of what America ought to be. This was the breakdown of classic Puritanism which I have called the movement from providence to pride.

We all know, of course, that Puritanism was a European product, brought here in its nearly finished state. We also know that Puritan orthodoxy, even in Europe, was not to outlive the seventeenth century; that many causes—among others, the growth of science, of rationalism, of materialism, of skepticism, and of evangelical religion—later led in Europe to the breakdown of what had once been a rounded theory of society. What was to be characteristic of American thought was not the fact that the Puritan theory broke down. Puritanism had a comprehensiveness, a brittleness, and a symmetry which destined it for a brief life anywhere. What was characteristic here was not *that* it broke down, but *how.*

The Puritan experience in America was to be distinguished by at least two features: first, an impressive success against great obstacles, the sudden building of new communities and new institutions; and second, a direct encounter with nature. Because the dogma which the Puritans brought with them was so sophisticated, complete, and articulate and because the America against which they struggled was so virginal, wild, and prehistoric, the pressures toward a sense of "givenness" appear with extraordinary clarity in the story of their American community. The anachronism which was to flavor much of American history—the Bible in the wilderness and the rifle against the tomahawk—would never be sharper. Moreover, the sense of having made something of nothing, the awe before a paleolithic landscape which could suddenly sprout civilized communities, would never be more poignant than it must have been in that age.

In the sin of "pride" the Puritans were to have a perfect word for describing the temptations of their success. It is, I believe, a French (and not an American) proverb that "Nothing succeeds like success." While we in the United States have been accused of having a "success-philosophy," the accusation can come only from a certain crudeness in approaching our history. It might be more accurate to say that our success has made us unphilosophical; that a soil where new institutions flourish is not likely to be fertile for metaphysics. Pride of accomplishment has perhaps always and everywhere been a satisfying substitute for a metaphysic of victory.

Of all this, nothing could be more vivid proof than the Puritan experience in its first generations in New England. The success of man's practical energies and the continuity of his institutions were to characterize American history and to make the American increasingly indifferent to cosmic dogmas while he came to believe that his task and his purpose were given by the land in which he lived. In this the Puritans were to foreshadow the way of American political thought.

If anyone had tried to make of whole cloth a philosophy to fortify a weak community on a wild continent, he could hardly have done better than to invent what the Puritans actually brought with them. A disillusioned, indolent, or cowardly Puritan was a contradiction in terms. Works like Norton's *Orthodox Evangelist* or the sermons of Thomas Shepard and John Cotton provided a marvelous combination: optimism and a sense of mission derived from faith that they were the chosen people of God; pessimism coming from a belief in original sin and the weakness of man. Thus they were sure of their success, but neither surprised nor disappointed by their failures.

This character of their thought is pretty obvious. What is perhaps less obvious is that if the Puritans had been able to conjure up a *land* to demonstrate the truth of their theories—a proving-ground, as it were, for their theology—they could hardly have done better than to create the America which they found in the years just after 1620. They saw themselves abandoning the idolatry of the Egyptians in order to rebuild Zion: God's chosen people being led into the wilderness. But for them the line between fact and symbol was never clear; although they possessed an elaborate theory of symbolism—of "types" and "antitypes," in their phrase—they always felt more comfortable if they could see in daily experience the literal counterparts of biblical doctrine. Into a wilderness, then, it was proper for them to be led: no metaphorical wilderness where the perils would be the seven deadly sins, but a wilderness of dark woods, howling wolves, treacherous swamps, and barbarous savages. Such a wilderness the New World provided.

For their purposes the emptiness and isolation of the place would be an advantage, if not actually a necessity. When the Pilgrims first left England, they had gone not to America, but to Holland, where for about ten years they had sought to reconstruct Zion. Before coming to America, they had thus already made an extensive experiment of building a purified community within a corrupt society. As William Bradford recalled their experience in Holland:

> That which was more lamentable, and of all sorowes most heavie to be borne, was that many of their children, by these occasions, and the great licentiousness of youth in that countrie, and the manifold temptations of the place, were drawne away by evill examples into extravagante and dangerous courses, getting the raines off their neks, and departing from their parents. Some became souldiers, others tooke upon them farr viages by sea, and other some worse courses, tending to dissolutnes and the danger of their soules, to the great greefe of their parents and dishonour of God. So that they saw their posteritie would be in danger to degenerate and be corrupted. [*History of Plymouth Plantation,* 1908]

All about them in Europe they had found heresy and corruption. Their best and only hope was to escape altogether from civilization to some place where they would feel no pressure to compromise and where their children would be safe from evil example.

That they would have to pay a price for this opportunity, at least the better-informed of their leaders were well aware. Bradford, for example, knew that America was

> vast and unpeopled . . . being devoyd of all civill inhabitants, wher ther are only salvage and brutish men, which range up and downe, litle otherwise then the wild beasts of the same.

To build Zion in their age, they could perhaps do nothing better than actually to seek out "a hidious and desolate wildernes, full of wild beasts and willd men."

From the point of view of Puritan morality, there would be many subsidiary advantages in their new situation. Where better could men obey God's commandment to fill the earth with his people and his truth? John White, among others, who labored hard from the English side to prepare for the planting of the Colony of Massachusetts Bay, rejoiced at the magnificent way in which men could now advance "the respect unto Gods honor . . . by this worke of replenishing the earth." Here in new parts of the world men could taste "the largeness of his bounty" and discover "the extent of his munificence to the sonnes of men." The hardships and poverty of the new land would actually enlarge the scope for social virtues:

> That the spirits and hearts of men are kept in better temper by spreading wide, and by pouring, as it were, from vessell to vessell . . . will [be] euident to any man, that shall consider, that the husbanding of unmanured grounds, and shifting into empty Lands, enforceth men to frugalitie, and quickneth invention: and the setling of new States requireth justice and affection to the common good: and the taking in of large Countreys presents a naturall remedy against couetousnesse, fraud, and violence; when euery man may enjoy enough without wrong or injury to his neighbour. [White, "Planters' Plea," in Peter Force, *Tracts,* 1947]

Not the least of the theological qualifications of the American continent would be the presence of the Indian savages. A completely uninhabited wilderness would not have served the mission of the Puritans so well as a land like America, peopled by a scattering of pagan tribes. In the first places, of course, the Indians would provide targets for their proselytizing zeal. The charter of the Massachusetts Bay Colony in 1629 declared that to

> wynn and incite the Natives of [the] Country, to the Knowledge and Obedience of the onlie true God and Sauior of Mankinde, and the Christian Fayth . . . in our Royall Intencon, and the Adventurers free Profession, is the principall Ende of this Plantacion.

Nor was this all. In a number of less obvious ways the Indians dramatized the social theory of the colonists.

Puritan theology, we should remember, depicted life on this earth as an unremitting struggle between God and Satan. Good Christians were soldiers in Christ's army battling against the forces of the Devil. Both in England and America, Puritans were, to be sure, quick to see this struggle in the minutiae of daily life. When Michael Wigglesworth sat in his study in Cambridge in Massachusetts Bay and heard the wind slamming his neighbor's door, he tortured himself over whether God had intended him to disturb his thoughts to help a neighbor. Was Satan seducing him by the comforts of his study chair? Such English works as Richard Baxter's autobiography and the numerous collections of "cases of conscience" show how a conscientious Puritan could find cosmic issues in a sneeze.

The struggle between Christ and Satan was the daily meat and drink of Puritans. In England the Puritans had fought their good fight by defending one side of a sophisticated theological debate. In America, however, the Devil would seek special means to harry and discredit God's chosen. "The Divell," Bradford conjectured, "may carrie a greater spite against the churches of Christ and the gospell hear [in America], by how much the more they indeaour to preserve holynes and puritie amongst them." In the New World, Satan had cohorts worthy of him: the wild Indians.

According to reports which most of the Puritans believed, the Indians were cannibals, polygamists, and idolators; they were idle, showed no respect for property, lightly broke their treaties, and delighted in torturing their enemies. However vividly the Puritan ministers may have painted Laud as the champion of Satan, they could not but see Satan with a new vividness when he was championed by a band of pillaging Indians. These, in White's phrase, were the very "bond-slaves of Sathan." No theological education, no prayer-book learning, no knowledge of history was required to see that the savage must be the soldier of Anti-Christ. As the Indians were so obviously the soldiers of darkness, the daily struggle of the New England Puritan was not merely an effort to survive; in fact, he could survive only by defeating Evil.

The Puritan missionaries to the Indians do not marvel—as we might—that the Indians were reluctant to abandon their superstitions for European science. To Puritan eyes the Indians seemed anything but weak: were they not equipped with the powers of Satan? Major General Daniel Gookin, who was for many years superintendent of Indians for the Massachusetts Bay Colony, tells of a savage whose wife, in the toils of a difficult childbirth, had been offered the assistance of the native medicine man. Gookin finally persuaded the Indian to renounce the aid of his witch doctor and, instead, to pray to God; he is, of course, full of praise for the young Indian. But Gookin does not praise the savage for his prudence in giving up the ineffective hocus-pocus of a witch doctor in order to save his wife by civilized methods. Not at all; Gookin does not for one moment doubt the power of Satan. He praises the converted Indian, rather, all the more because he is willing to give up the sure assistance of Satan and so risk the unpredictability of God's will. If, indeed, the Puritans had conceived themselves as carriers of a White Man's Burden, as engaged in civilizing the Indians, they might have been discouraged. But this was not their purpose; and the more hostile and obstinate the Indians, the more assured were the Puritans of the need to redouble their efforts.

The period I have been speaking about is what I shall call the "classic" age of New England Puritanism. It is the age dominated by first-generation immigrants, that is, until about 1660 or 1670. In interpreting their own history in this classic age in New England, the Puritans leaned especially heavily on their *doctrine of providence.* While not ostensibly a philosophy of history, this doctrine was at least a satisfactory substitute for one. And perhaps the most remarkable of those coincidences by which the New World at first confirmed the dogmas of Puritanism was the way in which life in America substantiated this particular notion. For them it was the doctrine of providence that held together the commonplace and the extraordinary, the understood and the mysterious, showing the place of all events in the divine design for their community. "Actual Providence," Norton explained, "is that transient acting of God, whereby he upholdeth, and infallibly governeth all things, and the several natures of things according to the immutable Counsel of his own Will unto their best end, namely, the Manifestation of his own Glory."

Providence, in its most general sense, included all the everyday ways in which God fulfilled his design. The more dramatic aspect of providence, however, was not in the familiar tenor of life but rather in the extraordinary interventions of God to attain his ends. These the Puritans were accustomed to call "special" or "remarkable" or "illustrious" providences; and the ministers of Massachusetts Bay Colony defined them in the following fashion:

> Such Divine judgements, tempests, floods, earthquakes, thunders as are unusual, strange apparitions, or whatever else shall happen that is prodigious, witchcrafts, diabolical possessions, remarkable judgements upon noted sinners, eminent deliverances, and answers of prayer, are to be reckoned among illustrious providences. [In Preface to I. Mather's *Remarkable Providences,* 1856]

Like all of us, the Puritan saw God's hand less vividly in the beating of his own heart than in the lightning and the thunder.

America in that earliest Puritan age actually offered the best possible stage to show men the hand of God in human experience. In America everything was extraordinary.

In the first place, there was something extraordinary about the appearance within the European orbit of a continent which for millennia had been unknown to the civilized world. Just then North America was discovered (in De Tocqueville's phrase) "as if it had been kept in reserve by the Deity and had just risen from beneath the waters of the Deluge" [*Democracy in America,* 1835]. What had been God's purpose in concealing the vast American continent from European eyes until so long after the Creation? Moreover, what was God's purpose in suddenly revealing this continent, in making it accessible in their particular epoch?

> What shall we conceive of that almost miraculous opening the passage unto, and discovery of these formerly unknowne nations, which must needs have proved impossible unto former ages for want of the knowledge of the use of the Loadstone, as wounderfully found out as these unknowne Countries by it. It were little lesse then impietie to conceive that GOD, (whose Will concurres with the lighting of a Sparrow upon the ground) had no hand in directing one of the most difficult and observeable workes of this age; and as great folly to imagine, that hee who made all things, and consequently orders and directs them to his owne glory, had no other scope but the satisfying of mens greedy appetites. [White, "Planters' Plea," in Force, *Tracts*]

But this was only the first of many providential facts which surrounded the early Puritan.

His very presence in America seemed nothing less than a remarkable providence. None of the first generation of Puritans of whom we are now speaking would have been in the New World unless he had survived the perils of a 3,000-mile sea voyage. Even supposing that romantic historians may have exaggerated, the perils of such voyages in the seventeenth century were far from negligible. An Englishman who found himself safely on American shores before 1650 must have been especially insensitive not to have seen something providential in his safe passage. God must have approved the Puritan mission in advance by giving favorable winds, stilling the sea, and moderating the weather. The collection of "illustrious providences" made by Increase Mather in 1684 in New England significantly opens with a chapter of "remarkable sea-deliverances." Every immigrant to early New England must at some time or other have felt the sentiments which William Bradford described at the first landing of the Pilgrims.

> Being thus arived in a good harbor and brought safe to land, they fell upon their knees and blessed the God of heaven, who had brought them over the vast and furious ocean, and delivered them from all the periles and miseries thereof, againe to set their feete on the firme and stable earth, their proper elemente. [*History of Plymouth Plantation*]

(pp. 36-49)

Just as the conditions of America in the first generation were admirably suited to confirm the Puritan beliefs, so the gradual removal of those conditions within the next generations was destined to undermine them. The firm establishment of a community in New England was marked by a growing sense of security, a decline of many of the fears and uncertainties which had nourished a desperate dependence on God. The second generation owed its presence in New England, not to God's happy guidance across the perils of an ocean, but to the simple accident of birth. Puritan immigrants who came after the mid-century were met, not by the Indian arrows which had greeted the first Pilgrims, but by the embrace of their countrymen. Glowing fireplaces and full storehouses were ready for them. Their welcome now seemed less from God—or from Satan—than from their fellow-Puritans.

The Indians were no longer such constant reminders of the powers of the Devil. The last great battle against them in the New England coastal settlements was King Philip's War (1675-76) when the Indians suffered disastrous defeat. Within a few decades, the savage population of Massachusetts Bay Colony had declined to an insignificant number. Puritan chroniclers record the fact with a mixture of sentimental remorse and hardheaded satisfaction. For, like all doctrinaires and fanatics, the Puritans had found it more difficult—and certainly less urgent—to convert their enemies than to exterminate them. Concern for their own young community had thus understandably stifled a lust for the souls of the unconverted. It is true that John Eliot, translator of the Bible into the Indian language, who was perhaps the most selfless, as he was surely the most successful, of the Puritan missionaries, had finally managed to convert a considerable band of Indians. But the Indians' only reward was deportation to a concentration camp on Deer Island.

As the fund of American experience increased, everyday events lost the magic of novelty and the mystery of the unexpected. More and more, life took on the air of the familiar, or even of the banal. The Puritans had now come to look for the bitter winter and the inspiriting spring of New England. The seasonal pattern of habits of the wild animals, the birds, and the fish was gradually discovered. Having learned the best ways of growing Indian corn, the Puritans saw more and more connection between their own efforts and the product of the soil. As they charted the Indian trails, named the hills, and followed the curves of the rivers, they built their own bridges and ferries and established the ways from one village to another. Now if one failed to reach his destination, he had to blame himself.

With remarkable rapidity the Puritans in New England built up their knowledge of the nature around them. The encyclopedic farmer's almanac displaced the catalogue of remarkable providences. As their interest in and mastery of natural history increased, New England Puritans—for example, Cotton Mather, John Leverett, Paul Dudley, John Winthrop, Jr., and Zabdiel Boylston—were enlisted in the Royal Society among the leaders of English science. In New England it was the clergy who propagated the new astronomy. The use of Charles Morton's *Compendium*

Physicae and the growing laboratories of Harvard College attest the serious interest in what they called "experimental natural philosophy." Encouraged by the growing enthusiasm of their age for the laws of nature, they added nearly every day to the data of their science something which a few years before had been the stuff of theology.

In 1684, when Increase Mather wrote the Preface to his collection of remarkable providences, he expressed his wish

> that the Natural History of New-England might be written and published to the world; the rules and method described by that learned and excellent person Robert Boyle, Esq., being duely observed therein. It would best become some scholar that has been born in this land to do such a service for his countrey.

Facts which formerly had been merely points of departure for the imaginative reconteur, or metaphors for sermons to exhort an isolated settlement, were gradually set in order. Now they had become useful knowledge. By the end of the seventeenth century the Puritans' familiarity with their environment, their increasing ability to predict the whims of the weather, and the gifts of the wilderness had seriously dulled—although it had not yet by any means destroyed—their sensitivity to the mysterious and the providential.

The development is nowhere clearer than in the striking change in the Puritan approach to their own history or, more precisely, in the growth of Puritan historical writing. The best early Pilgrim and Puritan accounts of themselves are contemporary chronicles, such as Bradford's history of Plymouth and John Winthrop's journal. These writings, and even lesser ones—like Johnson's *Wonderworking Providence of Sions Saviour in New England*—impress us with the Puritan's sense of his mission, his single-mindedness, his prudence, and his submission to the will of God. They are works of rare seriousness and dignity. But essentially they chronicle the fulfilment of a divine mission rather than the progress of a human enterprise. We are never allowed to forget that the principal protagonist is God, the enemy Satan; each is using men to attain his ends.

By the second or third generation in New England we note a change. It has sometimes been described as the appearance of a "modern" spirit in their historical writing. Now we begin to read works in which *men* are the protagonists: the reader's attention is focused on human successes and failures. Contemporary annals are replaced by retrospective history, dealing with causes and consequences. The discrete judgments of God—his dooms on the good and the evil—intelligible only in the light of cosmic and inscrutable purposes, now give way to the purposes of men.

At this period at the end of the seventeenth century, when the providential glow of the life of earliest New England was still a memory, there appeared the most important work of Puritan historiography, and indeed one of the greatest histories ever written in America. Cotton Mather's *Magnalia Christi Americana,* first published in 1702, was written while Puritan theology was sufficiently alive to give unity to a historical work; yet in its pages we encounter the first full flush of satisfaction at man's accomplishments in the New World. As Mather suggested in his title, he meant to focus on the achievements of Christ rather than on the providences of God. The *Magnalia* seems to tell us that God cannot be better glorified than by a display of the successes of the first two generations of his chosen people in the Wilderness. Here we begin to see the face of Pride. (pp. 53-7)

Mather is hardly to be blamed for pride in the work of his New England predecessors. Satisfaction was justified by the firm foundation of the churches and by the heroism of the New England fighters in "the wars of the Lord," as he called the battles against the Indians. It would have been surprising had Mather not sung the praises of Harvard College, which was already well established. He described his Alma Mater with his customary modesty, as "a river, without the streams whereof, these regions would have been meer unwatered places for the devil!" We could hardly ask for better evidence than Mather has provided us that, even for conservatives, the new security and prosperity of their community nourished a pride in the works of men. God, the providential guardian, who, for reasons best known to himself, had personally deflected the arrows of the Indians and had led the uncertain traveler by the hand from Boston to Cambridge—this God gradually slipped out of their vision. Instead, they began to see a beneficent Being who blessed their own human undertakings. They were moving from a sense of mystery to a consciousness of mastery; the two spirits could not well live together.

This movement was symbolized by a significant change in the character of New England holidays and religious festivals. For the first several decades after the arrival in New England, fast and thanksgiving days were unique occasions. If rain was lacking or an expected ship did not arrive, the magistrates would declare a day of fast to move God to their aid; if a good harvest was granted, a ship was saved from a storm, or the Indians were defeated in a battle, they would declare a day of thanksgiving and prayer. There was nothing regular or perfunctory about these occasions; they expressed the needs or the satisfaction felt by the community at a particular moment. A day of fast or thanksgiving in that earliest age did not mark the regular circuit of the calendar but was itself a symbol of the desperate unpredictableness of life in the wilderness.

By the third generation a significant, though not surprising, change had come over these institutions. Such occasions were now fixed by legislation, defined by the passage of a regular span of time or the recurrence of the season when the community had learned that it would be likely to have cause for thanksgiving. Inevitably, these holidays became symbols less of the prostration of the community before its Creator than of the solidarity of its members: a time for complacency. In this sense there could be nothing more un-Puritan than Thanksgiving Day, once the day had been fixed by law and the calendar rather than by the vicissitudes of life.

The sign of the times which was perhaps most characteristic of New England was the development of the so-called "Halfway Covenant." This doctrine signalized the acquiescence of the older divines in the decline of the sense of mystery and in the rise of a more naturalistic spirit in religion. Proposed by a New England Synod in 1662, it was not generally accepted in New England until some years later. The doctrine represented an abandonment of the strict concept of church membership which had characterized the first generation of Puritans.

According to that early doctrine, "membership" in the church (which they used in a special and technical sense) was one of the greatest mysteries. No one could be a member—that is, within the covenant himself—who had not had an experience of "regeneration" or of being saved. A child born of regenerate parents would, from that fact, be presumed to be holy and hence entitled to baptism; but this would not in itself give him full church membership. For that the personal "saving" experience was indispensable. This "saving" experience was neither the sure result of education nor a predictable response to any act of will. Rather it was an unforeseeable visitation of the spirit of God. Theologians might outline to the faithful some conditions which might prepare one to receive such an experience; and the faithful Puritan could, in a sense, prepare himself. But the experience itself remained mysterious. The arbitrariness with which God selected the men, the times, and the places for regeneration had become a symbol of that disparity between man's weakness and God's omnipotence which was at the heart of Puritan thought.

By the time of the second or third generation in New England, the Puritans, perhaps from an actual scarcity of such experiences, perhaps from a prudent unwillingness to leave the filling of church benches to the hand of providence, now redefined the concept of membership. Or, more precisely, they made an outspoken compromise on the way to abandoning the old mystery.

The Synod of 1662 proposed that henceforth those persons who had been baptized but had lacked the "saving experience" should be counted as "halfway" members of the church. Such membership would be sufficiently potent to be communicated in turn to their children also by the simple ceremony of baptism. In a word, the fact of individual membership (in the new diluted sense) and the size of the congregation would now admittedly be controlled by the community itself. By a devious and in some respects characteristically American route, they were finding their way back to one of those very doctrines from which they had wished to purify their English church. They had now come as close as they dared to making judgments for God. They had taken a long step in the direction of Solomon Stoddard (1643-1729), who a few years later was to argue in effect that all persons of good moral character be admissible to membership.

Men seemed more and more satisfied to show that they comprehended their world by the fact that they had come to master it. Philosophy—except to a lonely giant like Jonathan Edwards (1703-58)—seemed less impressive than institutions. Nor did the new spirit of mastery call forth any great philosophy of naturalism. Puritanism in earliest New England, as we have seen, had been rich in a sense of mystery. From one point of view, indeed, it had been little more than a way of formulating the unintelligibility of experience, of referring the most difficult issues—the salvation of the individual and the fate of the community—to the inscrutable and largely inaccessible purposes of God.

The declining sense of mystery which I have described carried with it an increasing directness in approaching all experience, a willingness to allow experience to give values. As the Puritan in the New World had come to feel that his enemies could be met and overcome, so he had come to feel less vividly the omnipresence of Satan. And as he came to discern and define his obstacles in the wilderness, so he was prepared to believe that even the fate of man's soul, the question of election itself—or at least of title to church membership—might not be entirely hidden from man.

No longer did he feel that he was encircled by enemies; rather he began to think of himself as confronting them. More and more of life seemed predictable, and the Puritan became ready to believe that perhaps the most important facts were intelligible to him, that he might read God's purpose in Nature's design. Once communities had become firmly established and wild men and wild animals had been exterminated from the gaps between the main coastal settlements, the Puritan community began to stand, or to feel that it stood, in a phalanx. With secure and prosperous communities behind them, men felt they could look outward from the larger centers to a definite line of battle in the West. Here, too, circumstances were to define the task.

There is no denying that the Puritan episode was in many ways untypical of later American experience: first, because the intellectual equipment of the earliest Puritans was so thoroughly European and, second, because the America they saw was virginal. By bringing Puritanism to America, they were, of course, starting the long process of importation of ideas from Europe. Their encounter with nature eventually helped disintegrate their original explicit philosophy. Their experience, of course, could not be precisely repeated in other frontier communities which were not equipped with any such explicit philosophy.

The mastery of nature depended on the ability to understand rather than on the ability to persuade. The Big Lie could not help against a snowstorm; it would kill no wolves and grow no corn. Therefore, it was less important to make a grand plan, to make generalities glitter, than to know what was what and how to control the forces of nature. In mastering the wilderness, in building institutions and communities, the second and third generation of New England Puritans became somewhat less anxious to dot all the *I*'s and cross all the *T*'s in their theology. They became more and more responsive to the values which seemed to emerge from their daily lives. The Puritan experience thus shows some persistent characteristics of American history which have encouraged belief in the implicitness of values. Already in that earliest age we see a growing sense of "givenness."

There is a subtler sense in which the Puritan experience symbolizes the American approach to values. For the circumstances which have nourished man's sense of mastery over his *natural* environment have on this continent somehow led him away from dogmatism, from the attempt to plan and control the *social* environment. In this our history may have been distinctive. The two other nations in recent times which seem to have made a fetish of technology started in reverse order. The Nazis and Communists started with blueprints for society and turned to technology as the only means to attain their ends. For our political thought it has been a happy fact that the opposite was true. Nature had to be mastered before society could even survive. (pp. 59-65)

. . . . .

We are accustomed to think of the Revolution as the great age of American political thought. It may therefore be something of a shock to realize that it did not produce in America a single important treatise on political theory. Men like Franklin and Jefferson, universal in their interests, active and spectacularly successful in developing institutions, were not fertile as political philosophers.

In the present chapter I shall offer some explanations of this fact and shall explore some of its significance for our later political life. I shall be trying to discover why, in the era of our Revolution, a political theory failed to be born. But my inquiry will not be entirely negative. I will seek those features of the Revolution, those positive ideas and attitudes, which actually have done much to reinforce our sense of "givenness."

We have been slow to see some of the more obvious and more important peculiarities of our Revolution because influential scholars on the subject have cast their story in the mold of the French Revolution of 1789. Some of our best historians have managed to empty our Revolution of much of its local flavor by exaggerating what it had in common with that distinctively European struggle. This they have done in two ways.

First, they have stressed the international character of the intellectual movement of which the French Revolution was a classic expression—the so-called "Enlightenment." They speak of it as a "climate of opinion" whose effects, like the barometric pressure, could no more be escaped in America than in Europe. As Carl Becker put it in his *Heavenly City of the Eighteenth-Century Philosophers:* "The Enlightenment . . . is not a peculiarly French but an international climate of opinion . . . and in the new world Jefferson, whose sensitized mind picked up and transmitted every novel vibration in the intellectual air, and Franklin of Philadelphia, printer and friend of the human race—these also, whatever national or individual characteristics they may have exhibited, were true children of the Enlightenment. The philosophical empire was an international domain of which France was but the mother country and Paris the capital."

Second, they have treated ours as only a particular species of the genus "Revolution"—of what should perhaps more properly be called *revolutio Europaensis.* Since the French Revolution has been made the model, from that European revolution historians have borrowed the vocabulary in which ours is discussed and the calendar by which it is clocked. "Thermidor," for example, is the name used in one of our best college textbooks to introduce its chapter on the federal Constitution.

It goes on:

> There comes a time in every revolutionary movement when the people become tired of agitation and long for peace and security. They then eliminate the radicals, trouble-makers and warmongers, and take measures to consolidate their government, hoping to secure what has already been gained through turmoil and suffering. *Thermidor* this time is called in leftist language, from the counter-revolution in France that overthrew Robespierre and ended the reign of terror. Thus, the establishment of Cromwell as Lord Protector was the Thermidor of the English Revolution in the seventeenth century; and the Stalin dictatorship and exile of Trotsky marks the Thermidor of the Russian Revolution. Every taking of the Bastille, it may be said, is inevitably followed by Thermidor, since human nature craves security, and the progress of a revolution must be stopped somewhere short of anarchy. [Morison and Commager, *Growth of the American Republic,* 1942]

The effect of all this has been to emphasize—or rather exaggerate—the similarity of ours to all other modern revolutions.

In so doing, historians have exaggerated the significance of what is supposed to have been the ideology of the Revolution. Such an emphasis has had the further attraction to some "liberal" historians of seeming to put us in the main current of European history. It has never been quite clear to me why historians would not have found our revolution significant enough merely as a victory of constitutionalism.

The most obvious peculiarity of our American Revolution is that, in the modern European sense of the word, it was hardly a revolution at all. The Daughters of the American Revolution, who have been understandably sensitive on this subject, have always insisted in their literature that the American Revolution was no revolution but merely a colonial rebellion. The more I have looked into the subject, the more convinced I have become of the wisdom of their naïveté. "The social condition and the Constitution of the Americans are democratic," De Tocqueville observed about a hundred years ago. "But they have not had a democratic revolution." This fact is surely one of the most important of our history.

A number of historians (J. Franklin Jameson and Merrill Jensen, for example) have pointed out the ways in which a social revolution, including a redistribution of property, accompanied the American Revolution. These are facts which no student of the period should neglect. Yet it seems to me that these historians have by no means succeeded in showing that such changes were so basic and so far-reaching as actually in themselves to have established our national republican institutions. When we speak of the Revolution therefore, we are still fully justified in referring to something other than what Jameson's disciples mean by "the American Revolution as a social movement." If we consider the American Revolution in that sense, it would not be a great deal more notable than a number of other social movements in our history, such as Jacksonianism, populism, progressivism, and the New Deal. Moreover, in so far as the American Revolution was a social movement, it was not much to be distinguished from European revolutions; and the increasing emphasis on this aspect of our history is but another example of the attempt to assimilate our history to that of Europe. (pp. 66-70)

The feature to which I want to direct your attention might be called the "conservatism" of the Revolution. If we understand this characteristic, we will begin to see the Revolution as an illustration of the remarkable continuity of American history. And we will also see how the attitude of our Revolutionary thinkers has engraved more deeply in our national consciousness a belief in the inevitability of our particular institutions, or, in a word, our sense of "givenness."

The character of our Revolution has nourished our assumption that whatever institutions we happened to have here (in this case the British constitution) had the self-evident validity of anything that is "normal." We have thus casually established the tradition that it is superfluous to the American condition to produce elaborate treatises on political philosophy or to be explicit about political values and the theory of community.

I shall confine myself to two topics. First, the manifesto of the Revolution, namely, the Declaration of Independence; and, second, the man who has been generally considered the most outspoken and systematic political philosopher of the Revolution, Thomas Jefferson. Of course, I will not try to give a full account of either of them. I will attempt only to call your attention to a few facts which may not have been sufficiently emphasized and which are especially significant for our present purpose. Obviously, no one could contend that there is either in the man or in the document nothing of the cosmopolitan spirit, nothing of the world climate of opinion. My suggestion is simply that we do find another spirit of at least equal, and perhaps overshadowing, importance and that this spirit may actually be more characteristic of our Revolution.

First, then, for the Declaration of Independence. Its technical, legalistic, and conservative character, which I wish to emphasize, will appear at once by contrast with the comparable document of the French Revolution. Ours was concerned with a specific event, namely, the separation of these colonies from the mother-country. But the French produced a "Declaration of the Rights of *Man* and the Citizen." When De Tocqueville, in his *Ancien Régime* (Book I, chap. iii), sums up the spirit of the French Revolution, he is describing exactly what the American Revolution was not:

> The French Revolution acted, with regard to things of this world, precisely as religious revolutions have acted with regard to things of the other. It dealt with the citizen in the abstract, independent of particular social organizations, just as religions deal with mankind in general, independent of time and place. It inquired, not what were the particular rights of the French cit-

izens, but what were the general rights and duties of mankind in reference to political concerns.

It was by thus divesting itself of all that was peculiar to one race or time, and by reverting to natural principles of social order and government, that it became intelligible to all, and susceptible of simultaneous imitation in a hundred different places.

By seeming to tend rather to the regeneration of the human race than to the reform of France alone, it roused passions such as the most violent political revolutions had been incapable of awakening. It inspired proselytism, and gave birth to propagandism; and hence assumed that quasi religious character which so terrified those who saw it, or, rather, became a sort of new religion, imperfect, it is true, without God, worship, or future life, but still able, like Islamism, to cover the earth with its soldiers, its apostles, and its martyrs.

In contrast to all this, our Declaration of Independence is essentially a list of specific historical instances. It is directed not to the regeneration but only to the "opinions" of mankind. It is closely tied to time and place; the special affection for "British brethren" is freely admitted; it is concerned with the duties of a particular king and certain of his subjects.

Even if we took only the first two paragraphs or preamble, which are the most general part of the document, and actually read them as a whole, we could make a good case for their being merely a succinct restatement of the Whig theory of the British revolution of 1688. Carl Becker himself could not overlook this fact. "In political theory and in political practice," he wrote parenthetically, "the American Revolution drew its inspiration from the parliamentary struggle of the seventeenth century. The philosophy of the Declaration was not taken from the French. It was not even new; but good old English doctrine newly formulated to meet a present emergency." To be understood, its words must be annotated by British history. This is among the facts which have led some historians (Guizot, for example) to go so far as to say that the English revolution succeeded twice, once in England and once in America.

The remaining three-quarters—the unread three-quarters—of the document is technical and legalistic. That is, of course, the main reason why it remains unread. For it is a bill of indictment against the king, written in the language of British constitutionalism. "The patient sufferance of these Colonies" is the point of departure. It deals with rights and franchises under British charters. It carefully recounts that the customary and traditional forms of protest, such as "repeated Petitions," have already been tried.

The more the Declaration is reread in context, the more plainly it appears a document of imperial legal relations rather than a piece of high-flown political philosophy. The desire to remain true to the principles of British constitutionalism up to the bitter end explains why, as has been often remarked, the document is directed against the king,

despite the fact that the practical grievances were against Parliament; perhaps also why at this stage there is no longer an explicit appeal to the rights of Englishmen. Most of the document is a bald enumeration of George III's failures, excesses, and crimes in violation of the constitution and laws of Great Britain. One indictment after another makes sense only if one presupposes the framework of British constitutionalism. How else, for example, could one indict a king "for depriving us in many cases, of the benefits of Trial by Jury"?

We can learn a great deal about the context of our Revolutionary thought by examining Jefferson's own thinking down to the period of the Revolution. We need not stretch a point or give Jefferson a charismatic role, to say that the flavor of his thought is especially important for our purposes. He has been widely considered the leading political philosopher of the Revolution. Among other things, he was, of course, the principal author of the Declaration of Independence itself; and the Declaration has been taken to be the climax of the abstract philosophizing of the revolutionaries. Because he is supposed to be the avant-garde of revolutionary thought, evidence of conservatism and legalism in Jefferson's thought as a whole is especially significant.

We now are beginning to have a definitive edition of Jefferson's papers (edited by Julian P. Boyd and published by the Princeton University Press), which is one of the richest treasures ever amassed for the historian of a particular period. This helps us use Jefferson's thought as a touchstone. Neither in the letters which Jefferson wrote nor in those he received do we discover that he and his close associates—at least down to the date of the Revolution—showed any conspicuous interest in political theory. We look in vain for general reflections on the nature of government or constitutions. The manners of the day did require that a cultivated gentleman be acquainted with certain classics of political thought; yet we lack evidence that such works were read with more than a perfunctory interest. To be sure, when Jefferson prepares a list of worthy books for a young friend in 1771, he includes references to Montesquieu, Sidney, and Bolingbroke; but such references are rare. Even when he exchanges letters with Edmund Pendleton on the more general problems of institutions, he remains on the level of legality and policy, hardly touching political theory. Jefferson's papers for the Revolutionary period (read without the hindsight which has put the American and the French revolutions in the same era of world history) show little evidence that the American Revolution was a goad to higher levels of abstract thinking about society. We miss any such tendency in what Jefferson and his associates were reading or in what they were writing.

On the other hand, we find ample evidence that the locale of early Jeffersonian thought was distinctly *colonial;* we might even say *provincial.* And we begin to see some of the significance of that fact in marking the limits of political theorizing in America. By 1776, when the irreversible step of revolution was taken, the colonial period in the life of Jefferson and the other Revolutionary thinkers was technically at an end; but by then their minds had been congealed, their formal education completed, their social habits and the cast of their political thinking determined. The Virginia society of the pre-Revolutionary years had been decidedly derivative, not only in its culture, its furniture, its clothes, and its books, but in many of its ideas and—what is more to our purpose—in perhaps most of its institutions.

It is an important and little-noted fact that for many American thinkers of the period (including Jefferson himself) the cosmopolitan period in their thought did not begin until several years *after* their Revolution. Then, as representatives of the new nation, some of them were to enter the labyrinth of European diplomacy. Much of what we read of their experiences abroad even in this later period would confirm our impression of their naïveté, their strangeness to the sophisticated Paris of Talleyrand, the world of the *philosophes.* In Jefferson's particular case, the cosomopolitan period of his thought probably did not begin much before his first trip abroad as emissary to France in 1784.

When John Adams had gone, also to France, a few years earlier on his first foreign mission, he thought himself fresh from an "American Wilderness." Still more dramatic is the unhappy career of John Marshall, who was an innocent abroad if there ever was one. The career of Franklin, who was at least two generations older than these Revolutionary leaders, is something of an exception; but even in his case much of his charm for the salons of Paris consisted in his successful affectation of the character of a frontiersman.

The importance of this colonial framework in America, as I have already suggested, was to be enormous, not only from the point of view of Revolutionary thought, but in its long-run effect on the role of political theory in American life. The legal institutions which Americans considered their own and which they felt bound to master were largely borrowed. Jefferson and John Adams, both lawyers by profession, like their English contemporaries, had extracted much of their legal knowledge out of the crabbed pages of Coke's *Institutes.*

Now there were the elegant lectures of Sir William Blackstone, published as the four-volume *Commentaries on the Laws of England,* appearing between 1765 and 1769. It was this work of the ultra-conservative interpreter of English law that for many years remained the bible of American lawyers and, for several generations of them, virtually their whole bookish education. Blackstone's *Commentaries,* as Burke remarked in his Speech on Conciliation, had even by 1775 sold nearly as many copies in America as in England. American editions were numerous and popular; despite copious emendations and contradicting footnotes, Blackstone's original framework was faithfully preserved. Lincoln (as Carl Sandburg describes him), sitting barefoot on a woodpile in Illinois, fifty years later, reading the volumes of the conservative English lawyer—which he called the foundation of his own legal education—is a symbol of that continuity which has characterized our thinking about institutions. For our present purposes, the significant fact is that such a work as the *Commentaries* and the institutions which it expounded could

continue to dominate the legal thinking of a people who were rebelling against the country of its origin.

During the very years when the Revolution was brewing, Jefferson was every day talking the language of the common law. We cannot but be impressed not only, as I have remarked, at the scarcity in the Jefferson papers for these years of anything that could be called fresh inquiry into the theory of government but also by the legalistic context of Jefferson's thought. We begin to see that the United States was being born in an atmosphere of legal rather than philosophical debate. Even apart from those technical legal materials with which Jefferson earned his living, his political pieces themselves possess a legal rather than a philosophical flavor.

A Summary View of the Rights of British America (July, 1774), which first brought Jefferson wide notice and which was largely responsible for his momentous choice on the committee to draft a declaration of independence, is less a piece of political theory than a closely reasoned legal document. He justifies the American position by appeal to the Saxon precedent: "No circumstance has occurred to distinguish materially the British from the Saxon emigration." It was from this parallel of the Americans with the Saxons, who also had once conquered a wilderness, that Jefferson draws several important legal consequences.

Jefferson's draft of the "new" Virginia Constitution of 1776 reveals a similar legalistic spirit: his Preamble comprised no premises of government in general, but only the same specific indictments of George III which were to be the substance of the Declaration of Independence. Jefferson actually describes the powers of the chief administrator as, with certain exceptions, "the powers formerly held by the king."

Jefferson's solid achievements in the period up to the Revolution were thus mainly works of legal draftsmanship. The reputation which he first obtained by his *Summary View,* he was to substantiate by other basic documents like the Virginia Constitution and by a host of complex public bills like those for dividing the county of Fincastle, for disestablishing the Church of England, for the naturalization of foreigners, and for the auditing of public accounts. Jefferson was equally at home in the intricacies of real-property law and in the problems of criminal jurisdiction. One of the many consequences of the neglect of American legal history has been our failure to recognize the importance of this legal element in our Revolutionary tradition. Jefferson's chef d'œuvre, a most impressive technical performance, was his series of Bills for Establishing Courts of Justice in Virginia. These bills, apparently drafted within about ten days in late 1776, show a professional virtuosity which any lawyer would envy.

The striking feature of these lawyerly accomplishments to those of us fed on clichés about the Age of Reason is how they live and move and have their being in the world of the common law, in the world of estates tail, bills in chancery, writs of supersedeas, etc., and not in the plastic universe of an eighteenth-century *philosophe.* Our evidence is doubly convincing, for the very reason that Jefferson was something of a reformer in legal matters. Yet even in his extensive projects of reform, he was eager to build on the foundation of the common law; for example, in his plan for the reform of the law of crimes and punishments. His tenacious conservatism appears in bold relief when we remind ourselves that Jefferson was a contemporary of Bentham, whose first important work, the *Fragment on Government,* also appeared in 1776.

But Jefferson did not found his reforms on any metaphysical calculus—rather on legal history and a continuity with the past. Even when he opposed feudal land tenures, he sought support from British sources. In the *Summary View* he had noted that feudal tenures were unknown to "our Saxon ancestors." "Has not every restitution of the antient Saxon laws had happy effects?" To have preserved the feudal tenures would actually have been, in Jefferson's words, "against the practice of our wise British ancestors. . . . Have not instances in which we have departed from this in Virginia been constantly condemned by the universal voice of our country?" (August 13, 1776; *Papers,* Vol. I, ed. Julian P. Boyd, 1950]. Jefferson asked: "Is it not better now that we return at once into that happy system of our ancestors, the wisest and most perfect ever yet devised by the wit of man, as it stood before the 8th century?"

It is worth noting that Jefferson, who was to be the principal political philosopher of the Revolution, was given leadership in the important technical project of legal codification and reform in his native state of Virginia. Had he died at the end of 1776, he would probably have been remembered as a promising young lawyer of reformist bent, especially talented as a legal draftsman. In both houses of the Virginia legislature he had received the highest number of ballots in the election of members of the committee of legal revisers. The gist of the report of that committee (which included Edmund Pendleton, George Wythe, and George Mason, three of the ablest legal scholars on the continent, all active in the Revolution) is significant for our purposes. Jefferson himself recalled some years later that the commission had determined "not to meddle with the common law, i.e., the law preceding the existence of the statutes, further than to accommodate it to our new principles and circumstances."

Jefferson's philosophic concern with politics by the outbreak of the Revolution (actually only the end of his thirty-third year) was the enthusiasm of a reflective and progressive colonial lawyer for the traditional rights of Englishmen. To be sure, Jefferson did go further than some of his fellow-lawyers in his desire for legal reform—of feudal tenures, of entails, of the law of inheritance, of criminal law, and of established religion—yet even these projects were not, at least at that time, part of a coherent theory of society. They remained discrete reforms, "improvements" on the common law.

Jefferson's willingness to devote himself to purification of the common law must have rested on his faith in those ancient institutions and a desire to return to their essentials. This faith shines through those general maxims and mottoes about government which men took seriously in the eighteenth century and which often imply much more than they say. Jefferson's personal motto, "Rebellion to

Tyrants Is Obedience to God," expresses pretty much the sum of his political theory—if, indeed, we should call it a "theory"—in this epoch. It was this motto (which Jefferson probably borrowed from Franklin, who offered it in 1776 for the Seal of the United States) that Jefferson himself proposed for Virginia and which he used on the seal for his own letters. But when we try to discover the meaning of the slogan to Jefferson, we find that it must be defined by reference less to any precise theology than to certain clear convictions about the British constitution. For who, after all, was a "tyrant"? None other than one who violated the sacred tenets of the ancient common law. Jefferson made his own view clear in the device which he suggested for the obverse of the United States seal: figures of "Hengist and Horsa, the Saxon chiefs from whom we claim the honor of being descended, and whose political principles and form of government we have assumed" (quoted by John Adams to Mrs. Adams, August 14, 1776 [*Familiar Letters*, 1875]).

In the Revolutionary period, when the temptations to be dogmatic were greatest, Jefferson did not succumb. The awareness of the peculiarity of America had not yet by any means led Jefferson to a rash desire to remake all society and institutions. What we actually discern is a growing tension between his feeling of the novelty of the American experience, on the one hand, and his feeling of belonging to ancient British institutions, on the other.

The tension was admirably expressed in Du Simitière's design for a coat of arms for Virginia. How large a hand Jefferson, who seems to have counseled Du Simitière, had in inventing the design is actually uncertain. But, regardless of authorship, the design eloquently portrays—indeed, almost caricatures—the current attitude. The indigenous glories of the New World were represented on the four quarters of the shield by a tobacco plant, two wheat sheafs, "a stalk of Indian corn full ripe," and "four fasces . . . alluding to the four gr[e]at rivers of Virginia." The background, the supporting and decorative elements—in fact, all parts of the arms that have any reference to institutions—emphasize the continuity of the British tradition. This was in August, 1776, after the date of the Declaration of Independence.

> Field a cross of St. george gules (as a remnant of the ancient coat of arms [showing] the origin of the Virginians to be English). . . . Supporters Dexter a figure dressed as in the time of Queen Elizabeth representing Sir Walter Rawleigh planting with his right hand the standard of liberty with the words MAGNA CHARTA written on it, with his left supporting the shield. Senester a Virginian rifle man of the present times compleatly accoutr[ed.]
>
> Crest. the crest of the antient arms of Virginia, the bust of a virgin naked and crowned with an antique crown. alluding to the Queen Elizabeth in whose reign the country was discover'd.
>
> Motto. "Rebellion to Tyrants is Obedience to God," or "Rex est qui regem non habet" [*Papers,* I].

It would be possible to multiply examples of the importance of the continuing legal framework in the thought of other leaders of the Revolution. Few would be more interesting than John Adams, another of the authors of the Declaration of Independence. During the Revolutionary era, he elaborated a theory of the British Empire and developed in detail the notion of an unconstitutional act. His thought in this era has been characterized by Randolph G. Adams as that of a "Britannic Statesman."

We begin to see how far we would be misled, were we to cast American events of this era in the mold of European history. The American Revolution was in a very special way conceived as both a vindication of the British past and an affirmation of an American future. The British past was contained in ancient and living institutions rather than in doctrines; and the American future was never to be contained in a theory. The Revolution was thus a prudential decision taken by men of principle rather than the affirmation of a theory. What British institutions meant did not need to be articulated; what America might mean was still to be discovered. This continuity of American history was to make a sense of "givenness" easier to develop; for it was this continuity which had made a new ideology of revolution seem unnecessary.

Perhaps the intellectual energy which American Revolutionaries economized because they were not obliged to construct a whole theory of institutions was to strengthen them for their encounter with nature and for their solution of practical problems. The effort which Jefferson, for example, did not care to spend on the theory of sovereignty he was to give freely to the revision of the criminal law, the observation of the weather, the mapping of the continent, the collection of fossils, the study of Indian languages, and the doubling of the national area.

The experience of our Revolution may suggest that the sparseness of American political theory, which has sometimes been described as a refusal of American statesmen to confront their basic philosophical problems, has been due less to a conscious refusal than to a simple lack of necessity. As the British colonists in America had forced on them the need to create a nation, so they had forced on them the need to be traditional and empirical in their institutions. The Revolution, because it was conceived as essentially affirming the British constitution, did not create the kind of theoretical vacuum made by some other revolutions.

The colonial situation, it would seem, had provided a *ne plus ultra* beyond which political theorizing did not need to range. Even Jefferson, the greatest and most influential theorist of the Revolution, remained loath to trespass that boundary, except under pressure: the pressure of a need to create a new federal structure. Mainly in the realm of federalism were new expedients called for. And no part of our history is more familiar than the story of how the framers of the federal Constitution achieved a solution: by compromise on details rather than by agreement on a theory.

There is hardly better evidence of this fact than the character of *The Federalist* papers themselves. Nearly everything about them illustrates or even symbolizes the way

of political thinking which I have tried to describe. *The Federalist or, The New Constitution* consists of essays written by Alexander Hamilton, James Madison, and John Jay and published one at a time in certain New York journals between late 1787 and early 1788. They had a simple practical purpose: to persuade the people of the state of New York to ratify the recently drawn federal Constitution. The eighty-five numbers were written, like any series of newspaper articles, to be read separately, each essay being a unit. Their object is summarized by Hamilton in No. 1:

> I propose, in a series of papers, to discuss the following interesting particulars:—The utility of the UNION to your political prosperity—The insufficiency of the present Confederation to preserve that Union—The necessity of a government at least equally energetic with the one proposed, to the attainment of this object—The conformity of the proposed Constitution to the true principles of republican government—Its analogy to your own State constitution—and lastly, The additional security which its adoption will afford to the preservation of that species of government, to liberty, and to property.

If, indeed, *The Federalist* may be considered a treatise on political theory, it differs from other important works of the kind, by being an argument in favor of a particular written constitution. In this it is sharply distinguished from the writings of Plato, Aristotle, Hobbes, Locke, Rousseau, and J. S. Mill, which give us either systematic theories of the state or wide-ranging speculation. The organization of *The Federalist* papers is practical rather than systematic: they proceed from the actual dangers which confronted Americans to the weaknesses of the existing confederation and the specific advantages of the various provisions of the new constitution.

While the individual essays are full of wisdom, we must not forget, as Sir William Ashley reminds us, that "*The Federalist* has come to stand out more distinctly in the public view because of the oblivion that has befallen the torrent of other controversial writings of the same period." *The Federalist* essays are too often treated as if they comprised a single logical structure. They were a collaborative work mainly in the sense that their authors agreed on the importance of adopting the new constitution, not in the sense that the authors start from common and explicit philosophic premises. Hamilton, Madison, and Jay differed widely in personality and in philosophic position: individually they had even favored some other institutions than those embodied in the Constitution. But they had accepted the compromises and were convinced that what was being offered was far superior to what they already had. To read *The Federalist* is to discover the wisdom of Calhoun's observation that "this admirable federal constitution of ours . . . is superior to the wisdom of any or all of the men by whose agency it was made. The force of circumstances, and not foresight or wisdom, induced them to adopt many of its wisest provisions" (*Works,* ed. R. K. Cralle).

The Revolution itself, as we have seen, had been a kind of affirmation of faith in ancient British institutions. In the greater part of the institutional life of the community the

Revolution thus required no basic change. If any of this helps to illustrate or explain our characteristic lack of interest in political philosophy, it also helps to account for the value which we still attach to our inheritance from the British constitution: trial by jury, due process of law, representation before taxation, habeas corpus, freedom from attainder, independence of the judiciary, and the rights of free speech, free petition, and free assembly, as well as our narrow definition of treason and our antipathy to standing armies in peacetime. It also explains our continuing—sometimes bizarre, but usually fortunate—readiness to think of these traditional rights of Englishmen as if they were indigenous to our continent. In the proceedings of the San Francisco Vigilance Committee of 1851, we hear crude adventurers on the western frontier describing the technicalities of habeas corpus as if they were fruits of the American environment, as natural as human equality. (pp. 81-98)

Daniel J. Boorstin, "The Puritans: From Providence to Pride" and "The American Revolution: Revolution without Dogma," in his The Genius of American Politics, *The University of Chicago Press, 1953, pp. 36-65, 69-98.*

Catherine L. Albanese

[In the following excerpt, Albanese assesses the influence of such Colonial ministers as Cotton Mather, Samuel Davies, and Jonathan Mayhew, as well as of statesmen John Adams and George Washington; their transformation of the Puritan ethic into a "humanocentric" civil religion, Albanese contends, led to America's reverence for its founding fathers and its belief in a divine destiny.]

With the publication in 1764 of the first volume of Thomas Hutchinson's *History of the Province of Massachusetts Bay,* a Royalist was ironically providing grist for the patriot mill. Ezra Stiles observed that the book had "contributed more than anything else to reviving the ancestral Spirit of Liberty in New England" [quoted in Wesley Frank Craven, *The Legend of the Founding Fathers,* 1956]. Cheerfully ignoring the lectures on loyalty which Hutchinson furnished, the patriots read instead of the marvellous deeds of their fathers. When five years later Hutchinson published a documentary appendix, the influential few who read it included Samuel Adams, who regularly sent letters to the newspapers, and a number of pamphleteers. "History," Hutchinson had written in contemplation of the planting of Massachusetts Bay, "affords us no instance of so great movements in so short a time. The same passion

Uniformed soldiers reenact the Battle of Trenton (N.J.), in which Washington scored a crucial victory.

still continues, and affords a prospect of the like happy effect for ages yet to come. [Thomas Hutchison, *The History of the Province of Massachusetts,* 1936] (p. 20)

That the truth of the colonists relied for its force upon an appeal to their past becomes even clearer in the records of their own consciousness which have come down to us. Taking themes which had been present in seventeenth- and early eighteenth-century election sermons, Americans shaped them to their own patriotic ends. Thus, Samuel Cooke in 1770 found it appropriate to preach before Royal Lieutenant-Governor Hutchinson that "our fathers supposed their purchase of the aboriginals gave them a just title to the land; that the produce of them, by their labor, was their property, which they had an exclusive right to dispose of; that a legislative power, respecting their internal polity, was ratified to them." To the query, "Our fathers—where are they?" Cooke could reply that they had "looked for another and better country, that is, an heavenly," and because they had found it, they heard no more "the voice of the oppressor." The implication for Hutchinson must have been unmistakable. Six years later, the election sermon was no longer preached before the royal representative. Now Samuel West declared that, when he considered "the dispensations of Providence towards this land ever since our fathers first settled in Plymouth," he found "abundant reason to conclude that the great Sovereign of the universe [had] planted a vine in this American wilderness which he [had] caused to take deep root" [*Election Sermon,* May 30, 1770].

In like fashion, George Duffield, preaching to a Philadelphia congregation in 1776, told them that "our forefathers, who first inhabited yonder eastern shores, fled from the iron rod and heavy hand of tyranny." In the patriots' cause, a "DIVINE AFFLATUS" had breathed. It was the "same spirit that inspired our forefathers' breasts when first they left their native shores and embarked for this then howling desert." Invariably, as the preachers told and retold the story, the fathers were memorable because they had suffered for the foundation of freedom, risking their lives to escape British tyranny, although it meant a liberty in the "howling wilderness." They pursued their goal and sought their freedom for the sake of the highest earthly reality—that of worshiping God in the manner the inner voice of conscience taught was most pleasing to him.

And invariably, as the preachers preached, there was a connection between the actions of the fathers and the present activity of their sons. Again, the spectre of British tyranny stood over them, and again they must face upheaval and the return to a state of nature, the "howling wilderness" of the war, in order to uphold the freedoms which the inner voice insisted belonged to them. Now, however, it was liberty itself which was the central issue and not, as in the past, liberty for the sake of religion. It was here that the analogy limped, and so it was here the preachers protested most vociferously. While some who lived out of a different myth might argue that British requests were reasonable, that the point was merely one of taxation and representation in Parliament, that there were complexities and subtleties in the dynamic of a political problem, the patriots brooked no response except the ringing truth of

their myth. And perhaps here was the area of stress where the patriots knew but did not know, for it must have been liminally apparent to some of them that they had grown sleeker and fatter than their image of their religion-loving fathers whose purported asceticism they no longer imitated. In fact, as we shall see, they were indeed aware of the place of stress—and they dealt with it with the venerable seventeenth-century solution of the jeremiad, by mourning the declension of the present and beating their breasts in sorrow that the austerity and innocence of former ages was gone.

Moreover, private letters agreed with public sermons. One correspondent [in a letter dated June 26] wrote back to England in 1775 that the Continentals were men "acting in defence of all those great and essential privileges which our forefathers ever held so dear." He added tellingly that "not a soldier dies of his wounds who does not believe he goes directly to heaven, notwithstanding all the anathemas of the general proclamation." Benjamin Rush admitted that his passion for liberty had been "early cultivated by my ancestors. I am the great grandson of an officer John Rush who fell fighting against King Charles 1st under Oliver Cromwell." Other correspondents who wrote to friends or relatives in England called the colonists "the descendants of Oliver Cromwell's army" and "the descendants of Cromwell's *elect.*" At the same time, a popular song of 1776 announced that "In story we're told/How our Fathers of old/Brav'd the rage of the wind and the waves" [from Broadside no. 2042, "Two Favorite New Songs at the American Camp," in *Broadsides, Ballads, etc, Printed in Massachusetts 1639-1800,* 1922], while John Dickinson's familiar "Liberty Song" began one stanza with a dedication to "Our worthy Forefathers."

In the public rituals in which the new religion of the Revolution was growing, both individual and collective consciousness were fused. Silas Downer, a Son of Liberty who spoke at the consecration of a Liberty Tree, evoked the well-worn theme at Providence in 1768.

> Our fathers fought and found freedom in the wilderness; they cloathed themselves with the skins of wild beasts, and lodged under trees and among bushes; but in that state they were happy because they were free—Should these our noble ancestors arise from the dead, and find their posterity trucking away that liberty, which they purchased at so dear a rate, for the mean trifles and frivolous merchandize of *Great-Britain,* they would return to the grave with a holy indignation against us. [*A Discourse Delivered in Providence . . . at the Dedication of the Tree of Liberty,* 1768]

In a Boston Massacre Oration for 1772, Joseph Warren told the populace that their "illustrious fathers" were the "zealous votaries" of freedom. They brought her "safe over the rough ocean and fixed her seat in this then dreary wilderness; they nursed her infant age with the most tender care; for her sake, they patiently bore the severest hardships; . . . neither the ravenous beasts that ranged the woods for prey, nor the more furious savages of the wilderness, could damp their ardor!" "No sacrifice," Warren underlined, "not even their own blood, was esteemed too rich a libation for her altar!" Three years later, with British officers in the aisles and his life in danger, Warren sounded the theme again for the same anniversary, this time linking it to the old Puritan motif of the Israel of God.

> Our fathers having nobly resolved never to wear the yoke of despotism, and seeing the European world, at that time, through indolence and cowardice, falling a prey to tyranny, bravely threw themselves upon the bosom of the ocean, determined to find a place in which they might enjoy their freedom, or perish in the glorious attempt. Approving heaven beheld the favorite ark dancing upon the waves, and graciously preserved it until the chosen families were brought in safety to these western regions. [*Boston Massacre Oration,* March 6, 1775]

It was no surprise that the official publication of *Rules and Regulations for the Massachusetts Army* (1775) began with a celebration of the virtues of the "venerable Progenitors" and a reminder of the "indispensable Duty" of their descendants in the present. A year earlier, the Continental Congress had passed the resolve which Massachusetts was echoing.

> It is an indispensable duty which we owe to God, our country, ourselves and posterity, by all lawful ways and means in our power to maintain, defend and preserve those civil and religious rights and liberties, for which many of our fathers fought, bled and died, and to hand them down entire to future generations. [September 17, 1774, in *Journals of Congress*]

If liberty was that highest good for which men died, it was in contrast with slavery that the colonists seemed to understand its meaning most forcefully. Songs enjoyed a propensity for being titled "Liberty Song," and not infrequently they contained verses similar to William Billing's "Hymn": "Let tyrants shake their iron rod,/And slavery clank her galling chains;/We fear them not; we trust in God—/New England's God for ever reigns." Oratory dwelt on the horrors and miseries of being enslaved, while newspapers and broadsides carried written reminders of the terrors of a slave existence. Enunciating the popular resolve, the Boston Committee of Correspondence declared that "the right of freedom being *the gift of* GOD AL-MIGHTY, it is not in the power of man to alienate this gift and voluntarily become a slave." At the height of the frenzy, Congress petitioned King George III [October 26, 1774] with a stern exhortation: "Had our Creator been pleased to give us existence in a land of slavery, the sense of our condition might have been mitigated by ignorance and habit. But, thanks to his adorable goodness, we were born the heirs of freedom."

It is worth scrutinizing the incongruity of these slaveholding patriots who trembled at the peril of becoming British "slaves." Their fears might be dismissed as overreaction or condemned in a moralistic denunciation of the hypocrisy believed to stand behind them. But neither approach is particularly helpful in understanding how it came to be that the language of slavery operated with such power in the myth. At the center of their being, the patriots seemed

to possess so graphic a sense of the meaning of slavery that it impelled them as a counterforce toward the fruits of liberty. One wonders if the memory of the sufferings of the fathers, though present, could have crystallized in such a sense. One wonders, in fact, if the popular descriptions of clanking chains and iron bonds could by any stretch of the imagination be applied to the ancestors. Rather, the patriots knew what slavery was because they *owned* slaves, clamped irons on the limbs of these unfortunates, and saw and heard their chains. Guilty before their fathers because they had left the legendary asceticism for the fat of the land, the patriots were also guilty before their black slaves. Through all the distance which the mythology of ownership and possession had created, the slaves tormented their masters with the remnants of humanness which managed to filter through.

Yet as the patriots played out their inner drama on a public stage, it was England which became, instead of a nurturing mother, an enslaving demon, corrupt and rotten at the core. Of course, there were good reasons for separation from England, and the British did not on every occasion tread lightly and angelically on colonial minds and lands. However, the power which "screwed the colonists to the sticking place" in their fight for the kind of world they wanted emerged out of the dynamic of the play of hidden forces within them. So, with incredible ease and speed, the British became "our unnatural Enemies, who have in a hostile Manner been endeavouring to enslave the United Colonies" [Broadside of the Massachusetts House of Representatives, April 19, 1776]. Abroad in England in 1772, Benjamin Franklin declared, "Had I never been in the American Colonies, but was to form my Judgment of Civil Society by what I have lately seen, I should never advise a Nation of Savages to admit of Civilization." As the Revolution progressed, a great outcry was raised over how the British looted and pillaged, burned the churches, horribly mistreated prisoners, raped the women, and tore sucking infants from their dying mothers' breasts. The forces of evil which England embodied were especially evident as a foil for the action of the God of Battles in the developing myth, and we shall have more to say about the demonization of the British when we confront Jehovah fighting for the American cause.

Particularly in New England, the fathers and sons who fought against slavery under a demonic England and found their liberty in a new land of freedom belonged to a chosen race. They were "our Israel," who, as Israel of old which was governed directly by God through Moses, knew no "divine right of kings." As in the days of the wilderness fathers, sermons on Old Testament themes predominated, while preachers announced the striking parallel between old and new: "Israel were a free, independent commonwealth, planted by God in Canaan, in much the same manner that he planted us in America" [Nathaniel Whitaker, "An Antidote against Toryism; or the Curse of the Meroz," in *The Patriot Preachers of the American Revolution,* 1868]. Yet in reality, the colonists were making *two* links as they used the language of "our Israel." They saw themselves in continuity with the first Israel in Canaan, but now they also and more importantly saw themselves in continuity with their fathers. John Winthrop's ringing declaration that "the eies of all people are vppon vs" had worked its way to the core of the collective soul.

"The eyes of the whole world are upon us in these critical times, and, what is yet more, the eyes of Almighty God," preached Phillips Payson in one election sermon [May 27, 1778]. For Mercy Otis Warren, reflecting later on events, America had stood as a "monument of observation, and an asylum of freedom."

> The eyes of all Europe were upon her: she was placed in a rank that subjected her to the inspection of mankind abroad, to the jealousy of monarchs, and the envy of nations, all watching for her halting, to avail themselves of her mistakes, and to reap advantages from her difficulties, her embarrassments, her inexperience, or her follies. [*History of the Rise, Progress and Termination of the American Revolution, Interspersed with Biographical, Political, and Moral Observations,* 1805]

In the tradition of its fathers, the favored nation saw with progressive clarity that its exemplary character led to millennial mission. The publication in 1774 of Jonathan Edward's chiliastic *History of the Work of Redemption* underlined the presence of the past in the revolutionary milieu. Warren seemed to echo the theologian when she wrote as an American patriot:

> The western wilds, which for ages have been little known, may arrive to that state of improvement and perfection, beyond which the limits of human genius cannot reach; and this last civilized quarter of the globe may exhibit those striking traits of grandeur and magnificence, which the Divine Oeconomist may have reserved to crown the closing scene, when the angel of his presence will stand upon the sea and upon the earth, lift up his hand to heaven, and swear by Him that liveth for ever and ever, that there shall be time no longer.

Long before the Revolution, a youthful John Adams had had intuitions which were similar. Writing to Nathan Webb, Adams reflected that "soon after the Reformation, a few People came over into this new world for conscience sake. Perhaps this, apparently, trivial incident may transfer the great seat of empire in America. It looks likely to me." It would take the consciousness of the nineteenth century to develop the "secular" version of the doctrine in its fulness, but the seeds were already present as the colonists began to shift the strongest ground of their argument from the rights of British subjects to the rights of humankind. For if the patriots were fighting for the rights which appropriately belonged to all, it was only a short and perhaps implicit deduction that they were fighting *for all.*

The importance of the mythological shift cannot be overestimated. In the switch in language from England to all humanity was buried a transposition which was changing a historical myth into a theological one. When patriots fought British tyrants, they were facing a particular, albeit demonic and corrupt, enemy who was trying to deprive them of particular rights which belonged to Englishmen. When they struggled for human rights in the name of all,

their efforts took on a universal and absolute character. Here was an answer to cover every opportunity and an argument to engage each particular. The patriots, as their fathers before them, were building on the strongest and surest foundation. It was true that the language of universal claims had a long history in the patriot past, familiar and comfortable from Puritan pulpits or from mid-eighteenth-century newspapers such as the *Independent Reflector.* But a transformation of symbol occurred in the context of events leading up to the Declaration of Independence. As the natural rights of humankind achieved ascendancy over the particular rights of British subjects, the myth of Revolution had touched a loadstone of power, and its magnetism became evident in the growing victory of the patriots over their unconverted brethren. Curiously, a theological myth of mission was linked to the philosophy of nature and natural rights. The amalgamation was only one of the "biformities" which made the American myth of origins a "two-in-one."

Chosen for an example and imbued with a deep sense of universal mission, Americans, as Israel of old and their fathers before them, inhabited a promised land. "When we view this country in its extent and variety," exulted Silas Downer, "we may call it the promised land, a good land and a large—a land of hills and vallies [*sic*], of rivers, brooks, and springs of water—a land of milk and honey, and wherein we may eat bread to the full." Other patriots agreed. Oratory echoed with the millennial theme in the land of plenty where, as in Israel's dreams of a future of bliss, each man would dwell under his own fig tree in the shade of his vines, while his wife would be a fruitful olive branch surrounded by her joyful children.

Yet there was a jarring note amid the beauties of Paradise. The patriots continually announced their fear of the blight which could hopelessly destroy the new Canaan, for an invasion of sin, bringing a degeneration and winding down of the world, could end the millennium. Here was sure evidence that the worldview of myth was at the core of patriotic awareness, for one recited a myth in order to bridge the gap between the profane world of ordinary events and the original world of myth in the strong and sacred time. The present world had come forth out of the power of the myth; but in and of itself, the world lacked power and would speedily return to an inert state. Only contact with living myth could close the separation, and hence the necessity of drawing strength from remembrance. If one could not be perfect as the fathers, the solution was to repent and to remember.

It was not surprising that the patriots throughout the Revolution were almost as worried about enslavement through their own lusts and excesses as they were about enslavement through British tyranny. If there were "deluges of the Old World, drowned in luxury and lewd excess," there could as easily be deluges of the new. John Witherspoon, New Jersey's preacher-delegate to the Congress in 1776, thought nothing "more certain than that a general profligacy and corruption of manners make a people ripe for destruction." A good form of government, he added, might "hold the rotten materials together for some time, but beyond a certain pitch, even the best constitution will be ineffectual, and slavery must ensue" [*The Dominion of Providence over the Passions of Men,* May, 1776]. Earlier in 1770, John Adams had seen a parallel between divine government and the human version in which the latter was "more or less perfect, as it approaches nearer or diverges further from an imitation of this perfect plan of divine and moral government." Yet, he warned an invisible audience in the pages of his diary:

> In times of simplicity and innocence, ability and integrity will be the principal recommendations to the public service, and the sole title to those honors and emoluments which are in the power of the public to bestow. But when elegance, luxury, and effeminacy begin to be established, these rewards will begin to be distributed to vanity and folly; but when a government becomes totally corrupted, the system of God Almighty in the government of the world, and the rules of all good government upon earth, will be reversed, and virtue, integrity, and ability, will become the objects of the malice, hatred, and revenge of the men in power, and folly, vice, and villany will be cherished and supported.

In this context, George Washington's order to his brigadiergenerals in 1777 was representative.

> Let vice and immorality of every kind be discouraged as much as possible in your brigade; and, as a chaplain is allowed to each regiment, see that the men regularly attend during worship. Gaming of every kind is expressly forbidden, as being the foundation of evil, and the cause of many a brave and gallant officer's and soldier's ruin.

Writing after the éclat of stirring events, Mercy Warren thought that few would deny that religion, viewed merely in a political light, is after all the best cement of society, the great barrier of just government, and the only certain restraint of the passions, those dangerous inlets to licentiousness and anarchy. For Warren and for most of the patriots, luxury and avarice were "totally inconsistent with genuine republicanism." Preachers such as David Tappan regularly inveighed against America's "crimes of the blackest hue" and the "turpitude and guilt of our national provocations" ["A Discourse Delivered in the Third Parish in Newbury, Massachusetts, on the 1st of May 1783"].

While some, like Nathaniel Whitaker, saw in Toryism a sin against forefathers, contemporaries, and posterity, others, like Samuel Langdon, viewed the cause of the troubles with England as rebellion against God and the loss of a "true spirit of Christianity." "Is it not a fact open to common observation, that profaneness, intemperance, unchastity, the love of pleasure, fraud, avarice, and other vices, are increasing among us from year to year? And have not even these young governments been in some measure infected with the corruption of European courts?" Yet, whether sin was a political or a personal reality, it always had a political effect. Citizens must be virtuous because their very communal existence as a state could be called into question by their vice. In one instance of a longstanding custom, the Massachusetts Provincial Congress at Watertown legislated against the "unnatural War" by

condemning "Prophanations" of the Sabbath; thus too the long tradition of congressional proclamations of fasts and thanksgivings. . . .

The most common interpretation of events among the patriots was to see "British oppression" as a visitation for sin, while war defeats required a revival of morality and religion in order to be changed to victory. So, for example, one broadside of 1777 lamented the "Dreadful Extortion and Other Sins of the Times" (committed against the patriots), offering "a serious EXHORTATION to all to repent and turn from the Evil of their Ways, if they would avert the terrible and heavy JUDGMENTS of the ALMIGHTY that hang over America at this alarming and distressing Day" ["Broadside, 1777," in *American Broadside Verse from Imprints of the Seventeenth and Eighteenth Centuries,* 1930]. In another interpretation, the political turmoil acted as a furnace to burn away the dross of sin and purge the new Israel from corruption. Benjamin Rush could write that he hoped the war would "last until it introduces among us the same temperance in pleasure, the same modesty in dress, the same justice in business, and the same veneration for the name of the Deity which distinguished our ancestors" [in a letter to John Adams, August 8, 1777].

Whether the actions of England were caused by sin or the cure of it, what emerged was a dualistic view of the world in which the past had been golden and the present stood in peril of decline. The jeremiad, as Perry Miller noted, paid the penny to Jehovah so that Americans could spend the rest of their dollar on their own pursuits. But the jeremiad was also a ritual for mythic remembrance. By clearly experiencing one's sinfulness, one implicitly understood what the opposite condition was about. And so by their lamentation, the patriots underwent a form of *anamnesis,* remembrancing the fathers in such a way that the sons really were present with these ancestors in the golden age of the beginning, *in illo tempore.*

Paradoxically, the jeremiad also looked toward the millennium, for the endtime of peace and plenty was an eschatological transposition of the time of beginning. That is, whether the sacred time of power was seen emerging out of an initial formlessness and chaos, or whether it came as final and perfect form after the world had erupted into the confusion and turmoil of the age before the millennium, it was still the time of the newness when the world experienced the strength of early vigor. In an early nineteenth-century expression, Hesper's words to Columbus in Joel Barlow's *Columbiad* captured the mythic sense.

> Here springs indeed the day, since time began,
> The brightest, broadest, happiest morn of man.
> In these prime settlements thy raptures trace
> The germ, the genius of a sapient race,
> Predestined here to methodize and mold
> New codes of empire to reform the old.
> A work so vast a second world required,
> By oceans bourn'd, from elder states retired;
> Where uncontaminated, unconfined,
> Free contemplation might expand the mind,
> To form, fix, prove the well adjusted plan
> And base and build the commonwealth of man.

As we shall see, the men and women who lived through the Revolution seemed to experience it as that kind of premonitory chaos and anarchy, that dissolution of forms, which would precede the coming of new and perfect form. The jeremiad, the golden age of the fathers, and the future age of the millennium were linked with the strongest of bonds as parallel mythologems of the myth.

But there were further links between their fathers' situation and their own to which the patriots did not allude. It is obvious that the patriots had appropriated the stories of liberty against tyranny and the new Israel in a regenerating wilderness from their understanding of their fathers. At the same time, the men of the Revolution had also received from their ancestors a tradition which had grown more and more comfortable with nature and its laws and increasingly certain that virtuous human activity was the key which would unlock not only the door to salvation but the door to the earthly paradise as well. This tradition is most clearly documented for the Puritan fathers whose past, because it was so well articulated, dominated the revolutionary consciousness, but there are hints that it was more quietly true in the middle and southern colonies. As Richard Merritt has shown [in his *Symbols of American Community, 1735-1775*, 1966], Massachusetts was the earliest articulator of the ideas which culminated in the Revolution, but "the Boston printers by themselves could not produce a symbol revolution." The middle colonies and the southern "nodded their assent" only when, through the processes of inner change, the concerns of the Puritan fathers had been linked to their own understandings and needs.

The records of Puritan experience reveal that the first generation had drawn heart and head together by linking the immediacy of a personal conversion process to reasonable and collective verification in the covenantal community. Yet the much-vaunted "synthesis" seemed to shatter not all at once, with the sudden appearance of revivalism and liberalism as opposing forces, but slowly and gradually. James W. Jones [in his *The Shattered Synthesis: New England Puritanism before the Great Awakening*, 1973] has shown that "throughout the seventeenth century there was an increasing tendency to equate the divine agency with natural causation and human volition. Gradually God's act became simply another name for what, in fact, was happening." Meanwhile, the Great Awakening suggested that perhaps the original Puritan focus on a direct experience of the divine, although it was greatly overshadowed by institutions like the "halfway covenant" and rituals like "owning the covenant," had never really died. Both sides of this Puritan heritage were present in the Revolution, which generated in effect a new and nontraditional religious synthesis, a veritable two-in-one. The lines of the growing crack in the old synthesis had not been so clear as might be supposed. In the mid-eighteenth century, would-be evangelicals could think like liberals when morality and human rights were concerned, and liberals could act as enthusiastically as their Calvinistic brethren.

The religion of nature was already incipiently challenging the ascendancy of the Calvinist God when John Norton began to teach that "God adapts himself to man to the ex-

tent of not dealing with man as with a brute creature." It was growing as Giles Firmin began to use human nature as the criterion for deciding what was and what was not correct theology. Ironically, Cotton Mather, that austere preacher of the sovereignty of God, himself helped the humanocentric process along. Mather was a moralist for whom the works of sanctification could be a sign that one was saved, and later Benjamin Franklin would state that Mather's *Essays to do Good* were formative in his (and by implication Poor Richard's) way of living. Moreover, if human nature was raised a notch by Mather's treatment of it, so too was the rest of the natural milieu. Mather indeed was "so enthralled by what he found in nature that he came perilously close to putting nature on a par with Scripture as a source of knowledge about God."

Similarly, Benjamin Colman placed God's sovereignty at the foundation of his theology, yet tied that sovereignty inextricably to God's role as creator of the beauties of the Newtonian cosmos. The God-who-acts was becoming the God whose will was expressed in the laws of nature, since, while humans were as nothing in the sight of God, their reasonable faculties could discover and use the harmonies of the cosmos. For Solomon Stoddard, as the century progressed, God's attractiveness was aesthetic, the effusion of his glory in nature which drew people toward the divine life. Stoddard's grandson, Jonathan Edwards, would himself have a great deal to say about the divine beauty as well as a keen appreciation of the loveliness of natural surroundings.

This sensitivity to the laws of nature as expressed in both human and cosmic form began gradually to take a political shape. With their understanding of themselves as a city on a hill, a theocracy in which God was the true ruler of the political state, the Puritans had always been inclined to treat civic realities as also sacred realities. But the tendency received expression in a manner which would be particularly serviceable for the formation of revolutionary mythology in the writings of John Wise. His *Vindication of the Government of the New England Churches* (1717), written to defend ecclesiastical polity, proved a blueprint for civil democracy and became decidedly influential when it was republished in 1772. Wise had seen himself as opposing Cotton Mather, but when he chose to place his argument from nature before his argument from Scripture in the text of the *Vindication*, he had advanced one side of Mather's thinking toward greater appreciation of the natural world. While it may be an overstatement to say that "some of the most glittering sentences in the immortal Declaration of Independence are almost literal quotations from this essay of John Wise" [as quoted by Morris in *Christian Life and Character of the Civil Institutions of the United States*, 1864] (since so many were by 1776 speaking in similar vein), the *Vindication* does present an early and emphatic version of the language of reason and nature which became so popular during the Revolution.

Wise, moreover, interwove his use of reason and nature with a mythic view of history. He saw the first three hundred years of the Christian church as an era of near-paradisal perfection, while the next twelve hundred betrayed the "commencement, and Progress of a Direful

Apostacy, both as to Worship and Government in the Churches." Yet if the world had wound itself down as it grew further away from the time of origins, it had experienced a mighty regeneration in the Reformation and the New England churches. In language which gloried in the restoration, Wise suggested that "the Churches in New-England; and the Primitive Churches are Eminently parallel in their Government." This perfection for Wise was bound up with early congregational polity which preserved the "Original [sic] State and Liberty of Mankind" and was "founded peculiarly in the Light of Nature." The Light of Nature, or alternately, "Light of Reason," was a "Law and Rule of Right" and an "Effect of Christ's goodness, care and creating Power, as well as of Revelation; though Revelation is Natures Law in a fairer and brighter Edition."

The eighteenth century continued to speak in the language of nature and natural religion, as Lemuel Briant asserted human "moral Agency" without trying to relate it to the sovereignty of God and made of Jesus of Nazareth a teacher more than a savior. When, in 1751, Justice Paul Dudley's will set up a fund for the Dudley lectureship on natural and revealed religion, Ebenezer Gay's lecture, "Natural Religion as Distinguished From Revealed," became a milestone for the developing liberal camp. "Revealed Religion is an addition to natural not built upon the Ruins but on the strong and everlasting Foundations of it," Gay had announced. One observer, John Adams, thought that Lemuel Briant and Ebenezer Gay were Unitarians sixty years early.

By the time Jonathan Mayhew and Charles Chauncy were both ministers, New England's preachers had already spent a good part of the century discoursing on such themes as the law of nature and the unalienable rights of human beings, equality, popular sovereignty and the nature of a just constitution, and even life, liberty, and property. Observers of the revolutionary era, many of them unfriendly to the patriots, came to the conclusion that independency in religion and politics went together. Joseph Galloway knew what cognitive consonance was when he wrote:

> This kind of popular independence in ecclesiastical, was so nearly allied to that in civil polity, it is scarcely possible to conceive that the human mind could hold the one and reject the other. That kind of reason which led to the one, as strongly inculcated the other; and the principle of either was the principle of both. [In David Ramsay, *The History of the American Revolution*, 1789]

If New England sounded the call to which the rest of the colonies responded, the clergy seemed to have the loudest voices. Peter Oliver [in his *Origin and Progress of the American Rebellion—A Tory View* (1781)] was contemptuous that the Boston clergy were "esteemed by the others as an Order of Deities." He pointed the finger of accusation especially at Mayhew, Chauncy, and Samuel Cooper, since, he said, they distinguished themselves in encouraging Seditions and Riots, until [sic] those lesser Offenses were absorbed in Rebellion." One newspaper correspondent identified among the "high sons of liberty" those

Thomas Jefferson's handwritten compilation entitled The Life and Morals of Jesus of Nazareth, *in four languages, with clipped copies of the New Testament from which he took the text.*

"ministers of the gospel, who, instead of preaching to their flocks meekness, sobriety, attention to their different employments, and a steady obedience to the laws of Britain, belch from the pulpit liberty, independence, and a steady perseverance in endeavoring to shake off their allegiance to the mother country." "The clergy of New-England," wrote David Ramsay [in his *The History of the American Revolution*, 1789], more tamely, "were a numerous, learned and respectable body, who had a great ascendancy over the minds of their hearers. They connected religion and patriotism, and, in their sermons and prayers, represented the cause of America as the cause of Heaven."

While it was true that the preachers tended to be an incendiary lot, it is important to emphasize that part of their rousing argument was couched in the language of natural rights and natural law. Beyond that, their sermons, both liberal and evangelical, suggested strongly that the proper (i.e., natural) behavior of human beings was virtue and the proper arena for the enactment of virtuous pursuits was public. And their message was spreading beyond New England's borders. One example was the sermonizing of the evangelical Samuel Davies, who, as president of the College of New Jersey (Princeton), touched the minds and lives of many of the young men of the Revolution, Benjamin Rush among them. In his *Religion and Public Spirit*, addressed to the graduates of the class of 1760, Davies used the model of King David, a public man whose excellence consisted in "two Things, PUBLICK SPIRIT and RELIGION.—Publick Spirit, *in serving his Generation,*—and

Religion, in doing this *according to the Will of God.*" For Davies, a religion without the presence of "public spirit" seemed more a vice than a virtue, for it was "but a sullen, selfish, sour and malignant Humour for Devotion, unworthy that sacred Name." Activity and righteousness, pragmatism and the need to make one's mark were blended in Davies's exhortations.

> But if you feel the generous impulses of a publick Spirit, you can never be altogether insignificant, you will never be mere Cyphers in the World, even in the obscurest and most sequestered Vale of Life. Even in the lowest Station, you will be of some Use to Mankind, a sufficient Recompense this for the severe Conflict of sixty or seventy Years.

Generally speaking, despite their Calvinistic doctrines, the Edwardseans who came out of the Great Awakening were preaching the virtuous life which was the external sign of the genuineness of the conversion experience. Revival techniques themselves might be called a step in the direction of "Arminian means," while the Anglicans of the southern colonies seemed already to have been preaching a species of de facto Arminianism for a long time. But it was above all the liberal clergy, now a distinguishable presence, who preached of natural rights and moral duties.

In Boston Jonathan Mayhew was holding forth from the pulpit of the West Church after 1747. As Charles Akers [in his *Called unto Liberty: A Life of Jonathan Mayhew,* 1964] has remarked, "The study of his life makes it easier to understand how a nation of orthodox Christians, led by such near-Deists as Benjamin Franklin, John Adams, and Thomas Jefferson, could undertake a revolution justified by the theory that all men 'are endowed by their Creator with certain unalienable rights.'" If "the liberals transformed the practical nature of Puritan theology into a theological precursor of American pragmatism," Mayhew's Arminian understanding of the process of salvation as contractual and moralistic was a strong enunciation of the position. Intellectual formulations and theological refinements were distasteful to Mayhew, who saw meaning and value elsewhere, in the life of activity. "It is infinitely dishonourable to the all good and perfect Governor of the world," he preached, "to imagine that he has suspended the eternal salvation of men upon any niceties of speculation: or that any one who honestly aims at finding the truth, and at doing the will of his maker, shall be finally discarded because he fell into some erroneous opinions." The pastor of the West Church was close here to the religion of righteous deeds on the field of battle and the stage of government, where individuals, as independent entities, gained their places in history.

Moral action, for Mayhew, was grounded not merely in Christian revelation but in the law of nature, a law he considered "obligatory upon all Mankind without exception; because it is promulg'd to all." Mayhew's sermon *Unlimited Submission* (1750) joined the language of natural rights and reason to the motifs of British tyranny and slavery oppressing the true lovers of liberty. This ringing defense of the Puritan and Glorious Revolutions against the canonization of King Charles I, who had died at Puritan hands,

became, as time progressed, a defense of the right of revolution per se. Some have seen its language in Thomas Jefferson's Declaration of Independence. It is difficult not to agree when one reads such passages as Mayhew's condemnation of Charles I for excessive and despotic taxation.

> He levied many taxes upon the people without consent of parliament; and then imprisoned great numbers of the principal merchants and gentry for not paying them. He erected, or at least revived, several new and arbitrary courts, in which the most unheard-of barbarities were committed with his knowledge and approbation. . . . He sent a large sum of money, which he had raised by his arbitrary taxes, into *Germany,* to raise foreign troops, in order to force more arbitrary taxes upon his subjects.

When the good news reached Boston, in 1766, that the Stamp Act had been repealed, Mayhew's famous sermon, *The Snare Broken,* celebrated the "natural right" that human beings had to their own persons and clearly named the twin sources for the consciousness out of which he spoke.

> Having been initiated, in youth, in the doctrines of civil liberty in general, as they were taught by such men as Plato, Demosthenes, Cicero and other renowned persons among the ancients; and such as Sidney and Milton, Locke and Hoadley, among the moderns, I liked them; they seemed rational. Having earlier still learned from the Holy Scriptures that wise, brave and virtuous men were always friends to liberty; that God gave the Israelites a king (or absolute monarch) in his anger, because they had not sense and virtue enough to like a free commonwealth, and to have himself for their king; that the Son of God came down from heaven to make us 'free indeed,' and that where the spirit of the Lord is, there is liberty; this made me conclude that freedom was a great blessing.

Mayhew's geographical and ideological neighbor was Charles Chauncy of the First Church in Boston. God, for Chauncy, gradually reshaped himself in the human image, a transformation which, as we shall see, was being carried out on the plane of activity in the American Revolution, as it more and more conveyed an implicit understanding of a deity found in the midst of human rational energy and control. By denying the imputation of Adam's guilt and the transmission of his sinful nature to others, Chauncy was teaching a kind of truth-in-activity. No human being who came into the world arrived as a "fallen creature who must be reclaimed but rather as a potentiality that must be actualized." The possibility now existed for a morality grounded, not in the traditional tenets of Christian teaching, but transportable to whatever new religious framework might be at hand. Such a framework would be provided in the emerging religion of the American Revolution. Humans for Chauncy controlled their own destinies as *separate* individuals; hence, an atomistic understanding grounded his view of human nature as much as it did the natural rights teaching of the public documents of the Revolution. Although it might be argued that God's benevolence got in the way of human autonomy in his teaching with its emphasis on the salvation of all, Chauncy, despite the theological problem, stood with Mayhew as a prime representative of one source of the moralism of the new religion. Like Mayhew, he had been true to his fathers.

> Moralism had been introduced to Boston long before Chauncy was born. No less a Puritan than Cotton Mather made man's duty and moral improvement the focus of his preaching. It was not the invention of the liberals; rather, they were the product of a long line of development in that direction. Chauncy's originality was that he redid all Puritan theology to arrive at a doctrine of man whereby man is able to make himself into whatever he becomes. [Charles H. Lippy, "Restoring a Lost Ideal: Charles Chauncy and the American Revolution," *Religion in Life,* Vol. 44, No. 4 (1975)]

At the same time, he was teaching an understanding of faith which also placed it close to the reason of the American Enlightenment. Again, in keeping with the tradition which had developed from the seventeenth-century fathers, Chauncy viewed faith as chiefly an assent of the mind and intellect to certain propositions. As the definition of faith grew more and more external, devotion to duty became a key to the genuineness of each given individual's assent.

By the end of the Revolution, many patriotic laymen could agree with Chauncy. The descendants of the fathers had appropriated and expanded that part of their past which struck the chord most in tune with the "secular" cultural milieu out of which the religion of the Revolution would emerge. The sons of the fathers had more and more seen the mighty acts of God in the unchanging laws of the Newtonian universe; they had seen the reasonableness of the divine plan in nature and the beauty and utility of reason. Above all, it seemed reasonable to these sons of the fathers who became the men of the Revolution to view human life in terms of regular and correct human activity, for the laws of nature could be found in the midst of the human community as well as in the harmony of the universe. Typically in 1768, Silas Downer, the High Son of Liberty, found that the people could not be "governed by laws, in the making of which they had no hand." Their privilege was *"inherent,"* not to be *"granted* by any but the Almighty," a "natural right which no creature can *give,* or hath a right to take away." By 1779, Samuel Stillman [in "A Sermon Preached before the Honorable Council and Honorable House of Representatives of the State of Massachusetts Ban" (May 26, 1779)] was only speaking conventionally when he affirmed the truth of human equality in the law of nature: "The sovereignty resides originally in the people."

While we have been emphasizing understandings of natural law, reason, and virtue which, part of the inherited Puritan worldview, expressed themselves in the American Revolution, we cannot ignore the "enthusiastic" elements . . . . Perry Miller [in his *Errand into the Wilderness; The Shaping of American Religion,* 1961; and *New England Mind*] has pointed to the parallels between revivalism and democracy, both of which require the "man in

the bench" to speak up and act his piece. Still more, the Calvinistic emphasis on the power of God found ready expression during the era of Revolution in the appeals to Jehovah, God of Battles. At the same time, contemporaries were linking the new events of the political sphere to the spirit and language of enthusiasm which had been used in the great revivals. It was not simply that "enthusiastic" clergy supported the Revolution with their sermons and their lives, but more that an *enthusiastic spirit,* which was recognized as such, gripped the populace which perpetrated the war. . . . Quite simply, people knew, and knew that they knew, that political uprisings were really grand revivals. One hears in their language the echoes of revivalistic ardor and millennial zeal, for Armageddon was surely close at hand when divine enthusiasm was unleashed by righteous patriots against demonic British soldiers.

Therefore, the patriots knit up in their new revolutionary myth both sides of an older union of head and heart. In a transformation of the old symbolism, they still spoke the language of nature and moral rectitude at the same time that they experienced the zeal of revolutionary rage in legions directed by the Lord of Hosts. The tension between the opposites held the myth together as a sacred story which shared the archetypal quality of all myth: the ability to express and sometimes to resolve contradiction. Structural analysis shows that both sides were present and both sides pulled their weight in the revolutionary story. Historical analysis indicates that the binary opposites which met in the revolutionary motifs were inherited in some measure from the fathers. While it would be emotionally and aesthetically pleasing at this point to launch into a happy-ever-after conclusion about the dualities being resolved into a final unity, the later history of the republic revealed that the myth expressed tension more than resolved it, kept two kinds of concerns in a highly charged balance more than dissolved them into one perfect form. In this respect, the new synthesis was more a statement of the opposites than a resolution of them.

Curiously, the mediating symbol which seemed still to be at hand was the old Puritan covenant, now transmuted into democratic form. Particularly in New England, one notices that when the colonists had dissolved themselves into a state of nature by renouncing their ties with England, they began to constitute themselves anew in covenantal relationships. The Committee of Correspondence at Boston formed a "solemn league and covenant" by which "the subscribers bound themselves in the most solemn manner, and in the presence of God, to suspend all commercial intercourse with Great Britain." Meanwhile, the committee for the town of Plainfield, New Hampshire, formulated a covenant oath which was typical of many in the area. "We the subscribers. . . . Do in the presence of God solemnly and in good faith covenant and engage with each other that from henceforth we will suspend all commercial intercourse with the said Island of Great Britain until the Parliament shall cease to enact laws imposing taxes upon the Colonies without their consent, or until the pretended right of taxing is dropped."

There was an obvious link between the sovereignty of the people and the covenant relationship, a link perhaps most succinctly expressed in the revolutionary era by John Wise's *Vindication.* "The first Humane Subject and Original of Civil Power is the People," Wise had written. "Let us conceive in our Mind a multitude of Men, all Naturally Free & Equal; going about voluntarily, to Erect themselves into a new Common-Wealth." How would they do it? For Wise, the answer was simple and easy: "They must Interchangeably each Man Covenant to joyn in one lasting Society, that they may be capable to concert the measures of their safety, by a Publick Vote." The laws of nature were respected in that humans were treated as the free and equal beings who they were; virtue had been attained because men had *acted* rightly and correctly in covenanting together; passion entered with the sense of need and determination to do something by creating a governmental structure. Finally, for Wise, it was clear that the Lord God must direct the enterprise in order for it to succeed.

Beyond this, the new synthesis was occurring in a form which did not render it easily discernible as religion for the patriots who became a part of it. Previous training had made it clear what religious realities were: they concerned God and his church, sin and grace, death and judgment, heaven and hell. The new revolutionary myth would certainly hold God within its compass—and indeed mold its understanding of him into another two-in-one. The myth would also chart a course of moral action for virtuous citizens. But much of the most colorful language from the traditional religious past was missing, and as the myth developed it became more humanocentric and less concerned with a heavenly realm. Thus, when the Puritan synthesis was partially fused again in the furnace of the Revolution, the amalgamation came in a transformed and "secular" condition as the civil religion of the new United States. The vertical was horizontalized; transcendence was flattened but did not disappear. For now the transcendent object of religion would become more and more America itself. A dynamic thrust had begun: a change which would continue along one gradient—the humanocentric—had been initiated.

Despite the inability of the patriots to recognize their new religion as religion because of the nontraditional language which mediated it, the evolving synthesis did provide a strong vehicle for carrying the values enshrined in the religious mythology of their fathers. The God-who-acted lived on in human beings who continued to imitate his endeavors, exerting themselves strenuously in righteous causes and deeds. Action therefore was, as in the past, a prime bearer of value. More than that, making history and taking one's role upon the public stage extended the life of the city on the hill with its exemplary and missionary import. Moral action was public action, part of the great drama of meaningful and significant events. Finally, right action was action that looked toward the future. Even in the era of the Revolution, the age of progress was at hand, since the patriots who worshiped their fathers seemed as concerned for the future of their sons.

But perhaps the most significant mythologem of the myth which the patriots took from their fathers and transformed unwittingly to their new concerns was the notion of the "fathers" itself. In 1775, Thomas Jefferson [in "Declaration of the Causes and Necessity for Taking Up Arms"] had eloquently summarized the myth of the fathers out of which the Revolution began.

> Our forefathers, inhabitants of the island of Great Britain, left their native land to seek on these shores a residence for civil and religious freedom at the expense of their blood, to the ruin of their fortunes, with the relinquishment of everything quiet and comfortable in life, they effected settlements in the inhospitable wilds of America.

A decade later, the Reverend Dr. Ladd was delivering an oration before the governor of South Carolina for the Fourth of July. "When we consider this as the natal anniversary of our infant empire," he told the governor and the other members of the audience, "we shall ever be led to call into grateful recollection the fathers of our independence: those to whom (under God) we are indebted for our political existence and salvation." The contrast was telling: within a decade the fathers who trod the wilderness had become the men of the Revolution. These fathers faced the social wilderness of the dissolution of governmental forms in the creation of the new order. Both sets of fathers were patriarchs. But as the civil religion grew with the early nineteenth century and beyond, it was clear that the revolutionary sons had supplanted their ancestral fathers to become the fathers of all America. (pp. 21-45)

> *Catherine L. Albanese, "Our Fathers Who Trod the Wilderness," in her* Sons of the Fathers: The Civil Religion of the American Revolution, *Temple University Press, 1976, pp. 19-45.*

CONSEQUENCES OF THE REVOLUTION

John Courtney Murray

[In the following excerpt, Murray examines the development of ethnic and religious pluralism in America as reflected in the Declaration of Independence and the Constitution of the United States.]

As it arose in America, the problem of pluralism was unique in the modern world, chiefly because pluralism was the native condition of American society. It was not, as in Europe and in England, the result of a disruption or decay of a previously existent religious unity. This fact created the possibility of a new solution; indeed, it created a demand for a new solution. The possibility was exploited and the demand was met by the American Constitution. (p. 27)

The first truth to which the American Proposition makes appeal is stated in that landmark of Western political theory, the Declaration of Independence. It is a truth that lies beyond politics; it imparts to politics a fundamental human meaning. I mean the sovereignty of God over nations as well as over individual men. This is the principle that radically distinguishes the conservative Christian tradition of America from the Jacobin laicist tradition of Continental Europe. The Jacobin tradition proclaimed the autonomous reason of man to be the first and the sole principle of political organization. In contrast, the first article of the American political faith is that the political community, as a form of free and ordered human life, looks to the sovereignty of God as to the first principle of its organization. In the Jacobin tradition religion is at best a purely private concern, a matter of personal devotion, quite irrelevant to public affairs. Society as such, and the state which gives it legal form, and the government which is its organ of action are by definition agnostic or atheist. The statesman as such cannot be a believer, and his actions as a statesman are immune from any imperative or judgment higher than the will of the people, in whom resides ultimate and total sovereignty (one must remember that in the Jacobin tradition "the people" means "the party"). This whole manner of thought is altogether alien to the authentic American tradition.

From the point of view of the problem of pluralism this radical distinction between the American and the Jacobin traditions is of cardinal importance. The United States has had, and still has, its share of agnostics and unbelievers. But it has never known organized militant atheism on the Jacobin, doctrinaire Socialist, or Communist model; it has rejected parties and theories which erect atheism into a political principle. In 1799, the year of the Napoleonic *coup d'état* which overthrew the Directory and established a dictatorship in France, President John Adams stated the first of all American first principles in his remarkable proclamation of March 6:

> . . . it is also most reasonable in itself that men who are capable of social arts and relations, who owe their improvements to the social state, and who derive their enjoyments from it, should, as a society, make acknowledgements of dependence and obligation to Him who hath endowed them with these capacities and elevated them in the scale of existence by these distinctions. . . .

President Lincoln on May 30, 1863, echoed the tradition in another proclamation:

> Whereas the Senate of the United States, devoutly recognizing the supreme authority and just government of Almighty God in all the affairs of men and nations, has by a resolution requested the President to designate and set apart a day for national prayer and humiliation; And whereas it is the duty of nations as well as of men to own their dependence upon the overruling power of God, to confess their sins and trespasses in humble sorrow, yet with the assured hope that genuine repentance will lead to mercy and pardon. . . .

The authentic voice of America speaks in these words. And it is a testimony to the enduring vitality of this first principle—the sovereignty of God over society as well as over individual men—that President Eisenhower in June, 1952, quoted these words of Lincoln in a proclamation of similar intent. There is, of course, dissent from this princi-

ple, uttered by American secularism (which, at that, is a force far different in content and purpose from Continental laicism). But the secularist dissent is clearly a dissent; it illustrates the existence of the American affirmation. And it is continually challenged. For instance, as late as 1952 an opinion of the United States Supreme Court challenged it by asserting: "We are a religious people whose institutions presuppose a Supreme Being." Three times before in its history—in 1815, 1892, and 1931—the Court had formally espoused this same principle.

The affirmation in Lincoln's famous phrase, "this nation under God," sets the American proposition in fundamental continuity with the central political tradition of the West. But this continuity is more broadly and importantly visible in another, and related, respect. In 1884 the Third Plenary [Roman Catholic] Council of Baltimore made this statement: "We consider the establishment of our country's independence, the shaping of its liberties and laws, as a work of special Providence, its framers 'building better than they knew,' the Almighty's hand guiding them." The providential aspect of the matter, and the reason for the better building, can be found in the fact that the American political community was organized in an era when the tradition of natural law and natural rights was still vigorous. Claiming no sanction other than its appeal to free minds, it still commanded universal acceptance. And it furnished the basic materials for the American consensus.

The evidence for this fact has been convincingly presented by Clinton Rossiter in his book, *Seedtime of the Republic* [1953], a scholarly account of the "noble aggregate of 'self-evident truths' that vindicated the campaign of resistance (1765-1775), the resolution for independence (1776), and the establishment of the new state governments (1776-1780)." These truths, he adds, "had been no less self-evident to the preachers, merchants, planters, and lawyers who were the mind of colonial America." It might be further added that these truths firmly presided over the great time of study, discussion, and decision which produced the Federal Constitution. "The great political philosophy of the Western world," Rossiter says, "enjoyed one of its proudest seasons in this time of resistance and revolution." By reason of this fact the American Revolution, quite unlike its French counterpart, was less a revolution than a conservation. It conserved, by giving newly vital form to, the liberal tradition of politics, whose ruin in Continental Europe was about to be consummated by the first great modern essay in totalitarianism.

The force for unity inherent in this tradition was of decisive importance in what concerns the problem of pluralism. Because it was conceived in the tradition of natural law the American Republic was rescued from the fate, still not overcome, that fell upon the European nations in which Continental Liberalism, a deformation of the liberal tradition, lodged itself, not least by the aid of the Lodges. There have never been "two Americas," in the sense in which there have been, and still are, "two Frances," "two Italys," "two Spains." Politically speaking, America has always been one. The reason is that a consensus was once established, and it still substantially endures, even in the quarters where its origins have been forgotten.

Formally and in the first instance this consensus was political, that is, it embraced a whole constellation of principles bearing upon the origin and nature of society, the function of the state as the legal order of society, and the scope and limitations of government. "Free government"—perhaps this typically American shorthand phrase sums up the consensus. "A free people under a limited government" puts the matter more exactly. It is a phrase that would have satisfied the first Whig, St. Thomas Aquinas.

To the early Americans government was not a phenomenon of force, as the later legal positivists would have it. Nor was it a "historical category," as Marx and his followers were to assert. Government did not mean simply the power to coerce, though this power was taken as integral to government. Government, properly speaking, was the right to command. It was authority. And its authority derived from law. By the same token its authority was limited by law. In his own way Tom Paine put the matter when he said, "In America Law is the King." But the matter had been better put by Henry of Bracton (d. 1268) when he said, "The king ought not to be under a man, but under God and under the law, because the law makes the king." This was the message of Magna Charta; this became the first structural rib of American constitutionalism.

Constitutionalism, the rule of law, the notion of sovereignty as purely political and therefore limited by law, the concept of government as an empire of laws and not of men— these were ancient ideas, deeply implanted in the British tradition at its origin in medieval times. The major American contribution to the tradition—a contribution that imposed itself on all subsequent political history in the Western world—was the written constitution. However, the American document was not the *constitution octroyée* of the nineteenth-century Restorations—a constitution graciously granted by the King or Prince-President. Through the American techniques of the constitutional convention and of popular ratification, the American Constitution is explicitly the act of the people. It embodies their consensus as to the purposes of government, its structure, the extent of its powers and the limitations on them, etc. By the Constitution the people define the areas where authority is legitimate and the areas where liberty is lawful. The Constitution is therefore at once a charter of freedom and a plan for political order.

Here is the second aspect of the continuity between the American consensus and the ancient liberal tradition; I mean the affirmation of the principle of the consent of the governed. Sir John Fortescue (d. 1476), Chief Justice of the Court of King's Bench under Henry VI, had thus stated the tradition, in distinguishing between the absolute and the constitutional monarch: "The secounde king [the constitutional monarch] may not rule his people by other laws than such as thai assenten to. And therefore he may set upon thaim non imposicions without their consent." The principle of consent was inherent in the medieval idea of kingship; the king was bound to seek the consent of his people to his legislation. The American consensus reaffirmed this principle, at the same time that it carried the principle to newly logical lengths. Americans agreed that they would consent to none other than their own legisla-

tion, as framed by their representatives, who would be responsible to them. In other words, the principle of consent was wed to the equally ancient principle of popular participation in rule. But, since this latter principle was given an amplitude of meaning never before known in history, the result was a new synthesis, whose formula is the phrase of Lincoln, "government by the people."

Americans agreed to make government constitutional and therefore limited in a new sense, because it is representative, republican, responsible government. It is limited not only by law but by the will of the people it represents. Not only do the people adopt the Constitution; through the techniques of representation, free elections, and frequent rotation of administrations they also have a share in the enactment of all subsequent statutory legislation. The people are really governed; American political theorists did not pursue the Rousseauist will-o'-the-wisp: how shall the individual in society come to obey only himself? Nevertheless, the people are governed because they consent to be governed; and they consent to be governed because in a true sense they govern themselves.

The American consensus therefore includes a great act of faith in the capacity of the people to govern themselves. The faith was not unrealistic. It was not supposed that everybody could master the technical aspects of government, even in a day when these aspects were far less complex than they now are. The supposition was that the people could understand the general objectives of governmental policy, the broad issues put to the decision of government, especially as these issues raised moral problems. The American consensus accepted the premise of medieval society, that there is a sense of justice inherent in the people, in virtue of which they are empowered, as the medieval phrase had it, to "judge, direct, and correct" the processes of government.

It was this political faith that compelled early American agreement to the institutions of a free speech and a free press. In the American concept of them, these institutions do not rest on the thin theory proper to eighteenth-century individualistic rationalism, that a man has a right to say what he thinks merely because he thinks it. The American agreement was to reject political censorship of opinion as unrightful, because unwise, imprudent, not to say impossible. However, the proper premise of these freedoms lay in the fact that they were social necessities. "Colonial thinking about each of these rights had a strong social rather than individualistic bias," Rossiter says. They were regarded as conditions essential to the conduct of free, representative, and responsible government. People who are called upon to obey have the right first to be heard. People who are to bear burdens and make sacrifices have the right first to pronounce on the purposes which their sacrifices serve. People who are summoned to contribute to the common good have the right first to pass their own judgment on the question, whether the good proposed be truly a good, the people's good, the common good. Through the technique of majority opinion this popular judgment becomes binding on government.

A second principle underlay these free institutions—the principle that the state is distinct from society and limited in its offices toward society. This principle too was inherent in the Great Tradition. Before it was cancelled out by the rise of the modern omnicompetent society-state, it had found expression in the distinction between the order of politics and the order of culture, or, in the language of the time, the distinction between *studium* and *imperium.* The whole order of ideas in general was autonomous in the face of government; it was immune from political discipline, which could only fall upon actions, not ideas. Even the medieval Inquisition respected this distinction of orders; it never recognized a crime of opinion, *crimen opinionis;* its competence extended only to the repression of organized conspiracy against public order and the common good. It was, if you will, a Committee on un-Christian Activities; it regarded activities, not ideas, as justiciable.

The American Proposition, in reviving the distinction between society and state, which had perished under the advance of absolutism, likewise renewed the principle of the incompetence of government in the field of opinion. Government submits itself to judgment by the truth of society; it is not itself a judge of the truth in society. Freedom of the means of communication whereby ideas are circulated and criticized, and the freedom of the academy (understanding by the term the range of institutions organized for the pursuit of truth and the perpetuation of the intellectual heritage of society) are immune from legal inhibition or government control. This immunity is a civil right of the first order, essential to the American concept of a free people under a limited government.

"A free people": this term too has a special sense in the American Proposition. America has passionately pursued the ideal of freedom, expressed in a whole system of political and civil rights, to new lengths; but it has not pursued

Franklin, Adams, and Jefferson—three of the principal architects of the new American nation.

this ideal so madly as to rush over the edge of the abyss, into sheer libertarianism, into the chaos created by the nineteenth-century theory of the "outlaw conscience," *conscientia exlex,* the conscience that knows no law higher than its own subjective imperatives. Part of the inner architecture of the American ideal of freedom has been the profound conviction that only a virtuous people can be free. It is not an American belief that free government is inevitable, only that it is possible, and that its possibility can be realized only when the people as a whole are inwardly governed by the recognized imperatives of the universal moral law.

The American experiment reposes on Acton's postulate, that freedom is the highest phase of civil society. But it also reposes on Acton's further postulate, that the elevation of a people to this highest phase of social life supposes, as its condition, that they understand the ethical nature of political freedom. They must understand, in Acton's phrase, that freedom is "not the power of doing what we like, but the right of being able to do what we ought." The people claim this right, in all its articulated forms, in the face of government; in the name of this right, multiple limitations are put upon the power of government. But the claim can be made with the full resonance of moral authority only to the extent that it issues from an inner sense of responsibility to a higher law. In any phase civil society demands order. In its highest phase of freedom it demands that order should not be imposed from the top down, as it were, but should spontaneously flower outward from the free obedience to the restraints and imperatives that stem from inwardly possessed moral principle. In this sense democracy is more than a political experiment; it is a spiritual and moral enterprise. And its success depends upon the virtue of the people who undertake it. Men who would be politically free must discipline themselves. Likewise institutions which would pretend to be free with a human freedom must in their workings be governed from within and made to serve the ends of virtue. Political freedom is endangered in its foundations as soon as the universal moral values, upon whose shared possession the self-discipline of a free society depends, are no longer vigorous enough to restrain the passions and shatter the selfish inertia of men. The American ideal of freedom as ordered freedom, and therefore an ethical ideal, has traditionally reckoned with these truths, these truisms.

This brings us to the threshold of religion, and therefore to the other aspect of the problem of pluralism, the plurality of religions in America. However, before crossing this threshold one more characteristic of the American Proposition, as implying a consensus, needs mention, namely, the Bill of Rights. The philosophy of the Bill of Rights was also tributary to the tradition of natural law, to the idea that man has certain original responsibilities precisely as man, antecedent to his status as citizen. These responsibilities are creative of rights which inhere in man antecedent to any act of government; therefore they are not granted by government and they cannot be surrendered to government. They are as inalienable as they are inherent. Their proximate source is in nature, and in history insofar as history bears witness to the nature of man; their ultimate source, as the Declaration of Independence states, is in

God, the Creator of nature and the Master of history. The power of this doctrine, as it inspired both the Revolution and the form of the Republic, lay in the fact that it drew an effective line of demarcation around the exercise of political or social authority. When government ventures over this line, it collides with the duty and right of resistance. Its authority becomes arbitrary and therefore nil; its act incurs the ultimate anathema, "unconstitutional."

One characteristic of the American Bill of Rights is important for the subject here, namely, the differences that separate it from the Declaration of the Rights of Man in the France of '89. In considerable part the latter was a parchment-child of the Enlightenment, a top-of-the-brain concoction of a set of men who did not understand that a political community, like man himself, has roots in history and in nature. They believed that a state could be simply a work of art, a sort of absolute beginning, an artifact of which abstract human reason could be the sole artisan. Moreover, their exaggerated individualism had shut them off from a view of the organic nature of the human community; their social atomism would permit no institutions or associations intermediate between the individual and the state.

In contrast, the men who framed the American Bill of Rights understood history and tradition, and they understood nature in the light of both. They too were individualists, but not to the point of ignoring the social nature of man. They did their thinking within the tradition of freedom that was their heritage from England. Its roots were not in the top of anyone's brain but in history. Importantly, its roots were in the medieval notion of the *homo liber et legalis,* the man whose freedom rests on law, whose law was the age-old custom in which the nature of man expressed itself, and whose lawful freedoms were possessed in association with his fellows. The rights for which the colonists contended against the English Crown were basically the rights of Englishmen. And these were substantially the rights written into the Bill of Rights.

. . . [Freedom] of speech, assembly, association, and petition for the redress of grievances, security of person, home, and property—these were great historical as well as civil and natural rights. So too was the right to trial by jury, and all the procedural rights implied in the Fifth- and later in the Fourteenth-Amendment provision for "due process of law." The guarantee of these and other rights was new in that it was written, in that it envisioned these rights with an amplitude, and gave them a priority, that had not been known before in history. But the Bill of Rights was an effective instrument for the delimitation of government authority and social power, not because it was written on paper in 1789 or 1791, but because the rights it proclaims had already been engraved by history on the conscience of a people. The American Bill of Rights is not a piece of eighteenth-century rationalist theory; it is far more the product of Christian history. Behind it one can see, not the philosophy of the Enlightenment but the older philosophy that had been the matrix of the common law. The "man" whose rights are guaranteed in the face of law and government is, whether he knows it or not, the Chris-

tian man, who had learned to know his own personal dignity in the school of Christian faith.

Americans have been traditionally proud of the earlier phases of their history—colonial and Revolutionary, constitutional and Federalist. This pride persists today. The question is, whether the American consensus still endures—the consensus whose essential contents have been sketched in the foregoing. A twofold answer may be given. The first answer is given by Professor Rossiter:

> Perhaps Americans could achieve a larger measure of liberty and prosperity and build a more successful government if they were to abandon the language and assumptions of men who lived almost two centuries ago. Yet the feeling cannot be downed that rude rejection of the past, rather than levelheaded respect for it, would be the huge mistake. Americans may eventually take the advice of their advanced philosophers and adopt a political theory that pays more attention to groups, classes, public opinion, power-élites, positive law, public administration, and other realities of twentieth-century America. Yet it seems safe to predict that the people, who occasionally prove themselves wiser than their philosophers, will go on thinking about the political community in terms of unalienable rights, popular sovereignty, consent, constitutionalism, separation of powers, morality, and limited government. The political theory of the American Revolution—a theory of ethical, ordered liberty—remains the political tradition of the American people.

This is a cheerful answer. I am not at all sure that it is correct, if it be taken to imply that the tradition of natural law, as the foundation of law and politics, has the same hold upon the mind of America today that it had upon the "preachers, merchants, planters, and lawyers who were the mind of colonial America." There is indeed talk today about a certain revival of this great tradition, notably among more thoughtful men in the legal profession. But the talk itself is significant. One would not talk of reviving the tradition, if it were in fact vigorously alive. (pp. 28-40)

Another idiom now prevails. The possibility was inherent from the beginning. To the early American theorists and politicians the tradition of natural law was an inheritance. This was its strength; this was at the same time its weakness, especially since a subtle alteration of the tradition had already commenced. For a variety of reasons the intellectualist idea of law as reason had begun to cede to the voluntarist idea of law as will. One can note the change in Blackstone, for instance, even though he still stood within the tradition, and indeed drew whole generations of early American lawyers into it with him. (Part of American folklore is Sandburg's portrait of Abraham Lincoln, sitting barefoot on his woodpile, reading Blackstone.) Protestant Christianity, especially in its left wing (and its left wing has always been dominant in America), inevitably evolved away from the old English and American tradition. Grotius and the philosophers of the Enlightenment had cast up their secularized versions of the tradition. Their disciples were to better their instruction, as the impact of the methods of empirical science made itself felt even in those areas of human thought in which knowledge is noncumulative and to that extent recalcitrant to the methods of science. Seeds of dissolution were already present in the ancient heritage as it reached the shores of America.

Perhaps the dissolution, long since begun, may one day be consummated. Perhaps one day the noble many-storeyed mansion of democracy will be dismantled, levelled to the dimensions of a flat majoritarianism, which is no mansion but a barn, perhaps even a tool shed in which the weapons of tyranny may be forged. Perhaps there will one day be wide dissent even from the political principles which emerge from natural law, as well as dissent from the constellation of ideas that have historically undergirded these principles—the idea that government has a moral basis; that the universal moral law is the foundation of society; that the legal order of society—that is, the state—is subject to judgment by a law that is not statistical but inherent in the nature of man; that the eternal reason of God is the ultimate origin of all law; that this nation in all its aspects—as a society, a state, an ordered and free relationship between governors and governed—is under God. The possibility that widespread dissent from these principles should develop is not foreclosed. (pp. 41-2)

> *John Courtney Murray, "E Pluribus Unum: 'The American Consenus'," in his* We Hold These Truths: Catholic Reflections on the American Proposition, *Sheed and Ward, 1960, pp. 27-44.*

Gordon S. Wood

[*In the excerpt below, Wood examines republicanism in Colonial America, suggesting that its adoption as a principle of authentic government depended upon the renewal of the moral spirit, encouraged by such leaders as John Adams, Thomas Paine, Benjamin Rush, and Samuel Stanhope Smith.*]

The changes the Americans intended to make in their politics and society were truly momentous—so momentous in fact that it is difficult to comprehend the swiftness and confidence with which they embraced republicanism. The Revolution was no simple colonial rebellion against English imperialism. It was meant to be a social revolution of the most profound sort. Different men of course participated with different degrees of enthusiasm, and their varying expectations of change were in fact a measure of their willingness to revolt, distinguishing a confident Richard Henry Lee from a more skeptical Robert Morris. There were doubts and apprehensions in 1776, many of them. Running through the correspondence of the Whig leaders are fearful suggestions of what republicanism might mean, of leveling, of licentiousness, of "the race of popularity." Yet what in the last analysis remains extraordinary about 1776 is the faith, not the doubts, of the Revolutionary leaders. All Americans who became committed to independence and republicanism were inevitably compelled to expect or to hope for at least some amount of reformation in American society, and for many the expectations were indeed high. Everyone was intensely aware of the special character of republicanism and the social and moral de-

mands it put upon a people. When American orators quoted the Whig poet laureate, James Thompson, on the blessedness of public virtue, the audiences knew what was meant. That the greatness, indeed the very existence, of a republic depended upon the people's virtue was "a maxim" established by the "universal consent" and the "experience of all ages." All these notions of liberty, equality, and public virtue were indelible sentiments "already graven upon the hearts" of Americans, who realized fully the fragility of the republican polity. Even the ancient republics, virtuous and grand as they were, had eventually crumbled. The only English experiment in republicanism had quickly ended in a predictable failure, capped by the tyranny of a dictator. The eighteenth century, moreover, offered few prototypes for America's grandiose venture: the only modern republics were tiny, insignificant states, in various stages of decline, paralyzed by surrounding absolutism, hardly fit models for this sprawling New World.

Nevertheless, Thomas Paine could exclaim in 1776 that it was only common sense for Americans to become republicans and have Americans heartily agree with him. Despite their keen awareness of the failure of past republics and of the unusual delicacy of republican government, Americans, observed Thomas Jefferson in the summer of 1777, "seem to have deposited the monarchical and taken up the republican government with as much ease as would have attended their throwing off an old and putting on a new suit of clothes." Looking back at the controversy with Britain from 1776, John Adams was likewise "surprised at the Suddenness, as well as the Greatness of this Revolution." "Is not the Change We have seen astonishing? Would any Man, two Years ago have believed it possible, to accomplish such an Alteration in the Prejudices, Passions, Sentiments, and Principles of these thirteen little States as to make every one of them completely republican, and to make them own it? Idolatry to Monarchs, and servility to Aristocratical Pride, was never so totally eradicated, from so many Minds in so short a Time" [Jefferson to Benjamin Franklin, Aug. 3, 1777, Boyd, ed., *Jefferson Papers,* II; Adams to Abigail Adams, July 3, 1776, and Adams to Richard Cranch, Aug. 2, 1776, Butterfield, ed., *Family Correspondence,* II]. Whatever the intensity of the Americans' grievances and whatever affinity the tenets of the republican ideology had for them, this ease of transition into republicanism remains remarkable and puzzling even today. For republicanism after all involved the whole character of the society.

But for Americans this social dimension of republicanism was precisely the point of the Revolution. Even the essential question raised in the debates Americans had with themselves in 1776 over the wisdom of independence was social: were Americans the stuff republicans are made of?—surely the most important and most sensitive issue in all of the Revolutionary polemics, for it involved not any particular economic advantages or political rights, but rather the kind of people Americans were and wanted to be. The question was not easily answered. Out of the Americans' investigation of this crucial issue flowed ambiguous and contradictory conclusions about the nature of their social character. On the one hand, they seemed to be a particularly virtuous people, and thus unusually suited for republican government; yet, on the other hand, amidst this prevalence of virtue were appearing dangerous signs of luxury and corruption that suggested their unpreparedness for republicanism. It was the kind of ambiguity and contradiction that should have led to a general bewilderment and hesitation rather than to the astonishingly rapid embrace of republicanism which actually occurred. Yet curiously the Americans' doubts and fears about their social character were not set in opposition to their confidence and hopes, but in fact reinforced them. Such was their enlightened faith in the comprehensive power of republican government itself that their very anxieties and apprehensions about the fitness of the American character for republicanism became in the end the most important element in their sudden determination to become republican. By 1776 republicanism had become not only a matter of suitability. It had become a matter of urgency.

Thomas Paine in his incendiary pamphlet, *Common Sense,* published early in 1776, touched off the argument that burned to the heart of the social issue. "The *time hath found us,*" he said, and this became his theme. Independence from Britain was not only desirable, it was necessary; and it was necessary now. The youth of America was no argument against independence; in fact, it was the most compelling reason for adopting republicanism. "History sufficiently informs us, that the bravest achievements were always accomplished in the non-age of a nation." If America delayed it would be too late. Fifty years from now, said Paine, trade and population would have increased so much as to make the society incapable of fighting for and sustaining republicanism. Wealth and distinctions would have created divisions and a jarring of interests among the people. "Commerce diminishes the spirit both of patriotism and military defence" and would eventually destroy America's soul, as it had England's. Years from now, "while the proud and foolish gloried in their little distinctions, the wise would lament that the union had not been formed before." The American people were ripe for revolution and republicanism. "It may not always happen that our soldiers are citizens and the multitude a body of reasonable men." "Virtue . . . ," said Paine, "is not hereditary, neither is it perpetual" [Thomas Paine, *Common Sense . . . , 1776*].

But not everyone thought that republicanism for America was a matter of common sense. Paine's argument immediately aroused several spirited and lengthy responses, the most important being Charles Inglis's *The True Interest of America Impartially Stated . . .* and James Chalmer's *Plain Truth,* both published in Philadelphia in the spring of 1776. Both of Paine's critics built their case against independence around a vigorous defense of the English monarchical constitution. Yet both grounded the core of their arguments on the social dangers of republicanism and on the inability of the American people to sustain a republican polity. Republics, they contended, had always been torn to pieces by faction and internal struggles, tumults from which America would never escape. "All our property throughout the continent would be unhinged," warned Inglis; "the greatest confusion, and the most violent convulsions would take place." Chalmers predicted a dreadful

anarchy resulting from republicanism, leading to a Cromwellian dictatorship. At the very least America would witness commercial chaos and agrarian laws limiting the possession of property. "A war will ensue between the creditors and their debtors, which will eventually end in a general spunge or abolition of debts, which has more than once happened in other States on occasions similar."

Paine, they charged, was flagrantly wrong in his estimate of the peculiar nature of American society. America was incapable of supporting republicanism: "A republican form of government would neither suit the genius of the people, nor the extent of America." American society was basically no different from that of the mother country. "The Americans are properly Britons. They have the manners, habits, and ideas of Britons." Hence any American experiment in republicanism would surely end as had the English attempt in the seventeenth century. The best governments and the wisest laws were ineffective "among a corrupt, degenerate people." Paine, they scoffed, had promised Americans the restoration of the golden age if they became republicans. But until Paine could give "some assurance that may be relied on, that ambition, pride, avarice, and all that dark train of passions which usually attend them" were absent from the American soul, his audience could only "doubt the truth of his assertions."

Other Americans also had doubts of the suitability of their society for republicanism. For William Smith of New York it called "for greater Sacrifices of private Liberty" than seemed possible or necessary. Were Americans capable of receiving a republican government? asked an anxious Virginian in June of 1776. "Have we that Industry, Frugality, Economy, that Virtue which is necessary to constitute it?" Laws and constitutions, after all, "must be adapted to the manners of the People." Several months earlier, in the fall of 1775, during the debates in the Continental Congress over the closing of all American ports to British trade, those opposed to the revolutionary course America was on had also brought into question the capacity of Americans to endure the hardships such economic restriction would cause. "A Republican Government is little better than Government of Devils," warned the Swiss-born John Joachim Zubly. "We must have Trade. It is prudent not to put Virtue to too serious a Test." "More Virtue is expected from our People," said Robert R. Livingston of New York, "than any People ever had." This kind of wholesale economic regulation by government would not work, declared John Jay in an argument that cut the Commonwealth assumptions to the core. "We have more to expect from the Enterprise, Activity and Industry of private Adventurers, than from the Lukewarmness of Assemblies." Americans needed goods, and individual entrepreneurs could best get them. "Public Virtue is not so active as private Love of Gain. Shall We shutt the Door vs. private Enterprise." But the revolutionary-minded in the Congress would hear none of this justification of selfishness. "We can do without Trade," said Samuel Chase. "I have too good an opinion of the Virtue of our People to suppose they will grumble." By closing all the ports "Merchants will not grow rich—there is the Rub. . . . We must give up the Profits of Trade or loose our Liberties." Such profits were no benefit anyway, added Richard Henry Lee, for "Money has debauched States as well as Individuals." Conventions and committees of the people could suppress whatever violations of the public good might arise [Smith, entry, Oct. 18, 1776, Sabine, ed., *Memoirs of Smith;* Alexander White to Charles Lee, June 27, 1776, *Lee Papers,* II; Adams, Notes of Debates in the Continental Congress, Oct. 1775, Butterfield, ed., *Diary of Adams,* II].

Probably the most trenchant public critique of this kind of Commonwealth thinking was written by one of Lee's enemies in Virginia, Carter Braxton, in his *Address to the Convention of . . . Virginia; on the Subject of Government . . .* published early in 1776. The advocates of republicanism, Braxton maintained, had confused and blended private and public virtue; the two must be separated. Man's happiness no doubt lay in the practice of private virtue: "In this he acts for himself, and with a view of promoting his own particular welfare." On the other hand, public virtue—"a disinterested attachment to the public good, exclusive and independent of all private and selfish interest"—had, said Braxton, "never characterized the mass of the people in any state." To be a true republican a man "must divest himself of all interested motives, and engage in no pursuits which do not ultimately redound to the benefit of society." This meant that ambition, wealth, luxury, influence—all had to be curbed. "To this species of Government everything that looks like elegance and refinement is inimical," resulting in all those sumptuary and agrarian laws for which the ancient republics were so noted. Such schemes, argued Braxton, were inapplicable for America. However sensible they may have been in naturally sterile countries which had only a scanty supply of necessities, "they can never meet with a favorable reception from people who inhabit a country to which Providence has been more bountiful." Americans will always claim the right to enjoy the fruits of their honest labor, "unrestrained by any ideal principles of Governments"; and they will always accumulate property for themselves and their children "without regarding the whimsical impropriety of being richer than their neighbours." "The truth is," concluded Braxton sententiously, "that men will not be poor from choice or compulsion," only "from necessity." Republicanism was an "ideal" principle—"a mere creature of a warm imagination" [Carter Braxton, *An Address to the Convention of. . . Virginia; on the Subject of Government . . .* (1776), in Force, ed., *American Archives,* 4th Ser., VI].

These were potent arguments, thrust upon Americans not only by discredited Tories but also by skeptical Whigs equally concerned with the defense of American liberties but convinced that the republican remedy was worse than the disease. Although these anti-republican writings could be casually dismissed (John Adams, for example thought Braxton's pamphlet was "too absurd to be considered twice"), the questions they raised were not the sort that could be ignored. Because of anti-republican arguments like these and because of their own self-doubts, Americans were compelled to explore the nature of their society. From this analysis involved in the Revolutionary polemics and from the Enlightenment portrait drawn of them,

Americans fashioned a conglomerate image of themselves as a distinct people with a social character possessed by few, if any, people before them. (pp. 91-7)

Of course, all the while Americans were well aware that their colonial society had not been all the Enlightenment believed it to be, that they had not really been free of the vices and luxury of the Old World. It was not enough that many European intellectuals considered them to be an especially egalitarian, virtuous people. Compared to Europe they did seem naturally republican, destined to be out from under a corrupt monarchy. But they could not believe that the future was simply a matter of becoming what nature had decreed, of accommodating a new political form to a society which had already become republican in spirit. Indeed, even to those who dwelt on America's distinctiveness, it appeared quite the contrary. America, declared some on the eve of the Revolution, "never was, perhaps, in a more corrupt and degenerate State than at this Day." "How have animosities been cherished . . . ! How has injustice abounded! And How prevalent has been every kind of iniquity!" [Samuel Buell, *The Best New-Yeear's Gift For Young People: Or, the Bloom of Youth Immortal by Piety and Glory,* 1775; Mansfield, *Sermon Preached November 23, 1775*]. In the eyes of many Americans, whether southern planters or New England clergymen, the society was far from virtuous and in fact seemed to be approaching some kind of crisis in its development. This prevalence of vice and corruption that many Americans saw in their midst did not, however, work to restrain their desire to be republican. It became in fact a stimulus, perhaps in the end the most important stimulus, to revolution. What ultimately convinced Americans that they must revolt in 1776 was not that they were naturally and inevitably republican, for if that were truly the case evolution, not revolution, would have been the eventual solution. Rather it was the pervasive fear that they were not predestined to be a virtuous and egalitarian people that in the last analysis drove them into revolution in 1776. It was this fear and not their confidence in the peculiarity of their character that made them so readily and so remarkably responsive to Thomas Paine's warning that the time for independence was at hand and that delay would be disastrous. By 1776 it had become increasingly evident that if they were to remain the kind of people they wanted to be they must become free of Britain. The calls for independence thus took on a tone of imperativeness. Only separating from the British monarchy and instituting republicanism, it seemed, could realize the social image the Enlightenment had drawn of them. Only this mingling of urgency and anxiety during their introspective probings at the height of the crisis could have given their revolutionary language the frenzied quality it acquired. Only profound doubts could have created their millennial vision of a new society, their idealized expectation that "on the morrow" there would be a "new thing under the sun, that hath not been already of old time" [Gordon, *Sermon before House of Representatives*].

When the Americans examined themselves in the years leading up to the Revolution, it became apparent that their society had been undergoing a drastic and frightening transformation. All the signs of the society's development by the middle of the eighteenth century, as described in the language of the day, became symptoms of regression. "To increase in numbers, in wealth, in elegance and refinements, and at the same time to increase in luxury, profaneness, impiety, and a disesteem of things sacred, is to go backward and not forward." Such apprehensions were not new to Americans. Since the seventeenth century they had warned themselves repeatedly against declension and social corruption. But never before had wealth and luxury seemed so prevalent, especially since the end of the war with France. Never before had Americans been so "carried away by the stream of prosperity" [Nathan Fiske, *Remarkable Providences to Be Gratefully Recollected, Religiously Improved, and Carefully Transmitted to Posterity* (1776); Jacob Duché, *The American Vine, a Sermon, Preached before the Honourable Continental Congress, July 20th, 1775* (1775)]. Throughout all the colonies and rising to a fever pitch by 1775-76 were strident warnings in newspapers, pamphlets, and sermons of the great social changes that seemed to be sweeping the land. (pp. 107-09)

By the 1760's the multiplication of wealth and luxury, the attempts to harden the social hierarchy, particularly the efforts of those who considered themselves socially superior to set themselves off from the rest of American society by aping the "Asiatic amusements" and "fêtes champêtres" of sophisticated English court life—all seemed to be part of the Crown's conspiracy to numb and enervate the spirit of the American people. On the eve of the Revolution, America was displaying all the symptoms (in the lexicon of eighteenth-century political science) of a state attacked by disease. The "Times of Simplicity and Innocence" of their ancestors seemed to be waning; "Elegance, Luxury and Effeminacy begin to be established." "Venality, Servility and Prostitution, eat and spread like a Cancer." England, it seemed, was encouraging American "dissipation and extravagance" both to increase the sale of her manufactures and geegaws and to perpetuate American subordination. "In vain," recalled David Ramsay in 1778, "we sought to check the growth of luxury, by sumptuary laws; every wholesome restraint of this kind was sure to meet with the royal negative." If Americans had not eventually revolted, concluded Ramsay, "our frugality, industry, and simplicity of manners, would have been lost in an imitation of British extravagance, idleness, and false refinements" ["Oration on Advantages of American Independence," Niles, ed., *Principles*].

The Crown actually seemed to be bent on changing the character of American society. Everywhere men appeared to be seeking the preferment of royal authority, eager to sell their country "for a smile, or some ministerial office." Throughout the society, particularly in the larger cities, an artificial inter-colonial aristocracy—springing ultimately from the honors and dignities bestowed by the Crown—was entrenching itself, consolidating and setting itself apart from the mass of American yeomen by its royal connections and courtier spirit of luxury and dissipation. Any distinction and title, any refinement, was sought by these aspiring aristocrats as long as it separated them from the rabble. "Even being a member of the Church of England," noted Arthur Browne, the famous Anglican minister at Newport and Portsmouth, "gave a kind of distinctive fashion."

Yet the would-be aristocrats themselves felt insecure. Their political and social position was too recent, too accidental, too arbitrary, too much the result of connections or marriage to command respect. It was with apology that Thomas Hutchinson wrote in 1765 that "altho' places and titles in the colonies are not hereditary, yet *caeteris paribus,* the descendants of such as have done worthily have some claim to be distinguished." By the middle of the eighteenth century royal officials on both sides of the Atlantic were anxiously concerned with the instability of American society; and the air was filled with proposals for reorganizing the imperial structure. What was especially needed, it seemed, was a strengthening of the aristocratic element in the society, those "most distinguished for their Wealth, Merit, and Ability," who needed "some few distinctions" annexed to their persons in order to maintain a proper subordination of rank and civil discipline in the colonies. By the 1760's various kinds of reforms were circulating, all generally pointing to the establishment in America of a "Nobility appointed by the King for life," which could eventually become hereditary. These plans seemed to be no idle tinkering by insignificant and uninfluential British officials. Not only were high colonial officials urging the creation of an American aristocracy, but ministers close to the Crown were doing the same. Perhaps nothing better indicates the gulf of thinking separating official England from the colonists than the ministerial pamphlet, *The Address of the People of England to the Inhabitants of America,* written by Sir John Dalrymple, "at the express requisition of lord *North,*" said one angry Virginian. "The deluded amongst you," wrote Dalrymple, "think that we assume airs of superiority over you even where they are needless." This was false, continued Dalrymple, in an argument that could not have been more frightening and rankling to Americans than if it had been so intended. Every honor of England was open to Americans. Indeed, said Dalrymple, "we should even be happy to see you ask the establishment of a Nobility, and of ranks amongst yourselves" so that American spirits could be exalted not only by the love of liberty but by the love of family as well [Purdie's Wmsbg. *Va. Gazette,* Sept. 22, 1775; Sir John Dalrymple, *The Address of the People of Great-Britain to the Inhabitants of America,* 1775].

This sort of suggestion only confirmed American apprehensions about what the Crown was up to, and in reaction the apparent equality of American society seemed more precious than ever. Anyone who read of these English proposals, warned one irate American Whig, "will then find how eagerly they wish to form distinctions amongst us, that they may create a few more tools of oppression. They wish to see us aspire to nobility, and are ready to gratify us whenever we do." At the present the ministry could depend only on the Crown officials and their dependents, plus a few Anglicans "who prefer basking in the sunshine of British royalty and court favour, to the simple practice of the pure religion of their forefathers." If Americans put off separating from the British only a few years longer, "until they raised a number of our first men to the different ranks of nobility," the society would be thoroughly corrupted. Then, Americans, "preserve your liberties if you can." This kind of American thinking transcended all particular trade or tax grievances: their very existence as a distinctive egalitarian people seemed at stake. (pp. 110-13)

Thomas Paine in his *Common Sense* had urged "those whose office it is to watch the morals of a nation, of whatsoever sect or denomination ye are of," to recognize the need for independence from Britain, that is, "if ye wish to preserve your native country uncontaminated by European corruption." But the admonition was hardly necessary. The American clergy were already deep in the process of working out—in an elaborate manner congenial to their covenant theology—the concept of the Revolution as an antidote to moral decay.

To a Calvinist clergyman the Enlightenment image of a virtuous society seemed extremely cloudy. "Others may, if they please, treat the corruption of our nature as a chimera: for my part," said John Witherspoon in a notable sermon delivered at Princeton in the spring of 1776, "I see it everywhere, and I feel it every day." All the exposed disorders and unhappiness of American society were rooted in the "envy, malice, covetousness, and the other lusts of man" [Witherspoon, *Dominion of Providence*, in *Works of Witherspoon*, III]. In their jeremiads the clergy scourged the people for their vices and warned them that England's Coercive Acts and the shedding of American blood were God's just punishments for a sinful people. "Have we not by our universal declensions, manifold offences, abuse of divine blessings provoked God into this severe controversy?" But the Americans, like the Israelites of old, were God's chosen people ("Where?—in what country, was it ever known that a people arose from paucity to populousness so fast?"), and bound to him by a "visible covenant" [Perry, *Sermon, May 11, 1775*]. Their very afflictions were a test of their peculiar blessedness, so that "God may prove us, whether we be wheat or chaff." "Such a season of declension" was their time of trial, the "day of the American Israel's trouble." It had always been the crafty policy of Israel's enemies, said the ministers in sermon after sermon centering particularly on the book of Nehemiah, to fall upon the "professing people" when they had forsaken their God and had sunk in sin. "Would the Britons have dared thus to magnify themselves against this people of the Lord of hosts, had they not been apprised of our declensions and abounding iniquities?" [Lyman, *Sermon Preached December 15th, 1774*].

Everywhere the clergy saw "Sins and Iniquities . . . very visible and apparent." And the sins were the same vices feared by a political scientist—infidelity, intemperance, profaneness, and particularly "pride and luxury in dress, furniture, eating, and drinking." Especially since the end of the French war it seemed that "luxury of every kind has flowed in faster than ever, and spread itself as a deluge all around us." Society appeared topsy-turvy: "Trade has flourished whereby money has flowed in apace, and raised many to the possession of opulent fortunes, whose fathers were glad to get their bread by the sweat of the brow." Pretension, ostentation, refinement—"shopkeepers and tradesmens daughters dressed like peeresses of the first rank"—all these were signs of social and moral deterioration [Ebenezer Baldwin, *The Duty of Rejoicing under Calamities and Afflictions . . . ,1776*].

Out of the language of their traditional covenant theology the ministers fashioned an explanation of the British tyranny as a divine punishment for the abominations of the American people. The prevalence of vices and immoralities among Americans had provoked their God. "Sin alone is the moral and procuring cause of all those evils we either feel or fear." Until the cause was removed the clergy could offer no relief from British oppression. Yet the Americans were still a peculiarly blessed and covenanted people; if they would but mend their ways and humbly acknowledge their God, good might come out of all this suffering. As Isaiah warned, God "sends his judgments abroad in the earth, that men may learn righteousness [*Affectionate Address*, iv; Josiah Stearns, *Two Sermons, Preached at Epping in the State of New Hampshire, January 20th, 1777*; Lyman, *Sermon Preached December 15th, 1774*]. In the sermons of the clergy the success of the Revolution thus became dependent on the repentance and reformation of the people. "We are now in an unusual way called upon to wash ourselves, to make ourselves clean, to put away the evil of our doings to do well, and to seek every kind of judgment." "SIN" itself, in bold capital letters, became the enemy. "May our land be purged from all its sins! May we be truly a holy people, and all our towns cities of righteousness!" Only then would God deliver them from the British [Gordon, *Sermon Preached before House of Representatives*].

A good Calvinist could never agree that the British connection was the main source of America's degeneration, for the "cause" of these "awful national Calamities . . . will never be removed, nor our Danger be over, 'until the Spirit is poured out from on High.' " Yet the clergy, like other colonial leaders, could not but be amazed at the extraordinary virtue and valor displayed by Americans under the British afflictions of 1774-75. Was it possible that this was "the Time, in which Christ's Kingdom is to be thus gloriously set up in the World?" The clergy, like many other Americans, felt the country "to be on the eve of some great and unusual events" and their language, ecstatic but not uniquely religious, took on a millennial tone. By 1776 it seemed to many of the ministers that decades of corrupt and vicious social behavior had at last caught up with the Americans, that now, here in this crisis with Britain, was the providential opportunity, not to be lost, for "a reformation in principles and practices," involving "a change of mind, and our entertaining different thoughts of past conduct." In this sense the Revolution became as much a rejection as an endorsement of previous American experience—raising some aspects of the way Americans had behaved to new heights of moral acceptability while at the same time repudiating the way they had exploited and maligned one another, out of their "vain appetites for wealth and honour," and the way they had bitterly fought to set themselves off one from another, "from a pique and jealousy of rank and place." Now in the midst of the unanimity and resolution of 1775 America appeared to be moving toward "a state of greater perfection and happiness than mankind has yet seen." With God's help they would build a harmonious society of "comprehensive benevolence" and become "the eminent example of every divine and social virtue." Out of the "perishing World round about" them they would create "a new World, a young World, a World of countless Millions, all in the fair Bloom of Piety [Gordon, *Sermon Preached before House of Representatives;* Brackenridge, *Six Political Discourses;* Williams, *Discourse on the Love of Our Country;* Duché, *American Vine;* Buell, *Best New-Year's Gift*].

Independence thus became not only political but moral. Revolution, republicanism, and regeneration all blended in American thinking. Further calamity, John Adams told his wife in July 1776, "will have this good Effect, at least: it will inspire Us with many Virtues, which We have not, and correct many Errors, Follies, and Vices, which threaten to disturb, dishonour, and destroy us." The repeated calls of the clergy for a return to the temperance and virtue of their ancestors made sense not only in terms of the conventional covenant theology but also, as many ministers enjoyed noting, in terms of the best political science of the day. As "pride," "prodigality, and extravagance" were vices, "contrary to the spirit of religion, and highly provoking to Heaven, so they also, in the natural course of things, tend to bring poverty and ruin upon a people." "The light of nature and revelation," social science and theology—perhaps for a final moment at the end of the eighteenth century—were firmly united. "Nothing is more certain," observed John Witherspoon in a common analysis of this fusion of piety and politics, "than that a general profligacy and corruption of manners make a people ripe for destruction." Yet when the character of the people was pure, when virtue and frugality were maintained with vigor, "the attempts of the most powerful enemies to oppress them are commonly baffled and disappointed. This will be found equally certain whether we consider the great principles of God's moral government, or the operation and influence of natural causes [Cumings, *Sermon, Preached on the 23d of November 1775;* Gordon, *Sermon Preached before House of Representatives;* Witherspoon, *Dominion of Providence,* in *Works of Witherspoon,* III]. The traditional covenant theology of Puritanism combined with the political science of the eighteenth century into an imperatively persuasive argument for revolution. Liberal rationalist sensibility blended with Calvinist Christian love to create an essentially common emphasis on the usefulness and goodness of devotion to the general welfare of the community. Religion and republicanism would work hand in hand to create frugality, honesty, self-denial, and benevolence among the people. The Americans would then "shew to the nations of the earth (what will be a most singular phenomenon) amidst all the jarring interests, subtlety, and rage of politics" that they "had virtue enough to think of, and to practice these things." The city upon the hill assumed a new republican character. It would now hopefully be, in Samuel Adams's revealing words, "the *Christian* Sparta."

The Americans' confidence in their republican future, bred from the evils and anxieties of the past, was not as illusory and as unjustified as it might on the face of it seem. Their new republican governments were to be more than beacons to the oppressed of the world, more than the con-

sequences of revolution. They were themselves to be the agencies of revolution. There was, the eighteenth century believed, a reciprocating relationship between the structure of the government and the spirit of its people. It was this belief in the mutual influence, the feedback and interplay, between government and society that makes eighteenth-century thinkers like Montesquieu so subtle and elusive. On one hand, there was no doubt that the nature of the government must be adapted to the customs and habits of the people. "A good form of government may hold the rotten materials together for some time, but beyond a certain pitch even the best constitution will be ineffectual, and slavery must ensue" [Witherspoon, *Dominion of Providence,* in *Works of Witherspoon,* III]. Yet, on the other hand, politics was not regarded simply as a matter of social determinism; the form of government was not merely a passive expression of what the spirit of the people dictated. The scheme of government itself had "a natural and powerful bias, both upon those who rule, and upon those who are ruled" [James Wilson, "Lectures on Law, Delivered in the College of Philadelphia in the Years 1790-1791," Wilson, ed., *Works of Wilson, I*]. Republicanism was therefore not only a response to the character of the American people but as well an instrument of reform. "If there is a form of government, then," John Adams asked of his countrymen in 1776, "whose principle and foundation is virtue, will not every sober man acknowledge it better calculated to promote the general happiness than any other form?" A republican constitution "introduces knowledge among the people, and inspires them with a conscious dignity becoming freemen; a general emulation takes place, which causes good humor, sociability, good manners, and good morals to be general. That elevation of sentiment inspired by such a government, makes the common people brave and enterprising. That ambition which is inspired by it makes them sober, industrious, and frugal." Adams could thus conclude that "it is the Form of Government which gives the decisive Colour to the Manners of the People, more than any other Thing." Societies differed, said Samuel West in the Massachusetts election sermon of 1776, and "men become virtuous or vicious, good commonwealthsmen or the contrary, generous, noble, and courageous, or base, mean-spirited, and cowardly, according to the impression that they have received from the government that they are under." "The strength and spring of every free government," said Moses Mather in 1775, "is the virtue of the people; virtue grows on knowledge, and knowledge on education" [Adams, *Thoughts on Government,* Adams, ed., *Works of John Adams,* IV; Adams to Mercy Warren, Jan. 8, 1776, Ford, ed., *Warren-Adams Letters,* I; West, *Sermon Preached May 29th, 1776,* Thornton, ed.; Mather, *America's Appeal*]. And education, it was believed was the responsibility and agency of a republican government. So the circle went.

Enlightened men could believe, as Samuel Stanhope Smith told James Madison sometime in 1777 or 1778, that new habitual principles, "the constant authoritative guardians of virtue," could be created and nurtured by republican laws, and that these principles, together with the power of the mind, could give man's "ideas and motives a new direction." By the repeated exertion of reason, by "recalling the lost images of virtue: contemplating them, and using them as motives of action, till they overcome those of vice again and again until after repeated struggles, and many foils they at length acquire the habitual superiority," by such exertions it seemed possible for man to recover his lost innocence and form a society of "habitual virtue." From these premises flowed much of the Americans' republican iconography—the "Pomp and Parade," as John Adams called it, the speeches and orations, the didactic history, even the "Painting, Sculpture, Statuary, and Poetry"—and the republicans' devotion to "the great importance of an early virtuous education [Adams to Abigail Adams, July 3, 1776, and same, Apr. 27, 1777].

Only this faith in the regenerative effects of republican government itself on the character of the people can explain the idealistic fervor of the Revolutionary leaders in 1776. Concentrating on the nicely reasoned constitutional arguments of John Adams or Jefferson in order to prove the moderation of the Revolution not only overlooks the more inflamed expressions of other Whigs but also misses the enthusiastic and visionary extravagance in the thinking of Adams and Jefferson themselves. Adams's hopes in 1776 were mingled with as much doubt and fear as those of any of the Revolutionaries, and he was aware as anyone of the vices and passions that drove men. Yet he could sincerely believe that the Revolution was "an Enterprise that is and will be an Astonishment to vulgar Minds all over the World, in this and in future Generations"—an intense conviction of success justified in 1776 by his extraordinary reliance, criticized acutely by Landon Carter, on the eventual ameliorating influence of republican laws and government on men's behavior. For Jefferson, faith in the future was always easier than for Adams, and he of all the Revolutionary leaders never seemed to lose heart. Like the Reverend John Joachim Zubly and others he believed that "when millions of free people at once turn their thoughts from trade, and the means of acquiring wealth, to agriculture and frugality, it must cause a most sensible alteration in the state" [in a letter from Adams to James Warren, Mar. 31, 1777]. In Jefferson's mind the Revolution was just beginning in 1776. The extensive reforms that he and other Virginians planned and in fact effected for their new state have never been fully appreciated and explored, even though Jefferson's autobiography clearly indicates that they intended to form "a system by which every fibre would be eradicated of ancient or future aristocracy; and a foundation laid for a government truly republican" [Jefferson, "Autobiography," Paul L. Ford, ed., *Writings of Thomas Jefferson,* 1892-99]. The Virginians' revision of laws, for example, although it may not have been, as Jefferson proposed to Edmund Pendleton in the summer of 1776, an immediate return to "that happy system of our ancestors, the wisest and most perfect ever yet devised by the wit of man, as it stood before the 8th century," was indeed, as the General Assembly realized, a work "which proposes . . . various and material changes in our legal code" [Jefferson to Pendleton, Aug. 13, 1776, Boyd, ed., *Jefferson Papers,* I]. Through extensive changes in inheritance, landowning, education, religion, administration, and law, designed to involve the people more personally in the affairs of government than at any time since the ancient Saxons, the Virginians hoped that their new republi-

can government would create the sources for its own sustenance.

The reforms were often foiled or compromised, the expectations smashed; yet the intentions were very real in 1776. For a young Virginian, who a decade later was to emerge as one of the greatest minds of the Revolutionary generation, the Revolution offered ecstatic prospects for a new kind of politics. In the spring of 1777 James Madison took his republicanism so seriously that he sought to promote by his own example "the proper reform" in the electoral practices of the state by doing away with all the personal soliciting and treating of voters that were corrupting Virginia's politics—practices that were "inconsistent with the purity of moral and of republican principles," but practices that were part of Virginia's experience for decades [Hutchinson and Rachael, eds., *Madison Papers,* I]. That Madison lost the election to the House of Delegates to a former tavern-keeper, that the republican hopes may have proved illusory, does not detract from the existence of these kinds of hopes in 1776, but indeed helps to explain in the years after Independence the increasing disenchantment of Madison and other Whigs with their Revolutionary assumptions and expectations. (pp. 114-22)

Indeed, it is only in the context of this sense of uncertainty and risk that the Americans' obsessive concern in 1776 with their social character can be properly comprehended. They knew only too well where the real source of danger

---

Alexis de Tocqueville on "The Trade of Literature" in America:

Democracy not only infuses a taste for letters among the trading classes, but introduces a trading spirit into literature.

In aristocracies readers are fastidious and few in number; in democracies they are far more numerous and far less difficult to please. The consequence is that among aristocratic nations no one can hope to succeed without great exertion, and this exertion may earn great fame, but can never procure much money; while among democratic nations a writer may flatter himself that he will obtain at a cheap rate a moderate reputation and a large fortune. For this purpose he need not be admired; it is enough that he is liked.

The ever increasing crowd of readers and their continual craving for something new ensure the sale of books that nobody much esteems.

In democratic times the public frequently treat authors as kings do their courtiers; they enrich and despise them. What more is needed by the venal souls who are born in courts or are worthy to live there?

Democratic literature is always infested with a tribe of writers who look upon letters as a mere trade; and for some few great authors who adorn it, you may reckon thousands of idea-mongers.

Alexis de Tocqueville, in his Democracy in America, *edited by Phillips Bradley, 1963.*

lay. "We shall succeed if we are virtuous," Samuel Adams told John Langdon in the summer of 1777. "I am infinitely more apprehensive of the Contagion of Vice than the Power of all other Enemies." Benjamin Rush in 1777 even expressed the hope that the war would not end too soon: "A peace at this time would be the greatest curse that could befall us. . . . Liberty without virtue would be no blessing to us." Several more military campaigns were needed, he said to John Adams, in order "to purge away the monarchical impurity we contracted by laying so long upon the lap of Great Britain." The Revolution with all its evocation of patriotism and the martial spirit would cleanse the American soul of its impurities and introduce "among us the same temperance in pleasure, the same modesty in dress, the same justice in business, and the same veneration for the name of the Deity which distinguished our ancestors" [in letters from Adams to Langdon, Aug. 7, 1777, and from Rush to Adams, Aug. 8, 1777]. (pp. 123-24)

> Gordon S. Wood, "Moral Reformation," in his The Creation of the American Republic, 1766-1787, *The University of North Carolina Press, 1969, pp. 91-124.*

Edmund S. Morgan

[In the following excerpt, Morgan examines the positive and negative aspects of national government under the Articles of Confederation.]

Nationalism has been the great begetter of revolutions. In Europe, in Asia, in Africa, we have seen it stir one people after another: they grow proud of their traditions, of their language, of their identity, and they strike for independence. In our case it was the other way round: we struck for independence and were thereby stirred into nationality; our nation was the child, not the father, of our revolution.

We did, of course, have some of the makings of a nation before 1776. We spoke, for the most part, the same language; we enjoyed common historical traditions; we occupied a continuous territory; we were almost all Protestants. We had even developed a certain self-consciousness, a pride in things American. Nevertheless, it was not this pride that drove the colonists to resist British taxation. All the colonial demands might have been satisfied within the limits of empire, had there been any disposition in London to satisfy them. Only as they saw every other means fail did Americans turn to independence.

Once they turned, however, the view proved fair beyond belief, and the means inexorably became an end, a goal that encompassed all previous ones. Independence, once sighted, seemed one with liberty and equality and inseparable from them—it is only the nationalism of other peoples that ever appears ugly or dangerous.

So American nationalism appeared to the British, who detected signs of it early in the dispute. It had been a commonplace that the colonies could not be kept forever, that sometime in the dim and—it was to be hoped—distant future they would attain independence. No one, least of all the Americans, wished the event to come in the eighteenth

century, but the British feared it and by meeting every protest against Parliament as a step toward it eventually brought about the very thing they feared. The British efforts to curb a supposed drive toward independence united Americans in a common sense of grievance and alarm, nourishing a sense of togetherness that grew steadily toward nationality.

The process, we can see now, began at the time of the Stamp Act when the colonists surprised themselves not only by the unanimity of their opposition to the tax but also by their ability to agree to a declaration of principles at the Congress in New York. After the meeting was over and repeal was on the way, Joseph Warren of Massachusetts wrote enthusiastically to a friend that the Stamp Act had accomplished "what the most zealous Colonist never could have expected! The Colonies until now were ever at variance and foolishly jealous of each other, they are now . . . united . . . nor will they soon forget the weight which this close union gives them."

In the years that followed, each time the colonists felt obliged to use the weight of union, the closeness of union was strengthened, for with each new contest they were discovering a wider agreement in principle. When the time came to cut loose from the mother country and set up government for themselves, they were ready to build upon a common core of political beliefs. They believed that government must protect property and not take it in taxes without consent, that government is the product of those who are governed by it and subject to alteration by them at any time. They knew that men are evil by nature and that governments are consequently prone to corruption. Together they watched the British government succumb to evil, and together they decided to do something about it.

By 1776 the consciousness that they belonged together had grown so strong that the phrase "United Colonies" had a singular as well as a plural meaning. When the Declaration of Independence substituted "States" for "Colonies," the singular meaning was still present, and it did not even occur to the colonists that they might establish thirteen separate governments and go their different ways. They must win independence together or not at all, and they must have some sort of central government to give expression to their existence as a nation.

Politicians argued for nearly a century over the question whether the national government was older or younger than the state governments. Historians still argue over it. But in 1776 Americans believed that the Declaration of Independence created the United States as well as the several states; and the Continental Congress which made the Declaration seemed as much a provisional government for the nation as the provincial congresses were for the states. The Declaration itself indicates as much when it says that "as Free and Independent States they have full power to levy war, conclude peace, contract alliances, establish commerce, and to do all other acts and things which independent States may of right do." Though given a plural wording, "Independent States" must have been intended to convey a singular as well as a plural meaning, for it was Congress, the central government of the nation, that levied war against Great Britain, contracted an alliance with France, and concluded peace.

When the members of the Continental Congress began to consider a declaration that would turn the United Colonies into the United States, they immediately took steps to prepare a constitution so that the new nation, as soon as it should be born, could be clothed in a properly defined and limited government. On June 12, 1776, a committee was appointed to draft such a document. Like most committees, it did not move as fast as history and was not able to report until a month later, after independence had already been declared. What it then proposed (in a report drafted by John Dickinson) was a formalization of the existing situation, with all the functions of the central government assigned to a congress composed of delegates annually appointed by the several states. The congress was to have exclusive authority over some matters and concurrent authority with the states over others, but there was very little indication of how it was to put its decisions into effect.

When the members of the existing Congress began to debate the Dickinson report, they soon found out that the forming of a national government posed problems which the previous history of America did not equip them to surmount. Most of them had had abundant political experience in local assemblies, but none of them had participated in the imperial administration—if they had, perhaps there would have been no revolution. Though they were rapidly learning the art of dealing with a continent rather than a colony, they had been at it for less than two years, during which their efforts had been directed exclusively toward opposing the British. Now when they were required to define the relations of the states to one another and to the nation, all the old divisive forces—the local quarrels and jealousies that had divided the colonies before 1763— reasserted themselves. To make matters worse, Congress discovered that it had inherited some of the hostility generated against imperial control during the preceding decade. Just as Americans continued to be suspicious of governors even when they were elective, so they continued to be suspicious of central authority even when it was their own.

During the summer of 1776 these obstacles blocked the efforts of Congress to work out the details of the proposed constitution. The members could not agree on an equitable way of apportioning either expenses or voting, and there were conflicting opinions about what should be done with the western territories to which some states laid claim. While they argued, the members had also to give their attention to the approaching Battle of Long Island and to the hundred other problems of conducting a government that was already in existence even though it had not been properly created. As these problems mounted, they temporarily put aside their constitution making and got on with the business of defeating Great Britain, arbitrarily assuming the powers they needed to get the job done.

They were aware, however, that they must tread lightly lest they inadvertently encourage the lingering suspicion of central government and dampen the national enthusi-asm that was necessary to sustain the war effort. They did not, for instance, venture to impose taxes, because, having been chosen by state legislatures or provincial congresses rather than by direct vote, they were not in the fullest sense representatives of the people. Yet they could not run a war without money, and so they turned to a method which they had devised as colonists for mortgaging their future: they assumed the authority to issue bills of credit (in other words, paper money). In this way they hoped to translate national enthusiasm into concrete economic support.

Paper money worked well at first, and the war could scarcely have been fought without it. But as time passed and the fighting dragged on, Congress learned what many governments have found to their sorrow before and since, that patriotism is more readily transformed into blood and death than it is into dollars and cents. Merchants and farmers did not have enough faith in the credit of the nation to accept its paper money at face value. Every month saw the bills worth less. In September 1779, Congress tried to halt the fall by resolving to issue no more, but as the bills continued to decline anyhow, in March 1780, it reversed its decision and put the presses to work again. By the following spring the bills were costing more to print than they were worth.

It was at this point, with the only independent source of income exhausted, that the United States at last acquired a constitution—though not one which would do much to bolster its credit. When Congress had resumed discussion of the proposed constitution in April 1777, the claims of the particular states were heard on its floors in a swelling chorus from people who often looked upon themselves more as watchdogs of local interests than as participants in a large enterprise. Such a man, for example, was Dr. Thomas Burke, congressman from North Carolina. Burke thought he discerned in the central government a grasping for power of the kind that signalled a degeneration into tyranny. Rather than risk erecting another tyranny in place of the one just destroyed, he favored dissolving Congress altogether as soon as the war should be won. National feeling was too strong to allow serious consideration of such a proposal, but Burke was able to win adoption of a strong states' rights clause which found its way into the finished constitution as Article 2: "Each State retains its sovereignty, freedom and independence, and every power, jurisdiction, and right, which is not by this confederation expressly delegated to the United States, in Congress assembled."

Esteem for the state governments and a corresponding distrust of the central government was rising all over the country. While the latter was losing its credit in the avalanche of paper, the states were able to begin the climb into comparative solvency by levying taxes. Most of them had constitutions by 1777, and as Congress groped its way down the uncharted path of national government, the state governments were entrenching themselves behind a growing body of legislation. They were in fact so jealous of their new strength that when Congress finally finished tinkering with the constitution on November 17, 1777, and presented it to them, they were not at all eager to ratify it.

It is true that the Articles of Confederation, as the document was called, assigned what appeared to be a formidable list of powers to the Congress, which remained the only department in the central government. Congress was to have exclusive authority over relations with foreign countries, including the determination of war and peace, over admiralty cases, over disputes between different states, over coining money and establishing weights and measures, over trade with the Indians outside the boundaries of particular states, and over postal communications. In addition, it was authorized to borrow money and to requisition the states for men and money. Decisions were to be made by a simple majority, with each state having one vote, except in specified important matters for which the consent of at least nine states was necessary.

Though these powers when set forth in black and white looked imposing, they hardly merited any alarm over states' rights or popular liberty; for they were actually no more than Congress had been exercising on a *de facto* basis since independence, and the states had nevertheless grown steadily stronger and popular liberties more extensive. Furthermore, the Articles carefully safeguarded the states against encroachment from the central government by leaving to them the power of the purse. Congress could requisition them for money, but if they refused, the Articles provided no means to enforce the demand or for that matter to enforce any congressional decision. Their own experience in thwarting colonial governors might have reassured the American people that with the power of the purse the states were also retaining the ultimate power of government. They were also guarded against each other: equal voting by states was intended to protect the small states from the large and the nine-state majority to protect the large from the small.

But in spite of all its safeguards the people who had to judge this constitution could not at first bring themselves to ratify it. They were conditioned by the preceding ten or twelve years to approach all government with caution. In Massachusetts and New Hampshire they went over the Articles clause by clause in town meetings while local sages pointed out defects and dangers. Elsewhere the state legislatures talked it up and down much as Congress had already done and sent in recommendations for amendment, mostly designed to limit further the powers assigned the central government.

In only one important respect were these powers considered insufficient. The states without western land claims, particularly Maryland and New Jersey, felt that Congress should have the authority originally assigned it by the Dickinson committee to limit those states (Georgia, the Carolinas, Virginia, Connecticut, and Massachusetts) whose charters had named the Pacific Ocean as a western boundary. The lands beyond the settled regions, it was urged, would be won by the joint efforts of all the states in the Continental Army. What was thus purchased by the blood of all should belong to all.

The people of Maryland and New Jersey feared that unless the United States took over the western lands, the states that claimed them would have an immeasurable economic and political advantage over the others. Through sale of these lands the government, say of Virginia, might enjoy a steady income without taxing her citizens at all. As a result people would move from Maryland to Virginia to avoid taxes and would thus increase further the tax burden of those who were left behind, until Maryland and the other landless states would be depopulated and bankrupt. Better that all states be put on an equal footing and the western lands be given to the United States.

In evoking the philosophy of equality the landless states were of course seeking to further their own interests, just as Americans had been seeking to further their own interests in resisting British taxation, and the dissenting churches in seeking to end the special favors shown to the Anglicans and Congregationalists. The arguments for a cession of western lands were not less cogent because those who offered them stood to benefit. It must be pointed out, however, that much of the support came from a group of men who stood to gain privately far more than they disclosed, far more than an equality of the states.

These men were land speculators who had formed companies to develop the territory in question. The Illinois-Wabash Company and the Indiana Company, with a membership drawn largely from Pennsylvania, Maryland, and New Jersey, had made purchases from the Indians in the Ohio Valley before independence and were now seeking a governmental validation of their titles. They knew that Virginia held the best claim to the lands: as the first colony to be founded her claim antedated all others, and it covered most of the Mississippi Valley north of the Carolinas. But Virginia made it plain that she did not intend to recognize Indian purchases made by outsiders; she had speculators of her own to please. If, however, the lands were ceded to the United States, the members of the Indiana and Wabash companies hoped that congressmen would prove more pliant than the Virginia legislators. There was good reason to hope too, because many influential congressmen already held shares of stock in the companies and showed a more than charitable disposition toward them.

The speculators and their propagandists worked hard for a revision of the Articles of Confederation to give Congress control of the area where their investments lay. Not only did they argue that conquest of the West by the Continental armies would entitle the nation to sovereignty over it, but they also maintained that since the West had formerly belonged to Great Britain it should now belong to Congress, because, as they claimed, the authority of Great Britain had devolved upon Congress. The speculators were most influential in Maryland, and to enforce their arguments persuaded Maryland not to ratify the Articles of Confederation unless amended to make the unbounded states give up their western lands.

Because of the urgency of union the other states agreed by early 1779 to ratify the basic document first and tackle the multitude of proposed amendments afterward. But Maryland held out. It is to the credit of the Virginians in this crisis that many of them recognized the validity of the principle Maryland was contending for, even while they called attention to the ulterior motives at work. And it is doubly fortunate that they discovered reasons closer to their own states' interests to justify limiting its size. There was a common assumption at this time that a republic could not cover more than a small territory and remain a republic. It was hoped that a confederation of republics might extend more widely, but a single republic, if spread too large, would prove weak and either fall prey to monarchical despotism or disintegrate into anarchy. Thomas Jefferson and Richard Henry Lee, both of whom expressed these views, thought that Virginia should voluntarily limit its own size. Thus through an attachment to the principles of republican government they reached much the same position that men with other reasons had been contending for.

Because of these views and also because the British armies were now pressing up from the Carolinas, making the need of confederation seem daily more desperate, the Virginians agreed on January 2, 1781, to cede their territory north and west of the Ohio. In doing so, however, they stipulated certain conditions that carried much further the principle of equality upon which Maryland had insisted. Maryland had been worried about its own inferiority to so

huge a sister state. Virginia was concerned about the future of the United States and of the people who should live in the territory it was resigning. Virginia gave it up only on condition that it be held as a common fund for the nation—thus providing the United States with a national domain—and on condition also that it be laid out in separate new states not more than 150 and not less than 100 miles square, to be admitted eventually to the union with the same "rights of sovereignty, freedom, and independence as the other States." Virginia by its cession cut itself down to a size more nearly that of its fellow states and gave all Americans an equal share in the possession of the West. At the same time, it guaranteed that future westerners should not become second-class citizens, that the United States should remain a union of equals without subordinate colonies of the British type.

Though Congress could not refuse these conditions, there was trouble over another of Virginia's stipulations, namely, that all Indian purchases in the area be declared void. The powerful land speculators were able to cause a shameful wrangle over this question, which delayed the acceptance of Virginia's offer for several years. It was apparent, however, that the land would ultimately belong to the United States. Maryland was thus left with no grounds on

The Battle of Yorktown (1781, here portrayed in a reenactment), which was the last major confrontation with the British before the end of the war in 1783.

which it could conscientiously refrain from joining in the Articles of Confederation. But, still in the clutch of the land companies, the legislators continued to delay. At this point they received a strong nudge—it might be called a kick—from the French Ambassador, La Luzerne, to whom Maryland had appealed for the protection of French naval forces against British raids in the Chesapeake. The Ambassador, exceeding his powers, suggested that naval aid would not be forthcoming unless Maryland ratified the Articles. In February 1781, Maryland did so, and on March 1 the Confederation was formally announced. (pp. 101-12)

The country gave signs of its social sanity by the speed with which the wounds of war were healed in the rehabilitation of colonists who had remained loyal to the King. If the American Revolution was in any sense a civil war, the Confederation did a much faster and much better job of reconstruction than the United States did after Appomattox. How many thousand loyalists departed for Canada or England is not known, but whatever their number their places were quickly filled. Of those who stayed behind, many suffered loss of property and, for a time, of political rights, but the end of the Confederation period saw them reabsorbed into the community on equal terms with no enduring heritage of bitterness.

The social health of the new nation was also apparent in the proliferation of intellectual activity following the war. National pride found expression in appeals for an American culture, and though the appeals were frequently more eloquent than the response, there was an astonishing production of historical writing, verse, painting, and even schoolbooks dedicated to magnifying America. New scientific societies were begun, notably the American Academy of Arts and Sciences at Boston, while the older American Philosophical Society breathed a new vigor. Companies of eager reformers sprang up everywhere and organized to improve agriculture, remodel penal codes, abolish slavery, prevent drunkenness, help immigrants, build libraries. The Americans were already embarked on their tireless, and to many Europeans tiresome, campaign to improve themselves and the world.

Although the perspective of nearly two centuries enables us to see the United States of the 1780s as a healthy, thriving young nation, there were many Americans at the time who thought otherwise. The achievements of the period . . . , except in western policy, were the work either of the state governments or of smaller groups or of individuals. Only in relation to the West could the national government point to any notable accomplishment, and only in relation to the West did it really have any power to act independently of the state governments. True, it had supervised the war and the negotiation of the peace, but those who had participated in the government during that time were aware of how heavily they had leaned on France. Congress had found it much easier to get both troops and money from France than from the states, a fact which dimmed the pride they felt in victory.

As for the peace, reliance on France had led Congress to impose a shameful set of conditions on its diplomats, namely, that they follow French dictates in everything except insistence on independence. Only by ignoring their instructions had the United States ministers been able to secure the terms which gave Americans land west of the Appalachians. Even at that it was not the strength of the United States but rather the rivalry of England and France that had made possible the negotiation of such favorable terms. England had been generous in an attempt to drive a wedge between the United States and its ally.

After the war, American diplomats in Europe felt for the first time the full meaning of their country's impotence. Jefferson, who took Franklin's post in France, found the job an excellent school of humility, and John Adams at the Court of St. James's was treated with studied contempt, while England steadfastly refused to grant a commercial treaty and clung to her trading posts in the Northwest area in direct violation of the peace treaty. Spain, left in undisputed possession of the Mississippi for three hundred miles from its mouth, closed the port of New Orleans to American commerce in the not unreasonable hope of detaching Kentucky and Tennessee. The American frontiersmen there could scarcely exist unless they could float their produce to market via the Mississippi, and yet Congress almost agreed to a proposed treaty negotiated by John Jay that would have yielded for twenty-five or thirty years whatever claim the United States had to navigation of the river through Spanish territory. In return eastern merchants would have obtained commercial privileges in Spain. Since the American claim was a very dubious one at best, the treaty was not a bad one, and it received a majority of votes in Congress, though not the necessary nine-state majority. It nevertheless antagonized the westerners, whose interests it seemed to sacrifice to those of eastern merchants.

In retrospect it is possible to see that the diplomatic failures of the Confederation period were the result of forces that lay beyond the control of the United States in its infant condition. Though independent, its three million people scarcely constituted a world power. No matter how their national government had been constructed, they could not have carried a big enough stick to command respect in Europe. But this thought, when it occurred to people at the time, was cold comfort. Men like Washington, Madison, Hamilton, Jay, John Adams, Robert Morris, men who had caught a vision of American greatness, wished to see it translated into fact without delay. As they struggled to operate the government they had created and repeatedly found themselves blocked by a lack of power, they became increasingly convinced that greatness would never attend a country whose government rested so helplessly on the capricious sufferance of thirteen superior state governments.

These men did what they could to make the national government under the Articles of Confederation as strong as that document and the prevailing temper of the state delegations would allow. Even before the Articles were formally put into operation, they moved to consolidate administrative responsibility by appointment of separate secretaries to manage each of the important activities with which the government must be concerned: foreign affairs, war, and finance. Hitherto the United States had no real executive departments, the matters requiring continuous attention being handled by various congressional committees. In January 1781, a Department of Foreign Affairs was created and in February the departments of Finance and War, each to be run by one man who would be responsible to Congress and hold office during its pleasure.

In selecting a Superintendent of Finance, Congress was fortunate in having available Robert Morris, a leading Philadelphia merchant. Morris was able to bring a semblance of order into the chaos he encountered upon undertaking the job. Though he had to beg and borrow from state governments and from foreign countries, and though he seems to have mingled private gain too closely with public, he kept the United States almost solvent during the remainder of the war. In order to assist him, Congress authorized the first national bank on May 26, 1781, thus exercising a power that was to be a matter of controversy for some time to come.

In appointing heads of the other departments, Congress made less fortunate choices. Robert R. Livingston, the first Secretary for Foreign Affairs, was elected with the active assistance of the French minister La Luzerne in August 1781, but resigned the following year and was not replaced by John Jay until 1784. Jay, like Livingston, was more ready to listen to the demands of other countries than was proper in a secretary whose business was to bargain with them. The office of Secretary at War was held successively by Benjamin Lincoln and Henry Knox, neither of them distinguished. Nevertheless, the very existence of secretaries whose sole business was to administer a department and who could be held responsible for its activities was a considerable advance in the creation of an effective national government. Each department developed a small staff of workers who became the first professional civil servants of the United States and in many cases continued to work in the same capacities under the new government after the Confederation ended.

But the creation of administrative departments did not in itself furnish the power to take necessary or desirable actions. After the Articles of Confederation were adopted, the more nationalistic congressmen began to feel out the possibilities of a more effective central government by suggesting that Congress had by implication the power to use whatever means were necessary to carry out its functions. As long as the war with England lasted, they frequently persuaded the other members to take bold actions, as in creating the national bank, laying an embargo on trade with England, or giving Washington authority to impress food and supplies. But the members were not yet ready to ask, nor would the states have been willing to grant, a general authority to execute laws. Once the war ceased and united action became less urgent, Congress became increasingly timid about asserting itself, and its strength ebbed rapidly. There was even a reversion in administration: Robert Morris resigned as Superintendent of Finance and a committee took charge again.

As Congress spoke in feebler tones, the state governments grew contemptuous of its authority. They violated the Articles of Confederation by ignoring the nation's treaties with foreign countries, by waging war with the Indians, by building navies of their own. They sent men with less vision and less ability to represent them and at times failed to send any, so that Congress could scarcely muster a quorum to do business. They refused to fill congressional requisitions any better than they had those imposed by Great Britain during their colonial days.

As in the years before Confederation, it was in financial matters that the impotence of the national government was most acutely felt. From 1780 when its paper money became worthless until 1787 when it began to realize a small income from the sale of public lands, the government was totally dependent, except for loans, on the unobliging states. Congress sought a remedy by proposing an amendment to the Articles of Confederation giving the United States the right to levy and collect a 5 percent duty on foreign imports. Amendment, however, required unanimous acceptance and in 1782 failed because Rhode Island, the smallest state of the union, flatly rejected it, while the other states attached various conditions to their acceptance. In the following year Congress tried again by coupling the proposal with a number of others designed to win favor for it. By 1786 every state but New York was ready to agree in some form, but New York's refusal was enough to defeat the scheme once more.

It had become clear, to the country's leaders at least, that Congress as then constituted could never perform its functions. When the Articles of Confederation were drafted, Americans had had little experience of what a national government could do for them and bitter experience of what an arbitrary government could do to them. In creating a central government they were therefore more concerned with keeping it under control than with giving it the means to do its job. Their state governments, they felt, should hold a leading rein on this new power. State governments were closer to home, closer to the people, and could be relied on to prevent Congress from getting the bit in its teeth and rushing into tyranny.

Time had by no means disappointed these calculations: Congress had never got out of hand. But anyone with half an eye for the nation's welfare could see by 1787 that the state governments had proved unworthy masters. They would not allow Congress to act whether action was needed or not. Congress had been safeguarded into impotency, its deliberations rendered as ineffective as those of a debating society, while the states grew ever stronger. Washington had seen what was happening and warned against it as early as 1780: "I see one head gradually changing into thirteen. . . . I see the powers of Congress declining too fast for the consequence and respect which is due to them as the grand representative body of America." In the summer of 1787 James Wilson sadly confirmed the fact:

> Among the first sentiments expressed in the first Congress one was that Virginia is no more, that Massachusetts is no more, that Pennsylvania is no more. We are now one nation of brethren. We must bury all local interests and distinctions. This language continued for some time. The tables at length began to turn. No sooner were the State Governments formed than their jealousy and ambition began to display themselves. Each endeavored to cut a slice from the common loaf,

to add to its own morsel, till at length the confederation became frittered down to the impotent condition in which it now stands.

As the state governments grew stronger, they grew, in the opinion of many of their leading citizens, more irresponsible not only toward the nation but toward their own people. The Revolution had begun because the British government violated the sacredness of private property. Now it seemed that some of the state governments were doing the same by failing to protect the investments of creditors. Rhode Island, where a wildly depreciating paper currency had been made legal tender, was the notorious example. Hordes of happy debtors there were paying off their obligations in worthless paper, leaving their creditors bankrupt. Or so the newspapers said, and from past experience everyone was ready to believe the worst of Rhode Island.

And so, in addition to the need for a government which could act effectively for the nation, there began to be felt the need for a central authority with power to meet this new threat to property rights. Without such an authority, it was feared by many, the whole country would degenerate into anarchy. Was not property the only real security for life and liberty? Those who felt this way saw a dreadful portent for the future in what had happened in Massachusetts in the autumn of 1786. Farmers in the western part of the state, hit hard by a combination of low prices and high taxes, rose in armed rebellion under Daniel Shays. Shays and his men closed the courts in Berkshire, Hampshire, and Worcester counties, thus ending suits at law and preventing creditors from collecting debts. They defied the state government; and if the loyal militia of the state had not come to the rescue, the United States arsenal at Springfield would have fallen to an armed mob, with the central government helpless to prevent it. Without men or money it would be equally helpless to cope with future, possibly worse, threats of anarchy.

The prospects of remedying the situation looked dim, for with the states so powerful and so irresponsible it was unlikely they would agree to give up their death grip on the central government. Even if the majority of them should be willing, one dissent was sufficient to prevent amendment of the Articles of Confederation. But while wise men shook their heads over Daniel Shays and talked hysterically of the advantages of monarchy or dictatorship, events were already stirring which would give the United States a government true to the principles of the Revolution and commensurate with the national vision of its greatest leaders. (pp. 120-28)

. . . . .

The year 1786 was the low point of the Critical Period. It was the year of Shays' Rebellion, the year of John Jay's proposed treaty with Spain, a year in which the depression in trade reached its lowest ebb. In the midst of discouragements Virginia took the lead in an attempt to breathe a little life into the national government. Virginia proposed an interstate convention to discuss a uniform regulation of commerce. If the delegates could agree on a set of recommendations, the states might then authorize Congress to carry them out. Several states expressed a readiness to take up Virginia's proposal, and the meeting was sched-

uled for Annapolis, Maryland, on the first Monday in September 1786.

Not much is known about the maneuvering that preceded the Annapolis convention, but there is evidence that some of the commissioners saw in it the opportunity to inaugurate a thorough overhaul of the Articles of Confederation. New Jersey sent a delegation empowered to consider not only commerce but "other important matters." New York sent Alexander Hamilton, an ardent nationalist, and Virginia sent James Madison, who wrote to Jefferson a month earlier that "Gentlemen both within and without Congress wish to make this meeting subservient to a plenipotentiary convention for amending the Confederation." (p. 129)

> *Edmund S. Morgan, in his* The Birth of the Republic, 1763-89, *third edition, The University of Chicago Press, 1992, 206 p.*

Reinhold Niebuhr on "the pursuit of happiness" in America:

The Declaration of Independence assures us that "the pursuit of happiness" is one of the "inalienable rights" of mankind. While the right to its pursuit is, of course, no guarantee of its attainment, yet the philosophy which informed the Declaration, was, on the whole, as hopeful that all men, at least all American men, could attain happiness as it was certain that they had the right to pursue it. America has been, in fact, both in its own esteem and in the imagination of a considerable portion of Europe, a proof of the validity of this modern hope which reached its zenith in the Enlightenment. The hope was that the earth could be transformed from a place of misery to an abode of happiness and contentment. The philosophy which generated this hope was intent both upon eliminating the natural hazards to comfort, security and contentment; and upon reforming society so that the privileges of life would be shared equitably.

Reinhold Niebuhr, in his The Irony of American History, *1952.*

RELIGIOUS INFLUENCES IN POST-REVOLUTIONARY AMERICA

Merrill Jensen

[In the following essay, Jensen discusses the separation of church and state, as well as the influence of the churches on such issues as slavery, criminal justice, and charitable organizations in post-revolutionary America.]

The political upheaval and change that was an integral part of the American Revolution made possible other changes in American society: changes that were sometimes an answer to ancient grievances, and sometimes a response to new conditions. The deep-rooted antagonism to established churches was expressed in the revolutionary constitutions and in laws disestablishing or removing the special privileges of established churches. Negro slavery, long hateful to some, was attacked anew as inconsistent with the idealism of the Revolution, and several states (invariably where slavery was unimportant), abolished slavery and the slave trade. The criminal codes, long as merciless as England's, were revised in the direction of humaneness. Prison reform was advocated and conditions were improved. The engrossment of the land was not stopped but the abolition of laws of entail and primogeniture did away with one legal foundation for great land holdings. British Crown lands and confiscated estates of Loyalists fell to the individual states and in turn were sold and granted, usually in smaller lots. In a measure, this contributed to the democratization of land holding, as did the opening up of the vast national domain west of the Appalachians.

On the practical side, Americans now got together as they had never done before in creating societies for social and economic improvement, digging canals, building bridges, and improving roads. They founded newspapers and magazines at a rate undreamed of before the war. All these and many more activities were a reflection of the new spirit and the new opportunities which were the result of the successful outcome of the American Revolution.

Religion had been a basic part of American thought and feeling from the beginning, and so had controversy about it. Some believed in a theocracy, as did the Puritans of Massachusetts Bay. Others, like Roger Williams and William Penn, believed that men should be free to worship as they pleased, or not at all if such was their desire. But such men and the colonies they founded were exceptional. By the time of the Revolution most colonies had state-churches, established by law and supported by the taxation of all the people, whatever their personal religious beliefs. In New England, aside from Rhode Island, the Congregational Church was so privileged. To the south the Church of England was supported by law and public money in most of the colonies.

There was ever mounting opposition to this union of church and state during the eighteenth century. The back country was settled by a multitude of religious sects that objected ever more violently to paying taxes for the support of churches they did not believe in and often actively hated. In addition there was the growing influence of ideas which did battle with authoritarian ones. These ideas had various names at various times but basic to most of them was the belief that the individual had the right to decide for himself what religion, if any, he should have, and the corollary that no state could support and enforce any one religion in preference to any other. For the most part, though not invariably, men who believed thus were believers in democracy. Beyond this most of them, whatever their political beliefs, were subscribers to the religious belief known as Deism. Thus Thomas Paine, John Adams, Thomas Jefferson, and Benjamin Franklin was each in his own way a Deist. Years after, in *The Age of Reason,* Paine was to formulate that creed in its clearest form. It was stat-

ed in another way by George Mason in the Bill of Rights of the Virginia Constitution of June 1776. In it he declared that "that religion, or the duty which we owe to our Creator, and the manner of discharging it, can be directed only by reason and conviction, not by force or violence; and therefore all men are equally entitled to the free exercise of religion, according to the dictates of conscience; and that it is the mutual duty of all to practice Christian forbearance, love, and charity towards each other." John Adams expressed their creed in a practical way when asked about the appointment of Anglican bishops in America after the Revolution. He saw no objection and thought it inconsistent with American character and the American constitution to raise political objections. He did not believe that "the Father of all" was confined by lines of distinction or differences of opinion. "When we can enlarge our minds to allow each other an entire liberty in religious matters, the human race will be more happy and respectable in this and the future stage of its existence" [To Rev. William White, London, 28 Feb. 178 (4 or 5), Joseph Reed Papers, NYHS].

The attack on established churches took many forms. The clearest example of the combination of back-country opposition and a leadership moved by high ideals of human freedom came in Virginia. There the Presbyterians who had gotten a measure of tolerance were less opposed to the Anglican establishment than were the Baptists who carried on a long and heartbreaking struggle. Their preachers were persecuted and Patrick Henry won some of his early fame as a lawyer by helping Baptist preachers out of jail. The Revolution was for such people a great opportunity. In 1774 they circulated petitions demanding freedom of conscience and disestablishment of the Anglican Church. Since the Baptists and other dissenters were a majority of the population of Virginia, and the planter leaders of the revolutionary movement needed support, dissenting petitions were listened to as never before. Leaders such as George Mason and Jefferson, who believed in freedom of conscience as a matter of conviction rather than of expediency, thus got far more help than otherwise they would have had.

The framing of the Virginia constitution was followed by new attacks on the Anglican Church. The battle was long, for the majority of the legislature, unlike their constituents, were Anglicans who wanted no change in the old aristocratic order. But Mason, Jefferson, and Madison kept up the fight. First they repealed the law requiring dissenters to pay taxes for the support of the Anglican Church. Then, in 1779, Jefferson wrote a bill calling for the separation of church and state. This was countered by a proposal that the state take over the support of all churches within its bounds. Patrick Henry, who had won much fame in fighting established churches, was now equally ardent for the "establishment" of all churches in the state, and Jefferson's bill was defeated. The fight went on until 1786 when James Madison was at last able to steer Jefferson's bill of 1779 through the legislature. The law was a striking achievement for its day and at the end of his life Jefferson regarded it as one of his three greatest services to his country.

The disestablishment of the Anglican Church in the remainder of the South was an easy matter, for it was a sickly institution. The laws favoring it were strong but the dissenters were vastly superior to the Anglicans in numbers, tenacity, and courage. There were only a half dozen Anglican ministers in North Carolina and most of them were Loyalists. The Constitution of 1776 declared that no church should be established in preference to any other and that no one could be compelled to pay for the upkeep of a church. The Georgia Constitution of 1777 provided religious freedom for all people in the state. The Anglican clergy in South Carolina were able men and most of them were Patriots, but there too the dissenters demanded and got the church disestablished. The Constitution of 1778 provided for civil and religious equality for all peaceable members of Protestant sects.

In New England the Congregational clergy had been leading propagandists for revolution. This gave them strength in maintaining their privileged position in Massachusetts, Connecticut, and New Hampshire. In Massachusetts the church was tax-supported by all citizens except Baptists, Quakers, and Episcopalians, who were required by law to support their own churches. Yet the Baptists led the opposition to this system. When the Constitution of 1780 was written it included an article dealing with religion that was confused if not self-contradictory. It declared that every man had the right to worship in the way and time most agreeable to his own conscience, and yet it insisted that all men must worship publicly at stated times. It declared that no sect should ever be subordinated to any other by law, yet it required that towns should tax for the support of ministers, leaving it up to the town fathers to grant taxes to dissenters for their own churches. The result was that the towns taxed one and all, and dissenters found it difficult to get their share. Congregationalist town fathers, especially in rural districts where Calvinist orthodoxy was to hold sway for many years to come, found it easy to avoid such payments. This was entirely in keeping with the narrow Calvinism of such men as Sam Adams who helped draft that part of the Constitution.

New Hampshire followed in the steps of Massachusetts, but Connecticut held out much longer against what its citizens regarded as the forces of iniquity. They allowed dissenters to escape payment of taxes to the established church if they presented the clerk of the local church with a certificate of church attendance signed by an officer of the dissenter's own church.

New York had a mixed lot of religious sects: Dutch Reformed, Presbyterian, Episcopalian, Quaker, Moravian, Baptist, and many others. The establishment of the Anglican Church was nominal at best, and disappeared with the outbreak of the war. The Constitution of 1777 made the break complete. New Jersey had no established church but had almost as many vigorous groups as New York, and its Constitution of 1776 provided for complete freedom of religion.

The situation in Maryland was unique. The Anglican Church was established by law. There were many dissenters, but there were also many wealthy Catholic leaders in the colony, and fear of the latter kept the dissenting sects quiet on the subject of the Anglicans, despite the fact that Anglican preachers in Maryland had a universally bad reputation. They were well paid out of public taxes, appointed by the governor, and often lived a life of riotous enjoyment. There was little objection to the disestablishment provided for by the bill of rights in the Maryland Constitution of 1776 which declared that no one could be compelled to go to other than a church of his own choice.

Despite the attacks on established churches and proclamations of religious freedom, many of the states were still much concerned with the maintenance of Christianity, particularly of the Protestant variety, and within it, of a belief in the Trinity. At the same time that Georgia and the two Carolinas refused clergymen seats in their legislatures, they limited governmental offices to Protestants. The New York Constitution of 1777 provided for freedom of religion but required that all foreigners who applied for citizenship must renounce allegiance to all foreign rulers in ecclesiastical matters as well as civil. Even in Pennsylvania, Delaware, and New Jersey, where there had always been religious freedom, holders of public office were required to measure up to certain religious marks. In Pennsylvania they were required to believe in the divine inspiration of the Old and New Testaments. Delaware barred Deists, Jews, and others by requiring all officials to believe in the Trinity. In New Jersey only Protestants could hold office.

The steps in the direction of religious freedom and the complete separation of church and state were thus halting, but the direction was sure and the purpose was clear. The multitude of dissenting sects and the liberal religious and political ideas of many revolutionary leaders did not disappear although often defeated in particular battles. It was perfectly plain by the end of the 1780's how much progress had been made. A bill of rights was a part of the price that had to be paid for the ratification of the Constitution of 1787. The first of those rights declared that Congress should never make any law "respecting an establishment of religion, or prohibiting the free exercise thereof. . . ." The orthodox were horrified of course. Many Americans then as now have never accepted the idea that people's minds should be and must be free.

There were forms of bondage other than spiritual from which some Americans of the revolutionary generation sought to free themselves or their fellow men. Negro slavery had long been opposed in the colonies. The Quakers had delivered the first protests against it. The independent small farmers in the South objected to a labor system with which they found it difficult to compete. Many planters such as William Byrd II, Thomas Jefferson, and others, objected to slavery although their way of life was in large part founded on it. Clergymen like George Whitfield preached against it and found support among the back countrymen. The equalitarian ideals of the Revolution itself caused more than one man to question their reality when faced with the fact of human bondage. Freedom from Britain made it possible to act, for the British government had consistently supported slavery and the slave trade. In the decade just before the Revolution several of the colonies, including some in the South, made serious efforts to stop the trade only to have all legislation vetoed in London. At the beginning of the war only Georgia and South Carolina were in favor of the slave trade, and in every colony there were believers in the abolition of slavery.

Within a few years after 1775, either in constitutions or in legislation, the new states acted against slavery. Within a decade all the states except Georgia and South Carolina had passed some form of legislation to stop the slave trade. Freeing the slaves was much more difficult except in those states where there were very few of them. Vermont abolished slavery in her Constitution of 1777. In 1780 the Massachusetts Constitution declared that all men were born equal and endowed with freedom. It was at once argued that this part of the bill of rights freed all the slaves held in the state, and the state supreme court agreed. New Hampshire followed this lead in its Constitution of 1784. Other states such as Connecticut, Pennsylvania, and Rhode Island passed acts for piecemeal abolition. There was no unanimity, however, even in New England. A writer calling himself "Not Adams" declared that ever since "that class of people called Negroes" began to imbibe the idea they were not slaves, they have been coming to Boston. This made it harder for the poor inhabitants of the town to make a living. No Negroes should be allowed in Boston, he said, except such as had been born there.

The concern with slavery led to the creation of many organizations which were the forerunners of the abolitionist societies of a later age. The first abolitionist society in America was organized in 1774. As with most Philadelphia societies during his lifetime, Franklin was president. Pennsylvania passed a law for the gradual abolition of slavery in 1780. This was largely the work of George Bryan, one of the democratic leaders in the state, and one of slavery's most tireless opponents. The law was evaded and when the Society re-emerged in 1784, it made prosecution of such evasion its main business. It was instrumental in having the law revised and for years was an active force in the abolition movement. By 1800 Pennsylvania had less than 2,000 slaves left, as a result of her gradual emancipation law and of the watchful vigilance of the Society.

In New York the "Society for the Promotion of the Manumission of Slaves and Protecting such of them that have been or may be Liberated" was organized in 1785 with John Jay, a slaveholder, as president, and Alexander Hamilton, as secretary. There was strong anti-Negro feeling in New York where a good many slaves had always been held, and the Society was unable to secure passage of a bill for gradual abolition. It kept up its agitation, however. In 1788 it agreed that its members would boycott all auction masters who sold slaves and to give business only to those who "shall uniformly refrain from a practice so disgraceful and so shocking to humanity" [*New York Journal, and Daily Patriotic Register,* 27 Nov. 1788]. It likewise concerned itself with building a school for the children of free Negroes. But despite all its efforts there were more than 20,000 slaves in the state in 1790.

The well publicized activities of the Philadelphia and New York societies led to the formation of others, usually with names as top-heavy. One was organized in Delaware in 1788 and between then and 1794 others were organized in Rhode Island, Connecticut, New Jersey, Maryland, and Virginia. Maryland had a very active movement for gradual abolition. A writer in Maryland declared that slavery was inconsistent with the principles of the Revolution and he pointed to the horrors of slavery in the South.

There was important opposition to slavery in the South during and after the Revolution. Washington, Jefferson, Madison, and Patrick Henry all hoped that slavery could be ended in some fashion. They were in a minority, although Virginia did pass laws making it easier to free slaves. Farther to the south there was bitter opposition to the idea of abolition and to any restriction on the slave trade. Tolerance soon disappeared from Virginia as well, and the law making it easy to free slaves was repealed and petitions for abolition were ignored. Economics and idealism met head on and the former won an easy victory.

Still another institution that was a source of both labor supply and immigration to America was the system of indentured servitude. Tens of thousands had come to the new world in this way, and although it had offered them opportunity to escape from the evil of poverty in Europe, their lot as "servants" was not a happy one. Very few people either during or after the Revolution, except the German societies, seem to have shown much concern over these people or the improvement of their lot. In New York an effort was made to get a group of citizens to liberate a shipload of white servants by paying their passage, taking in return small deductions from wages. It was argued that while immigration was necessary, the traffic in white people was contrary to the idea of liberty and to the feelings of many citizens. However, the only laws passed during the 1780's were simply to clarify their status rather than to change it, and the system did not die out for decades.

Americans were far more deeply concerned about their fellow men who lost their freedom through crime and debt. The accounts of the treatment of law breakers, the violence with which they were punished, and the jails into which they were thrown, have about them a nightmarish quality difficult to realize. This was as true in Europe as in America, and such conditions there brought about investigations and demands for reform which found their counterpart in America. The list of acts for which one could be punished was long and the penalties brutal. Death was common for robbery, forgery, housebreaking, and counterfeiting. In Pennsylvania in 1783, five men were put to death for one robbery. Two years later, a man in Massachusetts who made fifty counterfeit dollars, was set in the pillory, taken to the gallows where he stood with a rope around his neck for a time, whipped twenty stripes, had his left arm cut off, and finally was sentenced to three years' hard labor. Actually this was an improvement (from the public if not his point of view) for the usual punishment had been death.

Many Americans took such things casually. In 1787 Henry Jackson wrote to Henry Knox that one of his "late federal soldiers," only twenty-three years old, had been executed for burglary. He had thanked Jackson for his efforts to have him pardoned, insisted on his innocence to the last moment, and died with "astonishing firmness" [Boston, 25 Nov. 1787, Knox Papers, Massachusetts Historical Society]. During the war Justice William Atlee of the Pennsylvania supreme court was riding circuit. He wrote to his wife of a man who had been sentenced to death for burglary. That did not bother him, but a case coming up the next day did. A woman was to be tried for killing her husband and Atlee feared it would go hard with her. He hoped that she would be acquitted "to save us the disagreeable task of ordering her to be burned. What affects me much is that her son, a likely young man of about eighteen or twenty is an evidence against her for the death of his father. We shall doubtless have a tender scene with her at the bar and her child giving the fatal testimony which may bring her to the stake" [William Atlee to Mrs. Esther Atlee, York, 23 April 1778, *Atlee Papers,*].

Such punishments were abhorrent to those who believed in "reason" as a guide to man's actions. Some writers attacked the "dark and diffuse" laws of England and said that Americans should burn the vast "load of legal lumber" and have concise, intelligible, and rational laws [Philadelphia *Freeman's Journal,* 11 Feb. 1784]. Others, like Jefferson, were more moderate in their demands for legal reform. In 1776 he undertook to bring Virginia laws into line with republican government. The law should be shaped, said Jefferson, with "a single eye to reason and the good of those for whose government it was framed." He revised the criminal code, abolishing all death penalties except for treason and murder. His revision was not passed and after the war it failed again. Not until 1796, twenty years after Jefferson had begun the work, was he able to get it adopted by the State of Virginia.

There was a sharp demand for reform of the laws of Pennsylvania. William Penn at the beginning of the colony had drawn up a humane code but it had been vetoed by the British government. For a time the legislature had stuck to Penn's ideas but eventually it gave in and followed the English code. The Constitution of 1776 demanded a revision, but the death penalty for such crimes as robbery was not repealed for ten years. The demand did not stop with this law. Men like Dr. Benjamin Rush and William Bradford continued to propagandize for more humane criminal laws. Year in and year out, they wrote and spoke against capital punishment with such effectiveness that in 1794 Pennsylvania made a sweeping revision of her whole code, retaining the death penalty only for wilful murder. This code was to be a model for other American states for years to come.

One other side of the law in its relation to the individual gave concern to Americans. No "tank" in a twentieth century American city, however bad, can equal the horrors of an eighteenth century "gaol." All ages, all varieties of criminals, and both sexes were crowded together in filthy, often unheated jails. Food was poor at its best and at its worst, rotten. Jailers were of the lowest kind and made money robbing the inmates of their clothing and selling liquor to those who had means to buy. So bad was the jail in Philadelphia, said a grand jury in 1787, that it had become "a desirable place for the more wicked and polluted of both sexes" [*Pennsylvania Gazette,* 26 Sept. 1787]. In-

vestigations during the 1780's revealed conditions that were horrifying to some people. The infamous Newgate prison in Connecticut was established by thrifty Connecticut legislators. It was an old copper mine in which men lived in conditions that only a fevered imagination can visualize.

Conditions in Philadelphia were so bad that they led to the formation of the "Philadelphia Society for Assisting Distressed Prisoners" in 1776. The Society bought covered wheelbarrows which it sent through the streets daily carrying a sign "Victuals for the prisoners." British occupation put an end to the Society but in 1787 "The Society for Alleviating the Miseries of Public Prisons" was organized. In it were men such as Dr. Benjamin Rush, Tench Coxe, and Bishop William White of the Episcopal Church, who was its president for forty years. This Society investigated the prisons and made suggestions for their improvement. It proposed that the sale of liquor be stopped, that men and women be separated, that rooms be washed with lime, and many other things.

The jailers naturally opposed interference with their prerogatives. They objected to inspections: they said the criminals were too desperate. Once when Bishop White visited the jail, the chief jailer put on a show. He started by asking the visitors to give him their valuables for safekeeping. The prisoners were lined up in the common room facing loaded cannon beside which men stood ready to fire. The prisoners, unfortunately for the chief jailer's purpose, were so struck by the proceedings that they were quiet and polite while the good bishop questioned them. The Society did much to bring about the adoption of the new penal code. When regular prison inspectors were created by law in 1790, most of them came from its membership.

Prison reform in New York took a different turn. There it was concerned with those imprisoned for debt. No people in eighteenth century society were more luckless than those imprisoned for debt, and they were an astonishingly large part of the jail population. The idea of imprisonment for debt seems completely irrational in an age which has different notions of what is reasonable, but it seemed logical enough in the "age of reason." People were put in jail for small sums. In Boston, for instance, a woman was jailed for four months for failing to pay a fine of sixpence. No one ever explained how a debtor in jail was better able to pay his debts than a debtor out of jail and at work. But more and more people were questioning the sense of it all, particularly for people whose debts were small, and they demanded legislation to free debtors from jail sentences. In New York the "Society for the Relief of Distressed Debtors" was organized. Its twenty-four members were required to see that jailed debtors got food, fuel, and clothing to lighten the burdens of their stay in jail. Despite such activity and newspaper comment on the idiocy of the practice, dominant opinion for some years to come was that of the creditors who could see no fallacy in jailing a man when he failed to pay his debts.

The organization of societies for the abolition of slavery, the improvement of jails, and of the lot of debtors, was not an isolated phenomenon in the years after the war. Immigrant aid societies had been organized in most colonial towns by Scotch, Welsh, Irish, English, and German immigrants to take care of those who followed them. Library societies were formed in Philadelphia, New York, Providence, and Charleston, and in smaller towns before the middle of the eighteenth century. Marine societies were organized in New England and other towns.

All told, some thirty-odd such societies were organized during the colonial era, most of them in the four urban centers of Philadelphia, New York, Boston, and Charleston. Philadelphia had at least eleven, Charleston eight, New York six, and Boston three or four. Most of these societies were small and exclusive and concerned more with social affairs than with practical ones, but they were a focus for humanitarian ideals and intellectual interests. Most of them suspended activity at the outbreak of the war, but before it was over they began to revive and new societies began to appear, five of them in Boston alone. Between 1783 and 1786, eleven pre-revolutionary societies got going again and no less than eighteen new ones were formed. Between 1786 and 1789 fourteen more new societies were formed and most of the rest of the pre-revolutionary ones were reorganized. This was extraordinary activity: more societies were organized between 1776 and 1789 than in the whole colonial period. They were much more active; their meetings were more regular; and their influence spread wider and wider as in the case of the abolition and prison reform groups.

Perhaps the most intriguing of the new societies were the "humane" societies: one in Boston and one in Philadelphia. Their main concern was the rescue of those suffering from "suspended animation": that is, those who appeared to be dead but actually were not. The primary cause of "suspended animation" was drowning, but hanging, sunstroke, lightning, drinking laudanum, drinking cold water when overheated, and so on, were also recognized as causes.

These societies drafted first aid rules, published them in American papers, and posted them in likely spots. They offered rewards for lives saved. They provided special lifesaving equipment and stored it at wharves and taverns near the waterfront. Such equipment included bellows for inflating and deflating the lungs, drags, hooks, and medicines. An extraordinary device, long a favorite with the Massachusetts Humane Society, was the "fumigator," an instrument for pumping tobacco smoke into the rectum of a person supposed to be drowned. In addition, the Massachusetts Society erected huts at spots along the coast where shipwrecks were likely. These were stocked with food and firewood and proved useful, although prowlers soon broke in and ate the food and used the wood.

The marine societies cooperated closely with the humane societies during the 1780's. These organizations had appeared before the Revolution and had operated continuously. They were organizations of seamen, and particularly of pilots who were much concerned, not only with their present but their future. As early as 1786 it was proposed to build a hospital for disabled seamen in Boston and to place it under the direction of the marine society in that town. The marine society likewise worked with the humane society in the building of huts for the shipwrecked.

In Philadelphia there were two organizations: the "Society for the Relief of Poor and Distressed Masters of Ships, Their Widows and Children," and the "Society for the Relief of Widows of Decayed Pilots." In 1788 the legislature provided that the latter society should receive a quarter of the tonnage duties paid by shipowners.

Societies for specifically charitable purposes were organized as well. One of the first was the "Massachusetts Charitable Society" which had roots before the war but was not incorporated until March 1780. It was religious in spirit but professed to be nonsectarian for it declared that "charity is a principle that no particular persuasion can monopolize. . . ." It was interested in general charities and tried to raise money for a girls' school. A Black Friar's Society was organized in New York for both charitable and social purposes. In Philadelphia a "Corporation for the relief and employment of the poor" was organized. An "Amicable Society" was organized in Richmond for the purpose of relieving strangers in distress. As early as 1769 Charleston had a "Fellowship Society" which gathered funds, half for "the deplorable maniac" and the other half for the education of children.

The beginnings of temperance organizations are also to be found, and this alone, if nothing else, is adequate testimony to the optimism of a period in which the per capita consumption of liquor was enough to win the admiration of all other ages. Dr. Benjamin Rush, one of the most optimistic of joiners, declared in 1788 that now that traffic in slaves was over in Pennsylvania, his next task would be the correction of abuses of liquor. The next year a temperance society was actually organized in Litchfield, Connecticut, where the forty members agreed not to use liquor in their business and to serve only beer and cider to workingmen.

The immigrant aid societies were only partly humanitarian in purpose. They were also social clubs for immigrant groups. Inevitably they were political as well, for leading politicians in towns like Philadelphia made a point of belonging to all the groups, whatever the politicians' own origins might be. With few exceptions their activities were convivial. A French traveler in describing an initiation to the Irish Society of Philadelphia said that they were "initiated by the ceremony of an exterior application of a whole bottle of claret poured upon the head, and a generous libation to liberty and good living, of as many as the votary could carry off " [Marquis de Chastellux, *Travels in North America in the Years 1780, 1781, and 1782*, 2 Vols., 1787]. The chief exceptions were the societies organized by Germans in Philadelphia, New York, Charleston, and Baltimore. There were few social or political leaders among them and they had a pietistic streak that led some of them to forbid meetings in taverns. In Philadelphia the society demanded a bureau for the registration of German immigrants and the legislature set one up in 1785. For years thereafter it was manned by members of the society. They visited vessels coming into port to see that immigrants had not been mistreated; they got jobs for immigrants; they provided legal aid for indentured servants. They were concerned also with charity and education. They set up German language grammer schools and founded a library. They established scholarships to send poor German boys to the University of Pennsylvania and during the 1780's supported fifteen scholars in that school.

The societies whose main interests were humanitarian in origin were outweighed both in number and importance by organizations whose interest was in scientific investigation, the furtherance of knowledge, and in economic development. Important among these were the library societies, of which the oldest was the Library Company of Philadelphia, founded by Franklin in 1731. By the end of the Revolution it had 5,000 volumes and was open both to members and the general public. The Charleston Library Society was organized in 1743 and had an even bigger collection of books than the Philadelphia Company but all these were burned in 1778. It was reorganized in 1783 but it did not regain its former position for years. New England libraries found it difficult to get support. The Newport Library was burned; the Portsmouth Library gave up and sold its books in 1786. Others were too short of funds to perform any real service. Practically all of the library societies, except the one in Philadelphia, looked upon themselves as exclusive social clubs and had no desire to serve the public.

Of the scientific societies, the one with the widest reputation during the 1780's was the American Philosophical Society. Philosophy in the eighteenth century had a very broad meaning: it included natural and physical science, social science, and theology; in fact it took all knowledge for its field. The Philosophical Society did little before the war and it was reorganized in 1780. The act incorporating it declared that it was interested in the improvement of agriculture, the development of trade, "the ease and comfort of life, the ornament of society, and the increase and happiness of mankind" to the end that prejudices might be abolished, a humane and philosophical spirit be cherished, and that youth be stimulated to a "laudable diligence and emulation in the pursuit of wisdom" [*Laws and Regulations of the American Philosophical Society . . . ,* 1866]. Despite its high ideals its meetings were poorly attended at first, its funds were small, and it owed most of its reputation to two men: Benjamin Franklin and David Rittenhouse. Not until Franklin returned from France in 1785 did the Society get going actively. Its first volume of transactions was published and Franklin promoted it with all his old skill. He distributed the volume and saw to it that important people in both America and Europe were invited to join.

The most active of the societies during the Confederation was the American Academy of Arts and Sciences which was founded in Boston in 1780. John Adams was the driving force behind its formation. In Europe he discovered the high reputation of the American Philosophical Society, which was doubtless at that time due more to Franklin's prestige and his gift for advertising than to its achievements. When Adams returned to America he was perhaps the chief architect of the Massachusetts Constitution of 1780, which included a clause calling for state encouragement of scientific associations. With James Bowdoin as president, the American Academy got off to a flying start and published its first volume of *Memoirs* in 1785. It was concerned with both economic improvement and

scientific investigation. James Bowdoin's political career has too long obscured the fact that he was one of the leaders in the scientific thought of his day and one of the few men who had the courage to dispute scientific points with Franklin, and the capacity to come off with at least even honors. Other such societies were attempted in New York, Connecticut, and elsewhere, but with little result.

At the same time there was a rapid development of medical societies which had both humanitarian and scientific interests. The first ones were organized during the 1760's in New Jersey and Connecticut and were concerned primarily with establishing standards for medical practice. But in medicine, as in so many other things, Philadelphia was the center. The Philadelphia Hospital was founded in 1751. The American Medical Society was organized in 1773. Medical education began in 1765 when the College of Philadelphia, at the urging of Dr. John Morgan, began formal instruction in medicine. King's College in New York started medical training in 1767. Meanwhile, more and more American doctors were being educated in Europe, particularly at Edinburgh University. Between 1758 and 1788 no less than sixty-three Americans were graduated from it. The Revolution itself gave doctors an opportunity to "practice" as they never had before and, as Ramsay pointed out in his history, they learned more in one day on the battlefield than in months at home.

After the war Philadelphia continued to be a center of medical activity. The "Society for inoculating the Poor Gratis" had been organized in 1774 by doctors and others and was providing free vaccinations for all who applied at the state house. It disappeared during the war but in 1787 the dispensary was providing free medicine for the poor. During that year Brissot de Warville said that it had treated 1,647 people at a cost of £200. During the 1780's the College of Physicians was formed. It met for discussion of medical research and took an active interest in improving public health in such matters as street cleaning, quarantines, and in the creation of a "contagious" hospital.

The doctors of Boston organized the Massachusetts Medical Society in 1781. It was interested in standardizing fees but also in medical research. It founded a library in 1782 and by the 1790's was publishing research papers. It was soon in competition with the new medical school which Harvard established. Harvard announced the appointment of three professors of medicine in the fall of 1783. A curriculum was outlined, and the whole story was sent forth to the newspapers of the United States and was printed in many of them. Harvard and the Medical Society engaged in a bitter struggle over the examination and licensing of doctors to practice, but the competition seems not to have hurt either institution.

But great difficulties were encountered everywhere by medical schools in getting "materials" for training purposes. Adequate medical training called for the dissection of bodies, but the populace looked upon this as sacrilege. Antagonism developed until, in New York, it led to the "doctor's riots" of 1788 in which the militia was called out and several people were killed. While great advances were made in medicine, even greater distances were yet to be traveled. As always, popular opinion and much medical opinion was opposed to the "radicals." Barbers, druggists, and dentists were "doctors" and still practiced on the citizenry and the citizenry still found quacks more appealing than scientists. A certain Reverend W. M'Kee announced that at last he had found the cure for cancer. He got testimonials for his product which he had tried on the helpless denizens of the Philadelphia almshouse. Not only would it cure cancer but ulcers, scurvy, ringworm, and other dread afflictions. It was such charlatanry that led Dr. Lemuel Hopkins to write his biting ode to a man killed by a cancer quack:

> Here lies a fool flat on his back,
> The victim of a cancer quack;
> Who lost his money and his life,
> By plaster, caustic, and by knife.
> The case was this—a pimple rose,
> South-east a little of his nose,
> Which daily reddened and grew bigger,
> As too much drinking gave it vigor.
> A score of gossips soon ensure
> Full threescore different modes of cure;
> But yet the full-fed pimple still
> Defined all petticoated skill;
> When fortune led him to peruse
> A hand-bill in the weekly news,
> Signed by six fools of different sorts,
> All cured of cancers made of warts;
> Who recommend, with due submission,
> This cancer-monger as magician. . . .
> Go, readers, gentle, eke and simple,
> If you have wart, or corn, or pimple,
> To quack infallible apply;
> Here's room enough for you to lie.
> His skill triumphant still prevails,
> For death's a cure that never fails.

The Revolution had devastating effects on many established schools. School after school was abandoned, colleges were "purged" of those tainted with Loyalist sentiments, their endowments were ruined, and their student bodies decimated. Yet at the same time many revolutionary leaders were much concerned with the development of an educated people. Five of the new state constitutions declared that the state was responsible for education. John Adams said in his "Thoughts on Government" that "laws for the liberal education of youth, especially of the lower class of people, are so extremely wise and useful, that, to a humane and generous mind, no expense for this purpose would be thought extravagant." Jefferson, believing in education as an indispensable basis for democracy, tried to establish a public school system in Virginia with his "Bill for the More General Diffusion of Knowledge," but could not get it passed. New winds blew through old halls when, under Jefferson's prodding, the College of William and Mary set up chairs of law and modern languages. Once the war was over, men like Jefferson, John Adams, Benjamin Rush, and . . . Noah Webster, preached the idea of public education. Various states, including New York, Georgia, and North Carolina, set up university organizations, at least on paper. Private academies were being founded in every state as well as private colleges, some of them with public support. In 1786 the *Massachusetts Centinel* applauded the "encouragement of literature, and diffusion of knowledge" in the southern states and cited the money

and land given by the Pennsylvania legislature to Dickinson College, and the lands given for schools by North and South Carolina and Georgia. Elaborate plans for a public school system in Pennsylvania were set forth to the readers of the *Pennsylvania Gazette.*

In every other field concerned with the betterment of humanity, as with education, there was talk, argument, writing, and organization. No better example exists than in the concern of Americans with the improvement of transportation. Expansion westward before the Revolution produced demands for better means of getting back-country crops to market. Roads and bridges were an obvious answer that not everyone was willing to give. The first Americans had lived on or near water and water-borne transportation was an ideal they tried to project into the wilderness. Before the Revolution George Washington and his friend Thomas Johnson of Maryland made plans to clear the Potomac so that boats could go to and from the back country. The war was no sooner over than southerners once more took up the promotion of a water route to the West. Washington again led. Early in 1785 Maryland and Virginia gave identical charters to the Potomac Company. Virginia subscribed to a fifth of the stock. Maryland too supported the project as the years went on. It was an enormous undertaking primarily because too few people had any technical knowledge and they had to learn as they went along. Yet by 1815 some 338 miles of the Potomac had been opened.

There were many other projects in the South. The James River Company was chartered to improve navigation on the James at the same time the Potomac Company was chartered. It too was financed by both state and private subscriptions, and in time became a dividend paying company and still was when the state took over in 1820.

The Great Dismal Swamp Company, in which Washington was a heavy stockholder and manager, had been started before the war. Its purpose was to drain the Swamp and produce rice and naval stores. After the war it began digging a canal to connect the Swamp with the Elizabeth River in North Carolina. After many years this too was completed and is still in operation.

In 1786 South Carolina chartered a company to dig a canal between the Cooper and Santee rivers. The canal was not completed until 1800, but it was in use until 1858. There were other schemes both there and in North Carolina. Some of them achieved a little success and others remained only ideas on paper.

In the North the chief concern was with roads and bridges during the 1780's: their passion for canals was to come later. The most famous bridge company was The Proprietors of the Charles River Bridge, incorporated by the Massachusetts legislature in March 1785. There was heated argument in both prose and poetry on the subject of the bridge: its location, the materials of which it should be built, and the like. The bridge was completed by the summer of 1786 and was at once profitable and continued to be so until its monopoly was at last broken by the building of the Warren Bridge and by the decision of the United States Supreme Court in the "Charles River Bridge Case."

This bridge was followed by many others all through the North and most of them made money for their backers in a rapidly growing society.

The demand for improved transportation also resulted in better roads. Maryland, Virginia, and Pennsylvania all passed legislation to provide for roads to the westward although the great emphasis was not to come until the next decade. Stagecoaches had been few and far between in the years before the war but by the end of the 1780's mail was carried in stagecoaches from New Hampshire to Georgia. New "flying machines" were advertised in the newspapers and soon a flying machine promised to take passengers the ninety miles between New York and Philadelphia in one day. When it did, it was agreed that it was a wonder of the age and that perhaps the ultimate in speed had at last been reached.

But not quite, for the whole country was excited about balloons. Man's ancient dream of flying through the air had at last been realized by a Frenchman. Descriptions of balloon ascensions in Europe appeared in American newspapers. Illustrated articles describing a "machine, proper to be navigated through the air" likewise appeared. By midsummer 1784 it was reported that nothing was important unless it had the name balloon attached to it. Ladies and gentlemen of fashion wore balloon ornaments and even a farmer who came to town with vegetables cried: "fine balloon string beans." As always, a decent amount of fun was poked at the new fad. It was reported from New York that "Air-balloon dress is so much the fashion in this city, and so generally fancied, that some ingenious sempstresses have it in contemplation to establish a balloon petticoat, so constructed, as that every person may go up in it with safety" [*Pennsylvania Gazette*, 30 June, 21, 28 July, 8 Dec. 1784; *Massachusetts Centinel*, 12 May, 14 July 1784].

Poets likewise had a go at the new craze. Partly in fun and partly in prophecy was a poem called "The Progress of Balloons." After an invocation to the muses the poet declared:

> Let the Gods of Olympus their revels prepare,
> By the aid of some pounds of inflammable air
> We'll visit them soon—and forsake this dull ball,
> With coat, shoes and stockings, fat carcase and all.

The balloon was a French invention which would give them world power.

> At sea let the British their neighbors defy—
> The French shall have frigates to traverse the sky—
>
> If the English should venture to sea with their fleet,
> A host of balloons in a trice they shall meet,
> The French from the zenith their wings shall display,
> And souse on these sea dogs and bear them away.

Surveyors drawing meridians and parallel lines should build balloons and survey with ease. Astronomers can now go by balloon,

> And floating above, on our ocean of air,
> Informs us, by letter, what people are there.

A survey of the planets can be made and we can know at last what goes on on Venus, Mars, and the others.

> But now to have done with our planets and moons
> Come, grant me a patent for making balloons,
> For I find that the time is approaching—the day
> When horses shall fail, and the horsemen decay.

Post riders shall leave their "dull poneys behind and travel, like ghosts, on the wings of the wind." And stage drivers whose gallopers take you through the dirt at ten miles an hour,

> When advanc'd to balloons shall so furiously drive,
> You'll hardly know whether you're dead or alive.

> The man who from Boston sets out with the sun,
> If he has a fair wind gets to New York at one.
> At Gunpowder-Ferry drink whiskey at three,
> And at six be at Edenton ready for tea.

> (The machine shall be order'd we hardly need say,
> To travel in darkness as well as by day)
> At Charleston by ten he for sleep shall prepare,
> And by twelve the next day be the devil knows where.

After a fling at the ladies who would go forty miles high for their afternoon's airing, the poet concluded on a practical note:

> Yet more with its fitness for commerce I'm struck,
> What loads of tobacco shall fly from Kentuck
> What packs of best beaver—bar iron and pig,
> What budgets of leather from Bonocco-cheague.

> If Britain should ever disturb us again,
> (As they threaten to do in the next George's reign)
> No doubt they will play us a set of new tunes,
> And pepper us well from their fighting balloons.

> To market the farmers shall shortly repair,
> With their hogs and potatoes, wholesail, thro' the air,
> Skim over the water as light as a feather,
> Themselves and their turkies conversing together.

> Such wonders as these from balloons shall arise,
> And the giants of old that assaulted the skies,
> With their Ossa on Pelion shall freely confess
> That all they attempted was nothing to this.
> [*Massachusetts Centinel*, 15 Jan. 1785]

At the same time people were excited about balloons, they were little concerned with the development of steamboats, except to oppose them. Two inventors, a Virginia tavern keeper, James Rumsey, and a Connecticut Yankee, John Fitch, were bitter rivals. Both worked by rule of thumb and trial and error in developing a steamboat that would move against current and wind. Rumsey first tried a boat that moved by sticks forced against the bottom of the stream. He showed this to Washington when the great man visited the innkeeper's place in 1784. Thereafter Rumsey had the support of most of his fellow Virginians. He soon turned to jet propulsion: a steam engine which would pump water out the back of the boat and thus push the boat forward. Jet propulsion had the support of men like Franklin, while the paddle wheel was frowned upon.

John Fitch, wild and sensitive to the point of hysteria, worked on various ideas and fought bitterly with both backers and enemies. The great men of Virginia and men like Franklin supported Rumsey, for although he was an ex-tavern keeper, he was handsome, he had the manners of a gentleman, and was politically sound. Fitch was ugly, ill-clad, and had no manners. He had deserted his wife. He was an anti-Federalist and an extreme Deist. Each man sought and got monopolies for operating steamboats in the waters of various states. Fitch finally got a company behind him and during August 1787 ran a boat up and down the river at Philadelphia where members of the Constitutional Convention saw it. Rumsey's boat did not run until December 1787 and then only twice. But he was made a member of the American Philosophical Society. He was sent to England to get support, while Fitch continued to battle against odds that only a man with almost maniacal convictions could surmount. He won out, at least to the point where he had a boat running regular trips on the Delaware River during 1790. Seventeen years before Robert Fulton "invented" the steamboat that ran on the Hudson, Fitch's boat had run thousands of miles on the Delaware.

Fitch was convinced, though he found it difficult to convince anyone else, that the steamboat was the answer to the problem of travel on the Mississippi River. He got that conviction when he had been a surveyor in the West and had laid the groundwork for "John Fitch's Map." All his efforts came to nothing for himself. He died a suicide, poverty-stricken, and half insane, in a little Kentucky town. His rival, Rumsey, died in England, also without achieving any of the greatness or the profit that he had hoped for.

In this survey of the varied activities of Americans in the first years of independence one can realize something of the enthusiasm with which the citizens of the new nation worked at altering the pattern of society they had inherited from colonial times. It is true that much of what they did had earlier roots, but their achievements are also the result of a new freedom of choice and of a delight in national independence. This enthusiasm bolstered native optimism and furnished the motive power for new deeds in years to come. (pp. 129-53)

Merrill Jensen, "The Betterment of Humanity," in her The New Nation: A History of the United States During the Confederation, 1781-1789, *Alfred A. Knopf, 1950, pp. 129-53.*

COLONIAL LITERARY GENRES

Bernard Bailyn

[*In the essay below, Bailyn explores the art of the pamphlet during the Colonial period, contending that the American pamphlet lacked the literary excellence of its English counterpart, yet proved effective in promoting the cause of liberty and independence.*]

Whatever deficiencies the leaders of the American Revolution may have had, reticence, fortunately, was not one of them. They wrote easily and amply, and turned out in the space of scarcely a decade and a half and from a small number of presses a rich literature of theory, argument, opinion, and polemic. Every medium of written expression was put to use. The newspapers, of which by 1775 there were thirty-eight in the mainland colonies, were crowded with columns of arguments and counter-arguments appearing as letters, official documents, extracts of speeches, and sermons. Broadsides—single sheets on which were often printed not only large-letter notices but, in three or four columns of minuscule type, essays of several thousand words—appeared everywhere; they could be found posted or passing from hand to hand in the towns of every colony. Almanacs, workaday publications universally available in the colonies, carried, in odd corners and occasional columns, a considerable freight of political comment. Above all, there were pamphlets: booklets consisting of a few printer's sheets, folded in various ways so as to make various sizes and numbers of pages, and sold—the pages stitched together loosely, unbound and uncovered—usually for a shilling or two.

It was in this form—as pamphlets—that much of the most important and characteristic writing of the American Revolution appeared. For the Revolutionary generation, as for its predecessors back to the early sixteenth century, the pamphlet had peculiar virtues as a medium of communication. Then, as now, it was seen that the pamphlet allowed one to do things that were not possible in any other form.

> The pamphlet [George Orwell, a modern pamphleteer, has written] is a one-man show. One has complete freedom of expression, including, if one chooses, the freedom to be scurrilous, abusive, and seditious; or, on the other hand, to be more detailed, serious and "highbrow" than is ever possible in a newspaper or in most kinds of periodicals. At the same time, since the pamphlet is always short and unbound, it can be produced much more quickly than a book, and in principle, at any rate, can reach a bigger public. Above all, the pamphlet does not have to follow any prescribed pattern. It can be in prose or in verse, it can consist largely of maps or statistics or quotations, it can take the form of a story, a fable, a letter, an essay, a dialogue, or a piece of "reportage." All that is required of it is that it shall be topical, polemical, and short. ["Introduction," in *British Pamphleteers*, Vol. I, 1948-1951]

The pamphlet's greatest asset was perhaps its flexibility in size, for while it could contain only a very few pages and hence be used for publishing short squibs and sharp, quick rebuttals, it could also accommodate much longer, more serious and permanent writing as well. Some pamphlets of the Revolutionary period contain sixty or even eighty pages, on which are printed technical, magisterial treatises. Between the extremes of the squib and the book-length treatise, however, there lay the most commonly used, the ideally convenient, length: from 5,000 to 25,000 words, printed on anywhere from ten to fifty pages, quarto or octavo in size.

The pamphlet of this middle length was perfectly suited to the needs of the Revolutionary writers. It was spacious enough to allow for the full development of an argument—to investigate premises, explore logic, and consider conclusions; it could accommodate the elaborate involutions of eighteenth-century literary forms; it gave range for the publication of fully wrought, leisurely-paced sermons; it could conveniently carry state papers, collections of newspaper columns, and strings of correspondence. It was in this form, consequently, that "the best thought of the day expressed itself"; it was in this form that "the solid framework of constitutional thought" was developed; it was in this form that "the basic elements of American political thought of the Revolutionary period appeared first." And yet pamphlets of this length were seldom ponderous; whatever the gravity of their themes or the spaciousness of their contents, they were always essentially polemical, and aimed at immediate and rapidly shifting targets: at suddenly developing problems, unanticipated arguments, and swiftly rising, controversial figures. The best of the writing that appeared in this form, consequently, had a rare combination of spontaneity and solidity, of dash and detail, of casualness and care.

Highly flexible, easy to manufacture, and cheap, pamphlets were printed in the American colonies wherever there were printing presses, intellectual ambitions, and political concerns. But in their origins most of them may be grouped within three categories. The largest number were direct responses to the great events of the time. The Stamp Act touched off a heavy flurry of pamphleteering in which basic American positions in constitutional theory were staked out; its repeal was celebrated by the publication of at least eleven thanksgiving sermons, all of them crowded with political theory; the Townshend Duties led to another intense burst of pamphleteering, as did the Boston Massacre and the precipitating events of the insurrection itself—the Tea Party, the Coercive Acts, and the meeting of the first Continental Congress.

But if the writing of the pamphlets had been only a response to these overt public events, their numbers would have been far smaller than in fact they were. They resulted also, and to a considerable extent, from what might be called chain-reacting personal polemics: strings of individual exchanges—arguments, replies, rebuttals, and counter-rebuttals—in which may be found heated personifications of the larger conflict. A bold statement on a sensitive issue was often sufficient to start such a series, which characteristically proceeded with increasing shrillness until it ended in bitter personal vituperation. Thus East Apthorp's tract of 1763 on the Church of England's Society

for the Propagation of the Gospel, inflaming as it did New Englanders' fears of an American bishopric, was answered at once by Jonathan Mayhew in a 176-page blast, and then, in the course of the next two years, by no less than nine other pamphleteers writing in a melee of thrusts and counterthrusts. Similarly, a succession of seven or eight searing pamphlets followed Richard Bland's attack on the Reverend John Camm in the Two-Penny Act controversy in Virginia. Any number of people could join in such proliferating polemics, and rebuttals could come from all sides. Thomas Paine's *Common Sense* was answered not merely by two exhaustive refutations by Tories but also by at least four pamphlets written by patriots who shared his desire for independence but not his constitutional and religious views or his assumptions about human nature.

A third type of pamphlet—besides those that surrounded the great public events and those that appeared in polemical series—was distinguished by the ritualistic character of its themes and language. In the course of the Revolutionary controversy, the regular, usually annual, publication in pamphlet form of commemorative orations came to constitute a significant addition to the body of Revolutionary literature. In an earlier period such publications had consisted mainly of sermons delivered on election day in New England, together with a few of those preached on official thanksgiving and fast days, and public letters addressed to "freeholders and qualified voters" that appeared regularly on the eve of the annual elections. But from the mid-1760's on, celebrations of more secular anniversaries were added: the anniversary of the repeal of the Stamp Act, of the Boston Massacre, of the landing of the Pilgrims, and of an increasing number of fast and thanksgiving days marking political rather than religious events.

Such commemorative orations were stylized; but in the heat of controversy the old forms took on new vigor, new relevance and meaning: some of the resulting pamphlets of this type have remarkable force and originality. Massachusetts and Connecticut had been publishing sermons preached on election days for one hundred years before Independence; by 1760 these pamphlets had arrived not only at an apparent fulfillment in style but, in content, at a classically monitorial attitude to political authority as well. Yet Andrew Eliot's use of the familiar formulas in his election sermon of 1765 infused them with more direct power and gave them new point; for to proclaim from the pulpit in the year of the Stamp Act and before the assembled magistrates of Massachusetts that when tyranny is abroad "submission . . . is a crime" was an act of political defiance strengthened rather than weakened by the sanction of time and tradition the words had acquired. Similarly the title of John Carmichael's Artillery Company sermon, *A Self-Defensive War Lawful,* though it merely repeated a traditional phrase, was, in 1775, in itself provocative; and the concluding passage of the pamphlet constitutes a significant transition in which clichés about the duties of Christian soldiers acquire the fervor of battlefield prayers. And if one of the later commemorative celebrations, that of the Boston Massacre, quickly became the occasion for the outpouring of some of the most lurid and naive rhetoric heard in eighteenth-century America, another of them, a thanksgiving day appointed by the Continental Congress, inspired an obscure Salem parson to write, in the most dignified and moving prose, a paean to the promise of American life, and to devise an original blend of theological and constitutional principles. Everywhere in New England, clerical orators celebrating these anniversary events invoked the power of the ancient "jeremiad" to argue that "any vindication of provincial privileges was inextricably dependent upon a moral renovation" [Andrew Eliot, *A Sermon Preached before His Excellency Francis Bernard . . . ,* 1765].

Not all the pamphlets, of course, fall into these three categories. Some, like the *Votes and Proceedings of the Freeholders . . . of . . . Boston* (1772), written for circulation in pamphlet form, were in themselves political events to which other pamphleteers responded. Others, like Jefferson's *Summary View . . .* (1774), written as an instruction to the Virginia delegates to the first Continental Congress, were political "position" papers. And in addition there were literary pieces—poems like John Trumbull's *M'Fingal* and plays like Mercy Otis Warren's *The Blockheads* and *The Group*—which, though manifestly political, sprang from more deeply personal inspiration.

Expressing vigorous, polemical, and more often than not considered views of the great events of the time; proliferating in chains of personal vituperation; and embodying to the world the highly charged sentiments uttered on commemorative occasions, pamphlets appeared year after year and month after month in the crisis of the 1760's and 1770's. More than 400 of them bearing on the Anglo-American controversy were published between 1750 and 1776; over 1,500 appeared by 1783. Explanatory as well as declarative, and expressive of the beliefs, attitudes, and motivations as well as of the professed goals of those who led and supported the Revolution, the pamphlets are the distinctive literature of the Revolution. They reveal, more clearly than any other single group of documents, the contemporary meaning of that transforming event.

Important above all else as expressions of the ideas, attitudes, and motivations that lay at the heart of the Revolution, the pamphlets published in the two decades before Independence are primarily political, not literary, documents. But form and substance are never wholly separate. The literary qualities of the pamphlets are also important, not only in themselves but for what they reveal of the people who wrote them, their goals and style of mind.

These pamphlets form part of the vast body of English polemical and journalistic literature of the seventeenth and eighteenth centuries to which the greatest men of letters contributed. Milton, Halifax, Locke, Swift, Defoe, Bolingbroke, Addison were all pamphleteers at least to the extent that Bland, Otis, Dickinson, the Adamses, Wilson, and Jefferson were. But there are striking differences in the quality of the British and American polemical writings considered simply as literature.

The differences do not lie in the presence or absence of literary techniques. One of the surprising aspects of the American writings is the extent to which they include the stylistic modes associated with the great age of English pamphleteering. Of satire, the protean artifice that dominated the most creative pamphleteering of the time, one scholar has identified no fewer than 530 examples published in America during the period 1763-1783; a large percentage of these appeared originally, or were reprinted, in pamphlets. In addition to satire there is an abundance of other devices: elusive irony and flat parody; extended allegory and direct vituperation; sarcasm, calculated and naive. All the standard tropes and a variety of unusual figurations may be found in the pamphlet literature.

The results are at times remarkable. Who has ever heard of Ebenezer Chaplin? He was parson of the second parish of the town of Sutton, Massachusetts, in the years before the Revolution; in conventional form he preached regularly and published occasionally on the problems of the church. But in a sermon published as a pamphlet in 1773 he suddenly revealed a remarkably self-conscious literary bent. The sermon is entitled *The Civil State Compared to Rivers,* and in it Chaplin managed for the better part of twenty-four pages to sustain the single simile announced in the title; the figure winds steadily through the argument, dramatizing it, coloring it, raising the aesthetic level of the piece far above what could have been attained by direct exposition. It is a noteworthy literary invention, and it gleams amid the hundreds of artistically drab sermons of the period.

Similarly unexpected in its literary effects, though of a quite different genre, is Philip Livingston's *Other Side of the Question,* which appeared in the heavy bombardment of polemics of 1774. Where most of the writers in those exchanges used invective, Livingston used ironic ridicule, and he did so with such agility and lightness of touch that a device reminiscent of [Laurence Sterne's] *Tristram Shandy* fits in naturally; two scatological passages seem normal exaggerations of a smart and worldly style.

Effective in another way is the extended sham of a Christian catechism that was published anonymously in 1771 as an attack on sycophantic officemongering. No work of genius, it nevertheless gave a twist of originality to a familiar theme, exaggerating the abjectness of bought loyalty by its burlesque of sacred obligations. In a somewhat similar vein is what has been described as "the most ambitious and nearly successful of half a dozen Biblical imitations which appeared in the Revolutionary period," *The First Book of the American Chronicles of the Times,* a parody in six parts of an entire book of the Bible. It is so complete in its plot and characterization as to make identification of people and places an engaging puzzle. By its extensiveness and detail, by the sheer number of its imaginative touches, it attains a considerable effect.

In other ways, by other devices, literary effects were sought and achieved. The most commonly attempted was the satire associated with pseudonymous authorship. Governor Stephen Hopkins of Rhode Island, for example, fell upon the opportunity offered to him when his antagonist, Judge Martin Howard, Jr., characterized him as a "ragged country fellow"; he replied with an earthy, vicious attack which he justified by the argument that rags go together with a crude directness of speech. And Richard Bland, in what was probably the most intricate literary conceit written in the entire period, succeeded to such an extent in ridiculing his antagonist by reversing roles with him and condemning him from his own mouth that his victim was forced to reply weakly by explaining to his readers who was really who. Even the more common and transparent forms of pseudonymity provided an opportunity for literary invention. The pastoral pose was more useful to the Reverend Samuel Seabury, arguing the case for the agrarian interests in New York against nonimportation, than it had been to the most famous "farmer" of them all, John Dickinson; it provided not only a consistent point of view but figures of speech and the opportunity for fanciful self-characterization.

All sorts of literary twists and turns were used. Thomas Bradbury Chandler's *The American Querist,* one of the most popular of the Tory pamphlets, consisted of an even one hundred rhetorical questions aimed at the pretensions of the first Continental Congress; the queries were printed for emphasis as one hundred separate paragraphs spread across twenty-one octavo pages. Elephantine footnoting attached to nine stanzas of lampooning verse was the form one response took to Mayhew's extended attacks on the Society for the Propagation of the Gospel. Dramatic dialogues—*"Between the Ghost of General Montgomery, Just Arrived from the Elysian Fields, and An American Delegate"; "Between a Southern Delegate and His Spouse"*—were convenient frames for lurid caricatures, and since they made fewer demands on the skills of the dramatist, they were on the whole more successful than the half-dozen more fully evolved plays that were written for pamphlet publication.

And all the detailed linguistic tactics of the classic era of English pamphleteering were present. The pamphlets abound in aphorisms: a section of one sermon is in effect nothing but a mosaic of aphorisms. There are apostrophes, hyperboles, and vivid personifications. There are subtle transitions that seek to ease the flow of thought, and others contrived to interrupt it, to surprise and fix attention. Even the most crudely bombastic harangues contain artful literary constructions.

And yet, for all of this—for all of the high self-consciousness of literary expression, the obvious familiarity with cosmopolitan models and the armory of sophisticated belles-lettres—the pamphlets of the American Revolution that seek artistic effects are not great documents. Next to the more artful pamphlets of eighteenth-century England they are pallid, imitative, and crude. And the higher, the more technically demanding the mode of expression, the more glaring the contrast. There is nothing in the American literature that approaches in sheer literary skill such imaginatively conceived and expertly written pamphlets as Swift's *Modest Proposal* and Defoe's *Shortest Way with the Dissenters;* there is no allegory as masterful as Arbuthnot's *History of John Bull,* and no satire as deft as his *Art of Political Lying.* Indeed, there are not many of the American pamphlets that are as successful in technique as any number of the less imaginative, straight expository essays published in seventeenth- and eighteenth-century England, essays of which Shebbeare's *Letter to the People of England,* lamenting corruption and excoriating the mismanagement of Braddock's expedition,

may be taken as average in quality and Swift's *Conduct of the Allies* as a notable refinement. Why this should be so—why the more imaginative and self-consciously literary of the pamphlets of the Revolution should be manifestly inferior in quality to the English models—is an important even if not a wholly answerable question. For it helps locate and explain the qualities of these documents that are of the greatest distinction.

First and foremost, the American pamphleteers, though participants in a great tradition, were amateurs next to such polemicists as Swift and Defoe. Nowhere in the relatively undifferentiated society of colonial America had there developed before 1776 a group of penmen professional in the sense that Defoe or Franklin's friend James Ralph were professional: capable, that is, of earning their living by their pens, capable of producing copy on order as well as on inspiration, and taught by the experience of dozens of polemical encounters the limits and possibilities of their craft. The closest to having attained such professionalism in the colonies were a few of the more prominent printers; but with the exception of Franklin they did not transcend the ordinary limitations of their trade: they were rarely principals in the controversies of the time. The American pamphleteers were almost to a man lawyers, ministers, merchants, or planters heavily engaged in their regular occupations. For them political writing was an uncommon diversion, peripheral to their main concerns. They wrote easily and readily, but until the crisis of Anglo-American affairs was reached, they had had no occasion to turn out public letters, tracts, and pamphlets in numbers at all comparable to those of the English pamphleteers. The most experienced polemical writer in the colonies was probably William Livingston of New York, who, together with two or three of his friends, had sustained *The Independent Reflector* through enough issues in 1752 and 1753 to fill one good-sized volume. But Swift's formal prose work alone fills fourteen volumes, and Defoe is known to have written at least 400 tracts, pamphlets, and books: his contributions to a single periodical during a ten year period total 5,000 printed pages, and they represent less than half of what he wrote in those years. It appears to have been no great matter for a professional like James Ralph, who attained success as a paid political writer after years of effort in poetry, drama, and criticism and who late in life published an eloquent *Case of Authors by Profession or Trade,* to turn out, amid a stream of pamphlets and periodical pieces, a massive *History of England* whose bibliographical and critical introduction alone covers 1,078 folio pages.

No American writer in the half century between the death of Cotton Mather and the Declaration of Independence had anything like such experience in writing; and it is this amateurism, this lack of practiced technique, that explains much of the crudeness of the Revolutionary pamphlets considered simply as literature. For while the colonial writers were obviously acquainted with and capable of imitating the forms of sophisticated polemics, they had not truly mastered them; they were rarely capable of keeping their literary contrivances in control. All of the examples cited above for their literary qualities (and as self-conscious artistic efforts they are among the most noteworthy documents of the group) suffer from technical weaknesses. By virtue of its extended simile Chaplin's *Civil State* shines among the sermons of the time, but in the end the effect is almost overcome by insistence; the figure is maintained too long; it becomes obtrusive, and the reader ends more aware of it than of the thought it is supposed to be illuminating. The *Ministerial Catechism* lacks the verbal cleverness necessary to keep it from falling into a jog-trotting substitution-play of words. And while *The First Book of . . . American Chronicles* is a more intricate and extended burlesque, its diction, one critic [Bruce I. Granger, *Political Satire in the American Revolution, 1763-1783,* 1963] has noted, "has a synthetic ring and at one point a brief passage of French dialect is jarring." Most of the pseudonymous poses, including Hopkins' cited above, were transparent to begin with, and they were unevenly, even sloppily, maintained; often they were simply cast aside after the opening passages, to be snatched up again hurriedly at the end in a gesture of literary decorousness. Even Bland, as artful a litterateur as America produced in the period, was incapable of fully controlling his own invention. If his elaborate conceit threw his intended victim into confusion, it must have had a similar effect on many of its other readers, for at times the point is almost lost in a maze of true and facetious meanings. Chandler's *Querist* is notably original, but strings of syntactically identical questions can become monotonous unless their contents are unusually clever; fifty of them are almost certain to become wearying; Chandler's one hundred will exhaust the patience of any reader.

And these are among the strongest of the efforts made to attain literary effects. The weakest are, on technical grounds, quite remarkably bad. The poetry—or, more accurately, the versification—is almost uniformly painful to read. There is scarcely a single group of stanzas that can be read with any satisfaction as poetry. Most of the verses are a kind of limping jingle-jangle in which sense and sound are alternatively sacrificed to each other, and both, occasionally, to the demands of termination. The dramatic dialogues, whatever their political importance might be, as literary expressions are wooden and lifeless. And the plays, especially the verse plays, are almost totally devoid of characterization or any other form of verisimilitude.

But there is more than amateurism behind the relative crudeness of the artistic efforts in the American pamphlets. For if writers like Adams and Jefferson were amateur pamphleteers, their writings in other ways display formidable literary talents. Jefferson had an extraordinary gift for supple and elegant if abstract expression; it was well known and appreciated at the time. And Adams, seemingly so stolid and unimaginative an embodiment of prosaic virtues, had a basically sensuous apprehension of experience which he expressed in brilliantly idiomatic and figurative prose—but in diary notations and in letters. Neither, as pamphleteers, sought literary effects: Jefferson's sole effort is a straightforward if gracefully written political policy statement, and Adams' major piece is a treatise on government.

It is not simply a question of the presence or absence of literary imagination or technical skill but of their employment. The more deliberately artful writings were in a significant way—for reasons that reach into the heart of the Revolutionary movement—peripheral to the main lines of intellectual force developing through the period. They were peculiarly incongruous to the deeper impulses of the time, and they never attracted the major talents nor fully excited those that were drawn to them. Beneath the technical deficiencies of the belletristic pieces lies an absence of motivating power, of that "peculiar emotional intensity" that so distinguishes the political writing of Jonathan Swift. The American pamphlets are essentially decorous and reasonable. Not that they are all mild in tone, prissy, anemic, or lacking in emphasis. Vigor of one sort or another was common enough; at times, as in the frantic Tory outpouring of 1774-1775, there was something akin to verbal violence. And mud-slinging invective was everywhere; for in an age when gross public accusations were commonplace, it took a degree of restraint no one sought to employ to keep from depicting George Washington as the corrupter of a washerwoman's daughter, John Hancock as both impotent and the stud of an illegitimate brood, William Drayton as a disappointed office seeker whose fortune had been ruined by "the nicks of *seven* and *eleven,*" and Judge Martin Howard, Jr., as a well-known cardsharper.

But mere vigor and lurid splash are not in themselves expressions of imaginative intensity. Among all those who wrote pamphlets, in fact, there appear to have been only three—James Otis, Thomas Paine, and that strange itinerant Baptist John Allen—who had anything like the concentrated fury that propelled Swift's thought and imagination through the intensifying indirections of literary forms. And in all three cases there were singular circumstances. Otis' passion, the wildness that so astonished his contemporaries, already by 1765 was beginning to lack control: it would soon slip into incoherence. The "daring impudence," the "uncommon frenzy" which gave *Common Sense* its unique power, Paine brought with him from England in 1774; it had been nourished in another culture, and was recognized at the time to be an alien quality in American writing. And Allen too—in any case no equal, as a pamphleteer, of Paine—had acquired his habits of literary expression abroad.

The American writers were profoundly reasonable people. Their pamphlets convey scorn, anger, and indignation; but rarely blind hate, rarely panic fear. They sought to convince their opponents, not, like the English pamphleteers of the eighteenth century, to annihilate them. In this rationality, this everyday, businesslike sanity so distant from the imaginative mists where artistic creations struggle into birth, they were products of their situation and of the demands it made in politics. For the primary goal of the American Revolution, which transformed American life and introduced a new era in human history, was not the overthrow or even the alteration of the existing social order but the preservation of political liberty threatened by the apparent corruption of the constitution, and the establishment in principle of the existing conditions of liberty. The communication of understanding, therefore, lay at the heart of the Revolutionary movement, and its great expressions, embodied in the best of the pamphlets, are consequently expository and explanatory: didactic, systematic, and direct, rather than imaginative and metaphoric. They take the form most naturally of treatises and sermons, not poems; of descriptions, not allegories; of explanations, not burlesques. The reader is led through arguments, not images. The pamphlets aim to persuade.

What was essentially involved in the American Revolution was not the disruption of society, with all the fear, despair, and hatred that that entails, but the realization, the comprehension and fulfillment, of the inheritance of liberty and of what was taken to be America's destiny in the context of world history. The great social shocks that in the French and Russian Revolutions sent the foundations of thousands of individual lives crashing into ruins had taken place in America in the course of the previous century, slowly, silently, almost imperceptibly, not as a sudden avalanche but as myriads of individual changes and adjustments which had gradually transformed the order of society. By 1763 the great landmarks of European life—the church and the idea of orthodoxy, the state and the idea of authority: much of the array of institutions and ideas that buttressed the society of the *ancien régime*—had faded in their exposure to the open, wilderness environment of America. But until the disturbances of the 1760's these changes had not been seized upon as grounds for a reconsideration of society and politics. Often they had been condemned as deviations, as retrogressions back toward a more primitive condition of life. Then, after 1760—and especially in the decade after 1765—they were brought into open discussion as the colonists sought to apply advanced principles of society and politics to their own immediate problems.

The original issue of the Anglo-American conflict was, of course, the question of the extent of Parliament's jurisdiction in the colonies. But that could not be discussed in isolation. The debate involved eventually a wide range of social and political problems, and it ended by 1776 in what may be called the conceptualization of American life. By then Americans had come to think of themselves as in a special category, uniquely placed by history to capitalize on, to complete and fulfill, the promise of man's existence. The changes that had overtaken their provincial socieites, they saw, had been good: elements not of deviance and retrogression but of betterment and progress; not a lapse into primitivism, but an elevation to a higher plane of political and social life than had ever been reached before. Their rustic blemishes had become the marks of a chosen people. "The liberties of mankind and the glory of human nature is in their keeping," John Adams wrote in the year of the Stamp Act. "America was designed by Providence for the theatre on which man was to make his true figure, on which science, virtue, liberty, happiness, and glory were to exist in peace."

The effort to comprehend, to communicate, and to fulfill this destiny was continuous through the entire Revolutionary generation—it did not cease, in fact, until in the nineteenth century its creative achievements became dogma. But there were three phases of particular concentration: the period up to and including 1776, centering on the discussion of Anglo-American differences; the devising of the first state governments, mainly in the years from

1776 to 1780; and the reconsideration of the state constitutions and the reconstruction of the national government in the last half of the eighties and in the early nineties. In each of these phases important contributions were made not only to the skeletal structure of constitutional theory but to the surrounding areas of social thought as well. But in none was the creativity as great, the results as radical and as fundamental, as in the period before Independence. It was then that the premises were defined and the assumptions set. It was then that explorations were made in new territories of thought, the first comprehensive maps sketched, and routes marked out. Thereafter the psychological as well as intellectual barriers were down. It was the most creative period in the history of American political thought. Everything that followed assumed and built upon its results.

In the pamphlets published before Independence may be found the fullest expressions of this creative effort. There were other media of communication; but everything essential to the discussion of those years appeared, if not originally then as reprints, in pamphlet form. The treatises, the sermons, the speeches, the exchanges of letters published as pamphlets—even some of the most personal polemics—all contain elements of this great, transforming debate. (pp. 1-21)

> *Bernard Bailyn, "The Literature of Revolution," in his* The Ideological Origins of the American Revolution, *The Belknap Press of Harvard University Press, 1967, pp. 1-21.*

David Minter

[In the essay below, Minter discusses the development of the jeremiad, contending that this literary form derived from the scriptures was used by second- and third-generation Puritans to justify their secular pursuit of worldly goods.]

Long after the finest hours of the Puritan experiment, Americans continued to echo the rhetoric of design: they invoked the 'wise and glorious purposes' for which men had been 'placed' in the New World; they praised the 'new order' America had created 'to teach old nations'; and they celebrated the 'blessings' she was destined to 'shed . . . round the world'. In fact, however, life in both New England and Georgia proved confusing. Before the end of the seventeenth century the Puritans were forced to redefine their errand and revise their experiment; and within twenty years of its launching the Georgia project had gone so badly that its authors and trustees were forced to surrender their colony to the crown. Developments in both places forced men to acknowledge that the products of their actions failed to meet the specifications of their designs. By mid-century the builders of Massachusetts knew that they had met with considerable success—that they had established a strong plantation. Yet they found in apparent success what the Georgians found in obvious failure: that they had missed their grand self-designation.

Soon after the fate of the Georgia enterprise became apparent, men began to tell its story. The most interesting of the Georgia stories is the so-called 'Tailfer Book'—*A*

Philadelphia in 1775, with a frigate in the foreground and the Christ Church spire dominating the shore. The city had a population of 40,000 inhabitants during the Revolutionary period.

True and Historical Narrative of the Colony of Georgia (1740), by Patrick Tailfer, David Douglass, and Hugh Anderson, with comments by the Earl of Egmont. The work is deliberately satirical. As spokesmen for 'the few surviving Remains of the Colony of *Georgia*', as members of a small group that managed to escape back 'to a LAND OF LIBERTY', the authors offer their narrative as 'a true and impartial account' of Georgia 'from its first settlement, to its present period'. Their sole purpose is to recount and explain the 'shipwreck' met by the 'Plan' of the 'Projectors' of that 'unhappy colony'.

In prosperous Massachusetts, where failure took subtler, more disturbing form, and where loyalty precluded satire, spokesmen for the community followed a less direct path to a more thoroughly interpretive genre. By 1650 the Puritan model had been established in Massachusetts. The 'foundation', Peter Bulkeley asserted . . . [in his *The Gospel Covenant: or the Covenant of Grace Opened,* 1646], has been 'laid, by many skilfull builders'. What accordingly was required of later Puritans was that they hold fast, keeping 'the foundation . . . the same'. As defined by William Stoughton . . . [in his *New Englands True Interest: Not to Lie,* 1670], 'the solemn work' of the children and

grandchildren was 'not to lay a new Foundation, but to continue and strengthen, and beautifie, and build upon that which hath been laid'.

The work of caretaking and maintaining proved, of course, less heroic and more domestic than the work of designing and constructing a grand model. It also proved more confining and confusing. For New England the decisive event in the middle seventeenth century was England's official refusal to attend the New England model— her official decision to go her profligate way, whoring after toleration, ignoring the model city built specifically for her redemption. Then, to make bad matters almost unbearable, piety in the promised wilderness began to wane. 'O', Stoughton said, Election Day, April 1668, 'what a sad *Metamorphosis* hath there of later years passed upon us in these Churches and Plantations.' 'O *New-England*', he continued, 'thy God did expect better things from thee and thy Children'.

By smashing the New England dream of being a city upon a hill, England made the Puritan voice, in an unsought, unsettling sense, a voice crying alone in a wilderness. The already tame and domestic task of maintaining the celestial city became provincial as well. It was not as an isolated colony, nor as a tarnished model in a 'far remote, and vast Wildernesse', that New England could hope to fulfill her high self-designation. As the century progressed, bringing 'Ruine upon Ruine, Destruction upon Destruction'—as it became increasingly apparent that both the Puritan design and the Puritan understanding of 'Divine Expectations' were being 'frustrated'—the whole New England enterprise became problematical. Too much had failed to go according to plan. The sons and grandsons of the builders continued to celebrate the beauty of their fathers' vision—a vision of such *Divine Original and Native Beauty'* that it 'would dazzle the Eyes of Angels, daunt the Hearts of Devils, ravish and chain fast the Affections of all the Saints'; and they continued to praise the dedication of their fathers' action—the trials they had passed through, the tribulations they had overcome. But they did so in knowledge that men and events on both sides of the Atlantic were saying no to the Puritan design.

It was not merely that the second and third generations found it a sad fate 'to be styled *Children that are corrupters'* [Stoughton]. It was also that they were compelled to wonder whether New England were doomed to stand, not 'as a Citie upon an hill, [but] . . . desolate and forsaken' [Bulkeley]. Again and again they were forced to ask whether what they represented, what they had become, meant that their fathers had come 'flying from the depravations of Europe, to the American Strand' only to fail and fall short [Cotton Mather, *Magnalia Christi Americana,* Vol. 1, 1702]. Finding themselves in a changing world curiously in conspiracy against the original Puritan aim, later Puritans were forced, again and again, to seek some way to reshape their heritage and redefine what they were about.

The steady purpose and free enthusiasm of the builders depended upon unrepeatable experience, and it died when they died. 'The first generation', Stoughton said, 'have been ripened time after time . . . But we who rise up to tread out the footsteps of them that are gone before us, alas! what are we?' The second- and third-generation Puritans wanted to fulfill their caretaking assignment. But that assignment was theirs by accident of birth, not by decision to voyage, and they were in fact ill suited to it. They wanted to be about heroic tasks of their own, and that meant, within the historical context in which they found themselves, giving up being a model for England and becoming a strong and prosperous society. If their still young society could not be made the revealing, transforming model their fathers had said it must be, if New England could not renew the old, perhaps she could be significant simply as a thriving, dedicated land.

The initial difficulty the second- and third-generation Puritans faced in seeking out their own heroic course was a matter of loyalty. They could never bring themselves simply to ignore the task their fathers had bequeathed them; nor could they ever admit that in fact they were not keeping the foundations the same. But the subtler, potentially more divisive difficulty they faced derived from the very character of their fathers' experience. By teaching that 'the Successes and Events of [human] Undertakings and Affairs are not determined' by man's intent, that man's effort may be frustrated and disappointed despite 'the greatest Sufficiency' and the highest resolve, their fathers' experience questioned the wisdom of all heroic activity.

It was through strangely turned interpretation of their fathers' design that the Puritans sought first to remain loyal sons without remaining captive to their inherited task and second to master their problematical heritage. In tracing the course of their fathers' action—in telling their fathers' story—they sought not only to revise the logic of their own situation but also to redefine the fate of their fathers' design. They wanted to save their fathers as well as themselves from an inadequate fate. Interpretation became for them a way of taming 'a time and season of eminent trial' [Stoughton]. Through it they attempted to master failure—to deliver themselves from an inadequate fate; through it they attempted to salvage one of the failed 'Designs of men' and thereby move beyond human 'Defeat and Disappointment' [Vrian Oakes, *The Sovereign Efficacy of Divine Providence,* 1682].

The 'jeremiad' was the form Puritan interpretation took. On designated fast-days New Englanders congregated to repent that they had erred and strayed. Neither the theory—that sin was linked with judgment, judgment with repentance, repentance with forgiveness, forgiveness with hope, and hope with reform—nor the practice of public lamentation represented Puritan improvization. But the role such lamentation played in New England was special because the covenant the Puritans had made with God was special. Unlike the covenant of grace (with which it was, of course, not coextensive), their communal covenant had to do not with eternal salvation of the elect of God but with a pledge to perform a mission within the world. Faithful performance of this mission would lead to victory, and victory would be rewarded on earth, not in heaven: God specifically would bless New England, giving her peace and prosperity within, influence and praise without. Concomitantly, however, betrayal of the agreement would be met not with eternal fire but with present visitations of God's wrath—with plagues and droughts, wars and rumors of wars, with scorn and laughter, derision and infamy.

The jeremiad became, increasingly after 1650 and especially after 1660, the characteristic utterance of the Puritans. Again and again, as Perry Miller has shown, they told and retold the story of 'God's Controversy with New-England' [Perry Miller, *The New England Mind: from Colony to Province,* 1953]. The original intention of the jeremiad was to inspire reform. After cataloging calamities—droughts and plagues and savage raids—Puritan spokesmen label them tokens of God's displeasure with His people's failure faithfully to run their errand. Various 'sad affliction[s]'—'epidemical sickness' and 'Pekoat furies'—function within jeremiads as signs of providential chastisement of a recalcitrant and inconstant people. Having been reminded that only 'the singular pity and mercies' of their God can shield them from deserved annihilation, suffering them to live, the people are called to repent and reform [Thomas Shepard, *A Treatise of Liturgies,* 1653].

In its classic form, as defined by Perry Miller, the jeremiad was rooted in immediate difficulties. In July 1646, John Winthrop noted that great harm had been visited on grain crops by an invasion of caterpillars. 'In divers places', he said, churches observed a day of humiliation, whereupon 'presently after the caterpillars' disappeared. Later Puritans continued to link 'tokens of God's displeasure' with their having become 'a people so unworthy, so sinfull, that by murmurings of many, unfaithfulness in promises, oppressions, and other evils' they had 'dishonoured [God's] Majesty, expos[ing] his worke here to much scandall and obloquie'. Year after year election sermons reminded the folk that they had 'cause for ever to bee ashamed', and cause also to call upon God 'rather [to] correct us in mercy, then [sic] cast us off in displeasure, and scatter us in this Wildernesse'.

The Puritans tended, however, increasingly to blur the rationale of the jeremiad. More specifically, in a distinctly anthropocentric turn they began to treat consciousness of failure as the chief visitation of God's wrath. The burden of sensed defeat and faithlessness gradually displaced 'Pekoat furies' as a token of punishment for defeat and faithlessness. Distinctions between human acts of betrayal, divine judgment of betrayal, and human consciousness of both betrayal and judgment lost their sharpness. The Puritans continued of course to be disturbed by acts that rendered their city a defective model and by calamities that disclosed divine displeasure. But what most distressed them was knowledge that, despite careful and ostensibly successful building, they and their fathers had fallen short. At times, as a result, they appear most to lament the necessity of lamentation. But they were moved by more than longing to have that cup pass from them. They needed new assurance, yet were compelled—because their design had failed—to seek it surreptitiously.

There was accordingly, coincident with the generalizing and blurring of the logic of the jeremiad, a tendency to use it to relativize God's judgment. Early Puritans assumed that they must either keep and fulfill their commission or become not a dimmer beacon on a lower hill but a byword for infamous failure. Later Puritans found themselves in a situation defined by the curious intermingling of three elements: the crumbling of their design, the waning of their piety, and the waxing of their prosperity. And in an effort to overcome the incongruity of obvious prosperity amid felt declension, they not only defined consciousness of failure as punishment for failure; they also decided that to fail in a designation sublime was after all to fail with a difference. If the Puritans would but continue to gaze from their present peak to the serene summit of their ancestors' desire, and if they would but condemn their failure, New England still could be truly new. In lamenting their sad decline, New Englanders subtly thanked their God and notified the world that they yet were not as other men, that they, despite all, were a chosen people dedicated to perfection. Our churches are not perfect. Cotton Mather admitted, but they 'are very like unto those that were in the first ages of Christianity', which even Quakers and Roman Catholics knew better than lightly to criticize. We have failed, Mather also acknowledged, but we 'Nevertheless . . . have given great examples of the methods and

measures wherein an Evangelical Reformation is to be prosecuted' [Cotton Mather].

The Puritans thus used careful dissection rather to minimize than to stress the importance of their failings. By emphasizing the heights from which they had fallen, they underscored the height at which they yet stood. But this strange logic did not alone suffice. The Puritans also used the jeremiad to move completely beyond caretaking and correction. They continued, to be sure, to lament their failure. And they sought to avoid as well as repent 'sins against the purpose and Covenant' of their community; they felt, after all, no desire to adorn the Puritan edifice with 'hay and stubble, in stead of gold and precious stones'. But what they most needed—and what they finally found in the jeremiad—was a way of skirting the requirement that they persevere in what they called the 'old way' of New England.

That the caretaking generations had been left to make their way with 'a fixed unalterable' design through an era characterized by drastic change and seemingly dedicated to undermining their design—that they, in the name of all they held dear and holy, were required to remain loyal to a design that had failed—proved more than curious and perplexing. It constituted the most troublesome problem the second and third generations had to confront. And though they tried to avoid the implications of their failure, those implications became the elements of their characteristic nightmare. Why had the God who had sent His chosen few into a wilderness to build a model society, through them to give to the world a model for ordered and meaningful society, so soon permitted England to intensify her flirtation with social and religious pluralism? Why should New England be forced to suffer the knowledge that nothing had made her more anachronistic within the world she wanted to save, that nothing did more to chafe her relationship with that world, than her efforts—efforts prescribed by her covenant with her Lord God—to stem the tide of toleration? Why had her God bound her to a design so unalterable that it defined all adjustment and accommodation as betrayal? And why had her God sent her into a land that demanded and rewarded preoccupation, not with building and maintaining a model city and living model lives, but with hard work and close trading? The Puritans knew, of course, that trial, temptation, and uncertainty were the appointed lot of man: that it was not given man to know '*what* Afflictions shall come upon him' or what shall be 'the Time of his Death'; that he was called to 'follow the Lord, as it were blind-fold[ed]'. But the wilderness they knew, placed against an English backdrop, seemed to confront them not with trial but with insoluble dilemma: with choice between the disloyalty of compromise and revision and the failure of scorn and irrelevance.

Puritan orthodoxy possessed, it should be noted, one direct solution to the dilemma of the caretaking generations—that of radically applying to the pursuits of the first generation the wisdom set forth in Urian Oakes' sermon of 1677. Puritans knew, almost by right of birth, that mere men were never able 'infallibly' to determine the issue of their plans and activities; that God alone governed time and ordered history, and that God's ways were to man inscrutable. 'God is the Lord of Time, and Orderer, and Governour of all Contingences', Oakes insisted, including the 'Time and Chance that further or hinder the Designs of men'. Men accordingly should labor, Oakes continued, 'to be prepared and provided for Disappointments', for 'Changes and Chances', for 'Occurrents and Emergencies that may blast' their 'Undertakings'; for only with sound preparation could they hope in the face of 'such Frustrations' to keep 'Faith and Prayer . . . a going' and to avoid either flying 'out against God' or fainting and sinking 'in Discouragements'.

Radical application of this 'good Counsel to men of projecting Heads' would have permitted explanation of the failure of the Puritan design, which would in turn have justified revising or abandoning it. Indeed, such a step would have undone even the need of using the jeremiad to generalize and relativize judgment. But Puritans were no less the children of their fathers than of their God: they were no more capable of asserting that their fathers had misread God's commission than they were capable of flying out against the God who had placed them in their trying land. They used Oakes' good counsel to explain their own false starts. But in their effort to move beyond their appointed tasks and yet remain loyal to their fathers, they extended in two ways their already revised jeremiad.

On one side they used it to substitute tribute for action. They made humiliation a form of homage, lamentation a mode of loyalty. By decrying their failure, by contemning their disloyalty, they defined themselves as a dedicated people. Preaching, hearing, and reading jeremiads became tests of loyalty and acts of heroism. The ingenuity and eloquence the clergy could muster in detailing declension, the openness and remorse the people could summon in accepting judgment—these were strange tests of fortitude, courage, and devotion. But to the Puritans they were altogether necessary. For it was only by substituting formal repentance for active reform and loyal discourse for loyal action that the Puritans managed in good conscience slowly to move beyond caretaking and enter their changing world.

On the other side, however, they made the jeremiad a work of celebration. In it they not only confronted their 'great and dangerous *Declensions*'; they also celebrated, and in celebrating reclaimed, the great work of their fathers. Had the second and third generations been concerned solely with their own freedom, had they been less loyal sons, they should have felt no further need of the jeremiad. But because they wanted also to free their fathers' design from disappointment and defeat, they made their works of complex lamentation works of praise and celebration. In 1648 Thomas Shepard called 'all the Godly wise' to the task of celebratory interpretation: 'let us . . . consider and look back', he said, 'upon the season of this great enterprise'. In 1669, John Davenport, one of the last survivors of the first generation, extended the recitative jeremiad. But the form belonged to the second and third generations, who used it to re-order the entire New England experience.

By recalling 'the Considerable Matters, that produced and attended the First Settlement of Colonies', by telling of the 'more exemplary' among 'the *Actors*' in the settlement story, and by relating 'Memorable Occurrences, and amazing Judgments and Mercies', the makers of the jeremiads established a standard and defined the genius of dedicated action. Quoting Virgil's *Aeneid,* Cotton Mather stressed the importance of understanding what drove men eminent in piety to endure so many calamities and to undertake so many hardships. The explanation he offered was dedication to the Puritan design. The *'Actions'* that 'signalized' Puritan settlement and construction were authored by men so dedicated that they withstood 'temptations', overcame 'Disturbances', and confuted 'enemies'; their 'Methods' and their dedication together enabled them to weather 'out each horrible tempest'.

For latter-day Puritans, however, dedicated action took a different form. Deprived of the tasks of radical social and theological construction, they turned to construction of another sort. They reconstructed 'the Beginning' of the 'remarkable' work of their fathers. They defined 'the End and Design' that had inspired and informed that work. And they recounted and praised those of their fathers' *'Actions'* that seemed to them 'of a more eminent importance'. In short, they substituted the dedicated action of telling and retelling their inherited story for the dedicated action of pursuing their inherited task. Through their lamenting—recounting—celebrating jeremiads, they hoped to 'preserve and secure the interest of Religion in the Churches of . . . New-England'. But beyond renewing life at home, they sought to complete their fathers' 'Great Design'. They saw in their jeremiads analogues and extensions of the grand action from which they had derived. Having redefined action, and having moved to new unity by tracing grand action, the makers of jeremiads were able to proffer their works not as mere lament but rather as a mode of constructive activity, a form of creative endeavor.

The jeremiad accordingly became not simply a way of reviving 'religion' in New England, but more strangely a way of spreading 'abroad in the world, some small Memorials' of the New England story. The Puritan interpreters thus would salvage a design that had failed. Beyond 'Defeat and Disappointment', beyond the death of a dream, they reconstructed the story of New England. Whether that story would '*live* any where else or no', at least it would '*live*' in and through interpretations of her 'History'. By this indirection the Puritans were able to approximate the perfection they had missed. In 1730, a century after the inauguration of the Great Migration, Thomas Prince composed a sermon [called *The People of New England,* 1730] in which all things are duly ordered: New England is 'a Countrey' of 'Religion, good Order, Liberty, Learning and flourishing Towns and Churches'; wherefore it possesses 'a destinguishing Name in the World' and reflects 'singular Honour to the Persons and Principles of it's [sic] original Setlers' and the 'very grievous Trials . . . Hardship and Affliction' they endured. Echoing biblical passages of promise that had all along provided the model of Puritan hope, Prince envisaged and recorded perfection achieved only in vision and record.

> And now the WILDERNESS and the solitary Place is Glad for them: The Desart rejoices and blossoms as a Rose . . . The Glory of LEBANON is given to it, the Excellency of CARMEL and

SHARON; they see the Glory of the LORD and the Excellency of our GOD. The Waters of the Divine Influence break out in the Wilderness, and the Streams in the Desart: The parched Ground becomes a Pool; and the thirsty Land, Springs of Water: In the Habitations of Dragons where they lay, there grows up the Grass; and an High Way now is there, which is call'd the *Way of Holiness,* over which the Unclean do not pass, and the Wayfaring Men do not err therein.

Despite the 'great and dangerous *Declensions*' of 'transcendently guilty' men, both the Puritans' original design and the action to which it led are preserved and completed in the story that the jeremiads tell. Through poetic rendering, the work of the Puritan builders is redeemed: the wayfaring men within no longer err; those without now see the glory of the Lord; within the New England Way has become and without it is acknowledged as the Way of Holiness. And further, should 'the Plantation . . . soon after this, *come to nothing*', as another interpreter put it, its story nonetheless would survive in the lamentation and celebration of its telling.

The jeremiad thus became, to borrow from Wallace Stevens [in his *Collected Poems,* 1964], a 'poem that took the place of a mountain', an interpretation that embodied a failed design and so preserved and, in one sense, realized and perfected it. Through the jeremiad second- and third-generation Puritans 'recomposed' their heritage. Through it they were able to 'discover, at last, the view toward which they had edged', and to find, at last, 'A place to go in [their] own direction'. With it they became 'complete in an unexplained completion', and were able to accept their 'unique and solitary home'.

That the jeremiad became imaginative interpretation does not mean, of course, that any jeremiad is a literary masterpiece. None is. In their own way, however, the latter-day Puritans were true, though very imperfect and partial, poets: they followed, if not to the bottom, at least into the darkness of their night, there to order words of themselves and of their origins, there to seek a basis of renewal; in their tales of pleasing woe, they sang, as best they could, 'of human unsuccess / In a rapture of distress'. Their characteristic decision was, to be sure, rather to skirt than fully to explore the incongruity, first between the intent of the design and the result of the actions of their fathers, and second between the purposes to which they had been dedicated as children and the causes to which they were giving themselves as men. But in their jeremiads they acknowledge and, in their most interesting moments, attempt even to master these incongruities: they attempt, that is, to reconcile, by proclaiming them one, the intent and the achievement of their fathers and they attempt, while going about other business, to remain loyal to the purposes to which their fathers had dedicated them. (pp. 45-55)

> *David Minter, "The Puritan Jeremiad as a Literary Form," in* The American Puritan Imagination: Essays in Revaluation, *edited by Sacvan Bercovitch, Cambridge University Press, 1974, pp. 45-55.*

FURTHER READING

Bercovitch, Sacvan. *The American Jeremiad.* Madison: University of Wisconsin Press, 1978, 239 p.
 Discusses "the impact of Puritan rhetoric upon our culture" and how its religious symbols laid the foundation for the development of bourgeois culture in America.

Boorstin, Daniel J. *The Americans: The Colonial Experience,* Vol. I. New York: Random House, 1958, 434 p.
 Overview of the Colonial period, demonstrating the ingenuity, innovation, and versatility of the American colonials as they pursued a revolutionary course and won independence.

Brownson, O. A. *The American Republic.* New York: P. O'Shea, 1866, 439 p.
 Explains the development of the governing principles of the United States, from the early Colonial years to the drafting of the Declaration of Independence and the Constitution of the United States.

Dawson, Christopher. "The Birth of Democracy." In his *The Gods of Revolution,* pp. 32-50. New York: New York University Press, 1972.
 Explores Colonial America's interest in democratic ideals, contending that the writings of the French Enlightenment, in particular the philosophy of Jean-Jacques Rousseau, were instrumental in reshaping American Colonial government according to democratic principles.

Hatch, Nathan O. *The Sacred Cause of Liberty.* New Haven & London: Yale University Press, 1977, 197 p.
 Examines the religious influences that defined the Revolution as a sacred cause with a divine destiny.

Ketcham, Ralph. *From Colony to Country.* New York: Macmillan Publishing Co., 1974, 318 p.
 Explores "the changing ideas of loyalty, purpose, and national character that were part of the transition from colony to country in 1750-1820," focusing on the works of Benjamin Franklin, John Adams, Thomas Jefferson, James Madison, and Alexander Hamilton.

Kirk, Russell. "Salutary Neglect: The Colonial Order" and "Declaration and Constitution." In his *The Roots of American Order,* pp. 301-346, 393-440. Malibu, Calif.: Pepperdine University Press, 1978.
 Assesses the effect of British rule on Colonial politics and discusses the use of English common law in the Declaration of Independence and the Federal Constitution of 1787, which ensured an orderly society and a new relationship between church and state.

Knollenberg, Bernhard. *Origin of the American Revolution: 1759-1766.* New York: Macmillian Company, 1960, 486 p.
 Studies the American colonies before the Revolution and the causes that led to the Declaration of Independence in 1776.

Koch, G. Adolf. *Republican Religion: The American Revolution and the Cult of Reason.* New York: Henry Holt and Company, 1933, 334 p.
 Investigates the breakdown of the theocratically-centered colonial American governments, explaining

how the republic's subsequent toleration of religious diversity reshaped American attitudes.

May, Henry F. *The Englightenment in America.* New York: Oxford University Press, 1976, 419 p.

Examines the effect of Enlightenment thought on the American colonies and the post-revolutionary republic, suggesting that what resulted was a "compromise between a belief in moral certainties and a belief in the desirability of change and progress."

Miller, John C. *The Federalist Era: 1789-1801.* New York: Harper & Brothers, 1960, 304 p.

Discusses the development of Federalism, contrasting the political philosophies of Alexander Hamilton and Thomas Jefferson.

Wills, Garry. *Inventing America: Jefferson's Declaration of Independence.* Garden City, N.Y.: Doubleday & Company, 1978, 398 p.

Argues that Jefferson's original version of the Declaration of Independence reflected "eighteenth-century Scottish concepts of the moral sense."

————. *Explaining America: The Federalist.* Garden City, N.Y.: Doubleday & Company, 1981, 286 p.

Proposes that James Madison and Alexander Hamilton, among others, utilized the philosophical ethics of David Hume to construct a federalist form of constitutional government for the new republic.

Benjamin Franklin

1706-1790

(Also wrote under the pseudonyms Silence Dogood and Poor Richard Saunders) American statesman, autobiographer, essayist, and journalist.

INTRODUCTION

An outstanding figure of eighteenth-century literature and colonial politics, Franklin has come to embody the American ideal of the self-made man. He was an individual of myriad interests, the diversity of his activities and accomplishments attesting to the breadth of his learning. Franklin made significant discoveries in the field of electricity, and was integral in securing French aid during the American Revolutionary War. He acted as presiding officer of the Pennsylvania constitutional convention, served as colonial postmaster general, founded the American Philosophical Society, and performed numerous other social and political functions for the nascent United States of America. Although generally remembered as a scientist and a statesman, Franklin also earned great renown as a man of letters, producing the hugely popular *Poor Richard. An Almanack* and what most scholars consider his preeminent literary work, the *Autobiography*. The latter is often described as one of the finest examples of the genre.

Franklin was born in Boston, Massachusetts to Josiah and Abiah Folger Franklin. He received only two years of formal education as a child, but learned to read at an early age and pursued that activity voraciously. In 1718 he was apprenticed to his older brother James, editor of the *New-England Courant,* a newspaper which published a series of essays the younger Franklin had written under the pseudonym Silence Dogood. Following the *Courant*'s suppression by the Massachusetts government in 1723, Franklin left Boston, sailing first to New York and later to Philadelphia, where he hoped to establish himself in the printing trade. He also traveled to London, where he stayed for two years, and while there published a pamphlet entitled *A Dissertation on Liberty and Necessity, Pleasure and Pain* in 1725. Having returned to Philadelphia in 1726, Franklin bought a newspaper, the *Pennsylvania Gazette,* and in 1732 began to publish his highly successful *Almanack.* Produced annually until 1757, the *Almanack* sold as many as 10,000 copies per year, providing Franklin with considerable wealth and fame. He was chosen clerk of the Pennsylvania General Assembly in 1736, and was later made a full member. While he increased his political activity, Franklin also devoted time to his lifelong interest in science; his study of electrical phenomena, in particular, culminated in the discovery of several basic scientific principals on the subject, which he described in his *Experiments and Observations on Electricity* of 1751. Having earned a reputation for his keen wit and diplomatic

sense, he served as a mediator between the British government and the American colonies, spending all but two years between 1757 and 1775 in England. Franklin began work on his memoirs while living near the town of Twyford in 1771, but focused little attention on this project, instead spending much of his time in continued arguments for conciliation. Seeing that a peaceful solution between Britain and the American colonies was unlikely, he returned home; his stay, however was brief. During the American War of Independence Franklin was appointed ambassador to France, and while residing there he succeeded in winning the economic and military support of the French, who signed the 1778 Treaty of Alliance with the colonies. Franklin remained in France for nearly a decade, and continued to write prolifically. Moving in esteemed literary and cultural circles, he produced several lighthearted, satirical pieces known collectively as the *Bagatelles.* He returned again to America in 1785, hoping to continue work on his memoirs. Franklin died five years later, a renowned figure on both sides of the Atlantic.

In his long career Franklin produced a vast quantity of writings, the bulk of which appear in the form of letters, newspaper essays, and political pamphlets. For his series of fourteen satirical essays entitled the "Silence Dogood" papers, which discuss topics ranging from alcoholism and the value of a Harvard education to the importance of free speech, Franklin imitated the witty, colloquial style of Joseph Addison's and Richard Steele's *Spectator.* Franklin also dabbled in philosophical speculation, though he did so without a systematic approach or overriding vision. In *A Dissertation on Liberty and Necessity, Pleasure and Pain*—a deistic pamphlet that he was later to describe as one of the "errata" of his life—Franklin contends that free will does not exist; instead human beings are ruled by the desire to seek pleasure and avoid pain. With his series of almanacs printed under the title of *Poor Richard,* Franklin intended to instruct common people by conveying to them the compressed knowledge and wit of his many (typically borrowed and reworked) proverbs, along with innumerable charts, lists, and facts ranging from agricultural to cosmological. Among his political works, his "An Edict by the King of Prussia" —a clever satire of burdensome British colonial trade regulations—is representative of Franklin's use of humor to undercut his opponents. This same penchant for humorous writing is also discernible in his *Bagatelles,* a series of amusing essays containing Franklin's observations on topics both mundane and philosophical, which are listed among Franklin's finest literary creations. Perhaps his greatest work, Franklin's *Autobiography* not only details his life, but also reiterates the theme of the self-made man who, through conscious effort and the contemplation of virtue, exhorts himself to success.

The vast majority of Franklin criticism has tended to focus on his legitimacy as an artist, especially in relation to the *Autobiography.* D. H. Lawrence disliked Franklin's portrayal of himself in the work; he disapproved in particular of his "bold and arduous project of arriving at moral perfection," finding his words smug and priggish. Critics have since observed that the virtues of industry, prudence, and frugality that frequently appear as Franklin's aspirations in the *Autobiography* and in other writings have come to represent only a caricatured portrait of the man, and that it is only this caricature that writers such as Lawrence, Charles Angoff, and William Carlos Williams found so distasteful. Later commentators have claimed these critics failed to see that Franklin was merely adopting the deceptive pose of a naive narrator as a means of universalizing himself and creating an image of a fallible, but self-made man. Some critics have argued that Franklin's works lack artistic merit; many have objected, however, to that characterization, praising the simplicity and lucidity of his style. Scholars have acknowledged, however, that the vast majority of Franklin's writings were designed for utilitarian rather than literary purposes. His *Almanacks* are decidedly didactic, and his hoaxes, satires, and essays were typically written with some political end in mind. Nevertheless, Franklin's influential *Autobiography* is generally considered a classic of American literature, and Franklin himself—for the sheer weight and diversity of his political, social, scientific, and literary contributions—is viewed as an extraordinary figure in American history.

PRINCIPAL WORKS

A Dissertation on Liberty and Necessity, Pleasure and Pain (essay) 1725
A Modest Enquiry into the Nature and Necessity of Paper-Currency (essay) 1729
Poor Richard. An Almanack (almanacs) 1733-46
Plain Truth: or, Serious Considerations On the Present State of the City of Philadelphia, and Province of Pennsylvania (essay) 1747
Poor Richard Improved: Being an Almanack and Ephemeris (almanacs) 1748-57
Experiments and Observations on Electricity, Made at Philadelphia in America, by Benjamin Franklin, and communicated in several Letters to Mr. P. Collinson of London (non-fiction) 1751
The Interest of Great Britain Considered, With Regard to her Colonies, And the Acquisitions of Canada and Guadaloupe. To which are added, Observations concerning the Increase of Mankind, Peopling of Countries, &c. (essay) 1760
Cool Thoughts on the Present Situation of Our Public Affairs (essay) 1764
"An Edict by the King of Prussia" (essay) 1773
*The Way to Wealth, as clearly shewn in the Preface of An Old Pennsylvania Almanack, Intituled, Poor Richard Improved (essay) 1774
"Rules for Reducing a Great Empire to a Small One" (essay) 1793
†*Autobiography of Benjamin Franklin* (autobiography) 1868
The Complete Works of Benjamin Franklin, including his private as well as official and scientific correspondence. 10 vols. (essays, letters, and verse) 1887-89
The Papers of Benjamin Franklin. 29 vols. to date (essays and letters) 1959
The Political Thought of Benjamin Franklin (essays) 1965
The Bagatelles from Passy by Benjamin Franklin, Text and Facsimile (essays) 1967
The Complete Poor Richard Almanacs (almanacs) 1970

*Originally published as the preface to the 1758 edition of *Poor Richard Improved.*

†The first complete edition of Franklin's *Autobiography.*

CRITICISM

John Adams   (essay date 1811)

[*Adams is best known as the second president of the United States. Also an author and political thinker, he is remembered for his writings on the nature of government and for his voluminous correspondence with the great statesmen of his day. In the following excerpt, orig-*

inally published in the 15 May 1811 edition of the Boston Patriot, *Adams discusses Franklin's character and international reputation.*]

Mr. Jefferson has said that Dr. Franklin was an honor to human nature. And so, indeed, he was. Had he been an ordinary man, I should never have taken the trouble to expose the turpitude of his intrigues, or to vindicate my reputation against his vilifications and calumnies. But the temple of human nature has two great apartments: the intellectual and the moral. If there is not a mutual friendship and strict alliance between these, degradation to the whole building must be the consequence. There may be blots on the disk of the most refulgent luminary, almost sufficient to eclipse it. And it is of great importance to the rising generation in this country that they be put upon their guard against being dazzled by the surrounding blaze into an idolatry to the spots. If the affable archangel understood the standard of merit, that

> Great or bright infers not excellence,

Franklin's moral character can neither be applauded nor condemned, without discrimination and many limitations.

To all those talents and qualities for the foundation of a great and lasting character, which were held up to the view of the whole world by the university of Oxford, the Royal Society of London, and the Royal Academy of Sciences in Paris, were added, it is believed, more artificial modes of diffusing, celebrating, and exaggerating his reputation; than were ever before or since practised in favor of any individual.

His reputation was more universal than that of Leibnitz or Newton, Frederick or Voltaire, and his character more beloved and esteemed than any or all of them. Newton had astonished perhaps forty or fifty men in Europe; for not more than that number, probably, at any one time had read him and understood him by his discoveries and demonstrations. And these being held in admiration in their respective countries as at the head of the philosophers, had spread among scientific people a mysterious wonder at the genius of this perhaps the greatest man that ever lived. But this fame was confined to men of letters. The common people knew little and cared nothing about such a recluse philosopher. Leibnitz's name was more confined still. Frederick was hated by more than half of Europe as much as Louis the Fourteenth was, and as Napoleon is. Voltaire, whose name was more universal than any of those before mentioned, was considered as a vain, profligate wit, and not much esteemed or beloved by anybody, though admired by all who knew his works. But Franklin's fame was universal. His name was familiar to government and people, to kings, courtiers, nobility, clergy, and philosophers, as well as plebeians, to such a degree that there was scarcely a peasant or a citizen, a *valet de chambre,* coachman or footman, a lady's chambermaid or a scullion in a kitchen, who was not familiar with it, and who did not consider him as a friend to human kind. When they spoke of him, they seemed to think he was to restore the golden age. They seemed enraptured enough to exclaim

> Aspice, venturo lætentur ut omnia sæclo.

To develop that complication of causes, which conspired to produce so singular a phenomenon, is far beyond my means or forces. Perhaps it can never be done without a complete history of the philosophy and politics of the eighteenth century. Such a work would be one of the most important that ever was written; much more interesting to this and future ages than the *Decline and Fall of the Roman Empire,* splendid and useful as that is. La Harpe promised a history of the philosophy of the eighteenth century; but he died and left us only a few fragments. Without going back to Lord Herbert, to Hobbes, to Mandeville, or to a host of more obscure infidels, both in England, France, and Germany, it is enough to say that four of the finest writers that Great Britain ever produced, Shaftesbury, Bolingbroke, Hume, and Gibbon, whose labors were translated into all languages, and three of the most eloquent writers that ever lived in France, whose works were also translated into all languages, Voltaire, Rousseau, and Raynal, seem to have made it the study of their lives and the object of their most strenuous exertions, to render mankind in Europe discontented with their situation in life, and with the state of society, both in religion and government. Princes and courtiers as well as citizens and countrymen, clergy as well as laity, became infected. The King of Prussia, the Empress Catherine, were open and undisguised. The Emperor Joseph the Second was suspected, and even the excellent and amiable King of France grew impatient and uneasy under the fatiguing ceremonies of the Catholic church. All these and many more were professed admirers of Mr. Franklin. He was considered as a citizen of the world, a friend to all men and an enemy to none. His rigorous taciturnity was very favorable to this singular felicity. He conversed only with individuals, and freely only with confidential friends. In company he was totally silent.

When the association of Encyclopedists was formed, Mr. Franklin was considered as a friend and zealous promoter of that great enterprise, which engaged all their praises. When the society of economists was commencing, he became one of them, and was solemnly ordained a knight of the order by the laying on the hands of Dr. Quesnay, the father and founder of that sect. This effectually secured the affections and the panegyrics of that numerous society of men of letters. He had been educated a printer, and had practised his art in Boston, Philadelphia, and London for many years, where he not only learned the full power of the press to exalt and to spread a man's fame, but acquired the intimacy and the correspondence of many men of that profession, with all their editors and many of their correspondents. This whole tribe became enamoured and proud of Mr. Franklin as a member of their body, and were consequently always ready and eager to publish and embellish any panegyric upon him that they could procure. Throughout his whole life he courted and was courted by the printers, editors, and correspondents of reviews, magazines, journals, and pamphleteers, and those little busy meddling scribblers that are always buzzing about the press in America, England, France, and Holland. These, together with some of the clerks in the Count de Vergennes's office of interpreters, (*bureau des interprètes,*) filled all the gazettes of Europe with incessant praises of Monsieur Franklin. If a collection could be made of all the Gazettes of Europe for the latter half of the eighteenth century, a greater number of panegyrical paragraphs upon *"le grand Franklin"* would appear, it is believed, than upon any other man that ever lived.

While he had the singular felicity to enjoy the entire esteem and affection of all the philosophers of every denomination, he was not less regarded by all the sects and denominations of Christians. The Catholics thought him almost a Catholic. The Church of England claimed him as one of them. The Presbyterians thought him half a Presbyterian, and the Friends believed him a wet Quaker. The dissenting clergymen in England and America were among the most distinguished asserters and propagators of his renown. Indeed, all sects considered him, and I believe justly, a friend to unlimited toleration in matters of religion.

Nothing, perhaps, that ever occurred upon this earth was so well calculated to give any man an extensive and universal celebrity as the discovery of the efficacy of iron points and the invention of lightning-rods. The idea was one of the most sublime that ever entered a human imagination, that a mortal should disarm the clouds of heaven, and almost "snatch from his hand the sceptre and the rod." The ancients would have enrolled him with Bacchus and Ceres, Hercules and Minerva. His *Paratonnères* erected their heads in all parts of the world, on temples and palaces no less than on cottages of peasants and the habitations of ordinary citizens. These visible objects reminded all men of the name and character of their inventor; and, in the course of time, have not only tranquillized the minds, and dissipated the fears of the tender sex and their timorous children, but have almost annihilated that panic terror and superstitious horror which was once almost universal in violent storms of thunder and lightning. To condense all the rays of this glory to a focus, to sum it up in a single line, to impress it on every mind and transmit it to all posterity, a motto was devised for his picture, and soon became familiar to the memory of every school-boy who understood a word of Latin:—

Eripuit cœlo fulmen sceptrumque tyrannis.

Thus it appeared at first, and the author of it was held in a mysterious obscurity. But, after some time, M. Turgot altered it to

Eripuit cœlo fulmen; mox sceptra tyrannis.

By the first line, the rulers of Great Britain and their arbitrary oppressions of the Colonies were alone understood. By the second was intimated that Mr. Franklin was soon to destroy or at least to dethrone all kings and abolish all monarchical governments. This, it cannot be disguised, flattered at that time the ruling popular passion of all Europe. It was at first hinted that it was written in Holland; but I have long entertained a suspicion, from many circumstances, that Sir William Jones, who undoubtedly furnished Mr. Franklin with his motto,

Non sine Diis animosus infans,

sent him the *Eripuit cœlo,* and that M. Turgot only added the *mox sceptra.* Whoever was the author of it, there can be no doubt it was an imitation of a line in a poem on as-

tronomy, written in the age of Tiberius, though it ought not to be called a plagiarism,

Eripuit Jovi fulmen, viresque tonandi.

The general discontents in Europe have not been produced by any increase of the power of kings, for monarchical authority has been greatly diminished in all parts of Europe during the last century, but by the augmentation of the wealth and power of the aristocracies. The great and general extension of commerce has introduced such inequalities of property, that the class of middling people, that great and excellent portion of society upon whom so much of the liberty and prosperity of nations so greatly depends, is almost lost; and the two orders of rich and poor only remain. By this means kings have fallen more into the power and under the direction of the aristocracies, and the middle classes, upon whom kings chiefly depended for support against the encroachments of the nobles and the rich, have failed. The people find themselves burdened now by the rich, and by the power of the crown now commonly wielded by the rich. And as knowledge and education, ever since the Reformation, have been increasing among the common people, they feel their burdens more sensibly, grow impatient under them, and more desirous of throwing them off. The immense revenues of the church, the crowns, and all the great proprietors of land, the armies and navies must all be paid by the people, who groan and stagger under the weight. The few who think and see the progress and tendency of things, have long foreseen that resistance in some shape or other must be resorted to, some time or other. They have not been able to see any resource but in the common people; indeed, in republicanism, and that republicanism must be democracy; because the whole power of the aristocracy, as of the monarchies, aided by the church, must be wielded against them. Hence the popularity of all insurrections against the ordinary authority of government during the last century. Hence the popularity of Pascal Paoli, the Polish insurrections, the American Revolution, and the present struggle in Spain and Portugal. When, where, and in what manner all this will end, God only knows. To this cause Mr. Franklin owed much of his popularity. He was considered to be in his heart no friend to kings, nobles, or prelates. He was thought a profound legislator, and a friend of democracy. He was thought to be the magician who had excited the ignorant Americans to resistance. His mysterious wand had separated the Colonies from Great Britain. He had framed and established all the American constitutions of government, especially all the best of them, *i. e.* the most democratical. His plans and his example were to abolish monarchy, aristocracy, and hierarchy throughout the world. Such opinions as these were entertained by the Duke de la Rochefoucauld, M. Turgot, M. Condorcet, and a thousand other men of learning and eminence in France, England, Holland, and all the rest of Europe.

Mr. Franklin, however, after all, and notwithstanding all his faults and errors, was a great and eminent benefactor to his country and mankind.

Such was the real character, and so much more formidable was the artificial character of Dr. Franklin, when he en-

> **Franklin's reputation was more universal than that of Leibnitz or Newton, Frederick or Voltaire, and his character more beloved and esteemed than any or all of them.**
>
> —*John Adams*

tered into partnership with the Count de Vergennes, the most powerful minister of State in Europe, to destroy the character and power of a poor man almost without a name, unknown in the European world, born and educated in the American wilderness, out of which he had never set his foot till 1778. Thanks to the wisdom, virtue, dignity, and fortitude of congress, all their arts were defeated in America. And thanks to the intelligence, integrity, and firmness of Mr. Jay, they were totally disappointed at Paris. For, without his coöperation, no effectual resistance could have been made, as Mr. Jefferson and Mr. Laurens were not present.

A clamor will no doubt be raised, and a horror excited, because Franklin is dead. To this, at present, I shall say no more than that his letters still live, that his enmity to me is recorded in history, and that I never heard it was unlawful to say that Cæsar was ambitious, Cato proud, Cicero vain, Brutus and Seneca as well as Pompey, usurers; or that the divine Socrates gave advice to a courtesan in her trade, and was even suspected of very infamous vices with Alcibiades and other boys,—because they were dead.

Franklin had a great genius, original, sagacious, and inventive, capable of discoveries in science no less than of improvements in the fine arts and the mechanic arts. He had a vast imagination, equal to the comprehension of the greatest objects, and capable of a steady and cool comprehension of them. He had wit at will. He had humor that, when he pleased, was delicate and delightful. He had a satire that was good-natured or caustic, Horace or Juvenal, Swift or Rabelais, at his pleasure. He had talents for irony, allegory, and fable, that he could adapt with great skill to the promotion of moral and political truth. He was master of that infantine simplicity which the French call *naïveté*, which never fails to charm, in Phædrus and La Fontaine, from the cradle to the grave. Had he been blessed with the same advantages of scholastic education in his early youth, and pursued a course of studies as unembarrassed with occupations of public and private life, as Sir Isaac Newton, he might have emulated the first philosopher. Although I am not ignorant that most of his positions and hypotheses have been controverted, I cannot but think he has added much to the mass of natural knowledge, and contributed largely to the progress of the human mind, both by his own writings and by the controversies and experiments he has excited in all parts of Europe. He had abilities for investigating statistical questions, and in some parts of his life has written pamphlets and essays upon public topics with great ingenuity and success; but after

my acquaintance with him, which commenced in congress in 1775, his excellence as a legislator, a politician, or a negotiator most certainly never appeared. No sentiment more weak and superficial was ever avowed by the most absurd philosopher than some of his, particularly one that he procured to be inserted in the first constitution of Pennsylvania, and for which he had such a fondness as to insert it in his will. I call it weak, for so it must have been, or hypocritical; unless he meant by one satiric touch to ridicule his own republic, or throw it into everlasting contempt.

I must acknowledge, after all, that nothing in life has mortified or grieved me more than the necessity which compelled me to oppose him so often as I have. He was a man with whom I always wished to live in friendship, and for that purpose omitted no demonstration of respect, esteem, and veneration in my power, until I had unequivocal proofs of his hatred, for no other reason under the sun, but because I gave my judgment in opposition to his, in many points which materially affected the interests of our country, and in many more which essentially concerned our happiness, safety, and well-being. I could not and would not sacrifice the clearest dictates of my understanding and the purest principles of morals and policy in compliance to Dr. Franklin. When historians shall hereafter inform posterity that Mr. Adams was not beloved by his venerable colleague, it is to be hoped that they will explain this truth by adding, that Mr. Izard, Mr. Lee, Mr. Dana, and many other honest patriots were not beloved by him, and that Mr. Silas Deane and many others of his stamp were beloved by him.

What shall we do with these gentlemen of great souls and vast views, who, without the least tincture of vanity, *bonâ fide* believe themselves the greatest men in the world, fully qualified and clearly entitled to govern their governors and command their commanders as well as their equals and inferiors, purely for their good and without the smallest interest for themselves? Though it may be true, as Dr. Young says, proud as this world is, there is more superiority in it given than assumed, yet it is certain there is sometimes more assumed than the world is willing to give. (pp. 659-64)

John Adams, "Appendix B," in his The Works of John Adams, Second President of the United States: With a Life of the Author, Notes and Illustrations, Vol. I, *edited by Charles Francis Adams, Little, Brown and Company, 1856, pp. 649-64.*

William Cullen Bryant   (speech date 1874)

[Bryant is considered one of the most accomplished American poets of the nineteenth century. His poetic treatment of the themes of nature and mutability marks him as one of the earliest figures in the Romantic movement in American literature. In the following speech, originally delivered in 1874, Bryant discusses Franklin's accomplishments as a statesman and a poet.]

The illustrious printer and journalist whose birth we this evening commemorate is often spoken of with praise as an acute observer of nature and of men, as a philosopher, as an inventor, as an able negotiator, as a statesman. But in this latter respect, the capacity of statesman, he has not received all the praise which is his due. For he saw, as it seems to me, farther into the true province and office of a free government, and the duties of its legislators, than any man of his time. He saw and pointed out the folly of governing too much. He saw that it is not the business of a government to do what can be done by individuals. He saw that what the Government had to do was to restrain its citizens from invading each other's rights, and compel them to respect each other's freedom. He therefore condemned the corn laws—the laws against the importation of grain—a hundred years before the people of Great Britain became convinced of their folly and repealed them. He held also that it was not the policy of a state to put any limitations on paper credit—in other words, he was for free banking, believing that the intermeddling of the Government with that branch of commercial business could only lead to mischief. Franklin saw also the wisdom and humanity of mitigating the calamities of war by allowing trading vessels to pass and repass unmolested on the high seas in time of war, and, before he returned from Europe in 1785, he negotiated a treaty with Prussia which contained an article against privateering. Thus he anticipated by more than half a century the proposition which our Government has since made to Great Britain.

Franklin is not often spoken of as a witty man, but his wit was as remarkable as his statesmanship. I think that he would have had as much wit as Swift or as Voltaire if he had but cultivated this talent. Only his clear, practical good sense predominated, and he never showed himself in the capacity of a humorist save when some practical purpose was to be effected by it. Only twenty-four days before his death he composed the amusing parody of a speech delivered on the floor of Congress by Mr. Jackson in defence of slavery—a parody which evidently suggested to Sidney Smith the famous conservative oration of Noodle. I took up lately a French biographical account of Franklin, and there I found a list of some of the proverbs coined by him, and added to the common stock. Among these was one illustrating the difficulty which those who are in extreme poverty find in keeping to the strict line of rectitude. "It is hard," said Franklin, "to make an empty bag stand upright." **"The Petition of the Left Hand"** and the **"Dialogue between Franklin and the Gout"** are examples of his wit, which was all of the genuine sort. I suppose he never made a pun in his life, because he could see no use for it.

If I should say that Franklin was also a poet, this assembly, I suppose, would smile. Yet the poetic element was not wanting in his mental constitution, though he did not write verses, at least but rarely. You remember his tract written on seeing a fly crawl out from a glass of Madeira wine just drawn from the cask, where it had been immersed, perhaps, for years. That was a fine poetic thought which he wrought out from that circumstance, of being himself preserved in a state of suspended animation by some such means for a century or two, and being then recalled to life and the world and shown the mighty changes which had taken place in the interval in the aspect of things and the state of society—a new and strange world

in place of the one which he inhabited. But the most remarkable example of his possession of the poetic faculty was given when, in the year 1787, he sat in the convention which framed the Federal Constitution. As the convention finished its labors, the sun, emerging from a cloud, poured a flood of radiance into the hall where the assembly was held. You know that the ancients made the god of the sun, Phœbus Apollo, the god of poetry also, and the source of poetic inspiration. The aged philosopher, then in his eighty-second year, caught the inspiration, and, in a few well-chosen words, accepted and proclaimed the omen. I cannot give the precise words, because I have not been able lately to find the record of them, but they were in substance these: "Thus," he said, "are the clouds that lowered over our Republic in its infancy destined to pass away. Thus will the smile of Heaven be vouchsafed to our completed labors, and the sunshine of prosperity rest on our country!" My friends, may his words, in all the coming time, prove as prophetic as they are poetical. (pp. 329-31)

William Cullen Bryant, "Franklin as Poet," in his Prose Writings of William Cullen Bryant, Travels, Addresses, and Comments, Vol. 2, *edited by Parke Godwin, 1884. Reprint by Russell & Russell, Inc., 1964, pp. 329-31.*

D. H. Lawrence   (essay date 1923)

[*Lawrence was an English novelist, poet, and essayist noted for introducing the themes of modern psychology to English fiction. In his lifetime he was a controversial figure, both for the explicit sexuality he portrayed in his novels and for his unconventional personal life. Much of the criticism of Lawrence's work concerns his highly individualistic moral system, which was based on absolute freedom of expression, particularly sexual. Human sexuality was for Lawrence a symbol of the Life Force, and is frequently pitted against modern industrial society, which he believed was dehumanizing. In the following excerpt originally published in 1923, he inveighs against Franklin and the rigidly moralistic principles that he promulgated.*]

The Perfectibility of Man! Ah heaven, what a dreary theme! The perfectibility of the Ford car! The perfectibility of which man? I am many men. Which of them are you going to perfect? I am not a mechanical contrivance.

Education! Which of the various me's do you propose to educate, and which do you propose to suppress?

Anyhow, I defy you. I defy you, oh society, to educate me or to suppress me, according to your dummy standards.

The ideal man! And which is he, if you please? Benjamin Franklin or Abraham Lincoln? The ideal man! Roosevelt or Porfirio Díaz?

There are other men in me, besides this patient ass who sits here in a tweed jacket. What am I doing, playing the patient ass in a tweed jacket? Who am I talking to? Who are you, at the other end of this patience?

Who are you? How many selves have you? And which of these selves do you want to be?

Is Yale College going to educate the self that is in the dark of you, or Harvard College?

The ideal self! Oh, but I have a strange and fugitive self shut out and howling like a wolf or a coyote under the ideal windows. See his red eyes in the dark? This is the self who is coming into his own.

The perfectibility of man, dear God! When every man as long as he remains alive is in himself a multitude of conflicting men. Which of these do you choose to perfect, at the expense of every other?

Old Daddy Franklin will tell you. He'll rig him up for you, the pattern American. Oh, Franklin was the first downright American. He knew what he was about, the sharp little man. He set up the first dummy American.

At the beginning of his career this cunning little Benjamin drew up for himself a creed that should "satisfy the professors of every religion, but shock none."

Now wasn't that a real American thing to do?

"That there is One God, who made all things."

(But Benjamin made Him.)

"That He governs the world by His Providence."

(Benjamin knowing all about Providence.)

"That He ought to be worshipped with adoration, prayer, and thanksgiving."

(Which cost nothing.)

"But—" But me no buts, Benjamin, saith the Lord.

"But that the most acceptable service of God is doing good to men."

(God having no choice in the matter.)

"That the soul is immortal."

(You'll see why, in the next clause.)

"And that God will certainly reward virtue and punish vice, either here or hereafter."

Now if Mr. Andrew Carnegie, or any other millionaire, had wished to invent a God to suit his ends, he could not have done better. Benjamin did it for him in the eighteenth century. God is the supreme servant of men who want to get on, to *produce*. Providence. The provider. The heavenly storekeeper. The everlasting Wanamaker.

And this is all the God the grandsons of the Pilgrim Fathers had left. Aloft on a pillar of dollars.

"That the soul is immortal."

The trite way Benjamin says it!

But man has a soul, though you can't locate it either in his purse or his pocket-book or his heart or his stomach or his head. The *wholeness* of a man is his soul. Not merely that nice little comfortable bit which Benjamin marks out.

It's a queer thing is a man's soul. It is the whole of him. Which means it is the unknown him, as well as the known. It seems to me just funny, professors and Benjamins fixing

the functions of the soul. Why, the soul of man is a vast forest, and all Benjamin intended was a neat back garden. And we've all got to fit into his kitchen garden scheme of things. Hail Columbia!

The soul of man is a dark forest. The Hercynian Wood that scared the Romans so, and out of which came the white-skinned hordes of the next civilization.

Who knows what will come out of the soul of man? The soul of man is a dark vast forest, with wild life in it. Think of Benjamin fencing it off!

Oh, but Benjamin fenced a little tract that he called the soul of man, and proceeded to get it into cultivation. Providence, forsooth! And they think that bit of barbed wire is going to keep us in pound for ever? More fools they.

This is Benjamin's barbed wire fence. He made himself a list of virtues, which he trotted inside like a grey nag in a paddock.

1

TEMPERANCE

Eat not to fulness; drink not to elevation.

2

SILENCE

Speak not but what may benefit others or yourself; avoid trifling conversation.

The house in Boston where Franklin was born in 1706.

3

ORDER

Let all your things have their places; let each
part of your business have its time.

4

RESOLUTION

Resolve to perform what you ought; perform
without fail what you resolve.

5

FRUGALITY

Make no expense but to do good to others or
yourself—i.e., waste nothing.

6

INDUSTRY

Lose no time, be always employed in something
useful; cut off all unnecessary action.

7

SINCERITY

Use no hurtful deceit; think innocently and justly, and, if you speak, speak accordingly.

8

JUSTICE

Wrong none by doing injuries, or omitting the
benefits that are your duty.

9

MODERATION

Avoid extremes, forbear resenting injuries as
much as you think they deserve.

10

CLEANLINESS

Tolerate no uncleanliness in body, clothes, or
habitation.

11

TRANQUILLITY

Be not disturbed at trifles, or at accidents common or unavoidable.

12

CHASTITY

Rarely use venery but for health and offspring,
never to dulness, weakness, or the injury of your
own or another's peace or reputation.

13

HUMILITY

Imitate Jesus and Socrates.

A Quaker friend told Franklin that he, Benjamin, was generally considered proud, so Benjamin put in the Humility

touch as an afterthought. The amusing part is the sort of
humility it displays. "Imitate Jesus and Socrates," and
mind you don't outshine either of these two. One can just
imagine Socrates and Alcibiades roaring in their cups over
Philadelphian Benjamin, and Jesus looking at him a little
puzzled, and murmuring: "Aren't you wise in your own
conceit, Ben?"

"Henceforth be masterless," retorts Ben. "Be ye each one
his own master unto himself, and don't let even the Lord
put His spoke in." "Each man his own master" is but a
puffing up of masterlessness.

Well, the first of Americans practised this enticing list
with assiduity, setting a national example. He had the virtues in columns, and gave himself good and bad marks according as he thought his behaviour deserved. Pity these
conduct charts are lost to us. He only remarks that Order
was his stumbling block. He could not learn to be neat and
tidy.

Isn't it nice to have nothing worse to confess?

He was a little model, was Benjamin. Doctor Franklin.
Snuff-coloured little man! Immortal soul and all!

The immortal soul part was a sort of cheap insurance policy.

Benjamin had no concern, really, with the immortal soul.
He was too busy with social man.

1. He swept and lighted the streets of young Philadelphia.

2. He invented electrical appliances.

3. He was the centre of a moralizing club in Philadelphia,
and he wrote the moral humorisms of Poor Richard.

4. He was a member of all the important councils of Philadelphia, and then of the American colonies.

5. He won the cause of American Independence at the
French Court, and was the economic father of the United
States.

Now what more can you want of a man? And yet he is
infra dig., even in Philadelphia.

I admire him. I admire his sturdy courage first of all, then
his sagacity, then his glimpsing into the thunders of electricity, then his common-sense humour. All the qualities
of a great man, and never more than a great citizen. Mid-
dle-sized, sturdy, snuff-coloured Doctor Franklin, one of
the soundest citizens that ever trod or "used venery."

I do not like him.

And, by the way, I always thought books of Venery were
about hunting deer.

There is a certain earnest naïveté about him. Like a child.
And like a little old man. He has again become as a little
child, always as wise as his grandfather, or wiser.

Perhaps, as I say, the most complete citizen that ever
"used venery."

Printer, philosopher, scientist, author and patriot, impec-
cable husband and citizen, why isn't he an archetype?

Pioneer, Oh Pioneers! Benjamin was one of the greatest pioneers of the United States. Yet we just can't do with him.

What's wrong with him then? Or what's wrong with us?

I can remember, when I was a little boy, my father used to buy a scrubby yearly almanac with the sun and moon and stars on the cover. And it used to prophesy bloodshed and famine. But also crammed in corners it had little anecdotes and humorisms, with a moral tag. And I used to have my little priggish laugh at the woman who counted her chickens before they were hatched and so forth, and I was convinced that honesty was the best policy, also a little priggishly. The author of these bits was Poor Richard, and Poor Richard was Benjamin Franklin, writing in Philadelphia well over a hundred years before.

And probably I haven't got over those Poor Richard tags yet. I rankle still with them. They are thorns in young flesh.

Because, although I still believe that honesty is the best policy, I dislike policy altogether; though it is just as well not to count your chickens before they are hatched, its still more hateful to count them with gloating when they *are* hatched. It has taken me many years and countless smarts to get out of that barbed wire moral enclosure that Poor Richard rigged up. Here am I now in tatters and scratched to ribbons, sitting in the middle of Benjamin's America looking at the barbed wire, and the fat sheep crawling under the fence to get fat outside, and the watchdogs yelling at the gate lest by chance anyone should get out by the proper exit. Oh America! Oh Benjamin! And I just utter a long loud curse against Benjamin and the American corral.

Moral America! Most moral Benjamin. Sound, satisfied Ben!

He had to go to the frontiers of his State to settle some disturbance among the Indians. On this occasion he writes:

> We found that they had made a great bonfire in the middle of the square; they were all drunk, men and women quarrelling and fighting. Their dark-coloured bodies, half-naked, seen only by the gloomy light of the bonfire, running after and beating one another with fire-brands, accompanied by their horrid yellings, formed a scene the most resembling our ideas of hell that could well be imagined. There was no appeasing the tumult, and we retired to our lodging. At midnight a number of them came thundering at our door, demanding more rum, of which we took no notice.
>
> The next day, sensible they had misbehaved in giving us that disturbance, they sent three of their counsellors to make their apology. The orator acknowledged the fault, but laid it upon the rum, and then endeavoured to excuse the rum by saying: "The Great Spirit, who made all things, made everything for some use; and whatever he designed anything for, that use it should always be put to. Now, when he had made the rum, he said: 'Let this be for the Indians to get drunk with.' And it must be so."

> And, indeed, if it be the design of Providence to extirpate these savages in order to make room for the cultivators of the earth, it seems not improbable that rum may be the appointed means. It has already annihilated all the tribes who for merly inhabited all the seacoast. . . .

This, from the good doctor with such suave complacency, is a little disenchanting. Almost too good to be true.

But there you are! The barbed wire fence. "Extirpate these savages in order to make room for the cultivators of the earth." Oh, Benjamin Franklin! He even "used venery" as a cultivator of seed.

Cultivate the earth, ye gods! The Indians did that, as much as they needed. And they left off there. Who built Chicago? Who cultivated the earth until it spawned Pittsburgh, Pa?

The moral issue! Just look at it! Cultivation included. If it's a mere choice of Kultur or cultivation, I give it up.

Which brings us right back to our question, what's wrong with Benjamin, that we can't stand him? Or else, what's wrong with us, that we find fault with such a paragon?

Man is a moral animal. All right. I am a moral animal. And I'm going to remain such. I'm not going to be turned into a virtuous little automaton as Benjamin would have me. "This is good, that is bad. Turn the little handle and let the good tap flow," saith Benjamin, and all America with him. "But first of all extirpate those savages who are always turning on the bad tap."

I am a moral animal. But I am not a moral machine. I don't work with a little set of handles or levers. The Temperance-silence-order-resolution-frugality-industry-sincerity-justice-moderation-cleanliness-tranquillity-chastity-humility keyboard is not going to get me going. I'm really not just an automatic piano with a moral Benjamin getting tunes out of me.

Here's my creed, against Benjamin's. This is what I believe:

> "That I am I."
> "That my soul is a dark forest."
> "That my known self will never be more than a little clearing in the forest."
> "That gods, strange gods, come forth from the forest into the clearing of my known self, and then go back."
> "That I must have the courage to let them come and go."
> "That I will never let mankind put anything over me, but that I will try always to recognize and submit to the gods in me and the gods in other men and women."

There is my creed. He who runs may read. He who prefers to crawl, or to go by gasoline, can call it rot. (pp. 9-16)

And now I, at least, know why I can't stand Benjamin. He tries to take away my wholeness and my dark forest, my freedom. For how can any man be free, without an illimitable background? And Benjamin tries to shove me into a barbed wire paddock and make me grow potatoes or Chicagoes.

And how can I be free, without gods that come and go? But Benjamin won't let anything exist except my useful fellow men, and I'm sick of them; as for his Godhead, his Providence, He is Head of nothing except a vast heavenly store that keeps every imaginable line of goods, from victrolas to cat-o'-nine tails.

And how can any man be free without a soul of his own, that he believes in and won't sell at any price? But Benjamin doesn't let me have a soul of my own. He says I am nothing but a servant of mankind—galley-slave I call it—and if I don't get my wages here below—that is, if Mr. Pierpont Morgan or Mr. Nosey Hebrew or the grand United States Government, the great US, US or SOMEOFUS, manages to scoop in my bit, along with their lump—why, never mind, I shall get my wages HEREAFTER.

Oh Benjamin! Oh Binjum! You do NOT suck me in any longer.

And why, oh why should the snuff-coloured little trap have wanted to take us all in? Why did he do it?

Out of sheer human cussedness, in the first place. We do all like to get things inside a barbed wire corral. Especially our fellow men. We love to round them up inside the barbed wire enclosure of FREEDOM, and make 'em work. *"Work, you free jewel,* WORK!" shouts the liberator, cracking his whip. Benjamin, I will not work. I do not choose to be a free democrat. I am absolutely a servant of my own Holy Ghost.

Sheer cussedness! But there was as well the salt of a subtler purpose. Benjamin was just in his eyeholes—to use an English vulgarism, meaning he was just delighted—when he was at Paris judiciously milking money out of the French monarchy for the overthrow of all monarchy. If you want to ride your horse to somewhere you must put a bit in his mouth. And Benjamin wanted to ride his horse so that it would upset the whole apple-cart of the old masters. He wanted the whole European apple-cart upset. So he had to put a strong bit in the mouth of his ass.

"Henceforth be masterless."

That is, he had to break-in the human ass completely, so that much more might be broken, in the long run. For the moment it was the British Government that had to have a hole knocked in it. The first real hole it ever had: the breach of the American rebellion.

Benjamin, in his sagacity, knew that the breaking of the old world was a long process. In the depths of his own under-consciousness he hated England, he hated Europe, he hated the whole corpus of the European being. He wanted to be American. But you can't change your nature and mode of consciousness like changing your shoes. It is a gradual shedding. Years must go by, and centuries must elapse before you have finished. Like a son escaping from the domination of his parents. The escape is not just one rupture. It is a long and half-secret process.

So with the American. He was a European when he first went over the Atlantic. He is in the main a recreant European still. From Benjamin Franklin to Woodrow Wilson may be a long stride, but it is a stride along the same road.

There is no new road. The same old road, become dreary and futile. Theoretic and materialistic.

Why then did Benjamin set up this dummy of a perfect citizen as a pattern to America? Of course, he did it in perfect good faith, as far as he knew. He thought it simply was the true ideal. But what we *think* we do is not very important. We never really know what we are doing. Either we are materialistic instruments, like Benjamin, or we move in the gesture of creation, from our deepest self, usually unconscious. We are only the actors, we are never wholly the authors of our own deeds or works. IT is the author, the unknown inside us or outside us. The best we can do is to try to hold ourselves in unison with the deeps which are inside us. And the worst we can do is to try to have things our own way, when we run counter to IT, and in the long run get our knuckles rapped for our presumption.

So Benjamin contriving money out of the Court of France. He was contriving the first steps of the overthrow of all Europe, France included. You can never have a new thing without breaking an old. Europe happens to be the old thing. America, unless the people in America assert themselves too much in opposition to the inner gods, should be the new thing. The new thing is the death of the old. But you can't cut the throat of an epoch. You've got to steal the life from it through several centuries.

And Benjamin worked for this both directly and indirectly. Directly, at the Court of France, making a small but very dangerous hole in the side of England, through which hole Europe has by now almost bled to death. And indirectly in Philadelphia, setting up this unlovely, snuff-coloured little ideal, or automaton, of a pattern American. The pattern American, this dry, moral, utilitarian little democrat, has done more to ruin the old Europe than any Russian nihilist. He has done it by slow attrition, like a son who has stayed at home and obeyed his parents, all the while silently hating their authority, and silently, in his soul, destroying not only their authority but their whole existence. For the American spiritually stayed at home in Europe. The spiritual home of America was, and still is, Europe. This is the galling bondage, in spite of several billions of heaped-up gold. Your heaps of gold are only so many muck-heaps, America, and will remain so till you become a reality to yourselves.

All this Americanizing and mechanizing has been for the purpose of overthrowing the past. And now look at America, tangled in her own barbed wire, and mastered by her own machines. Absolutely got down by her own barbed wire of shalt-nots, and shut up fast in her own "productive" machines like millions of squirrels running in millions of cages. It is just a farce.

Now is your chance, Europe. Now let Hell loose and get your own back, and paddle your own canoe on a new sea, while clever America lies on her muck-heaps of gold, strangled in her own barbed wire of shalt-not ideals and shalt-not moralisms. While she goes out to work like millions of squirrels in millions of cages. Production!

Let Hell loose, and get your own back, Europe! (pp. 18-21)

D. H. Lawrence, "Benjamin Franklin," in his

Studies in Classic American Literature, *1923.*
Reprint by The Viking Press, 1964, pp. 9-21.

William Carlos Williams   (essay date 1925)

[*Williams was one of America's most renowned twenti-eth-century poets. Rejecting as overly academic the Modernist poetic style established by T. S. Eliot, he sought a more natural poetic expression, endeavoring to replicate the idiomatic cadences of American speech. In the following essay, he criticizes Franklin's practical-ness, contending that it is at odds with an apprehension of beauty.*]

"He's sort of proud of his commonness, isn't he?"

He was the balancer full of motion without direction, the gyroscope which by its large spinning kept us, at that early period of our fate, upon an even keel.

The greatest winner of his day, he represents a volup-tuousness of omnivorous energy brought to a dead stop by the rock of New World inopportunity. His energy never attained to a penetrant gist; rather it was stopped by and splashed upon the barrier, like a melon. His "good" was scattered about him. This is what is called being "practi-cal." At such "success" we smile to see Franklin often so puffed up.

In the sheer mass of his voluptuous energy lies his chief excuse—a trait he borrowed without recognition from the primitive profusion of his surroundings.

Relaxed in a mass of impedimenta he found opportunity for thought.

Franklin, along with all the responsible aristocrats of his period, shows the two major characteristics of a bulky, crude energy, something in proportion to the continent, and a colossal restraint equalizing it. The result must have been a complete cancellation, frustration or descent to a low plane for release, which latter alternative he chose shiningly.

He played with lightning and the French court.

The great force (which was in him the expression of the New World) must have had not only volume but a quality, the determination of which will identify him. It was in Franklin, as shown characteristically in this letter, a scat-tering to reconnoitre.

Poor Richard's Almanac was as important in founding the nation as Paine's *Age of Reason*—he adaged them into a kind of pride in possession.

By casting scorn at men merely of birth while stressing the foundation of estates which should be family strongholds he did the service of discouraging aristocracy and creating it—the qualifying condition being that he repelled that which was foreign and supported that which was native—on a lower level FOR THE TIME BEING. He sparred for time: he was a diplomat of distinction with positive New World characteristics.

His mind was ALL out of the New World. Feeling a strength, a backing which was the New itself, he could af-ford to be sly with France, England or any nation; since, to live, he had to be sly with the massive strength of that primitive wilderness with whose conditions he had been bred to battle: thus, used to a mass EQUAL to them, he could swing them too. So again he asserted his nativity.

Strong and New World in innate strength, he is without beauty. The force of the New World is never in these men open; it is sly, covert, almost cringing. It is the mass that forces them into praise of mediocrity to escape its compul-sions: so there is a kind of nastiness in his TOUCHING the hand of the Marchioness, in his meddling with the light-ning, a resentment against his upstart bumptiousness in advising London how to light its stupidly ill-lit streets.

There has not yet appeared in the New World any one with sufficient strength for the open assertion. So with Franklin, the tone is frightened and horribly smug—at his worst; it flames a little in de Soto; it is necessary to Boone to lose himself in the wilds; there are no women—Houston's bride is frightened off; the New Englanders are the clever bone-men. Nowhere the open, free assertion save in the Indian: this is the quality. Jones has to leave the American navy, we feel, to go to Russia, for release.

It is necessary in appraising our history to realize that the nation was the offspring of the desire to huddle, to pro-tect—of terror—superadded to a new world of great beau-ty and ripest blossom that well-nigh no man of distinction saw save Boone.

Franklin is the full development of the timidity, the strength that denies itself.

Such is his itch to serve science.

"Education" represented to these pioneers an *obscure* knowledge of the great beauty that was denied them, but of the great beauty under their feet no man seems to have been conscious, to appreciable degree; the foundation they must *first* appraise.

Nowhere does the full assertion come through save as a joke, jokingly, that masks the rest.

The terrible beauty of the New World attracts men to their ruin. Franklin did not care to be ruined—he only wanted to touch.

"I wish he hadn't gone fooling with lightning; I wish he'd left it alone—the old fool." Sure enough, he didn't dare let it go in at the top of his head and out at his toes, that's it; he *had* to fool with it. He sensed the power and knew only enough to want to run an engine with it. His fingers itched to be meddling, to do the little concrete thing—the barrier against a flood of lightning that would inundate him. Of course he was the most useful, "the most industri-ous citizen that Philadelphia or America had ever known." He was the dike keeper, keeping out the wilder-ness with his wits. Fear drove his curiosity.

Do something, anything, to keep the fingers busy—not to realize—the lightning. Be industrious, let money and com-fort increase; money is like a bell that keeps the dance from terrifying, as it would if it were silent and we could hear the grunt,—thud—swish. It is small, hard; it keeps the attention fixed so that the eyes shall not see. And such is humor: pennies—that see gold come of copper by adding together, shrewd guesses hidden under the armament of an humble jest.

Poor Richard.

Don't offend.

His mighty answer to the New World's offer of a great embrace was THRIFT. Work night and day, build up, penny by penny, a wall against that which is threatening, the terror of life, poverty. Make a fort to be secure in.

The terrific energy of the new breed is its first character; the second is its terror before the NEW.

As a boy, he had tentatively loosed himself once to love, to curiosity perhaps, which was the birth of his first son. But the terror of that dare must have frightened the soul out of him. Having dared that once, his heart recoiled; his teaching must have smitten him. But Franklin, shrewd fellow, did not succumb to the benumbing judgment and go branded, repentant or rebellious. He trotted off gaily to Philly and noticed Bettsy in the shop on Arch Street, the first day.

He is our wise prophet of chicanery, the great buffoon, the face on the penny stamp.

The shock his youth got went into the fibre of the Constitution: he joked himself into a rich life—so he joked the country into a good alliance: to fortify, to buckle up—and reserve a will to be gay, to BE—(on the side).

Poor Richard: Save, be rich—and do as you please— might have been his motto, with an addendum: provided your house has strong walls and thick shutters.

Prince Richard in the lamb's skin: with a tongue in the cheek for aristocracy, humbly, arrogantly (that you may wish to imitate me) touching everything.

To want to touch, not to wish anything to remain clean, aloof—comes always of a kind of timidity, from fear.

The character they had (our pioneer statesmen, etc.) was that of giving their fine energy, as they must have done, to the smaller, narrower, protective thing and not to the great, New World. Yet they cannot quite leave hands off it but must TOUCH it, in a "practical" way, that is a joking, shy, nasty way, using "science" etc., not with the generosity of the savage or scientist but in a shameful manner. The sweep of the force was too horrible to them; it would have swept them into chaos. They HAD to do as they *could* but it can be no offense that their quality should be *named*. They could have been inspired by the new QUALITY about them to yield to loveliness in a fresh spirit.

It is the placing of his enthusiasm that characterizes the man.

It is not to mark Franklin, but to attempt to appraise the nature of the difficulties that molded him, the characteristic *weight of the mass;* how nearly all our national heroes have been driven back—and praised by reason of their shrewdness in making walls: not in bursting into flower.

To discover the NEW WORLD: that there is something

there: what it has done to us, its quality, its weight, its prophets, its—horrible temper.

The niggardliness of our history, our stupidity, sluggishness of spirit, the falseness of our historical notes, the complete missing of the point. Addressed to the wrong head, the tenacity with which the fear still inspires laws, customs,—the suppression of the superb corn dance of the Chippewas, since it symbolizes the generative processes,— as if morals have but one character, and that,—SEX: while morals are deformed in the name of PURITY; till, in the confusion, almost nothing remains of the great American New World but a memory of the Indian. (pp. 153-57)

> *William Carlos Williams, in his* In the American Grain, *Albert & Charles Boni, 1925, 235 p.*

Charles Angoff   (essay date 1931)

[*A naturalized American citizen born in Russia, Angoff was a prolific writer of novels, plays, short stories, and literary criticism, who is most famous for his series of novels describing the Jewish experience in American life. Also a prominent journalist, he was associated with many American newspapers and magazines, and served as editor of the* American Mercury *and the* Literary Review, *among others. In the following excerpt, he acknowledges that Franklin's influence on American literature and thought was great, but contends that his works lack philosophical depth and poetic artistry.*]

Franklin made a relatively small contribution to the American argument during the Revolutionary period. He exerted a powerful influence, but it was "chiefly through the customary channels of diplomacy, and in a voluminous correspondence with friends and public men on both sides of the Atlantic; and his contemporary publications, comparatively few in number, carried weight because of their directness and sturdy common sense, and of the fame of their writer" [according to William McDonald in *The Cambridge History of American Literature,* 1927] rather than because of their intrinsic merit. He never knew precisely what all the noise was about, and the philosophical and theological pamphlets of such men as Mayhew, Cooper, Otis, and Lee always left him somewhat puzzled. Indeed, so doubtful was he of the principles involved that more than once he came pretty close to allying himself with the loyalists. But on each occasion luck was with him, and he chose the right side.

He was the first great fixer of American political history, and also, if John Adams is to be believed, its first great trimmer. He made friends of the English, he made friends of the French, he made friends of the Germans, he made friends of the Federalists, he made friends of the Republicans, and when he died the whole civilized world mourned him. Just where he stood on any one of the fundamental issues is still something of a mystery. He trusted the people, and he didn't trust them. He claimed to be a deist, but he contributed to all the churches in his neighborhood, and believed in the transmigration of souls. All his life long he preached a copy-book morality, but he himself was extremely careless in his personal affairs. He spent money lavishly, ate so much that he suffered from gout for years and years, and when he was married at the age of twenty-four brought to his wife, as a wedding present, an illegitimate son.

He wrote a great deal, but it was chiefly to make money, or to forget the pain of his gout. He knew his public well. He made a fortune as a newspaper and a magazine editor, and his *Poor Richard's Almanac* was an immediate success: it sold 10,000 copies within the first three months of publication. He did not produce one truly great work of the imagination, and his general style was surely not above the ordinary, but his work achieved an amazing popularity.

All this was probably a colossal misfortune to the United States, for, despite his good fellowship and occasional good sense, Franklin represented the least praiseworthy qualities of the inhabitants of the New World: miserliness, fanatical practicality, and lack of interest in what are usually known as spiritual things. Babbittry was not a new thing in America, but he made a religion of it, and by his tremendous success with it he grafted it upon the American people so securely that the national genius is still suffering from it. He extolled the virtues of honesty, industry, chastity, cleanliness, and temperance—all excellent things. But it never occurred to him that with these alone life is not worth a fool's second thought. Philosophy, poetry, and the arts spring from different sources.

Franklin was born in Boston on January 17, 1706. At the age of ten he was taken from school to assist his father, a tallow chandler and soap-boiler by trade. Three years later he was apprenticed to his older brother James, editor and publisher of the *New England Courant.* He began his career as a writer by slipping under the door of his brother's printing office an anonymous contribution, which was accepted. He was unable to get along with James, so in 1723 he ran away from Boston, first to New York, and then to Philadelphia, where he found work in the printing office of one Samuel Keimer, a Jew. The following year he went to London to get type to open an office of his own, but instead he spent the next two years in drinking and whoring. In 1726 he was penniless, so he returned to Philadelphia, where he opened a shop of his own, in which he did a great deal of the public printing of Pennsylvania, Delaware, and New Jersey. In 1728 he formed the Junto Club for group reading and debating, and for the purpose of helping reform the world.

In 1729 he bought from Keimer the *Universal Instructor in All Arts and Sciences and Pennsylvania Gazette,* which at the time had a subscription list of not more than 90. The paper in time became the leading public print between New York and Charleston. He wrote a number of essays for it, including **"A Meditation on a Quart Mug," "Dialogue Between Philocles and Horatio Concerning Virtue and Pleasure,"** and **"A Witch Trial at Mount Holly."** About this time he also wrote the pamphlet, *A Modest Inquiry into the Nature and Necessity of Paper Currency.* The argument in it was a wholly false one, but it got Franklin the job of printing most of the worthless paper money of Pennsylvania.

In 1732 he began the publication of *Poor Richard's Almanac,* which for twenty-five years was one of the most popular publications in the Colonies. Its average annual sale was more than 10,000 copies. In the same year he established in Philadelphia the first circulating library in America. In 1730 he married Deborah Read of Philadelphia. She died in 1774. In 1741 he began the second monthly publication in America, the *General Magazine and Historical Chronicle for All the British Colonies in America,* which died with the sixth number.

Franklin had very little schooling in his youth, but he made up for it by omnivorous reading. While still in his teens he read Plutarch, Bunyan, Defoe, Mather, Locke, Collins, Hume, and Shaftesbury. He early became interested in scientific matters, and kept that interest up till his dying day. Nothing was alien to his experimental mind. He was in the habit of writing about his experiments and general ideas to scientists and philosophers in Europe, and thus he earned the respect of many of them. He in this way became the friend, in England, of Collinson, Priestley, Price, Hume, Adam Smith, Robertson, Lord Kames, Mandeville, Joseph Banks, Bishop Watson, Burke, Chatham, and Lord Shelburne; and in France, of Turgot, Mirabeau, Quesnay, La Rochefoucauld, Lafayette, Vergennes, Condorcet, Buffon, Voltaire, Robespierre, Lavoisier, and D'Alembert. His electrical experiments he used to report in the form of letters to the English physicist, Peter Collinson, who later published all of them in London in 1751 under the title, *Experiments and Observations on Electricity, Made at Philadelphia in America, by Mr. Benjamin Franklin.* The following year Franklin showed the identity of lightning and electricity by his famous kite experiment, and he invented the lightning rod at the same time.

He began his active political life in 1736, when he was chosen clerk of the General Assembly of Pennsylvania; he retained the office till 1750. In 1737 he was made postmaster of the Colony. About the same time he organized a night watch, a fire company, the American Philosophical Society, and a sort of high high-school, which in 1779 became the University of Pennsylvania. In 1751 he helped establish a hospital in Philadelphia. By this time, because of his scientific discoveries, he had an international reputation, and was the foremost individual man in the Colonies. Harvard, Yale, Oxford, and St. Andrews gave him honorary degrees. He was elected a Fellow of the Royal Society, and was one of the eight foreign associates of the French Academy of Science. So great was his renown then that Lord Jeffrey, editor of the *Edinburgh Review,* said of him: "In one point of view the name of Franklin must be considered as standing higher than any of the others which illustrated the Eighteenth Century. Distinguished as a statesman he was equally great as a philosopher, thus uniting in himself a rare degree of excellence in both these pursuits, to excel in either of which is deemed the highest praise."

He was a member of the Colonial Congress held in Albany in 1754, at which he submitted a plan for colonial union. The Congress adopted the plan, but it was rejected by the colonial assemblies. In 1759 he wrote **"An Historical Review of the Constitution and Government of Pennsylva-**

nia," and then went to England as a representative of the Province. He returned to America in 1762, and in 1763 traveled in all the Colonies inspecting the postal service in each. He worked mightily against the Stamp Act, but when it was finally passed by Parliament he thought it would be enforced, and he suggested his friend John Hughes as stamp distributor of Pennsylvania. This was a great political blunder, and for the rest of his days it was brought up against him by his enemies. In 1766 he went to England again, and appeared at the bar of the House of Commons to answer questions in regard to the situation in America. In the political discussions at home in the next eight years he contributed several articles to the newspapers, but he was not one of the leaders. His course was too moderate for the extremists in either country. Nobody really knew precisely where he stood, so evasive was he. He kept up this caution even after he signed the Declaration of Independence, and it was largely on account of the lack of definiteness in his political opinions that John Adams, in a letter to his cousin, Samuel Adams, dated December 7, 1778, said of him:

> He loves his Ease, hates to offend, and seldom gives any opinion till obliged to do it. . . . You know that, although he has as determined a soul as any man, yet it is his constant Policy never to say "yes" or "no" decidedly but when he cannot avoid it.

Nevertheless, he managed to win back the confidence of the people at large after the Revolution, and in 1776 he was made president of the Constitutional Convention of Pennsylvania. In the same year he was chosen as envoy to France, where he showed great skill as a negotiator. He was also a great success socially. He was the star attraction in the salons of Mmes. Helvetius and Brillon. He set up a printing press of his own in Passy, and there printed a collection of writings since known as *The Bagatelles.* They included **"The Ephemera," "The Morals of Chess," "The Whistle,"** and **"The Dialogue Between Franklin and the Gout."** They were all written between 1778 and 1785 for the amusement of his friends in Paris. They were not a new literary form for him. In 1773 he published in the *Gentleman's Magazine* two similar things: **"An Edict by the King of Prussia"** and **"Rules by which A Great Empire May Be Reduced to A Small One."** Stuart P. Sherman, in a burst of enthusiasm [in his 1922 work, *Americans*], called them masterpieces of irony, adding that "Swift might have been pleased to sign" them.

On his return to this country in 1785 he took part in the debates of the Constitutional Convention, but it was hardly a prominent part. Franklin was very good in organizing post offices and fire departments, but he was completely lost when it came to drafting organic bodies of laws. Basic philosophical ideas were beyond him. He did not approve of the new Constitution, but he regarded it as the best obtainable and therefore signed it. His last act was the signing of an anti-slavery petition to Congress as president of the Pennsylvania Society for Promoting the Abolition of Slavery. He died in Philadelphia on April 17, 1790, at the age of eighty-four.

One American critic [John T. Morse in his *Benjamin Franklin,* 1889] has said, "Intellectually there are few men who are Franklin's peers in all the ages and nations." This opinion must be put down as an amiable exaggeration. Franklin had an excellent mind, but surely he was not a philosopher. Abstract ideas, save those of the corner grocery store, somehow irked him. He was not an original thinker, but he was one of the best eclectic thinkers who ever lived. He lived in an age of rationalism, and few other men of that time were so imbued with the ideas then afloat. The current French philosophy was in large part precisely to his taste. "In their youth, Voltaire and Franklin had both drunk at the same spring: the English radicalism of Gordon, Collins, and Shaftesbury. But Voltaire had developed it into a witty, dry and sharp-tongued philosophy, while Franklin had expanded it with good fellowship and sentimentality" [Bernard Faÿ, *Franklin: The Apostle of Modern Times,* 1929].

This good fellowship of his explains his strange brand of deism. He was not a believer, but there were many reservations to his unbelief. In Paris he refused to have any priests around him, and this caused much surprise in a land where every diplomat had his private chaplain. He told everybody that he could say his prayers himself. [According to Faÿ] "He considered the Church of Rome to be like raw sugar, the American churches like refined sugar, for they were less influenced by hierarchical systems or mysticism. He saw a certain advantage in the multiplicity of churches in the world, as that made for competition and competition made for trade, but he didn't think churches were of any importance in Heaven." He spoke of miracles with levity, but he had some belief in Pythagoreanism. In other words he was pretty much confused about the whole business. His main contribution to the religious question was little more than a good-natured tolerance influenced largely by his shrewd business sense. Nobody but Franklin could have reconciled deism with the practice of contributing money to all the denominations in Philadelphia.

On the few occasions when he tried to be philosophical about religion he made a sorry spectacle, as in the following celebrated letter to Dr. Ezra Stiles, president of Yale. The letter is dated March 9, 1790—a little more than a month before Franklin's death.

> You desire to know something of my Religion. It is the first time that I have been questioned upon it. But I do not take your curiosity amiss, & shall endeavor in a few words to gratify it. Here is my Creed. I believe in one God, Creator of the Universe: That he governs the World by his Providence. That he ought to be worshipped. That the most acceptable service we can render to him, is doing good to his other Children. That the Soul of Man is immortal, and will be treated with Justice in another Life, respect^g its Conduct in this. These I take to be the fundamental Principles of all sound Religion, and I regard them as you do, in whatever Sect I meet with them. As to *Jesus of Nazareth,* my Opinion of whom you particularly desire, I think the *System of Morals & his Religion as he left them to us, the best the World ever saw;* but I apprehend it has received various corrupting changes; and I have, with most of the present Dissenters in Engld,

some Doubts as to his Divinity: tho' it is a question I do not dogmatize upon, hav⁸ never studied it, & think it needless to busy myself with it now, when I expect soon an Opport^y of know⁸ the Truth with less Trouble. I see no harm however in its being believed, if that Belief has the good Consequence, as probably it has, of mak⁸ his Doctrines more respected & better observed, esp^y as I do not perceive that the Supreme [Being] takes it amiss, by distinguish⁸ the Believers, in his Gov^t of the World, with any particular Marks of his Displeasure. I shall only add respect⁸ myself, that hav⁸ experienced the Goodness of that Being in conducting me prosperously thro' a long Life, I have no doubt of its Continuance in the next, tho' without the smallest Conceit of meriting such Goodness.

Try to imagine Thomas Paine dismissing God and the churches in so flippant a way!

Franklin's most popular work was, and still is, his *Autobiography.* It was the longest of his writings, and the one he did most carelessly. He wrote it whenever he felt like it, and apparently cared very little if it was ever published. The greater part of it he composed while he was in England as agent for the United Colonies. Parts of it were printed in France between 1791 and 1798, but the complete *Autobiography* did not appear till 1868 under the editorship of John Bigelow, who copied it from the original MS., which he obtained in France.

John Bach McMaster the historian has called the book the greatest biographical work of any kind ever written in America, and has compared it to Defoe's *Robinson Crusoe* in literary merit. The book is very simply written, and is quite readable. But it is lacking in almost everything else necessary to a really great work of *belles lettres:* grace of expression, charm of personality, and intellectual flight. The essential commonplaceness of the man is in every line of it. He was incapable of dreaming, of doubting, of being mystified. The only mysteries he understood were those that lent themselves easily to experimentation. The mysteries of poetry, of philosophy, and even of religion were beyond him. Doing good, making money, and gaining the approbation of one's fellows were the only things that occupied him when addressing the public. Witness his "Scheme for Aiming at Moral Perfection":

> It was about this time I conceiv'd the bold and arduous project of arriving at moral perfection. I wish'd to live without committing any fault at any time; I would conquer all that either natural inclination, custom, or company might lead me into. . . .

> In the various enumerations of the moral virtues I had met with in my reading, I found the catalogue more or less numerous, as different writers included more or fewer ideas under the same name. Temperance, for example, was by some confined to eating and drinking, while by others it was extended to mean moderating every other pleasure, appetite, inclination, or passion, bodily or mental, even to our avarice and ambition. I

To the *Author* of the New-England Courant.

SIR,   [No 3

IT is undoubtedly the Duty of all Persons to serve the Country they live in, according to their Abilities; yet I sincerely acknowledge, that I have hitherto been very deficient in this Particular; whether it was for want of Will or Opportunity, I will not at present stand to determine: Let it suffice, that I now take up a Resolution, to do for the future all that *lies in my Way* for the Service of my Countrymen.

I HAVE from my Youth been indefatigably studious to gain and treasure up in my Mind all useful and desireable Knowledge, especially such as tends to Improve the Mind, and enlarge the Understanding: And as I have found it very beneficial to me, I am not without Hopes, that communicating my small Stock in this Manner, by Peace-meal to the Publick, may be at least in some Measure useful.

I AM very sensible that it is impossible for me, or indeed any *one* Writer to please *all* Readers at once. Various Persons have different Sentiments; and that which is pleasant and delightful to one, gives another a Disgust. He that would (in this Way of Writing) please all, is under a Necessity to make his Themes almost as numerous as his Letters. He must one while be merry and diverting, then more solid and serious; one while sharp and satyrical, then (to mollify that) be sober and religious; at one Time let the Subject be Politicks, then let the next Theme be Love: Thus will every one, one Time or other find some thing agreeable to his own Fancy, and in his Turn be delighted.

ACCORDING to this Method I intend to proceed, bestowing now and then a few gentle Reproofs on those who deserve them, not forgetting at the same time to applaud those whose Actions merit Commendation. And here I must not forget to invite the ingenious Part of your Readers, particularly those of my own Sex to enter into a Correspondence with me, assuring them, that their Condescension in this Particular shall be received as a Favour, and accordingly acknowledged.

I THINK I have now finish'd the Foundation, and I intend in my next to begin to raise the Building. Having nothing more to write at present, I must make the usual excuse in such Cases, of *being in haste,* assuring you that I speak from my Heart when I call my self, The most humble and obedient of all the Servants your Merits have acquir'd,
SILENCE DOGOOD.

The third of Franklin's "Silence Dogood" letters, published in his brother James's New-England Courant.

propos'd to myself, for the sake of clearness, to use rather more names, with fewer ideas annex'd to each, than a few names with more ideas; and

I included under thirteen names of virtues all that at that time occur'd to me as necessary or desirable, and annexed to each a short precept, which fully express'd the extent I gave to its meaning.

These names of virtues, with their precepts were:

1. Temperance.

Eat not to dullness; drink not to elevation.

2. Silence.

Speak not but what may benefit others or yourself; avoid trifling conversation.

3. Order.

Let all your things have their places; let each part of your business have its time.

4. Resolution.

Resolve to perform what you ought; perform without fail what you resolve.

5. Frugality.

Make no expense but to do good to others or yourself; *i.e.,* waste nothing.

6. Industry.

Lose no time; be always employ'd in something useful; cut off all unnecessary actions.

7. Sincerity.

Use no hurtful deceit; think innocently and justly and, if you speak, speak accordingly.

8. Justice.

Wrong none by doing injuries, or omitting the benefits that are your duty.

9. Moderation.

Avoid extreams; forbear resenting injuries so much as you think they deserve.

10. Cleanliness.

Tolerate no uncleanliness in body, cloths, or habitation.

11. Tranquility.

Be not disturbed at trifles, or at accidents common or unavoidable.

12. Chastity.

Rarely use venery but for health or offspring, never to dullness, weakness, or the injury of your own or another's peace or reputation.

13. Humility.

Imitate Jesus or Socrates.

Not a word about nobility, not a word about honor, not a word about grandeur of soul, not a word about charity of mind! Carlyle called Franklin the father of all the Yankees. That was a libel against the tribe, for the Yankees have produced Thoreau, Hawthorne, and Emily Dickinson. It would be more accurate to call Franklin the father of all the Kiwanians.

Franklin began his *Poor Richard's Almanac* in December, 1732. It was an imitation of the English *Poor Robin's Almanac.* It attained a great popularity at once. [According to Bigelow] "Three editions were sold within the month of its appearance. The average sale for twenty-five years was 10,000 a year. He was sometimes obliged to put it to press in October to get a supply of copies to the remote Colonies by the beginning of the year. It has been translated into nearly if not quite every written language, and several different translations of it have been made into the French and German." The most celebrated number was that for the year 1757, the last Franklin edited. It contained the well-known speech on thrift, called *Father Abraham's Speech at an Auction,* which was reprinted many times as *The Way of Wealth.* For some time it was used as a text in the French schools, under the title of *La Science du Bonhomme Richard.*

As to the purpose of the *Almanac* Franklin says the following:

In 1732 I first publish'd my Almanac, under the name of "Richard Saunders;" it was continu'd by me about twenty-five years, commonly call'd *Poor Richard's Almanac.* I endeavour'd to make it both entertaining and useful, and it accordingly came to be in such demand, that I reap'd considerable profit from it, vending annually near ten thousand. And observing that it was generally read, scarce any neighborhood in the province being without it, I consider'd it as a proper vehicle for conveying instruction among the common people, who bought scarcely any other books; I therefore filled all the little spaces that occurr'd between the remarkable days in the calendar with proverbial sentences, chiefly such as inculcated industry and frugality, as the means of procuring wealth, and thereby securing virtue; it being more difficult for a man in want, to act always honestly, as, to use here one of those proverbs, "It is hard for an empty sack to stand upright."

These proverbs, which contained the wisdom of many ages and nations, I assembled and form'd into a connected discourse prefix'd to the *Almanack* of 1757, as the harangue of a wise old man to the people attending an auction. The bringing of these scatter'd councils thus into a focus enabled them to make a greater impression. The piece, being universally approved, was copied in all the newspapers of the Continent; reprinted in Britain on a broadside, to be stuck up in houses; two translations were made of it in French, and great numbers bought by the clergy and gentry, to distribute gratis among their poor parishioners and tenants. In Pennsylvania, as it discouraged useless expense in foreign superfluities, some thought that it had its share of influence in producing that growing plenty of money which was observable for several years after its publication. . . .

Bigelow thinks that *Poor Richard* contains "some of the best fun as well as the wisest counsel that ever emanated from Franklin's pen." That is quite true, but absolutely considered the wisdom is of a low order. It points downward. True enough, it was addressed to the common man, but one does not always have to be a vulgarian when talking to the man in the street. Consider Jesus and Socrates and Confucius and Lao-Tze. Consider Montaigne. Consider even Krylov.

The following are representative epigrams in *Poor Richard:*

> A word to the wise is enough.
>
> God helps them that help themselves.
>
> Sloth, like rust, consumes faster than labor wears, while the used key is always bright, as Poor Richard says. But dost thou love life, then do not squander time, for that is the stuff life is made of, as Poor Richard says.
>
> The sleeping fox catches no poultry.
>
> Lost time is never found again, and what we call time enough always proves little enough.
>
> Sloth makes all things difficult, but industry all things easy.
>
> He that riseth late must trot all day, and shall scarce overtake his business at night.
>
> Laziness travels so slowly that Poverty soon overtakes him.
>
> Early to bed and early to rise, makes a man healthy, wealthy, and wise.
>
> He that hath a trade hath an estate, and he that hath a calling hath an office of profit and honor.
>
> At the working man's house hunger looks in but dares not enter.
>
> Industry pays debts, while despair increaseth them.
>
> Diligence is the mother of good luck, and God gives all things to industry. Then plough deep while sluggards sleep, and you shall have corn to sell and to keep.
>
> One today is worth two tomorrows.
>
> The cat in gloves catches no mice.
>
> Women and wine, game and deceit.
>
> Make the wealth small and the want great.
>
> What maintains one vice would bring up two children.
>
> Fools make feasts, and wise men eat them.
>
> If you would know the value of money, go and borrow some; for he that goes a borrowing goes a sorrowing.
>
> The proof of gold is fire; the proof of a woman, gold; the proof of a man, a woman.
>
> Three may keep a secret, if two of them are dead.
>
> Opportunity is the great bawd.

> Fish and visitors smell in three days.

Of *The Bagatelles,* which Franklin wrote while he was in France, little more can be said than for *Poor Richard.* Even after more than ten years of Parisian salon life he could not forget his two-penny philosophy. Mme. Brillon fell in love with him, and carried on a long correspondence with him, some of which he published on his private press in Passy. How did Franklin repay her for her eager caresses and elegant dinners? He wrote her a little story, entitled **"The Whistle,"** the moral of which was that one must always be careful not to spend too much money on trifles! She had sent him a description of what she would like to find in Paradise, and Franklin answered thus:

> I am charmed with your description of Paradise, and with your plan of living there; and I approve much of your conclusion, that, in the mean time, we should draw all the good we can from this world. In my opinion, we might all draw more good from it than we do, and suffer less evil, if we would take care not to give too much for *whistles.* For to me it seems, that most of the unhappy people we meet with, are become so by neglect of that caution.
>
> You ask what I mean? You love stories, and will excuse my telling one of myself.
>
> When I was a child of seven years old, my friends, on a holiday, filled my pockets with coppers. I went directly to a shop where they sold toys for children; and, being charmed with the sound of a *whistle,* that I met by the way in the hands of another boy, I voluntarily offered and gave all my money for one. I then came home, and went whistling all over the house, much pleased with my *whistle,* but disturbing all the family. My brothers, and sisters, and cousins, understanding the bargain I had made, told me I had given four times as much for it as it was worth; put me in mind of what good things I might have bought with the rest of the money; and laughed at me so much for my folly, that I cried with vexation; and the reflection gave me more chagrin than the *whistle* gave me pleasure.
>
> This however was afterwards of use to me, the impression continuing in my mind; so that often, when I was tempted to buy some unnecessary thing, I said to myself, *Don't give too much for the whistle;* and I saved my money.

Franklin perpetrated one more piece of literature that has somehow escaped the literary historians, but that surely deserves mention. That was his proposed new version of the Bible. Like the immortal authors of the Bay Psalm Book he did not like the King James version. He said:

> It is now more than one hundred and seventy years since the translation of our common English Bible. The language in that time is much changed, and the style being obsolete, and thence less agreeable, is perhaps one reason why the reading of that excellent book is of late so much neglected. I have therefore thought it well to procure a new version in which, preserving the sense, the turn of phrase and manner of expression should be modern. I do not pretend to

have the necessary abilities for such a work my-self; I throw out the hint for the consideration of the learned.

The following was his idea of how the first chapter of Job should read:

Verse 6. *King James version.*—Now there was a day when the sons of God came to present themselves before the Lord, and Satan came also amongst them.

Verse 6: *New version by Franklin.*—And it being *levee* day in heaven, all God's nobility came to court, to present themselves before him; and Satan also appeared in the circle, as one of the ministry.

Verse 7. *King James version.*—And the Lord said unto Satan: Whence comest thou? Then Satan answered the Lord, and said: From going to and fro in the earth, and from walking up and down in it.

Verse 7. *New version by Franklin.*—And God said to Satan: you have been some time absent; where were you? And Satan answered: I have been at my country-seat, and in different places visiting my friends.

Verse 8. *King James version.*—And the Lord said unto Satan: Hast thou considered my servant Job, that there is none like him in the earth, a perfect and an upright man, one that feareth God, and escheweth evil?

Verse 8. *New version by Franklin.*—And God said: Well, what do you think of Lord Job? You see he is my best friend, a perfectly honest man, full of respect for me, and avoiding everything that might offend me.

Verse 9. *King James version.*—Then Satan answered the Lord, and said: Doth Job fear God for naught?

Verse 9. *New version by Franklin.*—And Satan answered: Does your Majesty imagine that his good conduct is the effect of mere personal attachment and affection?

Verse 10. *King James version.*—Hast thou not made an hedge about his house, and about all that he hath on every side? Thou has blest the work of his hands, and his substance is increased in the land.

Verse 10. *New version by Franklin.*—Have you not protected him, and heaped your benefits upon him, till he is grown enormously rich?

Verse 11. *King James version.*—But put forth thine hand now, and touch all that he hath, and he will curse thee to thy face.

Verse 11. *New version by Franklin.*—Try him; only withdraw your favor, turn him out of his places, and withhold his pensions, and you will soon find him in the opposition.

This crime against beautiful letters was in perfect keeping with Franklin's general character. He had a cheap and shabby soul, and the upper levels of the mind were far be-

yond his reach. His one attempt at dignified philosophical speculation, **Dissertation on Liberty and Necessity** (1725), was so bad that even he was later ashamed of it. As for his scientific experiments, they have been vastly overrated. [According to Faÿ] "All that he invented was current supposition at the time; his work was rather in confirming and defining the scientific notions of others."

His writings enjoyed a vast popularity in his own day, and still do in ours, but that should not blind us to their inferior quality. All he had to say he borrowed from others, and what is worse, he was a bad borrower. The literature of England in the Seventeenth and Eighteenth Centuries was the most glorious in its entire history. There was the immortal King James version of the Bible, and there was the galaxy of stars beginning with Shakespeare and ending with Pope. Franklin read them all, but when he came to imitate and to borrow did he choose any of these? He rejected the entire lot, and instead picked *Poor Robin's Almanac*! And of the King James version his chief comment was that its style was "obsolete"!

To call Franklin "one of the greatest masters of English expression" [as did Bigelow] is the veriest nonsense. Almost any one of the Eighteenth Century New England theologians wrote better. Franklin, to be sure, was easier to understand, but there was far less in him worth understanding. His influence on the national letters, in the long run, was probably nil. [According to McMaster] "He founded no school of literature. He gave no impetus to letters. He put his name to no great work of history, of poetry, of fiction."

But by his international prominence and by the wide circulation of his two-penny philosophy he left a lasting impression on the national culture. In him [according to Van

---

Carl Van Doren on Franklin's greatness:

[Franklin] was not one of those men who owe their greatness merely to the opportunities of their times. In any age, in any place, Franklin would have been great. Mind and will, talent and art, strength and ease, wit and grace met in him as if nature had been lavish and happy when he was shaped. Nothing seems to have been left out except a passionate desire, as in most men of genius, to be all ruler, all soldier, all saint, all poet, all scholar, all some one gift or merit or success. Franklin's powers were from first to last in a flexible equilibrium. Even his genius could not specialize him. He moved through his world in a humorous mastery of it. Kind as he was, there was perhaps a little contempt in his lack of exigency. He could not put so high a value as single-minded men put on the things they give their lives for. Possessions were not worth that much, nor achievements. Comfortable as Franklin's possessions and numerous as his achievements were, they were less than he was. Whoever learns about his deeds remembers longest the man who did them. And sometimes, with his marvellous range, in spite of his personal tang, he seems to have been more than any single man: a harmonious human multitude.

Carl Van Doren, in his Benjamin Franklin, *1938.*

Wyck Brooks, in *America's Coming of Age,* 1915] "the 'lowbrow' point of view for the first time took definite shape, stayed itself with axioms, and found a sanction in the idea of 'policy'. " Thrift, industry, and determination were essential virtues in the building of the nation, but they were not, then or at any other time in history, of sufficient human dignity to build a life philosophy on. Franklin did precisely that for his private life, and by the force of his personality did more than any other man in his day to graft it upon the American people. The vulgarity he spread is still with us. (pp. 295-310)

> *Charles Angoff, "Pennsylvania: The Prose and Verse of Pennsylvania in the Years 1750-1810: Benjamin Franklin," in his* A Literary History of the American People: From 1750 to 1815, Vol. 2, *1931. Reprint by Tudor Publishing Company, 1935, pp. 295-310.*

Henry Seidel Canby   (essay date 1939)

[*Canby was a professor of English at Yale and one of the founders of the* Saturday Review of Literature, *of which he served as editor in chief from 1924-1936. He was the author of many books, including* The Short Story in English *(1909), a history of that genre, which was long considered the standard text for college students. In the following excerpt, he appraises Franklin's character and his place in American literature and culture, comparing him in particular to colonial writers Jonathan Edwards, Cotton Mather, and John Woolman.*]

Benjamin Franklin, the apostle of American common sense, was the publicity agent of the new American. In spite of his flashes of scientific intuition, his genius for statesmanship, and his easy sexual morals, Franklin was a good representative of the average American man—devoid of mysticism, little interested in theology, but determined to learn how to live in America. Broadly considered, this last might be said to be the theme of the most characteristic American literature ever since Franklin stated the problem in terms that if they were the lowest were, in their application, the broadest also.

Franklin is the practical man of common sense, who goes on and on after enthusiasms are dead. He is the New England farmer on weekdays, the New York trader, the fur purchaser opening new routes, the engineer, the employer of labor, the politician who keeps his eyes on earth. Yet unlike the thousands whose common sense told them that they must get a living whatever the preacher might say, he was enough of a philosopher to stand aside and look at his America with a speculative glance. Edwards, Mather, and Woolman deal with souls; he is concerned with the American man as man. (pp. 35-6)

Franklin began his career as a man determined to find and use opportunity; no sooner was he established than he undertook the broader task of making Pennsylvania a model modern state; and he concluded his extraordinary career as a specialist in world politics and the leader of the new school of bourgeois philosophy. This is the reason for the absorbing interest of his *Autobiography.* Written by one who had gained perspective by experience, it records the story of how an intelligent man was formed by, and reacted to, the new environment of America.

The Philadelphia in which he lived after 1723 was no citadel of the inner light, but the prosperous and somewhat cosmopolitan metropolis of the colonies, the center, if not of intellectuality except for some scientific thinking, certainly of liberal ideas on government and such worldly culture as was imported from abroad. In comparison, New England in the mid-century was provincial, and New York commercial. As a chief port of entry, with a broad stretch of fertile land between the sea and the higher mountains, the experiences of the immigrant were most evident here, and the note of thrift and promise, which was the prevailing tone of colonial America within the frontiers, was most sure to be struck. If Franklin became a political philosopher and a scientist, as a writer from the beginning to the end he was first of all a journalist, explaining first to Americans, and then to the nations of Europe, what American colonists must do in order to make themselves at home in their new environment. He had a scientist's imagination that projected beyond his own epoch, a scrupulously cultivated gift for words, an experience of men and cities perhaps more varied than any other individual in either hemisphere in his time, a lucidity, shrewdness, and intellectual curiosity as transcendent as the intellectual strenuosity of the Puritan divines. Possessing a genius for normality in spite of his abnormal powers, he was, as Carlyle said, the father of all the Yankees—of all the self-dependent, inventive Yankees, those "practical idealists" who came after him and made a character type for America. Franklin is still modern, whereas Edwards, and even Washington, need explanation.

His faculty of observation was fresh and original, and so was his scientific imagination, but his interest in ethics came with him from New England and his philosophy of life was strongly influenced by the Quakers among whom he lived. In this, as in other respects, the father of the Yankees was a good representative for America.

His ethics of common sense—implicit always, when not explicit, in *Poor Richard's Almanack*—are mere pragmatism in comparison with the Puritan code. "Honesty is the best policy" sums up his creed—and not a bad creed for a new country that could certainly not be conducted on the Quaker assumption that all its inhabitants were to become saints. His constant insistence upon the importance of doing right derives ultimately from his youth in New England, and the specific stimulus was apparently from Cotton Mather's book *Essays to Do Good,* which Franklin, characteristically, liked because the title seemed to offset the Calvinists' belief that good works in themselves were without value for the soul. His later Deism merely rationalizes a habit of judgment already formed. And indeed, when set against Mather's bigoted theology, his shrewd reasoning to prove that the good man is sure to prosper seems a justifiable materialism. But if Franklin's morals and his religion were determined by expediency, nevertheless they did not strain human nature, especially they did not strain his own, which in its moral vagaries might have supplied an argument to Puritan preachers against the relaxations of common sense. They were reasonable if not elevated, and applied to ethics in the religious life in general the logic of facts as he observed them in this world, rather than a logic based upon premises established by metaphysics.

Franklin had a scientist's imagination that projected beyond his own epoch, a scrupulously cultivated gift for words, an experience of men and cities perhaps more varied than any other individual in either hemisphere in his time. . . .

—Henry Seidel Canby

His ethical ideas seem more doubtful when compared with the only other religious doctrine he seems to have strongly felt. Whoever knows Quakerism detects in a hundred places in Franklin's works the results of living with the Friends in Philadelphia. There is no evidence that the reasonable, reconciling, tolerant spirit that made him so successful as a mediator, was born in him. His biographer, Smyth, describes him as self-willed, opinionated, and defiant in youth. Strong-willed he certainly was throughout life, but the cardinal principle of his political philosophy was tolerance when possible at home and abroad, whether it was the Germans to be assimilated in Pennsylvania, or the Revolution to be satisfactorily concluded. The Quaker principle of good will, the Quaker insistence upon the essential nobleness of right-minded man, are dominant principles with Franklin that made him popular in France and, aided by his shrewd amiability, set a fashion in a Europe growing tired of privilege and distrustful of rank. Yet the Quaker spiritual dependence, the Quaker mysticism, are utterly absent. In a very real sense, the moral ideas of Franklin represent Quakerism conventionalized, stylized, and Deicized, if the word may be permitted, in order to become immediately useful in the skeptical eighteenth century world. There is no reason for good will given in Franklin's writings except its success, no reason for loving one's fellow man except expediency. As the Quaker grew rich because of his unworldliness, which made him inevitably prudent in expenditure and reliable in business, and then grew worldly because he was rich, so the political ethics of Franklin, with its liberal, Quaker tinge, became the common-sense utilitarianism of American business ethics. If not the father of dollar philosophy and dollar diplomacy, he is at least the foster father—the American environment and American circumstance, which he so shrewdly and prophetically viewed, being presumably the ultimate cause.

His practical mind made Franklin an extraordinarily keen observer of the actual business of living in the colonies, and one of the wisest of commentators upon how to adjust oneself to the new environment, or indeed to any environment. A collection of his more important essays and letters not devoted to immediate political problems would show a series of advisory articles telling how to light

streets, how to avoid colds by air baths, how to get ready to immigrate, how to provide for universal peace. The spirit of the logical, inquisitive eighteenth century is strong in all this, and indeed Franklin, even before his diplomatic residence abroad, was a citizen of the world—yet it is constantly evident how strongly his keen and lucid mind was stimulated by the needs and possibilities of a new state where nature had to be conquered, and where experiments in new and better human relationships could be hopefully inaugurated. A journalist by taste and talent, he became, as they say now, a specialist in public relations. His science was always applied science, his great diplomatic achievements were gained by carefully applied publicity—if he could not speak, he wrote. It is questionable whether any pen did more to influence practical thinking in the latter eighteenth century than his, and this without any masterpiece of philosophical thought or literary expression. He was a first-class working intellect, smoothing the way by speech and writing, even more than by deeds, for the new republic.

If his place in American literature is as an influence rather than as a master, that is because he was a great statesman and a most articulate philosopher, but in no way a great artist, even in words. His style is trenchant, and carefully formed and imitated from models drawn from an earlier English period. The *Autobiography* is solid eighteenth century prose, cogent, luminous, strong, reflecting a remarkable mind. But the *Autobiography* is not quoted for its style, nor were the sententious epigrams of *Poor Richard's Almanack* borrowed everywhere because of their wit or form. School readers inevitably reprint the episode of the poor boy with the rolls under his arm while his future wife watched him from a doorway, because it is the typical narrative of successful men in America, and several generations drew from *Poor Richard* because his thrift was a keynote for a country still empty of capital, and "Do it yourself," "You can be what you will," "Try and see," were slogans for initiative and hope. The physical and political development of the United States is implicit in the writings of Franklin.

Cotton Mather, a generation behind him, seems insane by comparison, Edwards, only three years older, a man of another world. Franklin, a far more capacious intellect than Mather, and intellectually more flexible if not more powerful than Edwards, is the expected voice to say that America is by no means an experiment of the Puritan God, but a great economic proposition, to be conducted ethically, sensibly, with freedom for initiative, hard work, and every resource of invention in a community where every variety of human nature is to have its chance.

Regarded as a man of letters—and in his capacity of prime journalist for the colonies, he must be so regarded—Franklin is, indeed, an excellent example of a phenomenon peculiarly American. In his social ideas he was ahead of his time, in his literary expression behind it. As Edwards's style belongs to the seventeenth rather than to the eighteenth century, so Franklin in his style and in his forms of address belongs with Addison, Steele, and especially Defoe rather than with his own English decades. Yet his social philosophy is abreast of the early eighteen hundreds, and if the French, always intuitive in such matters, felt in him the exponent of a new order, it was because in what they called his simplicity (he was never simple) they saw the idea of a new community where intelligence, industry, and common sense would break through privilege into success.

It was his cool, practical advice, favorable to sensible living in a country poor in means but rich in ends, that gave prestige to worldly affairs (including science) in communities where eloquence had always belonged to the theologians. The brand of idealistic common sense that he stamped with his name has been staple in the United States ever since, and no philosophy was so thoroughly rubbed into the minds of youth in the young republic. Henry Adams praises it in the Pennsylvania of a century later, as the stabilizer of the Union. Never again after Franklin did it come so near literature as in his essays and his *Autobiography,* but it has been the substance of the best American journalism, and in its decadence has provided a solid philistinism from which indignant literary genius has rebounded into art.

Evil is evil, says Franklin in one oft-quoted passage of the *Autobiography,* not because it is forbidden, but because it is evil it is forbidden, the ugliness of evil and the advantage of virtue being proved by their results. As a proposition, this is not very different from Edwards's belief that the nature of evil is more important than its cause in predestination, yet the emphasis is entirely different. Edwards is concerned with the necessity of willing evil or good, Franklin with the results. And it might be added that Woolman's concern was neither with the practical results in this world nor with a practical necessity to prepare for the next by right willing, but with goodness itself, which must be apprehended before any attitude or course became of the slightest importance. These are the three strains of ethics, the three kinds of temperament that appear, reappear, blend, confuse, and create in the later American imagination, where they are further complicated by pioneer temperament and pioneer morals. Played upon by immense forces generated by immigration, settlement, and the establishment of a political and economic society under new circumstances and upon an unexploited continent, in a very real sense they condition the scope and ethical character of the literature of the first national century. (pp. 38-45)

> *Henry Seidel Canby, "The Colonial Background," in his* Classic Americans: A Study of Eminent American Writers from Irving to Whitman, with an Introductory Survey of the Colonial Background of Our National Literature, *Harcourt, Brace & Company, 1939, pp. 3-66.*

Max Farrand   (essay date 1949)

[*In the following excerpt, Farrand explores the literary and biographical contexts of the* Autobiography, *examining Franklin's purpose in writing his memoirs.*]

The Huntington Library is the fortunate possessor of the original and only known manuscript of Benjamin Franklin's *Autobiography,* the editing of which for publication presented an intricate problem in textual criticism. While I was seeking a solution to that problem over several years, these two questions persistently intruded: What led Franklin to write his memoirs? What are the qualities in those memoirs that have made them one of the great autobiographies of all literature and the first great American literary classic? (You may notice that the word "memoirs" is used, for that is what Franklin always called them. The *Oxford English Dictionary* gives the date of the first known use of the word "autobiography" as 1809, almost twenty years after Franklin's death.) (p. ix)

Many biographies of Franklin were, of course, examined; but the *Autobiography* is more than just the story of Franklin's life—it is also a part of our literary heritage. So, not long ago, having gathered several ideas for presentation, I made the fatal mistake of going to the shelves of a library where in one section were gathered a large number of histories of American literature. To my dismay I found, on looking through twenty or thirty different works, that almost everything which I intended to say had already been expressed far better than I could pretend to put it. More than that, everything that ever *could* be said about Franklin seemed already to have been put into print. But much of it was concealed in a flood of verbiage and was scattered through a mass of hopelessly second- and third-rate stuff. Like Gratiano's "two grains of wheat hid in two bushels of chaff: you shall seek all day ere you find them: and when you have them, they are not worth the search."

One is inclined to think we would be better off, so far as our *understanding* of Franklin is concerned, if nothing had been published except James Parton's *Life and Times of Benjamin Franklin* which appeared in 1864. Perhaps an exception might be made in favor of Sainte-Beuve's unrivaled essay on Franklin among his *Portraits.* Please notice that the word used was "understanding." There is no doubt that our *knowledge* concerning Franklin has greatly increased, especially in recent years, but the definition of "knowledge" in Webster's *Dictionary,* quoting Thomas Gray: "Knowledge and intelligence . . . alone do not constitute wisdom," is particularly applicable here.

Even the best of the recent lives—Carl Van Doren's readable and informative *Benjamin Franklin*—has not superseded Parton. Van Doren has brought together much material from hitherto inaccessible or inconveniently situated sources and has added some things that are new, and has told the story in an attractive, if not to say fascinating, manner. But in the preface he wrote, "In effect Franklin's *Autobiography* is here completed on his own scale and in his own words." It is perhaps the purpose of this essay to show that he attempted something beyond the power of any person except Franklin himself to achieve.

Apparently the correct thing to say about Franklin these days is that he was a child of the Enlightenment. If ever an agreement is reached upon what is meant by the "Enlightenment," we may then be able to concur in the opinion that Franklin was its child. Until such time, I, for one, prefer the late William P. Trent's way of putting it [in his *History of American Literature,* 1929]—Franklin "is, perhaps, the most complete representative of his century that any nation can point to." Such a statement may be equally vague, but to me at least it sounds more comprehensible. Trent gives as a further explanation of Franklin's immortality in the United States that "he is a typical and unapproachable product of what his countrymen are pleased to call 'true Americanism'."

I shall come back again and again to those estimates of Franklin as a product of the eighteenth century and the personification of what have come to be regarded as American characteristics. There are persons who blame him for some of our present traits and qualities.

Thomas Carlyle has been quoted as saying that Benjamin Franklin was the father of all the Yankees. Charles Angoff (*A Literary History of the American People,* 1931) protests that this "was a libel against the tribe, for the Yankees have produced Thoreau, Hawthorne, and Emily Dickinson." He then proceeds to castigate Franklin unmercifully and to make him primarily responsible for much that is common and vulgar in American life today.

Angoff has been cited deliberately, for he presents the point of view and even the considered judgment of some persons. But why lay this all up against Franklin? He was essentially a child of his times, as we all are of ours. He was a product of the eighteenth century. Some years ago a prominent Englishman expressed in conversation his irritation that many persons complained of the so-called "Americanization of England." "All that the United States has done," he said, "is to be about twenty years ahead of England. Industrialization is inevitable with all its faults and virtues. We [i.e., the English] are simply experiencing what the people of the United States have already gone through. That isn't Americanization." So Franklin should be regarded as the forerunner, rather than the originator, of some of our less admirable traits and practices.

Benjamin Franklin bears the reputation of having been a shrewd and a wise man. It might be adduced in support of that reputation that he showed those qualities at an early age in his choice of parents. Josiah Franklin, his father, lived to be eighty-nine years old, and Abiah Folger Franklin, his mother, lived to be eighty-five. In other words, he came of a long-lived and, it might be added, industrious stock.

This child, born in 1706, at the beginning of the eighteenth century, in humble circumstances, and reared in poverty, rose from such conditions to become one of the world's great figures and literally to stand before kings. The story has all the elements of success and romance that constitute the ideal of millions of Americans.

Fortunately, it is not necessary to go into the details of Franklin's life; they are well known to everyone. And so we may turn directly to the writing of the *Autobiography.* One point ought to be emphasized, because it is so frequently overlooked, and that is the conditions under which its composition was begun.

Franklin was, as is well known, on his second mission to England, and it should be remembered how happy he was in that country. When on his previous mission, he had written to one of his friends that he had spent in Scotland "six weeks of the densest happiness I have ever met with in any part of my life." After returning to America he wrote to Mary Stevenson in 1763:

> Of all the enviable Things England has, I envy it most its People. Why should that petty Island, which compar'd to America, is but like a stepping-Stone in a Brook, scarce enough of it above Water to keep one's Shoes dry; why, I say, should that little Island enjoy in almost every Neighbourhood, more sensible, virtuous, and elegant Minds, than we can collect in ranging 100 Leagues of our vast Forests? (*The Writings of Benjamin Franklin*)

Benjamin Franklin was a person of importance in his world, and no one knew it better than Franklin himself. He had succeeded beyond his greatest expectations. He was not disagreeably conceited—he was pleasantly, even delightfully, vain. Franklin appreciated that, too, for in the very beginning of his *Autobiography* he admits that his writing will

> perhaps not a little gratify my own *vanity.* . . . Most people dislike vanity in others . . . but I give it fair quarter wherever I meet with it, being persuaded that it is often productive of good to the possessor. . . . And therefore . . . it would not be altogether absurd if a man were to thank God for his vanity among the other comforts of life.

So it was in that humor, in 1771, when he was sixty-five, and on a fortnight's holiday at Twyford with his dear friend Jonathan Shipley, that he indulged himself in something he had long wanted to do—to tell the real story of his life and to give his own explanation of his success.

Certain facts of his career were common knowledge. Other facts were known to a few. In his memoirs Franklin is telling his son, and very probably expecting through his son to tell the world, the things about himself that other people did not know, and furthermore what lay back of those facts. Through the whole story runs an extraordinary analysis of the motives that inspired his several activities.

Even for such a piece of self-indulgence, Franklin carefully made out a list of topics to be taken up, which, in the copies now extant, covers three pages measuring seven by ten inches. The memoirs themselves were written on both sides of larger-sized sheets, approximately thirteen inches by eight, and were always inscribed in the same fashion— that is, in a long column on one half of the page, leaving the other half as a wide margin for additions and corrections.

When he had written a little more than eighty-six pages in this way, he stopped. From the outline he had prepared we know that he was not a third of the way through his undertaking—in fact, the story had come down only to 1730; he had not reached the point of his great successes,—but all that was written was evidently just what it purported to be: a story for his son and immediate family and, perhaps, if they saw fit, to be made public. It is Franklin at his best.

They are, as Van Doren has said, "the homeliest memoirs that had ever been written in the plainest language." But they are something more than that. They tell the story of a printer and shopkeeper who was infinitely bigger than his job but was not above it; of a tradesman who had risen to greatness but was not ashamed of his origin or of his station. He never shirked any of the menial tasks he had to perform. In fact he quickly saw their advertising value. Even as a youngster—who, again forecasting later American qualities, was to become the great "publicity artist" of his time—Franklin played up these menial tasks. A passage in the *Autobiography* is often quoted, but it will bear repetition here:

> In order to secure my credit and character as a tradesman, I took care not only to be in *reality* industrious and frugal, but to avoid all appearances of the contrary. I dressed plain and was seen at no places of idle diversion. I never went out a fishing or shooting; a book, indeed, sometimes debauched me from my work; but that was seldom, snug, and gave no scandal; and to show that I was not above my business, I sometimes brought home the paper I purchased at the stores, thro' the streets on a wheelbarrow.

. . . . .

And now to take up the qualities revealed in the memoirs that have made them famous. Franklin's first love was what his contemporaries called "philosophy" but what we call "science." One of the chief reasons he gave for retiring from active participation in the printing shop was to gain more time for his experiments. To speak of his scientific qualifications is stepping outside of my field, but the ideas used are common property. The line of thought here followed is taken from Lord Jeffrey, as refined by Sainte-Beuve, and adapted to our modern parlance with the help of a scientific friend whom the Franklin Institute has honored with its medal—Dr. Edwin P. Hubble.

Franklin was not a mathematician—that is, he was not a theorist. He was a natural philosopher, a physicist, keenly observant and everlastingly curious about the why and wherefore of natural phenomena. He made simple, searching, decisive experiments and then by his clear reasoning was able to offer convincing demonstrations.

The prime qualification of any person who would succeed in science or in scholarship is the ability to dissociate himself, his feelings, and his prejudices from the undertaking in hand, so that he may make thoroughly impartial and impersonal observations of facts; then, in the same spirit, to record those facts; and eventually, if possible, to find the explanation. To me, this is a leading intellectual quality of Franklin's: his ability to take a detached, impersonal, dispassionate point of view.

But Franklin was also interested in human behavior, and in his observations of how human beings acted he displayed one of the rarest of all qualities. His own doings were, of course, the ones about which he knew the most, and he observed and recorded them with complete detachment from self. He was not in the least morbidly introspective; if anything, he was whimsically amused. Benjamin Franklin was merely one of the curious human phenome-

na he was studying and whose acts he was recording. His ultimate aim was to explain how this person had been able to function so effectively. He succeeded, as almost no one else has ever done—a fact attested by the place accorded to the memoirs in the world's esteem.

An explanation has been offered to show why the *Autobiography* is so remarkable a human document. There still remains the question of why it is regarded as a literary classic. Franklin could always tell a good story, so it is not surprising that he should tell his own story extraordinarily well. That makes a good start. He also possessed a delightful sense of humor, and his display of it adds to the reader's enjoyment.

At this point the interpretation here presented diverges from much of the current opinion. The difference is mainly in the use of terms, but the most discriminating—and that means the best—critics apparently do not accept Franklin as one of the great "men of letters." Franklin was the essence of practicality, the embodiment of common sense. He was always constructive, but it is claimed, and with that claim I am inclined to agree, that he was not possessed by the genius which forces men to write whether they will or no, and which is necessary to produce great literature. Sainte-Beuve was apparently making the same point when he wrote:

> Here a reflection begins to dawn upon us. An ideal is lacking in this healthy, upright, able, frugal, laborious nature of Franklin—the fine flower of enthusiasm, tenderness, sacrifice,—all that is the dream, and also the charm and the honor of poetic natures. . . . He brings everything down to arithmetic and strict reality, assigning no part to human imagination.
> [*Portraits of the Eighteenth Century,* 1905]

His writings were generally journalistic and most of them were published in newspapers. To disregard them is perhaps to treat "literature" too exclusively as belles-lettres. There is no denying that Franklin influenced both his contemporaries and his successors in their writing, in ways that we think were for their betterment because they are ways that accord with our present-day standards. He may therefore be regarded as a "literary figure," but that hardly makes him a great man of letters if his sole lasting contribution to literature is the *Autobiography.* This would seem to be the substance of the opinion expressed by such recognized literary historians and critics as Henry A. Beers (*Initial Studies in American Letters,* 1891), William P. Trent (*History of American Literature,* 1929), and Stuart P. Sherman (in the *Cambridge History of American Literature*).

All these critics, however, are agreed upon the directness and simplicity of Franklin's style. It is from the *Autobiography* that we learn how Franklin used the *Spectator* as a model, and taught himself to improve his writing and to express his ideas clearly and concisely. Of course, the first essential is to think clearly, and that was one of Franklin's strongest points. But anyone who imagines that clarity and conciseness in expressing one's thoughts may be achieved and learned once and for all has another guess coming. Undoubtedly many have a gift in that direction.

had much to do with the wide acceptance of the results of his experiments in electricity. He also found a worthy opportunity for their advantageous use in giving the account of his own life.

There are the final qualities—the simplicity of presentation and the crystal clearness of the style—that, in the flood of memoirs deluging the eighteenth century, raised Benjamin Franklin's story to preëminence.

Some things the *Autobiography* does not reveal. Nothing is said about Franklin's social life. Apparently, to him there was little that was new or of interest in the story of a simple, frugal household. But nevertheless there were in his social life certain features which are of consequence to our forming a correct estimate of the man. Society with a capital "S" didn't know him. Aristocratic Philadelphia seems to have refused to recognize him socially, although it found him useful, and indeed essential, in public enterprise. That didn't bother Franklin. He cared less for Society than Society did for him. One thing, however, I doubt he was ever aware of having missed: it is a great pity that in his early, impressionable years Franklin was not privileged to have acquaintance and friendship with women of cultivation and refinement. What the effect might have been, we can only guess, but that it would have been of benefit to so observing and receptive a youth, eager to improve himself, seems beyond question.

The same social inexperience might account for Franklin's failure to develop the art of conversation. The lack is generally recognized, and many references might be quoted to that effect. He was a good listener, but his contribution to social conversation and even to more serious discussions consisted frequently in telling a good story, humorous and apt. And how characteristic that is of Americans today!

We also get no hint of one of Franklin's most lovable traits—his fondness for children and his delight in companionship with young people. (Van Doren has brought these out admirably in his biography.) His affectionate nature, his gentleness and whimsicality, are displayed to the best advantage in letters to his young friends. Theodore Roosevelt said of his own *Letters to His Children*, "I would rather have this book published than anything that has ever been written about me." So one wishes that Franklin's letters to young people might have been permitted to tell their own story, and to reveal his attractive and natural self, without that trace of the tradesman's expediency that alienates many people.

The first part of the *Autobiography* is the best, so far as self-revelation is concerned, not only because Franklin enjoyed writing it and let himself go, but also because "the child is father to the man" and the first part covers the character-forming years of his life. The later parts, however, have their own significance.

. . . . .

For more than ten years nothing was heard of what he had written. It is doubtful if more than a very few knew of its existence. In the meantime he had returned to America, and after the outbreak of the War for Independence he

"Au Genie de Franklin," by Jean Honoré Fragonard.

Practice improves one, but no person has yet been born who could write continuously and consistently in a clear and concise manner. Like poetry, such writing is the product of infinite pains.

The best way to learn to write, provided one is critical of one's own work, is to write and to keep on writing, which was Franklin's habit. It would seem that among the most helpful things he did for his own style was the composition of the maxims for *Poor Richard's Almanac.* In the compilation of these aphorisms Franklin borrowed freely from everywhere. As he himself said, "They were the wisdom of many ages and nations." But they were transmuted by him, pointed with his wit, and put into direct and simple English. They stand practically alone in the eighteenth century—the type of humor henceforth to be known as American.

There are people who complain of the broadness of some of the witticisms and the coarseness of some of the anecdotes. Just to see if there might be any relation between the two productions, I turned to Joe Miller's *Jest-Book,* the first edition of which was printed in 1739. There was no resemblance. In comparison with the *Jest-Book, Poor Richard* might well be used as a textbook in a young ladies' finishing school.

Franklin's method of composition and form of written expression, so laboriously acquired in his youth, developed in all his newspaper writing, and sharpened by the sayings he gathered and prepared for *Poor Richard,* undoubtedly had been sent as a commissioner to France. His incredible reception by the French and his astounding popularity, when he was the idol of Paris and crowds blocked the streets to see him, are too well known to bear repeating.

Just as the peace negotiations were drawing to a close, Abel James, a printer, wrote from Philadelphia that the manuscript of the memoirs commenced at Twyford had come into his hands. He begged Franklin to go on with them, and enclosed a copy of the outline as a reminder of what was still to be done. Franklin turned the letter over to his young friend Benjamin Vaughan, with a request for his opinion. Louis Guillaume le Veillard, the mayor of Passy, with whom Franklin had developed a warm friendship, was also consulted. They and others urged him to continue the story of his life.

But even after peace was concluded, it was not until 1784 that Franklin again took up the *Autobiography.* When he resumed writing he inserted Vaughan's reply along with James's letter. They make a disconcerting break in the flow of the narrative, but evidently were put in to justify the resumption of the story and to emphasize the change in the character of the memoirs. Franklin prefaced the letters with a note that the first part of the account of his life was written for the family and that the following was "intended for the public." What a difference there is! Franklin was now seventy-eight years old. He was not merely a man of consequence; he was one of the great figures of the world. Science may have been his first love, but the passion of his life was the improvement of others as well as of himself, and even in his greatness he never forgot it. Where this motive came from is not clear. It may have been from his New England Calvinistic training, but whatever its source, it certainly was one of the great forces in his life.

Accordingly, when Franklin again took up the *Autobiography,* he was no longer writing the simple story of his life, for the benefit of his son; he was consciously preaching virtue, as exemplified in his own practices and experience; he was writing to instruct youth. Through all of the second part one feels a more didactic purpose than was noticeable in the first installment.

The value of this part consists in the revelation of his methodical plan for "arriving at moral perfection" and in the calm way he describes his own deficiencies and limitations. He notes that he listed thirteen virtues and determined to give strict attention to the practice of each of them successively for a week at a time. His reference to this systematic plan of self-improvement as "a course complete in thirteen weeks, and four courses a year," sounds very modern.

Franklin returned to America in the summer of 1785. On the eve of sailing from Southampton he said in a letter to a friend: "I purpose, on my voyage, to write the remaining notes of my life, which you desire." Instead, he wrote three of his most extensive and useful essays: one on navigation, another on smoky chimneys, and the third a description of his smoke-consuming stove. So, for one reason or another, he kept putting off the continuation of his memoirs.

He had long been troubled with gout, and for several years

with a stone in the bladder. He has been quoted as having said that in the last two years of his life he had not had two months, in all, of freedom from pain. In December, 1787, he fell down the steps leading to his garden. He was badly bruised, his right wrist was sprained, and the shock was followed by a severe attack of the stone. Not long afterward he began to put his house in order for the end which he saw inevitably approaching, and made his will, which bears the date July 17, 1788.

. . . . .

The third installment of his memoirs was not begun until after he had made his last will and testament. When the continuation was taken up, Franklin made a note in the margin of the manuscript: "I am now about to write at home, August, 1788." He was well on in his eighty-third year and was suffering grievously—so much that he was forced at times to the use of opium. He was apparently engaged for several months in writing this part. He did the best he could, but he was an old man and his story shows the effects of his age. One misses, particularly, the spontaneity and the zest with which Franklin had commenced his memoirs. At Twyford he was writing almost gleefully, reliving his youth. In Philadelphia he was making a forced effort; only at times could he forget himself in the interest of the story he was telling.

This part of the *Autobiography* describes the emergence of a tradesman into a man of affairs, the growth of a citizen of local importance into a person of consequence throughout the colonies, and into a scientist of reputation not only in England but also on the Continent. There is a quality revealed in it that had not appeared so clearly before: Franklin's remarkable business ability. Many writers refer to Franklin's frugality, but frugality was more characteristic of Mrs. Franklin than it was of him. Franklin's success in his printing shop and other activities—so great that he could retire at the age of forty-two—was due not to economy but to his business efficiency. He was also quick to see and seize any opportunity. When those abilities were combined with an extraordinary insight into human nature, it is little wonder the achievements were remarkable.

Franklin knew that his life was nearly over and that he would never finish his memoirs. Accordingly, in 1789, he had his grandson, Benjamin Franklin Bache, make two "fair copies" of so much as had then been written. One was sent to Vaughan and the other to Le Veillard. The original manuscript, with its many corrections, was interlined, confused, and in places difficult to read. At some stage in the copying, changes were made. This statement is positive, for although neither of these copies is now to be found the evidence in support of it is convincing. To what extent these changes were made or approved by Franklin will probably never be known. Sometime before his death Franklin added seven and one-half pages to his memoirs. This is the fourth and last part, and for present purposes its chief significance is that it is not included in the copies sent to Vaughan and Le Veillard.

Franklin died in 1790. His grandson, William Temple Franklin, was made his literary executor. Years passed, and Temple Franklin failed to bring out the promised edition of his grandfather's works. He was probably absorbed in various land speculations from which he expected large profits. It was no small task to make selections from his grandfather's papers and edit them. He is said to have found particular difficulty in transcribing the manuscript of the most important of all the documents, the *Autobiography.* On one of his visits to Paris, in 1791 or 1792, he saw the fair copy that had been sent to Le Veillard and finally gave the original manuscript in exchange for it.

Temple Franklin's edition of his grandfather's works at last appeared, in 1817-1818, in London. In this edition the *Autobiography* was printed from Le Veillard's copy, transcribed by Benjamin Bache, in which the wording had been changed in many places. Also, as this copy was sent to France before the fourth part was written, it did not include that last section. The Temple Franklin edition became the accepted version of the *Autobiography* and remained so for fifty years; it was copied, reprinted, and translated hundreds of times.

When John Bigelow was American Minister to France in 1865 and 1866, he started inquiries that resulted in the location of the original manuscript, which he finally purchased. Bigelow was greatly excited over what he found. A comparison of the manuscript with the Temple Franklin version showed many variations, and revealed also the neglected fourth part. He at once started to prepare what he believed would be the definitive text of the *Autobiography,* and it was published in 1868. And so the entire autobiography was printed in English for the first time seventy-eight years after Franklin's death.

Bigelow retained possession of the manuscript of the *Autobiography* for some thirty years and then disposed of it to Dodd, Mead and Company, who in turn sold it to E. Dwight Church. In 1911 the manuscript passed, with the rest of the Church library, into Henry E. Huntington's collection.

All four parts of the original manuscript were written on folio leaves of approximately uniform size. Many years later these were mounted on guards and bound in boards, with a red-leather back. The binding is evidently of French workmanship—an inference that is confirmed by the French-style spelling, "Francklin" in the title on the spine.

The mere transcription of the text was not an easy task, because of numerous corrections and interlineations, but far more difficult was the problem of deciding what Franklin wished the final wording to be. It is doubtful if he himself knew. When he sent the copies to Vaughan and Le Veillard, he made the "earnest request" that they should read them critically. He asked them to help him decide whether or not the memoirs should be published and, if they were to be published, what changes should be made, for, he added pathetically, "I am now grown so old and feeble in mind, as well as body, that I cannot place any confidence in my own judgment." The changes of wording in the "fair copies" prepared by Bache were made, I am inclined to believe, under his grandfather's instructions. Temple Franklin's text was based on one of these copies. We also have two French translations that bear directly on the problem. One of them is of the first part only and

was evidently taken from a copy and not from the original. The other is of the entire *Autobiography,* and the translator had access to both the original and a copy. From these four basic texts the present edition of the *Autobiography* has been prepared. But the differences between this edition and previous versions are not great. They relate only to questions of style, occasionally touching the picturesque wording of a phrase or sentence.

The memoirs will stand as we know them—an unsurpassed story of how a printer and shopkeeper in Philadelphia rose to be one of the world's great figures, and "the most complete representative of his century that any nation can point to." Underlying the whole narrative runs a dispassionate self-analysis that could be made only by an impersonal, impartial scientist or scholar, and which has never been excelled, if it has ever been equaled. (pp. ix-xxvii)

> *Max Farrand, in an introduction to* The Autobiography of Benjamin Franklin: A Restoration of a "Fair Copy," *edited by Max Farrand, University of California Press, 1949, pp. ix-xxvii.*

Verner W. Crane   (essay date 1950)

[*Crane was an American educator, historian, and author, whose works include two monographs on Franklin and the collection* Benjamin Franklin's Letters to the Press, 1758-1775. *In the following excerpt from his introduction to the collection, he surveys Franklin's political and journalistic writings.*]

In his English writings Franklin rarely strayed from American themes—or from immediate issues. The *ad hoc* character of his letters to the press gives them historical and biographical interest but in each instance calls for exegesis. It is not difficult to understand and appreciate their qualities as propaganda. It is a nicer problem to determine by what scale to assess their ideas. When was Franklin setting out his own conceptions of empire and of American rights? When was he writing as the prudent advocate, tempering his views and even his reports of American sentiments to the prejudices of his readers, and to the self-interest and Whiggish principles of the so-called English friends of America?

It will be well to appraise them in the first instance as political journalism: that is, by his own definition, writings aimed to promote some opinions and oppose others. They were all timely, which is the essence of journalism. In Foote's *The Bankrupt,* one character, the printer, explained: "The conductor of a Newspaper, like a good cook, should always serve things in their season: who eats oysters in June? Plays and Parliament Houses are winter provisions." During four years, 1766 and 1768–70, twenty-seven of Franklin's pieces were written for printing in January, thirty-five for January-February issues. Within ten days in April, 1767, he sent in four considerable essays. "I have taken that Method," he wrote Galloway, "to answer all the groundless Charges, and state aright all the mistaken Facts that I heard urged in the Debates at the House of Lords, tho' I durst not mention those Debates."

Most summers he went on his travels, but in 1768, as he explained (again to Galloway) he found that "A Party is now growing in our Favour, which I shall endeavour to increase and strengthen by every Effort of Tongue and Pen." In August, accordingly, he printed five pieces, and seven others before the year was out. It was another of his shrewd observations on political journalism that it was "not only right to strike while the iron is hot," but practicable "to heat it by continually striking." Several of the newly discovered letters to the press are little pieces written to direct renewed attention to more carefully elaborated essays like the Canada tract, the essay on **"The Causes of the American Discontents,"** and the **"Rules for diminishing a Great Empire."**

Franklin began his political writing in 1758 with a piece of anti-proprietary propaganda in line with the object of his mission for the assembly. But his newspaper writings soon took on a much wider scope; and rarely thereafter did he print anything of his own in England merely in his capacity of Pennsylvania agent. Thus in 1759 he supported the assembly's case mainly through the printing and circulation of a number of tracts from other hands, while he himself turned in the newspapers to broader themes. Between 1758 and 1761 he printed a series of humorous or satiric letters to the press to support the vigorous prosecution of the war with France, and to oppose a weak peace. These minor essays in war propaganda provide an interesting setting for his major contribution in 1760 to the Canada-Guadeloupe controversy, in the famous Canada pamphlet. It was in the same character of the general advocate for the Americans in England that he printed in May, 1759, his admirably effective defense of the conduct of the provincial forces in the war, against slanders he had read in printed extracts of letters from the regular officers in America.

From 1765 to 1775 defense of the Americans—against both ignorance and misrepresentation—was a recurrent theme of his publicity. He directed one of his most amusing satires in 1765 at mendacious news reports of America. "The great Defect here is," he wrote Dr. Cooper in July, 1773, "in all Sorts of People, a want of attention to what passes in such remote Countries as America," and "an Unwillingness even to read anything about them if it appears a little lengthy." Franklin's newspaper defenses were seldom long, but they covered a good deal of ground. He defended Americans against "angry reflections" and very often against opprobrious epithets; against charges of inconsistency and intolerance and other charges that they sought independence; against "misrepresentation" by officials of a people who were denied actual representation in Parliament; he defended their ancestors, their virility, and even their diet. More rarely he defended his own conduct. A long "Vindication" that he began in 1774 he did not trouble to print or even to finish.

These were his defenses of all Americans, *vis à vis* Britain—or rather of the North Americans, for his few references to the West Indians were in another tone. Some were defenses of particular colonies, but not especially of Pennsylvania, which until 1769 stood rather well in the scale of English regard. As "A Friend to both Countries" he appeared in 1767 as a special friend to New York in its current troubles. One of his most famous essays was written in 1768 to defend the Bostonians in their quarrels with Bernard—nearly three years before he became the Boston agent. But he thought it well to explain to friends in Philadelphia that "as every offensive thing done in America is charged upon all," he had intervened "to palliate the matter a little for our own sakes," and also to give "some ease to our friends here," members of Parliament who had urged him to write.

Much of his writing was performed during the intensive campaigns for repeal by Parliament of obnoxious measures, as in the press campaign for repeal of the Stamp Act, 1765–66, and in the more prolonged but interrupted campaign for repeal of the Townshend Revenue Act, 1768–69 and 1769–70. Doubts were cast upon the zeal with which he had originally opposed the Stamp Act: doubts which have some basis in the confusions of his opinions and of his private projects in 1764–65. But the further charge, widely circulated in America, that he had not stirred himself to campaign for repeal was untrue. His English friends denied it. "All this while," wrote William Strahan to David Hall, January 11, 1766, he "hath been throwing out Hints in the Public Papers, and giving Answers to such letters as have appeared in them, that required or deserved an Answer."

As now recovered (there were likely other pieces not yet recognized), his Stamp Act essays throw a little light upon the complicated problem of the adjustment, the rather tardy adjustment, he was making in his private ideas of empire and American rights. They add much more to an understanding of his journalistic methods. For one thing they demonstrate that his performance in his famous examination before Commons—a brilliant performance on the whole, though evasive in some particulars—was of a piece with his current newspaper propaganda, and levied rather heavily upon it.

Except for his *Examination,* which was not printed in England until 1767, his Stamp Act pieces cannot compare for variety of interest or often in individual brilliance with the essays he wrote during the second prolonged crisis of empire, 1767-70. Many of these are new additions to the Franklin canon: they include pieces which throw fresh light on his relations with Hillsborough in 1768; a satirical essay which contains his most direct and elaborate analysis of American economic grievances; and the one substantial periodical series that he attempted in England. They present further examples of "ideological lag," especially in one essay of 1767. But they also sometimes reveal, despite their cautious tone and their deliberate suppression of the more divisive constitutional issues, striking glimpses of Franklin's radical private notions of Parliamentary power.

As Pennsylvania agent, Franklin's publicity task was complicated until 1769 by the cautious course of the Philadelphia merchants in regard to nonimportation. Once convinced, however, that Pennsylvania would come in, he undertook the congenial rôle of press agent in England for the Nonimportation League. To this function one may relate the major part of his letters to the press from January,

1769, until November, 1770, and by anticipation several of his earlier essays. In them he appears one of the most persistent American proponents of the tactics of trade withdrawal, even after the partial repeal of the Townshend duties.

After 1770, as the agent for four colonies, Franklin was more than ever the "ambassador" of North America, in the view of English friends and foes alike. It was his agency for the Massachusetts assembly, in particular, which now thrust him prominently into leadership. Much of his later newspaper writing, especially from 1773 to 1775, was directly related to this agency, and the problems it created for him: the personal problems involved in the Hutchinson letter affair and its sequels, his disgrace in the Cockpit and the deprivation of his crown office; and the larger political problems of the later crises, from the Tea crisis to the eve of war, in which he found himself the spokesman for the most radical and troublesome, and therefore the most distrusted, of the American communities. To this period belong the most vigorous of his satirical attacks on British policies and attitudes toward the colonies: the well-known satires of September, 1773, and two other satires of 1774, hitherto unidentified. Yet on the whole he wrote less, and reprinted more, in his final year in England than in the other great emergencies.

FRANKLIN'S POLITICAL IDEAS: EMPIRE AND AMERICAN
RIGHTS

In these essays Franklin had more to say about the views of the Americans than about his own ideas. Repertorial phrases are common: "These are their notions. They may be errors." Right or wrong, government should weigh them, for "Government must depend for its Efficiency either on Force or Opinion. . . . Free Government depends on Opinion, not on the brutal Force of a Standing Army." He called himself the "impartial historian of American facts and opinions," but he was more concerned to make ideas effective in action than to clarify the issues with ultimate precision. Indeed he thought it well not to look too closely at constitutional issues, and deplored "public Discussion of Questions that had better never have been started." He was the editor as well as the reporter of American opinions. His interpretations were dictated primarily by his strong sense of tactics. But they took color also from his own habits of thought.

Franklin was not, of course, a systematic political philosopher. His ideas have to be discovered in *ad hoc* pieces, arguments to immediate ends. They show inconsistencies, but also evolution, and quite early reveal that he was developing the elements of a respectable political theory. His political thinking was essentially pragmatic. Like his science it was based upon observation. From a reading of history, and from observation of societies that he knew— including an especially acute analysis of the dynamics of growth in American society—he had arrived at certain usable generalizations. One of these was his generalization about opinion and government. **"In Matters of General Concern to the People,"** he reminded Governor Shirley in 1754, "and especially where Burthens are to be laid upon them, it is of Use to consider as well what they will be apt to think and say, as what they ought to think." Another

was his doctrine that government should promote the general welfare. This was a very different approach from that of the American intellectuals of his time who began with principles of positive or natural law, though it led him in the long run to similar conclusions. No lawyer himself and no great admirer of the profession, Franklin was the least legalistic of American champions. It is not surprising that he sometimes fumbled constitutional distinctions. He also stood quite outside the tradition of the natural rights philosophy; he rarely appealed to Locke, seldom used the conventional language of natural law, compact, and fundamental right.

By the 1750's Franklin had reached a number of practical conclusions about the British empire in America. In his imperial ideas he took account both of the rapid growth of American population and of defense necessities in face of French power. At Albany in the summer of 1754, and in his later discussions at Boston with Governor Shirley, he proposed improvements in imperial machinery. His famous plan of intercolonial union was framed to concentrate the existing powers of the colonial assemblies "in certain points of the general welfare," namely in respect to Indian relations, new settlements, common defense. It failed. Had it succeeded, he later claimed, it would have made unnecessary those later measures which unhinged the empire.

His discussions with Shirley in December led farther afield. He showed himself at that time fully aware of the scope of probable American reaction to an alternative scheme of Parliamentary taxation. Their objections, he predicted, would run to the point of constitutional right as well as to equity, for they would say: "That it is supposed an undoubted right of Englishmen, not to be taxed but by their own consent given through their representatives." Americans recognized their subordination to Parliament as well as their allegiance to the King, and accepted Parliamentary legislation, which was mainly economic regulation. They did not complain of those "secondary taxes" which though nominally borne by Englishmen were actually shifted to their own shoulders through the restraints of the mercantilist system, by which "our whole wealth centers finally amongst the merchants and inhabitants of Britain." But in another letter to Shirley he revealed that he had begun to doubt the validity of the basic mercantilist principle of colonial subordination, on grounds of general welfare. In conversation Shirley had opened "the subject of uniting the colonies more intimately with Great Britain, by allowing them representatives in Parliament." At the time Franklin thought this would be satisfactory to Americans, but on condition that prior to union all acts restraining colonial trade and manufactures be repealed, and both peoples put on the same footing until the imperial Parliament should "think it for the interest of the whole to reenact some or all of them."

These positions which Franklin took in 1754 furnish an interesting measure of the American case of 1764-65, and a yardstick also for his own retreats and compromises during that later crisis. There was no revival of interest among the colonists in the plan of union they had so unanimously ignored a decade before. But Franklin listed this measure as a possible alternative to the projected Stamp Act. He also prepared arguments (fit only for the ears of ministers) for another alternative, discussed with Shirley, colonial representation in Parliament. In 1766 he began to write a pamphlet which would have led up to this solution. But American assemblies and the Stamp Act Congress rejected it, and in the London press Franklin fell into line. As for the predicted American arguments against Parliamentary taxation, they were woven into the petitions and resolves and pamphlets which made up the American case. In February, 1766, Franklin had his letters to Shirley printed in a London paper to show that current American arguments were not recently invented to rationalize new grievances. A few days later, in his famous examination at the bar of the House of Commons, he explored some of the same ground. But he now drew a different line to bound the power of Parliament. In 1754 he had drawn the line rather clearly between taxation and regulation. In 1766 he drew it between internal and external taxation.

Until the winter of 1765-66 Franklin had taken little part in the public discussion of the new imperial questions. But meanwhile he had been active in politics. His engrossing concern in 1764 was the bitter campaign to overthrow the proprietary government. It involved him in compromising alliances with conservatives like Joseph Galloway and John Hughes. Later in England he thought it necessary to find a ground of opposition to the Grenville measures upon which English Whig friends of America would rally. These were defensible expediencies. But he also tried to solve the crisis by over-ingenious expedients. He was the one American of distinction who rose to Grenville's bait, and sought to discover an acceptable counterproposal to the stamps. Even after the Pennsylvania assembly in October, 1764, had shelved its mysterious "Plan," he was willing to offer secretly to Grenville his own device of a General Loan Office, which also involved a tax. When the Stamp Act passed, he accepted it in too bland a spirit of resignation and busied himself to get the post of stamp-master in Pennsylvania for a henchman. His conduct aroused no little scandal at the time. Not all of it was deserved. Judged merely as politics, however, his course is hard to defend, for these schemes failed. And it was a sad lapse in the practical politician to lose touch as completely as Franklin did for a time with the main currents of American opinion.

His divergence had begun as early as the spring of 1764. It was from his friend Richard Jackson, the English lawyer who was the Pennsylvania agent and at the same time a member of Parliament and a private secretary to Grenville, that Franklin had received advance intelligence of the new British measures. Jackson soon convinced him that Parliament would inevitably establish some kind of American revenue; that the best hope was for moderate duties on trade; and that it would be easier to make a case in England against what Jackson called internal taxes (excises), such as stamps. Jackson had no doubt that Parliament, a "Universal Legislature," had constitutional authority to impose taxes of every sort in every part of the dominions. As for Franklin, he certainly never adopted Jackson's Whig doctrine of Parliamentary sovereignty. But he accepted his version of the facts, and his strategy. "If Money *must* be raised upon us," he replied in Febru-

ary, 1764, "I think your Plan the most advantageous to both the Mother Country and Colonies of any I have seen." In April, in his pamphlet *Cool Thoughts,* he pressed one of his arguments for royal government so far as to speculate that after a few years' experience Americans might become "very well satisfy'd" to be defended by British troops, and to provide in return "some Revenue arising out of the American Trade." He kept his composure even in face of the Sugar Act and the Currency Act, and discounted the mercantile murmurings. He took more comfort than he should from his conviction that the Sugar Act "will, if it hurts us, hurt you also, you will feel the Hurt and remedy it." These were his comments to Jackson. To Peter Collinson he wrote more sharply of the folly of the new duties and restraints upon trade—indeed of all artificial trade restrictions—but in the same sceptical tone of resignation to immediate evils. He saw no way of bringing Parliament suddenly around to a rational sense of the general welfare. Englishmen must learn for themselves that "what you get from us in Taxes you must lose in Trade. The Cat can yield but her skin."

"Your Objection to internal Taxes," he replied to Jackson, May 1, 1764, "is undoubtedly just and solid." He went on to develop his own favorite objection, which he restated (though without this limitation) as late as 1770. It was a practical objection, quite simply, to the inconvenience of a duplicity of taxation in legislatures so remote as Westminster and the colonial assemblies; and he linked it with his earlier endorsement of a consolidating union. "If you chuse to tax us, give us Members in your Legislature, and let us be one People."

Franklin certainly did not invent the unhappy distinction between internal and external taxation. But he continued to maintain it after the colonists in 1765 had dropped it from their official statements; and he defended it a number of times, rather confusingly, in his examination before the bar of the House of Commons in February, 1766. Rockingham liked it, and Pitt, and so it promised to be useful in securing the repeal of the Stamp Act. But Franklin evidently had convinced himself that it had other merits. He had brought it into harmony with the principle that the subject should not be taxed without his consent. Americans could refuse their consent to external taxes merely by refusing to buy the dutied goods. No doubt he was too sanguine that this remedy would suffice in face of any revenue duties which Parliament might choose to lay; and the distinction was a dangerous invitation to a reckless minister to experiment with new taxes on trade. But having adopted this argument Franklin showed his consistency both in the first and the second crisis, by supporting the American tactics of "industry and frugality." Nor was the argument a sudden improvisation when he found himself cornered before Commons by hostile questioners. He had already stated it, though very briefly, in a letter to the press.

It was Franklin more than any other American who convinced some Englishmen that this was the line Americans in general had adopted in their constitutional challenge to Parliamentary power. He did not discard it immediately [after] it had done its work in repeal, as he might prudently have done—and as he dropped his private proposal to successive ministries of the loan office scheme. He restated both the distinction and his supporting argument in a letter to the press so late as April, 1767. The "BENEVOLUS" letter was in effect an invitation to Charles Townshend to exploit what he regarded as the frivolous American distinction, and hence it was a major political *erratum*. He defended the distinction again, privately, against John Dickinson's cogent criticisms so late as 1768. But in this important letter to his son he also showed that he had advanced in imperial theory far beyond the half-way house of the Pennsylvania Farmer.

"From a thorough Enquiry," Franklin wrote in 1774, "(on Occasion of the Stamp Act) into the Nature of the Connection between Britain and the Colonies, I became convinced, that the Bond of their Union is not the Parliament, but the King." By 1774 it was clear enough that the Anglo-American conflict had come to turn upon the constitutional issue, broader than taxation, of Parliamentary sovereignty in the dominions. This had been openly exposed in the controversy of 1773 between Thomas Hutchinson and the Massachusetts assembly. By 1774 other American leaders, James Wilson, John Dickinson, Thomas Jefferson and John Adams, were beginning to publish their elaborate arguments against Parliamentary legislative power, though these tracts, with the resolves of the First Continental Congress, still made practical concessions. This was the one really significant advance in imperial doctrine that Americans made before they took their final step, revolutionary rather than constitutional, of declaring independence from their King. Englishmen had foreseen the issue much earlier than most Americans were ready to admit it. The Declaratory Act (1766) had been passed to close the door upon this constitutional heresy.

There is reason to believe that it was the resolutions of right which became the Declaratory Act, with the difficulties he had found in drawing a line between duties for regulation and duties for revenue, that turned Franklin's thinking, early in 1766, to this solution of the imperial enigma. The evidence to substantiate his later brief summary of his private conversion appears abundantly in the marginalia he entered in copies of controversial tracts between 1766 and 1770. Fragmentary as they are, they leave no doubt of the vigor of his privately considered doctrines. In them he sharply distinguished between the realm and the dominions; repeatedly asserted that Britain and the colonies were separate states, subject to the same king; claimed an amplitude of legislative power in the colonial assemblies; denied the imperial character of Parliament as then constituted; questioned its legislative authority in America; and cited appropriate precedents from other dominions, especially from the case of Ireland. There is evidence that in 1770 Franklin was planning a fuller argument which he promised to send to his Boston correspondent, Dr. Samuel Cooper, who was anxious to read the "treatise" but apparently never received it. These were not Whig views; they may even be called anti-Whig views. They were shared in England by a few Radical writers only: Joseph Priestley, David Hartley, Granville Sharp, Richard Price. These men were Franklin's friends; Price and Priestley were members of his favorite club, where such opinions may have been discussed. They were not the

announced doctrines of the Pennsylvania Farmer, nor the imperial formulas written into Massachusetts documents between 1768 and 1772. Franklin himself seems to have developed them more as a frame of reference than as a program of imperial reform, unless in a distant future. When he discussed desirable changes in the government of empire he usually referred to his dim hope, always growing dimmer, of a consolidating union, or otherwise urged a return to "the good old way." It was as a frame of reference to judge past and future "usurpations" that he began to communicate his private thoughts to confidants in America: first, to William Franklin, in 1768; and then in significant letters of counsel which he wrote to Massachusetts leaders after 1769.

It was not profitable, even as late as 1774, to air these ideas in the English press. There he was appealing to English Whigs, and he stuck rather closely to the more moderate American arguments. He often pointed out that the colonists submitted to laws enacted in England, as he did in December, 1765, in asserting that they had not the least desire for independence; and in April, 1767, when he denied the charge of English writers: "That the colonies contend the Parliament of Britain has no authority over them." "The truth is," he wrote in rebuttal, "that all acts of the British legislature, expressly extending to the colonies, have ever been received there as laws, and executed in their courts, the right of Parliament to make them being never yet contested, acts to raise money upon the colonies by internal taxes only and alone excepted." "None of the Dummers, the Otises, the Dickinsons, the Dulaneys," he wrote in 1770, "dispute, in their Writings, the Power of the British Government over the Colonies. All they oppose is the illegal and unconstitutional Application of it." And in the same series of essays, he met the Grenvillian charge that Americans were inconsistent in refusing to submit to British taxation, at the same time that they acknowledged obedience to British laws, by recalling Pitt's argument of 1766. All these and other similar admissions after 1765 he made in his capacity of the historian "of American facts and opinions," and obviously for tactical reasons in the contest for English opinion. Not only Franklin but most other Americans preferred until very late to keep close to the issue of taxation, where they could expound arguments which some at least of the English Whigs admitted were cogent. Moreover, as Franklin observed in a marginal note in 1769, "The Americans think, that, while they can retain the right of disposing of their own money, they shall thereby secure all their other rights. They have, therefore, not yet disputed your other pretensions." In 1769 an English pamphleteer wrote: "Our right of legislation over the Americans, unrepresented as they are, is the point in question. This right is asserted by most, doubted by some, and wholly disclaimed by a few." Franklin commented: "I am one of those few, but am persuaded the time is not far distant, when the few will become the many; for *magna est Veritas, et prevalebit.*"

For all his caution, his letters to the press occasionally reflected his secret opinions. The first guarded hint appears in a letter dated January 6, 1766, printed in the *Gazetteer*, January 11. The colonies may, "if the King pleases, be governed as *domains of the crown*," without Parliament.

Even in his *Examination* he asserted that "The Colonies are not supposed to be within the realm." The only conclusion he then drew was that, like Ireland, they were to be taxed by their own Parliaments. On the same occasion he declared that the colonies would consider the resolutions of right, embodied shortly in the Declaratory Act of 1766, "unconstitutional and unjust." His private comment was more emphatic: "the Parliament of Great Britain has not, never had, and of right never can have, without consent, given either before or after, power to make laws of sufficient force to bind the subjects in America in any case whatever, and particularly in taxation."

In 1768 he dropped other hints in the press. In one piece he wrote of "a new kind of loyalty" required of Americans, a loyalty to Parliament. In another, less certainly his, there is a denial that subjects of the King could be treated as "subjects of subjects." In a third he objected to the phrase, "the Colonies . . . belonging to Great Britain." "It would have been more rightly expressed, if you had said, 'to the King of Great Britain.' " In the first of two letters signed "A BRITON" the argument for internal legislative independence is more fully developed. William Franklin, who guessed the authorship of these pieces, no doubt recognized parallels with the confidential letter he had received a few months earlier. In November, 1769, in the answers that he wrote to Strahan's questions, he declared that "Submission to Acts of Parliament was no part of their original Constitution," though at present they consented and submitted to general regulations of commerce. Because he wrote the paper to persuade ministers to a total repeal of the Townshend Revenue Act of 1767 he argued that the asserted supremacy of Parliament could be best preserved by "a very sparing use of it, never, but for the evident good of the Colonies themselves, or of the whole British Empire, never, for the partial Advantage of Britain, to their Prejudice. . . . " Perhaps by that method the supremacy might be in time fully established; otherwise it would be lost in the dispute. Let Britain, if she pleased, keep up her claims, provided they are never exercised; let Americans enjoy *in fact* the right of granting their own money "with the Opinion now universally prevailing among us, that we are free subjects of the King, and that Fellow Subjects of one part of his Dominions are not Sovereigns over Fellow Subjects in any other part." When this paper was later printed in England, in 1774, these passages were singled out by ministerial writers who denounced as "a mere American chimera" the idea of a sovereignty without power to impose laws.

Meanwhile, copies had been sent over to America. One of them Franklin sent to Dr. Samuel Cooper in Boston, with a letter in which he opened up his private views, and advised that such expressions as "*the Supreme Authority of Parliament; the Subordinacy of our Assemblies to the Parliament,* and the like, (which in Reality mean nothing, if our Assemblies, with the King, have a true Legislative Authority)," be dropped from the American vocabulary. His letters to Cooper, with other letters of counsel to Thomas Cushing, deserve closer attention than they have received from historians. They led to his appointment as Massachusetts assembly agent in 1770; and they were evidently a principal channel by which the dominion doctrines

found their way into the American case. They were always accompanied by more moderate counsels in point of tactics. Wait for time and the rapid growth of American population and power—and for England's necessity in some new European crisis—to confirm essential American rights without destroying the empire by a premature contest.

The more firmly Franklin grasped the tenets of his private doctrine of empire, the more careful he became to avoid stirring these issues in public debate. This caution which looks so much like duplicity he could justify to himself on the higher grounds of the general interest of the empire. Nowhere is the basis of his self-imposed censorship so clearly stated as in the introduction to a letter to the *Public Ledger,* Nov. 19, 1774. Proofs of his authorship are not complete, but these views were certainly his own: ". . . it is certain that the Americans NEVER WILL acknowledge the legislative and TAXING power of the British Parliament, nor will the British Parliament ever relinquish that claim. All we can expect is, that the British Parliament will on some PRUDENTIAL considerations suspend the exercise of it; not that they will give up the PRINCIPLE. This question therefore ought by all means to be kept out of sight, because there is no hope of its ever being settled, and any discussions of it will certainly widen the breach." (pp. xxxiii-xlvi)

> *Verner W. Crane, in an introduction to* Benjamin Franklin's Letters to the Press, 1758-1775, *edited by Verner W. Crane, The University of North Carolina Press, 1950, pp. xi-lix.*

Walter Shear   (essay date 1962)

[*In the following essay, Shear argues that Franklin's portrait of himself in his* Autobiography *is incomplete and that the fragmented work only coheres in terms of its theme of self-interest.*]

In view of his recognized stature and the fact that Franklin claimed writing was a principal means of his advancement, his *Autobiography,* which is acknowledged as his major work, appears a rather pallid exercise. The major weakness seems to lie precisely where its strength should be—in the portrait of Franklin himself. Charles Angoff, who uses the *Autobiography* to attack Franklin as a person, argues, "The essential commonplaceness of the man is in every line of it." D. H. Lawrence was also disturbed by the unheroic hero he saw there. Even Carl Van Doren in his biography of Franklin felt restrained in his admiration of the book: "He (Franklin) had lived too long, and put off writing too late, to be able to do justice to himself in a book." Indeed, if one were to judge from the interrupted composition and the incompleteness of the work, one might well question Franklin's own enthusiasm for himself.

It is odd that in an autobiography the major defect should be the presentation of the main character himself, a portrait which, for all its sketches of the many facets of Franklin, remains on each page a one-dimensional view of the man. There seems to be no blood flowing through Franklin's veins despite the factual evidence of events themselves. The character is flat and the logical conclusion would seem to be that the book is a failure. Yet the fact remains that the quality of the style and the book itself fit the character extremely well. Apparently Franklin rejected the type of characterization developed by Defoe and Fielding, in which the characters took on an emotional dimension in their reactions to their environment. By responding in terms of particular situations, these characters inevitably absorbed some of the concreteness of their environment. Franklin knew this type of characterization—he mentions Defoe several times—but he rejects it because his view of himself is based on a different conception of the relationship between man and the world.

In describing his deception by Governor Keith and his subsequent voyage to England, Franklin is content to mention his responses to apparent favors in flat statements—". . . a very great honor I thought it"; "This was the second governor who had done me the honor to take notice of me, which, to a poor boy like me, was very pleasing." His disillusioning discovery of the real state of affairs after he arrives in London is expressed in a straightforward account of his awakening, a paragraph on Keith which is obviously the product of retrospective thought attempting to be as fair as possible, and the beginning of his adjustment to the London scene. The treatment of the entire incident suggests that it is a peculiar story involving someone Franklin did not know personally. This tendency to take a rather abstract view can also be seen in the narration of the great mistakes in his life, most of which seem to ignore the problem of evil since they are merely noted as errata and thus fall far short of the dimensions of real sin.

Ordinarily one might dismiss this approach as an error in composition, but the fact that Franklin seems rather deliberate prohibits an easy judgment. His approach can be accounted for. The detachment with which he defines his view of himself seems to spring from his conception of himself at the time he was writing. He was then the philosopher-statesman, not above worldly concerns but not hopelessly submerged in their trivia. In a sense the story is told by an aspect of Franklin rather than the entire man. (In this connection one might recall the fictitious writers he used—Silence Dogood, the Busy-Body, and Poor Richard.) Turning to deal with his own life, Franklin seems to have felt as Aristotle did that "poetry is something more philosophic and of graver import than history, since its statements are rather of universals, whereas those of history are singulars." It would be foolish to claim that Franklin's book does not contain history; obviously chronology is a key thread and occasionally a complicating one in the book's organization. But Franklin is also quite consistent in focusing his attention on what he had come to feel was one of the chief philosophic problems of the age, self-interest, and in doing so he as an historical character tends to be swallowed by philosophy as his self-interest becomes Everyman's.

The underlying basis for self-interest, vanity, is at first humorously presented to the reader as a careless self-revelation containing what proves to be one of the essential truths of the *Autobiography:* "Most people dislike

vanity in others, whatever share they have of it themselves; but I give it fair quarter wherever I meet with it, being persuaded that it is often productive of good to the possessor, and to others that are within his sphere of action. . . ." His mention of its being "often productive of good to the possessor" reveals that practicality governs his view of vanity, as indeed it proved a criterion for the vast majority of his observations. Men who cultivated humility and meekness were not apt to rise in the world; they might cultivate what they felt were beautiful souls, but they would never attain the worldly success that was his. Franklin seems to be aware that vanity is directly related to the diligence which he points out in his ancestors and parents and which he practiced all his life. When vanity took the form of ambition and when it was channelized as it was in his learning to write by imitating the *Spectator* papers, it could be of great benefit.

Man's vanity, however, was not always the source of all progress; Franklin was well aware of the ambiguity of its force. He is careful to demonstrate that many of his early troubles in Boston were the result of pride and its frequent manifestations, the penchant for careless and extreme self-expression. As a young man, perhaps just beginning to feel his mental strength, Benjamin was overly fond of arguing. He disputes on paper with a friend, John Collins, and later adopts the Socratic method of argumentation, which he says he delighted in and frequently employed. For the reader's benefit he immediately points out the errors of dogmatism and a disputatious temper, mistakes which he would only discover years later. That he was aware of his errors at the time seems doubtful, for, flattered by the praise of his Dogood letters, he begins to resent his brother's orders and to engage in such violent differences of opinion that his father is frequently called upon to serve as an arbitrator. While Benjamin claims that justice was often on his side, in the end these differences lead to his brother's dismissing him and effectively preventing him from getting employment at the other print shops in Boston. He confesses that his position was made worse because he had made enemies of powerful politicians and some "indiscrete disputations about religion began to make me pointed at with horror by good people as an infidel or atheist." Certainly his experiences in Boston were an impressive lesson in the ways of the world and the limitations of the self, and while Benjamin was to spend his life avoiding such errors, he learned this truth only gradually and sometimes painfully.

Later in Philadelphia he is wise enough to perceive that both Bradford and Keimer have weaknesses as printers, but he still has not discovered that his own true interest requires such prosaic practices as diligence and frugality. Instead his naivete makes him an easy victim of Keith's promises and flattery, both of which were an appeal to his major weakness, pride. One of the few good pictures of the proud Benjamin shows him in fine clothes and cultivating an appearance of wealth in a visit to his brother's shop.

His pride is justified, to some extent, because he has risen in the world, but it is unwise since it merely serves to needlessly anger his brother.

Thus the groundwork has been laid, through the selection

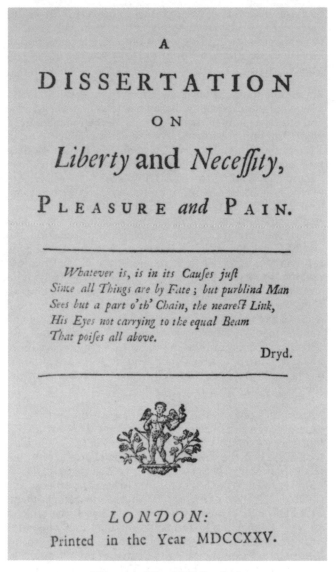

A

DISSERTATION

ON

Liberty and *Neceſſity,*

PLEASURE *and* PAIN.

Whatever is, is in its Cauſes juſt
Since all Things are by Fate ; but purblind Man
Sees but a part o'th' Chain, the neareſt Link,
His Eyes not carrying to the equal Beam
That poiſes all above.

Dryd.

LONDON:
Printed in the Year MDCCXXV.

Title page of Franklin's first book.

of relevant detail if not in its emphasis, for the philosophic quest which follows: the search for Franklin's true interest. This view of himself in relation to abstractions necessarily limits any character development or soul searching, yet it serves to endow the surface of the book with the moving symmetry of an ideological pattern. While many of the apparent possibilities of his governing passion lead to a dead end, there is always an opportunity for a new view of the subject and a calm assurance that the problem will eventually be solved. The movement is one of indefinite spatial extension, a journey in which the personal overtones of experience are subdued and the past is only a matter of abstract interest.

Displaying a loyalty to truth as well as to his ideological concerns, Franklin traces his deviation from a more perfect line of development. The discovery of one's true interest, as he later points out, demands a partial submission of the self to the dictates of systematic reason. Instead, Franklin, lured by Keith's promises, chooses at this point

to follow his inclinations, though he might have profited by the examples of the drinking of his friend Collins, the enthusiasms and gluttony of Keimer, and the careless morality of Ralph, all of whom regard personal gratifications rather than objective standards of conduct as prime goals in life. During this time Franklin abandons his vegetable diet—after he has "balanc'd some time between principle and inclination"—and, what is much more serious for a man who intends to make a living in business, he breaks into Vernon's money. Each incident here demonstrates the vanity of those human wishes that do not attempt to come to terms objectively with that formidable world that exists outside the self, and Franklin's disappointment in England is a fitting climax for such errors in judgment.

Thus far Franklin's imagination, taking the form of credulity, has mainly served to betray him. In London his mind begins to work more efficiently for him as his orientation to a more matter of fact relationship to reality makes him increasingly aware of certain approaches to life which he will be able to use in new and different situations. He still makes mistakes, but he begins to be more alert to their consequences and pays more attention to possible solutions to his difficulties. In his situation money becomes more of a key factor and, though he quite properly relies now on his own industry, an element he can be certain of, he spends too much. Forgetting Deborah, a mistake he will remedy later, he makes advances to Ralph's mistress and thus loses not only a friend but a debt owed him. However, looking about, he encounters a Roman Catholic lady who, intent on living the life of a nun in the midst of the world, provides a lesson for his extravagance, showing on "how small an income life and health may be supported." Her method of adjusting to the world—renunciation—and his own isolated and vulnerable position at this time provide a hint of the future direction of his thought and also define a position to which the self might retreat when the adversities of the world appear overwhelming.

Another change that gives Franklin new impetus is the shrewdness in his choice of acquaintances. One of his friends, the merchant Denham, offers him a promising job in Philadelphia and, though Denham dies soon afterwards, Franklin, now a man of some experience, is able to get a good position with Keimer.

Besides the increase in his self-confidence, Franklin's changing attitude toward reality includes a new willingness to adjust to the social world. During his London employment he has a difference with his fellow workers; however, he eventually conforms instead of rebelling, finally being "convinc'd of the folly of being on ill terms with those one is to live with continually." When back in Philadelphia he is obviously much more cognizant of the power of public opinion, perhaps to too great a degree since his anger at being *publicly* rebuked by Keimer brings about his dismissal. At this point he seems to have come to the conclusion that the force of society will inevitably overcome the individual who opposes it and in another instructive example he points out to the reader that Keimer's failings in business were the result of his failure to cultivate the public: ". . . he was an odd fish; ignorant of common life, fond of rudely opposing receiv'd opinions, slovenly to extreme dirtiness, enthusiastic in some points of religion, and a little knavish withal."

When Franklin enters business, he shows the concern for public appearance which he later mentioned in a letter to his sister: " . . . *appearances* should therefore be attended to, in our conduct towards them, as well as Realities." "In order to secure my credit and character as a tradesman, I took care not only to be in *reality* industrious and frugal, but to avoid all appearances to the contrary. I drest plainly; I was seen at no places of idle diversion. . . . I sometimes brought home the paper I purchas'd at the stores thro' the streets on a wheelbarrow." In his business experiences Franklin discovered the close association between public service and self-advancement: by meeting the needs of society, one might also satisfy the needs of the self. Apparently tending to his own business, he had seen that reciprocity was the key to the complex relationship between the individual and society. This transformation of the selfless activity into the self-satisfying becomes a major motif upon which many variations are played.

At this point the ***Autobiography*** breaks off, dividing into two rather distinct fragments. While the division is a serious defect from the point of view of history and the continuity of personality, the fragments fit rather nicely from the standpoint of thematic treatment as an additional exposition and extension of his concern with self-interest. Though the first section is more personal, Franklin had pointed out in a letter to the Duke de la Rochefoucauld that the earlier years would be "of more general use to young readers; as exemplifying strongly the effects of prudent and imprudent conduct in the commencement of a life of business." In the last two parts, especially the more abstract second part, the philosophic lessons become more sharply delineated. In fact, the concern with instruction is specifically mentioned in the third section where it is suggested that the ***Autobiography,*** along with most of his other writing, was an important part of his service to the public.

In resuming his book, Franklin shifts his theme into the area of religion, rather abruptly it seems and yet not without a felt attachment to the business world he had just described. At this time he was free from many of the pressures which had previously hampered him. He had money now and he had solved the problem of "that hard-to-be-governed passion of youth" through his marriage with Deborah Read. It was natural rather than hypocritical that he should relate religion to his theme with the blunt awareness of a man who was content to struggle with the world on its own terms—"nothing is so likely to make a man's fortune as virtue." His experience had taught him that the reasoning in books was not always applicable to life. Though generally considered a Deist, he is very explicit about his eventual disagreements with those he regarded as freethinkers. Evidently Franklin interpreted the arguments he had read for the natural sense of right and wrong as being justifications for following one's own inclinations and this approach to morality he had found inadequate. He now believed his London pamphlet, ***Dissertation on Liberty and Necessity, Pleasure and Pain,*** "Not

so clever a performance as I once thought it." From his experience he had seen that inclination, even with good intention, and abstract rules were not enough; there had to be systematic efforts in order to really live the life of reasonable virtue.

An examination of the virtues themselves reveals immediately why there existed a close association between virtue and interest: many of them reflected, perhaps deliberately, what Franklin considered good business habits—Order, Resolution, Frugality, Industry, Sincerity. The modern mind, naturally enough, is quick to accuse Franklin of calculation. According to D. H. Lawrence, " . . . if Mr. Andrew Carnegie, or any other millionaire, had wished to invent a God to suit his ends, he could not have done better. Benjamin did it for him in the eighteenth century." This sort of condemnation has a great deal of justification and yet it ignores Franklin's basic concern with what is good for man. He is trying to fit religion into life, not life into religion. In mixing the ideal and the ordinary—as demonstrated in the peculiar juxtaposition "Rise, wash, and address Powerful Goodness!"—Franklin tries to point out some of the necessary connections between daily life and Sunday theology. Having had some contact with the stricter religious communities, he knew that religion occasionally did as much harm as good. But he also knew how the world could play on a man to bring out his weaknesses and the pettiness in his character.

Most critics of Franklin's religion neglect the fact that he himself was well aware of the limitations of his virtues. He had seen too much of faith in action ever to be religion's fool. He rejects the role of the enlightened prophet for that of the philosophic observer. As F. L. Lucas states, " . . . he never fell into the folly of trying to be unreasonably reasonable. . . " (*Art of Living*). Because of this temperament Franklin tends to qualify his presentation of the table of virtue with such comment as: "something that pretended to be reason, was every now and then suggesting to me that such extream nicety as I exacted of myself might be a kind of foppery in morals, which, if it were known, would make me ridiculous. . . . " With this shift in point of view he puts everything he has said at a peculiar angle, thus avoiding bondage to his own abstraction and preserving his freedom to act in whatever way he deems most appropriate. From his new vantage point he is even able to see a certain humor in the relationship between virtues and the social pressures which may force a man to be virtuous against his will. Each shift, of course, creates a greater complexity in the pattern of the surface and with the final twist he pushes aside society's reverence for humility, saying, "I cannot boast of much success in acquiring the *reality* of this virtue, but I had a good deal with regard to the *appearance* of it," and returns once again to the world.

In the third section Franklin weaves in a complex fashion the religious, political, and individualistic threads of his theme as these concerns find their place in the broader expanse of society. Although the chronological order seems to introduce the disorder of time, Franklin's basic vision, outlined at the beginning of the section, constantly governs and controls events, permitting him to move easily through a great many different environments. His public point of view bears a direct correspondence to his own conception of himself: Just as the individual must determine his *true* interest, so single organizations and nations must find an interest larger than their particular causes if they are to be successful in their dealings with others. Blending his deep belief in benevolence and the good of all mankind with his basically practical vision, Franklin saw in his experience that one could best attain his interest by identifying it or merging it with this greater good of mankind. As he later demonstrates, those involved in social or political causes attain their ends by adjusting to the will of the majority and those who display selfishness or narrow self-interest are inevitably doomed to fail.

This mixture of the practical and the ideal is notably shown in the account of his projects. In serving God by doing good to man, Franklin not only stores up credits for heaven but also gains significant earthly rewards. Although the reference to his newspaper and ***Poor Richard's Almanack*** emphasizes their role as a service, a means for conveying instruction to the "common people," it is obvious that they helped to make Franklin a wealthy man. The rewards for public service were frequently many and diverse. As he made clear in his account of the Junto Club project, the expansion of their aims involved not only "the improvement of so many more young citizens," but "the promotion of our particular interests in business by more extensive recommendation, and the increase of our influence in public affairs." One of Franklin's first involvements with politics, being chosen clerk of the General Assembly, gained him a great deal of business besides being a service to the public, and his fire company was as much a benefit to himself as to the others involved. His most selfless action, declining a patent for his stove, probably served to win him some good will in the long run. A further benefit would seem to be the way in which the lesson of the double advantage aided Franklin in his later affairs. In analyzing his political theory, Gerald Stourzh claims Franklin set out "in search of schemes which would bring conveniences to all participants" (*Benjamin Franklin and American Foreign Policy*).

Franklin never refrained from doing favors for people because even the most apparently selfless deed was never really selfless: His account of a favor done for Whitefield reveals his predilection for strong social obligation as opposed to the idea of waiting for heavenly rewards. According to the proverb he quotes, there was also an advantage in being the recipient of a favor: *"He that has once done you a kindness will be more ready to do you another, than he whom you yourself have obliged."* Men were gathered together in society not merely to form an organization but to benefit one another and their very psychology contributed, or should contribute, to the progress and felicity of the whole. If his projects benefited many, they also gave him reputation and eventually an opportunity to raise himself to the status of a statesman. As he commented earlier in an explanation of the successful conduct of a project, "If it remains a while uncertain to whom the merit belongs, some one more vain than yourself will be encouraged to claim it, and then even envy will be disposed to

do you justice by plucking those assumed feathers and restoring them to their right owner."

Franklin's treatment of the Hemphill controversy also emphasizes his concern for good works, but it is, in addition, the first treatment of what becomes a major thematic aspect in the last section, the tendency for particular religious beliefs to run counter to the public good. Because he thought Hemphill's religious views were of use to the people, Franklin sided with him, and his later friendship with Whitefield was based on the same sort of regard for the ends of religion. His more negative attitude toward the sectarian aspects of religion, as shown in the account of his political differences with the Quakers, stems from his belief that such groups or factions would inevitably suffer if their principles were so static that they failed to respond to the needs of society. All his dealings with religious sects apparently confirm his idea. He claims that the number of Quakers who were strict pacificists were much less than had been expected, and he reinforces this attack on denominational peculiarity with the anecdote of James Logan. His later experience with the Moravians, who dismissed pacificism because of their vulnerable position on the frontier, also proved to his satisfaction that "common sense, aided by present danger, will sometimes be too strong for whimsical opinions." The religious views Franklin truly admires are those of the Dunkers, who, being aware of further possible improvement, have successfully avoided the dangers of sectarian pride: "This modesty in a sect is perhaps a singular instance in the history of mankind, every other sect supposing itself in possession of all truth, and that those who differ are so far in the wrong. . . ." With their fluid point of view the Dunkers would be able, in Franklin's eyes, to respond with society as a whole to any new situation or any new knowledge. Whatever the needs of a society were, the factions within that society would be forced to come to terms with them and in this condition of flux self-interest might have many guises.

Franklin expresses the pragmatic aspect of interest very simply: "The best public measures are . . . seldom *adopted from previous wisdom, but forc'd by the occasion."* Yet as he outlines his dealings with the British colonial administration, the difficulties which traditional ideas and methods presented for a nation's interest soon appear rather considerable and disconcertingly vital. Perhaps not without prejudice, Franklin views the rejection of the Albany Plan by both the Colonists and the British as a basic miscalculation:

> Look around the habitable world, how few
> Know their own good, or, knowing it, pursue!

Later he is able to insert a moral tale, the story of General Braddock, to illustrate how pride in past accomplishments can blind one to his own interest. Because of his experiences in Europe, Braddock believes he knows too much about warfare to listen to Franklin's advice. Dealing with the incident in great detail and stressing his service in a definite yet modest manner, Franklin follows the disaster to Braddock's last words, which form a rather ironic moral. In contrast to Braddock's narrowness and failure, Franklin's practical methods of providing for frontier defense are wholly concerned with the proper effecting of the common good: "This kind of fort, however contemptible, is a sufficient defense against Indians who have no cannon."

In his own political dealings Franklin attempts to avoid such egotistic blindness by refusing to become involved personally in political differences. Though he is publicly in constant opposition to Governor Morris, the two have very satisfactory personal relationships. Perhaps this restraint on Franklin's part was an effort at the sort of humility which would enable him to attain his long range interest since he noted that those who were constantly argumentative "get victory sometimes, but they never get good will, which would be of more use to them."

It becomes obvious that Franklin's practical outlook on life, acquired no doubt in his business struggles, eventually became a central factor in his political thinking. With the good of the whole as the objective in political affairs, the individual frequently had to abandon a personal view of situations and participants in order to deal more effectively with the problem. Practicality, success, and a temporary submersion of the self were all absolutely bound together in Franklin's social vision. On the level of the community of nations the British policy toward the Colonists ignored all these factors and the resultant indecisiveness and incompetence are clearly illustrated in the uncertainties of Lord Loudon. In describing Loudon's failure to serve the needs of the Colonies, Franklin focuses on one of the prime causes of the Revolution and foresees the ultimate rejection by the Americans of a force which could no longer see or serve its interests.

In the brief account of his early experiences with British politics Franklin indicates that the proprietaries suffer from this same blindness to colonial interests. He is dismayed when his conversation with Lord Grenville discloses the great differences in the English view of the colonial situation. In looking back at the situation he seems to be attempting a detached attitude but without much success. Although he states that "each party had its own ideas of what should be meant by *reasonable*," he shows no inclination to abandon claims he considers just, for he refers without qualification to "the selfishness of the proprietaries." If the *Autobiography* had not broken off here, the question of interest might have been viewed from an even more illuminating angle. Perhaps in view of the absolute conflict on the practical level Franklin might have argued that the American position promised the most advantage for both sides since, as Stourzh notes, "Franklin, when he celebrated the interest of mankind, never forgot the interest of America. . . . " At any rate his broad political views seem to be outlines even though the book remained incomplete at his death.

The *Autobiography* does not present the complete Franklin, but it does define a purposeful man in terms of his own key ideas. Though the book seems fragmented through its attention to the varied aspects of his life as well as by its interrupted composition, the focus on the problem of interest, or its more moral manifestation, pride, establishes a consistent point of view. Interest was the impulse to improvement and, though it needed to be controlled by sys-

tematic thinking, in this capacity it was an asset both to the individual and to all mankind. While the theme is presented in a simple and direct style, the movement of Franklin's thought displays the complexity resulting from the interaction of philosophy and ordinary life. It is in this complexity, the account of the sudden and sharp enlargements of understanding, that the book attains its classic status. Franklin as character fits into the philosophic texture as a growing and supple intelligence—not always avoiding the shocks of the world, but able to deal with this world, merge with it, and still retain the quality of observation necessary to record it. (pp. 71-86)

> *Walter Shear, "Franklin's Self-Portrait," in* The Midwest Quarterly, *Vol. IV, No. 1, Autumn, 1962, pp. 71-86.*

Richard E. Amacher   (essay date 1962)

[*Amacher is an American scholar and the editor of* Franklin's Wit and Folly: The Bagatelles *(1953). In the following essay from his* Benjamin Franklin *(1962), he discusses Franklin's personal essays, including the* Dogood *and* Busy-body *papers, and the* Bagatelles.]

Since the history of the personal essay as a genre is long and complicated, we may sketch it only briefly here. It begins in the late sixteenth century with the *Essais* of Montaigne (1580); but before Montaigne the French had developed a form known as the *leçon morale,* which often resembled a collection of sayings organized around a central topic or moral lesson. Montaigne developed this form into the essay by adding a highly personal element. In the early part of the seventeenth century Francis Bacon contributed elements of practicality and utilitarianism to the essay, stressing the original aphoristic quality in his style. Writers such as Joseph Hall, Thomas Overbury, John Earle, George Savile, and Jean de La Bruyère injected what were known as *Characters,* sketches of typical persons, vices, or virtues. In the eighteenth century Defoe, Steele, and Addison transformed the essay into a vehicle for their periodicals—*A Weekly Review of Affairs in France,* the *Tatler,* and the *Spectator.* Under their hands the essay attempted—under the dual headings of entertainment and instruction—to reform the age, refine the taste of the reader, and provide a wide variety of topics for conversation. *Humor* and *satire* received strong stress in a generally more informal style. This was the state of the essay by the time Franklin came to it in the early 1720's.

Three large groups of Franklin's essays—the **Dogood** papers, the **Busy-Body** papers, and the **Bagatelles**—must be considered. We will also treat some of the hoaxes . . . and the essay entitled **"On Conversation,"** which appeared in the *Pennsylvania Gazette* for October 15, 1730. We have selected the latter because it seems representative of the separate essays that Franklin composed and printed from time to time in his paper.

I *The Dogood Papers*

In the *Autobiography* Franklin tells how as a young apprentice he overheard the writers for his brother's *Courant* discussing their work.

I was excited to try my hand among them. But being still a boy and suspecting that my brother would object to printing anything of mine in his paper if he knew it to be mine, I contrived to disguise my hand; and writing an anonymous paper, I put it one night under the door of the printing house. It was found in the morning and communicated to his writing friends when they called in as usual. They read it, commented on it in my hearing, and I had the exquisite pleasure of finding it met with their approbation, and that in their different guesses at the author, none were named but men of some character among us for learning and ingenuity. . . . Encouraged . . . by this attempt, I wrote and sent in the same way to the press several other pieces, which were equally approved, and I kept my secret till my small fund of sense for such performances was pretty well exhausted, and then I discovered it, when I began to be considered a little more by my brother's acquaintances.

Evidence in possession of the Yale editors of the Franklin papers (I, 8) points to the fact that these writings were the *Dogood* papers, printed from April 2 to October 8 in the year 1722.

[The] *Courant* owed a more than sizeable debt to the *Spectator.* Similarly, it is easy to demonstrate a resemblance between the *Dogood* papers and the periodical essays composing the *Spectator.* In their use of a character mask of an observer at the same time belonging to and yet apart from society, in the characterization of this observer at the beginning of the essay, in their common purpose (to correct the follies of the age), and in their common desire to please, the *Spectator* and the *Dogood* essays agreed. The *Spectator* had his club; Silence Dogood had her lodger (a minister) and her neighbor (Rusticus). Other common techniques were the use of Latin mottoes, lay sermons, allegorical visions, eaves-droppers, street-strollers, and letters from correspondents. They even treated the same subjects: the excess of religious zeal, the extravagance of female fashions, the plight of widows, and alcoholism. In style the *Dogood* papers resembled the colloquial manner of the *Spectator,* but discarded the learned allusions and literary anecdotes, replacing them with homely sayings (*Dogood,* No. V) and with comic, and sometimes earthy, stories (No. XIII). Horner notes many resemblances between the *Spectator* papers of Addison and Steele and the *Dogood* papers of Franklin "in method, purpose, and matter." The bulk of the fourteenth *Dogood* paper, for example, is an extract of *Spectator* No. 185.

But although Franklin's debt to the *Spectator* for style and other matters was large, his more immediate models for the *Dogood* papers lay closer to home in the "homely and unsophisticated satire" of the Couranteers themselves— James Franklin, who is believed to have written under the pseudonyms of Abigail Afterwit and Timothy Turnstone; Mathew Adams, who wrote as Harry Meanwell; and a Mr. Gardner, who disguised himself as Fanny Mournful. The Couranteers, who had domesticated the *Spectator* brand of essay, had also supplied Franklin with a lively and more native humor.

The smallpox and the Indian wars had decimated the male population of Boston in the year 1722. The town abounded with widows. The choice of a young widow as a mouthpiece for the young printer's apprentice was therefore timely. The name "Silence" ill becomes the talkative nature of this young woman and therefore must be ironic. Dogood as a surname properly expressed Franklin's early didactic spirit. But he also may have thought Dogood an appropriate name for the deceased young minister who had married her. As for her character, she best describes it herself in the last paragraph of the second paper (April 16, 1722):

> I am an Enemy to Vice, and a Friend to Vertue. I am one of an extensive Charity, and a great Forgiver of *private* Injuries: A hearty Lover of the Clergy and all good Men, and a mortal Enemy to arbitrary Government and unlimited Power. I am naturally very jealous for the Rights and Liberties of my Country; and the least appearance of an Incroachment of those invaluable Priviledges, is apt to make my Blood boil exceedingly. I have likewise a natural Inclination to observe and reprove the Faults of others, at which I have an excellent Faculty. I speak this by Way of Warning to all such whose Offences shall come under my Cognizance, for I never intend to wrap my Talent in a Napkin. To be brief; I am courteous and affable, good humour'd (unless I am first provok'd,) and handsome, and sometimes witty, but always, Sir, Your Friend and Humble Servant, SILENCE DOGOOD.

Silence had her fling at the town of Boston every two weeks, as she had announced in her first letter, with only three exceptions. Two of the exceptions came at three-week intervals, but this was balanced somewhat by the appearance of the third after only one week.

In the first *Dogood* letter Franklin satirizes the tendency of people not to blame or praise anything they read until they know what kind of person the writer is and also their tendency to criticize a literary performance in terms of what they know about the author's circumstances— "whether he be *poor* or *rich, old* or *young, a Schollar* or a *Leather Apron Man,* etc." Taking this observation as a cue for a brief satiric character sketch of a typical sentimental heroine, Franklin then describes Silence as a poor girl whose father had been washed overboard from a ship by a "merciless wave" at the very moment he was rejoicing at her birth.

Eventually, because of her mother's poverty, Silence became a bound apprentice to a country minister, who "instructed her in all that Knowledge and Learning which is necessary for our Sex," including needlework, writing, arithmetic, etc. The minister, it seems, owned a library, and so Silence had spent a good deal more time in reading books than had most other girls of her day. Left an orphan by her mother's death, she declared that she really had "no affliction but what was imaginary, and created in my own Fancy; as nothing is more common with us Women, than to be grieving for nothing, when we have nothing else to grieve for."

The second letter tells of how the bachelor minister who had brought her up proposed to her and won her. "Whether it was Love, or Gratitude, or Pride or all Three that made me consent, I know not; but it is certain, he found it no hard Matter, by the help of his Rhetorick to conquer my Heart, and persuade me to marry him." After seven years of happy married life and the birth of three children, her husband passed to his heavenly reward. As a widow of several years she admits she "could be easily persuaded to marry again." But since good husbands are hard to find, she has decided to forego such intentions.

In the third letter she invites correspondence from members of the female sex. At the age of sixteen Franklin must have thoroughly enjoyed this prank on his female readers, for he tells them that he will look on such correspondence as favors and will acknowledge them "accordingly."

The fourth *Dogood* paper is probably the best known of all. It is the famous one dealing with "The Temple of Learning," a clever satire of Harvard College. It contrasts noticeably with the brevity of the third. Beginning with an appropriate Latin quotation from Cicero to the effect that he was neither talking Greek nor teaching Latin, Franklin shows Silence faced with the problem of whether or not to send her young son to college. She makes discreet inquiries of her "Reverend Boarder," Clericus, but he fails to satisfy her curiosity. Wandering into an orchard while she ruminates this problem, she falls asleep and dreams of the famous Temple of Learning to which every peasant desired to send at least one of his children. "Most of them [the peasants] consulted their own Purses instead of their Childrens Capacities: So that I observed, a great many, yea, the most part of those who were traveling thither, were little better than Dunces and Blockheads. Alas! Alas!"

At the entrance to the temple stand two porters—Riches and Poverty. Poverty refuses to admit anyone who has not gained the favor of Riches, so that many are turned away "for want of this necessary Qualification." Silence is careful to explain that she got in only as a *spectator*.

In the middle of a great hall on a throne raised above "two high and difficult steps sat LEARNING in awful State; she was apparelled wholly in Black, and surrounded almost on every Side with innumerable Volumes in all Languages. She seem'd very busily employ'd in writing something on half a Sheet of Paper, and upon Enquiry, I understood she was preparing a Paper, call'd, *The New-England Courant*." She was surrounded by English, Latin, Greek, and Hebrew. The latter three, who had been veiled by Idleness and Ignorance, only unveiled themselves to "those who have in this Place acquir'd so much Learning as to [be able to] distinguish them from *English*" and who consequently "pretended to an intimate acquaintance with them."

The whole tribe then began to climb the two "high and difficult Steps" to the throne; but most of them, aided by Madam Idleness and her Maid Ignorance, found the ascent too difficult and withdrew, while those who were assisted by "Diligence and a docible Temper" had to be dragged up the steps by those who had already made the ascent. "The usual Ceremonies at an End, every Beetle-Scull seem'd well satisfy'd with his own Portion of Learning, tho' perhaps he was *e'en just* as ignorant as ever."

After graduating from the Temple, some took to merchandising, others to traveling, "some one Thing, some to another, and some to Nothing; and many of them from henceforth, for want of Patrimony, liv'd as poor as Church Mice, being unable to dig, and asham'd to beg, and to live by their Wits it was impossible." The greater part, however, traveled along a well-beaten path to the Temple of Theology. This surprises Silence, until, as she writes, "I spy'd Pecunia [Money] behind a Curtain, beckoning to them." In the Temple of Theology, Silence also sees Plagiarism, "diligently transcribing some eloquent Paragraphs out of Tillotson's *Works, &c.*, to embellish his own."

Silence says she cannot help reflecting upon the folly of parents who, "blind to their Children's Dulness, and insensible of the Solidity of their Skulls, because they think their Purses can afford it," persist in sending their children to the Temple of Learning, where they learn little more than "how to carry themselves handsomely, and enter a Room genteely, [*sic*] (which might as well be acquir'd at a Dancing-School) and from whence they return, after Abundance of Trouble and Charge, as great Blockheads as ever, only more proud and self-conceited."

In the fifth *Dogood*, Silence defends the female sex against a charge that they are "the prime Causes" of a great many vices of men. But in the sixth *Dogood*, Silence attacks women for pride in clothing, particularly the hoop-petticoats then in fashion. "These monstrous topsy-turvy *Mortar Pieces*, are neither fit for the Church, the Hall, or the Kitchen; and if a Number of them were well mounted on Noddles-Island, they would look more like Engines of War for bombarding the Town, than Ornaments of the Fair Sex." She concludes her argument by saying that she has little hope of persuading her sex "utterly to relinquish this extravagant Foolery," but she would at least "desire them to lessen the Circumference of their Hoops, and leave it with them to consider, Whether they who pay no Rates or Taxes, ought to take up more room in the King's High-Way, than the Men, who yearly contribute to the Support of the Government."

The seventh *Dogood* paper is one of the earliest examples of literary criticism in American literature. It parodies the sentimental school of obituary verse rife in Franklin's Boston. Silence marches directly to the front firing line with her first sentence: "It has been the Complaint of many Ingenious Foreigners, who have travell'd amongst us, *That good Poetry is not to be expected in New-England.*" She then attacks, in the best tradition of eighteenth-century literary satire, the pious effusions of an elegy composed upon the death of a Mrs. Mehitabell Kitel—an actual person, according to Labaree and Bell. Silence remarks that the author of this elegy has "invented a new Species of Poetry, which wants a Name, and was never before known." Since this kind of poetry cannot in any sense be called either "Epic, Sapphic, Lyric, or Pindaric, nor any other Name yet invented, I presume," she says, "it may be called the Kitellic," in honor of the dead person. Such "Elegies which are of our own Growth (and our Soil seldom produces any other sort of Poetry) are by far the greatest part, wretchedly Dull and Ridiculous." Appropriately she then proceeds with systematic womanly vigor and pungency to offer, in her best household manner, a *recipe* for making a New-England elegy.

> *For the Title of your Elegy.* Of these you may have enough ready made to your Hands; but if you should chuse to make it your self, you must be sure not to omit the words *Aetatis Suae* [Latin for "his age"], which will Beautify it exceedingly.
>
> *For the Subject of your Elegy.* Take one of your Neighbours who has lately departed this Life; it is no great matter at what Age the Party dy'd, but it will be best if he went away suddenly, being *Kill'd, Drown'd,* or *Froze to Death.*
>
> Having chose the Person, take all his Virtues, Excellencies, &c. and if he have not enough, you may borrow some to make up a sufficient Quantity: To these add his last Words, dying Expressions, &c. if they are to be had; mix all these together, and be sure to *strain* them well. Then season all with a handful or two of Melancholly Expressions, such as *Dreadful, Deadly, cruel, cold Death, unhappy Fate, weeping Eyes,* &c. Hav-[ing] mixed all these Ingredients well, put them into the empty Scull of some *young Harvard;* (but in Case you have ne'er a One at Hand, you may use your own,) there let them Ferment for the Space of a Fortnight, and by that Time they will be incorporated into a Body, which take out, and having prepared a sufficient Quantity of double Rhimes, such as *Power, Flower; Quiver, Shiver; Grieve us, Leave us; tell you, excel you; Expeditions, Physicians; Fatigue him, Intrigue him;* &c. you must spread all upon Paper, and if you can procure a Scrap of Latin to put at the End, it will garnish it mightily; then having affixed your Name at the Bottom with a *Moestus Composuit* [composed in a state of melancholy], you will have an Excellent Elegy.
>
> N.B. This Receipt will serve when a Female is the Subject of your Elegy, provided you borrow a greater Quantity of Virtues, Excellencies, &c.

Dogood essays eight and nine were printed while Franklin had sole management of his brother's newspaper, his brother having been jailed for charging that the Massachusetts authorities were not exerting themselves sufficiently to capture a pirate ship said to be off the coast. The serious tone of these two essays contrasts sharply, therefore, with that of the others.

The eighth essay is in its entirety a long but important quotation from the *London Journal* for February 4, 1721. Franklin introduces this quotation by saying, "I prefer the following Abstract from the London Journal to any thing of my own, and therefore shall present it to your Readers this week without any further preface." The "Abstract," which we have further abridged, follows:

> Without Freedom of Thought, there can be no such Thing as Wisdom; and no such Thing as publick Liberty, without Freedom of Speech; which is the Right of every Man, as far as by it, he does not hurt or controul the Right of anoth-

er; and this is the only Check it ought to suffer, and the only Bounds it ought to know.

> This sacred Privilege is so essential to free Governments, that the Security of Property, and the Freedom of Speech always go together; and in those wretched Countries where a Man cannot call his Tongue his own, he can scarce call any Thing else his own. Whoever would overthrow the Liberty of a Nation, must begin by subduing the Freeness of Speech; a *Thing* terrible to Publick Traytors.
>
> . . . . .
>
> That Men ought to speak well of *their Governours* is true, while *their Governours* deserve to be well spoken of; but to do publick Mischief, without hearing of it, is only the Prerogative and Felicity of Tyranny: A free People will be shewing that they are *so,* by their Freedom of Speech.
>
> . . . . .
>
> Freedom of Speech is ever the Symptom, as well as the Effect of a good Government. . . .

From reading this particular essay, too, one might judge that Franklin knew Latin and Roman history rather well, for it contains numerous Latin quotations and historical allusions in support of the argument. Studied as a whole, the *Dogood* papers reveal interest in such writers as Cicero, Terence, Seneca, Pliny, and Tacitus, which we might expect in a neoclassical age.

The subject of *Dogood* nine is religious hypocrites and the harm they do when stationed in government offices; they are people who "ruin their Country for God's sake," as Franklin puts it. They skilfully deceive their countrymen in the name of religion and under pretext of legal procedure. Franklin felt very strongly against such public deceivers. "This Subject raises in me an Indignation not to be born," [*sic*] he says. While the satire is mainly political rather than religious or anticlerical, it is true that in this letter, as Davy says, Silence forgot that she had earlier characterized herself as "a Lover of the Clergy."

Franklin anticipates twentieth-century New Deal social legislation in *Dogood* ten. He makes Silence admit that the idea of insurance for widows, which she sponsors, is not her own, for it probably came from Defoe. The next letter goes beyond even New Frontier legislation; in it Silence advocates similar insurance for old maids.

In *Dogood* twelve Silence delivers herself of a temperance lecture. Moderate drinking, she doubts not, tends to be serviceable to those people who "want the Talent of a ready Utterance" in order to "discover the Conceptions of their Minds in an entertaining and intelligible Manner." Humorously she concedes that "much Study and Experience, and a little Liquor, are of absolute Necessity for some Tempers, in order to make them accomplish'd Orators." "But after all," she says, "it must be consider'd that no Pleasure can give Satisfaction or prove advantageous to a reasonable Mind, which is not attended with the *Restraints* of *Reason.*"

The thirteenth *Dogood* concerns what a casual stroller

might see during a night's walk in Boston. Silence, who takes such a moonlit stroll, hears herself talked about by persons pretending to know her; one says that she is a low character who keeps up a correspondence with a criminal who helps her in her writing. Another guesses that she is actually a man and, at that, a man needing more reforming "in himself, than spending his Wit in satyrizing others."

The last letter in the *Dogood* series concerns the case of Timothy Cutler, the rector of Yale College who was expelled for his Arminian and Anglican views. The Arminians liberalized certain Calvinistic doctrines such as predestination, and they believed that the human will constituted an element in the salvation of the soul. Since Franklin believed strongly in what he called "morality," the necessity of practical deeds in religion—voluntary effort, in short—he sympathized with Cutler and his two colleagues, who left for England to be ordained in the Anglican church. Broadly tolerant of all religions, Franklin censured any kind of "indiscreet Zeal" among Christian denominations.

Although Silence received at least two other invitations to continue her letters (one by James Franklin and another by an unknown assailant who twitted her on the depletion of her wit), the fourteenth *Dogood* marked the end of the series. In all, it was a remarkably original performance for a sixteen-year-old boy. The vernacular style and the use of the Widow Dogood as vehicle for a type of shrewd, middle-class humor distinguished these essays.

The *Dogood* papers were important in Franklin's career as a writer. They led to later *Dogoods*—such characters as his old Janus, the Busy-Body, Poor Richard, etc. Such characters marked the beginnings of the crackerbox tradition which makes up a really sizeable and significant part of Amreican humor.

In terms of Franklin's development as a writer the *Dogood* papers are important because they express the growth of Franklin's ability at satire: for at sixteen Franklin had achieved, as he says in the *Autobiography,* a reputation as "a young genius that had a turn for libelling and satyr." Had he remained in Boston, argues Davy, the growth of Franklin's "reputation for libelling and satire" might have called down upon his head a fate even worse than his brother's. From fear of such a fate he fled Boston, according to Davy. But, whatever the reason for Franklin's departure from Boston, his *Dogood* papers were "among the most literary essays which that period published."

II *The Busy-Body Papers*

The circumstances of publication of the *Busy-Body* papers are told in the *Autobiography.* There Franklin describes how in the year 1728 he happened to mention to a certain George Webb, who had applied for work, his plan to publish a newspaper in opposition to Bradford's *American Weekly Mercury.* Webb violated Franklin's confidence by relaying this plan to Samuel Keimer, another of Franklin's rivals. Keimer then beat Franklin to the public by immediately announcing that he himself planned to publish a newspaper. Franklin retaliated with the *Busy-Body* papers. A further circumstance of publication in connection

with the *Busy-Body* papers includes the fact that Keimer's first issue of his *Universal Instructor in all Arts and Sciences: and Pennsylvania Gazette* appeared December 24, 1728—before Franklin could begin his own paper with his partner, Hugh Meredith. The *Busy-Body* papers themselves, as Franklin explains in the *Autobiography,* he wrote as "Entertainment for Bradford's paper (*The American Weekly Mercury*), under the Title of the Busy Body which Breintnal [a Quaker member of the Junto] continued some Months." These papers stopped with the issue of September 25, 1729, at which time Franklin and Meredith bought out Keimer's bankrupt paper and forthwith abbreviated its title to *Pennsylvania Gazette.* According to a marginal note on the February 18, 1729 issue, possibly by Franklin himself, Franklin wrote only the first four, part of number five, and part of number eight of the *Busy-Body* papers. Labaree and Bell regard this note as true.

Keimer, however, had drawn Franklin's satire upon himself even before this incident because of his bad taste in publishing an article on abortions which he had taken from Chambers' *Cyclopedia.* Keimer's article appeared in the fifth issue of his own *Gazette* (January 21, 1729), and Franklin answered it—according to Labaree and Bell—in Bradford's *American Weekly Mercury* exactly one week later. This reply took the form of three letters under two pseudonyms, Martha Careful and Caelia Shortface. Both ladies objected to Keimer's indignity to their sex. Labaree and Bell think it significant that the *Busy-Body* papers appeared "the next week after Martha and Caelia had voiced their sex's sense of scandal and insult."

Franklin's manner of introducing his three letters from Martha and Caelia foreshadows his later strategy in the London press. "Having had several Letters from the Female Sex, Complaining of S. K.," he writes, "I have thought fit to Publish the Two following." (The "Two" refers to the ladies rather than to the letters, which are short and three in number.) In the first letter Martha Careful, writing in behalf of the rest of her "Agrieved Sex," threatens to take Keimer "by the Beard at the next Place" she and her friends meet him and "make an Example of him for his Immodesty." In Caelia Shortface's two letters to Keimer she, too, speaks for several of her acquaintances, threatening "That if thou proceed any further in that Scandalous manner, we intend very soon to have thy right Ear for it."

The first *Busy-Body* paper lives up to its officious-sounding name. In the form of a letter to Mr. Andrew Bradford, it bluntly tells him what is wrong with his paper. The Busy-Body speaks in the first person: "I have often observ'd with Concern, that your *Mercury* is not always equally entertaining . . . [and is] frequently very dull." He then states his purpose and character: "With more Concern have I continually observ'd the growing Vices and Follies of my Country-Folk. And tho' Reformation is properly the concern of every Man; that is, *Every one ought to mend One;* yet 'tis too true in this Case, that *what is every Body's Business is no Body's Business,* and the Business is done accordingly. I, therefore, upon mature Deliberation, think fit to take *no Body's Business* wholly into my own Hands; and, out of Zeal for the Publick

Good, design to erect my Self into a Kind of *Censor Morum* [Censor of Morals]."

He offers a word of encouragement to womankind: "Let the Fair Sex be assur'd, that I shall always treat them and their Affairs with the utmost *Decency* and Respect. I intend now and then to dedicate a Chapter wholly to their Service; and if my Lectures any Way contribute to the Embellishment of their Minds, and Brightening of their Understandings, without offending their *Modesty*, I doubt not of having their Favour and Encouragement."

He explains his aims—entertainment and instruction in morality, philosophy, and politics. "Sometimes I propose to deliver Lectures of Morality or Philosophy, and (because I am naturally enclin'd to be meddling with Things that don't concern me) perhaps I may sometimes talk Pol-

Title page of the first issue of Poor Richard's Almanack.

iticks. And if I can by any means furnish out a Weekly Entertainment for the Publick, that will give a Rational Diversion, and at the same Time be instructive to the Readers, I shall think my Leisure Hours well employ'd: And if you publish this I hereby invite all ingenious Gentlemen and others, (that approve of such an Undertaking) to my Assistance and Correspondence."

The first *Busy-Body* paper partook of the nature of an announcement. It included a seventeenth-century *character*. And it made some brief comments on the need of the age for correction (its purpose). The second paper, more like modern essays, confined itself to a single subject, *Ridicule*. But, it, too, had its characters—Ridentius, in all his folly; and his opposite, Eugenius, "who never spoke yet but with a Design to divert and please."

The third *Busy-Body* paper continues the same pattern as the second by setting up two characters to personify the subject matter. This time, however, the subject is *Virtue*. And the man representing it is Cato, a humble American farmer, "a man whom Fortune has placed in the most obscure Part of the Country." The other character, Cretico, plays the part of the "sowre Philosopher." He possesses cunning and craft, but he is "far from being Wise." Keimer apparently thought the character of Cretico applied to himself, for in the *Universal Instructor* (February 25, 1729) he warned Franklin against scandal and defamation.

Busy-Body four has a three-part structure. The first part invites correspondence. The second part, an amusing letter from a female shopkeeper, complains that her neighbor's children disrupt the shop on the occasions of the bothersome social visits of their mother. The disruptions take the form of the children's urinating on the "Goods" (dry goods) and mixing up the assortments of nails; the mother takes the attitude that no real damage is done by this kind of play: "Let them play a little," she remarks, "I'll put all to rights my self before I go." But of course things are never put to rights, and the shopkeeper complains that she finds "a great deal of Work to do after they are gone." In the third part Franklin (in his role as Busy-Body) writes a more formal discourse on the regulation of social visits: "It is a nice thing and very difficult, to regulate our Visits in such a Manner, as never to give Offence by coming too seldom, or too often, or departing too abruptly, or staying too long." He then refers to the Turkish custom of concluding visits by perfuming the beards of the males present when the host wants to bid his visitors good-by. The Busy-Body serves notice on his visitor that after providing French brandy and snuff for the men and citron-water for the ladies, he expects them to retire.

The fifth *Busy-Body* announces its purpose as "a Terror to Evil-Doers as well as a Praise to them that do well." The last part of this essay is a fairly long and serious defense of the Busy-Body against an attack on his character of Cretico (see the third paper) that appeared in Keimer's *Universal Instructor*.

The eighth and final *Busy-Body* that Franklin is known to have participated in calls attention to the fact that someone has written a key to the fourth *Busy-Body*, thereby converting "a gentle Satyr upon tedious and impertinent Visitants into a Libel on some in the Government." It also contains a letter from Titan Pleiades, an astrologer, who hopes to find a fortune buried in the earth. The astrologer proposes a union of Busy-Body, his correspondent who had the supernatural gift (see **Busy-Body,** No. 4), and himself, who with united endeavors might eventually become the three richest men of the province. (Titan Pleiades is obviously a humorous reference to Titan Leeds, the almanac maker whom Franklin later pilloried in *Poor Richard.*) Busy-Body replies to this letter with a general attack on all get-rich-quick schemes (including the romance of digging for buried pirate treasure) and their disastrous results to poor persons taken in by their proponents. He concludes with a characteristic Franklin ending, by relating the story of a father who gave his son a valuable piece of land and assured him that he had found a "considerable Quantity of Gold by Digging there" and that the son might do the same if he carefully observed the rule of never digging "more than Plow-deep."

These five essays comprising Franklin's part in the *Busy-Body* papers have sometimes been likened to commonplace books, because of their rather loose structure, their use of sayings, Latin epigraphs, letters, etc. There is a workday, didactic quality about them, too—an air of the print shop. Davy therefore calls the *Busy-Body* papers "a sort of Silence-Dogood-in-breeches series of essays" for the purpose of destroying the competition of Keimer's *Universal Instructor.* They succeeded in their purpose.

When we examine one of the separate essays Franklin contributed to his *Pennsylvania Gazette,* the successor of Keimer's paper, we shall see that at times he was certainly capable of writing a well-organized essay in the nineteenth- and twentieth-century manner. In his essay **"On Conversation"** (October 15, 1730) he begins with his customary quote from the classics (Terence's *Andria*). Immediately following this quotation he announces: "The Bounds and Manner of this Paper will not allow a regular and methodical Discourse on the Subject, and therefore I must beg Leave to throw my Thoughts together as they arise." Nevertheless he develops his essay quite methodically. First, he observes that to give pleasure in conversation is "an Art which all people believe they understand and practice, tho' most are ignorant or deficient in it." Then he analyzes the art of giving such pleasure into two parts—*"Complaisance* and *Good Nature." Complaisance* he defines as "a seeming preference of others to ourselves"; *Good Nature,* as "a Readiness to overlook or excuse their Foibles, and do them all the services we can." Following these definitions, he lists and explains seven errors of conversation, seven "Things which cause Dislike," proceeding generally from the most common as well as the most disagreeable to the less common and the less disagreeable—at least in the first part of the essay—and using such adjectives as "common," "disobliging," and "disagreeable" to make this progress clear.

The list includes the following: (1) *"talking overmuch";* (2) "seeming wholly unconcerned in Conversation, and bearing no other Part in the Discourse than a *No* or *Yes* sometimes, or an *Hem,* or perhaps a *Nod* only"; (3) "ever

speaking of ourselves and our own Affairs"; (4) *"Storytelling,"* especially those with "rambling Particulars"; (5) *"Wrangling* and *Disputing";* (6) "Raillery"; (7) and "Scandal." This list constitutes the middle, or main part, of the composition.

In the short transition paragraph that follows, Franklin explains in the first sentence that these are only "the most obvious" mistakes and that "whosoever avoids them carefully can never much displease." His conclusion recapitulates his main points. This essay **"On Conversation"** has the clear-cut beginning, middle, and end characteristic of Franklin's later method as a writer of essays.

III *The Bagatelles*

Franklin achieved his highest development as a writer of belles-lettres with a series of approximately fifteen essays known as the *Bagatelles.* These essays, most of which were composed as letters to Mmes. Brillon and Helvétius, were with some exceptions printed on his own private press during his residence in France (1776-1785). At the time, he lived in Passy, a suburb of Paris, where he enjoyed the social and intellectual company of a small group of sophisticated French people; among them, besides the two ladies mentioned, were his good friends the Abbé Morellet, the Abbé de la Roche, Cabanis, Le Veillard, and others.

Since we have treated at length both the social background and the excellent artistic quality of these works in our edition of these essays, entitled *Franklin's Wit and Folly: The Bagatelles* (1953), we refer the reader interested in a more detailed discussion of these aspects to this book. We shall say here merely that the bagatelles represent Franklin's brief and only excursion into the domain of belles-lettres. Here, as in no other of his works, we see him as an artist who has momentarily laid aside his constant watchword of *utility.* For once the essay in his hands becomes not a mere means to an end. The *Bagatelles* are little classics that must be judged among Franklin's finest creations.

The scholarly textual problems connected with the *Bagatelles* are legion and in a state of flux because of new discoveries. For this reason the readers would do well to consult Professor A. O. Aldridge's chapter about this subject in his book *Franklin and his French Contemporaries* (1957) as well as the excellent recent work of Professor Chinard, which we shall discuss below. In our discussion of the *Bagatelles* we present only the most representative of them and a few of the major problems that scholars, editors, and critics encounter in reading them. One of these problems concerns definition.

What is a *bagatelle?* As Franklin used the word in his letter to Mme. Brillon (April 8, 1784) it certainly included the "several other little things, of which some samples have been printed here in the house, solely for our friends." These, as Aldridge sees it, were distinct from the **"Information to Those Who Would Remove to America"** and the **"Remarks Concerning the Savages of North-America"** that Franklin alludes to in this same letter.

The **"Information"** was a serious kind of realistic real-estate brochure to inform French dandies—and others romantically contemplating moving to the New World—that they would have to work for a living in the new country. The **"Remarks"** satirized the exploitative attitude of the white man toward the American Indian, particularly "the Cheating of Indians in the Price of Beaver." It also pleaded for common courtesy and politeness towards people whose "manners differ from ours."

Franklin also tells Mme. Brillon in this letter that "if you have not lost **"The Handsome and the Deformed Leg,"** and **"The Morals of Chess"** [two other *Bagatelles*], you have with these here [what he was sending enclosed] a complete collection of all my Bagatelles which have been printed at Passy." He talks about the gout, apparently referring to probably the most famous of all the *Bagatelles,* the **"Dialogue between the Gout and Mr. Franklin,"** which he also enclosed. Conceivably Franklin could have written other *Bagatelles* elsewhere than at Passy, and conceivably Mme. Brillon may have been in possession of them; but, to the best of our knowledge, he nowhere refers to his other light essays as *Bagatelles.* The term *"bagatelles," as he used it,* then, meant the light-hearted or humorous essays which he wrote for the intimate company at Passy, or possibly for a few friends like Priestley in England during this period, and which he usually printed on his own private press.

Aldridge and Davy have hastened to point out that even such a qualified definition has serious shortcomings and that numerous other essays of earlier periods belong to this same genre—such as **"The Craven Street Gazette"** (written for Polly Stevenson), **"The Speech of Polly Baker,"** and **"Advice on Choosing a Mistress."** The canon of the *Bagatelles* should probably be revised to include the following, with the added stipulation that this list is by no means complete or final: **"The Dialogue Between Franklin and the Gout," "The Whistle," "The Ephemera," "The Elysian Fields," "The Flies," "Letter to Mme. La Freté (Bilked for Breakfast)," "Letter to the Royal Academy," "A Tale," "The Handsome and the Deformed Leg," "The Morals of Chess," "Two Extra Commandments"** (*Franklin Papers,* XLIII, 19½), **"To the Abbé de la Roche at Auteuil"** (containing the drinking song), **"Letter from Franklin to the Abbé Morellet"** (with drawings by W. T. Franklin), **"The Craven-Street Gazette," "On the Death of a Squirrel," "The Art of Procuring Pleasant Dreams," "On Early Marriages," "On the Choice of a Mistress"** (Letter to Cadwallader Colden), **"The Harrow," "A Petition of the Left Hand," "An Economical Project," "A Letter from China," "The Speech of Polly Baker,"** and **"The Witch Trial at Mount Holly."**

Besides the *Bagatelles* already mentioned in the list above there are, of course, numerous other nominations among Franklin's essays and letters: among others, the letter to Mrs. Thompson (February 8, 1777), the letters to Catharine Ray, and the letter to Jacques Barbeu-Duborg (London, April, 1773) about flies drowned in Madeira wine. (Thinking about the drowned flies leads him to speculate on various methods of embalming drowned persons and of reviving them. He says that he himself has "a very ardent desire to see and observe the state of America an hun-

dred years hence," but would prefer an ordinary death than being immersed in a cask of Madeira.)

One should list, too, among the supplementary *bagatelles* some of Franklin's drinking songs. (In this instance, of course, we have *bagatelles* which are in verse, not essay form.) We have Van Doren's word [in his *Benjamin Franklin*] that Franklin "was convivial in taverns"; as a young man, he liked rum "and Madeira, sang songs, and wrote some." His drinking songs, says Van Doren "are probably his best expressions in verse."

The hoaxes—some of them, at least—also fall into the category of *bagatelles*. **"The Proposed New Version of the Bible"** and the **"Parable Against Persecution,"** for example, were both used on numerous social occasions to divert Franklin's guests. According to his friend Priestley, the famous chemist and English clergyman, Franklin would lay the parable loosely in the Bible and read it. He would then read the first chapter of Job. Often the guests mistook the latter for Franklin's own work. In this guessing game he usually gave his auditors the choice of identifying the fifty-first chapter of Genesis (which does not exist) or his own imitation. Since his imitation was very accurate as to style, the guests often failed. The **"Proposed New Version of the Bible"** led Matthew Arnold far afield. Paul Elmer More thought Franklin intended "a satire on monarchical government" by it under pretext of modernizing the text.

To give the reader some idea of the great emotional range the *Bagatelles* cover, we select two, **"To the Royal Academy"** and **"The Elysian Fields"**; and in presenting them we reverse the usual order of the sublime and the ridiculous. In order to present Franklin's earthy satire of a certain scientific academy, probably of Brussels, we offer a few excerpts from this less well-known *bagatelle*. It was the custom for this academy to undertake investigation of research projects in mathematics and the natural sciences for a prize. Franklin starts his essay by proposing a rather unusual question for investigation by the academy.

> My Prize Question . . . *To discover some Drug wholesome & not disagreeable, to be mix'd with our common Food, or Sauces, that shall render the Natural Discharges, of Wind from our Bodies, not only inoffensive, but agreeable as Perfumes.*

> That this is not a chimerical Project, and altogether impossible, may appear from these Considerations. That we already have some knowledge of Means capable of Varying that Smell. He that dines on stale Flesh, especially with much Addition of Onions, shall be able to afford a Stink that no Company can tolerate; while that has lived for some Time on Vegetables only, shall have that Breath so pure as to be insensible to the most delicate Noses; and if he can manage so as to avoid the Report, he may any where give Vent to his Griefs, unnoticed. But as there are many to whom an entire Vegetable Diet would be inconvenient, and as a little Quick-Lime thrown into a Jakes [outdoor toilet] will correct the amazing quantity of fetid Air arising from the vast Mass of putrid Matter contain'd in such Places, and render it rather pleasing to the smell, who knows but that a little Powder of Lime (or

some other thing equivalent) taken in our Food, or perhaps a Glass of Limewater drank at Dinner, may have the same Effect on the Air produc'd in and issuing from our Bowels? This is Worth the experiment. . . .

For the Encouragement of this Enquiry, (from the immortal Honour to be reasonably expected by the Inventor) let it be reasonably considered of how small importance to Mankind, or to how small a Part of Mankind have been useful those Discoveries in Science that have heretofore made Philosophers famous. Are there twenty Men in Europe at this Day, the happier, or even the easier, for any knowledge they have pick'd out of Aristotle? What Comfort can the Vortices of Descartes give to a Man who has Whirlwinds in his Bowels! The Knowledge of Newton's mutual Attraction of the Particles of Matter, can it afford Ease to him who is rack'd by their mutual Repulsion, and the cruel Distensions it occasions? The Pleasure arising to a few Philosophers, from seeing, a few Times in their Life, the Threads of Light untwisted, and separated by the Newtonian Prism into seven Colours, can it be compared with the Ease and Comfort every Man living might feel seven times a Day, by discharging freely the Wind from his Bowels? Especially if it be converted into a Perfume. . . . And surely such a Liberty of *Ex-pressing* one's *Scent-iments,* and *pleasing one another,* is of infinitely more Importance to human Happiness than that Liberty of the Press, or of *abusing one another,* which the English are so ready to fight & die for.—In short, this Invention, if compleated, would be, as Bacon expresses it, *bringing Philosophy home to Mens Business and Bosoms.* And I cannot but conclude, that in Comparison therewith, for universal and continual UTILITY, the Science of the Philosophers abovementioned, even with the Addition, Gentlemen, of your *"Figure quelconque"* and the Figures inscrib'd in it, are, all together, scarcely worth a

FART-HING.

This *bagatelle,* as perhaps no other, is remarkable for both the quality and the quantity of its puns. Franklin was a lover of puns; and the following letter to Dr. Richard Price at Brighthelmstone, England (September 16, 1783), in connection with this letter to the academy and the balloon experiments at Versailles reveals one of his slyest:

All the conversation here at present turns upon the Ballons fill'd with light inflammable Air. . . .Inflammable air puts me in mind of a little jocular paper I wrote some years since in ridicule of a prize Question given out by a certain Academy on this side of the Water, and I enclose it for your Amusement. On second thoughts, as it is a mathematical Question, and perhaps I think it more trifling than it really is, and you are a Mathematician, I am afraid I have judg'd wrong in sending it to you. Our friend Dr. Priestley, however, who is apt to give himself *Airs,* and has a kind of Right to everything his Friends produce upon that Subject, may perhaps like to see it, and you can send it to him without reading it.

Anyone who thinks Dr. Price forwarded this letter to Dr. Priestley "without reading it" should consult a psychiatrist.

The *bagatelle* known as **"The Elysian Fields"** was written to Mme. Helvétius, a wealthy widow who but a few years before had lost her husband. At the time this letter was written (December 7, 1778), Franklin's wife had been dead nearly four years, and he had proposed to Mme. Helvétius. Like other examples noted, this essay has a clearly discernible beginning, middle, and end. With its elements of surprise and balanced irony it constitutes more of a complete *jeu d'esprit* than some of the other **Bagatelles.** In it Franklin tells how he had been so disturbed by her refusal to marry him that he had returned home, fallen on his bed, and, believing himself dead, had found himself in the Elysian Fields. He was asked if he "desired to see anybody in particular." "Lead me to the home of the philosophers," he had replied. Two, Socrates and Helvétius, lived in a nearby garden. Since he could talk no Greek and only a little French, Franklin desired to see Helvétius.

He received me with great courtesy, having known me for some time, he said, by the reputation I had there. He asked me a thousand things about the war, and about the present state of religion, liberty, and the government in France.— You ask nothing of your dear friend Madame H [elvétius]; nevertheless she still loves you excessively and I was at her place but an hour ago. Ah! said he, you make me remember my former felicity.—But it is necessary to forget it in order to be happy here. During several of the early years, I thought only of her. Finally, I am consoled. I have taken another wife. The most like her that I could find. She is not, it is true, so completely beautiful, but she has as much good sense, and a little more of Spirit, and she loves me infinitely. Her continual Study is to please me; and she has actually gone to hunt the best Nectar and the best Ambrosia in order to regale me this evening; remain with me and you will see her. . . . At these words the new Madame H—entered with the Nectar: at which instant I recognized her to be Madame F[ranklin], my old American friend. I reclaimed her. But she told me coldly, "I have been your good wife forty-nine years and four months, nearly a half century; be content with that. Here I have formed a new connection, which will endure to eternity.

Offended by this refusal of my Eurydice, I suddenly decided to leave these ungrateful spirits, to return to the good earth, to see again the sunshine and you. Here I am! Let us revenge ourselves.

Playfully, more like a father than a wooer, Franklin made love to young Mme. Brillon, one of the great beauties of France, and about thirty-five years his junior. "What highlights the correspondence [between Franklin and Mme. Brillon] is the thrust and parry of verbal courtship," says Granger [in *American Heritage,* X (June 1959)]. In one of her letters to "Papa" Franklin, as she called him, she wrote: "You combine with the best heart, when you wish, the soundest moral teaching, a lively imagination, and that drole roguishness which shows that the wisest of men allows his wisdom to be perpetually broken against the rocks of femininity." This is an apt description of Franklin's letters to her. In all, they exchanged a correspondence of over one hundred and fifty letters, several *bagatelles*, and poems between 1777 and 1789. Some of these letters, such as **"The Elysian Fields"** and **"The Ephemera,"** served as exercises in French composition for Franklin; and some scholars have had much to say about Franklin's bad French. Professor Chinard [in the *American Philosophical Society Library Bulletin*, CIII, No. 6, 1959], however, takes a different view: "His French [in **"The Elysian Fields"**] may not be of classical vintage, although it did not shock the purists of the time; but it was distinctly his. He knew exactly what he wanted to say and he said it in his own words, in his own way, in an easy and fluent manner." Like the style of several excellent French writers, Franklin's French style has "a deceptive simplicity."

Of all the *Bagatelles,* **"The Ephemera"** is undoubtedly the most charming. It is also one of the most philosophic. In it Franklin makes delicate fun of his omnivorous scientific and philosophic interest in the world of nature, his difficulties with the French language, the vivacious disposition of the French people to talk rapidly and "three or four together," and French excitability about matters of art, particularly music. Behind this surface humor, however, he plays skillfully on the transitoriness of life—his theme—and the vanity of human wishes.

In this tender allegory, for that is the form of **"The Ephemera,"** the old insect philosopher is Franklin himself, aged seventy-two; "the ever-amiable Brillante" is Mme. Brillon. The happy people who live securely under a wise government, equitable and moderate, are the French, who at the time were involved in a hot dispute about the respective merits of the composers Gluck and Picini. (On hearing that Franklin himself preferred Gluck to Picini, Marie Antoinette is reported to have said, "What can a man whose trade is to place [lightning] rods on buildings know of music?") "My Compatriotes, Inhabitants of this Bush," were the Americans in the wilds of a distant continent. The eighteen hours stand for the life of man. Employing his delicate symbolism of the insect world, Franklin touches on such distant and serious matters as the origin of the universe and the end of the world, the true value of time and of life, and the microcosm and the macrocosm.

Structurally considered, the beginning of **"The Ephemera"** explains the occasion and introduces the subject of the insects. With kind permission of the Cornell University Library, we quote from an original manuscript—a version of **"The Ephemera"** which Franklin wrote in English:

Passy Sept 20, 1778

You may remember, my dear Friend, that when we lately spent that happy Day in the delightful Garden and sweet society of the Moulin Joli, I stopt a little in one of our Walks, and staid some time behind the Company. We had been shewn numberless Skeletons of a kind of little Fly, called an Ephemere, all whose successive Generations we were told were bred and expired with

the Day. I happen'd to see a living Company of them on a Leaf, who appear'd to be engag'd in Conversation.—You know I understand all the inferior Animal Tongues: my too great Application to the Study of them is the best Excuse I can give for the little Progress I have made in your charming Language. I listened thro' Curiosity to the Discourse of these little Creatures, but as they in their national Vivacity spoke three or four together, I could make but little of their Discourse. I found, however, by some broken Expressions that I caught now & then, they were disputing warmly the Merit of two foreign Musicians, one a *Cousin* [a gnat], the other a *Musketo;* in which Dispute they spent their time seemingly as regardless of the Shortness of Life, as if they had been Sure of living a Month. Happy People! thought I, you live certainly under a wise, just and mild Government; since you have no public Grievances to complain of, nor any Subject of Contention but the Perfection or Imperfection of foreign Music.

Franklin then develops the longer middle part of the essay into the form of a soliloquy by an old, white-haired insect.

It was, says he, the Opinion of learned Philosophers of our Race, who lived and flourished long before my time, that this vast World, the *Moulin Joli,* could not itself subsist more than 18 Hours; and I think there was some Foundation for that Opinion, since by the apparent Motion of that great Luminary that gives Life to all Nature, and which in my Time has evidently declin'd considerably towards the Ocean at the End of our Earth, it must then finish its Course, be extinguish'd in the Waters that surround us, and leave the World in Cold and Darkness, necessarily producing universal Death and Destruction. I have lived seven of these Hours; a great Age; being no less than 420 minutes of Time. How very few of us continue so long!—I have seen Generations born, flourish and expire. My present Friends are the Children and Grandchildren of the Friends of my Youth, who are now, alas, no more! And I must soon follow them; for by the Course of Nature, tho' still in Health, I cannot expect to live above 7 or 8 Minutes longer. What now avails all my Toil and Labour in amassing Honey-Dew on this Leaf, which I cannot live to enjoy! What the political Struggles I have been engag'd in for the Good of my Compatriotes, Inhabitants of this Bush; or my philosophical Studies for the Benefit of our Race in general! For in Politics *what can Laws do without Morals!* our present Race of Ephemeres will in a Course of Minutes, became corrupt like those of other and older Bushes, and consequently as wretched. And in Philosophy how small our Progress! Alas, *Art is long and Life is short!* My Friends would comfort me with the Idea of a Name they say I shall leave behind me; and they tell me I have lived long enough, to Nature and to Glory: But what will Fame be to an Ephemere who no longer exists? And what will become of all History in the 18th Hour, when the World itself, even the whole *Moulin Joli,* shall come to its End, and be buried in universal Ruin?—

The old philosopher insect then closes with this remark which is in the usual gallant style of Franklin's letters to Mme. Brillon: "To me, after all my eager Pursuits, no solid Pleasures now remain, but the Reflection of a long Life spent in meaning well, the sensible Conversation of a few good Lady-Ephemeres, and now and then a kind Smile and a Tune from the ever-amiable BRILLANTE."

The handling of tone during the soliloquy is particularly effective. Seldom has pathos been more "delicately sustained," writes Professor Hornberger [in *The Literature of the United States*, I, 1953] The classical quotations from Horace, Hippocrates, and Caesar in this section suit the discourse of a philosopher, as do Franklin's classical periods. "The Ephemera" as Professor Chinard points out, is no mere *bagatelle;* it is "a work of art and a literary masterpiece." His recent study of the manuscripts of this work shows that Franklin took special care with style in its composition, that he pursued the exact word through frequent corrections and revisions, and that he made determined efforts to express nuances of thought and feeling. This so-called *bagatelle* is an answer, Chinard goes on, to critics like Sainte-Beuve who had argued that Franklin lacked imagination and was only a utilitarian, a practical experimenter.

Two other **Bagatelles** written to Mme. Brillon rank among the more popular of these productions—**"The Whistle"** and the **"Dialogue Between Franklin and the Gout."** Along with the **"Ephemera"** these enjoyed great popularity in the 1790's, being copied and recopied.

The essay as Franklin used it in the eighteenth century covered a rather broad range of subject matter, in form and in purpose. Some of these essays represent Franklin's most polished work as a writer. All of them are interesting and well worth studying, especially by students of writing. For students of history, too, they are often important as original source material not otherwise generally available. Franklin's essays constitute some of his most important work as a writer. The essay and the letter were the two forms he used more often than any other. (pp. 104-28)

Richard E. Amacher, in his Benjamin Franklin, *Twayne Publishers, Inc., 1962, 192 p.*

Robert Freeman Sayre   (essay date 1963)

[*An American educator and critic, Sayre is the author of* The Examined Self: Benjamin Franklin, Henry Adams and Henry James *(1964). In the following essay, he responds to Franklin's harshest critics, stressing that in the* Autobiography, *especially the section devoted to "moral perfection," Franklin was merely adopting a pose of naivete.*]

Despite the passage of years, the portrait of Benjamin Franklin most prominently hung in the imaginations of many educated and emancipated Americans is still that etched by D. H. Lawrence and other writers and critics of the twenties and thirties like William Carlos Williams and Charles Angoff. Their essays, particularly Lawrence's, have had a wide circulation, and they have put to flight the nineteenth-century conception of Franklin as a

model of virtue and industry. The "wisdom" of Poor Richard is now classified as smug opportunism. Franklin's pluralism is now looked upon as cynically noncontroversial. Franklin retains his mythic status as an "original" American, a prototype of the race, but that type is now regarded as a little old-fashioned, moralistic, plodding, and rather tiresome.

It is not the function of this [essay] to defend the man. That has been ably and recently done by I. Bernard Cohen [in his *Benjamin Franklin: His Contribution to the American Tradition,* 1953] and Alfred Owen Aldridge [in his *Franklin and his French Contemporaries,* 1957], and the publication of *The Papers of Benjamin Franklin* by the American Philosophical Society and Yale University will eventually confirm his own belief that "When a man's actions are just and honourable, the more they are known the more his reputation is increased and established." Neither does this [essay] aim to glue back together the dull and admonitory Victorian Franklin so conclusively smashed by the Jazz Age. The essence of the Lawrence-Angoff attack was that Franklin protected himself from experience behind a wall of maxims and moral dogma, a just and necessary criticism of the man as they had been taught him. What is needed is a defense and reappraisal of the *Autobiography,* or the four memoirs to which we give that name. It is this self-portrait, after all, by which Franklin will always be known and which provided the material for most of the iconoclasm; so it is appropriate that on it we should launch our counterattack. The very nature of the *Autobiography* disproves the notion that Franklin held a static, moralistic attitude toward his experience. Its three main sections demonstrate that he was continually reassessing his early life and past in the terms and style of his present. It reflects the ceaseless adventure of his personality and his always fresh receptivity to new points of view. The time has come for new criticism of it.

I

The detractions of Lawrence, Williams, and Angoff all employ two techniques. First they blame Franklin for faults and vulgarities which are not his but those of men we are encouraged to believe are his ethical heirs. Secondly, they abstract portions of his work and damn the whole by the part. Williams [in his *In The American Grain*] quotes the whole of **"Information to Those Who Would Remove to America,"** then follows it with five pages of "Notes for A Commentary on Franklin." Lawrence and Angoff, whose interests are more explicitly fixed on the *Autobiography,* quote most extensively from the portion dealing with the author's "Project of arriving at moral Perfection." Indeed, it is for this piece that the man and the self-portrait have suffered most, and it is here that reappraisals are most important, but first I shall deal with those aspersions in which Franklin is blamed for the sins of his supposed successors.

The attack on Franklin as moralistic and overly dedicated to the Goddess of "Getting Ahead" is, at bottom, not so much an attack on him as on the middle class. Thus Angoff [in his *Literary History of the American People,* 1931] corrects Carlyle for calling him the "father of all the Yankees" and says, "It would be more accurate to call Franklin the father of all the Kiwanians." [In his *Studies in Classic American Literature*, 1955] Lawrence similarly berates him for inventing a God perfectly suited to the ends of Andrew Carnegie. "God is the supreme servant of men who want to get on, to *produce*. Providence. The provider. The heavenly storekeeper. The everlasting Wanamaker." This is lively pamphleteering, but it is misdirected. About halfway through *Babbitt* Sinclair Lewis says that,

> If you had asked Babbitt what his religion was, he would have answered in sonorous Boosters' Club rhetoric, "My religion is to serve my fellow men, to honor my brother as myself, and to do my bit to make life happier for one and all."

This—a wretched degeneration of Franklin's "the most acceptable Service of God is doing Good to man"—is a far more accurate rendering of the public religion of the Kiwanians than anything that can be pejoratively extracted from Franklin. His religion, we can tell by his writings, was almost constantly on his mind. It impresses different people different ways, but it was not cunning, cocky, or selfish.

The failure of Angoff and Lawrence in understanding Franklin's statement of his creed in the famous letter to Ezra Stiles and in the opening of the third memoir is a failure of sophistication and humor. The eighty-four-year-old statesman was in his best form when he wrote President Stiles, and there is something benign in his replies to the minister's entreaties. If Yale College wants a portrait of him, then the artist "must not delay setting about it, or I may slip through his fingers." He states his beliefs simply and succinctly, holding them too privately to wish them publicized and too sacredly to wish any excitement made over them. If there is blasphemy about the long, careful, and yet easy sentence on the divinity of Jesus of Nazareth, it is a blasphemy invoked expressly to forestall the remark's being taken too seriously. To treat the creed as a hypocrite's, as Lawrence does, or to treat the letter as "flippant," as Angoff does, is to miss Franklin's sincere humility and grace. Like Stiles, these critics were comparatively provincial!

They were similarly obtuse before the Poor Richard aspect of Franklin. Carl Van Doren observed that the supposed "wisdom" of Poor Richard is hardly Franklin's. As well as the fact of the mask, it must also be remembered that the maxims are first and foremost folk sayings that go back hundreds of years. Not all are in support of industry and thrift. They are crazily contradictory. Lawrence is again fighting symbol rather than fact:

> I can remember, when I was a little boy, my father used to buy a scrubby yearly almanac . . . And . . . crammed in corners it had little anecdotes and humorisms, with a moral tag. And I used to have my little priggish laugh at the woman who counted her chickens before they were hatched, and so forth, and I was convinced that honesty was the best policy, also a little priggishly. The author of these bits was Poor Richard, and Poor Richard was Benjamin Franklin, writing in Philadelphia well over a hundred years before.

> And probably I haven't got over those Poor Richard tags yet. I rankle still with them. They are thorns in young flesh.

He criticizes himself, not Franklin. Angoff, recognizing that the wisdom is of a "low order," argues that "one does not always have to be a vulgarian when talking to the man in the street. Consider Jesus and Socrates and Confucious and Lao-Tze. Consider Montaigne. Consider even Krylov." This is flattering company for a seller of almanacs!

A fact that must constantly be attended in considering Franklin is the almost unequalled length of his active life and the multiplicity of his careers. The urbane letter to Stiles, for example, comes fifty-eight years after the first edition of the **Almanac.** Within these years are at least five complete careers: printer, civic leader, scientist, ambassador, patriot, and a whole host of sidelines and occasional interests. The scope of his achievement and the reach of his personality make the narrow specialist gasp. He was not a poet; but he was vastly creative. All this must be remembered in dealing with the **Autobiography.**

II

First of all, the modern critic of that work must recall that it was written in three (really four) different installments and that each reflects the place and time at which it was written. The memoirs are no more the same throughout than Franklin was the same when he wrote them. To realize this, each must be studied separately. I shall begin by taking up the first part, then the third and fourth sections, and finally the second one, since it, written at Passy, outside Paris, in 1784, provided Lawrence and Angoff with their most remarkable criticisms.

The first part, as is well known, was written in August, 1771, while Franklin was staying at the home of Bishop Shipley near Twyford in Hampshire. He at that time liked England, the Shipleys were good friends, and his life was comfortable. As Max Farrand has said [in *Meet Doctor Franklin*], this memoir in every way indicates this repose and contentment. Note the opening:

> Dear Son,
>
> I have ever had a Pleasure in obtaining any little Anecdotes of my Ancestors. You may remember the Enquiries I made among the Remains of my Relations when you were with me in England; and the Journey I took for that purpose. Now imagining it may be equally agreeable to you to know the Circumstances of *my* Life, many of which you are yet unacquainted with; and expecting a Weeks uninterrupted Leisure in my present Country Retirement, I sit down to write them for you.

This memoir is uniform in tone and masterfully organized. It adheres to a fairly strict chronological order, yet is also held together by several continuing themes—his ambition to be in business for himself, his education in writing, his struggle to repay the debt to Vernon, his regret over such "errata" as the effort to seduce his friend James Ralph's mistress, and his uneven progress toward marriage with Debbie Read. In some ways it is a short picaresque novel, with deceitful villains like Governor Keith, braggadocios like Samuel Keimer, and adventurous travels from Boston through New York and New Jersey to Philadelphia, back to Boston, to London, and back to Philadelphia. Franklin and the other "characters" occasionally masquerade and mistake one another or fail to distinguish between real and apparent natures. The hero is a bright, yet over-proud and ambitious, young man whose impatience to succeed makes him incompatible with his brother and vulnerable to the empty promises of Governor Keith. The narrator, on the other hand, is a skilled story teller and indulgent older man who is now amused by the slips and falls of his younger self and now ashamed and penitent. Moralistic commentary is actually very small; there is much more in Defoe and a good deal more in Richardson. Franklin moves too fast. Finding himself too involved in a record of the life of his parents, he abruptly reins himself in:

> By my rambling Digressions I perceive my self to be grown old. I us'd to write more methodically. But one does not dress for private Company as for a publick Ball. 'Tis perhaps only Negligence.

> To return. I continu'd thus employ'd.

Because of the reference to "private Company," the opening "Dear Son," and the occasional direct address to his son, many people persist in believing this part of the *Autobiography* to differ markedly from the other parts in being private and not intended for publication. It does differ markedly, but this is not how. William Franklin was at this time governor of New Jersey and about forty years old, considerably beyond paternal counsel. Robert Spiller is right in calling the various signs of a letter literary devices, techniques by which Franklin established his particular relationship to his material. He definitely designed it for publication, though not until after his death. Furthermore he enjoyed writing it, and he took in it, as he did with much of his writing, the opportunities it offered for self-examination and self-advertisement. The famous arrival in Philadelphia, "eating my Roll," is recognized to have enormous symbolic value, and the elder Franklin used it to its fullest advantage. He gives the exact itinerary of his walk through the town, the people he met, the things he did, the places he stopped, and the "Meeting House of the Quakers near the Market . . . the first House I was in or slept in, in Philadelphia." William Carlos Williams' comment that " 'He's sort of proud of his commonness, isn't he?' " should be a truism, not an insight. He was not only proud of it—loving to "gratify my own Vanity" and being willing to "give it fair Quarter wherever I meet with it"; he also knew how to manipulate and display it so as to make it work for him. It put other people at their ease. It was a self-imposed check on his social ambitions and at the same time gave great interest to his success. It was the foundation of his most famous and effective public character, "Benjamin Franklin of Philadelphia, printer."

In the third and fourth sections of the *Autobiography* he is decidedly the Philadelphian. The ambassador has returned a national hero, has participated in the Constitutional Convention, and the memoirs show it. The account of General Braddock's campaign, the offhand remarks

about working hours in London, and the impatience with Lord Loudon's delay of the ship Franklin sailed in to England in 1757 all reflect a post-Revolution Anglophobia which is entirely lacking from the first piece. This is in spite of the obvious fact that the first was written sooner after the events themselves occurred. Stylistically, the narrative control and the power of organization have been lost, or else they simply were not so available within the material, for the action is naturally that of a busier, more widely involved man. Yet the narrator is a more deceptively naive, more ultimately sophisticated man. He was back in Philadelphia when he wrote it, in August, 1788, and in one sense was an old Poor Richard. Practically every adventure is preceded or followed by a moral or principle: *"It is hard for an empty sack to stand upright."* "When Men are employ'd they are best contented." "Human Felicity is produc'd not so much by great Pieces of good Fortune that seldom happen, as by little Advantages that occur every Day." "The best public Measures are therefore seldom *adopted from previous Wisdom,* but *forc'd by the Occasion."*

So much for the wise saws and modern instances!

This old man is rich in many ways. Rich in the helter-skelter clutter of a busy, eventful, refreshingly earthy, confoundingly practical, and still ordered and thoughtful life. It is gloriously undignified: fire ladders, dirty streets, smoky lamps, stoves, bags and buckets, waggons, munitions, bonds and subscriptions, pigs and chickens, schools, evangelists, and dull assemblies. Where the memoir written at Twyford in 1771 was like a picaresque novel, this one is like portions of *Gargantua and Pantagruel.* Franklin has been called Rabelaisian for certain of his drinking songs and obscene hoaxes. He is much more like the other Rabelais of Renaissance energy, good-will, and boundless possibilities.

Mixed in with all this is a modest and shrewd politician. The earlier lessons about vanity and the manipulations of appearance and reality are now extended and employed in one project after another. While making his way as a printer, he had learned that it was necessary "not only to

A political cartoon drawn by Franklin for the Pennsylvania Gazette *of 9 May 1754, urging the uniting of the colonies.*

be in *Reality* Industrious & frugal, but to avoid all *Appearances* of the Contrary." In putting together the Philadelphia Public Library, he soon felt "the Impropriety of presenting one's self as the Proposer of any useful Project that might be suppos'd to raise one's Reputation in the smallest degree above that of one's Neighbours, when one has the need of their Assistance to accomplish that Project." This is policy of a most subtle sort. The projects undertaken were entirely in the public interest; people might have been expected to subdue their personal vanities and antagonisms. Franklin became attentive, however, both to how people *should* behave and also to how they *do* behave. Support for the public hospital from private subscription and from the Pennsylvania Assembly was obtained only after a system of matching public and private funds was devised. Then members of the Assembly "conceiv'd they might have the Credit of being charitable without the Expence." Pacifist Quakers, Franklin found, were not opposed to "the Defence of the Country . . . provided they were not requir'd to assist in it."

The actor in these projects became a master of compromise and held within himself an amazing combination of idealism, vision, and practicality. Of great interest is his receptivity to new ideas, to new possibilities, and to new roles for himself. Most autobiography is the account of an arrival, written by the figure who has arrived and who holds a fixed conception of himself. Compare, for example, Gibbon's picture of himself as the emerging author of *The Decline and Fall of the Roman Empire* in his *Memoirs of my Life and Writings.* Franklin, while in one sense always remaining "Benjamin Franklin of Philadelphia, printer," is also constantly becoming something else: from printer to public servant to scientist to ambassador and on to the patriot and retired philosophizer who is the author of the third and fourth sections of the *Autobiography.*

It is because of this flexibility and never-ending development of Franklin's character that I have been stressing the difference between the man writing and the man written about. The first memoir is a story of youthful adventure and self-discovery told by a sixty-five-year-old scientist, political journalist, and colonial representative. In a rare hour of country retirement he is recollecting and confessing his wilder days. The third and fourth are the work of an eighty-two-year-old national hero. Back at his remodeled Philadelphia residence he is reviewing the mass of the public projects of his thirties and forties and writing *memoirs* of a more conventional nature. In giving the account of his experience as a civic leader he is also composing a kind of handbook. It is full of the lessons he learned and of counsel for future committee men, militia officers, and good citizens.

III

The much abused second memoir requires an even closer attention to the place and time of its composition and to the differences between author and subject. Alfred Owen Aldridge's study of Franklin in France makes us more aware than ever of the great ambassador's uncanny sense for depicting himself both as he was and also as the various circles of his friends, his associates, and the public thought he was. The particular selections of his writings which

were available there before his arrival in December, 1776, combined with his first appearance in plain clothes and marten-fur cap to crystallize him in the French imagination as the rural sage, the "philosophical Quaker." A letter of Franklin's to Mary Stevenson Hewson, written from Paris on January 12, 1777, demonstrates his awareness of the effect he had created:

> My dear, dear Polly: Figure to yourself an old man, with grey hair appearing under a marten-fur cap, among the powdered heads of Paris. It is this odd figure that salutes you, with handfuls of blessings on you and your dear little ones.

This half-cultivated and half-imposed role of the rural philosopher was a pose, but it was not a deceitful pose. To think so is to be a little provincial and to rush to conclusions. Franklin's poses were chosen to reveal rather than to conceal: they were a means of presenting himself. The character of the philosophical Quaker, which could be abstracted from works so widely different as *The Way to Wealth,* his descriptions of the American Indians, and the reports of his electrical experiments, became another elaboration of "Benjamin Franklin of Philadelphia, printer."

At the same time the French experience developed in him a certain sophistication and gallantry few Americans are able to appreciate. Most are ignorant of it and continue to treat him as a moralistic pedant. On the other hand, if they knew the Franklin of the French bagatelles and hoaxes, the letters to Madame Helvetius and the chess games with Madame Brillon, they would respond with the Puritan horror of John and Abigail Adams! The delightful quality of moral pieces like **"The Morals of Chess," "Remarks Concerning the Savages of North America,"** and **"The Handsome and the Deformed Leg"** is that they season and age—*mellow* might be most apt—moral instruction with a sunny humor. The Passy Franklin could remain quite serious, but he mixed the seriousness with the style and artfulness of play. In this way he was both the rural philosopher in the plain Poor Richard sense and also the rural philosopher in a pastoral sense, a man who gave in simplicity the furthest and most natural expression of his worldliness and experience. The author of the second part of the *Autobiography* was a *naif.*

The major portion of the second memoir and the part of it that is best known and most attacked is the description of the project for attaining moral perfection. This is the passage by which many well-intentioned readers make Franklin such an admonitory exemplar and it is largely because of this passage that Lawrence and Angoff found him so detestable. In reading it, however, one must forget the pious, bifocaled Doctor Franklin and concentrate on the sly and straight-faced ironies which attend the recollections of youthful presumption. The man who writes, in 1784, is very different from the conscientious young tradesman of 1728-1730:

> It was about this time that I conceiv'd the bold and arduous Project of arriving at moral Perfection. I wish'd to live without committing any Fault at any time; I would conquer all that either Natural Inclination, Custom, or Company might lead me into. As I knew, or thought I

knew, what was right and wrong, I did not see why I might not *always* do the one and avoid the other. But I soon found I had undertaken a Task of more Difficulty than I had imagined.

At this point Franklin discusses the need of a method and his selection of the virtues to be acquired. "For the sake of Clearness," he decided "to use rather more Names with fewer Ideas annex'd to each, than a few Names with more Ideas; . . . " This would also have the advantage of allowing him to devote himself more completely to each virtue. "Temperance" might be more easily arrived at if it referred only to eating and drinking. Intemperance of other kinds could be resisted by "Moderation" and "Chastity."

The final list of thirteen and the famous precepts that accompanied each ("Eat not to Dulness / Drink not to Elevation." "Speak not but what may benefit others or yourself. / Avoid trifling Conversation." Etc.) are so familiar that they need not be repeated. It is more important to re-read the story of the attempt to practice the virtues.

> My Intention being to acquire the *Habitude* of all these Virtues, I judg'd it would be well not to distract my Attention by attempting the whole at once, but to fix it on one of them at a time, . . . *Temperance* first, as it tends to procure that Coolness & Clearness of Head, which is so necessary where constant Vigilance was to be kept up, and Guard maintain'd, against the unremitting Attraction of ancient Habits, and the Force of perpetual Temptations. This being acquir'd & establish'd *Silence* would be more easy, . . .

It all fitted together, each virtue being ingeniously conceived to facilitate the acquisition of the next! To keep score he invented the childlike plan of the "little Book in which I allotted a Page for each of the Virtues." Only Franklin could have done it. By comparison Robinson Crusoe's balance sheet of the "Evil" and "Good" in being castaway on his island is primitive: Franklin's "moral algebra" is complete with red-ink lines, columns, mottos, dots, abbreviations, and headlines. Children are absorbed by it, even D. H. Lawrence! ("It is rather fun to play at Benjamin.")

> I made a little Book in which I allotted a Page for each of the Virtues. I rul'd each Page with red Ink, so as to have seven Columns, one for each Day of the Week, marking each Column with a letter for the Day. I cross'd these Columns with thirteen red Lines, marking the Beginning of each Line with the first Letter of one of the Virtues, on which Line & in its proper Column I might mark by a little black Spot every Fault I found upon Examination to have been committed respecting that Virtue upon that Day.

The intricacy of "arriving at moral Perfection" makes it the most confounding of games, though the rules were still less difficult than the objective. The young man decided to "give a Week's strict Attention to each of the Virtues successively." If the "Temperance" line was kept clear of foul "Spots" during the first week, then he could turn ahead to "Silence," and so on, endeavoring all the while

to prevent back-sliding! Thirteen virtues, thirteen weeks: four courses a year. The beginning of the book was given over to bolstering mottos and prayers; the end contained the "Scheme of Employment for the Twenty-four Hours of a natural Day," which was brought into being by the requirements of the precept "Order." It, says Franklin, "gave me the most Trouble." No one but Franklin could have said so! None but the victims of his popularizers and mechanical disciples, however, could find it remarkable!

Now it is imprecise and invites misunderstanding to refer to this portion of the *Autobiography,* as a large number of Franklin critics and scholars have done, as his "Art of Virtue." He indeed refers to that never-written project here and reveals the "Design" of it in one paragraph of words for ambitious servants of power, but this is not that book and its title does not have the same meaning for the twentieth century that it had for the eighteenth century. If the modern meaning is in mind, one can only be glad he never wrote it. This part of the memoirs is something of a different kind. The author of this piece was parading himself as a *naïf.*

The role of the rural philosopher demanded a youthful experience like this, a "Project of arriving at moral Perfection." On the other hand, only the wiser, older man was aware just how "bold and arduous" it was. It is the combination of the apparently serious and conscientious youth and the gay, mellow gentleman of Passy that meet to produce this part of the *Autobiography.* Like the other sections, it is an exercise in self-examination and self-advertisement. As the first memoir was a picaresque tale of mistakes and travels told by an indulgent "father" and the third and fourth memoirs were accounts of public causes related by a civic leader and national hero, this is a *naïf* "Philosophical Quaker's" initiation into the trials of a moral life.

When Franklin has completed the chronicle of this project, he goes on to explain to "my Posterity . . . that to this little Artifice, with the Blessing of God, their Ancestor ow'd the constant Felicity of his Life down to his 79th Year." This is the high-flown recollection of a man plainly playing the role of the retired sage. It is the writer of memoirs who is speaking, the man who looks backwards and avails himself of the opportunity to distinguish the crises and decisive choices of his life. The list of thirteen virtues and his intricate system of practicing them is responsible for "that Evenness of Temper, & that Chearfulness in Conversation which makes his Company still sought for, & agreable even to his younger Acquaintance." This is as revealing a kind of acting as Robert Frost's pose as the octogenerian New England poet:

> I shall be telling this with a sigh
> Somewhere ages and ages hence:
> Two roads diverged in a wood, and I—
> I took the one less traveled by,
> And that has made all the difference.

The man who tells of this "bold and arduous Project of arriving at moral Perfection," then, is no dogmatist or facile believer in the possibilities of moral Perfection. It was a "bold and arduous Project."! Note the history of the young man's tribulations with it:

I was surpriz'd to find myself so much fuller of Faults than I had imagined, . . . To avoid the Trouble of renewing now & then my little Book, which by scraping out the Marks on the Paper of old Faults to make room for new Ones in a new Course, became full of Holes: I transferr'd my Tables & Precepts to the Ivory Leaves of a Memorandum Book, on which the Lines were drawn with red Ink that made a durable Stain, and on those Lines I mark'd my Faults with a black Lead Pencil, which Marks I could easily wipe out with a wet sponge.

Franklin is not telling sarcastic jokes on himself, but he is enjoying the natural ironies which the seventy-eight-year-old autobiographer watched quietly emerge in a detailed and truthful record of his youthful vanity. Lawrence's outbursts were the result of too flat and impoverished a reading: "The Perfectibility of Man! Ah heaven, what a dreary theme! The Perfectibility of the Ford car!" "I am a moral animal. But I am not a moral machine. I don't work with a little set of handles or levers." Franklin was not a moral machine either. Moral Perfection, instead, was a kind of game. Its very mechanic quality did not reduce its inventor to a slave of lines and squares ("that barbed-wire moral enclosure that Poor Richard rigged up"), it broke the more confining bonds of unconscious habit. And it broke them without morbid brooding and immobilizing self-consciousness. Faults and offences were black dots. They were committed and recorded and later wiped away. The "wet sponge" is no mighty symbol of foregiveness and should not be hyper-critically thought of as a travesty of such charity. Time brings second chances. In the rules Franklin prescribed for himself the cycle of time was arranged at thirteen weeks, a quarter of a year!

The gallant and *naïf* autobiographer described his Project with a thoroughness that is absorbing, meanwhile letting the ironies of its vanity and impossibility rise up where they might. There is as much education and moral instruction in them as in the pious, more traditional reading of the second memoir. Abel James and Benjamin Vaughan, in the letters that precede the Passy section, ask for serious and inspirational matter that will be a guide to youth. They are in a sense like Ezra Stiles in his letter requesting Franklin's opinion on Jesus of Nazareth: a little too holy. What Franklin returns is something that includes the instruction but also mellows it with the temperate wisdom of later experience. Too much of the game could result in "a kind of Foppery in Morals." In respect to "Humility" Franklin noted: "I cannot boast of much Success in acquiring the *Reality* of this Virtue; but I had a good deal with regard to the *Appearance* of it." He gave them more advice than they were capable of expecting. He was quite sincere, even in the midst of his ironies, but his gravity was not dreary; it was *naïf.* The Franklin of Passy had put aside moral Perfection ("but I always carried my little Book with me") and arrived at a worldly perfection of his humanity instead. (pp. 512-24)

> *Robert Freeman Sayre, "The Worldly Franklin and the Provincial Critics," in* Texas Studies in Literature and Language, *Vol. IV, No. 4, Winter, 1963, pp. 512-24.*

David Levin   (essay date 1964)

[*Levin is an educator and critic who has edited several works concerning American Enlightenment writers, including Cotton Mather, Jonathan Edwards, and Benjamin Franklin. In the essay below, he defends Franklin's* Autobiography *from the criticisms of those who disregard the author's humor, didactic purpose, and conscious creation of self.*]

It would be difficult to find a book that seems more widely understood, as a model of plain exposition of character, than *The Autobiography of Benjamin Franklin.* Everyone knows that this is the life of a self-made, self-educated man and that *Poor Richard's Almanac* was a best-seller. Everyone knows that the penniless sixteen-year-old boy who first walked down the streets of Philadelphia with his pockets bulging with shirts and stockings, and with two great puffy rolls under his arms, worked so diligently at his calling that for him the promise of Scripture was fulfilled, and he one day stood before kings. (He "stood before five," he wrote later, with characteristic precision, and sat down to dine with one.) We all know, too, that the Franklin stove and bifocals and the electrical experiments bear witness to Franklin's belief in life-long education, and that it was because of his ability to explain clearly and persuade painlessly—even delightfully—that his international reputation soared higher than his famous kite.

Too often, however, we forget a few simple truths about this great man and his greatest works. We forget the chief purposes for which he wrote his autobiography, and the social system that led him to conceive such aims. Remembering his plainness, his clarity, we overlook the subtlety of his expression, his humor, and his qualifying statements. Above all, we forget that he was a writer, that he had a habit of creating characters. And so he takes us in. Some of us forget that Poor Richard is just as clearly Franklin's creation as is Mrs. Silence Dogood, the fictitious character through whom young Benjamin had published in his brother's newspaper in Boston; many of us forget that *The Way to Wealth,* Franklin's brilliantly successful collection of economic proverbs, is a humorous *tale* narrated by Poor Richard, who at first makes fun of himself and then reports the long speech made by another fictitious character named Father Abraham; and most of us overlook the crucial distinction, especially in the first half of Franklin's autobiography, between the *writer* of the book and the chief *character* he portrays.

Please understand that I do not mean to call Franklin's autobiography a work of fiction. I must insist, however, that we refuse to let its general fidelity to historical fact blind us to the author's function in creating the character who appears in the book. Franklin's first entry into Philadelphia may serve as an example. We are apt to consider the picture of that boy as a natural fact of history, as if no conceivable biographer could have omitted it. It merges in our experience with the myth that Horatio Alger exploited a century later, and with dozens of other pictures of successful men at the beginning of their careers: the country boy walking into the big city, the immigrant lad getting off the boat and stepping forth in search of his fortune. So grandly representative is this human experience that our current critical fashion would call it archetypal. But it was Franklin the writer who elected to describe this picture, and who made it memorable. He was not obliged to include it. He *chose* to make it represent an important moment in his life, and he chose to depict his young former self in particular detail. His dirty clothes, his bulging pockets, and the huge rolls constitute nearly the only details respecting his personal appearance in the entire book. He might have omitted them, and he might have ignored the whole incident.

If we try to imagine what our view of Franklin might have been had he not written his autobiography, we will recognize that the author's conception of himself has considerably more literary significance than one can find in a single descriptive passage. Though the honest autobiographer refuses to invent fictitious incidents, he *actually creates himself as a character.* He selects incidents and qualities for emphasis, and discards or suppresses others. He portrays himself in relation to some other character (whom he also "creates" in this book), but refrains from portraying himself in relation to some others whom he once knew. He decides on the meaning of his life and the purpose of his book, and he selects traits, incidents, and characters accordingly. Obviously he cannot record everything that happened unless he spews forth every feeling, impulse, twitch that ever entered his mind or affected his senses. Indeed, the very conception of a happening requires some selection, some ordering of experience, and a point of view from which to perceive that order. D. H. Lawrence did not understand Franklin's autobiography, but he saw that it recognized a kind of order, and a view of the self, which imposed a planned control on natural feelings. "The ideal self !" he cried scornfully in his critique of Franklin.

> Oh, but I have a strange and fugitive self shut out and howling like a wolf or a coyote under the ideal windows. See his red eyes in the dark? This is the self who is coming into his own.
>
> The perfectibility of man, dear God! When every man as long as he remains alive is in himself a multitude of conflicting men. Which of these do you choose to perfect, at the expense of every other?
>
> Old Daddy Franklin will tell you. He'll rig him up for you, the pattern American. Oh, Franklin was the first downright American.

As we shall see later on, this gross caricature of "the sharp little man" reflects some imperfections in Franklin's ability to communicate with ages beyond his own, and as we shall see even sooner, it reflects an inability or unwillingness in Lawrence and many others to read carefully. For the moment, however, let us content ourselves with two observations in support of Lawrence's limited perception. First, Franklin's autobiography represents that kind of art in which the author tries to understand himself, to evaluate himself, to see himself, in a sense, from outside; it is a *portrayal* of the self rather than simply an *expression* of current feeling or an outpouring of those multiple selves that Lawrence celebrates. Old Daddy Franklin did indeed know what he was about. But the second observation must limit the praise in the first. The very terms in which Frank-

lin expresses his admirable self-awareness limit his communication in a way that obscures the identity of the author. The technique of humor, and the disarming candor about techniques of influence and persuasion—these occasionally make us wonder which of several selves Benjamin Franklin is.

Franklin's art is deceptive. At first there may seem to be none at all. The book, written at four different times from 1771 to 1790, the year Franklin died, is loosely constructed; it is almost conversational in manner. It begins, indeed, as a letter to Franklin's son. It is episodic, anecdotal. Clearly, however, its narrative order includes two major divisions: the first half of the book describes his education, as he strives for a secure position in the world and for a firm character; the second half concentrates on his career of *public* service, though the account breaks off well before the American Revolution.

That simple pattern itself illustrates the most important fact about Franklin's autobiography. He not only creates an attractive image of himself but uses himself as a prototype of his age and his country. There are three essential ways in which he establishes this story of the self-made man securely in the broadest experience of his time. If we examine them with some care, we may understand his purposes and his achievement more clearly.

The first context is that of Puritanism, represented here by Franklin's admiration for John Bunyan's *Pilgrim's Progress* and Cotton Mather's *Essays To Do Good.* Although Franklin says that he was converted to Deism by some anti-Deistic tracts in his Presbyterian father's library, we cannot overestimate the importance of his Puritan heritage, and his own account gives it due credit. (I refer, of course, not to the gross distortion suggested by the word "puritanical," the joy-killing and fanatical, but to that firm tradition that required every Christian to venture into this world as a pilgrim, doing right for the glory of God.) It is to this tradition that we owe Franklin's great proverb "Leisure is time for doing something useful," his emphasis on diligence in one's calling, the moral preoccupation that colors his view of ordinary experience. We see the Puritan influence in his insistence on frugality, simplicity, and utility as standards of value; and we see it just as clearly in his acceptance of public duty, his constant effort to improve the community, his willingness at last to serve the local and international community without pay. When we remember that the Protestant ethic combines the profit motive with religious duty, we should remember that in Franklin's day (as in John Winthrop's before him) it also obliged one to use one's fortune, and one's own person, in public service.

The Puritan tradition, indeed, gave Franklin a more purely literary kind of model. By the time he was growing up there existed in both old and New England a fairly large body of personal literature that emphasized objective self-examination and the need to keep an objective record of divine Providence as it affected an individual life. One recorded one's daily life in order to evaluate one's conduct and also to find evidence of God's will in the pattern of events. It was the Puritan custom, moreover, to improve every opportunity to find moral instruction and signs of universal meaning in particular experience. Franklin himself describes and exemplifies this custom in an anecdote (not in the *Autobiography,* but in a letter) of a visit that he made in 1724 to the old Puritan minister Cotton Mather. As Franklin was leaving, he wrote later, Mather

> showed me a shorter way out of the house, through a narrow passage, which was crossed by a beam overhead. We were talking as I withdrew, he accompanying me behind, and I turning partly towards him when he said hastily, "STOOP, STOOP!" I did not understand him till I felt my head against the beam. He was a man that never missed any occasion of giving instruction, and upon this he said to me: "You are young, and have the world before you; STOOP as you go through it, and you will miss many hard thumps." This advice, thus beat into my head, has frequently been of use to me, and I often think of it when I see pride mortified and misfortunes brought upon people by carrying their heads too high.

One of the most successful devices that Franklin uses in his autobiography is this kind of symbolic anecdote, or parable; what brings Franklin's practice closer to Puritan preaching than to the parables in the Bible is his careful addition of a conclusion that drives home the point—the application or use—for those who might otherwise misunderstand it.

Before turning from Puritanism to a second quality of eighteenth-century experience, we should pause for another minute over the name of John Bunyan. For the first half of Franklin's autobiography, as Charles Sanford has said, represents a kind of pilgrim's progress. As his pious contemporaries Jonathan Edwards and John Woolman published accounts of their growth in Christian grace, so Franklin, acknowledging the aid of Providence, narrates the progress of a chosen, or at least fortunate, and often underserving young man through a series of perils (including the valley of the shadow of death) to a relatively safe moral haven, if not to the Heavenly City. Others, we must remember, do not fare so well. A number of his early associates fall into one pit or another, and although Franklin tries to show what he did to save himself, so that others might profit by his example, he makes it perfectly clear that on several occasions he was so foolish that he too would have gone down had he not been preserved by Providence—or plain good luck.

It is this sense of the perils facing a young man in the free society of the new capitalism that brings me to the second of my three kinds of representativeness. Whether he was a Puritan or not, the young indentured servant, the young apprentice, the young artisan or farmer of Franklin's time had to walk a perilous way in the world. And if, like a great many Americans, he was leaving his childhood community as well as the restraints and comforts of his childhood religious faith, when he came forth to make his way in the world, he faced those dangers with very little help from outside himself. He had precious little help in the experience of others, for often his experience was new for the entire society. The mistakes he made did not entitle him to the protection of bankruptcy laws or of the less grand

comforts of our welfare state. They sent him to a debtor's prison, or subjected him to the permanent authority of a creditor. Franklin described plain economic fact as well as moral truth when he said, "It is hard for an empty sack to stand upright."

Thus one of Franklin's major purposes in the *Autobiography* was to instruct the young, not only by good example but by warning. Especially in his account of his youth, he presents himself repeatedly as the relatively innocent or ignorant young man in conflict with those who would take advantage of him. Much of the sharp dealing that annoys D. H. Lawrence and others occurs in this kind of situation. Franklin's older brother, exploiting and sometimes beating the young apprentice, tries to circumvent a court ruling against his newspaper by freeing young Benjamin and making him nominal owner of the paper; Benjamin takes advantage of the opportunity by going off to Philadelphia to strike out on his own. Samuel Keimer uses Franklin to train other printers so that Franklin's services may then be dispensed with; but Franklin plans to set up his own shop, and when he does, he prospers as Keimer fails.

As in the fiction of Daniel Defoe, whom Franklin admired, and Samuel Richardson, whom he was among the first American printers to publish, Franklin's *Autobiography* indicates clearly that the relations between the sexes concealed some of the chief dangers to the young freeman's liberty. Luckily, he concedes, he escaped the worst consequences of occasional encounters with "low women"; but in a society that frankly recognized marriage as an economic contract he was almost entrapped by a clever pair of parents who seem to have counted on hoodwinking the young lad because he had to bargain for himself in a matter that required cooler heads. Franklin's account of the episode is priceless:

> Mrs. Godfrey [his landlady] projected a match for me with a relation's daughter, took opportunities of bringing us often together, till a serious courtship on my part ensued, the girl being in herself very deserving. The old folks encouraged me by continued invitations to supper and by leaving us together, till at length it was time to explain. Mrs. Godfrey managed our little treaty. I let her know that I expected as much money with their daughter as would pay off my remaining debt for the printing house, which I believe was not then above a hundred pounds. She brought me word they had no such sum to spare. I said they might mortgage their house in the Loan Office. The answer to this after some days was that they did not approve the match; that on enquiry of Bradford [another printer] they had been informed the printing business was not a profitable one, the types would soon be worn out and more wanted; that Samuel Keimer and D. Harry had failed one after the other, and I should probably soon follow them; and therefore I was forbidden the house, and the daughter shut up. Whether this was a real change of sentiment or only artifice, on a supposition of our being too far engaged in affection to retract and therefore that we should steal a marriage, which would leave them at liberty to give or withhold what

they pleased, I know not. But I suspected the motive, resented it, and went no more. Mrs. Godfrey brought me afterwards some more favourable accounts of their disposition and would have drawn me on again, but I declared absolutely my resolution to have nothing more to do with that family.

This anecdote is not among the most popular with modern readers. It should be noticed, however, that people who owned their house outright did not ordinarily leave their daughter alone with a young man until they had some assurance of his economic eligibility for marriage, and that these parents were not worried about Franklin's ability to provide for their daughter until he demanded the usual dowry. We should notice, too, that the young Franklin who is described in this anecdote seems at last to have obeyed his own feelings of resentment rather than the economic interest that might have been served by allowing the girl's parents to re-open negotiations.

But although he always prospers, the innocent young man is not infallibly wise. Although he is never so roguish as Moll Flanders, his confession appears to be remarkably candid. He concedes that he was greatly deceived by the Governor of Pennsylvania, who sent him as a very young man to England, along with supposed letters of recommendation and letters of credit that never arrived. (That, by the way, was probably the greatest peril of Franklin's young life, and he confesses that he walked into it despite his father's clear warning.) He admits freely to motives and perceptions that we, along with most of his contemporaries, prefer to conceal. He thanks heaven for vanity, "along with the other comforts of life," and admits that it is useful to cultivate not only the reality but the *appearance* of industry and humility. It was effective, he says, to carry his own paper stock through the streets in a wheelbarrow, so that people could see how hard he was willing to work. A book, he confesses, "sometimes debauch'd me from my work, but that was seldom, snug, and gave no scandal."

This apparent honesty leads us to the heart of the book. My third kind of representativeness, the most important of all, can be summed up in a single statement that appears near the end of the *Autobiography*. "This," Franklin wrote, "is an age of experiments." It *was* an age of experiments, an age of empirical enlightenment, when every freeman might, if wary and lucky, learn by experience and test for himself. Franklin's greatest achievement in this book is that of characterizing himself repeatedly as a man of inquiry. He creates for us a convincing image of the inquiring man, self-educated, testing for himself, in morality, in business, in religion, in science. On almost every page we see some evidence of his willingness to learn. He contrives to reveal the vast range of his interests—from the pure science of electricity, to the effect of lading on the speed of merchant ships, to street-lighting and street-cleaning, to the value of learning modern romance languages before trying to learn Latin—all these he contrives to reveal in anecdotes of questioning and discovery. And in anecdote after anecdote, the plain questioning of Benjamin Franklin in action applies an experimental test to theories and assumptions. As a young journeyman printer in

England, he demonstrates to his fellow workmen that the customary beer is not necessary to the maintenance of strength; he drinks water, and carries more type than they can carry. Young Franklin and a friend agree that the one who dies first will prove the possibility of communicating from beyond the grave by getting in touch with the other who remains alive; but, Old Franklin the narrator reports, "he never fulfilled his promise." As a military commander at the start of the Seven Years' War with France, Franklin hears the zealous Presbyterian chaplain's complaint that the men do not attend religious services; he solves the problem by persuading the chaplain himself to serve out the men's daily rum ration just *after* prayers. " . . . and never," the narrator comments, "were prayers more generally and more punctually attended—so that I thought this method preferable to the punishments inflicted by some military laws for non-attendance on divine service."

Especially in the narrative of the early years, this wide-eyed freshness of perception is perfectly compatible with the young man's shrewdness, and it is nowhere more delightful than in his depiction of some of the other chief characters in the book. One of the most remarkable qualities in the book is the author's almost total lack of rancor. His brother James, Samuel Keimer, Governor Keith, and General Edward Braddock—all these people may be said to have injured him; yet he presents them all with the charitable curiosity of a man who was once interested in learning from his experience with them something about human nature. I refer here not to the kind of curiosity that can be so easily caricatured, the ingenious Yankee's humor that leads him to tell us how he measured reports of the distance at which the revivalist George Whitefield's voice might be heard. What I mean to admire is the humorous *discovery* of another person's strange faults. Consider the economy of this portrayal of Samuel Keimer, whose faults are balanced against those of the young Franklin:

> Keimer and I lived on a pretty good familiar footing and agreed tolerably well, for he suspected nothing of my setting up [for myself]. He retained a great deal of his old enthusiasm and loved argumentation. We therefore had many disputations. I used to work him so with my Socratic method and had trappaned him [that is, tricked him] so often by questions apparently so distant from any point we had in hand, and yet by degrees leading to the point and bringing him into difficulties and contradictions, that at last he grew ridiculously cautious and would hardly answer the most common question without asking first, "What do you intend to infer by that?" However, it gave him so high an opinion of my abilities in the confuting way that he seriously proposed my being his colleague in a project he had of setting up a new sect. He was to preach the doctrines, and I was to confound all opponents. When he came to explain with me upon the doctrines, I found several conundrums which I objected to, unless I might have my way a little, too, and introduce some of mine. Keimer wore his beard at full length, because somewhere in the Mosaic Law it is said, "Thou shalt not mar the corners of thy beard." He likewise kept

the seventh day Sabbath, and these two points were essentials with him. I disliked both but agreed to admit them upon condition of his adopting the doctrine of not using animal food. "I doubt," says he, "my constitution will bear it." I assured him it would and that he would be the better for it. He was usually a great glutton, and I wished to give myself some diversion in half-starving him. He consented to try the practice if I would keep him company; I did so, and we held it for three months. Our provisions were purchased, cooked, and brought to us regularly by a woman in the neighbourhood who had from me a list of forty dishes to be prepared for us at different times, in which there entered neither fish, flesh, nor fowl. This whim suited me better at this time from the cheapness of it, not costing us above eighteen pence sterling each per week. I have since kept several Lents most strictly, leaving the common diet for that, and that for common, without the least inconvenience, so that I think there is little in the advice of making those changes by easy gradations. I went on pleasantly, but poor Keimer suffered grievously, tired of the project, longed for the flesh pots of Egypt, and ordered a roast pig. He invited me and two women friends to dine with him, but it being brought too soon upon table, he could not resist the temptation and ate it all up before we came.

Franklin's acute awareness that Keimer is a ridiculously pretentious, affected character does not prevent him from expressing some unsentimental sympathy for his former victim, or from hinting broadly that he himself now disapproves of giving himself diversion at the expense of others—although he might relish the chance to repeat the same experiment. We must remember, in reading this anecdote, that Franklin has previously told us of his decision some years later to abandon the Socratic method, because it had sometimes won him victories that neither he nor his cause deserved. And we must notice that his rational skepticism, his testing by experience, extends even to reason itself.

In an age of reason Franklin was not afraid to admit the limits of reason, nor did he hesitate in his autobiography to illustrate those limits by recounting an experience in which young Franklin himself is the only target of his humor. He used this device on several occasions, but one of them is astonishing in its brilliance, for it not only establishes the author's attitude toward himself but phrases the issue in the key terms of eighteenth-century psychology. The battle in young Franklin is a battle between principle and inclination. The anecdote appears immediately before the vegetarian experiment with Keimer. During a calm on his voyage back from Boston to Philadelphia, Franklin says,

> our crew employed themselves catching cod, and hauled up a great number. Till then I had stuck to my resolution to eat nothing that had had life; and on this occasion I considered . . . the taking every fish as a kind of unprovoked murder, since none of them had or ever could do us any injury that might justify this massacre. All this seemed very reasonable. But I had for-

merly been a great lover of fish, and when this came hot out of the frying pan, it smelled admirably well. I balanced some time between principle and inclination, till I recollected that when the fish were opened, I saw smaller fish taken out of their stomachs. "Then," thought I, "if you eat one another, I don't see why we mayn't eat you." So I dined upon cod very heartily and have since continued to eat as other people, returning only now and then occasionally to a vegetable diet. So convenient a thing it is to be a *reasonable creature*, since it enables one to find or make a reason for everything one has a mind to do.

Franklin gives us, then, the picture of a relatively innocent, unsophisticated, sometimes foolish young man who confounds or at least survives more sophisticated rivals. Consistently, the young man starts at the level of testing, and he often stumbles onto an important truth. We see his folly and his discoveries through the ironically humorous detachment of a candid old man, whose criticism of the young character's rivals is tempered by the same kind of affectionate tolerance that allows him to see the humor of his own mistakes. The wise old writer expects people to act selfishly, but retains his affection for them. He leads us always to consider major questions in terms of simple practical experience, as when he tells us that he soon gave up converting people to belief in Deism because the result seemed often to be that they thus became less virtuous than before. Deism, he said, might be true, but it did not seem to be very useful. Because he assumed that at best people will usually act according to their conception of their own true interest, because all his experience seemed to confirm this hypothesis, and because metaphysical reasoning often turned out to be erroneous, he concentrated on demonstrating the usefulness of virtue.

It is right here, just at the heart of his most impressive achievement as an autobiographer, that Franklin seems to have made his one great error in communication. Many people, first of all, simply misunderstand him; he did not take sufficient account of the carelessness of readers. Many are completely taken in by the deceptive picture. So effective has Franklin been in demonstrating the usefulness of virtue through repeated anecdotes from his own educational experience, so insistent on effectiveness as a test of what is good in his own life, that many readers simply believe he has no other basis for deciding what is good. They simply conclude that the man who would say, "Honesty is the best *policy*" will be *dis*honest if ever dishonesty becomes the best policy. Readers wonder what the man who tells them candidly that he profited by *appearing* to be humble hopes to gain by *appearing* to be candid.

If I were to follow Franklin and judge chiefly by the results, I would give up trying to clarify the misunderstanding, for I am sure that many readers will refuse to follow me beyond this point. Yet it seems to me important to understand Franklin's intention as clearly as possible, if only to measure properly the degree of his miscalculation or his inadequacy. Let us examine one other brief passage from the *Autobiography*, a statement describing Franklin's own effort to propagate a new set of religious beliefs, to establish a new sect which he proposed, characteristically, to call The Society of the Free and Easy. "In this piece [a book to be called *The Art of Virtue*] it was my design to explain and enforce this doctrine: That vicious actions are not hurtful because they are forbidden, but forbidden because they are hurtful, *the nature of man alone considered;* that it was therefore everyone's interest to be virtuous who wished to be happy *even in this world.*"

I have stressed the qualifying phrases in this statement in order to emphasize the nature of Franklin's faith: *the nature of man alone considered;* everyone who wished to be happy *even in this world.* This doctrine of enlightened self-interest represents an important reversal—almost an exact reversal—of a sentence written by a sixteenth-century English Puritan named William Perkins, who in propounding the absolute sovereignty of God had declared: "A thing is not first of all reasonable and just, and then afterwards willed by God; it is first of all willed by God, and thereupon becomes reasonable and just." Yet Franklin's reversal does *not* say that discovering what is apparently to our interest is the only way of *defining* virtue. He, every bit as much as the Calvinist, believes that virtues must be defined by some absolute standard. Vicious actions, he says, *are forbidden*—by the benevolent authority of a wise God and by the universal assent, as he understood it, of wise men throughout history. But some actions *are* inherently vicious, whether or not they seem profitable.

Franklin's faith, then, professes that a true understanding of one's interest even in this world will lead one to virtue. Since the obvious existence of viciousness and folly in every society demonstrates that men do not yet practice the virtues on which most philosophers *have* agreed, finding a way to increase the practice of virtue—the number of virtuous actions—is a sufficiently valuable task to need no elaborate justification. And so the same Franklin who in the year of his death refused to dogmatize on the question of Jesus Christ's divinity because he expected soon to "have an opportunity of knowing the truth with less trouble," contented himself with questions of moral practice. His faith told him that the best way to serve God was to do good to one's fellow men, and he reasoned that just as all wise men preferred benevolent acts to flattery, so the infinitely wise God would not care very much to be flattered, but would prefer to have men *act* benevolently. He denied, however, that any man could ever *deserve* a heavenly, infinite reward for finite actions. He knew perfectly well the implications of his faith, but he saw no reason to worry very much about whether it was absolutely correct. For all his experience indicated that whether or not virtue and interest do coincide, no other argument but that of self-interest will persuade men to act virtuously, and even that argument will not always persuade them.

It is in this context that we must read Franklin's account of the thirteen-week course he gave himself in the Art of Virtue. D. H. Lawrence and other critics have overlooked the humorous self-criticism with which Franklin introduces the account. "It was about this time," Franklin says, "that I conceived the bold and arduous project of arriving at moral perfection. As I knew, or thought I knew, what was right and wrong, I did not see why I might not *always* do the one and avoid the other. But I soon found I had undertaken a task of more difficulty than I had imagined.

While my attention was taken up and care employed against one fault, I was often surprized by another." Franklin, you will remember, listed the chief instrumental virtues under thirteen headings and at first devoted a week to concentrating especially on the habit of practicing one of the thirteen virtues. He made himself a chart, and in the daily period that he allotted to meditating the question "What good have I done today?" he entered a black mark for each action that could be considered a violation of the precepts. He worked to achieve a clear page. At thirteen weeks for each completed "course," he was able, he says, to go through four courses in a year. As he was surprised, at first, to find himself so full of faults, so he was pleased to find that he was able to decrease the number of his faulty actions. He endeavors to persuade us by pointing out that this improvement of conduct made him happier and helped him to prosper. But he makes perfectly clear the relative nature of his progress. He compares his method of attacking one problem at a time to weeding a garden, a task that is never really completed. He tells us not only that he later advanced to taking one course each year (with four weeks for each virtue), but also that he bought a book with ivory pages, so that he could erase the black marks at the end of one term and begin the course anew. The task was endless. Wondering about D. H. Lawrence's reading of Franklin, we may echo his own uncomprehending words: The perfectibility of man, indeed!

In trying to clarify Franklin's beliefs, I have not meant to absolve him of all responsibility for the widespread misunderstanding of his work. As I have already suggested, he invites difficulty by deliberately appearing to be more simple than he is, by choosing the role of the inquisitive, experimental freeman. By daring to reduce metaphysical questions to the terms of practical experience, he sometimes seems to dismiss them entirely, and he draws our attention away from the books that he has read. Thus, although he alludes to the most influential philosophical and psychological treatises of his age, and although he certainly read widely in every kind of learning that attracted his remarkably curious mind, he does not give this theoretical groundwork any important place in the narrative of his life. He mentions that he read John Locke at a certain point, and the Earl of Shaftesbury, and he says that this sort of education is extremely valuable. But in the narrative itself he is plain Benjamin Franklin, asking questions prompted by the situation. Even as he recounts, much later in the book, his successful correspondence with some of the leading scientists of England and the Continent, he underemphasizes his learning and portrays himself as a fortunate and plain, if skillful and talented, amateur.

This effect is reinforced by another quality of Franklin's literary skill, the device of humorous understatement. I have already cited one or two examples, as in his statement about answering the question of the divinity of Jesus. Similarly, he refers to the discovery that an effective preacher was plagiarizing famous English sermons as "an unlucky occurrence," and he says that he preferred good sermons by others to bad ones of the minister's own manufacture. He repeatedly notices ridiculous incongruity by putting an apt word in a startlingly subordinate place and thus shocking us into a fresh, irreverent look at a subject that we may well have regarded in a conventional way. So he says that for some time he had been regularly absent from Presbyterian church services, "Sunday being my studying day"; and he remarks that enormous multitudes of people admired and respected the revivalist George Whitefield, "notwithstanding his common abuse of them by assuring them they were naturally 'half beasts and half devils'. " This is the method that Henry Thoreau later used in *Walden* when he declared that the new railroads and highways, which were then called internal improvements, were all external and superficial; it is the method Samuel Clemens employed through his narrator Huckleberry Finn, who says that at mealtime the widow Douglas began by lowering her head and grumbling over the victuals, "though there warn't really anything the matter with them." The device is often delightfully effective in negative argument, in revealing ludicrous inconsistency. But because it depends on an appeal to simple self-reliance, and often to a hard-headed practicality, it is not conducive to the exposition of positive, complex theory. The particular form of Franklin's wit, his decision to portray himself as an inquisitive empiricist, the very success of his effort to exemplify moral values in accounts of practical experience, his doctrine of enlightened self-interest, and the fine simplicity of his exposition—all these combine to make him seem philosophically more naïve, and practically more materialistic, than he is.

Yet this is a great book, and despite the limitations implicit in his pedagogical method, the breadth and richness of

Benjamin Wilson's portrait of Franklin, 1759.

Franklin's character do come through to the reasonably careful reader. One chief means, of course, is the urbane yet warm tone of the wise old narrator, who begins by conceding that one of his reasons for writing an autobiographical statement to his son is simply the desire of an old man to talk about himself. We should also notice that although his emotional life is clearly beyond the bounds of his narrative purpose, he expresses an unmistakable affection, even in retrospect, for his parents, his brother, and his wife. His judgment is nowhere firmer or more admirable than in his account of the self-satisfied young Benjamin's return to taunt brother James, his former master, with the signs of the Philadelphia journeyman's prosperity. His record of his wife's life-long usefulness to him is not in the least incompatible with genuine affection for her. And in one brief paragraph citing as an argument for smallpox vaccination the death of his own son, "a fine boy of four years old," he reveals that his serenity could be rippled by the memory of an old grief.

We must remember, finally, that Franklin was one of the most beloved men of his time. The first American who was called the father of his country, he had no reason to feel anxious about the quality of what our own public relations men would call his "image." He had retired at the age of 42 to devote the rest of his long life to public service and scientific study; he was known internationally as a faithful patriot who had for decades defended the popular cause in almost every political controversy; he had been a great success at the French court, and he was a member of the Royal Society in England. With these sides of his character known so well, he had no reason to expect that his instructive *Autobiography* would be taken as the complete record of his character, or of his range as a writer. The polished *Bagatelles* that he had written in France; the brilliant ironic essays that he had published in England during the years just before the Revolution; the state papers that he had written in all seriousness as an agent of the Congress—all these formed a part of his public character before he completed his work on the *Autobiography.* He could not foresee that, in a romantic age in which many writers believed capitalism and practical science were overwhelming the human spirit, a novelist like D. H. Lawrence would make him a symbol of acquisitive smugness; nor could he foresee that F. Scott Fitzgerald, lamenting in *The Great Gatsby* the betrayal of the great American dream, would couple Ben Franklin's kind of daily schedule with a Hopalong Cassidy book, and would imply that in the 1920s anyone who followed Franklin's advice would have to be a stock-waterer or a boot-legger.

What Franklin represented in his day, and what we should see in his greatest book, was something much more complex than this stereotype. He was deceptively simple, to be sure; but his life and his character testified to the promise of experience, the value of education, the possibility of uniting fruitful public service with simple self-reliance, the profitable conduct of a useful business enterprise, and the free pursuit of knowledge in both pure and practical science. His book remains an admirable work of art, and its author still speaks truth to us as an admirable representative of the Enlightenment. (pp. 258-75)

David Levin, "The Autobiography of Benjamin Franklin: The Puritan Experimenter in Life and Art," in The Yale Review, *Vol. LIII, No. 2, Winter, 1964, pp. 258-75.*

Bruce Ingham Granger   (essay date 1964)

[*Granger is an American scholar and critic who has written on the literature of the American Revolutionary era. In the following essay from his* Benjamin Franklin: An American Man of Letters, *he examines* Poor Richard's Almanack, *commenting on Franklin as a proverb stylist.*]

On December 28, 1732, the *Pennsylvania Gazette* announced as "JUST PUBLISHED, FOR 1733,"

> POOR RICHARD: AN ALMANACK containing the Lunations, Eclipses, Planets Motions and Aspects, Weather, Sun and Moon's rising and setting, Highwater, &c. besides many pleasant and witty Verses, Jests and Sayings, Author's Motive of Writing, Prediction of the Death of his friend Mr. Titan Leeds, Moon no Cuckold, Batchelor's Folly, Parson's Wine and Baker's Pudding, Short Visits, Kings and Bears, New Fashions, Game for Kisses, Katherine's Love, Different Sentiments, Signs of a Tempest, Death a Fisherman, Conjugal Debate, Men and Melons, H. the Prodigal, Breakfast in Bed, Oyster Lawsuit, &c. by RICHARD SAUNDERS, Philomat.

Poor Richard's Almanack was by no means the first such production in Pennsylvania, where farmers, artisans, and shopkeepers demanded a literature of action. As early as 1686 Samuel Atkins had tried his hand at the form, and Daniel Leeds took his place the next year. From the turn of the century the colony witnessed a steady flow of almanacs. When Franklin undertook his, no fewer than six others were being published at Philadelphia, several of them written and printed by men like Andrew Bradford, Samuel Keimer, and Thomas Godfrey whom he knew personally.

In his almanacs Franklin, the rising young editor, wrote with greater familiarity than he allowed himself in his more studied periodical essays; after all, as philomath he did not need to maintain the same dignity as in the *Gazette*. Considering *Poor Richard* "a proper Vehicle for conveying Instruction among the common People, who bought scarce any other Books," he "endeavour'd to make it both entertaining and useful." He approached his task in seeming earnest, thereby escaping the prosaic dullness that characterized most colonial almanacs. In 1737 "Philomath," expressing what was certainly Franklin's attitude, specified "the Talents requisite in *an Almanack Writer.*" Contending that "*Almanackorum scriptor nascitur non fit,*" he said that such a writer "*should be descended of a great Family, and bear a Coat of Arms*"; that he should possess "a Sort of Gravity, which keeps a due medium between Dulness and Nonsense, and yet has a Mixture of both. . . . He shou'd write Sentences, and throw out Hints, that neither himself, nor any Body else can understand or know the meaning of"; and that he "*shou'd not be a finish'd Poet, but a Piece of one,* and qualify'd to

write, what we vulgarly call Doggerel." "I could further prove to you, if I was to go about it," concluded Philomath, "That an *Almanack Writer* ought not only to be a Piece of a Wit, but a very Wag; and that he shou'd have the Art also to make People believe, that he is almost a Conjurer, &c."

I

In the prefaces to *Poor Richard's Almanack* and occasionally in the verse Franklin created his most famous American personae, the homespun Richard Saunders and his clacking wife Bridget. "I might in this place attempt to gain thy Favour," Richard informs the reader in the first number,

> by declaring that I write Almanacks with no other View than that of the publick Good; but in this I should not be sincere; and Men are now a-days too wise to be deceiv'd by Pretences how specious soever. The plain Truth of the Matter is, I am excessive poor, and my Wife, good Woman, is, I tell her, excessive proud; she cannot bear, she says, to sit spinning in her Shift of Tow, while I do nothing but gaze at the Stars; and has threatned more than once to burn all my Books and Rattling-Traps (as she calls my Instruments) if I do not make some profitable Use of them for the good of my Family. The Printer has offer'd me some considerable share of the Profits, and I have thus begun to comply with my Dame's desire.

His first almanac sells so well that at once he gains a measure of relief:

> My Wife has been enabled to get a Pot of her own, and is no longer oblig'd to borrow one from a Neighbour; nor have we ever since been without something of our own to put in it. She has also got a pair of Shoes, two new Shifts, and a new warm Petticoat; and for my part, I have bought a second-hand Coat, so good, that I am now not asham'd to go to Town or be seen there. These Things have render'd her Temper so much more pacifick than it us'd to be, that I may say, I have slept more, and more quietly within this last Year, than in the three foregoing Years put together (1734).

A prospering Richard assures his readers, "If the generous Purchaser of my Labours could see how often his *Fi'-pence* helps to light up the comfortable Fire, line the Pot, fill the Cup and make glad the Heart of a poor Man and an honest good old Woman, he would not think his Money ill laid out, tho' the Almanack of his Friend and Servant R. Saunders were one half blank Paper" (1737). Lest they suppose him grown wealthy, though, he reminds them that the printer, though "I do not grudge it him," "runs away with the greatest Part of the Profit" (1739).

From the outset the *Almanack's* purpose was wholly social. Like the Busy-Body, Richard professes and adheres to a neutrality in religion and politics. In 1746 he assures his public,

> Free from the bitter Rage of Party Zeal,
> All those we love who seek the publick Weal.

Indeed, other than his attacks on fellow philomaths like Titan Leeds and John Jerman, attacks for which Swift's Bickerstaff papers furnished a precedent, Franklin avoided polemics altogether, exhibiting instead that sweet reasonableness and moralistic bent so highly esteemed in the early eighteenth century.

As the Couranteers had entertained their readers with the age-old battle of the sexes, so now Franklin. To Richard's charge,

> She that will eat her breakfast in her bed,
> And spend the morn in dressing of her head,
> And sit at dinner like a maiden bride,
> And talk of nothing all day but of pride;
> God in his mercy may do much to save her,
> But what a case is he in that shall have her.
> [Dec., 1733]

Bridget retorts,

> He that for the sake of Drink neglects his Trade,
> And spends each Night in Taverns till 'tis late,
> And rises when the Sun is four hours high,
> And ne'er regards his starving Family;
> God in his Mercy may do much to save him,
> But, woe to the poor Wife, whose Lot it is to
>   have him.
> [Dec., 1734]

The lines of battle thus early drawn, Bridget cries out against Richard's aspersions on her character:

> What a peasecods! cannot I have a little Fault or two, but all the Country must see it in print! They have already been told, at one time that I am proud, another time that I am loud, and that I have got a new Petticoat, and abundance of such kind of stuff; and now, forsooth! all the World must know, that Poor Dick's Wife has lately taken a fancy to drink a little Tea now and then. A mighty matter, truly, to make a Song of! 'Tis true, I had a little Tea of a Present from the Printer last Year; and what, must a body throw it away? (1738).

When placed side by side with Mrs. Afterwit, Bridget seems the soul of modesty; in fact, her practicality, honesty, and industry call to mind rather the Widow Dogood. No matter, the battle raged on.

> My sickly Spouse, with many a Sigh
> Once told me,—Dicky I shall die:
> I griev'd, but recollected strait,
> 'Twas bootless to contend with Fate:
> So Resignation to Heav'n's Will
> Prepared me for succeeding Ill;
> 'Twas well it did; for, on my Life,
> 'Twas Heav'n's Will to spare my Wife.
> [Jan., 1740]

When he tells her that heaven will deny whatever she prays for, "Indeed! says Nell, 'tis what I'm pleas'd to hear; / For now I'll pray for your long life, my dear" (Sept., 1743). Finally, in what closes out this debate, there appeared an **"Epitaph on a Scolding Wife by her Husband,"** adapted from Dryden: "Here my poor Bridget's Corps doth lie, she is at rest,—and so am I" (Dec., 1744).

Although Richard Saunders has often been confused with his creator, the separate identity of the humble philomath grown affluent and his printer was clearly established from the opening number. So it is that Richard, in order to quash malicious rumors that there is no such man as he and that his productions are actually the work of the printer, publicly declares, *"That what I have written heretofore, and do now write, neither was nor is written by any other Man or Men, Person or Persons whatsoever"* (1736). So, too, that he holds the printer, not himself, accountable for most of the errata in one of the almanacs, remarking:

> Printers indeed should be very careful how they omit a Figure or a Letter: For by such Means sometimes a terrible Alteration is made in the Sense. I have heard, that once, in a new Edition of the *Common Prayer,* the following Sentence, *We shall all be changed in a Moment, in the Twinkling of an Eye;* by the Omission of a single Letter, became, *We shall all be hanged in a Moment,* &c. to the no small Surprize of the first Congregation it was read to (1750).

This confusion between the author and his persona arises in part from the fact that after 1738 Richard the honest philomath tends to be obscured by the emergence of Richard the moralizing philosopher, a confusion later compounded by the avowedly didactic purpose of the often reprinted **Autobiography.** "Besides the usual Things expected in an Almanack," declares Richard in 1739, "I hope the profess'd Teachers of Mankind will excuse my scattering here and there some instructive Hints in Matters of Morality and Religion." From this time, but especially beginning in 1748, the year Franklin expanded his pamphlet from twenty-four pages to thirty-six, didactic and practical essays become more numerous and play a more prominent role in the **Almanack.**

Any final estimate of the character of Richard must take into account the 1758 Preface, known familiarly as **The Way to Wealth,** a work allied to popular tradesman books like Defoe's *Complete English Tradesman* and English conduct books like John Barnard's *Present for an Apprentice.* While Franklin's first object in living was to master the art of virtue and while he undoubtedly gave general assent to the wisdom of Poor Richard, here it is so narrowly concentrated and cast in so precise a narrative frame that Franklin probably did not mean the work to be taken altogether seriously. But eighteenth-century France, identifying Franklin's attitude with Richard's, regarded it "as a work of sublime morality"; and since that time readers the world over have generally so interpreted it. Actually we see Richard, hearing himself quoted so liberally, enslaved by his own morality, a fact of which Franklin is clearly aware. Whereas the people at the auction, having approved the doctrine in Father Abraham's speech, "immediately practised the contrary, just as if it had been a common Sermon," Richard takes this prudential wisdom—and it is, of course, his own—so much to heart that he denies himself material for a new coat, even though the one he is wearing was secondhand when he bought it a quarter of a century before. And when he adds smugly, *"Reader,* if thou wilt do the same, thy Profit will be as great as mine," though we do not necessarily sympathize with the behavior of the others "at this Vendue of *Fineries* and *Knicknacks,*" we smile at the foolish caution that prevents him from making a reasonable purchase. Franklin, who prized frugality as highly as any man, is here warning his public not to fall victim to a narrow and unimaginative exercise of it.

At this point I should like to revise one judgment in John F. Ross's otherwise highly perceptive article [in *PMLA*, LV (1940)] on the character of Richard Saunders. Having distinguished carefully between the two Richards, Ross remarks:

> It is easy to see why Franklin let the original character go, and made no attempt to relate the maxims to the character of his star-gazer. He was interested in getting an almanac to press every fall, not in the depiction of character or the maintenance of literary consistency. . . . The early Richard was finally submerged by the famous farewell preface of 1758, wherein a shadowy Richard appears, only to introduce the speech of a wise old man, Father Abraham, who quotes maxim after maxim from the body of the almanacs. . . . That is, Franklin forced Richard to play a rôle.

Granted that as Franklin built a comfortable living in the 1740's, he began to conceive of Richard as the complete American tradesman. Granted, too, that by the 1750's the **Almanack** was selling at the impressive rate of 10,000 copies a year. I cannot accept the inference that he consciously forced Richard to play a rôle. It seems more probable that insofar as the conception of Richard underwent a change, it happened unconsciously. And if Franklin was not immediately concerned with maintaining literary consistency, how is it that the original Richard reappears in the 1750's—nowhere more memorably than in **The Way to Wealth,** where he is anything but "shadowy"? The enduring vitality of this, Franklin's most fully articulated persona, lies finally in the fact that over the space of twenty-five years the character of the indigent stargazer turned philomath is never totally submerged.

II

Balzac, in a statement that is true in spirit if not wholly in fact, once observed, *"Le canard est une trouvaille de Franklin, qui a inventé le paratonnerre, le canard et la république."* The earliest of Franklin's canards, recalling Swift's hoax on John Partridge, was perpetrated at the expense of a local rival, Titan Leeds. The equation: Richard Saunders is to Titan Leeds as Isaac Bickerstaff is to John Partridge: expresses the similarity in rhetorical strategy, though in certain respects Richard resembles Partridge more nearly than he does Bickerstaff. In the 1733 Preface Richard predicts the time of Titan's death to the minute and, when Titan protests that he did not die at that time, earnestly defends his prediction:

> Mr. Leeds was not only profoundly skilful in the useful Science he profess'd, but he was a Man of *exemplary Sobriety,* a most *sincere Friend,* and an *exact Performer of his Word.* These valuable Qualifications, with many others so much endear'd him to me, that although it should be so, that, contrary to all Probability, contrary to my Prediction and his own, he might possibly be yet

alive, yet my Loss of Honour as a Prognosticator, cannot afford me so much Mortification, as his Life, Health and Safety would give me Joy and Satisfaction (1734).

Titan's protests continuing, Richard retorts with pretended indignation:

> Having receiv'd much Abuse from Titan Leeds deceas'd, (Titan Leeds when living would not have us'd me so!) . . . I cannot help saying, that tho' I take it patiently, I take it very unkindly. And whatever he may pretend, 'tis undoubtedly true that he is really defunct and dead. First because the Stars are seldom disappointed. . . . Secondly, . . . for the Honour of Astrology, the Art professed both by him and his Father [Daniel] before him. Thirdly, . . . [because] his two last Almanacks . . . are not written with that *Life* his Performances use to be written with (1735).

In 1739, by Richard's account, the Bradfords, who continued to publish Titan's almanac, at last admit that he is dead. Whereupon Richard relates how, waking early one morning at his study table where he had fallen asleep, he discovered a letter from Titan confessing that he had indeed died at the time predicted, "with a Variation only of 5 min. 53 sec." Titan goes on to explain further:

> Finding you asleep, I entred your left Nostril, ascended into your Brain, found out where the Ends of those Nerves were fastned that move your right Hand and Fingers, by the Help of which I am now writing unknown to you; but when you open your Eyes, you will see that the Hand written is mine, tho' wrote with yours (1740).

Here for the first time Franklin employs a rhetorical strategy that colored later writings like Polly Baker's Speech and the fictitious controversy involving English news writers. He initiates, carries forward, and closes out this hoax, not through malice, but for the pleasure to be gained from exploiting the comic implications of the fiction. Once Richard has predicted the time of Titan's death, pseudological proofs follow hard upon one another, the principal strategy being to seize upon the victim's every protest of innocence and turn it back upon him. Thus, in reply to Titan's declaration, "Saunders adds another GROSS FALSHOOD in his Almanack, viz. that by my own Calculation I shall *survive* until the 26th of the said Month October 1733, which is as *untrue* as the former," Richard asserts, "Now if it be, as Leeds says, *untrue* and a *gross Falshood* that he surviv'd till the 26th of October 1733, then it is certainly *true* that he died *before* that Time" (1735). The climactic letter in which Titan admits to having died at the time predicted, "with a Variation only of 5 min. 53 sec.," bears final witness to Franklin's high sense of invention. This Swiftian hoax is part of a continuing, good-humored attack on astrology in the pages of the **Almanack.** Not so incidentally, the sophistry Richard here displays lends subtlety to his character.

Franklin, who took himself less seriously than did his rival philomaths, has Richard declare:

> The noble Art [of astrology] is dwindled into

Contempt; the Great neglect us, Empires make Leagues, and Parliaments Laws, without advising with us; and scarce any other Use is made of our learned Labours, than to find the best Time of cutting Corns, or gelding Pigs. This Mischief we owe in a great Measure to ourselves. . . . Urania has been betray'd by her own Sons; those whom she had favour'd with the greatest Skill in her divine Art, the most eminent Astronomers among the Moderns, the Newtons, Halleys, and Whistons, have wantonly contemn'd and abus'd her, contrary to the Light of their own Consciences (1751).

In the prefaces and essays such astrological lore as eclipses, weather predictions, and prophecies is constantly being held up to ridicule. Thus, Richard predicts two eclipses of the sun, "both, like Mrs. ——s's Modesty, and old Neighbour Scrape-all's Money, *Invisible*" (1734); and says of John Jerman's prediction, "He has done what in him lay (by sending them out to gaze at an invisible Eclipse on the first of April) to make *April Fools* of them all" (1744).

As for the weather, Richard asks that philomaths be allowed a few days' leeway, and, "if it does not come to pass accordingly, let the Fault be laid upon the Printer, who, 'tis very like, may have transpos'd or misplac'd it, perhaps for the Conveniency of putting in his Holidays" (1737). The year Bridget tampered with the almanac during her husband's absence she informs the reader, "Upon looking over the Months, I see he has put in abundance of foul Weather this Year; and therefore I have scatter'd here and there, where I could find room, some *fair, pleasant, sunshiny,* &c. for the Good-Women to dry their Clothes in" (1738). All in all, Richard is pleased to think that his weather predictions come to pass *"punctually* and *precisely* on the very Day, in some Place or other on this little *diminutive* Globe of ours" (1753).

Richard's "TRUE PROGNOSTICATION, for 1739" is a skillful abstracting of the "Pantagruelian Prognostication" at the end of the Urquhart-Motteux translation of *Gargantua and Pantagruel,* with vernacular additions and substitutions made out of regard for an American audience. In a passage taken almost verbatim from Rabelais, Richard predicts: "During the first visible Eclipse Saturn is retrograde: For which Reason the Crabs will go sidelong, and the Ropemakers backward. The Belly will wag before, and the A—— shall sit down first." The passage continues: "Mercury will have his share in these Affairs, and so confound the Speech of People, that when a Pensilvanian would say PANTHER, he shall say PAINTER. When a New-Yorker thinks to say (THIS) he shall say (DISS) and the People in New-England and Cape-May will not be able to say (COW) for their lives, but will be forc'd to say (KEOW) by a certain involuntary Twist in the Root of their Tongues." To Rabelais' prediction, "This Year the Stone-blind shall see but very little; the Deaf shall hear but poorly; and the Dumb shan't speak very plain," Richard adds, "And it's much, if my Dame Bridget talks at all this Year." For Rabelais' "Salt-eel" he substitutes the more homely expression "Cowskin"; for "Apes, Monkeys, Baboons, and Dromedaries," the more familiar "Cats, Dogs and Horses"; for "your Hops of Picardy," the more nearly

American "Orange Trees in Greenland"; and for "Wine" and "Herbs," the less exotic "Cyder" and "Turnips." In this burlesque Franklin exhibits skill in compressing and adapting a literary source to his own very different purpose.

III

In addition to prefaces and essays, colonial almanacs traditionally carried what Franklin advertised as "pleasant and witty Verses, Jests and Sayings," that is, proverbial matter and poetic borrowings. B. J. Whiting has defined the proverb [in *Harvard Studies and Notes in Philology,* XIV (1932)] as "an expression which, owing its birth to the people, testifies to its origin in form and phrase. It expresses what is apparently a fundamental truth . . . in homely language, often adorned, however, with alliteration and rhyme; it is usually true, but need not be." Judging by Swift's *Complete Collection of Genteel and Ingenious Conversation,* two dialogues burlesquing proverbial expressions of the day, and by Lord Chesterfield's admonition that his son avoid "old sayings, and common proverbs; which are so many proofs of having kept bad and low company," it seems safe to accept Robert Newcomb's assertion [in his unpublished dissertation] that during the first part of the eighteenth century "the educated Englishman's attitude toward the proverb was not very favorable." As an artisan's son Franklin had no such reservations, however; from the time Silence Dogood announced that *"a Woman's Work is never done,"* proverbial expression was an essential component of his style.

Franklin filled the little spaces of his almanacs with what Richard calls *"moral* Sentences, *prudent* Maxims, and *wise* Sayings, many of them containing *much good Sense* in *very few* Words, and therefore apt to leave *strong* and *lasting* Impressions on the Memory of young Persons" (1747). These proverbs were gleaned principally from Thomas Fuller's *Gnomologia* (1732), *Introductio ad Prudentiam* (1727), and *Introductio ad Sapientiam* (1731); Lord Halifax's *Character of King Charles the Second: and Political, Moral, Miscellaneous Thoughts and Reflections* (1750); George Herbert's *Outlandish Proverbs* (1640); James Howell's *Lexicon Tetraglotton* (1659); and Samuel Richardson's *Collection of Moral and Instructive Sentiments* (1755). Such sayings, especially those that appear in the early numbers of the **Almanack,** usually reflect Richard's interests.

While most of Richard's comic sayings are given verbatim from the original source, on occasion Franklin, yielding to a coarseness that was native to him, modifies them in the direction of the obscene or bawdy.

> A good friend is my nearest relation. [Fuller, *Gn.,* No. 151]
> > Relation without friendship, friendship without power, power without will, will without effect, effect without profit, and profit without vertue, are not worth a farto. [**Poor Richard's Almanack,** Apr., 1733]

> A Fort which begins to parley is half gotten. [Howell, *It. Prov.*]

> The Woman who hearkens, and the town which

treats, the one will yield, the other will do. [Howell, *Fr. Prov.*]
> Neither a Fortress nor a Maidenhead will hold out long after they begin to parly. [**PRA,** May, 1734]

The pun, a recognizable feature in the proverb, is so habitual to Franklin that he will introduce one where none is present in the original.

The good wife is made by the man. [Howell, *Sp. Prov.*]
> Good wives and good plantations are made by good husbands. [**PRA,** Aug., 1736]

The comic element present in such sayings further vivifies Franklin's most vital comic creation and goes far toward counteracting the stereotype of Richard the prudential moralist that persisted throughout the "inner-directed" nineteenth century and still lingers today.

As a proverb stylist who often recast what he borrowed, Franklin was guided by such neoclassic ideals as perspicuity, elegance, and cadence. In accommodating foreign sayings to an American audience, he habitually familiarizes and simplifies the diction.

Nor wife, nor wine, nor horse ought to be praised. [Howell, *It. Prov.*]
> Never praise your Cyder, Horse, or Bedfellow. [**PRA,** Mar., 1736]

A yeoman upon his legs is higher than a prince upon his knees. [Fuller, *Gn.,* No. 488]
> A Plowman on his Legs is higher than a Gentleman on his Knees. [**PRA,** May, 1746]

Go neither to the Physician upon every distemper, nor to the Lawyer upon every brabble, nor to the pot upon every thirst. [Howell, *Sp. Prov.*]
> Don't go to the doctor with every distemper, nor to the lawyer with every quarrel, nor to the pot for every thirst. [**PRA,** Nov., 1737]

He tightens the syntax of many sayings and expresses the meaning in a narrower compass, sometimes employing alliteration or rhyme.

That cheese is wholesomest which comes from a Miser. [Howell, *Sp. Prov.*]
> The misers cheese is wholesomest. [**PRA,** Feb., 1737]

As soon as men have understanding enough to find a fault, they have enough to see the danger of mending it. [Halifax, *Misc.*]
> Men take more pains to mask than mend. [**PRA,** Apr., 1757]

A ship under sail, a man in complete armor, a woman with a great belly are three of the handsomest sights. [Howell, *Eng. Prov.*]
> A Ship under sail and a big-bellied Woman, Are the handsomest two things that can be seen common. [**PRA,** June, 1735]

But since Franklin does not believe in economy for its own sake, he may see fit to expand the original saying. Such expansion is usually the result of supplying the saying with an introduction (often a personification), clarifying its sense by extending it, or appending a moral close.

He is a greater Liar than an epitaph. [Howell, *It. Prov.*]
> Here comes Glib-tongue: who can out-flatter a Dedication; and lie, like ten Epitaphs. [**PRA,** Dec., 1742]

Happy those who are convinced so as to be of the general opinions. [Halifax, *Polit.*]
> Singularity in the right, hath ruined many: Happy those who are Convinced of the general Opinion. [**PRA,** Oct., 1757]

A quiet Conscience sleeps in Thunder. [Fuller, *Gn.,* No. 375]
> A quiet Conscience sleeps in Thunder, But Rest and Guilt live far asunder. [**PRA,** July, 1747]

When all sins grow old covetousness grows young. [Herbert, No. 18]
> When other Sins grow old by Time, Then Avarice is in its prime, Yet feed the Poor at Christmas time. [**PRA,** Dec., 1757]

To secure precision he modifies sayings in the direction of concreteness.

The tongue talks at the head's cost. [Herbert]
> The Tongue offends, and the Ears get the Cuffing. [**PRA,** Nov., 1757]

Slander would not stick, if it had not always something to lay hold of. [Halifax, *Misc.*]
> Act uprightly, and despise Calumny; Dirt may stick to a Mud Wall, but not to polish'd Marble. [**PRA,** Sept., 1757]

Revisions like these all make for greater perspicuity.

Such ornament as Richard's sayings possess is consistent with the responsible use of rhetoric enjoined by the Port-Royalists and Locke. Franklin at times introduces a metaphor into an original saying, at others amplifies or gives greater precision and consistency to one already present.

Nothing can be humbler than Ambition, when it is so disposed. [Halifax, *Moral*]
> Nothing humbler than *Ambition,* when it is about to climb. [**PRA,** Nov., 1753]

Who riseth late, trots all day, because he is behind hand with business. [Howell, *Sp. Prov.*]
> He that riseth late, must trot all day, and shall scarce overtake his business at night. [**PRA,** Aug., 1742]

That which is given shines, that which is eaten stinks. [Howell, *Fr. Prov.*]
> What's given shines, What's receiv'd is rusty. [**PRA,** July, 1735]

Sometimes he supplies an example to point up and color a saying.

Necessity has no law. [Howell, *Eng. Prov.*]
> *Necessity* has no Law; I know some Attorneys of the name. [**PRA,** Oct., 1734]

However elegantly Franklin dresses up Richard's sayings, he carefully avoids making a show of rhetoric.

Cadence, which John Hughes defined as "a Disposing of

the Words in such Order, and with such Variation of Periods, as may strike the Ear with a sort of musical Delight," is markedly present in the sayings Franklin recasts. Frequently he strives for a more balanced expression, or one that is less mechanically balanced.

> It is better to have an egg today than an hen tomorrow. [Howell, *It. Prov.*]
> An Egg today is better than a Hen to-morrow. [**PRA,** Sept., 1734]

> Thou shouldst grace thy House; not thy House thee. [Fuller, *Prud.,* No. 1796]
> Grace then thy House, and let not that grace thee. [**PRA,** Apr., 1739]

> A Man had as good go to Bed to a Razor, as to be intimate with a foolish friend. [Halifax, *Moral*]
> To be intimate with a foolish Friend, is like going to bed to a Razor. [**PRA,** Sept., 1754]

> When one Knave betrayeth another, the one is not to be blamed, nor the other to be pitied. [Halifax, *Moral*]
> When Knaves betray each other, one can scarce be blamed, or the other pitied. [**PRA,** Feb., 1758]

To strengthen the rhythm of the sentence he often employs alliteration.

> A Melon and a woman are hard to be known. [Howell, *Sp. Prov.*]
> Men and Melons are hard to know. [**PRA,** Sept., 1733]

> Men should do with their hopes as they do with tame fowl, cut their wings that they may not fly over the wall. [Halifax, *Moral*]
> Cut the Wings of your Hens and Hopes, lest they lead you a weary Dance after them. [**PRA,** Feb., 1754]

Having early achieved a flexible command of the English sentence, Franklin knows how to refine the syntax of his source and make it more euphonious.

> Who goes far to marry, either goes to deceive, or to be deceived. [Howell, *Sp. Prov.*]
> He that goes far to marry, will either deceive or be deceived. [**PRA,** Mar., 1735]

> Do not Do it if thou wilt not have it known. [Howell, *It. Prov.*]
> Do not do that which you would not have known. [**PRA,** Feb., 1736]

> Resolving to serve well, and at the same time to please, is generally resolving to do what is not to be done. [Halifax, *Polit.*]
> To serve the Publick faithfully, and at the same time please it entirely, is impracticable. [**PRA,** Oct., 1758]

The skill with which Franklin shaped his proverbial borrowings suggests that by the time he launched the *Almanack,* in his twenty-seventh year, he was on his way to becoming one of the great makers of the English sentence. Whereas proverbs merely serve to fill up the spaces in the almanacs, in his letters public and private and in the *Autobiography* they form an integral part of the work. Franklin's proverbial manner of expression was undoubtedly one reason the genteel critic Joseph Dennie [in *The Port Folio* (Philadelphia), I (Feb. 14, 1801)] charged him with being "the founder of that Grubstreet sect, who have professedly attempted to degrade literature to the level of vulgar capacities, and debase the polished and current language of books, by the vile alloy of provincial idioms, and colloquial barbarism, the shame of grammar, and akin to any language, rather than English." As a Boston critic had deplored the plain prose of the *Dogood* papers, so Dennie's social bias ruled out proverbial expression. How infinitely poorer and less idiosyncratic Franklin's style would be without it!

"The Verses on the Heads of the Months . . . not many of them are of my own Making," confesses Richard. "If thou hast any Judgment in Poetry, thou wilt easily discern the Workman from the Bungler. I know as well as thee, that I am no *Poet born;* and it is a Trade I never learnt, nor indeed could learn. . . . Why then should I give my Readers *bad Lines* of my own, when *good Ones* of other People's are so plenty?" (1747). More numerous and frequently of greater length than poems of his own composition are those Franklin borrowed from seventeenth- and eighteenth-century English sources, notably Dryden, Pope, Swift, Gay's *Fables,* Young's *Love of Fame,* Savage's *Public Spirit,* and two miscellanies, Sir John Mennes and James Smith's *Wits Recreation* (1640) and the anonymous *Collection of Epigrams* (1735-1737). In fact, over a twenty-five-year period (1733-1758) most of the genres popular in the early eighteenth century—epigrams, topographical poems, georgics, satires, odes, fables, epistles—appeared in the pages of ***Poor Richard's Almanack.***

Generally speaking, Franklin made few changes in his poetic borrowings; thus Savage's *Public Spirit,* cut and revised, runs at the heads of the months in 1752. Consider, though, the case of an *Almanack* poem for January 1734:

> From a cross Neighbour, and a sullen Wife,
> A pointless Needle, and a broken Knife;
> From Suretyship, and from an empty Purse,
> A Smoaky Chimney and a jolting Horse;
> From a dull Razor, and an asking Head,
> From a bad Conscience and a buggy Bed;
> A Blow upon the Elbow and the Knee,
> From each of these, *Good L—d deliver me.*

These lines are abstracted from the first third of "A Letany," in the "Fancies and Fantasticks" section of *Wits Recreation:*

> From a proud Woodcock, and a peevish wife,
> A pointlesse Needle, and a broken Knife,
> From lying in a Ladies lap,
> Like a great fool that longs for pap,
> And from the fruit of the three corner'd tree,
> Vertue and goodnesse still deliver me.

> From a conspiracy of wicked knaves,
> A knot of villains, and a crew of slaves,
> From laying plots for to abuse a friend,
> From working humours to a wicked end,
> And from the wood where Wolves and Foxes be,
> Vertue and goodnesse still deliver me.

From rusty Bacon, and ill roasted Eeles,
And from a madding wit that runs on wheels,
A vap'ring humour, and a beetle head,
A smoky chimney, and a lowsie bed,
    A blow upon the elbow and the knee,
    From each of these, goodnesse deliver me.

From setting vertue at too low a price,
From losing too much coyn at Cards and Dice.
From surety-ship, and from an empty purse,
Or any thing that may be termed worse;
    From all such ill, wherein no good can be,
    Vertue and goodnesse still deliver me.

This poem, addressed to a seventeenth-century English audience, ranges widely and bawdily through the manifold layers of London life. Franklin, writing for less sophisticated American readers, retains only those portions of it that do not conflict with his purpose; lines 2-3, the first half of line 4, line 7, and most of line 8 in his poem are taken over verbatim from his source. Because his eye is fixed on the emerging characters of Richard and Bridget Saunders, he sees fit to eliminate the whole of the second stanza and the bawdy reference in lines 3-5 of his source and invents such details as "cross Neighbour," "jolting Horse," and "dull Razor" in order to strengthen the domestic atmosphere. The same consideration governs his substitutions: "buggy" is a more homely, alliterative description of a bed than "lowsie." In drawing upon "A Letany" (many details of which were alien to the American scene) to create a far shorter poem that would appeal to his immediate public, Franklin shows himself in this instance to be a workman, not a bungler.

In 1792, the year Robert Bailey Thomas launched the now famous *Farmer's Almanac,* Reverend William Smith praised **Poor Richard's Almanack** [in *Eulogium on Benjamin Franklin . . .* (Philadelphia, 1792)] as "the Farmers' Philosopher, the Rural Sage, the Yeomens' and Peasants' Oracle." Among the countless almanacs that flourished in colonial times Franklin's stands in the first rank, both for the matter that Smith admired and for its manner of expression. No other American philomath created and developed within his pages such original types as Richard and Bridget Saunders; in subtlety no other equaled Franklin's hoax on Titan Leeds. Although Moses Coit Tyler has called Nathaniel Ames's *Astronomical Diary and Almanack* (1726-1764) "in most respects better than Franklin's," the best that can be said for it is that it had a much larger subscription. Certainly Ames's sayings fall short of Franklin's in respect to perspicuity, elegance, and cadence. What finally assured the general excellence and favorable reception of **Poor Richard** is the fact that here, as on so many later occasions, Franklin seems to be relaxing after the day's labor and enjoying himself. (pp. 51-75)

> *Bruce Ingham Granger, in his* Benjamin Franklin: An American Man of Letters, *1964. Reprint by University of Oklahoma Press, 1976, 264 p.*

Alfred Owen Aldridge (essay date 1967)

[*The editor of* Comparative Literature Studies, *Aldridge is an American educator and author. Among his studies of the eighteenth century are* Man of Reason: The Life of Thomas Paine *(1959),* Benjamin Franklin: Philosopher and Man *(1965), and* Benjamin Franklin and Nature's God *(1967). In the essay below, taken from the lattermost work, he investigates Franklin's moral philosophy.*]

Many critics . . . have been supercilious about Franklin's materialistic morality, viewing his system as a Horatio Alger formula for getting rich. But sneering does not invalidate. Also, we must remember that Franklin's prudential schemes form only a small part of his complete moral system. Franklin was actually a philosopher, not only in the eighteenth-century sense of an experimenter with natural science, but in the broader sense of one who reflects maturely on all the problems of existence. He looked at fundamental ethical problems as they were related to the doctrines of liberty and necessity, the chain of being, the ontological basis of the universe, and the nature of God. And the system he evolved was fundamentally altruistic. The contrary image of Franklin as a self-seeking materialist has sprung up because not all of his works were known in the nineteenth century and because his maxims of thrift and sobriety have always had far greater circulation than his reflective works.

Even in his *Autobiography* Franklin focused his discussion of morality upon the prudential virtues and thus contributed to the impression that his ethical vision extended no further than to commercial maxims. Actually he was acquainted with Shaftesbury and other idealistic moralists from the time of his early youth and was fully aware of the speculative ethical problems of the age. In his letters and other personal documents Franklin showed himself acutely concerned with altruistic virtues. His multitudinous private benefactions and philanthropic projects are even more compelling proof of his ethical consciousness. Yet the popular mind has been unable to assimilate the two facets of Franklin's personality. Paradoxically, moral altruism is generally considered to be a part of Franklin's life, but not his thought.

Even though Franklin failed to make a precise list and definition of the altruistic virtues, he praised them separately in scattered letters and other works and exemplified them in his life. In his **"Articles of Belief and Acts of Religion,"** for example, he begged God to help him to "have Tenderness for the Weak, and a reverent Respect for the Ancient; [and to] . . . be kind to my Neighbours, good-natured to my Companions, and hospitable to Strangers; . . . honest and Openhearted, gentle, merciful and Good, chearful in Spirit, rejoicing in the Good of Others."

When Franklin spoke of virtue in general, it is sometimes difficult to know whether he understood only the prudential virtues or whether he included the social ones as well. In a statement such as, "Nothing so likely to make a man's fortune as virtue," he probably meant only the prudential ones. But what did he imply by the statement, *"Virtue alone is sufficient to make a Man Great, Glorious and Happy"?*

The great importance Franklin attached to virtue is revealed in one of his sayings which has come down to us through the recollections of Cabanis. Franklin "constantly repeated that [morality] was the single rational design of individual happiness as it was the sole guarantee of public happiness. One day when he had already spoken at length on this point, he finished by telling us . . . : 'If rascals knew all the advantages of virtue, they would become honest out of rascality' " [A. O. Aldridge, *Franklin and His French Contemporaries*]. This is typical of Franklin. Just at the moment when he was presumably supporting altruistic virtue, he seemed to nullify his idealism by adding that virtue pays material dividends. Yet it does not really diminish the nobility of a moral system to point out that it may at the same time be personally and socially advantageous.

Franklin's writings show that he fully understood the theoretical implications of ethical thought as well as the practical utility of rules of personal conduct. He may not have had a high opinion of that kind of abstract morality which seems to have no relationship to practical behavior, but he realized that general principles have to be formulated in order that practice might be based upon them.

Evidence of the intellectual basis of Franklin's system of ethics may be found in the pages of the *Pennsylvania Gazette,* a newspaper which Franklin began to edit in 1728. Franklin remarked in his **Autobiography** that he considered his newspaper a "Means of Communicating Instruction," and that for this reason he sometimes published moral pieces of his own which had been first composed for reading in the Junto. Two of the pieces which he identified as his own writing belong in the realm of speculative rather than practical ethics and stem directly from the Platonic systems of Shaftesbury and Hutcheson. Franklin's pieces comprise a dialogue concerning the character of a man of sense and a discourse on the relation of self-denial to virtue.

His dialogue, stylistically modeled on a paraphrase of Xenophon which Franklin had published some time earlier, concerns an eternal problem of human relations, whether great abilities or high morals are the more desirable attainments. In it, Franklin analyzed the mental equipment of a man of reason in order to demonstrate the pre-eminent importance of moral qualities. He showed himself in agreement with Bacon, who had declared in his essay "Of Great Place" that one should prefer an ignorant man with integrity to a dishonest man with ability.

A random comment of Franklin's interlocutor, Socrates, elicits the statement of his companion, Crito, that a certain gentleman of the city is "esteem'd a *Man of Sense,* but not very honest." In the remainder of the dialogue, Socrates by means of appropriate questions persuades Crito to declare that a man who is not honest cannot be a man of sense.

The next moral essay which Franklin wrote for the *Gazette* was designed to prove against Mandeville "*That* SELF-DENIAL *is not the* ESSENCE OF VIRTUE." The problem is an ancient one, to decide which man has the greater virtue, the temperate man with no inner temptations to evil who follows the path of virtue undisturbed, unopposed, and unruffled, or the continent man with strong urges to commit evil who resolutely persists in the path of

virtue but must constantly overcome vicious inclinations. In the eighteenth century, the problem had been stated in Shaftesbury's *Characteristics* and resolved in favor of the temperate man. Previous philosophers had more generally held the contrary opinion.

At the outset Franklin condemned as obscure and erroneous the opinion that "without *Self-Denial* there is no Virtue, and that the greater the *Self-Denial* the greater the Virtue." He proposed as more intelligible the contrary of the proposition, that he who cannot deny his injurious inclinations lacks the virtue of resolution or fortitude. Franklin's conclusion, like that to his dialogue on a man of sense, is the most vigorous part of the piece.

> The Truth is, that Temperance, Justice, Charity, &c. are Virtues, whether practis'd with or against our Inclinations; and the Man who practises them, merits our Love and Esteem: And Self-denial is neither good nor bad, but as 'tis apply'd: He that denies a Vicious Inclination is Virtuous in proportion to his Resolution, but the most perfect Virtue is above all Temptation, such as the Virtue of the Saints in Heaven: And he who does a foolish, indecent or wicked Thing, meerly because 'tis contrary to his Inclination, (like some mad Enthusiasts I have read of, who ran about naked, under the Notion of taking up the Cross) is not practising the reasonable Science of Virtue, but is lunatick.

This conclusion is obviously a vindication of the philosophy of Shaftesbury against the aspersions of Bernard Mandeville. Shaftesbury, defining virtue as natural affection, had argued that love of virtue could enable a man completely to banish contrary impulses and that in so doing he would become more virtuous, not less. Mandeville, who maintained that man's basic impulses were brutish, cowardly, and selfish, insisted that self-denial was a necessary ingredient of virtue and ridiculed Shaftesbury for expecting a natural "goodness in his Species."

Franklin's exposition of the concept that virtue does not depend upon resistance to an innate contrary principle of evil offers a striking parallel with the thought of Jonathan Edwards, who devoted a large section of his *Freedom of*

Victor Hugo's illustration of the building where Franklin lived while in Passy, France.

the Will to proving the same thing. Specifically, Edwards demonstrated first that the moral excellence of God and Christ exists in a pure form without any contrary force and is still praiseworthy, and second that the virtuous behavior of Christ was necessary but still worthy of reward.

In his "Miscellanies," Edwards affirmed in a blunt style remarkably similar to Franklin's that it would be utterly preposterous to assume that "if a man be naturally a very ill-natured man, and from that ill nature does often treat his neighbors maliciously and with great indignity, his neighbors ought to excuse and not to be angry with him so far as what he does is from ill nature."

The philosophic preoccupations of Franklin's mind are revealed not only in his newspaper essays, but also in a series of questions for discussion which he drew up for his intellectual club, the Junto. In morals, as well as in science, Franklin realized that the theoretical is the generating force which makes the practical possible even though it is the practical which creates the welfare and happiness of mankind.

The idea for the Junto—Franklin's association of tradesmen for mutual improvement—had come to him from the New England Puritan, Cotton Mather. In his *Essays to Do Good* (1710), Mather had proposed voluntary associations for the promotion of religion and morality and prescribed for them a structure and order of business. Franklin drew up similar rules for his secular organization, requiring that every member in turn produce moral or philosophical queries for general discussion and once in three months deliver an original essay on any subject he pleased.

In one of the topics he proposed for general discussion Franklin touched on one of the most fundamental ethical problems of the century, "Whether Men ought to be denominated Good or ill Men from their Actions or their Inclinations?" In other words, are acts to be judged by their results or their motives? Believers in absolutes of good and evil such as Shaftesbury argued that motives alone should be considered. Relativists such as Mandeville argued that results were more important. Franklin's opinions for the Junto are not on record, but we have seen that in the *Gazette* he decided unequivocally for Shaftesbury.

Franklin also proposed a number of queries concerning the respective value of riches and virtue. He was quite aware that wealth and goodness are not necessarily companion qualities even though his "prudential" writings do not show this comprehension. He asked:

> Which is best to make a Friend of, a wise and good Man that is poor; or a Rich Man that is neither wise nor good? Which of the two is the greatest Loss to a Country, if they both die?

> Which of the two is happiest in Life?

> Does it not in a general Way require great Study and intense Application for a Poor Man to become rich and Powerful, if he would do it, without the Forfeiture of his Honesty?

> Does it not require as much Pains, Study and Application to become truly Wise and strictly Good and Virtuous as to become rich?

> Can a Man of common Capacity pursue both Views with Success at the same Time?

> If not, which of the two is it best for him to make his whole Application to?

Franklin also asked the question, which some of his critics have accused him of ignoring, whether there is any "Difference between Knowledge and Prudence? If there is any, which of the two is most Eligible?"

And he took note of some of the ethical problems of political association long before he himself engaged in any form of government. He wondered:

> Is it justifiable to put private Men to Death for the Sake of publick Safety or Tranquility, who have committed no Crime?

> As in the Case of the Plague to stop Infection, or as in the Case of the Welshmen here Executed. . . .

> If the Sovereign Power attempts to deprive a Subject of his Right, (or which is the same Thing, of what he thinks his Right) is it justifiable in him to resist if he is able?

In the commonplace book in which these queries are preserved, Franklin gave no answers. He attempted an answer, however, to a much more basic ethical question, one which every human being must consider: "Wherein consists the Happiness of a rational Creature?" His answer: "In having a Sound Mind and a healthy Body, a Sufficiency of the Necessaries and Conveniences of Life, together with the Favour of God, and the Love of Mankind." Significantly, Franklin at this time considered man's relation to God equally important as his relation to his fellow men.

He gave an even more detailed answer to another purely ethical query based on fundamental religious and metaphysical concepts. "Can a Man arrive at Perfection in this Life as some Believe; or is it impossible as others believe?" Franklin found his answer in the theory of the Great Chain of Being. "The Perfection of any Thing," he argued, is the highest point of development which "the Nature of that Thing is capable of." Although in the notion of the chain of being each species is ranked according to its closeness to or remoteness from God, individuals of every species are at the same time capable of various degrees of perfection within that species. Thus, according to Franklin's scheme, "an Horse is more perfect than an Oyster yet the Oyster may be a perfect Oyster as well as the Horse a perfect Horse. And an Egg is not so perfect as a Chicken, nor a Chicken as a Hen; for the Hen has more Strength than the Chicken, and the C[hicken] more Life than the Egg: Yet it may be a perfect Egg, Chicken and Hen." Applying the notion to mankind, Franklin concluded that "a Man cannot in this Life be so perfect as an Angel, . . . for an Angel by being incorporeal is allow'd some Perfections we are at present incapable of, and less liable to some Imperfections that we are liable to." And it may also be true that "a Man is not capable of being so perfect here as he is capable of being in Heaven." But man is nevertheless capable of reaching the maximum degree of perfection which his rank in the scale of being permits. To assert the contrary would be nonsense. "It is as if I should say, a Chicken in the State of a Chicken is not capable of being so perfect as a Chicken is capable of being in that State. In the above Sense if there may be a perfect Oyster, a perfect Horse, a perfect Ship, why not a perfect Man? that is as perfect as his present Nature and Circumstances admit?" A few years later Alexander Pope expressed essentially the same idea in his *Essay on Man.*

> If to be perfect in a certain sphere,
> What matter, soon or late, or here or there.

This was Franklin's answer to the Calvinistic doctrine of "the total depravity and corruption of man's nature." Franklin's view of mankind was neither optimistic nor pessimistic but could be extended in either an optimistic or pessimistic direction. If one believes that the majority of mankind live up to their potentiality as a species in the chain of being, this is an optimistic view; if one believes that the majority of mankind fail to do so, this is pessimistic. During the remainder of his life Franklin shifted from one view to the other according to his prevailing mood. He frequently varied his opinion concerning moral progress or perfectibility, but he never wavered from his conception of man occupying a mid-way station in the Great Chain of Being.

Toward the end of his life Franklin graphically presented his conception of the chain of being in the guise of an oriental tale, a highly popular literary genre of the eighteenth century developed by such authors as Addison, Goldsmith, and Voltaire. In keeping with the tradition, Franklin used an oriental philosopher, the good magician Albumazar, to convey his moral lesson. One night Albumazar was visited by one of the spirits of the first rank, Belubel the strong. "His height was seven leagues, and his wings when spread might overshadow a kingdom." Belubel laid himself gently down between the ridges of the mountain range, using the tops of the trees in the valley as his couch. Albumazar "spoke to him with rapturous piety of the wisdom and goodness of the Most High; but expressed his wonder at the existence of evil in the world, which he said he could not account for by all the efforts of his reason."

Belubel, in reply, advised the wise mortal not to value himself upon that quality called reason. "If thou knewest its origin and its weakness, it would rather be matter of humiliation."

Then Belubel called upon the magician to contemplate

> the scale of beings, from an elephant down to an oyster. Thou seest a gradual diminution of faculties and powers, so small in each step that the difference is scarce perceptible. There is no gap, but the gradation is complete. Men in general do not know, but thou knowest, that in ascending from an elephant to the infinitely Great, Good, and Wise, there is also a long gradation of beings, who possess powers and faculties of which thou canst yet have no perception.

Although Franklin did not round out his tale with a moral tag such as is usually found in the genre, his meaning is clear enough. Man exists in the scale of being just above the elephant, and his intellectual faculties are inadequate to enable him to understand the moral problems of the

universe. This must certainly be taken as Franklin's final opinion concerning the problem of evil.

His moral tale illustrates not only the Great Chain of Being, but also the equally common eighteenth-century doctrine that "purblind Man" is in error if his pride causes him to overlook the limitations of his reason.

On still another occasion Franklin used his oyster and horse to illustrate the scale of being. In one issue of the *Pennsylvania Gazette* (August 1, 1734), he had published a dismal monologue by an English clergyman, Joshua Smith, "On the Vanity and Brevity of Human Life." Then he wrote twin repudiations which he printed in the next issue: a humorous and somewhat ribald parody and a parallel meditation reflecting a cheerful outlook. In introducing his parody, he remarked that he not only disliked to view the dark side of things but considered gloomy philosophy unjust. "The World is a very good World, and if we behave our selves well, we shall doubtless do very well in it. I never thought even *Job* in the right, when he repin'd that the Days of a Man are *few* and *full of Trouble;* for certainly both these Things cannot be together just Causes of Complaint; if our Days are full of Trouble, the fewer of 'em the better." Smith's gloomy meditation Franklin compared to the perverse lamenting of a child that he cannot have his cake and eat it too. His irony is worthy of Swift.

> [Smith:] *All the few days we live are full of Vanity; and our choicest Pleasures sprinkled with bitterness:*
> [Franklin:] All the few Cakes we have are puffed up with Yeast; and the nicest Gingerbread is spotted with Flyshits!
> [Smith:] *The time that's past is vanish'd like a dream; and that which is to come is not yet at all.*
> [Franklin:] The Cakes that we have eaten are no more to be seen; and those which are to come are not yet baked. . . .
> [Smith:] *But the longer we live, the shorter is our life; and in the end we become a little lump of clay.*
> [Franklin:] And the more we eat, the less is the Piece remaining; and in the end the whole will become Sir-reverence! [a turd]

In his conclusion Franklin dismissed all such insignificant meditations. "I am for taking *Solomon's* Advice, *eating Bread with Joy, and drinking Wine with a merry Heart.* Let us rejoice and bless God, that we are neither Oysters, Hogs, nor Dray-Horses; and not stand repining that He has not made us Angels; lest we be found unworthy of that share of Happiness He has thought fit to allow us."

Franklin's companion address on the benevolence of the universe emphasizes smiles and pleasure. "Most happy are we, the sons of men, above all other creatures, who are born to behold the glorious rays of the sun, and to enjoy the pleasant fruits of the earth." After a life of using our reason in doing good, we are rewarded with "the sweet sleep of death, pleasant as a bed to a weary traveller after a long journey."

During the same period that Franklin was drawing up his queries for the Junto, he also wrote for his private use a series of **"Observations on Reading History."** Here he expressed an opinion of human nature which seems at variance with the Shaftesburian direction of his thought in other writings. Starting with the principle that all the great affairs of the world are carried on by parties, he observed

> That while a Party is carrying on a general Design, each Man has his particular private Interest in View. . . . That few in Public Affairs act from a meer View of the Good of their Country, whatever they may pretend; and tho' their Actings bring real Good to their Country, yet Men primarily consider'd that their own and their Country's Interest was united, and did not act from a Principle of Benevolence. That fewer still in public Affairs act with a View to the Good of Mankind.

In one sense there does not seem to be much benevolent altruism in these views, and the statement that men act according to their own particular interest seems to reflect the "selfish" system of Hobbes and Mandeville. Indeed, in 1737 Franklin was inclined to consider Hobbes's notion somewhat "nearer the Truth than that which makes the State of Nature a State of Love." There is a paradox here which can be understood only by considering a "great and extensive Project" which Franklin envisaged in the final paragraphs of his observations on history.

> There seems to me at present to be great Occasion for raising an united Party for Virtue, by forming the Virtuous and good Men of all Nations into a regular Body, to be govern'd by suitable good and wise Rules, which good and wise Men may probably be more unanimous in their Obedience to, than common People are to common Laws.

> I at present think, that whoever attempts this aright, and is well qualified, cannot fail of pleasing God, and of meeting with Success.

In his *Autobiography* Franklin revealed that he hoped to organize this party of virtue under the name of The Society of the Free and Easy, in a sense a Junto for the whole world, but the project was never carried out.

The paradox may be resolved in this way: Franklin agreed with Mandeville that observation of society indicates that the majority of men indeed act upon primarily selfish motives. But this is true only for society as it is now constituted—not necessarily as it must remain for all time. Franklin also agreed with Shaftesbury that man possesses benevolent instincts which can be nurtured and developed. There *can* be a perfect man just as there *can* be a perfect oyster. Franklin's Party for Virtue was designed to organize the existing altruists, to increase their number, and to bring the commonality of men closer to the Shaftesburian ideal. Franklin consequently emphasized the existing division between common men and good and wise men, a consequence of Shaftesbury's theories rather than Mandeville's.

Franklin's opinion of human nature is obviously an important part of his religion. Although in theory he shared the benevolent philosophy of Shaftesbury and the English latitudinarian divines, he veered during his moments of disillusion toward the views of Mandeville and exponents of Calvinistic depravity. "Whatever may be the Musick of the Spheres," he wrote in *Poor Richard* for 1735, "how great soever the Harmony of the Stars, 'tis certain there is no harmony among the Stargazers; but they are perpetually growling and snarling at one another like strange Curs."

Most famous of Franklin's gloomy observations are those in which he similarly contrasts the inanimate "Works of Nature" with the animate or moral part. The more he discovered of the former, he affirmed, the more he admired them; the more he learned of the latter, the more he became disgusted with them. In one of his most extreme passages, he expressed the rhetorical hope "that moral Science were in as fair a way of Improvement" as physical science, "that Men would cease to be Wolves to one another, and that human Beings would at length learn what they now improperly call Humanity."

In the midst of the Revolution, Franklin expressed revulsion at man's perverse attitude toward procreating and killing his own species:

> Men I find to be a Sort of Beings very badly constructed, as they are generally more easily provok'd than reconcil'd, more disposed to do Mischief to each other than to make Reparation, much more easily deceiv'd than undeceiv'd, and having more Pride and even Pleasure in killing than in begetting one another; for without a Blush they assemble in great armies at NoonDay to destroy, and when they have kill'd as many as they can, they exaggerate the Number to augment the fancied Glory; but they creep into Corners, or cover themselves with the Darkness of night, when they mean to beget, as being asham'd of a virtuous Action. A virtuous Action it would be, and a vicious one the killing of them, if the Species were really worth producing or preserving; but of this I begin to doubt.

This is indeed a very gloomy view—but not as deep-seated as it appears. Franklin was not actually presenting sentiments which had originated in his own despondent heart—instead he was paraphrasing a passage from the French essayist Montaigne, who had written:

> Every one avoids seeing a Man born, every one runs to see him die. To destroy a Man, a spacious Field is sought out, and in the Face of the Sun; but to make him, we creep into as dark and private a Corner as we can. 'Tis a Man's Duty to withdraw himself from the Light to do it; but 'tis Glory, and the Fountain of many Vertues to know how to destroy what we have done: The one is Injury, the other Favour.

This passage comes from a long essay "On Some Verses of Virgil," dealing principally with sex. Franklin's temporary pessimism may have been as much affected by his reading as by any of the events of the war or the diplomatic crisis.

Franklin once wrote to his sister that "Mankind were Devils to one another," but he meant by this merely that man's greatest sufferings come from other men rather than from other animals. He had been led into this reflection by recalling a printer's widow he had known during his first visit to London when he was nineteen. This lady, Elizabeth Ilive, had held the doctrine of pre-existence and by the terms of her will obliged her son to deliver a public discourse "the purport of which was to prove, that this world is the true Hell, or place of punishment for the spirits, who had transgressed in a better state, and were sent here to suffer for their sins in animals of all sorts." This theory was supported by the assumption that "though we now remembered nothing of such a preëxistent state, yet after death we might recollect it, and remember the punishments we had suffered, so as to be the better for them; and others, who had not yet offended, might now behold and be warned by our sufferings."

In a letter to his sister, December 30, 1770, Franklin seemed partly convinced by this reasoning.

> We see here, that every lower animal has its enemy, with proper inclinations, faculties, and weapons, to terrify, wound, and destroy it; and that men, who are uppermost, are devils to one another; so that, on the established doctrine of the goodness and justice of the great Creator, this apparent state of general and systematical mischief seemed to demand some such supposition as Mrs. Ilive's, to account for it consistently with the honor of the Deity.

But Franklin held back from any positive affirmation because our reasoning powers lack the materials necessary to inform us about our existence either before or after this life. "Revelation only can give us the necessary information, and that, in the first of these points especially, has been very sparingly afforded us."

Since Franklin's sister seems to have been completely unreceptive to the doctrine of pre-existence, Franklin tried to show in a subsequent letter that it was not entirely nonsensical. He explained that "it had been invented with a good Intention, to save the Honour of the Deity, which was thought to be injured by the Supposition of his bringing Creatures into the World to be miserable, without any previous misbehaviour of theirs to deserve it." But Franklin himself did not accept this reasoning. In Biblical symbols, he denominated the doctrine "an officious Supporting of the Ark." When God has "thought fit to draw a Veil, our Attempting to remove it may be deem'd at least an offensive Impertinence. And we shall probably succeed little better in such an Adventure to gain forbidden Knowledge, than our first Parents did when they ate the Apple."

Seeking to remove some of the sting from his comparison of men to devils, he added: "Upon the whole, I am much disposed to like the World as I find it, & to doubt my own Judgment as to what would mend it. I see so much Wisdom in what I understand of its Creation and Government, that I suspect equal Wisdom may be in what I do not understand: And thence have perhaps as much Trust in God as the most pious Christian." In his final sentence, Franklin virtually separated himself from the body of Christianity, perhaps without realizing it, almost wistfully portraying himself as on the outside, looking in.

His propensity to like the world as it is explains the view of mankind which he held most of the time—whenever his natural cheerful disposition was not overcome by temporary clouds of gloom. In France during a conversation with English friends at the close of the American war, he reprobated the maxim that all men are equally corrupt. "A man," he affirmed, "who has seen nothing but hospitals, must naturally have a poor opinion of the health of mankind."

Although Franklin is usually considered as one of the outstanding rationalists of the eighteenth century, his faith in pure reason diminished as he grew in years. He made his most positive assertion of the supreme importance of reason in his Junto lecture on providence in the course of which he repudiated "Art and Ornament," "Flourishes of Rhetorick," "the false Glosses of Oratory," and "a musical Accent in delivery." "I know," he affirmed, "that no Authority is more convincing to Men of Reason than the Authority of Reason itself."

In contrast to this confident rationalism, the spirit Belubel in Franklin's oriental tale warns us against placing a high value on human reason, which because of its origin and weakness is rather a matter of humiliation. Franklin once complained to his sister that reason sometimes not only fails to help us prevent evil but even actually misleads us. Occasionally he was "almost tempted to wish we had been furnished with a good sensible Instinct instead of it."

To one of his friends he suggested that reason may be best fitted for some people, instinct for others. "As those Beings, . . . who have Reason to regulate their Actions, have no Occasion for Enthusiasm. However, there are certain Circumstances in Life, sometimes, wherein 'tis perhaps best not to hearken to Reason." One of Franklin's best examples of the deficiencies of reason is the man who knows the theory of swimming but loses his head in deep water.

To a close friend in France, he once wrote that reason must be a thing quite uncertain "since two people like you and me can draw from the same principles conclusions diametrically opposite. This reason seems to me a guide quite blind. A good and certain instinct would be worth much more to us. All the inferior animals together do not go so far astray in a year as a single man in a month—although this man pretends to act according to reason." This paradoxical view of the irrationality of human reason, Franklin supported in a witty anecdote which he related to John Adams in 1775:

"Man, a rational Creature"! said Franklin.

> "Come, Let Us suppose a rational Man. Strip him of all his Appetites, especially of his hunger and thirst. He is in his Chamber, engaged in making Experiments, or in pursuing some Problem. He is highly entertained. At this moment a Servant Knocks, "Sir dinner is on Table." "Dinner! Pox! Pough! But what have you for dinner?" "Ham and Chickens." "Ham"! "And must I break the chain of my thoughts, to go down and knaw a morsel of damn'd Hogs Arse"? "Put aside your Ham." "I will dine tomorrow."

(pp. 58-74)

Alfred Owen Aldridge, in his Benjamin Franklin and Nature's God, *Duke University Press, 1967, 279 p.*

Roger J. Porter   (essay date 1979)

[*In the following essay, Porter examines Franklin's concealment of self in his* Autobiography.]

Naive critics of autobiography seek to find in the work a faithful mirror of lived experience; when they do not, they turn to biographies for greater authenticity. More knowing critics acknowledge the made-up, story-telling aspect of narrative; all autobiographers, they believe, create fictions of one sort or another, however verifiable individual moments in their accounts may be, however "true" large swaths of recorded experience. The motives behind such imaginative discourse vary, of course, from Nabokov's complex epistemology to James' ineluctably novelistic mind. Perhaps the most common instance of this need to shape a story is the compensatory one: the autobiographer creates an order in his or her book that was absent in the life; if the person failed to make the life into the desired work of art, predictable and composed with a discernible order, then the artful form of the writing will stand in its place. Here is a succinct expression of this view by a recent critic [Peter Glassman in *The Hudson Review* XXX, No. 1 (Spring 1977)]:

> The act of writing autobiography offers itself as an occasion not for celebration, but for commencing one's existence as a personality. I believe that most autobiographers create their discourse in order to conceive and sustain a self other than that which they have established—or which they have failed to establish—in their engagement of actual experience. The autobiographer, I believe, typically undertakes to press the resources of language in ways in which he has been unable to press the resources of history. He endeavors to elaborate from words that sense of reality, that feeling of freed individuation, which the components of his desperately mediated life have not permitted him experientially to develop. For such beings the act of writing autobiography declares itself not as a first but as a last emotion of life; not as a hymn to peace and plenty, but as a final, extraordinarily inventive attempt at therapy.

Such a theory would not seem to work for a man as successful, confident and self-confessedly exemplary as Franklin. No one in our national life has more grandly "press[ed] the resources of history"—statesman, diplomat, writer of laws, inventor, scientist, educator, essayist, editor, printer, philosopher, public benefactor. Franklin's motive for writing does not seem to be sparked by any uncertainty about the mysteries of the self (the "dark forests" that D. H. Lawrence lamented Franklin had excluded from his account), or by a desire to explore the meaning of life in the act of writing, or by an urge to tell his story because he doubts the actualness of his inner being. On the contrary, no autobiographer begins with more assurance and self-congratulation:

> Having emerg'd from the Poverty and Obscurity in which I was born and bred, to a State of Affluence and some Degree of Reputation in the World, and having gone so far thro' life with a considerable Share of Felicity, the conducing Means I made use of, which, with the Blessing of God, so well succeeded, my Posterity may like to know, as they may find some of them suitable to their own Situations, and therefore fit to be imitated.

And yet Franklin's *Autobiography* is a work which creates that very sense of confidence and ease only by revealing the constant surveillance that Franklin needed to apply to his life and the constant effort *in the writing* that makes the life appear as frictionless and effortless as possible. James Cox has remarked that Franklin's account is notable for its absence of crises and dramatic turning points; in fact, Franklin speaks, appropriately for a printer, of various "faults" which he calls merely "errata," and would, if he could live his life again, correct in a "second edition" (that is, another life). Difficult moments in the life are smoothed over by the application of tact, generosity, or, in textual terms, euphemisms. Potentially explosive episodes in the work which beg for exploration and analysis are passed by with a rhetorical equanimity and comic self-irony that belie the problem of self-evaluation they inevitably raise. To be exemplary is not to chance too much in the realm of introspection; the risks are taken mostly in the social and political domains, where private fears may be skirted or at least held in check, and where civic government coincides with self-government.

Where does the reluctance to probe the self originate? To begin with, such introspection represents for Franklin an indulgence that runs contrary to the more pressing needs of a rough and tumble existence that threatened to overwhelm the precarious civilization of Philadelphia in the early eighteenth century. Franklin several times mentions incidents involving relatives, friends and acquaintances who suddenly experienced a frightening loss of stability in their lives. His friend James Ralph leaves family and country only to become totally dependent on Franklin's charity in order to avoid financial ruin; one friend succumbs to drink and wastes his life; another becomes hostile and excessively belligerent, and is disgraced in his dealings with Philadelphia's citizenry; a third quits civilization for the Barbados never to be heard from again. Amidst these cautionary tales of horror Franklin assures us that the only way to avoid a similar fate is through the proper application of discipline, tact, and control. In a culture that provided greater order and leisure than Franklin experienced, one might turn inward without feeling he was squandering his mental energies; but where life was chancy and chaos threatened at every turn, or at least where one tended to perceive matters that way, self-questioning was doubtless irrelevant and certainly distracting. Instead of engaging in a romantic exploration of private values Franklin turned to the more public world—first of collective wisdom and shared moral assumptions, later of public service and community enlightenment.

The centerpiece of the *Autobiography* is Franklin's project of arriving at moral perfection, and everyone is familiar with the lined pages of his notebook, the days of the week across the top, and the initials of the thirteen virtues, such as temperance, order, frugality and industry, down the side, and the "little black spots" marking every fault against those virtues committed that day. This plan may stand for an entire conception of self in the **Autobiography**—life as a grid, where external behavior is primary, where faults and virtues may be plotted and balanced, and where the self, or at least its darker urges, may be transformed into whatever can be of value. The entire autobiography is an exercise in dramatizing the application of these virtues to the smoothing over of difficult moments in the life, and the success that ensues from keeping unruly emotions at bay. But Franklin cannot tell too much. Like Plato on the arts, he believes that too much revelation of what cannot be managed will harm *someone*. His strategy is not merely to convert inner passion into usable history, but to show how control, rules, and effort may be employed to give the appearance of effortlessness. Franklin's progress in eliminating vices is charted by the erasure of the black marks—significant again for a printer, for whom black smirches on a clean page would be anathema, and who tells us how proud he is for having returned borrowed books "soon and clean." The eradication of the black marks becomes a metaphor for life and writing: if the darker, difficult aspects of experience are not dwelt upon, they will appear hardly to have been there at all.

I do not wish to linger on the psychoanalytic possibilities of Franklin's obsession with sweeping the streets clean of dirt, or his absolute loathing of and preoccupation with the removal of mud, dust, slush and mire, or the grime and smoke on the insides of gaslight globes which inhibited the lighting of Philadelphia's streets. He is pleased to "enlighten" all the city with his new inventions, whether a better globe, a stove, or electricity. Nevertheless, getting rid of dirt, black marks and even savage Indians is, in Franklin's calculus, all the same: the removal of what threatens to inhibit culture. His fear of what cannot be controlled and contained is manifestly great. Here is a passage describing his experience with Indians who had been given rum as a reward for signing a peace treaty.

> We found [the Indians] had made a great Bonfire in the Middle of the Square. They were all drunk Men and Women, quarrelling and fighting. Their dark-color'd Bodies, half naked, seen only by the gloomy Light of the Bonfire, running after and beating one another with Firebrands, accompanied by their horrid Yellings, form'd a Scene the most resembling our Ideas of Hell that could well be imagin'd. There was no appeasing the Tumult, and we retired to our Lodging. At Midnight a Number of them came thundering at our Door, demanding more Rum; of which we took no Notice. The next Day, sensible they had misbehav'd in giving us that Disturbance, they sent three of their old Counsellors to make their Apology. The Orator acknowledg'd the Fault, but laid it upon the Rum; and then endeavor'd to excuse the Rum, by saying, *"The great Spirit who made all things made every thing for some Use, and whatever Use he design'd any thing for, that Use it should always be put to; Now, when he made Rum, he said,* LET THIS BE FOR INDIANS TO GET DRUNK WITH. *And it must be so."*

> And indeed if it be the Design of Providence to extirpate these Savages in order to make room for Cultivators of the Earth, it seems not improbable that Rum may be the appointed Means.

Franklin provides justification for his belief by recourse to providence and cosmic order; what underlies his position is fear of violence and savagery, and apparently not just that of others but his own. On numerous occasions Franklin recounts his own anger and violent urges, but backs off from any attempt to explore them in depth. There are several such episodes, but Franklin mentions them almost in passing, as if seeking to create the impression that the elicited passions need not be considered too strenuously. In one significant account he pitches overboard into the Delaware a drunken friend who has refused to help row their boat. Franklin will not take him back into the boat until the man is exhausted and waterlogged; but Franklin will not dwell on his own capacity for violence, and he quickly moves on to other matters. He must keep control of himself, grease the paths of his march to success and, in the actual writing, convey an image of one who has avoided the "dangerous Time of Youth and the hazardous Situations I was sometimes in. . . ." Nature or natural inclination must always be tamed by nurture and cultivation; what are prized are the clean book of the life and the immaculate, unspotted page of the virtues. Life is a kind of morality play for Franklin; overcoming and concealment are two ways of projecting an image of the successful self. Too much revelation is not unseemly in a puritanical sense, but it must be suppressed if he would avoid charges of egotism and make his way as a socially compliant being.

Franklin's book dwells on escapes of various kinds, and here we may see his characteristic complexity: escaping from dangers that promise to narrow his existence allows him on the one hand to avoid disorder and on the other to keep his world open and flexible. Too much fluidity is detrimental to Franklin's purpose: fluids in fact are his great enemy, and nothing terrifies him more than a drunken Dutchman who falls into the sea and almost drowns. Later he describes himself as a "graceful and easy" swimmer, and as making his way in the world "swimmingly"; he even speaks of a friend whose frugality barely allowed him to "keep his Head much longer above Water." When his father discouraged Franklin from writing verses "I escap'd being a poet," which in his formulation meant being a beggar. Poverty and obscurity are fates worse than death for him; obscurity and darkness must be set against enlightenment in his world. His discipline allows him to achieve freedom, whether by escaping a liaison with several thieving prostitutes on a boat, or by eluding financial ruin through his famous industry. Yet too much rigidity is no less harmful: escaping a tyrannical brother whose indenturing of Franklin threatened to cut off his freedom allowed Franklin to expand his world. Caution and control must always be exercised; the threat of ruin lies all around him.

Above all Franklin wishes to give us the impression that a rational life can be constructed with will. There are no problematics about his identity, no modern impulse to take the self *as* a problem, because introspection would be the mark of a man sidetracked into self-consciousness. For Franklin too much dwelling on the self is the most seductive threat of all, worse than those thieving prostitutes because it robs one of the ability to project oneself actively into the world. Cultivation of the self is justified only as a way of expanding its gains in public terms: the project to arrive at moral perfection does not stop in the realm of the private—soon after its formulation Franklin plans to create an organization to disseminate and inculcate its methods, a mutually self-helping group called the "Society of the Free and Easy." It is the ease of being in the world that Franklin seeks to communicate to us; not in the sense that life is providentially secure or even arbitrarily fortunate, but that through accommodation and energy he can achieve anything he wishes.

This is doubtless why the book never rises to an emotional climax or crescendo, but is accretive in its structure. What I mean is that for Franklin all experiences weigh equally, no single activity is more laden with significance for him than any other. Because both street cleaning and diplomatic negotiation are crucial enterprises for Franklin, he gives us the impression of a man who marches through life with a sense of dedication and ease. The writing itself softens whatever anxiety, self-doubt, fear or turmoil he might have felt about himself. These fears, as I've suggested, are present, particularly in the images of men disappearing or going under or remaining in obscurity. But the fears do not seem to Franklin to be paramount, or at least he does not wish to convey such an impression to us. It is the witty and outwitting side of himself that he offers, a comic compliance with circumstances that allows him to transcend them. But "transcendence" is probably not the best term to apply to Franklin; the very fact of an accretive style, a structuring of successive moments, and a book written over a period of eighteen years and on two continents says something about his disarmingly casual approach to the self. Like the book he writes, a concern with his inner being can be taken up momentarily and dropped at leisure; to suggest too much urgency or intensity or "transcendence" would be to acknowledge either a private or public anxiety he is, ironically, at great pains to dispel, or a lofty aim that is at odds with his insistence on the matter-of-fact and the every-day.

The writing, in its unadorned chronicling style, testifies to the desire to suppress individualism or at least not to assert an identity so particularized and distinct that it will run counter to the democratic ideal in which the common man with the proper will may achieve whatever Franklin has. The book ends with events in 1757, and it may be that an account of the later career, when Franklin's preeminence was so lofty, would throw off the balance between open-eyed youth and rising public figure, and make of the protagonist a hero too formidable to imitate. And so too, just as the worst sin of *living* is isolation from others, so the worst sin—or erratum—of *writing* would be the cultivation of a style so formal, singular and idiosyncratic that it would counteract his implied democracy. Franklin's fear of rhetoric is not unlike his fear of claiming too much for himself; he practices a simple, inelegant, almost storytelling style. A simple formlessness can signify freedom for Franklin (his very name means, of course, "free

Franklin on his diplomatic mission to France, wearing a fur hat he used to cultivate the impression that he was a simple backwoodsman.

man"); tied to no formal narrative convention, he seems to make up his story as he goes, just as he is the American hero as self-made man. And as Cox has noted, Franklin can stop where he wants to because he is not trapped by a need to see his life whole. I would add that it does change from one vantage point or perspective to another; it is all of a piece, and each piece resembles every other.

Franklin's style never lets us see the pressures generated within the self. Everywhere the matter-of-fact tone belies any inner struggle he must have confronted in his choice of behavior. He scrupulously avoids the language of subjectivity because it would raise issues that might divert his own and possibly the reader's attention from greater imperatives, namely the need to counteract the dangers he saw all around him. There is no sense of urgency, no pressure to strike out at an unyielding reality, but nevertheless we are struck by how much sheer activity the *Autobiography* contains, how much it is a record of constant business and busyness. Stylistically this continuous acting takes the form of paragraphs consisting of one declarative sentence after another, as one public activity follows close on the heels of the next: I wrote, I discovered, I suggested, I advocated, I established, I formed, I planned, and so on.

But in all of this reporting Franklin never gives us the impression that he struggled against a resistant and raw world; his tone suggests a fellow enormously pleased with himself and delighted by the public's reception of his character and work. He is always knowing and ingenuous at the same time, a combination that permits him to take things as they come. Here is the characteristically insouciant speaker:

> In order to secure in Credit and Character as a Tradesman, I took care not only to be in *Reality* Industrious and frugal, but to avoid all *Appearances* of the Contrary. I drest plainly; I was seen at no Places of idle Diversion; I never went out a-fishing or shooting; a Book, indeed, sometimes debauch'd me from my Work; but that was seldom, snug, and gave no Scandal: and to show that I was not above my Business, I sometimes brought home the Paper I purchas'd at the Stores, thro' the Streets on a Wheelbarrow. Thus being esteem'd an industrious thriving young Man, and paying duly for what I bought, the Merchants who imported Stationary solicited my Custom, others propos'd supplying me with Books, and I went on swimmingly. In the mean time Keimer's Credit and Business declining daily, he was at last forc'd to sell his Printing-house to satisfy his Creditors. He went to Barbadoes, and there lived some Years, in very poor Circumstances.

The obvious openings for a discussion about appearance and reality, image and interior selfhood, are never seized. In fact the content of the passage is appropriately conveyed by a poise that cannot afford much self-contemplation. Its very success depends upon our not asking too many questions. And yet that is exactly what we are inclined to do. We are impatient with the frictionless bearing of the work; it all works so easily because Franklin himself seems to have. Every setback becomes a lesson in how to turn things around in the future, every criticism can be corrected in the next edition. We are left not so much with the self-congratulating, pompous Franklin of Lawrence's caricature, but a speaker who knows how fragile the self really is. The satisfaction that comes from his ability to keep secret his inner conflicts leads to his own ironic tone, where an ability to mock his own formulae for success keeps the *Autobiography* from being as egotistical as might otherwise be the case.

Franklin, I am contending, knew that he had an abundant capacity for vanity, aggression, and luxuriant pleasure. But his constant fear, expressed directly or by implication, is that the exercise of these impulses would render his life meaningless. It is not, as has often been claimed, Puritan caution or Quaker reticence that lies behind these fears, but instead a cagey, wily view of himself, and what amounts almost to a pleasure in the act of mock-self-effacement, in secrecy and cunning. He engages the reader even as he refuses to give much away. Franklin takes Philadelphia and then the *Autobiography* for his stages, and he tries out a series of roles, enjoying the theatrical posturing and shifting of costume. The *Autobiography* is, in essence, the performance of a skilled and splendid conman. Just when we think we know Franklin he escapes our grasp; at one moment we can say that Ben Franklin is a

rank optimist and proud booster of civic virtues; the next moment that he has a dark vision of human rapacity and sees how much manipulation is necessary to effect even minimal social gains. But the autobiography will not settle into any comfortable conclusions about human action and personal awareness. Over and over we have the voice of an ironist whose strategy is to undercut himself even as he applauds himself. We often wonder where the real Franklin is.

Here, in a passage that closes Part II of the *Autobiography,* Franklin shows how emotions may get out of hand; what is important for my purpose is not so much Franklin's need to subdue passion, but the ironic way he survives with credit whether he does or does not subdue:

> In reality there is perhaps no one of our natural Passions so hard to subdue as *Pride.* Disguise it, struggle with it, beat it down, stifle it, mortify it as much as one pleases, it is still alive, and will every now and then peep out and show itself. You will see it perhaps often in this History. For even if I could conceive that I had compleatly overcome it, I should probably [be] proud of my Humility.

Even as he suggests his failings whichever way he has it, Franklin manages to have it—in the positive sense—both ways. A man as clever as Franklin in this passage is hard to trust, but not hard to admire. Finally, I want to say that Franklin knows that the self as a concept is something that can be created as much in the writing as in the long process of living. The two are related in that the life has prepared the writer to compose the self; but for Franklin this

---

Carl Becker on Franklin as a child of the Enlightenment:

Great men are often hampered by some inner discord or want of harmony with the world in which they live. It was Franklin's good fortune to have been endowed with a rare combination of rare qualities, and to have lived at a time when circumstances favored the development of all his powers to their fullest extent. He was a true child of the Enlightenment, not indeed of the school of Rousseau, but of Defoe and Pope and Swift, of Fontenelle and Montesquieu and Voltaire. He spoke their language, although with a homely accent, a tang of the soil, that bears witness to his lowly and provincial origin. His wit and humor, lacking indeed the cool, quivering brilliance of Voltaire or the corrosive bitterness of Pope and Swift, were all the more effective and humane for their dash of genial and kindly cynicism. He accepted without question and expressed without effort all the characteristic ideas and prepossessions of the century—its aversion to "superstition" and "enthusiasms" and mystery; its contempt for hocus-pocus and its dislike of dim perspectives; its healthy, clarifying scepticism; its passion for freedom and its humane sympathies; its preoccupation with the world that is evident to the senses; its profound faith in common sense, in the efficacy of Reason for the solution of human problems and the advancement of human welfare.

Carl L. Becker, in his Benjamin Franklin: A Biographical Sketch, *1946.*

lesson takes the specific form of circumspection, guile and, in both senses of the word, craft. In the deliberate act of frustrating our desires and thus keeping us at bay, "now and then peep[ing] out and show[ing]" himself, Franklin asserts that autobiography is not merely a retrospective genre but a continuous engagement between self and audience, an artful construction that matches that of the life itself. (pp. 229-38)

Roger J. Porter, "Unspeakable Practices, Writable Acts: Franklin's 'Autobiography'," in The Hudson Review, *Vol. XXXII, No. 2, Summer, 1979, pp. 229-38.*

Donald H. Meyer (essay date 1987)

[*Meyer is an American historian, educator, and author specializing in American intellectual history. In the following excerpt, he details Franklin's approach to religion, claiming that he "represents western man entering a new era of intellectual consciousness."*]

Franklin's approach to religion starts with a cultural heritage that includes Calvinist roots, his Boston background and "Leather-Apron" origins, and an intellectual milieu to which Franklin was extremely receptive. Although he was to become a diplomat, scientist, "founding father," international celebrity and all-around sage, Franklin never entirely transcended his identity as one of the "middling sort," who, starting out as a Boston printer's apprentice, was already engaged, as a teenager, in bitter disputes with that town's forever defensive Puritan establishment. The man who consciously projected the self-image of order, moderation, and good-natured tolerance emerged from what seems a caldron of contradictions: Franklin was a vehemently anti-Puritan Puritan, a proud working man with terrible status anxieties, a freethinker with second thoughts, a Deist who (sometimes) believed in prayer, Providence, and public worship, a natural philosopher who never had the time to do what he really wanted to, an amiable and always humble inquirer who had some pretty strong opinions on "merely speculative" matters and was capable of an almost Old-Testament sense of outrage. Franklin gives new dimensions to the word "contrareity."

In his *Autobiography* Franklin speaks of an early propensity alike toward "handiness" and "bookishness." It is easy to treat this admission casually, even though both qualities are well illustrated in the course of Franklin's life. Franklin's extraordinary experiments in electricity show him to be closer to Michael Faraday than to the Newton of the *Principia Mathematica* in his scientific style. It would seem that he was compensated for his lack of mathematical skill with a marvelous sense of the spacial, an instinctive trust in fact and a corresponding suspicion of mere assertion, and a knack for experimental precision that allowed him to transform the study of electrical phenomena from a curiosity into an exact science. When Franklin proved the conservation of charge in a Leyden Jar (a primitive capacitor) with the cork suspended midway between the two oppositely charged poles, his combination of economy of detail and richness of concept stirs

our admiration. Perhaps it is his idea of seriousness, or his redefinition of the serious, that puts Franklin in a different world from that of many of his contemporaries and of the great thinkers of the past. His is a definition of the serious that is based not on the results of logical argument and "bookish" learning only, but on something as mundane as "handiness" and an infinite caring for detail and meticulous mechanical procedure. Franklin combined the craftsman's skill in handling things with the philosopher's ability to interpret new relationships, and herein lay his great intellectual strength.

It was in the period from the dawning of the Renaissance to the time of Francis Bacon, we are told, that the mechanic and the craftsman received more than condescending notice from the scholar, and the serious philosopher began to adopt the methods of the artisan—realizing that altering nature might be essential to understanding it, and that the understanding of nature as it actually works might be worthwhile. It was no accident that God, in this period, was frequently described as a "clockmaker" and a master mechanic of the universe. The rise of modern science dates from this time and, in good measure, from this development. Franklin as scientist is surely within the tradition of the craftsman-scholar; and Franklin, as philosopher in the broader sense of that term, carries on in this tradition, applying new methods and a new way of seeing things to old questions. Cannot life be approached in the sensible, careful, and dependable way of the mechanical "arts"? Cannot life's "higher" concerns—even religious or "ultimate concerns"—be similarly treated and settled? The question sounds a little naive today. But Franklin lived in a time when many thinkers were starting to realize that for centuries the "Schoolmen," as Locke sometimes called them, had obfuscated and confused simple truths about religion, morality, and the nature of things in general. Theology, like natural philosophy, had been the province of men whose wisdom and judgment had been beyond questioning. But now any intelligent and "handy" person could understand the principles of the Leyden Jar or the Franklin Stove, and Franklin himself delighted in encouraging popular experimentation. An assertion that could not be submitted to this kind of public scrutiny was hardly to be taken seriously. One could quickly see the advantages of his new wood stove, Franklin had announced in 1744, by investigating the matter for oneself, come to understand the "Properties" and the "Principles" involved, examining them "separately and particularly," then make the necessary "comparisons." Why cannot something similar be done in the realm of faith? Has God hidden Himself like a prankish child, leaving clues that only a few close friends could ever figure out? Surely, such is not the God whose workmanship the great Newton had demonstrated to be so exquisitely orderly and rational! Why cannot religion be straightforward and rational, as everything else is? The real significance of this question lies in its second clause. It is only reasonable to suppose that the same kind of thinking that explains the physical universe would explain, equally well, the spiritual universe.

This attitude carried over to institutions. Franklin may have been a democrat "to the core," as some of his admirers contend, but he was a bookish handiman before he became a democrat, and his instinct for craftsmanship is as evident in his attitude toward social organization as it is in his approach to science and invention. Like physical things, institutions were subject to critical scrutiny, testing, alteration. They were to be judged, like conduct, on the basis of their utility, which involved both the nobility of their purpose and their efficiency in achieving it. Churches, like states, came within this category; and, for Franklin, the purpose that the churches were to serve involved mainly the public good and the general welfare.

In his defense of the Reverend Samuel Hemphill against the charge of heterodoxy by the Presbyterians, Franklin made it clear that the primary function of the preaching ministry is not saving souls—since church members are presumably saved already (Franklin was never much bothered by the difference between "true" Christianity and what Kierkegaard called "Christendom")—but in promoting socially beneficial conduct and right attitudes. In his *Autobiography* he reports that he was inclined to respect the teachings of all "sects," at least insofar as these teachings set forth the "essentials of every religion," namely, the acknowledgement of a creator-deity who is providentially active in the affairs of men and who rewards (or punishes) our conduct in this world or the next. He added, however, that he regarded these different teachings with varying "degrees of respect" as he found them "more or less mixed with other articles which without any tendency to inspire, promote, or confirm morality, served principally to divide us and make one unfriendly to one another." Franklin's rule in judging the doctrines of any sect was simple and broad, but inflexible. First, do they conform to the essential principles of every religion, principles which Franklin regarded as basic and universal? Second, insofar as they go beyond these basic principles, do they thereby encourage or undermine public morality and social tranquility? The utilitarian judgment is only half the test, applying only to those doctrines that claim more than the "essential" truths of religion. When the teachings of a sect go beyond the "truths" we all "know" they become matters of "speculation," and, as such, are to be handled not on the basis of truth or falsity but of social utility or worthlessness, perhaps mischief. In his public writings, like the *Autobiography,* Franklin liked to stress the positive side of his attitude, which makes him seem genially tolerant of just about anything. And, when dealing with a person's private convictions, Franklin probably really was this way. He had cordial relations with many among the Quakers, Dunkards, Moravians, and Baptists of Pennsylvania, and established a warm friendship with the great evangelist George Whitefield. But when convictions became institutionalized in a specific sect, and that sect managed to establish itself in a position to exert real social influence, Franklin's attitude could be considerably less tolerant.

His attitude toward the Presbyterians, at least until the last quarter of his life, is a case in point. He seems to have feared and distrusted this sect more than any other, mainly because the Presbyterians seemed to have more influence on the society he knew and were, therefore, capable of doing more mischief with their peculiar doctrines. Franklin claimed to have found the Calvinist doctrines of

predestination, election, and reprobation "unintelligible," sometimes "doubtful." In fact, he probably considered them quite mad—although beyond all proof or refutation. When people, holding such doctrines, form what amounts to a religious establishment they become a potential threat to the public good. It is little wonder that Franklin reacted with what seems at first glance uncharacteristic outrage when a heterodox preacher, like Hemphill—who, it turned out, was a plagiarist as well—was dismissed from his pulpit. Franklin was doing more here than speaking in behalf of better sermons or fighting for free speech: he was attacking what he considered a social menace—institutionalized ignorance equipped with the power to enforce its standards and its views on the wider society. The key to spiritual truth like the key to material progress is the open society, in which rational individuals can test conflicting claims for themselves, just as the prospective buyer of a Franklin stove might "make the Comparison" between the "old and the new Methods" of home heating. Any institution that has the power to prevent or restrict this kind of "Comparison" is dangerous. Franklin's tolerance applied to individuals, not to powerful social institutions. Institutions were the machinery that ran society. They were to be studied, used, repaired when necessary, redesigned, even junked when the circumstances demanded it. Machines control things, but they must never be permitted to control people.

Machines should not control people, but Franklin's attitude of intelligent handiness applied to people as well as to things, ideas, and institutions. The problem here is that man, though rational, may be overcome by his emotions, which have to be kept under control. Franklin always wanted to write a treatise on the "Art of Virtue," not a philosophy, as we commonly understand it, dealing with ethical theory, but a book on method and technique. The often criticized discussion of the subject in his *Autobiography,* with its list of virtues, charts, job descriptions, progress reports, and schemes for behavior modification gives us some idea of what he had in mind. In a famous letter to Joseph Priestly of 19 September 1772, Franklin even tried to quantify the act of decision-making, as though to make our moral choices more rational and exact. His plans for dieting and for the budgeting of time (time being money), even his measured surrender to "venery" for the sake of health or offspring, reveal a man anxious to control himself and direct his life in a rational, that is, workmanlike, manner—not denying his passions, but properly disciplining and mastering them. Like many of his contemporaries, Franklin condemned "zeal" and "enthusiasm"—excessive devotion to a cause and what Yeats would call "passionate intensity." In his defense of poor Hemphill, Franklin exhibited considerable passion himself in railing against "Ignorance and Error, Bigotry, Enthusiasm, and Superstition," condemning "the hellish Fires of furious Zeal and Party Bigotry," and accusing Hemphill's accusers of promoting "Enthusiasm, Demonism, and Immorality in the World." Bigotry, Ignorance, Superstition, Error—these were clearly not the proper tools for arriving at the truth, either in matters of religion or of natural philosophy. We might differ in our "religious Speculation" as we do "in Astronomy or any other Part of natural Philosophy" in peace and "Brotherly Love," Franklin advised.

We might then be able to achieve "those two invaluable Blessings, full Liberty and Universal Peace," that would in turn open up "the Ways of Truth," so that perhaps one day Christians might come to agree more than, as now, they differ. The point here is not that Franklin could be zealous in his denunciation of zeal: to wax enthusiastic occasionally is as human as to practice occasional venery. What deserves our attention, rather, is his concern for opening the *ways* of truth. The enemy was anything that blocked these "Ways"—and the plural form is noteworthy—be they coercive institutions, "Party Bigotry," or "furious Zeal." The ways are many, and must be kept free and clear. Truth is one, but perhaps of less immediate concern to Franklin than keeping open the approaches to it. One can muddle along without the most efficient heating system, but as fully functioning human beings we cannot get along in a society where the possibilities of discovery are systematically denied or limited. That this commitment to openness might itself imply a judgment about ultimate truths—that free choice among "Ways" might itself determine "Truth"—perhaps never occurred to Franklin.

Franklin is usually pictured as a Deist—one who believes in a god, but who insists that this god is known primarily through reason and the study of nature, without recourse to special revelation; and who thinks of God not in personal terms, but more abstractly, as creator of the universe and, perhaps, its moral governor. Everyone seems to agree, however, that Franklin is rather hard to pin down. In 1745, for example, commenting on the Massachusetts expedition against Fort Louisbourg, he could facetiously speculate on the efficacy of mass prayer, calculating the mechanical advantage of combined prayer power, and concluding that perhaps "works" count a bit more than "faith" when it comes to attacking fortified towns. Yet, during the Constitutional Convention in 1787, he proposed opening each session with a prayer in the conviction that "GOD governs in the Affairs of Men," and that, without God's help, the creators of the American republic would have no more success than the builders of the Tower of Babel. Inconsistencies of this sort are frustratingly common in Franklin.

A simple but important reason for such inconsistencies is the fact that Franklin approached religion with the instincts of a layman and the mindset of a secular philosopher. As a layman, Franklin had no specialized training in the language and logic of theology: he was an amateur, though perhaps better acquainted with "polemic divinity" than he liked to admit. As secular philosopher, Franklin was committed to no particular doctrine, only to the search for truth regardless of where it led. To say that he was committed only to the "search for truth" makes it all sound quite smug, as though everyone else was practicing some kind of deception. Perhaps it would be more accurate to say that Franklin sought "truth" as opposed to "saving truth." He represents a relatively new phenomenon in western thought. The notion of the concerned layman, interested in religion as an intellectual problem, stems mainly from the Reformation and the growing conviction that religious thought is no longer the exclusive province of a handful of scholarly monks. The idea of the secular philosopher investigating something out of mere curiosity is older, of course; but the *combination* of concerned layman and secular philosopher turning his attention to matters of ultimate concern was relatively new to the West in Franklin's time. Now, no one, not even Benjamin Franklin, can shrug off his cultural background entirely. Franklin retained many of the prejudices and presuppositions of the Calvinist-Protestant heritage. But when he approached theological questions it was neither as what we today would call an "expert" nor as an apologist. He carried fewer pieces of theological baggage than any theologian, and he had less of a burden of pious concern than a lay believer. He could therefore afford to be flexible to the point of intellectual playfulness and rational to the point of irresponsibility if his curiosity, interest, logic, and whims led him in such a direction. Franklin represents western man entering a new era of intellectual consciousness.

Perhaps his most playful and scandalous theological work is his *Dissertation on Liberty and Necessity, Pleasure and Pain* (1725), which he published in England, at age nineteen, then later renounced as one of the "errata" of his life. In this early piece, Franklin took the basic assumptions of Deism and Lockean psychology and pushed them to their logical conclusions, denying free will, moral agency, and the very idea of moral distinction. The work, as Alfred Owen Aldridge rightly concludes, is implicitly atheistic, one might even say nihilistic. In a clockwork cosmos of the kind young Franklin describes, everything is so perfect and thoroughly accounted for that, in the final analysis, nothing counts for anything. It is a world of right without wrong, Yin without Yang: it is morally frozen and existentially pointless. If there is a God, and that God is all-good, all-wise, and all-powerful, said Franklin, there is no freedom, no evil, no surprise. God has created a machine universe characterized by perfect "Order and Regularity" and little else. One may admire this universe for a while, then forget it entirely, since it will do what God intends it to do and nothing more. Franklin was being playful here, examining ideas and testing postulates mainly to see where certain assumptions lead. He may also have thought that this line of argument would provide one with a measure of metaphysical consolation, although his concluding remark to the effect that his idea might meet with an "indifferent Reception" and his homely advice that we cannot change geese into swans by wishful thinking suggest that our cosmic comfort was not uppermost in his mind. In any event, Franklin soon repudiated these speculations as being, if not illogical, morally unrealistic. He used, in fact, the pragmatic test: supposing a proposition to be true, what would be the consequences of acting upon it? Franklin concluded that his theory, though possibly true, was not very useful.

Franklin's *Dissertation* is itself an index of his secular rationalism. He felt no theological restraints in pushing his logic to its conclusion and in punctuating that conclusion with an exclamation point: "Our *Geese* are but *Geese* tho' we may think 'em *Swans*." But his renunciation of this conclusion is a clear mark of his empiricism: the empirical test of a moral proposition being its utility, Franklin found that as a philosophy of life the argument of the *Dissertation* was a failure. People actually making their way through the interrelationships of social life are, in fact, influenced by their moral cosmology and may behave the worse for believing their behavior counts for nothing.

Franklin was already rewriting his theology on the tedious voyage back from England in the summer of 1726, and in 1728 he drew up his **"Articles of Belief,"** in which he presented a revised version of the universe and of man's place in it. In the **"Articles"** one still has a sense of the immensity of the universe and of the puniness of humankind, but here Franklin's starting-point and his conclusions are different. In the *Dissertation* he started with God as the "First Mover," and reasoned deductively from that premise. In the **"Articles"** he also began by acknowledging God, the "one supreme, most powerful Being," but quickly shifted to the human perspective, looking up and out from "this little Ball on which we move," into the infinitude of deep space, finding his "narrow Imagination" quite overwhelmed by the cosmic prospect before him. His concern seems no longer cosmic description but basic comprehension, and he is less concerned with the workings of an enormous machine than with seeing himself emotionally in some kind of relationship with a vastness that seems beyond human conceptualization. His attitude is less one of curiosity than of awe and wonder. Still, Franklin was not the man to be entirely overwhelmed, even by cosmic emotion. A person is obliged to deal with the object of his wonder analytically, as he would deal with the problem of divine omniscience or of evil in the universe. But the question now is how we are to respond to something and not merely what we are to think of it. What is our personal relationship to God, and in what frame of mind do we properly approach the Creator of the Universe?

The "polytheism" of Franklin's **"Articles of Belief"** is a puzzle. Does it reflect his eighteenth-century devotion to classical thought and the ancient gods? Or is it an application of the idea of the Great Chain of Being, featuring subordinate gods to stand between the Supreme Being and man, just as the higher primates do between human beings and the lower animals? Franklin's position is clear in any case. It is inconceivable that an infinite God could have much regard for "such an inconsiderable Nothing as Man," or feel any need for human devotion and worship. On the other hand, as rational beings, we feel the need, the "Duty," in fact, to pay homage "to Something." Franklin, apparently, felt ridiculous offering praise To Whom It May Concern, and yet he seems to have had no patience with or understanding of the Christian idea of God Incarnate in some time-space embodiment. He concludes, therefore

> that the Infinite has created many beings or Gods, vastly superior to Man, who can better conceive his Perfections than we, and return him a more rational and glorious Praise.

"It may be," he speculates, "that these created Gods are immortal; or it may be that after many Ages, they are changed, and others supply their Places." In any event, "I conceive that each of these is exceedingly wise and good, and very powerful," and each has his own sun and planetary system, of which he is creator and ruler. "It is that particular Wise and good God, who is the author and owner of our System, that I propose for the object of my praise and adoration." What seems significant here is not the source of Franklin's idea but his reason for and way of proposing it. "It may be," "I conceive that," "I propose." His tone is clearly hypothetical and conjectural, in line with the tactic of humility set forth in the *Autobiography,* but suggesting as well the tentative, deliberate approach of the experimental inquirer. And his reasoning lies clearly with economy of explanation: given the facts as we know them, what is the simplest, most sensible explanation available to us to account for them? Franklin proposes a kind of cosmic bureaucracy, a rationalized, well-organized chain of divine command with an Infinite Being acting through the agency of less-than-infinite deistic intermediaries. This explanation fits in well with Franklin's theistic premise, with the classical idea of a Chain of Being, and with good sense; and it is presented not with the urgency of a manifestation of the sacred but with the unflappable casualness of one proposing a better way of explaining an electrical discharge. Does this mean that Franklin was not serious about religion? Not at all. His statement of belief was followed by a service of adoration, petition, and thanksgiving, nothing in which suggests flippancy. It is just that Franklin had a different idea of religious "seriousness" from the traditional one. The feeling of awe and reverence that he experienced before the Great Mystery of Being was more controlled and subdued than that experienced by Moses at Sinai or Isaiah before God's Throne. It is the Holy scaled down to what Franklin would consider its proper proportions—met with fear and trembling, perhaps, but not ecstacy or any emotion beyond all controlling. Religion was too serious a matter to be permitted to drive one to distraction. Faith is too important to be left to the passions: we should serve it with our highest not our lowest proclivities.

The God who created and who governs our solar system is "vastly superior" to man in wisdom, goodness, and power, and yet is "not above" caring for us, being pleased by our praise and worship, and of being our "Friend." Since the time of Copernicus the universe had grown infinitely distant. Franklin's created, finite deity lived within human reach and was more like the God of Abraham, Isaac, and Jacob—in accessibility if not in transcendence. The Infinite God filled Franklin's intellectual need for a Creator of the Universe, a Prime Mover. The more finite God of this world system seems to have satisfied his more personal need for a friend behind phenomena, a deity we may address as "Thou" and recognize as our "Father." It is unclear whether Franklin needed to feel this in any deeply personal way. But it seems to have been important to his idea of human nature and the human condition, particularly when man is regarded not in his solitude but in his social life and moral relations. Franklin's **"Articles of Belief"** are followed by a prayer of "Adoration," then a "Petition," asking mainly for strength and guidance, and prefaced by a prayer that explicitly avoids any request for particular "Temporal Blessings" (since, in our ignorance, we cannot really know what is best for us), and instead begs help in "my Continued Endeavors and Resolutions of eschewing Vice and embracing Virtue." One gets the impression that Franklin demands a nearby God who is a "Friend" not so much to console and support us in times of crisis, nor even to underwrite the moral order by punishing vice and rewarding virtue, but to inspire and cheer us in our noblest aspirations. Franklin's God relates to man primarily as a hope for transcendence, ever encouraging us to surpass ourselves in our moral life.

This moral life, furthermore, has to be understood in the broadest possible way. It is not to be narrowly identified with Franklin's list of specific virtues, for these were clearly instrumental virtues, enumerated only as a means or technique for improving one's attitude and conduct. It is, rather, our social existence regarded holistically, involving a network of human interrelationships, both public and private, in which we live to grow to the full measure of our humanity by always pushing beyond all measure, all limit. "Man's Perfection," Franklin said in 1731, "is in Virtue." And, although he maintained, in his *Autobiography,* that he had developed a plan (albeit a "bold and arduous" one) for arriving at moral perfection, it seems clear that Franklin never regarded perfection as an attainable (*i.e.,* measurable) goal in life; not only because we always fall short or slide back into one vice while trying to overcome another, but because human perfection is by definition always one step beyond whatever measure has been attained. Franklin was empiricist enough to know that we can meaningfully evaluate our performance only if we establish a standard of measurable achievement. But he was Calvinist enough to realize that perfection is an open-ended concept that points beyond all measure, beyond all quantifiable limits. It is true that Franklin insisted that the idea of a "perfect Man" is no more absurd than that of a perfect horse or perfect oyster—defining "perfection" as the best something is capable of being. Here he was arguing against Calvinists who insisted on human depravity and idealists who held up unrealizable standards. My point is simply that Franklin, in his more strenuous mood, did look beyond the actual, state-of-the-art best to see human life in terms of possibility and relentless striving. Religion offered Franklin not just reassurance for the moral status quo but hope for moral possibility in the making. He repudiated his own *Dissertation* for this very reason. The universe described therein saw to the punishment of horse thieves but offered no encouragement to the seeker after righteousness. To put it another way, the perfect man, unlike the perfect oyster, seeks always to outdo himself. For it is the built-in imperative of a moral nature that makes us human beings in the first place.

In 1732 Franklin delivered an address to his Junto, **"On the Province of God in the Government of the World."** In it he argued that, on the basis of our knowledge of God's wisdom, goodness, and power, we may safely infer that, although God allows for free agency and the regular operation of the "Course of Nature," He is nonetheless free to intervene from time to time at His pleasure. Our sense of moral justice supports the belief in a God who is both able and willing to answer our prayers. Our faith in God's Providence is "the Foundation of all true Religion," serving as a "Powerful Regulator of our Actions," giving us "Peace and Tranquility within our own Minds," and rendering us "Benevolent, Useful, and Beneficial to others." The faith in Providence, in other words, provides a basis

alike for social discipline, moral inspiration, and spiritual comfort—all resting on the conviction that humankind is part of a larger pattern of conscious purpose and active concern in the universe.

Franklin's thoughts on prayer and immortality tie in with his understanding of divine Providence. He put aside his early idea of a soulless, clockwork universe, but one suspects that he was never able entirely to shake off all the doubts expressed in the *Dissertation.* In any event, all his later utterances in behalf of prayer and immortality reveal as much doubt as faith, and seem more expressions of hope than of firm conviction. Franklin wanted to believe in both the efficacy of prayer and the afterlife, again for spiritual as well as moral and social reasons. He longed for the feeling that the universe was somehow responsive to human needs and longings, and that human life had meaning that was not confined to earthly existence nor defined by biological description. If God be truly all-wise, good, and powerful, and if God be truly the "Author" of our life, then surely God must be concerned with His handiwork, attentive to its details, and prepared to correct and amend it one day, to produce "a new & more perfect Edition." This is the thrust of Franklin's famous epitaph for himself, which, in both its playful wording and hopeful tone, perfectly captures his temper of tough-minded but resolute optimism, of spiritual secularity.

Franklin's attitude toward prayer appears to be a mixture of social pragmatism and spiritual instrumentalism. That is, he believed in public prayer and public worship as a basis for social unity and moral harmony among people, and in private devotion as a means of integrating one's spiritual energies. In making his proposal for public prayer before the American Constitutional Convention in 1787, Franklin evoked the image of the Tower of Babel and warned that, without God's help, the Americans will be "divided" by "little, partial, local interests," and their "Projects will be confounded." In the 1770s Franklin had taken part in developing a *Liturgy on the Universal Principles of Religion and Morality,* the purpose of which was to provide "a form of social worship composed of the most enlarged and general principles, in which all men may join who acknowledge the existence of a supreme Intelligence and the universal obligations of morality," including Jews, Christians of all sects, and Mohammadens. According to the organizer of this project, David Williams, Franklin had "with some emotion" declared that he "never passed a Church, during Public Service, without regretting that he could not join in it honestly and cordially. He thought it a reproach to Philosophy that it had not a Liturgy and that it skulked from the public Profession of its Principles." Franklin's own private "Petition" of 1728, as we have seen, sought neither material things nor special circumstances but concentrated, instead, on the cultivation of desirable virtues and habits of mind—justice, generosity, tenderness, integrity, and the like. Prayer and worship, whether public or private, are treated as efficacious not in affecting events or provoking divine intervention in external affairs but, in the case of public worship, in drawing people together in a common bond of cosmic loyalty and humility, and, in the case of private devotion, summoning inner strength and resolve, and bringing one's spiritual energies to a focus. Our cosmic piety and cosmic loyalty inspire us in our highest endeavors and give us peace both within and among ourselves.

Franklin's views on the afterlife, like those on prayer and worship, have an "as if" quality to them. When formally declaring himself, as he did in his famous letter to Ezra Stiles a few weeks before his death, Franklin showed no hesitation in affirming "That the soul of Man is immortal, and will be treated with Justice in another Life respecting its Conduct in this." Franklin expressed himself less formally and less confidently in a letter to George Whatley in 1785. There, after wryly noting the futility of our life's wishes, he yet observed that he had "some reason to wish" for improvement "in a future State." Observing God's economy in the natural world in both the proliferation of life and the conservation of matter, Franklin announced his inability to believe in the "Annihilation of Souls" and the "daily Waste of Millions of Minds." And, returning to his favored printer's metaphor, he declared that "with all the inconveniences human Life is liable to, I shall not object to a new Edition of mine." Franklin's views on the afterlife are not consistent and are often quite tentative. He speaks, sometimes, in the conventional terms of rewards and punishments; yet he is capable of affirming universalism, the belief that all will be saved. But the doubts of the **Dissertation** are never entirely dispelled. "My Esteem and Respect for you," he wrote Jan Ingenhousz in 1785, "will be everlasting"—concluding his lengthy letter on how to cure smoky chimneys—"if Consciousness and Memory remain in a future State." The conditional qualification is important and characteristic of Franklin.

Recalling his early speculations about the nature of God and the universe, Franklin wrote Benjamin Vaughan in 1779 that the "great uncertainty I found in metaphysical reasonings disgusted me, and I quitted that kind of reading and study for others more satisfactory." In 1757, having read a deistical manuscript submitted by a young man apparently hostile to Christianity, Franklin advised that the manuscript be burned and not even shown to another person. His reasoning offers no surprises. First, the manuscript denies the idea of specific Providence, that is, God's intervention in the world at His pleasure. To Franklin this amounted to an attack on all religion, for it removed all possibility of a real relationship with God, either in worship, in prayer, or in obedience through fear of divine wrath. Humankind cannot relate to a remote diety. Characteristically, Franklin refused to enter into any discussion of the truth or falsity of the writer's position: it was sufficient to observe that the work would win few converts and serve mainly to bring "Odium" upon its writer. Second, by implicitly denying religion, the work undermines morality among common folk who lack education and sophistication. For where is the motive (as far as most people are concerned) to seek virtue and shun vice once that of religion is removed? Here we have both the key to Franklin's religion and a clue to his temper of mind in approaching religious matters.

The idea of divine Providence was central to Franklin's religious thinking, despite the many doubts he had about it. Franklin's God had to be more than an unmoved mover.

He had to be in some way responsive to our entreaties, protective of our best interests, and moved by our efforts to do good. Franklin's God gave moral rationality to the universe and, as importantly, brought to it the warmth of personality. Beyond this Franklin was reluctant to go, for it lead into that realm of "great uncertainty" that so frustrated and "disgusted" him. Franklin's temper of mind here appears to resemble that of the agnostics of the nineteenth century who argued not only that *they* did not know the answers to the ultimate questions, but that such things were entirely unknowable by *anyone;* and that speculation about such matters was futile because no conclusive answers were possible. Franklin allowed his own hopes and cosmic needs to take him so far and no further: he believed in all-powerful God who was benignly interested in His creation and both able and willing (occasionally) to intervene, notably in human affairs. Beyond this, speculation was useless.

It was worse than useless, in fact. For the great mass of people, religious faith was essential as a backstay for morality. Any speculation that served to undermine this faith might undermine morality as well, and with it the entire social order. This kind of reasoning seemed almost axiomatic to a large number of eighteenth-century thinkers beside Franklin. The social order stood at the top of a great pyramid, supported by public and private morality, and resting on the base of religious faith. To chip away at the base was to risk toppling the entire structure.

Ultimately, we can only understand Franklin's religion by looking beyond it. To call him a "Deist" is fair enough; but it does not really explain very much, either about the man or about his age. Franklin's disgust at "metaphysical reasonings" and the "great uncertainty" surrounding them is as central to our understanding as his specific affirmations of belief in Providence, in prayer, in the afterlife. Religion, as Clifford Geertz has reminded us, is "never merely metaphysics," for it involves the entire conduct of life; but it is "never merely ethics either." It is neither a body of "truths" to be believed nor a system of commands to be obeyed. It is, rather, a "world-view" by which "reality" is defined, in recognition of which and loyalty to which the people of a given culture perform the rituals, observe the rules, and acknowledge the symbols which give their lives significance. But what happens when this very complicated process starts to become self-conscious and when, because of social and cultural change, a people begins to observe its own beliefs and practices critically or from an entirely new point of view? And what happens when this "new point of view" is not just different, but actually raises to the level of a moral imperative the critical examination of all assumptions—not merely those involving the tenets of the faith itself, but the ontological presuppositions underlying those tenets? This is exactly the situation that faced the western world in the seventeenth and eighteenth centuries. Both the regulatory institutions and the reigning beliefs that had given order and purpose to western society and culture for hundreds of years were losing their legitimacy—the result of the Protestant Reformation, the rise of capitalism, global exploration, technological progress, and the Scientific Revolution that began with Copernicus. These are developments we have learned to connect with modernity, the first self-consciously cultural manifestation of which we identify with the eighteenth-century Enlightenment. And it has long been customary to associate Franklin with the American Enlightenment, in perhaps its most dramatic manifestations.

The word "Enlightenment" is, in a way, misleading, especially when we use it in connection with Franklin's religion. It suggests illumination, awakening, or instruction as opposed, presumably, to darkness, sleep, or ignorance. This, in fact, is how many eighteenth-century people liked to think of themselves. They saw themselves as putting aside the "supersitition," "mystery," and "ignorance" of the "Dark Ages" as they stepped into the "light" of "reason." We are left with images of children growing up, of blind men gaining their sight, or of prisoners released from a dungeon. And this invites the question raised by Krutch in his *Modern Temper:* just what have we "gained" with our "freedom"? Have we not lost more in our forsaken sense of purpose and our relinquished ability to transcend the world of things than we have gained in clarity, objectivity, and logical precision? In our mastery of means have we not lost sight of ultimate ends? It is perhaps more useful, if not more accurate, to think of modernity not so much as growing up or lighting up or coming forth, but as a lateral move from one world-view to another, a process of replacing one set of beliefs, values, and rituals with a different set.

Eighteenth-century thinkers believed in truth no more passionately than those of the Middle Ages, and were no more opposed to superstition and corrupting influences than were their predecessors. But they were less committed to tradition and creeds, and they were more attached to the idea of simplicity and economy of explanation. Their idea of truth was more open-ended because they gave closer, more critical attention to the process by which "truth" was arrived at. This process they came increasingly to identify with the method of science and what David Hume called "the Experimental Method of Reasoning," which had been so successful in describing the physical universe by resolutely refusing to "go beyond experience." By focusing on experience, systematically studied and critically analyzed, modern people developed the habit of equating the real with the material, and of regarding what is beyond the senses or immaterial as unreal. For medieval people, on the other hand, the unseen world could be every bit as "real" as the material world. Medieval people possessed what Carolly Erikson describes as a "visionary imagination," which allowed them to regard their world as "enchanted," the supernatural as "real," and the entire universe as part of a wider pattern of theological meaning. When John Locke decided that the best way to approach the profound questions of religion and morality was not head-on but through an investigation of the meaning of knowledge itself—ultimately tracing knowledge to "sensations"—he not only revolutionized philosophy, but he also demonstrated how fundamentally the western imagination had shifted its focus. He showed how closely western people had joined truth "to temporal existence, to the world of individual variables." All that was really needed was a system of thought to rationalize and describe the scope of the new imagination.

This new system of thought was taking shape in the eighteenth century. In the seventeenth and eighteenth centuries, according to Norman Fiering, western people moved from a theological to a moral universe—from an age dominated by the language and metaphors of theology to one that looked to moral philosophy to provide the basis for discourse and communication, the images and concepts by which people made sense out of their world. In the English-speaking world, says Fiering, we may trace the emergence of moral philosophy from its former status as a (rather suspect) branch of theology to independence, then to cultural dominance. And moral philosophy proved to be inseparable from *natural* theology—the effort to establish God's existence and attributes through the empirical study of the natural world—"since it invariably involved a kind of moral teleology of the universe." This provided cosmic purpose and moral rationality to a universe being drained of spiritual meaning by science and, more fundamentally, disenchanted by a shift in mentality—in which the unseen became increasingly unreal, the supernatural was viewed with suspicion, and all "metaphysical reasonings" were plagued with "great uncertainty."

British and American moral philosophy owed much to Anthony Ashley Cooper, the Third Earl of Shaftesbury, for its central inspiration. Shaftesbury made the so-called moral sentiments central to his ethical system, in effect basing morality on human nature itself. This meant that, just as natural theology allowed one to establish the existence and attributes of God, so moral philosophy allowed

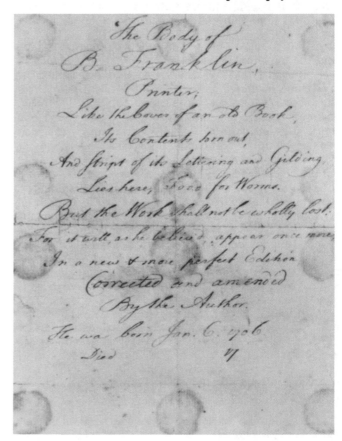

A copy of Franklin's epitaph, written circa 1728.

one to make a rational case for the moral order of the universe. If Franklin truly shifted his religious position from "scientific deism" to "humanitarian deism," no longer looking for proof of God in the physical universe, but searching instead into the human heart, the shift was neither a fundamental nor an original one. Many, beside Franklin, realized that the "scientific deism" of natural theology needed the "humanitarian deism" of moral philosophy (including the emphasis it placed on man's moral nature) to make the case for value and righteousness in the universe. The indicative statements of physics cannot establish norms or duties: they describe a universe that is value free. Moral philosophy, on the other hand, probing into the deepest recesses of human nature—and doing so in an empirical or "experimental" way—finds here the most convincing proof of the morality of existence. As Franklin observed in his *Autobiography,* he became convinced:

> that vicious actions are not hurtful because they are forbidden, but forbidden because they are hurtful, the nature of man alone considered. . . .

Franklin could not blindly accept the authority of revelation; nor could he find in the brute facts of the physical universe the germs of virtue. But in man's moral nature was the empirical link which, for Franklin, joined both the world of fact to the world of value and the method of science to the moral demands of religion. Franklin could, relieved, abandon the vagaries of metaphysical reasonings because moral philosophy ("the nature of man alone considered") joined world-view to ethos, translating the Divine Imperative into empirical terms. Together, natural theology and moral philosophy furnished the basis for a new way of interpreting experience—a new cosmic perspective to replace that which had formerly been provided by traditional theology and sustained by the visionary imagination of a vanished—or vanishing—age.

Benjamin Franklin—a self-made man in an age when the "self" (as distinct from society) had scarcely been defined—did not have a visionary imagination. Franklin's might be called a *graphic imagination,* an engineering, manipulative, hands-on approach to the world that could grasp the meaning of smokeless chimneys and improved heating devices, but was impatient with the fabulous, the theophanous, the unworldly. Yet, his graphic imagination could extend, by means of the new "experimental method of reasoning," to the invisible world of electrical "fluids," suggesting hypotheses, devising experimental situations to test them, and making intelligent inferences. Had he, like Newton, understood higher mathematics, Franklin might have explored the invisible world even more extensively. But the invisible world of the new physics was nothing like that invisible world to which the saints and martyrs of the past had consecrated their lives. It was a world of precise measurements, repeatable experiments, and public verifiability. The "miracles" of science were miracles only in a figurative sense; and herein lay a world of difference. The inventor of the Franklin stove participated in a universe of discourse in which science increasingly provided the standard of rationality, and reason was exalted as the proper instrument of good sense and clear thinking. This kind of thinking accompanied Franklin when he moved from science to religion. Franklin did not approach religion with the attitude of a scientist: he approached both science and religion with nothing more esoteric than the frame of mind of a no-nonsense workman who saw no reason why alert intelligence and solid common sense should not work as effectively on one area as in the other. And this frame of mind was not just a function of Franklin's snuff-colored mediocrity. It was an expression of his culture and its alteration in imaginative perception. To Franklin's way of thinking, what had been lost in making this move had probably not been worth having in the first place. (pp. 150-65)

> *Donald H. Meyer, "Franklin's Religion," in* Critical Essays on Benjamin Franklin, *edited by Melvin H. Buxbaum, G. K. Hall & Co., 1987, pp. 147-67.*

Ormond Seavey   (essay date 1988)

[*In the following essay, Seavey discusses the* Autobiography *as a vehicle for Franklin to display his "mode of consciousness," which posterity could both learn from and imitate.*]

We know Franklin most of all through his *Autobiography.* It is difficult to conceive of him outside the terms which that book dictates, so persuasive is the image offered there. As a result, our responses to Franklin are in large measure responses to a text. We know him not so much as we know Lincoln but more as we know Gatsby; he is a character in a book. He was determined that he should endure in that way, as the protagonist of his own text, and this is probably the first thing to understand about him.

Autobiographies are quite often a somewhat accidental comment or a momentary reordering of their authors' lives. In Franklin's case his life story was a natural and necessary culmination of a lifetime of preoccupations with self-creating. Henry Adams leaves out almost his entire career as a historian, and Gibbon treats his memoirs as an indulgence to which he is entitled after completing *The Decline and Fall.* But Franklin wrote nothing else so long and complex as his *Autobiography,* and he spent the final months of his life trying to pack in as much more material as he possibly could. That he wrote such a book explains both his distinctiveness and his representativeness in eighteenth-century America.

Franklin's preoccupation with controlling and preserving his own story stands out in particular when he is compared to his associates among the Founding Fathers, the leaders of the Revolution, and the early Republic. Washington, Adams, Jefferson, Madison, and Hamilton made no comparable effort to characterize their own personalities for the benefit of posterity. They saw themselves as contributors to a history of thought and action; they were satisfied to be known for military campaigns, legislative enactments, diplomatic negotiations, and state papers. Where they preserved autobiographical records of themselves, they located their lives in a narrative of public events, not in a comprehensive pattern of experiences centering around themselves. They had played their parts in a large drama that lacked a central character or a clear plot line.

Like his associates in the Revolution, Franklin was committed to a life of action, but his *Autobiography* shows that for him events continually became occasions for self-discovery and self-expression. He describes his quarrels with his older brother as a foreshadowing of his later opposition to arbitrary tyranny. He represents his civic and political accomplishments as manifestations of a particular kind of self. The Franklin who helps to found the Pennsylvania Hospital is the canny negotiator for the public good; the Franklin who serves as unofficial quartermaster for the army of General Braddock is the helpful and sensible American confronting the obtuse and imperious Britisher. Ideology was less important for him than it was for the other Founding Fathers because he always subordinated ideology to the demands of experience—not simply for the sake of being more pragmatic and *doing* more but also so as to allow himself the greatest field of self-expression. It might be said that Franklin was drawn to public life for reasons similar to those which drew Whitman to poetry (and away, incidentally, from the politics of the 1850s): public life and poetry offered them occasions to play to the largest possible audiences, to exhibit themselves as embodiments of national traits. Whitman achieved this end by opening himself up to the varied human possibilities he saw in the country; Franklin displayed himself to the nation by engineering a set of reflections of his own qualities. The lightning rod showed his practical inventiveness and his love of gadgets; the Library Company of Philadelphia became for thousands an access to a self-directed education like his own; the French alliance set the seal of international approval on an America whose highly visible embodiment was Franklin himself.

As the *Autobiography* reveals, Franklin's personality was not just an element in his success. It was the success itself. That image of a self had to be carefully preserved for posterity. Jefferson left his personality for the biographers to describe, but Franklin was determined to forestall any possibility that his historical image might get out of his control. As a careful student of character and a master at manipulating audiences, he had worked all his life at the creation of himself and at the presentation of that self—not as ordinarily vain people do, with continual but discontinuous displays of themselves, but more as an artist, who must think continually about the comprehensive effect of his work as a whole. Both in his actions and in his writings, Franklin was aiming at a certain large effect, of which the *Autobiography* was to be the fullest realization.

In other words, Franklin saw himself as an exemplar of a particular mode of consciousness, which the *Autobiography* makes available for imitation. On the first page of his text he makes his intentions quite clear. "Having emerg'd from the Poverty and Obscurity in which I was born and bred, to a State of Affluence and some Degree of Reputation in the World, and having gone so far thro' Life with a considerable Share of Felicity, the conducing Means I made use of, which, with the Blessing of God, so well succeeded, my Posterity may like to know, as they may find some of them suitable to their own Situations,

and therefore fit to be imitated." The "conducing Means" entail something more subtle than a collection of directly imitable activities, like pushing his wheelbarrow through the streets of Philadelphia or being careful to repay borrowed money. A mode of consciousness has generated those activities, and it is that consciousness which his "posterity" is invited to adopt.

By "mode of consciousness" I am referring to a self-consistent assemblage of beliefs, attitudes, and mental reflexes, distinguishable from "personality type" in that its style and signature reflect some engendering cultural situation. D. H. Lawrence in particular saw Franklin as the advocate of such a mode of consciousness, and whatever might be said about the tone of his well-known essay in *Studies in Classic American Literature,* that central perception about Franklin is correct. (Lawrence himself, it has often been pointed out, saw himself as the representative of a certain mode of consciousness.) The concept of the mode of consciousness is useful in describing certain recurring patterns of cultural behavior. When Perry Miller refers to "the Augustinian strain of piety" at the beginning of his great exposition of American Puritanism in *The New England Mind,* he is noting the kinship between the inner lives of the Puritans and the mode of consciousness set forth in Augustine's *Confessions.* Emerson describes Montaigne as the exemplar of a particular response to the varying appeals of ultimate reality and immediate experience; that response can be somewhat unsatisfactorily labeled "skepticism," but its fullest articulation appears in Montaigne's own renditions of the world in the *Essais.* Though the figures who originate or exemplify modes of consciousness are highly aware of the distinctiveness and dimensions of their casts of mind—and aware as well of the possibility that others might imitate them—they are also responding to their own deeper or unconscious impulses, in ways that link their thought and expression to certain emotional states. Thus, for example, a restlessness with transient earthly pleasures is symptomatic of Augustine and his inheritors; a contented disorderliness exemplifies the disciples of Montaigne. Each style can be related to a pattern of inner life. Franklin's own mode of consciousness, in turn, arose from a set of unconscious energies which are partially discernible in the *Autobiography.*

Franklin also insists that his own consciousness has connected him with a certain body of people. It has been an *American* consciousness. In the words of Benjamin Vaughan, his English editor, "All that has happened to you is also connected with the detail of the manners and situation of a *rising* people." The *Autobiography* records both his own consciousness and his sense of identity—a second term in need of definition here. The term "identity" obviously implies a relationship of resemblance, in this case between self and group, but this recognition of connection also involves the self's own most basic awareness of its own distinctiveness. The two processes are reciprocal and mutual: as one discovers affective ties to a human community, one discovers who one is. The particular nature of the identification with a group is a further aspect of identity. In orthodox psychoanalytic terms identification means the absorption of something into the subject, whether that something be a role, a loved one, or a group association. Identification is thus distinguishable from object-choice: in object-choice one *has* something; in identification one *is* something. Naturally in the case of group identity the stronger the incorporation of the group into the ego ideal, the less accessible that incorporation is to conscious direction by the ego.

In the case of Franklin, the question of group identity included the problems he faced as a writer addressing an audience. His first audiences were small, the reading publics of Boston and then Philadelphia, and the group identities available to him were similarly circumscribed. Eventually it became possible to be an American and to address an American audience, but neither that identity nor that audience had much meaning while he was first writing and coming into maturity in the 1720s. Creating the audience and the possibility for identity as something more than a colonist (the inhabitant of a single colony, itself by definition a society of marginal people) required a sequence of political events, the most important being the American Revolution. But those events were brought about to a great extent by writing, by pieces in newspapers and resolutions of committees and legislatures, by correspondence among men and factions that were widely scattered. All his life Franklin was engaged in this sort of writing. His own identity as a writer demanded an audience proportioned to his sense of himself; he could not think of his early successes as a ballad writer or author of clever periodical letters in Boston as substantial or satisfying for long, because he knew how few people were reading his work and how slight an impact he was having. The *Autobiography* represents the culmination of his efforts to create an audience, a "posterity" to which he could be attached, in the deliberate, mastering ways by which writers connect themselves to their readers.

If the *Autobiography* remains our principal access to Franklin's life, it also serves as an obstacle that must be removed or neutralized before we can gain any closer access to him. It is an elaborate fabrication, truthful in its details yet subtly misleading in its overall plan. As a literary creation, the *Autobiography* must be examined in terms of its genre, its structure, and its rhetoric, which together impose certain alterations in the record of his experience.

The basic distortions in the *Autobiography* derive from the very act of organizing the materials of his experience and giving them shape and direction. The *Autobiography* asserts that Franklin's life was in marvelously good order, certainly beyond what his readers could ever have experienced. At the beginning of his narrative he compares his life to a book which he has written himself. What another might have called faults, sins, or mistakes he refers to as "*errata*"—mistakes in type, errors of presentation. The Philadelphia that he describes as the backdrop to his activities appears as the perfect complement to his own notion of himself; it honors the appearance of industriousness, it forms itself into committees and organizations to do good, it responds generously to appeals to its good will. The city appears as an extension of Franklin himself, a field on which he could display his own personality. He lacks the sense, common to others who have recorded their own

lives extensively and persuasively, that the world is frustrating and mysterious, that their lives have only intermittently been under their own control. Writers as different as Augustine and John Stuart Mill have attested to such a feeling. Franklin, by contrast, insists on his capacity to adjust to his surroundings and to resolve the apparent dilemmas of his experience.

Franklin considered setting forth his ideas about the way life should be led in a straightforward expository form. He was accustomed to that sort of writing, and in various shorter versions he had set down what he called **"Hints to Those Who Would Be Rich"** or **"Advice to a Young Tradesman"**; he even had a title in mind for his projected work: *The Art of Virtue*. But he ended up incorporating that project in his *Autobiography,* so that the whole record of his experience might stand as proof of the soundness of his teaching.

All autobiographies, even the most honest, distort the lives they describe, in the same way that depictive art distorts the material depicted. Many of the distortions are introduced by the implied presence of a reader in the text, because readers necessarily impose certain expectations. Any reader will require that the narrative should hold together, based around a single figure whose perceptions will determine what is presented. That central figure must be recognizable as a personality, not so much for consistency of perspective as for a believable pattern of inconsistencies. The Franklin who advocates planning out one's life also confesses several times to his own tendencies for disorder; the confessions serve to make his personality, and even his message, more believable. Readers also expect the described events to be true, by an inner if not a literal standard; autobiographies fail more from the author lying to the reader than from the author lying to himself. Franklin professes to understand himself thoroughly; the work would founder if the reader felt any real acknowledgment from him of the limits of that understanding or any palpable concealment of the inner truth about himself. Finally, the reader cannot be satisfied with the fact that all lives are different and lived on their own terms; readers wonder what general category of life this will be—the confessions of a saint, for example, or the memoir of a politician or soldier, or the adventures of a scoundrel. Even unsophisticated writers respond to these expectations by projecting a pattern on their recollections; Franklin was in no way unsophisticated, and he had a comprehensive design for the description of his life that operates from the first page.

The consistency of Franklin's purpose in the *Autobiography* is somewhat masked by the rather casual and offhand way he appears to treat the project. The book may seem at first glance to have problems of unity and coherence. He wrote it in several installments, probably of concentrated effort in each case, in between long interruptions; Franklin began the work in 1771, purportedly as a letter to his son, and was still working on it almost nineteen years later. In the meantime he had broken with his son, the American Revolution had taken place, and his fame had grown to immense proportions. The disruptions are indicated in the text of the life: in 1771 he is on vacation at Twyford, the estate of the Bishop of St. Asaph, while in 1784 he is at Passy in the suburbs of Paris, moved to continue, he says, by the advice of friends. These disjunctions give the *Autobiography* its appearance of artlessness, as if the project were one pottered around with in spare moments. As he puts it himself, "I shall indulge the inclination so natural in old Men, to be talking of themselves and their own past Actions, and I shall indulge it, without being troublesome to others who thro' respect to Age might think themselves oblig'd to give me a Hearing, since this may be read or not as any one pleases."

It would be foolish to accept this good-humored description of his motives or to believe that the sporadic surges of writing in the *Autobiography* led to a mixed presentation. Franklin understands that the reader's attention is best engaged by casual and subtle means, and he is determined to secure that attention. Unlike old men who talk about themselves out loud, Franklin says he will indulge that inclination by writing. He juxtaposes hearing and reading as if the reader is in some way freer, less under obligation to be attentive than the hearer. The reader can easily put the book down, whereas the hearer cannot graciously walk away from an interminable story. But the reader once engaged can be exposed to the writer for much longer, and the written word can be more deeply coercive. Franklin is not, after all, telling a story so much as he is setting forth a mode of consciousness; he does not want to be in front of his audience talking but rather inside their heads.

Despite its artless appearance the *Autobiography* makes large, uncompromising claims for its own importance. Franklin's rhetorical strategy is to assume rather than to demonstrate his basic claims; the reader is not offered this consciousness to accept or reject it but is instead invited inside to see how everything works. Rather than asserting overtly that his life has been the exemplary American life, Franklin introduces letters into the text from two friends who say more than he could have dared to, and he permits those letters to stand as the explanation for why he resumed writing. The consistency of his perspective through large changes of condition is a given, just as it is a given that his life is susceptible to being imitated by others. The *Autobiography* leads its readers to believe that it is perfectly natural to be Benjamin Franklin; anyone else, at any later date, can do it too. He says that his motive for writing is an old man's self-indulgence, to which he then adds the motive of vanity. But self-indulgence and vanity are quickly transformed from their usual meanings; self-indulgence turns out to be an aspect of self-direction, and vanity operates for the benefit of the public as a whole. What he appears at first to be excusing in himself he is in fact advocating. Confession is converted to assertion without any change in the inflection of presentation.

The force of Franklin's rhetoric of self-presentation depends upon the reader's impression that he is not alone, that he has been a representative or exemplary figure. As David Levin [in the *Yale Review*, L111 (Winter 1964)] and Daniel Shea [in his *Spiritual Autobiography in Early America*, 1968] have noted, the *Autobiography* is oddly reminiscent of the tradition of spiritual autobiography, with its tendency to identify the authorial self as sinner or saint rather than as someone to be known primarily on his or her own terms. In Franklin's case, saint and sinner are replaced by the category of man in general. He arrives at a creed that he claims to share with every other believer anywhere. He bequeaths his project for the advancement of virtue to the world as a whole. Always he is careful not to locate himself in any limiting pattern of unreproducible events and circumstances, and that stance is intended to associate him with all of humanity. Though the reader sees him throughout as a somewhat detached observer of his surroundings, that detachment is shared by all the other recognizable figures of his story except his parents; everybody else picks up and moves on to another place or changes jobs or spouses. Franklin maintains a balance between alienation and full identification in his relationship with others, and that balance seems related to his successes. He is continually introducing himself—to governors, employers, merchants of Philadelphia, the readers of Boston—rather than coping with circumstances where he has long been known; he manages to escape the limitations of his own past circumstances and define the terms under which he will live. When he needs an outlet for his sexuality, he gets married to someone he had discarded earlier; when he is stranded in London, he finds work as a printer and soon convinces some of his fellow employees to adopt his own diet. Throughout he presents his accomplishments not just as the product of one particular personality but as the natural human response to his circumstances.

The belief in the existence of natural human responses—those of the reasonable man, who is also the sentimental man—was an an article of faith in the eighteenth century, and Franklin found in that belief another means of translating his own particular experience into a sort of universal language. The *Autobiography* will appear to be only a charming story of material success if its deep connection with the Enlightenment is not understood. However much as he may have remained detached from his social surroundings, Franklin readily adjusted to the climate of opinion in the Enlightenment. His own version of the age, to be sure, left a good deal out; it was not the same Enlightenment as Voltaire's or Hume's or even Jefferson's. The problems of epistemology that concerned his contemporaries never bothered him. Intrigued as he was with natural science, it was a sort of game for him, though for others like Diderot or d'Alembert it provided a philosophical foundation. Franklin was never seriously involved in the *philosophes'* campaigns against religious fanaticism; believers were around him everywhere in America, and he sought nothing more than to get along with them all. Franklin never allowed those differences of emphasis to develop into differences of theory because he was determined to embrace all the positive possibilities of his age. The *Autobiography* registers little awareness that the eighteenth century was a domain with its own constraining peculiarities; instead he calls it "the Age of Experiments," a field of possibilities, and those experiments he could not undertake himself he felt sure would be undertaken by others.

The Enlightenment collaborated in the portrait of Franklin in the *Autobiography,* and its part in the process of recreating Franklin will need to be described further. Certain

Enlightenment assumptions about the self seemed to explain or validate his life. It promised, above all, that one could know oneself better—and that there was, perhaps, more of the self that was worth knowing than one could have known in previous ages and that one's relationship to society was newly comprehensible and subject to conscious adjustments. These, of course, are the premises upon which the *Autobiography* was written. (pp. 3-11)

> *Ormond Seavey, in his* Becoming Benjamin Franklin: The "Autobiography" and the Life, *The Pennsylvania State University Press, 1988, 266 p.*

Kenneth Dauber   (essay date 1990)

[*In the excerpt below, Dauber describes Franklin's Autobiography as "America's primary epic," and argues that the work marks a dramatic shift in the traditional relationship between writer and reader.*]

At the threshold of America stands "B. Franklin, Americain." This is the inscription on one of the popular medallions struck in Franklin's honor on the occasion of his ambassadorship to France, and it is especially appropriate. Franklin, abroad and at home, for better and for worse, has been our most enduring exemplar. The picture on the medallion represents the general sense of him well. Here is Franklin, perfectly attired in studded shirt and closed collar—and with a fur cap on his head! The tensions of American culture, that natural paradise that yet aspires to the vanguard of Western civilization, appear together in one figure. Down-home earthiness meets urbane sophistication, native sagacity cosmopolitan wit. Franklin spans America's diversity. He gave it electricity, daylight savings time, a new stove, its first public library, the idea for the union of its colonies, a university, a fire department, government borrowing from the people, bifocals, and on and on. "One might enumerate the items of high civilization," says Henry James in a famous passage, "which are absent from the texture of American life," and there follows a list ranging from "sovereign," "church," and "army," to "novels," "Epsom," and "Ascot." Franklin, then, would seem to have gone far toward providing such items himself, to have created America's civilization single-handedly, and all of it, from "high" to low, with everything in between. Businessman, scientist, statesman, man of letters, his genius was in no one field above any other, but in his having worked so many fields, in his having *been* America in all of its variousness.

This identification of Franklin with his nation is remarkable, and I take it to be the beginning of any uniquely American studies. Both personal and national, "American" appears before us undivided, referring equally to the general and to the particular. No division need, or even should, be undertaken. No a priori objection that we confuse different senses of American should be raised. Indeed, it is only by refusing to raise it that we can really investigate what "American," in Franklin's sense, means. We must resist the seductions of presumably more rigorous analysis. We must not separate out independent elements of our identification, even if only to put them together

again in some deeper resolution. If we speak of Franklin as American, it is as describing neither the fortuitous circumstance of his having lived in America, nor yet some idea of a fundamental characteristic he shares with others who lived with him. American, in Franklin, means neither something accidental nor something essential. For, in the wide range of his national activities, Franklin is not a part of America's variety and not its principle, but variety at its very level.

Here, we must not be misled by a habit of what we take to be disinterested investigation. Too typically we place Franklin at a kind of arm's length away from us. We eye him skeptically, afraid of being taken in. We remove ourselves from our own observations of him, as if disinterest would not affect observation with interests of its own. We insist, for example, that an individual cannot really be his community except in some too near view from which we must be careful to distance ourselves. But we do not see that, for Franklin, only a community of individuals would even be an American community and that our distance, accordingly, displaces Americanness from the very perspective in which it signifies. Let us not be so ready to assume, a priori, such an ostensible objectivity that we would do better to interrogate. If our failure to divide "American" appears to be naive, if it is parochial or, even, ideologically motivated, at least it is the ideology of America itself. Let us render our subject in its own language. Let us develop our reflections in the terms of what we reflect about. Or, if reflection itself means division, separating ourselves from what we reflect about, we may even admit the inescapability of terms of separation. But let us, reflecting not only *on* America, but *as* American, give our very division, as it were, an "undivided" account.

> **Businessman, scientist, statesman, man of letters, Franklin's genius was in no one field above any other, but in his having worked so many fields, in his having *been* America in all of its variousness.**
>
> **—*Kenneth Dauber***

We have said that Franklin had no preeminent genius, that he is given to us as dispersed across his nation. And yet, since this Franklin is given to us primarily through his own writings, we cannot help suspecting that he was preeminently the writer through whom we learn of his other eminences, author of a self too designedly American and concealing the real man behind the model we have thus far accepted. *The Autobiography of Benjamin Franklin* is a work of art, we usually say. It is a fiction its author would foist upon us out of some ulterior, however benevolent, motivation, an artifact to be rejected or, even, accepted. As we should note, however, it would thus fill the gap of some divide between us which it simultaneously begets. It would resolve only such an opposition of Franklin to his world which consideration of it as art actually creates.

Here would be the equivalent at a formal level of the a priori approach, but registered for us, now, in the order of its generation. It is a descent from "American" in its irreducibility, from an identity of American writing with American reading. It is a departure from a certain simultaneity of producing and processing American works—a "fall," let us call it, whose significance we must undertake to evaluate.

THE IDEA OF AUTHORSHIP

I can remember, when I was a little boy, my father used to buy a scrubby yearly almanac with the sun and moon and stars on the cover. And it used to prophesy bloodshed and famine. But also crammed in corners it had little anecdotes and humorisms, with a moral tag. And I used to have my little priggish laugh at the woman who counted her chickens before they were hatched, and so forth, and I was convinced that honesty was the best policy, also a little priggishly. The author of these bits was Poor Richard, and Poor Richard was Benjamin Franklin, writing in Philadelphia well over a hundred years before.

And probably I haven't got over those Poor Richard tags yet. I rankle still with them. They are thorns in young flesh.

Because although I still believe that honesty is the best policy, I dislike policy altogether; though it is just as well not to count your chickens before they are hatched, it's still more hateful to count them with gloating when they *are* hatched. It has taken me many years and countless smarts to get out of that barbed wire moral enclosure that Poor Richard rigged up. Here am I now in tatters and scratched to ribbons, sitting in the middle of Benjamin's America looking at the barbed wire, and the fat sheep crawling under the fence to get fat outside and the watchdogs yelling at the gate lest by chance anyone should get out by the proper exit, Oh, America! Oh, Benjamin! And I just utter a long loud curse against Benjamin and the American corral.

Moral America! Most moral Benjamin. Sound, satisfied Ben!

These are D. H. Lawrence's words, in a well-known passage whose sentiments are shared by many of us. Franklin's moralisms are absurdly simplistic. His conventional virtues are a falsification of life. Our presumed identity of "American" is roundly denied, for Franklin stands condemned as the representative of just that public America that, privately at least, Americans have always opposed. It is the opposition of the romantic in us to the formalism of neoclassicism, of a certain warm idealism to cold, practical calculation. It is the classic division of self and society, the individual and rules in general. It is the historic division in the renaissance of transcendentalist and Yankee, earlier of heart and head, and earlier still, as scholars of the colonial period tell us, of antinomian and Puritan orthodoxy. What is particularly significant about Lawrence's formulation of the division, however—where he offers us something beyond the standard formulation—is the opportunity he provides us to see it in the making. For Lawrence, unmistakably the partisan, does not assert the division so much as he reenacts it. He intentionalizes the American division, removing it from the plane of ostensibly disinterested statement and placing it inside a context it creates for itself.

This creativity is nowhere more evident than in Lawrence's virulence. He insists on taking everything Franklin says as a personal affront. His hostility seems so much in excess of what Franklin warrants that it is manifestly self-generated. It is not a response to some prior hostility, the result of an attempt by Franklin to tyrannize him. But it is read back into, in order to deny, Franklin's utter obliviousness to the Lawrence for whom his work was proving so tyrannical. It is Franklin's "satisfaction" that Lawrence cannot stand, his "priggishness" or "gloating," which are but aggressive terms for what, to an indifferent observer, might just as easily appear as an innocent or, at worst, naive contentment. Franklin's disinterest looms everywhere as a silent rebuke. His monumental imperturbability, his almost divine detachment in the face of Lawrence's mere mortal's struggles, are unbearable. For Franklin does not so much oppose Lawrence's aspirations as he fails to understand or, for that matter, even care to understand them, and it is this that Lawrence cannot abide. "Benjamin" and "Benjamin's America" were ignoring him, and they were doing so successfully, were building a literature and a nation based upon ignoring him. Writing in another age and with another temperament, writing, most of all, as a European between the wars at a period when the balance of world power seemed to be shifting across the Atlantic, Lawrence could not but see in Franklin the negation of everything he hoped to achieve. Here was success, mastery, a man with a command of himself and his art that Lawrence, striving romantic and suffering Englishman, could never really hope for. By inscribing Franklin within a context motivated by his private pains, therefore, Lawrence turns Franklin's very completeness inside out. Independence becomes arrogance, simple self-sufficiency an act of aggression against others. Franklin, as he claims later, cut a "hole in the side of England," inventing, for that purpose, what Lawrence calls a "dummy" American, a crude, almost invulnerable mechanical soldier against which the more natural and human European could not hope to stand. Lawrence's opposition *to* Franklin is thus successfully transferred. It becomes the opposition *of* Franklin.

More important for our purposes, however, as Lawrence continues, the opposition becomes, finally, opposition actually *in* Franklin. This is a critical development evident in Lawrence's focus, in the passage we quoted, on the proposition that honesty is the best policy. For such a proposition need not be construed, as Lawrence construes it, hypocritically. To a sympathetic reader, indeed, to an audience, let us say, before the "fall" to which we have alluded, sharing the writer's presuppositions and, in a sense we will elaborate later, written into the work from the start, it expresses but a simple democratic faith. Policy, no calculating means to an end, might be seen as the functioning of man in a society where power is disseminated universally, as the operation of a citizen of a nation in which the operation of all the citizens is what determines events. But Lawrence is not a sympathetic reader, and so, unable to join with the work in agreement, he projects his opposition to it onto it, where it appears as a putative opposition of honesty to policy. Alienated and objectifying his alienation from Franklin in Franklin, he makes all but inevitable paradox, contradiction, the binary oppositions of formal analysis. He creates, simultaneously, a method of analysis and the work as object to be analyzed, which, however, no matter how much analysis may then explain it, will enshrine forever its separateness from him. Indeed, he creates the *Autobiography* as a classic, which it has become all the more for Americans, and even for those who rather follow than struggle against it.

Accordingly, we may freely note that Franklin was from the beginning America's glorious achievement, the *Autobiography* its indisputably great work of art. Even Emerson could admire Franklin, and Melville, who did not completely trust him, seemed to be fond of him nevertheless. Yet the axis of Lawrence's bias, if not the bias itself, was the axis of American writers of the nineteenth century as well. As an Englishman, Lawrence inverts things, but the terms are the same. This is why, in fact, *Studies in Classic American Literature* was so important to a generation rediscovering itself and why it remains so popular. For hostility to America we must substitute hostility to Europe, for insecurity about the continued significance of an English fiction substitute insecurity about an emergent American fiction. The bind in which American writers found themselves after the War of 1812 has been well documented. Called upon, in a burst of nationalism at the new country's "victory," to produce at last works of art representative of what was uniquely American, they struggled to free themselves of the forms of an English fiction which was their inevitable literary model. Here, and even more intensely than in Lawrence, is a literature asserting itself only in opposition to another literature. It is writing striving for self-determination but dependent by definition, writing in a love-hate relationship under the shadow of writing which has not yet learned to love or to hate, which is innocent of designs against it or of the need of designing itself. Thus Americans, too, though they did not oppose Franklin, mistook him in striving toward him. They would reproduce him in a world and in a medium that inescapably transform him. The *Autobiography* is, as it were, a part of American literature's prehistory. It is what American writers were after all along but could never achieve precisely because they were after it.

It is important to insist on the literary formulation of the problem here. For although what is at issue is a cultural shift, yet Lawrence's use of textual terms folds literature back onto culture, making it integrated with, rather than a representation of, culture. The significance of this will become apparent as we continue. But we may note here, at any rate, Lawrence's description of Franklin's presence as a function of his dispersion throughout his materials. Franklin is inescapable. He appears all over, even in almanacs Lawrence's father picks up thousands of miles away from America over a hundred years after Franklin lived. Lawrence's attempt to set Franklin up as legislator of tyrannies thus takes the form of setting him up as an "author," as he calls him. And yet the fact remains that Franklin does not seem to authorize anything. In the maxims he repeats there is articulated but a conventional wisdom without voice, sentiments arising from no person and no passion, which always were and always will be and which, accordingly, cannot be effectively resisted. The would-be maker of books cannot escape the retailer of old saws, and he must struggle desperately to hold Franklin accountable, to fix his responsibility for what he says so that he has someone and some thing from which he can escape. Behind the maxims is Poor Richard, and behind Poor Richard is Benjamin Franklin, as if behind Franklin there were not the folklore in which all—Franklin, Poor Richard, and maxims—was properly dissolved.

The result is the emergence as a problem of a question never raised until after Franklin, the idea of authorship itself. It is a death and a birth, the end of writing continuous with reading and the beginning of the work as an object. Literature as process, we may say, becomes literature as a series of artifacts—models if one is partial to them, constraints if one is not. They are things independent, unities susceptible of formal analysis. And both writer and reader must struggle with them, writer and reader who are no longer one in the activity of producing and receiving meaning, but eternally at odds, striving to assert either their ownership of or independence from works which resist them both.

EPIC

Let me state my thesis plainly. *The Autobiography of Benjamin Franklin* is America's primary epic. It is like the *Iliad* in Greek culture, by which I mean not that the *Autobiography* and the *Iliad* share any thematic or even, necessarily, structural elements, but that they exist in comparable relationships to their audiences. The *Autobiography* is an epic as [George] Lukács has best defined it, a work continuous with its readership, neither inferior to it as representing it nor superior as holding out an ideal to which it may aspire. In a manner to be elaborated in the course of this [essay], rather, it is, at least from the point of view of its rhetoric, its culture itself: coextensive with it, showing no marks of a world outside it or, insofar as such marks may appear, assimilating them back into it in a way that abolishes the world's independent existence. The *Autobiography* is, thus, a true original. It does not, in a Lawrentian sense, propose anything personal, anything new, but, in the sense of Poor Richard's maxims, it re-presents as its own whatever propositions are available. It begins with its culture and ends with it, effectually obliterating all beginnings and endings before itself and itself as a beginning or ending. It presents itself as being, it presents itself as having always been, and it is impossible, except with hindsight, to see how it might ever cease to be. This is an almost theological conception of originality, a conception of some primal All out of which everything emerges. And, indeed, the *Autobiography,* I am maintaining, would be just such an original, except that, since it is an original writing rather than an original Being, an action and not an existence, rhetoric rather than metaphysics is involved, words and not the Word. . . . We know that Franklin began writing the *Autobiography* at some particular point and stopped writing it at another. We are certain that he selected some things to include in it and left others out and, given our best documentary evidence, that he either misremembered many events he does record or even deliberately altered them. And yet, because there are no signs within the text itself of such discontinuities between it and the world, we must either forsake such external knowledge or risk misinterpretation. The world exists but in the terms in which he writes it. Or, as we have put it, the work becomes the world and meaning wholly a rhetorical matter.

Two letters from friends, traditionally printed at the beginning of part 2 of the *Autobiography,* may serve to clarify the situation. These are letters urging Franklin to continue his story of himself. They argue the usefulness of the project and set forth its value to the general well-being. Yet though Franklin, as the editors of the Standard Yale Edition tell us, meant to include them in the completed work, we should not make the mistake of attributing to him the motives they espouse. There is a pietism about the letter of Abel James, for example, a too insistent high-mindedness, that would turn the *Autobiography* into an agent of a transcendent morality: "I know of no Character living nor many of them put together, who has so much in his Power as Thyself to promote a greater Spirit of Industry and early Attention to Business, Frugality and Temperance with the American Youth." The virtues enumerated are all Franklinian virtues, but the tone is not, the superciliousness, the smugness of the didact betraying a habit of imposing himself quite dissimilar to the sufficiency of a Franklin content simply to relate his beliefs. Hence, as in "Spirit of Industry" and "American Youth," we see

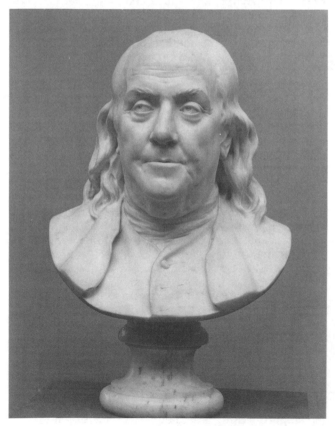

Benjamin Franklin, sculpture by Jean Antoine Houdon, 1778.

the hypostatization, by a true believer in the Virtues as gods, of what in Franklin are but qualified human attributes.

In the letter of Benjamin Vaughan, on the other hand, there is an apocalypticism, the reverse of smugness, but which turns the *Autobiography* equally into an instrument of what transcends it, into a stay against some primal Hobbesian chaos:

> For the furtherance of human happiness, I have always maintained that it is necessary to prove that man is not even at present a vicious and detestable animal; and still more to prove that good management may greatly amend him; and it is for much the same reason, that I am anxious to see the opinion established, that there are fair characters existing among the individuals of the race; for the moment that all men, without exception, shall be conceived abandoned, good people will cease efforts deemed to be hopeless, and perhaps think of taking their share in the scramble of life, or at least of making it comfortable principally for themselves.

Here is a fundamental pessimism at odds with Franklin's benignity, an intensity, a pressure, simply incompatible with the even, almost unmotivated style of the *Autobiography,* written with the expectation of "a Weeks uninterrupted Leisure in my present Country Retirement." It is not that Franklin writes only for amusement. There is *utile* as well as *dulce* in his work, as he states in the opening pages. But all purposes are, finally, subordinated to the fundamental nonpurpose of restating his life: "since such a[n actual] Repetition is not to be expected, the next Thing most like living one's Life over again, seems to be a *Recollection* of that life; and to make that Recollection as durable as possible, the putting it down in Writing." We shall return to the issue of "writing," too, as well as to that of rhetoric. . . . But we should note, here, that "Recollection," so far from presenting us with the psychological cause of the *Autobiography,* reconstitutes all causes, psychological or otherwise, within the *Autobiography* as part of its manifest content. Thus where Vaughan writes, "you are ashamed of no origin; a thing the more important, as you prove how little necessary all origin is to happiness, virtue, or greatness," Franklin admits, "I would not however insinuate that my Ambition was not flatter'd by all these Promotions. It certainly was. For considering my low Beginning they were great Things to me." Franklin need not "prove" anything. Motives of all sorts, even the motive of concealing motives, become simple facts. And this is why Franklin may include the two exhortatory letters in his text in the first place. Nothing Franklin writes about exists outside his text, not his friends, not his culture, not the influences on him, not even himself. This is true epic status, and alongside it all autobiographies, all narratives for that matter, autobiographical or not, with which we might be tempted to compare it are reduced to the status of either the personal alone, or more dangerously, the personal eliding itself in the impersonal.

The Puritan autobiographies of Franklin's era and before are, perhaps, the clearest example. For the sake of comparison we may take, as representative, *A Personal Narra-*

tive of Jonathan Edwards, Franklin's opposite number in what we have called the standard division of American intellectual history. For Edwards, as Perry Miller, for example, would have it, is a protoromantic, an explorer, albeit in religious terms, of inwardness and of that universal truth which resides within. Presumably, he thus represents a concern wholly at odds with Franklin's neoclassic outward interests, as manifested in, say, Franklin's argument, in connection with the death of his son from smallpox, of the importance of inoculation where we would expect some mention of private grief, or in his discussion of his marriage from its financial side to the almost complete exclusion of matters of the heart. The difference between the men, however, lies not in the fact that one emphasizes insides and the other outsides, as if those terms were objectively specifiable and we could assign writers to the rule of one or the other, but in their acceptance of those terms in the first place, in their construction of the work in such a way as to admit or deny the possibility of anything existing outside it. In Edwards' *A Personal Narrative,* a self anterior to the work journeys through the length of the work to find itself. The work is not wholly an instrumentality, as it is for Abel James and for Vaughan. Indeed, in the course of Edwards' search, the instrument becomes an end. Edwards becomes a searcher, a man defined by the very progress he has set out upon. He lives the life of his means to discover his life, self and work becoming, in the progress of the work, coextensive. But self and work do not begin so, and the resulting difference between where Edwards begins and where he ends allows for a mystification impossible in the Franklin who begins and ends in the same place.

To some extent this is because all endings tend to become theological. As Frank Kermode has explained so well, they provide teleologgies for events which, read sequentially, are experienced in a far different way. The course of events is recreated, the substantiality of any particular destroyed by the structuralization of the final cause in which it is dissolved. But in Edwards, the difficulty is compounded because the progress toward a telos is his subject. Precisely the discrepancy between first and second readings, as it were, is at issue:

> My affections seemed to be lively and easily moved, and I seemed to be in my element when engaged in religious duties. And I am ready to think, many are deceived with such affections, and such a kind of delight as I then had in religion, and mistake it for grace.

One senses, here, an immersion in the particularity of events, in the search itself, rather than in its goal, so that it is all the more poignant when what the text itself leads us to be interested in observing is taken away as unworthy of interest. The work fades from view. The unity achieved is projected beyond it. The progress toward unity creates the illusion that more is united than really is. Before the work is the self; at its end is the self at one with its world. Forgotten is the fact that the self's world is only the work, the only world Franklin ever admits. The self becomes a typological self, the work "symbolic." Language as words becomes language as the Word. The community that language began by consolidating is dissolved into a visionary unity transcending community, transcending writing, destroying the stability of the very rhetoric from which Franklin will not let us extricate him.

Franklin stands opposed to Edwards, then, not because he is a neoclassical denier of self and Edwards a romantic explorer of it, but because he refuses even to admit a self discontinuous with his denials or explorations and so obviates the very terms which Edwards finds so problematic. Indeed, Franklin opposes neoclassicism equally with romanticism, as a look at a true neoclassical autobiography will make clear. No such American work of quality comparable to Franklin's or Edwards' exists, but Gibbon's *Autobiography,* written at very nearly the same time as Franklin's, should serve just as well.

In Gibbon, too, we find discontinuity, though of a somewhat more difficult sort to get at. Gibbon, as well as Edwards, seeks unity. He would explain himself as a man like other men. But rationalist, child of the Enlightenment that he is, he cannot combine what is peculiar to him and general to humanity in the typological mode of an Edwards. Presumably, he would proceed to write on the basis of what he shares with us all: "A lively desire of knowing and of recording our ancestors so generally prevails, that it must depend on the influence of some common principle in the minds of men." But such a procedure denies the very individuality he wishes to integrate with "common principle":

> I shall not expatiate more minutely on my economical affairs which cannot be instructive or amusing to the reader. It is a rule of prudence, as well as of politeness, to reserve such confidence for the ear of a private friend, without exposing our situation to the envy or pity of strangers. . . . Yet I may believe and even assert that in circumstances more indigent or more wealthy, I should never have accomplished the task, or acquired the fame, of an historian; that my spirit would have been broken by poverty and contempt; and that my industry might have been relaxed in the labour and luxury of a superfluous fortune. Few works of merit and importance have been executed either in a garret or a palace. A gentleman, possessed of leisure and independence, of books and talents, may be encouraged to write by the distant prospect of honor and reward: but wretched is the author, and wretched will be the work, where daily diligence is stimulated by daily hunger.

Unity, here, is possible only at the level of the norm, the abstract, even the statistical average. Only by maintaining himself there can Gibbon succeed, and he must, as a result, keep out by conscious effort such portions of his life as are of purely personal concern. The result is a gap between self and world and a work that fills the gap, but fills it by denying such parts of Gibbon or his world as are not normalizable. The rhetoric of Gibbon's *Autobiography* is a rhetoric of exclusion. It is never in danger of mystification, for what lies beyond it is held always in view. But it is in constant danger of trivializing itself and can never be an epic. Self and work neither begin together nor end together, but *extend* together in a middle which exists by virtue of its place between a beginning and an end that are never, as they are in Franklin, obliterated. To use the term we have already introduced, if the mode of Franklin is "re-collective," the mode of Gibbon is retrospective. It exists in the context of a priority to which it must always refer. The lessons in it are all, already, learned. The work is past, or, at least, refers to incidents in the past, and it is, as a result, a constant reminder of limitation, of incomplete-ness, of the failure to fulfill all that its author desires. Franklin's recollection, on the other hand, is a constant success. It exists in a continuous present that can never admit of limitation. Neither pointing beyond his life nor a mere record of it, it is his life itself, at once the fulfillment of what, accordingly, may never even become his desire.

WRITING

Franklin's way of indicating this, as we have seen, is to refer to his life quite overtly in literary terms, calling it, as in the passage quoted above, his "Writing." As numer-ous critics have noted, this is, in fact, one of his most strik-ing stylistic habits. The regrettable actions of his youth he terms "errata." The epitaph he composes for himself re-fers to his body as "the Cover of an old Book" with "Its contents torn out." Even a repetition of his life, were he to be given the chance of it, would be but a "second Edi-tion to correct some Faults of the first." As we now can see, however, more than metaphor is involved here, more than the employment of a "natural figure of speech for the former printer," as the Yale editors put it. Franklin means quite literally what he says, and in particular, his insis-tence on the printed nature of his *Autobiography,* on the fact that it is not a story told but one inscribed on paper, more than confirming the epic unity of life and work for which we have been contending points to the difference of Franklin's epic, its particularly American way of uniting terms united quite otherwise in Homer. For by giving us his life in writing, to continue quoting,

> I shall indulge the Inclination so natural in old Men, to be talking of themselves and their own past Actions, and I shall indulge it, without being troublesome to others who thro' respect to Age might think themselves oblig'd to give me a Hearing, since this may be read or not as any one pleases.

Franklin distinguishes writing from speaking, here, for the openness of choice it provides, the freedom of "as any one pleases." Thus although we have been arguing that the au-thor and audience of the *Autobiography* are continuous, yet the dependence of that continuity on deliberation needs to be insisted upon. The immediacy of Homer's oralness, its necessity—prior to compulsion, it is true, but precisely, therefore, beyond either authorial or audience control—is casually, perhaps, but categorically rejected. Franklin's work *is* a work after all, to modify somewhat our earlier position. And yet it remains a work which is still no object, a work, rather, because it is made. Never natural, it is sustained by the decision to write it and the decision to read it which Homer's song, rather performed than made, simply cannot admit.

Such a work, it remains true to say, does not at all intrude itself *between* writer and reader. It does not admit the pos-sibility of alienation, say, that independent of it stands an-

other world which is its boundary, which, even initially, defines it as a romantic inside or a neoclassical outside, as something that may be compared with an objective or sub-jective reality not included in it. But in a purely positive way, excluding nothing, Franklin's work is founded on choice. The community it embraces is the product of willed association. It is a community of readers and writ-ers freely assenting to each other, bound by a sort of secu-lar covenant differing from theological or romantic cove-nants because not compelled by truth, and differing from neoclassical social "contracts" because not based upon natural law. At its heart is not even rational self-interest, as the Enlightenment theorists of contracts would have it, but nonrational choice, devotion based on a purely arbi-trary predilection, "as any one pleases." To put this in yet a different way, to triangulate Franklin's position on yet another plane, though he is not innocent in the manner of traditional oral epics, he is not self-conscious in the man-ner of traditional written ones, either. Franklin's epic is in-nocent and self-conscious both. Neither assuming the con-tinuity of oral communities nor attempting in writing to restore to a community the continuity it has forever lost, Franklin's *Autobiography* is created by a community which thereby creates itself. Franklin's world is wholly rhetorical, as we have said. But as we may now see, neither the Homeric extension of rhetoric to the status of what we might call the natural, nor yet the Virgilian and Miltonic restriction of it to the mechanics of mere suasion, will do for Franklin. Franklin's rhetoric is sufficient unto itself, and it embraces a community, accordingly, neither as-sumed nor cajoled but agreed upon, a community which, reading itself, makes itself.

Let us consider, by way of comparison, three great invoca-tions in the three sorts of epic we are discussing. "Sing, O goddess," Homer begins, simply, directly, the author in perfect agreement with an audience he need not even, therefore, address. And yet, properly speaking, no author and no audience exist in Homer, for the collective memory in which they proclaim themselves, invited but uncon-trolled, has been exalted above the level of culture to be-come the voice of the god. Choice, here, can never be more than a secondary phenomenon, a sort of resistance to or acquiescence in inevitability. Assent, so complete as to have suffered, as it were, a repression by generalization, appears in such places to which it manages a return as but a bowing to destiny. The single exception, perhaps the only chink in Homer's armor, will be recalled as proving the rule, the objection of Thersites to Agamemnon's con-duct of Greek affairs. For Thersites' animadversions are reiterated later by Achilles, by the always reliable Nestor, and by Odysseus, who rebukes Thersites by beating him. Yet Thersites, speaking "idly and in no orderly wise," as-serts himself while all others, even the heroes, "sat them down and were stayed in their places." Speaking not, as does, say, Achilles, the mere division of Greek culture against itself, he speaks outside the culture altogether and as refusing to authorize it. He is the one example in the *Iliad* of a man who "pleases"—merely because he is, self-ishly, arbitrarily, *not* pleased—not to listen to Agamem-non, and Homer can understand him but as unnatural, "ill favored . . . bandy-legged . . . lame . . . warpen." The ugly violence in Homer, lurking beneath the heroic violence, surfaces in Thersites' beating, the negation of enemy by conqueror, the assimilation of Trojan to Greek culture that is at bottom the absolute refusal to admit of difference. The potential tyranny of "good order," the coercion necessary if all are to be "stayed in their places," emerges, a denial of culture by promoting it to nature, where difference is a meaningless term.

On the other hand, "Of Arms and the Man I Sing. . . . Help me, O Muse," writes Virgil. As Lukács has noted, only a memory of Homer's continuity is present in the *Aeneid,* and this is implicit already in the necessity Virgil finds of writing what Homer did, indeed, "sing." For the "voice" of the *Aeneid* is not the Muse's but Virgil's who in invoking the Muse's assistance would, though but a man, yet claim a god's power. Authorship, as we move from Homer to Virgil, has become a problem, a burden. It is evident biographically in Virgil's dissatisfaction with his epic and in the epic itself, as it strains after an authority it can never quite achieve. The labor of the *Aeneid* is a labor of justification, of aligning what is felt as an ultimately irreconcilable difference. Less direct, perhaps, than Milton's attempt to justify the ways of God to man, it is an attempt to justify the ways of man, Roman ways, *as* God's. Culture is precisely *not* nature, here, and choice, threatening to remind us of this, is so threatening that it must be denied even Homer's secondary operation. Heroes are not allowed even to seem to decide, but ask the gods in advance what has been decided for them. The readers, upon whose assent culture's elevation to nature depends, must be persuaded to deny themselves. This is why, in fact, the absence of direct appeal to the reader in Virgil's invocation is something other than the similar absence in Homer. For while Homer as it were honestly takes his audience for granted, Virgil attempts to make his audience take itself for granted. Rhetoric has become propaganda, the criticism traditionally offered against the *Aeneid,* and with reason.

How different from both Homer and Virgil is Franklin's "Dear Son." For however trivial the words may seem, they constitute as genuinely epic an invocation as either of the two more heroic openings we have discussed. What is invoked in an epic is its sustaining force, the source of its truth, and Franklin's readership is precisely such a source, though sustaining the *Autobiography* as much by its limits as by its extent. The audience overleaped in Homer and denied in Virgil is given full play. Instead of the god we have a man. In place of vision we have social exchange. Presenting the *Autobiography* as a letter, Franklin assures that the experience he relates will remain never more than a cultural transaction.

Of course the manifest fictiveness of the letter form, the fact that Franklin is not "really" writing to his son, needs to be considered. Yet this is no more than any other fiction of the *Autobiography* presupposes a nature on which the *Autobiography,* because a fictionalization of it, thereby covertly depends. For what is fictionalized is not, in fact, reality, but the work itself, the "real" letters which, as we have discussed, are included within the work. "Dear Son," accordingly, but exposes more clearly the *Autobiography*'s status as its own reality. It is part of the *Autobiogra-*

phy's epic rhetoric. Indeed, the presence of both real *and* fictive letters is but a more striking example of what we called earlier the *Autobiography*'s originality. An epic which does not imitate prior epics, it rather stands in for them, as in this case by its use of a conventional invocation whose conventionality is derived from itself. In the *Autobiography* the major problem of composing an epic in modern times is thus solved. The fall of epic discourse into conventionality is internalized. The fate of the *Iliad,* its socialization, which, after all, is what enabled us to see its invocation as a mystification in the first place, is precluded because accepted from the start. The *Autobiography* becomes the foundation of a new literature forever free of the myth of a fall. Or, rather, the literature proceeding from the *Autobiography* is fallen from a union of man with men instead of the gods. Its paradise is the wholly rhetorical one of writer and readers in agreement, of a culture of perfect assent. (pp. 3-21)

> *Kenneth Dauber, "Benjamin Franklin and the Idea of Authorship," in his* The Idea of Authorship in America: Democratic Poetics from Franklin to Melville, *The University of Wisconsin Press, 1990, pp. 3-38.*

FURTHER READING

Biography

Aldridge, Alfred Owen. *Benjamin Franklin: Philosopher and Man.* Philadelphia: J. B. Lippincott Co., 1965, 438 p.
    Reveals "Franklin as a man first and as a universal genius second."

Clark, Ronald W. *Benjamin Franklin: A Biography.* New York: Random House, 1983, 530 p.
    Recent biography of Franklin.

Parton, James. *Life and Times of Benjamin Franklin.* 2 vols. New York: Mason Brothers, 1864.
    Standard Franklin biography for more than a century.

Sainte-Beuve, C. A. "Benjamin Franklin (1704-1790)." In his *Portraits of the Eighteenth Century: Historic and Literary,* pp. 311-75. New York: G. P. Putnam's Sons, 1905.
    Discussion of Franklin's life by the foremost French literary critic of the nineteenth century.

Van Doren, Carl. *Benjamin Franklin.* New York: Viking Press, 1938, 788 p.
    Premier twentieth-century biography of Franklin.

Criticism

Aldridge, Alfred Owen. "Benjamin Franklin and Philosophical Necessity." *Modern Language Quarterly* 12, No. 3 (September 1951): 292-309.
    Comparative analysis of Franklin's *A Dissertation on Liberty and Necessity, Pleasure and Pain* and William Wollaston's *The Religion of Nature Delineated.*

———. "Form and Substance in Franklin's *Autobiography.*"

In *Essays on American Literature in Honor of Jay B. Hubbell,* edited by Clarence Gohdes, pp. 47-62. Durham, N. C.: Duke University Press, 1967.

> Examines the literary merit and influence of Franklin's *Autobiography,* claiming that its value is "psychological rather than artistic."

Baender, Paul. "The Basis of Franklin's Duplicative Satires." *American Literature* XXXII (November 1960): 267-79.

> Explores Franklin's method of persuasion in his political satires "Exporting of Felons to the Colonies," "An Edict by the King of Prussia," and "On the Slave Trade."

Conkin, Paul K. "Benjamin Franklin: Science and Morals." In his *Puritans and Pragmatists: Eight Eminent American Thinkers,* pp. 73-108. New York: Dodd, Mead & Co., 1968.

> Investigates the religious, scientific, and ethical thought of Franklin, describing him as a product of the Enlightenment.

Dawson, Hugh J. "Fathers and Sons: Franklin's 'Memoirs' as Myth and Metaphor." *Early American Literature* XIV, No. 3 (Winter 1979-80): 269-92.

> Argues that the "discovery of identity" in terms of the father-son relationship gives Franklin's *Autobiography* its "coherence and special meaning."

Ensor, Allison. "The Downfall of Poor Richard: Benjamin Franklin as Seen by Hawthorne, Melville, and Mark Twain." *Mark Twain Journal* XVII, No. 3 (Winter 1974-75): 14-18.

> Assesses the strong, negative perception of Franklin among many nineteenth-century writers.

Gallagher, Edward J. "The Rhetorical Strategy of Franklin's *Way to Wealth.*" *Eighteenth-Century Studies* 6, No. 4 (Summer 1973): 475-85.

> Claims that Franklin's *Way to Wealth* is a prime example of his rhetorical skill because of the subtlety of its didacticism.

Griffith, John. "The Rhetoric of Franklin's *Autobiography.*" *Criticism: A Quarterly for Literature and the Arts* 13 (Winter 1971): 77-94.

> Asserts that, despite certain stylistic shortcomings, the *Autobiography* is a classic work of literature.

Ketcham, Ralph L. "Benjamin Franklin: *Autobiography.*" In *Landmarks of American Writing,* edited by Hennig Cohen, pp. 21-32. New York: Basic Books, 1969.

> Stresses the importance of the *Autobiography* in shaping the American national character.

More, Paul Elmer. "Benjamin Franklin." In his *Shelburne Essays, Fourth Series,* pp. 129-55. New York: Knickerbocker Press, G. P. Putnam's Sons, 1911.

> Describes Franklin's intellect as "enormously energetic, but directed to practical rather than literary ends."

Sanford, Charles L. "An American *Pilgrim's Progress.*" *American Quarterly* VI, No. 4 (Winter 1954): 297-310.

> Examines affinities between Franklin's *Autobiography* and John Bunyan's seventeenth-century Puritan allegory.

Sayre, Robert F. "Benjamin Franklin and American Autobiography." In his *The Examined Self: Benjamin Franklin, Henry Adams, Henry James,* pp. 3-43. Princeton, N. J.: Princeton University Press, 1964.

> Discusses Franklin's *Autobiography,* especially as a precursor of the genre in American literature.

Spiller, Robert E. "Franklin on the Art of Being Human." *Proceedings of the American Philosophical Society* 100, No. 4 (31 August 1956): 304-15.

> Argues the relative merits of Franklin's pragmatic humanism.

Stourzh, Gerald. *Benjamin Franklin and American Foreign Policy.* Chicago: University of Chicago Press, 1954, 335 p.

> Analysis of Franklin's approach to international politics.

Van Gastel, Ada. "Franklin and Freud: Love in the *Autobiography.*" *Early American Literature* 25, No. 2 (1990): 168-82.

> A Freudian-feminist analysis of Franklin's *Autobiography* which contends that the literary persona Franklin created "exemplifies modern man in his acts of sublimation."

Patrick Henry

1736-1799

American orator and statesman.

INTRODUCTION

Renowned for his skills as an orator, Henry was the foremost critic of British policy in eighteenth-century colonial America. He amassed widespread public support both for himself, politically, and for American independence, earning the designation "Trumpet of the Revolution." Elected in 1776 to his first of five two-year terms as Governor of Virginia, he regained national political prominence in the years following the war, leading opposition to the proposed federal constitution. While Henry's most famous orations were not transcribed, he was afforded a legacy in American lore with the publication of William Wirt's adulatory biography *Sketches in the Life and Character of Patrick Henry* (1817), which offers re-creations of the speeches based largely on reminiscences Wirt solicited from Henry's acquaintances. Despite the lack of an authoritative source to substantiate Wirt's composition, there was near-unanimous agreement among his contemporaries that Henry was a remarkably passionate and eloquent speaker. Scholar M. E. Bradford has thus asserted that Henry was "*the* characteristic American spokesman during the Revolution" and that he "*made* a revolution, though he did not write about one."

Henry was born and raised in Hanover County, Virginia. His father, a Scottish immigrant who had become moderately wealthy both through speculation and marriage, was also a community leader, acting as a county judge and as a vestryman in the local Anglican church. Although Henry received little formal education, he is believed to have read Roman classics by Homer, Cicero, and Livy. After attempts at farming and operating a general store, he turned to an informal study of law in 1760, and was eventually admitted to the bar, principally on the basis of his argumentative skill. He first gained fame in the Parsons' Cause case of 1763, successfully arguing the state's case against a clergyman's claim for remuneration. Henry was elected in 1765 to the Virginia House of Burgesses, where he immediately caused a sensation by leading vehement opposition to the newly imposed British Stamp Act. One of the first Colonial leaders to advocate armed resistance to British rule, Henry was elected to represent Virginia in the First Continental Congress at Philadelphia in 1774; addressing the delegates there, he proclaimed, "I am not a Virginian, but an American." He reached the apex of his stance against British rule in his famous "Liberty or Death" speech, delivered in March 1775. The following year, Henry was elected to his first term as governor of Virginia, replacing his longtime British adversary, Lord Dunmore. After declining nomination to the 1787 Phila-

delphia Constitutional Congress—of which he remarked, "I smell a rat"—, Henry led opposition to the proposed federal constitution. Following its eventual passage, he returned to the private practice of law until his retirement in 1794. Becoming increasingly reactionary in his politics, Henry opposed the liberal Republican Party of Thomas Jefferson, favoring the conservative Federalist Party against which he had earlier fought. In his later years he declined ambassadorships to Spain and France as well as the offices of Secretary of State and Chief Justice of the Supreme Court. Henry was coaxed out of retirement by public election to the Virginian General Assembly in 1799, but died before beginning his term.

Excluding the transcripts of his speeches in the Virginia Convention of 1788 and his arguments in the British Debts case of 1791, what is known of Henry's work is largely attributed to the reconstructions of William Wirt. He kept no diary and neither the colonial courts nor the Burgesses kept a comprehensive log of daily proceedings. Wirt expressed his frustration at the lack of source material in 1815: "It is all speaking, speaking, speaking. 'Tis true he could talk:—'Gods! how he *could* talk!' but there is no acting 'the while.' . . . And then, to make the matter worse, from 1763 to 1789 . . . not one of his speeches lives in print, writing or memory." Accepted texts of Henry's most famous speeches are often credited more to Wirt than Henry. The so-called "Caesar-Brutus" speech concerns the fifth of six resolutions debated in the House of Burgesses regarding the newly imposed Stamp Act. The oration compares King George III to the Roman statesman who warns darkly of Caesar's fate, and concludes, according to popular legend, with the words "If this be treason, make the most of it!" While the authorship of the pro-liberty Virginia Resolves, as the resolutions were called, has been attributed to Henry in varying degrees, critics have questioned the amount of original thought present in Henry's version. Although the fifth motion, which claimed that the colonists were not subject to any taxation other than that imposed by the Burgesses, passed on the initial vote, it was later expunged. However, the complete set of resolutions were published by various papers throughout the colonies, and Henry—whom the British claimed "set fire to a continent"—became recognized as a leader of the American cause. Another renowned oration, his "Liberty or Death" speech at the Virginia Convention of 1775, advocated preparations for armed resistance to the British in order to put the colony in a "position of defense." Wirt has been accused of taking many liberties in his reconstruction, and the words are almost universally viewed as not Henry's alone; but the speech has endured amid continued criticism, and, as scholar Charles L. Cohen has noted, "it stands among the most celebrated American utterances, an oratorical classic."

Henry's skills as a speaker have been widely acknowledged. In his poem *The Age of Bronze,* Lord Byron called Henry "the forest born Demosthenes / Whose thunder shook the Philip of the seas." Thomas Jefferson, upon first hearing him, remarked, "He appeared to me to speak as Homer wrote." However, doubts have persisted regarding Henry's intellectual ability. In a reminiscence to William Wirt, Jefferson observed that Henry "could not draw a bill on the most simple subject which would bear legal criticism, or even the ordinary criticism which looks to correctness of style and idea: for indeed there was no accuracy of idea in his head." But, according to contemporary scholar Lois J. Einhorn, Henry was undaunted by such negative evaluations for he "flatly asserted that reason had little place in the discussion of political issues." Irving Brant has likewise noted that "Henry's rule of conduct was simple: always be on the popular side and never too far ahead." Instead of appeals to logic or reason, "The secret of [Henry's] eloquence," wrote Jared Sparks, "unquestionably rested in his power of touching the springs of passion and feeling."

PRINCIPAL WORKS

"The Parsons' Cause" (oration) 1763
" 'Caesar-Brutus' Speech" (oration) 1765
"Virginia Resolves" (manifesto) 1765

" 'Liberty or Death' Speech" (oration) 1775
"Speeches concerning the Proposed Federal Constitution" (orations) 1788
"The British Debts Case" (oration) 1791

CRITICISM

Patrick Henry (speech date 1788)

[*The following excerpts are taken from the debates of the Virginia Convention of 1788 concerning ratification of the proposed national constitution. Henry vehemently opposed its passage, objecting that the Constitutional Convention had no right to claim "We the people," that a national government would curtail the liberty of its citizens, and additionally, that the document lacked a bill of rights.*]

Mr. Chairman, the public mind, as well as my own, is extremely uneasy at the proposed change of government. Give me leave to form one of the number of those who wish to be thoroughly acquainted with the reasons of this perilous and uneasy situation, and why we are brought hither to decide on this great national question. I consider myself as the servant of the people of this commonwealth, as a sentinel over their rights, liberty, and happiness. I represent their feelings when I say that they are exceedingly uneasy at being brought from that state of full security, which they enjoyed, to the present delusive appearance of things. A year ago, the minds of our citizens were at perfect repose. Before the meeting of the late federal Convention at Philadelphia, a general peace and a universal tranquillity prevailed in this country; but, since that period, they are exceedingly uneasy and disquieted. When I wished for an appointment to this Convention, my mind was extremely agitated for the situation of public affairs. I conceived the republic to be in extreme danger. If our situation be thus uneasy, whence has arisen this fearful jeopardy? It arises from this fatal system; it arises from a proposal to change our government—a proposal that goes to the utter annihilation of the most solemn engagements of the states—a proposal of establishing nine states into a confederacy, to the eventual exclusion of four states. It goes to the annihilation of those solemn treaties we have formed with foreign nations.

The present circumstances of France—the good offices rendered us by that kingdom—require our most faithful and most punctual adherence to our treaty with her. We are in alliance with the Spaniards, the Dutch, the Prussians; those treaties bound us as thirteen states confederated together. Yet here is a proposal to sever that confederacy. Is it possible that we shall abandon all our treaties and national engagements?—and for what? I expected to hear the reasons for an event so unexpected to my mind and many others. Was our civil polity, or public justice, endangered or sapped? Was the real existence of the country threatened, or was this preceded by a mournful progression of events? This proposal of altering our federal government is of a most alarming nature! Make the best of this new government—say it is composed by any thing but inspiration—you ought to be extremely cautious, watchful, jealous of your liberty; for, instead of securing your rights, you may lose them forever. If a wrong step be now made, the republic may be lost forever. If this new government will not come up to the expectation of the people, and they shall be disappointed, their liberty will be lost, and tyranny must and will arise. I repeat it again, and I beg gentlemen to consider, that a wrong step, made now, will plunge us into misery, and our republic will be lost. It will be necessary for this Convention to have a faithful historical detail of the facts that preceded the session of the federal Convention, and the reasons that actuated its members in proposing an entire alteration of government, and to demonstrate the dangers that awaited us. If they were of such awful magnitude as to warrant a proposal so extremely perilous as this, I must assert, that this Convention has an absolute right to a thorough discovery of every circumstance relative to this great event. And here I would make this inquiry of those worthy characters who composed a part of the late federal Convention. I am sure they were fully impressed with the necessity of forming a great consolidated government, instead of a confederation. That this is a consolidated government is demonstrably clear; and the danger of such a government is, to my mind, very striking. I have the highest veneration for those gentlemen; but, sir, give me leave to demand, What right had they to say, *We, the people?* My political curiosity, exclusive of my anxious solicitude for the public welfare, leads me to ask, Who authorized them to speak the language of, *We, the people,* instead of, *We, the states?* States are the characteristics and the soul of a confederation. If the states be not the agents of this compact, it must be one great, consolidated, national government, of the people of all the states. I have the highest respect for those gentlemen who formed the Convention, and, were some of them not here, I would express some testimonial of esteem for them. America had, on a former occasion, put the utmost confidence in them—a confidence which was well placed; and I am sure, sir, I would give up any thing to them; I would cheerfully confide in them as my representatives. But, sir, on this great occasion, I would demand the cause of their conduct. Even from that illustrious man who saved us by his valor, I would have a reason for his conduct: that liberty which he has given us by his valor, tells me to ask this reason; and sure I am, were he here, he would give us that reason. But there are other gentlemen here, who can give us this information. The people gave them no power to use their name. That they exceeded their power is perfectly clear. It is not mere curiosity that actuates me: I wish to hear the real, actual, existing danger, which should lead us to take those steps, so dangerous in my conception. Disorders have arisen in other parts of America; but here, sir, no dangers, no insurrection or tumult have happened; every thing has been calm and tranquil. But, notwithstanding this, we are wandering on the great ocean of human affairs. I see no landmark to guide us. We are running we know not whither. Difference of opinion has gone to a degree of inflammatory resentment in different parts of the country which has been occasioned by this perilous

innovation. The federal Convention ought to have amended the old system; for this purpose they were solely delegated; the object of their mission extended to no other consideration. You must, therefore, forgive the solicitation of one unworthy member to know what danger could have arisen under the present Confederation, and what are the causes of this proposal to change our government. (pp. 21-3)

. . . . .

Mr. Chairman, it is now confessed that this is a national government. There is not a single federal feature in it. It has been alleged, within these walls, during the debates, to be national and federal, as it suited the arguments of gentlemen.

But now, when we have heard the definition of it, it is purely national. The honorable member was pleased to say that the sword and purse included every thing of consequence. And shall we trust them out of our hands without checks and barriers? The sword and purse are essentially necessary for the government. Every essential requisite must be in Congress. Where are the purse and sword of Virginia? They must go to Congress. What is become of your country? The Virginian government is but a name. It clearly results, from his last argument, that we are to be consolidated. We should be thought unwise indeed to keep two hundred legislators in Virginia, when the government is, in fact, gone to Philadelphia or New York. We are, as a state, to form no part of the government. Where are your checks? The most essential objects of government are to be administered by Congress. How, then, can the state governments be any check upon them? If we are to be a republican government, it will be consolidated, not confederated.

The means, says the gentleman, must be commensurate to the end. How does this apply? All things in common are left with this government. There being an infinitude in the government, there must be an infinitude of means to carry it on. This is a sort of mathematical government that may appear well on paper, but cannot sustain examination, or be safely reduced to practice. The delegation of power to an adequate number of representatives, and an unimpeded reversion of it back to the people, at short periods, form the principal traits of a republican government. The idea of a republican government, in that paper, is something superior to the poor people. The governing persons are the servants of the people. There, the servants are greater than their masters; because it includes infinitude, and infinitude excludes every idea of subordination. In this the creature has destroyed and soared above the creator. For if its powers be infinite, what rights have the people remaining? By that very argument, despotism has made way in all countries where the people unfortunately have been enslaved by it. We are told, the sword and purse are necessary for the national defence. The junction of these, without limitation, in the same hands, is, by logical and mathematical conclusions, the description of despotism.

The reasons adduced here to-day have long ago been advanced in favor of passive obedience and non-resistance. In 1688, the British nation expelled their monarch for attempting to trample on their liberties. The doctrine of divine right and passive obedience was said to be commanded by Heaven—it was inculcated by his minions and adherents. He wanted to possess, without control, the sword and purse. The attempt cost him his crown. This government demands the same powers. I see reason to be more and more alarmed. I fear it will terminate in despotism. As to his objection of the abuse of liberty, it is denied. The political inquiries and promotions of the peasants are a happy circumstance. A foundation of knowledge is a great mark of happiness. When the spirit of inquiry after political discernment goes forth among the lowest of the people, it rejoices my heart. Why such fearful apprehensions? I defy him to show that liberty has been abused. There has been no rebellion here, though there was in Massachusetts. Tell me of any country which has been so long without a rebellion. Distresses have been patiently borne, in this country, which would have produced revolutions in other countries. We strained every nerve to make provisions to pay off our soldiers and officers. They, though not paid, and greatly distressed at the conclusion of the war, magnanimously acquiesced. The depreciation of the circulating currency very much involved many of them, and thousands of other citizens, in absolute ruin; but the same patient fortitude and forbearance marked their conduct. What would the people of England have done in such a situation? They would have resisted the government, and murdered the tyrant. But in this country, no abuse of power has taken place. It is only a general assertion, unsupported, which suggests the contrary. Individual licentiousness will show its baneful consequences in every country, let its government be what it may.

But the honorable gentleman says, responsibility will exist more in this than in the British government. It exists here more in name than any thing else. I need not speak of the executive authority. But consider the two houses—the American Parliament. Are the members of the Senate responsible? They may try themselves, and, if found guilty on impeachment, are to be only removed from office. In England, the greatest characters are brought to the block for their sinister administration. They have a power there, not to dismiss them from office, but from life, for malpractices. The king himself cannot pardon in this case. How does it stand with respect to your lower house? You have but ten. Whatever number may be there, six is a majority. Will your country afford no temptation, no money to corrupt them? Cannot six fat places be found to accommodate them? They may, after the first Congress, take any place. There will be a multiplicity of places. Suppose they corruptly obtain places. Where will you find them, to punish them? At the farthest parts of the Union; in the ten miles square, or within a state where there is a strong hold. What are you to do when these men return from Philadelphia? Two things are to be done. To detect the offender and bring him to punishment. You will find it difficult to do either.

In England, the proceedings are openly transacted. They deliver their opinions freely and openly. They do not fear all Europe. Compare it to this. You cannot detect the guilty. The publication from time to time is merely optional in them. They may prolong the period, or suppress it altogether, under pretence of its being necessary to be kept secret. The yeas and nays will avail nothing. Is the publication daily? It may be a year, or once in a century. I know this would be an unfair construction in the common concerns of life. But it would satisfy the words of the Constitution. It would be some security were it once a year, or even once in two years. When the new election comes on, unless you detect them, what becomes of your responsibility? Will they discover their guilt when they wish to be reëlected? This would suppose them to be not only bad, but foolish men, in pursuit of responsibility. Have you a right to scrutinize into the conduct of your representatives? Can any man, who conceives himself injured, go and demand a sight of their journals? But it will be told that I am suspicious. I am answered, to every question, that they will be good men. In England, they see daily what is doing in Parliament. They will hear from their Parliament in one thirty-ninth part of the time that we shall hear from Congress in this scattered country. Let it be proposed, in England, to lay a poll tax, or enter into any measure, that will injure one part and produce emoluments to another, intelligence will fly quickly as the rays of light to the people. They will instruct their representatives to oppose it, and will petition against it, and get it prevented or redressed instantly. Impeachment follows quickly a violation of duty. Will it be so here? You must detect the offence, and punish the defaulter. How will this be done when you know not the offender, even though he had a previous design to commit the misdemeanor? Your Parliament will consist of sixty-five. Your share will be ten out of the sixty-five. Will they not take shelter, by saying they were in the minority—that the men from New Hampshire and Kentucky outvoted them? Thus will responsibility, that great pillar of a free government, be taken away.

The honorable gentleman [James Madison] wished to try the experiment. Loving his country as he does, he would not surely wish to trust his happiness to an experiment, from which much harm, but no good, may result.

I will speak another time, and will not fatigue the committee now. I think the friends of the opposition ought to make a pause here; for I can see no safety to my country, if you give up this power. (pp. 395-99)

. . . . .

Mr. Chairman, the necessity of a bill of rights appears to me to be greater in this government than ever it was in any government before. I have observed already, that the sense of the European nations, and particularly Great Britain, is against the construction of rights being retained which are not expressly relinquished. I repeat, that all nations have adopted this construction—that all rights not expressly and unequivocally reserved to the people are impliedly and incidentally relinquished to rulers, as necessarily inseparable from the delegated powers. It is so in Great Britain; for every possible right, which is not reserved to the people by some express provision or compact, is within the king's prerogative. It is so in that country which is said to be in such full possession of freedom. It is so in Spain, Germany, and other parts of the world. Let us consider the sentiments which have been entertained by the people of America on this subject. At the revolution, it must be admitted that it was their sense to set down those great rights which ought, in all countries, to be held inviolable and sacred. Virginia did so, we all remember. She made a compact to reserve, expressly, certain rights.

When fortified with full, adequate, and abundant representation, was she satisfied with that representation? No. She most cautiously and guardedly reserved and secured those invaluable, inestimable rights and privileges, which no people, inspired with the least glow of patriotic liberty, ever did, or ever can, abandon. She is called upon now to abandon them, and dissolve that compact which secured them to her. She is called upon to accede to another compact, which most infallibly supersedes and annihilates her present one. Will she do it? This is the question. If you intend to reserve your unalienable rights, you must have the most express stipulation; for, if implication be allowed, you are ousted of those rights. If the people do not think it necessary to reserve them, they will be supposed to be given up. How were the congressional rights defined when the people of America united by a confederacy to defend their liberties and rights against the tyrannical attempts of Great Britain? The states were not then contented with implied reservation. No, Mr. Chairman. It was expressly declared in our Confederation that every right was retained by the states, respectively, which was not given up to the government of the United States. But there is no such thing here. You, therefore, by a natural and unavoidable implication, give up your rights to the general government.

Your own example furnishes an argument against it. If you give up these powers, without a bill of rights, you will exhibit the most absurd thing to mankind that ever the world saw—a government that has abandoned all its powers—the powers of direct taxation, the sword, and the purse. You have disposed of them to Congress, without a bill of rights—without check, limitation, or control. And still you have checks and guards; still you keep barriers—pointed where? Pointed against your weakened, prostrated, enervated state government! You have a bill of rights to defend you against the state government, which is bereaved of all power, and yet you have none against Congress, though in full and exclusive possession of all power! You arm yourselves against the weak and defenceless, and expose yourselves naked to the armed and powerful. Is not this a conduct of unexampled absurdity? What barriers have you to oppose to this most strong, energetic government? To that government you have nothing to oppose. All your defence is given up. This is a real, actual defect. It must strike the mind of every gentleman. When our government was first instituted in Virginia, we declared the common law of England to be in force.

That system of law which has been admired, and has protected us and our ancestors, is excluded by that system. Added to this, we adopted a bill of rights. By this Constitution, some of the best barriers of human rights are thrown away. Is there not an additional reason to have a bill of rights? By the ancient common law, the trial of all facts is decided by a jury of impartial men from the immediate vicinage. This paper speaks of different juries from the common law in criminal cases; and in civil controver-

sies excludes trial by jury altogether. There is, therefore, more occasion for the supplementary check of a bill of rights now than then. Congress, from their general powers, may fully go into business of human legislation. They may legislate, in criminal cases, from treason to the lowest offence—petty larceny. They may define crimes and prescribe punishments. In the definition of crimes, I trust they will be directed by what wise representatives ought to be governed by. But when we come to punishments, no latitude ought to be left, nor dependence put on the virtue of representatives. What says our bill of rights?—"that excessive bail ought not to be required, nor excessive fines imposed, nor cruel and unusual punishments inflicted." Are you not, therefore, now calling on those gentlemen who are to compose Congress, to prescribe trials and define punishments without this control? Will they find sentiments there similar to this bill of rights? You let them loose; you do more—you depart from the genius of your country. That paper tells you that the trial of crimes shall be by jury, and held in the state where the crime shall have been committed. Under this extensive provision, they may proceed in a manner extremely dangerous to liberty: a person accused may be carried from one extremity of the state to another, and be tried, not by an impartial jury of the vicinage, acquainted with his character and the circumstances of the fact, but by a jury unacquainted with both, and who may be biased against him. Is not this sufficient to alarm men? How different is this from the immemorial practice of your British ancestors, and your own! I need not tell you that, by the common law, a number of hundredors were required on a jury, and that afterwards it was sufficient if the jurors came from the same county. With less than this the people of England have never been satisfied. That paper ought to have declared the common law in force.

In this business of legislation, your members of Congress will loose the restriction of not imposing excessive fines, demanding excessive bail, and inflicting cruel and unusual punishments. These are prohibited by your declaration of rights. What has distinguished our ancestors?—That they would not admit of tortures, or cruel and barbarous punishment. But Congress may introduce the practice of the civil law, in preference to that of the common law. They may introduce the practice of France, Spain, and Germany—of torturing, to extort a confession of the crime. They will say that they might as well draw examples from those countries as from Great Britain, and they will tell you that there is such a necessity of strengthening the arm of government, that they must have a criminal equity, and extort confession by torture, in order to punish with still more relentless severity. We are then lost and undone. And can any man think it troublesome, when we can, by a small interference, prevent our rights from being lost? If you will, like the Virginian government, give them knowledge of the extent of the rights retained by the people, and the powers of themselves, they will, if they be honest men, thank you for it. Will they not wish to go on sure grounds? But if you leave them otherwise, they will not know how to proceed; and, being in a state of uncertainty, they will assume rather than give up powers by implication.

A bill of rights may be summed up in a few words. What

do they tell us?—That our rights are reserved. Why not say so? Is it because it will consume too much paper? Gentlemen's reasoning against a bill of rights does not satisfy me. Without saying which has the right side, it remains doubtful. A bill of rights is a favorite thing with the Virginians and the people of the other states likewise. It may be their prejudice, but the government ought to suit their geniuses; otherwise, its operation will be unhappy. A bill of rights, even if its necessity be doubtful, will exclude the possibility of dispute; and, with great submission, I think the best way is to have no dispute. In the present Constitution, they are restrained from issuing general warrants to search suspected places, or seize persons not named, without evidence of the commission of a fact, &c. There was certainly some celestial influence governing those who deliberated on that Constitution; for they have, with the most cautious and enlightened circumspection, guarded those indefeasible rights which ought ever to be held sacred! The officers of Congress may come upon you now, fortified with all the terrors of paramount federal authority. Excisemen may come in multitudes; for the limitation of their numbers no man knows. They may, unless the general government be restrained by a bill of rights, or some similar restriction, go into your cellars and rooms, and search, ransack, and measure, every thing you eat, drink, and wear. They ought to be restrained within proper bounds. With respect to the freedom of the press, I need say nothing; for it is hoped that the gentlemen who shall compose Congress will take care to infringe as little as possible the rights of human nature. This will result from their integrity. They should, from prudence, abstain from violating the rights of their constituents. They are not, however, expressly restrained. But whether they will intermeddle with that palladium of our liberties or not, I leave you to determine. (pp. 445-49)

> *Patrick Henry, in excerpts in* The Debates in the Several State Conventions, on the Adoption of the Federal Constitution, Vol. III, *edited by Jonathan Elliot, revised edition, J. B. Lippincott Company, 1836, pp. 21-3, 395-99, 445-49.*

Thomas Jefferson (letter date 1805)

[*The third president of the United States, Jefferson is best known as a statesman whose belief in natural rights, equality, individual liberties, and self-government found its fullest expression in the American Declaration of Independence. Here, in two August 1805 letters solicited by William Wirt for his biographical study of Henry, Jefferson reflects on his personal knowledge of the Virginia orator.*]

[I] feel every disposition to comply with your request respecting Mr Henry: but I fear to promise from a doubt whether my occupations would permit me the time requisite to recollect and commit to paper the facts respecting him which were within my own knolege; as we had a very familiar intercourse for upwards of 20 years, & ran our course nearly together. During this our political principles being the same, we acted in perfect concert until the year 1781. I witnessed the part he bore in nearly all the great

questions of that period, & perhaps could recollect some anecdotes not uninteresting. He was certainly the man who gave the first impulse to the ball of revolution. Were I to give his character in general terms, it would be of mixed aspect. I think he was the best humored man in society I almost ever knew, and the greatest orator that ever lived. He had a consumate knolege of the human heart, which directing the efforts of his eloquence enabled him to attain a degree of popularity with the people at large never perhaps equalled. His judgment in other matters was inaccurate, in matters of law it was not worth a copper: he was avaritious & rotten hearted. His two great passions were the love of money & of fame: but when these came into competition the former predominated. If the work you propose is not destined to come out speedily I will endeavor to recollect what may be of use to it. (pp. 386-87)

. . . . .

My acquaintance with Mr. Henry commenced in the winter of 1759-60. On my way to the college I passed the Christmas holidays at Colo. Dandridge's in Hanover, to whom Mr. Henry was a near neighbor. During the festivity of the season I met him in society every day, and we became well acquainted, altho' I was much his junior, being then in my 17th. year, & he a married man. The spring following he came to Williamsburg to obtain a license as a lawyer, and he called on me at College. He told me he had been reading law only 6 weeks. Two of the examiners however, Peyton & John Randolph, men of great facility of temper, signed his license with as much reluctance as their dispositions would permit them to shew. Mr. Wythe absolutely refused. Rob. C. Nicholas refused also at first, but, on repeated importunities & promises of future reading, he signed. These facts I had afterwards from the gentlemen themselves, the two Randolphs acknoleging he was very ignorant of law, but that they perceived him to be a young man of genius & did not doubt he would soon qualify himself.

He was, some time after, elected a representative of the county of Hanover, & brought himself into public notice on the following occasion which I think took place in 1762 or a year sooner or later. The gentlemen of this country had at that time become deeply involved in that state of indebtment which has since ended in so general a crush of their fortunes. Robinson, the Speaker, was also Treasurer, an officer always chosen by the assembly. He was an excellent man, liberal, friendly, & rich. He had been drawn in to lend, on his own account, great sums of money to persons of this description, & especially those who were of the assembly. He used freely for this purpose the public money, confiding, for its replacement, in his own means, & the securities he had taken on those loans. About this time however he became sensible that his deficit to the public was become so enormous as that a discovery must soon take place, for as yet the public had no suspicion of it. He devised therefore, with his friends in the assembly, a plan for a public loan office to a certain amount, from which monies might be lent on public account, and on good landed security, to individuals. This was accordingly brought forward in the House of Burgesses, and had it succeeded, the debts due to Robinson on these loans would have been transferred to the public, & his deficit thus compleatly covered. This state of things however was not yet known: but Mr Henry attacked the scheme, on other general grounds, in that style of bold, grand & overwhelming eloquence, for which he became so justly celebrated afterwards. He carried with him all the members of the upper counties, & left a minority composed merely of the aristocracy of the country. From this time his popularity swelled apace; & Robinson dying about 4 years after, his deficit was brought to light, & discovered the true object of the proposition.

The next great occasion on which he signalised himself was that which may be considered as the dawn of the revolution, in March 1774. The British parliament had passed resolutions preparatory to the levying a revenue on the Colonies by a Stamp tax. The Virginia assembly, at their next session, prepared & sent to England very elaborate representations addressed in separate forms to the King, Lords, & Commons, against the right to impose such taxes, the famous Stamp act was however passed in Jan. 1765 and in the session of the Virginia assembly of May following, Mr Henry introduced the celebrated resolutions of that date. These were drawn by George Johnston, a lawyer of the Northern neck, a very able, logical & correct Speaker. Mr Henry moved, & Johnston seconded these resolutions successively. They were opposed by Randolph, Bland, Pendleton, Nicholas, Wythe & all the old members whose influence in the house had, till then, been unbroken. They did it, not from any question of our rights, but on the ground that the same sentiments had been, at their preceding session, expressed in a more conciliatory form, to which the answers were not yet received. But torrents of sublime eloquence from Mr Henry, backed by the solid reasoning of Johnston, prevailed. The last however, & strongest resolution was carried but by a single vote. The debate on it was most bloody. I was then but a student, & was listening at the door of the lobby (for as yet there was no gallery) when Peyton Randolph, after the vote, came out of the house, and said, as he entered the lobby, "by God, I would have given 500 guineas for a single vote." For as this would have divided the house, the vote of Robinson, the Speaker, would have rejected the resolution. Mr Henry left town that evening, & the next morning before the meeting of the House, I saw Peter Randolph, then of the Council, but who had formerly been clerk to the house, for an hour or two at the Clerk's table, searching the old journals for a precedent of a resolution of the house, *erased,* while he was clerk, from the journals, by a subsequent order of the house. Whether he found it, or not, I do not remember; but, when the house met, a motion was made & carried to erase that resolution: and, there being at that day but one printer, & he entirely under the control of the Governor, I do not know that this resolution ever appeared in print. I write this from memory: but the impression made on me, at the time, was such as to fix the facts indelibly in my mind.

I came into the legislature as a Burgess of the county of Albemarle in the winter of 1768. On the accession of L. Botetourt to the government, and about 9 years after Mr Henry had entered on the stage of public life. The

exact conformity of our political opinions strengthened our friendship: and indeed the old leaders of the house being substantially firm, we had not after this any differences of opinion in the H of Burgesses, on matters of principle; tho' sometimes on matters of form. We were dissolved by Ld. Botetourt at our first session, but all were re-elected. There being no division among us, occasions became very rare for any display of Mr. Henry's eloquence. In ordinary business he was a very inefficient member. He could not draw a bill on the most simple subject which would bear legal criticism. Or even the ordinary criticism which looks to correctness of stile & idea: for indeed there was no accuracy of idea in his head. His imagination was copious, poetical, sublime; but vague also. He said the strongest things in the finest language, but without logic, without arrangement, desultorily. This appeared eminently & in a mortifying degree in the first sessions of the first Congress, which met in Sep. 1774. Mr Henry & Richard Henry Lee took at once the lead in that assembly, & by the high style of their eloquence, were, in the first days of the session, looked up to as primi inter pares. A Petition to the king, an Address to the people of Great Britain and a Memorial to the people of British America were agreed to be drawn. Lee, Henry & others were appointed for the first, Lee, Livingston & Jay for the two last. The splendor of their debut occasioned Mr Henry to be designated by his committee to draw the petition to the King, with which they were charged; and Mr Lee was charged with the Address to the people of England. The last was first reported. On reading it, every countenance fell & a dead silence ensued for many minutes. At length it was laid on the table for perusal & consideration till the next day, when first one member & then another arose, & paying some faint compliments to the composition, observed that there were still certain considerations, not expressed in it, which should properly find a place in it. At length Mr Livingston (the Governor of New Jersey) a member of the Committee rose & observed that a friend of his had been sketching what he had thought might be proper for such an address, from which he thought some paragraphs might be advantageously introduced into the draught proposed; and he read an Address which Mr Jay had prepared de bene esse as it were. There was but one sentiment of admiration. The Address was recommitted for amendment, and Mr Jay's draught reported & adopted with scarce an alteration. These facts were stated to me by Mr. Pendleton & Colo. Harrison of our delegation, except that Colo. Harrison ascribed the draught to Govr. Livingston, & were afterwards confirmed to me by Govr. Livingston, and I will presently mention an anecdote confirmative of them from Mr Jay & R. H. Lee themselves.

Mr. Henry's draught of a petition to the King was equally unsuccessful, & was recommitted for amendment. Mr. John Dickinson was added to the committee, & a new draught prepared by him was passed.

The occasion of my learning from Mr. Jay that he was the author of the address to the people of Great Britain requires explanation by a statement of some preceding circumstances. The 2d. session of the 1st. Congress met on their own adjournment in May 1775. Peyton Randolph was their President. In the mean time L. North's concilatory propositions came over, to be laid by the Governors before their legislatures. Ld. Dunmore accordingly called that of Virginia to meet in June. This obliged Peyton Randolph, as Speaker, to return our other old members being at Congress, he pressed me to draw the answer to L. North's propositions. I accordingly did so, & it passed with a little softening of some expressions for which the times were not yet ripe, & wire-drawing & weakening some others to satisfy individuals. I had been appointed to go on to Congress in place of Peyton Randolph, & proceeded immediately, charged with presenting this answer to Congress, as it was the first which had been given, and the tone of it was strong, the members were pleased with it, hoping it would have a good effect on the answers of the other states. A Committee which had been appointed to prepare a Declaration to be published by Genl. Washington on his arrival at the army, having reported one, it was recommitted, & Dickinson & myself added to the Committee. On the adjournment of the house, happening to go out with Govr. Livingston, one of the Committee, I expressed to him my hope he would draw the Declaration. He modestly excused himself, & expressed his wish that I would do it. But urging him with considerable importunity, he at length said "you & I, sir, are but new acquaintances; what can have excited so earnest a desire on your part that I should be the draughtsman? Why, Sir, said I, I have been informed you drew the Address to the people of Great Britain; I think it the first composition in the English language, & therefore am anxious this declaration should be prepared by the same pen. He replied that I might have been misinformed on that subject." A few days after, being in conversation with R. H. Lee in Congress hall, a little before the meeting of the house, Mr Jay observing us, came up, & taking R. H. Lee by a button of the coat, said to him pretty sternly, "I understand, Sir, that you informed this gentleman that the Address to the people of Great Britain, presented to the Committee by me, was drawn by Governor Livingston." The fact was that the Committee having consisted of only Lee, Livingston who was father-in-law of Jay, & Jay himself, & Lee's draught having been rejected & Jay's approved so unequivocally, his suspicions naturally fell on Lee, as author of the report; & rather as they had daily much sparring in Congress, Lee being firm in the revolutionary measures, & Jay hanging heavily on their rear. I immediately stopped Mr Jay, and assured him that tho' I had indeed been so informed, it was not by Mr Lee, whom I had never heard utter a word on the subject.

I found Mr Henry to be a silent, & almost unmedling member in Congress. On the original opening of that body, while general grievances were the topic, he was in his element, & captivated all with his bold and splendid eloquence. But as soon as they came to specific matters, to sober reasoning and solid argumentation, he had the good sense to perceive that his declamation, however excellent in its proper place, had no weight at all in such an assembly as that, of cool-headed, reflecting, judicious men. He ceased therefore in a great measure to take any part in the business. He seemed indeed very tired of the place, & wonderfully relieved when, by appointment of the Virginia Convention to be Colonel of their 1st regiment, he was permitted to leave Congress about the last of July.

How he acquitted himself in his military command will be better known from others. He was relieved from this position again by being appointed Governor, on the first organization of the government. After my services as his successor in the same office, my appointment to Congress in 1783, mission to Europe in 84 & appointment in the new government in 89 kept us so far apart that I had no farther personal knolege of him.

Mr. Henry began his career with very little property. He acted, as I have understood, as bar-keeper in the tavern at Hanover C. H. for some time. He married very young; settled, I believe, at a place called the Roundabout in Louisa, got credit for some little store of merchandize, but very soon failed. From this he turned his views to the law, for the acquisition or practice of which however he was too lazy. Whenever the courts were closed for the winter season, he would make up a party of poor hunters of his neighborhood, would go off with them to the piney woods of Fluvanna, & pass weeks in hunting deer, of which he was passionately fond, sleeping under a tent, before a fire, wearing the same shirt the whole time, & covering all the dirt of his dress with a hunting shirt. He never undertook to draw pleadings, if he could avoid it, or to manage that part of a cause, & very unwillingly engaged but as an assistant, to speak in the cause, and the fee was an indispensable preliminary, observing to the applicant that he kept no accounts, never putting pen to paper, which was true. His powers over a jury were so irresistible, that he received great fees for his services, & had the reputation of being insatiable in money. After about 10 years practice in the County courts, he came to the General court, where however, being totally unqualified for any thing but mere jury causes, he devoted himself to these, & chiefly to the criminal business. From these poor devils, it was always understood that he squeezed exorbitant fees of 50, 100, & 200 L. From this source he made his great profits, and they were said to be great. His other business, exclusive of the criminal, would never, I am sure, pay the expences of his attendance at the court. He now purchased from Mr Loxax the valuable estate on the waters of Smith's river, to which he afterwards removed. The purchase was on long credit, & finally paid in depreciated paper, not worth oak leaves. About the close of the war he engaged in the Yazoo speculation, & bought up a great deal of depreciated paper at 2 & 2/6 in the pound to pay for it. At the close of the war, many of us wished to re-open all accounts which had been paid in depreciated money; & have them settled by the scale of depreciation. But on this he frowned most indignantly; & knowing the general indisposition of the legislature, it was considered hopeless to attempt it with such an opponent at their head as Henry. I believe he never distinguished himself so much as on the similar question of British debts, in the case of **"Jones & Walker."** He had exerted a degree of industry in that case totally foreign to his character, & not only seemed, but had made himself really learned on the subject. Another of the great occasions on which he exhibited examples of eloquence, such as probably had never been exceeded, was on the question of adopting the new constitution in 1788. To this he was most violently opposed, as is well known; &, after it's adoption, he continued hostile to it, expressing, more than any man in the U. S. his thorough contempt and hatred of Genl. Washington. From being the most violent of all anti-federalists however, he was brought over to the new constitution by his Yazoo speculation before mentioned. The Georgia legislature having declared that transaction fraudulent and void, the depreciated paper which he had bought up to pay for the Yazoo purchase was likely to remain on his hands worth nothing. But Hamilton's funding system came most opportunely to his relief, & suddenly raised his paper from 2/6 to 27/6 the pound. Hamilton became now his idol, and abandoning the republican advocates of the constitution, the federal government, on *federal* principles, became his political creed. Genl. Washington flattered him by an appointment to a mission to Spain, which however he declined; and by proposing to him the office of Secretary of state, on the most earnest solicitation of Gen. Henry Lee, who pledged himself that Henry should not accept it. For Genl. Washington knew that he was entirely unqualified for it; & moreover that his self esteem had never suffered him to act as second to any man on earth. I had this fact from information; but that of the mission to Spain is of my own knolege; because, after my retiring from the office of Secretary of State, Genl. Washington passed the papers to Mr. Henry through my hands. Mr. Henry's apostacy, sunk him to nothing, in the estimation of his country. He lost at once all that influence which federalism had hoped, by cajoling him, to transfer with him to itself, and a man who, through a long & active life, had been the idol of his country, beyond any one that ever lived; descended to the grave with less than its indifference, and verified the saying of the philosopher, that no man must be called happy till he is dead. (pp. 387-96)

> *Thomas Jefferson, in a letter to Mr. Wirt of August, 1805, in* The Pennsylvania Magazine of History and Biography, *Vol. XXXIV, No. 4, October, 1910, pp. 387-96.*

William Wirt (essay date 1817)

[*A successful lawyer in post-revolutionary Virginia, Wirt made a name for himself as a prosecutor in the 1807 trial of Aaron Burr, who was charged with treason. He subsequently served as Attorney General for both the State of Virginia and the United States, holding the latter position from 1817 to 1829. Wirt also enjoyed success as a biographer and essayist, publishing a popular series of essays on American society entitled* The Letters of the British Spy *(1803) in addition to his widely read* Sketches of the Life and Character of Patrick Henry *(1817). In the following excerpt from the latter work, Wirt presents what has become the definitive version of Henry's famous "Liberty or Death" speech.*]

The morning of the twenty-third of March was opened, by reading a petition and memorial from the assembly of Jamaica, to the king's most excellent majesty: whereupon it was—"Resolved, That the unfeigned thanks and most grateful acknowledgments of the convention be presented to that very respectable assembly, for the exceeding gener-

ous and affectionate part they have so nobly taken in the unhappy contest between Great Britain and her colonies; and for their truly patriotic endeavours to fix the just claims of the colonists upon the most permanent constitutional principles:—that the assembly be assured, that it is the most ardent wish of this colony, [and they were persuaded of the whole continent of North America,] to see a speedy return of those halcyon days, when we lived a free and happy people."

These proceedings were not adapted to the taste of Mr. Henry; on the contrary, they were "gall and wormwood" to him. The house required to be wrought up to a bolder tone. He rose, therefore, and moved the following manly resolutions:—

"Resolved, That a well-regulated militia, composed of gentlemen and yeomen, is the natural strength and only security of a free government; that such a militia in this colony would for ever render it unnecessary for the mother-country to keep among us, for the purpose of our defence, any standing army of mercenary soldiers, always subversive of the quiet, and dangerous to the liberties of the people, and would obviate the pretext of taxing us for their support.

"That the establishment of such militia is, *at this time,* peculiarly necessary, by the state of our laws, for the protection and defence of the country, some of which are already expired, and others will shortly be so: and that the known remissness of government in calling us together in legislative capacity, renders it too insecure, in this time of danger and distress, to rely that opportunity will be given of renewing them, in general assembly, *or making any provision to secure our inestimable rights and liberties, from those further violations with which they are threatened.*

"Resolved, therefore, *That this colony be immediately put into a state of defence, and that be a committee to prepare a plan for imbodying, arming and disciplining such a number of men, as may be sufficient for that purpose.*"

The alarm which such a proposition must have given to those who had contemplated no resistance of a character more serious than petition, non-importation, and passive fortitude, and who still hung with suppliant tenderness on the skirts of Britain, will be readily conceived by the reflecting reader. The shock was painful. It was almost general. The resolutions were opposed as not only rash in policy, but as harsh and well nigh impious in point of feeling. Some of the warmest patriots of the convention opposed them. Richard Bland, Benjamin Harrison, and Edmund Pendleton, who had so lately drunk of the fountain of patriotism in the continental congress, and Robert C. Nicholas, one of the best as well as ablest men and patriots in the state, resisted them with all their influence and abilities.

They urged the late gracious reception of the congressional petition by the throne. They insisted that national comity, and much more filial respect, demanded the exercise of a more dignified patience. That the sympathies of the parent-country were now on our side. That the friends of American liberty in parliament were still with us, and had, as yet, had no cause to blush for our indiscretion.

Hanover Court House, where Henry began his legal and political career.

That the manufacturing interests of Great Britain, already smarting under the effects of our nonimportation, co-operated powerfully toward our relief. That the sovereign himself had relented, and showed that he looked upon our sufferings with an eye of pity.

"Was this a moment," they asked, "to disgust our friends, to extinguish all the conspiring sympathies which were working in our favour, to turn their friendship into hatred, their pity into revenge? And what was there, they asked, in the situation of the colony, to tempt us to this? Were we a great military people? Were we ready for war? Where were our stores—where were our arms—where our soldiers—where our generals—where our money, the sinews of war? They were nowhere to be found.

"In truth, we were poor—we were naked—we were defenceless. And yet we talk of assuming the front of war! of assuming it, too, against a nation, one of the most formidable in the world? A nation ready and armed at all points! Her navies riding triumphant in every sea; her armies never marching but to certain victory! What was to be the issue of the struggle we were called upon to court? What *could* be the issue, in the comparative circumstances of the two countries, but to yield up *this country* an easy prey to Great Britain, and to convert the illegitimate right which the British parliament now claimed, into a firm and indubitable right, *by conquest!*

"The measure might be brave; but it was the bravery of madmen. It had no pretension to the character of prudence; and as little to the grace of genuine courage. It would be time enough to resort to measures of *despair,* when every well-founded *hope* had entirely vanished."

To this strong view of the subject, supported as it was by the stubborn fact of the well-known helpless condition of the colony, the opponents of these resolutions superadded every topic of persuasion which belongs to the cause.

"The strength and lustre which we have derived from our connexion with Great Britain—the domestic comforts which we had drawn from the same source, and whose value we were now able to estimate by their loss—that ray

of reconciliation which was dawning upon us from the east, and which promised so fair and happy a day:—with this they contrasted the clouds and storms which the measure now proposed was so well calculated to raise—and in which we should not have even the poor consolation of being pitied by the world, since we should have so needlessly and rashly drawn them upon ourselves."

These arguments and topics of persuasion were so well justified by the appearance of things, and were moreover so entirely in unison with that love of ease and quiet which is natural to man, and that disposition to hope for happier times, even under the most forbidding circumstances, that an ordinary man, in Mr. Henry's situation, would have been glad to compound with the displeasure of the house, by being permitted to withdraw his resolutions in silence.

Not so Mr. Henry. His was a spirit fitted to raise the whirlwind, as well as to ride in and direct it. His was that comprehensive view, that unerring prescience, that perfect command over the actions of men, which qualified him not merely to guide, but almost to create the destinies of nations.

He rose at this time with a majesty unusual to him in an exordium, and with all that self-possession by which he was so invariably distinguished. "No man," he said, "thought more highly than he did of the patriotism, as well as abilities, of the very worthy gentlemen who had just addressed the house. But different men often saw the same subject in different lights; and, therefore, he hoped it would not be thought disrespectful to those gentlemen, if, entertaining as he did, opinions of a character very opposite to theirs, he should speak forth *his* sentiments freely, and without reserve.

"This," he said, "was no time for ceremony. The question before this house was one of awful moment to the country. For his own part, he considered it as nothing less than a question of freedom or slavery. And in proportion to the magnitude of the subject, ought to be the freedom of the debate. It was only in this way that they could hope to arrive at truth, and fulfil the great responsibility which they held to God and their country. Should he keep back his opinions at such a time, through fear of giving offence, he should consider himself as guilty of treason toward his country, and of an act of disloyalty toward the Majesty of heaven, which he revered above all earthly kings.

"Mr. President," said he, "it is natural to man to indulge in the illusions of hope. We are apt to shut our eyes against a painful truth—and listen to the song of that siren, till she transforms us into beasts. Is this," he asked, "the part of wise men, engaged in a great and arduous struggle for liberty? Were we disposed to be of the number of those, who having eyes, see not, and having ears, hear not, the things which so nearly concern their temporal salvation? For his part, whatever anguish of spirit it might cost, *he* was willing to know the whole truth; to know the worst, and to provide for it.

"He had," he said, "but one lamp by which his feet were guided; and that was the lamp of experience. He knew of no way of judging of the future but by the past. And judging by the past, he wished to know what there had been in the conduct of the British ministry for the last ten years, to justify those hopes with which gentlemen had been pleased to solace themselves and the house? Is it that insidious smile with which our petition has been lately received? Trust it not, sir; it will prove a snare to your feet. Suffer not yourselves to be betrayed with a kiss.

"Ask yourselves how this gracious reception of our petition comports with those warlike preparations which cover our waters and darken our land. Are fleets and armies necessary to a work of love and reconciliation? Have we shown ourselves so unwilling to be reconciled, that force must be called in to win back our love? Let us not deceive ourselves, sir. These are the implements of war and subjugation—the last arguments to which kings resort.

"I ask gentlemen, sir, what means this martial array, if its purpose be not to force us to submission? Can gentlemen assign any other possible motive for it? Has Great Britain any enemy in this quarter of the world, to call for all this accumulation of navies and armies? No, sir, she has none. They are meant for us: they can be meant for no other. They are sent over to bind and rivet upon us those chains which the British ministry have been so long forging. And what have we to oppose them? Shall we try argument? Sir, we have been trying that for the last ten years. Have we anything new to offer upon the subject? Nothing. We have held the subject up in every light of which it is capable; but it has been all in vain. Shall we resort to entreaty and humble supplication? What terms shall we find, which have not been already exhausted?

"Let us not, I beseech you, sir, deceive ourselves longer. Sir, we have done everything that could be done, to avert the storm which is now coming on. We have petitioned—we have remonstrated—we have supplicated—we have prostrated ourselves before the throne, and have implored its interposition to arrest the tyrannical hands of the ministry and parliament. Our petitions have been slighted; our remonstrances have produced additional violence and insult; our supplications have been disregarded; and we have been spurned, with contempt, from the foot of the throne.

"In vain, after these things, may we indulge the fond hope of peace and reconciliation. *There is no longer any room for hope.* If we wish to be free—if we mean to preserve inviolate those inestimable privileges for which we have been so long contending—if we mean not basely to abandon the noble struggle in which we have been so long engaged, and which we have pledged ourselves never to abandon, until the glorious object of our contest shall be obtained!—we must fight!—I repeat it, sir, we must fight!!! An appeal to arms and to the God of hosts, is all that is left us!

"They tell us, sir," continued Mr. Henry, "that we are weak—unable to cope with so formidable an adversary. But when shall we be stronger. Will it be the next week or the next year? Will it be when we are totally disarmed, and when a British guard shall be stationed in every house? Shall we gather strength by irresolution and inac-

tion? Shall we acquire the means of effectual resistance by lying supinely on our backs, and hugging the delusive

---

Henry's legal performance in the case of John Hook:

The versatility of talent for which Patrick Henry, the American orator and patriot, was distinguished, was happily illustrated in a trial which took place soon after the war of independence. During the distress of the republican army consequent on the invasion of Cornwallis and Phillips, in 1781, Mr. Venable, an army commissary, took two steers for the use of the troops from Mr. Hook, a Scotchman, and a man of wealth, who was suspected of being unfriendly to the American cause. The act had not been strictly legal, and on the establishment of peace, Hook, under the advice of Cowan, a gentleman of some distinction in the law, thought proper to bring an action of trespass against Mr. Venable, in the District Court of New London. Mr. Henry appeared for the defendant, and is said to have conducted himself in a manner much to the enjoyment of his hearers, the unfortunate Hook of course excepted. After Mr. Henry became animated in the cause, he appeared to have complete control over the passions of his audience: at one time he excited their indignation against Hook; vengeance was visible in every countenance: again, when he chose to relax and ridicule him, the whole audience was in a roar of laughter. He painted the distress of the American army, exposed almost naked to the rigor of a winter's sky, and marking the frozen ground over which they marched with the blood of their unshod feet. "Where was the man," he said, "who had an American heart in his bosom, who would not have thrown open his fields, his barns, his cellars, the doors of his house, the portals of his breast, to have received with open arms the meanest soldier in that little band of famished patriots? Where is the man? There he stands; but whether the heart of an American beats in his bosom, you, gentlemen, are to judge." He then carried the jury, by the power of his imagination, to the plains around York, the surrender of which had followed shortly after the act complained of. He depicted the surrender in the most glowing and noble colors of his eloquence: the audience saw before their eyes the humiliation and dejection of the British, as they marched out of their trenches; they saw the triumph which lighted up every patriotic face; they heard the shouts of victory, the cry of "Washington and liberty!" as it rung and echoed through the American ranks, and was reverberated from the hills and shores of the neighboring river. "But, hark!" continued Henry; "what notes of discord are these which disturb the general joy, and silence the acclamations of victory? They are the notes of John Hook, hoarsely bawling through the American camp, 'Beef! beef! beef!'"

The court was convulsed with laughter; when Hook, turning to the clerk, said, "Never mind, you mon; wait till Billy Cowan gets up, and he'll show him the la.' But Mr. Cowan was so completely overwhelmed by the torrent which bore upon his client, that when he rose to reply to Mr. Henry, he was scarcely able to make an intelligible or audible remark. The cause was decided almost by acclamation. The jury retired for form sake, and instantly returned with a verdict for the defendant.

Kazlitt Arvine, in his Cyclopædia of Anecdotes of Literature and the Fine Arts, *1851.*

phantom of hope, until our enemy shall have bound us hand and foot? Sir, we are not weak, if we make a proper use of those means which the God of nature hath placed in our power.

"Three millions of people armed in the holy cause of liberty, and in such a country as that which we possess, are invincible by any force which our enemy can send against us. Besides, sir, we shall not fight our battles alone. There is a just God who presides over the destinies of nations, and who will raise up friends to fight our battles for us. The battle, sir, is not to the strong alone; it is to the vigilant, the active, the brave. Besides, sir, we have no election. If we were base enough to desire it, it is now too late to retire from the contest. There is no retreat but in submission and slavery! Our chains are forged. Their clanking may be heard on the plains of Boston! The war is inevitable—and let it come!! I repeat it, sir, let it come!!!

"It is vain, sir, to extenuate the matter. Gentlemen may cry, peace, peace—but there is no peace. The war is actually begun! The next gale that sweeps from the north will bring to our ears the clash of resounding arms! Our brethren are already in the field! Why stand we here idle? What is it that gentlemen wish? What would they have? Is life so dear, or peace so sweet, as to be purchased at the price of chains and slavery? Forbid it, Almighty God!—I know not what course others may take; but as for me," cried he, with both his arms extended aloft, his brows knit, every feature marked with the resolute purpose of his soul, and his voice swelled to its boldest note of exclamation—"give me liberty, or give me death!"

He took his seat. No murmur of applause was heard. The effect was too deep. After the trance of a moment, several members started from their seats. The cry, "to arms!" seemed to quiver on every lip, and gleam from every eye. Richard H. Lee arose and supported Mr. Henry, with his usual spirit and elegance. But his melody was lost amid the agitations of that ocean, which the master-spirit of the storm had lifted up on high. That supernatural voice still sounded in their ears, and shivered along their arteries. They heard, in every pause, the cry of liberty or death. They became impatient of speech, their souls were on fire for action. (pp. 89-95)

> *William Wirt, in his* Sketches of the Life and Character of Patrick Henry, *revised edition, Thomas, Cowperthwait & Co., 1841, 306 p.*

Rev. Dr. Archibald Alexander   (essay date 1850)

[*A widely respected theologian and scholar, Alexander was praised for both his intellect and his skill as an orator. In the following essay, he recalls his encounters with Henry, praising the Virginia rhetorician's eloquence.*]

From my earliest childhood I had been accustomed to hear of the eloquence of Patrick Henry. On this subject there existed but one opinion in the country. The power of his eloquence was felt equally by the learned and the unlearned. No man who ever heard him speak, on any important occasion, could fail to admit his uncommon power over the minds of his hearers. The occasions on which he made his greatest efforts have been recorded by Mr. Wirt, in his Life of Henry. What I propose in this brief article

is to mention only what I observed myself more than half a century ago.

Being then a young man, just entering on a profession in which good speaking was very important, it was natural for me to observe the oratory of celebrated men. I was anxious to ascertain the true secret of their power; or what it was which enabled them to sway the minds of hearers, almost at their will.

In executing a mission from the Synod of Virginia, in the year 1794, I had to pass through the county of Prince Edward, where Mr. Henry then resided. Understanding that he was to appear before the Circuit Court, which met in that county, in defence of three men charged with murder, I determined to seize the opportunity of observing for myself the eloquence of this extraordinary orator.

It was with some difficulty I obtained a seat in front of the bar, where I could have a full view of the speaker, as well as hear him distinctly. But I had to submit to a severe penance in gratifying my curiosity; for the whole day was occupied with the examination of witnesses, in which Mr. Henry was aided by two other lawyers.

In person, Mr. Henry was lean rather than fleshy. He was rather above than below the common height, but had a stoop in the shoulders which prevented him from appearing as tall as he really was. In his moments of animation, he had the habit of straightening his frame, and adding to his apparent stature. He wore a brown wig, which exhibited no indication of any great care in the dressing. Over his shoulders he wore a brown camlet cloak. Under this his clothing was black; something the worse for wear. The expression of his countenance was that of solemnity and deep earnestness. His mind appeared to be always absorbed in what, for the time, occupied his attention. His forehead was high and spacious, and the skin of his face more than usually wrinkled for a man of fifty. His eyes were small and deeply set in his head, but were of a bright blue colour, and twinkled much in their sockets. In short, Mr. Henry's appearance had nothing very remarkable, as he sat at rest. You might readily have taken him for a common planter, who cared very little about his personal appearance. In his manners he was uniformly respectful and courteous. Candles were brought into the court house, when the examination of the witnesses closed; and the judges put it to the option of the bar, whether they would go on with the argument that night or adjourn until the next day. Paul Carrington, jun., the attorney for the state, a man of large size, and uncommon dignity of person and manner, as also an accomplished lawyer, professed his willingness to proceed immediately, while the testimony was fresh in the minds of all. Now for the first time I heard Mr. Henry make any thing of a speech; and though it was short, it satisfied me of one thing, which I had particularly desired to have decided; namely, whether like a player he merely assumed the appearance of feeling. His manner of addressing the court was profoundly respectful. He would be willing to proceed with the trial, but, said he, "My heart is so oppressed with the weight of responsibility which rests upon me, having the lives of three fellow citizens depending, probably, on the exertion which I may be able to make in their behalf, (here he turned to the prisoners behind him,) that I do not feel able to proceed tonight. I hope the court will indulge me, and postpone the trial till the morning." The impression made by these few words was such as I assure myself no one can ever conceive, by seeing them in print. In the countenance, action, and intonation of the speaker, there was expressed such an intensity of feeling, that all my doubts were dispelled; never again did I question whether Henry felt, or only acted a feeling. Indeed, I experienced an instantaneous sympathy with him in the emotions which he expressed; and I have no doubt the same sympathy was felt by every hearer.

As a matter of course the proceedings were deferred till the next morning. I was early at my post; the judges were soon on the bench, and the prisoners at the bar. Mr. Carrington, afterwards Judge Carrington, opened with a clear and dignified speech, and presented the evidence to the jury. Every thing seemed perfectly plain. Two brothers and a brother-in-law met two other persons in pursuit of a slave, supposed to be harboured by the brothers. After some altercation and mutual abuse, one of the brothers, whose name was John Ford, raised a loaded gun which he was carrying, and presenting it to the breast of one of the other pair, shot him dead, in open day. There was no doubt about the fact. Indeed, it was not denied. There had been no other provocation than opprobrious words. It is presumed that the opinion of every juror was made up, from merely hearing the testimony; as Tom Harvey, the principal witness, who was acting as constable on the occasion, appeared to be a respectable man. For the clearer understanding of what follows, it must be observed that the said constable, in order to distinguish him from another of the name, was commonly called 'Butterwood Harvey;' as he lived on Butterwood Creek.

Mr. Henry, it is believed, understanding that the people were on their guard against his faculty of moving the passions and through them influencing the judgment, did not resort to the pathetic, as much as was his usual practice in criminal cases. His main object appeared to be, throughout, to cast discredit on the testimony of Tom Harvey. This he attempted by causing the law respecting riots to be read by one of his assistants. It appeared in evidence, that Tom Harvey had taken upon him to act as constable, without being in commission; and that with a posse of men he had entered the house of one of the Fords in search of the negro, and had put Mrs. Ford, in her husband's absence, into a great terror, while she was in a very delicate condition, near the time of her confinement.

As he descanted on the evidence, he would often turn to Tom Harvey—a large, bold looking man—and with the most sarcastic look would call him by some name of contempt; "this Butterwood Tom Harvey," "this *would-be-constable*," &c. By such expressions, his contempt for the man was communicated to the hearers. I own I felt it gaining on me, in spite of my better judgment; so that before he was done, the impression was strong on my mind that Butterwood Harvey was undeserving of the smallest credit. This impression, however, I found I could counteract, the moment I had time for reflection. The only part of the speech in which he manifested his power of touching the feelings strongly, was where he dwelt on the irruption of the company into Ford's house, in circumstances so perilous to the solitary wife. This appeal to the sensibility of husbands—and he knew that all the jury stood in this relation—was overwhelming. If the verdict could have been rendered immediately after this burst of the pathetic, every man, at least every husband in the house, would have been for rejecting Harvey's testimony; if not for hanging him forthwith. It was fortunate that the illusion of such eloquence is transient, and is soon dissipated by the exercise of sober reason. I confess, however, that nothing which I then heard so convinced me of the advocate's power, as the speech of five minutes, which he made when he requested that the trial might be adjourned till the next day.

In addition to this, it so happened that I heard the last public speech which Mr. Henry ever made. It was delivered at Charlotte, from the portico of the court house, to an assembly in the open air. In the American edition of the *New Edinburgh Encyclopaedia* an account of this speech and its effects is given, so charged with exaggeration as to be grossly incorrect. There is more truth in the statements contained in Mr. Wirt's memoir. In point of fact, the performance had little impression beyond the transient pleasure afforded to the friends of the administration, and the pain inflicted on the Anti-federalists, his former political friends. Mr. Henry came to the place with difficulty, and was plainly destitute of his wonted vigour and commanding power. The speech was nevertheless a noble effort, such as could have proceeded from none but a patriotic heart. In the course of his remarks, Mr. Henry (as is correctly stated by Mr. Wirt) after speaking of Washington at the head of a numerous and well appointed army, exclaimed, "And where is the citizen of America who will dare to lift his hand against the father of his country, to point a weapon at the breast of the man who had so often led them to battle and victory?" An intoxicated man cried, "I could." "No," answered Mr. Henry, rising aloft in all his majesty, and in a voice most solemn and penetrating, "No; you durst not do it; in such a parricidal attempt, the steel would drop from your nerveless arm!"

Mr. Henry was followed by a speaker afterwards noted in our national history; I mean John Randolph of Roanoke; but the aged orator did not remain to witness the debut of his young opponent. Randolph began by saying that he had admired that man more than any on whom the sun had shone, but that now he was constrained to differ from him *toto coelo*. But Randolph was suffering with the hoarseness of a cold, and could scarcely utter an audible sentence. All that is alleged in the Encyclopaedia, about Henry's returning to the platform and replying with extraordinary effect, is pure fabrication. The fact is as above stated: Henry retired to the house, as if unwilling to listen, and requested a friend to report to him any thing which might require an answer. But he made no reply, nor did he again present himself to the people. I was amidst the crowd, standing near to Creed Taylor, then an eminent lawyer, and afterwards a judge; who made remarks to those around him, during the speech, declaring among other things that the old man was in his dotage. It is much to be regretted that a statement so untrue should be perpetuated in a work of such value and celebrity.

Patrick Henry had several sisters, with one of whom, the wife of Colonel Meredith of New Glasgow, I was acquainted. Mrs. Meredith was not only a woman of unfeigned piety, but was in my judgment as eloquent as her brother; nor have I ever met with a lady who equalled her in powers of conversation.

At an early period of my ministry, it became my duty to preach the funeral sermon of Mr. James Hunt, the father of the late Rev. James Hunt, of Montgomery county, Maryland. The death occurred at the house of a son who lived on Stanton river: Mr. Henry's residence, Red Hill, was a few miles distant, on the same river. Having been long a friend of the deceased, Mr. Henry attended the funeral, and remained to dine with the company; on which occasion I was introduced to him by Captain Wm. Craighead, who had been an elder in President Davies's church. These gentlemen had been friends in Hanover, but had not met for many years. The two old gentlemen met with great cordiality, and seemed to have high enjoyment in talking of old times.

On the retrospect of so many years I may be permitted to express my views of the extraordinary effects of Henry's eloquence. The remark is obvious, in application not only to him but to all great orators, that we cannot ascribe these effects merely to their intellectual conceptions, or their cogent reasonings, however great: these conceptions and reasons, when put on paper, often fall dead. They are often inferior to the arguments of men whose utterances have little impression. It has indeed been often said, both of Whitefield and of Henry, that their discourses, when reduced to writing, show poorly by the side of the productions of men who are no orators. Let me illustrate this, by the testimony of one whom I remember as a friend of my youth. General Posey was a revolutionary officer, who was second in command, under Wayne, in the expedition against the Indians; a man of observation and cool judgment. He was in attendance on the debates of that famous convention in which there were so many displays of deliberative eloquence. He assured me, that after the hearing of Patrick Henry's most celebrated speech in that body, he felt himself as fully persuaded that the Constitution if adopted would be our ruin, as of his own existence. Yet subsequent reflection restored his former judgment, and his well considered opinion resumed its place.

The power of Henry's eloquence was due, first, to the greatness of his emotion and passion, accompanied with a versatility which enabled him to assume at once any emotion or passion which was suited to his ends. Not less indispensable, secondly, was a matchless perfection of the organs of expression, including the entire apparatus of voice, intonation, pause, gesture, attitude, and indescribable play of countenance. In no instance did he ever indulge in an expression that was not instantly recognised as nature itself: yet some of his penetrating and subduing tones were absolutely peculiar, and as inimitable as they were indescribable. These were felt by every hearer, in all their force. His mightiest feelings were sometimes indicated and communicated by a long pause, aided by an eloquent aspect, and some significant use of his finger. The sympathy between mind and mind is inexplicable. Where

the channels of communication are open, the faculty of revealing inward passion great, and the expression of it sudden and visible, the effects are extraordinary. Let these shocks of influence be repeated again and again, and all other opinions and ideas are for the moment absorbed or excluded; the whole mind is brought into unison with that of the speaker; and the spell-bound listener, till the cause ceases, is under an entire fascination. Then perhaps the charm ceases, upon reflection, and the infatuated hearer resumes his ordinary state.

Patrick Henry of course owed much to his singular insight into the feelings of the common mind. In great cases, he scanned his jury, and formed his mental estimate; on this basis he founded his appeals to their predilections and character. It is what other advocates do, in a lesser degree. When he knew that there were conscientious or religious men among the jury, he would most solemnly address himself to their sense of right, and would adroitly bring in scriptural citations. If this handle was not offered, he would lay bare the sensibility of patriotism. Thus it was, when he succeeded in rescuing the man who had deliberately shot down a neighbour; who moreover lay under the odious suspicion of being a tory, and who was proved to have refused supplies to a brigade of the American army.

A learned and intelligent gentleman stated to me that he once heard Mr. Henry's defence of a man arraigned for a capital crime. So clear and abundant was the evidence, that my informant was unable to conceive any grounds of defence, especially after the law had been ably placed before the jury by the attorney for the commonwealth. For a long time after Henry began, he never once adverted to the merits of the case or the arguments of the prosecution, but went off into a most captivating and discursive oration on general topics, expressing opinions in perfect accordance with those of his hearers; until having fully succeeded in obliterating every impression of his opponent's speech, he obliquely approached the subject, and as occasion was offered dealt forth strokes which seemed to tell upon the minds of the jury. In this case, it should be added, the force of truth prevailed over the art of the consummate orator. (pp. 205-13)

> *Rev. Dr. Archibald Alexander, "Reminiscences of Patrick Henry," in* The Virginia Historical Register and Literary Notebook, *Vol. 3, No. 2, April, 1850, pp. 205-13.*

Lynchburg *Daily Virginian* (essay date 1859)

[*In the following reprint of an article originally published in the 31 August 1859 edition of the* Daily Virginian, *the unnamed reporter relates a portion of a lecture presented by Hugh Blair Grigsby to the students at the College of William and Mary. Grigsby—a noted scholar and American historian who followed George Washington and John Tyler as chancellor of that school—comments on the influence of classical Roman literature on Henry's thought and speech.*]

It has been common to suppose that Patrick Henry, "the natural orator," as he is properly called, was very slightly, if at all, indebted for his wonderful eloquence to those sources of mental culture which are held in highest esteem as at once the models of taste and the instruments of learning. It seems, however, that this opinion is unfounded, and that the American Demosthenes is no exception to the great law which affirms that "the gods give nothing to men without labor." From an interesting and instructive Oration delivered by Mr. Hugh Blair Grigsby, before the students of William and Mary College, on the 4th of July last, we cite the following statement in reference to the literary style and early classical proficiency of Patrick Henry:

One instance of the application of philology to . . . the history of Virginia is within my own experience and may not be without interest to the students of William and Mary. From a critical examination of the fragments of the speeches and writings of Patrick Henry which have come down to us, and by a careful collation of them with those of his prominent contemporaries, I was convinced that our Patriot Prophet had received a regular and [thorough] training in the Latin classics, and that he had received that training in early life. There was to be seen in his style a *"curiosa felicitas"* and a *"callida junctura,"* a purity and a tact which could not have been the result of chance, or they would have been equally apparent in the works of his rivals; and it was evident, so finely were these characteristics interwoven in the general texture of his style, that he must have studied [the] ancient authors in early life; as such results rarely appear so conspicuously in the productions of those who become acquainted with the classics at a more advanced age. This was the argument of internal evidence—an argument which was satisfactory to me, but which, without an infinitely minute exposition of details that none but a philologist could comprehend, would not be conclusive to others. It would thus be regarded rather as an opinion than a demonstration; and I must therefore, sustain my conclusion, for the benefit of others, from the facts of Henry's early life. His father was a teacher, and a native of Scotland, and he was educated in that country when Latin was taught with substantial skill, but many years before the sun of Greek literature had risen in the Scottish horizon. Now, the Scotch teach Latin at the tenderest age. I am myself of Scottish descent on the maternal side, and was taught by Scottish teachers, and I can hardly remember a time when I could not read Latin, or at least when I was not familiar with the grammar. But the father of Henry was not only a teacher and a Scotchman, but he was an admirable Latin Scholar; for we are told in the diary of Samuel Davies, himself a fine scholar, that the father of Henry was more familiar with his Horace than with his Bible. Hence the conclusion was irresistible that, if the father of Henry taught his pupils the classics, he would, like the rest of his countrymen, teach them early and, as he was proved to have been thoroughly skilled in them, that he would teach them well; and, further, that if he taught the children of other people Latin, he would at the same time teach his own. This was the argument from probability, which I did not need to enhance my own conviction, but which might be necessary to gain the

assent of others. Here, then, was a fact ascertained in the life of Patrick Henry which was not only not known, but which ran counter to the opinions and statements of all his contemporaries and biographers. But was my conclusion true after all? It was strictly true in both respects, that our great orator had learned the Latin classics, and that he had learned them in early life; for in the recently published dairy [sic] of John Adams, under the date of September,

---

Irving Brant on Henry and his adversarial relationship with Jefferson and Madison:

To the task on which his fame is built—incitement to revolution—Patrick Henry brought three superb qualifications: a gift of oratory so powerful in its appeal to the emotions that it swept reason from its seat, a sense of timing so perfect that it made audacity safe and an intense dislike of aristocratic airs and privileges. To his political activities he brought these same attributes plus an ambition which did not aim primarily at office-holding but could only be satisfied by the triumph of his will over the will of others. Had Henry possessed military genius commensurate with his ambition and his power of evoking loyalty, he could conceivably have furnished the American Revolution with a man on horseback. Had he been correspondingly gifted as a constructive statesman, he could have dominated the continent as he did Virginia. In either event American history would have followed a more nationalistic channel. Henry was temperamentally compelled to use his talents to the utmost. The narrow limits of the constructive use to which they could be put, after they had served their purpose of revolutionary incitement, made their actual use mainly destructive.

It was inevitable that Madison and Jefferson, both of whom entered public life as admirers and followers of Patrick Henry, should have found themselves afterward in chronic disagreement with him. The extent to which he ruled the waking hours and troubled the dreams of his Virginia associates is almost inconceivable today. Whatever was attempted, in the perfection of infant republican institutions, the first question had to be: Will Patrick Henry oppose it? And the query as to action usually was: How can we slip it past him?

In 1784, when Madison reported to Jefferson in Paris that the hostility of Henry would block the calling of a state constitutional convention, Jefferson replied, partly in a transparent "figure" cipher: "If one could be obtained I do not know whether it would not do more harm than good. While Mr. Henry lives another bad constitution would be formed and forever on us. What we have to do I think is devotedly to 252.746 for his death." That Madison and Jefferson agreed perfectly in their estimate of Henry at this time is shown by Jefferson's comment three months later: "Your character of the 446 magistrate is precisely agreeable to the idea I had formed of him. I take him to be of unmeasured ambition but that the men he uses are virtuous."

Irving Brant, in his James Madison: The Virginia Revolutionist, *1941.*

1774, we have it from the lips of Henry himself that *before* fifteen he had read Virgil and Livy—a degree of proficiency which, even in this day, except under favorable auspices, is rarely attained at so early an age; for, between the grammar and Livy, as was observed by my venerable friend, Bishop Meade, our old teachers, even those with whom I studied, introduced nearly the entire series of classical authors.

—— *Washington Intelligencer*
(pp. 453-54)

"Appendix I," in Patrick Henry: Practical Revolutionary *by Robert Douthat Meade, J. B. Lippincott Company, 1969, pp. 453-54.*

Judy Hample   (essay date 1972)

[*In the following essay, American scholar Hample argues that while the text of Henry's "Liberty or Death" speech is clearly the work of biographer Wirt, it has played such a large role in subsequent scholarship that it is now "culturally authentic" as Henry's voice calling for revolution.*]

In March of 1775, Virginia delegates convened in Saint John's Church in Richmond to consider the escalating tensions between Great Britain and her colonies. During the fourth session, on March 23rd, Patrick Henry introduced a series of resolutions and supported them with an oration calling for the colonists to arm themselves for war with Great Britain. That fiery speech, culminating in the declaration, "I know not what course others may take, but as for me, give me liberty, or give me death," is traditionally referred to as Henry's **"Liberty or Death" speech.**

The textual authenticity of **"Liberty or Death"** has long plagued scholars. One rhetorical critic used **"Liberty or Death"** as an example of "a vast literature of fictionalized speeches." He further observed that "we shall have to accept most of our speeches of the past as fiction, to be read and studied much as we would a fictionalized biography." If these generalizations are correct, the critic must determine why and how such "fiction" has persisted for two hundred years, why, despite the scholarly evidence, generation after generation of scholars and laymen have sustained the legend of **"Liberty or Death."**

This essay will argue that while **"Liberty or Death"** lacks textual authenticity, it has consistently had cultural authenticity for over two hundred years. At the time Henry addressed the Convention, he was responding to a particular rhetorical situation. The original words and ideas used in that message were never recorded. The first part of this study will show how a text was generated to replace the oral tradition of **"Liberty or Death."** The second part of this study will examine why the text was created and why its influence has continued for two hundred years.

Textual Authenticity

The textual authenticity of **"Liberty or Death"** was first questioned in 1855 by the Virginia historian Hugh Blair Grigsby. In a footnote in *The Virginia Convention of 1776,* Grigsby states that despite his belief that the outline of arguments and expressions is authentic, Wirt's version of **"Liberty or Death"** is apocryphal. The version referred to here is found in William Wirt's biography, *Sketches of the*

Life and Character of Patrick Henry. Wirt's biography was the first life of the Virginia orator and contains the first textual account of the **"Liberty or Death"** oration.

Thirty years after the speech was delivered, Wirt began collecting materials for his biography. The book was not published until 1817, however, because of complications in securing materials. Since Wirt had neither seen nor heard Henry speak, he planned to rely upon newspaper accounts, Henry's private papers, and the recollections of friends to aid him in writing the life of the patriot. As Wirt tried to rely on these sources for information, he discovered several gaps: there were no newspaper accounts of any of Henry's speeches; Henry's private papers contained no manuscripts or notes of any of his orations; and Henry's acquaintances were able to recall little of the verbatim language of Henry's speeches. A number of prominent Virginia gentlemen provided Wirt with information about Henry based upon their personal observations. Among them were Spencer Roane, Edmund Winston, Nathaniel Pope, John Tyler, St. George Tucker, Edward Carrington, Samuel Meredith, and Thomas Jefferson.

Based on the information Wirt received, he concluded that Henry's life was really monotonous because it was all "speaking, speaking, speaking. 'Tis true he *could* talk!" Despite Henry's devotion to public speaking, Wirt determined that between 1763 and 1789—the high point of Henry's career—"not one of his speeches lives in print, writing or memory. All that is told me is that, on such and such an occasion, he made a distinguished speech." Further complicating matters, Wirt's correspondents confirmed that David Robertson's accounts of Henry's speeches in the debates on the Constitution were far inferior to anything which Henry ever delivered. Consequently these speeches would serve as poor models should Wirt decide to create the **"Liberty or Death"** text himself. Wirt ultimately did rely upon Robertson for accounts of the debates on the Constitution and the **British Debts case.**

Discovering that Henry had left no manuscript, that there existed no stenographic recording of the speech, and that Henry's acquaintances were able to recall only scanty portions of **"Liberty or Death,"** Wirt contemplated adopting the plan of Botta, the Italian historian of the Revolution: that of inventing speeches for the Founding Fathers. In correspondence with Tucker, Wirt says, "I have sometimes a notion of trying the plan of Botta . . . but I think with Polybius, that this is making too free with the sanctity of history." Tucker responds to Wirt's idea by telling him that the Botta plan might be effective for recreating some of Henry's orations. However, he continued, it would not suffice in reconstructing **"Liberty or Death"** because the "Spur of the occasion" supplemented "the orator's Talent" so extensively that no one, including Wirt, could adequately recreate the event.

Ultimately Wirt was left no alternative but to rely on the testimony of the best available witnesses and attempt to reconstruct **"Liberty or Death."**

Several of Wirt's correspondents mention aspects of Henry's public speaking style and technique. However, only two accounts to which Wirt had access have survived and offer textual content—those of St. George Tucker and Edmund Randolph. A third account will be examined in this section because of its relationship to the believability of the first two accounts. It should be noted that Wirt may have had access to accounts other than these three and that since his 1817 writing, these materials have been lost. We have already observed, from Wirt's own correspondence, the inadequate and incomplete data with which he had to deal. These accounts give insight into the degree of incompleteness of the textual materials.

Although the extent of his contribution is vague, St. George Tucker's description of the speech appears to have been Wirt's greatest asset in rebuilding the **"Liberty or Death" speech.** In a letter to Tucker, Wirt states, "I have taken almost entirely Mr. Henry's speech in the Convention of '75 from you, as well as your description of its effect on you verbatim." Tucker is the only source Wirt acknowledges as contributing to the speech contained in the biography. The original correspondence in which Tucker described the speech for Wirt has been declared lost by the College of William and Mary Library in which the Tucker papers are located. At the time of Tyler's writing, the letter was available to him. According to Tyler's report of the letter, the substance of Tucker's contribution is the part of the speech beginning with the phrase, "Let us not, I beseech you, sir, deceive ourselves longer" and concluding with "An appeal to arms, and to the God of hosts, is all that is left us." This constitutes only two paragraphs, or less than one-fifth, of the speech as we know it today. By way of clarification, Tucker adds that the occasion impressed him with Henry's powers so much that "in vain should I attempt to give any idea of his speech." In a footnote to the biography, Wirt quotes Tucker's description of the setting when Henry delivered the phrase "we must fight":

> 'Imagine to yourself,' says my correspondent, (judge Tucker,) 'this sentence [We must fight. . . .] delivered with all the calm dignity of Cato, of Utica—imagine to yourself the Roman senate, assembled in the capitol, when it was entered by the profane Gauls, who, at first, were awed by their presence, as if they had entered an assembly of the gods!—imagine that you heard that Cato addressing such a senate—imagine that you saw the handwriting on the wall of Belshazzar's palace—imagine you heard a voice as from heaven uttering the words, *We must fight!* as the doom of fate, and you may have some idea of the speaker, the assembly to whom he addressed himself, and the auditory, of which I was one.'

A second account, Edmund Randolph's description of Henry's **"Liberty or Death"** oration, first appeared in *The Richmond Enquirer* in 1815, and it was later published in Randolph's *History of Virginia.* The only phrase which Randolph attributes to Henry is "peace when there was no peace." Wirt had seen a manuscript of Randolph's *History* and he was a patron of the *Enquirer*.

These accounts, consisting of two paragraphs from Tucker and one phrase from Randolph, constituted Wirt's material for construction of **"Liberty or Death."** In addition, it is necessary to consider a third possible account: one by Nathaniel Pope. In Wirt's estimation, Pope was "indefatigable in collecting information from every quarter," and his sources were "the purest" and "his authority for every incident was given, with the most scrupulous accuracy." In correspondence with Wirt, Pope states: "You have already received in detail the celebrated speech delivered in the Convention held in the Church in Richmond (1775) in favor of taking up arms against Great Britain—." But an examination of collected papers of William Wirt, Patrick Henry, and Nathaniel Pope has not revealed such a description.

There are two probable explanations. First, Pope may have been referring to Tucker's description. Since Pope was assisting Wirt in this project, it is reasonable that they would continually inform one another of new materials. Unfortunately the manuscript is undated and the Tucker correspondence is lost so there is no opportunity to compare dates. Second, perhaps Pope's reference is to a speech manuscript prepared by Judge John Tyler. In Moses Coit Tyler's biography [*Patrick Henry,* 1898], reference is made to a John Roane who, in conversation with Edward Fontaine in 1834, "verified the correctness of the speech as it was written by Judge Tyler for Mr. Wirt." All attempts to uncover a Tyler manuscript have failed. However, if such a manuscript had been prepared by Judge Tyler, this could explain Pope's reference to a detailed description.

There is reasonable evidence for rejecting the notion of Tyler authorship. First, a letter attributed to Judge John Tyler exists in the papers which Wirt used in writing the biography. The letter is partially mutilated and illegible, but clearly no manuscript of any speech is included. Second, Roane was over ninety years old at the time he made this statement. While age alone does not discount his assertion, it weakens his credibility in that he is recalling events occurring thirty and sixty years previously. Third, Roane's statement, even if accurate, does not necessarily mean that Tyler wrote the speech out word for word. Fourth, Wirt acknowledges Tucker's contribution to the speech and mentions Tyler's assistance on the whole biography. There would appear to be no reason why Wirt would not have acknowledged Tyler's help on the speech as well. Fifth, Wirt says he took the speech from Tucker.

Because the Tyler theory of authorship cannot be substantiated, and because of the incomplete text furnished by Randolph and Tucker, it seems reasonable to conclude that Wirt wrote the speech himself using these accounts as a basis. As an accomplished rhetorician, Wirt was capable of writing such a speech. Some believed that his eloquence was surpassed only by that of Henry himself. In addition to his oral skills, Wirt enjoyed a literary reputation as a Virginia essayist. When the editor of *Port Folio* magazine asked Wirt to submit a section from the Henry biography to use as advertising for the forthcoming book, Wirt submitted *only* the **"Liberty or Death"** oration. It was, according to Wirt, "a sample of my work."

CRITICS' RELIANCE UPON WIRT'S RECONSTRUCTION

Since Wirt's 1817 publication, no other text of **"Liberty or Death"** has appeared. Biographers, historians, and

Henry arguing the Parsons' Cause *in Hanover.*

rhetoricians have consistently relied upon Wirt's version while simultaneously labeling it as inauthentic. Not surprisingly, laymen have also relied on Wirt's version alone.

Biographers of Henry have played the most instrumental role in perpetuating the Wirt text. The five outstanding scholarly lives of Henry all rely on Wirt's text. Moses Coit Tyler, the first biographer of note after Wirt, includes Wirt's version in his book, saying the speech appears "substantially as it was given by Wirt in his 'Life of Henry.' " Tyler continues to point out that Wirt does not mention where he obtained his version, and that attempts to discover that version as a whole, before Wirt's writing, have all failed.

Tyler's biography was immediately followed by that of William Wirt Henry, grandson of Patrick Henry. [Entitled *Patrick Henry: Life, Correspondence, and Speeches,* 1891, this work] includes the speech exactly as it appears in Wirt. [Henry] prefaces the account with the observation that "Mr. Wirt has been able to give a condensed account of Mr. Henry's speech, gathered from the recollections of the hearers, principally from Judge John Tyler and Judge St. George Tucker."

The third major Henry biography [*Patrick Henry,* 1929] was written by George Morgan. Morgan used Wirt's text verbatim.

The most analytical interpretation of Henry comes from Robert Meade [in his *Patrick Henry: Practical Revolutionary,* 1969]. Meade includes Wirt's version except that "I have omitted some of the 'sirs' which Wirt used so copiously and divided one of his lengthy paragraphs." Meade prefaces the text with the statement that "no manuscript of Henry's speech exists," but refers to the text in Wirt as the "traditional account" of the speech.

The most recent Henry biography [*Patrick Henry,* 1974] by Richard Beeman does not include a text of **"Liberty or Death."** Beeman does, however, refer to Wirt's having reconstructed the speech.

In numerous anthologies of great speeches, Wirt's version of **"Liberty or Death"** has been reprinted. In addition rhetorical critics have undertaken an analysis of Henry's speeches. In his dissertation and critical essay on Henry [published in *A History and Criticism of American Public Address,* W. N. Brigance, ed.], [Louis A.] Mallory did an extensive stylistic comparison of **"Liberty or Death"** and other Henry speeches. While this article is beneficial in many respects, the stylistic comparison is almost worthless. Since Wirt says that none of Robertson's accounts of Henry's speeches are accurate, it seems needless to compare the styles. Even Mallory relied upon Wirt's version of the speech. In his conclusion, Mallory observes that the speech is incomplete.

The biographers, anthologists, and rhetoricians systematically point to the values of Wirt's version despite its textual inauthenticity. Tyler, for instance, urges that Wirt's version "certainly gives the substance of the speech as actually made by Patrick Henry on the occasion named." Furthermore, Tyler commends the form of Wirt's version because its basis is testimony gathered from "all available living witnesses." Morgan bases his belief in the speech's authenticity upon the credibility of Judges John Tyler and St. George Tucker. Since these were Wirt's authorities for the speech and "Two more reliable men than Tucker and Tyler it would be hard to name," Morgan says that "we need not be concerned as to the authenticity of Wirt's report." Meade views Wirt's version as based on a few helpful sources plus many bits of information. He believes that the general substance and many phrases of the speech are amply proved by existing evidence. All this, in addition to the fact that Thomas Jefferson—a prepublication critic of Wirt's biographical manuscript—never corrected Wirt, lends credibility to Wirt's version.

Biographers, historians, and rhetoricians have all given exclusive attention to Wirt's version of **"Liberty or Death."** Although the text is inauthentic, it is the only account we have available.

> You never heard anything more infamously insolent than P. Henry's speech: he called the K——a Tyrant, a fool, a puppet and a tool to the ministry. Said there was no Englishmen, no Scots, no Britons, but a set of wretches sunk in Luxury, they had lost their native courage and (were) unable to look the brave Americans in the face . . . This Creature is so infatuated, that he goes about I am told, praying and preaching amongst the common people.
>
> —*James Parker, in a letter to Charles Stewart, 6 April 1775.*

CULTURAL AUTHENTICITY

"Liberty or Death," as we have already observed, was created to fill a vacuum in the history of ideas. With the aid of eye-witness accounts and testimony, Henry's first biographer generated the speech text. Even though his data are still questioned today, it is primarily the tradition of the **"Liberty or Death"** oration "which to-day keeps alive, in millions of American homes, the name of Patrick Henry, and which lifts him, in the popular faith, almost to the rank of some mythical hero of romance." Although this appraisal was made by Tyler in 1888, it is still valid today. Tyler had observed "thousands of pilgrims" traveling to the "patriotic shrine" seeking a glimpse of the spot on the floor where Henry supposedly stood when he uttered his words of liberty. Even today the oration is celebrated and

portions of it are memorized. The purpose of this section of the paper is to examine some motives which prompted creation of the speech, sustained its immediate impact and continue to propagate the legend of Henry's oratory.

MORALISM

Most of what we know of Henry's oratory is derived from his first biographer, William Wirt. Wirt's motivations for writing a life of the Virginia patriot also influenced his decision to include **"Liberty or Death"** in the biography.

At least four explicit motives stimulated Wirt. First, Wirt's *Sketches* were an attempt to characterize and preserve the Virginian tradition that Patrick Henry was the oratorical leader of the Revolution. In an earlier essay [*The Letters of the British Spy*], Wirt had observed: "The Virginians boast of an orator of nature . . . . and he is the only orator of whom they do boast, with much emphasis . . . . I regret that I came to this country too late to see (him)." Second, Wirt viewed Henry as a patriotic model for youthful Virginians which would help deter the moral decline of Southern society. Third, Wirt was devoted to the study of eloquence. Henry symbolized the supremely eloquent and sublime leader. In Wirt's estimation, "Mr. Henry seems to me a good text for a discourse on rhetoric, patriotism, and morals. The work might be made useful to young men who are just coming forward into life: this is the highest point of expectation; nor do I deem the object a trifling one, since on these young men the care and safety of the republic must soon devolve." Finally, Wirt hoped that the moral life of a commonly acclaimed hero would be instrumental in securing him a fortune and a national literary reputation. In correspondence with Wirt, Jefferson argued that Henry was "the greatest orator that ever lived." Other friends and acquaintances, such as Francis Gilmer and St. George Tucker, concurred in Jefferson's estimation, and held that **"Liberty or Death"** was Henry's best effort. It ought to be preserved, they argued, because speeches are the "only avenue by which future generations could glean demonstrations of the speaker's ability" and "those who leave no such reports . . . sink into immediate oblivion."

Persuaded of the overwhelming need for models of Henry's eloquence, but finding no available text, Wirt was forced to rely upon the contributions of Tucker, Randolph, and Tyler. The speech was created out of a desire to provide a model for youths in Virginia—to give moral instruction to society. That Wirt offered the **"Liberty or Death"** text merely as a model, and not a verbatim account, is supported by the fact that the speech is presented in the form of a third-hand account, a report. For instance, " 'He had,' he said, 'but one lamp by which his feet were guided: and that was the lamp of experience. He knew of no way of judging of the future, but by the past.' " Wirt never intended for the text to be viewed as a verbatim account. Had Wirt not been convinced that a general decline in manners and morals was occurring in Virginia and the nation, **"Liberty or Death"** might have been completely lost.

ROMANTICISM

While a moralistic biographer was largely responsible for

the creation of the **"Liberty or Death"** speech, it was immediately sustained by a postrevolutionary romanticism that permeated early nineteenth-century society. Two expressions of this romanticism were especially germane to the immediate effects of the speech: first, there was a renewed interest in the classical past; and second, the important contributions to the Revolution tended to be interpreted in terms of individuals. Wirt's biography viewed "Revolutionary times in Virginia as a golden age, an age of heroes. '*Those* were the times,' he seemed to be repeating, 'and those were the giants such time produced.' "

With a thirty-year perspective and a vivid imagination, Wirt's correspondents confirmed this romantic tradition. In Tucker's account (noted earlier in this essay), he compares Henry to Cato of Utica addressing the Roman Senate. Edmund Randolph [in the *Richmond Enquirer,* 2 September 1815] says that "Henry was thought in his attitudes to resemble Saint Paul while preaching at Athens and to speak as man was never known to speak before." Randolph also emphasizes the contributions of Henry the individual to the Revolution: "It was Patrick Henry, born in obscurity, poor, and without the advantages of literature, rousing the genius of his country and binding a band of patriots together to hurl defiance at the tyranny of so formidable a nation as Great Britain."

Accounts of **"Liberty or Death"** made public after Wirt's biography was published tend to support this romantic attraction to glorious heroism. Three specific accounts offer textual structure and confirm Henry's use of the phrase, "Give me liberty or give me death." Importantly, it is difficult to determine whether these witnesses are recalling **"Liberty or Death"** as delivered in 1775 or as published by Wirt in 1817.

The first of these descriptions was obtained from Henry Stephens Randall, who obtained if from a clergyman, who heard it from an aged friend, who heard the speech. Randall's description [in his *Life of Thomas Jefferson,* 1858] compares Henry's effectiveness with the shout of a leader who turns back the rout of battle. The only part of the speech which Randall recalls is the famous last line, "Give me liberty, or give me death." The account's value lies in the explication of Henry's delivery of that line.

> Henry rose with an unearthly fire burning in his eye. He commenced somewhat calmly—but the smothered excitement began more and more to play upon his features and thrill in the tones of his voice. The tendons of his neck stood out white and rigid "like whipcords." His voice rose louder and louder, until the walls of the building, and all within them, seemed to shake and rock in its tremendous vibrations. Finally, his pale face and glaring eye became "terrible to look upon." Men "leaned forward in their seats," with their heads "strained forward," their faces pale, and their eyes glaring like the speaker's. His last exclamation—"Give me liberty or give me death"—was like the shout of the leader which turns back the rout of battle!

The old man from whom this tradition was derived added that, when the orator sat down, he himself " 'felt sick with excitement.' Every eye yet gazed entranced on Henry. It

seemed as if a word from him would have led to any wild explosion of violence. 'Men looked beside themselves.' " Since Wirt offers no such detailed description of Henry's delivery, Randall's account is the result of a vivid imagination or a vivid oral tradition about Henry's speech delivery.

The second postpublication description is ex-President Tyler's. This account was preserved in the diary of William Winston Fontaine (Henry's great-grandson). Tyler related a description which his father had given him.

> Mr. Henry was holding a paper cutter in his right hand: and when he came to that part of his speech in which he said: "I know not what course others may take." He cast a glance at these (opposing) gentlemen, and bending his head forward, and with stooping shoulders, and with submissive expression of countenance, he crossed his wrists, as if to be bound: then suddenly straightening up, a bold, resolute purpose of soul flashed over his countenance, and then struggling as if trying to burst his bonds, his voice swelled out in boldest, vibrant tones: "Give me liberty!" Then wrenching his hands apart, and raising aloft his hand with the clenched paper-cutter, he exclaimed: "Or give me death!" and aimed at his breast, as with a dagger and dropped to his seat.

The effect was "electrical," and the members of the House were "still as death." At this point, Fontaine indicates that the remainder of Tyler's description was taken from Wirt's account. In this instance, Tyler vividly portrayed Henry's symbolic use of a paper cutter to reinforce his concluding demand.

The third description is to be found in an 1834 manuscript of a conversation between Edward Fontaine and John Roane. According to Fontaine, Roane was "more than ninety years old; but his mind was very little impaired by age, & his memory was perfect in retaining past events." Roane argues that Henry's "voice, countenance, & gestures, gave an irresistible force to his words which no description could make intelligible to one who had never seen him, nor heard him speak." Roane's description of the conclusion of the oration demonstrates the vividness and reality of the tradition of the speech.

> When he said: "is peace so sweet, or life so dear as to be purchased at the price of chains & slavery," he stood in the attitude of a condemned galley slave leader with fetters, awaiting his doom. His form was bowed; his wrists were crossed; *his manacles were almost visible* as he stood like an embodiment of helplessness & agony. After a solemn pause, he raised his eyes and chained hands towards Heaven, & prayed in words & tones which thrilled every heart—: "Forbid it—Almighty God!!!" He then turned toward the timid loyalists of the House who were quaking with terror at the idea of the consequences of participation in proceedings which would be visited with the penalties of treason by the British Crown & he slowly bent his form yet nearer to the earth and said: "*I know not what course others may take,*" and he accompanied the words with his hands still crossed while he

seemed to be weighed down with additional chains. The man appeared transformed into an oppressed, heart broken, & hopeless felon. After remaining in this posture of humiliation long enough to impress the imagination with the condition of the colony under the *iron heel* of *military despotism,* he arose proudly, and exclaimed: "but as for me"—& the words hissed through his clenched teeth, while his body was thrown back, & every muscle and tendon was strained against the fetters which bound him; and with his countenance distorted by agony and rage, he looked for a moment like Laocoon in a death struggle with coiling serpents. Then the loud, clear, triumphant notes: "give me *Liberty!!!* electrified the assembly! It was not a prayer, but a *stern demand,* which would submit to no refusal or delay! The sound of his voice as he spoke these memorable words was like that of a Spartan Paean on the field of Plataea: and as each syllable of the word *Liberty* echoed through the building, his fetters were shivered; his arms were hurled apart: & the links of his chains were scattered to the wind! When he spoke the word *Liberty* with an emphasis never given it before, his hands were open & his arms elevated and extended; his countenance was radiant; he stood erect and defiant; while the sound of his voice & the sublimity of his attitude made him appear a magnificent incarnation of Freedom, & expressed all that can be acquired or enjoyed by nations & individuals invincible & free. After a momentary pause, only long enough to permit the echo of the word Liberty to cease, he let his left hand fall powerless to his side, & clenched his right hand firmly, as if holding a dagger with the point aimed at his breast. He stood like a Roman Senator defying Caesar, while the unconquerable spirit of Cato of Utica flashed from every feature, & he closed the grand appeal with the solemn words: *or give me death!* Sounded with the awful cadence of a hero's dirge—*fearless of death, & victorious in death;* and he suited the action to the word by a blow upon the left breast with the right hand which seemed to drive the dagger to the patriots heart!

Notice that once again the classical references to Caesar and Cato of Utica are used to generate instant comparison and understanding in the hearer's mind. The similarity of the Roane and Tucker accounts in their classical comparisons is striking.

The accounts by Randall, Tyler, and Roane share several commonalities: they emphasize the declaration of liberty or death as the high point of the speech; their descriptions of Henry's delivery indicate that it was very dramatic; and they all indicate that Henry began the speech in a calm manner and built tension and emotion throughout the speech. The resemblances among these descriptions would seem to attest either to the validity of Wirt's account or to the consistency in the established tradition of **"Liberty or Death."**

Postrevolutionary romanticism seems justified as an explanation for the institutionalization of **"Liberty or Death"** for a last reason. Despite the fact that unfavorable accounts of the speech exist, the tradition which has

emerged has been univocal and favorable. One unfavorable reaction is recorded in the diary of James Parker of Edinburgh, Scotland [and reprinted in *Magazine of History,* March 1906]. Parker, who was present in St. John's Church in the Convention, offers a radically different interpretation of Henry's speech:

> You never heard anything more infamously insolent than P. Henry's speech: he called the K——a Tyrant, a fool, a puppet, and a tool to the ministry. Said there was no Englishmen, no Scots, no Britons, but a set of wretches sunk in Luxury, they had lost their native courage and (were) unable to look the brave Americans in the face. . . . This Creature is so infatuated, that he goes about I am told, praying and preaching amongst the common people.

An editor's note following the excerpt clarifies: "Mr. Parker was always we observe, very hopeful for the success of the British Cause, and 'P. Henry's' name must to him have been Anathema." The derogatory references to the king are consistent with Robertson's account of Henry's **"Stamp Act"** speech. While Parker's perception of the speech may be the most accurate reflection of Henry's oratorical form, it has not sustained influence. It is the image of Patrick Henry as the patriot, the classical reincarnation of virtue, justice, and good will who provided "the first impulse to the ball of revolution" which has been sustained.

Aged men recalled youthful victories and saw things as they wished they had been—a society full of classical virtue, eloquence, and personal strength. This common experience of Henry's peers in recalling his great oration served to legitimize the tradition. An image of Patrick Henry, created by an ambitious biographer, was confirmed in the hearts and minds of Virginians.

SYMBOLISM

The rhetorical tradition associated with **"Liberty or Death"** was shaped by the moral purposes of a biographer, confirmed and legitimized by a post-revolutionary romanticism, and continues to exist today because of its symbolic value for our culture. With the aid of biographers and rhetoricians, the "Demosthenes" of the age still symbolizes eloquence and patriotism. In 1834, Judge Roane referred to **"Liberty or Death"** as an oration often declaimed by schoolboys. One hundred and fifty years later, practically every child of school age knows that Patrick Henry is the man who asked for liberty or death.

The scholarly biographies of Henry, especially those of Tyler, Henry, Morgan, and Meade have adopted Wirt's image of Henry as a great orator and have attempted to expand and explicate that characterization. Even biographies of other Revolutionary leaders, such as Henry S. Randall's *Life of Thomas Jefferson,* have extensively examined the details of Henry's oratory. Fictional and juvenile biographies with such titles as *Patrick Henry: Voice of Liberty, With Patrick Henry's Help,* and *Son of Thunder, Patrick Henry* typify attempts, initiated by Wirt, to offer a model for youthful emulation. Fictional caricatures such as *Give me Liberty; The Story of an Innocent Bystander* and *A Lighter of Flames* symbolize the American spirit of liberty.

In the late 1800's, an article by Edward Pollard in *Galaxy* magazine [September 1870] argued that Henry was nothing more than a stump speaker. A number of tracts and speeches were offered as responses. One of the more popular of these orations was delivered by Charles May in 1876. May paid tribute to Henry as "The Orator of the Revolution" and insisted that "as an orator he was supreme, and towers above all others." Other public declaimers have labeled Henry as the "greatest orator who had appeared in the history of the colonies" and the person "who lit the fires of the Revolution, and called armies up from the valleys and down from the mountains' heights to battle the birthright of man." "The words of that speech will echo in history as long as the guns of Lexington and Bunker Hill."

Literary historians, such as Moses Coit Tyler, have characterized Henry as an "orator of unexampled power" and the finest orator of the Revolution. By others, Henry's **"Liberty or Death"** speech has been labeled an "immortal oration," "his most noted speech," the speech "which stamped him as among the greatest orators of all ages," and the occasion for a height of sublimity never attained by any other orator. Accolades such as "The Trumpet of the Revolution," "the outstanding spokesman of the American Revolution," "the redhaired Demosthenes of Hanover County," and "the ability to sway the minds of the cultured and ignorant with equal ease," have promoted the image of Henry as an oratorical genius. More recently, a special Bicentennial issue of *Time* refers to Patrick Henry as the man "who became famous last year by shouting 'Give me liberty or give me death!'" In short, Henry symbolizes the American spirit of speaking out against injustices and defending the basic principles of human rights.

We have seen how the rhetorical tradition of **"Liberty or Death"** was created and has been perpetuated. A moralistic biographer generated the tradition in order to furnish youthful Virginians with an example of sublime eloquence. A postrevolutionary romanticism influenced and sustained the tradition through reliance upon the classical past and emphasis on individual contributions. As a symbol of the American spirit, Henry has been viewed as "the unequalled and ever-inspiring orator of liberty." In 1888, Moses Coit Tyler observed that it would

> be an odd thing, and a source of no little disturbance to many minds . . . if we should have to conclude that an apocryphal speech written by Wirt, and attributed by him to Patrick Henry fifteen years after the great orator's death, had done more to perpetuate the renown of Patrick Henry's oratory than had been done by any and all the words actually spoken by the orator himself during his lifetime.

It is evident that Wirt is directly responsible for Henry's reputation as an orator having been initially preserved. But that reputation would have vanished into the pages of history were it not for the fact that our society promotes an emphasis on moral virtue, tradition, heroism, and eloquence—just as Wirt's did. (pp. 298-310)

*Judy Hample, "The Textual and Cultural Au-*thenticity of Patrick Henry's 'Liberty or Death' Speech," in The Quarterly Journal of Speech, Vol. LXIII, No. 3, October, 1972, pp. 298-310.*

M. E. Bradford   (essay date 1975)

[*A scholar noted for his work on the literature of the American South, Bradford has published several studies on the social and political climate of revolutionary and post-revolutionary America. In the following excerpt, from the text of an address originally given in 1975, he presents Henry's political theory, attempting to wrest the orator's reputation from the "rationalist neo-Federalist scholars" who have portrayed him as a "simple-minded demagogue."*]

Even before the first of our bicentennial celebrations began, it was altogether predictable that their emphasis should fall more upon the *what* than the *why* of events transpiring during and prior to our original War for Independence. According to those responsible, no controversy could follow from this procedure. There is, however, a danger in submitting to such probability and neglecting to redress the balance of emphasis toward interpretation. For, try as we will, there is no honest way of making our salute to the revolutionary forefathers into a non-partisan event.

What they attempted and achieved embodied a political intention and a theory of the politically good. And no less than the New Left distortions of the People's Bicentennial Commission, the supposedly value-free and "factual" accounts of our received historiography which stand behind the rites and ceremonies of our official and federally sponsored celebrations obscure that intent and theory. Standing in the way of the recovery of legitimate precedent which I here recommend is, of course, the Second American Revolution of our Civil War. But that is another study.

The more immediate obstacles to our understanding of what American colonials intended by their official separation from the mother country are the unrepresentative sentiments of intellectually interesting but sometimes deviant revolutionaries, such as James Madison, Thomas Jefferson, Benjamin Franklin, and Thomas Paine. In their stead, we should concentrate upon the thoughts and actions of less curious men, such as John Dickinson, John Adams, and the taciturn Cincinnatus of Mount Vernon. And especially we should concentrate upon the thoughts and actions of that trumpet-voice of the Revolution—Patrick Henry of Virginia.

The great difficulty which we confront in reconstructing the thoughts of such active men as the Virginia Demosthenes is a paucity of detailed records and a shortage of that idol of scholars, written documents. For it is a paradox of intellectual history—a paradox rooted in human nature—that the men positioned on the outer fringes of the great events of an age write the most and the most interestingly about them, and the men at their center almost nothing at all. Or at least since the Renaissance it has been the rule that the modernist and secular philosophers of change have left us a record of their speculations upon happenings with which they had very little to do. Letters, tracts, and pamphlets have furnished them with an outlet which the public world of action did not provide. Yet thanks to the scholars, usually men of their own kidney, they have had a final victory through interpretation, a victory which stands between us and the actual deeds of more moderate and less ingenious men.

It is reasonable to claim that Patrick Henry was *the* characteristic American spokesman during the Revolution, the epitome of Whig sentiment in that era. As a young man he first threw down the gauntlet of constitutional challenge in the celebrated **"Parson's Cause"** (1763). His **"Stamp Act Resolves"** (1765) energized American resistance to usurpation in the thirteen colonies and led to the inter-colonial communication and cooperation which issued finally in the Continental Congress. And before the Second Virginia Convention of 1775, he drew his countrymen after him to face up to the logic of their situation and prepare for war.

After that peroration, for liberty or death, and after its general acceptance, not only by those present in St. John's Church but by a plurality of all Americans determined to resist the imposition of the royal prerogative through force, the Declaration of Independence was anticlimactic. Yet even in that development, Henry played a major role. For the document which young Jefferson composed in Philadelphia, effacing himself and speaking for representatives of the Commonwealths there assembled, had behind it the instructions of the various colonial legislatures: particularly the instructions of the Virginia Assembly drawn in the late spring of 1776 by or under the influence of their chief of men. I quote here the precise language of that instrument in the draft of Patrick Henry:

> As the humble petitions of the Continental Congress have been rejected and treated with contempt; as the parliament of G. B. so far from showing any disposition to redress our grievances, have lately passed an act approving of the ravages that have been committed upon our coasts, and obliging the unhappy men who shall be made captives to bear arms against their families, kindred, friends, and country; and after being plundered themselves, to become accomplices in plundering their brethren, a compulsion not practiced among prisoners of war except among pirates, the outlaws and enemies of human society. As they are not only making every preparation to crush us, which the internal strength of the nation and its alliances with foreign powers afford them, but are using every art to draw the savage Indians upon our frontiers, and are even encouraging insurrection among our slaves, many of whom are now actually in arms against us. And as the King of G. B. by a long series of oppressive acts has proved himself the tyrant instead of the protector of his people. We, the representatives of the Colony of Virginia do declare, that we hold ourselves absolved of our allegiance to the Crown of G. B. and obliged by the eternal laws of self-preservation to pursue such measures as may conduce to the good and happiness of the united colonies; and as a full declaration of Independency appears to us to be

> the only honourable means under Heaven of obtaining that happiness, and of restoring us again to a tranquil and prosperous situation;

> Resolved, That our delegates in Congress, be enjoined in the strongest and most positive manner to exert their ability in procuring an immediate, clear and full Declaration of Independency.

The changes made by Edmund Pendleton and certain other delegates in the resolution conveyed to Philadelphia are not significant. And in that summer, no Virginia Whig would presume to contradict such instructions or rewrite them to mean something contrary to what their author intended.

Thus Patrick Henry *made* a revolution, though he did not write about one. And we would be generally at a loss to know what he intended through that making, except for the preserved recollections of his contemporaries and a very few documents: that is, had he not been drawn in debates over the federal Constitution (1788) to reconsider those designs and purposes in public, with a stenographer at hand. In my opinion, there are few instruments more valuable to the student of our national beginnings than Volume III of Jonathan Elliot's *The Debates in the Several State Conventions on the Adoption of the Federal Constitution.* It is, of course, true that Henry stood in opposition to adoption in Virginia. But it is noteworthy that no Federalist opponent of his masterful performance disputes his interpretation of the history from which he argues. Nor do they deny him when he advances the prospect of certain innovations in the American system as hostile to and violations of the Revolutionary model. It is rather their point that the Constitution will be a means for preserving and perfecting a generally agreed upon heritage.

The Henry who was a better prophet than his antagonists is once again the subject of another essay. It is sufficient for our present purposes that he said a great deal about the Revolution in those heated Richmond debates, about its significance for the men who brought it to completion—many of whom were present; that they found his remarks to be unexceptionable; and that, together with the aforementioned recollections and occasional documents, they make available the original American precedent—a precedent from which we presently diverge at our great peril.

What counts most about Henry's teaching in those Richmond orations is that it discourages in our generation all attempts to subsume the American struggle for independence under the general category of "revolutions of dogma and abstract theory"—revolutions such as have convulsed the Old World periodically since the decade of our own achievement of political identity. According to his son-in-law, the eloquent Judge Spencer Roane, the mature Henry "detested the projects of theorists and bookworms. His prejudices against statesmen of this character were very strong." And these wise prejudices did suffer from considerable provocation during his thirty-five year experience of every sort of American politician, but more, at the end of his life, from over the seas. Patrick Henry did not think well of the rebellion they made in France. He wrote a friend of our original ally that "her conduct has made it the interest of the great family of mankind to wish the downfall of her present government." In fact, he thought so ill of it that to oppose the spread of such influence on these shores he made common cause with his old enemies, the Federalists. If "everything that ought to be dear to man is covertly but successfully assailed . . . under the patronage of French manners and principles [and] under the name of philosophy," what could an Old Whig constitutionalist do but disapprove?

In recommending corrections in the Federal Constitution of 1787, Governor Henry, speaking for the Virginia legislature, offered counsel "not founded in speculative theory but deduced from principles which have been established by the melancholy example of other nations, in different ages." And even in the most "radical" performance of his career he declared, "I have but one lamp by which my feet are guided; and that is the lamp of experience." In mixing the argument from consequences with the appeal *ad verecundium* (from tradition), Henry is far removed from the school of strict reason, from the world of the *philosophe*, but at the same time, at the very heart of the original American political tradition.

Stated briefly, this commitment to historic rights, inherited rights available at law and passed on in a historic continuum (organic compact), as property is passed from father to child, identifies Henry as an American subspecies of the English "country Whig". True enough, he did employ the conventional language of contract theory and make an occasional bow toward "natural rights". But that the fundamental and indefeasible rights of man could be even partially achieved outside the complex negotiation that is the common fortune of a given people located in a given place over a number of generations did not occur to him as a serious possibility. Nor did he by "equal liberty" mean anything like what natural rights theory assumes: anything more elaborate than the necessity for self-defense and self-preservation. For Henry's "liberty" allowed him to propose on the eve of his fourth term as governor a pluralistic religious establishment for the support through law and taxation of Virginia's principal denominations.

And, when the high-toned Edmund Randolph during the ratification debates spoke of the "short work" made of the bushwhacker Josiah Philips by his upcountry neighbors as proof that a federal power was needed to secure equal rights, Henry replied scornfully that his friends understood their business better than any uniformitarian jurisprudence and "beautiful legal ceremony" could guarantee. As we know, "Fair liberty" was all his cry. And of government he declared that the "security of liberty should be its direct and only end." By these injunctions he signified nothing more complicated than a desire to see his countrymen free to be themselves and to generate their own culture, out of the dialectic of their own experience according to what he called their "genius". And by that last word—"genius"—he specified an assumption, or set of assumptions, around which we may reconstruct his view of what the Revolution was all about.

Each nation has its own genius. And history is the touchstone of any systematic effort toward its identification. In the Richmond debates Henry spoke from little else but

history—particularly from the British and the English colonial record of which our new republic was to be, in his understanding, a consummation. Consider the following language and ask yourself, "Can it be otherwise construed?"

> When the American spirit was in its youth, the language of America was different: liberty, sir, was then the primary object. We are descended from a people whose government was founded on liberty: our glorious forefathers of Great Britain made liberty the foundation of every thing. That country is become a great, mighty, and splendid nation: not because their government is strong and energetic, but, sir, because liberty is its direct end and foundation. We drew the spirit of liberty from our British ancestors: by that spirit we have triumphed over every difficulty.

And again:

> We entertained, from our earliest infancy, the most sincere regard and reverence for the mother country. Our partiality extended to a predilection for her customs, habits, manners, and laws.

> From that noble source have we derived our liberty: that spirit of patriotic attachment to one's country, that zeal for liberty, and that enmity to tyranny, which signalized the then champions of liberty we inherit from our British ancestors. And I am free to own that, if you cannot love a republican government, you may love the British monarchy; for, although the king is not sufficiently responsible, the responsibility of his agents, and the efficient checks interposed by the British Constitution, render it less dangerous than other monarchies, or oppressive tyrannical aristocracies.

Against the new and insufficiently prescriptive Constitution he advanced over and over again, with the English precedent in hand. "How are the state rights, individual rights, and national rights, secured? Not as in England; for the authority quoted from Blackstone would, if stated right prove, in a thousand instances, that if the king of England attempted to take away the rights of individuals, the law would stand against him. The acts of Parliament would stand in his way. The bill and declaration of rights would be against him. The common law is fortified by the bill of rights." Finally, he summarized these objections in one sentence. Of the Philadelphia instrument, he maintained, "There is not an English feature in it."

We are reminded of the language employed by Edmund Burke in his "Speech on Conciliation with America" (1775) to describe his kinsmen over the sea: "The temper and character which prevail in our colonies are, I am afraid, unalterable by any human art. We cannot, I fear, falsify the Pedigree of this fierce people, and persuade them that they are not sprung from a nation in whose veins the blood of freedom circulates. The language in which they would hear you tell them this tale would detect the disposition; your speech would betray you." The affinity in perspective on a common inheritance linking these two statemen brings me to the crux of my argument concerning Henry on revolution.

Seen in this light, what happened in the thirteen North American colonies between 1774 and 1782 was not so much a revolution as a counterrevolution: a struggle by the colonials to preserve a regime both extant and well affirmed from threats to its felicity issuing from other components of the total British polity. Like the architects of 1787, who would have (according to an apparent majority of Americans) established a government not checked by the necessary and specific restrictions on its coercive powers, it was George III, his ministers, and their supporters who were guilty of a "radical" usurpation against the rule of interdependence for the common good. Once the prospect of military force in implementing these doctrines became an ingredient in this confrontation, war was bound to come. For once the sword is drawn, nothing can answer but the sword, or so says honor—hence the language in Virginia's 1776 instructions to the Continental Congress, the language of Henry quoted above; and hence the Declaration of Independence itself which, as we are so often urged to forget, should be read in the light of such representative Whig expressions of opinion. Men, in their composite character as collectivies, have inalienable rights to observe the "eternal law" of self-preservation, to protect life, property, and hope of a future. One people has the right to expect this of government as much as another—in that sense, are equal to them. And certainly, one group of Englishmen expects as much as any other Englishmen.

But compulsion aside, how precisely are the English authorities to be taken as usurpers against law, usage, and custom? And how shall rebellion take on the sanction of preservation? For, in Henry's view, as in the Declaration, "light and transient causes" will not serve; revolt is not an end in itself. First of all, as part of a sequence of developments in the evolution of the English Constitution, beginning with the 1628 Petition of Right and, after royal and parliamentary excesses, brought to a partial settlement in the 1689 Bill of Rights. Yet, as Americans discovered, a further step toward community under the sovereignty of law (charters, statutes, and unwritten prescription—all determining stations and roles) was required. As a young lawyer, Henry had foreseen this exigency. For in the **Parson's Cause** he had argued, "A king by annulling or disallowing laws of this salutary nature, from being the father of his people degenerates into a tyrant and forfeits all right to his subject's obedience."

American colonials had developed their government within the legal context of the established English political forms, minus a titled nobility and a full religious hierarchy. Remove also an offending king and only the prescriptive law remains. But (since another executive will be provided, and judges for their support) with additional writing down, add specificity to forestall those old enemies, inference and construction. And ban the more obvious infringements of fiat, called under the crown "expansions of the prerogative." However, if executive authority, representatives, and people are, in all their roles and stations, determined by a clear and limited set of agreements and laws; and if they come to love that bond, their genius may then flourish and their virtue (*qua* public spirit, reinforced by a sense of joint investment) be expected to grow. To how these improvements should be drawn history was

once again the key, experience followed by meditation. In it good citizens might find "the voice of tradition." Henry was always proud of his part in keeping the common law in a free Virginia proud of the heritage it made manifest, and also proud of his part in abstracting from the political system which antedated that freedom all prospect of future obstructions to its fruitful operation. His constant aim was to release what he, as a very social man, knew better than any of his contemporaries—that "genius" of this shore, this commonwealth, of which I spoke before, and to which I must now return in summarizing Henry's social theory.

Genius, as used in the eighteenth century, is an imprecise term. It can mean several things, but in a political context will usually signify a quality rooted in nature and place. As in the Latin *genus loci,* or resident spirit of a stream or wood, it could not be known save through its activities. And the genius of a people is likewise signified. A spare structure or supporting institutional framework could encourage its revelation—or a large *a priori* political machinery prevent that unfolding. Henry, even in 1775, wanted union and had once declared, in the context of war, that where our foreign enemies were concerned he did not think of himself as a Virginian, but as American. And he seriously wished to see the Articles of Confederation strengthened in keeping with the genius of the entire country.

But in his view, that was an entity which touched upon only a small portion of our common life; and likewise state law in the Old Dominion. Virginia had a "government suited to the genius of her people"—a government "formed by that humble genius," a spirit which included the genius of their ancestors. And its success proved of those who formed it that they, "perhaps by accident, did what design could not do in other parts of the world." It is only thus that liberty, a condition, is the end of official government, for by its operation is genius released, and a culture permitted to develop from its roots, upward.

Henry's antithesis of "design" and "accident" is central to his political teaching. For design is what he perceived in the Federalist model for our United States, an "energetic" plan framed to organize and dragoon its citizens toward the achievement of some externally determined end. Further, it was obvious that such design would eventuate in the divinization of the state: a condition where men live for government, not the other way around, and government either *for* ideology or to enact some monstrous private will. I will not here take you through his particular objections to Madison's crafty composition. It suffices to say that they were all directed toward liberty and away from an extrinsic *telos,* all finally productive of what we now know as the Bill of Rights. His America did not exist to pursue certain military, economic, moral, or philosophical objectives. To borrow language from a group of his most articulate political descendants, he scorned the notion of a culture "poured in from the top," whatever the rationale. Rather, his social-political vision was what Michael Oakeshott has called "nomocratic" and Eric Voegelin "compact."

Political manners, divorced from any purpose outside of

sustaining their devotees in relation to each other, would produce identity for *a posteriori* description by the wise: grown identity, as good husbandry of soil makes a tree bear fruit, but does not plumb the mystery of that tree. Not the glory, nor the power, nor the wealth which the Federalist (as had King George) promised could be the mainspring of the republic which Henry envisaged. Nor could it be the right to live outside the *societas* which a quasi-Roman notion of normative national law might guarantee: the anticommunity of atomistic individuals who become a "herd" (a word Henry despised) by overdoing their effort to be the opposite. What was needed must come from within, from persons in relation to persons, all knowing who they are.

It should now be possible for us to understand why there has been something like a conspiracy of silence concerning the political theory of Patrick Henry, its ancient antecedents, and its obvious relevance to disruptions in American life today. Our scholars, most of them rationalists and neo-Federalists, had a vested interest in producing Henry's present reputation: that he was a simple-minded country politician turned demagogue, a Populist trimmer whose talents happened to serve his more far-sighted contemporaries when the Revolutionary crisis came. That Madison was the fellow to read, and Jefferson before him—or certain selected Boston radicals, as reprinted under the auspices of the Harvard University Press. In any case, Henry's rhetoric could be explained as a product of the shifting circumstances of his private life and developments in the regional economy of the districts where Henry's will was "omnipotent": Henry's rhetoric, but not that of his political antagonists. To the degree that this obfuscation has been successful and Henry replaced in the center of our bicentennial attentions by more speculative politicians who in some way augur the present dispensation of things, to that extent we have been deprived of the political paradigm which the occasion requires us to seek.

We should not feel free to forget that the Revolution was made against power, uninformed of the conditions which it administered and untouched by the consequences of that remote administration, particularly in view of what we have learned of power since. Nor should we ignore the evidence that there was a republicanism abroad in the land which owed more to Lord Coke and Roman history than to Mr. Locke. Henry's politics as here reconstructed will, I hope, help prevent such mistakes.

But to practice a more complete piety and to make the precedent here considered into a living force, more than theoretical study is required. The best way to know from the inside the kind of America Patrick Henry hoped to leave us intact is to plunge submissively into state and county histories, reminiscences, and letters—into the bygone world of country and village and town as managed by ordinary citizens according to the *mos majorum* and their own particular lights. From such studies and from the evidence of American literature, as opposed to the more conventional searchings after nuance and refinement in the record of political thought, we can approach that interior knowledge: for there is theory in the private history of free Americans living *privately* in communities, within the ambit of family and friends: living under the eye of God out of the memory of their kind. Theory is evident for such students as are prepared to begin in the proper places and to seek out the proper contemporary guides in framing language for the translation of actions into thought—theory usually better than the disembodied kind.

Patrick Henry, as available in Elliot and in his other scattered remains, when framed by the early history of Virginia and the upper South, is such a guide. For, as we all recognize, his wisdom was longest preserved in its place of origin and from the perspective of our day seems almost inseparable from two hundred years of Southern testimony in "opposition". Yet it is not, nor was it ever, meant for local consumption alone—not just for the electors of Hanover, Louisa, Goochland, Prince Edward, and the other counties west of Richmond or on the "south-side" of the James. Assuming (as does my presence here) that Henry's America *of* the Revolution has a lesson for us all, Andrew Lytle, in his recently published *A Wake for the Living,* has recovered its image in a condensed and dramatic re-creation. Most of what is argued here from Henry is implicit in Lytle's family chronicle, and especially the separation of the public and private spheres, the horror of a totally politicized world. Toward the book's end, Lytle recalls the incident of a young colonel who asked of Robert E. Lee what the General could say to history in defense of his command decisions. Out of a world view identical with Henry's, Lee replied, "I will take the responsibility."

The authority for such decisions comes only from the virtue of unequal men unequally accountable to God, respectful of the prescription, guided by manners, and free through that combination to exercise responsible choice: only from the leader of a people whose genius remains intact because that "jewel . . . the public liberty" has been guarded with "jealous attention." If we consider the example of Patrick Henry with such distinctions in mind, we will have some idea of how far from our beginnings we have come—and some idea of the hard way back. (pp. 97-109)

M. E. Bradford, "According to Their Genius: Politics and the Example of Patrick Henry," in his A Better Guide Than Reason: Studies in the American Revolution, *Sherwood Sugden & Company Publishers, 1979, pp. 97-110.*

J. Michael Bordelon (essay date 1976)

[*In the following excerpt, Bordelon discusses Henry's politics and his standing as an anti-Federalist in post-revolutionary America.*]

[Mr. Madison] tells you of the important blessings which he imagines will result to us and mankind in general from the adoption of this system. I see the awful immensity of the dangers with which it is pregnant. I see it. I feel it. I see beings of a higher order anxious concerning our decision. When I see beyond the horizon that bounds human eyes, and look at the final consummation of all human things, and see those intelligent beings which inhabit the ethereal mansions reviewing the political decisions and revolutions which, in the progress of time, will happen in America, and the consequent happiness or misery of mankind, I am led to believe that much of the account, on one side or the other, will depend on what we now decide. Our own happiness alone is not affected by the event. All nations are interested in the determination. We have it in our power to secure the happiness of one half of the human race. Its adoption may involve the misery of the other hemisphere.

[Here a violent storm arose, which put the house in such disorder that Mr. Henry was obliged to conclude.]

Patrick Henry at Richmond,
Virginia, on June 24, 1788

Willmoore Kendall once suggested that of all the objectives enumerated in the Preamble to the Constitution that of forming a more perfect union has been the most difficult to achieve. Over the past two hundred years union has proved to be both the most troublesome and the most dangerous objective we have agreed upon as a people because it has often threatened to interfere with the nation's ability to accomplish its other well-announced ends. That threat became a reality in 1861 when the Civil War temporarily suspended the normal operations of government for the American polity. But there have always been some Americans who have argued that forming a more perfect union is not compatible with the nation's other chosen objectives. Throughout American history prominent figures have arisen who have advocated loose formal bonds of association while simultaneously warning against the tendency toward "consolidation," or centralization, which has always been their fear. But by and large these other Americans have generally been regarded, both in their time and ours, as somehow outside the mainstream of American political thought. At best they have been considered a little odd, and at worst they have been castigated as downright heretical and un-American.

One of the first of these "disunionists" was Patrick Henry, who used all of his forensic talents to persuade Virginia to reject ratification of the Constitution. This part of Henry's career is little known to those only passingly familiar with American history since in the popular mind he is best remembered for his leadership in the American Revolution, particularly for his **"give me liberty or give me death" speech** in 1775. The Henry of the history books is thus the Henry of the Revolution, the man who proclaimed in 1774 that "The distinctions between Virginians, Pennsylvanians, New Yorkers, and New Englanders, are no more. I am not a Virginian, but an American." But considering that the patriotic Henry of the Revolution is regarded so much more highly than the "short-sighted," provincialist Henry who opposed the Constitution and the Jeffersonian Republicans, it is worthwhile to note that a study of his experience as a rebellious colonial in the War for Independence helps to explain his less admired later political choices.

Henry first achieved renown in the **Parson's Cause** in 1763 when he launched a bitter attack against the established Anglican clergy who enjoyed the support of the Crown against the colonies. In the years that followed he was in the forefront of the struggle for independence, arguing resistance with a temerity that shocked many of his contemporaries. During those years of loosening bonds with the Mother Country, he and his fellow Americans became intimately acquainted with the dangers and difficulties of being governed according to a system operated by remote control. And no one was quicker or bolder than Henry in pointing out the inequities of such a system. But his legendary powers of speech were by no means the only talents he offered to the American cause. Although Jefferson intimated as much in his long canonical interviews with William Wirt, it is clearly an injustice to claim that Henry contributed to the cause of national independence solely with his tongue. Jefferson's comments have been the basis for an often repeated assertion that Henry possessed no great mental powers other than his ability to speak. But the education and literary talents of the Trumpet of the Revolution have always been matters of controversy and, despite Jefferson's calumny, there is reason to believe that Henry ably assisted in some of the important paperwork in proclaiming independence.

Certainly, during his tenure as wartime governor of Virginia, Henry proved himself to be a man of more than oratorical abilities. For example, when he learned of the desperate circumstances of the Continental Army at Valley Forge, he responded with a vigor and promptness uncharacteristic of either the Continental Congress or the other states. He quickly authorized agents to purchase provisions from around his state for shipment to the beleaguered army and took a personal hand in eliminating the red tape that might well have impeded the project's execution. During those same dark days of 1778 he learned of a plot to overthrow Washington as Commander-in-Chief, which information he immediately forwarded to the grateful General. As governor of Virginia Henry thus had ample opportunity to observe a link between the nation's interest and the patriotism of both its leaders and ordinary citizens.

After the War had been successfully concluded he continued to strengthen his already close ties to his native state. Through his extensive family connections and through several changes in residence he became acquainted with much more of Virginia than just the limited section he had known as a youth. His affection for his homeland could hardly have been diminished by his election to the governorship. Indeed, Henry's popularity in Virginia during the last quarter of the eighteenth century rivaled Washington's and was clearly superior to Jefferson's, excepting the last few years.

Several scholars have suggested that Henry was a radical democrat, the candidate of the people who led the opposition to English misrule faster and farther than would have the more conservative and well-established Virginia families had they been in complete control. In much the same manner he is also represented as a man of the West who boldly stepped forward and assumed a place of leadership more prominent than the Tidewater aristocracy would have liked. Although there may be some truth to these conceptions, the conclusion that Henry was one of the "radical" leaders of early American democracy is simplistic and thus misleading. The man who so admired Livy's Roman history could hardly have been blind to the dangers of popular envy or unaware of a tendency on the part of the many to be swayed on occasion by sentiment and passion. Like the other Founding Fathers, Henry scarcely fits the description of an unthinking democrat. He rarely found himself in league with Jefferson, who supported the more ostensibly democratic and libertarian movements of the day. During the course of his career he was generally on good terms with such leaders as Washington, John Adams, and John Marshall, none of whom can be described as ultra-democratic. He likewise enjoyed a strong rapport with the Antifederalist George Mason, one of Virginia's most blue-blooded citizens, whose aristocratic background nevertheless did not prevent him from supporting the Revolution and writing Virginia's Declaration of Rights. By no means, then, can it be argued that Henry always aligned himself with radical democrats. Nor did he always support the popular side of issues, since, for instance, he favored repatriating the Tories after the Revolution. He was also indifferent to certain restrictions upon the electorate, and, in his most unpopular decision, even opposed the Democratic-Republican party in the 1790's— the party embraced by so many of his former friends.

But even though one should bear in mind those qualifications which indicate that he was no blind worshipper of the god Demos, it is likewise foolish to rush to the conclusion that Henry was undemocratic. He enjoyed an unmatched popularity with the common people of Virginia. Since he believed that the final authority on political matters should be the people themselves, he was ultimately committed to popular government. As his speeches at the Virginia ratifying convention indicate, Henry deplored the failure of the Constitutional system to ensure that the representatives would be sufficiently responsible to the people.

But he was far from endorsing plebiscitary democracy. He preferred a system which combined the merits of rule by the many with those of rule by the few. Although he believed that the people should be the ultimate source of power and authority, he also believed that they should be led by men of integrity and sound judgment. A well-ordered popular government would thus be based on a certain degree of mutual trust. The legislators should never be contemptuous of the people's judgment nor fail to regard seriously their expressed desires. On the other hand, the people should not be excessively jealous about limiting the powers of their elected officials through a host of minutely detailed restrictions, but should instead demonstrate an ability to understand what is good for them if it is presented to them in coherent form by a capable *aristoi*. Henry thus advocated a system later commonly adopted in the South, suggesting that the region's political leadership assume positions of elected stewardship in which they would be permitted a degree of discretion in performing their duties of office, but who would nonetheless still remain ultimately responsible to their constituents.

The discretionary use of governmental power became a point of controversy in the Virginia ratifying convention

Lawrence Sully's portrait of Henry, c. 1795.

when a significant difference of opinion developed between Henry and Edmund Randolph over the hanging of a notorious outlaw with the bare minimum of legal form. The incident had taken place several years earlier when Henry had been governor of Virginia. Randolph began the disagreement by recounting an instance of a breakdown of the normal processes of government. He declared that a desperado, Josiah Philips, had been "attained very speedily and precipitately, without any proof better than vague reports. Without being confronted with his accusers and witnesses, without the privilege of calling for evidence in his behalf, he was sentenced to death and was afterwards actually executed." That Randolph's charges were apparently incorrect in some points of fact has been suggested by a number of later scholars.

Several of these authorities have reached the same conclusion as William Crosskey, who has argued [in his *Politics and the Constitution in the History of the United States,* 1965] that "the Philips case was deliberately misrepresented by Edmund Randolph." It is significant however, that even if the event did not take place as Randolph represented it, Henry chose to defend the procedure as it was described and did not defend his action by denying the deed. Instead [as quoted in *The Debates on the Adoption of the Federal Constitution,* Jonathan Elliot, ed.] he maintained the propriety of the unusual operation:

> That man [Philips] was not executed by a tyrannical stroke of power. Nor was he a Socrates. He was a fugitive murderer and an outlaw—a man who commanded an infamous banditti, and at a

time when the war was at the most perilous stage. He committed the most cruel and shocking barbarities. He was an enemy to the human name. Those who declare war against the human race may be struck out of existence as soon as they are apprehended. He was not executed according to those beautiful legal ceremonies which are pointed out by the laws in criminal cases. The enormity of his crimes did not entitle him to it. I am truly a friend to legal forms and methods; but sir, the occasion warranted the measure. A pirate, an outlaw, or a common enemy of all mankind may be put to death at any time.

Few Antifederalists would have been concerned about the summary form of justice meted out to the outlaw Philips because the decision had been made by citizens whose dedication to the public well-being could scarcely be questioned. Since these guardians of the public order could be depended upon to make trustworthy choices, there was no need to hold them rigorously to observing "those beautiful legal ceremonies" so carefully put aside by Henry. This was especially true if the accused were an outsider who was not only alien to their established order, but who in fact conducted himself as an outlaw, an enemy to their community, one whose actions "did not entitle him to" the same treatment that a local citizen would receive. Obviously the rights of an alien against the local community were not conceived to be the same as those of a local citizen against the national government. In the latter case trial by jury was regarded by Henry and a host of other Antifederalists as absolutely indispensable for the preservation of individual liberty. Such protections were necessary because men in high national office would no longer be affected by the unwritten customs of their people, but would be far removed from such influences and involved in the more abstract and legalistic processes of big government. As a general rule, the Antifederalists trusted an official less the further removed he was from his home locality, and consequently they sought to place as many restrictions as possible on the politicians serving in the federal city. But they were much less concerned with the letter of the law restricting the activities of government officials when they could be sure that those officials would be men of their own kind, sharing the common interests and views.

Such a relationship between governors and governed could not exist, however, without considerable personal contact between a nation's political leaders and the people they represented. Such personal contact between rulers and ruled would of course be lost in a leviathan commonwealth. Consequently, along with the other Antifederalists Henry agreed with Montesquieu that large nations cannot be democratic. This was chief among his objections to the form of union devised at Philadelphia in 1787. According to the argument, great nations cannot prosper under popular government. When nations grow so large that they can be described as "empires," they suffer from a variety of ills. They are governed by ignorance, corruption, confusion, and force. Just as the Parliament in far-off London was unable to legislate capably for the colonies, so also would a domestic national government operating from a distant capital be incapable of discerning and rectifying the problems of the various parts of the nation it supervised. The "ten miles square" set aside to be the national capital would be so far removed from the nation's particular regions that the legislators would lose contact with their constituents and thus would neither be familiar with the people's problems nor sympathetic with their needs. In addition, the politicians produced by this system would also be highly susceptible to corruption since they would be elected at great intervals and placed hundreds or even thousands of miles from those whom they governed.

Furthermore, the affairs of such a leviathan commonwealth would be too complicated for either the people or their representatives to comprehend them. Governing an "empire" would be a work "too great for human wisdom." The law-makers would be unequal to their task simply because it would be beyond their powers as mortal men. It would be impossible to legislate equitably for all the various parts of an "empire" since territories far apart from each other must inevitably have different customs and interests. Each state would have its own particular character, or "genius," which a wise legislator would not ignore. Thus, Henry informed the Convention, "After all your reforms in government, unless you consult the genius of its [the country's] inhabitants, you will never succeed; your system can have no duration." The government of Virginia had been found to be compatible with the happiness of its people, but the same would not be true of a government which must tend to an empire. Up to then, he said, Virginia had been able to govern herself adequately because "The system of laws under which we have lived has been tried and found to suit our genius." But since the national government must attempt to keep the interests of all the states in view, it would be obliged to rule in accordance with a general interest that might fit no particular state very well.

Furthermore, Henry predicted, under the new system no single state or region would be safe from hostile combinations of the other states. The unhappy experience which Americans had just suffered a few years earlier with an unsympathetic English government would be repeated if Virginia committed herself to obeying the edicts of a distant national authority which would be dominated by congressmen representing the other states. And in Henry's view such conflicts might well be unavoidable considering the extensive territory of the United States. If the bonds of union were not tied too firmly, distinct differences might exist from state to state or from section to section without causing friction. But the prospects of friction from these differences were to him an insuperable objection to the rigid kind of national union which he predicted would result from adopting the Constitution. Accordingly, Henry [again quoted by Elliot] warned that in adopting the Constitution Virginians would be threatened with the loss of liberty:

> When the people of Virginia, at a future day, shall wish to alter their government, though they should be unanimous in this desire, yet they may be prevented therefrom by a despicable minority at the extremity of the United States . . . It is not the particular government of Virginia: one

of the leading features of that government is, that a majority can alter it, when necessary for the public good. This government is not a Virginian, but an American government. Is it not, therefore, a consolidated government?

To those who might have suggested that he was unnecessarily suspicious in doubting the capacity for justice in Virginia's sister states, Henry replied that an instance of such sectional selfishness had already occurred, but fortunately nothing had come of it. Less than two years prior to Virginia's ratifying convention, John Jay had negotiated a treaty with Spain and recommended that the Mississippi River be surrendered to Spanish rule in exchange for trading rights largely beneficial to the Northeastern states. When the matter appeared before the Congress, seven Northern states supported the measure, but all of the enraged Southern states opposed it; and the motion was defeated according to the rules of the Articles of Confederation which were then in effect. But, Henry suggested, if the Constitution were ratified and the incident were to recur, the Southern states would have no adequate defense against loss of the Mississippi.

Other, less foreseeable, unpleasantries might also be visited upon Virginia in the same manner. Nor was Henry at a loss to suggest some of these other potential sources of friction between the states. Slavery, he warned, could conceivably become an object of interference by combinations of other states hostile to the peculiar institution. He thus concluded that it was better for each state to regulate its own internal affairs, and commit itself to the national government to the least extent possible.

By consolidating too closely under one national banner, Henry predicted, the citizens of the particular states would lose their basic freedoms. It was true, he conceded to the Federalists, that the nation might achieve a certain grandeur. But the price would be too dear. "No matter whether the people be great, splendid, and powerful," he argued, "if they enjoy freedom." He believed that the purpose of government is not so much to enhance the glory and wealth of the nation as to preserve freedom since "the most valuable end of government is the liberty of the inhabitants." The people are not free, however, if they cannot govern themselves as they wish, consistent with their own special "genius." Only if they are able to live according to their established way of life can the people be happy, enjoying what they have tried and found acceptable to themselves.

Henry thus argued that forming "a more perfect union" could easily conflict with securing the blessings of liberty for the nation's intractably various citizens. As long as the people of widely separated areas retain their own particular customs and views, it is foolish to expect any semblance of perfection in an artificially contrived union. The seeds of discord are imbedded wherever there are pronounced differences of any kind between peoples. Since the character of any nation is determined by a variety of circumstances peculiar to itself (differences of climate, soil, religion, and history), one cannot expect homogeneity among widespread regions. In legislating for a territory encompassing a variety of regions it is foolish to ignore

their differences, and it is madness to attempt to form them into a single entity. Henry thus maintained that the statesman should be extremely cautious in any attempt to form a more perfect union when union did not already exist on the basis of the much more natural ties of human attachment and interest.

Unlike the Federalists, he saw no identity between liberty and the strength of union; in the "consolidation" he foresaw under the Constitution he feared that he and his fellow citizens would be swallowed up by Leviathan. Nor did he agree that the first and last aims listed in the Preamble should be mentioned as if they were of equivalent value. In his opening speech at the Virginia ratifying convention, he boldly stated the crucial difference between Federalists and Antifederalists when he announced that "The first thing I have at heart is American liberty: the second thing is American union." Ultimately this priority would not let him agree to the Federalist system because he felt that vigorous national efforts to overcome the futility of union would inevitably deprive the people of the liberties they already enjoyed as a matter of custom.

The prestige of Washington's name, the convention's knowledge that eight states had already ratified the Constitution, and some shady dealing by Edmund Randolph helped to secure a narrow victory for the Virginia Federalists. It was Henry's bitterest defeat, one of the few times in his career that he actively supported a losing cause, and he attempted to mitigate the effects of the loss by supporting efforts to amend the Constitution's most radical defects. Nevertheless, he accepted the defeat gracefully, declared that he would be a "peaceable citizen," and offered no resistance to the new system.

Indeed, not only was Henry as good as his word, he was even better. Although the Bill of Rights was by no means all that he and the other Antifederalists had desired, he was mollified to some extent by the passage of those first ten amendments. In the course of the next decade he gradually became more and more accommodated to the Federalists. In time he became convinced the Federalist leaders were competent statesmen whose policies were not leading the nation to destruction. He was particularly reconciled to Washington, but he also had a special regard for John Adams and John Marshall. Henry's reapproachment with the Federalists was so complete that during his second term as President, Washington offered him the positions of Secretary of State, Chief Justice of the Supreme Court, and Minister to Spain—the last being of special significance when one remembers Henry's earlier objections to bartering away the Mississippi according to Jay's suggestions of 1786.

At the same time that Henry was growing friendlier with the Federalists, he found himself increasingly at odds with the Jeffersonians. Jefferson and Henry had a long string of differences dating back at least to 1781, when Jefferson was accused of negligence and cowardice for his wartime conduct as governor of Virginia; after the investigation was concluded, Jefferson continued to harbor suspicions that Henry had instigated the inquiry. Their differences were aggravated in the 1780's when Jefferson and Madison collaborated in defeating in the Virginia legislature a measure Henry had sponsored providing financial support for the Christian religions in the state. In fact, there is reason to believe that Jefferson and his lieutenant conspired to get Henry elected governor, thereby removing him from the legislature and enabling them to defeat the bill in his absence. Matters were not helped any by the fact that Henry believed that Jefferson was a Deist, while, in the decade following the Constitution's ratification, he himself grew increasingly orthodox.

These differences became pronounced when the two Virginians manifested opposite attitudes toward the French Revolution. Jefferson and his followers were at first pro-French and generally shared the Enlightenment sentiments which often went hand-in-hand with the Revolution. On the other hand, Henry was especially appalled at the atheism which appeared to be an integral part of the new French doctrines. He was disturbed to learn, for example, that the French extremists had erected a statue to a Goddess of Reason. He predicted that the French people did not have sufficient virtue to be able to establish and maintain a popular government. When he learned that Napoleon's early successes were being celebrated by some American admirers of the French cause, he asserted that the French people were not capable of sustaining a democracy, and he predicted that the very man whose victories they were then cheering might well become the next master of France.

In Henry's understanding, which he and the other Antifederalists may well have borrowed from Montesquieu, democratic nations require a virtuous citizenry if they are to be viable. But Henry did not necessarily learn this point from Montesquieu. While he was still in his teens he had read Livy's history of Rome, and he was so affected that he resolved to read the work annually thereafter. And the point might have been driven home even more emphatically during his years as governor of Virginia when he could not help but note the numerous occasions in which the national interest depended upon the virtue and unselfishness of the citizens. For a nation to be well-governed, he might have reasoned, it must be ruled for its good and not for the private interest of the ruler. But in a democracy the ruler is the people. Thus, the syllogism concludes, for a democratic nation to be well-governed, the citizens must be public-spirited, exercising self-restraint and ruling for the nation's benefit rather than for their own selfish interests.

Montesquieu represented this self-restraint, or virtue, as equivalent to patriotism, but Henry apparently thought that few men will be virtuous from intellectual conviction alone, without the sanctions of revealed religion to assist them in the preservation of character. Washington shared this opinion and, although he was no match for Henry as a speaker, he proved no less outspoken on the subject. In his Farewell Address of 1796 [quoted by Norine D. Campbell, in her *Patrick Henry, Patriot and Statesman*], Washington advised the American people that they should be wary of ignoring the benefits of religion to themselves and to their country:

> Of all the dispositions and habits which lead to political prosperity, religion and morality are in-

dispensable supports. In vain would that man claim the tribute of patriotism, who should labor to subvert these great pillars of human happiness, these props of the destinies of men and citizens. The mere politician, equally with the pious man, ought to respect and to cherish them . . . And let us with caution indulge the supposition, that morality can be maintained without religion. Whatever may be conceded to the influence of refined education on minds of peculiar structure, reason and experience both forbid us to expect, that national morality can prevail in exclusion of religious principles.

Henry obviously agreed with the Father of Our Country on this point since he included in his will the same admonition which he bequeathed to those who inherited the nation he and Washington had done so much to establish: "Righteousness alone can exalt them [the American people] as a nation. Reader! whoever thou art, remember this; and in thy sphere practice virtue thyself, and encourage it in others." (pp. 99-114)

J. Michael Bordelon, "Visions of Disorder: Patrick Henry and the American Founding," in The Occasional Review, *No. 4, Winter, 1976, pp. 99-120.*

The only recorded eye-witness account of Henry's "Caesar-Brutus" speech:

May the 30th. Set out Early from halfway house in the Chair and broke fast at York, arived at williamsburg at 12, where I saw three Negroes hanging at the galous for haveing robed Mr. Waltho of 300 ps. I went imediately to the assembly which was seting, where I was entertained with very strong Debates Concerning Dutys that the parlement wants to lay on the american Colonys, which they Call or Stile stamp Dutys. Shortly after I Came in one of the members stood up and said he had read that in former times tarquin and Julus had their Brutus, Charles had his Cromwell, and he Did not Doubt but some good american would stand up, in favour of his Country, but (says he) in a more moderate manner, and was going to Continue, when the speaker of the house rose and Said, he, the last that stood up had spoke traison, and was sorey to see that not one of the members of the house was loyal Enough to stop him, before he had gone so far. upon which the Same member stood up again (his name is henery) and said that if he had afronted the speaker, or the house, he was ready to ask pardon, and he would shew his loyalty to his majesty King G. the third, at the Expence of the last Drop of his blood, but what he had said must be atributed to the Interest of his Countrys Dying liberty which he had at heart, and the heat of passion might have lead him to have said something more than he intended, but, again, if he said any thing wrong, he beged the speaker and the houses pardon. some other Members stood up and backed him, on which that afaire was droped.

"Journal of a French Traveller in the Colonies, 1765," in The American Historical Review, *July, 1921.*

David A. McCants (essay date 1981)

[*In the following essay, American educator and critic McCants examines Henry's role in the Stamp Act debate. He claims that while the "Caesar-Brutus" speech has drawn much attention, the oration was only one aspect of Henry's involvement as a leader and strategist in the controversy.*]

About mid-May, 1764, the colonies learned that the House of Commons had proposed a Stamp Act. Opposition surfaced quickly. Economic burdens, especially those resulting from the recently concluded Seven Years War, caused some to oppose revenue acts in general. More significant, though, was the threatening precedent posed by the Stamp Act. It was the first direct, internal tax levied by Parliament. As such, it violated the constitutional principle requiring legislative consent to any tax. The colonies protested the Stamp Act proposal through their London agents and by legislative remonstrances to the King, Lords, and Commons. Parliament refused to hear the petitions and approved the Stamp Act on March 22, 1765. The act was to be effective November 1.

By adopting the Virginia Resolves in a debate that occurred May 29-31, 1765, the Virginia House of Burgesses was the first to declare resistance to Parliament's decision. At the center of the debate was Patrick Henry, newly elected by the freeholders of Louisa County in a special election. A well established Piedmont attorney and plantation owner, Henry entered the Assembly in the third week of the session, almost simultaneously with the notice that the House of Commons had not heeded the lobbying and appeals of the colonial legislatures. Publication of the intemperate Virginia Resolves in the colonial press stimulated resistance in other colonies. Over the next several months other legislatures and an intercolonial Congress, called by Massachusetts, echoed the Virginia Resolves. Public protests which began with rioting in Massachusetts were followed by the formulation of nonimportation agreements and the development of an organized intercolonial resistance movement by the Sons of Liberty. Final vindication of the colonial position occurred March 18, 1766, when George III approved repeal of the Stamp Act.

The Stamp Act debate impelled democrats throughout the colonies to rebel against the authority of the British Parliament; in addition, it established Henry as a political leader and orator of unequalled excellence. It is, therefore, disappointing that the record of this momentous debate—including the performance of its principal—is so scanty that Douglas Southall Freeman speculated [in his *George Washington,* 1951] that "perhaps four-fifths of what has been written about the proceedings . . . is guesswork." Reconstruction of the debate requires guesswork because the historical records are slight and of uncertain reliability.

The official account is meager because the *Journal* of the House of Burgesses recorded only the texts of approved resolutions in amended form. In keeping with the custom of the time, it did not report the order of speeches, the substance of speakers' remarks, or the texts of amendments. Committees of the Whole of the Virginia Assembly—and the Stamp Act debate on May 29 was conducted in Committee of the Whole—did not keep journals.

Unofficial accounts—also meager—are suspect because only one witness—an unidentified French traveller—is known to have written down any of what he saw or heard at the time. All other accounts were written as recollections or secondhand reports. Henry, who preserved none of his speeches and wrote few recollections, did leave a brief notice of the debate which was found with his will. The accounts of [fellow burgess] Paul Carrington, assemblyman, and the accounts of John Tyler and Thomas Jefferson, spectators, were written as much as fifty years after the event. What appear to be reliable secondhand reports—by Commissary William Robinson, Governor Fauquier, and newspapers in London, Bristol, and Glasgow—have the advantages of contemporaneousness but are exceptionally brief.

Legislative procedures, personal indifference to historical preservation, and poor memory limit the thoroughness with which the debate can be reconstructed but do not warrant rhetoricians' neglect of this controversy. The purpose of this essay is to re-examine the incomplete and dubious records of the Stamp Act debate, especially those elements central to understanding the role of Patrick Henry. The chronology of the debate, Henry's role as speaker and parliamentary strategist, and reconstruction of the peroration to Henry's **"Caesar-Brutus"** speech constitute the principal topics of investigation. The study enlarges our understanding of Henry's role in this vigorously contended, narrowly determined debate by emphasizing his role as the debate's fomenter and strategist; by explaining how the House's rules afforded him numerous opportunities to influence the debate oratorically; by affirming the radical arguments of the **"Caesar-Brutus"** speech; and by reconstructing its oft-quoted conclusion.

On May 29, George Johnston of Fairfax County moved, seconded by Patrick Henry, that the House form a Committee of the Whole to consider the "steps necessary to be taken in consequence of the resolutions of the House of Commons of Great Britain relative to the charging certain Stamp duties in the colonies and plantations in America." Upon approval of the motion, Speaker John Robinson surrendered the chair to Attorney-General Peyton Randolph as provided by the House's rules. In the Committee of the Whole Henry proposed and Johnston seconded the resolves, each of which was moved, debated, and approved separately by small majorities. Later that day the Attorney-General reported the Committee's resolves to the House, and the House ordered that the report be received the next day. How many resolutions were moved, how many were approved, who spoke to the resolutions, what arguments were advanced on May 29 is uncertain.

On May 30, the House received the resolutions as ordered the previous day. Attorney-General Randolph read the resolutions, delivered them "in at the table, where they were again twice read, and agreed to by the House, with some amendments." Four approved resolutions then follow in the record:

> *Resolved,* That the first adventurers and settlers of this his Majesty's Colony and Dominion of

Virginia brought with them, and transmitted to their posterity, and all other his Majesty's subjects since inhabiting in this his Majestey's said Colony, all the liberties, privileges, franchises, and immunities, that have at any time been held, enjoyed, and possessed, by the people of Great Britain.

Resolved, That by two royal charters, granted by King James the First, the Colonists aforesaid are declared entitled to all liberties, privileges, and immunities of denizens and natural subjects, to all intents and purposes, as if they had been abiding and born within the realm of England.

Resolved, That the taxation of the people by themselves, or by persons chosen by themselves to represent them, who can only know what taxes the people are able to bear, or the easiest method of raising them, and must themselves be affected by every tax laid on the people, is the only security against a burdensome taxation, and the distinguishing characteristic of British freedom, without which the ancient Constitution cannot exist.

Resolved, That his Majesty's liege people of this his most ancient and loyal Colony have without interruption enjoyed the inestimable right of being governed by such laws, respecting their internal polity and taxation, as are derived from their own consent, with the approbation of their Sovereign, or his substitute; and that the same hath never been forfeited or yielded up, but hath been constantly recognized by the Kings and people of Great Britain.

But what of those amendments to which the *Journal* [*of the House of Burgesses of Virginia, 1761-1765*] refers? Minor changes, which strengthened the resolutions, can be identified by comparing Henry's copy of the resolutions with the *Journal,* as Freeman has done. The dating of these changes, however, cannot be established. Major amendments may have been approved on the thirtieth. These are suggested by press reports that seven resolves were debated. The additional resolves read as follows:

Resolved therefore, That the General Assembly of this Colony, with the consent of his Majesty, or his substitute, have the sole right and authority to lay taxes and impositions upon it's [*sic*] inhabitants; And, That every attempt to vest such authority in any other person or persons whatsoever, has a manifest tendency to destroy [Henry's copy includes "British as well as"] American freedom.

That his Majesty's liege people, inhabitants of this Colony, are not bound to yield obedience to any law or ordinance whatsoever, designed to impose any taxation upon them, other than the laws or ordinances of the General Assembly as aforesaid.

That any person who shall, by speaking, or writing, assert or maintain, that any person or persons, other than the General Assembly of this Colony, with such consent as aforesaid, have any right or authority to lay or impose any tax whatsoever on the inhabitants thereof, shall be deemed, an enemy to his Majesty's Colony.

Whatever may have been the substance of the amendments, the debating of amendments on May 30 suggests that the Burgesses were sufficiently divided or intense in their convictions that they would not allow the recommendations of the House meeting in Committee of the Whole on May 29 to become the decisions of the House May 30 without contest.

On May 31, at least one of the resolutions was expunged, and, according to Carrington, "*actually* erased" from the manuscript *Journal* of the House. Most likely the fifth resolution was expunged. The specific action of expunging, as with the amendments of the thirtieth, cannot be reliably established, however. What is clear is that on this third day of the debate the opponents of the **"Virginia Resolves"** parliamentarily tested their strength and won a small victory. How did this happen? Henry left Williamsburg on May 30. Perhaps he—and others—expected the Assembly to return to routine business and by their absence sufficiently altered the House's composition to reflect a change of attitude toward a resolution passed the previous day by a single vote.

Moses Coit Tyler [in his *Patrick Henry,* 1887] believed that Henry regarded writing and championing the Virginia resolutions "the one most important thing he ever did." Certainly he would have been justified in such a self-evaluation, not just because the debate had significant personal and political consequences, but because of the completeness with which he participated. Henry framed the resolutions, co-directed the parliamentary moves on the floor of the House, and spoke in behalf of the resolutions. Thus, the pride he felt may derive as much from the comprehensive nature of his role in the **"Stamp Act"** debate as the magnitude of the debate's effects.

That Henry was elected to the House of Burgesses to lead the opposition to the Stamp Act is an exciting but unsubstantiated contention. His leadership is more properly attributed to personal initiative and the powerful articulation of his convictions in oratory than to political organization. Henry's own memorandum about the debate supports such a view. A sealed paper, left for his executors to open, contained the first five resolutions and the following narrative:

The within resolutions . . . formed the first opposition to the Stamp Act. All the colonies, either through fear, or want of opportunity to form an opposition, or from influence of some kind or other, had remained silent. I had been for the first time elected a Burgess a few days before, was young, inexperienced, unacquainted with the forms of the House, and the members that composed it. Finding the men of weight averse to opposition, and the commencement of the tax at hand, and that no person was likely to step forth, I determined to venture, and alone, unadvised, and unassisted, on a blank leaf of an old law-book, wrote the within. Upon offering them to the House, violent debates ensued.

Two prominent students of this period of American history believe that Henry exaggerated his role as author of the resolves. Irving Brant discredits Henry's originality; Edmund Morgan questions Henry's independency. Brant [in his *James Madison,* I, 1941] considers the resolutions "a condensed and vigorous paraphrase" of the memorials adopted by the House of Burgesses, December 1764. He observes that in places they "parallel, word for word" and that they contain "not a vital thought" which cannot be found in the other. Also, he chastises Henry for not admitting his debt. Direct parallels between the **"Virginia Resolves"** and the December memorials are immediately apparent; the absence of original thoughts is also evident. Brant's critique, however, misleads in two respects:

One, it assumes that Henry tried to conceal, or did not wish to admit, the similarities of language and thought. The only evidence for such a conclusion is negative. What seems more probable is that Henry expected, indeed that he wanted, the similarities to be recognized. Henry, the rhetor, prepared the **"Virginia Resolves"**; the rhetor typically argues from matters of belief and principle to which the audience subscribes. The parallels—especially of thought—represent a strategy of invention.

Two, Brant's critique misrepresents the resolves as a paraphrase. The significant condensation and alteration of tone which Brant observed are not characteristic of paraphrasing. The December memorials, collectively, are about six times as long as the five resolves. Moreover, they represent three genres of political discourse—Address, Memorial, and Remonstrance—which differ not only from one another but also from the genre of Resolution.

The Virginia House of Burgesses approved an "Address" to the King. The status difference between sovereign and subjects is accentuated by the impersonal and exalted modes of address; the power difference is accentuated by the supplicative tone; and reaffirmation of submission to the royal prerogative is expressed in the close. The Burgesses approved a "Memorial" to the Lords. The apologetic tone, the expressions of humility, and the flattery of the Lords honor the Lords' hereditary position; the statement of reasons, like the classical *narratio,* is adapted to predispose the Lords to a particular view but does not confront them with demonstration. To the Commons the Burgesses sent a "Remonstrance," which is a protest or reproof. Claims are asserted; arguments are amplified evidentially; the proposed recourse requested of the Commons is explicit; firmness of tone masks urgency, however.

The "Resolution" Henry drafted, addressed to an audience of peers facing a common threat, is neither supplicative nor solicitous; its style (the categorical terms, the direct expression) and form (highly compressed thought, climactically ordered reasons-and-consequent structure) coalesce to set forth the firmest determination of opinion, in this case a declaration of resistance to British authority as defined in the Stamp Act. In the manner typical of resolutions, the exclusivity of the Assembly's power to tax and the unequivocal condemnation of the Parliament's usurpation is expressed as a unanimously held belief, the truth of which is final and incontestable.

Henry's resolves are as original and as fitting to their con-

text as any of the December memorials. Brant underestimates the originality and significance of the condensation Henry executed, mistakenly labels a document with a different temper and purpose a paraphrase of three quite dissimilar documents, and overlooks the rhetorical significance of inventional similarities between the **"Virginia Resolves"** and the December memorials.

Edmund Morgan [in *Maryland Historical Magazine,* June 1951] believes that the **"Virginia Resolves"** were group written. The evidence upon which the claim is based is truly slim, an account Edmund Pendleton prepared for James Madison in 1790. Like other accounts of the Stamp Act debate, this one was written many years after the events. Like some of the other accounts, it is not first hand. And, like so much of the other accounts, it is neither full nor specific. That there was a meeting of Stamp Act opponents is confirmed by Paul Carrington. And both Carrington and Pendleton offer similar enumerations of those present. Also, both connect the meeting and the development of the resolves, but neither reports any details of what took place in the meeting.

Of the authorship of the resolutions Carrington wrote that "who held the pen I never knew or heard." Pendleton, not really more informed, wrote "that some Gentlemen . . . met and formed those Resolutions." Pendleton's account hardly creates reasonable doubt that Henry was not the sole author of the resolves. The order of events is not definitely known; Pendleton's words do not convincingly support one interpretation of the order of events. Perhaps those in attendance agreed to support resolves Henry composed during the meeting. Or, perhaps the group came to no agreement and Henry subsequently developed the resolves and shared them with Johnston, and possibly others, whose views he knew. In the absence of specific information about the order of events from a reliable source, Henry's limited claim—he claims only authorship of the resolutions as an independent action—stands.

Most likely Henry and Johnston planned the debate cooperatively, Henry having played the important role of framer of the **"Virginia Resolves."** Various sources link them in this episode in significant ways: both attended the meeting, they alternated roles of mover and seconder in the business on the floor May 29 and 30, and Johnston supported the resolves with speeches in the debate. In addition, there is testimony that it was Johnston, with great difficulty, who persuaded Henry to speak in the debate. These little noticed evidences of shared leadership with Johnston, including activities in the formative stages of the debate, enlarge our understanding of the roles Henry filled in the debate.

It is not known how often, in what order, or at what length Henry spoke. The rules of the House limited each member to speaking once. Indeed, the rules provided fines for speaking more than once on the same question. This limitation, however, was in practice not restrictive: One, the rules allowed members to speak to the same bill during different readings. Detailed consideration followed second reading; however, bills could be debated on first reading; and they could be debated and amended on third reading. Two, the rules provided for full and free discussion in committee, usually following second reading. The Stamp Act resolutions were considered in three readings and in Committee of the Whole. Further, since each of the re-solves was moved and seconded separately, each was probably debated successively. The procedures, therefore, allowed Henry numerous opportunities to enter the debate.

The order of speakers and the sequencing of issues cannot be reconstructed in significant detail. Accounts by Jefferson and Carrington suggest that the debate occurred in at least two parts, the first four resolutions sparking different objections than number five, and that Henry entered the debate on both issues. Both report that the opponents of the resolves considered the first four resolutions to be quite similar to the objections presented in the December memorials and argued that the House should take no further action until a response had been received. Carrington then says: "Mr. Henry, however, thought otherwise and went on to support his resolutions in a manner beyond my powers of description. . . . the first four were agreed to without violent opposition. But when the 5th and last came to be considered . . . Mr. Henry's manly eloquence surpassed everything of the kind I had ever heard before." Jefferson does not so clearly suggest that Henry spoke more than once, but he does contrast the debate on the first four resolutions and the fifth, terming the debate on the fifth "most bloody."

One of the misleading impressions perpetuated by writings about the debate may be the notion that all that Henry said must have been contained in a single, extended address which culminated in the **"Caesar-Brutus"** line. This impression is the direct result of scarcity of information about what took place and lack of understanding about the forms of legislative debate in colonial America. Unfortunately, it has contributed to Henry's larger-than-life reputation as one who rescued lost or neglected causes by brilliant, single oratorical efforts. This is a distortion of Henry's unquestionable superiority as an orator and his legislative acumen.

Neither Jefferson, Carrington, nor Tyler, the three witnesses who recalled the **"Caesar-Brutus"** line, could recall the topics of this speech, delivered presumably during the debate on the fifth resolution, May 29. Thus, little is reliably known about what Henry said in any of the debate. The only outline of the speech on the fifth resolution is the discredited one in John Daly Burk's *History of Virginia.* Extant evidence yields reliable knowledge only about the theme of the speech and the sources of its controversiality.

The most complete statement of Henry's position by a contemporaneous source is the secondhand report of Commissary Robinson, cousin of Speaker John Robinson. According to Robinson [quoted in *Historical Collections Relating to the American Colonial Church,* William Stevens Perry, ed.], Henry "blazed out in a violent speech against the Authority of parliament and the King" and offered "several outrageous resolves." Robinson's statement, which points up the tenor of the debate and the theme of Henry's speech, is confirmed by a variety of sources. Henry, for example, said that the resolutions prompted " 'violent debates' " and that " 'many threats were uttered, and [that] much abuse [was] cast' " on him.

Jefferson, as already cited, characterized the debate on the final resolution as "most bloody." The French traveller perceived the debate as "very hot." Newspaper reports confirm the incendiary nature of the debates. A Bristol dispatch, composed in Virginia, said that the Burgesses spoke freely in the House of the enslaving character of the Stamp Act. Governor Fauquier received word that Henry used "very indecent language" in the debate and that he carried the "young hot and giddy" members. What generated such an animated debate? Henry's "outrageous resolves," as Robinson termed them, were undoubtedly viewed as an attack on the authority of the Parliament and the King. In addition, the resolves—or interpretations of them by Henry and probably others—must have been viewed as an appeal for resistance which was seditious, if not treasonous.

Which resolution justified such a heated debate and ominous interpretation? Was it the fifth? Jefferson believed not. He believed, in recollection, that it was the sixth resolution that sparked the most violent debate. If, as some believed, the sixth and seventh resolutions were never moved, the question whether the fifth resolution justified such a heated debate remains. Freeman believes that the fifth resolution did justify major controversy. The language and content of the first four resolutions are quite similar to that of the memorials addressed to the King, Lords, and Commons in 1764. But the fifth, Freeman argues [again in his *George Washington*], because it was stated as consequent of the first four resolves, quite specifically and somewhat boldly asserted that *any* Parliamentary tax was tyrannous and thus unequivocally implied the right and duty of resistance. Resolutions six and seven explicitly called for resistance. But Henry's opponents might very well have anticipated such appeals in the debate on resolution five, provoking Henry's **"Caesar-Brutus"** threat and a decision to withhold resolutions six and seven.

The testimonies of Jefferson, Carrington, Tyler, Pendleton, and the French traveller support the view that Henry's speech constituted sedition. The resolutions may have been considered seditious, too. Certainly they were more direct and bold than the House's protests of 1764, which may be sufficient to explain why conservatives who supported Stamp Act protestations in 1764 did not support Henry's resolves. Too, the chronology of events had altered the psychological situation. In 1764, the Burgesses protested a bill; in 1765, Henry appealed for resistance to the law. Henry claimed to have been aware of the daring in his move. He told Judge John Tyler that he "was convinced of the rectitude of the cause" and his "own views." He was prepared, if necessary, he said, to seek "safe retreat from tyranny" in the back country. Optimistic that "a united sentiment and sound patriotism" would prevail, he also was convinced that "if the people would not die or be free, it was no consequence what sort of government they lived under."

The defiant peroration of the **"Caesar-Brutus"** speech, as published by William Wirt [in his *Sketches of the Life and Character of Patrick Henry,* 1841], was provided by Judge John Tyler, who, standing next to Jefferson, observed the debate from the House door. According to Tyler, Henry said: "Caesar had his Brutus—Charles the First, his Cromwell—and George the Third—*may profit by their example.* If *this* be treason, make the most of it." Wirt acknowledged that he had heard such variations of these words that he wondered if it was all fiction. He published the line after Jefferson vouched its authenticity. Three major variations occur across a variety of reports. These raise questions about the accuracy of Wirt's version, the audacity of Henry's threat to the Crown, and the legitimacy of his title as oratorical patriot of the American revolution.

One variation includes allusion to Tarquin as well as to Caesar and Cromwell. Henry, according to Commissary Robinson [as quoted in Perry], compared "his Majesty to a Tarquin, a Caesar, and a Charles the First . . . not sparing insinuations that he wished another Cromwell would arise." The *London Gazeteer and New Daily Advertiser,* and the French traveller, also report the reference to Tarquin. All three sources probably wrote their reports very close to the date of the debate. Moreover, the French traveller witnessed the debate. Thus the version Tyler provided Wirt is often amended to read: "Tarquin and Caesar had each his Brutus, Charles the First his Cromwell, and George the Third—may profit by their example! If this be treason, make the most of it."

The second variation pertains to Henry's retort to the cries of treason which greeted his comparisons. The variation shows Henry to be less daring than the traditional version. The version preserved by Edmund Randolph [in his *Histo-*

P.H. Rothermel's idealization of Henry's Caesar-Brutus Speech *in the Virginia House of Burgesses.*

ry of Virginia, 1970] reads: " ' . . . and George the Third, may he never have either.' " The version preserved by Edmund Pendleton, who, like Randolph, was not an observer, says that Henry did not name George III. Similarly, the version published in the *London Gazeteer* does not name George III. These reports in concert with that of the French traveller, whose version also implies George III was not mentioned, create serious doubt about the directness, although not the meaning, of Henry's statement.

The French traveller's account constitutes the strongest challenge to the authenticity of the traditional version. The diarist implies that Henry did not mention George III by name; in addition, he says that Henry apologized. Some critics, most notably Edmund and Helen Morgan [in *The Stamp Act Crisis: Prologue to Revolution,* 1953], conclude that this combination of facts proves that Henry's legendary daring is just that—legend. However, the reasoning is tenuous. By all estimations Henry spoke boldly. Even the French traveller's report supports the conclusion that Henry's advocacy was daring. Henry's meaning was clear even if there is a dispute about the exact language of his attack upon the King. He was interrupted with cries of treason, and later entries by the French traveller show that the speech was being widely discussed and that the public did not consider it weak.

In part, the Morgans' argument seems to be based upon a curious juggling of evidence. They say that the diary entry of May 31 (which the diarist probably misdated for May 30) makes it clear that the House did debate resistance in the form suggested by the seventh resolution. Thus, they conclude that on May 30 the House was ready "to go much farther in asserting their rights than has generally been supposed." What logic justifies drawing conclusions which enlarge the House's daring while deflating Henry's? Perhaps an open division in the House on the question of resistance at once emboldened Henry and tried his patience, and led to a show of defiance which Brant termed the "one false step" in Henry's oratorical career. Wirt judged Henry to be "throughout life, one of the most perfectly and uniformly decorous speakers that ever took the floor of the house. He was respectful even to humility; and the provocation must be gross indeed which would induce him to notice it." Specious arguments that the House's petitions might yet win a hearing, or abusive attacks which Henry may have viewed as stemming from his threat to the established leadership or their deficient patriotism in a critical moment, just might provoke misstep by a fervent lover of liberty.

The apology constitutes the third variation. According to the diarist, Henry, having been interrupted by the Speaker,

> stood up again . . . and said that if he had afronted the speaker, or the house, he was ready to ask pardon, and he would shew his loyalty to his majesty King G. the third, at the Expence of the last Drop of his blood, but what he had said must be atributed to the Interest of his Countrys Dying liberty which he had at heart, and the heat of passion might have lead him to have said something more than he intended, but, again, if

he had said any thing wrong, he beged the speaker and the houses pardon.

Only the French traveller reported the apology; however, it seems highly likely that it occurred. The absence of references to it by other sources, though, in no way detracts from Henry's image: the situation required apology.

In the first place, apology was conventional. Bernard Mayo [in his *Myths and Men,* 1959] speaks succinctly about the convention. "Many quibblers," he says, "contend that this gesture of respect takes the fire out of his speech. Actually it was conventional down to 1776, even after a year of bloody fighting, to damn Parliament and affirm loyalty to 'His Most Gracious Majesty'—but decidedly unconventional to threaten him with the fate of the decapitated Charles the First." Apology was the "required behavior of a loyal member of the house," according to Mary Patterson Clarke [in her *Parliamentary Privilege in the American Colonies,* 1943]. Indeed, had Henry apologized on his knees, she says, he would have been following the "best liberal traditions of his day," because in 1765 the colonials acknowledged that "most assemblies were called by the king's writ, were acting in the king's name, and were bound by innumerable ties of law and sentiment to England of which the king was a personification."

In the second place, apology was required for self protection and to save the House from censure. Henry risked personal and public safety with his original use of the severed head symbol. The symbol was first used to allay opposition to Charles I and the divine right of kings theory. In the years preceding the American revolution Whig orators and pamphleteers helped strip Charles I of his martyr's image. Among these was Jonathan Mayhew, who gave a new twist to the symbol when in 1750 he linked Charles' name and fate with a reigning monarch. Mayhew's comparison is favorable to George I; Henry linked the name and fate of Charles I with reigning monarch George III—unfavorably. The comparison constituted an intolerable threat upon the King; it risked Henry's personal position *and* the security of the House.

Clarke argues that representation was viewed as the central feature of the English constitution. In America, the Assembly embodied that concept. Through the Assembly the colonials practiced self-determination. The House could not allow Henry or any other member to endanger its existence or sovereign powers. Thus the Assembly, like the House of Commons, claimed—and exercised—the authority to discipline its members. Even if Henry did not believe that his remarks were treasonous, it is hard to believe that he would have welcomed exclusion from the Assembly—the only agency for change in the colony—or desired to damage the status of the "palladium of liberty!"

How sincere was the apology? If Henry apologized to protect his person, to protect the Assembly, or to observe polite convention, then it is probable that the obsequiousness of his words was evident in his delivery. Meade [in his *Patrick Henry: Patriot in the Making,* 1957] notes that "it was an age when gentlemen would bow politely even before attempting to run each other through in a duel." He reasons, therefore, that "if Henry did speak any apologetic words, they were doubtless uttered almost tongue in cheek to give

him some legal protection." He suggests that the French traveller, lacking familiarity with such assemblies, Virginia language, and customs, might have misunderstood Henry's performative language.

Henry detractors reason that the failure to report the apology represents a conspiracy to mythicize Henry's image. If so, then pro- and anti-Henry representatives worked equally diligently toward this end, for only one source—the most neutral—reported the apology. Those who wrote accounts of the debate many years later did not recall the broad outlines of the argument even. Why, then, should they be expected to recall the apology? Moreover, even if the reporters recalled the apology, successful American prosecution of the Revolution had eliminated the need—personal and corporate—to pay obedience to the King. Thus, an insincere apology might quite honestly not be reported, though recalled. What the apology reveals is that Henry in a tension-filled moment maintained his wits and that his oratory is more aptly compared to thunder than to fire.

The record-keeping procedures of the Virginia Assembly in the eighteenth century seriously limit the thoroughness with which the Stamp Act debate can be reconstructed. Because the *Journal* reports only the texts of approved resolutions in amended form, reconstruction of the chronology of the debate, the texts of amendments, the roles of participants, the order of speeches, and even the debaters' arguments must be derived from other sources. In the case of this debate these materials are invariably disappointingly brief and, because of such factors as personal and political partisanship, vagaries of memory, and hearsay reporting, of different degrees of reliability. Conclusions about the debate, and Henry's role in it, must be carefully weighed against the quality of the evidence.

The most salient facts reported by the *Journal* are the duration of the debate (May 29-31), consideration of the resolves in Committee of the Whole on the first day, and the final text of the amended resolves. These facts sustain inferences about the fullness and freedom of the debate, as well as the controversiality of the resolves. The expunging of at least one resolution on May 31, recollected many years later by Paul Carrington (a burgess) and Thomas Jefferson (an observer), and reported secondhand by Governor Francis Fauquier a few days after the debate, also sustains the conclusion that the resolves were vigorously contested in a full and free debate among a sharply divided house. Evidence from the unofficial sources, however, is inadequate for determining such specific issues as the number of resolves introduced May 29, the points at issue in the debating of amendments on May 30, and the substance of the expunging on May 31.

Henry played a variety of roles in the debate. He wrote the resolves, in cooperation with George Johnston planned the strategies for the debate on the House floor, and served as the chief advocate. The image of Henry that emerges from an identification of role relationships in the debate is much more complex than that of orator. Henry's reputation as an orator—as much as his political persuasion—may have influenced his election to the House and the ready welcome he received from the liberal Burgesses. But the varied leadership roles he played in the debate suggest that he employed his boldness and initiative to organize party interests as well as hurl oratorical challenges to the opposition. Identification of role relationships in the debate reveals a multifaceted Henry, not the one-dimensional orator, who, through a singular, personal effort mobilizes support for a controversial decision.

The House's rules afforded Henry numerous opportunities to enter the debate. Henry could have spoken during any of the three readings and during the deliberations in Committee of the Whole. Moreover, each of the resolutions was debated separately. Given the nature of legislative debate, Henry's loquaciousness, and Jefferson and Carrington's accounts of the debate's partitioning, it is reasonable to conclude that Henry entered the debate at several points, perhaps speaking to each resolution in turn. What has been dubbed the **"Caesar-Brutus"** speech, the date and timing of which is not reliably known, likely climaxed the debate and Henry's participation as debater.

Although only the theme, not the topics of the **"Caesar-Brutus"** speech, is identifiable, evidences from both primary and secondary sources, and sources friendly and unfriendly to Henry, confirm that Henry's speech constituted a bold and defiant attack on the authority of king and Parliament. The likelihood that Henry did not mention George III by name and apologized when greeted with cries of treason in no way detract from the daring of his oratory. Apologies which are self-serving or conventional deny the significance of apology; implied comparisons are not necessarily less forceful than explicit ones. Meaning is determined in part by social context: the insincerity of Henry's apology and the force of his comparison inhere in the setting and timing of his sensational conclusion. (pp. 205-27)

> *David A. McCants, "The Role of Patrick Henry in the Stamp Act Debate," in* The Southern Speech Communication Journal, *Vol. XLVI, No. 3, Spring, 1981, pp. 205-27.*

Lois J. Einhorn   (essay date 1981)

[*In the following excerpt, American scholar Einhorn examines assumptions concerning humankind and the role of reason in Henry's arguments at the 1788 Virginia Convention.*]

HENRY'S ASSUMPTIONS ABOUT THE ROLE OF REASON

In Henry's world there was little need to reason logically and test thought because there were few areas of knowledge and decisionmaking in which people had to deliberate in order to choose. Henry presented himself as a man of absolutes. Although he never fully explained his criteria for judging right and wrong, good and bad, true and false, he did seem to believe that such criteria existed and were or ought to be obvious. His absolutism explains perhaps why it was incomprehensible to him that Governor Edmund Randolph changed his position concerning the proposed Constitution. "What alteration," Henry asked, "has a few months brought about? The eternal difference between right and wrong does not fluctuate. It is immuta-

ble." An illustration of Henry's absolutism is his rejection of the theory of concurrent powers. It was outside the realm of possibility in Henry's thinking for both the federal government and the states to have such powers as those of taxation and the regulation of the militia. *Either* the federal government *or* the states had to possess the powers *exclusively* (or at least the powers of one had to be superior to those of the other).

Henry's style also showed a preference for the absolute. He frequently used what Kenneth Burke [in his *A Rhetoric of Motives,* 1969] calls "god-terms" and "devil-terms." "Liberty" and "freedom" were god-terms; "tyranny" and "monarchy" were devil ones. Henry also often used adjectives and adverbs that suggested extremes such as the following words taken from one short sample: "best," "extremely," "entire," "absolute," "every," "fully," "great," "highest," and "utmost." Henry's frequent use of absolute language and his infrequent use of qualified language meant that his listeners merely needed to accept or reject his pronouncements; they did not have to reason.

Henry's preference for explicit language also left little need for the application of reason. He demanded that meanings be expressed fully, leaving nothing to implication. Ambiguity and room for different interpretations were, to Henry, invitations to abuse power. He argued, for example, that under the "sweeping clause," Congress might pass any law it chose under the pretense that it was "necessary and proper" to carry out some specified power. He saw the lack of a Bill of Rights as sure proof that the proposed government was a conspiracy to enslave the people. To the Federalist argument that the rights were secure because they were implied, Henry retorted, "Even say it is a natural implication,—why not give us a right . . . in express terms, in language that could not admit of evasions or subterfuges?"

Henry's heavy reliance on rhetorical questions also suggests an absolutist stance. Rhetorical questions assume that listeners will provide the "correct" answers as these answers are implied in the questions. If the device works, listeners have little need to exercise reason.

Henry flatly asserted that reason had little place in the discussion of political issues. He scorned reasoning, particularly deductive reasoning, as both too technical and too devious for use in political argument. With regard to religious liberty, for example, Henry exclaimed, "There is many a religious man who knows nothing of argumentative reasoning; . . . who cannot go through all the labyrinths of syllogistic, argumentative deductions, when they think that the rights of conscience are invaded. This sacred right ought not to depend on constructive, logical reasoning." At another point, Henry declared, "Nations who have trusted to logical deduction have lost their liberty."

Henry's scorn of logic helps explain his organizational choices. He arranged most of his speeches topically around such themes as liberty, consolidation, and the danger of giving various powers to the central government. He rarely presented these topics in a systematic order; in fact, at one point he admitted that he found his "mind hurried on from subject to subject." Henry's lack of continuity resulted in "shotgun attacks" filled with inconsistencies which Madison quickly pointed out. For example, Madison noted that Henry claimed that the people were happy and secure under the Confederation *and* acknowledged that the states sent delegates to the general Convention because the people were distressed. Henry's inconsistencies, however, were irrelevant to anyone who accepted his basic assumptions about the role of reason in political decision making. From Henry's perspective, there was no need to pursue a systematic line of reasoning with thematic consistency because logical consistency was not a valid standard for judging political ideas.

What were Henry's criteria for making political decisions? He was not entirely clear here, but he gave the impression that a "good reason" was one that evoked a strong "feeling." At one point, he said, "It is a fact that the people do not wish to change their government. How am I to prove it? It will rest on my bare assertion, unless supported by an internal conviction in men's breasts." "Internal conviction" made an individual argument a "good" one. Henry, then, advocated basing political decisions on the strength of the feelings of the ordinary citizen he claimed to represent. (pp. 335-38)

> *Lois J. Einhorn, "Basic Assumptions in the Virginia Ratification Debates: Patrick Henry vs. James Madison on the Nature of Man and Reason," in* The Southern Speech Communication Journal, *Vol. XLVI, No. 4, Summer, 1981, pp. 327-40.*

Charles L. Cohen   (essay date 1981)

[*In the following essay, American scholar Cohen maintains that the biblical book of* Jeremiah *was the principal inspiration for Henry's "Liberty or Death" speech.*]

On March 23, 1775, Patrick Henry delivered an oration so powerful that Colonel Edward Carrington, standing outside the Henrico church and listening through an open window, reportedly exclaimed, "Right here I wish to be buried"—a desire his widow later satisfied. Another listener remembered feeling "*sick* with excitement." In 1816, William Wirt, soon to be appointed attorney general of the United States, published what purports to be that speech, a short, trenchant excursus on British perfidy and the necessity for armed resistance that culminates in the famous words "give me liberty, or give me death!" Wirt's text has stirred later generations much as Henry's oratory transported contemporaries. Modern critics have lauded the speech as "packed with rhetorical dynamite," "mesmeric," "one of the great revolutionary declamations of history." It stands among the most celebrated American utterances, an oratorical classic.

The **"Liberty or Death"** speech has served as the vehicle for countless schoolchildren who, mimicking Henry's alleged histrionics by stabbing themselves with make-believe paper cutters, have sought glory in countless elocution contests. Historians of the Revolution have put it to less melodramatic uses, primarily to advance the case for Henry's forensic powers and to give an example of his

prowess. These words, we are told, carried a close vote at the Virginia Convention of March 1775 in favor of a militia bill Henry supported. However, since Hugh Blair Grigsby raised an inquisitive eyebrow in the mid-nineteenth century, scholars have disputed the attribution to Henry. Some give the text no credence, alluding to it, if at all, only to contradict its authenticity, while others, wholly or partially skeptical about its verisimilitude, cite it for literary purposes; "liberty or death" adds dramatic tension to their narratives. What, then, have historians of the Revolution learned from this source? Nothing, if it is spurious, whatever its uses for comprehending the early national period. Little, if it is genuine, for no one disputes Henry's reputation, and proof of his effect on the convention's vote depends on evidence of his audience's reaction. All things considered, the speech has not yielded much information about Revolutionary Virginia. Have all its possibilities been explored?

The fate of the address epitomizes the truth in Mark Twain's observation that everyone praises a classic but no one reads it. The **"Liberty or Death"** speech has seemed uninformative because until now its message has escaped critical analysis. Fresh examination of its contents reveals new wine in an old bottle. The piece accuses the British of luxury, corruption, and desire to subvert American liberties, stock charges among the colonists. More significantly, it conveys these clichés through repeated references to the book of Jeremiah. A few scholars have noted the biblical citations without commenting on their fundamental importance for interpreting the address, the deepest meaning of which emerges from its sustained evocation of Judah's prophet. To understand the role of the scriptural allusions is to put the speech in a new perspective: it is a political harangue suffused with religious imagery. Its rhetoric suggests that the person who delivered it was both a radical and a sermonizer, an implication that bears on the question of authenticity because not everyone who has been suggested as the possible author fits both of these categories. Reevaluating the speech's authenticity in light of its content illuminates other issues: how the text took shape, the purpose of the rhetoric in the convention, and the patriots' method of communicating revolutionary ideas. In other words, knowing what the address *says* helps explain what it *is,* and this knowledge in turn yields further insights. Far from being a mere classic, the **"Liberty or Death"** speech proves to be a valuable document, notable as much for what it reveals about the political culture of late eighteenth-century Virginia as for its grandiloquence.

The oration published by Wirt repeats the sentiments of the Real Whig revolutionary ideology that historians have so thoroughly explored. Clearly, according to the speaker, a monstrous conspiracy exists to deprive the colonists of their liberties. History proves the point: the one sure guide is "the lamp of experience"; there is "no way of judging of the future but by the past"; the last ten years show little in the British ministry's conduct to justify hopes "with which gentlemen have been pleased to solace themselves and the house." Redress cannot be had from a corrupt ministry that receives petitions with an "insidious smile." One need look only as far as the "warlike preparations which cover our waters and darken our land," the "martial array" that augurs all the dangers of a standing army and whose purpose surely is "to force us to submission." There can be no mistake about Britain's intent; the navies and armies "are meant for us," dispatched "to bind and rivet upon us those chains which the British ministry have been so long forging," sent to destroy American rights and reduce the colonists to "submission and slavery" with chains whose "clanking may be heard on the plains of Boston!" Americans will have to fight "to preserve inviolate those inestimable privileges for which we have been so long contending." In 1,217 words, the speech compacts the central Real Whig themes of British corruption and conspiracy against liberty, along with colonial fear of enslavement and concern for the maintenance of traditional privileges claimed as British subjects.

To exhort listeners to action, the speech imbues its analysis with religious fervor. Through invocations of religious significance, appeals to God, and adept use of the Bible, a political address becomes a lay sermon. The "great and arduous struggle for liberty" is not a mundane but a "holy cause"; it concerns one's "temporal salvation." Repeatedly, the speaker enlists God in the Revolutionary crusade: the futility of petitioning leaves only "an appeal to arms and to the God of hosts"; the colonists must employ "those means which the God of nature hath placed in our power"; they do not fight alone because "a just God who presides over the destinies of nations" will provide friends for their cause. Prayerfully, the orator asks "Almighty God" to forbid backsliding into "chains and slavery." Biblical references punctuate the address. The speaker is "willing to know the whole truth" of America's situation, "whatever anguish of spirit it might cost." The war has actually begun, so "why stand we here idle?" The insidious ministerial smile casts a spell that requires two citations to exorcise: the colonists should know that "it will prove a snare to your feet" and should not allow themselves "to be betrayed with a kiss." In addition, and fundamentally, the speaker quotes Jeremiah to create the rhetorical substructure of his entire argument. At the outset, he wonders if his hearers comprise those "who having eyes, see not, and having ears, hear not"; and at the beginning of the famous peroration, he asserts, "Gentlemen may cry, peace, peace—but there is no peace." These allusions serve as proof texts, scriptural foundations for Revolutionary preachments that transform Jeremiah's admonitions to Judah into a message for dilatory patriots. Across 2,400 years, the prophet warns Virginia of impending doom.

Like the colonists in 1775, Hebrews of Jeremiah's day also faced a national crisis. Assyria had destroyed the northern kingdom of Israel in 722/721 B.C.E. and deported its inhabitants; after the battle of Carchemish in 605 B.C.E., Babylonia threatened Judah, the southern kingdom, with the same fate. Under these troubling circumstances, Jeremiah spoke of Judah's imminent demise. His message was ominous: Judah had sinned, and retribution would follow. "For the children of Judah have done evil in my sight, saith the Lord: they have set their abominations in the house which is called by my name, to pollute it . . . Therefore, behold, the days come, saith the Lord, that it shall no more be called Tophet, nor the valley of the Son of Hin-

nom, but the valley of slaughter: for they shall bury in Tophet, till there be no place." The intelligence left little to imagination, including even the avenue of approach, "for evil appeareth out of the north, and great destruction." Of course, there was always an alternative: Judah might avoid annihilation if the people repented, for if the Hebrews returned to God, "I will not cause mine anger to fall upon you: for I am merciful saith the Lord, and I will not keep anger for ever." Unfortunately, the Judeans seemed set in their ways, and Jeremiah disgustedly evaluated their prospects of redemption: "Can the Ethiopian change his skin, or the leopard his spots? then may ye also do good, that are accustomed to do evil."

One major obstacle to Judah's redemption lay in the activities of the cultic prophets, members of the ruling religious establishment whose pronouncements to the laity displayed an understanding of events that differed strikingly from Jeremiah's. Charismatic prophets like Jeremiah who appeared at irregular intervals may or may not have played a regularly accepted role within the official cult. It is clear, however, what Jeremiah thought of the professional prophets and the ecclesiastical hierarchy in general: "both prophet and priest are profane; yea, in my house have I found their wickedness, saith the Lord." Among their transgressions, the prophets erred by disregarding God's word; at a moment when only a moral revolution could save Judah, they blindly assured the populace that no danger threatened. They continued to cry "peace" when "there is no peace." Such false optimism could have only the most dire consequences: "they say, sword and famine shall not be in this land; by sword and famine shall those prophets be consumed." And the catastrophe Jeremiah announced came to pass: "the Chaldeans burned the king's house, and the houses of the people, with fire, and brake down the walls of Jerusalem."

Bluntly and forcefully, the patriot speaker states his case that Judah's destruction exemplifies Virginia's probable fate. The "lamp of experience" illumines a text that has force not merely as one historical precedent among many but as an instance of God's very actions in sacred history. The military power of a British Nebuchadnezzar waits on the horizon at Boston, its preordained location to the north. Despite the obvious danger, many of Virginia's established leaders, assembled in the convention, refuse to acknowledge the state of affairs. Urging conciliation, they cry "peace" when in fact "our brethren are already in the field!" and so manifest themselves as false prophets. If Virginians prove to resemble Judeans, if they are disposed to have eyes that do not see and ears that do not hear, then they will suffer Judah's fate. The impact of the speech, the full power of its revolutionary argument, depends on educing Jeremiah. The oration links a sacred past with an uncertain present, clothes revolutionary sentiment with divine authority, and invests the speaker with charisma. Judah's prophet of doom interprets the crisis with a Virginia accent.

Virginians were not the first Americans to hear Jeremiah comment on their trials. From the seventeenth century, Puritans and their descendants (both natal and adopted) invoked the prophet to castigate their own moral shortcomings within a rhetorical form known as the jeremiad. This genre of public address rested on the foundation of a covenant between God and His chosen people wherein He promises to be their God if they obey His commandments. Unfortunately, the members of the elect nation seldom live up to their responsibilities. As they turn away from God, He berates and punishes them for their misdeeds. Nevertheless, prophetic rehearsal of the people's sins reaffirms God's gracious providence and love. While announcing immediate disaster, it anticipates future reformation. In the final analysis, affliction makes eventual fulfillment of God's promises surer.

The **"Liberty or Death"** speech deviates from this pattern in several particulars. The oration never interprets history within the framework of a covenantal relationship. It does not claim a special election for Virginia, whose destiny involves that of other colonists, "our brethren . . . already in the field!" Nor does it single out the colonies as a whole: God governs "the destinies of nations," and nothing suggests a unique covenant with America. The received text sounds Jeremiah as an alarm yet lacks a catalog of sins to be repented and so leaves the question of the people's virtue essentially untouched. It does not refer to the achievements and wisdom of an earlier generation but instead emphasizes what "three millions of people armed in the holy cause of liberty" can do in their own behalf if they recruit God in the effort. Resistance will advance the cause of liberty but not, at least explicitly, the Kingdom of God. The oration misses the engine of doom and promise that runs the classical model. At most it is a truncated version, perhaps a jeremiad manqué, for not every use of Jeremiah need constitute a jeremiad. The oration employs the prophet to chastise those who endanger Virginia's safety and to inform listeners of a deadly historical parallel.

With its effective mixing of Revolutionary and biblical themes, the **"Liberty or Death"** speech resembles the sermons of New England's "Black Regiment." Virginia's Anglican clergy, however, refrained from similar discourses. Divided between sympathy for the colonists and loyalty to the church hierarchy, lacking centralized organization to support a unified front, and forensically inept, they did not have the requisite motivation, opportunity, and style. Political preachments in the Old Dominion emanated from another quarter. The fact that the speech combines political and biblical themes raises anew the question of authorship and adds another dimension to discussion of its authenticity. If the clergy could not produce such an effort, then the most likely candidate should be a Bible-thumping patriot. Orator, statesman, radical, and lay preacher, Patrick Henry fits the role.

As noted, the question of the genuineness of Wirt's printed text has occasioned intense historical interest, and the most comprehensive study of the problem refutes the attribution to Henry. Stephen Taylor Olsen [in *American Rhetoric: Context and Criticism,* Thomas W. Benson, ed.] has used a computer to compare fifteen linguistic-stylistic features of the **"Liberty or Death"** speech with writings by Henry, Wirt, and the Virginia jurist St. George Tucker, who years later provided Wirt with information about the speech and a recollection of Henry's magnetism. Primari-

ly on the basis of marker word tests, which measure habits of word selection, Olsen finds that the odds favor Tucker as author over Henry by 21.25 to 1 and over Wirt by 6.29 to 1. He concludes that Tucker probably composed the speech sometime between 1805, when Wirt first asked him for information about Henry's eloquence, and 1815, when Wirt thanked him for his response.

Olsen's sophisticated analysis shows convincingly that Tucker wrote the document that Wirt published, but the conclusion that Tucker invented the speech on his own does not necessarily follow. The techniques of linguistic-stylistics measure the form and structure of compositions but say little about content, about how the individual "building blocks" cohere to create meaning within a passage. The computer can do what the false prophets could not: Jeremiah's voice is stilled, his embassy dissipated, his words employed solely to determine significant differences between vocabulary choices. When one reads the speech in full and recognizes its scriptural citations, the feeling that Tucker alone wrote it diminishes and the impression of Henry's influence reappears.

Tucker was an unlikely figure to couch Revolutionary rhetoric in biblical language. For example, the treatment of republican themes in the **"Liberty or Death"** speech contrasts with their presentation in Tucker's poem *Liberty,* written in 1780-1781 and published several years later. The central figure in the poem is a goddess from the pantheon of Revolutionary America's classical mythology:

> DAUGHTER of Heaven, who, with indignant eye,
> On pomp and pageant royalty look'st down,
>
> . . . . .
>
> Fair LIBERTY! inspire thy votary's lay,
> And gladden with thy meed life's miserable way.

The work traces Liberty's trials through the history of Greece and Rome, Europe, Britain, and ultimately "Columbia," where, if the people

> From BRITAIN's ills a further Lesson learn,
> Nor let *Corruption's* deadly poison spread;

the goddess will find her final repose and:

> COLUMBIA thus shall live to deathless Fame,
> Unrivall'd or by ROME, or BRITAIN's vaunted
>   name!

The poem reeks of classical allusions, and its universe, circumnavigated by "Fair LIBERTY," has little in common with the world of Israel's God. When Tucker does invoke an incident from the Old Testament, his purpose is strictly metaphorical. The Declaration of Independence collapsed the British empire as the noise of trumpets rocked Jericho:

> The tottering City trembles at the sound,
> And her devoted walls fall thundering to the
>   ground:
> So trembled BRITAIN at the awful sound,
> And felt her empire to the Center shake.

Crediting Liberty for having "inspir'd" the proclamation of Columbia's freedom, Tucker passes up an opportunity to argue from Joshua 6:16 ("the Lord hath given you the city") that Jericho's destruction, and by extension the empire's fall, manifest God's providence. The poem conforms to what William Gribbin has labeled, for a later period, the "secular" version of republicanism. The speech, on the other hand, exhibits a "theocentric" style. If Tucker constructed the text entirely on his own, he adopted an uncharacteristic ideological voice.

Nothing in Tucker's life suggests that he was particularly animated by religious convictions. Henry, however, had early assumed a posture of piety and was quite accustomed to citing scripture. His father sat on the vestry in Hanover County, his mother converted to Samuel Davies's New Light Presbyterianism, and his uncle (and namesake), the rector of St. Paul's Church in Hanover County, presided over his early religious education. As a speaker, Henry was influenced by preachers such as George Whitefield and especially Davies. Whitefield had preached in Hanover in 1745, and Henry in his teens escorted his mother and sisters to hear Davies's sermons though he was still a member of his uncle's parish. Henry accounted Davies the greatest orator he ever heard and could easily have learned styles of evangelical fervor and political sermonizing from Virginia's leading dissenter.

The mien of an evangelical, nurtured in the youth, was second-nature in the adult. Henry absorbed a persona as well as a style: at first glance, according to Charles Thomson, he resembled "a Presbyterian clergyman, used to haranguing the people." More strikingly, he also spoke and acted like one. Edmund Randolph declared that Henry's "figures of speech, when borrowed, were often borrowed from the Scriptures," and compared him at the convention to Saint Paul preaching at Athens. James Parker, a merchant who disliked both Henry's posturing and his politics, wrote some days after the convention, "This Creature is so infatuated, that he goes about I am told, praying and preaching amongst the common people." The effects must have been impressive. To Virginians and New Englanders alike, Henry was "the Demosthenes of the Age," to George Mason "by far the most powerful speaker I ever heard," to Thomas Jefferson a debater so engaging that the *Summary View of the Rights of British America* may have been written with the hope that Henry would transform its prose into moving and persuasive speech. A skilled orator versed in biblical lore, Henry would not have hesitated to make Jeremiah's anger his own.

Of course, Henry's proclivity for sermonizing hardly proves that he uttered the published address, and a "smoking pistol," irrefutable evidence such as notes for the speech written in his hand, has never been found. Nor does an extensive secondhand record exist, a lacuna explained in part by Henry's talent. His hypnotic orations virtually precluded efforts to do anything but listen entranced, as Jefferson could testify [quoted in G. T. Curtis's *Life of Daniel Webster*]: "Although it was difficult, when [Henry] had spoken, to tell what he had said, yet, while speaking, it always seemed directly to the point. When he had spoken in opposition to my opinion, had produced a great effect, and I myself had been highly delighted and moved, I have asked myself, when he ceased, 'What the devil has he said?' and could never answer the inquiry." Wirt, who made extensive researches among Henry's con-

temporaries, noted that hearers "can only tell you, in general, that they were taken captive." When Henry argued the **"British Debts Case"** in 1791, his most brilliant passages overwhelmed the court stenographer, who could not reproduce them satisfactorily. Direct evidence for his earlier speeches is fragmentary at best. However, fragments are useful. Even if Henry hypnotized his audience, it need not follow that he totally obliterated their memories: it is easier to remember a felicitous phrase than a line of argument. The biblical references in the **"Liberty or Death"** speech identify parts of it with Henry, forcing reconsideration of how the text assumed its present form.

Years later, Edmund Randolph [in his *History of Virginia*] recounted one piece from the convention speech in a manuscript history. While today the words that give the speech its name strike us most forcefully, he and another listener singled out a different phrase: "Washington was prominent, though silent. His looks bespoke a mind absorbed in meditation on his country's fate, but a positive concert between him and Henry could not more effectually have exhibited him to view than when Henry with indignation ridiculed the idea of peace 'when there was no peace' and enlarged on the duty of preparing for war." The agreement between Wirt's report of the text and Randolph's recollection on this point is of utmost importance. Randolph concurred that Henry quoted Jeremiah 6:14, and that he thus drew a connection between Virginia and Judah. If not a smoking pistol, this passage constitutes at least a spent cartridge. Considered together with the rhetoric of the address and the facts of Henry's life, Randolph's remark strongly suggests that the heart of the **"Liberty or Death"** speech originated with Henry. If so, and if Olsen's claim for Tucker's authorship of the text be also granted, then Olsen's theory of composition must be recast. The debate has sometimes proceeded as if a single mind brought forth the text fully formed, like Zeus giving birth to Athena, yet in all likelihood the document manifests the efforts of two progenitors who worked at different times. Tucker remembered bits of what Henry said, added his own elaborations, and sent the completed product to Wirt. Olsen's contention that the speech should be "analyzed, interpreted, and criticized as a piece of early-nationalist period rhetoric, not as a piece of American revolutionary rhetoric," oversimplifies a complex creative evolution. The recorded speech underwent a protracted course of development.

How Randolph arrived at his account is problematic, since he did not attend the convention. He did not get his information from Wirt; in fact, Wirt borrowed some items from Randolph. It is possible that Randolph exchanged particulars with Tucker, but there is no proof of this, and it is unnecessary to suppose that he must have obtained his knowledge of Henry's words from a written source. A culture as enamored of print as ours, one habituated to writing things down immediately, may forget that other people have kept (and keep) their most important records in their heads and made them accessible through talk. Colonial Virginians favored oral over written modes of communication, and they preserved their history with their tongues. Although Henry's oratory did not survive in verbatim transcripts, accounts of his artistry, descriptions of his evangelistic style, and pieces of his speeches circulated in Virginia for years because he was an enormously popular figure. A week after his speech attacking the Stamp Act, inhabitants of Louisa County were buzzing "a great deal" about "the Noble Patriot" and pledged "the last Drop of their blood" in his defense. His eloquence served as a standard of excellence; the highest compliment the elders of Hanover County could pay a speaker in the late eighteenth century was to refer to Henry's triumph of 1763 over James Maury and contend that *"he is almost equal to Patrick, when he plead against the parsons."* Every witness Wirt approached could give him "some part" of the **"Liberty or Death"** speech. Though ordinarily ephemeral, important oral transmissions may eventually be written down. Jeremiah's words survived in a scroll dictated to his amanuensis, Baruch; Henry had scribes who, without his knowledge, performed a similar service for him. Tucker was one. Working within an oral tradition that independently passed on Henry's most memorable passages, Randolph was another. Both preserved the reference to Jeremiah.

One final point helps to locate the genesis of the speech in historical time and to explain some of the reasons for Washington's "meditation." Recall the situation Virginia faced early in 1775. The Revolutionary crisis had entered its final stage in the preceding year. When news of the Boston Port Act reached the colony in May 1774, the House of Burgesses proclaimed a fast day. In response, Governor Dunmore dissolved the assembly. The dismissed Burgesses met under Peyton Randolph and called a convention for August. This body established an association binding subscribers to severe nonimportation and nonexportation agreements, elected delegates to the Continental Congress, and authorized Randolph to call a future convention if necessary. Concurrently, the counties formed volunteer military companies and began to organize committees that enforced first the colony-wide association and later the Continental one. Meanwhile, months passed without the assembly reconvening. Dunmore's campaign against Indians in the Ohio Valley postponed one expected session. On orders from the British secretary of state, Lord Dartmouth, the governor further prorogued the assembly until May 1775, whereupon Randolph called another convention. Yet despite the colonial preparatory measures, the harder line assumed by British policymakers, and the increased tension, many Virginians, including Randolph himself, still hoped for reconciliation and decried force as unnecessarily provocative. When the second convention met in March, Henry introduced resolutions calling for the colony to "be immediately put into a posture of Defence." Meeting resistance from more conciliatory members, he made his famous address. In this context, the purpose of Henry's use of Jeremiah little resembles a paean to a timeless American ideal, the guise in which the speech has often wafted through the auditoria of the nation's schools. The prophetic imagery was a tough, partisan effort designed to sway opinion in favor of the militia bill. Attacking the conciliators, Henry equated them with the false prophets of Judah, whose equanimity in the face of danger resulted in ruin, derogating his adversaries with one of the most damning names he could devise.

Henry leveled another accusation as well. Virginia's patriotic movement coincided with an evangelical revival. The demeanor of the revivalists—moralistic, austere, unrefined—challenged the gentry's mores in every way, but the two movements each represented an ideological search for "psychic relief from the oppression of guilt, anxiety, and perceived disorder." In Henry, they fused. Participating in the social and political life of the gentry while committed to the revivalists' sober preoccupation with virtue, Henry [according to Isaac Rhys in *The American Revolution: Explorations in the History of American Radicalism,* Alfred F. Young, ed.] could "communicate in popular style that passion for a world reshaped in truly moral order, which lay at the heart of both the revolutionary evangelical and Revolutionary patriot movements." By uniting biblical imagery and Revolutionary ideas, he succeeded both in rebuking his political opponents among the gentry as lovers of ease and security, and in furthering his political aims. Henry was one of many Americans who comprehended political events in religious terms, unique only in the ability to publicize his insights. The broader significance of the **"Liberty or Death"** speech lies in the way it instances the importance of religious as well as political currents in the colonists' Revolutionary thought. The Bible could teach Virginians a provocative lesson; Jeremiah could unmask a devious conspiracy as effectively as "Cato" in the *Independent Whig.*

In the end, Virginia did heed Henry's words, readied for war, and so escaped Judah's fate. The Hebrews rewarded Jeremiah with curses, threats, and ostracism. Virginians elected Henry governor five times. Sometimes a prophet is not without honor even in his own country. (pp. 702-17)

> *Charles L. Cohen, "The 'Liberty or Death' Speech: A Note on Religion and Revolutionary Rhetoric," in* The William and Mary Quarterly, *third series, Vol. XXXVIII, No. 4, October, 1981, pp. 702-17.*

Richard R. Beeman   (essay date 1987)

[*Beeman is an American historian specializing in the study of eighteenth-century Virginia. In the following excerpt, he portrays Henry as a populist who emerged out of the larger movement of ideological republicanism.*]

Part of the key to an understanding of Henry's role in the evolution of American political thought and conduct lies in a clearer understanding of the ideological context in which all of the political battles of the Revolutionary era were fought. In the era in which William Wirt wrote of Henry's accomplishments, the ideological battle lines of the period seemed fairly clearly drawn. In dealing with the events leading up to 1776, one spoke of patriots and tories, and in dealing with the events of the postrevolutionary period, one talked of aristocrats and democrats, with the assumption being that patriots and democrats eventually won the ball game in America.

This mode of analysis, though occasionally appearing in more sophisticated guise, dominated historical interpretations of Virginia's and America's Revolutionary history up until the 1960s, but at that time—and continuing with considerable vigor into the present day—historians began moving away from those simple categories and have begun to talk about a common political language, common to groups both in England and America but with particular vitality in America—a language that the Americans themselves called "republicanism." The central concerns of republican ideology—the restraint of the ceaselessly aggressive tendencies of government power, the preservation of both liberty and the public virtue, and the cultivation of talent and virtue in political leaders—were timeless in their application to the problems of governance at any point in human history, but they were, in the way in which they were formulated by Americans of the Revolutionary era and in the logic they imposed on those who assumed the reins of government after the Revolution, nevertheless peculiar to a world that is now very distant from our own.

In its classical form, republicanism was often a system in which the individual's liberty was confined to those things that the society at large defined as useful. It was a mode of thought particularly obsessed with the maintenance of "virtue" in both leaders and followers and one that granted to the state broad powers to make certain that its citizens behaved virtuously. It was a mode of thinking that did not necessarily look askance at laws supporting religious observances or regulating individual economic activity for the common good. It was a view of government perhaps best summed up by John Adams of Massachusetts when he wrote to Mercy Otis Warren that "there must be a positive Passion for the public good [and] the public Interest . . . or there can be no Republican Government, *nor any real liberty.*" The public passion "must be Superior to all private Passions. Men must . . . be happy to sacrifice . . . their private Friendships and dearest Connections, when they stand in Competition with the Rights of Society." This was a brand of republicanism that had relatively little faith in direct, democratic involvement by the people in the affairs of government. Some measure of popular control over government was necessary in order to check the tendencies of government officials to become corrupted by excessive power, but this view of the role of the popular voice was essentially a negative one. As Bernard Bailyn has phrased it [in his *Ideological Origins of the American Revolution*]:

> [Though] 'republic' and 'democracy' were words closely associated in the colonists' minds, . . . they evoked a mixed response of enthusiasm and foreboding. For if 'republic' conjured up for many the positive features of the Commonwealth era and marked the triumph of virtue and reason, 'democracy'—a word that denoted the lowest order of society as well as the form of government in which the commons ruled—was generally associated with the threat of civil disorder and the early assumption of power by a dictator.

One way to conceive of this republican ideology is as a huge umbrella overarching all that Americans thought and did during the last half of the eighteenth century. This conception of republicanism as a unifying umbrella works pretty well during the period leading up to independence, for Americans were to an amazing extent united in their opposition to Great Britain and united in the language they used—in their conviction that the British were corrupted by excessive power, in their determination to preserve their personal independence, and in their commitment to liberty. But after independence, when people such as Henry and Madison and Jefferson began to do battle over some of the principal issues relating to the internal polity of the newly independent American nation, it is obvious that this republican umbrella, however much it may have provided Americans with a common political language, did not provide them with common solutions to the most fundamental problems of government and politics. It is plain, looking at those postrevolutionary debates, that this classical republican language was not by itself sufficient to lead Americans out of the eighteenth century and into a future in which individual liberties and more explicitly democratic political impulses figured more prominently. Although it may be true that all (or at least most) Americans embraced the corporate and communal precepts of classical republicanism on the eve of the Revolution, it is just as clear that Americans were increasingly confronted with a range of competing conceptions of government and politics after the Revolution.

As a consequence, we have seen other historians in recent years search for alternative ideological traditions that engaged the loyalties of Americans of competing political goals. The list of intellectual and behavioral traditions from which Americans of the postrevolutionary generation might have drawn is growing longer nearly every day. Classical republicanism, agrarian republicanism, classical liberalism, possessive liberalism, Mandevillian laissez-faire doctrine, Scottish common sense philosophy, French physiocratic political economy—one could go on and on about the forces working to change the way Americans thought about the world around them, but most of these developments did, in my view, tend to lead Americans toward a society in which values of the individual, of individual liberty, and of liberalism were much more prominently stressed.

My own initial conception of Henry's place within the constellation of republican ideas was that he was, in contrast to his rivals Madison and Jefferson, subject to very few—indeed, probably none—of the newer, more modern intellectual currents that were working to modify traditional republican thought. And, while Jefferson and Madison were moving on to embrace a more egalitarian, more libertarian, and more modern liberal faith, Henry seemed to me stuck in a classical republican mode of thought that left him ill-equipped to cope with some of the changing realities of the postrevolutionary era.

To some extent, it is hard to avoid an argument that proceeds along those lines, for there are many ways in which Henry does seem to fit comfortably in the classical republican mold. His rhetoric against the British could have come right out of a textbook for classical republican behavior. Ministerial plots to rob the Virginians of their liberties, a corrupt king joining in the plot to enslave Americans, constant reminders of the aggressive and corrupting nature of arbitrary, unchecked power—Henry seems beset by virtually all of the quintessential (and, to some extent, quintessentially paranoid) classical republican fears during the struggle with England.

Henry was, moreover, as committed as any good republican could be to the maintenance of civic virtue once the Revolution was under way, and he was sorely distressed when that virtue seemed to be falling into disrepair. As wartime governor, when the financial contributions of the states to the war effort seemed to lag and when individual self-interest seemed everywhere to be triumphing over the public good, he even suggested that George Washington be made a temporary dictator so that America could weather its revolutionary crisis. This concern for order and for public virtue led him also to oppose Jefferson's and Madison's bill for complete separation of church and state. Henry called instead for a general assessment for the support of all Protestant denominations in the state. The precise reasoning behind his position favoring state-supported religion is unfortunately unclear, but it is certain that he was deeply disturbed by what he saw as the decline in virtue and morality among his fellow Virginians in the decade immediately following the Revolution. Over the course of the 1780s he expressed concern about the decline of many Episcopal parishes in Virginia, the flight of Episcopalian ministers from the state, and, more generally, the tendency of many Virginians to ignore their public responsibilities, whether those responsibilities meant paying tithes for the support of the poor or honoring their financial and military obligations to the state. All of these changes were interpreted by Henry as an indication that some agency to restore and promote the public virtue was much needed. Henry did not feel that the Episcopal church alone should be charged with that task, but he did believe—in true classical republican fashion—that it was the job of the church and state, working hand-in-hand, to promote virtue among the citizenry, and the institution of a statewide public levy for the support of all Protestant religion seemed to him one way of doing so.

Similarly, it seems also clear that Henry's deathbed support of the Federalist party in 1798 and 1799 was prompted at least in part (with the other part being generated, I suspect, by a thoroughgoing personal animus against Jefferson) by a renewed concern for both the maintenance of order and the public virtue. Referring to the "calamitous" course of the French Revolution, he expressed great fear that the American experiment in republicanism would degenerate into similar violence and anarchy. And, like many traditionally minded politicians, he was not able to distinguish the Republicans' mounting attacks on the Federalist administration as being different from disloyalty. Although his precise views on the infamous Alien and Sedition Acts are a little cloudy, it does seem clear that he was outraged by the intensity and tone of Jefferson's and Madison's assaults on such men as John Marshall, John Adams, and even George Washington.

So here we have Henry, the traditional, classical republican, useful in his own time and place—namely, in Virginia, prior to the Revolution, when the country needed an alert sentinel to sound the alarm against corrupt English practices—but increasingly out of step when it came time to build a new nation on new principles.

But if Henry was, consistently—perhaps too consistently and too conservatively—a classical republican in his commitments to fighting corruption and maintaining order and the public virtue, he did also, consistently and unambiguously, display a faith in and a comfortableness with democratic politics that mark him as distinctly unrepublican, untraditional, and very modern in his political beliefs. And it is here that I would like to state the central proposition of this essay, namely, that though Madison and Jefferson are justly honored for a myriad of contributions to what we might call the growing liberal faith in America—their contributions to the cause of religious freedom, their support of doctrines of free trade and their opposition to anything that smacked of corporate economic privilege, their egalitarian and expansive view of the uses of America's western domain—they nevertheless couched their proposals on those issues in a language and set of assumptions that were, if not actively antidemocratic, at least explicitly elitist. By contrast, though his formal political thought lacked the learned and contemplative character of Madison's and Jefferson's views on government and society, Patrick Henry, by the strength of his faith in the popular voice—in populism—would contribute, sometimes quite unintentionally, in a powerful way to America's ultimate destiny as a liberal democracy.

Much of the evidence for Henry's populistic bent is in fact of a singularly negative sort, drawn from the utterances of those individuals who found themselves in political combat with Henry and who, almost invariably, came up on the short end of the debate. That their resentment of his "demagoguery" and his "appeals to the passions of the people" is so marked is, in fact, powerful testimony to how little reconciled most people were to a democratic style of politics.

If we listen to Anglican minister James Maury, who confronted Henry in the young lawyer's debut on the public stage in Virginia in the **"Parson's Cause,"** we get one perspective on the matter. Henry, defending the vestrymen of Louisa County (who, in effect, represented the citizens of the county) against Maury's claims for salary owed him by the vestry, went well beyond the narrow legal facts of the case to appeal directly to the passions of the jury and argued that it was the citizens of the colony, and not the bishop of London or Board of Trade back in London, who had the right to set ministers' salaries.

This was in fact an argument that should have carried very little legal weight, for the facts of the case were unambiguously on Maury's side, but Henry, pleading the case before a hometown jury, won a resounding victory for the vestrymen. Maury could barely believe it. Calling Henry a "little petty fogging Attorney," he accused him of demagoguery, of stacking the jury with what he called "the vulgar herd," and "in saying what he had . . . to render himself popular."

The charge that Henry sought "to render himself popular" by his political conduct was uttered again and again throughout Henry's career, as if politicians were not supposed to tap the popular sentiment. It was a charge voiced by Governor Francis Fauquier in 1765, when he first encountered the "angry young lawyer" during the Stamp

B.H. Latrobe's "Attempt at the Features" of the aged Patrick Henry.

Act Crisis. It was a charge uttered by Henry's antagonists in the House of Burgesses when Henry's radical Stamp Act Resolves gained passage. It was, most emphatically, a charge uttered by Virginia's royal governor, Lord Dunmore, who in 1775 issued a proclamation castigating Henry for his traitorous and outrageous acts.

And when James Madison and Thomas Jefferson found themselves pitted against Henry's enormous popular appeal within Virginia during the 1780s, they too would complain about Henry's populistic excesses. Although always convinced that they had "the young men of talent and education on their side," Madison and Jefferson were infuriated that so many individuals from the West in particular (which was, after all, their political territory as well) would allow their "passions" to be inflamed by Henry's politicking. Their denunciations of Henry's ability to unleash passion, precisely the same sort of denunciation uttered by Fauquier and Dunmore a decade or so earlier, suggest that neither Madison nor Jefferson—nor most of the rest of America—was prepared for the sort of popular politics that Henry was unleashing.

Indeed, I would argue that one of the principal factors underlying James Madison's energetic efforts in behalf of a stronger central government in the 1780s was his conviction that the individual state governments, subject to the whims and passions of the populace, could not be trusted, and that those observations came not from a dispassionate reading of Greek or Roman or even eighteenth-century American history, but rather from a direct, immediate, and painful experience in confronting the popular power amassed by Patrick Henry in Virginia during the 1780s.

The aspect of Henry's popular appeal that is best known to us is, of course, his oratory. As a number of scholars have observed, oratory served an important function within the traditional sort of republican society outlined above. It was not only a mark of learning, but also of gentility, of one's ability to control, through the use of reason, one's passions. A mastery of the ancient philosophers, a facility with classical allusion—these were the marks of a gentleman. Jefferson, in fact, was not a good public speaker and shunned the speakers' platform, but he did nevertheless have an appreciation for the traditional gifts of oratory, for that sort of oratory was compatible with his lifelong reverence for learning and for the ordered presentation of ideas. Madison, though he too was not a particularly good public speaker, did nevertheless subscribe to this classic style and by the sheer weight of his considerable learning was able to hold his own in public debate.

But how different was Henry's style! Jefferson, when he derided Henry for being all tongue and no head or heart, gave his opinion of the connection between Henry's oratorical gifts and his depth of learning. And, indeed, Jefferson was correct—the intellectual substance of Henry's oratory was not likely to inspire awe in his listeners, whether they be gentry or ordinary planters. But it was the ordinary planters whom Henry was able to reach with an effectiveness absolutely unparalleled up to that time. As Edmund Randolph noted [in his *History of Virginia*, IX, 1970], Henry's oratory was "vehement," "not always grammatical, and sometimes coarse in language, [but] he taught his hearers how to forget his inaccuracies by his action, his varying countenance and voice." Or, as Jefferson put it more pointedly [quoted in G. T. Curtis's *Life of*

Daniel Webster], "Although it was difficult when [Henry] had spoken to tell what he had said, yet, while speaking it always seemed directly to the point. When he had spoken in opposition to my opinion, had produced a great effect, and I myself had been highly delighted and moved, I have asked myself, when he ceased, 'What the devil has he said?' and could never answer the inquiry."

Rhys Isaac has labeled Henry's oratorical style "evangelical," in that it bore striking resemblance to the highly emotive preaching styles coming into currency with the rise of evangelical religion in Virginia. Though Henry himself was not a member of an evangelical sect, his Virginia Piedmont constituents were, and there seems little doubt that both the style and the substance of his speeches appealed to that constituency. Charles Thomson, the secretary of the First Continental Congress, likened Henry to a "Presbyterian clergyman used to haranguing the people," and Edmund Randolph noted that Henry's "figures of speech, when borrowed, were often borrowed from the Scriptures," and from the Old Testament in particular. Although it is difficult to gauge the precise influence of those religious movements on Henry's style, there can be no doubt that Henry's rhetorical style, like that of the evangelicals, was consciously and purposefully egalitarian. In both the style and content of their rhetoric, he and his evangelical counterparts involved listeners in speeches in a way unprecedented in politics in the past.

Our two most famous and controversial examples of his speeches are those before the House of Burgesses denouncing the Stamp Act and then later, in 1775, his **"Give Me Liberty or Give Me Death"** speech. Those speeches are deservedly renowned for the passions they aroused in his listeners—but his audience in both of those cases was composed of Henry's fellow burgesses, all members of the elite. What seems even more striking to me are Henry's stump speeches, whether at Hanover County Court House whipping up popular sentiment to march to Williamsburg to protect the colony's supply of gunpowder from Governor Dunmore or at the county seat in Prince Edward denouncing the proposed federal Constitution and asking the citizens of that county to rally around him in his opposition to that document (which they did, emphatically). These were the speeches of a man who felt not a trace of discomfort in using the arts of oratory to persuade, to cajole, and indeed, if necessary, to raise passions on issues he felt were important.

If we compare Henry's attitude toward the stump speech and the political campaign with Madison's, we get a better idea of the distinctiveness of Henry's mode. Madison, for his part, was still clinging to the model of the disinterested, virtuous statesman, a species of public servant who volunteered to serve in office and who rose to positions of service through superior learning and virtue. The thought of justifying one's claim to political leadership was a troublesome one to him, troublesome even when the beliefs that he stood for were under attack. Thus, we find Madison throughout his career complaining about the necessities of exerting himself in order to obtain election. Writing immediately following his successful campaign for a place in the Virginia ratifying convention of 1788, he confessed that he

was "obliged . . . to mount for the first time in my life, the rostrum before a large body of the people, and to launch into a harangue of some length in the open air and on a very windy day." Some months later, as he battled for his political life in a contest for a seat in the First Federal Congress (an election in which he was actively opposed by Henry's supporters), he nevertheless persisted in refusing to come home from New York to his congressional district because "it will have an electioneering appearance which I have always despised and wish to shun." In the end, he was forced to do so, for to fail to campaign would surely have cost him the election, but he made it clear that the currying of popular favor was not his idea of what a disinterested statesman was supposed to do.

To some extent these differences between Henry and Madison were functions of temperament. James Madison would have found it difficult at any age to stand up on a table in a tavern and entertain the assembled throng with his fiddle, as Henry did on more than one occasion. Indeed, Jefferson considered Henry's passion for "fiddling, dancing and pleasantry" the major factor in his political popularity, and he may not have been far from the mark, for Henry was, in his social and electoral conduct, one of the people in ways that his more formal and reserved rivals never could be. Henry, far from disdaining "an electioneering appearance," may have never been more at home than when he was in that guise.

It would be wrong, however, to account for Henry's populistic faith simply by reference to his congeniality and to the fact that he was a good fellow to go drinking or carousing with, though I am sure that gives us a part of the answer. That democratic faith ultimately went well beyond his own personal relationships and his comfort with the voters of his own district. It ultimately came to inform his view of the proper relationship between voters and candidates everywhere, and of the obligations of those candidates to be faithful servants to their constituents. In this respect, it seems most appropriate to turn now to that aspect of his public life for which he is likely to receive the least praise in the next several years, namely, his opposition to the proposed federal Constitution in 1787.

James Madison's progressive contributions to our science of government are well documented and justifiably praised. His tough-minded assessment of the weaknesses of the Articles of Confederation in areas of commerce, taxation, and defense; his notion, articulated in Federalist 10, of minimizing the harmful effects of faction by spreading government over a large territory; and his concern for constructing a government that would protect the "diversity in the faculties of men" are just a few insights for which Madison is justly famous. But we should not forget that there was one other aspect of Madison's defense of the need for a strong central government that was hardly progressive. Over and over again Madison underscored the need to "remove the government physically" from the people in order to insulate the "best and the brightest" within America from the popular clamor. In the Constitutional Convention of 1787, for example, he was explicit about the need to make the Senate the repository of talent and virtue, a sort of American version of the House of

Lords, removed from popular pressures. And even in Federalist 10, the literary contribution that has earned him a reputation as one of America's first "modern" and "realistic" political theorists, he speaks of the need to "refine and enlarge the public views, by passing them through the medium of a chosen body of citizens, whose wisdom may best discern the true interest of their country." He felt that one of the virtues of a large republic, in which each representative served a much greater number of citizens, was that demagogic candidates (like Henry, one suspects) would be unable "to practice with success the vicious arts, by which elections are too often carried."

For Patrick Henry, this tendency to remove public servants from the oversight of the people they served was itself proof of the defective character of the proposed Constitution. When Edmund Randolph, one of his opponents in the Virginia ratifying convention, argued that "there is a certain listlessness and inattention to the interest of the community—and [such] indecision or faction in numerous bodies, that I would rather depend on the virtue and knowledge of some few men, than on ever so many," Henry seethed with indignation. And when Francis Corbin, a Virginia federalist who had spent much of his time during the Revolution in England rather than in Virginia fighting for independence, opined that "it was of little importance whether a country was ruled by a despot with a tiara on his head, or by a demagogue in a red cloak [and] a caul-bare wig" (Henry's customary attire), Henry exploded with one of his most eloquent defenses of his populistic faith. "I am," he said, "a plain man, and have been educated altogether in Virginia. My whole life has been spent among [farmers] and other plain men of similar education, who have never had the advantage of that polish which a court alone can give, and which the gentleman over the way has so happily acquired." Henry went on to lament the fact that he had been caught up in the "toils of the revolution" while Corbin was "acquiring a foreign education, . . . *basking in the beams of royal favor at St. James'.*" And, bowing in mock obsequiousness to his opponent, Henry proclaimed that he had no intention "to vie with the gentleman in these courtly accomplishments, . . . yet such a bow as I can make, shall ever be at the service of the people."

In the end, Henry's criticisms of the unresponsive structure of the new government were ineffectual. Madison, who had given much more thought to matters of nation building than Henry had, was able to counter virtually all of Henry's specific charges about the new government's tendency toward "consolidation" and, in Federalist 10, managed to turn aside Henry's fears about the excessive size of territory to be governed by asserting that the spaciousness of the American republic was in fact a deterrent to tyrannical government. Indeed, it must be said, when all is said and done, that Henry as a theoretician of governmental structures—be it on the state or national level— was far inferior to Madison; but Henry did, in his denunciations of the proposed federal government, hit upon a fact that the federalists often tried hard to hide: namely, that the new government was designed by many of its principal advocates to ensure rule in America by a wealthy, virtuous elite, that it was, by a process that Madison himself called

the "filtration of talent," intended to sift out the clamorous voices of the populace at large and replace them with only the most sober, reasonable, and virtuous. Such a commitment would in practice have amounted to rule by the affluent and privileged few.

In some important senses, events would overtake Patrick Henry's political philosophy and render much of it irrelevant. In particular, the invention of national political parties would serve to bring the national government ever closer to the people, ever closer to popular scrutiny. But there is a great irony even to these developments—an irony that serves to underscore Henry's contribution to our political heritage. That democratic and nationalizing party system would have its beginnings in the 1790s, when James Madison and Thomas Jefferson, horrified at the threats posed to Virginia interests by the policies of the government that Madison had been so instrumental in creating, proceeded to adopt precisely the sort of democratic electioneering devices pioneered by Patrick Henry— stump speeches at town meetings and direct, emotional appeals to the people—in the creation of the Jeffersonian Republican party.

Many of the ideals of that party—the protection of individual liberties such as freedom of the press and of religion, the opposition to entrenched privilege—constituted in many respects an invaluable blueprint for America's liberal future, but I would insist that the democratic component of that liberal future owed far more to Jefferson's and Madison's longtime rival than the two men were ever willing to admit. (pp. 303-16)

Richard R. Beeman, "The Democratic Faith of Patrick Henry," in The Virginia Magazine of History and Biography, *Vol. 95, No. 3, July, 1987, pp. 301-16.*

David A. McCants   (essay date 1990)

[*In the following excerpt, McCants argues that Henry approached the crisis which inspired his "Liberty or Death" speech in the manner of an evangelical preacher, focusing on religious and moral rather than political concerns.*]

In at least two respects Henry was a radical: he took more extreme positions in the conflict with Great Britain than did most of his contemporaries, and he advanced his positions with the new, ultraegalitarian rhetoric of experimental religion. These two interacting strains of his intellectual and political composition explain to a large degree his popularity with the people and his controversiality among the Tidewater elite. They also explain the significant, but specialized, roles that he played most effectively in the conflict that led to American independence. Henry's communication skills served better in some situations than others as a survey of his communication activity during the period of his headship of the popular movement in Virginia and his ascendancy in the Virginia assembly will illustrate.

Eighteen months elapsed between the Stamp Act debate and the next session of the House of Burgesses. But when the House did meet, November 1766, the influence of Patrick Henry's treasonous behavior was evident in the composition of the new House. Henry took center stage among this liberal majority, and his behavior solidified his leadership position. The issue was the separation of the office of speaker and treasurer. The death of Speaker-Treasurer John Robinson had revealed the misconduct of using public funds for private loans. Richard Henry Lee introduced the resolution to separate the offices. Henry supported him. Henry's speech reinforced his image as a bold, decisive leader who acts to reclaim fairness and trust from the abuses of privilege and power. The decision to separate the offices, supported even by some of the House's conservatives, rendered the judgment that the union of the two offices had been an erroneous policy. The separation, and especially the addition of a stipend for the speaker which augmented the speaker's dependence on the House, increased the influence of the House and strengthened Henry's position among the enlarged number of moderates and liberals in the assembly.

Henry served in the House of Burgesses (first from Louisa County, later from Hanover County) and the Virginia Convention, successor to the House of Burgesses, from 1765 to 1776. From 1766 on, he was appointed to important committees of the assembly. In committee and on the floor of the House, as opportunity afforded, he advanced liberal political and economic positions. His concept of freedom made him an advocate of the independence of the Virginia assembly and toleration for religious dissenters. He adopted antislavery views early but did not publicly advance them prior to the Revolution. His concept of democracy made him an advocate of trial by jury and government by representative bodies. British threats to trial by peers and the imposition of taxes without representation roused him. Henry's economic views, as well as his political views, were based on concepts of freedom and democracy. A free-soil advocate, he envisioned an economy built upon farms and manufactures. In his vision, the free farm would replace the plantation built upon slave labor, and home manufactures would replace imports. Henry believed that a free economy would promote political democracy and economic strength. A key means to this end in his legislative agenda was support of western land development.

The conflict with England was at a low level between 1767 and 1773, the year of the Townshend Acts and the year of the creation of a standing Committee of Correspondence. Unless the extant evidence is misleading, Henry did not deliver any major speeches in those years. While it seems likely that the Townshend Acts, which gave "no taxation without representation" to our lexicon, would have prompted a Henry speech, the record is silent. Other disturbing English actions, however, were forthcoming: actions such as the retention of the tax on tea to symbolize the principle of parliamentary taxation, stepped-up efforts to control smuggling, and creation of a new court of inquiry with power to transport offenders to England for trial. This accumulation of grievances led to a motion in the Virginia assembly in 1773 to create a standing committee of correspondence, and notice of Henry's speech on this occasion has survived. Henry [according to biographers

R. D. Meade and W. W. Henry] delivered such a rousing speech that some of the citizenry ran to the Capitol's cupola and removed the royal flag.

Patrick Henry participated as a debater, a committee member, and sponsor of legislation, including the routine bills related to organizational maintenance and constituent affairs. His special talent, however, was the mobilization of opinion—popular feeling—for action. He had limited interest in the legislature's responsibility for managing public affairs or a committee's responsibility for designing the parts of a public plan. Whether a public day of fasting and prayer to show sympathy for the beleaguered citizenry of Boston would develop animosities among Virginians toward British soldiers was the kind of question that intrigued Henry. Henry grappled with how to motivate, not how to manage. Henry knew how to read the temper of an audience. He knew, for example, when he was too far in front of the public or legislature. Knowing for a long time that he was far in front of opinion on the inevitability of war and independence, he withheld advocacy of that position until he judged the exigency compelling.

In the most celebrated speech of his career, delivered 23 March 1775, during the meeting of the Virginia Convention, a revolutionary assembly, Henry advocated arming the colony. For the first three days, the members dealt with details of organizing the convention and approved reports of the actions of the First Continental Congress, which had met the previous fall. It was rumored that Henry would propose that the convention assume the functions of government. On the fourth day, Henry did just that, though with more finesse than had been anticipated. Instead of broad empowerment, Henry called only for the establishment of a militia and the development of a plan of defense. The rationale for the assumption of legislative authority as expressed in the resolution was based upon the importance of addressing military needs in the face of uncertainty about when the House of Burgesses would be convened. By a five-vote margin, Henry achieved in the convention what he had been unable to achieve at Philadelphia: agreement to fight.

Receptivity to Henry's views had been growing. Whig principles were not only more widespread but were more influential in the legislature because of the shift in power from Tidewater to Piedmont counties. Whig loyalties were to the British Constitution, not the Crown, and Whigs subscribed to the doctrine of government by compact. Only thoroughgoing Tories wholeheartedly subscribed to competing views of government set forth in the Jamaican Petition to which the convention was framing a response when Henry moved his resolutions on revolution. Indeed, not only were Whig opinions strong in Virginia but the delegates were in a belligerent mood. The conflict with Great Britain had stepped up, and the British Ministry's militancy seemed unrelenting. Confinement of the British-American conflict to the economic sphere seemed less and less likely to more and more people. The changing opinion and the vote in the convention, however, belie the profound impact of the **"Liberty or Death"** speech.

The **"Liberty or Death"** speech affected everyone. According to Edmund Randolph, the convention sat in silence for several minutes before anyone assumed the floor, and the public audience that spilled onto the grounds of St. John's Church, Richmond, was affected as much as the delegates. The effects of the speech were intense. Thomas Marshall, a member of the convention, told his son, Chief Justice John Marshall, that the speech was "one of the most bold, vehement, and animated pieces of eloquence that had ever been delivered." The speech so overpowered Colonel Edward Carrington, who listened from a window at the east end of the church, almost opposite Henry, that he begged to "be buried at this spot!" Judge St. George Tucker, the principal source for the report of what Henry said that day, struggled to find a metaphor that characterized the novelty and the magnitude of the effect that he experienced. An accumulation of images—imagine experiencing the dignity of the Roman senate, the magic of the handwriting on the wall of Belshazzar's palace, and a voice from heaven—in the end gave only "some idea" of his response, he said. The effect of the speech also persisted. When the House of Burgesses met June 1775, every member was clothed in homespun and had "Liberty or Death" sewed or painted on his coat breast. The speech was preserved by the oral tradition, and even in the twentieth century is one of our nation's most familiar and revered pieces of literature.

In the canon of American literature the **"Liberty or Death"** speech is a hymn on liberty and patriotism, a stand-alone piece assigned for memorization by children to instill national pride and chosen by others for declaiming in contests to demonstrate gifts of dramatic interpretation. To Henry's auditors, the **"Liberty or Death"** speech was persuasion, not catechetical celebration or graceful entertainment, although highly romantic, emotional, and dramatic. The best cues regarding the sources of the great and peculiar impact of the **"Liberty or Death"** speech are in the criticisms of its contemporaries, who speak of its religious inspiration. The rural, oral tradition of the speech said that Henry's eyes burned with an "unearthly fire." Edmund Randolph, reporting what was the common opinion, said that "Henry was thought in his attitudes to resemble Saint Paul while preaching at Athens and to speak as *man* was never known to speak before" [italics added]. Such cues suggest that analysis of the **"Liberty or Death"** speech as an instance of deliberative oratory may neither plumb its depth nor probe its character.

Analysis of the **"Liberty or Death"** speech as a stock deliberative oration proceeds along the following lines: The speech begins with a carefully developed introduction, the principal purpose of which is to conciliate the audience towards the speaker. In the body of the speech, the speaker establishes agreement about the danger faced by the colony, proposes a response for dealing with that danger, and counters objections about the merits of the plan. Specifically, the speaker argues that the danger is the lack of preparedness to meet an imminent military danger; that the duty is to raise arms; and that confidence can be had in victory because of national physical and spiritual resources and prospects for international assistance. The speech closes with an appeal for action—ostensibly an affirmative vote for Henry's motion—based upon the exam-ple of a dramatic personal avowal of patriotism by the speaker. The standard reading usually takes notice of the profusion of religious language in the speech to explain its zealously righteous tone.

A close reading of the speech reveals that Henry represents the crisis in religious or moral instead of political or military terms. This suggests that the speech may be sermonic instead of deliberative. It prompts reconsideration of its purpose, invention, and plan, and it implies that religious language, instead of being an overlay—perhaps by a later hand—for emotional effect or an anachronistic motive, is inherent to the genre. Reconsideration suggests that this singular oration was the result of Henry's superior realization of the evangelical style in the secular sphere of a newly incorporated rhetorical community.

The purpose of preaching, according to evangelical rhetorical theory, was to convince sinners to accept the offer of salvation set forth in the Christian gospel. To accomplish this end the preacher had to convince the people of their sinfulness, extract from them a commitment to accept the grace of Jesus, and assure them that the promise of salvation was genuine. According to Barbara Larson [in her *Prologue to Revolution: The War Sermons of the Reverend Samuel Davies*], New Light preacher Samuel Davies commonly developed all three steps in a single sermon. Application of the New Light paradigm to the **"Liberty or Death"** speech illuminates the parallels between evangelical preaching and the **"Liberty or Death"** speech; in addition, the type and extent of the similarities provides a basis for concluding whether the responses of Henry's auditors resulted from perceiving the **"Liberty or Death"** speech as a sermon in the evangelical tradition.

The main function of the speech's introduction was to promote a conciliatory attitude towards Henry. Given Henry's reputation for being violently provocative and his reputation for being ahead of others on the issue of military resolution of the conflict with Great Britain, the step seems like a strategic choice. The introduction, however, does serve other functions. Henry plants motivating appeals based upon "the magnitude of the subject," which, he says, is "nothing less than a question of freedom or slavery," and he forecasts that the subject has religious, as well as political, dimensions, when he posits dual criteria for measuring responsible behavior: loyalty to God and country. Not until the body of the speech does Henry clearly posit the relation of civic behavior to religious duty or the sinfulness of the neglect of public responsibility. This principle is, however, the foundation of the speech, and the thesis of the speech is expressible as follows: The willingness of the redeemed to confront England militarily will ensure God's blessings of liberty on the American colonies.

Henry's first task is to convince the audience that something more serious than lack of military preparedness threatens their liberty: namely, their unwillingness to admit the imminence of military subjugation. The danger to the colony, as represented by Henry, inheres in man's proclivity to deny his corruption, "to indulge in the illusions of hope." Henry depicts man's self-deceit and reliance on false gods in the following: "We are apt to shut our eyes against a painful truth—and listen to the song of that siren, till she transforms us into beasts." Continuing, he asked, "Were we disposed to be of the number of those, who having eyes, see not, and having ears, hear not, the things which so nearly concern their temporal salvation?" By these words he brought the audience to the same bar of self-trial that Jesus raised for the apostles when they did not understand the feeding of the multitude (Mark 8:19-21), and he forecast a final judgment of slavery for those who refused to admit the need to know the truth about themselves.

Evangelical preachers frequently roused guilt in sinners with scathing denunciations. Henry denounced kindly, if not gently, by presenting the British Ministry (the Devil) as more despicable than his fellow delegates. Henry admonishingly inquired

> what there had been in the conduct of the British ministry for the last ten years, to justify those hopes with which gentlemen had been pleased to solace themselves and the house? Is it that insidious smile with which our petition has been lately received? Trust it not, sir; it will prove a snare to your feet. Suffer not yourselves to be betrayed with a kiss.
>
> Ask yourselves how this gracious reception of our petition comports with those warlike preparations which cover our waters and darken our land. Are fleets and armies necessary to a work of love and reconciliation? Have we shown ourselves so unwilling to be reconciled, that force must be called in to win back our love? Let us not deceive ourselves, sir. These are the implements of war and subjugation—the last arguments to which kings resort.
>
> I ask gentlemen, sir, what means this martial array, if its purpose be not to force us to submission? Can gentlemen assign any other possible motive for it? Has Great Britain any enemy in this quarter of the world, to call for all this accumulation of navies and armies? No, sir, she has none. They are meant for us: they can be meant for no other. They are sent over to bind and rivet upon us those chains which the British ministry have been so long forging.

While reminding of the longstanding nature of the conflict, its severity, and present martial manifestations, the main function of the passage is to provoke guilt for behavior that is jeopardizing liberty. Reproof is given sharpness through a series of images that represent the Virginia gentry as stupid, victims of self-deception. Henry mocks the conceit that has allowed them to be comfortable with their opinions about resolution of the conflict, the defective intelligence that has prevented them from recognizing British duplicity, and the slothfulness that has favored the British military buildup in the colonies, ironically expressed by Henry as "the last arguments to which kings resort."

The evangelical preacher, having convinced the sinner of the need for salvation, next sought to remove the burden of the guilt of sin by involving the penitent in a life of commitment to Christ. Henry sought a similar commitment.

Henry offers relief from the guilt of jeopardizing liberty by assumption of the commitment to fight, a commitment as public and as sacrificial as accepting the call to a life of Christian piety and discipline. Henry reviewed the misdirected paths that the colonists had pursued. Said Henry:

> Shall we resort to entreaty and humble supplication? What terms shall we find, which have not been already exhausted?
>
> Let us not, I beseech you, sir, deceive ourselves longer. Sir, we have done everything that could be done, to avert the storm which is now coming on. We have petitioned—we have remonstrated—and we have supplicated—we have prostrated ourselves before the throne, and have implored its interposition to arrest the tyrannical hands of the ministry and parliament.

He reviewed the increasingly dehumanizing responses of the British Ministry and king that their illusions had encouraged. Said Henry: "Our petitions have been slighted; our remonstrances have produced additional violence and insult; our supplications have been disregarded; and we have been spurned, with contempt, from the foot of the throne." Repentant of the pursuit of false gods, including the foolishly naive, perhaps insane, hope for peace and reconciliation, Henry's audience awaited instruction in how to live a redeemed life. Henry offered release with the following:

> If we wish to be free—if we mean to preserve inviolate those inestimable privileges for which we have been so long contending—if we mean not basely to abandon the noble struggle in which we have been so long engaged, and which we have pledged ourselves never to abandon, until the glorious object of our contest shall be obtained!—we must fight!—I repeat it, sir, we must fight!!! An appeal to arms and to the God of hosts is all that is left us!

Henry's audience did not expect the living of the faith to be easy. The personal and societal hardships of war did not need to be mentioned to be manifest; however, Henry in evangelical style, prudently challenged the audience with the glory of the goal, expressed as the "inestimable privileges" of freedom and understood by his audience to include the broad guarantees of the British Constitution.

Faithfulness to the commitment requires assurance of reward. New Light preachers of Henry's day accomplished this step of the evangelical sermon by contrasting the rewards of the repentant and the terrors of the unrepentant expressed in visions of the final judgment and the life after death. The military victory that Henry forecast was based upon the assurance of God. When Henry said that "an appeal to arms and to the God of hosts, is all that is left us," he meant the appeal to arms to which God calls us is the way of truth. God, according to Henry, had provided for victory. Naysayers, who tell us "we are weak," and cowards, who tell us to persist in "hugging the delusive phantom of hope," deny God's promise, Henry argued. "Sir, we are not weak," said Henry, "if we make a proper use of those means which the God of nature hath placed in our power." Henry enumerated the means: three million people, dedicated to a holy cause, supported by a plenteous country, and allies who will fight by our side. Henry clinched the argument of assurance with "the battle, sir, is not to the strong alone; it is to the vigilant, the active, the brave," a sentence evocative of Ecclesiastes 9:11. Faithfulness, in other words, not superior arms, would ensure the blessings of liberty. The alternative, the destiny of those "base enough to desire it"—the unrepentant—was "submission and slavery" in "forged" chains, the "clanking" of which "may be heard on the plains of Boston!"

The final sentence of the speech is Henry's personal avowal of preference for physical death to political servitude. It is an appeal for others to follow his example and to engage the enemy physically. Henry was undoubtedly a patriot filled with courage. Henry's determination and confidence, however, were grounded in evangelical theology. When, like Jeremiah (Jeremiah 6:14), he says, "gentlemen may cry, peace, peace—but there is no peace. The war is actually begun!" he is restating his argument about being convicted of the sinfulness of self-deceit. When he says "Our brethren are already in the field! Why stand we here idle?" he is restating the call to commitment. When he says "Is life so dear, or peace so sweet, as to be purchased at the price of chains and slavery? Forbid it, Almighty God!" he is restating God's assurance to the redeemed. In this context, "I know not what course others may take; but as for me, give me liberty, or give me death" submerges patriotism in prophecy.

Henry's colleagues in the convention knew that they were hearing something new. Edmund Randolph confidently asserted [in his *History of Virginia*] that "those who had toiled in the artifices of scholastic rhetoric were involuntarily driven into an inquiry within themselves, whether rules and forms and niceties of elocution would not have checked his native fire." The speech's composition was vivid, personal, and dramatic. It appealed strongly to the senses; indeed, every passage stimulated the emotions in a cumulative way as Henry unrelentingly pursued the exhortative goal of his speech. The informal division of the subject, the popularized demonstration, and amplification by homely and familiar references, especially references to the Scriptures, fused in the rhetorical style of evangelical religion to explicate the passionate drama inherent to the salvation theology of experimental religion. Perhaps the scene—St. John's Church—mutely amplified the message as well. Certainly Henry's delivery did. John Roane, an auditor, described at length the delivery of the speech's conclusion that Henry dramatized, portraying himself as a condemned galley slave, manacled in physical and psychological humiliation, who is transformed into the incarnation of freedom, invincible even in death. If Henry's "voice, countenance, and gestures" did give "irresistible force to his words," as Roane contended [in M. C. Tyler's biography of Henry], then the force of that passage really must have posed a personal moral summit for every member.

Henry masked the novelty of the rhetoric of sensation by observing some of the rules and customs appropriate to gentry-dominated communication settings. Otherwise, his conservative colleagues might not have heard him out so

patiently. His oration, on the surface at least, satisfied the conventions of deliberative oratory. It proposed a solution to a serious problem. Although the speech was personal and general, the resolution that it sustained was objective and specific as to the action proposed and the reasons for it. Although the speech prompted affective responses and little edification, the responses arose from audience-supplied evidences of personal experience with a decade of British misrule. Furthermore, Henry behaved decorously: he behaved with decency, dignity, and propriety. Initially, Henry humbled himself with his praise of his colleagues' patriotism and legislative acumen. Besides establishing modesty he established his worth, which he based upon the willing exercise of thought and the unrestrained exercise of speech in behalf of the public welfare. And throughout the speech he behaved mannerly. Henry addressed the chair formally, speaking to "Mr. President" or "Sir." Observance of this convention, which Henry reiterated at intervals throughout the speech, helped him to present an objective and deliberate manner, though animated by great feeling. At the same time, it increased the focus of audience attention upon him. He appealed to and observed the gentlemanly code of fair play. He kindly reminded his colleagues, as he begged for a fair hearing, that serious situations provoke differences that are in no wise indications of disrespectfulness, and when he judged his colleagues to be out of right relation with the truth, he did so without offense to any individual member.

Henry's sermon induced a communal experience based on the evangelical paradigm of conviction, commitment, and assurance. In the **"Liberty or Death"** speech, he transformed the relation of God and man into the relation of God and nation. He represented the relationship to be reliant upon the moral or religious virtue of every citizen, and he articulated his vision of society by a fusion of rhetorical strategies agreeable to the new rhetorical community formed from evangelical and scholastic traditions. (pp. 55-63)

> *David A. McCants, in his* Patrick Henry, The Orator, *Greenwood Press, 1990, 173 p.*

FURTHER READING

Biography

Beeman, Richard R. *Patrick Henry, A Biography.* New York: McGraw-Hill Book Co., 1974, 229 p.
   Imparts "a more complete understanding of the society in which Henry operated."

Bradford, M. E. "Patrick Henry: The Trumpet Voice of Freedom." In his *Against the Barbarians, and Other Reflections on Familiar Themes,* pp. 83-99. Columbia: University of Missouri Press, 1992.
   Brief chronological biography highlighting important debates in which Henry participated.

Campbell, Norine Dickson. *Patrick Henry: Patriot and Statesman.* New York: Devin-Adair Co., 1969, 438 p.
    Standard biography wherein Henry is hailed as "the man who gave meaning to America."

Henry, William Wirt. *Patrick Henry: Life, Correspondence, and Speeches.* 3 vols. New York: Burt Franklin, 1891.
    Important biographical source by Henry's grandson.

Morgan, George. *The True Patrick Henry.* Philadelphia: J. B. Lippincott Co., 1907, 492 p.
    Frequently cited biographical source.

Criticism

Gewehr, Wesley M. *The Great Awakening in Virginia, 1740-1790.* Durham, N. C.: Duke University Press, 1930, 292 p.
    Describes the religious atmosphere in Virginia during the Revolutionary period and the role of the church in the transformation of American social institutions.

Grigsby, Hugh Blair. *The Virginia Convention of 1776, A Discourse.* Richmond, Va.: J. W. Randolph, 1855, 206 p.
    Examines the convention which framed the first constitution of Virginia and elected Henry as the state's governor.

Gummere, Richard M. *The American Colonial Mind and the Classical Tradition.* Cambridge, Mass.: Harvard University Press, 1963, 228 p.
    Discusses the influence of classical ideas and legend on colonial American thought.

Isaac, Rhys. "Preachers and Patriots: Popular Culture and the Revolution in Virginia." In *The American Revolution: Explorations in the History of American Radicalism,* edited by Alfred F. Young, pp. 124-56. DeKalb: Northern Illinois University Press, 1976.
    Details the parallel growth of patriotism and evangelicalism in colonial Virginia.

Kenyon, Cecelia M. "Men of Little Faith: The Anti-Federalists on the Nature of Representative Government." *William and Mary Quarterly* Third Series XII, No. 1 (January 1955): 3-43.
    Seminal discussion of Anti-Federalist thought. According to critic Gordon S. Wood, Kenyon's article "dramat-ically altered the direction of scholarly writing on the constitution."

Mallory, Louis A. "Patrick Henry." In *A History and Criticism of American Public Address,* edited by William Norwood Brigance, pp. 580-602. New York: Russell & Russell, 1960.
    Highlights Henry's political career, focusing especially on his skills as an orator.

Mayo, Bernard. "The Enigma of Patrick Henry." *The Virginia Quarterly Review* 35, No. 2 (Spring 1959): 176-95.
    Reviews the biographical sources on Henry, especially Wirt's initial study.

McCants, David A. "The Authenticity of James Maury's Account of Patrick Henry's Speech in the Parsons' Cause." *The Southern Speech Communication Journal* XLII, No. 1 (Fall 1976): 20-34.
    Evaluates the plaintiff's description of Henry's speech in the Parsons' Cause case.

———. "The Authenticity of William Wirt's Version of Patrick Henry's 'Liberty or Death' Speech." *The Virginia Magazine of History and Biography* 87, No. 4 (October 1979): 387-402.
    Examines Wirt's reconstruction of Henry's speech.

Olsen, Stephen T. "Patrick Henry's 'Liberty or Death' Speech: A Study in Disputed Authorship." In *American Rhetoric: Context and Criticism,* edited by Thomas W. Benson, pp. 19-65. Evansville and Carbondale: Southern Illinois University Press, 1989.
    Analyzes the debate concerning authorship of the "Liberty or Death" speech. Tracing the history of the controversy, Olsen evaluates the data both as historian and computer scientist, employing statistical stylistics.

Sparks, Jared. Review of *Sketches of the Life and Character of Patrick Henry,* by William Wirt. *The North American Review and Miscellaneous Journal* VI, No. 3 (March 1818): 293-324.
    Early review of Wirt's biography.

Francis Hopkinson

1737-1791

(Also wrote under the pseudonym Peter Grievous) American statesman, prose writer, poet, and composer.

INTRODUCTION

Hopkinson was a prominent Colonial statesman and political satirist whose humorous attacks on the British are believed to have helped maintain American esprit de corps during the Revolutionary War. A multifaceted figure, Hopkinson was also a noted poet, composer, painter, and inventor. In addition, he made significant contributions to American public life by attending the Second Continental Congress, signing the Declaration of Independence, and by holding several important political and judicial positions.

Hopkinson was born in 1737 to a distinguished Philadelphia family. His father, Thomas, was a judge and a friend of Benjamin Franklin, and his mother, Mary Johnson, was from a notable British family. In 1751 he enrolled in the Academy of Philadelphia, which later became the University of Pennsylvania, where he actively participated in the artistic and literary life of the college. Upon graduation in 1757, he studied law under Benjamin Chew, the Attorney General of Pennsylvania, and he was admitted to the bar in 1761. He became collector of customs for the port of Salem, New Jersey, but because of strong negative reaction to the Stamp Act, a tax on paper that was considered unfair, he was forced to resign. His fortune rose in 1768 when he married Ann Borden, heiress of Joseph Borden, the leading citizen of Bordentown, New Jersey. Through the patronage of Lady North, the wife of the English Prime Minister, Hopkinson was appointed collector of customs at New Castle, Delaware in 1771. This position offered him financial security and considerable leisure, thus enabling him to live as a country gentleman in Bordentown, where he devoted himself to art and music. During the Revolutionary War, he participated in the Second Continental Congress and was appointed to various administrative and judicial positions. From 1776 to 1778 he served as chairman of the Navy Board, and from 1778 to 1781 he attempted to manage the national debt as treasurer of loans. Appointed judge of the Admiralty Court in 1780, he decided many sensitive cases concerning captured British vessels, and at the end of his first year, he was impeached on the charge of having accepted a bribe, but was later fully exonerated in court. In addition to his professional duties, he also supported the war effort by writing numerous ballads and satires in verse and prose. After the war, he became a Federalist, a supporter of the new constitution, and was appointed to the district judgeship of Eastern Pennsylvania by George Washington in 1789. He died suddenly of apoplexy in 1791.

Hopkinson's writings were posthumously collected and published in three volumes as *The Miscellaneous Essays and Occasional Writings of Francis Hopkinson* (1792), though it is uncertain that all his writings have been discovered. Hopkinson wrote for serial publications, newspapers, and journals. His satirical essays and stories are regarded by commentators as his most successful literary endeavors. These works, which were occasionally modeled on the writings of such British satirists as Joseph Addison, Sir Richard Steele, and Jonathan Swift, also served as effective political propaganda during the Revolutionary War. For example, in the allegorical tale *A Pretty Story* (1774), Hopkinson lampoons the deterioration in relations between Britain and the Colonies by narrating the conflict between a greedy stepmother and the sons of a respectable farmer. One of his most famous poems, "The Battle of the Kegs" (1778), ridicules the excessive reaction of the British to Hopkinson's failed attempt to destroy their fleet by using kegs filled with gunpowder.

In addition to his literary endeavors, Hopkinson was, in the words of Oscar Sonneck, "the first native American composer of songs of whom we know, and his song 'My Days Have Been So Wondrous Free' is the earliest secular

American composition extant, dating back to 1759." Hopkinson composed numerous secular and sacred works, and in 1781 he saw his *The Temple of Minerva* performed before George Washington. This was a mythological allegory in which the goddess Minerva joins personifications of France and the United States in an alliance against Britain. Sonneck claims that this work, for which Hopkinson wrote both the words and music, must "be considered as our first attempt at 'grand opera.'" Hopkinson was also an inventor of note who improved the design of the harpsichord by replacing the traditional quill picks, which were used to pluck the strings, with tongues of leather and cork. This innovation enhanced the sound and made the instrument easier to repair. While in England, Hopkinson studied drawing and painting with an old college friend, Benjamin West; and when he returned to the colonies, he became a well-known designer, helping to fashion the seal of his alma mater, as well as those of the state of New Jersey and the American Philosophical Society. In addition, Hopkinson is generally recognized as having been the designer of the American flag.

In assessing Hopkinson's significance, scholars have focused more on his historical role in the founding and administration of the young republic than on the intrinsic merits of his literary works. Many commentators argue that Hopkinson was a dilettante whose interest in a broad range of disciplines deprived him of excellence in any single area. Others, however, emphasize that he did not aspire to be anything more than a well-rounded man of letters for whom the arts were a means of self-enrichment. Nevertheless, scholars concur that Hopkinson's contributions as a satirist, composer, and designer have earned him a modest but important place in the cultural history of the United States.

PRINCIPAL WORKS

An Exercise (poetry, music, and prose) 1761
Science: A Poem (poetry) 1762
A Collection of Psalm Tunes (hymns) 1763
Errata; Or, The Art of Printing Incorrectly (satire) 1763
A Psalm of Thanksgiving (hymn) 1766
A Pretty Story (allegory) 1774; also published as *The Old Farm and the New Farm: A Political Allegory,* 1857
Consolation for the Old Bachelor (satire) 1775
A Prophecy (satire) 1776
Art of Paper War (satire) 1778
The Battle of the Kegs (poetry) 1778
A Camp Ballad (poetry) 1778
Date Obolum Belisario (poetry) 1778
A Tory Medley (songs) 1780
The Temple of Minerva (opera) 1781
The New Roof (allegory) 1787
Account of the Grand Procession (essay) 1788
An Ode (song) 1788

Seven Songs for Harpsichord and Piano Forte (songs) 1788
Judgments in the Admiralty of Pennsylvania (legal decisions) 1789
An Oration (satire) 1789
The Miscellaneous Essays and Occasional Writings of Francis Hopkinson (essays, music, speeches, legal decisions, and poetry) 1792
Colonial Love Lyrics. Six Songs by Francis Hopkinson (songs) 1919
*The First American Composer. Six Songs by Francis Hopkinson (songs) 1919

*This collection includes "My Days Have Been So Wondrous Free."

CRITICISM

Carl Holliday (essay date 1912)

[*In the following excerpt, Holliday evaluates Hopkinson's humorous writing during the War of Independence and praises the keenness of his intellect, the sharpness of his wit, and the audacity of his humor.*]

[For a time], the Tories considered the American Revolution a huge joke. Not so to many of the colonial fathers. Indeed, some fun-makers were sorely needed by several of those solemn-faced founders of our nation. To them life was a little too earnest; they took themselves perhaps a trifle too seriously. Only a few of these greater men dared to risk their reputation for solidness by joking *openly* whenever they felt like it; and naturally these choice spirits stand out conspicuously because of their very loneliness. Among the common folk there was, of course, much rough humor and satire; but we speak now of the moulders of the Commonwealth. Of those conspicuous for their audacity in being funny in public one of the most daring in his defiance toward the ancient idea that all great people must be solemn was Francis Hopkinson. (p. 145)

The average reader of to-day knows Francis Hopkinson through one piece, **"The Battle of the Kegs."** And, if he had written nothing else, he is worthy of remembrance for that sly bit of sarcasm. Undoubtedly it was the most popular ballad written in Revolutionary days. It was copied in every colony; it was recited at social functions; and public speakers, when wishing to have the laugh on the British, quoted stanzas from it. The incident which caused the poem was laughable in itself, and Hopkinson measured up to his opportunity. Kegs charged with powder were floated down the river to destroy the British fleet lying before Philadelphia, with the result that the English soliders spent the day bravely *shooting kegs!* (p. 149)

It is characteristic of Hopkinson [that there is really no bitterness in the poem]. Always more amused than angered, he simply had a good-humored laugh over the follies of his opponents. Evidently he kept in mind the words of his contemporary Robert Burns—

O wad some Pow'r the giftie gie us

To see oursels as others see us!—

and did his utmost to help the Tories and British in their efforts along this line. Yet, it was not lack of serious principle that caused him to assume this good-natured levity. There were times when Hopkinson did not mince words. Hear his expressions in a letter to Joseph Galloway, a man who had proved himself a hypocrite:

> Now that you have gained the summit of your ambitious hopes, the reward of your forfeited honor, that dear-bought gratification, to obtain which you have given your name to infamy and your soul to perdition—now that you sit in Philadelphia, the nominal governor of Pennsylvania, give me leave to address a few words of truth to your corrupted heart. Retire for a moment from the avocations and honors of your new superintendency, and review the steps by which you have mounted the stage of power—steps reeking with the blood of your innocent country.
>
> When the storm was gathering dark and dreary over this devoted country, when America stood in need of all the exertions which her best patriots and most confidential citizens could make, you stepped forward—you offered yourself a candidate, and, with unwearied diligence, solicited a seat in the American Congress. Your seeming sincerity and your loud complaints against the unjust usurpations of the British legislature gained the confidence of your country. You were elected; you took your seat in Congress—and let posterity remember that while you were vehemently declaiming in that venerable senate against British tyranny, and with hypocritical zeal urging a noble stand in behalf of the liberties of your country, you were at the same time betraying their secrets, ridiculing their economy, and making sport of their conduct. . . .
>
> The temporary reward of iniquity you now hold will soon shirk from your grasp. . . . This you know, and the reflection must even now throw a gloom of horror over your enjoyments, which the glittering tinsel of your new superintendency cannot illumine. Look back, and all is guilt—look forward, and all is dread! When the history of the present time shall be recorded, the names of Galloway and Cunningham will not be omitted; and posterity will wonder at the extreme obduracy of which the human heart is capable, and at the unmeasurable difference between a traitor and a Washington.

If further proof were needed that this dainty-looking, art-loving gentleman could on occasion wield a sarcastic pen dipped in fluid bitterness, we might well turn to his **"Letter Written by a Foreigner on His Travels,"** in which he causes his "foreigner" to say concerning England:

> The extreme ignorance of the common people of this civilized country can scarce be credited. In general they know nothing beyond the particular branch of business which their parents or the parish happened to choose for them. This, indeed, they practise with unremitting diligence, but never think of extending their knowledge farther.

> A manufacturer has been brought up a maker of pin-heads. He has been at this business forty years and, of course, makes pin-heads with great dexterity; but he cannot make a whole pin to save his life. He thinks it is the perfection of human nature to make pin-heads. He leaves other matters to inferior abilities. It is enough for him that he believes in the Athanasian Creed, reverences the splendor of the court, and makes pin-heads. This he conceives to be the sum-total of religion, politics, and trade. He is sure that London is the finest city in the world; Blackfriars Bridge the most superb of all possible bridges; and the river Thames the largest river in the universe. It is in vain to tell him that there are many rivers in America, in comparison of which the Thames is but a ditch; that there are single provinces there larger than all England; and that the colonies . . . are vastly more extensive than England, Wales, Scotland and Ireland, taken all together—he cannot conceive this. He goes into his best parlor, and looks on a map of England, four feet square; on the other side of the room he sees a map of North and South America, not more than two feet square, and exclaims: 'How can these things be! It is altogether impossible!' . . . Talk to him of the British constitution, he will tell you it is a glorious constitution; ask him what it is, and he is ignorant of its first principles; but he is sure that he can make and sell pin-heads under it. . . .

This, however, was not the usual Francis Hopkinson. He preferred not to hiss, but to laugh his opponent out of court. If ever you enter one of the greater libraries of our country, ask for his *Pretty Story* (printed the very day the first Continental Congress met), and enjoy some very gentle yet very real humor. You will find it to be a lively little allegory telling the story of the disturbance between the mother country and the colonies down to the year 1774. England is represented by the Old Farm, America by the New, while the Nobleman is the King, and his Wife is Parliament. A few bits from it, to show its flavor:

> Once upon a time, a great while ago, there lived a certain Nobleman, who had long possessed a very valuable Farm, and had a great number of children and grand-children. Besides the annual profits of his land, which were very considerable, he kept a large shop of goods; and being very successful in trade, he became, in process of time, exceeding rich and powerful, insomuch that all his neighbors feared and respected him. . . . Now, it came to pass that this Nobleman had, by some means or other, obtained a right to an immense tract of wild uncultivated country at a vast distance from his mansion house. But he set little store by this acquisition, as it yielded him no profit; nor was it likely to do so, being not only difficult of access on account of the distance, but was also overrun with innumerable wild beasts very fierce and savage,—so that it would be extremely dangerous to attempt taking possession of it.
>
> In process of time, however, some of his children, more stout and enterprising than the rest, requested leave of their Father to go and settle

on this distant tract of land. [Then follows a list of the rules laid down by the king for the conduct of the settlers and the promises made by him. The new land showed prospects of becoming an earthly Paradise; but at length troubles began to come, as in every Paradise. The Nobleman's Wife began to cast envious looks towards the new home, and after a time issued an edict] setting forth that whereas the tailors of her family were greatly injured by the people of the New Farm, inasmuch as they presumed to make their own clothes, whereby the said tailors were deprived of the benefit of their custom, it was therefore ordained that for the future the new settlers should not be permitted to have amongst them any shears or scissors larger than a certain fixed size. In consequence of this, our adventurers were compelled to have their clothes made by their Father's tailors; but out of regard to the old Gentleman, they patiently submitted to this grievance. . . . She [the Wife] persuaded her Husband to send amongst them, from time to time, a number of the most lazy and useless of her servants, under the specious pretext of defending them in their settlements and of assisting to destroy the wild beasts, but in fact, to rid his own house of their company, not having employment for them, and at the same time to be a watch and a check upon the people of the New Farm.

The story then declares that the Nobleman's Steward had debauched the Nobleman's Wife and had persuaded her to wear two padlocks on her lips so that when he opened one she could cry only "No," and when the other, only "Yes." The Steward then persuaded the Nobleman, who was now in his dotage, to place a heavy tax on several articles to be bought only at his shop, notably Water-Gruel [tea]. But the settlers would have none of it, and allowed the gruel to sour by the roadside. And

one of the new settlers, whose name was Jack [Boston], either from a keener sense of the injuries attempted against him, or from the necessity of his situation, which was such that he could not send back the Gruel because of a number of mercenaries whom his Father had stationed before his house to watch and be a check upon his conduct,—he, I say, being almost driven to despair, fell to work and with great zeal stove to pieces the casks of Gruel which had been sent him and utterly demolished the whole cargo. . . . The old Gentleman fell into great wrath, declaring that his absent children meant to throw off all dependence upon him, and to become altogether disobedient. His Wife also tore the padlocks from her lips, and raved and stormed like a Billingsgate. The Steward lost all patience and moderation, swearing most profanely that he would leave no stone unturned until he had humbled the settlers of the New Farm at his feet, and caused their Father to trample on their necks. Moreover, the Gruel Merchants roared and bellowed for the loss of their Gruel; and the clerks and apprentices were in the utmost consternation lest the people of the New Farm should again agree to have no dealings with their Father's shop. Immediately an

immense padlock was fastened upon Jack's gate, and an overseer was sent to Jack's home to "break his spirit."

Jack appealed to his neighbors for supplies, and "seasonable bounty was handed to Jack over the garden wall, all access to the front of his house being shut up." Moreover, Jack's Family held consultations about the matter; but the Overseer "wrote a thundering prohibition, much like a Pope's Bull, which he caused to be pasted up in every room in the house; in which he declared and protested that these meetings were treasonable, traitorous, and rebellious, contrary to the dignity of their Father and inconsistent with the omnipotence of their Mother-in-Law; denouncing also terrible punishments against any two of the Family who should from thenceforth be seen whispering together, and strictly forbidding the domestics to hold any more meetings in the garret or stable.

"These harsh and unconstitutional proceedings irritated Jack and the other inhabitants of the New Farm to such a degree that . . . Caetera desunt"

Hopkinson refuses to prophesy what will happen; he leaves it to the gentlemen who were just then assembling in the hall of Congress not far from the book-stall where the *Pretty Story* was being exhibited.

If you will look into the story for yourself, you will see how well sustained, how interesting at all points, how full of bright surprises the genial narrative is. There is a flavor of French vivacity and French simplicity about it that charms one. We should not be surprised, therefore, to find that this man wrote some of the daintiest lyrics of early days—in some instances, exquisite little things that might well be revived and made popular through musical setting.

But the times were rather adverse toward love-lyrics and nature poems, and Hopkinson's talent was turned to the more immediately useful field of satirical verse. There were during those dangerous days, undoubtedly, numerous fickle creatures—"the summer soldier and the sunshine patriot," as Tom Paine's *Crisis* called them—men who were valiant patriots when the Americans held the city and zealous Tories when the British came to town; and just such a sharp pen as Hopkinson's was needed for such people. The neat fable, **"The Birds, the Beasts, and the Bat,"** leaves no doubt as to his opinion of such turncoats.

> A war broke out in former days—
> If all is true that Æsop says—
> Between the birds that haunt the grove
> And beasts that wild in forests rove.
>
> . . .
>
> From every tribe vast numbers came
> To fight for freedom, as for fame.
>
> . . .
>
> The bat—half bird, half beast—was there,
> Nor would for *this* or *that* declare,—
> Waiting till conquest should decide
> Which was the strongest, safest side.
>
> . . .
>
> The birds in fierce assault, 'tis said,
> Amongst the foe such havoc made—

That, panic-struck, the beasts retreat
Amazed, and victory seemed complete.
The observant bat, with squeaking tone,
Cried, 'Bravo, Birds! The day's our own;
For now I am proud to claim a place
Amongst your bold aspiring race.'

. . .

But now the beasts, ashamed of flight,
With rallied force renew the fight;

. . .

Enraged, advance—push on the fray
And claim the honors of the day.
The bat, still hovering to and fro,
Observed how things were like to go.

. . .

'Push on,' quoth he, 'Our's is the day!
We'll chase these rebel birds away,
And reign supreme—for who but we
Of earth and air the lords should be?'

. . .

Now in their turn the beasts must yield
The bloody laurels of the field.

. . .

Once more the bat with courtly voice,
'Hail, noble birds! Much I rejoice
In your success and come to claim
My share of conquest and of fame.'
The birds the faithless wretch despise:
'Hence, traitor, hence!' the eagle cries;
'No more, as you just vengeance fear,
Amongst our honored ranks appear.'
The bat, disowned, in some old shed
Now seeks to hide his exiled head;
Nor dares his leathern wings display
From rising morn to setting day.

. . .

It was true. Many a Tory, in the end, felt inclined "in some old shed . . . to hide his exiled head." And to good-natured Hopkinson their futile efforts to destroy patriotism before that fatal day, were just as laughable as their final predicament. This scene of the Loyalist wits' venting their spleen upon the unmoved structure of American liberty reminded him very much of a wasp endeavoring to sting a church-steeple! Hear some lines from his fable, **"The Wasp"**:

Wrapt in Aurelian filth and slime,
An infant wasp neglected lay;
Till having dosed the destined time,
He woke and struggled into day.

. . .

'In copious streams my spleen shall flow,
And satire all her purses drain;
A critic born, the world shall know
I carry not a sting in vain.'

This said, from native cell of clay,
Elate he rose in airy flight;
Thence to the city changed his way,
And on a steeple chanced to light.

'Ye gods!' he cried, 'what horrid pile
Presumes to rear his head so high?
This clumsy cornice—see how vile:

Can this delight a critic's eye?'

With poisonous sting he strove to wound
The substance firm, but strove in vain;
Surprised he sees it stands its ground,
Nor starts through fear, nor writhes with pain.

Away the enraged insect flew;
But soon with aggravated power,
Against the walls his body threw
And hoped to shake the lofty tower.

Firm fixed it stands, as stand it must,
Nor heeds the wasp's unpitied fall:
The humbled critic rolls in dust,
So stunned, so bruised, he scarce can crawl.

Is it not clear how genuinely useful such a man was in those discouraging times? Many of the colonial leaders seemed instinctively to look to Francis Hopkinson whenever any faction or individual became too prominent in hostility, and Hopkinson seldom failed to squelch the troublesome party. How skilfully, for example, he checked that malicious enemy of independence, Provost Smith of the College of Philadelphia. The provost was writing in the *Pennsylvania Gazette* his dangerous *Letters of Cato to the People of Pennsylvania.* The people were more than interested—they were aroused; for the papers were strong in argument and forceful in style. An answer was needed and that right early. Hopkinson came to the rescue with **"A Prophecy."** An ancient seer had a vision of what would occur, and did occur, in Philadelphia in 1776, and Hopkinson, it seems, interviewed the seer. It turned the laugh on the college president. After speaking of a tree sent over by the king of certain islands—a tree which proved exceedingly rotten at the core, the narration states that a proposal was made by a prophet (Dr. Franklin), to cut it down.

And the people shall hearken to the voice of their prophet, for his sayings shall be good in their eyes. And they shall take up every man his spade and his axe, and shall prepare to dig up and cut away the shattered remains of the blasted and rotten tree, according to the words of their prophet.

Then a certain wise man shall arise and shall call himself Cato; and he shall strive to persuade the people to put their trust in the rotten tree and not to dig it up or remove it from its place. And he shall harangue with great vehemence, and shall tell them that a rotten tree is better than a sound one; and that it is for the benefit of the people that the North wind should blow upon it, and that the branches thereof should be broken and fall upon and crush them.

And he shall receive from the king of the islands fetters of gold and chains of silver; and he shall have hopes of great reward if he will fasten them on the necks of the people, and chain them to the trunk of the rotten tree. . . . And he shall tell the people that they are not fetters and chains, but shall be as bracelets of gold on their wrists, and rings of silver on their necks to ornament and decorate them and their children. And his words shall be sweet in the mouth, but very bitter in the belly.

. . .

And it shall come to pass that certain other wise men shall also stand up and oppose themselves to Cato; and shall warn the people not to trust in the allurements of his voice, nor to be terrified with his threats, and to hearken to his puns no more. . . . And they shall earnestly exhort the people to despise and reject the fetters of gold and the chains of silver which the king of the islands would fasten upon them.

. . .

And in process of time the people shall root up the rotten tree, and in its place they shall plant a young and vigorous tree, and shall effectually defend it from the winds of the North by an high wall. . . . And the young tree shall grow and flourish and spread its branches far abroad; and the people shall dwell under the shadow of its branches, and shall become an exceedingly great and powerful and happy nation. . . .

Hopkinson's was a never ceasing pen for the American cause. We have touched only here and there in his works, and some of his best efforts must be left unnoticed. It would be pleasant to linger, for instance, over his **"First Book of the American Chronicle"** or his odd **"Specimens of a Modern Law Suit,"** wherein a man is brought to trial for paring his nails on Friday. It would be interesting, too, to look over his mock advertisement of the Tory editor, James Rivington, for whom circumstances had "rendered it convenient . . . to remove to Europe." Rivington had, for *immediate* sale, various books, maps, and patent medicines, some of which, according to Hopkinson, were as follows:

The History of the American War; or the Glorious Exploits of the British Generals, Gage, Howe, Burgoyne, Cornwallis, and Clinton.

The Right of Great Britain to the Dominion of the Sea—a Poetical Fiction.

The State of Great Britain in October, 1760, and in October, 1781, compared and contrasted.

Tears of Repentance; or the Present State of the Loyal Refugees in New York, and elsewhere.

The Political Liar: a Weekly Paper, published by the Subscriber [Rivington], bound in Volumes.

The Battle of Saratoga, and the Surrender at York: Two elegant Prints, cut in Copper, and dedicated to the King.

Microscopes for magnifying small objects, furnished with a select set ready fitted for use. Amongst these are a variety of real and supposed successes of the British Generals in America.

Pocket Glasses for Short-sighted Politicians.

Vivifying Balsam: excellent for weak nerves, palpitation of the heart, over-bashfulness, and diffidence. In great demand for the officers of the army.

Sp. Men. Or the genuine Spirit of Lying. Ex-

tracted by distillation from many hundreds of 'The Royal Gazette of New York.'

Anodyne Elixir, for quieting fears and apprehensions. Very necessary for Tories in all parts of America.

Few, indeed, were the men who served the American cause better than this "pretty, little, curious, ingenious gentleman," Francis Hopkinson. When he picked up his quill, well might the Tories lay in a supply of "Anodyne Elixir, for quieting fears and apprehensions." For to his task Hopkinson brought as keen an intellect, as great a degree of culture, and as forceful and witty a style as could be found in America, and his opponents often feared his good-humored ridicule far more than the violent and bitter expressions of some of his fellow patriots. (pp. 152-69)

Carl Holliday, "Philip Freneau, 'The Human Wasp'," in his The Wit and Humor of Colonial Days, *1912. Reprint by Frederick Ungar Publishing, 1960, pp. 145-69.*

George Everett Hastings   (essay date 1926)

[*Hastings was an American scholar and educator best known for his* The Life and Times of Francis Hopkinson (1926). *In an excerpt from this work, he delineates Hopkinson's achievements in law, art, poetry, music, and political satire. Hastings further praises Hopkinson's versatility and balance, and claims that his sense of humor may at times have bordered on genius.*]

Hopkinson's professional standing is indicated by the positions that he held. He was appointed judge of admiralty in 1779, and was reappointed in 1780 and 1787. In 1780 he was impeached for misconduct in office, but after a trial before the Supreme Executive Council of the State of Pennsylvania he was completely exonerated. In 1789 Washington appointed him judge of the newly established United States District Court of the Eastern District of Pennsylvania. In 1790 the University conferred upon him the degree of LL.D.

Hopkinson's legal knowledge was evidently respected by his associates. In the summer of 1789, when Congress was reorganizing the judiciary system of the country, his advice was sought by those who framed the bill establishing the new courts. On July 3 Robert Morris informed him that some of his suggestions had been presented to the Senate "with effect." Morris evidently sympathized with Hopkinson's ambition to be a judge in the new federal court, for he wrote:

I have coupled a sentiment with my Friendship for you, that justifies me to myself for any Attempt I can make to serve you; it is that by promoting your Views in the Judiciary line I shall promote the Services of that Country which sent me here.

Washington's statement that in nominating persons to fill offices in the Judicial Department he had chosen characters that would "give stability and dignity to our national Government," was not a mere compliment. Hopkinson's reputation among his contemporaries amply justified his appointment; moreover, his prestige has not diminished with the passing of time. Judge Thomas Bee, of South Carolina, who in 1810 published a book of *Reports of Cases Adjudged in the District Court of South Carolina,* considered Hopkinson's decisions so important that he republished twenty of them as an appendix to his work. An examination of the Supreme Court decisions handed down since Hopkinson's day shows that his judgments have frequently been cited by eminent jurists. *Shepard's Federal Citations* contains more than one hundred references to his decisions—one made as recently as 1904. His reputation among lawyers of the present is summed up in these words of Hampton L. Carson, Esq.:

> It is a high tribute to the judicial knowledge, impartial conduct and correct judgment of Judge Francis Hopkinson, of the Admiralty Court of Pennsylvania, that out of forty-nine cases, in which he has reported his decrees, and the reasons upon which they were based, but nine appeals were taken, and in eight of these he was sustained.

Though Hopkinson's legal essays grew out of a personal quarrel, and though they discuss problems of local and temporary interest, they contain material that is of permanent value. By protesting against the attempts of judges to dominate juries, he called attention to a peril that is ever present in a democracy—the danger that one department of government may usurp the powers of another. In his "Specimen of a Modern Law-Suit" he satirizes the redundancy of legal phraseology, the slowness of court procedure, and the absurdity of judges and lawyers who regard the observance of technicalities as being more important than the administration of equity and justice.

Hopkinson's scientific work was more ingenious than important. His improvements of the harpsichord and candlestick were useful in their day, but since the harpsichord has been superseded by the piano, and since the candlestick has become an object of ornament rather than use, they have given him no great permanent fame as an inventor. Of more value to science than his investigations was the help and encouragement that he gave to the American Philosophical Society, an institution that has been an important factor in American scientific progress.

Abundant evidence has already been produced to show that Hopkinson's musical abilities were highly esteemed by his contemporaries. That the popular opinion was shared, at least to some extent, by musicians is suggested by the fact that "*William Brown,* in 1787, composed and published 'Three Rondos for the Pianoforte,' which he *Humbly dedicated to the Honorable Francis Hopkinson, Esqr.*"

The permanent value of Hopkinson's work as a composer has been justly estimated by Mr. Sonneck [O. G. Sonneck in his *Francis Hopkinson,* 1905]:

> As a composer Francis Hopkinson did not improve greatly during the thirty years which separate this song collection [*Seven Songs*] from his earliest efforts. His harmony is still faulty at times, and he possesses not an original musical profile. To claim the adjective of beautiful or im-

portant for these songs or his other compositions would mean to confuse the standpoint of the musical critic with that of the antiquarian. But even the critic who cares not to explain and pardon shortcomings from a historical point of view will admit that Hopkinson's songs are not without grace and that our first poet-composer obeyed the laws of musical declamation more carefully than a host of fashionable masters of that period. Artistically, of course, he resembles his contemporaries. His musical world, like theirs, was an untrue Arcadia, populated with over-sentimental shepherds and shepherdesses, or with jolly tars, veritable models of sobriety and good behavior, even when filling huge bumpers for drinking-bouts. Then again we notice in Francis Hopkinson's music the studied simplicity of that age for which treble and bass had become the pillars of the universe.

> This and much more is antiquated to-day. But why should we criticize at all our first "musical compositions"? It becomes us better to look upon these primitive efforts as upon venerable documents of the innate love of the American people for the beauties of music and as documents of the fact that among the Signers of the Declaration of Independence there was at least one who proved to be a "SUCCESSFUL PATRON OF ARTS AND SCIENCES."

The publication in 1905 of Mr. Oscar G. Sonneck's *Francis Hopkinson, the First American Poet-Composer* brought about a very considerable revival of interest in Hopkinson's musical compositions. In 1919 two albums, each containing six of Hopkinson's songs, edited for modern use by Mr. Harold Vincent Milligan, were published by the Arthur P. Schmidt Company, of Boston. The first volume, which bears the title *The First American Composer. Six Songs by Francis Hopkinson,* contains "My Days Have Been So Wondrous Free," from the 1759 manuscript volume now owned by the Library of Congress, and the following selections from *Seven Songs:* "O'er the Hills Far Away," "Beneath a Weeping Willow's Shade," "Come, Fair Rosina," "My Generous Heart Disdains," and "The Traveller Benighted and Lost." The second, *Colonial Love Lyrics. Six Songs by Francis Hopkinson,* includes "The Garland" and "With Pleasure Have I Passed My Days," from the 1759 volume; "Give Me Thy Heart," from the *Columbian Magazine* of August, 1789; and "See, Down Maria's Blushing Cheek," "Enraptured I Gaze," and "My Love Has Gone to Sea," from *Seven Songs.* In 1920 the "Ode from Ossian's Poems," edited and harmonized by Mr. Carl Deis, was published by G. Schirmer, Inc., of New York.

Since the appearance of the volumes of Mr. Milligan and Mr. Deis, selections from Hopkinson's musical works have frequently appeared on concert programs. The first modern singer to use one of Hopkinson's songs in a public recital was Miss Kitty Cheatham, who, according to a letter which she wrote to Mr. Edward Hopkinson on February 19, 1926, sang "My Days Have Been So Wondrous Free" in the State College at Winona, Minnesota, "just precedent to the publication of Mr. Milligan's collection. This event," continues Miss Cheatham, "is important, because it was I who *first* sang the beloved little song *in public* there, in its arranged form." Since that time, the song has appeared frequently on Miss Cheatham's programs. On April 18, 1925, she sang it in Carnegie Hall, New York, and on July 9, 1925, in Aeolian Hall, London. Recently she has been broadcasting it over the radio. On the evening of May 28, 1919, the New York Symphony Orchestra gave a "Hopkinson Memorial" concert, "tendered to Mr. Harold V. Milligan," at which Miss Litta Grimm, soprano, sang **"My Days Have Been So Wondrous Free."** At this concert Mrs. Florence Scovel Shinn, a great-granddaughter of the composer, and Mr. Edward Hopkinson, a great-grandson, were among the guests of honor. On February 15, 1923, at the Town Hall, New York, Mr. Milligan himself appeared as pianist in a recital entitled "Three Centuries of American Song," in which two selections from Hopkinson's works were rendered. During the last six years the Pennsylvania Society of Colonial Dames of America has sponsored three recitals in which some of Hopkinson's songs were sung. Two of these performances were given in Philadelphia, on November 12, 1919, and April 27, 1922; the third was given at Merion, on October 15, 1925. Selections from Hopkinson appeared on the programs of the Matinée Musical Club of Philadelphia, for January 20, 1920, and February 3, 1925. Since Hopkinson's songs are written with harpsichord accompaniments, Miss Frances Pelton-Jones, the harpsichordist, has made liberal use of them in her recitals, notably those given at Peoria, Illinois, on April 17, 1920, and in New York on January 23, 1920, and January 29, 1924. In addition to Hopkinson's own compositions, Miss Pelton-Jones has used selections from the harpsichord repertoire compiled by him and played in his own concerts.

"My Days Have Been So Wondrous Free" appears more frequently on concert programs than any of Hopkinson's other songs. This is probably due to the fact that it is the oldest American song known. On the programs that the author of this work has seen, it appears eleven times. On these programs **"The Garland"** and **"My Generous Heart Disdains"** appear each three times; the **"Ode from Ossian's Poems"** and **"O'er the Hills Far Away,"** twice; and **"The Traveller Benighted and Lost"** and **"My Love Has Gone to Sea,"** once. The concerts and recitals mentioned here are only a few of those at which selections from Hopkinson's works have been rendered. All persons who make any pretense to having a musical education now know that Hopkinson was the first American poet-composer, and most of them are familiar with some of his songs. His musical reputation, therefore, is now secure, and is likely to grow rather than diminish as time goes on.

Several of Hopkinson's pictures have been preserved. Mr. Edward Hopkinson has three of his pastels: a copy of Titian's "Judgment of Paris"; a copy of "Danae and the Shower of Gold"; and a picture of a nude figure, probably copied from an unidentified original, since it is labeled "classic subject." None of these is particularly noteworthy. Mrs. Francis Tazewell Redwood has a pastel portrait of his infant son [James], a photograph of his portrait of his sister, Mary Morgan, and a life-size pastel of himself. The first of these is a stiff and amateurish piece of work, but the others are surprisingly good, especially the portrait

of himself, which is evidently copied from the painting made by R. E. Pine. Mr. Edward Hopkinson has another excellent copy that Hopkinson made of this same portrait. The *American Historical Record* for March, 1874, contains a picture of Jacob Duché, which is accompanied by this explanatory note:

> The above engraving of the portrait of Mr. Duché is from a drawing of him, in chalk, by Francis Hopkinson, and now in the possession of John A. McAllister, of Philadelphia, who received it from Richard Willing Oswald, a grandson of Colonel Eleazer Oswald, of the Continental Army. The grandmother of Mr. Oswald (whose family had possessed the picture for more than half a century), who died in Philadelphia in 1866, at the age of ninety-two years, and who was a friend and frequent visitor of Parson Duché, pronounced it the best likeness of him she had ever seen.

Hopkinson, of course, never pretended to be more than an amateur in art; nevertheless, his work, particularly the two copies of the Pine portrait, shows that he possessed natural ability and that he had had a considerable amount of training.

In heraldry Hopkinson has, in the opinion of the author, the unique distinction of being the designer of the American flag.

Hopkinson's verse may be divided into three main groups: (1) occasional lyrics, such as elegies, birthday pieces, complimentary addresses, and college exercises; (2) "political ballads," written to check the despondency and arouse the fighting spirit of his countrymen during the Revolution; (3) songs for which he composed music.

The poems of the first group have little interest except to the biographer and historian. The subjects are ephemeral, the ideas commonplace, the treatment stiff and conventional. They have the virtues of clearness and simplicity, and they never offend the ear with lame meters and faulty rhymes; but they contain no haunting lines that linger in the memory of the reader and refuse to be forgotten.

The political ballads accomplished very effectively the purpose for which they were written. As they were published and republished in many papers throughout the Colonies, they were undoubtedly read by many people; and since they are in spirit uniformly good humored, courageous, and hopeful, they must have had a very salutary effect upon the minds of the readers. On one occasion, at least, a song of Hopkinson's was sung by the soldiers at the front.

One evidence of the effectiveness of Hopkinson's work is the response it drew from the enemy. The *Pennsylvania Ledger* would not have gone to so much trouble to correct the exaggerations of **"The Battle of the Kegs,"** and the New York *Royal Gazette* would not have published the coarse parody on *The Temple of Minerva* if Hopkinson's verses had not injured the British morale. Another evidence is the praise his efforts received from the American leaders. Franklin carefully preserved as long as he lived the autograph copies of **"Date Obolum Belesario"** and **"The Battle of the Kegs"** that Hopkinson sent him. On

March 6, 1780, he wrote, "I thank you for the political *Squibs;* they are well made. I am glad to find such plenty of good powder." Jefferson, on July 6, 1785, showed his interest and appreciation by asking Hopkinson to send him a copy of **"The Battle of the Kegs."**

That Hopkinson's influence was generally recognized is indicated by an anonymous poem, "On the Present Prospects of America," which appeared in the *Pennsylvania Packet* on August 2, 1788. In this rather uninspired production the author first asks whether the muses are going to fail to celebrate such an important event as the adoption of the Constitution, and then answers his own question as follows:

> Honor forbids—and mid the wastes of time,
> Protects from ruin that auspicious rhyme,
> Which sang **The Roof,** as yet to song unknown,
> And mingled all its praises with his own.
> On that gay bosom, still, Oh Muses, smile,
> Whose nervous verse adorned the stately pile,
> Still as it rises, let his incense rise,
> And let him taste the joy that never dies!

In short, there is little or no exaggeration in the following assertion, which appears in the biographical sketch written for the *Columbian Magazine* by Dr. Rush:

> It only remains to add to this account of Mr. Hopkinson, that the various causes which contributed to the establishment of the independence and federal government of the United States, will not be *fully traced,* unless much is ascribed to the irresistible influence of the *ridicule* which he poured forth, from time to time, upon the enemies of those great political events.

The songs, which make up the third group of Hopkinson's verse, may be dismissed very briefly. As lyrics they are in general superior to his occasional poems. In one or two instances, indeed, they show glints of real poetic beauty. As the work of the "first American poet-composer," moreover, they have a historical value which is unique.

Hopkinson's prose is much more distinguished than his verse. Schooled under such masters as Arbuthnot, Swift, Addison, Steele, and Fielding, he early acquired a style that combined simplicity, clearness, and vigor. These qualities are found even in his private letters, which are fully as interesting as any of his other writings. The prominence of the persons to whom many of them were written and the importance of the events narrated in them give them unusual historical value. The number and variety of subjects discussed make them appeal to many classes of readers; and their cordiality, humor, and freedom from affection give them charm.

Hopkinson's literary essays, though too much like the English periodical essays to be very original, and too light in substance to be very significant, are well constructed, sprightly, and entertaining. It is to be regretted that the Revolution put an end to the career of the *Pennsylvania Magazine,* in which most of them were published, and thus removed the author's incentive to continue this sort of writing, and that his later absorption in public affairs prevented his returning to this promising field, except on rare occasions.

With regard to Hopkinson's discussions of educational problems Dr. Rush made this comment:

> Sometimes he employed his formidable powers of humour and satire in exposing the formalities of technical science. He thought much, and thought justly upon the subject of education. He often ridiculed in conversation the practice of teaching children the English language by means of grammar. He considered most of the years which are spent in learning the Latin and Greek languages as lost, and he held several of the arts and sciences which are still taught in our colleges, in great contempt. His specimen of modern learning, in a tedious examination, the only object of which was to describe the properties of a "salt-box," published in the American Museum for February 1787, will always be relished as a morsel of exquisite humour, while the present absurd modes of education continue to be practised in the United States.

The fact that Dr. Rush agreed with Hopkinson's educational theories probably caused him to overestimate their value. Few Latin teachers would agree with Hopkinson that "the Grammar should be the last Book put into the Learner's Hands," and most would question the practicability of his oral method of teaching the language. In general, however, his views have been adopted by educators in this country. Latin, though it still survives in a few sheltered spots, is dying by inches; Greek is now doubly a dead language; and at every educational convention some professor of pedagogy belabors the lifeless corpse of English grammar.

The effect of Hopkinson's satire on newspaper squabbles is thus described by Dr. Rush:

> Newspaper scandal frequently for months together, disappeared or languished, after the publication of several of his irresistible satires upon that disgraceful species of writing. He gave a currency to a *thought* or *phrase* in these effusions from his pen, which never failed to bear down the spirit of the times, and frequently to turn the divided tides of party-rage, into one general channel of ridicule or contempt.

The accuracy of this statement can be verified. An examination of the Philadelphia press for the year 1780 shows that the newspaper quarrel between Dr. William Shippen and Dr. John Morgan came to an end on December 23, the day on which Hopkinson's **"Proposal for Establishing a High Court of Honour"** was published.

The bulk of Hopkinson's prose consists of political tracts written on a wide variety of subjects and employing many forms, of which the letter, the allegory, and the account of some fictitious discovery are perhaps the most conspicuous. Dr. Rush, who was evidently not very accurate in his use of dates, asserts that

> . . . . he began in the year 1775, with a small tract which he entitled "a pretty story" in which he exposed the tyranny of Great Britain in America, by a most beautiful allegory, and he concluded his contributions to his country in this way with the history of "a new roof," a per-

formance, which for wit, humour, and good sense, must last as long as the citizens of America continue to admire, and to be happy under, the present national Government of the united states.

What has already been said of the influence of Hopkinson's political ballads may be said with equal justice of the influence of his prose tracts.

After the publication of *The Miscellaneous Essays* in 1792 there appeared in the August number of the *Columbian Magazine* a review which contained this comment:

> We are informed, in a note prefixed to the first volume, that the several pieces were prepared for the press by the author, before his death; and that they are now published from his manuscripts, in the dress in which he left them. But had he lived to superintend the publication of them himself, we think it probable that he would either have revised or expunged some of them, which were written to answer purposes of a temporary nature; and others, in which particular characters are severely satirized. In our opinion, these cast a shade over the splendour of his works. In justice to the memory of Mr. H. we shall state one fact, which supports our opinion, that sundry alterations would have been made, had he lived to revise his literary productions. The editor of a daily paper, which was established in this city some time after the publication of Mr. Hopkinson's celebrated allegory of **"The New Roof,"** applied to him for a correct copy of the performance, which he proposed to insert in his gazette. Mr. H. complied with his request; but was particularly careful to strike out the concluding observations, in which he had burlesqued the ravings of a declamatory writer, in the public papers. This was certainly a judicious and laudable omission. For, besides that the name of the declamatory writer alluded to had become publicly known, the force and beauty of the allegory were diminished, by a conclusion which was beneath the dignity of that inimitable performance, and which had no immediate connection with it. And yet the allegory is now published in its original form; and accompanied with the essay which is the subject of the burlesque.

The reviewer's criticism is, on the whole, manifestly just. It is surprising that Hopkinson should have included in his collection a protest against the method of conducting a local election held in 1785 and an attack on a bill passed by the Pennsylvania legislature in 1786, and should have omitted a number of spirited Revolutionary ballads and the essay **"Affectation."** Nevertheless, there is little ground for the reviewer's assumption that Hopkinson, had he lived to superintend the publication of *The Miscellaneous Essays,* would have omitted or revised some of the material that appears in the collection, for the three volumes were printed from manuscripts which the author had carefully prepared for publication. Moreover, the fact that these manuscripts are almost free from deletions and corrections indicates that he had selected, revised, and arranged his material to his own satisfaction before transcribing it in the bound volumes in which has it been preserved.

All the pieces selected for *The Miscellaneous Essays* were carefully revised by the author. The poems were slightly changed here and there; the literary essays were somewhat condensed; and the political tracts were toned down, so as "to blunt somewhat the edge of their sarcasms" [quoted from Moses Coit Tyler, *The Literary History of the American Revolution,* II, 140]. In general, the revised works are not superior to the originals; in many cases, indeed, they are decidedly inferior. The political writings suffered most in revision. The satirist who revises his works for the purpose of sparing the feelings of those he has attacked cultivates benevolence at the expense of his satire. Therefore, the student who would know the real Hopkinson must read his works in the newspapers and magazines in which they first appeared. Such was the view of Benson J. Lossing, who, when he republished *A Pretty Story* under the title *The Old Farm and the New Farm,* used the original version.

By his contemporaries Hopkinson was considered a genius of the first rank. Dr. Rush's biographical sketch, which has already been referred to several times, contains this estimate:

> This gentleman possessed an uncommon share of genius of a peculiar kind. He excelled in music and poetry, and had some knowledge in painting. But these arts did not monopolize all the powers of his mind. He was well skilled in many practical and useful sciences, particularly mathematics and natural philosophy, and he had a general acquaintance with the principles of anatomy, chemistry, and natural history. But his *forte* was *humour* and *satire,* in both of which he was not surpassed by Lucian, Swift, or Rabelais. These extraordinary powers were consecrated to the advancement of the interests of patriotism, virtue, and science.

Along with Dr. Rush's tribute to his friend there appeared two elegiac poems inscribed to Hopkinson's memory. One, entitled **"An Elegy,"** after referring most flatteringly to the professional reputation and private character of the deceased, continues:

> What knowledge was withheld from him, whose
>   mind
> For universal science was designed?
> He charmed the eye, and dignified the heart,
> Blending the limnist's with the poet's art.
> Fancy was ever present in his mind;
> Whilst truth, wit, music, every thought refined.
> Be harmony *his* meed, whose merits claim
> From worldly harmony a lasting fame.
> And be this line upon his tomb-stone writ—
> *The friend of virtue—and the friend of wit.*

The other, "Lines Sacred to the Memory of the Honourable Francis Hopkinson," which, according to a note, was "written immediately after returning from the interment of his remains," ends with these words:

> Yet let the bust be raised—and sculpture's art
> Due tribute, science, to they son impart.
> Youth on the trophy shall with rapture gaze,

Soaring to virtue on the wings of praise.
Painting! exert they imitative powers;
Display the sage reclined in learning's bowers;
Thou mournful muse! (since hushed is humour's
    vein)
Pour thy sad plaint in elegiac strain
And be this truth upon his marble writ—
He shone in virtue, science, taste, and wit.

The writer who published the review of *The Miscellaneous Essays* in the *Columbian Magazine* gives this general estimate of Hopkinson's work:

> The leading characteristics of Mr. Hopkinson's writings are, extraordinary versatility of genius, combined with extensive science; brilliancy of imagination, connected with a sound judgment and good taste; and genuine humour, uncontaminated by that low and trifling species of wit, which can yield pleasure to none but vulgar and frivolous minds.

Dr. Rush's sketch and the elegies contain some of the hyperbole usually found in such writings, but the review of *The Miscellaneous Essays* is a fair and impartial estimate of Hopkinson's rank and influence. Of the qualities enumerated, humor and versatility are the most conspicuous. Hopkinson's humor has individuality and charm. Among Revolutionary satirists he is conspicuous for his unfailing good nature. While others assailed the enemies of America with insult and abuse, he harried the foe with good-humored raillery. That he should have preserved his lightness of touch among such serious people as the American patriots and in such a grave crisis as the Revolution is in itself a distinction—perhaps even a mark of genius. To hail one of our writers as the American Lucian, Swift, or Rabelais is not the practice of modern critics. Hopkinson had qualities that may remind the reader of these or other satirists, but he had many other qualities that were original. In fact, he was too versatile to be tagged with any single word or phrase. In attainment he was an artist, a musician, and a scientist of acknowledged ability; a jurist of the first rank; and a distinguished man of letters. In character he was a man of clean life and firm integrity, a sincere and loyal friend, a fearless patriot, and a Christian gentleman. (pp. 459-74)

> *George Everett Hastings, in his* The Life and Works of Francis Hopkinson, *The University of Chicago Press, 1926, 516 p.*

Dixon Wecter   (essay date 1940)

[*Wecter is best known for his* The Age of the Great Depression 1929-1941 (1948). *In this excerpt, he publishes four previously unknown letters between Hopkinson and Benjamin Franklin and reviews the relationship between the two men from 1765 to 1787.*]

Benjamin Franklin's emergence as the first great American literary artist, and the more modest station of Francis Hopkinson [whom Moses C. Tyler (*The Literary History of the American Revolution,* New York, 1897) placed] among "the three leading satirists on the Whig side of the American Revolution," need not obscure the splendid versatility—so characteristic of the eighteenth-century intellect—which both possessed. Hopkinson indeed is in some respects a younger and a minor Franklin: man of business, scientist and amateur inventor, littérateur, patriot, statesman, and savant, with an ample fund of curiosity and good humor which he employed freely in the daily affairs of life. The editing of four hitherto unknown letters from Hopkinson to Franklin and of one satire by Hopkinson known before solely in mutilated form, gives occasion to review perhaps the most stable friendship found in the early literary annals of Philadelphia. The disparity of thirty-one years between their ages was perhaps more than balanced by the fact that Francis Hopkinson inherited the intimacy Franklin had bestowed upon Thomas Hopkinson, the poet's father, who had also set family precedents in being Judge of the Admiralty for Pennsylvania, a keen experimenter with electricity, and a zealous member of the Library Company and of the American Philosophical Society.

Educated as "the first scholar" of the Academy of Philadelphia which Franklin had sponsored, young Hopkinson wrote from Philadelphia on December 13, 1765, his first known letter to the sage, now in London, thanking him for an act of friendship. Franklin had reported indirectly to the Bishop of Worcester that his lordship's American kinsman was "a very ingenious young Man . . . daily growing in esteem for his good Morals & obliging Disposition." After hearing this favorable report the Bishop in the late spring of 1766 invited his Philadelphia relative to visit him, and Hopkinson accepted with alacrity. His elation was momentarily dashed upon finding when he reached London on July 22, 1766, that Franklin was absent in Germany, but in a short time his old friend returned and was "very kind" to him, as the young aspirant after place and fortune wrote on September 23 to his mother. Hopkinson's hopes in England seemed to bear little fruit, and from the episcopal pomp of Hartlebury Castle he wrote Franklin a long letter on May 31, 1767, telling of his pleasant times but looking forward to his departure in September for "dear Philadelphia." From his next letter to Franklin, written in Philadelphia on March 28, 1768, we surmise that the latter had advised Hopkinson to follow a mercantile career rather than the mirage of preferment. Although such counsels were dutifully received, Hopkinson wrote again to Franklin on April 23, 1770, soliciting his influence with the poet's relative by marriage, Lord North, in obtaining the Collectorship of Customs at Philadelphia; two years later Hopkinson reaped some reward from his cheerful persistence.

No letters between Hopkinson and Franklin appear to have survived from the crucial middle period of this decade—while Franklin in London was under fire as the representative par excellence of American discontent, steering a devious course between loyalties and interests which finally led him back to Philadelphia in 1775. Hastings has suggested that Hopkinson's immediate attachment to the American cause, in the face of his numerous Tory connections, may have come from Franklin's persuasion. Certainly the Revolution marked a new era in Hopkinson's life, evoking the satiric vein which began with *A Pretty Story* (1774), and arousing the patriotic statesmanship which made him a delegate from New Jersey to the Continental Congress, a signer of the Declaration of Independence, Chairman of the Continental Navy Board, and Treasurer of Loans. In this last official capacity he wrote his next known letter to Franklin in Paris, on September 18, 1778. A personal letter followed on October 22 of this same year, to tell Franklin of Hopkinson's flight from Bordentown to escape the plundering British; the hardships of war had not expelled all scientific curiosity from his mind, and in this same letter he reported borrowing Franklin's electrical apparatus from Mrs. Bache. This is a subject to which Hopkinson recurs in one of the letters below. Franklin's answer from Passy on June 4, 1779, assured him of sympathy over his losses from British vandalism, and among other interesting details disclosed the fact that he had named Hopkinson as one of the executors of his will. Hopkinson's next letter appears to be that written on September 5 of this year, enclosing "a few of my political Squibs." Holograph copies of **"The Battle of the Kegs"** and **"Date Obolum Bellesario"** by Hopkinson have long been listed among the Franklin Papers accessible to students; from the new MSS transcribed below it appears that the poet favored Franklin with other productions as well. Franklin's pleasure in receiving such patriotic *jeux d'esprit* is expressed in his letter to Hopkinson on March 6, 1780. Hopkinson's next letter to the philosopher at Passy is found among the Bache Papers, lately acquired by the American Philosophical Society, Philadelphia; it is written on a single page, and addressed on the back "Honourable / Doctor Franklin / forwar'd by / M^r. Foulk."

Philad^a. 22^d. April 1780

Dear Sir,

This Letter will be presented by M^r. Foulk the Son of Judah Foulk of this City whom you may remember. I beg leave to recommend him to your Notice, he is a worthy young Man in his private Character—whether Whig or Tory I cannot say—his Connections are for the most part of the latter Denomination.—I wrote to you by M^r. Gerard who is I hope safe arrived at Paris long before this,—We are very anxious here for the Fate of Charles Town—the present Time is probably the very Crissis [sic] of Decision respecting that City. The Southern Post arrived last Evening the British had got their Ships over the Bar—the heavy ones I mean—which was deemed impracticable—& were making their approaches to the City—we sanguine Whigs however are not without Hopes of Relief from the French or Spanish Ships in the West Indies.—Affairs in Ireland look well for us—a Cork Paper of January has found its Way here, & revived our Hopes from that Quarter—May God defend the Right & defeat the wicked purposes of those who would oppress & enslave their fellows!—

Your Family & Friends are all well, as also are mine.

I am ever
Your truly affectionate
F. Hopkinson

Hopkinson wrote Franklin again in August, 1780, and en-

trusted his letter to Henry Laurens, former President of the Continental Congress, who was bound for Europe. Captured by the British on September 3, 1780, off Newfoundland, Laurens attempted to destroy a sack of private letters by throwing it overboard; but his captors fished out the bag and later treated the letters with undeserved solemnity and pomp—such as Hopkinson imagined in writing again to Franklin on July 17, 1781. His correspondent acknowledged receipt of this letter in replying on September 13, to which the third Hopkinson letter of the present series is in turn a direct answer. Before Franklin's September letter had reached Philadelphia Hopkinson wrote the second of our series:

Philad^a. Oct. 3^d. 1781

My dear Sir,

Unwilling to engage too much of your Attention I write but seldom & yet have been unlucky in the few Instances wherein I have endeavour'd to amuse you & gratify myself. My letters have for the most part miscarried. I wrote pretty fully by M^r. President Lawrence [sic], who you know was taken with his Papers—My Bagatelles were no Doubt paraded in great form on Lord G.: Germain's or Ld. North's Tables—& much Good may they do them.

I again enclose you a few of my Performances, comic & serious.—The Oratorial Affair, is I confess not very eloquent Poetry but the Entertainment consisted in the Music—& went off very well—In short the Musician crampt the Poet.

This will be delivered to you by my good friend M^r. Thomas Barclay who is to reside in France as Consul for the United States; he is a Gentleman who will recommend himself on Acquaintance more effectually that I can do in a Letter; he has a particular Esteem for you; & will be much gratified in your Notice; and particularly obliged by your friendly advice & assistance in his Department.

I write no News—M^r. Barclay will give you a full Account of our Situation—I will only say that a very few weeks will leave the British very little Strength or Hold in America.

Sincerely wishing you Health and Happiness I am ever

Your Affectionate
F Hopkinson

write to me when you can
& inform me of Philosophical
Discoveries & Improvements.

The last two letters of our series were written on the same day, a little less than two months later. No intervening letters in the Franklin-Hopkinson correspondence appear to be on record. With the end of the Revolutionary War at last in sight, Hopkinson naturally turned his thoughts to the venerable friend, who, as most of his compatriots believed, had by his own skill achieved the French Alliance and thus assured victory to the American cause. Other letters among the Franklin and the Bache Papers testify to a similar feeling among correspondents of Franklin that personal congratulations were in order upon Cornwallis's surrender. Hopkinson wrote as follows:

Philad^{a.} Novr. 30th. 1781

My dear Sir,

Happening to be in your Parlour & finding Pen Ink Paper ready, that is to say, a bad Pen, a little Ink to be squeez'd out of an almost dry Piece of Cotton & this same Quarter of a Sheet of Paper which is all the house affords, I set down to brighten the Chain between us.—I wrote to you by Mr. Barclay who is I hope long since safe in Paris.—I heartily congratulate you on the glorious Conclusion of the Campaign. The Capture of Lord Cornwallis with near 10,000 Men is an Event honourable to the allied arms of France & America, & cannot avoid attracting the respectful Notice of the Neutral Powers. We are all in anxious Expectation of the Effects this will produce in Europe—& particularly impatient to know how the Court of London will digest this military Pill—Cornwallis will hasten home to justify himself & accriminate Clinton—he may shake Hands with Burgoyne & say Brother, Brother we are back in a Box. How many more Lords & Generals do they mean to send over?—Do they imagine our Washington's Brows are not yet sufficiently crown'd with Laurels?—or do they mean to continue the annual Tribute of a Sprig of that glorious plant, by sending over all of their Nobles to lay it at the feet of our virtuous & victorious Heroe—But my Paper is almost full—I shall enclose, if I can, an Advertisement I wrote for Rivington, who curses me for doing him this kindness.

Yours ever
F: Hopkinson

Philad^a Novr. 30th. 1781

My dear Sir,

I this morning wrote a short Letter to you which I left on Mr Bache's Table, since then, I have the Pleasure of your favour of Sepr. 13th. I need not assure you that this is a great Gratification to me. I always value your Letters at something above Par. First on account of their *intrinsic* Worth, & secondly because they have not, like our Continental Currency, been depreciated by *undue Emissions.*—Since you have found out such a useful Employment for your Enemies it is a great Pity your whole Stock should be reduced to *two.* What will become of you, if these should fail & become your friends out of pure Spite! In Case such a Misfortune should happen, I will endeavour to supply you from hence. Men who are perhaps not Enemies to you in particular, but to all good Men, good Measures & good Manners. Some are so unhappy as to outlive their friends: you are, I think, in a fair Way of outliving your Enemies, for if it were not for the beneficent Firmness of Monsieur L'E's et L'Zd's you would be exposed to the Friendship & Flattery of the whole Alphabet.—I am not in this Predicament—I have Enemies who have struck deeply at my Character—Enemies whom noth-

ing less would satisfy than Infamy affixed to my Name upon Record, & Beggary to my Children. I have thro' Life & thro' the trying Circumstances of the present war maintained at all Events an unspotted Integrity. My present (I will not call it Poverty but) want of Wealth is a Proof that I have not taken advantages which the Times afforded & which without Vanity, my abilities enabled me to do to enrich myself at the Expence of those Feelings of Right & Wrong which our Maker hath given us, & which are the merest Marks of the divine Will. Nevertheless I have been impeach'd by the Assembly & publickly tried before the Council as a corrupt Judge, an Extortioner & a violator of the Laws of my Country.—This happen'd about a Year ago: tho' I have hitherto avoided troubling you with the Detail, yet as you have mention'd the good Effects that may be derived from our Enemies, I am unavoidably led to give you this Anecdote, which I shall endeavour to explain to you in as few words as possible.—

On the Death of Mr. Geo. Ross I was without any Sollicitation voluntarily appointed Judge of the Court of Admiralty. I found the whole Business of this important Department in a State of utter Confusion. I determined to rescue this Court from a State of Prostration & Irregularity by mild but steady Measures. I found much opposition to my Design, from those whose temporary Interests would set Law aside, & whom Negligence & Habit had indulged in undue Advantages. My friend Mr. Matthew Clarkson was Marshal of the Court. From a State of extreme Poverty, he was by this lucrative Office plunged in surrounding Wealth. He was not like Tantalus prohibited to taste of Blessings so near. On account of our ancient friendship I indulg'd him to the utmost limits of Propriety—perhaps further—I at least restored him to the rights & powers of his office, which he had not enjoyed before. The Owners of Privateers having wrested those out of his hands, whilst he contented himself with such pecuniary Emoluments as he could make, a Case happen'd where some Owners of a Vessel that had been recaptur'd did by the advice of Lawyers, force the Vessel out of his Hands, in order to avoid the Interposition of the Court of Admiralty. In doing which they raised a Tumult, disturb'd the Peace of the City & most grossly insulted him in Person.

He call'd loud for Vengeance against the Rioters—he demanded Protection from the Judge—I suffered 3-4 days to pass that the first heat of this Transaction might cool. I then summon'd the offending Parties before me. I reproved & fined them for the offence but with great Moderation. And I called upon the Lawyer who had advised this illegal Conduct & reprimanded him for his Indiscretion. This Lawyer happen'd to be Mr. Serjeant the Attorney General. Most people thought, amongst whom were the Judges of the Supreme Court, that I should have sent him to Goal [*sic*]. But I always wish that any Punishments I have the Power to inflict may fall short of the Expectations of others rather than exceed them—The offending Parties by means [not *is blotted and apparently canceled*] easily ascertained pacified the Marshal & induced him not to execute the Writ against them. This was a Prostitution of office which I could not put up with. I thought it my Duty to Complain to Council. The Council as well as the mercantile Part of the City had long wish'd a favourable opportunity of changing the Marshal because they thought it an office too lucrative to remain long in the hands of one Person; & because Covetousness had too visibly possess'd the whole Soul of Mr. Clarkson. He was heard in his Defence & removed from the office—what was the Consequence! He united with Mr. Serjeant, whom before he had held in avowed Abhorrence, & with him plann'd my Destruction. They look'd over the Docket of the Court & found a Cause wherein they thought I had taken more fees than the Law strictly allowed; they found out a Case where a Prize had come in laden with Salt, an Article much wanted at that Time & greatly monopolised: I permitted the Captors to have the Salt sold before condemnation provided the Marshal might sell it in small parcels for the Accommodation of housekeepers, & retain the Monies in his hands till Condemnation,—for which Indulgence I neither did nor was to receive fee or Reward—but I had neglected to have the Cargoe viewed by 3 Men who were to swear that it was a perishable article, agreeably to the Law; & they discover'd also that a Person whom I had greatly befriended in the Days of his Youth had sent me out of Gratitude a Quarter Cask of Wine (I am sorry to say it was bad Wine) for which however I neither promised nor granted any official Favour. These Discoveries served for Articles of Impeachment. And I was accordingly impeached & tried before the Council: to the great Amusement of the City for a full week. I was however, notwithstanding the most strenuous Exertions, acquitted of the whole, by the *unanimous* Voice of Council. It appeared on examining the Charge of Extortion that I had taken £80 less than the Law would have justified; & that there was no Corruption in the Cases charged. I should not perhaps, have troubled you with this Narration, but that you are pleased to say my Squibs afford you some Entertainment; & the enclosed Fable would have been unintelligible without this Anecdote which occasioned it. It is the only Vengeance I have taken of these my unrighteous Enemies.—

You ask me for the Names and Writers in our Papers. They are too numerous & equivocal to be ascertained. I only know that Mr. Jay the ——[*sic*] Brother of a good Man at Madrid is reputed to be a considerable Writer in a Paper call'd the *Freeman's Journal*. A Paper fill'd with abuse without the nutritious Aliment of Truth or the vigorous Seasoning of Wit. Mr. Serjeant is also supposed to be a writer in and a foster Father of the Freeman's Journal. If I have Time I will enclose you a poetical account of the Rise of this Freeman's Journal.

I have your Gimcrack Instruments in safe Preservation, & they afford me great Amusement. I have many new Ideas floating in my Brain, in

Consequence of the Experiments I make; but have not Time, or what is more likely, not Genius sufficient to form them into a System for your Amusement. I have given Mr. Bache a Receipt for every article I have borrowed; & I shall call on Mr. Combe for those you mention: but fear he will plead the Act of Limitations against your Claim & mine.

I beg my Compliments to your Grand Son, for whom I have a high Esteem.

I am, dear Sir, with all Sincerity
Your ever affectionate friend
Fras Hopkinson

P.S. I this morning sent you Mr. Rivington's Advertisement: I now enclose his Answer in which I have been so good as to assist him.—

This letter, directed at the bottom "Dr. Franklin," covers four pages; it is accompanied by the two enclosures which the writer promised. The first, **"The Dog & the Scunk,"** is a commentary upon Hopkinson's impeachment in which, quite obviously, the disgruntled dog is Clarkson and the skunk with whom he forms an alliance of hate against the lawabiding cat is Sergeant. In view of Franklin's own partiality to animal fables as well as to Francis Hopkinson, it is probable that he relished this none too squeamish *jeu d'esprit*. Hitherto this fable has been known solely in mutilated form in Hopkinson's two-volume notebook, and with the exception of a short excerpt from that MS apparently has never been published. (pp. 200-11)

[The Bache MSS contains Hopkinson's second satire promised in the letter to Franklin], **"The Rise of the F—n's J—l: an old Scene reviv'd."** This parody of the Witches in *Macbeth* presents the scribblers for the *Freeman's Journal* in the act of plotting libels and concocting "th' infernal Ink." The author published it some five months after making this copy for Franklin, in the *Pennsylvania Packet* on April 2, 1782, under the signature of "Calumniator," and followed it two weeks later by an uninspired sequel which does not appear here. Under the title **"The Rise of the Freeman's Journal / an abusive libellous Paper printed / in the Year 1781"** the poem as sent to Franklin was recopied in Hopkinson's notebook now in the Huntington Library, with only the most trivial changes. Eight lines of the poem and a summary of its contents are printed by Hastings. Under these circumstances it seems hardly worth while to transcribe and collate the poem here.

A few more words suffice to tell of the remaining correspondence between Hopkinson and Franklin. The former wrote Franklin again on October 18, 1782, as we gather from the philosopher's reply of December 24 in that year. In the interim, possibly by reason of the many diplomatic and social demands upon him at this time, Franklin evidently had offered no comment on Hopkinson's long account of his impeachment as written above. Therefore in March, 1783, his Philadelphia correspondent returned to the subject:

I have written many Letters to you, which I fear have miscarried. One in particular I am anxious about, in which I gave you a Narrative at length of a most unhappy Circumstance—no less than a Combination to ruin me forever by some whom from my Youth up I had esteemed as my most confidential Friends, & on whom I had without Remission conferr'd such Acts of Kindness as I was capable of—You are no Stranger to the Feelings that must occur on such an Occasion.

Certainly it appears that time, as well as the decision of the Supreme Executive Council, vindicated Hopkinson of the charges made against him, and he continued in a rather distinguished judicial career under Washington's express approval. He wrote one more letter to Franklin in Paris, on May 24, 1784, discussing several pet scientific and civic projects, and we may suppose that he was one of the enthusiastic fellow townsmen who in mid-September, 1785, greeted the "arrival of that great philosopher, that great politician, that truly benevolent citizen of the world, Dr. Franklin." On March 27, 1786, Franklin wrote to Hopkinson concerning John Fitch's scheme for the propulsion of boats, and at some undetermined date probably within the year 1786, Hopkinson penned a note requesting Franklin to return "my *Law Suit*"—a satire against the writer's enemy Thomas McKean which had been submitted for criticism. On September 17, 1787, Hopkinson appealed to Franklin for help against the proposed abolition of his salary as Judge of the Admiralty and on December 24 of the same year he addressed Franklin respecting the affairs of the American Philosophical Society under the signature "Vires Acquirit Cedendo." This appears to complete the list of the known Hopkinson-Franklin correspondence.

John Adams on Hopkinson:

At this shop [Peale's] I met Mr. Francis Hopkinson, late a Mandamus Counsellor of New Jersey, now a member of the Continental Congress, who, it seems, is a native of Philadelphia, a son of a prothonotary of this county, who was a person much respected. The son was liberally educated, and is a painter and a poet. I have a curiosity to penetrate a little deeper into the bosom of this curious gentleman, and may possibly give you some more particulars concerning him. He is one of your pretty, little, curious, ingenious men. His head is not bigger than a large apple, less than our friend Pemberton, or Dr. Simon Taft's. I have not met with anything in natural history more amusing and entertaining than his personal appearance; yet he is genteel and well-bred, and is very social.

I wish I had leisure and tranquillity of mind to amuse myself with these elegant and ingenious arts of painting, sculpture, statuary, architecture, and music. But I have not. A taste in all of them is an agreeable accomplishment. Mr. Hopkinson has taken in crayons with his own hand a picture of Miss Keys, a famous New Jersey beauty. He talks of bringing it to town, and in that case I shall see it I hope.

John Adams, quoted in The Life and Works of Francis Hopkinson, *by George Everett Hastings, University of Chicago Press, 1926.*

Their letters reveal the kindliness and sympathy of Franklin for his younger friend who shared many tastes, curiosities, and political opinions with him. On the other side, Hopkinson's replies bear witness to his deep admiration for a man concerning whom he had written with grave playfulness on the eve of the Revolution [in his **"A Prophecy: Written in 1776"**]: "Then a prophet shall arise from amongst this people, and he shall exhort them, and instruct them in all manner of wisdom, and many shall believe in him; and he shall wear spectacles upon his nose; and reverence and esteem shall rest upon his brow." (pp. 215-17)

> *Dixon Wecter, "Francis Hopkinson and Benjamin Franklin," in* American Literature, *Vol. 12, No. 2, May, 1940, pp. 200-17.*

Gilbert Chase   (essay date 1955)

[*Chase is an eminent American musicologist and educator who has served as a consultant to the Library of Congress on Spanish and Latin American music. In the following excerpt, the critic assesses Hopkinson's stature as a composer, arguing that "it is not so much for his music that we value him, as for his attitude toward music."*]

On October 11, 1760, the *South Carolina Gazette* carried the announcement of "A Concert of Vocal and Instrumental Music" to be given in Charleston with the assistance of "the Gentlemen who are the best performers, both in Town and Country." In the eighteenth century professional musicians were not considered gentlemen. Hence this announcement, like many others of similar tenor that appeared in newspapers throughout the colonies, refers to the participation of those "gentlemen amateurs" who practiced music because they loved it and who played in public because there were not in those days enough professional musicians in any American community to make up a "full band." As a rule they played in semiprivate subscription concerts such as those sponsored by the St. Cecilia Society of Charleston, but when a worthy member of the musical profession gave a public "benefit" concert—that is, according to the custom of those times, a concert for his own benefit—then the Gentlemen from Town and Country rallied gallantly to his assistance with their fiddles, flutes, and hautboys. French horns, clarinets, and even an occasional bassoon, were not unknown; but these were not regarded as particularly genteel instruments.

That the gentlemen amateurs had no prejudice against performing in the theater is indicated by the following announcement in the *Pennsylvania Gazette* of Philadelphia for November 30, 1769: "The Orchestra, on Opera Nights, will be assisted by some musical Persons, who as they have no View but to contribute to the Entertainment of the Public, certainly claim a Protection from any Manner of Insult." This implies that the professionals, being paid for their pains, had no recourse save to suffer the abuse of the public if their efforts failed to please, while the amateurs claimed immunity from criticism by virtue of their voluntary service. Besides, *they* were Gentlemen. (pp. 84-5)

In the month of September, 1766, [Hopkinson] . . . on a visit to relatives in England, attended a performance of Handel's *Messiah* at Gloucester. He had the misfortune of being afflicted by a large and painful boil, which just then was at the height of tension and inflammation. Listening to the music, he no longer felt any pain. The boil even broke while he was at the concert, without his perceiving it. Yet, as he told his friend Thomas Jefferson long afterward, had he been alone in his chamber he "should have cried out with Anguish." And, in a characteristic speculative vein, he added: "May not the Firmness of Martyrs be accounted for on the same principle?"

Whatever Francis Hopkinson may have thought about the Firmness of Martyrs, there can be no question about his belief in the Power of Music, for he repeatedly proved it both by word and deed. Some seven years before his English journey he had written a **"Prologue in Praise of Music,"** in which these lines occur:

> Such pow'r hath music o'er the human soul,
> Music the fiercest passions can controul,
> Touch the nice springs that sway a feeling heart,
> Sooth ev'ry grief, and joy to joy impart.
> Sure virtue's friends and music are the same,
> And blest that person is that owns the sacred
>   flame.

If "the sacred flame" be taken to symbolize devotion to music rather than creative genius, then Francis Hopkinson was abundantly blessed with that gift. At the age of seventeen, when he began to take up the study of the harpsichord, he wrote an **"Ode to Music"** that fully reveals his enthusiasm for the divine art:

> Hark! Hark! the sweet vibrating lyre
> Sets my attentive soul on fire;
> Thro' all my frame what pleasures thrill,
> Whilst the loud treble warbles shrill,
> And the more slow and solemn bass,
> Adds charms to charm and grace to grace.

And so on for four more stanzas, rising to a grand pæan of praise for "th' admir'd celestial art." To demonstrate Hopkinson's fidelity to the Muse, we need only quote the concluding lines of his poem titled **"Description of a Church,"** in which he describes the effect made upon his sensibilities by the sound of the organ:

> Hail heav'n born music! by thy pow'r we raise
> Th' uplifted soul to arts of highest praise:
> Oh! I would die with music melting round,
> And float to bliss upon a sea of sound.

The final couplet almost matches the emotional mysticism of Fray Luis de León—and this from the pen of an eighteenth-century American lawyer, businessman, and public official!

This was the Age of Reason and of Good Taste, but it was also the Age of Sentiment and of Enthusiasm. A "rational" man like Francis Hopkinson could indulge his sensibilities to the full while keeping a firm hand on practical matters. Although as a poet he wrote about music like an enthusiast (which in eighteenth-century parlance meant a "crackpot"), he could also class it with "reading, walking, riding, drawing &c." as agreeable pastimes that "season the Hours with calm and rational Pleasure." If Hopkinson let himself go in his feelings toward music, it was precisely because he considered it a "calm and rational pleasure"

that even in its most ecstatic moments would not lead him from the path of Virtue and Reason. It thus contrasted with those moral dangers that he mentions in a letter to his mother from London: "You can have no Idea of the many Powerful Temptations, that are continually thrown out here to decoy unwary Youth into Extravagance and Immorality."

Being by this time fairly well acquainted with the habits of the gentleman amateur, the reader will not be too surprised at finding a Philadelphia lawyer playing the harpsichord and dabbling in verse, or even trying his hand at painting, which was Hopkinson's third avocation. Born in Philadelphia on September 21, 1737, son of a distinguished father and a pious mother, Francis Hopkinson graduated from the College of Philadelphia, was admitted to the bar, and became prominent in the political, religious, educational, and artistic life of his native city. A staunch patriot, he cast his fortune and the power of his pen with the cause of the American Revolution, was a delegate to the Continental Congress and a signer of the Declaration of Independence. In 1779 he was appointed Judge of the Admiralty from Pennsylvania, and he took an active part in the Constitutional Convention of 1787, influencing its decisions with a humorous political pamphlet titled **"The History of a New Roof."** During the war he wrote his famous satirical poem, **"The Battle of the Kegs,"** which became immensely popular. It was set to music and widely sung.

John Adams met Hopkinson in the studio of the artist Charles Willson Peale at Philadelphia in 1776 and wrote about the meeting to his wife: "He is one of your pretty, little, curious, ingenious men. His head is not bigger than a large apple. . . . I have not met with anything in natural history more amusing and entertaining than his personal appearance; yet he is genteel and well-bred, and is very social." Adams envied the leisure and tranquillity of mind that enabled Hopkinson to "amuse" himself with "those elegant and ingenious arts of painting, sculpture, statuary, architecture, and music."

Besides playing the harpsichord and the organ, which many other gentlemen amateurs also did, Francis Hopkinson composed a number of songs, which was a less common accomplishment. That Hopkinson himself was fully aware of the distinction to be derived from this achievement is indicated by the dedication (to George Washington) of his *Seven Songs for the Harpsichord* (1788), in which he says: "However small the Reputation may be that I shall derive from this Work I cannot, I believe, be refused the Credit of being the first Native of the United States who has produced a Musical Composition." Let us see on what grounds he rested his claim to be regarded as America's first native-born composer.

It is not known for certain whether Hopkinson was self-taught in composition or whether he took lessons from one of the professional musicians who were active in Philadelphia. There is a strong probability that he studied with the English organist James Bremner, with whom he long maintained ties of friendship and upon whose death he wrote a touchingly sincere elegy. During his college days, young Hopkinson had already distinguished himself as a poet, as a performer, and, it would seem, as a composer. In the winter of 1756-1757 the students at the College of Philadelphia produced an adaptation of *The Masque of Alfred the Great* which, according to a newspaper report, included "an excellent Piece of new Music by one of the performers." The piece of music in question was a song, **"Alfred, Father of the State,"** and in all likelihood Francis Hopkinson was its composer.

In 1759 Hopkinson began to copy out in a large book, in his neat and methodical manner, a collection of songs, operatic airs, cantatas, anthems, hymns, and duets, by various celebrated European composers, including Handel, Pergolesi, Purcell, and Arne. The completed collection contained over a hundred pieces in a volume of more than two hundred pages, and scattered among them were six songs signed with the initials "F. H." The first of these is **"My Days Have Been So Wondrous Free"** (a setting of Thomas Parnell's "Love and Innocence"), which has attained a somewhat unwarranted notoriety as the first known secular song composed by an American. The others are **"The Garland," "Oh! Come to Mason Borough's Grove," "With Pleasures Have I Past [*sic*] My Days," "The Twenty-Third Psalm,"** and **"An Anthem from the 114th Psalm."** All of them are written in two parts—the ubiquitous eighteenth-century "treble and bass." The common procedure was for the accompanist to fill in the harmony at the harpsichord. It is curious to notice that the anthem includes a figured bass, a rarity in early American music.

The inclusion of the psalm and anthem in this collection points to Hopkinson's lifelong interest in church music. There is strong evidence to indicate that he was the compiler of *A Collection of Psalm Tunes, with a few Anthems and Hymns* . . . published at Philadelphia in 1763 for the United Churches of Christ Church and St. Peter's Church. Hopkinson served as organist at Christ Church during the absence of James Bremner, and he also instructed the children of the two churches in "the art of psalmody." In 1786 he wrote **"A Letter to the Rev. Dr. White on the Conduct of a Church Organ,"** which contains some interesting observations on "the application of instrumental music to purposes of piety." Arguing for the dignity of church music, he writes: "It is as offensive to hear lilts and jigs from a church organ, as it would be to see a venerable matron frisking through the public street with all the fantastic airs of a *Columbine*."

During the 1780s, pro-French sentiment was at its height in Philadelphia. Hence we are not surprised to find the following notice in the *Freeman's Journal* for December 19, 1781:

> On Tuesday evening of the 11th inst. his Excellency the Minister of France, who embraces every opportunity to manifest his respect to the worthies of America, and politeness to its inhabitants, entertained his Excellency General Washington, and his lady, the lady of General Greene, and a very polite circle of gentlemen and ladies, with an elegant Concert, in which the following ORATORIO, composed and set to music by a gentleman whose taste in the polite arts is well known, was introduced and afforded the

most sensible pleasure. *The Temple of Minerva:* An ORATORICAL ENTERTAINMENT.

The gentleman whose taste in the polite arts was so well known was, of course, our friend Francis Hopkinson.

A few weeks after this performance, the *Royal Gazette* of New York published the libretto of *The Temple of Minerva,* together with a grossly indecent parody by a Philadelphia correspondent, titled *The Temple of Cloacina.* Hopkinson's reply, published in the *Pennsylvania Gazette,* described the circumstances under which he first saw the parody, in thoroughly Rabelaisian terms. Such was the obverse of eighteenth-century elegance and taste!

On October 25, 1788, Hopkinson wrote to his friend Thomas Jefferson:

> I have amused myself with composing Six easy & simple Songs for the Harpsichord—Words & Music all my own. The Music is now engraving. When finished, I will do myself the Pleasure of sending a Copy to Miss Jefferson. The best of them is that they are so easy that any Person who can play at all may perform them without out much Trouble, & I have endeavour'd to make the Melodies pleasing to the untutored Ear.

The work was published before the end of the year and was advertised as follows in the *Pennsylvania Packet:* "These songs are composed in an easy, familiar style, intended for young Practioners on the Harpsichord or Forte-Piano, and is the first work of this kind attempted in the United States."

The letter to Jefferson mentions six songs, the title of the book is *Seven Songs,* and the collection actually contains eight, with the last song bearing a note to the effect that it was added after the title page was engraved. Here is the complete contents, which consists of first lines:

> Come, fair Rosina, come away
> My Love is gone to the sea
> Beneath a weeping willow's shade
> Enraptur'd I gaze when my Delia is by
> See down Maria's blushing cheek
> O'er the hills far away, at the birth of the morn
> My gen'rous heart disdains
> The traveller benighted and lost

Hopkinson dedicated the volume to George Washington in a letter from which we quoted the passage in which he claims credit for being the first native American composer. He expresses the hope that "others may be encouraged to venture on a path, yet untrodden in America, and the Arts in succession will take root and flourish amongst us." Washington, who was fond of music though he played no instrument, replied in an amiable and humorous letter in which he laments his inability to do anything in support of the music, for "I can neither sing one of the songs, nor raise a single note on any instrument to convince the unbelieving."

There is no point in attempting a detailed analysis and critique of Hopkinson's music. His songs are typical of hundreds written during the eighteenth century and show no creative individuality whatever. However quaint and innocuous they seem to us now, we must not assume that they were without emotional effect either for Hopkinson or his listeners. Writing to Jefferson about the collection, Hopkinson said: "The last Song, if play'd very slow, and sung with Expression, is forcibly Pathetic—at least in my Fancy. Both Words & Music were the Work of an hour in the Height of a Storm. But the Imagination of an Author who composes from his Heart, rather than his Head, is always more heated than he can expect his Readers to be."

That at least one listener found this song "forcibly Pathetic" is indicated by Jefferson's reply: "Accept my thanks . . . and my daughter's for the book of songs. I will not tell you how much they have pleased us, nor how well the last of them merits praise for its pathos, but relate a fact only, which is that while my elder daughter was playing it on the harpsichord, I happened to look toward the fire, & saw the younger one all in tears. I asked her if she was sick? She said 'no; but the tune was so mournful.' "

"The Battle of the Kegs"

Gallants attend, and hear a friend
Trill forth harmonious ditty;
Strange things I'll tell, which late befel
In Philadelphia city.

'Twas early day, as Poets say,
Just when the sun was rising;
A soldier stood on a log of wood
And saw a sight surprising.

As in a maze he stood to gaze,
The truth can't be deny'd, Sir;
He spy'd a score of kegs, or more,
Come floating down the tide, Sir.

A sailor too, in jerkin blue,
This strange appearance viewing,
First damn'd his eyes in great surprize,
Then said—"some mischief's brewing:

"These kegs now hold the rebels bold
"Pack'd up like pickl'd herring,
"And they're come down t'attack the town
"In this new way of ferrying."

The soldier flew, the sailor too,
And scar'd almost to death, Sir,
Wore out their shoes to spread the news,
And ran 'til out of breath, Sir.

Now up and down throughout the town
Most frantic scenes were acted;
And some ran here and others there,
Like men almost distracted.

Some fire cry'd, which some deny'd,
But said the earth had quaked;
And girls and boys, with hideous noise,
Ran thro' the streets half naked.

Sir William he, snug as a flea,
Lay all this time a snoring;

Nor dreamt of harm, as he lay warm
In bed with Mrs. *Loring.*

Now in a fright he starts upright,
Awak'd by such a clatter;
First rubs his eyes, then boldly cries,
"For God's sake, what's the matter?"

At his bed side he then espy'd
Sir Erskine at command, Sir;
Upon one foot he had one boot
And t'other in his hand, Sir.

"Arise, arise," *Sir Erskine* cries,
"The rebels—more's the pity!
"Without a boat, are all afloat
"And rang'd before the city.

"The motley crew, in vessels new,
"With Satan for their guide, Sir,
"Pack'd up in bags, and wooden kegs,
"Come driving down the tide, Sir.

"Therefore prepare for bloody war,
"These kegs must all be routed,
"Or surely we despis'd shall be,
"And British valour doubted."

The royal band now ready stand,
All rang'd in dread array, Sir,
On every slip, in every ship,
For to begin the fray, Sir.

The cannons roar from shore to shore,
The small arms make a rattle;
Since wars began I'm sure no man
E'er saw so strange a battle.

The *rebel* dales—the *rebel* vales,
With *rebel* trees surrounded;
The distant woods, the hills and floods,
With *rebel* echoes sounded.

The fish below swam to and fro,
Attack'd from ev'ry quarter;
Why sure, thought they, the De'il's to pay
'Mong folks above the water.

The kegs, 'tis said, tho' strongly made
Of *rebel* staves and hoops, Sir,
Could not oppose their pow'rful foes,
The conqu'ring British troops, Sir.

From morn to night these men of might
Display'd amazing courage;
And when the sun was fairly down,
Retir'd to sup their porridge.

One hundred men, with each a pen
Or more, upon my word, Sir,
It is most true, would be too few
Their valour to record, Sir.

Such feats did they perform that day
Against these wicked kegs, Sir,
That years to come, *if they get home,*
They'll make their boasts and brag, Sir.

Francis Hopkinson, in Comical Spirit of Seventy-Six: The Humor of Francis Hopkinson, *edited by Paul M. Zall, The Huntington Library, 1976.*

Hopkinson composed only one more song before his death in 1791. Titled **"A New Song,"** it was a gay love lyric in which the poet asks, "What's life without the Joys of Love?"

Francis Hopkinson was correct in assuming that his historical priority would secure him a permanent place in the annals of America's music. It is not so much for his music that we value him, as for his attitude toward music. He represented the Golden Age of American culture, in which men of affairs, successful in business and in the conduct of government, thought it no shame not only to love music and practice it in private, but also to make public their love of the "Divine Art." Men like Jefferson, Franklin, and Hopkinson, in helping to create a nation that recognized man's inalienable right to the pursuit of happiness, did not overlook the aid and comfort that music can give in this unceasing quest. (pp. 97-105)

> *Gilbert Chase, "Gentlemen Amateurs," in his* America's Music: From the Pilgrims to the Present, *McGraw-Hill Book Company, Inc., 1955, pp. 84-105.*

Paul M. Zall (essay date 1976)

[*Zall is an American scholar who has written extensively on the eighteenth century and English Romanticism. In the following excerpt, he surveys Hopkinson's career and analyzes his comic spirit. Zall finds that most of Hopkinson's essays have more in common with the "often absurd yet subtly persuasive discourse" of Swift or Franklin than with the lofty language of Addison and Steele.*]

This first modern edition of comical works by Francis Hopkinson is intended to help revive a spirit that graced our nation at its birth. In the crucial period between the convening of the first Continental Congress in 1774 and the ratification of the Constitution in 1789, Hopkinson played the role later to be assumed by such national jesters as Will Rogers and Art Buchwald—relieving the tensions of an anxious age with an effervescent mixture of tomfoolery and common sense. While his contemporary writers argued for revolution and federalism with sermons or harsh satires, Hopkinson used fantasy and good humor that appealed alike to radicals, conservatives, and the vast undecided majority in between whose support proved decisive in the end. Midway in the war, when British marauders went out of their way to lay waste his home, he received it as a tribute to his powers: "I have not Abilities to assist our righteous Cause by personal Prowess & Force of Arms, but I have done it all the Service I could with my Pen." He had been kept out of combat by his tiny size (John Adams described his head as "not bigger than a large Apple"), but what he lacked in heroic deeds was made up in words that inspired his countrymen to go on with a war they thought would never end. And when at last the war did end, his good humor and good sense lightened the darkest hours of the emerging nation.

If today too few know Francis Hopkinson it is because his comic spirit has slept for two hundred years, deep in the files of the newspapers of his time. Selections of his work that sometimes appear in textbooks come not from those files but from a collection of his *Miscellaneous Essays* (1792), far different from the writings his contemporaries first read. In a deliberate attempt to elevate his earlier works above their rude origins in the popular press, he had polished and bowdlerized them all, suppressing the lively roughshod spirit that had been their true strength. So as to restore that spirit, this edition presents the best of Hopkinson's comic works as they first appeared in rough-and-ready dress, modernizing only typography and editorial conventions, and adding commentary for the convenience of modern readers who would wish to meet Hopkinson as his contemporaries knew him. (pp. 1-2)

By some happy accident of history, Hopkinson's career coincided with the dramatic development of America as a newspaper-reading nation. He was not a practicing newspaperman, but rather a multi-talented gentleman of modest means and boundless energy, busily pursuing the various projects that led to his signing the Declaration of Independence, composing America's first secular songs, designing the Stars and Stripes, inventing a metronome, and suffering as the first American judge to be impeached. In that busy life, dashing off essays to the press was a necessary means to promoting his projects, and he followed the rule of his lifelong friend Benjamin Franklin, who never embarked upon a philanthropic venture without first preparing "the Minds of the People by writing on the Subject in the Newspapers." When Franklin transferred this technique to preparing the minds of the people for revolution, Hopkinson followed faithfully.

By that time, Franklin had helped to develop a national press and a nation of readers who now reacted less as colonists and more as Americans. In Hopkinson's youth nearly half the space in a local newspaper would have consisted of local news and advertising, the other half of reprints from the British press. Citizens of Philadelphia thus knew more about what was happening in Cornwall than about what was going on in North Carolina. Franklin had helped to change the scope, content, and influence of American newspapers, chiefly through his own practice in *Poor Richard's Almanac* and the *Pennsylvania Gazette*—with "Poor Richard" appealing to common people, who scarcely read anything else, and the columns of the *Gazette* to more learned readers, including those raised to that rank through the *Almanac*. Franklin also entered partnerships with former apprentices as they set up shops along the seaboard and into the frontier, providing capital and counsel, and then, as postmaster general, establishing a swift, efficient postal system that made an intercolonial news service possible for a national press. Thus, on the eve of the Revolution, when Hopkinson launched his career in political propaganda, he could be confident of being read on the farthest frontiers. Fifteen years later, as he closed that career, the number of newspapers in America had increased from about forty to well over sixty, as many in proportion to the population as there would be on the eve of World War II. This unbridled growth had its dangers, since the press could carry counterpropaganda in wartime and irresponsible libel in peace, but in promoting his program of political and cultural change Hopkinson found a national press ideal.

Given this scope, he appealed to a broad spectrum of readers. With a fine talent for parody, he could imitate Addison and Steele for the genteel, Swift or Sterne for the middle class, Franklin for apprentices and farmers—or any other popular model who could be turned to the purposes of propaganda. In the custom of the day, he wrote anonymously and switched styles so skillfully that even newspaper publishers might not know who had written the work he sent them. Sometimes he would promote one argument and then, under a different pseudonym, demolish it in the next edition. This could have been harmless fun another time, but in an age when newspaper warfare was waged in dead earnest, the act of writing on politics incurred the risk of brutal retaliation, and Hopkinson early learned that a press powerful enough to mold national opinion could also destroy private character. Nevertheless, he was driven by a sense of cultural mission and zeal for the nationalism that would make a new culture possible, and he ran the risk of character assassination even though a good name was his only hedge against financial ruin.

His sense of mission and his good name had come to him, along with £900, as a legacy from his father, Thomas Hopkinson, who had been one of Franklin's "Junto," the small band of enterprising young men who had dedicated their lives to doing good. Francis was in fact the first fruit of the Junto's plan to educate young Americans toward a culture that would some day surpass Britain's, since it would be rooted in the humanist tradition but would also draw sustenance from modern science and technology. Thomas Hopkinson had served with Franklin as a founding trustee of the academy they established as a seedbed for this culture, and his son had been the first to be enrolled. The academy soon grew to a college, and Francis Hopkinson was in the first graduating class, but his father did not live to see him through, dying in 1751 at the age of forty-two. The obituary Franklin wrote for the *Pennsylvania Gazette* told how Judge Hopkinson had overcome a painful shyness (inherited by his son) to make his way in the world from an obscure scrivener's shop to a succession of highly sensitive judicial posts where he combined "the Wisdom of a Philosopher" with "the innocence of a Child" (14 November 1751). He left the bulk of his comfortable estate to his widow so that she could raise their six children to fulfill the dream they shared of a new culture on America's shores.

Mary Johnson Hopkinson fulfilled her husband's wishes with a little help from Franklin and marvelous management of her own. Three of her four daughters wed cultivated young men, and the fourth chose to remain with her mother in the heart of Philadelphia's lively culture. The younger son entered training to become an Episcopalian minister, and only the eldest child, Francis, gave her any trouble. After graduating, then studying law with the provincial attorney general and passing the bar, he still felt too diffident, too easily discouraged by competition, to practice law and much preferred to practice the organ instead. His moral character was fine and his disposition lively, but Mrs. Hopkinson worried because he could not decide on a choice of life.

For a while he tried writing. As an undergraduate he had shown some talent in genteel verses commemorating the death of George II and then the accession of George III, and as an alumnus he wrote commencement odes for the college every year, all of which appeared in the newspapers to popular acclaim. He was thus encouraged to publish as a pamphlet a long poem praising the college education he had received, dedicating it to every member of the faculty and of the first graduating class by name. Entitled *Science,* the poem concluded with a rousing prophecy of a new culture when "Fair Science" should soften "with reforming Hand/ The native rudeness of a barbarous Land," and proved so popular that it was immediately pirated.

Only a week after *Science* appeared, Hopkinson was advertising a warning to beware a spurious edition filled with "gross Errors" and "Absurdities" published by Philadelphia's leading Presbyterian printer, Andrew Steuart. But Hopkinson's advertisement appeared directly above Steuart's own advertisement offering the pamphlet at one-sixth the list price—even less if purchased in large lots (*Pennsylvania Gazette* 18 March 1762). And a month later, the *New York Mercury* reprinted Hopkinson's warning as a part of what had been Steuart's advertisement but now carried the name of Hugh Gaine of New York as publisher. The copyright law of the time offered no help against this flagrant piracy, so Hopkinson suffered in silence until Steuart published a Latin grammar for the college.

Then Hopkinson rushed into print with a list of 151 mistakes to be found in Steuart's 137 pages, but Steuart merely shrugged it off with a pamphlet entitled *Ass in the Lyon's Skin*—the title alluding to both the Aesop fable and the fact that Hopkinson's latest project was a collection of psalm tunes to compete with those earlier collected by James Lyon. Steuart otherwise left the debate to the college faculty who had been responsible for proofreading the grammar. They showed that Hopkinson's criticism was of no importance, and that the only Latin words he had used, he had misused. He replied in manuscript verses that circulated on the campus satirizing the "learned professors" as asses. They retaliated with similar satire, but written in Latin, mocking his psalm tunes—"What a novelty surpasses the marvels of old bards, Now a dull ass composes songs."

Apparently caught up in the excitement of pamphleteering, Hopkinson now turned to take on two-thirds of the population of Pennsylvania with an attack on Presbyterians, Baptists, and Quakers who had raised objections to a project of his, promoting instrumental music during church services. But as soon as his pamphlet, *The Lawfulness of Instrumental Musick,* was advertised in the *Gazette* for 28 April 1763, there also appeared an advertisement for a "Second Edition" published by Steuart, except that this time the "Second Edition" was not a reprint but a parody, ridiculing Hopkinson's pamphlet and his passion for the organ. Worse, it raised the specter of scandal, for a concluding note alluded not only to his tiny physique but to the entertaining probability that he had been consorting with an actress: "The ingenious Francis Hopkinson, ESQUIRE, stood so high in the good Graces of Mrs. *Douglass,* and the rest of the strolling Stage-Players, that HE prevailed on them to perform a Play, the profits arising therefrom, purchased the College Organ." Hopkinson had indeed persuaded the players to give a benefit performance that had enabled the college to buy an organ, but the slightest hint that there had been anything between him and Mrs. Douglass could be read as covert blackmail, a warning to keep quiet or risk his reputation. A gentleman of his modest means could hardly afford that risk, since he had to husband his good name if he wished to follow the common course for young men in his position—marrying a wealthy heiress of reputable family. Such a warning was sufficient to discourage a writing career, and Hopkinson kept quiet for the next ten years.

During those ten years he searched for a way of life both genteel and secure enough to allow him to cultivate his cultural interests. Thanks to Franklin, he was appointed customs collector for the small port of Salem, New Jersey in 1763-64. There his income depended entirely on whatever customs he could collect from veteran smugglers running a lively trade in heavily taxed sugar, rum, and molasses, and Hopkinson's activity consisted of writing notices in the newspapers, warning everyone that the law said duties had to be paid on these commodities. To supplement the meager commission he was able to earn, he took on a task congenial to his tastes, adapting the Psalms for the hymnal of the Dutch Reformed Church in New York. He spent the next two years arduously adapting the common meter of the English psalter (alternating lines of eight and six syllables) to a meter more amenable to Dutch (ten-syllable couplets), all for a fee of £145. This fee, however, would enable him to seek his fortune in England when his post at Salem vanished.

That post was swamped in 1765 by widespread public agitation against the Stamp Act. As new taxes on legal paper and newspapers provoked unprecedented united action by the colonists, local customs collectors like Hopkinson became scapegoats and fled their posts in the face of rising violence. Hopkinson then opened an office in Philadelphia as a conveyancer of deeds, a venture also bound to fail since it depended upon using legal paper that was taxed and thus boycotted by patriots and those who feared retribution from patriots. Consequently, in the spring of 1765, Franklin, who had been asked to wangle an invitation for Hopkinson to visit relatives in England, had to confess that the young man of twenty-seven still lived with his mother, not having established himself in "any material Business as yet."

It was at the appeal of Mrs. Hopkinson that Franklin had searched out English cousins of hers who could provide her son with some kind of security. Franklin had uncovered one cousin who could prove ideal. He was the influential James Johnson, once chaplain to George II and now the Bishop of Worcester, famous for generosity to relatives and known to be the sole support of at least seven of them. Succumbing to Franklin's perseverance, he invited Hopkinson for a year's visit.

Hopkinson set sail from Philadelphia in May 1766. On the night of his departure the city's skies blazed in celebration of the repeal of the Stamp Act, a stunning victory for the American press that had rallied Americans as Americans to apply pressure on British agents until, with a change of ministry in London, Parliament had capitulated. Thus Hopkinson sailed off to the mother country with great expectations reflected in the glow of a new colonial self-esteem. But the closer he came to his mother's cousin's castle, the more his innate shyness dampened those expectations. He found the castle crawling with sycophants whose fawning seemed to be more highly valued than an American cousin's obliging disposition. Too honest to use their means, he saw little to be expected from this visit except the opportunity to meet influential people who might someday be of use. Still homesick after a year's absence, he happily returned to Philadelphia in the fall of 1767, and followed Franklin's advice to take up shopkeeping.

He opened a drygoods store that also sold port wine, and within a year prospered enough to take a wife, beautiful Ann Borden, heiress of Joseph Borden, the leading citizen of Bordentown, New Jersey. For four years, Hopkinson continued to prosper, tending his shop, indulging his passion for music, raising a family. But by 1771 the American press had whipped up renewed agitation against Parliament's tax policies—this time against import duties on such building materials as glass and painter's lead. A series of patriotic "non-importation agreements" shut off Hopkinson's supplies, while concurrently a cartel of Quaker merchants undercut his prices and set up competing shops in his neighborhood. Facing financial disaster, he begged the aid of the proprietary governor, John Penn, whom he had met at his cousin's castle. Penn charitably gave him enough money to clear his debts, along with a little property outside of town.

At the same time, more substantial help came from another of the influential people he had met in England, the wife of Prime Minister North himself, who secured for him a political sinecure as collector of customs at New Castle, Delaware. This post was far superior to the one he had held at Salem ten years earlier, for New Castle was a bustling way station between Philadelphia and Baltimore, and the port employed a large customs staff, so that the collector's presence was seldom required. The political climate there was calm, especially after the government finally repealed all duties except those on tea. Since pilots on the Delaware River refused to board ships carrying tea, none berthed at New Castle, and Hopkinson was spared the trouble brewing at Boston.

In his new prosperity, then, he moved his little family to Bordentown, to a comfortably large house across the road from his wife's ancestral home. There, a country gentleman relieved from the need to earn a living, he launched his career in politics. In a colony where the governor was William Franklin, Benjamin's son, and in a county where Joseph Borden was baron, Hopkinson's rise was sure and swift. He was named justice of the peace for the county and, in April 1774, a member of the prestigious Governor's Council. He had been writing squibs for his father-in-law's personal quarrels and so had become fair game for local satirists, who greeted his appointments with scurrilous comments about the *"pretty, little, musical, poetical witling"* soaring to power on a bridal veil (*Pennsylvania Packet,* 11 April 1774). But Hopkinson's concerns now transcended petty personal politics and he would not stoop to reply.

Parliament's harsh repression of Boston in the spring of 1774 provided the radicals one more proof of the need for American autonomy, and when, in the course of the summer, a call went out for a Continental Congress to plan concerted action, Hopkinson popularized their arguments in a sprightly pamphlet called *A Pretty Story.* It told a tale of the foul deeds perpetrated on a hardy band of pioneers far from their father's farm by their stepmother and her steward—bringing the parable down to the closing of Boston Port and leaving the conclusion to depend on the pioneers' next move. The pamphlet appeared in three editions between August and the close of the year, but Hopkinson also had more practical politics on his mind. Angered by the conservative stand taken by New Jersey's delegates to the first Congress, he and his fellow radicals set about ensuring that their own voices would be heard in the second.

On the eve of the second Congress, they finally gained control of the Governor's Council as well as of the Assembly, and hastily revised the constitution, enabling them to elect representatives of their own. With Hopkinson in the van, the new delegation hurried down to Philadelphia in time to swing the vote for the Declaration of Independence. And though that measure put his patrons, the governors, out of office and dissolved his sinecure, Hopkinson burned with a patriotic zeal for the Revolution that consumed his interests for the next half-dozen years. From 1776 to midsummer 1778, he headed the vital Navy Board with powers equivalent to those of a secretary of the navy, and for the next three years he tackled the really impossible task of managing the national debt, trying to keep track of interest and payments on loans from allies in a day when even ardent patriots had no confidence in Congressional currency.

Yet, despite these wracking duties, he somehow found time to write as if he had been a practicing journalist. During 1775-76, while the political pot had bubbled in New Jersey, he had tossed off a half-dozen sprightly essays, light social satire, for the *Pennsylvania Magazine,* edited by his neighbor Tom Paine until wartime shortages put it out of business. After that, every year saw at least three or four political satires along with countless (because anonymous) serious pieces, all adjusted to patriotic expediency. He aimed his satires first at homebred Tories because he saw them as a subversive threat capable of undermining the new government; and then at the British forces whose presence was awesome until Hopkinson pilloried their leaders on parodies of their own proclamations. When the British occupied Philadelphia in the winter of 1777–78, he went into exile with the government, of course, but so did the friendly newspapers—the *Gazette* and the *Packet*—for which he had been writing since the demise of the *Pennsylvania Magazine,* and so he was able to publish vigorously as ever, a brilliant beacon for American patriots in their darkest hour.

In one instance his official and artistic lives coalesced. As chairman of the Navy Board, he perpetrated a masterful feat of psychological warfare by floating a few water-proofed kegs of gunpowder from Bordentown down the Delaware River to Philadelphia harbor where they served as mines, putting the British occupation troops into such panic that they subsequently shot at anything afloat—or so said the ballad Hopkinson published, **"The Battle of the Kegs."** Neither the ballad nor the newspaper accounts of this explosive event said anything about the fact that the kegs had been fabricated by his father-in-law or that the plan had been Hopkinson's own. It was enough for him that the ballad proved popular and lifted morale when at its lowest ebb. (He would have delighted in knowing that the ballad was sung again in 1969, and that an enterprising Marine lieutenant re-created the feat it celebrated by floating kegs down the Mekong Delta during the Viet Nam conflict.)

As the Revolutionary War wound down, Hopkinson turned his satiric sights on those Tories allowed to roam freely in Philadelphia, where they threatened internal security, even breaking into the State House to steal congressional secret papers. Worse were those who maintained regular traffic with Tories exiled in New York. There they conducted regular counterinsurgency raids, sending bands of marauders to terrorize New Jersey, counterfeiting Continental money, spreading false rumors, and waging a full-scale propaganda war to undermine public support for Washington's goal of unconditional surrender by the British forces. Hopkinson hit the Tories with squib upon squib, but to no avail. Public officials who could have curbed them went complacently on indulging their claims to postwar prosperity and political position. His voice cried in a wilderness: "Most of our Writers," he complained to Franklin, "have left the great Field of general Politics . . . to skirmish & bush-fight in the Fens & Thickets of Party Dispute. . . . "

Hopkinson himself fell into party disputes aplenty, but, for the immediate postwar years, kept them apart from his satires. In 1780 he was appointed judge of the Admiralty Court, a post similar to one his father had held with honor decades before. Politically this appointment was amazing because it came from George Bryan, political boss of Pennsylvania and Hopkinson's sworn political enemy. Bryan's party of Presbyterians called themselves Constitutionalists because they were sworn to uphold the state constitution (not to be confused with the later Federal Constitution that they would violently oppose). Bryan had designed the constitution to ensure that his party, though a minority in numbers, would control the state government. By virtue of one provision, any citizen desiring to hold property or public office or even to vote had first to take a loyalty oath forswearing all enemies, past and present, of the Revolution. Quakers found any oath anathema on religious grounds, and many Episcopalians found this one intolerable because it meant renouncing friends and relatives who had chosen to remain British subjects. Thus this so-called Test Act had decimated the Episcopalian-Quaker coalition that had ruled Pennsylvania before the war. Now Hopkinson and a small group of friends formed an opposition party, calling themselves Republicans, dedicated to defeating Bryan, repealing his Test Act, and making the constitution more democratic. In view of this,

Bryan's naming Hopkinson to the bench was like inviting the fox to tend the henhouse.

Bryan's motive is now unfathomable, but whatever he intended, he placed Hopkinson high in state government for a seven-year term (renewed at the end of that term when the Republicans assumed control). In the Admiralty Court Judge Hopkinson, like his father before him, was charged with deciding claims and counterclaims, often of a highly sensitive kind. Many of his cases related to British ships captured as prizes of war, making him vulnerable to charges of favoritism and, since his fees derived from commissions, venality. By the end of his first year he was impeached by the assembly for allegedly offering a citizen a post in return for a suit of clothes (and then appointing someone else); accepting a bribe of a cask of wine; and illegally authorizing the sale of a prize ship. When the case reached the state supreme court it was thrown out at once, but only after having acquired a widespread publicity that would haunt Hopkinson's future.

For the moment, however, his recourse was to his muse, and he expressed his rage in manuscript verses reminiscent of those he had written about the college professors in his youth. Now he confided to his notebook an allegory about a dog named "Chance" and a lawyer named "Skunk" who team up to ruin the household cat. The dog had been dismissed from the house for upsetting the parlor,

> And yelping creep'd beneath a ruin'd Shed
> To hide his Head:
> There on a Dung heap sat
>   Whining,
>   Repining,
> And cursing his hard Fate.

The skunk persuades him to seek vengeance on the cat who now enjoys the family's favor alone. They falsely accuse her of upsetting the parlor, but "Puss" is quickly acquitted and their villainy exposed. Unpublished, this saga remained in Hopkinson's notebook, perhaps because such personal satire was felt to be beneath a judge's dignity.

Despite their political differences, Hopkinson served Bryan well, for by virtue of his judicial post he also sat on the state's supreme court and on the High Court of Errors and Appeals, a sort of super-supreme court that monitored government operations as a whole. In addition, his office entitled him to a place on the Board of Trustees of what was now the University of Pennsylvania, after the charter of the college had been revoked because the previous board (of which Hopkinson had also been a member) had shown too little zeal for the Revolution. Bryan, nominally vice-president of the state's Executive Council, sat alongside him on these various courts and boards, where (in the absence of rumor to the contrary) we must assume they got along famously.

At least Hopkinson seldom satirized Bryan in the newspapers. His best effort in this respect was a connect-the-dots puzzle which, when filled out, was said to be a caricature of George Bryan shaping Pennsylvania in his own physiognomy. Hopkinson treated the Bryan-controlled assembly with similar whimsy. One satire featured a wooden post delivering a legislative oration against a recent ordi-

nance banishing trees from the streets of Philadelphia. Inspired by the post's speech, public reaction forced repeal from an assembly that normally would listen only to George Bryan.

Hopkinson's satire was not restricted to local politics. When Congress, frightened by a mob of veterans demanding back pay, fled Philadelphia, they regrouped at Princeton. There they found the site too small and too inconvenient, so they voted to hold alternate sessions at new sites to be selected near Trenton in the north and Annapolis in the south. Hopkinson greeted this decision with a proposal that they build an assembly hall upon a huge pendulum that would swing back and forth from site to site. When this plan received no congressional response, he proposed another by which they would meet in an enormous wooden horse, mounted on wheels so that it could be trundled up and down the Delaware shores.

This kind of whimsy was in calculated contrast to the tone of other postwar political essays in the newspapers. Franklin congratulated him for ignoring those "Pieces of Abuse" that had been clogging Philadelphia papers. These had grown so noisome that Franklin feared for the image they created of American civilization and so would censor the newspapers that he passed on to his Parisian friends. He took the occasion to lecture Hopkinson on the responsibility of a newspaper publisher to consider himself "in some degree the Guardian of his Country's Reputation, and refuse to insert such Writings as may hurt it." If people insisted on abusing one another in print, "let them do it in little Pamphlets"—"It is absurd to trouble all the world with . . . Matters so unprofitable and so disagreeable."

Hopkinson hardly needed to be told that. In one of his wartime satires he himself had made the same point another way, having a Tory lament the freedom of the press and the pen: "It is true they break no bones and shed no blood, but they can instigate others to do both; and, by influencing the minds of the multitude, can perhaps do more towards gaining a point than the best rifle gun or the sharpest bayonet." The press that had helped to create a nation could also undermine it at home and abroad. And now Hopkinson saw the newspapers increasingly being used for perpetuating petty quarrels that degenerated into vile name calling contests ("liar," "rascal," "s—poke"). Their numbers too were increasing: an estimated sixty new newspapers began publishing in the mid-eighties, and with greater frequency also. In September 1784, the *Pennsylvania Packet* began daily publication with such success that others followed. And from this turmoil Hopkinson could not long stand aloof, for he himself became a popular target of newspaper abuse.

When unconditional surrender came at last, Hopkinson sent off two hilarious squibs at James Rivington, long the fountainhead of Tory propaganda in America. A prosperous bookseller and publisher of the court-subsidized *New York Royal Gazette,* Rivington still carried on scot-free with *Rivington's Gazette.* For the *Packet,* then, Hopkinson composed a public notice that Rivington would hold a "going out of business sale" and included a catalog of bogus books whose titles celebrated British defeats on land

and sea and in diplomacy. The next week he published a mock reply from Rivington complaining about the notice and protesting that he had always been a true patriot. To Hopkinson's surprise, Rivington had friends in Philadelphia who counterattacked in Rivington's paper with a travesty of the cantata, *The Temple of Minerva,* which Hopkinson had produced in honor of Washington. They called their version *The Temple of Cloacina,* printing it in parallel columns with excerpts from the original that lent themselves to scatological parody.

With good-humored detachment, Hopkinson replied with a lively tale of traveling across darkest Philadelphia in search of a copy of Rivington's paper. The only copy he could find, having been used for toilet tissue, slipped out of his grasp and was lost for good. Rivington reprinted the opening paragraph of that tale with a new version ("second edition") even more scatological than the travesty had been—as an example of patriot belles-lettres. Hopkinson's patriot defenders rushed to his defense, hurling turd for turd as they came, until, above his own signature, he asked Rivington for a truce. Rivington mocked the gesture and the patriots exploded, more at Hopkinson for making the appeal than at Rivington for rejecting it. Led by the *Freeman's Journal* and then the *Independent Gazetteer,* the rabidly patriotic press would watch him warily for the next ten years of his life.

Their attacks struck at his patriotism, his personality, even his purse. His overture to Rivington reminded extremist patriots about the old friendship with ex-Governor William Franklin who was now exiled in New York where, it was alleged, he masterminded the counterinsurgency raids against New Jersey and thus made Hopkinson culpable by old association. That recollection in turn brought to mind Hopkinson's penchant for attaching himself to the wealthy and powerful, regardless of party, and they conjectured in print about the attachment being homosexual. They raised questions about his moral integrity, resurrecting the record of his impeachment and questioning his qualifications for serving in his various public posts. Ironically, those posts were pinching his private purse, since on an income that seldom rose over 500 pounds a year he could not hope to educate his five children as he himself had been educated, but his dignity as a judge prevented his engaging in trade of any kind. Still, the newspaper satirists hinted at his venality, and watched him very closely.

His dignity also kept him from counterattacking on his own behalf, but once he tried curbing the scurrility of *Le Courier de l'Amerique,* America's first French newspaper, then only two months old and already notorious for vicious attacks on the government of France, our closest ally. As a trustee of the University, he wrote to the *Pennsylvania Packet* under a favorite pseudonym, "A.B.," accusing the *Courier* of un-American activities in subverting the Franco-American alliance. He warned that newspapers had "the most direct access to the minds of the people" and thus such irresponsibility as the *Courier* displayed could weaken the alliance at home as well as in the French court. He focused his complaint on the *Courier's* mocking remarks about a large collection of French books

that Louis XVI, in a magnanimous gesture, had just donated to the University. And he reported the abominable conduct of the *Courier's* editors when a respectable trustee of the University asked them to print a more accurate estimate of the collection—one he had already written for them. The respectable trustee even offered to pay for the insertion if necessary. But editor Boinod refused to publish it without the author's name. The author refused to sign it. Boinod remained recalcitrant. Thus, "A.B." had turned to the *Packet* which had freely printed the review and the prefatory letter (10 August 1784).

But in its next issue the *Packet* also printed Boinod's side of the story, including a re-creation of the impacted interview in which the respectable trustee is identified as Judge Hopkinson and Boinod as the champion of a free press:

> "I cannot," said he, "insert your complimentary paragraph unless it be signed."
>
> "But why? our American papers never refuse such things: you are bound to do it." . . .
>
> "Never shall we expose ourselves to such an infamy."
>
> "You will not insert this article," continued Mr. Hopkinson in a pet: "take care, think well on it; I will do you all the harm in my power; I will make you lose immediately five subscribers."
>
> "O sir, it is not five, a hundred or one thousand subscribers, nor any power on earth, which can intimidate or cause us to deviate from the truth—"

And thus Boinod held firm while Hopkinson fled in a pet. The *Courier* would go on attacking the French for another two months until the postmaster general imposed an exorbitant tax that put it out of business. Whether Hopkinson had anything to do with official suppression, his sally against the *Courier* was enough to reinforce the enemy's image of him as an unprincipled fool or knave or both.

For his part, Hopkinson refused to reply directly to such libels but instead kept up a good-humored burlesque of newspaper warfare on a broad front, and especially of the pathetically petty quarrels that spotted the columns of the Philadelphia press: disgruntled clients accusing lawyers of not pursuing cases with sufficient enthusiasm; musicians criticizing each other's talents; grizzled veterans disputing the prowess of others in the war. For these skirmishes, Hopkinson offered such ingenious weapons as preprinted blank forms adaptable to all arguments since they required only inserting antagonists' names and appropriate epithets; or, a sample sheet of type faces from which they could select models suited to the tone of their quarrel—the larger the letter, the louder the voice. Such nonsense laughed a quarrel or two off the pages of the press. Some quarrels succumbed to the technique Hopkinson had used with British generals in wartime, merely reprinting their own words out of context, in all their naked absurdity. But for every fool flushed out in this way, legions would leap into his place.

Hopkinson's anxiety about the quality of the press was somewhat relieved when, in 1787, two new magazines appeared in Philadelphia where there had been none since the *Pennsylvania Magazine* expired in 1776. The *Columbian Magazine* patterned itself after Britain's popular *Gentleman's Magazine* and featured miscellaneous essays, reviews, and engraved illustrations. The *American Museum* was quite different, a reprint journal, republishing pieces that had already appeared in American newspapers or pamphlets but deserved wider circulation and preservation as samples of indigenous culture. Hopkinson offered his wholehearted support, even filling in as temporary editor of the *Columbian* for two months. As editor, he promoted recent fiction and verse, and reported on the latest discoveries in science and technology, illustrating them with detailed engravings, trying hard to administer sweetness and light as an antidote to the national cultural blight engendered by the newspaper press. He also reprinted several of his wartime poems, and composed an original essay on spring cleaning in reply to one of his earlier essays on the subject that the *Museum* had reprinted in its inaugural issue. Both essays revived the urbane, sprightly wit that had brightened the *Pennsylvania Magazine,* and now seemed to signal a renaissance of good humor and philosophical calm.

But Hopkinson had one more newspaper war to wage. Though fifty and suffering from gout, he girded his loins with the fervor of old to do battle for the Federalist cause. In September 1787 the Constitutional Convention proposed to Congress the federal system of checks and balances we have today, and Congress quickly turned the proposal over to the states for ratification. For the next six months Federalist and anti-Federalist propaganda swamped the national press. In Pennsylvania, George Bryan led the anti-Federalists, crying that the new plan would rob Americans of the God-given rights the Revolution had wrested from other tyrannical forms of government. One of his writers even hinted at treason to the Old Cause on the part of such Federalists as George Washington and Franklin, who was now head of the state's Executive Council. This charge incensed Hopkinson, for Washington was his idol and Franklin a second father.

Hopkinson counterattacked with a political allegory, **"The New Roof,"** about the need to protect the national edifice from erosion. He tried to revive the spirit that had informed *A Pretty Story* in 1774, but his temper had thinned with age and unremitting attacks from the newspaper satirists. Towards the close of **"The New Roof "** his comic detachment dissolved, and he lashed out against Bryan's villainous writer, caricatured as an otherwise harmless religious fanatic whipped into a frenzy by Bryan's warnings about the impending rape of American citizens, foaming at the mouth with seditious libel. Not satisfied with that caricature, he sent a straightforward letter to the most licentious of the anti-Federalist newspapers, the *Independent Gazetteer,* paying for its insertion in order to expose the villainous writer by name and as a henchman of Bryan's in a conspiracy to libel the nation's leaders.

The anti-Federalist response was predictably swift and as scurrilous as any he had suffered in the years since Steuart's writers had silenced him a quarter-century ago, but

Hopkinson endured. They accused him of being a lifelong leech on the rich and powerful, of betraying his patrons and his party for pay or public office. They caricatured his tiny body, called him a pet monkey, a homosexual, a toady, and a thief. They even threatened to reopen his impeachment at a time when, they pointed out, should the Constitution be adopted, his office would be abolished and he would have to seek another. One writer pointed out that he had never been able to make a living without someone else's help. "Scarcely a Day passes," Hopkinson sighed, "without my appearance in the Newspapers in every scandalous Garb that scribbling Vengeance can furnish." It was as though his enemies had been storing up their venom for just such a time as this.

Still, he managed to regain his composure and, instead of replying in kind, began again to write the kind of good-humored parody that depended on comic detachment, leaving the anti-Federalists to drown in their own diatribes. When a newspaper publisher asked permission to reprint **"The New Roof,"** Hopkinson gave him a version that left out the caricature in which his comic spirit had turned to gall. There was no longer need to waste that spirit on anti-Federalists, since theirs had become a lost cause after June 1788 when nine of the states ratified the Constitution, making it the law of the land.

To make the Federalist victory sweeter still, Hopkinson was called upon to produce a spectacular pageant for the Fourth of July, celebrating both the Constitution and the Declaration of Independence. It was a gala day, with long lines of marchers arrayed by occupation, swirling through the streets singing a song he had written called **"The New Roof,"** and following a float also called **"The New Roof,"** with a wooden dome thirty-six feet high spanning thirteen columns—three left unfinished to signify states still to ratify the Constitution. That float was drawn by ten white horses to a place of honor in front of the State House where fifty-four years earlier his father and Franklin had helped lay the cornerstone. This was Hopkinson's shining hour—to him ample compensation for the years of misunderstanding, mistrust, and abuse from a people he had tried to serve so faithfully.

Exhilarated, he published a detailed description of every element in the Grand Federal Procession held on that day, and then wrote a sparkling parody of his own description, pretending that the anti-Federalists had held their own "Grand Antifederal Procession" in which all his old political enemies passed in review as skunks, dogs, and miscellaneous monsters. He kept this cathartic exercise in manuscript; having written it down, he had flushed the gall out of his system. Before the summer was over, Bryan's forces publicly conceded defeat, accepting the new Constitution as harbinger of "a new era in the American world," and thus tacitly acknowledging fulfillment of the political dream Hopkinson had spun in *A Pretty Story* fourteen years earlier.

In his last years, Hopkinson kept busy as ever, publishing a volume of secular songs dedicated to General Washington, and a collection of the decisions he had handed down in the Admiralty Court. The new Constitution abolished that court, and for a year he was once again without "any material Business" until President Washington appointed him district judge of the United States. Fifty-two and crippled now by gout, he was still able to compose music and dabble in such inventions as a device for twilling harpsichords. He served as treasurer of the American Philosophical Society until a few months before his death, and also as alderman for his ward in Philadelphia. His evenings passed most pleasantly in company with Franklin, another invalid, whose death preceded his own by one year and a month. Hopkinson suffered a serious stroke that crippled him further but still did not keep him from attending ceremonies at the University in September 1790 to receive the honorary degree of Doctor of Laws.

On 9 May 1791, he was dead at the age of 53, succumbing to a final stroke. Notwithstanding Hopkinson's long years of service to the nation and his reputation as well, the local newspapers all but ignored his passing, paying more attention to the concurrent death of a slave who had displayed a prodigious memory for mathematics. The *Packet,* for which he had written so much, reported: "Died suddenly on Monday morning last, the Hon. Francis Hopkinson, Esq. District Judge of the United States, for the state of Pennsylvania. The interests of science and patriotism, will long deplore the loss of this valuable citizen" (11 May). His old antagonist, the *Independent Gazetteer,* copied that first sentence exactly, but left out the last (14 May). A new paper, the *Mercury,* at least copied it all and added a eulogy (12 May)—

> Hopkinson! thy memory shall endure,
> As long as worth exists, or praise secure.
> With wit, law, science, every heart be warm'd;
> Whilst blended with the bard, the Patriot
>   charm'd.

A month earlier, the *Mercury* had devoted an entire column to the obituary of George Bryan.

The only comparable obituary for Hopkinson appeared in the May issue of the *Columbian,* now called the *Universal Asylum.* Written by Dr. Benjamin Rush, who had served with Hopkinson in the Revolution and the newspaper wars, the obituary stressed his achievement in writing propaganda for his country in its time of need. Rush took for granted that his readers already knew of Hopkinson's achievements in law and science and music. But since so much of the propaganda had been anonymous, few could have realized "the irresistible influence of the *ridicule* which he poured forth" upon the enemies of revolution and, later, federalism; upon absurdities in science and education; and upon an irresponsible press:

> Newspaper scandal frequently for months together, disappeared or languished, after the publication of several of his irresistible satires. . . . He gave a currency, to a *thought* or *phrase* in these effusions from his pen, which never failed to bear down the spirit of the times, and frequently to turn the divided tides of party-rage, into one general channel of ridicule or contempt.
> (6:292–93)

One measure of how far Rush was right may be found in the preface to Clement Biddle's *Philadelphia Directory,* re-

printed in the *Mercury* during the week that Hopkinson died.

> Biddle reviewed the city's progress over the past ten years—a very remarkable revolution in respect to the healthiness of its inhabitants" had cut the death rate dramatically. He listed a dozen factors contributing to that revolution and almost every one, at some time, had been a favorite project of Hopkinson's which he had promoted in his "irresistible satires": public sanitation, "life saving" measures, even cultivation of what we now call urban "green belts." But even more satisfying from Hopkinson's perspective was Biddle's boast of a concurrent cultural revolution, "the general diffusion of knowledge among all classes of people from our libraries, our numerous societies, monthly, weekly, and daily publications" (7 May 1791). Hopkinson had been a leader in this revolution, through energetic service for the Library Company of Philadelphia, the American Philosophical Society, and the University, as well as through his essays which he would garnish with allusions to standard authors and to recent developments in science, art, music, or literature, teasing casual readers with cultural carrots, leading them to liberal learning through laughter. Thus, as he lay dying, he could have found fulfillment of the mission prophesied thirty years earlier in his poem **Science,** with its promise of "Fair Science" softening "with reforming Hand / The native rudeness of a barbarous Land."

There still remained the rudeness of the newspaper press that, while making it perilous, had also made his mission possible. Before he died, Hopkinson had managed to tame the rudeness of at least his own newspaper writings, subduing them with a "reforming Hand" to a uniform gentility. In his obituary, Rush would have placed him with the great satiric spirits of the Western World—Swift, Rabelais, and Lucian, all of whom he imitated and sometimes well. But the next year in the *Universal Asylum* a reviewer of the posthumous **Miscellaneous Essays** complained that the satires were so personal and topical that they damaged the whole collection (8:110). The irony was that Hopkinson had already twice tried to make them more universal, once sometime before the close of 1782, in a two-volume notebook now at the Huntington Library and, sometime later, in five notebooks which are now at the Library of the American Philosophical Society. Those revisions removed his work even farther from the company of Swift, Rabelais, and Lucian and placed it closer to that of Addison and Steele, a company more proper for a state and then a federal judge, perhaps, but hardly in keeping with the Hopkinson his contemporaries once knew.

One glaring instance of the kind of revision he made is the omission of the entire "Preface" to **A Pretty Story** with its monolog by the madcap "Peter Grievous" teasing his readers; e.g., "Or, if you like not this, you may suppose that the following Sheets were found in the Cabinet of some deceased Gentleman; or that they were dug out of an ancient Ruins, or discovered in a . . . Hail Storm. In short you may suppose just what you please." This is the raucous tone of a man speaking to men—dramatic, colloquial, improvisational, a tone familiar to his contemporary readers from the popular *Tristram Shandy* and thus rousing their expectations of a comical turn. But the omission strips this antic voice from the original narrative and leaves it a more serious antique allegory of chiefly antiquarian charm.

Just as deplorable were those revisions that heightened the style while sacrificing the sense, as in this sample from the second chapter of *A Pretty Story,* which at first read:

> After some Time, however, by Dint of indefatigable Perseverance, they found themselves comfortably settled in this new Farm; and had the delightful Prospect of vast Tracts of Land waving with luxuriant Harvests, and perfuming the Air with delicious Fruits, which before had been a dreary Wilderness, unfit for the Habitation of Men.

In the notebooks of 1782 the passage is substantially the same except for added emphasis on the contrast between what the land was before and after the colonists came: " . . . with delicious Fruits where at their first Coming nothing saluted the Eye but a dreary & unmeasurable Wilderness." But in the later notebook, used as copy text for the *Miscellaneous Essays,* the paragraph is radically concise:

> After some Time, however, by their indefatigable Perseverance, they found themselves comfortably settled, & had the delightful Prospect of Fields waving with luxuriant Harvests & Orchards glowing with the Fruits of their Labour.

Printers of the *Miscellaneous Essays* discarded Hopkinson's practice of capitalizing nouns and also touched up his punctuation to remove the ambiguity that had the fields waving with luxurious orchards. Otherwise, this is the way the passage appeared in its final version (1:71). The revision does make it more concise and coherent, and does make the images more precise, since orchards at harvest time would glow rather than perfume the air. But the paragraph is so refined that it loses its function of contrasting the colorful fields with the dreary wilderness.

Revisions of this kind are so pervasive that they make it seem as though Hopkinson had worked through everything he had written, trying to raise it all to one uniform standard of melodious style. He had provided negative and positive samples of this standard in an oration to University students in 1785; first, positive:

> Some have a happy talent of expression, whereby they compensate the want of sentiment, by the melody of their style; their language, ever flowing like a wave of the sea, and their periods closing in such musical cadence, that the ear is fascinated by the magic of sound, and the mind lulled in a pleasing repose.

For contrast, he gave this negative example, "as offensive to the ear as the sharpening of a saw":

> Others, without giving to grammar rules offence, shall arrange so unskillfully their words, breaking, as it were, and interrupting the sense, or rather nonsense, they mean to inculcate, by

> frequent (and oft-times unnecessary) parenthesis, that the ear stumbles through the rugged paragraph, as the feet would stumble in scrambling through a street, when the pavement had been broken up, over bricks, stones, and posts, mixed together confusedly.
>
> (*Miscellaneous Essays,* 2:39)

It did not seem to matter whether this rough style was appropriate in its place. He polished it all, consistently transforming lively, disjointed speech patterns into the coherent, literary style that lulls the mind "in a pleasing repose."

In doing so, he violated the nature of such essays as **"Consolation for the Old Bachelor,"** that pretends to be the monologue of "a tradesman in this city," given to such locutions as, "We were all tumbled hickledy-pickledy into the dirt." Speaking of stopping at Trenton to have lunch, he says in the original:

> Here we dined—my wife found fault with every thing; ate a very hearty dinner—declaring all the time there was nothing fit to eat. Miss *Jenny* crying out with the tooth-ach, her mother making sad lamentations—all my fault, because I did not make the glazier replace a broken pane of glass in her chamber window—

The revision makes him sound almost like Sir Roger de Coverley:

> Here we dined. My wife found fault with every thing; and whilst she disposed of what I thought a tolerable hearty meal, declared there was nothing fit to eat. Matters, however, would have gone on pretty well, but Miss *Jenny* began to cry with the tooth-ach—sad lamentations over Miss *Jenny*—all my fault, because I had not made the glazier replace a broken pane in her chamber window.
>
> (1:24)

The revision makes the passage more melodious and gives it tighter coherence, but also sacrifices psychological accuracy—since the point of the narrative is to illustrate the hubbub and confusion reflected in the style of the original version. In other words, the style of the original had been an image of what it was talking about.

This kind of violence is done even to a dramatic monologue such as **"Nitidia's Answer,"** published originally in the *Columbian* while Hopkinson served as editor: "He had spilt a quantity of vitriol, and burnt a great hole in my carpet" becomes "He had spilt a quantity of vitriol upon my carpet, and burned a hole in it" (2:164); "My carpet . . . was destined to be most shamefully dishonoured in the afternoon, by a deluge of nasty tobacco juice—Gentlemen smoakers love segars better than carpets" becomes "My carpet . . . was destined to be shamefully dishonoured in the afternoon by a deluge of filthy tobacco juice—Gentlemen smokers and chewers, love segars and pigtail better than carpets" (2:167) where psychological accuracy is once again shamefully dishonored in the cause of logical coherence and melodious style.

The cumulative effect of such revisions drains these humorous essays of the lively, colloquial, sometimes vulgar qualities that made them seem to spring from the circumstances that first excited them. By sacrificing that air of improvisation and spontaneity, Hopkinson achieved a higher style but he violated the integrity of the essays themselves. He tried to raise the language to the level of the essays of Addison and Steele, yet only about a third of his own essays were the kind they had written—the "dream" allegories, some of the character sketches, and the letters from "foreigners" among the earlier works. The large majority, early and late, were patterned rather after Swift or Lucian or Franklin, with their self-deluded narrators and wily "projectors" reveling in ironic, nonsequential, often absurd yet subtly persuasive discourse, and relying upon psychological as opposed to logical coherence. The logical coherence that Hopkinson later imposed upon them was as inappropriate for them as scatology was for a judge of the state or federal courts.

Knowing his work in earlier versions, his contemporaries saw Hopkinson as the "inimitable master of wit and humor" (*Packet,* 12 February 1787). But even in 1960, in some cases reading the revisions alone, so discriminating a critic as Bruce Granger [in his *Political Satire in the American Revolution,* 1960] could see him as "the foremost essayist of the Revolution." This could be owing to Hopkinson's having relied for effect less on style than on character and situation and idea. Put another way, if we say humor is the perception of the ridiculous, and wit is its expression, then Hopkinson focused on humor.

These humorous essays convey a charm in distinct contrast with the angry, Juvenalian satires produced by such now more familiar contemporaries as Philip Freneau, and with the coolly dispassionate satires by Franklin such as the "Edict of the King of Prussia." Hopkinson's were more like Franklin's bagatelles, more playful than critical, as though illustrating a principle he lightly tossed off in the essay called **"Common Amusements"**: "The miseries, misfortunes, and sufferings of our fellow creatures can never be proper subjects of ridicule; but the passions, follies, and excentricities of mankind are surely lawful occasions of laughter." For him, both the source and end of humor lay in the lively interplay of words, images, feelings, and ideas. The mark of the true humorist is his "amazing facility in associating ludicrous ideas to the most ordinary and seemingly the most barren incidents of life."

In some of the purely playful essays he could exploit ambiguity of language for its own sake, as in Nitidia's puns and "switches"—where we are led to expect the sentence to end one way but find it switching to another: "When one is about a thorough cleaning—the first dirty thing to be removed is one's husband." More often, he focused on the ambiguity of language as a common root of "the passions, follies, and excentricities" of men who mistake the letter of language for its meaning. Thus, the catalog of Rivington's merchandise lets irony run riot, and **"The Art of Paper War"** tortures the medium to fit the message.

But at its best, Hopkinson's humor focuses on the incongruous images and absurd ideas abounding in everyday life. Typically his essays exploit familiar objects in new relations, as the giant pendulum or wooden horse show up Congressional folly. The more imaginative essays still are those which, like Swift's, set up a spokesman for some outrageous argument and have him maintain it in the face of common sense or common humanity—letting him demonstrate its absurdity out of his own mouth, unconsciously revealing himself to be a fool or moral monster. Thus Admiral Collier and General Tryon declare solemnly that the only reason they have set fire to people's homes is to provide light for reading proclamations by night, and Rivington swears that the reason he printed so many monstrous lies was his conviction that only the British would have been stupid enough to believe them.

With perceptions of this order and the skills to convey them, Hopkinson could have succeeded Franklin as the nation's foremost satirist, and become the American Swift or Rabelais or Lucian, for he shared their moral concerns. In filibustering before the assembly, the wooden post speaks of man's pride in being a rational creature: "When nature gave one man the power to *reason,* she gave another the power to *laugh* at him." Man is ridiculous when he uses reason to deceive himself; contemptible when he uses reason to deceive others: "To over-reach, deceive, ruin and destroy . . . to conceal or embarrass truth, to establish falshood, to lead the blind out of his way and the lame into a ditch." Into the mouth of his madman in **"The New Roof "** Hopkinson puts the moralist's paradox: "Oh God! what a monster is man!—A being possessed of knowledge, reason, judgment and an immortal soul—what a monster is man!" Still he wrote less as a moralist than as a satirist, and less as a satirist than a humorist who preferred to laugh at moral ambiguities rather than lament what man has made of man.

He called the best of his later essays **"Some Thoughts on the Diseases of the Mind; with a Scheme for Purging the Moral Faculties,"** and there proposed that "an intimate connection" between the disorders of the body and the soul caused most of man's miseries. An insatiable rage for slander and abuse, often the subject of earlier essays, is here diagnosed as a natural "disease peculiar to free governments," requiring a free press as a vent "for the morbid minds of the people to get rid of their impurities, and the opportunity of keeping up a free circulation of ideas, so necessary to the mental health of man." As a public health measure, then, he proposes that two newspapers—one weekly, one daily—be set aside exclusively for venting slander and abuse, leaving other papers free to circulate ideas, information, and entertainment: "All the filth in the city would be carried off by the commissioned papers," and the time would come when it would be "as shocking to good manners for a man to vent his spleen in one of the public *news* papers . . . as it would be to commit an indecent evacuation in a private parlour, or a public assembly." He could easily have treated the problem of an irresponsible press as a serious moral issue, yet typically preferred to treat it as another instance of man's "passions, follies, and excentricities"—the province of the true humorist that he chose, out of diffidence or conviction, to be. (pp. 2-31)

Paul M. Zall, in an introduction to Comical Spirit of Seventy-Six: The Humor of Francis Hopkinson, *edited by Paul M. Zall, The Huntington Library, 1976, pp. 1-32.*

The manuscript of the first American secular song, "My Days Have Been So Wondrous Free."

William D. Andrews   (essay date 1977)

[*Andrews places Hopkinson in the context of the thriving culture of the middle colonies, New York, New Jersey, and Pennsylvania, and examines several of his major satirical works. The critic praises Hopkinson's humor, which, he claims, is good-natured rather than bitter.*]

Several decades before the Revolution, the cultural center of the American colonies shifted south from Boston to Philadelphia, which by the time of the war was in both its size and the quality of its intellectual life second in the British empire only to London itself. The great political events of the last third of the eighteenth century which occurred in the middle colonies—meetings of the Continental Congresses, signing of the Declaration of Independence, drafting of the Constitution—symbolized not merely the triumph of American nationalism but also the maturation of the colonies of New York, New Jersey, and Pennsylvania. The life of the mind as it was lived in New England in the seventeenth century and after influenced ideological developments that culminated in the Revolution, but the middle colonies and the South provided organizers and penmen who planned goals and strategy and popularized them, through writing, among other colonials. The importance of the middle colonies in the Revolution is of course partly due to mere geography: central location made Philadelphia the logical seat of the Continental Congresses and the Constitutional Convention. More significant than geography, though, was the cultural life of the middle colonies which nurtured the men and women and the ideas which encouraged separation from England and the establishment of a new nation.

Philosophy and art—both of which played key roles in the making of the Revolution—enjoyed hospitable receptions in New York, New Jersey, and Pennsylvania. Although hardly alien in either New England or the South, they were especially cultivated by residents of the middle colonies, where an atmosphere of openness and tolerance endorsed the pursuit of thought and art and encouraged

their growth and communication through literature. The instruments of literary and intellectual development were widely available in the middle colonies in the form of lending libraries (like Franklin's Library Company, founded in 1731 in Philadelphia); colleges (King's, now Columbia, founded in New York in 1754; the College of New Jersey, now Princeton, in 1746; the College of Philadelphia, now the University of Pennsylvania, in 1751); publishers of newspapers, magazines, and books; and philosophical and literary societies (like the Junto and American Philosophical Society in Philadelphia), which brought together persons of like interests for the purpose of sharing ideas and supporting one another's work. Such institutions are themselves insufficient to explain the growth of cultural life in the middle colonies, but their presence—and the presence of theaters, private libraries, collections of scientific instruments, studios of painters, and so forth—reflects the commitment of residents of the area to the life of the mind. Active and successful in trade and agriculture, residents of the middle colonies had ready access to the instruments of culture and the desire and capacity to make profitable use of them.

The flourishing of culture in New York, New Jersey, and Pennsylvania in the middle decades of the eighteenth century serves as necessary background to an understanding of an important writer of the American Revolution, Francis Hopkinson (1737–91). (Hopkinson was a native of Philadelphia and lived for a time in New Jersey. (pp. 127-28)

Chief among his contributions to the Revolution were his writings—ballads and satires in verse and prose. In a letter to Franklin of October 22, 1778, Hopkinson remarked that "I have not Abilities to assist our righteous Cause by personal Prowess & Force of Arms, but I have done it all the Service I could with my Pen—throwing in my mite at Times in Prose & Verse, serious & satirical Essays &c." His literary and musical talents served Hopkinson especially well in the writing of ballads like his famous **"The Battle of the Kegs"** (1778), an eighty-eight line poem based on a real incident of war. The Navy Board commissioned Asa Bushnell to invent floating mines in the form of kegs of gunpowder which were sent down the Delaware River in January of 1778 to sink British ships in the Philadelphia harbor; but because the ships were drawn to the docks to avoid ice floats, the kegs missed their mark and exploded harmlessly in the river. Hopkinson exploited the humor of this failure in **"The Battle of the Kegs,"** turning it against the British reaction rather than the colonists' miscalculations. (pp. 130-31)

Satirical treatment of British pomposity in thinking they had repelled the attack gave **"The Ballad of the Kegs"** its contemporary fame. It was set to music and song by colonial soldiers and reprinted in newspapers and as a broadside.

"A Camp Ballad" (1778), another of Hopkinson's popular verses also sung by soldiers, took a more serious attitude toward the war, depicting the bold actions of colonists to overcome the loss of freedom threatened by England:

> MAKE room, oh! ye kingdoms in hist'ry renowned

Whose arms have in battle with glory been
    crown'd,
Make room for America, another great nation,
Arises to claim in your council a station.

Her sons fought for freedom, and by their own
    brav'ry
Have rescued themselves from the shackles of
    slav'ry.
America's free, and tho' Britain abhor'd it,
Yet fame a new volume prepares to record it.

The sentiments in these ballads, conventionally patriotic, probably explain less well their contemporary popularity than do the clever phrasing and Hopkinson's musical gift, which fashioned memorable songs to rouse and entertain the embattled colonists. His ballads had a contemporary use and fame in excess of their inherent literary merit, but they retain their interest to historians as reflections of American popular attitudes during the Revolution.

The most pleasing and probably most effective of Hopkinson's writings on the Revolution, a work that deserves extended consideration, is his transparent political allegory, *A Pretty Story Written in the Year of our Lord 1774, by Peter Grievous, Esq; A.B.C.D.E.* Published in Philadelphia on September 5, 1774, during the meeting of the First Continental Congress, *A Pretty Story* attracted sufficient attention to warrant a second edition the same year in Philadelphia and an additional reprinting in Williamsburg; it was issued in 1857 as a plea for unity in a nation heading toward civil war, under the title by which it is sometimes known, *The Old Farm and the New Farm. A Pretty Story* is a tale of "a certain Nobleman, who had long possessed a very valuable Farm, and had a great Number of Children and Grandchildren." The reader quickly discovers that the Nobleman is the allegorical representation of the king of England. His wife, "sole Mistress of the Purse Strings," represents Parliament. His children, who settle the New Farm, an "immense Tract of wild uncultivated Country at a vast Distance from his Mansion House," are the American colonists. Despite the rights guaranteed them in the Great Paper (Magna Carta) and their deep love of their father the Nobleman, the settlers are subjected to harrassment and financial control by the father's Steward (Lord North), who "had debauched his [the Nobleman's] Wife, and by that Means gained an entire Ascendency over her." Loving appeals to their father bring no relief to the settlers as the Steward and wife continue their campaign to control the New Farm and use its wealth for their own ends. The Steward's motives in this endeavor include his lust for power, but he is principally governed by simple hatred: "Now the Steward continued to hate the new Settlers with exceeding great Hatred, and determined to renew his Attack upon their Peace and Happiness." Such a view of the Steward conformed to the prevalent colonial attitude toward Lord North, but Hopkinson's depiction of him as a nearly satanic figure is especially striking since North was Hopkinson's relative by marriage.

Reprisals against the settlers of the New Farm continue, despite their protests. A particularly vexing tax on *"Water Gruel"* (tea) leads to confrontation with one of the settlers, Jack (Massachusetts), who destroys the commodity in his port rather than pay the hated tax. Because of his disobedience the gate to Jack's home is padlocked (the Boston Port Bill), and an Overseer (General Gage) is sent to enforce the laws of the Old Farm as interpreted by the Steward. Jack's brothers rally to his cause but are prohibited by the Overseer from meeting to express their grievances and solidarity with Jack. *A Pretty Story* ends inconclusively after the description of the Overseer's prohibition of assembly: "These harsh and unconstitutional Proceedings irritated *Jack* and the other Inhabitants of the new Farm to such a Degree that * * * * * * *." *"Caetera defunt,"* "the rest is lacking," are the last words of the piece, an indication of Hopkinson's belief that his allegorical depiction of the events of the 1760s and 1770s would lead to action, probably dramatic action, by the Continental Congress just then meeting to consider such matters as the Boston Port Bill and General Gage's suppression of dissent.

No one in Hopkinson's day could miss the meaning of *A Pretty Story;* its allegory was, by design, bald. More than that, the piece addressed familiar political events in a literary form equally familiar to Hopkinson's contemporaries. Modeled in part upon John Arbuthnot's *The History of John Bull* (1712), a popular British political allegory, *A Pretty Story* derives also from Hopkinson's familiarity with the satires of such other British writers as Joseph Addison, Richard Steele, and Jonathan Swift. Well versed in the conventions of satire and allegory practiced by his transatlantic cousins, Hopkinson, like so many American writers of his day and after, added to British forms the urgency of American experience, thus creating a work which resembles contemporary British writing on the surface—in its dependence on form and style—but at core addresses the American situation unmistakably and powerfully. *A Pretty Story* thus deserves to be remembered not only for its significance as a literary document of the Revolution but also because it shares with so much later, and better, American literature a critical distinguishing characteristic: the use, and modification, of English conventions to fit the special requirements of the American experience.

The allegory also reveals much about Hopkinson's view of the Revolution. Blame for British mistreatment of the colonies was directed squarely at Lord North, the real-life steward whose "exceeding great Hatred" toward the prosperous and happy settlers of the New World motivated British actions. Hopkinson absolved George III, pictured in *A Pretty Story* as a dear but ineffectual old father, and laid the failure of Parliament to check North's rule on its having been "debauched" by the minister. Greed and lust for power on the part of the ministry, resulting in unjustifiable hatred of the colonists, appeared to Hopkinson as the explanation for British conduct. To him the whole sad affair boiled down to politics and the pettiness of those who practiced it at the highest levels of the imperial government. Abstract questions of liberty and slavery which moved such other revolutionary writers as Freneau played no part in Hopkinson's view of the cause of the revolt as it is revealed in *A Pretty Story.* To Hopkinson the Revolution was the result of power-hungry politicians acting for their own purposes. At them he aimed his satire, the literary weapon British writers of the eighteenth century honed so finely for their attacks on ministers and bishops, poetasters and pretenders. Hopkinson's effective use of satire, couched in allegory, reflected his fundamental belief that the Revolution was the reaction of men against men, of wronged colonists against their transgressors, and not the result of cosmic forces or the reflection of national destiny.

Hopkinson's distinguished friend Dr. Benjamin Rush observed "that the various causes which contributed to the establishment of the independence and federal government of the United States, will not be *fully traced,* unless much is ascribed to the irresistible influence of the *ridicule* which [Hopkinson] poured forth . . . upon the enemies of those great political events." *Ridicule* describes precisely Hopkinson's contribution to the polemics of the Revolution. His writings were never bitter; good-natured himself, prone to humor and wit, Hopkinson turned these qualities against the enemies of *causes* he supported—he seldom had personal enemies. Behind the Revolution he perceived only the failings of particular individuals, British ministers like Lord North, and not the corruption of a whole nation or the movement of destiny. Decency, which Hopkinson had in abundance, required action, defense of principles and property when they were threatened. But Hopkinson's writing, though pointed and vigorous, never partook of invective and never lost its essentially humorous quality. In the justness and good nature of his revolutionary writings Hopkinson probably represented faithfully the sentiments of the majority of his fellow patriots. Certainly in his love of place, his commitment to the cause of independence, and his willingness to employ art to support politics he shares much with later Americans, writers and others, who lived in a society made possible by the revolution Hopkinson lent his literary talent to advance. (pp. 132-35)

> *William D. Andrews, "Philip Freneau and Francis Hopkinson," in* American Literature, 1764-1789: The Revolutionary Years, *edited by Everett Emerson, The University of Wisconsin Press, 1977, pp. 127-44.*

FURTHER READING

Granger, Bruce. *Political Satire in the American Revolution,* *1763-1783.* Ithaca, N.Y.: Cornell University Press, 1960, 314 p.

> Places Hopkinson's major works in the context of American political satire written between 1763 and 1783.

———. "Early Philadelphia Serials." In his *American Essay Serials Franklin to Irving,* pp. 41-69. Knoxville: University of Tennessee Press, 1978.

> Examines the humorous essays that Hopkinson wrote under the pseudonym Old Bachelor.

Hastings, George Everett, "Francis Hopkinson and the Anti-Federalists." *American Literature: A Journal of Literary History, Criticism and Bibliography* 1 (March 1929-January 1930): 405-18.

> Provides the background and text to two unpublished satires by Hopkinson relating to the ratification of the Constitution.

Howard, John Tasker. "Our First Composer." In his *Our American Music: Three Hundred Years of It,* pp. 37-57. New York: Thomas Y. Crowell Company, 5th ed., 1954.

> An overview of Hopkinson's achievements as a composer.

Marble, Annie Russell. "Francis Hopkinson: Man of Affairs and Letters." *New England Magazine* XXVII (September 1902): 289-302.

> Assesses Hopkinson's artistic achievements, granting him an important place in our nation's literary history.

———. "Francis Hopkinson: Jurist, Wit, and Dilettante." In her *Heralds of American Literature,* pp. 19-58. Chicago: University of Chicago Press, 1907.

> Provides a survey of Hopkinson's life and career.

Sonneck, Oscar, G. T. "Francis Hopkinson; The First American Composer." In his *Francis Hopkinson and James Lyons,* pp. 76-116. 1905. Reprint. New York: Da Capo, 1967.

> Gives a detailed account of Hopkinson's contribution as a composer and as an inventor of an improved method of quilling the harpsichord, as well as background on his musical education and the musical life in Colonial Philadelphia.

Tyler Moses Coit. *The Literary History of the American Revolution.* 2 vols. New York: G. P. Putnam's Sons, 1897.

> Contains an account of Hopkinson's role as the "humorous champion of American independence," as well as separate discussions of *A Pretty Story* and "A Prophecy."

Additional coverage of Hopkinson's life and career is contained in the following source published by Gale Research: *Dictionary of Literary Biography,* Vol. 31.

William Penn

1644-1718

English essayist and nonfiction writer.

INTRODUCTION

Penn was the founder of the colony of Pennsylvania and one of history's greatest champions of religious tolerance, civil liberty, and political freedom. A devoted follower of Quakerism, he tirelessly defended his faith during a time in England when religious nonconformists were routinely arrested and persecuted for their beliefs. Despite government censorship, Penn published over 150 essays, pamphlets, and broadsides espousing toleration and supporting the Quaker cause. His province of Pennsylvania, established as a haven for Quakers, quickly became one of the most prosperous of the original thirteen American colonies, due in large part to its implementation of the progressive measures outlined in Penn's *Frame of the Government of the Province of Pennsylvania in America,* which guaranteed freedom of worship, association, and expression. Penn is thus generally credited with introducing liberal, humane democracy to the New World.

Born in London, Penn was the son of Sir William Penn, an admiral and naval hero during Cromwell's Commonwealth and the reign of Charles II. Penn's upbringing was privileged, and throughout his life he maintained close personal and political ties to England's ruling aristocracy. From the time of his youth, however, he also demonstrated a tendency to rebel, especially against religious authority. In 1662, much to his father's displeasure, Penn was expelled from Christ Church College, Oxford, for refusing to attend chapel and conform to Anglican rites. Five years later, while administering his family's holdings in Ireland, he was briefly imprisoned for attending a Quaker meeting in Cork. The Quakers, formally known as the Society of Friends, are a religious group that began to attract a large following in the mid-seventeenth century; their nonconformist theology appealed to Penn's spiritual restlessness. Quakers believe that the presence of God is manifest as an "Inner Light" within each individual, and divine will can be known without the aid of churches, clergy, or sacraments. In the seventeenth century, an age when religion and state power were closely integrated, the Quakers' refusal to swear oaths, give tithes, and attend the Church of England was viewed as a particularly subversive form of political dissent. Quakers were forbidden to hold public office, and were persecuted under a wide variety of penal laws, such as the Quaker Act of 1662.

Passionately devout, educated, and wealthy, Penn quickly became one of the most prominent Quaker activists. He wrote prolifically on toleration and Quaker theology— mainly argumentative tracts and pamphlets designed to stir controversy and extend the religious debate into the

public sphere. For his essay *The Sandy Foundation Shaken,* which argues that the doctrine of the Holy Trinity is not supported by Scripture, he received eight months imprisonment in the Tower of London. In 1670 he was arrested again on inflated charges of inciting a riot. This time, however, the jury refused to convict Penn, despite being sequestered "without meat, drink, fire, and tobacco" until they came to a verdict the magistrate found acceptable. The jurors were later fined and imprisoned when they remained defiant. On appeal, however, the sentences were thrown out, setting a precedent in English law for the independence of the jury. Penn rose to the jurors' defense in his memoir of the trial, *The Peoples Ancient and Just Liberties Asserted.* In 1681, in exchange for a £16,000 debt owed to Penn's family by Charles II, he was granted a charter for the colony of Pennsylvania, named by the king in honor of Admiral Penn, who had died in 1670. Penn wrote his *Frame of the Government* for the province the following year, establishing a legislature controlled by the freemen of the colony and a *Charter of Liberties* modeled on Quaker principles. In 1682 he visited Pennsylvania for the first time, and signed a treaty with the Native American population that has been praised for its fairness and honesty and is celebrated in the paintings of Benjamin West and Edward Hicks. Penn was forced to return to England in 1684, however, in order to settle a boundary dispute with Lord Baltimore, the proprietor of Maryland.

Legal difficulties also cut short his second visit to America (1699-1701). Meanwhile, Penn's financial situation steadily deteriorated. Defending his colony in the English courts was an extremely costly enterprise, and, to make matters worse, he was secretly being defrauded by a close associate. In 1708 Penn was assigned to a debtors prison in London. His appeal to the colonial assembly for a loan was ignored, even though the majority of his debts were incurred while working on the colony's behalf. He was released only after several English Quakers took up a collection. Penn suffered a debilitating stroke in 1712, and died six years later in London.

Penn rarely wrote for literary or artistic effect; most of his writing had a practical purpose and was prompted by specific problems or circumstances. His works, therefore, taken as a whole, do not express a carefully developed political philosophy, and his prose style has been criticized for being hurried, difficult to read, and overly polemical. Critics generally recognize four of Penn's works as having genuine literary merit: *No Cross, No Crown,* a detailed defense of Quaker beliefs and customs that remains a classic of Quaker literature; *An Essay Towards the Present and Future Peace of Europe,* a proposal for a peacekeeping parliament of European nations that is considered an important early document of international legal theory; *Some Fruits of Solitude,* a collection of aphorisms regarded by critics as Penn's most thoughtful and consciously artistic work; and *The Great Case of Liberty of Conscience,* a philosophical treatise likened to Mill's *On Liberty* that has been described by critic J. H. Powell as "the most elaborate discussion of toleration the Stuart period produced."

Penn's *Frame of the Government* is valued by historians as an important contribution to the development of constitutional democracy in America. The *Frame* established representative government, outlined progressive trade and penal laws, provided for its own amendment, and, most significantly, guaranteed freedom of worship and minority rights. Many commentators note that while Penn intended his colony to be a Quaker homeland, he also believed that a truly open, tolerant society depended upon the inclusion of a wide variety of ethnic and religious groups. In the view of historian Caroline Robbins, "The conviction that absence of uniformity brought strength rather than confusion lay behind Penn's emphasis on the rights of dissenters, of Indians, of people of different origins." The freedoms established under Penn's liberal constitution attracted a large and diverse population to the province and helped fuel an economic expansion that made Pennsylvania one of the most prosperous English colonies in the New World.

Scholars point out that few of the ideas expressed in Penn's writings were entirely new or original. His views were heavily influenced by both Quaker philosophy and the enlightened thinkers of his age, including John Locke and Algernon Sidney. But Penn was far ahead of his time in putting liberal ideals into action. His unprecedented democratic experiment in America, historians note, appears even more remarkable when considered in the context of the age in which he lived. Europe in the seventeenth century was dominated by political totalitarianism and religious persecution; Penn's reforms were not the products of his time. As the economist and historian Jonathan Hughes suggests, "Penn's colony succeeded primarily because of its institutions, and those reflected the intellectual man, the interior world of William Penn, not the models in the world around him."

PRINCIPAL WORKS

The Sandy Foundation Shaken   (essay)   1668
Truth Exalted   (essay)   1668
Innocency with Her Open Face   (essay)   1669
No Cross, No Crown   (essay)   1669
The Great Case of Liberty of Conscience, Once More Briefly Debated and Defended by the Authority of Reason, Scripture, and Antiquity   (essay)   1670
The Peoples Ancient and Just Liberties Asserted in the Tryal of William Penn, and William Mead   (essay)   1670
Quakerism a New Nick-Name for Old Christianity   (essay)   1672
The Christian Quaker and His Divine Testimony Vindicated   [with George Whitehead]   (essay)   1674
England's Present Interest Discovered with Honour to the Prince and Safety to the People   (essay)   1675
Some Account of the Province of Pennsylvania in America   (nonfiction)   1681
Charter of Liberties   (nonfiction)   1682
The Frame of the Government of the Province of Pennsylvania in America   (nonfiction)   1682
A Perswasive to Moderation to Dissenting Christians, In Prudence and Conscience: Humbly Submitted to the King and His Great Council   (essay)   1685
An Essay Towards the Present and Future Peace of Europe   (essay)   1693
Some Fruits of Solitude, in Reflections and Maxims Relating to the Conduct of Human Life   (aphorisms)   1693
A Brief Account of the Rise and Progress of the People Called Quakers   (nonfiction)   1694
Primitive Christianity Revived in the Faith and Practice of the People Called Quakers   (essay)   1696
William Penn's Plan for the Union of the Colonies   (nonfiction)   1697
The Quaker a Christian   [with John Everett and Thomas Story]   (essay)   1698
More Fruits of Solitude   (aphorisms)   1702
A Collection of the Works of William Penn. 2 vols.   (essays, letters, nonfiction)   1726
The Papers of William Penn. 5 vols.   (documents, essays, letters, nonfiction, poetry)   1981-1986

CRITICISM

Samuel M. Janney　(essay date 1852)

[*In the excerpt below, Janney discusses Penn's political activities, including his association with the Whig party, his access to the royal court, and his involvement in the management of New Jersey.*]

In the year 1679, William Penn became so deeply interested in the political affairs of the kingdom, as to employ his pen and his personal influence in an election for members of Parliament.

It had not been usual for members of the society of Friends to take an active part in the choice of their rulers; some of them did not even exercise the elective franchise, and they were precluded by their religious principles from holding any office under the government which required the administration of an oath, or gave the least countenance to the practice of war.

The king having issued writs for the election of a new Parliament in the early part of this year, a contest ensued between the court and country parties, which, for the deep interest it excited, was then almost without a parallel in British history.

There was in the minds of a great part of the nation a profound disgust with the measures pursued by the king and his ministers; they saw that he had sacrificed the interest and honour of the kingdom, by his alliance with France; and although it was not then generally known that he received an annual pension from Louis XIV as the reward of his perfidy, yet there was a settled conviction that he intended to betray the Protestant cause. The pretended popish plot contributed to augment the prejudices against him, and the blood that had already been shed on that account seemed rather to inflame than allay the popular fury.

At this time originated those party names of Whig and Tory, which have ever since been adhered to, and are now familiar to every reader.

[Hume notes in his *History of England,*] "The court party reproached their antagonists with their affinity to the fanatical conventiclers, who in Scotland, were known by the name of Whigs; the country party fancied a resemblance between the courtiers and the popish banditti in Ireland, who had received the appellation of Tories." The Whigs in England were then the staunch asserters of constitutional freedom; the Tories professed to be a conservative party, who supported the king's prerogative, and at that time all the influence of the court was exerted in favour of their election.

William Penn, although he could not approve of all the measures of either party, was by his principles drawn into sympathy and co-operation with the Whigs; among whom the distinguished Algernon Sidney was his intimate friend, whose virtues, talents, and liberal views he greatly admired.

Just before the election, Penn issued a pamphlet entitled ***England's great Interest in the Choice of this Parliament.***

In this work he alludes to the very peculiar circumstances in which the nation was then placed on account of the sudden and surprising dissolution of the last Parliament, "the strong jealousies of the people" and the "universal agitation that prevailed." He considers it a most important crisis in the affairs of the nation, and states the work of the new Parliament to be, 1st. The discovery and punishment of the plot; 2dly. To remove and bring to justice the evil counsellors of the king and arbitrary ministers of state; 3dly. To detect and punish the pensioners of the former parliament who had sold their influence to the court; 4thly. To secure frequent parliaments as the only true check upon arbitrary ministers, and therefore feared, hated, and opposed by them; 5thly. Security against popery and slavery, and relief for Protestant dissenters; 6thly. That in case this be done, the king be released from his burdensome debts to the nation, and eased in the business of his revenue.

He states the great importance of choosing "wise men, fearing God and hating covetousness." "We must," he says, "not make our public choice the recompense of private favours from our neighbours; they must excuse us that; the weight of the matter will very well bear it; this is our inheritance, all depends upon it, and, therefore, none must take it ill that we use our freedom about that which in its constitution is the great bulwark of all our ancient English liberties."

> We, the commons of England, are a great part of the fundamental government of it, and *three rights* are so peculiar and inherent to us, that if we will not throw them away for fear or favour, for meat and drink, or those other little present profits that ill men offer to tempt us with, they cannot be altered or abrogated. The first of these fundamentals is, right and title to your lives, liberties, and estates. In this every man is a sort of little sovereign in himself; no man has power over his person to imprison or hurt it, or over his estate to invade or usurp it. Only your own transgression of the laws (and those of your own making too) lays you open to loss, which is but the punishment due to offences, and should be in proportion to the fault committed. So that the power of England is a legal power which truly merits the name of government. That which is not legal is tyranny, and not properly a government. The second fundamental that is your birthright is *legislation.* No law can be made or abrogated without you. Your third great right and privilege is executive; that is, you share in the execution and application of those laws that you agree to be made. No man, according to the ancient laws of the realm, can be adjudged in matters of life, liberty, and estate, but it must be by the judgment of his *peers;* that is, twelve men of the neighbourhood, commonly called a jury; though this has been infringed by two acts made in the late long Parliament: one against the Quakers in particular, and the other against dissenters in general, called, 'An act against seditious conventicles.'

He then proceeds to declare the kind of men fitted for the high trust of a seat in Parliament:

They should be honest and capable; men of industry and improvement; possessed of liberal principles, and sincerely attached to the Protestant religion; for implicit faith and blind obedience in religion will also introduce implicit faith and blind obedience in government. So that it is no more the law in the one than in the other, but the will and power of the *superior* that shall be the rule and bond of our subjection. This is that fatal mischief popery brings with it to civil society, and for which such societies ought to beware of it, and all those that are friends to it.

William Penn would probably have confined his exertions in favour of civil liberty to the issuing of this address, had not his feelings been deeply interested for the success of his friend Algernon Sidney, then a candidate for Parliament.

He believed that the success of this enlightened patriot would greatly promote the cause of civil and religious liberty, and he not only used his influence among his friends to obtain votes for him, but he accompanied him to the hustings at Guilford, where Sidney was then a candidate against Dalmahoy, who was then one of the court party.

While Penn was in the act of encouraging his friends, he was stopped by the Recorder, who, in order to make him odious, branded him with the name of Jesuit, and would have tendered him the oaths; but this having been shown to be illegal, he then proceeded to use force, and "turned him out of court."

Though Sidney had the majority of votes, Dalmahoy was returned, under the plea that the former was not a freeman of Guilford. (pp. 150-54)

Although the court party by unfair means succeeded at Guilford, it was not so throughout the kingdom, for all the influence and patronage of the government could not prevent the return of a Parliament still more disaffected toward the court than the last. About two months after the assembling of Parliament, the king, finding he could not carry his measures, nor protect his prime minister from impeachment, suddenly dissolved it, and issued writs for a new election.

This gave another opportunity for bringing forward Algernon Sidney, and William Penn again became one of his supporters.

He proposed to him to become a candidate for Bamber, which was in his own county, and he interested himself in paving the way for him in that borough. The following is one of his letters to Sidney:

> DEAR FRIEND—I am now at Sir John Fagg's, where I and my relations dined. I have pressed the point with what diligence and force I could; and to say true, Sir John Fagg has been a most zealous, and, he believes, a successful friend to thee. But, upon a serious consideration of the matter, it is agreed that thou comest down with all speed, but that thou takest Hall-Land in thy way, and bringest Sir John Pelham with thee, which he ought less to scruple, because his having no interest can be no objection to his appearing with thee; the commonest civility that can be

is all [that is] desired. The borough has kindled at thy name, and takes it well. If Sir John Temple may be credited, he assures me it is very likely. He is at work daily. Another, one Parsons, treats to-day, but for thee as well as himself, and mostly makes his men for thee, and perhaps will be persuaded, if you two carry it not, to bequeath his interest to thee, and then Captain Goreing is thy colleague; and this I wish, both to make the thing easier and to prevent offence. Sir John Pelham sent me word, he heard that thy brother Henry Sidney would be proposed to that borough, or already was, and till he was sure of the contrary, it would not be decent for him to appear. Of that thou canst best inform him. That day you come to Bramber, Sir John Fagg will meet you both; and that night you may lie at Wiston, and then, when thou pleasest, with us at Worminghurst. Sir John Temple has that opinion of thy good reasons to persuade, as well as quality to influence the electors, that, with what is and will be done, the business will prosper; which, with my true good wishes that it may be so, is all at present from thy true friend,

> WILLIAM PENN.

Sir JOHN FAGG salutes thee.

From this letter it appears that the interest of Sir John Pelham was expected to be exerted in favour of Algernon Sidney; but he was engaged by the ministry to sustain Algernon's younger brother Henry, who belonged to the court party. The polls closed with a double return. Algernon thought himself elected, and claimed his seat, but on the meeting of Parliament his election was declared void.

Soon after the election of this Parliament, Penn issued another publication, intended to allay persecution, and promote the prosperity of the kingdom; it bears the title of ***One Project for the Good of England; that is, our civil union is our civil safety.***

This work was dedicated to the Parliament, and ably maintains the position that the *civil* interests of all *Protestants,* whether dissenters or members of the Established Church, are the same. They can unite in denying the supremacy of the pope, and of all other foreign potentates. "The civil interests of English Protestants being thus the same, and their religious interest too, so far as concerns a negative to the usurpation and error of Rome, I do humbly ask," he says, "if it be the interest of the government to expose those to misery that have no other interest than the government? Or if it be just or equal that the weaker should be prosecuted by the more powerful Protestants?"

He proceeds to show that nothing can be better calculated to build up the church of Rome, and enable her to regain her ascendency in England, than for Protestants of different persuasions to weaken and destroy one another.

The commercial and manufacturing interests of the kingdom were also impaired by persecution, for it wasted the estates and deranged the business of industrious citizens. Having shown the many evils resulting from the penal laws enacted to secure uniformity in religion, and the ill success that must always attend them, he then brings forward his "Project for the good of England," which is a new test in the form of a declaration to be subscribed without an oath. This declaration contains an acknowledgment of King Charles the Second, as lawful king of the realm, and denies the authority of the Pope or See of Rome to depose him or absolve his subjects from their allegiance.

It denies the claim of the pope to be Christ's vicar, disclaims the doctrines of purgatory and transubstantiation, and declares the worship of the Catholic church to be superstitious and idolatrous. This tract, as well as that which immediately preceded it, was issued without the author's name, and with the signature of Philanglus.

In estimating the character and principles of Penn, these political tracts, and the part he took in favour of the election of Algernon Sidney, are worthy of especial attention. They show most conclusively that he was not only opposed to the papal predilections of the king, but deeply interested in promoting the success of the Whigs, and especially of the patriotic Sidney, a republican in principle, who was more feared and hated by the court than almost any other man in the kingdom. Yet in the face of all this evidence, his enemies of that day, in order to subject him to public odium, persisted in calling him a Jesuit; and even in this age, when we are enjoying the benefits of his tolerant and liberal principles, he has been held up to public reprobation as a courtier whose sympathies were all on the side of arbitrary power.

It is true that he enjoyed ready access to the king, and that he often made use of this privilege to plead the cause of suffering humanity, not only in procuring the release of his imprisoned brethren, but in securing pardon and protection to those of other religious persuasions.

How then shall we account for the favour he enjoyed at court? There is only one way, and that is so singular as to be considered incredible by men of the world. He was an honest, sincere-hearted man, one of the very few of that class who ever appeared at the court of Charles II, and that monarch, profligate as he was, had the discernment to discover, and the good sense to appreciate, those sterling qualities which stood out in bold relief, when contrasted with the fawning sycophants by whom he was surrounded. The favour he showed to Penn was a memorable instance of the homage that vice pays to virtue.

As to Penn himself, we cannot doubt that his pure spirit was disgusted with the licentiousness of the court, for we find in many of his writings that he attacked with boldness and energy the profligate manners of the age, and his domestic life was so exemplary as to be above the reach of calumny.

His motives, then, in appearing at court, were of the noblest character; he felt it his duty to use his influence for the promotion of individual happiness and national prosperity. But in doing this, it must be conceded, that his example was not without danger, if followed by others of less independence and firmness of character. It was said, by the Divine Teacher, "they that wear soft clothing are in king's houses," and it is generally found that the pliancy of their principles corresponds with the softness of their apparel.

Public honours and sumptuous living have a wonderful influence in subduing that sternness of purpose with which the young disciple sets out in pursuit of spiritual good. If he permit himself to be seduced, in the least degree, from this purpose, by the disguised flattery of the world, he incurs the risk of gradually losing his hold upon better things, the desires that appeared to be subdued spring up afresh, and he must either retrace his steps by a timely retreat, or go forward and make shipwreck of the faith.

Among the few who have maintained their integrity while mingling with the incumbents of high political station, William Penn affords a most remarkable instance, and yet the professors of religion should hesitate to expose themselves to the temptations incident to such an intercourse without an imperative necessity.

His circumstances were peculiar: born to the possession of wealth and rank, introduced in early life to the society of the most distinguished men, possessed of great learning and talents, he had the power to render effectual relief to thousands who were suffering under the iron rod of persecution; and he could not exert the influence he possessed, without appearing at court and exchanging civilities with men whose principles were as opposite to his own as darkness to light. Nor can it be supposed that the king considered him as a partisan of the court, for his political writings, as well as the course he pursued at the hustings in Guilford, had identified him with the Whigs.

There is another point in which the professors of religion, and especially ministers of the gospel, should closely examine themselves, before they venture to follow the example of Penn,—the share he took in obtaining votes, and speaking at the hustings to promote the election of Algernon Sidney. It cannot be denied that the political arena, both in England and America, is a most unfavourable field for the growth of religious principles. Men of all parties who mingle in the strife generally attendant on elections are too much in the habit of using means, to promote the success of their candidates, which are not consistent with Christian principles. And, moreover, the very excitement which prevails at such times is unfavourable to that quiet contemplative spirit which peculiarly becomes the station of those "who minister about holy things."

In considering the course that Penn pursued in the election at Guilford, justice to his memory requires that we should bear in mind the motives that prompted him, and the very important objects he had in view. He says, in one of his letters to Sidney, "Thou, as thy friends, had a conscientious regard for England, and to be put aside for such base ways is really a suffering for righteousness." "Thou hast embarked thyself with them that seek, and love and choose the best things, and number is not weight with thee."

It was, therefore, with a view to promote the highest interests of his country, and the progress of religious liberty, that he departed from the line of conduct generally adopted by his brethren in religious profession.

William Penn had for some years previous to this time been concerned as a trustee in the management of West New Jersey, which continued to prosper, and to attract toward its shores a constant stream of emigration; but in the year 1680, much dissatisfaction was excited among the colonists by the exaction of a duty on imports and exports, imposed by the Governor of New York, and collected at the Hoarkills, a town at the capes of the Delaware, since called Lewistown.

This duty being considered an onerous and illegal exaction, the trustees complained to the Duke of York, then proprietary of the province of New York, who referred the consideration of it to commissioners to examine the subject, and report to him. The argument submitted by the trustees on behalf of the colony is remarkable for its ability, and some of the views it exhibits, as well as the diction in which they are conveyed, bear evident marks of William Penn's style of thought and expression.

After showing that the duke had granted to [Lord] Berkley, and that he had transferred to the trustees of [Edward] Byllinge, his title, not only to the soil, but to the government of West New Jersey, for which they had paid a valuable consideration, and that in the conveyance the *powers of government were expressly granted,* he proceeds to prove that the power of taxation claimed by the duke's agents was a flagrant violation of English liberty. "To give up this," he says, (the power of making laws,)

> is to change the government, to sell, or rather resign, ourselves to the will of another: and that for nothing. For under favour we buy nothing of the duke, if not the right of an undisturbed colonizing, and that as Englishmen, with no diminution, but expectation of some increase, of those freedoms and privileges enjoyed in our own country; for the *soil is none of his,* 'tis the natives', by the *jus gentium,* by the laws of nations, and it would be an ill argument to convert to Christianity, to expel instead of purchasing them out of those countries.

> If then the country be theirs, it is not the duke's, he cannot sell it; then what have we bought? We are yet unanswered on this point, and desire you to do it with all due regard to the great honour and justice of the duke. If it be not the right of colonizing, then which way have we our bargain, that pay an arbitrary custom, neither known to the laws of England nor the settled constitution of New York, and those other plantations?

> This very tax, of five per cent., is a thing not to be found in the duke's conveyances; but an after business, a very surprise to the planter! and such an one as, could they have foreseen, they would have sooner taken up in any other plantation in America. Customs, in all governments in the world, are laid upon trade, but this upon planting is unprecedented. Had we brought commodities to these parts to sell, made profit out of them, and returned to the advantage of traders, there had been some colour or pretence for this exaction; but to require and force a custom from persons for coming to their property, their own terra-firma, their habitations, in short, for coming home, is without a parallel; this is paying custom, not for trading, but landing; not for merchandising, but planting; in very deed, for hazarding; for there we go, carry over our fami-

lies and estates, and adventure both for the improvement of a wilderness, and we are not only told we must pay hereafter out of our gains and improvements, but must pay out of our poor stock and principal, (put into goods,) five pounds in the hundred, and not as they are there worth, but as they here cost, and this for coming to plant; so that the plain English of the tragedy is this: we twice buy this moiety of New Jersey, first of Lord Berkley, and next of the natives, and what for? the better to mortgage ourselves and posterity to the duke's governors, and give them a title to our persons and estates, that never had any before. But pray consider, can there be a house without a bottom, or a plantation before a people? if not, can there be a custom before a trade? Besides, there is no end of this power, for since we are, by this precedent, assessed without any law, and thereby excluded our English right of common assent to taxes, what security have we of any thing we possess? we can call nothing our own, but are tenants at will, not only for the soil, but for all our personal estates; we endure penury and the sweat of our brows to improve them, at our own hazard only. This is to transplant not from good to better, but from good to bad; this sort of conduct has destroyed governments, but never raised one to true greatness, nor ever will in the duke's territories, whilst there are so many countries equally as good, in soil and air, surrounded with greater freedom and security.

This remonstrance was so effectual, that the commissioners reported favourably, and the duty was remitted.

In the following year, Penn became interested in the property and government of East New Jersey, of which Elizabethtown was the capital.

Sir George Carteret, the former proprietary of this province, having died, it was sold under his will to pay his debts, and Penn became the purchaser, on behalf of himself and eleven other persons.

The twelve proprietaries soon after admitted twelve others into copartnership with them, and to these twenty-four proprietaries the Duke of York made a fresh grant of East New Jersey, bearing date the 14th of March, 1682: they instituted a government, called the Council of Proprietors, whose meetings were held twice in the year, at Perth Amboy. All the proprietaries, except two, were members of the society of Friends, and in the year 1683, Robert Barclay, of Urie, in Scotland, a noted member and writer of the society, was made Governor of East New Jersey for life, and Thomas Rudyard, of the same society, residing in the colony, was Deputy Governor. West New Jersey having become quite populous, Edward Byllinge was chosen Governor by the proprietaries in England, and he commissioned Samuel Jennings, a minister in the society of Friends, to act as Deputy Governor. These two provinces, East and West New Jersey, continued in a prosperous state for many years; but much inconvenience having arisen from the large number of proprietaries, they agreed to surrender the government to the British crown, which was done in the reign of Queen Anne, by an instrument dated the 15th of April, 1702. (pp. 155-62)

Samuel M. Janney, in his The Life of William Penn, *revised edition, Lippincott, Grambo & Co., 1852, 576 p.*

G. K. Chesterton　(essay date 1932)

[*Regarded as one of England's premier men of letters during the first half of the twentieth century, Chesterton is best remembered as a witty essayist and the author of such fiction as his "Father Brown" mysteries and his fantasy* The Man Who Was Thursday (1908). *His works reflect his pronounced Roman Catholic beliefs and are characterized by his humor, frequent use of paradox, and chatty, rambling style. In the following essay, Chesterton contrasts Penn and the Quakers with the Puritans and suggests that Quakers were the true fundamentalists.*]

The Americans have established a Thanksgiving Day to celebrate the fact that the Pilgrim Fathers reached America. The English might very well establish another Thanksgiving Day; to celebrate the happy fact that the Pilgrim Fathers left England. I know that this is still regarded as a historical heresy, by those who have long ceased to worry about a religious heresy. For while these persons still insist that the Pilgrim Fathers were champions of religious liberty, nothing is more certain than the fact that an ordinary modern liberal, sailing with them, would have found no liberty, and would have intensely disliked almost all that he found of religion. Even Thanksgiving Day itself, though it is now kept in a most kindly and charming fashion by numbers of quite liberal and large-minded Americans, was originally intended, I believe, as a sort of iconoclastic expedient for destroying the celebration of Christmas. The Puritans everywhere had a curious and rabid dislike of Christmas; which does not encourage me, for one, to develop a special and spiritual fervour for Puritanism. Oddly enough, however, the Puritan tradition in America has always celebrated Thanksgiving Day by often eliminating the Christmas Pudding, but preserving the Christmas Turkey. I do not know why, unless the very name of Turkey reminded them of the Prophet of Islam, who was also the first Prophet of Prohibition.

It is not, however, in connexion with either Thanksgiving Day or Christmas Day, that I recur for a moment to the somewhat controversial question of the Pilgrim Fathers. It is merely to note anew that there has always seemed to me too much emphasis on the Pilgrim Fathers, as compared with many others who were at least as truly Fathers of the Republic. There has certainly been in recent times a considerable combination between Puritanism and Publicity. The Puritans may not always have approved of the stage; but for all that they got a great deal of the limelight. Somebody managed to make the *Mayflower* as legendary as the Ark or the Argo; indeed, it is legendary in more ways than one, so far as the aim and atmosphere of the expedition are concerned. But I doubt whether most people even know the names of the ships in which many of the other devoted or heroic colonists of America sailed; I, for one, most certainly do not. I will not insist especially on the very noble example of Lord Baltimore and the founders of the State of Maryland; who established the first sys-

Penn at about the age of Twenty-two.

tem of religious toleration in history; for there I might be accused of favouring my own religious sympathies and ideas. But I am at least detached and impartial in the subsequent and somewhat similar story of the founding of the State of Pennsylvania. And whatever ship brought the great Quakers to that settlement has a rather better right than the *Mayflower* to be called, in the language of Mr. Ford, a Peace Ship.

These reflections occurred to me when I was recently standing in the city of Philadelphia; on which looks down the great statue of William Penn, whose unmarked grave lies a mile or two from my own house at home. And it struck me as very strange that all the millions of men, with modern humanitarian sympathies, have said so little of the immense superiority of that intellectual and spiritual leader to the clamorously advertised Calvinists of the *Mayflower*. I gravely fear that a great many of them do not even see much difference between the two. Among the most curious of all curiosities of literature, or of legend, I have actually heard a sort of romantic rumour (which I have never been able either to trace or test) that portions of the timber of the *Mayflower* were found in some strange way attached to the old Quaker meeting-house that stands beside Penn's grave. I cannot imagine what the story could possibly mean; or how the incident can possibly be supposed to have come about; unless indeed some enthusiastic American globe-trotter merely threw fragments of *Mayflower* furniture (said to be rather suspiciously common in the States) at any house that had any connexion with any founder of any American State. Anyhow, he might just as well have said that Sir Walter Raleigh sailed in the *Mayflower* as connect William Penn and his people with the fanaticism that filled that famous vessel. He might as well have hung the first Calvinistic meeting-house with rosaries and relics and scapularies, belonging to the Catholic Calverts, as pretend to have patched up the house of the first Friends with the relics of their mortal enemies and persecutors, the old Puritans. An American Puritan in the seventeenth century would have regarded a Quaker very much as an American Puritan in the twentieth century would regard a Bolshevist. And though Bolshevists are supposed to be fierce and Quakers were supposed to be meek, they were at least alike in this; they were what modern America would call Radical; in the sense of going to the real root of the question, and answering it rightly or wrongly. In short, they were really Fundamentalists; and most Fundamentalists are not Fundamentalists. For whatever we think of the thing now called Fundamentalism, it is not fundamental. It is not particularly fundamental to throw a big Bible at people's heads (or rather a particular translation of the Bible, with a lot of books left out as Apocrypha) any more than to throw the Encyclopædia Britannica or the Institutes of Calvin. Even if it be a truth, it is not a first principle. But it is fundamental, and it is a first principle, right or wrong, to go back as William Penn did to the doctrine of the Inner Light. For William Penn really was a great man and not merely a seventeenth-century sectarian; his thoughts; whether we think with him or no, have a meaning in the twentieth-century or any century; and he founded something much larger than Pennsylvania and much greater than Philadelphia; a faith that has not yet failed.

I think I know why Penn has been thrown into the shade by the Pilgrim Fathers. It was his politics; and for some they are still a dreadful secret. I was once asked by some worthy modern pacifists, of the Nonconformist culture, to lecture on something in one of the oldest meeting-houses of the Society of Friends. I agreed to lecture upon William Penn; and with secret and malignant joy drew up an elaborate plan for a eulogium on that Quaker hero. I set myself specially to express boundless admiration for all those parts of his life and opinion which his modern Puritan admirers do not admire. I proposed to praise extravagantly his loyal and devoted sympathy with the House of Stuart. I intended to point out eagerly, how worthy he was of the gracious and glorious friendship of a man like Charles the Second. I meant to rub in every detail of his diplomatic and political support of the admirable political designs of James the Second. I intended to insist on the intellectual amity, almost amounting to intellectual alliance, which so often bound him to Cavaliers and even to Catholics. In short, it was my evil intention to praise him for everything for which Macaulay blamed him. Then, I thought, when I have explained how intimately identified was Penn with the Royalists, and especially with the Papists—then surely all the Nonconformist ministers would be frightfully pleased. Then should I be acclaimed and admired by all the modern Puritans for my perfect understanding of the great seventeenth-century sectary. Then should I become the idol of all the people who glorify the Pilgrim Fathers and talk enthusiastically about the *Mayflower*. Then it

would be admitted that I also was a grand grim old Puritan, like all the rest of them. Unfortunately, I fancy I must have boasted of my intention, and some rumour of it must have reached them. For I received at the eleventh hour a hurried request to give a lecture on Dickens. And from this we may learn that, if Dickens was an enemy of the Puritans, he was not so much of an enemy as Penn. (pp. 160-65)

G. K. Chesterton, "And What about the Quakers?" in his Sidelights on New London and Newer York and Other Essays, 1932. Reprint by Books for Libraries Press, 1968, pp. 160-65.

Bonamy Dobrée (essay date 1932)

[*A highly regarded English historian and critic, Dobrée distinguished himself as both a leading authority on Restoration drama and as an author of biographical studies which seek through vivid depiction and captivating style to establish biography as a legitimate creative form. In the following excerpt from his biography of Penn, Dobrée examines Penn's early life and works, focusing on* The Sandy Foundation Shaken *and* No Cross, No Crown.]

The extraordinary vigour which Penn displayed [in his early years as a Quaker] is a natural enough result of conversion. 'In this state of the new man, all is new.' Instead of his impulses being scattered, all the springs of action—his love of activity, of putting in order, of dominating, even; his combativeness, his intellectual authoritarianism, all the complex volitions of a variously gifted man—were centred about one point. . . . [He] had surrendered to God, and, in the happy transformation which followed, all the fields of his consciousness were fused together, directed to a single end. His personal energy proceeded from one node; he was unified with the religious life and ready to face anything for its sake. (p. 40)

[Penn] had a gift of words which he liked to use. The words were abundant, they flowed with a large generosity he had no desire to quench or refine upon; he was no castigator of prose. He was popular as a preacher, expounding with a pleasant voice, a little too plangent for a room, perhaps, but excellent for a Meeting-House. He was not torn by the vehemence of Fox, who used to have to retire from the room shattered by his own outbursts; and when he held forth to the unlearned, he always used words that were plain and phrases which the simplest could understand. Beyond this we cannot say what his 'openings' were like at this time; most probably they resembled the **'Letter to the Churches of Jesus'** which he wrote during his travels in Holland and Germany, discourses not likely to induce ecstasies, but calm exhortations to Friends to 'stay their minds in the light of the Lord for ever; and let the awe, fear, and dread of the Almighty dwell in them'; a little rhetorical, perhaps, to an austere taste that dislikes needless multiplication of synonyms; but then it is the function of rhetoric to move, and therefore the business of the preacher to use it as an instrument.

But 'enlarging' at Meetings, discussing among Friends, was not enough; to remain happily where no strife is may be regarded as a form of self-indulgence; and Penn unceasingly felt that he must battle against the abundant errors of other men. 'In his love of controversy, of printing, indeed,' [Francis] Jeffrey summed up, 'this worthy sectary . . . not only responded in due form to every work in which the principles of his sect were indirectly or directly attacked—but whenever he heard a sermon that he did not like—or learned that any of the Friends had been put in the stocks;—whenever he was prevented from preaching—or learned the edifying particulars of the death of a Quaker, or of a persecutor of Quakers, he was instantly at the press with a letter, or a narrative, or an admonition—and never desisted from the contest till he had reduced the adversary to silence.'

Penn's first essay in pamphleteering was a tract called *Truth Exalted,* a 'short but sure testimony' against all religions but his own, which is proved to be the only true and original one, by which the Light is again come upon the earth. The style is richly polemical, the denunciations tremendous, the massed battalions of rhetorical questions pungent with heavenly gunpowder. 'Come answer me first, you Papists,' he cried, demanding Biblical authority for Popes, dogmas, practices of all, even the most innocuous, kinds; for 'cardinals, archbishops, deans, prebends, Jesuits, Franciscans, Ursulines, Capuchines, Benedictines, with other such like lazy nuns and friars. . . . '

'Come now, you that are called Protestants, however denominated or distinguished,' he drove on, turning to other adversaries, taxing them with being greedy to persecute. 'Come and tell me now, ye of the Church of England that say the scriptures are your rule,' he pursued, turning his heaviest guns on the chief enemy; ' . . . what precedent do you find for litanies, responses, singing, choristers, organs, altars, bowing, surplices, square caps, hoods, rochets, fonts, baby-baptism, holy days (as you call them) with much more such like dirty trash, and foul superstition?' Where, indeed? But Penn never waited for an answer. He rushed on, growing ever more exalted, terrifically, orientally, prophetic.

> Woe unto you protestants, that are mighty to drink strong drink, that give your neighbours drink, and put the bottle to them that they may be drunk; that put far away the evil day, and cause the seat of violence to come near; that lie upon beds of ivory, and stretch yourselves upon your couches; that eat the fat of the flock, and drink the sweet of the vine; that anoint yourselves with the chief ointments; that chant to the sound of the viol, and invent to yourselves instruments of music, but consider not the afflictions of Joseph. How sport you away your precious time, as if ye were born not to die, at least never to be judged? O what swearing, what uncleanness, what drunkenness, what profanation, what vanity, what pride, what expense, what patching, what painting, what lascivious intrigues, what wanton appointments, what public unclean houses, what merry masks, what lustful insinuating treats at your plays, parks, mulberry gardens, with whatever else may please the lustful eye, and gratify the wanton mind!

We do not know what reception the book met with among sober Quakers: did they smile, we wonder, at the youthful extravagance? Did they criticise the kaleidoscopic style, the breathlessly accumulating periods? We fear not. [Samuel] Pepys, on his part, found it such a 'ridiculous nonsensical book' that he was 'ashamed to read in it.' What was all this stuff about chanting to the sound of the viol? He often did it himself, and—well, there is no need to proceed further in the argument.

This was Penn's earliest unprovoked attack on backsliders, and he soon followed it up with his first entry into controversy. At this period, since there was a slight relaxation in the hunt after Nonconformists, the sects, finding that time moved lazily, turned their attention to mending each other's views, or, alternatively, clapper-clawing each other to shreds for heretics. Controversy in those days was hardly urbane; if you thought a man a fool, you said so without more ado; indeed, you did not hesitate to call him worse things. A son of Belial is a son of Belial, and it is your duty to say so. Penn revelled in the work; he could sling words with anybody, good gnarled stones from a catapult. And now a Norfolk 'priest' named Jonathan Clapham saw fit to open the vials of grotesque wrath on the Quakers in *A Guide to True Religion,* which their new champion, to win his spurs, answered in *The Guide Mistaken,* of which we can repeat here that it was 'an extremely fierce and personal piece of writing,' which stigmatised Clapham as 'peevish and hypocritical'; he marched on 'without fear, wit or wisdom.' More interesting, because of what it led to, was the public debate with Vincent.

Thomas Vincent, sometime student of Christ Church, and thus possibly influenced by Owen, went 'under the notion of a presbyter,' to use Penn's phrase; and, having thus been ejected from his living at the Restoration, now decorated a pulpit in Spitalfields. Because the Quakers had seduced many of his congregation from his 'inventions, carnal observations, will-worship, and vain conversation'—Penn once more—he grew rabid against them. 'His peevish zeal transported him not only beyond the moderation of Christianity, but the civility of his education, venting his folly and prejudice much to this purpose, that he had as lieve they should go to a bawdy-house as to frequent the Quakers' Meetings.' He plainly told his flock that, if they seceded from him to the Friends' damnable doctrines, they would indeed be damned. The Quakers asked for a public dispute to be arranged, which was done, after some demur. A day was settled, the time to be two o'clock. But by one o'clock Vincent had packed the room with his own followers, so that only a very few of the opposite faction could squeeze in. Penn appeared with George Whitehead, 'a man of excellent qualities, if somewhat pedestrian talents,' and then Vincent opened the ball with a discourse. 'The manner of it was so gross,' Penn recorded, 'that I do not know how to represent it better, than by the levity and rudeness of some prize; laughing, hissing, shoving, striking, and stigmatising us with the opprobrious terms of confident fellow, impudent villain, blasphemer, etc.' But, after all, had Penn any right to complain?

Vincent upheld three main doctrines: (1) the trinity of separate persons, in the unity of essence: (2) God's incapacity to forgive, without the fullest satisfaction paid him by another: (3) a justification of impure persons from an impu-tative righteousness (that is, a man might be as wicked as he pleased, but he would be saved by the righteousness of Christ being imputed to him). These are difficult points; one must walk warily to slip past the ever-open arms of heresy; a stumble on either side of the razor edge may plunge us into the most white-hot depths of hell. These, the first point especially, were snares in the Quaker fold, as they have been to more sinuous minds than theirs, and we shall hear of them again. On this occasion Vincent fab-ricated absurd syllogisms; and when the Friends tried to be a little more subtle, he accused Penn of Jesuitism; for in England, any departure from the downright object, that all plain men-in-the-street may see, is apt to incur that charge: it stuck to Penn for a great part of his life. Vincent talked, he talked for hours, he talked till it was dark, and still he did not stop. At last, horror-struck at the abomina-tion of the Quaker heresy, he fell on his knees in prayer, and, 'with many strangely affected whines,' denounced the Friends as blasphemous. He then got up and walked away, calling upon his flock to follow him, a quite usual method of controversy in those days. You made your statement, and then departed, as though to imply that no answer could possibly be forthcoming to cloud the light which had so brilliantly radiated from you. But a number of peo-ple stayed, whereupon Vincent's supporters put out the candles. This strategy, however, failed, for Penn and Whitehead went on propounding in the dark: till in the end Vincent 'came very palely down the stairs (having a candle in his hand),' and ordered everyone to disperse, which they did on his promising another public debate. But this never took place; Vincent could not waste his time, he said, in such terribly blasphemous nonsense.

Penn's public activities were not limited to squabbling with obscure divines; they were to take him into higher spheres. The fall of the Church-minded Clarendon and the advent of the Cabal having put new hope into the Dissent-ers, the Quakers resolved to approach Buckingham, who was said to favour toleration. Although he was only Mas-ter of the Horse, he was actually much in the position of first minister and now at the height of his power; no one foresaw his miserable end 'in the worst inn's worst room.' So Penn, with Whitehead, [Thomas] Loe, and [Josiah] Coale, attended this brilliant high personage, who benign-ly promised help; but since he was 'everything by starts and nothing long,' no good came of it. It was Thomas Loe's last effort: he was suddenly taken ill at the interview, and, worn out by his battlings, soon collapsed irremedia-bly. When the crisis of his illness approached, Penn, him-self prostrate with a fever, staggered up, and 'though in a sweat,' hurried to his first teacher's bedside. He described the death scene in a manner that is a little too edifying; but perhaps this is understandable, for Loe made a special ap-peal to him. Taking Penn by the hand he said, 'Dear heart, bear thy cross; stand faithful to God, and bear thy testimo-ny in thy day and generation: and God will give thee an eternal crown of glory that none shall ever take from thee.' Then he passed away in a great stillness.

The work, however, did not stop, but it was a reduced dep-utation that made a second attempt to soften authority, this time through the medium of Sir Henry Berwick, Sec-

retary of State. Penn begged him to look more closely in-to the doctrines and behaviour of the Friends; it would then be found that they deserved better things in their own country than 'stocks, whips, gaols, dungeons, præmunires, fines, sequestration, and banishment.' Again nothing happened. What was to be done? Was no reason-able appeal of any use? Penn framed within himself a scheme to obtain toleration; but before he could do any-thing, he was thrown into prison.

It was due to his intense desire to testify: he could not bear to let the Vincent controversy rest where it was. Since the Presbyterian would not give him a hearing, he yielded to a passion for self-justification which never forsook him, and in hot haste scribbled off a book in which he told the story of the disputation, and with that genius for good sell-ing titles which he always displayed (though he gave his books away), he sent it into the world as *The Sandy Foun-dation Shaken.* So far good, but he followed it up with a second part, in which he made a statement of the Quaker faith as he saw it. This was undoubtedly a mistake, not only from his, but from the Quaker, point of view; for in it he tried to express in terms of every day what can only be explained, and that with extreme fastidiousness, in the language of theology. The attitude of the Friends to all such vexed questions should have been, 'No doubt; but that sort of thing does not interest us.' What had they to do with the intricacies of *homoousian* or *homoiousian,* the diphthong which centuries before had caused the East to run with blood, or all the knotty statements of the Athana-sian Creed? To formulate a doctrine, to evolve dogmas, is really foreign to the Quaker standpoint; and indeed, on the score that Penn was too much given to theology, the Soci-ety of Friends has a little tempered its admiration of their great leader. In *The Sandy Foundation Shaken,* Penn pro-ceeded to set forth what seems to the layman an admirably lucid statement of the Unitarian point of view: in it the mind is freed from consideration of essences and sub-stances. To the world, certainly, it seemed a shockingly undermining work. It was 'a most blasphemous book . . . which says much in derogation of our Saviour's deity'; it was a 'horrid and blasphemous piece against the Holy Trinity.' Pepys, who thought the fat pamphlet so well written that it could not come from his young acquain-tance, and that it was too deep to be safe for the vulgar to read, regarded it as a 'book against the Trinity'; while [John] Evelyn, from popular report, referred to it as 'a blasphemous book against the Deity of our Blessed Lord.' 'Pulpits rang,' Penn himself recorded, 'of how the Quakers had unmasked themselves.' The question had better have been left well alone.

The handle Penn had left temptingly unguarded for au-thority to seize on was that he had not obtained the Bishop of London's licence to publish the book. Though this was a formality not at this time insisted upon, Bishop Hench-man, who had a weakness for Presbyterians, caused the printer to be clapped into the Gatehouse Prison; where-upon Penn surrendered himself to Lord Arlington, the other Secretary of State, to be forthwith sent to the Tower. But hardly had he got there than Arlington dashed after him with a paper he said had been found in his house just after Penn's visit, a paper full of treason. Penn easily exculpated himself from this extra charge, and Arlington went off, professedly satisfied, promising to use his influence to secure the young man's release. Nevertheless, Penn was mewed up in the Tower for more than seven months.

The whole affair is somewhat mysterious; not so much that Penn was called to account, but that he should have been imprisoned so long and so severely. For though it was 'conjectured and reported' that he was kept by the heels, 'not on any religious matter, but for some points deeply concerning the safety of the King'—which was obvious nonsense—he was not treated as a political prisoner, comfortably housed, and allowed to see his friends; but was alternately frozen and stifled in a room under the tiles, and allowed to see no one but his father, or such people as were officially sent to reason with him. Penn himself supposed that Henchman was egged on by the Presbyterians; Hepworth Dixon violently incriminates Arlington, in pages of ill-informed scorn, crammed with picturesque statements for which he gives no authority. We know little for certain, except that on the 16th December, four days after Penn's incarceration, the Council approved Arlington's action, and two days later issued a warrant to Sir John Robinson, Lieutenant of the Tower, to keep Penn 'close prisoner . . . until his Majesty's pleasure shall be further signified.' Arlington himself can have had no animus against Penn. Being at this time a secret, and later an avowed, Roman Catholic, he cherished no love for the Church of England, and thus, presumably, no hatred against those who dissented from it. [Mabel Richmond Brailsford, in her *The Making of William Penn*, 1930] ingeniously suggests that Arlington treated the business merely as a matter of routine, and that his private secretary, Sir John Williamson, was the villain of the piece; for Williamson, a sometime student at Saumur, seems to have hated the Quakers, since a correspondent at Deal could write to him at this time; 'News also to some Quakers here is that their Saint Penn is taken. He is devilishly cried up among that perverse sullen faction.' But here again proof is lacking.

And, moreover, Penn was the son of far too distinguished a man for a subordinate, however trusted and however officious, to vent his spleen upon in that way; and perhaps one must look for a curious remark made by [Samuel] Sewell to throw further light on the matter. Recording Penn's imprisonment, he adds, 'some thought it was not without his father's being acquainted with it, perhaps to prevent a worse treatment.' Worse treatment to whom? If to the Admiral, it suggests that Sir William sacrificed his son to save his own skin; if to Penn, that he was threatened with transportation. The Court, indeed, was full of the Admiral's enemies; he was not smiled upon by the Cabal, and the Navy Office had been purged of his friends: but by now he had himself retired, or rather occupied only a minor post, with a seat on the Board. Since he had survived one impeachment there would be no point in attacking him again, though, of course, spite takes a long time to exhaust itself. Perhaps, as Miss Brailsford suggests, the Admiral was not unwilling to see whether a dose of rigorous prison might not cure his son of intemperate religion:

he knew what the Tower was like. As for a worse treatment threatening Penn, that can only be sheer conjecture.

At all events, there Penn was, harshly used, cut off from all communication with the outer world, subsisting on rough, meagre prison fare, and so wretched that, through either physical disorder or nervous strain, he once more lost his hair; and though the more rigid of his sect looked askance at him for sinking to the vain adornment, he ever afterwards used a wig to cover his baldness. Fox, however, excused him. It was 'a little civil border,' he explained in a letter to a querying Friend, 'thin, plain and short . . . a very short civil thing,' he repeated. 'He wears them to keep his head and ears warm, and not for pride.' Nor was it an expensive wig; it only cost five shillings. 'And,' he added in a postscript, 'he's more willing to fling it off if a little hair come, than ever he was to put it on.'

For three months the prisoner had no word from his father, who, indeed, was too ill to leave his room. At last permission was obtained for Penn's servant to see him, and 'to speak with him in the presence of a keeper.' This man, though a Quaker much in Penn's confidence, brought him no news of his friends, no message from his father; only a threat from the Bishop of London that Penn should either recant or die a prisoner. 'All is well,' he answered; 'I wish they had told me so before, since the expecting of a release put a stop to some business; thou may'st tell my father, who I know will ask thee, these words: that my prison shall be my grave before I will budge a jot; for I owe my conscience to no mortal man; I have no need to fear, God will make amends for all.' No doubt the servant delivered the message; but also, seeing that Penn was likely to prove an unprofitable master, he proceeded to visit a rich Socinian, friendly to the Quakers, and pitifully beg the loan of forty pounds from him for the prisoner (say two hundred pounds at the present value of money): he then disappeared—another witness to Penn's complete inability to read character. Penn repaid the sum, but his enemies used the incident against him.

Immured, abandoned, apparently hopelessly lost, Penn turned with extraordinary courage to the 'business' his expectation of release had put a stop to, the writing of the work for which he is most famed, and which has ever since been one one of the standard works of Quakerism. This apology, which, remembering Loe's deathbed words, he called *No Cross; No Crown,* deserves a place, not only in the literature of religion, but in literature without qualification. Free from any vituperation, except for a sentence in the Preface, afterwards deleted, unencumbered by learned authority (the references are to the Bible only), it is an exhortation to men to look into themselves, and to realise that 'Christ's Cross is Christ's way to Christ's Crown.' It deals with 'the nature and *discipline* of the Holy Cross of Christ,' and thus is no mere exercise in 'uplifting' literature. As a piece of Christian homiletics it may be below what Jeremy Taylor could do, but it is far above anything Bunyan wrote, because, while as frank and whole in the faith, it is far more intelligent. After all, Penn was familiar with the world; the knew what it thought and felt, and so knew exactly where to attack it. The prose is not chastened; he did not spare words: even in its first form it is a bulky sermon—it was enlarged in later editions—so that no mere statement of its scope will suffice: all one can hope to do is to give a taste of its quality by quoting a short extract:

> So I say to thee, unless thou believest, that he that stands at the door of thy heart and knocks, and sets thy sins in order before thee, and calls thee to repentance, be the Saviour of the world, thou wilt die in thy sins, and where he is gone, thou wilt never come. For if thou believest not in him, it is impossible that he should do thee good, or effect thy salvation: Christ works not against faith, but by it. It is said of old, 'he did not many works in some places, because the people believed not in him.' So that if thou truly believest, thine ear will be attentive to his voice in thee, and the door of thine heart open to his knocks. Thou wilt yield to the discoveries of his light, and the teaching of his grace will be very dear to thee.

It is suave, it is fervent without being strained, and it expresses the most profound and unalterable conviction.

A second part is more learned; it is, indeed, a compendium of erudition, an anthology of accounts of edifying actions, or equally edifying deaths, and no one can deny that it is broad enough in its scope. The brave examples range as far back as that of Penelope, the wife of Ulysses; while the later editions contain an account of the last words of Sir William Penn. To us, the work would be better without these 'testimonies': they are unreadable; but people in that age could absorb such florilegia without the suspicion of a smile or a doubt as to their relevancy.

In due course the Admiral came to see his son: he was now eager to get him out of prison, and implored him to recant. But Penn stood firm: life as anything else but a Quaker seemed impossible to him. Since threats would not do, other tactics were tried: learned divines were despatched to him to straighten out his theological path; it was no good. The only person who made the least impression on him, and that on his heart rather than on his mind, was the learned and gracious Dr. Stillingfleet, afterwards Bishop of Worcester.

> But as I told him, and he told the King, that the Tower was the worst argument in the world to convince me; for whoever was in the wrong, those who used force for religion could never be in the right—so neither the Doctor's arguments, nor his moving and interesting motives of the King's favour and preferment, at all prevailed; and [here is a charming touch] I am glad I have the opportunity to own so publicly the great pains he took, and the humanity he showed, and that to his moderation, learning, and kindness, I will ever hold myself obliged.

But seeing that there was obviously a misunderstanding somewhere, for Stillingfleet could find nothing dangerous in him, Penn, to clear himself of false accusations and wrenchings of his meaning, produced another pamphlet, ***Innocency with her Open Face,*** to show how mistaken people had been in the meanings they ascribed to his offenceless words in ***The Sandy Foundation Shaken.*** To the candid lay mind, this work does not really make matters any better, at least as far as sound views on the Trinity are concerned: for though the divinity of Christ is indeed strenuously upheld, it is equally insisted that Christ is God without distinction or separation of persons. Penn always succeeded in keeping clear of Arianism, that pitfall for the Unitarian; but, we ask ourselves, was he not here in grave danger of a still worse heresy, a new kind of monotheism: or even—the horrid suspicion flits across the brain—of being a Sabellian? Coleridge bluntly calls him as much. But no; it is error to accuse Penn of theology; it was merely that he took too literally the phrase 'being of one substance.' But substance, what did that mean? And what had Vincent said—essence? Well, at all events, there was justification by works as opposed to the doctrine of imputed righteousness; there could be no mistake about that; he could safely stick to it. Indeed, it seems to the uninstructed that Penn did not recede an inch from his former position. Of most weight, surely, was the appeal at the end that the harrying of Christians by Christians should cease. It is a straightforward, simple document, too simple, indeed, for the matter in hand, and Penn did not rely on that alone to argue his freedom. On July 1, 1669, he wrote to Arlington pleading for release, a long letter, not quite so unadorned as his apologetic pamphlet; indeed, here and there it is made a little turgid for a busy man to read, with its references to Socrates Scholasticus, the Emperors Jovianus and Sejanus, and to Tacitus on Lingonius. Yet it contains some shrewd hits. 'I beseech thee to intreat the King, on my account, not to believe every man to be his enemy, that cannot shape his conscience to the narrow forms and prescripts of men's inventions . . . ' Would this not make persecutions seem absurd? At the same time he insisted upon his right to be tried before being condemned, for all the hearing he had so far had was from Henchman's emissaries. Did they represent the law? At last, after a weary period, his pamphlet, his letter, a favourable report from Stillingfleet, and, it is said, the intercession of the Duke of York (this sounds like the Admiral's doing), procured him his release, the order for which was signed on July 28th. Gossip had it that 'Penn, the author of the late heretical book, having renounced his opinions by his hand, is to be delivered to his father, and by him to be transported.' (pp. 40-53)

> *Bonamy Dobrée, in his* William Penn: Quaker and Pioneer, *Houghton Mifflin Company, 1932, 346 p.*

William I. Hull   (essay date 1937)

[*In the following excerpt, Hull discusses Penn's early years as a writer, which were characterized by his controversial pamphlets and fiery polemics.*]

Controversy was the native element of seventeenth century Englishmen. Their political disputes they fought out by Civil War and Revolution. Their religious disputes added fervour and bitterness to their political controversies, and were themselves fought out by wars of pamphlets and oral debates. The Quakers, although they abjured hard blows on fields of military combats, were no whit behind their contemporaries in hurling hard words and heavy literature at the heads of their adversaries. This fervent warfare was due, of course, to no peculiar contentiousness of Englishmen; but in that century of ultra-serious religiosity, they devoutly believed that their souls' salvation and that of every other human being depended upon the triumph of their own religious views over those of others. They believed, too, that the survival of their religious or ecclesiastical organizations was at stake, and that the ability to give and return hard knocks in theological logic constituted one of the chief characteristics of the fittest in their struggle to survive.

William Penn, in his youthful ardour and with the zeal of a new convert, performed his first service for Quakerism by plunging eagerly into this war of controversy. During the first seven years after his 'convincement,' he published at least forty-two books and pamphlets! The quality of many of these was as striking as their quantity and their titles. Among them are found such titles as *Truth Exalted; The Guide Mistaken, and Temporizing Rebuked; The Sandy Foundation Shaken; Innocency with her Open Face; Truth rescued from Imposture; A Seasonable Caveat against Popery; The Malicious Aspertions, Erroneous Doctrines and Horrid Blasphemies of Thomas Jenner and Timothy Taylor; The Spirit of Truth vindicated against . . . a late Malicious Libel; The New Witnesses proved Old Hereticks; Plain-Dealing with a traducing Anabaptist; A Winding-Sheet for Controversie Ended; The Devil's Champions Defeated; The Ignorance and Calumny of H. Hallywell; Reason against Railing, and Truth against Fiction; The Counterfeit Christian Detected; Naked Truth needs no Shift; Libels no Proofs; Saul smitten to the Ground.*

There is no murmuring in the text of these writings; they live up to the thunder of their titles. Indeed, the controversialist aspect of Penn's life has been a source of embarrassment to most of his biographers, whether Quaker or non-Quaker, and they have touched but lightly upon the character of his polemical writings and debates. From the time of his first biographer [Joseph Besse]—who said of him that 'he never turned his back in the day of battle'—, down to Clarkson, Dixon, and Janney, in the middle of the nineteenth century, they ignore or condone their bitterness. Janney, for example, gently comments:

> Many of his publications were of a controversial nature, a species of writing which, though needful at times for the correction of errors and the advancement of truth, is seldom interesting or edifying to succeeding generations, especially when tinctured with party zeal, or imbued with the prejudices of the age. He was, perhaps, as clear of these faults as any writer of his day; and if the impartial reader of his works shall find, in his controversial writings, some expressions more harsh than should be expected from his enlarged views and liberal feelings, it must be remembered that all men are liable to be influenced by the spirit of the age in which they live. [*Life of William Penn*]

Not so with our twentieth century critics. They have fallen blithely upon this defect, this Achilles Heel, in the great man's character, and have assailed it with vituperations

that nearly match his own. A vigorous fighter was Penn; no gently ambling polemist like Isaac Penington; he denounced and affirmed with intemperate violence; with frenetic activity, he sailed over a choppy sea of interminable wranglings, ruffled by the perverse winds of doctrine; he was garrulous, arrogant, bluntly positive, tart, virulent, truculent, abusive, maledictory, even scurrilous; he descended to the low and muddy level of popular controversy, to the worst kind of religious journalism; he had heated, vulgar debates with common ranters, with little dignity and a surprising disregard of good manners; disregarding Quakerly gentleness, he made bitter and malicious attacks upon his enemies; he talked frothily about false prophets, impostors, gross perversions, black slanders, vile forgeries, plain contradictions; he wrote with no imagination, no humour, no courtesy, no subtlety, no artistry or grace of utterance! Such is the modern indictment; and there is much in Penn's printed words to substantiate at least some of its items.

His *Seasonable Caveat against Popery*—written when he was only twenty-six, but after long meditation following his residence in France—was decidedly 'severe,' as his apologists call it. Attacking the Papacy as 'the ancient enemy,' he accuses it of promulgating the doctrines of the Devil, which were as false and immoral as their infernal parent. The fundamental doctrine of transubstantiation he denounced as contrary to both the Bible and to reason: 'If this Doctrine were true, their Lord would be made by their Priest; for till he says the Words, there is no Real Presence; and so the Creature (and sometimes a sad one too) makes his Creator, which is nothing short of wretched Blasphemy. The Lord they Adore and Reverence, they Eat.' The other cardinal doctrines of the papacy—including its subordination of the Bible, its practical repudiation of the trinity, its justification by merits, its communion in one kind for the laity and in both kinds for the clergy, its prayers in Latin for the dead and to the saints, and its ecclesiastical hierarchy—are disputed as being contrary to the Bible and to primitive Christianity. To support his arguments, Penn cites a learned array of quotations from the Fathers of the Church, leading schoolmen and obscure Roman Catholic apologists, and from the popes themselves. But his most severe denunciation of popery is because of its contravention of the moral law in its worship of images; its subordination of children's obedience to parents, to their obedience to the church; its massacre of 'heretics'; its theft of enormous wealth; and its 'Dispensations of public Stews, especially at Rome, where the Pope's Revenue is not a little greatened by those ungodly Licenses.' In short, that 'by reason of its Latitude in Point of Indulgence, the Popish Religion is an open Sanctuary for refuge to all loose and debauch'd Livers.'

After quoting such a denunciation, it is right that Penn's specific and emphatic distinction between popery and papists, between Catholicism and Catholics, should be stressed. While he attacked without quarter what he believed to be false and pernicious doctrines, he insisted that 'the great number of Romanists [who] may be abused Zealots' should be tolerated. Accordingly, in his preface, addressed 'To the English Protestant Reader,' he declares: 'I design nothing less than incensing of the Civil Magistrate against them (were such a Thing possible), for I profess my self a Friend to an Universal Toleration of Faith and Worship.' But in this same preface, he expresses the fear lest the 'Romanish Emissaries' should even then desire to restore the Inquisition; and in his 'Questionary Postscript,' he demands an assurance that the Catholics of England 'would allow a Toleration, were they powerful,' and questions whether or not they could be believed, 'since it's one of their most sacred Maxims, Not to keep Faith with Hereticks.' Nevertheless, despite these questionings, he remained true to his inmost principle of toleration for the Catholics (which was a very rare virtue in his century, and not too well ingrained in ours) both in England and in his colony over seas.

As a typical Protestant of the Quaker 'left wing,' Penn had no soft, condoning words for his fellow-Protestants of the right wing. His first book, *Truth Exalted,* written while a prisoner in Newgate, bears upon its title-page the provocative and imperious words: 'A short but Sure Testimony against all those Religions, Faiths, and Worships, that have been formed and followed in the *Darkness of Apostacy* . . . Presented to Princes, Priests and People, that they may Repent, Believe, and Obey. By William Penn, whom Divine Love constrains in an Holy Contempt, to trample on *Egypt's Glory,* not fearing the *King's Wrath,* having beheld the MAJESTY OF HIM Who is Invisible.' This is a vigorous attack upon all religions based upon 'Rites, Duties and Ceremonies,' and was doubly offensive to partisans of the church and the monarchy because it not only scorned them, but also exalted Quakerism as 'that Glorious Light which is now Risen, and Shines forth in the Life and Doctrine of the Despised Quakers, as the Alone Good Old Way of Life and Salvation.' Papists, Episcopalians, 'Separatists of divers Names' he takes severely to task for their rites and practices of many kinds, which he enumerates and condemns as coming not from the Bible, but from 'the Devil (that subtil Serpent);' and in a 'Cautionary Postscript,' warns the People of England of the 'Calamity, Pining and Distress' which are about to descend upon them for their sins of commission and omission, and specifically for the cruel and wholesale persecution of the Quakers. With a final reference to the salvation of those 'who have forsaken either Father, Mother, Sister, Brother, House, Land [his own recent experience] Husband or Wife' for the blessed testimony of the Light, he signs himself: 'I am not of this World, but seek a Country Eternal in the Heavens. William Penn.'

This book was read by Penn's friend Pepys, who states in his Diary: 'So to supper, and after supper to read a ridiculous nonsensical book set out by Will Pen for the Quakers; but so full of nothing but nonsense, that I was ashamed to read in it.' And after two and three-quarter centuries, a recent critic condemns it as the 'noisy taunting . . . of a bawling fanatical Puritan, distressingly uncouth.' It was probably not a best seller, even at first, unless among the Quakers; but it was speedily followed by another which demolished a book called *A Guide to the True Religion.* This book was written by an Anglican rector, named Jonathan Clapham, and it stated the essential articles of the true Christian creed as held by the Church of England and denounced all others, especially those of the Papists, So-

cinians, and Quakers, the doctrines of the last of whom he called 'wicked and damnable.' Penn was stung by its severity towards the Quakers, and he replied to it in a fierce attack called *The Guide Mistaken.* The falsity of the Guide's religion, his uncharitable accusations, his hypocrisy, and his contradictions are 'confuted, reprehended, detested, and compared.'

Some Presbyterians enjoyed Penn's attack on the Anglicans and attended a Quaker meeting to hear more of it; there, they were 'convinced' of the Truth as the Quakers saw it and desired to unite with their society. But their pastor, Thomas Vincent, denounced the Quakers' doctrines in unmeasured terms. This denunciation led to a hot debate between him and Penn, and to Penn's next pamphlet, *The Sandy Foundation Shaken.* In the latter, Penn took up the refutation of the doctrines of the trinity, of eternal damnation without a plenary satisfaction, and of the justification of sinners by imputed righteousness. His reasoning was so cogent that the minister demanded Penn's punishment, which led to his imprisonment in the Tower; and even Pepys declared: 'So home, and there Pelling [his apothecary, book-providing friend] hath got me W. Pen's book against the Trinity. I got my wife to read it to me, and I find it so well writ as, I think, it is too good for him ever to have writ it; and it is a serious sort of book, and not fit for every body to read. So to supper and to bed.' Pepys' contemporary diarist, Evelyn, was more severe and denounced it as 'a blasphemous book against the Deity of our Blessed Lord.'

The Sandy Foundation Shaken having caused Penn's imprisonment, his next pamphlet helped to cause his release. This was entitled—appropriately for its imprisoned author—*Innocency with her Open Face.* This was not a retraction of the views stated in the former book, but an amplification of them clothed in much of the orthodox theological phraseology of the time.

Besides his controversial books and pamphlets, Penn wrote numerous letters which were also distributed in print. Some of these were quite as full of heat as the former. In a letter from Newgate in 1671, addressed to 'My ingenious Friend,' a Roman Catholic who had written him a resentful letter, he begins by saying: 'I am perswaded I was cooler when I read thy Letter than thou wast when thou writ'st it . . . ; scolding I utterly abhor, and have been ever bred a Step above so great Rudeness.' But he proceeds to condemn his correspondent's letter as 'an Earnest of a Romish Smithfield Bargain,' and expresses amazement that 'so ingenious Person as thyself should ever play the Bigot for a Religion that never yet dare stand the Test of being read in known, I mean in Vulgar Languages.' A few years later (1675), he wrote another letter to a Roman Catholic, in which he denounced the Church of Rome for having lost its chastity, and become 'the Great Whore that look'd like the Lamb's Bride, Christ's Church, but was not.'

To doctors of divinity, noblemen, persecuting justices of the peace and those with whom he had oral debates, Penn's scathing letters went. The Vice Chancellor of Oxford University incurred his resentment when on a visit to the Quakers in his old college town, a few weeks after his own imprisonment (due chiefly to the persecution of university-trained men) about eight years after his own expulsion from the Oxford world of learning. This university head had set up a system of espionage, blackmail, 'ragging' by the students and cruel imprisonment, against the Quakers, whose chief offence in his eyes was their rejection of human learning and ordination as a necessary qualification for gospel ministry. The letter which Penn wrote to the Vice Chancellor was couched in 'terms unworthy of a Christian gentleman today,' as one friendly biographer [John Stoughton] characterized it; or in 'the downright and somewhat unaccountable language of the time,' as another equally friendly one [Mrs. Colquhoun Grant] describes it. Possibly thinking of him as clothed in a little brief authority, Penn addressed him as 'Poor Mushroom, Wilt thou war against the Lord? . . . Dost thou think to escape His fierce Wrath and dreadful Vengeance for thy ungodly and illegal Persecution of his poor Children? . . . He hath decreed to exalt Himself by *us,* and to propagate His Gospel to the Ends of the Earth. . . . Repent of thy proud, peevish, and Bitter Actings.'

Other, anonymous authors fared severely at his hands. One published what Penn called 'A pretended Answer to the Tryal of W. Penn and W. Mead, &c. writ and subscrib'd S.S.;' and he wrote from Newgate prison a reply to it entitled **Truth rescued from Imposture, or A Brief Reply to a meer Rhapsody of Lies, Folly and Slander.** On the title-page of this, he placed the provocative texts: 'A Fools Lips enter into Contention, and his Mouth calleth for Strokes (Prov. 18.6); A Whip for the Horse, a Bridle for the Ass, and a Rod for the Fool's Back (Prov. 26.3).' One of the most infamous of all Men; his Fardle of Impostures and Abuse; scurrilous, false, ridiculous, peevish: such are the harsh words with which Penn opens his thirty-five folio pages of indignant affirmations and bitter personalities.

Of **A Brief Answer to a False and Foolish Libel,** Penn says: 'Reader, the Petulancy of some Adversary or other has given occasion for this little Treatise.' He then answers one by one the accusations of the anonymous author against the Quakers, which he denounces as 'the Mistakes of his Ignorance and the Reflections of his Malice.'

To an anonymous author who wrote an attack upon the Quakers, entitled *The Spirit of the Quakers Tried,* Penn wrote a reply entitled **The Spirit of Truth Vindicated,** in which he condemned the attack as full of 'error and envy,' 'a late malicious libel,' and its author as 'filled with nothing but disingenious [sic] Reflection, empty Stories, and unprofitable Cavils about a few Scriptures.' Although he said he 'designed not to be long,' Penn wrote sixty-one folio pages of refutation and confutation!

Other anonymous authors of attacks on the Quakers in several issues of a London magazine called *The Athenian Mercury,* Penn answered in a pamphlet entitled **The New Athenians no noble Bereans.** This was written a score of years after his first controversial works; and there is pathos in the fact that the new Athenians [Londoners], like those of old, could not be convinced of the truth, no matter how plainly and frequently he might state it. Unlike the nobler Bereans, they continued to charge all the old famil-

Penn's father, Admiral Sir William Penn.

iar falsehoods upon the Quakers; and Penn, who was then experiencing his own persecution upon false charges, wrote more sorrowfully than bitterly in reply. Seven years later still, a pamphlet entitled *A brief Discovery* was published by Norfolkshire clergymen (Dr. Edward Beckham and others), repeating and even exaggerating the old charges which had been denied and disproved so often, but which they denounced as 'the Blasphemous and Seditious Principles and Practices of the People called Quakers: taken out of their Most Noted and Approved Authors.' In reply to this, Penn deemed it wise, in spite of his many previous answers, to circulate among the members of Parliament a brief document denying the charges; for the obvious intention of the clergy was to procure the repeal of the Toleration Act so far as the Quakers were concerned.

The Anglican clergy received most of Penn's controversial attention, because they had naturally been the most numerous opponents of the Quakers. Besides those already mentioned, Rev. Samul Grevill, whom Penn styles 'a pretended Minister of the Gospel,' wrote a 'Discourse'—against a Quaker book by Alexander Parker, entitled *A Testimony of the Light Within.* Penn called this discourse 'Un-Gospel-like,' and replied to it in **Urim and Thummim** maintaining the doctrine of salvation from sin by the Christ Within. A Lincolnshire rector, John Stillingfleet, wrote *Seasonable Advice* as to the methods by which the

'Unlearned Members of the Church of England' could get rid of Quakers in their parishes. A Quaker physician, Daniel Phillips, replied to this book in *Vindiciae Veritatis,* for which Penn wrote a preface. Two Anglican ministers, named Thomas Jenner and Timothy Taylor, attacked 'the Manifold Damnable Errors—, Vain Principles, pernicious Practises, and Blasphemies of the Quakers (denying the Lord that bought them)'; to this 'Rapsody of Slander and imposture,' Penn replied in **A Serious Apology for the . . . Quakers, against the Malicious Aspertions, Erronious Doctrines, and Horrid Blasphemies** of the two authors. The Quaker authors, Penn and George Whitehead, wrote this **Serious Apology,** which fact Penn explains by saying: 'Nor would I have the Man conceit it was his Strength of Argument that necessitated Two to answer it; since the Meanest had been more than enough. I am asham'd and troubl'd,' he continues, 'that any Man should live so long, and to so little Purpose. He recommends his Discourse with Sixty Six Years of Age, as if we ought to infer Verity from his Antiquity; not considering, *Bis pueri senes,* and that his Age gives but a more just Reflection upon his Folly, whose best Apology will be his Doting. Certainly he must have been very envious in his Youth, in whom the Flames of Wrath are so unquenchable in old Age.'

Penn himself records the fate of his rival's (Jenner's) book as follows:

> T. Jenner, a Presbyter-Independent Priest of Ireland, writ a Book against us for Gain; for he went from House to House of many sufficient, and some great Men, to present them; some gave him a Crown, some two Crowns, some a Piece; Among others, he had the Confidence and Avarice to go to the Lord Lievt. of that Kingdom [to present one]: His Secretary carried it to him; he turning it over, observed many black Charges of foulest and most pernicious Errors to Religion and Civil Government [as laid down]: The Parson still stayed [for an Alms] the Secr. thought he had favoured him sufficiently [in delivering his Book]: but not understanding the Priest's Aim, that is Lucre (the Old Priest's Sin) was prest to tell his Lord, that he waited for His Excellencies Answer: The Secretary was so civil as to answer his Desire; but when the Lord-Lievt. understood his Drift, he returned the Book to the Parson, with this Account, That he was sorry to hear that the Quakers held such ill Principles [if what he writ of them was True] but the Tares and the Wheat must grow together, till the Day of Judgment [or the Time of Harvest]. So the Parson was corrected for his Baseness, and disappointed of the Great Bone he crept thither for.

Besse adds in his biography the information that 'the Answer our Author gave to these Men, met with a General Acceptation, and it was reported, that Jenner vext himself to Death at it in a little Time after.' Reverend Jeremiah Ives, another Presbyterian, made of the Quakers 'A Sober Request' about the same time, which Penn 'proved in the Matter of it to be False, Impertinent and Impudent.'

The Anglican clergy often joined hands with the Presbyterians in attacks upon the Quakers. Among the Presbyterian writers, John Faldo, a chaplain in Cromwell's army and pastor of a congregation in London, was especially successful in procuring Anglican and Independent assistance in his attacks upon them. These included *Quakerism no Christianity,* which Penn answered in **Quakerism a New Nick-Name for Old Christianity;** Faldo replied in *A Vindication of Quakerism no Christianity,* and Penn rejoined in **The Invalidity of John Faldo's Vindication;** this brought forth *A Challenge,* which Penn answered, and *A Curb for William Penn's Confidence,* which Penn also answered. Faldo then called to his aid twenty-one clergymen of several faiths, who endorsed by their Epistolary Preface a new edition of *Quakerism no Christianity,* and Penn levelled **A Just Rebuke** against these 'One and Twenty Learned and Reverend Divines (so called).' The debate had now lasted four years, and Penn evidently decided it was useless to continue it; but Faldo replied to **A Just Rebuke** by another pamphlet entitled *XXI Divines Cleared of the Unjust Criminations of Will. Penn* (1675), which was brought out in a second edition twenty-three years later (a half-dozen years after Faldo's death).

Meanwhile (in 1676), John Cheyney, an Anglican minister in Lancashire, took up the cudgels against Penn's **Quakerism a Nick-Name for Old Christianity,** and wrote *A Skirmish made upon Quakerism;* to this Penn did reply, in **The Skirmisher Defeated.** Cheyney published eight more attacks upon the Quakers within the next year; but Penn left these to be answered by sundry other Quakers, who entered valiantly into the lists.

The animus of John Faldo in this long controversy is described by Penn's first biographer as follows: 'He perceiving some of his Hearers drawing off to the Quakers, and being sensible that every Sheep he lost carried away Wool on his Back, was grievously incensed: At length he gave his Fury Vent in a Book.' Faldo's books give evidence of his 'Fury' in such phrases as: 'A Thorow Quaker no Christian;' 'their many Usurped and Unintelligible Words and Phrases;' 'their near approach to Popery and their bold Blasphemy;' 'William Penn's false insinuations and jugglings;' 'the Snake in the Grass . . . or the Quakers no Christians.' Penn on his side did not lack for such hard verbal missiles as: 'the Synagogue of Satan;' 'Enemies to the Cross of Christ, and are at best but Carnal, Historical and meerly Outside-Christians;' 'all the Hideous, Devilish Falsities Satan's utmost Interest can furnish them withal;' 'the Foulest Charges of one of our greatest Enemies;' 'Forgery is his own beloved Crime;' 'Froth, Railing, Barks of Malice: Curs yelping at the Moon.' Penn was in such deadly earnest that he did not see the humour of declaring, in the very midst of such taunts of his own: 'My Rejoynder [shall be] without those insolent Checks, frequent Abuses and very vain and gingling Taunts he has cramb'd his Pamphlet with. . . . My Religion will not allow of a like Return in Vindication.'

An even sharper thorn in the side of Penn the Controversialist, than Faldo the Presbyterian, was a Baptist preacher named Thomas Hicks. This opponent published *A Dialogue between a Christian and a Quaker,* in 1673; and in the same year, a second edition and a *Continuation of the*

Dialogue. Penn, while wrestling at the same time with Faldo, immediately replied to Hicks's attacks upon the 'Quakers' perilous and pernitious errors concerning The Person of Christ, etc.' He entitled his reply to the two pamphlets *Reason against Railing, and Truth against Fiction,* in which he roundly rebuked (through sixty-two folio pages) the 'Dis-ingenuity, Prophaneness and Forgeries' of the accuser. Hicks replied in *The Quaker Condemned out of his own Mouth;* and Penn rejoined in *The Counterfeit Christian Detected and the Real Quaker Justified,* in which he denounced and disproved, by an appeal to 'God and Scripture, Reason and Antiquity', the 'Vile Forgeries, Gross Perversions, Black Slanders, Plain Contradictions, and Scurrilous Language of T. Hicks an Anabaptist Preacher.' Five of Hicks's partisans came to his aid in answering Penn's rejoinder in a pamphlet entitled *The Quakers Appeal Answered;* and Penn called to his aid George Whitehead in writing *The Christian Quaker,* while a half-dozen other Quakers replied independently to Hicks's various pamphlets.

The most important of these writings of Penn was his part of *The Christian Quaker,* which was devoted chiefly to his view of the divinity of Christ. . . . His pamphlet controversy with Hicks led to a debate with the London Baptists in general, and with several other Baptists leaders. Among these were John Morse of Watford, who wrote Penn a letter in January, 1673, which Penn included in his reply, entitled *Plain Dealing with a Traducing Anabaptist;* Henry Hedworth, whose *Spirit of the Quakers Tried* and *Controversy Ended* were answered by Penn in *The Spirit of Truth Vindicated* and *A Winding-Sheet for Controversie Ended;* Henry Hallywell, whose *Account of Familism as it is Revived and Propagated by the Quakers* was answered by Penn in *Wisdom Justified of her Children;* and finally, twenty-five years later, John Plimpton of Dublin, whose *A Quaker no Christian* was replied to by Penn and his two travelling companions, Thomas Story and John Everet, in a pamphlet entitled *The Quaker a Christian.*

In these charges and counter-charges, familiar epithets were used by the contestants, the accusation of Familism being chiefly resented by Penn, who charged ignorance and calumny, slanderous reflections, invective spirit, ungodly sly way of defaming, etc., etc., upon his equally tart opponents.

Amidst the wrangle and jangle of controversial contradictions, there occur from time to time, like oases in a desert, really splendid passages such as the following from Penn's *Wisdom Justified of her Children.* Since Hallywell, whose attack Penn is answering, addressed his book to a knight and baronet, Penn addressed his to the justice of the peace in the County of Sussex, to whom he says: 'I come not to you for Protection (a Thing he and his Cause wanted), but for Impartiality and Justice: Truth is sufficient to patronize and defend her own Cause from the Lash of Envy, without the weak Auxiliaries of Human Force; She gives Sanctuary to all that take to her for Refuge, but is all-sufficient to her own Relief from the deepest Pressure and most inveterate Prosecutions of her implacable Enemies.' Here is a passage worthy of Milton and his *Areopagitica!*

Two of Penn's literary opponents were not the 'inconsiderable wranglers' whom he had mostly to deal with, namely, Roger Williams, the founder of the Baptists in New England, and Richard Baxter, a leading Presbyterian divine. Williams was aroused by the invasion of his realm by George Fox and three other Quaker missionaries, and after a four days' debate with Fox's companions at Newport and Providence, Rhode Island, in 1676, wrote a book against Fox (who had 'slily' escaped from the debate), entitled *George Fox Digged out of his Burrowes.* After Fox returned to England, he and John Burnyeat visited Penn and wrote at his house at Worminghurst a reply to Williams, entitled *A New-England Fire-Brand Quenched,* Penn himself participating in the quenching. The relative importance of the founders of Rhode Island and Pennsylvania in the eyes of Penn's biographers, may be estimated by [Thomas] Clarkson's reference to the great Rhode Islander as 'a person of the name of Williams, then a settler in New England.'

In a preface to his book, Williams told Richard Baxter that 'through your sides, the Devil by the Clawes of this wily Fox hath tore at the heart of the Son of God.' This was the same year in which Faldo had called to his aid against Penn twenty-one clergymen, of whom Baxter was one. Incited, therefore, by Williams and Faldo, or perhaps because of the inroads which Quakerism was making among his own parishioners in Penn's neighbourhood, Baxter not only challenged Penn to a debate, but wrote him several denunciatory letters and signed a letter in support of Faldo's attack upon Penn, which called forth Penn's *Just Rebuke.* After the debate, Penn's five letters to Baxter appear to have closed the controversy between them, although they both continued—Baxter until his death in 1691, and Penn until his paralysis in 1712—to expound their respective doctrines in numerous publications.

Baxter, in common with many other learned men of the time, stressed the alleged resemblance of the Quakers to the Papists, while others confused them with extreme Protestant sectarians like the Familists and Muggletonians. The leaders of the last named were John Reeve and Ludovic Muggleton, who claimed to be reincarnated Moses and Aaron, respectively, and to be the last two witnesses foretold in Revelation XI:3, who would prophcsy in sackcloth clothes twelve hundred and sixty days. Reeve 'prophesied' through his pamphlets for nearly twice the appointed time, between 1652 and 1658, while Muggleton continued to pour forth his 'prophecies' until his death in 1698; and their followers reprinted their fulminations for another century.

The Quakers came within the range of the Muggletonians' fire as early as 1656, when *A Divine Looking Glass* was published; and this was followed by sundry other pamphlets, including *The Neck of the Quakers Broken: or, Cut in Sunder by the two-edged Sword of the Spirit which is put into my* [Muggleton's] *Mouth.* Thirty-five Quakers replied, among them William Penn, who wrote *The New Witnesses proved Old Hereticks.* In this, Penn proves the Muggletonian 'mysteries' to be 'mostly ancient Whimsies, Blasphemies and Heresies'; and he regarded them as the most 'compleat Monster on the Stage of Controversie . . . the blackest Work that ever fallen Men or Angels could probably have set themselves upon.' Penn paid Muggleton two visits and records, in several pages towards the end of the treatise, the very extraordinary conversation which ensued between them. Muggleton and his followers are finally dismissed by Penn as having no part in the peace possessed by genuine believers in it, who will 'possess the Habitations of true Peace when Muggleton and his obstinate Brats shall howl in the Lake that burns with Brimstone and Fire for ever and evermore. W.P.'

Muggleton wrote an Answer to Penn's *New Witnesses* (1673), in which he proved Penn to be 'an ignorant Spaterbrained Quaker, who knows no more what the true God is, nor his secret decrees than one of his Coach-horses doth, nor so much;' and he had already, in their conversation, declared: 'W.P. I say thou art a Damned Devil; remember Thomas Loe, who was the wickedest Devil that ever I knew, who never went out of his Bed after I Curst him.' This was Muggleton's farewell and benediction to Penn; and it may have been due to his excessive scurrility that Penn became increasingly courteous in his later controversies, so that he was able to say to a denunciatory justice of the peace: 'However differing I am from other Men . . . , I know no Religion that destroys Courtesie, Civility and Kindness.'

In fact, Penn's days of religious controversy through the press were nearly over. In 1675, at the age of thirty-one, he began his great work as colonizer and governor; and almost at the same time, entered upon his outstanding political championship of religious toleration. In the midst of these large and exacting tasks, he had only a minor interest in, and but little leisure for, the hot controversies of his youth.

The student of Penn's character and career, after reading of and through the bitter controversial pamphlets which were hurled from his pen, naturally seeks an explanation of this apparent inconsistency; and for it, various explanations are offered and varied excuses are advanced. Some of these accusing explanations are as follows:

Penn was rude and uncouth by nature, rough in speech as well as in writing. His treatment of so eminent a man as Baxter—thirty years his senior—is illustrative of this obnoxious trait, which crops out in much of his later writings. He was in fact only a skirmisher, a scribbler, a propagandist, giving no sign of any real greatness in his eccentric, noisy early manhood before his spirit had been tempered by the Tower and Newgate to a softer wisdom. Against this is placed his appeal to Baxter to believe that the Quakers wait upon God that they may have their hearts replenished with his Divine love and life in which to forgive their opposers and those that despitefully use them.

One biographer [C. E. Vulliamy] opines that he had inherited from his middle-class ancestors certain qualities which are not associated with good breeding! Another [Mabel Richmond Brailsford] thinks that the example of George Fox, George Whitehead (who at the age of thirty had written twenty-nine Quaker polemics), and other vehement champions of Quakerism was responsible for

Penn's extravagances! The lime-light of leadership accounts for his kaleidoscopic style, his breathlessly accumulating periods. The love of battle, especially in one who had so recently laid aside the sword and assumed the pen, showed itself in his worldly passion for controversy and caused him to use spontaneously the metaphors of war in his Bible Battles. He was in fact still Ensign Penn and not yet entirely Quaker Penn.

A feeling of personal revenge, a sense of wrong for the undeserved contempt and ostracism from the respect due to his ability, integrity, and social rank, made him virulent in his attacks on his own and his Quaker comrades' enemies. Penn's defenders would naturally reply to this, that if revenge entered into his writings at all it was for his persecuted comrades of the Quaker faith. In his *Truth Exalted* (1668), for example, he cites 'the many Thousands now of late that have been club'd, bruised, imprisoned, exiled, poisoned to Death by stinking Dungeons, and ruined in their outward Estates, contrary to Law, Christian or Humane: Therefore well may I take up the Lamentation and Reproof that was of old [Isaiah, 29:21, etc.].'

The spirit of the age of controversy is relied upon by others to account for Penn's severe polemics. Contentiousness was the common infirmity of his contemporaries. Frankness of expression was also a characteristic of the century. A spade was not only called a spade, but a damned old shovel; and 'damnation' had very positive meaning then. 'Fool,' 'blasphemous wretch,' 'Son of Belial' were verbal coins in universal exchange. Theological opinions were held in such deadly earnest that thunderous epithets naturally accompanied the whirlwind of controversy. It was marred by spiteful personalities, as the drama was stained by indecency, the most exalted literature (that of Milton, for example) was spotted by the crudest taunts, and even sermons were filled with sarcastic slurs and tremendous personal denunciations. Penn therefore entered unquestioningly into this battle of give and take, and proved himself quite equal to forging and hurling weapons as deadly as those of his opponents.

His unquestioning conviction of the validity of the Quaker interpretation of 'the Truth' made him absolutely certain that his opponents not only erred, but were the agents of the Devil in spreading false and pernicious doctrines. This, too, was characteristic of the age; but in Penn's case it was accompanied by an ardent desire both to confute false doctrine and to convert its victims (even the most uncompromising of them, like Ludovic Muggleton) to the true way of life and death. The sects contemporary with the Quakers, even those most extreme like the Familists and Muggletonians, Roman Catholics and Jesuits, were so often and so maliciously confused with them that their champion struck hard blows to shatter this harmful illusion. Throughout all the din of controversy, his supreme desire endured, not for victory over opponents, but for their conversion to the beneficent influences of the Light. He sincerely believed that he was engaged in a battle of reason against railing, and his method of attack was shaped by his defence of truth against rant.

That Penn was divinely commissioned to defend his young and bitterly persecuted sect, he had no doubt; for he regarded Quakerism as a genuine movement to restore primitive Christianity and the true interpretation of the New Testament. His was a struggle not only to prove that Quakerism was the fittest, but to enable it to survive in the bitter struggle for existence. When every man's hand was against it, and its principles were assailed from *every* quarter, an Ishmaelitish policy was the most promising one; hence Penn became 'the sword of the Quakers,' sharpened, unsheathed, and perpetually ready to do battle against their implacable foes. The Quakers, too, regarded him as a champion, endowed with many advantages and raised up by the Lord to wield sword and shield in their defence at a time when so many of their older leaders had been cut off by persecution.

It was not only against hostile sectarians that Penn turned his weapons; he was equally forward to denounce persecutors in the seats of power. Numerous magistrates became the object of his denunciation; and in the light of the system of 'justice' which disgraced the period, it might well be agreed that only swords as sharp as his would avail. Indeed, it has seemed to some students of Penn that by his ruthless attacks he was deliberately seeking persecution and the martyr's crown. To have lived in peace and quietness at such a time would have seemed to him, as to the early Christians, a species of self-indulgence.

The years of Penn's most numerous and most violent controversial writings were years of comparative freedom from persecution by the government, and the many religious sects utilized the opportunity of turning savagely upon one another. The rapid increase of the Quakers at the expense of the other congregations led not only to virulent spoken and written attacks upon them, but even to demands by the sectarians themselves that the persecuting hand of the state should continue to be laid heavily upon the dangerous Quakers. Such is the familiar reaction from persecution to tyranny. But throughout the fury of this contest, it is heartening to find Penn remaining steadfastly loyal to his great principle of religious toleration. He proved himself indeed as fervent a champion of toleration as he was of the other fundamental principles of Quakerism; and it is due largely to his success in procuring toleration, that we of today can view with charitable indifference attacks upon our several religious faiths which would have caused Penn to fly to such methods of defending them as we may now be inclined to condemn as inconsistently violent. (pp. 137-54)

> *William I. Hull, in his* William Penn: A Topical Biography, *Oxford University Press, Inc., 1937, 362 p.*

Irvin Goldman   (essay date 1939)

[*In the following essay, Goldman analyzes the Quaker concept of the Inner Light as expressed in Penn's writings, arguing that Penn "is especially prone to confuse the Light with common reason or instinct."*]

An ethical spirit of individualism was groping its way through the events and circumstances of seventeenth-century England and America. It manifested itself not in a tendency toward ethical anarchy, but in a disposition to find in every individual the equipment for an independent perception of universal ethical truth. Every kind of dissent, political or religious, from the Reformation to the eighteenth century, was in its beginning a substitution in some measure of a faculty of the individual as an ethical norm in place of the authority of tradition and convention. Puritanism, though caused by circumstances to become frozen into an orthodoxy as tyrannical as that from which it revolted, was in essence an expression of ethical individualism. Within the Anglican Church rational theology, and later Platonism and natural theology, were manifestations of the same spirit. Quakerism was the most determined upheaval, and it asserted itself in a final resort to inner norms not only in religion but in politics.

Wherever the state of nature was regarded as a more or less primitivistic state, it was usually praised specifically for the absence of convention, political and religious authority, and dependence resulting from economic inequality. The Cambridge Platonists, the Quakers, and occasionally even the Puritans interpreted primitive life and character in terms of certain concepts of the ethical self which indicated an unconscious quest for an ethical and religious certainty no longer to be found in the authoritarian standards of the past. Accordingly all forms of ethical individualism were encouraged by the widely penetrating notion that the New World offered an opportunity for men to start new religious and civil communities completely purged of all the error, hypocrisy, and tyranny of emasculated Old World society.

The Inner Light of the Quakers is not much nearer a natural ethics than the most orthodox of Christian doctrine. But, like Platonism, Quakerism was receptive to various conceptions of natural ethics because it made the individual, rather than society or external revelation, the measure of truth. Once make the individual a direct recipient of ultimate truths and at once every conceivable phenomenon of the human mind stands a good chance of being taken for the inner voice of God. The best Quaker theologians at times clearly saw the danger, and fought wisely to prevent it. But even these theologians, in trying to convince sceptics that there is an inner light, illustrated and fortified their doctrine with such arguments and authorities as to lay open frequently a way to the belief that in order to be happy and virtuous, one need only turn loose his reason or emotion, or even his instincts. It was more than the mere wiles of a controversialist that led Daniel Leeds to declare that the Quakers were fundamentally like the "Heathen Deists"; it was more than an adversary's trick for James Keith, after his apostasy from Quakerism, to write a pamphlet on the deism of William Penn.

It goes without contradiction that of all seventeenth century Quakers William Penn had the broadest education and was the most keenly alive to the various currents of thought in his day. And there could be no serious contradiction to the statement that Penn had more influence than any other man upon the thinking of the middle colonies of America in the seventeenth century. Although he came to America but twice, and stayed less than two years each time, during the interval between visits and during much of his time after the second one, he was busy in En-

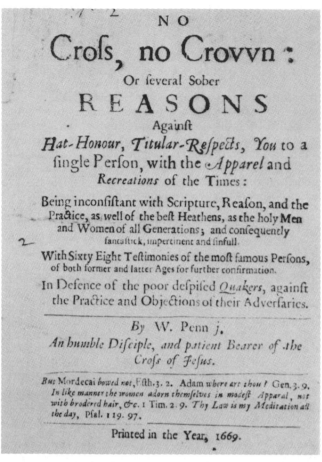

Title page for No Cross, No Crown, *1669.*

gland with the affairs of Pennsylvania. Several times he expected to return to America and was prevented by complications at home. His theological and political views became the basis for the constitution of Pennsylvania, and inspired the expressions of the Philadelphia Yearly Meeting of Quakers for several years. He was associated with John Locke in planning the government for Carolina; he had a hand in the settlement of New Jersey before he established the colony in Pennsylvania; and his authorship of the New Jersey charter is regarded by one commentator as "beyond doubt." He was not only largely responsible for Quaker settlements in the middle colonies, but it was he who stimulated the immigration of the like-minded Mennonites and Dunkers from Germany. And a contemporary adversary, Daniel Leeds, tells us of the influence of Penn's writings in America. He reports that the **Sandy Foundation Shaken** is "a precious Book with the Quakers." In England, he says, Quakers keep the book hidden for fear of the law; "But here, having the power in their own hands, they are bold with it." They announce in their meetings where copies are made available to the public.

The influence of Penn's writing in England was considerable. Miss Mabel R. Brailsford, one of his best biographers, declares that the **Sandy Foundation Shaken** "was hotly discussed, even in the most unlikely circles. The worldly Pepys, who was not charitably inclined towards

the Penn family, was moved to admiration when Pelling brought 'W. Penn's book against the Trinity,' to his house." When his wife read it to him, he found it "so well writ, as, I think it is too good for him ever to have writ: and it is a serious sort of book, and not fit for everybody to read." **No Cross, No Crown** has seen fifty-three editions, most of them of course coming in the seventeenth and eighteenth centuries.

Penn, unlike most of the Quakers, made use of his learning in his controversies. He studied the ancients at Christ Church, and under Amiyraut at Saumur, France, he studied extensively the early Christian fathers. In addition, Penn "knew and admired the prose of Bacon, Herbert of Cherbury, Cowley, Boyle, and the Cambridge Platonists." He was, according to [Luella M. Wright in her *Literary Life of the Early Friends,* 1932], a contributing member of the Royal Society. The teaching of Amyraut may be one explanation of Penn's tendency at times to confuse the Inner Light with natural powers. Amyraut believed that man should

> build upon the foundation laid by nature, the instruction given him by revelation; and to that end, while not neglecting the light which may reach him from without, it is the human conscience—his own conscience above all, which he must study and interrogate. The Laws of God are every where printed upon the heart of man, who is himself their true commentary.

1. Penn's Conception of the Light

Though it would not reveal the whole man, a strong case could be made for Penn's absolute orthodoxy as a Quaker. Several times he asserts his distrust of mere human nature. Though men have the Light of Christ to condemn their evil, he says, "yet they love darkness, they love the lusts and imaginations of their vain hearts, better than this holy light." "I say, is Adam silent in you? Is the spirit of man silent in you? Is thy soul, O man! *passive* and *quiet,* retired from all images, ideas, figures, or self-apprehensions, that thou mayest hear and discern, what God, through his Son, will speak unto thee?" "Man must die to his own will, inclinations, imaginations, and fleshly conceits."

It is obvious, then, that in his cautious moments Penn makes a clear distinction between the ethical faculties of man as a created being and the understanding which he has as direct illumination from God. He declares, after Barclay, that the Light is in man, but not of him. He disagrees with those who think the Light is a part of man's created nature:

> If by natural be meant a created thing as man is, or anything that is requisite to the composition of man, I deny it . . . But if by natural is only intended that the light comes along with us into the world; or that we have it as sure as we are born or have nature; and is the light of our nature, of our minds and understandings, and is not the result of any revelation from without, as by angels or men; then we mean and intend the same thing. For it is *natural* to man to have a *supernatural* light, and for the *creature* to be lighted by an uncreated light. . . .

Penn sometimes uses the Calvinistic language of the "yoke," the "daily cross," the "self-denying life." In his strictly Quaker utterances, Penn is fully conscious of a distinction between natural and supernatural elements of man's ethical constitution.

2. Penn's Platonic Bent

But in defending the doctrine of the Inner Light Penn sometimes uses the language and the method of the Platonists. Like the Cambridge Platonists, he refers often to the beliefs of "Gentiles" or heathen to show that the light is universal. This is especially true in *The Christian Quaker,* in which he declares, "For my part, I am of the mind that many thousands of Christians, at least so reputed, . . . believe not God so clearly, nor are able to give better reasons for what they do believe of him," than the Gentiles. A later section will show that Penn, like Culverwel, uses the American Indians to show the universality of the Light in a way that comes close to primitivism. In *The Christian Quaker* Penn uses the language of Platonists often in support of his doctrine. In one passage he seems conscious of translating the language of Platonism into Quaker terms. He observes that Gentiles believed the fundamentals of religion "because God had imprinted the knowledge of himself on their hearts; or, in our Quaker language, that he had lighted all mankind with a divine light." Many are the Platonists of various times whom he quotes. Here are a few of the quotations:

> Plato: The LIGHT and SPIRIT of God are as wings to the soul, or as that which raiseth up the soul into a sensible communion with God above the world, which the mind of man is prone to slug or bemire itself withal.

> Plotinus: Man hath a divine principle in him, which maketh the true and good man.

> Philo: . . . the divine reason we have from God is an infallible law; not a moral rule given by this or that mortal; . . . being engraven by the eternal nature in the minds of men.

> Clement of Alexandria: Man cannot be void of divine knowledge, who naturally, or as he cometh into the world, partaketh of divine inspiration; as being of a more pure essence, or nature, than any other animal.

> Origen: An immutable law; which with the knowledge of good and evil, is engraven upon the heart, and grafted into the soul, of man.

> Augustine: There is a *superior* and *inferior* reason. The inferior is a mere rational creature, or that understanding which distinguisheth a man from a beast. But the *superior* reason is a LIGHT, or, as it were, a power in mankind dictating, revealing, and enjoining divine, eternal, and entirely good things.

In this work Penn mentions "above all" (though he does not quote him) "Dr. Cudworth."

Penn not only finds Platonists helpful in supporting his doctrine, but he shows that he accepts fully the basic doctrine of the Platonists that something of the essence of God is diffused in the souls of men. "God is every where, not only very near us, but infused," he quotes from Minutius Felix. Man should be governed by "that divine, infinite, and eternal nature, which is God universally diffused or sown through the whole race of man." Defending Fox against an opponent who accused him of believing the "soul is a part of the essence and being of God," Penn (not improving matters much) explains Fox's meaning: "That the life God breathes into the soul of man, by which man comes to live to God, is something of the Divine Being; not that the soul, as a created capacity, without that inspiration, is a part of God, or of his Divine Being." This difficult distinction would be for the layman a distinction without a difference; for in either case the "soul is a part of the essence and being of God," no matter how it gets to be so. In another place Penn's acceptance of Platonism is still more clearly shown. In a defense of the Duke of Buckingham's "Book of Religion and Worship," a surprising venture for any Quaker, Penn quotes Buckingham:

> That Man only, of all other Creatures, having had Conceptions, at least, Suspicions of a *Deity,* and another World; It is probable there is *something nearer a Kin to the Nature of God in Man,* than in any other Animal whatsoever; and that *Instinct of a Deity,* ought to be our Guide and Director, in chusing the Best Way for our Religious Worship of God.

The Duke's adversary had declared that this "Instinct" would as readily plead for Pythagoras' *Golden Verses* as for St. Paul's *Epistles.* Penn retorts that it would be no dishonor to the Instinct that Pythagoras is so far approved by it. It is well known, says Penn, "how Fruitful the Doctrine of Idea is, to the Defence of the Duke's Instinct."

3. Reason as a Guide

As a Quaker Penn believes the Light is not a part of man's nature except in the sense that no man is without it. His Platonic vein leads him to the conclusion that there is diffused in man's spiritual nature the very essence of divine being; so that (all human propensions being ultimately of divine origin) any arbitrary distinction between the natural and the supernatural ethical propulsions would be meaningless. But in his rationalistic moments Penn seems unaware of the importance of considering reason as synonymous with the Light, and encourages the conclusion that the natural reason as a created power is the ultimate criterion in ethical matters.

Penn's defense of such a treatise as Buckingham's is in itself evidence that he did not always take care to distinguish clearly between the natural instinct or the natural reason and the Inner Light. When his Quakerism needed defense, he was sometimes careful to show a difference; but when he was expressing his doctrine positively there is not only a failure to distinguish, but occasionally even a patent confusion. Where the definition is made, it is theoretical rather than practical, and needs the aid of concrete illustration; as when Penn says, "our natural rational faculty is our *sight,* but not our *light:* that by which we discern and judge what the divine light shews us, viz. *good* from *evil,* and *error* from *truth.*" Light is to reason what the sun is to the eye. Even when he is conscious of the supernatural quality of the Light he, like the Cambridge Platonists, sanctions the use of the term *Reason* for it. When the adversary of the Duke of Buckingham says that the Divine Instinct can be nothing but reason, and that reason is an "arrant Strumpet," Penn immediately comes to the defense of reason:

> Now the little Skill I have in Books, tells me . . . : That Superstition and Idolatry are the most Unreasonable Things in the World; that they could never Bribe Her [Reason] at any Time; and 'till Sensuality had darkened and overlaid Men's Reason, It was impossible for Superstition and Idolatry to obtain that Empire, that in Prejudice of Reason, they have at any Time got upon the Belief of any Part of Mankind.

We must not condemn Reason because of "all the ill Things, that Men pretending to it, have committed." The adversary's own resort to Reason "shews the Nature and Power of Reason, that it will rise to it's own Evidence and Vindication, even in the most Unreasonable Men."

In two of his ablest early tracts on Quaker doctrine [*Sandy Foundation Shaken* and *The Christian Quaker*], Penn with utter frankness appeals largely to reason to establish his doctrine of the Inner Light. He sees the full consequences of the Reformation, and is willing to accept Luther's attack on tradition "at the bar of his private judgment." Even if the Scriptures told nothing on the subject of imputed righteousness, he says, the idea would be so repugnant to "right reason" that "who had not veiled his understanding with the dark suggestions of unwarrantable tradition, or contracted his judgment to the implicit apprehensions of some over-valued acquaintance, might with great facility discriminate to a full resolution in this point." His refutation of the doctrine of imputed righteousness is thus grounded upon neither Scripture nor Inner Light, but upon a rational conception of Deity. Like Channing, he feels that, although "the ways of God to man" may not all be understandable, there can be nothing in God's nature that actually repels man's reason. He refuses to believe "That it was unworthy of God to pardon, but not to inflict punishment on the innocent, or require a satisfaction where there was nothing due." Such a belief "entirely deprives God of that Praise which is owing to his greatest love and goodness."

It is hard to believe that at heart Penn was greatly concerned about differences between the Light and the rational faculty. A series of quotations which he uses in *The Christian Quaker* should be sufficient to show his indifference:

> Plutarch: [The light is] a law not written in tables or books, but dwelling in the mind always, as a living rule, which never permits the soul to be destitute of an interior guide. . . . To debase this ancient faith of mankind, and natural belief, which is planted in all reasonable souls, is to overthrow the strong and everlasting foundation of virtue.

> Lactantius: That law is pure and unspotted REASON (not inconsonant with, nor unintelligible by, NATURE) diffused through all the world; in itself unchangeable and eternal.

> Zeno: The chief good therefore is to square our lives according to the knowledge given us from the Eternal Being, when the soul, entering into the path of virtue, walketh by the steps and guidance of right reason, and followeth God.

The Great Case of Liberty of Conscience (1670) explains the process by which Christian faith is acquired, and the basic faculty employed is reason. In order to believe,

> we must first will; to will, we must judge; to judge any thing we must first understand: if then we cannot be said to understand any thing against our understanding; no more can we judge, will, or believe against our understanding. . . . take away understanding, reason, judgment, and faith, and, like Nebuchadnezzar, let us go graze with the beasts of the field. . . . the understanding can never be convinced, nor properly submit, but by such arguments as are rational, persuasive, and suitable to its own nature. . . . it is faith, grounded upon knowledge, and consent, that makes a Christian.

To Protestant opponents Penn says, "Your best plea [against Papists in the Reformation] was, conscience, upon principles the most evident and rational to you: do not we Quakers the like?"

Wisdom Justified of her Children (1673) gives equally strong evidence of Penn's trust in the reason. An enemy has said that the Quakers deny the use of reason. Penn heatedly replies,

> This man dares swagger for *reason,* and yet cries out, *heresy,* as soon as he sees it. *His* reason is, *the authority of his church;* the *say-so* of some university doctor; finally *the works of some learned man*: and offer never so much reason and conscience against them, and your reason is *sophistry,* and conscience, *enthusiasm.* . . . God is the fountain as well of reason as light: and we assert our principle not to be without reason, but most reasonable.

Penn is ready to acknowledge a conception of God himself as the spirit of pure reason—a conception which Gerrard Winstanley, the Digger, had promulgated earlier in the century. He quotes a translation by Tertullian of John I:1, "In the beginning was reason, and that reason was with God, and that reason was God; by that were all things made." To Penn this "seems no foreign interpretation."

> . . . so that it is very evident by our adversary's denying and the Quakers asserting an unerrable principle to be in man, and the refusal of the one, and the readiness of the other, to be governed thereby, that not the Quakers, but their enemies, are unreasonable, both in their faith and practice.

According to *England's Present Interest Considered* (1675), there are fundamental laws of human conduct which

> immediately spring from synteresis (that eternal principle of truth and sapience, more or less disseminated through mankind) [and which are] as the cornerstones of human structure, the basis of reasonable societies, without which all would

run into heaps and confusion; to wit . . . 'To live honestly, not to hurt another, and to give every one their right,' (excellent principles, and common to all nations).

In essence this is identical with the Law of Nature of the Stoics. Apparently it can be relied upon for theological as well as moral truth. Like the latitudinarian Jeremy Taylor, Penn believes that men of all sects could agree on the fundamentals of "general" and "practical" religion, such as the ten commandments and the sermon on the mount,

and this being the unum necessarium [an expression almost certainly borrowed from Taylor], that one thing needful, to make men happy here and hereafter, why, alas! should men sacrifice their accord in this great point, for an unity in minute or circumstantial things, that perhaps is inobtainable.

The "sum and perfection" of Christian religion is reduced to a single commandment: "Thou shalt love the Lord thy God with all thy heart and with all thy soul and with all thy mind; Thou shalt love thy neighbor as thyself." Penn quotes Taylor in *Good Advice to the Church of England* (1687): "No man speaks more unreasonably, than he that denies to men the *use* of their *reason* in choice of their *religion*."

The ablest defense of reason that Penn offers is in his *Address to Protestants of all Persuasions* (1679). Even a Tom Paine could subscribe to most of these ideas:

Since man is a reasonable creature, and that the more reasonable he is in his religion, the *nearer* to his own *being* he *comes* to the wisdom and truth of his Creator, that did so make him; a religion without reason, imposed by an unaccountable authority, *against reason,* sense and conviction, cannot be the religion of the God of *truth* and *reason:* for it is not to be thought that he requires anything that carries any violence upon the *nature* of his *creature,* or that gives the *lie* to that *reason* or *sense* with which he first endowed him. In short, either convince my *understanding,* by the light of truth and power of *reason,* or bear down my infidelity with the force of miracles: for not to give me understanding or faith, and to press a submission that requires *both,* is most unreasonable.

Penn believes the fundamental error of Catholicism is that it subjects understanding to the obedience of faith, failing to see that "a man can never be certain of that about which he has not the liberty of examining, understanding, or judging." Penn could "see no reason why we should trust any man, or men, against the *eyes* of our *understanding,* any more than we ought to confide in them against the sense and certainty of the eyes of our bodies."

4. The Lessons of Nature

It is in keeping with Penn's faith in reason that he should find the observation of nature a valuable source of our knowledge of duty to God and man. In the introduction to *The Christian Quaker* there is an apologetic note which suggests that Penn is conscious of the radical nature of his opinions: "Socrates, That good heathen, if, without of-

fence to the professors of Christianity, I may say so, not only confesseth to ONE GOD, but, I am of opinion, they will think he gives good reason why he doth so." Socrates' "reason why he doth so" is strongly deistic in tone:

That God, not chance, made the world, and all creatures, is demonstrable from the reasonable disposition of their parts as well for use as defence; from their care to preserve themselves, and continue their species. . . . That God takes care of all creatures, is demonstrable from the benefits he gives them of light, water, and fire, seasonable production of fruits of the earth. . . . That God, notwithstanding he is invisible, hath a being; from the instances of his ministers, invisible also, as thunder and wind; and from the soul of man, which hath something with, or partakes of the divine nature.

Impatient at the scholasticism of the English universities, Penn advocates the introduction of scientific studies into the curriculum; for "*Nature* is an excellent book, easy, useful, pleasant, and profitable."

In his defense of the Duke of Buckingham, Penn is led to consider whether matter is eternal, or whether God actually created the world out of nothing. He concludes that even if we concede the eternity of matter,

the Wisdom and Power of that Being which dispos'd and fram'd it into the Glorious and Regular Thing we all see it is, shew Him to be what we call GOD, and *Us* that we should fear Him . . .

The Built and Skill then of the World thus proving the Supreme Intelligence, and at the same Time, that He is the Object of the Adoration of His Creatures, we are naturally brought to the Duke's next Point . . . viz. That Man only, of all other Creatures, having had Conceptions, at least, Suspicions of a Deity, and another World; It is probable there is something nearer a Kin to the Nature of God in Man, than in any other Animal whatsoever; and that Instinct of a Deity, ought to be our Guide and Director.

5. Primitivism

It is clear that Penn does not always regard the Light as a supernatural power. There are times when his speculation upon the innate ethical discernment of the individual leads him to the idea that primitive man has a better ethical guide than has a product of a traditional culture. If "the best Heathens, as well as Jews and Christians," have appealed from authority and tradition to some "divine principle in man, planted by himself," civilization has little to offer that would make a man wiser or better. By an attempt to force belief or disbelief,

Mankind is hereby robbed of the use and benefit of that instinct of a Deity, which is so natural to him, that he can be no more without it, and be, than he can be without the most essential part of himself. . . . What shall we say, but that such as invalidate the authority of this heavenly instinct, (as imposition and restraint evidently do) destroy nature, or that privilege which men are born with, or to.

One almost unequivocal expression of a theory of natural ethics appears in **One Project for the Good of England** (1679), which was written not long before Penn had personal contact with the American savages:

> I beseech you, let *Nature* speak, who is so much a better Friend to Human Society, than False or Froward *Opinion,* that she often rectifies the Mistakes of a Prejudiced Education, that we may say, how *Kind,* how *Gentle,* how Helpful does she teach us to be to each other, till that *Make-bate* OPINION (falsly called *Religion*) begins the Jangle, and Foments to Hatred.
>
> All the Productions of Nature are by Love, *and shall Religion propagate by Force*? If we consider the poor *Hen,* she will teach us Humanity. Nature does not only learn her to hatch, but to be tender over her Feeble Chickens, that they may not be a Prey to the *Kite.* All the *Seeds* and *Plants* that grow for the Use and Nourishment of Man, are produced by the kind and warm Influence of the *Sun.* Nothing but *Kindness* keeps up *Human Race*: Men and Women don't get Children in *Spite,* but *Affection.* 'Tis wonderful to think by what friendly and gentle Ways Nature produces, and Matures the Creatures of the World; and that Religion should teach us to be *Froward* and *Cruel,* is lamentable: This were to make her the *Enemy* instead of the *Restorer* of Nature. . . . What shall we say then, but that even *Nature* is a truer Guide to Peace, and *better informs us to preserve Civil Interest, than False Religion,* and consequently, that we ought to be true to the Natural and Just Principles of Society, and not suffer one of them to be violated for *Humour* or *Opinion.*

We are here given to understand that man has by nature sentiments of humanitarianism. It is as clear an expression of humanitarianism, I believe, as any to be found before Shaftesbury.

In actual practice the Quakers were probably the most humanitarian of all the colonists, but as a rule they did not theorize much about sentiments of beneficence. However, there are in Penn a few more striking passages which deserve to be quoted. He makes liberty of conscience, which is dear to the hearts of all Quakers, a requisite of the "natural affection" which exists in a "state of nature." By restraint of conscience, he writes,

> All natural affection is destroyed: for those who have so little tenderness, as to persecute men that cannot for conscience-sake yield them compliance, manifestly act injuriously to their fellow-creatures, and consequently are enemies to nature; for nature being one in all, such as ruin those who are equally entitled with themselves to nature, ruin it in them, as in liberty, property, &c. and so bring the state of nature to the state of war; as the great Leviathan of the times, as ignorantly as boldly, does assert.

Penn's **Address to Protestants** has an argument against luxury which offers as a main objection to extravagance the "abusing the providence of God" by failing to take care of the poor. There is another discussion of luxury in

No Cross, No Crown in which Penn makes self-denying charity something more than the duty of Christians:

> Well, my friends, if there were no God, no heaven, no hell, no holy examples, no Jesus Christ, in cross, doctrine and life to conform unto; yet would charity to the poor, help to the needy, peace among neighbors, visits to the sick, care of the widow and fatherless, with the rest of those temporal good offices already repeated, be a nobler employment, and much more worthy of your expence [*sic*] and pains.

Finally, the clearest statement of humanitarian theory in Penn, again in conjunction with a discourse on luxury, is not presented in his own words, but in a quotation from Charron's *Of Wisdom:*

> . . . the immoderate desire to get riches, is a gangrene in our souls, which, with a venomous heat consumeth our natural affections, to the end it might fill us with virulent humours. So soon as it is lodged in our hearts, all honest and natural affection, which we owe either to our parents or friends, or ourselves, vanisheth away.

It is not surprising to find Penn, after quoting Charron, calling avarice the "moth of the soul."

Penn has much more to say on the anti-luxury theme, and on this subject he seems to have been profoundly impressed also by Cowley's bucolic essays. He probably takes more seriously than Cowley himself the idea that a life in the country, close to nature, is the most contented, inspirational, and virtuous life to be found. The following passage from Cowley is quoted in **No Cross, No Crown,** very early in Penn's writing; but he refers again to the passage twenty-five years later.

> What a brave privilege is it, to be free from all contentions, from all envying, or being envied, from receiving and from paying all kind of ceremonies! We are here among the vast and noble scenes of nature; we are there among the pitiful shifts of policy: we walk here in the light, and open ways of the divine bounty; we grope there in the dark and confused labyrinths of human malice: Our senses are here feasted with the clear and genuine taste of their objects; which are all sophisticated there . . . Here pleasure looks, methinks, like a beautiful, constant, and modest wife; it is there an impudent, fickle, and painted harlot. Here, is harmless and cheap plenty: There, guilty and expenceful luxury. The antiquity of this art is certainly not to be contested by any other. The three first men in the world were a Gardener, a Ploughman, and a Grasier. . . . We are all born to this art, and taught by nature to nourish our bodies by the same earth out of which they were made, and to which they must return, and pay at last for their sustenance. Behold the Original and Primitive Nobility of all those Great Persons, who are too proud now not only to Till the ground, but almost to tread upon it. We may talk what we please of lilies and lions rampant, and spread eagles in fields d'or, or d'argent; but if heraldry were guided by Reason, a Plough in a Field Arable would be the most noble and ancient arms.

In *Some Fruits of Solitude* (1693) Penn advised the reader to choose "God's trades before men's":

> Adam was a gardener, Cain a ploughman, and Abel a grasier or shepherd. These began with the world, and have least of snare and most of use. When Cain became murderer, as a witty man [Cowley] has said, he turned a builder of cities and quitted his husbandry.

Penn's conception of the natural life of savages in America before he had experience with them was conditioned by such views, and also by the reports of travellers. The universality of the Inner Light, he says, is "a matter of fact, which I have already proved, and the most barbarous of nations now inhabited, are a clear demonstration of what I say." Criticizing finery in dress and manners, he writes,

> Nay, such are the remains of innocence among some Moors and Indians in our times, that they do not only traffick in a simple posture, but if a Christian (though he be an odd one) fling out a filthy word, it is customary with them, by way of moral, to bring him water to purge his mouth.

The Quakers did not readily give up their preconceptions of the savages when they came to America. James Dickinson [in *Journals of the Lives, Travels,* [etc.] . . . *of Thomas Wilson and James Dickinson,* 1847] tells how he undertook to explain to an Indian how he could know God.

> I asked, If he did not find something, when he told a lie, swore or wronged any, that let him see he should not do so. . . . I told him the great God, that made the Indians, and all things, was a spirit and a great light; and appeared in the Indians' hearts in order to teach them to be good, and forsake evil.

John Richardson [in *An Account of the Life of that Ancient Servant of Jesus Christ, John Richardson,* 1791] tells that he and Penn had a talk with the Indians about religion. They found that the savages believed some of the basic doctrines of Christianity. He concludes that since they have not the Scriptures, their knowledge "must be by an inward sensation, or by contemplating upon the works of God in the creation," or by oral tradition. When he preached to them, they declared what he said was good. When asked how they knew it was good, "they replied, and smote their hands on their breasts, *The good man here (meaning in their hearts) told them what I said was all good.*"

Penn finds that, though "These poor people are under a dark night" with respect to the traditions of religion, "they believe a God and immortality without the help of metaphysics." Penn admires especially the expansive virtues of hospitality and generosity. He can see in their simple mode of living greater happiness and less guile than in the life of the Europeans:

> . . . give them a fine gun, coat or other thing, it may pass twenty hands before it sticks; light of heart, strong affections, but soon spent; the most merry creatures that live, feast, and dance perpetually; they never have much, nor want much. . . . They care for little, because they want but little, and the reason is, a little contents them. In this they are sufficiently revenged on us; if they are ignorant of our pleasures they are also free from our pains. They are not disquieted with bills of lading and exchange, nor perplexed with Chancery suits and Exchequer reconings. We sweat and toil to live; their pleasure feeds them.

Such reflections convince Penn that the Indians have remaining in them a distinct knowledge "between good and evil."

It would be impossible for Penn or anybody else to weave into a coherent pattern all the motley threads of thought which he picks from patristic literature, from the Bible, from Jeremy Taylor, Cowley, Charron, and the Cambridge Platonists, as well as from Fox and Barclay. Penn the Platonist can bolster Penn the Quaker so long as both can keep clear of rationalism. But any kind of ethical individualism is in constant danger of allowing supernatural sanctions to identify themselves with the natural reason. Penn sometimes drifts in this direction, and more often allows his readers to drift.

Penn, like other Quakers and mystics of the American colonies, begins with a conception of a divine light in every individual which is capable of guiding him in all matters of religion and morality. He does not regard this light as a natural faculty, but the shifting of ethical authority from tradition and convention to an individual criterion is in itself a step toward a conception of natural ethics. It is because of this trust in an individual sanction that the Quakers can go as far as they do in advocating separation of church and state and in standing firmly for a more democratic state. However, in questions involving one's duty to God, they intend always to resort to a supernatural faculty. But even in their own minds the Quakers are not always clear in their distinctions between the supernatural and the natural faculties. Penn is especially prone to confuse the Light with common reason or instinct.

We have seen that Penn held three ideas which predisposed him to advocate a more or less primitivistic mode of living: (1) Every man, however humble, ignorant, or simple, has a Light within him which, if heeded, will conduct him to true religion. (2) Every man, however uncivilized, has natural faculties of reason, emotion, instinct, or conscience which are capable of leading him to virtue. (3) Living close to nature and contemplating the beauty and order of nature can bring a man to a more devout appreciation of the glory and wisdom of the Creator. The tendency of each of these ideas is to minimize the value of tradition (even if it be revelation), convention, and all kinds of external authority, and to magnify the importance of all that is natural. Penn at some times permits these ideas to sway his judgment of the Indian savages. There is nowhere a frank admiration of the "noble savage" of eighteenth-century thought; but we can see the Quaker mind being well seasoned for the acceptance of such an idea. (pp. 337-52)

Irvin Goldman, "Deviation toward Ideas of Natural Ethics in the Thought of William Penn," in Philological Quarterly, *Vol. XVIII, No. 4, October, 1939, pp. 337-52.*

J. H. Powell (essay date 1944)

[*In the following essay, Powell provides an overview of Penn's writings and political philosophy.*]

This autumn [of 1944] marks the three-hundredth anniversary of the birth of William Penn, which occurred, according to our present way of reckoning dates, on October 24, 1644. Penn lived seventy-four years, and except for the last six, when mental and physical decay overtook him, he lived boldly, dangerously, and effectively. He was not one of that rare company of universal spirits whose achievements are the timeless truths of history, for he dwelt in the court, the council chamber, the market place, and even the jails rather than in the scholar's cloister or the philosopher's den. He was of the world, worldly. His days were spent with issues, with men, with policies. He played the game of political intrigue with consummate skill and remarkable success; he devoted much of his energy to developing and defending his extensive private fortune, which he never ceased to regard as one of his major responsibilities; and like any mercantilist he looked upon government as a means of attaining material prosperity and national power. Yet supporting his worldliness was a complex and highly vocal spiritual life.

Widely read, extensively educated, endowed with a keen intellect, Penn regarded information and ideas as weapons rather than as ends, as tools rather than as products. He had no desire for philosophic detachment nor any intention of rising above conflict. Indeed, he lustily entered into the most critical struggles of his age and fought with intelligence, understanding, and impressive courage. He was a man of action, espousing great causes in seventeenth-century England's long travail, and as the passage of time gives a permanent meaning to discrete instances of transitory conflict, so his various victories have lifted his name out of the turmoil of forgotten issues and won for him an enduring place in the history of human liberty.

It is as a man of action that Penn is remembered: as the rich and well-born youth who became the champion of religious dissent, as the one-time soldier who became a Quaker minister, as the moderate Whig who steered his course between the extremes of Shaftesbury and the schemes of Charles II, as a proprietor of West Jersey and the founder of Pennsylvania, as the missionary traveler in Holland and France and Germany, as the loyal companion who cheerfully accepted imprisonment as the price of his loyalty, as the dissident defender of Catholic King James, as the instigator of the Gracechurch trial, a landmark in the development of civil law. Pennsylvanians knew him as a practical and capable administrator motivated by exalted ideals of social justice; Montesquieu hailed him as the "modern Lycurgus."

Those who lived closest to him respected Penn for all these attributes and activities, but in their estimates they included a word which it would not occur to a modern person to use. They called him "scholar." In their candid way the Quakers did not spare him criticism for the deficiencies with which his temporal affairs were managed; nor was the failure of his mind overlooked in the memorials that the Reading Yearly Meeting spread upon its minutes when he died. He was greatly praised, however, as a man and a friend—"learned without vanity; apt without forwardness; facetious in conversation, yet weighty and serious—of an extraordinary greatness of mind, yet void of the stain of ambition"—and the highest encomium of all with which the Friends climaxed their tribute was reserved for his books:

> . . . he may, without straining his character, be ranked among the learned, good, and great; whose abilities are sufficiently manifested throughout his writings, which are so many lasting monuments of his admired qualifications, and are the esteem of learned and judicious men of all persuasions.

These writings, once thought to be "lasting monuments," are all but forgotten now. Even special students of the seventeenth century rarely consult them, and such were the prose fashions of Penn's time that today's general readers would find enforced perusal of many of them a cruel and unusual punishment. Yet they were very important to Penn, and they constitute a major part of his achievement. Surprisingly enough, this unusually busy man found time to produce, apart from an enormous quantity of letters and documents, more than fifty separate pamphlets and books, which formed a pair of large folio volumes of nearly two thousand pages when most of them were first collected in 1726. With this considerable amount of writing as a tangible literary legacy to posterity Penn cannot be entirely understood unless he is regarded as a man of thought as well as a man of action.

To be sure, the purpose of these writings was frequently to stimulate action. Most of the titles are controversial tracts associated with the obscure quarrels of early Quakerism, in which a modern reader's interest can be only oblique at best. Argumentative tracts are properly suspect as serious literature. But Penn was not at any time a trivial man, and his tracts, however occasional their motivation, were produced never in light mood but always with the highest seriousness of purpose. Special pleading undisguised though they were and created for the moment, they nevertheless evoked the deepest thought and most ardent application. "The end of Controversie," Penn once remarked, " . . . is the advancement of the Truth."

Indeed, it is their controversial, argumentative character which gives these writings their significance for us. From them we get the picture of a shrewd man defending in debate the things of life he valued. We see Penn drawing ideas from his reading, his experience, and doubtless also from conversations and correspondence and using these ideas as an advocate for a cause. We see at times the twisting and torturing of an argument of the opposition to suit his own purpose. And since we perceive no great original ideas or unique interpretations—for Penn was not an original thinker—we have in these works a fruitful example of the manner in which the thoughts of previous ages and the ideologies of many conflicts become pawns in social struggles.

Of contentiousness and argumentation there is such an abundance that those with a taste for polemics would find the pages full of excitement. But even sincere admirers of

The Tower of London as it appeared when Penn was imprisoned there in 1668.

Penn could scarcely regard them as great literature. They gain their effect cumulatively. Read as a whole, they take one inside Penn's mind and disclose the kind of a world in which and for which he lived. Of the half-a-hundred tracts only a handful are worth consideration individually as separate books. ***No Cross, No Crown*** (1668) is a blast against luxury, a preachment to the Quakers on simplicity and virtue in the most rigorous, austere mood of contemporary Puritanism. It has been occasionally reprinted and has had a long vogue as a handbook of moral teaching. Its importance rises above the Sunday-school level when its doctrines of frugality are articulated with the ideas of human nature and political obligations Penn expressed elsewhere. The connection between Puritanism and the economic theories of mercantilism has never been satisfactorily made; it raises worthwhile speculations concerning this connection to reflect that Penn was advocating for moral reasons the same sumptuary standards that the national planners, for quite different reasons, were recommending.

The Great Case of Liberty of Conscience Debated (1670) is the most elaborate discussion of toleration that the Stuart period produced. The ***Rise and Progress of the People Called Quakers*** (1694) is an acceptable history of the first decades of the Society of Friends which can be read as a single piece with profit and with some gratification, for it is the most accomplished in style of all Penn's works. His ***Letter to Lord Arlington,*** written from his cell in the Tower in July, 1669, is a trenchant bit of political argument that touches the greatest issues of civil liberty. The political student will find ***England's Present Interest Dis-*** ***cover'd*** (1675) a suggestive collection of current constitutional and legal doctrines regarding private property and its free enjoyment. It is an epitome of the Whig view of English history, flavored with the author's extensive reading in theological literature.

But far outshining all the rest, competent to be judged apart from the whole structure of his thought, are the productions of Penn's fiftieth year, his year of sequestration, when his political activities were suspended, his colonial enterprise seized, his personal freedom jeopardized, and his sect imperiled. In the tensions of the revolution of 1688 Penn had never forsaken his loyalty to James II, though he was three times called before the council to defend himself. In 1691 an informer betrayed his presence at the funeral of George Fox, and he narrowly escaped arrest. The next year (October, 1692) the government of Pennsylvania was removed from his control. For two years Penn lived in complete retirement, watched but not molested by the government. He was free on sufferance, only because the king had no particular reason to place him in custody. He found these two years uneasy and trying. All he had wished for was still at stake, but he could not fight openly without risking imprisonment, banishment, or even the execution that had been the lot of Russell and Sidney— any of which fates would destroy his hopes for domestic and colonial improvement.

In these two years Penn did his most remarkable writing. The man of action was forced to live the life of contemplation, to sustain the elevation of the spirit for a longer period and with less of the animating exercise of the sinews of power than ever before or (in his active life) ever again. What he wrote in this period may be regarded as the best of which he was capable, for he was then freest from the immediate pressures of conflict. For a brief span of months his motives were didactic, not political. Out of enforced detachment, of what seems to have been at times a desperate hermitage, he brought forth "this sweet, dignified, and wholesome book," as Robert Louis Stevenson called it, *Some Fruits of Solitude in Reflections and Maxims Relating to the Conduct of Human Life.*

"Man being made a Reasonable, and so a *Thinking* Creature," Penn wrote, "there is nothing more Worthy of his Being, than the *Right* Direction and Employment of his Thoughts; since upon This, depends both his Usefulness to the Publick, and his own present and future Benefit in all Respects." For the right direction and employment of thought he compiled his book of maxims, a work which is like La Rochefoucauld's *Maximes* in form and is reminiscent in places of Franklin's homely apothegms, with both of which it has frequently been compared. But Penn was in spirit neither cynical nor homely. He was appealing to the highest in men, with an ingenuousness that left no room for scorn. "His heart is on his sleeve," Edmund Gosse remarked; "he will take you aside, although he sees you for the first time, and tell you everything." He described his "Enchiridion" as "the Fruit of Solitude: *A School few care to learn in, tho'* None *instructs us better.*" The hustle and bustle of life concerns us so much, he said, that we miss the right way of happy living, "And till we are perswaded to stop, and step a little aside, out of the noisy Crowd and Incumbering Hurry of the World, and Calmly take a prospect of Things, it will be impossible we should be able to make a right Judgment of our Selves or know our own Misery."

Few books of the seventeenth century afford more genuine pleasure than this one, for few open such a window into the writer's soul. Its strength does not lie in its wisdom, for its insights are not exceptional. The maxims are the kind of thing a busy, successful man with no illusions about himself might say in looking back over his career. But they are said with such charm and such modest confidence, so ingratiatingly, so amiably, that Penn captures his readers in a conversational intimacy bridging the ages. The little volume is quiet and reposeful, strangely relaxed for one of Penn's robust moods—a book of philosophical poise from a man usually discovered in the front ranks of civil strife.

"There are some Men like Dictionaries," Penn tells us; "to be lookt into upon occasions, but have no Connection, and are little entertaining." Such men's knowledge is miscellaneous, and, while it may be wide, it is unified by no systematic formulation of the principles by which life moves. The *Fruits of Solitude* needs no unifying system of philosophy, for it serves itself as an expression of simple and enduring belief that gives system, meaning, depth, and stature to the manifold activities of Penn's varied career. The essence of conviction which, crudely understood, had guided action is here developed into rule and precept. We learn what Penn thought of education, of studies, of teaching; what he considered the true office of worship and the highest

purpose of religion. We discover that he preferred the country to the city, that he liked his art to be functional, that he thought government officials should be paid, and that he believed conversation to be dull when it was disputatious. We have forty maxims on government and many more on the characters of governors. We have forty maxims on government and many more on the characters of governors. As in Castiglione's *Courtier,* with which the *Fruits of Solitude* is worthy to be compared, the ideal social man and the ideal prince are both described. The one must rule with justice, the other live with honor. Freedom was the goal of the state, but obligations waited upon freedom. Penn was not fearful of power: "Where the Reins of Government are too *slack,* there the Manners of the People are *corrupted:* And that destroys Industry, begets Effeminacy, and provokes *Heaven* against it." Oppression would drive desperate people to rebellion; but "Where the State intends a Man no affront, he should not Affront the State."

Penn reached the plane of universals in his thinking, but throughout the maxims he used sentences so peculiar to his age that they jerk us back over the years and make us realize that we are reading a work of other times. He described the prevailing mercantilist idea of the division of employments in the state and wondered which calling should be favored. He had confronted the serious problem of labor shortage in his Pennsylvania affairs, and his preoccupation with this national difficulty led him to endorse a sort of job-freezing program: "As it is not reasonable that Men should be compell'd to serve; so those that have Employments should not be endured to leave them humorously." This topicality, this inability to remove himself from the problems of his age, was characteristic of the man. It would have been strange indeed had he, even in retirement, abandoned his intense convictions on current issues.

It was this same responsiveness to the stimuli about him that had guided Penn's hand in another work of his retirement, produced a few months earlier—*An Essay Towards the Present and Future Peace of Europe By the Establishment of an European Dyet, Parliament, or Estates.* This is a work that has a peculiar appositeness in 1944, two hundred and fifty years after its appearance and three hundred after the birth of its author.

In 1693/4 Europe was wallowing in the sixth year of a great war. England, led by her Dutch king, was the spearhead of opposition to Louis XIV and had committed the resources of all her empire to the struggle. "He must not be a Man, but a Statue of Brass or Stone," Penn declared, "whose Bowels do not melt when he beholds the Bloody *Tragedies* of this War, in *Hungary, Germany, Flanders, Ireland,* and at Sea: the Mortality of sickly and languishing Camps and Navies, and the mighty prey the Devouring Winds and Waves have made upon Ships and Men since 88." In his house by the side of the road, as "the Fruit of my solicitous Thoughts, for the Peace of Europe," he wrote the little essay that in spite of a certain quaintness stands as one of the bold and significant books in the history of peace thought. He examined the benefits of peace, which, he said, were never appreciated until men smarted under the vices and penance of war. Peace preserves property, encourages trade, fosters expenditures, excites industry, stimulates manufactures, and "gives the Means of Charity and Hospitality, not the lowest Ornaments of a Kingdom or Commonwealth." War, on the other hand, "like the Frost of 83, seizes all these Comforts at once, and stops the civil Channel of Society." Of all the means of peace only one—law—was sure. Law could keep peace between government and people; it could do the same between nations. As peace was the result of law, so law was the result of government. Therefore international government, "an Expedient against *Confusion* . . . the *Prevention* or *Cure* of *Disorder,* and the Means of *Justice,* as that is of Peace . . . ," ought to be created which would serve all peoples and all nations.

Penn proposed an international legislature, "a *General Dyet, Estates,* or *Parliament,*" which would make laws for all sovereignties and have powers stronger than any government or league could resist. He outlined many of the details of a constitution, letting his mind roam over the numerous facets of his idea. Some of these details are curious and colorful. The representatives were to meet in a round room, with many doors, so that no questions of precedence would arise. Voting was to be secret, so that the delegates, he almost suggests, could take their bribes from the highest bidders but still vote as they pleased. A three-fourths majority would be required for all measures, so that corruption of the assembly would be at least expensive if not impracticable. The records would be kept in a chest with a separate lock for every ten representatives, and there would be a clerk also for each ten representatives. No state would be allowed to refrain from voting on any issue, thus to prevent alliances and cabals, he hoped; and debates would be either in Latin or in French, "the first would be very well for *Civilians,* but the last most easie for Men of Quality."

There were some arguments against the plan, Penn recognized. Great states would oppose it; smaller states would hesitate to surrender their sovereignties; and, since armies would decay, careers for younger sons would be restricted. But the real benefits would far outweigh these objections. Blood would no longer be spilled; Christendom would become a peaceful example to the heathen; money would be saved; the ravages of war would give way to the prosperity of peace; international amity would result; the Turk would be repelled by a united Europe; and princes could choose wives for love rather than for politics. And so, Penn concluded, "till the *Millenary* Doctrine be accomplished, there is nothing appears to me so beneficial an Expedient to the Peace and Happiness of this Quarter of the World."

The great plans for world peace have come from a strange assortment of pens. In Dante, in Pierre Dubois, in the whole magnificent achievement of medieval Christendom the memory of the Roman Imperium, one state, one church, had been preserved. But the awful devastation of the sixteenth- and seventeenth-century national wars brought new motives and new problems to those who dreamed of peace. Penn, like Newton, stood on giant shoulders. Emeric Crucé in 1623 had proposed that all nations send ambassadors to a European parliament at Ven-

ice to settle those commercial jealousies which caused wars. Hugo Grotius, believing world peace to be the end for which international law should exist, had outlined a vast system of arbitration among nations. A hundred years earlier old Professor Vitoria at Salamanca had pleaded the rights of the people rather than of the sovereign as the basis of enduring peace. And the duc de Sully, while forging absolutism in France, had produced his *Great Design* of the federation of the fifteen Christian states of Europe, with a council empowered to raise an international police force. All or at least most of these proposals were known to Penn. As their propounders had been moved by the contemplation of other wars, so Penn in writing his *Essay* was moved by the prolonged struggle of his time against Louis of France; and in like manner the Abbé de Saint Pierre, Leibnitz, Kant, Bentham, and later Woodrow Wilson and still later Clarence Streit were prompted to formulate for their warring worlds their various designs for peace. Penn made no claim to originality. Indeed, he declared that he was only urging what Sully had proposed and what the federated history of the Dutch Provinces had proved could be done—merely putting an old idea "into the Common Light for the Peace and Prosperity of *Europe.*"

But new or old, the ideal of the universal dominion of peace and the erection of effective machinery to establish it was a worthy cause to champion. Penn's advocacy has won him the "esteem of learned and judicious men of all persuasions."

Penn was at his best in the two works of his retirement under discussion. Had he never written anything else, his reputation as both thinker and stylist would doubtless have been greater than it is and we should regret the paucity of his production. But we have so much from his pen that we have now to regret that he did not in the balance of his writing maintain the intensity and depth of the *Essay,* the charm and breadth of the *Fruits of Solitude.* I propose not to examine any other work in detail but rather to try from a survey of the whole of his writing to draw a few general conclusions as to his literary and intellectual habiliments, his notions of the political structure of liberty, and the pattern of his thinking on man and the state.

Penn was not an original thinker; this we have already perceived in the *Essay,* and it may be seen throughout his other works as well. But it does not follow that he was the eclectic representative of the dominant ideas of his age. He was a man with a cause who approached his cause with a bias. To compare his writings with John Locke's is to recognize the great gulf which could separate two Whig leaders with many goals in common. Penn was the proponent of a very particular point of view, a much more restricted one than Locke's and one with which very few of the leading minds of his time could have precise agreement. He was a theological student of considerable attainment, but he was disputing political questions, for which his reading had not thoroughly equipped him. A study of the books in his library and a careful listing of all the authors whose works he quoted or to whom he referred produces a very long but a very curious collection of writers. One concludes that Penn must have been a voracious reader but not a systematic or a selective one; that he did not know a surprising number of the principal works of political thought but that he did know a surprising number even of obscure books on ancient and modern religions, travel, and science, sometimes of indifferent merit. He combined with rather undiscriminating reading habits a thorough familiarity with the history of English law and the leading constitutional texts. As a result of his miscellaneous learning and of the fact that his ideas were tempered in controversy the several recurring motifs running through his works omit some of the leading typical ideas of his times, while they include some that seem scarcely of general application. Perhaps this is one reason why Penn did not influence the thought of the eighteenth century as extensively as did Locke.

Another reason lies in the fact that Penn was essentially a conservative thinker, seeking to preserve the interests of a man of property in a political order based on property, convinced that the English monarchy was the safest guarantee of property that existed. He believed that the "men of estates" gave stability to society. He even attributed the success of Pennsylvania to its beginnings by men of wealth. He was by no means the only Quaker of great property; indeed, there were some forty other conspicuously rich Friends who associated with him as investors in colonial adventures. But the spectacle of a wealthy courtier involved in dissent with the most radical of sects remained incomprehensible to many. "I vow Mr. Penn I am sorry for you," said Sir John Robinson, lieutenant of the Tower, as he committed Penn to prison. "You are an ingenious gentleman, all the world must allow and do allow you that, and you have a plentiful estate. Why should you render yourself unhappy by associating with such a simple people?" Had Sir John known history better or understood human nature more thoroughly than he did, he could have answered his own question, for society has never been without its rich adherents of the lower classes. Motives of philanthropy and benevolence, of enthusiasm and sympathy, are difficult to explain, but they exist. Yet first of all Penn was a man of estate with property to maintain. He wished on the one hand to secure equality and recognition for the Society of Friends but on the other to receive a guaranty of the inviolability of his property, a sort of security in which toleration and economic liberty prevailed side by side harmoniously. With these two criteria, toleration and security, the one economic but full of ethical content, the other ethical but big with political and economic implications, he measured society. They were the large values he formed from groups of small values. Somehow he succeeded in ejecting incompatible elements and in welding the two together in a social program. In the homeliest terms, he ate his intellectual cake and had it too.

There was every reason why the seventeenth-century Quaker should have been on the most advanced fringe of social thinking. His religious belief, his social position, his economic status, and the disabilities he suffered might well have placed him among the group whose aim was the reform of political institutions and the creation of an equalitarian state. But the clouds of Penn's property interest that he trailed with him into the Society of Friends moderated his religious radicalism. There was nothing of the Leveller in his thinking; nothing of the equalitarianism of Overton, the communism of Walwyn, or the socialism of Chamberlen; nothing of the enthusiasm for realism and reform that had always animated "honest John" Lilburne. Penn belonged rather in the same realm with a man like Samuel Hartlieb, who also desired reform within the existing governmental and economic system. His program, placed along side that of Overton, Lilburne, or even the inoffensive Hartlieb, seems no radicalism but only a practicable, pragmatic, and rather mild liberalism.

There were, Penn declared, three fundamental rights of man in society—property, consent to laws, and jury service. *"The First of these Three Fundamentals is Property, that is, Right and Title to your own Lives, Liberties and Estates:* In this, every Man is a Sort of *Little Sovereign* to himself: No Man has Power over his Person, to Imprison or hurt it, or over his Estate to Invade or Usurp it." The English government was a legal entity, with legal power only. Law allowed it a certain scope. If it went beyond the law, it was exercising not legal power but tyranny and was not then truly a government at all. "Now the Law is Umpire between the *King, Lords and Commons,* and the *Right and Property is One in Kind through all Degrees and Qualities in the Kingdom:* Mark that." The laws of England, Penn observed, gave the most protection to property that there was throughout the world.

Thus Penn founded his political thinking on the subject's right to property and his right to share in government in order to protect his property. One's estate was conferred upon him by the "great Charters of Nature and Scripture," not by the State and certainly not by religious opinions. Was it not wrong therefore to deprive a man of his possessions because of his religion? " . . . my plain and honest Drift has all along been neither more or less than this," he asserted, "to show that *Church Government* is no real Part of the old English Government; and to disentangle property from Opinion." Penn asked the restoration of the traditional rule of the laws of England, whose cry had ever been *"Property more sacred than Opinion, Civil Rights not concerned with Ecclesiastical Discipline, nor forfeiture for Religious Non conformity."*

In a generation that had produced social radicalism of all kinds, invariably associated with religious radicalism, Penn embraced the latter without the former. A mystic like Peter Waldo of old, devoted like him to the primitivistic concepts of original Christianity, he nevertheless retained an affection for property interests more reminiscent of de Montfort than of Waldo, more suitable to a Hampden, a Pym, a Shaftesbury, or milord Bishop of London than to a latter-day mystic. At least it is certainly less than accurate to claim, as an historian has recently done, that Penn "was in advance of his time in the lengths to which he was willing to go in liberalizing the government and in safeguarding the rights of the people." It will not lessen our regard for the benevolent motives which actuated him to realize that he was truly far behind, rather than in advance of, many of his contemporaries in the "lengths to which he was willing to go" in governmental reform. Penn's ideal state was a paternalistic government assuring to subjects the "possession and enjoyment of their own." But the paths to social happiness were not so narrow as such paternalism, and we cannot but believe that the large body of literature which came from the lower-class movements of the midcentury strife and had its descendants in the restoration years made more thorough recommendations for political reform and met more intimately the serious issues of poverty, labor, and food than did the writings of William Penn, cast as they were within a frame of reference limited by the interests of a property-owning middle class. It may well be argued that Penn's program was similar to that of the great defenders of property rights who were his contemporaries, such as Locke; it may be advanced also that his ideas were more nicely calculated to secure at least some support than the extremist pamphlets of the Levellers and reformers, which would frighten a landed and mercantilist parliament into more severe repressive measures. This is probably true. It is true too that Penn is a more important character for us today than any of his more radical contemporaries. But shall we say the reason is that he reached closer to the truth or grappled more intelligently with problems at stake than did other writers or that he proposed solutions which could be worked out within the social framework already existing, solutions which the entrenched elements in society to which he belonged could adopt without prejudice to their dominant position?

If his characteristic defense of property was Penn's first political principle, his second was his nationalism. "I love *England,*" affirmed the Quaker, "I ever did so, and . . . am not in her Debt. I never valued *Time, Money,* or *Kindred,* to serve her and do her Good. No Party could ever bypass me to her *Prejudice,* nor any *Personal Interest* oblige me in her Wrong." He proposed that national feeling ought to cure religious disagreements. "I am sure it has been my Endeavour," he said, "that if we could not all meet upon a *Religious Bottom,* at least we might upon a *Civil One,* the Good of England." This was the end all religions could strive together to foster, but only by obliterating doctrinal differences could it be served. "Certain it is, that there are few Kingdoms in the World more divided within themselves, and whose Religious Interests lye more seemingly cross to all Accommodations, than that we Live in." Penn addressed a book to the question, "What is most Fit, Easy and Safe at this Juncture of Affairs to be done, for quieting of Differences, allaying the Heat of contrary Interests, and making them subservient to the Interests of the Government, and consistent with the Prosperity of the Kingdom?"

Penn felt that England had the freest government in all the world. Since "it hath pleased Almighty God to cast our Lot in a Kingdom, whose *Constitution* is more than ordinarily careful of the Liberty and Property of its freeborn Inhabitants," what foolhardiness was it which desired the overthrow of the established institutions and organizations of the nation? To be an Englishman was "to be a *Freeman,* whether *Lord* or *Common.*" This was the government which stemmed from the Great Charter of Liberties, this was the government which protected the rights of men, this was the government that stood between English Protestants and French Catholics, between English merchants and Dutch men-of-war. To renounce it was to lose all, to undermine it was to undermine the foundations of landlordism, mercantile wealth, private property, and all else which Penn meant by the word *liberty.*

The freedom of Englishmen came from the constitutional limitations which confined government to its proper sphere and preserved the private rights of all the subjects. Penn accepted without question the conventional doctrine of the social contract and the rights of nature which had attained general currency in the crises of the seventeenth century, but he accepted it with some peculiar reservations. While he did not embrace fully the discredited theories of the divine right of kings, he did assert that government was divinely ordained. Yet he was placed in the inconsistent position of opposing government as power when he sought to win civil rights for the Quakers. The reconciliation he made among the contradictory theories of the natural rights of men, the divine origin of government, and the oppressiveness of government as power is a foggy part of his thought, but it is nevertheless the key to his political philosophy. Government, he said, was indeed the mandate of God, but the all-important element was the purpose of that mandate: to achieve the good of the whole. Government was an expedient, necessary but not innately desirable, forced upon men to control the anarchy of nature. Every man had a royalty of his own which he lost by combining in government; yet by entering society he received protection in exchange for sovereignty. "And if he be Servant to others that before was free, he is also served by others that formerly owed him no *Obligation.* Thus while we are not our own, every Body is ours, and we get more than we lose, the Safety of the *Society* being the Safety of the *Particulars* that constitute it. So that while we seem to submit to, and hold all we have from *Society,* it is by *Society* that we keep what we have."

This philosophy was the familiar theory of the social contract. But when he came to the problem of political obligations, Penn departed in a measure from convention. The government on its side had duties of justice as well as of protection, and the maintenance of justice was the spirit of true government. The Quakers, he said, were enemies not to government in general but only to injustice wrought by governments or by anyone else.

> . . . we believe *Government* to be *God's Ordinance,* and . . . that this *Present Government* is established by the *Providence* of *God* and *Law* of the *Land,* and that it is our Christian Duty readily to obey it in all its *Just Laws,* and wherein we cannot comply through *Tenderness* of *Conscience,* in all such Cases, not to revile or conspire against the *Government,* but with *Christian Humility* and *Patience* tire out all Mistakes about us, and wait their better Information, who, we believe, do as undeservedly as severely treat us, and I know not what greater Security can be given by any People, or how any *Government* can be easier from the Subjects of it.

It will be noted that Penn did not claim the right of revolution, though the sentence just quoted might easily have ended with the assertion of this right of nature instead of promising "Christian Humility and Patience." The ques-

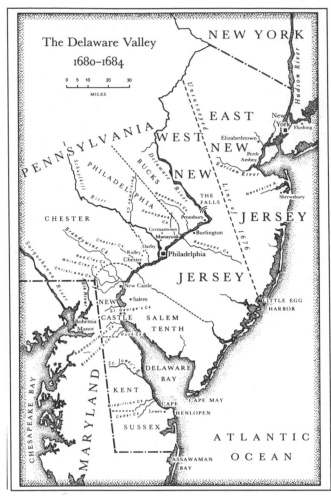

The Delaware Valley, 1680-1684.

the rule of law he was defending. Law must be supreme. It governed ruler and ruled alike. It was the glory of the English king that he was a prince by right, not might; by law, not power. "He has Power, but from and according to Law, not that he makes his Will and Power Law." These were the two alternatives in government: will and power, "Condition and Contract. The one rules by *Men,* the other by *Laws.*"

Laws were of two kinds: fundamental, durable, indissoluble, and immutable; or superficial, temporary, alterable, and circumstantial. The latter were "Acts, Laws, or Statutes" made by men to meet specific immediate problems. The former—"all those Laws, that constitute the ancient Civil Government of *England,* and which make up those two words, *English Men*"—were defined generally as springing from "that Eternal Principle of Truth and Sapience, more or less disseminated through Mankind, which are as the Corner-Stones of Humane Structure, the Basis of reasonable Societies, without which all would run into Heaps, and Confusion; namely . . . To live Honestly, not to Hurt another, and to give every one their Right."

Specifically Penn enumerated three privileges which were "the proper *Birth-right* of *English* Men":

> I. *An Ownership, and Undisturbed Possession: That what they have, is Rightly theirs, and no Body's else.*
> II. *A Voting of every Law that is made, whereby that Ownership or Propriety may be maintained.*
> III. *An Influence upon, and a Real Share in that Judicatory Power that must apply every such Law, which is the Ancient Necessary and Laudable Use of Juries . . .*

These three privileges had been fundamental with the primitive Britons, he learned from *"Caesar, Tacitus,* and especially *Dion";* the Saxons had preserved them in the principles of their government, and the Normans had shrewdly incorporated them in the great charters of the constitution. He cited "that great Father of the Laws of England, Chief Justice Cook" to support his arguments: "The Laws of *England* were never the Dictates of any Conqueror's Sword; or the *Placita* of any King of this *Nation;* or (saith he) to speak impartially and freely, the Results of any *Parliament* that ever sate in this land." Freedom had always been part of the English government; the governors were entrusted to preserve it, and "All Trusts suppose such a fundamental Right in them for whom the Trusts are as altogether indissolvable by the Trustees. The *Trust* is the *Liberty* and *Property* of the People; the Limitation is, that It should not be invaded, but invoidably preserved, according to the Laws of the Land."

The second privilege, consent of the governed, was necessary to preserve ownership and control of property against state power. Penn demonstrated its antiquity but was interested chiefly in pointing out to "superiours" that it was to their interest to foster consent. " . . . as *paradoxal* as any may please to think it, 'tis the great Interest of a *Prince,* that the People should have a Share in the *making of their own Laws;* where 'tis otherwise, they are no *Kings* of *Free-Men,* but *Slaves,* and those their *Enemies* for mak-

tion was so much in the air that we have the uneasy feeling that he was shying away from the logical results of his argument. But more was at stake than the syllogistic perfection of a logical system of politics. Penn was not only pleading the Quaker cause; he was also pleading the cause of property, to which revolution was abhorrent. He was trying to convince a timid governing class that Quakerism could be tolerated without danger to governmental institutions, that it could quietly exist within a state governed as England was governed. The question of majority will, the definition of general will, the matter of consent—these and many other aspects of his belief would have to be examined to throw the clearest light on his "stopping at the half-way house." Yet the Quakers did constitute a danger to the ruling Anglican and Presbyterian interests, a danger greater than differences in religious dogma; so our ultimate judgment of Penn will rest on whether we believe the kind of argument he used or the threatening gesture he might have used to be the stronger persuasive for his cause.

At any rate Penn felt his obligation to the state more important than those limitations his sphere of private rights imposed upon the state. He contended that this obligation was to the state as law, not as sovereign or prince. It was ing them so." He quoted from Ulpian and from Gratian and on the latter commented:

> It is then (saith he) that human Laws have their due Force, when they shall not only be devised, but confirm'd by the Approbation of the People. 1. It makes Men *diligent,* and increaseth *Trade,* which advances the Revenue; for where Men are not *free,* they will never seek to improve, because they are not sure of what they have. 2. It frees the Prince from the *Jealousie* and Hate of his People; and consequently, the Troubles and Danger that follow; and make his *Province* easy and safe. 3. If any Inconveniency attends the Execution of any Law, the *Prince* is not to be blam'd; 'tis their own Fault that made, or at least consented to it.

Privileges were necessary for the preservation of property, for if the great ancient and fundamental laws of nature so often accepted and ratified in England "shall not be to our great Pilots, as Stars of Compass for them to steer the Vessel of the Kingdom by, or *Limits* to their *Legislation,* no Man can tell how long he shall be *secure of his Coat, enjoy his House, have Bread to give to his Children, Liberty to work for Bread, and Life to eat it."

The above extracts have been chosen to convey the spirit of Penn's writings as well as the content; they cannot help but convey also the conclusion that the author did not have a well developed or carefully integrated political theory. There is much that is casual in his thinking, and there are some irreconcilable contradictions. There is a curious mixture of serious and trivial matter, and there is a strange marshaling of great moral principles side by side with the most worldly arguments. The mixed character of his appeal, combining worldliness, policy, and interest with the highest spiritual aspirations, is the hardest aspect of his writing for a modern reader to accept sympathetically. It seems to throw doubt on his sincerity, and it raises questions regarding his motives. The tone of his works led Mr. Russell-Smith to remark [in his *The Theory of Religious Liberty in the Reigns of Charles II and James II,* 1911] that Penn looked at the whole question of toleration from the point of view of policy rather than of religion. But I think one could as easily maintain the opposite position, namely, that toleration was the great lodestone of Penn's thought, that in his writings Penn was addressing particular audiences whom he knew well, to whose interests he tuned his arguments; that in the course of his pleading for toleration he developed as much of the current political ideology as was helpful to his cause and consonant with Quaker belief; and finally that he failed to formulate a systematic political theory beyond that point because it was not necessary to his argument. If this position be tenable, Penn's political theory may be regarded as a by-product of his advocacy of free worship.

Still, in those underlying assumptions that direct belief Penn had made basic intellectual commitments other than toleration. Even if we consider freedom of worship as the great goal for which he consciously strove, we must acknowledge that in his mind toleration was not an ideal separate from the stable government of the English monarchy or separate either from the stability of property interests

which that monarchy represented. His toleration was a nationalistic, middle-class ideal. Penn desired not freedom of worship in the abstract but freedom of English worship under English institutions. The significant thing about his motives seems to be that it was toleration he wanted, rather than revolution. "It is not my Purpose to dispute for Liberty of Conscience," he declared, "but to recommend it."

When we turn to the writings addressed directly to the issue of toleration, we meet with a familiar William Penn. This was the cause he made so peculiarly his hall mark, especially in ***The Great Case of Liberty of Conscience Debated.*** He argued for religious freedom on three grounds: reason (the rights of man), scripture (the rights of Christians), and history (the rights of Englishmen). Offended at the persecution of his sect, he warned that such injustices as had been suffered could not be endured much longer. ". . . we who are nick-nam'd Quakers," he said, "have under every Revolution of Power and Religion been the most reviled, contemned and persecuted, as if God indeed had set us forth in these last Days as a Spectacle to the World, to Angels and to Men; and treated as if, by being what we are, our common Right and Interest in humane Societies were forfeited." But even more important was the fact that toleration was theologically necessary to Quakers because of the doctrine of the Inner light. Penn stated this doctrine simply in syllogistic form. "Every man ought to Fear, Worship and Obey God. No Man can do it aright, that knows him not. No Man can know him, but by the Discovery he makes of himself. No Discovery can be made without Light: Nor can this Light give that Discovery, if imperfect or insufficient in Nature; therefore all have a *Sufficient Light* to this Great End and Purpose, *viz.* To Fear, Worship, and Obey God; and this Light is Christ." The Divine Principle in man went by many names. To follow the guidance of that principle freedom of worship was necessary. By intolerance and repression mankind was "robbed of the Use and benefit of that *Instinct* of a *Deity,* which is so natural to him, that he can be no more without it, and be, than he can be without the most essential part of himself . . . such [rulers] as *invalidate* the Authority of this *Heavenly* Instinct *(as Imposition and Restraint evidently do) destroy Nature, or that Privilege which Men are born with, and to.*"

What the Quakers demanded, Penn argued, was not unreasonable. By toleration they meant a liberty of the mind—the right to believe what doctrines they wished—and a liberty of worship—the right to act on their beliefs. Their coming together to worship would be without danger to the government or laws of the land and would result in their moral improvement and thus the moral improvement of the state. Religion, the noblest end of man's life, was the best bond of human society.

Penn directed his arguments at many targets. First, he exhibited that toleration would be advantageous to the king. The Declaration of Indulgence had granted toleration and had benefited the crown by doing so. Indulgence was no dangerous or obsolete thing, even though the declaration was gone. It was, on the contrary, prudent because it preserved concord. No kingdom divided against itself could stand. Toleration by indulgence made the prince "peculiarly *Safe* and *Great. Safe,* because all Interests, for Interests Sake, are bound to love and court him. *Great,* in that he is not govern'd or clogg'd with the Power of his Clergy, which in most Countries is not only a Co-ordinate Power, a Kind of Duumvirateship in Government, *Imperium in Imperio,* at least an Eclipse to Monarchy, but a Superior Power, and rideth the Prince to their Designs, holding the Helm of the Government, a steering not by the Laws of Civil Freedom, but certain Ecclesiastical Maxims of their own, to the Maintenance and Enlargement of their Worldly Empire in their Church." It well became the prince to tolerate dissenting sects because thereby he not only promoted religion, "the noblest end," but actually fostered its civil function, to bind society together. A prince who ruled with temperance, mercy, justice, meekness, and fear of God was assured of respectful and loyal subjects. And in the year 1686, with a Catholic king in England, Penn added that toleration was a security to the royal family.

Second, Penn held that it was to the larger interests of the nation to tolerate freedom of worship. Here he was striking at the controlling groups in the parliament. He admonished them again and again that there could be no conviction except by the spirit, that to enact sincere conformity by law was impossible, for "as no Man can inherit the Kingdom of God, *unless he be born of the Spirit,* so no Ministry can beget a Soul to God, but that which is *from the* Spirit." Intolerance would vitiate both peace and plenty, those twin goals for which government was instituted among men, because civil society could not exist if it was not the will of all that it should exist. Penn pleaded for equal rights for all dissenting groups, for an equilibrium attained by the pushes and pulls of many sects against each other. This balance would be the means of "overpoizing faction." Thus he conceived of a sort of federation of religions within the state, all parts of which were bound to the state by self-interest, the churchman for his bounty, the dissenter for his very existence which, "being the last of Tyes, and the strongest Obligation, the Security is greatest from him, that is fancy'd most unsafe to *Tolerate.*"

Third, Penn attempted to prove that it was the best policy for the established Church of England itself to tolerate dissenters and maintain a balance among religions. There were three "church interests" in the kingdom—Anglican, Roman Catholic, and Protestant—and he believed that the two dissenting groups should be played off against each other by the established church so that neither might become too strong in itself. Both dissenting interests would benefit, for strife would be governed if not ended.

Fourth, Penn strongly urged the advantage toleration brought to the commerce and industries of the nation—a new argument introduced in the years following the Restoration. In language designed to appeal to the business instincts of merchants, ship-owners, and colonial factors whose influence in Parliament was appreciable he warned of the results of intolerant and repressive measures and denied that toleration would lead to revolutions or civil strife. History had proved the opposite to be true. On toleration the empire stood safe; on intolerance it stood shaking, like a house built upon the sands. If intolerance per-

sisted, there would certainly be two dire results: impoverishment of the people and emigration of part of the producing class to other lands. If, on the other hand, toleration was adopted, prosperity would ensue and immigration of artisans and laborers into the country would be encouraged; for toleration fostered the useful arts and industry, attracted people to a country "where the Sweat of the Brow is not made the Forfeit of Conscience," and engendered tranquillity, which would "at a Time when our Neighbouring Monarch is wasting his People, excite those Sufferers into the King's Dominions, whose Number will encrease that of his Subjects, and their Labour and Consumption, the Trade and Wealth of his Territories."

Finally, Penn appealed to the moral interest of all in society. He pointed out that the Quakers were a useful, productive, universally law-abiding, exemplary element in the civil state, instructed by their theological doctrines in respect for their superiors and obedience to law and devoted to simple living, virtue, and industry in the community. They should be protected in order to preserve the profit of trade and commerce. The kingdom had been weakened by five sins against nature—drunkenness, fornication, luxury in living, profuse gaming, and profaneness. The teachings of the Quakers would eliminate these vices by a return to primitive Christianity, simplicity in living, and ancient virtue. The modern Christians could have none of the Quakers' character so long as they persevered in their vanity, superstition, and intemperance; in these respects it was the Catholic and the Anglican, not the Quaker, who undermined the moral foundations of the state.

Penn did not recommend the life of a recluse; that would have seemed barren to Restoration mercantilist and Quaker moralist. The Christian life was of a different nature. "What a World should we have, if every Body for fear of Transgressing, should Mew himself up within Four Walls?" The Quakers carried goodness and righteousness into all their activities, thus forming the part of society which should be valued most, for never was the hand of God raised against a righteous nation. "Kingdoms are rarely as short lived as Men, yet they also have a Time to die: But as Temperance giveth Health to Men, so *Virtue* gives Time to Kingdoms; and as *Vice* brings Men betimes to their Grave, so Nations to their Ruin."

The ultimate problem of political thinking, which Penn frequently had to tackle, concerned the fundamental nature of human nature. To Penn's contemporaries this question was particularly significant, since by the social-contract theory government was assumed to be the result of an escape from primitive anarchy. If in his natural, presocial condition man had been essentially good, then the civil state was a dissent from his goodness; but if he had been bestial and savage, the state was an ascent to a higher, nobler plane. Though Penn nowhere developed his ideas on this subject systematically, he often expressed them, and there are ample indications throughout his works that he felt man's lot in society to be richer, more productive, and morally better than his life in presocial nature. He spoke of the freedom that comes through obedience and of the elevated condition of the social man, using terms that remind one of the idealistic position of English writers of a much later period.

But Penn had as his principal concern man in society and the motives that move most men most of the time to do what they do. Very early in his work he hit upon an idea (fully explained in a tract of 1679) which he continued to develop throughout the rest of his writing. This was the concept of "interest," the belief that the individuals and the groups struggling with one another in society formulated certain persisting and identifying values which they sought to effectuate either consciously or unconsciously and which could be relied upon to predict their reactions to any given situation. Men had interests as individuals and in groups as well. Some were primary, some derived. The elementary ones they all had in common. "Civil Interest" was the basis of all civil government (a sort of will of all). "National Interest" was the support of the nation.

> *Interest* will not lye: Men embarked in the same Vessell, seek the Safety of the *Whole* in their *Own,* whatever other Differences they may have. And *Self-Safety* is the highest worldly Security a Prince can have; for though all Parties would rejoyce their own Principles prevailed, yet every one is more solicitous about its own Safety, than the other's Verity. Wherefore it cannot be unwise, by the Security of All, to make it the Interest as well as the Duty of All, to advance that of the Publick.

Interest was a mutable thing in life. It could change in substantial ways, but it always functioned in the same way, as the sure determinant of individual action.

> As I take all Men to be unwillingly separated from their Interests, and consequently ought only to be sought and discours'd in them, so it must be granted me on all Hands, *That Interests change as well as Times, and 'tis the Wisdom of a Man to observe the Courses, and humour the Motions of his Interest, as the Best Way to preserve it.* And lest any ill-natured, or mistaken Person, should call it *Temporizing,* I make this early Provision; *That I mean, no immoral or corrupt Compliance.* . . . For upon the Principle I now go, and which I lay down, as common and granted in Reason and Fact, with all Parties concern'd in this Discourse, that Man does not change, that *Morally* follows his Interest under all its Revolutions, because to be true to his Interest, is his First Civil Principle. . . .

Penn declared that the foundation of governments was the interest in government that men had and that when the government went beyond its function of fostering the interests of individuals, it overreached its own interest. He explained his terms thus:

> The Word INTEREST has a good and bad Acceptance; when it is taken in an ill Sense, it signifies a Pursuit of Advantage without regard to Truth or Justice; which I mean not: The good Signification of the Word, and which I mean, is a Legal Endeavour to keep Rights, or augment honest Profits, whether it be in a private Person or a Society. By GOVERNMENT, I understand a Just and Equal Constitution, where Might is not Right,

> but Laws rule, and not the Wills or Power of Men; for that were plain Tyranny.

The good of the whole was the "rise and end" of government, but how could a man determine that good? Penn answered that he should consult his own interest: he certainly would believe that an undisturbed possession of his property was a "good" for him, and "the Construction he makes for himself will serve his Neighbour, and so the whole Society." Hence the preservation of property was one part of the good of the whole which government existed to enhance. When property ownership was insecure, the government would be unstable. Where the line between obedience and interest could be drawn Penn did not know, but eventually the latter would triumph, even over the government.

In preserving the good of the whole (particularly property ownership) governments were but consulting interests they had apart from individuals or rather interests they had as the sums of individuals, for the "whole" would unite with the government in a general will for the good of the government. The interests of the subjects were the most potent force in society; the state was an instrument for directing them. Poring over English history, Penn proved by many examples the power of interest as a factor in government. All persuasions of religion were governed by their interests; they supported the rulers and the kind of a state which best served the interests they most highly prized.

But interest as a principle operated not alone in government. Several of the maxims in the *Fruits of Solitude* were designed to illustrate its importance in private life. "Interest has the *Security,* tho' not the *Virtue* of a Principle. As the World goes 'tis the surer side; For Men daily leave both Relations and Religion to follow it. 'Tis an odd Sight, but very evident, That Families and Nations, of cross Religions and Humours, *unite* against those of their *own,* where they find an *Interest* to do it. We are tied down by our *Senses* to this World; and where that is in Question, it can be none with Worldly Men, whether they should not forsake all other Considerations for it." Even art and literature were affected by interest. The biographer of the bishop of London, Penn remarked, concealed the bishop's sentiments in favor of toleration because it was to his interest to do so.

In Penn's use of the word *interest* we have what the writer conceives to be the most revealing indication of his notions of human motives. The term was employed so frequently, in so many contexts, that it became a sort of ubiquitous periapt in his writings. No consideration of his political thought would be complete without a notice of it. First let us observe that Penn did not mean by the term a materialistic determinism. The great business of man's life, he believed, was to glorify God. He abominated pride, luxury, avarice, and what he called "constancy to the world." He preached against display and against pleasure. But he did not despise commerce. The perfection of the Christian life extended, he felt, "to every honest Labour or Traffick used among Men." To acquire and enjoy property was decent and Christian. Interest, therefore, was not economic, though it did not exclude economic pursuits.

What Penn appears to have meant is that men act according to their notions of their own good, and if these notions are properly qualified by understanding, by moral goodness, and by regard for truth and justice, each man's good will result in the good of society as a whole. This was an optimistic concept, for Penn believed the generality of men capable and desirous of attaining goodness. It was an individualistic concept, which regarded society as the sum of the true, valid, or good interests of all individuals in it. Thus, by the way, it seems comparable to the "invisible hand" doctrine of Adam Smith, with the basic economic assumptions of Smith replaced by basic moral assumptions concerning the nature of human nature.

Of course the concept was uncompleted, and there was the possibility of a serious inconsistency, for men's property interest might frequently not coincide with their other social interests and with their interest to live frugally. An interest to "augment honest profits" has not always proved compatible with "a legal endeavor to keep rights." But inconsistencies in social theory were resolvable in Penn's mind by an appeal to the problem of evil, on which the Quaker had some very strong convictions.

Inchoate though it be, this notion of interest gives continuity to Penn's thought and suggests the heights that the author might have reached had he spent his energies principally in the philosopher's study. Dealing as we are with the works of a very busy man, who must be known as much through his actions as through his ideas, we are not unjustified in attributing to Penn a deeper consciousness and a more thorough understanding of political philosophy than he elaborated in his books. To place the writings alongside the public achievements and the private charac-

ter of the man is to appreciate the full magnitude and variety of the colorful canvas of life Penn painted. The nationalist—not in the grand manner but in the manner of the landowning, trading, entrepreneurial middle-class Englishman; the colonial proprietor; the Quaker leader; the staunch advocate of Whig programs of liberalism—is part and parcel of the man of thought. All taken together amply support the deliberate judgment of Lord Acton, that Penn was the "greatest historical figure of his age." (pp. 233-59)

> *J. H. Powell, "William Penn's Writings: An Anniversary Essay," in* Pennsylvania History, *Vol. XI, No. 4, October, 1944, pp. 233-59.*

William Wistar Comfort   (essay date 1944)

[*In the following excerpt, Comfort presents a detailed examination of Penn's* Frame of the Government of the Province of Pennsylvania.]

When William Penn sat down to write a frame of government and a constitution for his new province, he had plenty of available inspiration. Anyone with his interests would be familiar with the outstanding efforts to create an ideal government: the Old Testament, Plato with his ideal Republic, Lycurgus and his laws, Rome, Venice, the French absolute monarchy, the government of the Netherlands—all these were doubtless present in Penn's mind before he had any occasion to make use of them. In England there was More's *Utopia* (1516), Hobbes's *Leviathan* (1651), and James Harrington's *Oceana* (1656). A detailed examination of Penn's resulting efforts would reveal the possible origin of this or that idea which he incorporated in his own work. Especially is this true of More's and Harrington's ideal governments. But they were only two of many plans of government which had been conceived in western Europe since the Renaissance and the Reformation had liberated thought from the domination of the medieval church and Roman Empire. Democratic government had been the dream of political philosophers even under tyranny. None of these philosophers, however, had had a chance to do more than theorize; none of them had had to face the realities in a government for which he was personally responsible. In this unique situation Penn found himself. He must choose carefully and determine wisely what would be practicable. He must devise a government whose laws should be consonant with those of England, and still rest lightly upon a colony of lovers of religious liberty, in a wilderness three thousand miles away. Moreover, his laws must satisfy one fundamental condition, and that condition was a new one in human history: these laws must conform to the Quaker philosophy of life. (p. 132)

Already in 1671, in *A Serious Apology for the Principles and Practices of the People called Quakers,* Penn had found occasion to distinguish between "fundamental" and "superficial" laws:

> By the first we understand the determinations of right reason regarding moral and just living, with certain privileges that in the first constitu-

---

An excerpt from the preface to *The Frame of the Government*

I know what is said by the several admirers of monarchy, aristocracy, and democracy, which are the rule of one, a few, and many, and are the three common ideas of government, when men discourse of that subject. But I choose to solve the controversy with this small distinction, and it belongs to all three: any government is free to the people under it (whatever be the frame) where the laws rule, and the people are a party to those laws, and more than this is tyranny, oligarchy, or confusion.

But lastly, when all is said, there is hardly one frame of government in the world so ill designed by its first founders, that in good hands would not do well enough; and [hi]story tells us, the best in ill ones can do nothing that is great or good; witness the Jewish and Roman states. Governments, like clocks, go from the motion men give them; and as governments are made and moved by men, so by them are ruined too: wherefore governments rather depend upon men, than men upon governments. Let men be good, and the government can't be bad; if it be ill, they will cure it. But if men be bad, let the government be never so good; they will endeavor to warp and spoil it to their turn.

William Penn, in his preface to The Frame of the Government of the Province of Pennsylvania, *1682.*

---

tion are agreed upon as essentials in government: as meers, bounds and landmarks of truth, equity and righteousness, that as well confine rulers as people. By the second we understand certain temporary laws, proclamations or customs, that relate to more trivial matters, and that receive alteration, with the reason of them, according to that maxim *cessante ratione cessat lex,* of which the people and rulers are judges.

This distinction between general moral and religious principles of permanent validity and laws affected by circumstances and temporary expediency Penn will maintain in his later distinction between his "frames" and "laws." (pp. 132-33)

. . . [Application] of the four essentials of Quakerism . . . may be expected as follows: The equality and sanctity of all men in the divine sight will show in a democratic frame favorable to personal liberty; the universality of grace will appear in his trust of the natives and of his colonists; the search for absolute perfection will be the ideal pursued by Penn; the belief in continued revelation will be reflected in the revisions of his constitutions, as new light is granted. In addition to these fundamental principles, he will study the constitutions of other British colonies and seek to avoid their limitations. He will confer with men of light and leading, like his friend Algernon Sidney. He will accept some ideas and reject others. It was a stupendous undertaking and, as it turned out, of far-reaching consequence to future Americans. For Penn's "Holy Experiment" is not to be a feudal aristocratic state, like that of the Carolinas planned by Locke; or a narrow-minded Puritan commonwealth like Massachusetts; or a mercantile adventure like New York; or a private preserve of the Anglican Church like Virginia. West New Jersey and Pennsylvania were to offer the best chance a Quaker has had to apply his religion to the government of a state. Pennsylvania was for seventy years a Quaker exhibit, not perfect, but interesting and unique. The problem before Penn was a hard one, and not every Quaker would have solved it in the same way. But no other Quaker ever had to solve it. The ideal political liberty of the people was complicated by Penn's interests as proprietor, and by the claims of the Crown as eventual feudal overlord.

The period of Penn's life when he must have been quite constantly occupied with constitutions and laws for his provinces beyond seas lasted from 1676 to 1701. The first date is that of the Concessions and Agreements of West New Jersey, in which he was then concerned; the latter date is that of the final revision of the **Pennsylvania Charter** during Penn's lifetime and, indeed, before the American Revolution. The intervening period saw a succession of frames, charters, laws, privileges, liberties, and concessions, of which [Francis N.] Thorpe has published the significant documents. Unlike the fixed feudal law for control by a privileged landowning class in the Carolinas, intended by Locke to endure for all time, Penn's ideas evolved progressively in response to new conditions and popular demands. It is the natural result of belief in a "continuing revelation," which was a feature of Quaker philosophy. [William I. Hull, in his *William Penn*] has pointed out that "this series of documents gradually developed from the

grant of a charter by a superior power, into a genuine constitution originating with and formulated by the people themselves, with the coöperation of the proprietor. That it met the needs of the Pennsylvanians is evidenced by the fact that it endured until 1776, when the colony was converted into a state."

Provisions for religious and civil liberty in West New Jersey were recognized by Penn to be something new, and he hoped they would serve as a precedent. They have done so in America: "There [in West New Jersey] we lay a foundation for after ages to understand their liberty as men and Christians, that they may not be brought in bondage, but by their own consent; for we put the power in the people." This is what George Bancroft had in mind when he said in his eulogy of Penn: "Penn did not despair of humanity, and though all history and experience denied the sovereignty of the people, dared to cherish the noble idea of man's capacity for self-government." The difference in the situation of the two parts of New Jersey as compared with Pennsylvania is obvious. The ownership of New Jersey involved a changing personnel, originally consisting of Lord Berkeley and Sir George Carteret; but as time went on, it increased to twenty-four proprietors before it was turned over to the Crown in 1702. Pennsylvania, on the other hand, was the property of an individual, William Penn, who had the declared right to dispose of his holdings as he pleased, through gift or sale, and to divide it into counties, towns, and manors, as time might determine. However, the spirit of the earlier frames of government are in both cases closely identical, as they breathe the religious faith and political philosophy of the same man. What we may fairly call the peculiar Quaker provisions are the same in both. We shall note them all in the following summary of the more characteristic laws.

Beginning with the fundamental laws of West New Jersey agreed upon in 1676, we find it declared (chap. XVI) "that no person . . . shall be any ways upon any pretence whatsoever, called in question . . . for the sake of his opinion, judgment, faith or worship towards God in matters of religion." Chap. XVII provides for jury trial of any inhabitant by "twelve good and lawful men of his neighborhood." We hark back to the Penn-Mead trial a few years before, when we read, after provision for three justices who shall sit with the jury, "that the said Justices shall pronounce such judgment as they shall receive from, and be directed by the said twelve men in whom only the judgment resides, and not otherwise" (chap. XIX). Thus was the function of the jury protected henceforth in American law, as was also the equivalent of a legal affirmation for an oath (chap. XX). Furthermore, it is provided that "no person shall be compelled to fee any attorney or councillor (*sic*) to plead his cause, but that all persons have free liberty to plead his own cause." Moreover, no prisoner shall be obliged to pay prison fees under any condition (chap. XXII). All court hearings are to be open to the public "that justice may not be done in a corner nor in any covert manner," but "that all and every person and persons inhabiting the said Province, shall, so far as in us lies, be free from oppression and slavery" (chap. XXIII).

Confining ourselves still to the Province of West New Jersey, we find in 1681 that it was provided that for no Governor or Council at any time hereafter shall it be lawful "to make or raise war upon any accounts or pretence whatsoever, or to raise any military forces within the Province aforesaid, without the consent of the General Free Assembly for the time being" (Art. III). Thus, originally as in Pennsylvania, so long as the Quakers predominated in the popular Assembly, any war-party executive was stymied. Indeed, without the consent and concurrence of the General Assembly, no law could be made or enacted (Art. IV), nor could the Assembly be prorogued or dissolved without its own consent (Art. V), nor could any tax be levied or raised without its consent (Art. VI). All officers of state, or trust, shall be nominated and elected by the Assembly and shall be accountable to it (Art. VII). Most important is the provision that "Liberty of conscience in matters of faith and worship towards God, shall be granted to all . . . and that none of the free people of the said Province shall be rendered uncapable (*sic*) of office in respect of their faith and worship" (Art. X). This is a more liberal statement than that in *The Fundamental Constitutions for the Province of East New Jersey* of 1683, to which we may now turn. Art. XVI reads: "All persons living in the Province who confess and acknowledge the one Almighty and Eternal God, and hold themselves obliged in conscience to live peaceably and quietly in a civil society, shall in no way be molested or prejudiced for their religious persuasions and exercise in matters of faith and worship; nor shall they be compelled to frequent and maintain any religious worship, place or ministry whatsoever." So far we see the Quaker testimony against a state church and against tithes. But the same Article further provides "that no man shall be admitted a member of the great or common Council, or any other place of public trust, who shall not profess faith in Christ Jesus," and solemnly declare that he will not seek the ruin or prejudice of any who may differ in judgment from him. Art. XX of the East New Jersey Constitutions provides that marriages shall be esteemed lawful "where the parents or guardians being first acquainted, the marriage is publicly intimated in such places and manners as is agreeable to men's different persuasions in religion, being afterwards still solemnized before creditable witnesses, by taking one another as man and wife, and a certificate of the whole, under the parties' and witnesses' hands, being brought to the proper register for that end, under a penalty if neglected." Thus the legal validity of the Quaker marriage ceremony without priest or justice of the peace was recognized. Witnesses in court "shall there give and deliver in their evidence by solemnly promising to speak the truth, the whole truth and nothing but the truth to the matter in question" (Art. XXI). Here we have, with the usual penalty for perjury, that legal substitution of the affirmation for the oath, for which Friends, and Penn in particular, so long contended. And this same substitution was allowed for a sufficient engagement of all the officers of the state from the governor down to the justices of the peace in their affirmation of loyalty to the King of England and to the Proprietors (Art. XXIV). Thus the hated Test Act of contemporary England, involving the oath of allegiance and supremacy, when demanded, was never transferred as a requirement to Penn's provinces in America.

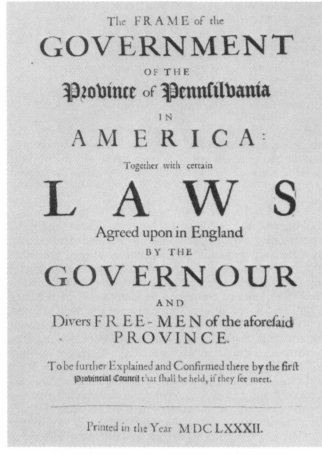

The FRAME of the
GOVERNMENT
OF THE
Province of Pennsilvania
IN
AMERICA:
Together with certain
LAWS
Agreed upon in England
BY THE
GOVERNOUR
AND
Divers F R E E - M E N of the aforesaid
PROVINCE.

To be further Explained and Confirmed there by the first Provincial Council that shall be held, if they see meet.

Printed in the Year M DC LXXXII.

Title page to The Frame of the Government of the Province of Pennsylvania, *1681.*

That is all that is of significance for us in the early laws of the Jerseys. Penn had incorporated certain inalienable privileges to be enjoyed without further sufferings: freedom of conscience and worship; popular government through the concurrent approval of all laws, including taxation, by the General Assembly; guarantee of trial by jury and freedom of the accused from unjust fees and court abuse; no state religion or exaction of tithes; validity of Quaker marriages; and the acceptance of an affirmation for an oath in law and in declarations of loyalty. There was already some advantage to the Quakers in having their leader associated with a fresh start in America.

The circumstances under which Penn became the sole proprietor and first governor of Pennsylvania gave a somewhat different color to the frames of government he progressively developed for that province between 1681 and 1701. Whereas his experience with East and West New Jersey had been as only one of several proprietors, he was now the only one. Pennsylvania was, moreover, a personal grant from the King—a fact of which we are reminded in the first charter granted by Charles II in 1681, "favouring the petition and good purpose of the said William Penn, and having regard to the memory and merits of his late Father in divers services, and particularly to his conduct, courage, and discretion under our dearest Brother James Duke of York, in that signal battle and victory fought and obtained against the Dutch fleet etc." After stating the geographical limits of the territory, this charter grants Penn full liberty for the making and execution of laws, permission to trade with the natives, license to lade and freight ships between Pennsylvania and England, subject to any present or future customs and other duties imposed by English law. Further, it authorizes the erection of ports to which officers of the commissioners of customs shall at all times have free admittance, all customs and subsidies in such ports to be enjoyed by William Penn, saving such as by Act of Parliament may be appointed to the Crown.

In this very generous charter there are three features that may be specially noted. The first is the power "to remit, release, pardon, and abolish, whether before judgment or after, all crimes and offences whatsoever committed . . . against the said laws, treason and wilful and malicious murder only excepted, and in those cases to grant reprieves until our pleasure may be known therein etc." In view of the scores of crimes punished with death under the contemporary code in England, this limitation of capital punishment to treason and murder is a marked concession to Quaker concern for the sacredness of human life. The second provision to remark is that "the said laws be consonant to reason." This is one of Penn's contentions. . . . (pp. 133-38)

Beside these two important provisions attributable to Penn, the Crown on its part made one significant reservation that the said laws "be not repugnant or contrary, but as near as conveniently may be agreeable to the laws and statutes and rights of this our kingdom of England"; to insure this, all laws made and published in Pennsylvania "shall within five years after the making thereof, be transmitted and delivered to the Privy Council . . . and if any of the said laws, within the space of six months . . . be declared by us . . . inconsistent with the sovereignty or lawful prerogative of us . . . that thereupon any of the said laws shall be adjudged and declared to be void by us." It should be said that the Crown did not abuse the right of veto which it thus reserved.

Penn must have made his own reservations in accepting for himself and his heirs and assigns the power "to levy, muster and train all sorts of men, of what condition soever, or wheresoever borne, in the said Province of Pennsylvania, for the time being, and to make war, and to pursue the enemies and robbers aforesaid, as well by sea as by land, even without the limits of the said Province, and by God's assistance to vanquish and take them, and being taken to put them to death by the law of war, or to save them, at their pleasure, and to do all and every other thing which to the charge and office of a Captain-General of an army belongeth or hath accustomed to belong, as fully and freely as any Captain-General of an army hath ever had the same." Reflecting upon these powers in his country house or in a London office, Penn must have thought they were less likely to be called for than in fact they were. It was not long before he was bedeviled by complaints from non-Quakers that the Quaker Assembly refused to chase away *vi et armis* the pirates and smugglers who entered Delaware Bay, or under other circumstances to furnish military quotas in the wars in which England was engaged with France.

The King also covenanted that there should be no taxes or impositions laid upon the dwellers in Pennsylvania for their lands, tenements, goods, or chattels, or upon goods imported or exported "unless the same be with the consent of the Proprietary, or chief governor, or Assembly, or by Act of Parliament in England." The last clause was pregnant with possibilities before 1776. At the instance of the Church authorities in England, it was provided for this Quaker province "that if any of the inhabitants of the said Province, to the number of twenty, shall at any time hereafter be desirous, and shall by any writing, or by any person deputed for them, signify such their desire to the Bishop of London for the time being that any preacher or preachers, to be approved of by the said Bishop, may be sent unto them for their instruction, that then such preacher or preachers shall and may be and reside within the said Province, without any denial or molestation whatsoever." It was not long before the Anglicans in Philadelphia were entirely able, under this toleration, to take care of themselves, and to thwart the original Quaker peace principles upon which Pennsylvania was founded. If the Quakers had received the same toleration in Massachusetts as the Anglicans did in Pennsylvania, there would not have been four hangings of Quakers to the credit of the Bay State.

Another contrast between Pennsylvania and New England is offered by the treatment of witchcraft. The Puritans seem to have been obsessed by witches. But the only trial for witchcraft of which we hear in Pennsylvania concerned a Swede in 1683, at which the Governor himself presided. The evidence was not convincing to the jury, which brought in a verdict of "guilty of the common fame of being a witch, but not guilty in the manner and form as she stands indicted." That was the simple disposition of witchcraft by a Quaker jury. As Graham remarks, "witchcraft and Quakerism do not belong to the same kind of universe." Thus progress in toleration was gradually registered in America.

A final personal tribute of royal confidence in Penn is to be found in the statement that, if any contest about the sense or meaning of anything in this charter should arise in court, "such interpretation be made thereof and allowed in any of our courts whatsoever, as shall be adjudged most advantageous and favorable unto the said William Penn, his heirs and assigns," provided only that allegiance to the Crown be in no way prejudiced.

There are some interesting features in the Concessions to the Province agreed upon in July 1681 by Penn and his first purchasers of land. Beside the provisions concerning land surveys, apportionments, etc., we may note the agreements for the protection of the Indians from all unfair practices in trade, for mixed juries of "six planters and six natives" in trials of natives, and for equal liberty for the Indians "to do all things relating to improvement of their ground." It was not contemplated that the Indians should be driven out of the inhabited territory, or be excluded from it, but that they should come and go at their pleasure and own their own land. This freedom prevailed for some years, while the sight of Indians trading in the settlements was common. This desire to treat the Indians justly as brothers was found only in the colonies where the Quaker element could exert its influence.

A year before Penn himself went to Pennsylvania, he dispatched two missives from which a few extracts will testify to his kindly nature. The first is addressed to the Indians of the province:

> My friends, there is a great God, and Power, which hath made the world and all things therein, to whom you and I, and all people owe their being and well-being, and to whom you and I must one day give an account for all that we have done in the world. This great God has written his law in our hearts, by which we are taught and commanded to love, and to help, and to do good to one another. Now this great God hath been pleased to make me concerned in your part of the world; and the King of the country where I live hath given me a great province therein; but I desire to enjoy it with your love and consent, that we may always live together as neighbours and friends; else what would the great God do to us, who hath made us (not to devour and destroy one another, but) to live soberly and kindly together in the world? . . . I have great love and regard toward you, and desire to win and gain your love and friendship by a kind, just, and peaceable life; and the people I send are of the same mind, and shall in all things behave themselves accordingly; and if in any thing any shall offend you or your people, you shall have a full and speedy satisfaction for the same, by an equal number of just men on both sides, that by no means you may have just occasion of being offended against them.

To the few Europeans—Dutch, Swedes, and English—already settled in those lands, he wrote:

> I have to let you know that it hath pleased God in his Providence to cast you within my lot and care. It is a business that, though I never undertook before, yet God has given me an understanding of my duty, and an honest mind to do it uprightly. I hope you will not be troubled with your change and the King's choice, for you are now fixed, at the mercy of no Governor that comes to make his fortune great; you shall be governed by laws of your own making, and live a free, and, if you will, a sober and industrious people. I shall not usurp the right of any, or oppress his person; God has furnished me with a better resolution, and has given me his grace to keep it. In short, whatever sober and free men can reasonably desire for the security and improvement of their own happiness, I shall heartily comply with, and in five months resolve, if it pleases God, to see you.

Some private letters of Penn at the time he was granted the charter show more informally what was engaging his attention. To some of his intimate friends he wrote in 1681:

> I have been these thirteen years the servant of truth and Friends, and for my testimony sake

lost much, not only the greatness and preferments of this world, but 16000 pounds of my estate, that had I not been what I am I had long ago obtained . . . For the matters of liberty and privilege, I purpose that which is extraordinary, and to leave myself and successors no power of doing mischief; that the will of one man may not hinder the good of an whole country.

A group of Penn's friends formed the Free Society of Traders, purchasing twenty thousand acres of land, and receiving from the Proprietary certain rights and privileges within this tract. Penn himself was an individual member of this Society, which published a prospectus inviting others to take shares in the enterprise and outlining the conditions of settlement which had been agreed upon. In addition, another proposal came before Penn from a group of men who desired to secure a concession for trade with the Indians. Regarding their proposal, he wrote to Robert Turner in 1681:

> I did refuse a great temptation last Second Day, which was 6000 pounds, and pay the Indians, for six shares, and make the purchasers a company, to have wholly to itself the Indian trade from south to north, between the Susquehanna and Delaware rivers, paying me 2½ per cent acknowledgment or rent: but as the Lord gave it me over all and great opposition, and that I never had my mind so exercised to the Lord about any outward substance, I would not abuse his love, nor act unworthy of his providence, and so defile what came to me clean.

Next in order of time comes Penn's *Charter of Liberties* of April 20, 1682, in which he grants and confirms to the freemen, planters, and adventurers those liberties, franchises, and properties to be held, enjoyed, and kept by them. If, as some believed, Algernon Sidney collaborated as a friend with Penn in drafting his constitution, it is interesting to point out here what Sidney may have disapproved. Sidney was a republican and counseled, it is supposed, against any proprietary reservations and privileges; he would like to see Penn go to the extreme of democracy. The only document surviving in the case is a letter from Penn to Sidney, dated October 13, 1681, regretting the report that he and Sidney had fallen out, and that Sidney had said, "I had a good country, but the basest laws in the world . . . and that the Turk was not more absolute than I." No one in his senses could say such a thing as that. We do not know what satisfaction, if any, Penn received from one for whom he says he had felt "more true friendship than I have been guilty of to any man I know living." Any rift between two such noble men is regrettable, but if Sidney differed from the Proprietor on any important points, it would be on the following: "Art. 6. In this Provisional Council the governor or his deputies shall or may always preside and have a treble voice." And still less democratic was the provision that all bills shall be prepared and proposed by the governor and Provincial Council, to be passed or rejected as the General Assembly shall see meet (Art. VII). Though the Provincial Assembly was elected by popular suffrage of the qualified freemen, yet this provision for the initiation of legislation only through the Governor and an upper house was essentially opposed to popular government. It is hard to see what else Sidney could have objected to. But it was precisely these provisions favoring the proprietary interests which were soon challenged in Pennsylvania. This charter also provided for another concern of the Quakers: "The Governor and Council shall erect and order all public schools" (Art. XII). This was soon done, and the Overseers of the William Penn Charter School in Philadelphia still preserve the name and the disposition of certain funds for educational and charitable purposes. The rest of the document is taken up with the necessary ordering of government.

We come now to the most significant of all the early documents connected with the history of Pennsylvania, *The Frame of Government of Pennsylvania*—1682—"together with certain laws agreed upon in England by the Governor and divers freemen of the aforesaid province; to be further explained and confirmed there, by the first provincial Council, that shall be held, if they see meet." This document, and especially the Preface, expresses Penn's own conception of government more clearly than does any other single declaration. In the Preface, after recognition of the supreme authority of God, Penn continues in a series of eloquent announcements:

> This settles the divine right of government without exception, and that for two ends: first, to terrify evil doers; secondly, to cherish those that do well; which gives government a life beyond corruption, and makes it as durable in the world, as good men shall be. So that government seems to me a part of religion itself, a thing sacred in its institution and end.

His conception of a free government is thus stated:

> Any government is free to the people under it (whatever be the frame), where the laws rule, and the people are a party to these laws, and more than this is tyranny, oligarchy, or confusion.

Again,

> . . . governments, like clocks, go from the motion men give them; and as governments are made and moved by men, so by them they are ruined too. Wherefore, governments rather depend upon men, than men upon governments. Let men be good, and the government cannot be bad; if it be ill, they will cure it. But, if men be bad, let the government be never so good, they will endeavour to warp and spoil it to their turn. I know some will say, let us have good laws, and no matter for the men that execute them: but let them consider, that though good laws do well, good men do better; for good laws may want [i.e., lack] good men, and be abolished or evaded by ill men; but good men will never want good laws, nor suffer ill ones. . . . That, therefore, which makes a good constitution, must keep it, *viz.:* men of wisdom and virtue, qualities, that because they descend not with worldly inheritances, must be carefully propagated by a virtuous education of youth; for which after ages will owe more to the care and prudence of founders, and the successive magistracy, than to their parents, for their private patrimonies.

Penn's Utopia was to depend upon a good foundation and a succession of righteous magistrates, rather than upon the hazards of individual privileges. In conclusion:

> We have to the best of our ability, contrived and composed the frame and the laws of this government, to the great end of all government, *viz:* to support power in reverence with the people, and to secure the people from the abuse of power; that they may be free by their just obedience, and the magistrates honourable, for their just administration: for liberty without obedience is confusion, and obedience without liberty is slavery.

Pennsylvania lawmakers and judges might well be guided by these principles in the discharge of their responsibilities.

The twenty-four laws which accompany the frame may be regarded as something tentative, to be approved in Pennsylvania, or revised as may seem best. With slight verbal changes, these twenty-four laws are identical with those issued a few days before, but now appearing with the benefit of Penn's personal preface. "Agreed upon in England" on May 5, 1682, by the Governor and the same freemen, were forty laws later ratified by the Pennsylvania Assembly in December 1682, immediately after Penn's arrival. Some of these laws are worth attention. For example, any bribery or promise of reward in money or in kind in connection with an election shall be punished upon both parties concerned (III); there shall be no levy of public tax, custom, or contribution, but by a law, for that purpose made (IV); all courts shall be open, and justice shall neither be sold, denied, nor delayed (V); persons may plead their own cause in court (VI); all court pleadings and processes shall be short, and in English (VII); legal fees shall be moderate in accordance with a fixed scale (IX); all prisons shall be workhouses, one in each county (X). Here we see the first steps in the development of the famous Pennsylvania prison system, in which the Quakers had a great part. Remembering his own experiences, Penn specified that "all prisoners shall be bailable by sufficient sureties, unless for capital offenses" (XI); that all persons wrongfully imprisoned or prosecuted shall receive double damages against the informer or prosecutor (XII); that all prisons shall be free as to fees, food, and lodging (XIII). The nine laws referring to courts and prisons all reflect directly the sufferings of Friends in contemporary England. Further, Quaker marriages are provided for (XIX); affirmation instead of oath-taking in court is provided for (XXVI); "all children, within this province, of the age of twelve years, shall be taught some useful trade or skill, to the end none may be idle, but the poor may work to live, and the rich, if they become poor, may not want" (XXVIII). This provision reflects all the early Quaker pronouncements in favor of a practical education. The ancient Quaker testimony against "tale-bearing and detraction" is discovered in Penn's law "that all scandalous and malicious reporters, backbiters, defamers and spreaders of false news, whether against Magistrates or private persons, shall be accordingly severely punished, as enemies to the peace and concord of this province" (XXX).

The religious qualifications for the suffrage and for office-holding are more strict in this Constitution than in that of the Jerseys already considered. It is provided in Pennsylvania that all office-holders and those who have the right to vote for the same "shall be such as profess faith in Jesus Christ" (XXXIV); the next law, however, specifies "that all persons living in this province, who confess and acknowledge the one Almighty and eternal God, to be the Creator, Upholder and Ruler of the world . . . shall, in no ways, be molested or prejudiced for their religious persuasion, or practice, in matters of faith and worship, nor shall they be compelled, at any time, to frequent or maintain any religious worship, place or ministry whatever" (XXXV). Thus was all possibility of the transfer of the odious tithes to Pennsylvania forever denied. The XXXVII law decreed that all the grosser forms of immorality should be severely punished, and also "all prizes, stage-plays, cards, dice, May-games, gamesters, masques, revels, bull-baitings, cock-fightings, bear-baitings, and the like." This is the Quaker counterpart of the New England Blue Laws against idle and dissipating practices, and the reaction against those worldly amusements which Penn had already flayed thirteen years earlier in *No Cross, No Crown.* The document ends with the statement that these laws may not be altered without the consent of the Governor and "six parts in seven of the freemen, met in provincial Council and General Assembly" (XXXIX), and that all other matters not provided for shall be referred to the determination of the same authority (XL).

Another *Frame of Government* dates from April 2, 1683, made necessary by changed circumstances and opinions. The Duke of York deeded to Penn his territory, consisting of the three southern counties now forming the State of Delaware. As soon as Penn arrived in America, the inhabitants of these southern counties, or "territories," as they were called, had requested to be included in the government of Pennsylvania. It was found, moreover, that the number of representatives in the Governor's Council and the General Assembly provided for in the earlier documents was much too large for the present population. The new *Frame,* therefore, had to incorporate the appropriate changes made necessary by these two factors. The *Frame* of 1683 refers to "this province and territories thereunto annexed," making six counties in all. Here, too, each county is to be represented in the Council by three persons, totaling eighteen, instead of twenty-four from each of three counties, totaling seventy-two, as previously provided. Similarly, the large number of two hundred Assemblymen to be elected by the three original counties is now reduced to six from each of six counties, totaling thirty-six. We thus have a Governor's Council of eighteen, and a General Assembly of thirty-six members. It was intended that the three lower counties or territories should be fully incorporated in the government of Pennsylvania, and their inhabitants of foreign birth were straightway naturalized as well as those of Pennsylvania. Very significant also is the abolishment of the treble vote reserved to the Governor, as we have seen in the earlier Frames—a provision likely disapproved by Sidney in the first place. An Act was also passed at this time, incorporating the Quaker faith in arbitration of civil disputes, by providing at every county court for three peacemakers, who should serve as arbitrators and determine, if possible, differences between individuals without bringing them into court. Quakers

have always been shy of courts, if any other way of settling differences could be found. Their historic association with courts in England had not left with them a happy memory. To the present day, the two Philadelphia Yearly Meetings inquire annually of their members whether "we endeavor to settle disagreements between individuals" and "where differences arise, are prompt endeavors made to end them?"

It is interesting to observe that Penn translated and published for the benefit of his colonists in distant America the Latin text of Magna Charta with later comments upon it, followed by an abstract of the charter granted to him by Charles II. This little handbook for the use of legislators and electors is entitled *The Excellent Privilege of Liberty and Property Being the Birth-right of the Free-born Subjects of England.* Though the perfect copy, thought to be unique, of the original edition in the Haverford College Library bears no date or place of publication, it is considered to be a publication of Bradford in Philadelphia in 1687.

In 1696, the government of Pennsylvania having been restored to Penn in 1694 and his cousin William Markham acting for him as deputy governor, a new *Frame of Government* was made necessary as a matter of form. It contains new provisions regarding qualifications for the suffrage, and a lengthy restatement of the acceptability of a solemn affirmation instead of an oath "upon any lawful occasion." Provision is here also made for the daily compensation and travel allowance of members of Council and Assembly. The number of members is further reduced to two from each of the six counties for the Council, and four for the Assembly. This provision for a Council of twelve and an Assembly of twenty-four members continued in force until 1701.

Meanwhile, the Proprietor was continually harassed by standing grievances: the desire of the "territories" first to be associated in the government of Pennsylvania, and later to be separated from it; the insistence of the popular Assembly upon the right to initiate legislation, regardless of the charter reservation of this power to the Governor and Council; the difficulties about providing subsidies for military defense of Pennsylvania and the adjoining colonies; disputes about the requirement of oaths in legal matters; the reluctance of the people to pay their quitrents, upon which Penn counted to reimburse himself for the heavy expenses of government; the inadequacy of his deputy governors appointed by himself; the danger that the Crown, egged on by the Anglican Church party, would take over the government of the province again, as it had already done for two years; and later, the temptation in days of discouragement to sell the government to the Crown.

These were the main causes for anxiety in Penn's mind during the unexpectedly long absence from his province which he was compelled to spend in England from 1684 until 1699. There was a well-nigh irreconcilable opposition between his own financial interests as Proprietary, his feudal obligations to the Crown, and the democratic aspirations of the people represented by their Assembly— aspirations with which in spirit he was not unsympathetic. It is significant that Penn during his lifetime was never able to secure his financial rights in Pennsylvania, and died many thousand pounds poorer than he was before 1682: the next two generations of the family secured the advantages of his large investment, through better management and the increased value of lands during the eighteenth century. It is also significant that over the period 1682-1701 the popular party made steady gains in its pretensions and its acquired privileges. It was largely due to the tact and fidelity of Penn's secretary and personal representative, James Logan, that after 1701 the proprietary interests fared as well as they did. Logan's personal opponent for years was David Lloyd, a somewhat factious but determined political leader in the Quaker Assembly. Lloyd championed popular rights against those of the proprietary party very effectively. It may be fair to say that Penn did not so much object to granting the wishes of the popular party as he objected to the ungrateful spirit in which the popular demands were made, coupled with the continued refusal of the Assembly to provide for his financial requirements. Ingratitude was one trait that he could not overlook. The harshest language used by Penn in his correspondence with Logan refers to those men by whose ingratitude he was stung.

Many of the problems just mentioned were in Penn's mind when he was finally able to return to America with his wife and daughter in 1699. Fifteen years had elapsed since his last visit. Physical and political conditions in the province were much altered since 1684: Philadelphia was now a young city, Meetings had been settled, roads opened, estates laid out in the adjoining counties, prosperity had come, and most important of all, democratic demands had come to a focus. The *Charter of Privileges* of 1701 was the fruit of this visit, and remained the law of the province until 1776.

Penn's address to the Provincial Council on April 1, 1700, contains some notable expressions of generosity and confidence: "If in the constitution by charter there be any thing that jars, alter it. If you want a law for this or that, prepare it. I advise you not to trifle with government; I wish there were no need of any, but since crimes prevail, government is made necessary by man's degeneracy. Government is not an end, but a means; he who thinks it to be an end, aims at profit—to make a trade of it—but he who thinks it to be a means, understands the true end of government." Again, "At the late election in Philadelphia, I was grieved to hear some make it a matter of religion. It [government] is merely a human and moral thing relating to society, trade, traffic, and public good, consisting in virtue and justice; where these are maintained, there is government indeed." Finally, "I have been now nineteen years your Proprietor and Governor, and have at my charge maintained my Deputy, whereby I have much worsted myself and estate. I hope it will be no wonder to any here, to hear me make this mention of it." It was in this spirit on Penn's part that the final charter granted by him was discussed for over a year.

In this last *Charter of Privileges* of 1701, the first article again declares the dependence of good government upon freedom of conscience in terms which are here rehearsed:

Because no people can be truly happy, though

under the greatest enjoyment of civil liberties, if abridged of the freedom of their consciences, as to their religious profession and worship: And Almighty God being the only Lord of conscience, Father of lights and spirits; and the Author as well as Object of all divine knowledge, faith and worship, who only doth enlighten the minds, and persuade and convince the understandings of people, I do hereby grant and declare that no person or persons, inhabiting in this province or territories, who shall confess and acknowledge one Almighty God, the Creator, Upholder and Ruler of the world; and profess him or themselves obliged to live quietly under the civil government, shall be in any case molested or prejudiced, in his or their person or estate, because of his or their conscientious persuasion or practice, nor be compelled to frequent or maintain any religious worship, place or ministry, contrary to his or their mind, or to do or suffer any other act or thing contrary to their religious persuasion.

All public officers must "profess to believe in Jesus Christ, the Saviour of the world," must promise allegiance to the King as sovereign, and fidelity to the Proprietary and Governor. The Assembly is given full power to choose a Speaker and its own officers, to judge of qualifications of its own members, to sit upon its own adjournments, appoint committees, prepare bills in order to pass into laws, etc. This marks the final triumph of popular government. In this document there is no provision for a Governor's Council, with its former power of initiation of legislation. By letters patent, however, Penn established a Council of ten members, mostly Quakers, "to consult and assist, with the best of their advice, the Proprietary or his deputies, in all public affairs and matters relating to government." Thus the function of the Council was henceforth purely advisory, and to it Penn appointed ten of his most substantial and intimate friends: Edward Shippen, John Guest, Samuel Carpenter, William Black, Thomas Story, Griffith Owen, Phineas Pemberton, Samuel Finney, Caleb Pusey, and John Blunston. The "territories" were granted liberty to dissolve their union with the "province" at any time within three years; in case they did so, the numbers of the Assembly (24) were to be maintained by the election of four additional members from each of the three counties of Philadelphia, Chester, and Bucks. This charter of October 1701 also incorporated the city of Philadelphia, and gave the city two members in the Assembly. This charter, having been considered for fifteen months previously, gave great satisfaction to the inhabitants. It was granted by Penn on the eve of his departure for England, necessitated by the outbreak of war with France, and the fear that fresh efforts would be made to deprive him of his government. The "territories" separated within two years, but shared a governor with Pennsylvania while supporting a government of their own until the Revolution; finally, they became the State of Delaware.

We have seen in the Penn-Logan correspondence what the analysis of the situation was in Pennsylvania, as seen by others, between 1701 and 1710. Penn's own explanation of his troubles, and a fanciful cure for them, are found in a letter of February 17, 1705, to Judge Mompesson:

There is an excess of vanity that is apt to creep in upon the people in power in America, who, having got out of the crowd in which they were lost here [i.e., in England], upon every little eminency there, think nothing taller than themselves but the trees, and as if there were no after superior judgment to which they should be accountable; so that I have sometimes thought that if there was a law to oblige the people in power, in their respective colonies, to take turns in coming over for England, that they might lose themselves again amongst the crowds of so much more considerable people at the custom-house, exchange, and Westminster Hall, they would exceedingly amend in their conduct at their return, and be much more discreet and tractable, and fit for government. In the mean time, pray help to prevent them not to destroy themselves. . . . Let them know and feel the just order and decency of government, and that they are not to command but to be commanded according to law and constitution of English government.

Thus spoke the Founder in one of his firmer moments.

In the preceding pages we have seen the solicitude of Penn for the moral and religious welfare of his province, and the gradual evolution of the people's part in the government. The official documents contain, of course, the usual provisions which are common to all democratic governments, and have not been repeated here. It is not too much to say that the *Charter of Privileges* of 1701 represents the final form given by Penn to the preceding theories of closet-philosophers which he had had the rare opportunity to sift and test. Religious toleration, civil liberty, and popular government had reached a new high as the result of his Holy Experiment.

It is true that under the Proprietary government of colonial Pennsylvania after Penn's death and under the earlier constitutions of the State of Pennsylvania, there was a falling away on some minor points from Penn's ideals. But the present constitution of the State has incorporated all the rights of the Quaker citizen for which Penn sought to make provision in the documents we have examined.

There is a statesmanlike proposal of Penn which has not been mentioned. It concerned not only Pennsylvania, but all the British colonies in America, and was submitted by request to the Lords of Trade in February 1697. It is called a *Plan for the Union of the Colonies,* and is the earliest of those colonial projects which foreshadow the later confederation of the colonies in 1776. Penn's plan contained measures that the colonies "may be made more useful to the Crown, and one another's peace and safety with an universal concurrence." The plan contained provisions for the periodic meeting of delegates from all the colonies from Massachusetts to the Carolinas, with a King's Commissioner as chairman, who in time of war should be commander-in-chief, to adjust matters of complaint or differences between provinces: such as the return of debtors and fugitives from justice, and the righting of injuries arising from disputes over commerce, etc. Further, the delegates were to devise plans for protection against public enemies by placing military quotas for the good and benefit of the whole. As has been said, "all these matters, placed at the disposition of the central body, found their place in the Articles of Confederation."

Under the pressure of the existing war with France, Penn violates in this plan his personal conscience by proposing military defense of the colonies upon a coöperative basis. In this case he could not speak for Pennsylvania and his Quaker convictions alone, but had to submit a plan which might secure the adherence of all concerned. He doubtless knew that he was proposing to the Lords of Trade "all that the traffic would bear." As Professor Hull, with his enthusiasm for arbitration, remarks of this plan, Penn's early proposal for mixed juries of whites and Indians to try the latter, his three arbitrators provided in each county court to settle individual differences, his proposal for a congress of European nations made in 1693, and now this plan for an orderly settlement of differences between provinces, "are interesting stepping-stones towards the peaceful international settlement of international disputes."

One other subject should claim our attention in this [essay], and that is Penn's treatment of Negro slavery. Penn's life covered the period of the earliest agitation in America against the evils of Negro slavery. The trade in African Negroes had been encouraged by England in order to provide labor in her new colonies where it was scarce. Slavery was not an evil with which the first generation of Quakers in England had any experience. When George Fox first encountered slavery and its effects in Barbados in 1671, his expressed concern went no further than that masters should care for the religious training of their slaves, should treat them humanely, and eventually set them free. Penn's Free Society of Traders, an association of Quaker colonists for Pennsylvania, provided that Negro slaves should be set free after fourteen years, when they should be allotted land, stock, and tools, and pay two-thirds of their produce to the Free Society of Traders: "if they agree not to this, to be servants till they do." This was in 1682. The earliest protest against the institution of slavery was in 1688 from the German Quakers in Germantown, Pennsylvania. The superior Meetings in Philadelphia were not then ready to consider the subject, but a few years later the sentiment spread to the extent of discouraging the importation of Negro slaves, while a concern for their spiritual welfare and the regularization of their marriages took hold of some Philadelphia Friends. A will of Penn, written in 1701, provided for the freedom of his own blacks, thus showing his intentions at that time. In 1705 a tax was laid by the Assembly upon imported Negroes. First the slave trade from Africa, and then slavery itself, was discountenanced by Friends with increasing vigor, until the labors of Ralph Sandiford, John Woolman, Anthony Benezet, and Benjamin Lay cleared Quakers in Pennsylvania of the curse about 1780. Thus Penn personally did not take much part in the suppression of slavery, but it is to the Quakers during the eighteenth century that the earliest effective efforts to abolish the institution must be credited in those colonies where their influence was strong.

It will be recalled that Penn was considering for years the expediency of selling his government to the Crown. *The Charter [of Privileges]* of 1701 offered a stumbling-block

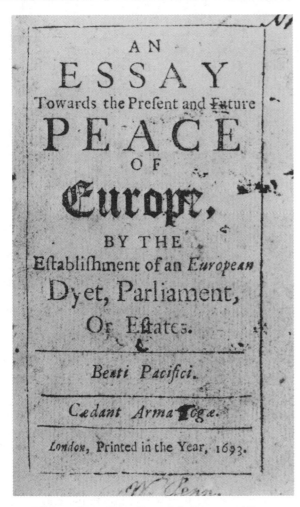

Title page for An Essay Toward the Present and Future Peace of Europe, *1693.*

to the consummation of this sale. The fact that he had handed over his political prerogatives to the people reduced the value of such a purchase in the eyes of the Crown. The Crown was not eager to buy the government of a Quaker province which had had its popular rights permanently guaranteed by this charter of 1701. The Church party, however, was anxious to gain control there, and continued to urge the purchase, while accusing Penn's government of incompetence. Colonel Robert Quarry, the British revenue officer, was a thorn in Penn's side because of the charges he preferred against the Proprietor to the Lords Commissioners of Trade and Plantations, and because of his prejudice against the interests of the Proprietary party. On the other hand, David Lloyd headed the Quaker party that claimed the province was losing its privileges and immunities through Penn's administration of government. For years after 1704 he continued to bait Penn by his representations to the small party of English Quakers who were suspicious of Penn's contacts with the world. Lloyd's conduct seemed to Penn and Logan little short of treason.

Harried by the conflicting representations of the Anglican and the Quaker party, Penn dragged on his negotiations

with the Crown until 1712. Then he was stricken, and the question of a sale was permanently dropped. The last few years of Penn's invalid life witnessed a better spirit in Pennsylvania, and a better attitude toward the financial obligations to the Proprietor. The controversies between the Assembly and the deputy governors were less bitter, and the country was flourishing. Sales of land and better collections cleared the family debt. It is unfortunate that Penn did not live to appreciate fully the period of bloom in the province between 1710 and 1740. (pp. 138-54)

> *William Wistar Comfort, in his* William Penn, 1644-1718: A Tercentenary Estimate, *University of Pennsylvania Press, 1944, 185 p.*

Jonathan Hughes   (essay date 1965)

[*Hughes is an American economist and historian. In the following excerpt, he assesses the uniqueness and legacy of the* Frame of the Government of the Province of Pennsylvania.]

The Quakers had had long contact—a great deal of it most unpleasant—with the rising new English colonies on the North American mainland. In fact, George Fox himself visited America in 1671-73, and was present in 1672 at the first meeting of the Baltimore Friends. But the Quakers generally had little hope for toleration in the existing colonies. Roger Williams, to be sure, protected the Quakers in Rhode Island, but he objected to their doctrine.

As for the other colonies, the future of the Friends was all too obvious. Among the New England bigots persecution was savage. When the first preaching Quakers, two women, landed in Boston in 1655, their books were burned; they were imprisoned, stripped naked and examined for signs of witchcraft. Quakers were commonly tied to carts' tails in Massachusetts, stripped to the waist and "whipped out" of the colony. In 1658, an act was passed in Boston against the "pernicious sect" which permitted the arrest without warrant of Quakers, and their being jailed without bail and banished from the colony on pain of death. Corded whips, starvation, holes in tongues, ears cut off, such constituted the Massachusetts treatment of Friends. In Boston, three, including one woman, were hanged for the crime of their religious convictions. At one point it took an order from Charles II to New England's government to get the Quakers out of the jails. Virginia officially persecuted Quakers. They were nearly driven out of Maryland; Penn interceded personally with Lord Baltimore on their behalf.

What was needed was a Quaker colony. The older colonies held no hope. In 1664, New Netherland had fallen to the English and had been given by Charles to his brother. The seacoast was mainly inhabited. But West New Jersey had earlier been occupied and William Penn had been instrumental in drawing up the initial laws governing that settlement. In 1677 some 230 colonists had gone there and their establishment was successful. The town of Burlington, planned and run on Quaker principles, thrived. Moreover, a Quaker leader, Josiah Coale, had corresponded with Fox about the possibility of settling the Susquehanna Valley.

By 1680 it was likely that Penn could press his advantages at court to get a grant of land for several reasons. First and foremost, the Stuarts had been active in the continuation of Cromwell's empire building and the Restoration colonization had been largely done through the establishment of proprietorships. The proprietaries established after 1660 had not been entirely successful, but there was no need for Penn to repeat the errors of others, and his family had long been able to count on royal patronage.

On June 1, 1680, Penn applied to King Charles for a grant of land. In just nine months, on March 4, 1681, the deed for Pennsylvania was signed. Penn was a well known Whig and warmly supported Algernon Sidney (who, convicted of treason by a kangaroo court, was beheaded in 1683) in his two bids for Parliament in 1679 after the fall of the Cavalier Parliament. Charles obviously could not have made Penn the grant as a public favor. But the Penns' great service to the Stuarts warranted such a thing and a way was found. The Stuarts owed debts to their thousands of supporters, which largely were never paid. James, the Duke of York, had indeed earlier paid some of his main debts with grants of land after the fall of New Netherland. The royal obligations were for loans, wages never paid, gifts promised and so forth. The Stuart debt to Admiral Sir William Penn was reckoned as "at least" £11,000 (some have placed it as high as £16,000). Beyond such information, the reasons why Charles and James did Penn this great favor are not known. This is tantamount, unfortunately, to not knowing at all why the grant was made. With the rising Tory and Anglican reaction in sight it has been suggested that the King simply wanted to save Penn's head. Considering the fate of Algernon Sidney, this hypothesis may not be too far-fetched. Penn himself thought that those around the King considered the Pennsylvania land grant a bargain: " . . . the government at home was glad to be rid of us at so cheap a rate as a little parchment to be practiced in a desert 3,000 miles off. . . . "

By July, 1681, the Concessions were signed by Penn which stated the ground rules for settling the new land. Penn's "Holy Experiment" had begun.

There was no doubt from the beginning that Penn intended to grant his people liberty and assure it to their descendants. He was now a great feudal proprietor, like Lord Berkeley and Baltimore and others before him. While he hoped for profit, his immediate object was to let his ideals find expression in a new land and government. In April, 1681, he had written to Friends in Ireland: "For the matters of liberty and privilege, I purpose that which is extraordinary, and to leave to myself and my successors no power of doing mischief, that the will of one man may not hinder the good of an whole country." In every major document relating to the colony's government which Penn signed, he repeated that pledge.

Within two years, in his great *Frame of Government* and *Charter of Liberties,* Penn had given the savage political world of the 17th century the spectacle of representative government with religious freedom. For Europe, Pennsylvania was a rude awakening. For America the effects were equally profound. Penn dealt honestly and compassionately with the Indians. As Trevelyan noted succinctly, in the new colony ". . . was founded the most strange settlement of all: Charles II's government, at the moment of the strongest Tory reaction in England, permitted William Penn, the Quaker courtier and organizer, to found Pennsylvania . . . as a refuge for persecuted Friends in the wilderness, where they practised the unwonted principles of just dealing with the redskins."

Penn made two great formal contributions to American political tradition and practice. The first concerned Quaker settlers in New Jersey. The West New Jersey Concessions and Agreements, the charter under which that region was settled by English, was drawn up by trustees of an estate who included Penn. It foreshadowed the great *Frame of Government* and *Charter of Liberties of Pennsylvania.* The West New Jersey concessions included representative government; freedom from arrest except under proper warrant and from conviction save by "twelve men of the neighborhood"; no detainment in prison for debt (debt to be worked out by the debtor, the man not to "lie in prison") and, of course, complete religious freedom.

The second fundamental contribution made by Penn was the body of laws he gave to his colony of Pennsylvania. Some rules were established in 1681 for the first settlers under his charter, and then in the spring of 1682 he completed and signed the original versions of the *Frame of Government* and the *Charter of Liberties.* These two sets of laws established the great tradition of American constitution making. On March 4, 1681, King Charles signed the deed granting the proprietary colony of Pennsylvania to William Penn. The great and "Holy Experiment" in self-government and individual liberty was foreshadowed in April, 1681, when Penn wrote to those already established in his lands (mainly Swedes, Finns and Dutch): "You shall be governed by laws of your own making, and live a free, and if you will, a sober and industrious people. . . . " Penn held to this promise. In fact, compared to the condition of government in Penn's England, the Pennsylvania settlers found a democratic utopia beyond the Delaware.

To appreciate fully what Penn did for his colonists, and eventually for the new nation, it must be emphasized that the grant of land called "Pensilvania" was considered by Penn to be entirely his own. Only the surviving incumbrances of feudal landholding rights, or the power of the King, stood between him and the treatment of his fief as he saw fit. Penn's charter had never been submitted to Parliament and he considered that he might end it at his own pleasure if he so desired. His proprietary rights were held directly from King Charles with the remaining trappings of feudal landholding arrangements. The onerous and hated "quit rents" imposed by Penn upon Pennsylvania in his Concessions of 1681 were the proprietor's just and legal feudal dues as lord of the province. In addition to his own enterprises, the quit rents were to be a primary source of income to repay him (in perpetuity) for his investment. As in England, the titles of smallholders were not entirely clear.

This was reasonable enough in the 17th century. Quit rents were an outcome of centuries of feudal development and allowed the purchaser of land to be "quit and free," for a single annual cash payment, of such feudal services as "boon" and "week" work. In keeping with feudal usage, Penn himself owed fealty to the King and had to pay quit rents of his own. They were nominal:

> . . . William Penn, his heires and assignes fore ever to bee holden to Us, Our heires and Successors, Kings of England, as of Our Castle of Windsor in Our County of Berks . . . by fealty only for all Services . . . Yielding and paying therefore to Us, Our heires and Successors, Two Beaver Skins, to bee delivered at Our said Castle of Windsor on the First Day of January in every Year. . . .

Charles also reserved 20 percent of the gold and silver for himself, should any be found.

The rents Penn imposed were not high—about one shilling per 100 acres. But as lord of Pennsylvania, his *seigneurie,* the rents were his right. That the American colonists didn't pay them carefully and dealt abruptly with the whole feudal apparatus after 1776—the quit rents, entails, primogeniture and the rest—is eloquent evidence of what ordinary people thought of the last remains of feudalism, however generously imposed.

Nor were the quit rents all. A further hangover from the Middle Ages is found in the Concessions of 1681—a system of quality control in the markets. "There shall be no buying and selling, be it with an Indian, or one another, of any goods to be exported, but what shall be performed in public market . . . where they shall pass the public stamp or mark." While it is true that the Quakers were traditionally in favor of morality in business dealings, this requirement was a hangover from the Middle Ages when markets were subject to such controls. The business community of the late 17th century doubtless had little enthusiasm for such "government interference."

Yet in spite of his arbitrary powers, Penn made good his promise. The people were given a remarkable (if imperfect) government, and made their own laws. They had privileges and liberties Englishmen did not have in England. Penn must certainly be ranked as history's most enlightened feudal lord.

Even in 1681 Penn made provisions for unfree men to become free: he granted land which indentured servants might take over after their term of service had been worked off. He foresaw that the society of freemen must be enlarged from below if it would prosper, doubtless a result of his experience with the Quakers, who were largely men of the humbler classes.

Almost a year after the Concessions, in April and May of 1682, in the *Charter of Liberties* and in the *Frame of Government of Pennsylvania,* a more complete set of laws together with a statement of Penn's philosophy of government were signed. The province was to be governed by a Governor, a Council and a General Assembly. Penn's democracy worked downward (among its chief defects were the difficulty of amendment and the lack of provision for initiative). The Governor and Council were to prepare laws to submit to the General Assembly, which had the right to approve or reject them. The General Assembly, composed of all freemen at first, and thereafter of their representatives, was to choose the Council members.

Of the seventy-two-member Provincial Council, the proprietary (in the person of the Governor) was to have a triple vote—three against seventy-two votes—otherwise Penn was satisfied to allow his egalitarian democracy to work. Tenure of office in the original Council was staggered, with members rotating off. Once the Council was established, one-third would be elected each year. Experience would remain among the incumbent members. Once off, a councilman was ineligible to serve in the following year " . . . so all may be fitted for the Government and have Experience of the Care and burthen of it." The Assembly had the power of impeachment but, like Parliament, could itself be dismissed by the Governor and Council.

The original laws of Pennsylvania contained some remarkable provisions for those, or any, times. The economic provisions were in accord with King Charles' general policies of attempting to encourage trade and the arts. The Governor and Council were charged to provide schools and to "Reward the Authors of usefull Science and, Laudable Inventions." In actual practice, all schools were run either by the churches or by private individuals. Trades were seen as a method of forestalling sloth and crime. All children of 12 were to be taught a trade or skill " . . . to the end none may be idle, but the poor may work to live and the rich, if they become poor, may not want." Taxes could be raised only by due legal processes. In the Concessions provision was made, along with the well known schemes to lay out the city and to entice whole families and their servants (extra grants of land were made to encourage the wealthy to bring their servants), to have one acre of every five not cleared but left uncut to preserve oak and mulberries for ships and silk.

With an eye to the notorious penal abuses in England, Pennsylvania's laws and prisons were laudably liberal. There were to be no Fleets, Newgates or Towers. All prisons were to be workhouses. And all prisons were to be free to the inmates. There were only two capital offenses, treason and murder (compared to scores in England—more than 200 as late as the 18th century). Except for those two offenses, all prisoners were bailable. Courts were to be open, justice " . . . neither sold, denied or delayed." Juries were to consist of twelve peers, and in case of a capital offense there was to be both a grand jury of twelve to make the indictment and a different jury of twelve to try the case. The state would not confiscate property. For capital offenders one-third of the estate went to *next of kin of the victim* and two-thirds to next of kin of the criminal.

It was to be a religious society, no doubt of that. Sunday "according to the good example of the primitive Christians" was to be set aside and no common daily labor performed. There was to be religious liberty for all. Roger Williams had provided a refuge for English dissenters from Puritanism and Lord Baltimore's fief had provided toleration for a time. But in Penn's *Charter* the breakthrough to religious freedom for Christians was intended to be complete and unequivocal (as in Rhode Island, religious liberties were not always recognized in practice). He *invited* settlers of all Christian sects: Article XXXV of the *Charter of Liberties,* laws agreed to in England by Penn and certain of his settlers, set a tremendous mark in an age of nearly universal religious totalitarianism.

> That all persons living in this province, who confess and acknowledge the one Almighty and eternal God, to be the Creator, Upholder and Ruler of the world; and that hold themselves obliged in conscience to live peaceably and justly in civil society, shall in no ways, be molested or prejudiced, for their religious persuasion, or practice, in matters of faith and worship, nor shall they be compelled at any time, to frequent or maintain any religious worship, place or ministry whatever.

These laws were written by an Englishman, ascribed to by Englishmen, at a time when the English King was ruling without Parliament, when England was still trembling from the terrors of the Popish Plot, when religious persecution was raging, the prisons filled and when, in the fight between the Tories and the Whigs, religious nonconformism was again to be linked by association with treason. On the Continent, Protestants were soon to be harried again when Louis XIV revoked the Edict of Nantes in 1685. It was not a time in England, or in Europe, of toleration in religious matters or of liberalism in politics. Yet in this storm of the products of the totalitarian mind Penn wrote his great liberal constitution. As we have seen, it would have been possible in England to believe these things by 1681—if one had a very great power to be eclectic and knew just what one wanted to believe. It would be difficult to find a more striking example of the power of idealism to choose its own and to be untouched by the rest of the world around it. In Penn's *Frame of Government* his serene vision was made explicit. The origin of government was seen to be divine with two main functions:

> . . . first, to terrify evil doers; secondly, to cherish those who do well; which gives government a life beyond corruption, and makes it as durable in the world, as good men shall be. So that government seems to me a part of religion itself, a thing sacred in its institution and end. For, if it does not directly remove the cause, it crushes the effects of evil, and is as such . . . an emanation of the same Divine Power, that is both author and object of pure religion . . . I know what is said by the several admirers of *monarchy, aristocracy* and *democracy,* which are the rule of one, a few, and many, and are the three common ideas of government, when men discourse on the subject. But I chuse to solve the controversy with this small distinction, and it belongs to all three: *Any government is free to the people under it . . . where the laws rule, and the people are a party to those laws,* and more than this is tyranny, oligarchy, or confusion. . . . Governments, like clocks, go from the motion men give them; and as governments are made and moved by men, so by them they are ruined too. Wherefore governments rather depend upon men, than men upon governments. Let men be good, and the government cannot be bad; if it be ill, they will cure it. But if men be bad, let the government be

never so good, they will endeavor to warp and spoil it to their turn. . . . we have . . . to the best of our skill, contrived and composed the *frame* and *laws* of this government, to the great end of all government: *To support power in reverence with the people, and to secure the people from the abuse of power;* that they may be free by their just obedience, and the magistrates honourable, for their just administration; for liberty without obedience is confusion, and obedience without liberty is slavery. . . .

In spite of such philosophical predecessors as Penn had, such a document written in the year 1682 was an astonishing performance—especially for a feudal lord. The spirit of it permeated American political tradition. Channing, the historian, studying the various manuscript drafts of Penn's *Frame,* ruled that it was entirely Penn's own doing. He could find no support for the theory that other minds (John Locke and Sir William Petty have been candidates for the honor) were involved. Channing's examination of the *Frame* "failed to reveal any steps of progress in the formulation of that remarkable document: nor did it give any reason for supposing that Penn received any important suggestions from outside sources."

Penn early saw the prospects of union in the North American colonies, and in 1697 was author of the first known *Plan of Union.* It was also a scheme for representative government. The colonies were to send picked representatives at least once every two years "to debate and resolve of such measures as are most advisable for their better understanding and the public tranquility and safety." The presiding officer was to be a commissioner of the Crown. This deliberating body was to be a "congress" and was to devote itself to intracolonial affairs. In time of war the commissioner was the commander of the colonial forces.

Carlyle, in a famous essay, once noted that "the Time" often cried out for the appearance of a "Great Man," but "the Time, calling its loudest, had to go down to confusion and wreck because . . . the Great Man . . . would not come when called." In Penn's case we have the opposite. No one seemed in 1681 to be calling for a colonizer who was also a great democratic lawgiver. Indeed, the wonder is that he appeared at all. Colonization and economic innovations one might expect in the later years of Charles II's reign. These were certainly "in the air" in the times. But a *political* vision like Penn's was an unlooked-for piece of good fortune. Or so it would seem. In Penn's life one finds some explanation of this, of the unique forces which, in combination with his historical environment, made Penn's great contribution to America possible. He was a singular individual in almost every respect.

After years of indifferent success in their colonization schemes, the Stuarts had granted a charter which would not only soon attract thousands from Britain and Europe, but would absorb settlers from other colonies as well. Virginia and New York during the late 1680's were losing young men of military age to Pennsylvania; army garrisons were threatened by desertions to the Quaker settlements, and Maryland's border had to be patrolled to intercept deserters from the British fleet. Moreover, Pennsylvania attracted men of wealth as well as those of poverty.

Her institutions were free, her land rich and the new colony was soon a success in the New World.

Pennsylvania's freedom reflected the great liberal mind of her proprietor. Penn represented the best of the 17th century. It was, to be sure, the century of the Stuarts, the Puritans, the Popish Plot, of witch hunts, massacres, Judge Jeffreys, judicial murders, of political executions and all the horrors of a dark age. But it was also the age of Coke and Selden; of Eliot, Pym and Hampden; of Locke, Mandeville and Petty; of Bunyan and Milton. In law, government, philosophy and letters the Age of Enlightenment was beginning to stir even in the darkness of religious and political totalitarianism. As we noted earlier, the founding of the Royal Society in 1660 witnessed the rise of science. Penn was elected a member in 1682 just before his departure for America.

Penn and his colony were the vanguard of a new age. By 1689, an act of religious toleration was passed by Parliament, and that Parliament's power in the British constitution was forever established in 1688 when William and Mary came over from Holland. William Penn, born in 1644, who was imprisoned for his religious beliefs, who once saw a woman burned alive for hers, lived into the age of Swift and Pope. The times were violent, but fast-changing. Penn had greatly contributed to the change. The Cavalier Quaker, a man of his times, grasped an opportunity. The "times" favored his effort. The growing commercial progress of England, the rising spirit of independence among England's common people, the triumph of British naval and mercantile sea power, the growth of a new American empire, all these were in his favor. But that was not all. Others failed to build great colonies in the same time and circumstances. Penn's colony succeeded primarily because of its institutions, and those reflected the intellectual man, the interior world of William Penn, not the models in the world around him.

Such a story ought to have a glorious ending. Unfortunately, history is not always so accommodating. Penn's tumultuous career contained several disastrous episodes after the successful establishment of his colony in America. First let us consider the colony itself.

Penn's lands contained about a thousand white inhabitants when he received the charter from Charles II. The people there were mostly Swedes and Dutch, with a sprinkling of English, Finns, Germans, Welsh and others. Penn gave them full rights as citizens in the new colony. The boundary with Maryland was an almost immediate source of contention between Penn and Lord Baltimore. This was due largely to initial ignorance in England about the true survey lines (originally Penn was to have from 40 degrees latitude north, which would have excluded much of the present site of Philadelphia). Penn met in America with Lord Baltimore in an attempt to settle favorably, but the dispute was finally thrown back into litigation in Britain, a slow and costly process. For years the boundary dispute dragged on and, at one period, Maryland actually armed a fort in Pennsylvania to protect its own borders.

Penn was in his colony twice, first from October, 1682, until October, 1684. His second visit was from December, 1699, until November, 1701. There is no doubt that he was completely taken with his colony. He had provided for it well. His city was laid out in squares and with spacious dimensions, possibly as a reaction to his having witnessed plague and fire sweep London, alerting him to the ill effects of urban congestion. Probably in December, 1682, his famous treaty with the Indians was negotiated (Penn, a considerable linguist, prided himself with having learned their language, which he thought to be similar to Hebrew). The treaty was not broken during Penn's lifetime and, when it finally was, it was not broken first by the Indians.

The site of Philadelphia contained perhaps ten buildings when Penn arrived. Land sales went well and, in the first three years, fifty ships brought in settlers under the terms of the Concessions of 1681. About two-thirds of the settlers up to 1700 were English, and another 20 percent Welsh and Irish. There was also immigration from the Low Countries and Germany. Partly this was the fruit of Penn's missionary work for the Quakers, and partly the result of the Revocation of the Edict of Nantes in 1685.

During his first trip Penn built his estate, Pennsbury, to which he was devoted. He went back to England in the fall of 1684 to defend his boundaries against Lord Baltimore and did not return for fifteen years. On his second visit in 1699-1701 he revised the *Frame* according to the wishes of his colonists. On this trip he was accompanied by his second wife, Hannah Callowhill Penn, and several of his children, of whom one, John, "the American," was born during that trip. It was on this visit that Penn drew up a proposal for union of the North American colonies. By 1699 Philadelphia had 5,000 citizens and was second only to Boston in the New World. The colony thrived on exports of grains and fruits, timber, hides, etc. Penn went back to England again in 1701 to fight to keep his charter; a new war with France was brewing, and there was agitation to turn Pennsylvania into a Crown colony. Penn never saw his colony again.

Penn loved his colony, would have liked to live there himself and urged his family to do so. But Pennsylvania made him a poor man. His own estimate of his loss in the venture was £30,000. His Irish estates were seized by the Crown when Penn was an outlaw, and at the time his health failed he was negotiating with Queen Anne's government to sell his proprietary grant back to the Crown, since the settlers would not pay their quit rents and Penn's debts were mounting. He tried to borrow £10,000 from settlers in Philadelphia (interest free) and was refused.

Moreover, he was systematically swindled over the years by his steward, a man named Ford, to whom he was in danger of losing all his property in America. When Ford's widow sued Penn in chancery, and won the case, Penn could not pay and went to debtor's prison, in 1708. A settlement was finally made with a payment of £7,600 to the Ford family. The sum was raised by the Friends against a new mortgage upon Penn's American estate.

When Penn died on July 30, 1718, he was not penniless, although he came close enough. His heirs, Tories in 1776, were awarded £500,000 by the Crown for their loss after the American Revolution, though the Penn properties taken by the Americans were valued at about £1,000,000, an enormous sum in those days.

The long-run effects of Penn's life have been profound—beyond measure perhaps—and, one hopes, may yet have their greatest days ahead. Penn was an advocate of justice, law and individual liberty. The world as yet has no surfeit of these. Penn's achievements all represent decisions made in his life on the basis of his "abstract" beliefs, uncompromised by advantages or convenience. For some modern Americans it is useful to note that in no case did Penn make his great decisions on the basis of "practical" or "common sense" or "expedient" considerations. A famous court case illustrates the point.

In August, 1670, Penn was arrested for causing a riot, as he was preaching in the street in London outside the Friends meetinghouse, the doors having been barred by soldiers. The trial, called "Bushell's Case" after one of the jurors, began in September. Penn urged the jury not to have their verdict dictated by the bench. He argued heatedly and persuasively from the prisoner's box, challenging the court on every point; and then, locked in the bale dock at the back of the courtroom, he shouted out his defense to the jury. Penn having reminded them of their rights as Englishmen, they were convinced and would not bring in a verdict satisfactory to the bench even after being locked up for two nights. When the verdict of "Not guilty" was finally brought in, the jurors were placed in Newgate Prison and fined. Four of the "phenatique jurymen" refused to pay, appealed their case eventually and won it in Common Pleas under Chief Justice Vaughan's ruling that no jury could be punished for its verdict. "It is absurd, a jury should be fined by the judge for going against their evidence. . . ." Penn's father paid his fine to get him out of Newgate. The principle of a free jury remains to this day.

Penn's beliefs were not easy to hold. He suffered a great deal for them. Not only did Pennsylvania, his "Holy Experiment," ruin him financially, but he was jailed at least four times for his religious beliefs, and his loyalty to his sovereigns caused him to be outlawed. Penn's criminal record is a useful reminder of the reality which lies behind the words in history. The phrase "suffered for his religious beliefs" is not just a way to "pad" books. In 17th-century England it meant filthy prisons, public humiliation and exorbitant fines and bails, threats of a life in prison and worse.

In September, 1667, Penn was jailed in Cork, Ireland, under the Conventicle Act. In December, 1668, he was arrested (age 24) and placed in the Tower of London for publishing a religious pamphlet, *The Sandy Foundation Shaken,* without license from the Bishop of London (under the same law which earlier had induced Milton to write *Areopagitica*). Penn lay in the Tower under threat of life imprisonment until the following spring. In August, 1670, he was again arrested under the Conventicle Act and from this arrest came the ruling against punishment of juries for their verdicts. In February, 1671, Penn was in Newgate Prison for preaching in London. Just before leaving for America in 1682 he was again threatened with arrest for the same offense.

In addition to these problems involving his beliefs, William Penn, friend of the Stuarts, was sought under a warrant of "suspicion of High Treason" in 1689 which was issued by William and Mary. He was not apprehended, but as a fugitive from the King's justice, he now lost the income from his Irish lands, estimated at as high as £12,000 or £13,000, and was reduced to poverty. In July, 1690, he was arrested on a similar charge and placed in the Tower. In February, 1691, another warrant for treason was out for Penn, and he "disappeared" for three years (a perjuring informer was involved in this case, and Penn wisely did not risk arrest). He was finally pardoned in December, 1693.

Broken by his expenses and lack of financial return from his colony, and swindled by his own employees, Penn went to debtors prison for some months beginning in January, 1708. He thus shared to the full the experience of his co-religionists *and* the political losers of the era. He was no stranger to prisons.

Some have argued that Penn's important achievements as statesman and lawgiver ought rightly to be separated from his career as a Quaker leader. This is difficult to understand. It is true that Penn was a shrewd and sophisticated politician and courtier, and a man of action in a debauched age. But his use of these facets of his personality were surely the means, the ends being consistently, so far as we know, peace, justice, mercy, toleration and the rule of law. Penn, heir to a fortune and friend of the Stuarts, used his personal wealth, his estates and his influence to organize his great experiment in Pennsylvania. The profit motive was there to be sure, but the organization of that particular profit-making venture could have been much different than it was, and that is the only important point. Penn's legacy to Americans was the work of a statesman and politician all right, but it was also the work of a tolerant and democratic pacifist.

Those who argue that Penn's career as statesman and lawgiver are best understood in isolation from his career as an early leader of the Quakers are presuming that in Penn's own mind the two were separate. That was clearly not the case. In the turbulent 17th century whose statesmen were Straffords, Lauds, Cromwells and Clarendons, totalitarian doctrines and actions ruled. The democratic peace-loving beliefs and policies of Penn obviously grew out of his own extraordinary motives and choices among the infinity of alternatives open to him. As Trevelyan noted, in 1689 when the British first tried religious toleration as national policy, they were experimenting on new and novel ground. By that time Penn had already occupied the greater part of his life in pursuit of that end. His was an idealism which had been acquired by choice, not inherited.

The Penn family's loyalties to the Stuarts proved their fortune, but almost cost William Penn his own fortune if not indeed his life. Charles II's reign closed ingloriously with a battle between the Crown and Parliament over religion and the line of succession. Charles, cavalier to the end, after medical science failed to save him ("they opportunely blooded and cupped him, and plied his head with red-hot frying pans"), apologized for lingering so long, and finally expired in the arms of Rome on Feb. 5, 1685. Charles having no legitimate son, the succession went to his brother James, the Duke of York.

Penn's close association with James II was much to his advantage until the King fled in 1688. If Penn was indeed a close adviser, it could only be said that even the best advice could not save James from his ill-fated course. Penn went on a personal mission for the King to Holland in a vain attempt to gain the approval of William and Mary for James' policies of religious toleration. James' efforts to free his Catholic co-religionists from persecution in England were supported by Penn, it is suggested, because the Quakers, also a proscribed sect, gained from any move toward religious toleration. Through James, Penn got George Fox once more out of prison, and saved at least one Friend from the gallows. Penn is supposed by some to have influenced James to grant the indulgences which released thousands of dissenters from prison.

Penn stuck with the Stuarts to the end, was accused of being secretly a Jesuit and, in 1688, when William and Mary came to England, he was high on the list of Stuart favorites destined to suffer.

By 1693, when three members of the peerage, Lords Rochester, Ranelagh, and Sidney procured Penn's pardon from King William, Pennsylvania had been temporarily taken over by the Crown. Penn got his charter back only on the promise that his colony would contribute to King William's war with the French. The colony continued for years to cause Penn great difficulties and there seems little doubt that he would have sold it to Queen Anne's government if his health and mental powers had not failed him. Penn's widow was a good manager of the colony but his sons by that marriage, John and George, were thoroughly disliked in the colony. When the end came for the proprietary government in 1776, Penn's grandson Richard was Governor under the revision of the government which had been negotiated and signed by Penn.

Penn's contribution to American development was one of many achievements in his long, complicated and eventful career. His affairs were vast for a man of any age. He was involved in his country's life at all levels, from the royal entourage to the lowest levels of governmental proceedings, the magistrates' courts where he and his co-religionists were hailed for their nonconformism. As a loyal supporter of the Stuarts he lived through the political upheavals of his time. As a pioneer practitioner of the Quaker faith his affairs were inextricably entangled in the great and bloody religious revolution which gripped England from the Act of Supremacy to the Toleration Act. As an absentee landlord he participated in the economic subjugation of Ireland by the English. As Proprietor of Pennsylvania he was a great figure in the extension of the British Empire which had consciously been started by Cromwell.

Penn was thus a complex and forceful representative of a revolutionary age. Yet his greatest achievement, the founding of Pennsylvania, displayed a kind of ultimate simplicity in Penn's character. Perhaps as a counterpart to his ineptness in business affairs, he was naive to the point of childishness in his straightforward belief in man's goodness, and in his abilities to know and understand the good, the true and beautiful. Penn's "Holy Experiment" was a portent of the *ideal* in America's future tradition—men of all classes, races and religions striving to live in harmony, governed by laws of their own making, with equality for all before the bar of justice.

Penn the man of action was also a man of peace. Following his ideals undid him in his own time, but they created a great force for the future. There is no paradox here. A cynical age might view Penn and his "peaceable people" with a smile, yet in affairs of war, we have the examples of Washington and the American cause at Valley Forge and of Churchill in the summer of 1940 to teach us that simple faith can achieve great things. Such was true in the case of Penn. In American liberty and freedom Penn lives on. Some historians, for example, S. E. Morison and H. S. Commager, consider that the ability of the United States to resist the totalitarianisms of a modern dark age is due more to Penn's resistance to an earlier totalitarianism than to the efforts of any other man. The experience of individual liberty has been nearly universal with our people and human freedom is a cherished ideal among Americans. Imperfectly realized, unequally distributed, liberty is still "natural" to Americans and autocracy is still "foreign." It is a great legacy. (pp. 50-65)

> *Jonathan Hughes, "William Penn and the Holy Experiment," in his* The Vital Few: American Economic Progress and Its Protagonists, *Houghton Mifflin Company, 1965, pp. 22-66.*

Harry Emerson Wildes   (essay date 1974)

[*Wildes was an American educator and critic. In the following excerpt, he provides a brief overview of Penn's relations with Native Americans.*]

Penn took pains to cultivate good race relations. It was a matter dear to his heart. Other American provinces had mistreated their Indians, not because of viciousness or hostility, but through ignorance and misunderstandings; naturally, the Indians had responded in kind. Penn, in common with other well-meaning leaders, laid the cause of conflict to failure to recognize that all men, as children of a common God, were, or should be, brothers. The Holy Experiment, he believed, must show the way to peace, harmony, and cooperation.

Himself a member of a minority group whose unusual customs were misinterpreted and distrusted by the authorities, Penn was determined that no one in his province, whatever his race, religion, or background, should suffer discrimination or persecution. All Pennsylvanians, whatever their origins, were to be equally protected by laws passed by a free legislature democratically elected. This did not necessarily imply that everyone was to be wholly equal to all others, for certain rights, suffrage for example, must be exercised only by those capable of wise and mature judgment, but any limitation imposed applied equally to everyone. No free white citizen should own a privilege denied a black man of equal status. No Quaker should possess a power denied on religious grounds to any other Christian. A fully naturalized Frenchman should stand on precisely the same footing as a citizen of English birth. Wholly unrestricted manhood equality had not yet dawned in any country, but Pennsylvania under William Penn came closer to that goal than any other region in his day.

Penn came to America with rather sketchy ideas about the Indians. Certainly he had listened to George Fox and to Josiah Coale, perhaps also to others, as they talked about their travels in America. As a frequenter of the court he would have met officials returned to report on colonial conditions. He may have known, or at least have seen, an Indian or two. His insatiable appetite for ransacking libraries would have led him to inform himself about Sir Walter Raleigh's ill-fated settlement at Roanoke, as well as about the luckier adventures in Virginia, Carolina, New England, and, of course, New Jersey. None of the sources, except the very recent Quaker experiences, were beyond criticism. Officials would have had axes to grind. Indians, in whom Penn would have been far more interested, would not have commanded sufficient English to discuss the topics with which Penn would have been most concerned.

From what Penn had read or heard or seen of Indians, he had formed a highly favorable opinion of them. They were quiet folk, much like typical Quakers, serious, reserved, and taciturn, qualities Penn admired. They were dignified, not frivolous, nor were they given to vain jesting as were so many people of the world. They prized their honor and never forgot a discourtesy, but they were more considerate than European snobs, for never would an Indian act rudely to another. Penn did not use the term "nature's gentlemen" to describe the Indians, but he would have approved of it. Since he was no devotee of poetry, he may not have read John Dryden's lines about noble savages running wild in the woods, but he would have accepted the description.

Penn, shocked and dismayed by the wickedness that he believed lay all about him, saw in unspoiled America man's best, perhaps his only, hope for earthly redemption. He looked upon the Indian almost as a man of Genesis, living in an isolated world untouched by civilized corruption. In this naïve belief he broke new ground. According to general report, the Indians were rude and barbarous, benighted, and perhaps subhuman. Some said they were thievish, treacherous, and murderous. Penn, willing enough to believe that white men of his generation were decadent, had a higher opinion of the aborigines. Europeans had been corrupted by the evil institutions of their times; they had rejected the good teachings of ancient days and had drifted from the paths of virtue, but the Indians remained unspoiled.

No one could argue that Penn understood the Indians. All the evidence was against him. But secure in his faith that the Indians might very possibly be pursuing some form of the ancient laws of Jehovah, as they interpreted those laws, he thought it possible that those Indians might really be survivors of the Ten Lost Tribes of Israel. All those derogatory rumors stemmed from the casual and unreliable reports of chance visitors, some of whom, at least, had been seeking only adventure, profit, or rich land that would cost them nothing but would yield enormous wealth. Virtually none were high-minded scholars looking for the truth. Penn intimated that few indeed had ever tried to understand the Indian's social structure, his psychology, or his ethics.

Penn envied the Indian's simplicity and his freedom from the corruption of the supposedly civilized world. Theirs was the way of life that God intended man to live, a life close to the heart of nature, where everyone was free and equal, each willing and anxious to help his fellows, to share the good and to work together to avoid the evil. Theirs was not the selfish world where men thought only of private gain. They did not practice cutthroat competition, seek public office to exact gratuities, or cheat each other. They did not draw up lengthy contracts, swear solemn oaths that they would perform what they promised, and then tear up the agreements if thereby they could save a shilling or two. The Indians were honest men who needed no police, no lawyers, and no jails. Apparently they had never heard of taxes.

Though the Indian religion left something to be desired, it did hold promise. To a Quaker mind it was unilluminated, but there were faint gleams of light. Their beliefs and practices were far from being as "dark" as Penn considered some European forms of worship. The Indians did not recognize the One True God, at least not by that name; but with a little coaching, they would come to realize their Great Spirit's true identity. They were not fanatic; they did not demand conformity. Certainly they did not punish those who disagreed for conscientious reasons.

Their simplicity and innate goodness extended even to their speech. Indians avoided verbosity, restricting their talk to a Quakerish Yea-Yea or Nay-Nay; but when they did speak they were fervent and eloquent, their sentences notable for imagery and charm. Penn resolved that he would learn their tongue.

William Penn was not maudlin in his admiration, however. The Indians had faults, though some of them could be excused. "They live by their pleasures," said Penn, but he was quick to add, "I mean hunting and fishing." Unhappily, they drank too heavily; this vice was not entirely their own fault, for they had been a temperate people corrupted by the Swedes and Dutch and, to Britain's shame, by English traders who had dealt with them. They did not always keep their word, but maybe this was due to ignorance. Indian chiefs had "sold" the same lands over and over again, but white men must remember that Indians knew nothing of European systems of land titles. What had really happened was that foreigners had "bought" something that the Indians had never sold: not the exclusive ownership of any territory but merely an equal right to live and hunt and farm together with the tribesmen.

Reared in a monarchial and aristocratic culture, Penn did not realize that primitive tribesmen had little concept of a stratified society. Quite understandably he assumed that Indian spokesmen were kings or at least noblemen with powers similar to those of English monarchs: the right, for instance, to make binding treaties, to commit their people to specific actions, to barter away the tribal land. Thus, Penn undertook to purchase territory, not realizing that the price that he would pay would not be used for tribal benefit but would be accepted as presents to the "kings" to be used for their personal enjoyment. As such prices were usually paid in goods rather than by cash, it was indeed strange that neither Penn nor others connected the transfer of so many articles of clothing, so many pairs of shoes, or so many blankets; so many axes, knives, or scissors; so many guns or so many rounds of ammunition; even so many gallons of liquor, with the number of chiefs attending the conferences at which the goods were given.

Penn's misconceptions were not peculiar to him; they were shared by virtually every European who had done business with the Indians. Each wave of immigrants had bought and paid for the land on which the people settled, and each, after the first arrivals, had been dismayed to learn that the same land had been previously sold, sometimes several times, to others. The Indians, however, had not been guilty of fraud; rather, they had been hospitable, freely admitting strangers to equal enjoyment of the land.

Though Penn, like others, anticipated exclusive possession of farm and residential tracts, he had no thought of exploitation of the Indians. He assured the red men of his firm intention to avoid the harassment to which other foreigners had subjected them; he expressed his anxiety to avoid animosity by treating them with kindliness and justice. If disputes should occur, the conflicts would be resolved by fair trials before impartial courts. "If anything should offend you or your people," he promised, "you should have a full and speedy satisfaction for the same by an equal number of just men on both sides."

He, no more than any other European, ever stopped to wonder whether Indians had any real idea of precisely what he meant, and the Indians were too polite to request an explanation. It was exactly what he had told his European colonists, and it was said for exactly the same reasons. Penn well understood that his province, unlike most of the others and to a greater degree than any, was polyglot, with peoples of various stocks, whose backgrounds, languages, and customs varied widely. His plans of settlement, he suspected rightly, would entail inconveniences, some relocations, and perhaps serious culture clashes; unless the matter was delicately handled, strong antagonisms might arise. In fairness and justice the disputes must not be arbitrarily settled by any one group, however overriding that group's authority might be, but must be ended by mutual agreement. The Swedes, Hollanders, and non-Quaker English should have as strong a say as should the Friends and, unusual as the practice might be, so should the Indians.

Penn therefore instructed his officials, when dealing with the Indians, to treat them as equals and not to assume that because a chief might happen to understand a few words of broken English he could negotiate in that alien tongue. Everything that might be said to Indians, Penn insisted, should be translated by just such a competent interpreter as Lasse Cock, his own interpreter.

Statue of Penn at Philadelphia's City Hall. Erected in 1892, the bronze casting stands 37 feet tall and weighs 52,400 lbs.

Early in November Penn, with a small group of Friends, rode up to Shackamaxon, a mile or two north of the city where a few Quakers had already established a meeting. His major purpose was to attend services at the home of Thomas Fairman, and as Shackamaxon was a favorite Indian council grounds, he hoped to meet some of their people. He would transact no business on a First Day, but the acquaintances would be helpful at further conferences.

As usual, Penn was lucky; it so chanced that Chief Tamamend of the Lenni Lenape, who American Revolutionists later adopted as Tammany, the patron saint of the young democracy, was visiting the council grounds. According to legend, Penn here pledged to Tamamend and to leaders of tribes from as far west as the Susquehanna, that Indians and Quakers would always live side by side in mutual harmony and perpetual peace. The legend apparently originated with John Oldmixon, author of English histories, who possibly misread the date of a letter in which Penn described a later conference held on the same grounds or who may have confused Penn's Shackamaxon meeting with an earlier meeting there by Markham. Whatever the cause of the error, Shackamaxon in November 1682 has long been commemorated as the occasion when Penn and the Indians, standing under a giant elm, concluded a solemn treaty pledging that Indians and Quakers would remain forever friendly. Penn said:

The Great Spirit who made me and you, who rules the heavens and the earth and knows the inmost thoughts of man, knows that I and my friends have a hearty desire to live in peace and friendship with you. It is not our custom to use weapons. . . . We are met on the broad pathway of good faith and good will . . . all is to be openness, brotherhood and love. . . . I will not do as the Marylanders did, that is, call you children and brothers only, for parents are apt to whip their children too severely, and brothers sometimes will differ. Neither will I compare the friendship between us to a chain, for the rain may rust it, or a tree may fall and break it, but I will consider you as the same flesh and blood with the Christians and the same as if the one body were to be divided into two parts."

Whether Penn actually delivered such a speech, translated into Indian by Lasse Cock, is immaterial; there is no question that he would have endorsed every word of it. Nor is it important whether, when the speech was ended, Penn did or did not join the Indians in feasting on roasted acorns and hominy. It is questionable, however, whether he then played with them, "hopping and jumping higher than any of them" (as the legend has it), for that sort of activity, which he would have termed "carnal frivolity," was not in his character.

The famous Benjamin West painting, wherein Penn, clad in anachronistic costume, stands between Deputy Governor Markham and West's ancestor Robert Pearson, is historically incorrect. Certainly the Penn of the portrait, fat and pudgy at thirty-eight, would have offered no athletic competition to the lithe young Indians of the background, nor, if the picture were accurate, could the ancient lady half a century later have described the Proprietor as "the handsomest man she had ever met."

As Indians were averse to indoor gatherings, the sharp frosts of a Pennsylvania winter prevented further conferences until spring. Penn did not find the cold too severe; he was pleasantly surprised that it was no worse. At a season when, in England, he would have seen the Thames frozen, with thousands of people on the ice, booths and huts erected upon it, and even some enterprising merchants roasting oxen on the frozen surface, Pennsylvania, he assured his London friends, was reasonably comfortable. Once in a while, he admitted, there might be ships caught in the ice, but there were no coaches rolling up and down upon the river such as he would have seen upon the Thames. Even though the temperature might be low, there was none of the "foul, thick, black weather the northeast winds bring to England." The climate might be "dry, cold, piercing and hungry, yet I remember not I wore more clothes than in England."

After "a sweet spring, no gusts but gentle showers and a fine sky," Penn and his entourage, including Lasse Cock, met the Indians again at Shackamaxon on June 23, 1683. Because this was a formal occasion, the conclusion of a treaty of lasting peace and friendship, the one that was never sworn to and never broken, Penn dignified the occasion by wearing the impressive sky-blue sash he had worn at New Castle. The Indians arrived in full regalia, Tamamend crowned by a chaplet and carrying a small horn as a symbol of authority. Addressing Penn as "Onas," which they explained was Indian for a pen or quill, they presented him with a wampum belt showing a hatted man holding an Indian by the hand. Both the belt and the sash are preserved at the Historical Society of Pennsylvania.

Thus the Indians again welcomed Penn's colonists to residence while Penn, in return, distributed useful European articles. These were the usual household articles, the customary knives, axes, fishhooks, needles, and other steel goods, together with such woolens as blankets, knee-length stockings, and the long mantles which were then called matchcoats. It is doubtful that Penn included rum or other grog in this list of gifts; himself a moderate consumer of wine and beer, he was far more careful than other colonial leaders about supplying liquor to the Indians. In buying some New Jersey land, Fenwick, for instance, had paid two matchcoats and forty gallons of rum. Penn, however, realized that Indians were particularly susceptible to hard liquors, unknown to them before the coming of the white men. The Indians when drunk, Penn saw, were easily cheated; for sixpence worth of liquor they would part with furs that they would not sell for five shillings' worth of any other commodity. Penn would have liked to impose total prohibition on the sale of rum to red men, and one or two chiefs, even before Penn's arrival, had proposed as much to Lasse Cock, but white men would not cooperate. Indians then proposed that drunken Indians suffer the same punishments as drunken Europeans, but this scheme proved unworkable because Indians had no cash to pay the five-shilling fine imposed. Law enforcement broke down entirely when a sheriff, hunting through the woods to find some culprits, became hopelessly lost and had to be rescued, apparently by the very Indians he had been sent to arrest.

Despite the tokens of friendship distributed at Shackamaxon, the tribesmen were not entirely happy in their new alliance. Tamamend, realizing that the white men acted as though Indians no longer had the right to hunt on the land, was quoted as having threatened to burn their houses. "He has played the rogue," Holme reported. Tamamend had contended that the Indians had never parted with any land and so the whites should move away.

Penn did not hear of this development until after he had returned to England, but he took a firm stand. He had given Indians, he said, the equivalent of at least £1000. "Tamine [*sic*]" he told Holme, "sold all and if the Indians do not punish him we will and must." Apparently Chief Tamamend needed no chastisement. For the rest of Penn's life no further misunderstandings developed.

Actually, the conflict had been exaggerated, for only three days after Tamamend's threat, a Hollander, writing from Germantown, assured his friends in Europe that Indians were friendly. "We live together with them very quiet and peaceful. We travel day and night through the forest without the slightest fear." The testimony reinforced German assurances. "The so-called Indians or savages," a leading German reported, "are kindhearted, honest folk who, upon a time, in that great day of judgment will stand up with those of Tyre and Sidon to shame the false-mouthed Christians."

White conduct toward the Indians was not above reproach. The common trader practice of making the tribesmen drunk, the easier to cheat them, was bad enough but certain scoundrels went farther. Arming themselves with bottles of rum the young Europeans, identified only as the "servants" of a prominent Philadelphian, visited nearby Indian villages, invited the natives to drinking parties and then not only lay with the squaws but, afterward, beat up both men and women. When the red men complained the Provincial Council took appropriate action; it ordered that the laws against *selling* liquor to Indians be strengthened and enforced. Though the Indians identified the culprits no punishment was inflicted. (pp. 176-82)

> *Harry Emerson Wildes, in his* William Penn, *Macmillan Publishing Co., Inc., 1974, 469 p.*

Hugh Barbour   (essay date 1979)

[*An American educator and theologian, Barbour is a member of the Society of Friends and has written extensively on Quakers. In the following essay, he traces the development of Penn's thought, maintaining that Penn fused humanism with Quaker eschatology to build "a new ethic of social reform."*]

William Penn intended no new synthesis of thought. His practical social reforms, combining the Quakers' radical hope for the total transforming of men, ethics and society by God's Spirit with a humanist's trust in reason and conscience already at work in all men universally, were a new stance for Quakers. But Friends noted mainly his exuberance and pragmatism and his uncritical openness about ideas. In Europe and America as a whole, he was best known in his own time for his practical career: he was the man of peace with the Indians, the founder of Pennsylvania, the champion of toleration. For these he was later celebrated in the paintings of "the Peaceable Kingdom" and the writings of Voltaire.

But Penn's ideas, developing gradually (if not always clearly) in his laws and tracts, raised important issues for Quakers and Protestants generally. We will focus on Penn's approaches to *history,* to *toleration,* and to *theology and ethics.* In granting legal rights to Indians and a vote to all Pennsylvania citizens, as also in his reform ideals for England, Penn was accepting truth from whatever source it might come, and yet he was confident he must and could remake men and society, at least by convincing consciences. It is this union of humanism and eschatology which seems to typify Protestant liberals. Such folk expect to cooperate in society for concrete goals with reasonable men though they differ in belief. Yet they have a vision of history and an urgency about social reform rarely found in secular humanists, or even in utopians' visions of a golden past.

The humanist movement had combined a revived love of classical learning, rationalism and universalism with an intensified concern for ethics and moral reform. Interest in both the Stoics and the New Testament was reborn after 1000, and for men as diverse as Erasmus, Thomas More, Henry More and Grotius ethical concern predominated. Yet the same men usually separated their personal faith from natural law, which had retained a certain autonomy. Even medieval scholastics had identified Greek virtue with the decalogue. Truth, even moral truth, was thus universal, while salvation was not, in the diverse orthodoxies of Rome, Wittenberg, Geneva or Deventer. At the same time, humanists tended to turn away from the medieval view of sacred history: purity was timeless, or belonged before man's fall.

But the millenarians, Hussites, early Anabaptists, and the radical Puritans and Quakers shared with all manner of Calvinists a more drastic vision of history. For them, God's absolute power over nature and history was coupled with his total rejection of evil. The radicals' vision of history as a judgment and revolution, however, arose out of thorough inner changes in their own heart and life, quite as much as out of political struggle or class conflict. Yet their ethic turned into sectarian separatism only after persecution or failure: their first hope was for the remaking of the world. In Geneva and in the Puritan Commonwealths of England and New England they could unite contemporary and sacred history. But the religious radicals usually credited little truth to the ungodly, and rejected pagan antiquity and all its works.

Many men fail to fit such oversimplified images of humanist and radical. Nor should other Protestant liberals of Penn's lifetime, such men as Comenius, Milton, Walwyn the Leveller, Gottfried Arnold and perhaps even Cotton Mather, be isolated from the diverse thought-worlds with which each interacted. Yet these men professed a dynamic, often unstable, blend of ground-beliefs which identifies them as vigorous hybrids of the humanist and the religious radical: they learned truth from wise men of every age, faith and culture, and praised the classical philosophers as warmly as did secular humanists. Yet simultaneously they held a positive view of history and believed in the Kingdom of God and his power to change men.

William Penn's ideas cannot be claimed as unique. Yet Penn drew a unique intensity in both his universalism and his radicalism from his Quaker community, from its wrestling with "the Light within," and from his own experience of the unity of world truth and the radical depth of evil. He was no mere blender of ideas.

Upon the Quakers, moreover, Penn's influence was clearly crucial. The early Quakers' experience of God's Light had begun as judgment, not as man's self-affirmation. It was a radical extension and internalizing of Puritan concerns for conversion, inner selflessness and "visible sainthood." In the 1650s, George Fox and his brethren had stirred mass meetings in the relatively unchurched North and West of England, turning them from their Bibles to the answering voice within. By 1660 he had taught some 50,000 Friends, as he called them, to sit in silence under the inwardly searchlighting truth which showed up every act or impulse of self-will or self-righteousness. Naturally, they quaked, struggled and despaired for months, upheld meanwhile by fellow-quakers alert to self-made escapes, until finally a "new man" was born within, able to respond freely to positive leadings of the Light, and joy broke through. The Light was also the Spirit of Christ, whose power and judgment Friends had found to be loving. This overwhelming power would surely sweep through and overcome the world. Each man's "day of Visitation" could then be seen as part of a cosmic conquest of evil, "the Lamb's War," for which he too was now recruited, to confront evil in other men. Like the Hebrew prophets, Friends hoped for total repentance, even by those in power, and for the transformation of national life.

The Restoration of Charles II, however, began two decades of persecution under the Clarendon Code, during which some hundreds of imprisoned Quakers died. In face of the worldly court and its triumphant immorality, Quaker confidence in "the Lamb's War" gradually faded. The Quaker community remained committed to their ethical *"Testimonies,"* now as badges of loyalty rather than as challenges to convict other men's pride. But Friends might easily have retired into a radically separatist ethic like the Anabaptists', as indeed John Woolman later urged Quakers to withdraw from power amid the Seven Years War. Thanks to Penn, however, Friends never lost sight of social justice and concern for legislation.

Universalism had indeed always been part of Quaker experience. From the first, Friends affirmed that every man or woman in each culture is directly reached by the Spirit of God, and can know moral as well as factual truth directly. Early Quakers never assumed that by nature men universally followed that Light, much less were inherently good. Yet they affirmed, unlike Thomists, humanists and Puritans that the Light was not merely "natural" since it was enough to save men from evil. It was the Light of Christ. To see how William Penn built upon both ethical radicalism and universalism a new ethic of social reform, we need to study how these outlooks entered his life, and some areas and ways he let them interact.

Unlike most other Friends, Penn was a humanist before he was a Quaker. An admiral's son, an activist, he was by nature eclectic. He learned the Latin classics at Chigwell School, and many of the Greeks in Latin; the schoolboy's philosophers, especially Socrates and the Stoics, remained his lifelong favorites. Then as later, he read and loved Jeremy Taylor and other Anglican humanists. Penn's schooling taught him to enjoy reading, and to keep a "commonplace book" for noting ideas and quotations. He went on to learn ethics and toleration from John Owen at Oxford and the Huguenot professor Moise Amyraut at Saumur, but not their Calvinist theology or arguments on the Trinity. Penn briefly studied law at Lincoln's Inn; later he could quote Coke's *Institutes* and three Plantagenet statutes in one sentence in his self-defence at his Old Bailey trial of 1670. Penn quoted every one available. On toleration he regularly cited Grotius and Pufendorf and the histories of a dozen nations, along with early church fathers and the Romans. Like most Quakers and Englishmen, he amassed Bible quotations, too often from memory. In his earliest edition of *No Cross, No Crown*, written as a twenty-four-year-old prisoner in the Tower of London, Penn cited nineteen classical authors, ten church fathers, twenty-five recent continental writers, and nine Englishmen, by way of presenting forty-three ancient and twenty-two modern instances of simple living or holy dying. For his second edition in 1682, he added ninety-one more, mostly Greek

kings, virtuous women and dying Englishmen, and climaxed with the cases of his own father and his friend Princess Elizabeth of the Rhine. Many of Penn's quotations were second- or fourth-hand.

Penn, one must admit, was a culture snob, even in using the customary appeal to authorities. But Penn also shared deeper outlooks of the humanists: that the world is one and is rational; that we are taught about it by philosophers of all faiths and eras; that between thoughtful men, nothing human is alien.

Meanwhile, Penn was also a young radical Quaker. In his lonely Irish winter of 1666-67 he too wrestled to search his motives and to renounce worldly pomp and honor along with self-seeking. Penn's fullest picture of the experience "when about Two and Twenty Years of Age . . . God took me by the Hand, and led me out of the Pleasures, Vanities and Hopes of the World . . . with the Terrors of the Lord," was given in an early tract of *Counsel and Advice* to others:

> Friends who are sensible of the Day of your Visitation, . . . and have cried in your Souls, "How long, O Lord": Live and Abide in that Light and Life which hath visited you, . . . and made Sin exceeding sinful to you. . . . O love his judgments. . . . Part with all that is for judgment, . . . the vain Fashions and Customes of this World. . . . The Enemy will attend you in this holy march. . . . He will aggravate your Sins, and plead the impossibility of their Remission: he will act the Advocate for the Justice of God, that he might cast you into Despondency. . . . Even Jesus was tempted and tried, . . . Yea . . . cryed out in the Agony of the Cross, "My God, my god, why hast thou forsaken me?" Nevertheless he gloriously Triumph'd over all. . . .

From inner experience, Penn first and last was always centrally concerned about morality, and was drawn to the uncompromising Friends. But public morals was a bitter issue in 1667, when the Court and the royal mistresses had undone the work of three generations of Puritans. In that year, George, Duke of Buckingham, the king's best friend and worst corrupter, forced Lord Clarendon out of office and became the leader of the ruling "cabal." Only weeks later, he killed his mistress' husband, Lord Shrewsbury, in a duel and at once procured a royal pardon. Within weeks "the jolly Duke of Bucks" had installed the widow in his own home, forcing his good-humored wife back to her father's. Buckingham's thousands of pounds a year for clothes may be reflected in Penn's famous attack:

> When the pale faces are more comiserated, the pinched bellies relieved, and naked backs clothed, . . . it will be early enough for you to plead the "indifferency" of your pleasures. But that the sweat and tedious labor of the husbandman, early and late, cold and hot, wet and dry, should be converted into the pleasure, ease and pastime of a small number of men, that the cart, the plow, the thrash should be . . . laid upon nineteen parts of the land to feed the inordinate lusts and delicious appetites of the twentieth, is . . . blasphemous. [*No Cross, No Crown*]

Penn also fully shared the early Quakers' sense that God's cosmic plan and power were fulfilled in their movement. He wrote to Vice-Chancellor Peter Mews of Oxford University, who had been harassing Friends:

> Poor mushroom, wilt thou War against the Lord, and lift up thy self in Battel against the Almighty? Canst thou frustrate His Holy Purposes and bring His Determinations to nought? . . . Dost thou think to escape His Wrath . . . for thy ungodly and illegal Persecution of His poor Children?

This leads us, however, to closer study of Penn's interpretation of history, the first of the areas in which it is possible to see him fusing universalism and radicalism.

. . . . .

To trace changes in his view of *history* is not always simple. In theology, he inherited a series of doctrinal disputes with Presbyterians, Baptists and Anglicans from the Quakers before him; these debates and some of Fox's specific lines of argument Penn kept up most of his life. Second, he liked his own writings, especially on ethics and doctrine. Some works he reissued unchanged; in others only minor changes and additions reflect his new views. Third, Penn tried to revive after the Toleration Act of 1689 the old ethical zeal and perspective among Friends. Specifically, he wrote as a preface to Fox's *Journal* the survey later printed alone as **The Rise and Progress of the People Called Friends** (1694). Here, and in **Primitive Christianity Revived** (1696), what looks like radicalism is found on careful reading to be, like Mennonite "Restitutionism," closer to sectarian separatism and conservatism than to an ethos of world conquest. Penn's later tracts stressed Quakerism more as a pattern than as a present power.

Changes in the view of history in Penn's earlier years, while he believed God was still actively working out his purposes, are found mainly in how and where he sees God working. His first view of world history underlies an unpublished tract of 1670, "God's Controversy Proclaimed," and its more careful parallel after his first mission to Holland the following year:

A Trumpet sounded in the ears of the Inhabitants of both the High & Low Dutch Nation

O ye Inhabitants of these Countries, the Spirit of the Lord is upon me, & by the same I am necessitated to proclaim the Great & Dreadfull Day of the Lord, which is already come unto many, & hasteneth to come upon all Nations. . . . In what nation upon Earth is Pride, Vain Glory, Worldly Pomp, & suchlike Vanities found more to abound, than in your streets? Repent, and mind God. . . . Nothing shall deliver you out of his hand,. . . . neither your stately buildings, deep Consultations, great Traffiques, nor manyfold Inventions, . . . whose works [are] being reproved by the light which God hath caused to shine into every one's heart.

Therefore to you all, howsoever named, Papists, Protestants, Lutherans, Calvinists, Socinians,

Mennists, Behemenists, Armininians, this is the Visitation . . . of God to you all: . . . As men come to believe in the Light, to receive & obey it, their Minds diligently waiting upon it, & being thereby taught, they shall . . . sensibly experience that the End of Christ's coming is . . . to make an End of trangression in the hearts of men. . . . Whether you hear or forbear, . . . yet I have clear'd my Conscience before the Lord, & am thus far clear of the Charge of your blood.

By 1678, however, Penn's humanism or liberalism can be seen in his sympathy for all England, and in his inclusion of English hopes, as much as Quaker destinies, within God's plans. Panic pervaded England: men feared violent capture of power by Catholics after Titus Oates' witch hunt had precipitated a real Catholic plot and murder; King Charles' cousin and secret ally, Louis XIV, was beginning the Huguenot persecutions leading up to the Revocation of the Edict of Nantes in 1685. Penn felt called to interpret those times to Friends:

> I have not only long beheld . . . the Lusts, Pleasures, Wantonness, Drunkenness, Whoredoms, Oaths, Blasphemies, . . . but for some time I have had a deep Sense that the Overflowing Scourge of God's Wrath was just ready to break out upon the [English] People. . . . And in the midst of his judgments, this I received for you [Friends] from the Lord as his . . . counsel: TO THY TENTS, O ISRAEL; TO THY TENTS, O ISRAEL; [but] GOD IS THY TENT: TO THY GOD, O ISRAEL. . . . And my witness is that ye are the People through whom this Heavenly Seed of Righteousness must clearly and stedfastly shine unto others, in this Uneven and Rough Times that are coming. . . . We are the People above all others that must stand in the Gap, and pray for the putting away of the Wrath, so that this Land be not made an utter Desolation.
>
> Be therefore encouraged to wait upon the Lord. . . . For he will not cast off this Land, as he did Sodom; he hath a Right Seed, a Noble People in it, that he yet will gather: Many Sheep there be, not yet of our Fold, [whom] the foul Weather and the Storms will but help to Jesus the Light within. . . . [Yet] let us be careful not to mingle with the Crowd, lest their Spirit enter us, . . . and we fall into the same Temptations of Fear. . . . They must come to us, we must not come to them. . . . Yet can we not be insensible of their infirmities, as well as we shall not be free from some of their Sufferings. . . . We must make their case our own, and travail alike in Spirit for them as for ourselves, . . . that in Truth, Righteousness and Peace they may be established, and the land . . . shall yet be called THE ISLAND SAVED BY THE LORD. [*To the Children of the Light*]

Here the dynamic of "sacred history" and universal human concern blend not as manifest destiny but as a call to national reform. Even while giving Friends a "saving remnant theology" like Isaiah's, Penn did in fact "go to the people" for their sake as well as the Quakers'. He did not feel inconsistent in campaigning for his agnostic friend Algernon Sidney in the two Parliamentary elections of

1679 despite the misgivings of many Friends, since it seemed the best hope in a generation for achieving toleration through Parliament.

. . . . .

Penn's efforts for *toleration* continued throughout his career. Thus his universalism, humanism, and newly-formed liberalism must rather be seen in the changes in his arguments for toleration. Penn at all times used a wide repertoire of approaches to toleration, tailored to his immediate audience. Thus his new insights are seen mainly by contrasting his arguments with early Friends', and by noticing his shifts of emphasis. From the beginning, but increasingly, Penn argued from pragmatic, economic, rational grounds, or from the value of conscience in general, more than from the claims of the Spirit or the Quaker Light.

There is a long pedigree for each of the main lines of reasoning about toleration. Different and characteristic arguments had been used by humanists, by Baptists and sectarians, and even by Calvinists and Catholics long before Quakers arose. These can be classified into at least eight main groups; and Penn himself can be quoted for examples of each: First, theological or even theocratic arguments rest on the divine authority a persecuted group claims for its beliefs or for its own existence. Calvinists made such claims for their biblical doctrines, Catholics for both church and papacy. A subgroup of theocrats argues more subjectively that true faith is inward, being compelled only by the Word of God, however this may be given to men. This was once the special argument of Baptists and others stressing conversion of the heart. Coercion only makes hypocrites: "it defeats the work of Grace, which alone can beget faith" [Penn, *Great Case of Liberty of Conscience*]. A third subset of theocrats stresses ethics, since the saints must be allowed to act outwardly as divine authority commands, "which we sin if we omit," as John Clarke told Cotton in Boston, and Penn told the Cavalier Parliament. The authority of the Spirit was the dominant, sometimes the only argument used by the earliest Friends.

A second group of arguments can be called humanist. One form of this is the rationalist's confidence that truth can and must be found by free inquiry and debate. Persecution is "destructive of the noble principle of reason"; and reason here is conceived as personal, individual understanding. As Penn grew older, he moved farther this way; increasingly he identified reason and conscience. "It would certainly be most unreasonable to judge a man . . . that receives his religion without the suffrage of his own reason." Another form of humanist argument diverges here, for the skeptic knows that all men are ignorant and fallible. Persecution would imply an "evident claim to the infallibility which Protestants, . . . to avoid the Papists, have denied to all but God himself." A third humanist argument was ethical: the test by which a group is shown to be unjustly persecuted is their morality. Penn could be bitter about the suffering of the virtuous: "Licentious Persons see Men of Vertue molested for Assembling with a Religious Purpose to Reverence and Worship God, and . . . inferr it is better for them to be as they are." Thus Penn had no objection to blue laws limiting "conscience to keep within the bounds of Morality, and that it be nei-

ther Frantick nor Mischievous, but a Good Subject, a Good Child, a Good Servant, in all the affairs of life." a humanitarian appeal for sympathy for sufferers was often linked to this argument, protesting the "unspeakable pressure of nasty prisons, and daily confiscations of our goods, to the ruin of intire families, ... whilst there have been none more inoffensive." Such sympathy by non-Quakers was perhaps the strongest motive for the eventual Toleration Act of 1689. A persecuted sect that has separated itself from society, intrenched its own moral discipline, and despaired of the world, may come to feel that the true church must always be the suffering few, and adopt its own version of these arguments. Yet rational, skeptical and even ethical arguments really assume that other values carry more weight than salvation or known truth.

This is clearest in the third main group of arguments, which we may call pragmatic. The basis increasingly has shifted from the beliefs of those persecuted down to the principles already accepted by the persecutors or by all men in common. These pragmatic arguments may include appeals to civil law, to history, and to great rulers and empires of the past, or the "birthright of English freedom." More often they show how persecution injures the state by arousing "frequent tumultuary disturbances," and will cause national "poverty by the destruction of many thousand families" economically or by their exile abroad. Such thinking usually assumes a separation of church and state. It bases government purely on "civil interest," as Penn hoped to do in England, if not in Pennsylvania.

Our special interest in this list of arguments is to notice that Penn tended to move down from the theocratic towards the pragmatic, and carried Quaker thought with him. Over the years Penn was merely shifting his balance of stress, since he already had used every type of argument in *The Great Case of Liberty* in Newgate jail in 1670, and used most of them again in his *Address to Protestants* a decade later. In comparison with other Quaker writers, the contrast is clearer. Edward Burrough and other early Friends who wrote on toleration insisted on God's own Spirit and infallibility as the basis of Quakerism, a claim Penn ceased to make after *The Continued Cry of the Oppressed* in 1675. By 1661 his father-in-law Isaac Penington was already stressing the second approach, the inward nature of faith and the need to conquer evil inwardly. Persecution he saw as a persecutor's "transferance" against the Children of Light of his own anger at the Light's reproach within him. Penn always preferred the more conservative version of this argument: the perils of hypocrisy under coercion. Penn's favorites and specialties, moreover, were the legal and pragmatic arguments. In 1675, *England's Present Interest* presented massive documentation showing that "fundamental" English law, as distinct from Acts of the Cavalier Parliament, treated all loyal citizens equally, regardless of their religion. In 1679, Penn added to his *Address to Protestants* a rather longer Part II arguing against persecution:

> By sacrificing Men's Property, look what Number they cut off from themselves and the Government, not only rendering thereby a great Body of People useless, but provoking them to be dangerous. It tends to the utter Ruin of Thou-

sands of Traders, Artificers and Husbandmen; it must needs increase the Poor of the Nation.

In the political arena Penn was also pragmatic in switching allies for toleration: in 1679 he supported the Whigs in Parliament, and opposed political freedom for Catholics. In 1686, when Whig power and Parliament seemed broken and Catholic James II had become king, Penn came out in *A Perswasive to Moderation* in favor of royal power to establish toleration for everyone by decree. Even the new argument was pragmatic: "It should be the Interest of a Dissenting Prince to indulge Dissent. . . . Interest will not Lye. . . . Who should give Ease like the Prince that has wanted it." In the previous year, Penn had even written a *Defence of the Duke of Buckingham's Book.* The aging former rake, shorn of power, had written a short statement for Deism but also for toleration. An anonymous churchman who replied to it accused the Duke of getting his ideas from "the Pensilvanian," whose rebuttal in turn did not praise the Duke's past morality but his present appeal to "the instinct of reason." Penn has been fiercely attacked, by Whigs in his own day and historians since, for trusting and supporting James II and Buckingham. The key point argued, both for and against Penn, is that he took seriously their commitment to the truth of their own beliefs.

Thus Penn changed the Quaker idea of conscience in his toleration tracts. Earlier Quakers had made absolute claims for the *Divine Light within* men's conscience, and for the Truths which it showed. Penn gave absolute value to conscientiousness, alongside a humanistic awareness that men's actual consciences grow and differ. Penn also increasingly identified conscience with understanding, with reason, and even with nature. His absolute claim for men's relative conscience implies the individualism and pluralism which we also associate with liberalism, and undergirds its characteristic motif of individual freedom.

Penn's praise of conscience raises the question of his beliefs about man and the source of evil. Penn did not polarize the spiritual and the physical to the extent that the Cambridge Platonists and even Robert Barclay did at this time. Like all Friends, Penn used this contrast when arguing against reliance on the letter of Scripture, on the physical sacraments, or even on Jesus' physical body and its resurrection. But for Penn, the contrast of inner and outer is based on conflicting sources of motivation, of conscience against temptation. The deeper dualism of self against God, however, which had been basic for Fox, for most early Friends, and even for Penn the young radical, was breached by the time he wrote the second *No Cross.* Though he could still say that "the Way of God is a Way

Penn's Treaty with the Indians, *by Benjamin West, 1772.*

of Faith, as dark to Sense as mortal to Self," more often he spoke of the Light as enabling *man* to resist Satan, to watch against Temptation endlessly, and to bear willingly the inward cross which is to check one's lust and self-will. By the time that Penn issued *Some Fruits of Solitude* in 1693 and *More Fruits* in 1702, he had moved still farther. His ethic still kept the force of *No Cross,* and more compactly: "Excess in Apparell is another costly Folly. The very Trimming of the vain World would cloathe all the naked one." And, with new maturity: "Never marry but for love! but see that thou lov'st what is lovely." But though more kindly than the maxims of Ecclesiastes and Marcus Aurelius, Penn's fruits are increasingly rationalist and humanist. By this time even Penn's hope that all Pennsylvanians would share the Light enough to agree in his ideals was being shaken by endless haggling with the colonists. In the *Fruits,* inward retirement has become the retired life of the country gentleman, for whom public life itself is the chief temptation. Yet Penn was thereby also recognizing his debt to the Stoic aphorists, and to his conscientiously non-Quaker allies toward toleration, whom he continued to trust even in debt and despondency.

. . . . .

We are thus led, finally, to consider changes in Penn's *theology.* Its relation to his ethical and social liberalism is obscured by two intruding factors which unfairly suggest a theological migration from extreme liberalism to conservative orthodoxy.

There is no denying that in Penn's later writings such as *A Key Opening a Way* (1693), he laid more emphasis on Christ and his death than in his earlier books, and indeed more in the 1694 edition than in that of the year before. In the interim, Penn, who had written many tracts to defend Quakers from charges of unorthodoxy thrown down by Puritans and Baptists, had faced new attacks from George Keith, a Quaker and teacher at Penn's own school in Philadelphia, who had been Penn's companion in Germany and Robert Barclay's only equal as a Quaker theologian. Keith had even turned against him Penn's own title of "Christian Quaker," and Penn felt challenged to vindicate his right to it. But we have also seen the role of Gethsemane and God's forgiveness in Penn's own experience. They play an increasing role also in his later sermons. The atonement was a balance he needed against the disappointments of Pennsylvania and English politics as well as his own failures. Liberal openness to the Light's power in every man's experience needed this counterpoise. Christ is central in Penn's later theological tracts.

Second, Penn's Christology had looked like extreme liberalism in his first active year as a Quaker, when he was thrown in the Tower of London for his tract *The Sandy Foundation Shaken,* attacking the doctrine of the Trinity. Debating against four strong Puritan pastors, Penn defended the traditional Quaker assertion that the word Trinity, like the word sacrament, was unbiblical. Although he was charged with Socinian heresies regarding Christ, recent scholars have concluded that Penn was merely inept and indiscreet. Admittedly the Unitarians Thomas Firmin and Henry Hedworth denounced Penn after his retractions as a renegade to their cause. But John

Owen and Edward Stillingfleet, who wrote against both Penn and the Unitarians, were among the best theological minds of their age, and their charge had actual grounds. Hedworth and Firmin belonged to a group led by an earnestly ethical Puritan classical scholar, John Biddle, who had already been gracefully exiled to Scilly by Cromwell to save him from worse penalties for denying the divinity of Christ and the Holy Spirit. A series of English translations of works by the Polish Socinians John Crellius, Joachim Stegman, Samuel Przypkowski and Sozzini himself began to appear in the 1650s, probably translated by Biddle and his disciple John Knowles and published by Firmin. Penn himself owned Crellius' *Two Books on the One True God the Father* (1665) and seems to have used Biddle's own tract *The Testimonies of Ireneus, Justin Martyr, Tertullian,* etc. He used the same arguments as Biddle's *Apostolical & True Opinion Concerning the Holy Trinity* (1653). These sources Penn did not cite by name. Thus Penn's assertion that he "had never read any one Socinian Book in all my Life, if look't into one, at that time," may be a verbal quibble, may reflect honest ignorance that these books were in fact Socinian, or may show that some of the arguments came to him orally. He did admit to knowing the life of Sozzini in some detail and to agreeing with some of his doctrines.

But Penn had already made clear that it was the Puritan ethics of the Socinians which he admired, rather than their theology, in his earliest controversial tract, *The Guide Mistaken* (1668). Here he took Jonathan Clapham, a conforming ex-Puritan, to task for denying salvation only to papists, Socinians and Quakers:

> It's not my business [wrote Penn] to apologize for *Papists:* I am not of their kin. As for the *Socinian,* I know him to have wit and learning enough to encounter a more redoubtable adversary than mine; and however he has exposed himself to the just censure of some, his exemplary life and grave deportment I must acknowledge to be very singular. And if his cause receive no greater foil than this person's bare reproaches, . . . the discreet world will sooner acquiesce in the stronger arguments of Socinus and his quaint adherents.

Thus when Stillingfleet visited Penn in the Tower, perhaps carrying with him his own *Six Sermons* on the atonement and against Crellius (which Penn later quoted), the future bishop had no trouble in getting Penn to recognize that theologically, like most early Quakers, he was a Sabellian (rolling the Father, the eternal Word or Christ-Spirit, and the Holy Spirit, into one God), rather than a Socinian denying the divinity of Christ.

If Penn turned to the Socinians, then, for radical ethics rather than for liberal theology, we must look for his theological liberalism not in his Christology but in his interpretation of the Light within men. The early Friends had held together their universalism regarding the Light's outreach and their radical moral judgment upon the pride and self-will ruling in every man's heart by an exuberant trust in the Spirit's power to bring any man to the Truth. Except in the universality of a guilty conscience, most men were not assumed already to possess much truth. But it was important for Penn to be able to affirm those concrete elements of truth which men had already known. His pragmatic appreciation of conscientious non-Quaker reformers as allies, and his sense of the authority of classic Greek and Roman writers, needed theological undergirding. He quoted the righteous pagans from the beginning, in ethical appeals like *No Cross.* But Penn needed to affirm as a Friend that the pagan's moral knowledge came to him by revelation from God's Spirit within him, and was potentially saving rather than merely by nature.

Penn made his key link as he wrote **The Christian Quaker,** which began as a joint reply by Penn and Whitehead to the Baptist Thomas Hicks in 1674. This rapidly grew into a massive volume, so systematic that Penn eventually reprinted his section of it without mention of Hicks in 1699. Penn's main section focused on Quaker claims for the universality and sufficiency for salvation of the "Light within," which became henceforth Penn's favorite phrase for what Fox called "the Light of Christ." Like earlier Quakers, Penn cited Bible verses to prove that the Old Testament patriarchs knew and were saved by this Light. But he also quoted the Greeks on four topics of specific religious truth: the existence of God, man's inward knowledge of God, the nature of virtue, and the immortality of the soul. This section on "Gentile Divinity" owes its structure to Lord Herbert of Cherbury's *De Religione Gentilium.*

The right fully to baptize the Greek sages, Penn took from Clement of Alexandria. Penn may have worked directly from the Latin of *Stromateis,* sensibly ignoring Clement's claims that Plato and Pythagoras plagiarized from the text of Moses' Pentateuch. But the idea of using Clement and other early Fathers to show the seamless unity of Gentile and Christian truth probably came to Penn from Henry More's *Defense of the Philosophick Cabbala.* Penn, like the Cambridge Platonists, did not make a dispensational contrast between the revelation given to Old Testament prophets and the wisdom of the Greek sages.

This brings us into the wider issue of how far Penn was influenced by the Cambridge Platonists in his Christian humanism and universalism. Penn clearly owed much to other latitudinarians such as Stillingfleet, Sanderson, Jeremy Taylor and Wilkins, and found earlier writers with the same liberal Spirit: he quoted William Dell, Bishop Jewel, Walter Cradock and Grotius endlessly, along with the essentially Protestant works of Luther, Beza, and Foxe's *Martyrs.* In the humanist culture of Restoration England, where even the Duke of Bucks expounded Deism, exclusive lines are hard to draw. As to personal contacts, we can only know that Henry More in 1675 had only recently met George Keith and failed to meet Penn. Evidence of other personal contacts by Friends is more tenuous.

The ideas of Cambridge Platonists—their love of erudition, their sense of the universality of men's awareness of truth, and their teachings on inspiration and prophecy— are so similar to Penn's that even without citation we must assume he was influenced. With the Platonists Penn shared a sense of the centrality of moral truth, and that "a well-grounded assurance of Divine love is . . . for a man to overcome himself and his own will," and Penn

would have agreed with them that "God only is such an almightly goodness," that mere justification is never true holiness. Fox had said so too. Equally centrally, the Cambridge Platonists rooted religion in a direct, intuitive knowledge of God: "besides . . . outward revelation of God's will to men, there is also in *Inward impression* of it on their Minds and Spirits. . . . We cannot divine things but in a divine light: God only, who is the true light." And this light is ethical so that he who does good will know Truth. The Platonists' insistence on identifying this intuitive understanding with reason may have led Penn to feel free to identify the Quaker's Light with reason, despite earlier Friends' judgment upon human understanding and learning as the fruit of pride. Like them, Penn contrasted the light of reason with the passions of the world.

Yet, for More, unlike the Friends, "Natural Conscience . . . is a Fear and Confusion of Minde arising from . . . some mischief that may befall a man. . . . because he has done. . . . this or that Evil against his Conscience." Penn also entirely resisted the Platonists' tendency to see God's own nature in the spirit of man, or to talk of moral transformation as the deification of man. Penn's pragmatism and activism and his preference for aphorism over abstract discourse contrasted sharply with the Cambridge scholars. Penn was of course no philosopher and never considered the nature of ideas either in the Platonists' sense or in Locke's. He rarely considered the existence of God or the reality of Spirit, as Barclay and the Platonists did. He was not their direct disciple.

Unlike other Friends, Penn learned from all the Christian humanists to revere universal human understanding and the concrete wisdom of alien men as containing divine truth. Yet Penn's ethical radicalism was rooted in the Quaker understanding of the dynamic interaction of God's Spirit and the proud ego, of man's inward resistance to truth and to social justice. Penn thus also shared the Puritan vision of history. Penn's liberalism represented a challenge for social reform which the Platonists never achieved, and a sense of historical urgency which they feared. Eighteenth-century Europe would accept humanistic rationalism and universalism and even return to a Platonic "Chain of Being," but it also turned eagerly to a new doctrine of progress. In this new thought-world Penn remained a stronger influence than the timeless saints.

Admittedly, except for the model of Pennsylvania, Penn had little influence on the American Revolution. His books were rarely quoted by the Puritan liberals whose ideas became the mainstream of "the Kingdom of God in America." In the nineteenth century, American liberal religion, especially the Unitarians and Transcendentalists, picked up many of the themes of the Cambridge Platonists. Through Rufus Jones this interpretation of mysticism became a standard picture of normative Quakerism. Yet even the mystical tradition of Rufus Jones, like the Quietist tradition symbolized by Woolman, retained among Friends Penn's sense of responsibility for reform and social justice and his sense of climactic history. Today's Quakers are still faced by Penn's dilemma, how to recognize and affirm truth insofar as it may be shown

PENN

in any man, and yet to respond to man's need for moral challenge and social transformation. Friends should at least be able today to avoid Penn's too easy identification of truth with reason. For Quakers and all Protestants, both Penn's teaching that the *logos,* the "Word-God," is the Light of conscience as well as natural law, and his political practice and rough-sketched theories renew the challenge to unite reforming zeal with universal human understanding. (pp. 156-73)

Hugh Barbour, "William Penn, Model of Protestant Liberalism," in Church History, *Vol. 48, No. 2, June, 1979, pp. 156-73.*

Caroline Robbins on Penn's political philosophy:

The most original aspect of Penn's political philosophy may be found in arguments for a balance of disparate elements in state or community. Others theorized on the matter in his day, but he had a chance to experiment practically. Differences, he wrote, to Henry Bennet, later Lord Arlington, in 1669, did not always make trouble; kingdoms containing a balance of parties had remained secure. Only civil disobedience, lack of industry, or disloyalty could justify correction. Force created hypocrites; diversity could not be prevented or suppressed. No one group monopolized all the wisdom, wealth, numbers, sobriety, and resolution. Physicians varied medicine given according to the admixture of distempers. Divers languages, laws, customs, and religions did not result in mutiny among Italy's invaders. Hannibal's army, containing a variety of men, suffered fewer disturbances than the more uniform hosts of Rome. The conviction that absence of uniformity brought strength rather than confusion lay behind Penn's emphasis on the rights of dissenters, of Indians, of people of different origins. He tried to provide in the province for their varied needs.

Caroline Robbins, in Aspects of American Liberty: Philosophical, Historical, and Political, *1976.*

Mary Maples Dunn (essay date 1986)

[Dunn is an American historian. In the following essay, she explores Penn's personality and temperament.]

It is a commonplace to observe that William Penn regularly inhabited two worlds—the world of power, privilege, and authority, and the peculiar egalitarian, spiritual, and persecuted world of the Friends. Historians are suspicious of applications of psychology to actors so long departed from the scene, and yet one must ask questions about the inner world of William Penn—about his emotional make-up and personality—if we are to understand how he was able to move between these spheres, what tension or conflict existed for him, and what this ambivalence contributed to his development, his ideas, and his public behavior.

It is not easy to understand William Penn's personality—too much of the evidence we have for his life is contained in public papers. Few personal and intimate materials have survived; we have nothing written by him before he was sixteen, and very little before he converted to Quaker-

ism. About twenty-six hundred Penn documents have survived the vicissitudes of three centuries, but only seventy-five of these are private family letters. It is possible, if the person who vandalized the Penn papers in 1870 was a disgruntled, illegitimate, and disinherited member of the family as has been suggested, that family papers were the special target of wanton destruction. It is also possible that the family placed greater value on the public papers. William Penn's son, Thomas Penn (1702-1775), who arranged and filed the family papers, was primarily interested in documents which related to his proprietary claims and revenues. It would not be surprising to learn that he was little interested in his father's family by his first wife; whatever the reason, the only letter from Gulielma Penn to William Penn survives because it was intercepted and preserved in the Public Record Office. Nor would it surprise those engaged in the study of women to discover that he was more interested in his grandfather than his grandmother. Whatever Thomas Penn's central concerns, the fact is that the largest number of personal papers which have been preserved are exchanges between William Penn and his father, and between William Penn and Hannah Penn, the second wife and mother of Thomas. We know that everyone in the family was literate, and we know from references in the extant Penn papers that much family correspondence was exchanged which is now lost.

Pictures may be worth a thousand words, but we have only two portraits of Penn, and they may be misleading. One is of a handsome boy in armor, the other of a complacent fat man. Neither carries any suggestion of the belligerent, activist Quaker. We must therefore look at his social experience and what we know of his behavior in order to arrive at or infer the emotional determinants and habits which are such an important part of personality.

Emotional habits are formed very early. We know about William Penn's early emotional development that as a youth he exhibited a strong mystical streak. By his own account, he had mystical experiences by the time he was twelve or thirteen. There was no pattern for this in his family; he said, pathetically, "I had no Relations that inclined to so solitary & Spirituall a Way; I was as a Child alone." His father was an energetic warrior, and a man who was capable of changing sides in the civil war. If he had dreams, they were dreams of a rather worldly glory, of social and political success for his son. The mysticism of the son may have been an early attempt to escape from the authority of his father, or from his father's dreams. We can be reasonably certain about Penn's relationship with his father because the collection of their correspondence is revealing, large for a set of personal papers (containing eight letters from son to father, and nineteen from father to son), and because their fairly stormy relations have been documented in other ways. We may begin with the inference that they never knew each other particularly well.

William junior could have seen but little of his father when he was a young boy; his mother and his older sister were his chief companions until he was eleven. His father left London in command of the *Fellowship* just days before his birth in October 1644 and was at sea with the Irish squadron until August of 1645. William senior may then have visited London, but he was stationed at Milford Haven until January 1646, when he set sail for Ireland where he stayed until August. He was in England for two months before he was given command of the *Assurance* in which he was at sea for the next year. He was rear admiral of the Irish fleet in 1648 and vice admiral in 1649. In 1650 he was at Deptford, fitting a new ship, the *Fairfax;* in December he went on cruise in the Azores and Mediterranean, and did not return to England until March 1652. From May 1652 until July 1653 he was pretty consistently in action in the Dutch war; he then spent perhaps a year at home until December 1654 when he sailed for the West Indies, where he remained until August 1655. He retired to his Irish estates in October 1655. He was then with his son a great deal, until the boy went up to Oxford at sixteen. The father certainly missed much of young William's development and was not there to observe and influence the boy as he learned to negotiate his way within the family. The son did not see enough of his father to absorb the father's standards of manliness and success, and he may have viewed his father, on the sailor's occasional visits home, as an interloper who deprived him of his usual measure of his mother's attention.

A Freudian would no doubt be tempted to interpret the mysticism and other later escapes from the standards of the father in powerfully psychoanalytical terms, and it is indeed very difficult to avoid thinking about William junior's early religious life as a rejection of authority. In fact, between the ages of seventeen (when he was expelled from Oxford) and twenty-two (when he converted to Quakerism) we see the double strand of religion and rebellion constantly coming together. At Oxford he joined forces with others of puritan persuasion to object to the prayer book and to ritual which seemed too popish (for example, wearing the surplice). He could not have been very surprised when he was sent down in 1662, although in later years he looked back at himself with pity and referred to his experience as "my persecution at Oxford," a "hellish darkness and debauchery." But he seemed to relish "the bitter usage I underwent when I returned to my Father, whipping, beating, and turning out of Dores." This may suggest feelings of guilt about what he was doing, or even about what he was thinking, and the Oxford conflict was followed by several years in which he tried to be the good son. He went to France to study; he acted enthusiastically as his father's envoy to Charles II; he went to Ireland to manage the family estates, and he even helped put down a mutiny there in 1666; he made friends with rich and worldly men. It is certain, then, that Penn knew the kind of man his father wanted him to be.

Penn became a Quaker in 1667, and his father was, predictably, furious. The son could share with Quakers powerful feelings of possession by the spirit and enjoy a certain freedom to interpret and act on those feelings in an individual way. But he must also have taken a lot of pleasure in the ways in which Quakers flouted social conventions. For example, they used the familiar "thee" with everyone, including duke and king. This may seem merely quaint today, but in the seventeenth century it was very important to know to whom one must use the formal form of the personal pronoun (one's social superiors) and to whom

one might use the familiar form (intimates or inferiors). Pronouns were a part of the system by which people identified their places in society. Therefore to use "thee" indiscriminately was a way of defying social authority, structure, and values, and perhaps defying the father.

This overturning of language convention is matched by an attack on the dress code of seventeenth-century England. "Hat honour" was important in Penn's day in the same way that pronouns were. Hats were off in the presence of superiors, and Penn's refusal to doff his hat before judge and king must have given him little frissons of fun. The importance of hat behavior is demonstrated in an amusing legend. According to the story, Penn was once at the court of Charles II, and of course, unlike the other courtiers, he was wearing his hat. The king therefore swept off his own hat, explaining to Penn that "only one person wears a hat here." The story is a nice one because it illustrates the meaning of the hat, Penn's entree at court, his stubborn independence—and Charles's wit. But Penn kept his hat and his head in more serious circumstances, too. In one of his many court appearances, he was fined for contempt of court because he refused to take off his hat. Actually, according to his testimony, his hat was forcibly removed when he came into court and was returned by order of the bench. The judge then asked him to remove it, which Penn declined to do "Because I do not believe that to be any Respect." The upshot was the fine for contempt about which Penn wryly observed, "not we, but the Bench should be fined." We may observe that Penn was willing to use the hat as a means of defiance of authority at a high level.

Quakerism even gave Penn good religious grounds for disobeying his parents. His father was angry when he converted, but he could justify disobedience by insisting that he was compelled to follow the divine light. In an unpublished essay on marriage, he argued that parents' consent to a true marriage (that is, one made by God) should be sought but was not necessary, a position at great variance with the accepted wisdom of the propertied classes. Penn married after his father died, and his bride was an heiress as well as a devout Quaker. Nevertheless, he considered the point an important one to make.

Becoming a Quaker in 1667 was therefore neither socially acceptable nor acceptable in an elder son, and relations between the admiral and his son William were really bad almost all of the time after the expulsion from Oxford until the father's death. And even at the end there was plenty of tension. Admiral Penn was very ill for some months before he died on 16 September 1670. During most of that August and the first week of September, his son was in Newgate prison and at the center of the Penn-Mead trial, which was to prove a benchmark case in the history of religious liberty and trial by jury. William junior wrote to his father frequently. He was at some pains to tell him, among other things, of the judge's public slurs on the reputation of the admiral (surely not pleasant reading for a dying man), and of his own defense of his father; the mayor, he said, would "see me whipped himself, for all I was Penn's son, that starved the seamen. . . . I told him I could very well bear his severe expressions to me concerning myself, but was sorry to hear him speak those abuses of my father, that was not present." On 9 September, as the case wore down and all that remained was the fine for contempt of court for having refused to take off his hat in the courtroom, he wrote that however much he wanted to see his father, whose condition was much worse, he could not agree to paying the fine in order to be released. It was a matter of principle. But he did very shortly relent, the fine was paid, and he went home to his dying father. In a final burst of filial piety, he erected a monument to his father at St. Mary Redcliffe, Bristol, including all his military panoply and naval pennants. A display so un-Quakerly in its composition forces the observer to ponder on the son's inner conflicts.

William Penn was, then, a religious rebel or rebellious religious. In his early years as a Friend, he was persistently contentious; the rebellious and religious strains continued to be central in his personal development until at least 1678. He engaged others of every religious stripe, from conservative churchmen to rather mad sectarians, in religious debate. This took a number of forms; he wrote a great many tracts for publication, he engaged in public and private debates, he courted arrest in order to extend the debate into the civil sphere. In many ways, his language was sharper and more interesting at this stage of his life than at any other—he clearly relished the quarrel with authority (or with his father) at every turn. He became powerful in the use of invective, and he was not very polite. Consider this furious borrowing from the Book of Revelation in a letter to Ludowick Muggleton, a man who thought he had been chosen by God to say who would be saved and who damned; and he damned more than a few Quakers.

> Boast not, thou Enemy of God, thou Son of Perdition, and Confederate with the unclean Croaking Spirits reserved under the Chaines of Eternal Darkness; . . . on you I trample in his Everlasting Dominion, and to the bottomles Pit are you sentenc'd, . . . where the Endles wormes shall gnaw, and tortur your Imaginary Souls to Eternity.

He was only slightly more polite to Richard Baxter, the most noted Presbyterian of the day. Penn accused him of "tedious Harangues," "Envye, and artifice," and "virulent, and imperious . . . behaviour."

This aggressive, argumentative, and conflicted young man is an attractive character, and those qualities were the source of some of his most enduring accomplishments. During his first imprisonment in 1669 he began to develop his ideas on the principle of liberty of conscience and the need for government to balance different religious interests. In a letter written in 1669 from the Tower of London to Henry Bennett, earl of Arlington, this part of the inner conflict between his two worlds, and his solution to it, rings clear: "What if I differ from some religious apprehentions publiquely Impos'd am I therfore Incompatible with the well-being of humain Societys? Shall it not be remembred with what successe Kingdoms & commonwealths have liv'd by the discreet ballanceing of Partys?" His later struggles for liberty of conscience, or at least a toleration, led him to understand the nature of constitutional guarantees of civil rights, which he was able to real-

ize in the creation of a new society or "holy experiment" in America. But his rebelliousness had its darker side, too, particularly as he moved into middle age. It placed real obstacles in the way of developing close relationships with men of his own class; and yet it was never successful enough to allow him to establish true friendships with those who were coreligionists but not gentlemen. He was not even equal in contest; one opponent, Richard Baxter, objected that Penn spoke out against tithes which supported poor but serious ministers "while hee swims himselfe in wealth." The effect was to create a real emotional and social distance between him and others.

Penn used his well-born acquaintances to advantage. This is particularly evident in the acquisition of the charter to Pennsylvania, but a useful example is also found in George Villiers, second duke of Buckingham. Buckingham was notorious for his profligate life but also known for his belief in religious toleration. Penn tried on several occasions to secure Buckingham's support for persecuted Friends, or for Penn's own political campaigns for liberty of conscience. When Buckingham was attacked for writing a pamphlet on religious liberty in 1685, Penn wrote two tracts in his defense. Penn probably realized that his association with this member of the Restoration elite was not quite appropriate for a simple Friend of the truth, since he went out of his way to have his letters to Buckingham destroyed, and suggested that he hoped only to help Buckingham improve his record before the duke died by giving him a chance to be of service to the kingdom.

Buckingham, in his private life, carried to an extreme attitudes and behaviors which made up the social ethos of the Restoration elite. It was hardly a world in which a young Quaker convert could feel at home; if his Quakerism was a barrier between him and his social equals, for companionship he had to look to Quakers. But because of differences in social station, an uncomfortably large number of those early Quaker friendships acquired a patron-client character, and many were eventually destroyed by quarrels. The clients did not take kindly to that role. Consider the break with Thomas Rudyard, who had been a close associate for many years, and a companion on Penn's travels in England, Holland, and Germany. Penn had employed Rudyard as a lawyer, and they worked closely in provoking and prompting cases of conscience. Rudyard developed many of the arguments in the famous Penn-Mead trial when they went into print; he was also Penn's closest collaborator in devising a constitution for Pennsylvania. Indeed, the two men worked as partners in that effort, jointly composing many of the drafts for the constitution. Yet by 1684, when Rudyard had become a landowner in Pennsylvania, Penn complained about his un-Quakerly habits and refused to make him master of the rolls in Pennsylvania. A few months later, they were in sharp disagreement about the assignment of waterfront lots in Philadelphia, and Rudyard signed a remonstrance against Penn. Philip Ford, a faithful steward for many years, is another excellent example of the faults of the patron-client relationship between Friends. Ford, who spent years in service to Penn, also silently built up a case of indebtedness which allowed Ford's heirs to sue Penn for £20,000 and send him to debtor's prison. Ford's wife, Bridget

Ford, who was generally present when loans were negotiated, was particularly resentful and angry for what she seemed to think were a rich man's failures to live up to promises, and it is entirely possible that Penn behaved toward Ford with a patrician's lack of understanding for the middle-class creditor.

The fact that Penn had few really intimate friendships is without a doubt a key to his bad judgment about people, or perhaps it is the other way around, and his bad judgment contributed to his failure to find true friends. In any case, he made many inappropriate appointments to office in Pennsylvania; that is, he misjudged both the candidates and the Pennsylvanians they would govern. His judgment rested principally in a form of *noblesse oblige*—he appointed people to office; expected them to do their duty; considered it inappropriate to check up on them; and then broke with them in anger and disappointment when they failed. A case in point is Penn's secretary, Philip Theodore Lehnmann, who worked for Penn from 1672 to 1685. He left behind in Pennsylvania vitally important papers which would have supported Penn's claim to Maryland territory when Penn returned to London from Pennsylvania in 1684. As Penn put it, "I am now here wth my finger in my mouth," and he was so angry that he fired Lehnmann. The appointment of John Blackwell, a puritan Cromwellian who had moved to Massachusetts, as governor of Pennsylvania, 1688-89, was a fascinating case in which Penn seemed to allow full rein to the authoritarian side of his character, but when Blackwell engaged in vigorous dispute with the colonists in order to secure Penn's authority and collect his rents, Penn failed to support Blackwell, dismissed him, and allowed the Provincial Council, as a whole, to act as his deputy governor.

There were exceptions. Penn found in George Fox a substitute father of sorts, who called forth a respect and affection which Penn did not easily hold for men. Letters to "Dear George" have a personal and intimate quality which, despite ritual effusions of Quaker love, does not often appear in Penn's correspondence. Penn was also capable of a special intimacy with women, especially with well-born women who had similar religious beliefs. It has been observed by others that well-born and well-educated women in the seventeenth century were often attracted to radical sects, in which they were more open to religious experience and participation than they could be in the more structured and organized traditional churches which enjoined silence on women. Between these women and Penn there were no barriers of authority or class, and they could establish good rapport. We see this first in respect to his marriages.

Penn married twice, both times probably as much for money as for love. His first wife, Gulielma Springett, was an heiress; her father, Sir William Springett, was a puritan of a rich London family. She was educated, deeply religious, and intelligent. In short, they were equals in family, class, wealth, and religion, and they could talk to each other. Penn's understanding of his passion for Gulielma may be inferred from the unpublished essay on marriage, probably written shortly before they were betrothed. In it he describes a transcendent understanding of love which is the will and pleasure of the Lord, and which in the first instance could only be recognized by the couple themselves, who must refer their case to the "Light" before going to their parents. He was confident that the Lord would not approve or bless an unsuitable match and defined suitability as "station" or class, education, and life style, as well as temperament.

Penn's second marriage was less clearly suitable. His bride, Hannah Callowhill, was the only child of a wealthy merchant, and Penn was accused of marrying her for her money. She was twenty-five to his fifty-one when they married, and she had not been easily convinced that he was the love of her life. Her family wanted them to live in Bristol, and although he said he liked "a citty less then a little house," he agreed to give up his very large house in the country and insisted that he believed "lowness as well as plainness" to be important parts of his character. But his letters to her during the courtship were very loving and tender: "My hand is the messenger of my heart, that most entirely loves thee, . . . And if thou Couldst believe, in how little a house I could live with thee, at least thou wouldst think I placed my happiness more in thee than any outward conveniences." Although she wrote many letters to him, only those of a later period were preserved, and they too speak of an affectionate relationship. They were both Quakers, and used to money and comfort. She was an educated woman who wrote easily, kept careful accounts, and was not unduly deferential to her husband, although she was careful of his interests.

This rapport with women is also observable in 1677, when Penn traveled to Holland and Germany and was frequently entertained by sectarian women. One of the most important was Elizabeth, Princess Palatine; others were Anna Maria, Countess von Hoorn, and Anna Maria von Schurman, the Labadist and daughter of Lord Sommelsdiijk, who had been one of the richest men in the Netherlands. To these women, Penn was able to open his heart and life; with a little prompting he told the princess and her followers the story of his conversion and the troubles and trials which followed in his life, in a session which began at three in the afternoon and went on until eleven at night, with just one break, for supper. One could speculate that he might have had a more emotionally satisfying career had he been able to maintain friendships like these; but in fact, Penn was probably not capable of a continuous relationship.

Penn had another quality which underlines the way he maintained emotional distances from other people. He was a tremendously restless person, constantly traveling. He once called himself "a wayfareing man" and referred to his life as a pilgrimage. This could be seen as the quintessential Anglo-American quality, but one he had in common with his sailor father, too. In any selected year before 1712, when he had a debilitating stroke, he is found on the move. His roving went far beyond what was normal for the Quakers (except for George Fox) who traveled extensively in an informal ministry. It began, perhaps, with the Grand Tour after he was expelled from Oxford; and continued with his trips on family business to Ireland. Throughout his life he made the usual circuit from town for business, back to his house in the country, and so on. His wife and children remained in the country, and like his father, he was an absentee father a good deal of the time. Even the patient Gulielma complained in a low-key way to Margaret Fox, and Hannah once wrote "I cannot with any Satisfaction endure thy absence much Longer." He journeyed frequently in the Quaker ministry—to Germany, Holland, all over England; he traveled to Pennsylvania.

He loved a whirlwind life. His journal of his trip to Holland and Germany is revealing—it was a rough trip of three months. Sometimes he traveled for as long as twenty-four hours in an open cart, or walked for ten or twelve miles. He was forced out of some towns, detained in others. He loved every minute and recorded distances, inns, miles, weather, prayers, with real gusto. If we look at the whole year of 1677 (from March to March) we find him in March in London and in Arundel, Sussex; in May in London; in June in Bristol; in July in Harwich and then on to Holland and Germany where he was constantly on the move until November when he returned; in November he was in Warminghurst and London; in December in London; in January in Buckinghamshire and Bristol; in February in Bristol; but in March back in London again. Twenty years later, in 1698, he was just as active: February found him in London, March in Bristol and London, April in Bristol, May in Dublin, June in Waterford and Cork; he was in Cork in July and in August but in September and October was in Bristol; in November he returned to London. This ceaseless activity extended itself to his political life, too. He went out on the hustings for the Whigs (and especially for Algernon Sidney) in 1678-79; he was equally busy in the task of getting his colonial charter; and when he returned from his first trip to Pennsylvania he hustled for James II. One wonders if there was any calm at the center of the hurricane, or if he had to keep on the move to avoid meeting even himself.

As Penn got older, the distance between him and his Quaker associates widened, and his affinity for the ways of his father became more pronounced. He was always happy to live well. Warminghurst, his house in Sussex, was a grand gentleman's country seat, large enough to entertain meetings of several hundred Friends. Pennsbury, his Pennsylvania estate, was designed to suit proprietary status. He spent liberally to support his station—for example, between 1672 and 1674 he ordered three coaches built; ordered food to set a luxurious table, and clothes and silver fit for a gentleman. After he became proprietor of Pennsylvania he came more and more to enjoy authority. His notes to his secretary, James Logan, were often curt and peremptory, for example, and he was impatient with people who disagreed with him. But his letters were also dipped in self-pity for what he saw as lack of appreciation and misunderstood benevolence. He could refer to himself as the "Old kind abused landlord" without self-consciousness.

It is easy to conclude that he had come full circle, and that in the end, despite all the resistance, he became the man his father wanted him to be. In a way he was successful

Penn's home in Philadelphia.

far beyond even his father's dreams—he held title to a province as large as England and was a landlord on a colossal scale. In short, we could conclude that class allegiance outweighed the hostility to authority which was generated in his youth. But in terms of historical significance, this was not the measure of his success. He had deeply seated emotional responses to the authority of others; this created in him an inner conflict which enabled him to set checks to his own excesses in the handling of power and to make significant contributions to the spiritual and political development of Englishmen and Americans. He conceived of and established a society without military defenses, with freedom of religion, with a criminal code humane beyond anything known to Englishmen, with a written constitution containing guarantees of rights and checks on the power of the proprietor. The vision that made these things possible came from his resistance; the situations in which vision could become reality came from the wealth and status that led to influence and grants of favor. He was a man whose greatness was greater than the sum of his parts. (pp. 3-12)

> *Mary Maples Dunn, "The Personality of William Penn," in* The World of William Penn, *edited by Richard S. Dunn and Mary Maples Dunn, University of Pennsylvania Press, 1986, pp. 3-14.*

Caroline Robbins   (essay date 1986)

[*Robbins is an American historian who served from 1967 to 1979 as chairperson of the Committee on the Papers of William Penn. In the following essay, she evaluates Penn's later writings (1689-1702), focusing on* An Essay Towards the Present and Future Peace of Europe, A Brief and Plain Scheme How the English Colonies . . . May Be Made More Useful to the Crown, *and* Some Fruits of Solitude.]

The name of William Penn immediately recalls the great Quaker founding father of Pennsylvania. Yet the image evoked thereafter may well vary with the particular situation in which his life and work be considered. From December 1688 when James II fled to France until Penn's return late in 1701 from a second and last sojourn in America, frustrated ambition and declining vigor dominate many accounts. After that return, illness became more frequent and financial embarrassments greater. Old age developed quickly, and actual disability extended from about 1712 to 1718.

Any study of Penn in his fifties, our present concern, has often focused on familiar biographical detail, and, as remarked by a friend in 1696 after the death of Springett, the favorite son, Penn's portion was always "to have wormwood mingled with his drink." Suspicions of popery and Jacobitism, sparked by association with the now exiled monarch, led the new government to suspend his authority in the American province. The deaths, not only of Springett and of his beloved wife Gulielma, but also of several close Quaker friends, induced deep sorrow. Penn's secret retirement, brought on by constant harassment in the early nineties, resulted in distinct coolness from other Friends. Such a retreat from persecution was frowned on,

even forbidden to Quakers. Querulous criticism and demands for help from the colonists produced no satisfactory result before, during, or after disbarment from the Proprietary.

With authority restored, and distrust diminished, Penn made a fortunate second marriage and resumed activities—controversy, travel, agitation for further Quaker privilege, and preaching. He was one of those who in 1697 informed Peter the Great at Deptford about the Quaker faith. Before the second Atlantic voyage of 1699, he revisited his long-neglected Irish estates without greatly improving their yield, and communed with Friends in that island. The American stay of less than two years was unrewarding. The *Charter of Privileges* he felt obliged to sign in October 1701 on the eve of departure abandoned or reversed much of his original plan. No wonder that he then began those never completed negotiations for the sale of the colony.

These aspects of Penn's career will be disregarded here. Examination of the extraordinary quality of intellectual achievement during this period of frustration may suggest some illumination of an enigmatic and elusive personality. Complete coverage of works then written will not be given, but a glance at a few pieces on history, on relations between states and between colonies, and some discursive and general reflections may suggest characteristics not always remembered.

Originally published in 1694 as a preface to George Fox's *Journal,* Penn's *Rise and Progress of the People called Quakers,* appearing separately in the same year, immediately developed a life of its own. Brief, it showed a certain freshness. "Great Books . . . grow Burthensome," he averred in an introductory epistle. Six short chapters offered a summary relation of former dispensations of God up to the emergence of the Quakers, whose fundamental principles, discipline, ministry, and organization were outlined. The sixth and final chapter exhorted Friends to maintain integrity and urged those as yet unconvinced to find salvation in this faith.

The fifth chapter concentrated upon the "First Instrument" of God, George Fox, and resembled the "characters"—pen portraits—popular at the time. Penn had already written tributes to deceased associates like Josiah Coale, Thomas Loe, Robert Barclay, and John Burnyeat, the last two of whom died in the same year as Fox, 1690. Writing but a preface he dwelt briefly on biographical detail, mentioning by name a few early Friends as well as persons like Judge John Bradshaw, the regicide, who deflected persecution. Taking up after 1675 when Fox's *Journal* narrative ended, and he was often with Fox, Penn succinctly suggested his continued services to Quakers near and far, as well as to the movement as a whole. For example, Fox helped persuade doubters that regularity and organization were necessary and not in the least like the rules and demands of the established church they had left.

Intimate traits received frank and affectionate commentary. Not "Notional or Speculative," Fox was "no Man's Copy." An original, sometimes even appearing "Uncouth and Unfashionable," he was ignorant of "Sophistical Science." Although Fox spoke at times in abrupt and broken sentences, his prayers and sermons revealed a "profound" understanding which with "an Innocent Life" opened to many, including the unlearned, the true religion. Often as he had been in his company, Penn declared, he had never observed him out of place, nor unequal to any occasion. The *Journal* of this great man "by whom God was pleas'd to gather this People" should be widely studied. Penn concluded by apostrophizing his late friend: "Many sons have done Virtuously in this Day; but, Dear George, Thou excellest them All."

While *The Rise and Progress* had a crispness not often found in other Quaker writings, *An Essay towards the Present and Future Peace of Europe,* published in 1693 and also a product of retirement, was in a very different vein. Twice reprinted before Penn's death, it has always attracted readers. The argument was secular and was offered to an audience of warring states. Penn wrote that he welcomed constructive criticism of remedies put forward to ameliorate the "incomparable miseries" of war-torn Europe, seldom in his lifetime free from hostilities for more than a few months. Conflict, Penn believed, despite the claims of men like Oliver Cromwell, did not bring peace, but only disorder, impoverishment, and devastation.

Peace, eminently desirable, could only be brought about by justice, and justice by government—"chief expedient against confusion." A European or even Imperial assembly, diet, parliament, or estates, composed of representatives of each sovereign state, the number of deputies being proportionate to size, could prevent war. Meetings taking place at intervals could be held in a round room to avoid disputes over precedency. A record to keep all informed of proceedings would be kept in Latin and French, the languages most commonly known. Decision would be reached by ballot, three-quarters of the whole constituting a majority. Liberty and orderliness of debate would be the concern of a presiding officer, chosen by turn from each of the anticipated ten areas—Penn would have welcomed Russia and Turkey but did not expect their immediate cooperation. To the chair all speeches would be addressed; and no absenteeism would be allowed.

Penn expected objections. The stronger powers would never agree; this, he hoped, might be overcome by the united strength of the rest. Disuse of soldiering might be feared as conducive of effeminacy; education could surely remedy this. In a peaceful world younger sons could find ample employment as merchants, husbandmen, or "ingenious naturalists." Loss of sovereignty might be resented but would not be felt in domestic affairs. The enormous benefits of a warless Europe—or even universe—would be discovered in the absence of bloodshed, a greater reputation accorded Christian realms, an economy of money, prevention of destruction, a greater ease and safety for travel and traffic, and a freedom for princes to marry for other than reasons of state. If the Turks did not join, Christendom even so would be more secure against threat. Some interested in the quest for peace have read these reflections thoughtfully; others have termed Penn naive. Yet

it may be questioned whether that epithet might not be applied to any designers of international leagues or unions that depend upon the ultimate rationality of man.

The Quaker cited earlier examples—that of the United Provinces recently described by Sir William Temple. Penn had also studied a plan often attributed to Henry IV of France, but probably mainly the work of Maximilien de Béthune, duc de Sully, influenced by *The New Cyneas* of Eméric Crucé. Penn, who credited Henry with its authorship, may have read *The Grand Design,* when it was published in France in the mid-seventeenth century. But the European arrangements proposed by Penn incorporated in them the old Gothic representative tradition. A friend and avowed disciple, John Bellers, also moved by the recurrence of war, resumed the elder Quaker's theme in *Some reasons for an European State* (London, 1711), adding some sensible remarks about disarmament as a necessary ingredient of peace. He further presented a plan for a council where ecclesiastics might discuss matters about which they agreed, rather than those about which they differed. The same warring conditions decided Charles St. Pierre to bring out in Paris in 1712 his thoughts about making peace perpetual in Europe. He wanted a treaty of alliance insuring through its signatories—"a confederation of kings"—that withdrawal from the pact would entail loss of power and even territories by the warmongers. Penn was apt to be overoptimistic, but in these reflections upon a desired peaceful world, as in others about political behavior, he often anticipated modern prejudice and thinking.

Penn was, of course, involved in colonial enterprise long before the nineties. One of three trustees for Edward Byllynge's West New Jersey settlement (until he obtained the Pennsylvania Charter in 1681), he acquired holdings there, and after the death of Sir George Carteret in 1680, others in East New Jersey. For Pennsylvania he wrote promotional literature, drafted frames and laws, and described prospects and qualifications for would-be emigrants. Such establishment overseas, he felt compelled to argue, was a benefit to the home country, rather than (as often stated) a drain on population and wealth. Colonies were, he declared, "the seeds of nations," following the thoughts already outlined by Jan de Witt, Josiah Child, Francis Bacon, and others. One of Penn's statements justifying colonization was reprinted in *Select Tracts relating to the Colonies,* probably to promote the currently proposed Georgian colony. Penn continued to be expansionist, issuing a broadside in 1690 advocating development of the Susquehanna area, about whose strategic and cultural value he had remarked during the first American visit.

Penn had surely not anticipated the lack of enthusiasm for the regime he had so carefully outlined on obtaining Pennsylvania. A few months among the colonists seems not to have taught him the arts of management. Yet he observed difficulties outside the realm of domestic politics. By the nineties the increase of piracy in western waters and war in Europe and over the Atlantic area added complications not only in places affected but also in those not actually involved. Penn turned his thoughts about America and Europe to interrelationships. Two plans, one solely of his own devising, the other drawn up in concert with two colonial governors, offered suggestions. He had remained in touch with the colonists and in 1695 received a letter, often referred to, from Peter de la Noy of New York declaring that the American colonies needed reorganization. This was an idea long current and evoking various schemes from 1643 on, but none having lasting effect. De la Noy may have prompted Penn's decision to write.

In December 1696 Penn presented to the newly reactivated Board of Trade *A Brief and Plain Scheme how the English Colonies in the North Parts of America . . . may be made more useful to the Crown and one another's Peace and Safety with a Universal Concurrence.* The Board, interested, asked Penn to bring it back in more formal fashion. This he did in February 1697. In 1698 it was printed in London along with some suggestions by others in Charles Davenant's *Discourses on the Publick Revenues and the Trade of England.* Penn's tract provoked commentary in ensuing years largely from defenders of the rights of their own particular area. Only a brief summary of the seven points of *A Brief and Plain Scheme* is necessary. A meeting of two deputies from each of the ten settlements should be held once a year or, in wartime, more often. This assembly should be presided over by the king's commissioner, specifically named, and should meet in a central location. This was likely to be New York, whose governor could indeed be appointed chair, "after the manner of Scotland," and also, if needed, act as general of the agreed upon forces. Quotas of men and money should be determined in concert. Penn, although head of a Quaker colony, was obliged by the promise required when given back the province, to see the navigation laws enforced and a due measure of assistance afforded the war effort. He was anxious to see this fairly undertaken. His proposal for setting quotas was probably the most important point. Moreover, discussions about treatment of debtors, would-be bigamists fleeing one colony for another, and the convicted trying to escape the sentences of their own courts, were recommended. Commercial injuries could be adjudicated. If the Board of Trade had carried out the policy, very much in the air of the later years of the seventeenth century, of putting all colonies under royal control, it might have implemented some of these ideas, or others similar to them.

In New York in the first week of October 1700 the governors of Virginia and New York, together with Penn, debated schemes very like these, with a common body to adjust border disputes between states, unify coinage, deal with marital and financial defectors, and regulate laws of naturalization and marriage. Also put forward were plans for common encouragement of timber exportation, and a fairer distribution of loot seized from pirates. Neither project aimed at any amalgamation of the several settlements; both were directed to the improvement of relations between them. Penn's vigorous defense of proprietary rights, vowing that colonies like his cost Westminster less than those where a royal governor ruled, was in vindication of the property rights needed to bring him revenue. But he hoped for easier contacts of one colony with another, and by mutual agreement, to obtain fair treatment for Pennsylvania and lessen tensions between states.

Nothing significant transpired. Neither the Board of Trade nor, it must appear, the majority of colonists were prompted to further action for a good many years, and then under different circumstances. But Penn, frequently insensitive to the wishes of Pennsylvanians about their domestic government, and often unfortunate in his choice of assistants, nevertheless revealed real understanding of difficulties present or likely to develop among the various American units. He offered what might be deemed a federal method of solving those problems. Desirable concessions should be possible if agreed upon together. In neither European nor American matters did he think in terms of a force able to impose peace and concord upon the rest. He was ahead of most contemporaries. Even where a union was being implemented in Britain, only a few like Andrew Fletcher and Robert Molesworth were far-sighted enough to think of equal cooperation between all sectors—Ireland, Wales, Scotland, and England—of what was to become the United Kingdom, ruled in fact only or chiefly from one capital city. As noted, Penn had read Temple, but otherwise he reveals little or no attention to ancient or modern federations.

The preface to one of Penn's most popular works, *Some Fruits of Solitude in Reflections and Maxims relating to the Conduct of Human Life,* explained the little book as in part "the Result of serious Reflection," in part "the Flashings of Lucid Intervals." God, Penn declared, had blessedly given him retirement—time he could never before have called his own. Before troubles induced retreat, he had been extremely busy. During this relief he could "turn over the Leaves" of past activities and write for the "moral instruction of readers." There is nothing of which "we are apt," he wrote, "to be so lavish as of Time, and about which we ought to be more Solicitous. . . . Time is what we want most, but what, alas! we use worst." Man should keep "a ledger" to what end he employs it. Penn would have agreed with George Savile, marquis of Halifax, that "Mispending a man's time is a kind of self-homicide, it is making life to be of no use."

Though frankly admonitory, the manner and style of both parts of *Fruits of Solitude* (hereafter cited as A and B [with numbered references to maxims as listed in his *Works*]) are different in arrangement and mode from Penn's other tracts. They were professedly in a style grown increasingly popular from the days of Michel Montaigne and were fashionable in the latter half of the seventeenth century. In such works as *Moral Reflections and Maxims* (1665) by François, duc de la Rochefoucauld, *The Pensées* (c. 1662) by Blaise Pascal, and the *Maxims* of George Savile (written contemporaneously but not published until 1750) may be found examples of the manner of *Fruits of Solitude.* Penn had studied Montaigne and may also have read when in France the works of Pascal and de la Rouchefoucauld. Most aphorists used the term *moral* but usually remained cynical or defensive commentators, analysts, and apologists rather than the admonitor that was Penn.

Significantly, Penn began by reflecting upon ignorance. Men are, he thought, more likely to observe the beauties of Windsor Castle and Hampton Court than to study the living, walking tabernacle of their own bodies, and the stately volume of the world in which they live (A, 1-3). Nature, whose "rules are few, plain and most reasonable" is "very legible" and deserves further investigation (A, 9-11). If man be "the index or Epitomy of the World," he has only to scan himself "to be learn'd in it" (A, 17). "God's works," nature, meant a great deal to Penn. To him nature could instruct if read properly, whereas for La Rochefoucauld, "Nature gives merit, and Fortune sets it at work"; indeed, nature "marked out to every man at birth the bounds of his virtues and vices." But for Penn it was the reality declaring God's power and wisdom. The country provides "the Philosopher's *Garden* and *Library,*" a sweet retreat where all can learn its easily legible lessons (A, 223). Countrymen, to be sure, often neglect their opportunities and fail to realize that while cities are but man's handiwork, the country is God's provision for food, study, life, and learning. Penn's enjoyment of the beauties as well as the uses of nature is apparent throughout his work but especially in *Fruits of Solitude* and in his description of Pennsylvania to the Free Society of Traders. He not only noted animal and vegetable products likely to be useful to potential settlers but also remarked upon the flowers which could enrich even a London garden.

Keenly aware of the deficiencies of contemporary education, Penn wrote that "the first Thing obvious to Children is what is *sensible*"—that is, what is seen, heard, and felt. Instead, memory is strained with words, grammar, and strange tongues to produce scholars rather than men (A, 4-6). Natural genius in the young for "*Mechanical* and *Physical* or natural Knowledge" is neglected. Languages are useful, but the child would prefer making tools and playthings (A, 6-8). Regrettably, books by naturalists and mechanics were not translated into Latin and adapted to a youthful pace, thus making familiar a foreign vocabulary (A, 15).

In *The Advice of William Penn to his Children,* written about 1699 and published posthumously in 1726 by Jane Sowle, Penn counseled his family to read less and meditate more. But he urged the study of manuals suitable to the offspring of the ruling class likely to serve as justices, sheriffs, and coroners, and such other works generally serviceable on clerkships and wills. As we have seen, he himself had read widely. But as *Fruits of Solitude* suggest, he attached as much importance to solitary, observant inquiry and reflection.

As for recreation, both old and young are limited in Penn's view to conversation with godly friends, and occupation in garden or laboratory (A, 58), although Robert Barclay would have added the reading of history. Possibly Barclay's emphasis on history was reflected in Penn's admiration for the *Memorials* of Sir Bulstrode Whitelocke for which he wrote a preface in 1709 declaring "I take history then, to represent us as in a glass the whole world at one view . . . a sort of pre-existence." England regrettably had produced no Livy or Tacitus to provide such a "glass in which we should see that true understanding and admiration of the wisdom of the Creator" we need.

"Man being made a Reasonable and so a Thinking Creature," there is nothing, Penn wrote, "more worthy of his Being, than the right Direction and Employment of his Thoughts" (B, 63). Pascal in the same vein had thought man only a reed, yet "a thinking reed." But the Quaker's admonitions were perhaps more explicit. "Manage thy Thoughts rightly, and thou will save time. . . . Always remember to bound thy Thoughts to the present Occasion" (B, 68-69). Avoid *"Vulgar Errors"* (A, 155). Remember that though there is truth in rhetoric it may also lead to error (A, 138-39). "Inquiry is *Human;* Blind Obedience, *Brutal*" (A, 156). Reason should prevail: "Tis quite another Thing to be *stiff* than Steady in an Opinion" (B, 155). Without reason man is a beast; the wise man governs himself by the reason of his case. "A reasonable Opinion must ever be in Danger, where Reason is not Judge" (B, 161). Reason is common to all. "It is for want of examining it by the same light and measure that we are not all of the same mind" (B, 169). The inference was to utilize both the Light within and judicious inquiry before making decisions.

Not only must the wise man apply intelligence to his problems, he must also value sense above wit. "A man may be a fool with wit," wrote La Rochefoucauld, "but never with judgment." Or, as Penn phrased it, "Less Judgment than Wit is *more Sail than Ballast*" (A, 171). Wit is "fitter for Diversion than Business" (A, 170). The wise man must take everything into account and be neither officious, captious, nor critical (B, 59-60).

As well as reflecting on education and continuing inquiry, Penn of course emphasized personal virtues: moderation in food, drink, and dress. Excessive avarice should be avoided, but careful management, expenditure never exceeding income, is essential. Penn apparently never followed this admonition himself; as La Rochefoucauld said, "Tis easier to be wise for other people than for ourselves." A marriage for love and companionship is better than a union based on money. A good wife should never be treated as a servant but regarded as an equal partner. Wives and friends should be carefully selected. Men are often, Penn surmised, more concerned about the breed of animals than of posterity, the children of the next generation. Both marriage and friendship should be sought with those of similar tastes with whom intercourse of soul rather than of sense can be enjoyed (A, 79-82). Unprofitable society should be eschewed; only that likely to reward, pursued (A, 128, 133). He cautioned that people can be "Witty, Kind, Cold, Angry, Easy, Stiff, Jealous, Careless, Cautious, Confident, Close, Open," but in the wrong time and place (A, 159). Wisdom never adventured where the probability of advantage did not exceed that of loss (A, 264). Yet society must be had. "Tis a great folly to set up for being wise by oneself."

Fruits of Solitude and the *Advice* reveal the social thinking of Penn as one of the gentry. Children should all be treated alike save the eldest who deserves a double portion. The young should be obedient (A, 174) and grateful (A, 177). A structured society, accepted as a matter of course by Penn and contemporaries, demands servants. They should not be domineered over and must be treated considerately. In turn they should be faithful, hardworking, careful, and trustworthy (A, 192-200). The good servant serves God in serving his master and receives double wages—to wit, both here and hereafter (A, 207). In remarking that Indians were shocked at men being called servants, a term they used only for dogs (B, 268), Penn declared that the Almighty had made all men of the same physical elements but had arranged them in ranks, some subordinate and dependent. This same inequality can be found from king to scavenger and in stars, trees, fishes, birds, and so on. Yet the mighty were not created to serve their own pleasure but to promote the public good (B, 255-66).

Remarking that men love change, Penn declared that this is because they, like the whole world, are composed of changeable elements. All subsist by revolution. Yet they often cannot bear to reflect on the last, greatest, and best alteration (A, 487). Death being the way and condition of life, we cannot really live if we are unable to die. Life never ends, simply changes from time to eternity (A, 503). By contrast Pascal found death easier to accept without thinking about it. Men cannot escape death, reflected La Rochefoucauld, but submit to it out of insensibility and custom rather than of resolution. "The sun and death are two things that cannot be steadily lookt on."

Rather more generally Penn considered public life, reli-

Portrait of Penn by Henry Inman, 1832.

gion, and the obligations they entail. "A Private Life is to be preferred," the honor and gain of public office bearing no proportion to the comfort of them (A, 370). Yet the public must be served, and those that do so deserve reward (A, 377). They will also be accountable to God (B, 262). Penn recognized as legitimate many governments. A free government, whatever its form, is that where "the laws rule and the people are a party to those laws." Like clocks, governments are valuable for the motion men give them. Men likewise are esteemed for their proper "going" (A, 254). Pascal on the other hand discovered the power of kings in the folly of the people. He refused to take politics, even that of Plato and Aristotle, seriously. The governor of Pennsylvania was much more concerned, if not with form, then with character. In his preface to the 1682 *Frame of Government,* Penn had written that government is to secure men from the abuse of power. Liberty without obedience brings confusion, but obedience without liberty, slavery. In *Fruits of Solitude* he distinguished between rex and tyrannus, one ruling by law, the other by absolute power (A, 330-69). Good princes should cultivate wisdom, seeking love rather than fear, and never straining their authority too far. The universal aim is happiness. Perhaps this echoed good Bishop Richard Cumberland; the end of government should be to bring felicity to all (A, 350). The ambition of a people could shake a regime; maladministration, that of a tyrant (A, 331). Let the people think they govern, and they will be governed (A, 337). The prince with the assistance of ministers and councilors carefully selected for their interest and ability should work for the general good (A, 353-62).

Government is ruined by three things: looseness, oppression, and envy (A, 363). When reins are slack, manners are corrupted, effeminacy begotten, and industry destroyed (A, 364). Oppression results in a poor country and a desperate population (A, 365). Envy disturbs society and clogs "the Wheels" (A, 367). Good officials should have clean hands, assiduity, dispatch, impartiality, and capacity. Delay, for example, is often more injurious than injustice (A, 380-95). Justice should be blind, with the same scale for rich and poor (A, 408). Penn differentiated between impartiality, indifference, and neutrality. Where right or religion calls for decision, a neuter must perforce be either coward or hypocrite (A, 432).

Luxury should be discouraged, if necessary by sumptuary laws (B, 227). Exertion is wholesome for both body and mind, besides supplying the want of parts (A, 57, 233). Only a miserable nation can offer no better employment for the poor than the production of superfluities. Liberality and frugality mixed well together: the very trimmings of the vain world would clothe all the naked (A, 50, 52-54, 73). Superfluities abolished might make possible almshouses, and excess would at the same time disappear (A, 53).

True godliness, Penn believed, does not turn men out of the world but enables them to live more profitably by exciting the endeavors of others in it. Religion is, after all, the fear of God demonstrated in good works. Pure and undefiled religion is to visit the fatherless and widowed in charity and piety. There is neither use nor necessity for endless investigation, as Penn may have felt Pascal's inquiry into truth to be. "Men may tire themselves in a Labyrinth of Search, and talk of God: But if we would know him indeed," wrote the Quaker, "it must be from the Impressions we receive of him" (A, 511). The less form in religion, the better since "God is a Spirit" (A, 507) and value lies not in *"verbal Orthodoxy"* (A, 472).

Pious and devout souls are everywhere of one religion (A, 519). The truly pious loves his particular persuasion for its devotion (A, 519-20). Public worship may truly be valuable but God who is everywhere at once might be better served "in resisting a Temptation to Evil, than in many formal Prayers" (A, 473, 478). Conformity may be reasonable where conscience is not against it, but a weakness in religion and government "where it is carried to things of an indifferent Nature" (B, 249, 251). Penn condemned censoriousness (A, 41). "They have a Right to censure, that have an Heart to help: The rest is Cruelty not Justice" (A, 46). To have religion solely upon authority, and not from conviction, is "like a *finger watch,* to be set forwards or backwards, as he pleases that has it in keeping" (A, 523). Conscience and charity are all important. Where love prevails, "we shall all be *Lovely,* and in *Love* with *God,* and *one* with *another"* (A, 556).

These achievements of the years of frustration provide glimpses of Penn's character that are not, perhaps, as sharply revealed in the years of greater activity and influence. His writing of Quaker history focuses clearly on essentials. Similarly, *An Essay* and the *Brief and Plain Scheme* deal briskly with the secular alignment of states and colonies, while *Some Proposals for a Second Settlement* pursues the potential for colonial expansion. Not many contemporaries, as noticed, examined methods of federal union. Penn perceived the difficulties and concessions reconciliation would make necessary, though the extent of the task was not fully comprehended. Concordance was urgent if disagreements and war were to be prevented. That implementation did not follow his suggestions in no way renders them less illuminative of his thinking. And if inclined to underestimate a general reluctance to take positive steps, he nonetheless understood the essential role of frequent consultation by some kind of representative assembly.

Wide reading and travel influenced Penn throughout life. One result may be seen in his curiosity about Indians, and another in recognition of the special needs of both earlier settlers and later immigrants lacking the British background of his Quaker purchasers. *Fruits of Solitude* displays acquaintance with other than legal, political, and controversial literature. Penn was very little of a cynic. He was, in spite of his troubles, convinced that men could be talked or cajoled into reasonableness, good government, and charity in religion. Successful in missionary work, he was the reverse in convincing the Pennsylvanians of the virtues of laws and frames proposed. Quite possibly this sprang from a failure to understand human beings as such.

Penn, like Barclay, was not a leveler. Every person had an appointed rank and good relations between social categories were important. Save for his Quaker belief in religious liberty and in greater forebearance toward malefactors, he was very much the conscientious and reflective Englishman, born to service and a share in government. His love of the beauties of the wonderful world in which he lived led to a simple interpretation of natural laws easily discovered and leading to peace among men. In his treasured retreat, Penn contemplated a better life and seldom delved deeply into the matter of obstacles likely to stand in the way of achieving it.

Fox, the "great instrument" of Quakerism, and Barclay, its first philosopher, rightly occupy the highest place in the esteem of the Society of Friends. Penn, although dedicated, was distracted by vicissitudes of fortune different from those caused by persecution shared by all early members. He had charisma and showed fierce energy in argument with unbelievers but was often guilty of hasty judgment about those of whom he disapproved. Farsighted about larger issues, he seemed unable at times to cope with smaller problems. Great complications in social relationships, a continued association with the rich and powerful, his role as proprietor placing him in the ruling class of the day—all these factors help to blur the Quaker image, even when so much of his activity directly concerned the Friends.

Yet in spite of frustrations and disappointments, Penn remains the greatest of colonial founding fathers. His interest in boundaries, in peaceful relations with the natives, in an open-door policy for would-be emigrants, and his perception of certain intercolonial problems, and of the harm wrought by European disunity, all reveal him to be capable, not only of legal argument and religious persuasion, but also of constructive thinking about questions still of universal concern. In the writings of the years of Penn's last major exertions may be traced what the late Frederick Tolles once called a "final distillation" of thought and character. (pp. 71-82)

> Caroline Robbins, "William Penn, 1689-1702: Eclipse, Frustration, and Achievement," in The World of William Penn, *edited by Richard S. Dunn and Mary Maples Dunn, University of Pennsylvania Press, 1986, pp. 71-84.*

FURTHER READING

Brailsford, Mabel Richmond. *The Making of William Penn.* London: Longmans, Green and Co., 1930, 267 p.
  Biography focusing on Penn's early life.

Bronner, Edwin B. *William Penn's "Holy Experiment": The Founding of Pennsylvania, 1681-1701.* New York: Temple University Press, 1962, 306 p.
  Investigates "the religion, the philosophy, the economic life, and the social life of the people in Pennsylvania" during Penn's proprietorship.

Dunn, Mary Maples. *William Penn: Politics and Conscience.* Princeton, N.J.: Princeton University Press, 1967, 206 p.
  Studies Penn's political career.

Du Ponceau, Peter S., and Fisher, J. F. "A Memoir on the History of the Celebrated Treaty made by William Penn with the Indians under the Elm Tree at Shackamaxon, in the year 1682." In *Memoirs of the Historical Society of Pennsylvania,* Vol. III, Part II, pp. 141-204. Philadelphia: McCarty and Davis, 1836.
Details Penn's treaty with the Native Americans of Pennsylvania.

Endy, Melvin B., Jr. "William Penn the Quaker." In his *William Penn and Early Quakerism,* pp. 93-149. Princeton, N.J.: Princeton University Press, 1973.
Discusses Penn's conversion to Quakerism and his leadership within the Society of Friends.

Fantel, Hans. *William Penn: Apostle of Dissent.* New York: William Morrow and Company, 1974, 298 p.
Biography of Penn focusing on his politics.

Illick, Joseph E. *William Penn the Politician: His Relations with the English Government.* Ithaca, N.Y.: Cornell University Press, 1965, 267 p.
Contends that Penn's success in establishing his Quaker colony of Pennsylvania was due largely "to his influence with prominent statesmen."

Kunze, Bonnelyn Young. "Religious Authority and Social Status in Seventeenth-Century England: The Friendship of Margaret Fell, George Fox, and William Penn." *Church History* 57, No. 2 (June 1988): 170-86.
Examines the relationships between Penn and two fellow Quaker leaders. Kunze argues that "religious authority [in the Quaker Movement] rested to a significant degree on social status."

Nash, Gary B. *Quakers and Politics: Pennsylvania, 1681-1726.* Princeton, N.J.: Princeton University Press, 1968, 362 p.
Analyzes the connection between the structure of Quaker society in Pennsylvania and the nature of their politics.

Peare, Catherine Owens. *William Penn: A Biography.* London: Dennis Dobson, 1956, 448 p.
Includes primary and secondary bibliographies.

Philips, Edith. "The Utopia of Penn." In her *The Good Quaker in French Legend,* pp. 91-132. Philadelphia: University of Pennsylvania Press, 1932.
Traces the influence of Penn and Quakerism in French thought.

Robbins, Caroline. "The Efforts of William Penn to Lay a Foundation for Future Ages." In *Aspects of American Liberty: Philosophical, Historical, and Political,* pp. 68-80. Philadelphia: American Philosophical Society, 1977.
Examines Penn's contribution to the formation of American political thought and institutions.

Wildes, Harry Emerson. *William Penn.* New York: Macmillan Publishing Co., 1974, 469 p.
Biography focusing on Penn's personality.

For further information on Penn's life and career, see *Dictionary of Literary Biography,* Vol. 24.

George Washington

1732-1799

American statesman and political writer.

INTRODUCTION

Washington, who has been hailed as "the first American" and "the father of our country," led the American forces during the Revolution, presided over the Federal Constitutional Convention that adopted the American Constitution, and was the first president of the United States. One of the most influential leaders of his time, Washington was also a prolific writer; his collected works amount to more than eight thousand documents, including his *Farewell Address,* a speech on domestic and foreign policy which has influenced the course of political thinking well into the twentieth century.

Born in Westmoreland County, Virginia, on 22 February 1732, Washington was the fourth son of Augustine Washington and the first child of Mary Ball, whom Augustine had married the previous year. In 1743 his father died and shortly thereafter Washington was withdrawn from school. As he matured, the majority of his time was spent in the company of his older half-brothers, particularly Lawrence, a captain in the American Regiment and proprietor of Mount Vernon. Despite his limited education, Washington was highly skilled in mathematics and at fifteen found employment as a surveyor for Thomas Lord Fairfax. He then entered the Virginia military, where he quickly rose to the rank of major, but did not distinguish himself as a soldier until 1753 when Governor Dinwiddie sent him on an expedition to the Ohio valley where Washington met with the invading French. This journey, in addition to Washington's subsequent attempts to build a fort along the Ohio River, resulted in *The Journal of Major George Washington.* Published in Williamsburg in 1754, it is one of the first authentic accounts of life in the Western frontier and was widely read throughout the colonies as well as in England and France. The following year, Washington, at twenty-three, became commander-in-chief of the Virginia forces, but because he was a colonist, was treated poorly by lower-ranking British officers and consequently resigned his commission in December 1758. That same year, he was elected to the House of Burgesses. On 6 January 1759 Washington married Martha Dandrige Custis, the wealthy widow of Colonel John Custis, and, two years later, inherited Mount Vernon from Lawrence, who had died in 1752. A respected, prosperous, and influential citizen, Washington was gradually and somewhat reluctantly drawn into politics as relations with England worsened. In August 1774 he was a delegate to the Williamsburg Convention and later served in the first and second Continental Congress in September 1774 and May 1775. On 15 June 1775 Washington was unanimously

elected commander-in-chief of the Continental Army, a position he held for the duration of the American Revolution, without accepting payment from Congress. At the close of the war it was suggested that Washington become king, but he refused and immediately resigned his commission to Congress on 23 December 1783. In May 1787 Washington, who had spent the past several years managing Mount Vernon, became a delegate to and president of the Federal Constitutional Convention in Philadelphia. Following the ratification of the Constitution, Washington was unanimously elected president of the United States on 4 March 1789 and was inaugurated in New York City on 30 April 1789. Washington had contemplated retirement after his first administration and, with the aid of James Madison, he began writing a farewell address to the American people. Nevertheless, he was persuaded to continue in the office for a second term and was unanimously re-elected in 1792. Tired of public life, Washington decided to retire after his second term, despite public enthusiasm for a third. In revising his 1792 address to the people, Washington sought guidance from Alexander Hamilton, and together they constructed Washington's famous *Farewell Address.* The speech was never read aloud, but upon Washington's orders it appeared in *Claypoole's American*

Daily Advertiser on 19 September 1796. Washington returned to Mount Vernon, but on 3 July 1798 he was appointed lieutenant general and commander of the United States Army, serving until his death on 14 December 1799.

Following Washington's death, a large portion of his papers was either lost or destroyed by family members and early biographers. Martha Washington burned all but a select few of the letters Washington sent her throughout their marriage, and Washington's nephew Bushrod Washington, who was entrusted with the majority of Washington's collection, sent several pieces to friends and acquaintances throughout America and Europe. Jared Sparks, an early biographer and editor of Washington's works, also disseminated numerous torn pages and clippings from the collection. In fact, Sparks's damage to the Washington's collected works was so great that large segments of important documents, such as Washington's first inaugural address, have never been fully recovered.

Washington's writings consist of diaries, journals, letters, and state papers. Overall, his prose style is simple, assertive, straightforward, and highly disciplined. Because he lacked the formal training of his contemporaries, Washington's writings are considered unique in that they allude to common sources such as the Bible and popular literature of his time, especially Joseph Addison's *Cato*. Highly erratic, Washington's diaries simply record how his time was spent and, although they are not the works of a literary diarist by any means, his diaries are considered important for historical purposes, offering insight into Washington's daily activities and some detail about the time in which he lived. His *Journal,* like his diaries, tends to focus on daily events, especially those involving action, but offers little insight into his character. Although Washington is purely objective throughout the *Journal,* historians have detected some elements of Romanticism in this work which are absent from his more mature writings. Of Washington's later works, critics have noted that his letters and state papers are most indicative of his true character and philosophy. Here, Washington reveals his dedication to an American republic comprised of an indissoluble union bound by a strong federal government; in his Circular Letter to the States, Washington argued that "without an entire conformity to the spirit of the Union, we cannot exist as an Independent Power." Critics have contended that his most notable literary achievement is the *Farewell Address*. A testament of American policy, it argues against geographic and political factionalism and long-term foreign alliances. Though the document was written by Hamilton from Washington's notes, Washington edited and rewrote large portions of the text, replacing Hamilton's wordiness with his own simple and direct style.

Nineteenth-century criticism regarding Washington tended to focus almost entirely on his character and, in most instances, accounts of his achievements were grossly exaggerated, elevating him to the status of a patriot-hero of mythic proportions. Sparks, when editing Washington's works, altered some of the original wording so that Washington would appear flawless. Moreover, Parson Mason Locke Weems, an early biographer, created several anecdotes about Washington's childhood which were so popular that he expanded his 1800 biography into nearly seventy editions, adding such tales as the "cherry tree fable," wherein a young and infallibly honest Washington admits to chopping down his father's favorite tree. Twentieth-century Washington scholarship has been more objective in its estimation of his character. Many historians and scholars, while they recognize his admirable traits, have attempted to humanize Washington; in his 1948 biography, Douglas Southall Freeman noted that "acceptance of Parson Weem's fables seems to have kept Americans from realizing that to proclaim perfection was to deny growth. . . . More Americans will be relieved than will be shocked to know that Washington sometimes was violent, emotional, resentful—a human being and not a monument in frozen flesh." Recent trends in Washington criticism have focused primarily on his philosophy and overall contribution to the founding of the American government. Several scholars, who use the *Farewell Address* as the centerpiece of their argument, have maintained that Washington was merely a figurehead whose works reflect the philosophy of the Madison and Hamilton, both of whom wrote the majority of Washington's state papers, including the *Farewell Address*. Others, such as Harold W. Bradley, have argued that Washington, while he may not have been a political philosopher, did give "more than casual thought to the fundamental issues of political principle . . . in the years preceding and following the framing of the constitution." Similarly, Glenn A. Phelps has asserted that Washington's private letters, written prior to his relationships with Madison and Hamilton, "reveal a man with a passionate commitment to a fully developed idea of a constitutional republic on a continental scale, eager to promote that plan wherever and whenever circumstances or the hand of providence allowed." Critics have generally agreed, however, that although Washington may not have been the greatest thinker of his time, he was—due to his tremendous popularity with the American people—the most influential statesman in colonial America and essential to the success of the new government. "If there ever was an indispensable leader at a critical moment in history," wrote Saul K. Padover, "it was George Washington. In the formative years of the American republic, roughly between 1776 and 1796, the man, the moment, and the crisis coincided."

PRINCIPAL WORKS

The Journal of Major George Washington, Sent by the Hon. Robert Dinwiddie, Esq., His Majesty's Lieutenant-Governor and Commander in Chief of Virginia, to the Commandant of the French Forces on Ohio . . . (journal) 1754

Farewell Address (speech) 1796

The Diaries of George Washington. 6 vols. (diaries) 1976-79

The Papers of George Washington. 5 vols. (speeches and letters) 1983-

---

CRITICISM

George Washington   (letter date 1783)

[*Written upon his resignation from the American forces, this famous circular letter to the state governors, known as "Washington's Legacy," contains the centerpiece of Washington's statesmanship. In it, he argues for an indissoluble national union, payment of public debts, continuance of a national military, and suppression of sectional rivalries.*]

Sir:

The great object for which I had the honor to hold an appointment in the Service of my Country, being accomplished, I am now preparing to resign it into the hands of Congress, and to return to that domestic retirement, which, it is well known, I left with the greatest reluctance, a Retirement, for which I have never ceased to sigh through a long and painful absence, and in which (remote from the noise and trouble of the World) I meditate to pass the remainder of life in a state of undisturbed repose; But before I carry this resolution into effect, I think it a duty incumbent on me, to make this my last official communication, to congratulate you on the glorious events which Heaven has been pleased to produce in our favor, to offer my sentiments respecting some important subjects, which appear to me, to be intimately connected with the tranquility of the United States, to take my leave of your Excellency as a public Character, and to give my final blessing to that Country, in whose service I have spent the prime of my life, for whose sake I have consumed so many anxious days and watchfull nights, and whose happiness being extremely dear to me, will always constitute no inconsiderable part of my own.

Impressed with the liveliest sensibility on this pleasing occasion, I will claim the indulgence of dilating the more copiously on the subjects of our mutual felicitation. When we consider the magnitude of the prize we contended for, the doubtful nature of the contest, and the favorable manner in which it has terminated, we shall find the greatest possible reason for gratitude and rejoicing; this is a theme that will afford infinite delight to every benevolent and liberal mind, whether the event in contemplation, be considered as the source of present enjoyment or the parent of future happiness; and we shall have equal occasion to felicitate ourselves on the lot which Providence has assigned us, whether we view it in a natural, a political or moral point of light.

The Citizens of America, placed in the most enviable condition, as the sole Lords and Proprietors of a vast Tract of Continent, comprehending all the various soils and climates of the World, and abounding with all the neces-

saries and conveniencies of life, are now by the late satisfactory pacification, acknowledged to be possessed of absolute freedom and Independency; They are, from this period, to be considered as the Actors on a most conspicuous Theatre, which seems to be peculiarly designated by Providence for the display of human greatness and felicity; Here, they are not only surrounded with every thing which can contribute to the completion of private and domestic enjoyment, but Heaven has crowned all its other blessings, by giving a fairer oppertunity for political happiness, than any other Nation has ever been favored with. Nothing can illustrate these observations more forcibly, than a recollection of the happy conjuncture of times and circumstances, under which our Republic assumed its rank among the Nations; The foundation of our empire was not laid in the gloomy age of Ignorance and Superstition, but at an Epocha when the rights of mankind were better understood and more clearly defined, than at any former period; the researches of the human mind, after social happiness, have been carried to a great extent; the Treasures of knowledge, acquired through a long succession of years, by the labours of Philosophers, Sages and Legislatures, are laid open for our use, and their collected wisdom may be happily applied in the Establishment of our forms of Government; the free cultivation of Letters, the unbounded extension of Commerce, the progressive refinement of Manners, the growing liberality of sentiment, and above all, the pure and benign light of Revelation, have had a meliorating influence on mankind and increased the blessings of Society. At this auspicious period, the United States came into existence as a Nation, and if their Citizens should not be completely free and happy, the fault will be intirely their own.

Such is our situation, and such are our prospects: but notwithstanding the cup of blessing is thus reached out to us, notwithstanding happiness is ours, if we have a disposition to seize the occasion and make it our own; yet, it appears to me there is an option still left to the United States of America, that it is in their choice, and depends upon their conduct, whether they will be respectable and prosperous, or contemptable and miserable as a Nation; This is the time of their political probation; this is the moment when the eyes of the whole World are turned upon them; this is the moment to establish or ruin their national Character forever; this is the favorable moment to give such a tone to our Federal Government, as will enable it to answer the ends of its institution; or this may be the ill-fated moment for relaxing the powers of the Union, annihilating the cement of the Confederation, and exposing us to become the sport of European politics, which may play one State against another to prevent their growing importance, and to serve their own interested purposes. For, according to the system of Policy the States shall adopt at this moment, they will stand or fall; and by their confirmation or lapse, it is yet to be decided, whether the Revolution must ultimately be considered as a blessing or a curse: a blessing or a curse, not to the present age alone, for with our fate will the destiny of unborn Millions be involved.

With this conviction of the importance of the present Crisis, silence in me would be a crime; I will therefore speak to your Excellency, the language of freedom and of sincerity, without disguise; I am aware, however, that those who differ from me in political sentiment, may perhaps remark, I am stepping out of the proper line of my duty, and they may possibly ascribe to arrogance or ostentation, what I know is alone the result of the purest intention, but the rectitude of my own heart, which disdains such unworthy motives, the part I have hitherto acted in life, the determination I have formed, of not taking any share in public business hereafter, the ardent desire I feel, and shall continue to manifest, of quietly enjoying in private life, after all the toils of War, the benefits of a wise and liberal Government, will, I flatter myself, sooner or later convince my Countrymen, that I could have no sinister views in delivering with so little reserve, the opinions contained in this Address.

There are four things, which I humbly conceive, are essential to the well being, I may even venture to say, to the existence of the United States as an Independent Power:

1st. An indissoluble Union of the States under one Federal Head.

2dly. A Sacred regard to Public Justice.

3dly. The adoption of a proper Peace Establishment, and

4thly. The prevalence of that pacific and friendly Disposition, among the People of the United States, which will induce them to forget their local prejudices and policies, to make those mutual concessions which are requisite to the general prosperity, and in some instances, to sacrifice their individual advantages to the interest of the Community.

These are the Pillars on which the glorious Fabrick of our Independency and National Character must be supported; Liberty is the Basis, and whoever would dare to sap the foundation, or overturn the Structure, under whatever specious pretexts he may attempt it, will merit the bitterest execration, and the severest punishment which can be inflicted by his injured Country.

On the three first Articles I will make a few observations, leaving the last to the good sense and serious consideration of those immediately concerned.

Under the first head, altho' it may not be necessary or proper for me in this place to enter into a particular disquisition of the principles of the Union, and to take up the great question which has been frequently agitated, whether it be expedient and requisite for the States to delegate a larger proportion of Power to Congress, or not, Yet it will be a part of my duty, and that of every true Patriot, to assert without reserve, and to insist upon the following positions, That unless the States will suffer Congress to exercise those prerogatives, they are undoubtedly invested with by the Constitution, every thing must very rapidly tend to Anarchy and confusion, That it is indispensable to the happiness of the individual States, that there should be lodged somewhere, a Supreme Power to regulate and govern the general concerns of the Confederated Republic, without which the Union cannot be of long duration. That there must be a faithfull and pointed compliance on the part of every State, with the late proposals and demands of Congress, or the most fatal consequences will ensue, That whatever measures have a tendency to dis-

solve the Union, or contribute to violate or lessen the Sovereign Authority, ought to be considered as hostile to the Liberty and Independency of America, and the Authors of them treated accordingly, and lastly, that unless we can be enabled by the concurrence of the States, to participate of the fruits of the Revolution, and enjoy the essential benefits of Civil Society, under a form of Government so free and uncorrupted, so happily guarded against the danger of oppression, as has been devised and adopted by the Articles of Confederation, it will be a subject of regret, that so much blood and treasure have been lavished for no purpose, that so many sufferings have been encountered without a compensation, and that so many sacrifices have been made in vain. Many other considerations might here be adduced to prove, that without an entire conformity to the Spirit of the Union, we cannot exist as an Independent Power; it will be sufficient for my purpose to mention but one or two which seem to me of the greatest importance. It is only in our united Character as an Empire, that our Independence is acknowledged, that our power can be regarded, or our Credit supported among Foreign Nations. The Treaties of the European Powers with the United States of America, will have no validity on a dissolution of the Union. We shall be left nearly in a state of Nature, or we may find by our own unhappy experience, that there is a natural and necessary progression, from the extreme of anarchy to the extreme of Tyranny; and that arbitrary power is most easily established on the ruins of Liberty abused to licentiousness.

As to the second Article, which respects the performance of Public Justice, Congress have, in their late Address to the United States, almost exhausted the subject, they have explained their Ideas so fully, and have enforced the obligations the States are under, to render compleat justice to all the Public Creditors, with so much dignity and energy, that in my opinion, no real friend to the honor and Independency of America, can hesitate a single moment respecting the propriety of complying with the just and honorable measures proposed; if their Arguments do not produce conviction, I know of nothing that will have greater influence; especially when we recollect that the System referred to, being the result of the collected Wisdom of the Continent, must be esteemed, if not perfect, certainly the least objectionable of any that could be devised; and that if it shall not be carried into immediate execution, a National Bankruptcy, with all its deplorable consequences will take place, before any different Plan can possibly be proposed and adopted, So pressing are the present circumstances! and such is the alternative now offered to the States!

The ability of the Country to discharge the debts which have been incurred in its defence, is not to be doubted; an inclination, I flatter myself, will not be wanting; the path of our duty is plain before us; honesty will be found on every experiment, to be the best and only true policy; let us then as a Nation be just; let us fulfil the public Contracts, which Congress had undoubtedly a right to make for the purpose of carrying on the War, with the same good faith we suppose ourselves bound to perform our private engagements; in the mean time, let an attention to the chearfull performance of their proper business, as Individuals, and as members of Society, be earnestly inculcated on the Citizens of America, then will they strengthen the hands of Government, and be happy under its protection: every one will reap the fruit of his labours; every one will enjoy his own acquisitions without molestation and without danger.

In this state of absolute freedom and perfect security, who will grudge to yield a very little of his property to support the common interest of Society, and insure the protection of Government? Who does not remember, the frequent declarations, at the commencement of the War, that we should be compleatly satisfied, if at the expence of one half, we could defend the remainder of our possessions? Where is the Man to be found, who wishes to remain indebted, for the defence of his own person and property, to the exertions, the bravery, and the blood of others, without making one generous effort to repay the debt of honor and of gratitude? In what part of the Continent shall we find any Man, or body of Men, who would not blush to stand up and propose measures, purposely calculated to rob the Soldier of his Stipend, and the Public Creditor of his due? and were it possible that such a flagrant instance of Injustice could ever happen, would it not excite the general indignation, and tend to bring down, upon the Authors of such measures, the aggravated vengeance of Heaven?

If after all, a spirit of disunion or a temper of obstinacy and perverseness, should manifest itself in any of the States, if such an ungracious disposition should attempt to frustrate all the happy effects that might be expected to flow from the Union, if there should be a refusal to comply with the requisitions for Funds to discharge the annual interest of the public debts, and if that refusal should revive again all those jealousies and produce all those evils, which are now happily removed, Congress, who have in all their Transaction shewn a great degree of magnanimity and justice, will stand justified in the sight of God and Man, and the State alone which puts itself in opposition to the aggregate Wisdom of the Continent, and follows such mistaken and pernicious Councils, will be responsible for all the consequences.

For my own part, conscious of having acted while a Servant of the Public, in a manner I conceived best suited to promote the real interests of my Country; having in consequence of my fixed belief in some measure pledged myself to the Army, that their Country would finally do them compleat and ample Justice; and not wishing to conceal any instance of my official conduct from the eyes of the World, I have thought proper to transmit to your Excellency the inclosed collection of Papers, relative to the half pay and commutation granted by Congress to the Officers of the Army; From these communications, my decided sentiment will be clearly comprehended, together with the conclusive reasons which induced me, at an early period, to recommend the adoption of the measure, in the most earnest and serious manner. As the proceedings of Congress, the Army, and myself are open to all, and contain in my opinion, sufficient information to remove the prejudices and errors which may have been entertained by any; I think it unnecessary to say any thing more, than just to

observe, that the Resolutions of Congress, now alluded to, are undoubtedly as absolutely binding upon the United States, as the most solemn Acts of Confederation or Legislation. As to the Idea, which I am informed has in some instances prevailed, that the half pay and commutation are to be regarded merely in the odious light of a Pension, it ought to be exploded forever; that Provision, should be viewed as it really was, a reasonable compensation offered by Congress, at a time when they had nothing else to give, to the Officers of the Army, for services then to be performed. It was the only means to prevent a total dereliction of the Service, It was a part of their hire, I may be allowed to say, it was the price of their blood and of your Independency, it is therefore more than a common debt, it is a debt of honour, it can never be considered as a Pension or gratuity, nor be cancelled until it is fairly discharged.

With regard to a distinction between Officers and Soldiers, it is sufficient that the uniform experience of every Nation of the World, combined with our own, proves the utility and propriety of the discrimination. Rewards in proportion to the aids the public derives from them, are unquestionably due to all its Servants; In some Lines, the Soldiers have perhaps generally had as ample a compensation for their Services, by the large Bounties which have been paid to them, as their Officers will receive in the proposed Commutation, in others, if besides the donation of Lands, the payment of Arrearages of Cloathing and Wages (in which Articles all the component parts of the Army must be put upon the same footing) we take into the estimate, the Bounties many of the Soldiers have received and the gratuity of one Year's full pay, which is promised to all, possibly their situation (every circumstance being duly considered) will not be deemed less eligible than that of the Officers. Should a farther reward, however, be judged equitable, I will venture to assert, no one will enjoy greater satisfaction than myself, on seeing an exemption from Taxes for a limited time, (which has been petitioned for in some instances) or any other adequate immunity or compensation, granted to the brave defenders of their Country's Cause; but neither the adoption or rejection of this proposition will in any manner affect, much less militate against, the Act of Congress, by which they have offered five years full pay, in lieu of the half pay for life, which had been before promised to the Officers of the Army.

Before I conclude the subject of public justice, I cannot omit to mention the obligations this Country is under, to that meritorious Class of veteran Non-commissioned Officers and Privates, who have been discharged for inability, in consequence of the Resolution of Congress of the 23d of April 1782, on an annual pension for life, their peculiar sufferings, their singular merits and claims to that provision need only be known, to interest all the feelings of humanity in their behalf: nothing but a punctual payment of their annual allowance can rescue them from the most complicated misery, and nothing could be a more melancholy and distressing sight, than to behold those who have shed their blood or lost their limbs in the service of their Country, without a shelter, without a friend, and without the means of obtaining any of the necessaries or comforts of Life; compelled to beg their daily bread from door to door! Suffer me to recommend those of this discription, belonging to your State, to the warmest patronage of your Excellency and your Legislature.

It is necessary to say but a few words on the third topic which was proposed, and which regards particularly the defence of the Republic, As there can be little doubt but Congress will recommend a proper Peace Establishment for the United States, in which a due attention will be paid to the importance of placing the Militia of the Union upon a regular and respectable footing; If this should be the case, I would beg leave to urge the great advantage of it in the strongest terms. The Militia of this Country must be considered as the Palladium of our security, and the first effectual resort in case of hostility; It is essential therefore, that the same system should pervade the whole; that the formation and discipline of the Militia of the Continent should be absolutely uniform, and that the same species of Arms, Accoutrements and Military Apparatus, should be introduced in every part of the United States; No one, who has not learned it from experience, can conceive the difficulty, expence, and confusion which result from a contrary system, or the vague Arrangements which have hitherto prevailed.

If in treating of political points, a greater latitude than usual has been taken in the course of this Address, the importance of the Crisis, and the magnitude of the objects in discussion, must be my apology: It is, however, neither my wish or expectation, that the preceding observations should claim any regard, except so far as they shall appear to be dictated by a good intention, consonant to the immutable rules of Justice; calculated to produce a liberal system of policy, and founded on whatever experience may have been acquired by a long and close attention to public business. Here I might speak with the more confidence from my actual observations, and, if it would not swell this Letter (already too prolix) beyond the bounds I had prescribed myself: I could demonstrate to every mind open to conviction, that in less time and with much less expence than has been incurred, the War might have been brought to the same happy conclusion, if the resources of the Continent could have been properly drawn forth, that the distresses and disappointments which have very often occurred, have in too many instances, resulted more from a want of energy, in the Continental Government, than a deficiency of means in the particular States. That the inefficiency of measures, arising from the want of an adequate authority in the Supreme Power, from a partial compli-

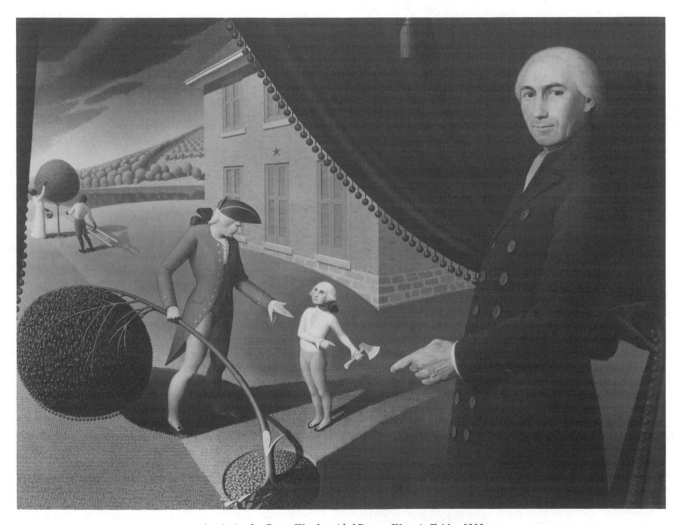

A painting by Grant Wood entitled Parson Weem's Fable, *1939*

ance with the Requisitions of Congress in some of the States, and from a failure of punctuality in others, while it tended to damp the zeal of those which were more willing to exert themselves; served also to accumulate the expences of the War, and to frustrate the best concerted Plans, and that the discouragement occasioned by the complicated difficulties and embarrassments, in which our affairs were, by this means involved, would have long ago produced the dissolution of any Army, less patient, less virtuous and less persevering, than that which I have had the honor to command. But while I mention these things, which are notorious facts, as the defects of our Federal Government, particularly in the prosecution of a War, I beg it may be understood, that as I have ever taken a pleasure in gratefully acknowledging the assistance and support I have derived from every Class of Citizens, so shall I always be happy to do justice to the unparalleled exertion of the individual States, on many interesting occasions.

I have thus freely disclosed what I wished to make known, before I surrendered up my Public trust to those who committed it to me, the task is now accomplished, I now bid adieu to your Excellency as the Chief Magistrate of your State, at the same time I bid a last farewell to the cares of Office, and all the imployments of public life.

It remains then to be my final and only request, that your Excellency will communicate these sentiments to your Legislature at their next meeting, and that they may be considered as the Legacy of One, who has ardently wished, on all occasions, to be useful to his Country, and who, even in the shade of Retirement, will not fail to implore the divine benediction upon it.

I now make it my earnest prayer, that God would have you, and the State over which you preside, in his holy protection, that he would incline the hearts of the Citizens to cultivate a spirit of subordination and obedience to Government, to entertain a brotherly affection and love for one another, for their fellow Citizens of the United States at large, and particularly for their brethren who have served in the Field, and finally, that he would most graciously be pleased to dispose us all, to do Justice, to love mercy, and to demean ourselves with that Charity, humility and pacific temper of mind, which were the Characteristicks of the Divine Author of our blessed Religion, and without an humble imitation of whose example in these things, we can never hope to be a happy Nation. (pp. 239-49)

> *George Washington, in a letter to the state governors on June 14, 1783, in* George Washington: A Collection, *edited by W. B. Allen, Liberty Classics, 1988, pp. 239-49.*

John Marshall   (essay date 1804-07)

[*Highly regarded as the architect of American Constitutional law, Marshall—who played a vital role in both Washington's and John Adam's administrations—is best known for his service as Chief Justice of the United States from 1801-1835. In the following selection, originally published in his* The Life of George Washington *(1804-07), Marshall estimates Washington's character and political standing.*]

General Washington was rather above the common size, his frame was robust, and his constitution vigorous—capable of enduring great fatigue, and requiring a considerable degree of exercise for the preservation of his health. His exterior created in the beholder the idea of strength, united with manly gracefulness.

His manners were rather reserved than free, though they partook nothing of that dryness, and sternness, which accompany reserve when carried to an extreme; and on all proper occasions, he could relax sufficiently to show how highly he was gratified by the charms of conversation, and the pleasures of society. His person and whole deportment exhibited an unaffected and indescribable dignity, unmingled with haughtiness of which all who approached him were sensible; and the attachment of those who possessed his friendship, and enjoyed his intimacy, was ardent, but always respectful.

His temper was humane, benevolent, and conciliatory; but there was a quickness in his sensibility to any thing apparently offensive, which experience had taught him to watch, and to correct.

In the management of his private affairs he exhibited an exact yet liberal economy. His funds were not prodigally wasted on capricious and ill examined schemes, nor refused to beneficial though costly improvements. They remained therefore competent to that expensive establishment which his reputation, added to a hospitable temper, had in some measure imposed upon him; and to those donations which real distress has a right to claim from opulence.

He made no pretensions to that vivacity which fascinates, or to that wit which dazzles, and frequently imposes on the understanding. More solid than brilliant, judgment, rather than genius, constituted the most prominent feature of his character.

Without making ostentatious professions of religion, he was a sincere believer in the Christian faith, and a truly devout man.

As a military man, he was brave, enterprising, and cautious. That malignity which was sought to strip him of all the higher qualities of a General, has conceded to him personal courage, and a firmness of resolution which neither dangers nor difficulties could shake. But candour will allow him other great and valuable endowments. If his military course does not abound with splendid achievements, it exhibits a series of judicious measures adapted to circumstances, which probably saved his country.

Placed, without having studied the theory, or been taught in the school of experience the practice of war, at the head of an undisciplined, ill organized multitude, which was impatient of the restraints, and unacquainted with the ordinary duties of a camp, without the aid of officers possessing those lights which the Commander-in-chief was yet to acquire, it would have been a miracle indeed had his conduct been absolutely faultless. But, possessing an energetic and distinguishing mind, on which the lessons of experience were never lost, his errors, if he committed any, were quickly repaired; and those measures which the state of things rendered most adviseable, were seldom, if ever, neglected. Inferior to his adversary in the numbers, in the equipment, and in the discipline of his troops, it is evidence of real merit that no great and decisive advantages were ever obtained over him, and that the opportunity to strike an important blow never passed away unused. He has been termed the American Fabius; but those who compare his actions with his means, will perceive at least as much of Marcellus as of Fabius, in his character. He could not have been more enterprising, without endangering the cause he defended, nor have put more to hazard, without incurring justly the imputation of rashness. Not relying upon those chances which sometimes give a favourable issue to attempts apparently desperate, his conduct was regulated by calculations made upon the capacities of his army, and the real situation of his country. When called a second time to command the armies of the United States, a change of circumstances had taken place, and he meditated a corresponding change of conduct. In modelling the army of 1798, he sought for men distinguished for their boldness of execution, not less than for their prudence in counsel, and contemplated a system of continued attack. "The enemy," said the General in his private letters, "must never be permitted to gain a foothold on our shores."

In his civil administration, as in his military career, ample and repeated proofs were exhibited of that practical good sense, of that sound judgment, which is perhaps the most rare, and is certainly the most valuable quality of the human mind. Devoting himself to the duties of his station, and pursuing no object distinct from the public good, he was accustomed to contemplate at a distance those critical situations in which the United States might probably be placed; and to digest, before the occasion required action, the line of conduct which it would be proper to observe. Taught to distrust first impressions, he sought to acquire all the information which was attainable, and to hear, without prejudice, all the reasons which could be urged for or against a particular measure. His own judgment was suspended until it became necessary to determine; and his decisions, thus maturely made, were seldom if ever to be shaken. His conduct therefore was systematic, and the great objects of his administration were steadily pursued.

Respecting, as the first magistrate in a free government must ever do, the real and deliberate sentiments of the people, their gusts of passion passed over, without ruffling the smooth surface of his mind. Trusting to the reflecting good sense of the nation for approbation and support, he had the magnanimity to pursue its real interests, in opposition to its temporary prejudices; and, though far from being regardless of popular favour, he could never stoop to retain, by deserving to lose it. In more instances than one, we find him committing his whole popularity to hazard, and pursuing steadily, in opposition to a torrent which would have overwhelmed a man of ordinary firmness, that course which had been dictated by a sense of duty.

In speculation, he was a real republican, devoted to the constitution of his country, and to that system of equal political rights on which it is founded. But between a balanced republic and a democracy, the difference is like that between order and chaos. Real liberty, he thought, was to be preserved, only by preserving the authority of the laws, and maintaining the energy of government. Scarcely did society present two characters which, in his opinion, less resembled each other, than a patriot and a demagogue.

No man has ever appeared upon the theatre of public action, whose integrity was more incorruptible, or whose principles were more perfectly free from the contamination of those selfish and unworthy passions, which find their nourishment in the conflicts of party. Having no views which required concealment, his real and avowed motives were the same; and his whole correspondence does not furnish a single case, from which even an enemy would infer that he was capable, under any circumstances, of stooping to the employment of duplicity. No truth can be uttered with more confidence than that his ends were always upright, and his means always pure. He exhibits the rare example of a politician to whom wiles were absolutely unknown, and whose professions to foreign governments and to his own countrymen, were always sincere. In him was fully exemplified the real distinction, which forever exists, between wisdom and cunning, and the importance as well as truth of the maxim that "honesty is the best policy."

If Washington possessed ambition, that passion was, in his bosom, so regulated by principles, or controlled by circumstances, that it was neither vicious, nor turbulent. Intrigue was never employed as the means of its gratification, nor was personal aggrandizement its object. The various high and important stations to which he was called by the public voice, were unsought by himself; and, in consenting to fill them, he seems rather to have yielded to a general conviction that the interests of his country would be thereby promoted, than to an avidity for power.

Neither the extraordinary partiality of the American people, the extravagant praises which were bestowed upon him, nor the inveterate opposition and malignant calumnies which he encountered, had any visible influence upon his conduct. The cause is to be looked for in the texture of his mind.

In him, that innate and unassuming modesty which adulation would have offended, which the voluntary plaudits of millions could not betray into indiscretion, and which never obtruded upon others his claims to superior consideration, was happily blended with a high and correct sense of personal dignity, and with a just consciousness of that respect which is due to station. Without exertion, he could maintain the happy medium between that arrogance which wounds, and that facility which allows the office to be degraded in the person who fills it.

It is impossible to contemplate the great events which have occurred in the United States under the auspices of Washington, without ascribing them, in some measure, to him. If we ask the causes of the prosperous issue of a war, against the successful termination of which there were so many probabilities? of the good which was produced, and the ill which was avoided, during an administration fated to contend with the strongest prejudices, that a combination of circumstances and of passions, could produce? of the constant favour of the great mass of his fellow citizens, and of the confidence which, to the last moment of his life, they reposed in him? the answer, so far as these causes may be found in his character, will furnish a lesson well meriting the attention of those who are candidates for political fame.

Endowed by nature with a sound judgment, and an accurate discriminating mind, he feared not that laborious attention which made him perfectly master of those subjects, in all their relations, on which he was to decide: and this essential quality was guided by an unvarying sense of moral right, which would tolerate the employment, only, of those means that would bear the most rigid examination; by a fairness of intention which neither sought nor required disguise: and by a purity of virtue which was not only untainted, but unsuspected. (pp. 325-29)

> *John Marshall, "An Estimate of Washington,"* in Virginia Reader: A Treasury of Writings, from the First Voyages to the Present, *edited by Francis Coleman Rosenberger, E. P. Dutton & Company, 1948, pp. 325-29.*

Thomas Jefferson   (letter date 1814)

[*The third president of the United States, Jefferson is best known as a statesman whose belief in natural rights, equality, individual liberties, and self-government found its fullest expression in the American Declaration of Independence. A skilled writer noted for his simple yet elegant prose, he profoundly influenced the direction of American politics. In the following excerpt from a letter addressed to Dr. Walter Jones, Jefferson provides what critics regard as the most accurate and penetrating portrait of Washington.*]

You say that in taking General Washington on your shoulders, to bear him harmless through the federal coalition, you encounter a perilous topic. I do not think so. You have given the genuine history of the course of his mind through the trying scenes in which it was engaged, and of the seductions by which it was deceived, but not depraved. I think I knew General Washington intimately and thoroughly; and were I called on to delineate his character, it should be in terms like these.

His mind was great and powerful, without being of the very first order; his penetration strong, though not so acute as that of a Newton, Bacon, or Locke; and as far as he saw, no judgment was ever sounder. It was slow in operation, being little aided by invention or imagination, but sure in conclusion. Hence the common remark of his officers, of the advantage he derived from councils of war, where hearing all suggestions, he selected whatever was best; and certainly no General ever planned his battles more judiciously. But if deranged during the course of the action, if any member of his plan was dislocated by sudden circumstances, he was slow in re-adjustment. The consequence was, that he often failed in the field, and rarely against an enemy in station, as at Boston and York. He was incapable of fear, meeting personal dangers with the

calmest unconcern. Perhaps the strongest feature in his character was prudence, never acting until every circumstance, every consideration, was maturely weighed; refraining if he saw a doubt, but, when once decided, going through with his purpose, whatever obstacles opposed. His integrity was most pure, his justice the most inflexible I have ever known, no motives of interest or consanguinity, of friendship or hatred, being able to bias his decision. He was, indeed, in every sense of the words, a wise, a good, and a great man. His temper was naturally high toned; but reflection and resolution had obtained a firm and habitual ascendency over it. If ever, however, it broke its bonds, he was most tremendous in his wrath. In his expenses he was honorable, but exact; liberal in contributions to whatever promised utility; but frowning and unyielding on all visionary projects and all unworthy calls on his charity. His heart was not warm in its affections; but he exactly calculated every man's value, and gave him a solid esteem proportioned to it. His person, you know, was fine, his stature exactly what one would wish, his deportment easy, erect and noble; the best horseman of his age, and the most graceful figure that could be seen on horseback. Although in the circle of his friends, where he might be unreserved with safety, he took a free share in conversation, his colloquial talents were not above mediocrity, possessing neither copiousness of ideas, nor fluency of words. In public, when called on for a sudden opinion, he was unready, short and embarrassed. Yet he wrote readily, rather diffusely, in an easy and correct style. This he had acquired by conversation with the world, for his education was merely reading, writing and common arithmetic, to which he added surveying at a later day. His time was employed in action chiefly, reading little, and that only in agriculture and English history. His correspondence became necessarily extensive, and, with journalizing his agricultural proceedings, occupied most of his leisure hours within doors. On the whole, his character was, in its mass, perfect, in nothing bad, in few points indifferent; and it may truly be said, that never did nature and fortune combine more perfectly to make a man great, and to place him in the same constellation with whatever worthies have merited from man an everlasting remembrance. For his was the singular destiny and merit, of leading the armies of his country successfully through an arduous war, for the establishment of its independence; of conducting its councils through the birth of a government, new in its forms and principles, until it had settled down into a quiet and orderly train; and of scrupulously obeying the laws through the whole of his career, civil and military, of which the history of the world furnishes no other example.

How, then, can it be perilous for you to take such a man on your shoulders? I am satisfied the great body of republicans think of him as I do. We were, indeed, dissatisfied with him on his ratification of the British treaty. But this was short lived. We knew his honesty, the wiles with which he was encompassed, and that age had already begun to relax the firmness of his purposes; and I am convinced he is more deeply seated in the love and gratitude of the republicans, than in the Pharisaical homage of the federal monarchists. For he was no monarchist from preference of his judgment. The soundness of that gave him correct views of the rights of man, and his severe justice devoted him to them. He has often declared to me that he considered our new constitution as an experiment on the practicability of republican government, and with what dose of liberty man could be trusted for his own good; that he was determined the experiment should have a fair trial, and would lose the last drop of his blood in support of it. And these declarations he repeated to me the oftener and more pointedly, because he knew my suspicions of Colonel Hamilton's views, and probably had heard from him the same declarations which I had, to wit, "that the British constitution, with its unequal representation, corruption and other existing abuses, was the most perfect government which had ever been established on earth, and that a reformation of those abuses would make it an impracticable government." I do believe that General Washington had not a firm confidence in the durability of our government. He was naturally distrustful of men, and inclined to gloomy apprehensions; and I was ever persuaded that a belief that we must at length end in something like a British constitution, had some weight in his adoption of the ceremonies of levees, birth-days, pompous meetings with Congress, and other forms of the same character, calculated to prepare us gradually for a change which he believed possible, and to let it come on with as little shock as might be to the public mind.

These are my opinions of General Washington, which I would vouch at the judgment seat of God, having been formed on an acquaintance of thirty years. I served with him in the Virginia legislature from 1769 to the Revolutionary war, and again, a short time in Congress, until he left us to take command of the army. During the war and after it we corresponded occasionally, and in the four years of my continuance in the office of Secretary of State, our intercourse was daily, confidential and cordial. After I retired from that office, great and malignant pains were taken by our federal monarchists, and not entirely without effect, to make him view me as a theorist, holding French principles of government, which would lead infallibly to licentiousness and anarchy. And to this he listened the more easily, from my known disapprobation of the British

---

American Revolutionary statesman Henry Lee eulogizes Washington:

First in war, first in peace, and first in the hearts of his countrymen, he was second to none in the humble and endearing scenes of private life. Pious, just, humane, temperate, and sincere; uniform, dignified, and commanding, his example was as edifying to all around him as were the effects of that example lasting.

To his equals he was kind; to his inferiors condescending; and to the dear object of his affections, exemplarily tender. Correct throughout, vice shuddered in his presence and virtue always felt his fostering hand; the purity of his private character gave effulgence to his public virtues.

Henry Lee, from an address delivered on the death of Washington, 1799.

---

treaty. I never saw him afterwards, or these malignant insinuations should have been dissipated before his just judgment, as mists before the sun. I felt on his death, with my countrymen, that "verily a great man hath fallen this day in Israel." (pp. 1318-21)

Thomas Jefferson, in a letter to Dr. Walter Jones on January 2, 1814, in his Writings, *The Library of America, 1984, 1600 p.*

Stuart Sherman   (essay date 1924-25)

[*In the following excerpt, originally published in 1924-25, Sherman examines the contents of Washington's diaries, arguing that they provide little insight into Washington, his contemporaries, or the significant events of his time.*]

Let us be plain about this. There is a little batch of diaries, perhaps half a dozen, which are of vivid interest throughout—to anybody. But for hundreds of pages an unprepared and incurious reader will regard Washington as the "dumbest" diarist who ever employed the line-a-day method. There is nothing which Greville would have called a "character" in all the four volumes, and upon all the famous men that he met in half a century he utters only with the utmost rarity a two-line judgment. In general, neither births nor deaths nor weddings nor funerals nor good fortune nor calamity nor pestilence nor hurricane betrays him into the recording of the faintest emotion of elation or sorrow or hope or regret. He almost never attempts a picture or reports a conversation. Of himself as a dramatic object of consciousness he seems to have been aware on only two or three occasions in the course of his life. There is virtually no indication that he ever felt the slightest curiosity regarding the "subjective" condition of any other being. He seems to have been absolutely uninitiated into the pleasure of associating ideas. And these characteristics make great tracts of the record—months and years of it—as dry as chopped straw, as dry as Aristotle or Euclid, as dry as the fossil teeth of a dinosaur.

Nevertheless the only way to give this man a chance to reconstitute for us his character and career is to take a clear week and plow straight through the diaries systematically from end to end, going just as slowly and working the imagination just as hard through the long desert places as in the occasional astonishing oases.

We start from an oasis. The first diary begins early Friday morning, March 11, 1748, when in his sixteenth year George Washington set out with his neighbor, young George Fairfax, on a jolly surveying and turkey-shooting expedition in the wild lands of Lord Fairfax beyond the Blue Ridge. At sixteen George had high spirits and a sense of humor, such as he seldom betrayed during the next fifty years. He relishes the joke on himself when, in a backwoods lodging, he strips "orderly" for bed, to find himself lying on a little matted straw under one threadbare blanket "with double its weight of vermin such as lice, fleas, etc." He gets up, dresses and lies, "as my companions," outdoors by a fire. Next day: "We cleaned ourselves (to get rid of the game we had catch'd the night before)." The next week, meeting thirty-odd Indians with a scalp, the boys give them some liquor: "it elevating their spirits put them in the humor of dancing." Then follows the first and last description of a dance in all George's four volumes.

If I were bent on making merely a readable article about the diaries, my cue would be to dwell at length on this first batch of them, written when the young fellow admitted finding a charm in the whistling of bullets. Then I should pass swiftly to the diary kept during Washington's attendance at the Continental Congress in 1775, and I should pause there and say that the diarist disappointed me bitterly in that emergency. Specimen entries during the month of May are here presented:

> 12. Dined and supped at the City Tavern.
>
> 13. Dined at the City Tavern with the Congress. Spent the evening at my lodgings.
>
> 14. Dined at Mr. Wellings and spent the evening at my lodgings.
>
> 15. Dined at Burnes and spent the evening at my lodgings.

Something happened; for Washington was made commander-in-chief; but the incident gets no more space or comment in this singular journal than planting turnips back of the garden. During a considerable period of the war he was too busy to write at all.

On entering Philadelphia for the Constitutional Convention in 1787 he was for a few moments impressed with his reception by his old officers and by his own conduct and appearance. But his memoranda of the sessions are perfectly barren. We learn the names of a great number of Philadelphia ladies and gentlemen with whom he "drank tea"—at one place he "drank tea in great splendour"; we learn that he sat to Mr. Peale for his portrait, attended charity concerts, visited Morris at his country place, went trout fishing and rode away from his fishing companion to visit the site of one of his old cantonments.

What did he feel on August 19, 1787, standing on the old camp ground from which he had marched to his winter quarters in Valley Forge? I do not know. All that he says is: "traversed my old incampment, and *contemplated on* the dangers which threatened the American Army at that place." All that he says of the faintest color, when the great business of the four months' convention is over, is that the members adjourned to the City Tavern, dined in good humor and he, after he had finished up some odd jobs with the secretary of the convention, "retired to meditate on the momentous work which had been executed." Those eleven words indicate about the extent to which the soul of the man will expand and flow—on paper.

The diaries of the first years of the Presidency seem, relatively speaking, of an absorbing interest to one who is trying to press nearer to the man. Of course, there was a big budget of national business without guiding precedents: diplomatic missions to be established, Moroccan affairs, Indian affairs, national militia, finance, ratification of state constitutions, Quaker slavery agitation, Spain and France threatening the flanks of the new nation, problems of uniting the seaboard and the Western frontier by land and water and by the ties of commerce. But, after all, this was

nothing but national housekeeping, of which Washington had mastered the principles at Mount Vernon, in the Virginia House of Burgesses, and in the army. He conducts business now with Cabinet officers instead of overseers; but he goes at it in precisely the same thorough, methodical, orderly, realistic fashion. An able, unagitated executive.

What strikes the student of the diaries is that the Presidential office made Washington conscious of himself and of Mrs. Washington as parts of a dramatic exhibition, which they were "putting on" for the edification of their countrymen. The Father of His Country obviously gave anxious thought to all the details of the visible spectacle when he made his appearance to deliver his first message before the two houses of Congress; and the diarist records the picture—his equipage and his costume, his entrance and his exit—with evident feeling that the little show, now set up to rival the performances at Versailles and the Court of St. James, came off fairly well.

One feels this new self-consciousness of his with almost pathetic poignancy in his notes on the success of his Tuesday levees and of Mrs. Washington's Friday teas. He is particularly sensitive about the "Fridays." One day: "The visitors to Mrs. Washington were respectable, both of gentlemen and ladies"; another day, "not numerous, but respectable"; another, "rainy and bad; no one but the Vice-President." On the 29th of December, 1789: "Being very snowing, not a single person appeared at the Levee"; but on the following New Year's Day, thank goodness, "all the respectable citizens" turned out, and the Federal Union once more seemed secure.

When one considers what George Washington had been through without turning a hair—such things as having two horses shot under him and his clothes riddled with bullets in a single battle, and when one considers the events in which he participated without leaving a word of them in his daily record, one is almost justified in guessing that the very deeps of his nature must have been troubled on those Fridays when he set down for everlasting remembrance the reason why the attendance at Mrs. Washington's tea was light.

The two of them liked it superficially when there was a big gathering of "respectable" persons, but inwardly I think they both hated the officializing of their social intercourse, and were unspeakably happy, when the second heavy term was over, to be back again in the easy casual coming to and from of their Virginia kinsmen and neighbors.

I have been dwelling on what, as it seems to *us*, must have been the high spots in Washington's life. How did they seem to him? Well, there is no emphasis or proportioning in the diaries to suggest that Washington himself regarded his soldiership and statesmanship as *living* and the rest of life as débris and dross. On the contrary, the Revolution and the two Presidential terms dwindle and sink in this long record—sink into troublesome but by no means overwhelming incidents in the half century. So far as the record goes, the planting of a consignment of Chinese flower seeds in his garden made a vastly greater impression upon him than meeting Benjamin Franklin in Philadelphia; and

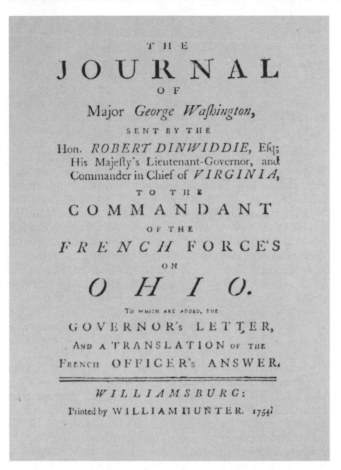

THE

JOURNAL

OF

Major *George Washington,*

SENT BY THE

Hon. *ROBERT DINWIDDIE,* Efq;
His Majefty's Lieutenant-Governor, and
Commander in Chief of *VIRGINIA,*

TO THE

COMMANDANT

OF THE

FRENCH FORCES

ON

OHIO.

To WHICH ARE ADDED, THE

GOVERNOR's LETTER,

AND A TRANSLATION OF THE

FRENCH OFFICER's ANSWER.

WILLIAMSBURG:
Printed by WILLIAM HUNTER. 1754.

Title page of Washington's Journal *recording his 1753 journey to the Ohio country.*

I am certain that he took more pleasure in making inventories of his stock, servants and tools in preparation for the spring planting than he did in making inventories of his regiments in preparation for the spring fighting. It is only when his public life is set in his private that one can see it as he saw it.

All that one knows about Washington gets a new value when one comes at it faithfully in its place amid the long routine of his country life. The first obvious reward of reading straight through the diaries is that one receives an almost oppressive sense of *lapsing time,* filled with the ordinary "inanities" of existence—so important an element in "artistic illusion." One gets the sense of streaming time not merely or mainly in the crowded years of war and statecraft but most richly and sumptuously in the long, quiet, orderly flow of the years on the Mount Vernon estate in the '60s and the early '70s, when one follows the crops and the weather, the first haul of shad in the river, the breeding stock and the litters of puppies, the blossoms in orchard and garden, the harvesting of hay and wheat, of apples and of ice, and the fleeing of hunted foxes, or of ducks in the swampland, day by day, month by month, season by season, year by year—up at sunrise, breakfast with guests who have spent the night, then off on horseback to visit "my mill," "my ferry," "my fishlanding," "my swamp," "my sick people," or to see what Cupid and

Sambo, "my Negroes," two or three hundreds of them, are doing on "my" remoter plantations.

"A better farmer ne'er brushed dew from lawn," as Byron remarked of George III. Our "Farmer George," as you see, had a lively sense of property. He liked branding his stock "G. W." It expanded his sense of being. And he enjoyed all the details of good husbandry. Twice he made actual experiment with tallow and spermaceti candles and recorded in fractions his demonstration that tallow is cheaper. And so on.

The last diary ends on December 13, 1799—a snowy day with the mercury falling from 30 to 28 and a northeast wind blowing. On that day the Father of his Country developed an acute sore throat from the previous day's exposure, having come in from the farms with his neck wet and snow hanging in his hair. On the next day he died very quietly under the bleedings and blisters and wheat-bran cataplasms of the attending physicians. He expressed a desire not to be put in the vault till he had been three days dead. Beyond that he betrayed no anxiety about the hereafter. (pp. 304-10)

> Stuart Sherman, "George Washington as Diarist," in his Critical Woodcuts, *Charles Scribner's Sons, 1926, pp. 296-310.*

Joseph Charles (essay date 1942)

[*In the following essay, originally a chapter from his 1942 doctoral dissertation posthumously published in 1956, Charles addresses Washington's role in the development of the American party system, maintaining that he contributed to its formation by allowing himself to be manipulated by members of the Federalist party for political gain.*]

If we ask how Hamilton attained and kept the influence which he had from 1789 to 1801, the answer is that it was primarily because of his standing with Washington. Such an answer does not call into question the genius and magnetism of Hamilton, nor his single-minded devotion to the interest of the country as he saw it. His extraordinary endowments, however, were so frequently devoted to purposes which were contrary to tradition and popular feeling that his possession of them does not account for the almost incredible influence which remained at his command until after the election of 1800. In his dissertation, *Some Presidential Interpretations of the Presidency* [1932], Norman Small describes Hamilton's customary procedure in getting his measures put into effect in the following terms:

> . . . by shielding his political maneuvres behind the cloak of the President's reputation, Hamilton not only carried out his program with little interference, but practically deprived his opponents of a means of protest; for the latter refused to risk popular condemnation by an attack which, though directed against the Secretary, would have unavoidably included the President. Thus proceeding boldly in pursuit of his policies Hamilton submitted reports to Congress, expounding in detail both the reason why and the manner in which the financial recommendations contained in the President's messages should be

adopted, saw to it that party associates in accord with his opinions were appointed to committees deliberating on his measures, and finally when a doubt arose as to the fate of his program, rounded up his political adherents in order to secure a majority vote in favor of his bills. In fact the conduct of the Federalists in Congress was invariably predetermined by the decisions reached in their own secret party meetings at which Hamilton presided.

According to this view, Washington's recommendation of Hamilton's measures was not the only thing necessary to get these measures adopted, but it was the most essential. The President's approval, helpful in getting measures through Congress, also provided the best possible protection for them against popular criticism.

The influence of Washington himself, from the establishment of the new government to his death, is of an importance which all who have studied the period have acknowledged. Affection for him and complete trust in him were at times during this period probably the only sentiments which were shared without important reservations by the mass of the people throughout the country. These sentiments were called into service to support government policy at every important crisis from 1793 on, and provided on these occasions the most important check on criticism of the government's course.

There can be little doubt as to the effectiveness of Washington's influence; the questions arise when one begins to examine the relation of Washington himself to the use made of his influence. How much did he understand of the things being done in his name? How did those who made the greatest use of him actually regard him? Was he a responsible executive, making his own decisions after consulting his advisers, or was he something of a figurehead? Was he a sick, tired old man who went grimly through the ceremonies laid out for him, or was he an actual leader of his people, whose own deepest convictions and ultimate aims were expressed in the policies he was shaping?

A final answer to such questions as these can never be given; if the true answer were susceptible of discovery and proof, it could not be a simple one. Yet they are of the greatest importance for a study of this period, and whatever evidence we can find as to the nature of the influence which Washington exerted should be applied to them.

A legendary figure from the Revolution on, Washington reached the final stages of his apotheosis with the adoption of the Constitution and the establishment of the new government. Samuel Henshaw, writing to Sedgwick in June, 1789, about the deplorable character of the Massachusetts Lower House, of which he was a member, stated, "I thank God we have a Federal government. I have had the honor to move an address to the President. . . . It is not so sublime and sentimental as I could wish—but it is as good as ought to be expected from such a mixed medley as compose our General Court." Sedgwick wrote soon after this [in a letter to Ephraim Williams in June 1789], "Today I dined with the President and as usual the company was as grave as at a funeral. All the time at table the silence more nearly resembled the gravity of [illegible] worship

than the cheerfulness of convivial meeting." All the descriptions of Washington in office, but particularly those written during the first months of his Administration, when there seems to have been a conscious effort to set the tone for the new government, stress the formality of his bearing. A court etiquette was drawn up and strictly observed, and if the operations of the government had reflected the atmosphere which surrounded Washington, monarchy would have been only a little way ahead.

The genuine respect and gratitude which the people bore Washington and their realization of the momentous step being taken with the establishment of a new government offered an adequate basis for a certain degree of solemnity on state occasions. Apparently, however, this spontaneous regard of the masses of the people for Washington did not reach the heights of the "sublime and sentimental," and some who were most interested in the setting up of the new government deliberately strove to increase the influence of Washington in every way possible. He was to be lifted above the level of criticism, and the measures of the new government were to be linked inseparably to him. In 1793 Jefferson recalled an observation that Madison had made to him early in 1790, "that the satellites & sycophants which surrounded him had wound up the ceremonials of government to a pitch of stateliness which nothing but his personal character could have supported, & which no character after him could ever maintain." Except that Hamilton, one of the chief movers in this political strategy, was no man's sycophant or satellite, Madison's judgment was accurate prophecy; and Hamilton himself would probably have admitted that to increase Washington's hold on the popular imagination was a necessary part of his plans. Certainly no one ever described the relation between them better than Hamilton did when after Washington's death he wrote, ". . . he was an *Aegis very essential to me.*"

The isolation which was imposed upon Washington by the ceremonious manner in which he lived enhanced the importance of those believed to be in his confidence, while it rendered him more dependent than he otherwise would have been upon his advisers. Under the circumstances, the utterances of such men as Hamilton and Robert Morris, whose advice he was known to value, were doubtless believed by many to reflect the views of the President, while the opinions which such men gave Washington were probably regarded by him as those both of Congress and of the solid men of business. The stage setting for the new Administration, certainly so far as John Adams had a share in it, had probably not been designed with any such purpose as this in mind, but that this state of things was among the more important effects of Washington's exalted position there seems no reason to doubt.

The very serious illness of Washington in his first year of office, from which he had not been expected to recover, must have interfered seriously with his comprehension of the fundamental measures which were being discussed at that time. This illness, incidentally, made a deep impression upon those who were depending upon Washington's prestige for the establishment of a government to their tastes. Christopher Gore's estimate of his importance to the Union at this time is shown in one of his letters to King, written May 30, 1790:

> These things [desire for discrimination between original holders and speculators], my dear friend, make me truly anxious that some men shou'd be bound to this government by strong pecuniary ties, and which ties are not obvious to the public view. Suppose a possible event, the dissolution of the President, wou'd not, unless some chain of more & stronger links than now binds the Union shou'd hold us together, the American people cease to exist as a nation—and let me ask what other chain so binding as that of involving the interests of the men of property in the prosperity of the government. . . .

We have Madison's word for it that Washington himself believed the state of his health in these first years in office to be such that he should not be required to serve a second term:

> He then entered on a more explicit disclosure of the state of his mind; observing that he could not believe or conceive himself any wise necessary to the successful administration of the government; that on the contrary he had from the beginning found himself deficient in many of the essential qualifications, owing to his inexperience in the forms of public business, his unfitness to judge of legal questions, and questions arising out of the Constitution; that others more conversant in such matters would be better able to execute the trust; that he found himself also in the decline of life, his health becoming sensibly more infirm, and perhaps his faculties also; that the fatigues and disagreeableness of his situation were in fact scarcely tolerable to him; that he only uttered his real sentiments when he declared that his inclination would lead him rather to go to his farm, take his spade in his hand, and work for his bread, than remain in his present situation. . . .

Washington made these remarks to Madison at a time when the worst trials of the Presidency still lay ahead of him. In 1792 party strife had hardly begun in earnest; the decisions which the conduct of England and France forced upon this country in 1793 marked the first serious and long continued dissension in the Cabinet. In his procedure with the Cabinet on difficult questions, Washington seems to have regarded himself only as chairman of a board. At first he depended upon the advice of senators and members of the Supreme Court, but he later learned that they, and particularly the latter, did not regard it as a function of their offices to advise him upon questions of every kind. He then asked the written opinions of his department heads, and later began to have these department heads meet with him, but he took very little part in the discussions. He did not give his opinion unless the Cabinet of Hamilton, Knox, Randolph, and Jefferson was evenly divided. On the rare occasions when it was needed, his own opinion became the deciding one, but there is no indication that when these men were divided three to one, Washington ever followed the advice of the lone member, even though that advice happened to coincide with his own opinion. There was no parallel here with the procedure of Lincoln, who after getting the opinion of each

member of his Cabinet, is said to have remarked, "Eight ayes, one nay; the nays have it."

As a general, Washington had shown more than customary dependence upon his staff. In a field in which he felt that he knew less than he did of warfare, he depended even more upon his advisers, and as the conflict between Jefferson and Hamilton grew more and more bitter and was taken up in pamphlets and newspapers, Washington probably suffered more than he ever had on any battlefield.

After Jefferson had withdrawn from the Cabinet, no one among Washington's intimate advisers represented a point of view sharply opposed to Hamilton's and there was little disagreement until in the summer of 1795 the question of ratifying the Jay Treaty arose. Washington's relation to the struggle between the two slowly emerging parties changed after Jefferson's withdrawal, and this change coincided with or brought about an important change in the struggle itself. Until Jefferson had withdrawn, each party had been represented at court and could have a hearing. The appeal of each side had to be to reason and, in order to move Washington, had to be put in terms which a mind in close sympathy with that of the average man of the time could grasp. When after Jefferson's retirement there was no longer any opportunity for the point of view of one side to be so expressed, there was no longer any necessity for the other side to strive to express itself in the same way. Each was then exposed to a temptation which it had not had to face before. Secret societies, subversion, and defiance seemed the only course possible to many who disapproved of government policies, since an opposition party had yet to be formed, much less to be vindicated in popular opinion. Reliance upon authority, the *fait accompli,* and, ultimately, force was the obvious answer to such procedure. From the point of view of the historian it does not matter whether force provoked subversion or subversion, force; the important thing for the development of parties is the way in which the attitudes of supporters and opponents of the Administration aggravated each other. It is obvious that if the course indicated by Shays' Rebellion, the Whiskey Rebellion, and Fries' Rebellion was to be followed, written constitutions would go for little and the actual mode of government would follow the old patterns of tyranny or disorder. At the time of these disorders substantial groups felt that they had no effective voice in the government, while many conservatives wished to see the disaffected areas treated like conquered provinces. This was one of the gravest problems of the period, yet Washington seems never to have thought of it in these terms. More than any other man of his time, he tried to prevent the growth of parties, holding that there was no necessity or place for them in our form of government. Had he been successful in this, the main effort of his declining years, it is most doubtful that representative government in this country would have outlived him for long. He thought that republicanism was in grave danger from the tactics and behavior of the opposition party, but he apparently did not perceive any danger to these principles from Administration policies.

Small says of Washington's attitude in the last years of his Presidency:

In fact his observation as to the rapidity with which the populace was aligning itself with political factions and injecting itself into their violent yet petty disputes, tended to diminish his faith in the ability of people to discern its own good, and to confirm him in his opinion that he must henceforth endeavor to guide, rather than to reflect opinion.

If Washington's conception of his duty changed, if he came to believe that he should "guide rather than reflect opinion," a very important question is raised. In what direction did he wish to guide it? His state of mind at this time may be seen in a letter concerning the Jay Treaty which he wrote to Knox in September, 1795:

> Next to a conscientious discharge of my public duties, to carry along with me the approbation of my Constituents, would be the highest gratification my mind is susceptible of; but the latter being subordinate, I cannot make the former yield to it; unless some criterian more infallible than partial (if they are not party) meetings, can be discovered as the touch stone of public sentiment. If any power on earth could, or the great power above would, erect the standard of infallibility in political opinions, there is no being that inhabits this terrestrial globe that would resort to it with more eagerness than myself, so long as I remain a servant of the public. But as I have found no better guide hitherto than upright intentions, and close investigation, I shall adhere to these maxims while I keep the watch; leaving it to those who will come after me to explore new ways, if they like; or think them better.

This letter shows that although Washington regarded the opposition to the Jay Treaty as the work of a "party," he did not regard the support of the Treaty as also being the work of a party. His desire to have a standard of political infallibility made known to him is also characteristic. Finally, while there can be no doubt of the purity of his intentions, there must be considerable doubt as to the nature and thoroughness of the close investigation of which he speaks. In the early years of his Presidency he received information about the state of public feeling from a wide variety of persons, but after 1794 he seems to have sought advice only from a closely restricted circle in sympathy with Administration policies. This change was in a sense to be expected. As parties began to form and opinion became more and more divided, people naturally consorted more with their own kind than heretofore, but the more Washington followed this tendency, the more bitterly he denounced parties. He is to be blamed, not for allying himself with a party, but for not knowing that he had done so, and for denouncing those opposed to his party as opposed to the government. He was most in the grip of party feeling at the time when he was being represented as being above it.

It may be said that Washington was no more dependent upon Hamilton in the last years of his Presidency than he had been in the early ones, and that the two men were as thoroughly of one mind throughout this whole period as they are usually represented. It can be shown, however, that in the earlier years Washington had questioned Ham-

ilton upon some of the most fundamental points of the latter's policy and that Hamilton had had to resort to evasion, if not outright deception, to answer. Washington wrote him a long letter in August, 1792, in which he sent him objections to the course the government was following, objections which had been put to him by George Mason of Virginia. Among the most searching of these was the following charge:

> The funding of the debt has furnished effectual means of corrupting such a portion of the Legislature as turns the balance between the honest voters whichever way it is directed.

Hamilton answered:

> As far as I know there is not a member of the Legislature who can properly be called a stock-jobber or a paper-dealer. . . . As to improper speculations on measurers depending before Congress, I believe never was any body of men freer from them.

In the vote on Assumption, the most important measure of that time on which there is a record of the yeas and nays, we find material to challenge Hamilton's statements. Of the fourteen senators who favored Assumption, at least ten held securities. Of the thirty-two members of the House who favored it, at least twenty-one held securities. Further, these security holders were the men nearest Hamilton. Can we believe that he did not know of the holdings of Strong, Ellsworth, Johnson, King, Schuyler (his own father-in-law), Read, Robert Morris, and Charles Carroll in the Senate, or of those of Ames, Sedgwick, Wadsworth, Laurance, Benson, Boudinot, Clymer, Fitzsimmons and William L. Smith, the members of the House who were most intimate with him? Some of these men were also very close to Craigie and Duer and were almost certainly among those whose chief interest in the financial measures before Congress lay in the promise of large profits for themselves. Can we believe that Hamilton did not know as much as Andrew Craigie of the speculations of congressmen in government securities, of their desire to postpone the funding of the debt until they were in the position to take full advantage of it? Whether these men could properly be called stockjobbers or paper dealers is beside the point, and that Hamilton did not consider their speculations on measures pending before Congress "improper" does not conceal the fact that he did not choose to state what he must have known of them to Washington, letting the latter decide whether it was proper or not.

In 1794 Hamilton was charged in the House of Representatives with having used money appropriated by that body for a purpose other than that which had been designated. There was no charge that the use of the money had been improper in any other respect, but the law declared that money must be used for the purpose for which it had been appropriated. He claimed that he had had specific consent from Washington, both verbally and by letter, for the use to which he put the money. Washington answered the letter in which Hamilton sought to remind him of the spoken consent as follows:

> I cannot charge my memory with all the particulars which have passed between us, relative to

the disposition of the money borrowed. Your letters, however, and my answers, which you refer
to in the foregoing statement . . . speak for
themselves, and stand in need of no explanation.

As to verbal communications, I am satisfied,
that many were made by you to me on this subject; and from my general recollection of the
course of proceedings, I do not doubt, that it was
substantially as you have stated it in the annexed
paper, that I have approved of the measures,
which you, from time to time, proposed to me
for disposing of the Loans, upon the condition,
that what was to be done by you, should be
agreeable to the Laws. [letter to Hamilton, 8
April 1794]

Hamilton stated that this letter was not satisfactory, and
letters from Washington which gave more specific approval of Hamilton's operations with the funds in question
were apparently produced. The significance of this incident for our present purpose does not rest on Hamilton's
use of the funds, but on the light it throws upon the relation between Hamilton and Washington. It is natural that
Washington trusted Hamilton without knowing too much
about the details of the transactions which he was called
on to approve, but that he would afford Hamilton the
means of clearing himself before an investigation while entertaining the misgivings as to the legality of his conduct
which his letter to Hamilton suggests, is one of the points
which cause us to ask whether we see Washington at his
best during the years of his Presidency.

From this time on, Washington and Hamilton became
more and more "of one mind," at least in appearance. We
cannot know the means by which this unity was reached,
but the results of it were strikingly apparent. In the fall of
1794, Washington denounced the Democratic societies,
charging them with responsibility for the Whiskey Rebellion though many of these societies had condemned it; and
many gave yet another instance of their loyalty to the government by dissolving soon after Washington's attack
upon them.

The Jay Treaty is the most striking example of a measure
which could not have been passed without the fullest use
of Washington's prestige, and it was, of all the measures
of his Administration, the one he was most reluctant to
accept. Although he deliberated long and anxiously before
signing it, and although he wrote to Hamilton soon after
he signed it [on 31 August 1795] that "it would seem next
to impossible to keep peace between the United States and
Great Britain," yet it was only by the use of his prestige
that the people of the country could be brought to accept
the Treaty. William Plumer has recorded that no arguments for the Treaty were so effective as the statement that
Washington had accepted it, and that it must, therefore,
be for the best interests of the country. In March, 1796,
the House of Representatives was deliberating upon the
question of appropriating the necessary money to put the
Jay Treaty into effect, and they voted sixty-two to thirty-
seven to ask the President for the papers which would explain the negotiations for the Treaty. Washington refused
their request sharply, and the address in which he did so
was widely circulated and used to discredit the House of

Representatives. Christopher Gore wrote [to Rufus King
on 14 April 1796] of the reception which Boston gave the
address, "The President's answer has been universally
pleasing here, some have become so enamoured with the
thing that they have had it printed in white satin and are
having it framed and glazed."

The main burden of Washington's *Farewell Address,*
much of which was written by Hamilton, is the condemnation of parties. Even the famous passages against foreign
influence and alliances are important in that connection,
as the French were at that time exerting themselves to get
Jefferson elected in the hope that the Jay Treaty would not
go into effect if he were made President. This warning, so
frequently quoted to give the sanction of Washington to
any kind or degree of isolationism, seems to have come
mainly from Hamilton, whose measures and policies did
more than those of any other man in the country to involve us in the current of European affairs. There is no reason to believe that isolationism was the policy which Hamilton wished us to pursue, since the whole tenor of his policies was in the opposite direction. His words in this part
of the address were political propaganda, an effort to appeal to two of the desires strongest throughout the country
at that time, the desires for peace and for an independent
foreign policy. Such an appeal also turned attention and
resentment away from the situation in which the Jay Treaty had placed us. It was praiseworthy to warn against foreign influence in our politics; but, under the circumstances, to point the warning in only one direction and to
warn against parties themselves on the eve of a Presidential election, in the terms which Hamilton put into Washington's mouth, was to become the tool of a party without
apparently being aware of it.

Hamilton did not cease to use Washington when the latter
had retired from office. As soon as he had news of the
XYZ Affair, which brought us to the verge of war with
France, he asked Washington [in a letter dated 19 May
1798] to make a tour of the Southern states, where his
presence might provide the occasion for demonstrations
of loyalty. Though Washington did not yield to Hamilton's request on this point, he did support Hamilton's
claims to be second in command in the provisional army,
against Adams's determination not to alter the precedence
which Knox and C. C. Pinckney had had over Hamilton
during the Revolution. Commenting on this matter later,
Adams said that he was only Viceroy under Washington
and that Washington was Viceroy under Hamilton [as
quoted in Manning Julian Dauer's *The Adams Federalists,*
1954]. This was the most notable instance during his Presidency in which Adams was thwarted by the prestige of
Washington, but he put up with opposition from his Cabinet largely because he did not feel that he could challenge
ministers who had been appointed by Washington. Had
they chosen to resign over a question of policy, as they
threatened to do early in 1797, they could have placed
Adams in an impossible position. It was not until he had
been driven so far that he himself threatened to resign and
turn the Presidency over to Jefferson, not until the questions at issue seemed to him to justify such a step, that
Adams ventured to challenge his ministers.

The way in which Adams was weakened at this time by popular feeling for Washington may be indicated by the fact that in Pennsylvania some of the farmers who defied the tax collectors during Fries' Rebellion in 1799 believed that Washington himself was coming to lead them. Actually, most of Adams's Administration was only a continuation of earlier policies, but because of the differences between the two men and because the country had been prosperous in the early 1790's and was not so in the later years of the decade, Adams was blamed personally by many for all the difficulties of the country during his Administration.

At the time of Washington's death, December, 1799, the High-Federalist leaders were trying desperately to find some way of dropping Adams from their ticket in the coming election. Gouverneur Morris had decided that the only solution was that Washington should run again. The letter in which he tried to persuade him to do so was either at Mt. Vernon or on its way there when Washington died. People were deeply stirred by his death, and the publications dealing with it in one way or another make up more than 400 titles of about 2,200 which came off the press in this country in 1800.

Even after Washington's death, the High-Federalists continued to use popular feeling toward him as a weapon against Adams. In the pamphlet which Hamilton wrote against Adams in the fall of 1800, his main argument for C. C. Pinckney was that he had many points of resemblance to Washington. The Republicans were likely to regard Washington's prestige as their greatest stumbling block, but to the very considerable extent that the Washington legend was used to thwart and undermine John Adams, Washington was for practical purposes their ally. In the early days of the Revolution John Adams had put Washington and Jefferson on the road to fame, but his prestige and authority as President were gravely menaced by the figures he had helped to create.

The way in which Washington was regarded by some of his more eminent contemporaries only adds to the enigma of his character. One of the most measured and penetrating comments upon him was written by Jefferson in a private letter in 1814, which, since it is long and may be found in his collected works, will not be quoted here. When we reflect upon the magnificent tribute which Jefferson pays Washington here and the regard which many other Republican leaders held for Washington in spite of the fact that they were opposed to him politically, and then remember Hamilton's remark at the time of Washington's death, "He was an *Aegis very essential to me,*" a statement which Benjamin Rush made about Washington's reputation takes on new interest. Rush wrote to Adams [in April 1812], "The detractors from the fame of most military men have been their enemies—the detractors from that of your character Washington are his personal friends, most of whom have lived in his family and received favors from him." Liston, the British Ambassador, who moved almost exclusively in Federalist circles, wrote only a little more than a month after Washington's death, "Notwithstanding this ostentatious display of regret and veneration, I find a great proportion of his appar-

ent friends and intimate acquaintances more inclined to depreciate his merit than to exalt his fame, and he seems already to be in a great measure forgotten by the multitude." It is doubtful if Liston had a sufficient knowledge of the facts to justify the latter part of his statement, but there could hardly be a better authority than he for the first part.

Timothy Pickering was one of the men who tried to exploit Washington's prestige but who did not regard him highly except in a moral sense. Years after Washington's death he wrote, "No man, however well-informed, was willing to hazard his own popularity by exhibiting the real intellectual character of the immensely popular Washington." He thought that Washington's prudence and want of decision had been due to his realization of his own deficiencies and that while it was patriotic for those who were aware of his defects to have been silent on this point so as not to undermine public confidence, there was no reason why they should remain silent longer. "But who originated the great measures of Washington's administration? Certainly not Washington." Pickering gave Hamilton almost all of the credit and thought that if it had not been for Hamilton, Jefferson would have had an influence with Washington similar to that which Hamilton exerted.

The description which Liston gave of the memorial ceremonies held throughout the country on February 22, 1800, illustrates some of the ways in which the official custodians of Washington's reputation used it after his death.

> The day was solemnized by crowded meetings in places of worship,—processions of the legislature and other publick bodies, and the delivery of funeral orations, preceded by prayers adapted to the occasion.
>
> The leading men in the United States appear to be of the opinion that these ceremonies tend to elevate the spirit of the people, and contribute to the formation of a *national character*, which they consider as much wanting in this country. And assuredly, if self-opinion is (as perhaps it is) an essential ingredient in that *character* which promotes the prosperity and dignity of a nation, the Americans will be gainers by the periodical recital of the feats of their Revolutionary war, and the repetition of the praises of Washington. The hyperbolical amplifications, the Penegyricks in question have an evident effect especially among the younger part of the community, in fomenting the growth of that vanity, which to the feelings of a stranger had already arrived at a sufficient height.
>
> The orators upon this occasion (who are generally attached to the ruling system of politics) have wisely seized the occasion to raise the publick esteem for the federal constitution, and to strengthen the hands of the administration of Mr. Adams, by dwelling upon the strong and unequivocal approbation which the late president gave to both. It is further to be remarked, to the honour of these gentlemen, that they have in general expressed themselves with less animosity and indecorum respecting Great Britain

than used to prevail in discourses of an analogous nature on former occasions.

The question of his relation to the development of political parties is not the vantage point from which a final estimate of Washington in the last decade of his life can be best given, however important the question is for the purposes of this study. In such a discussion we deal almost exclusively not with the elements of his greatness, but with the weaknesses which he probably would not have exhibited in his prime. Further, if we concentrate upon his political significance Washington himself is obscured and crowded out by the legendary figure which was so cleverly manipulated. An aged military hero who symbolizes national unity and independence becomes one of the most dangerous figures possible to representative government if he gets into the hands of a group who protect with the magic of his name whatever furthers their ends, and then use the denunciations of him which follow as a further political weapon. A political opposition must be very solidly based in order to survive the attacks which can be made upon it in this state of affairs. The extent to which this description fits the use made of Washington in his declining years is still to be decided, but the decision must be based upon a more scholarly approach and a much larger body of material than can be found in any of his biographies. The political exploitation of Washington's name in the first decade of the new national government has misled posterity even more completely than it did his contemporaries, and perhaps the most interesting question of these crowded years is how much Washington himself knew and what he really thought about the important policies and events of the 1790's. (pp. 37-53)

> *Joseph Charles, "Hamilton and Washington," in his* The Origins of the American Party System: Three Essays, *The Institute of Early American History and Culture, 1956, pp. 3-53.*

Harold W. Bradley (essay date 1945)

[*An American editor and historian, Bradley is the author of* The United States: 1492-1877 *(1972). In the following essay, he discusses the political ideas expressed in Washington's private correspondence after 1783, noting how his "thinking was dominated by his intense nationalism and his fear of sectional rivalries."*]

It has become an axiom among historians that the period of the establishment of national government in the United States was one in which the republic was blessed with a remarkable group of political leaders, among whom were a few men with unusual insight into the problems and institutions of government. Foremost among these political giants were Alexander Hamilton and Thomas Jefferson, who not only founded and led political parties but who succeeded in impressing upon those parties their own views upon the nature and function of government and the appropriate relationship between government and the citizen. Second to Hamilton and Jefferson in the quality of leadership, but equal to them in the realm of political thinking, were John Adams and James Madison. These four men constituted a quartet which has not been surpassed and perhaps has not been equaled in the history of

political thought in the United States. The enduring quality of their contributions to political practice and theory has led historians to dismiss with little consideration the ideas of the man who more than any other was at the center of political activity during the early years of the republic. All too often, President Washington appears in history only as a dignified and colorless figure moving mysteriously in the political background, supporting the program of Hamilton, succumbing to the influence of his Secretary of the Treasury, and associated in the popular mind with the Hamiltonian concepts of government.

There is historical justification for thus subordinating the role of Washington in his own administration. He may have been "first in war, first in peace, and first in the hearts of his countrymen," but quite conspicuously he was not first in politics. He did not wish to be a politician and he did not seek to become a molder of political forces. His warning in the *Farewell Address* against "the baneful effects of the spirit of party generally" was doubtless the heartfelt expression of his own disillusionment after nearly eight years of active political life. But it was a warning which he might have uttered with as much sincerity at the opening of his presidency as at its close. If Washington deliberately avoided the role of political leader, he would seem equally miscast as a political philosopher. He was neither a phrase maker nor an original thinker. His public papers and his private correspondence are filled with pleasant platitudes reflecting the accepted virtues of his day. Thus, when about to assume the presidency, he assured Lafayette that nothing more than "harmony, honesty, industry and frugality" were needed "to make us a great and happy people" [Washington to Marquis de Lafayette, 29 January 1789]; and in his first inaugural he declared that "there is no truth more thoroughly established than that there exists . . . an indissoluble union between virtue and happiness; between duty and advantage." Six years later, while bitter political strife swirled about him, he informed a correspondent that "in politics, as in religion" the principles upon which he acted were "few and simple," and of these the most important was "to be honest and just . . . and to exact it from others" [Washington to Dr. James Anderson, 24 December 1795].

One may search the public papers of Washington without finding a concise statement of political philosophy. The greater part of the eight annual messages to Congress were devoted to matter-of-fact descriptions of the state of the Union. Among the topics discussed in those messages, foreign relations and Indian affairs received the most attention. Of the great issues of domestic policy which divided the nation during his first administration, only the enforcement of the excise laws was given more than perfunctory notice in the reports to Congress. These messages contain frequent references to the economic conditions of the day. In his recommendations to Congress, agriculture, commerce, and manufactures were almost invariably linked together, as indeed they had come to be in his thinking. He urged Congress and his fellow countrymen to support religion, morality, education, and science, and he suggested the establishment of a national university with the observation that existing institutions lacked the funds necessary to command "the ablest professors in the different departments of liberal knowledge." It is also evident from his public papers that Washington, as President, favored a strong constitutional government which would be responsive ultimately to the public will but which would not be subject to the whims or caprice of a temporary majority. These were cautious statements on a conservative philosophy; under close scrutiny they do not appear to have been Hamiltonian. They were, instead, the guarded public expressions of political ideas which Washington had stated freely to his friends in private correspondence during the years of relative leisure at Mount Vernon from 1783 to 1789.

The practical figure of the first President seems curiously remote from the realm of abstract ideas. Washington, however, appears to have fancied himself as something of an amateur philosopher—at least in the field of political thought. His private correspondence is filled with allusions to the delights of the philosophically minded—a category in which obviously he included himself. Perhaps a better clue to his self-analysis is his description of himself, in a letter to Lafayette [dated 15 August 1786], as "a Philanthropist by character, and . . . a Citizen of the great republic of humanity at large." This self-portrait of the prosaic Virginia farmer sitting in his home above the Potomac and passing philosophical judgments upon the policies and aspirations of men on both sides of the Atlantic is one which may amaze the historian. It suggests, however, a mind which had thought carefully if not profoundly upon the fundamental political issues of his day. The product of this thought may be found scattered through hundreds of letters to intimate friends or even to casual correspondents.

A survey of this correspondence and of his official career indicates that the dominant note in the political thinking of Washington, both before and after 1789, was his unwavering belief that only a strong central government, able to determine and enforce national policies, would enable the United States to assume its appropriate position among the nations of the world. This conviction was the product of experience rather than of meditation. As commander of the army, Washington felt a natural sympathy for the plight of his unpaid men, and while counseling them against rash measures he urged Congress and the states to recognize the services of the army by making provision for the payment of the money due the soldiers. It was the states, he believed, which were delinquent in this matter rather than Congress, and he felt for the states the same distrust that he felt for private debtors who refused to honor their obligations. Furthermore, Washington by his very position as commander of the army had been compelled to transcend local interests to become a national figure concerned with national aspirations and national policies. The members of Congress were the representatives of the states, but he had been the repository of national hope and of such national power as could be created. The inevitable conflict between a civilian Congress responsible to local feeling and the commander of an army in the field had confirmed him in his suspicion of too much local autonomy. With reason, and probably with some emotion, he informed Hamilton, in March, 1783, that no man in the country could be "more deeply impressed" with the neces-

sity of strengthening the federal government because no man had felt more keenly "the bad effects" of a diffusion of his correspondents and of the historian, but his satisfaction with the Constitution of 1787 seems to offer a clue to his views as to the proper spheres of state and federal authority.

Washington returned to Mount Vernon at the close of 1783, content with the prospect of ending his career as a gentleman farmer and amateur philosopher. He retired to private life with foreboding that the eight years of struggle might yet prove to have been futile, but these gloomy thoughts were balanced by the conviction that with "a little political wisdom" the United States might become as "populous and happy" as its territory was extensive [Washington to Sir Edward Newenham, 10 June 1784]. Although he traveled little in the next three years, he did not lose contact with the outside world. Scarcely a week passed that invited or uninvited guests did not come to Mount Vernon to share his hospitality, for which they paid with idle gossip or news of events on either side of the ocean. More important among his sources of information was an extensive correspondence with men of prominence in this country and in Europe. To a privileged few of these correspondents he freely confessed his growing fear that the potential greatness of the new republic was being sacrificed on the altar of pride and jealousy of thirteen quarreling states. When the delicate problem of national and state finances led to a demand for the issuance of paper money and then to the threat of civil war in some of the states, the residue of optimism with which he had returned to Mount Vernon disappeared. As he read re-

Considered the first authentic painting of Washington, this portrait was done by Charles Willson Peale at Mount Vernon in 1772.

ports of Shays' Rebellion and of the paper money struggle in Rhode Island, his faith in the wisdom and rectitude of the people was severely shaken. To correspondents who turned to him for counsel, he indicated his own wish that the powers of the central government should be greatly strengthened, though he thought that proposals which would virtually eliminate the powers of the individual states were too radical to be acceptable to the majority of the people [Washington to Henry Knox, 3 February 1787]. He noted [in a letter dated 1 August 1786 to John Jay, the Secretary of Foreign Affairs] that "even respectable characters" contemplated the establishment of a monarchy "without horror." He would not approve so drastic a step until all other measures failed; but in a letter to Madison, written at the close of March, 1787, he indicated a tacit acquiescence in this remedy if the proposed increase in the powers of Congress should fail to produce an efficient government which could command the respect of the people.

Recent historical studies have suggested that the years from 1781 to 1787 were less critical than John Fiske supposed. Washington, however, would have subscribed without reservation to the statement that they were indeed the "critical period." Alarmed by what he regarded as painful evidence that the nation was on the verge of disintegrating in disorder and dishonor, he welcomed the call for the Philadelphia Convention and he accepted the new constitution with unfeigned satisfaction as the only alternative to anarchy. He did not regard the proposed constitution as perfect, frankly confessing that it contained much which did not meet his "*cordial* approbation" [from a letter to Governor Edmund Randolf, 8 January 1787]. There is no clue as to what provisions he would have altered, nor is there any clear evidence as to whether he agreed with those who regretted that even greater power had not been granted to the federal government. It is apparent, however, that he did not favor conferring unlimited power upon any political authority, including presumably the central government. [In a letter dated 10 November 1787, he] assured his nephew, Bushrod Washington, that no man was "a warmer advocate" of "proper restraints and wholesome checks in every department of government"; and in writing to Lafayette [on 7 February 1788] he defended the Constitution as one which contained "more checks and barriers against the introduction of Tyranny" than any yet devised by men. Eight years later, in the *Farewell Address,* he asserted that "the efficient management" of public business required "a government of as much vigor as is consistent with the perfect security of liberty." In view of the political situation in 1796, it is probable that this rather vague statement of principle was intended as a warning against any weakening of the federal authority rather than as a plea for an increase in its powers.

Washington's views on other great issues of his day were generally less emphatic and occasionally reflected inconsistencies. This is particularly true of his judgments as to the validity of the democratic processes. During his last year in the army and the first year of his retirement at Mount Vernon he avoided a direct commitment upon this delicate problem. He did indeed assert, [in a letter to Harrison dated 4 March 1783], that Congress was "in fact . . . the People," and he argued that it could not be dangerous to increase the powers of Congress, for its members were "the creatures of the people," to whose wishes they were completely amenable [Washington to Gordon, 8 July 1783]. More significant, perhaps, was his advocacy of short sessions of Congress which would permit the delegates to return to their homes and mingle with their constituents. Such a procedure would be reciprocally beneficial, for the Congressmen could explain national problems to their fellow citizens and in turn they would become "better acquainted" with the sentiments of the people whom they represented [Washington to Jefferson, 29 March 1784]. In 1786, he modified this theme somewhat in a letter [dated 30 September 1786] to his nephew, Bushrod Washington. He declared that he did not question the thesis that representatives "ought to be the mouth of their Constituents," nor would he deny the right of the latter to give instructions to their delegates in the legislature. He contrasted, however, the position of representatives in state legislatures with those in Congress. The latter were compelled to deal with national issues upon which the people were often poorly informed, and they must consider the welfare of the entire nation rather than the interests of a single locality. If Congressmen, therefore, were bound by instructions from their constituents, great national issues would be decided on the basis of local interests and insufficient knowledge. This was a middle-of-the-road doctrine. It fell far short of the views of the democratically inclined anti-Federalists, but it reflected none of the indifference to the wishes of the public commonly attributed to the Federalists.

By the summer of 1785, Washington's faith in the wisdom of the people was being shaken by the refusal of individual states to cooperate with Congress in forming a national policy. The people, he several times complained, "must feel" before they would see or act [Washington to G. W. Fairfax, 30 June 1785]. The news of the insurrection in western Massachusetts drove him still farther along the road of disillusionment, and in apparent despair he wrote to John Jay [on 1 August 1786] that "we have probably had too good an opinion of human nature in forming our confederation," and added that experience taught that men would not "adopt and carry into execution measures . . . calculated for their own good, without the intervention of coercive power." In a similar mood, he addressed to David Humphreys [on 26 December 1786] the rhetorical inquiry, "What, gracious God, is man! that there should be such inconsistency and perfidiousness in his conduct?"

The state of the nation in 1786 had temporarily destroyed Washington's belief in the ultimate wisdom of the people, but his disillusionment was not permanent, and the events of 1787 and 1788 largely restored his faith. He returned to Mount Vernon from the Philadelphia Convention still fearing that "the multitude are often deceived by externals" [Washington to Madison, 10 October 1787], but when by August, 1788, eleven states had ratified the Constitution, Washington became confident that "the People when rightly informed will decide in a proper manner" [Washington to Charles Pettit, 16 August 1788]. His recent skepticism was conveniently forgotten, and he proudly informed Lafayette [in a letter dated 19 June 1788] that he had never believed that the United States would become "an awful monument" to the doctrine that "Mankind, under the most favourable circumstances . . . are unequal to the task of Governing themselves." In March, 1789, he believed that it would be "necessary . . . to conciliate the good will of the People" inasmuch as it would be impossible "to build the edifice of public happiness, but upon their affections" [Washington to Samuel Vaughan, 21 March 1789]. He had returned to a qualified belief in democracy, and with this belief he entered the presidency. Apparently he held similar views after eight months in that office, for in January, 1790, he declared that he had always believed that "an unequivocally free and equal Representation of the People in the Legislature, together with an efficient and responsable [*sic*] Executive, were the great Pillars on which the preservation of American Freedom must depend" [Washington to Catherine Macaulay Graham, 9 January 1790]. As he approached the period of conflict within the cabinet between Hamilton and Jefferson, he stood midway between the two antagonists in his views on democracy.

The vicissitudes of the presidency provided a serious test of Washington's wavering views concerning democracy. The unexpected bitterness of the opposition to the policies of his administration, the disillusioning breach with Jefferson, and his growing dependence upon Hamilton were factors which might have shaken a stronger faith than his in the efficacy of democratic institutions. It is clear that he was distressed by that inescapable adjunct of democratic government, the rise of partisan opposition to the government in power. When this political division invaded his cabinet, he urged both Hamilton and Jefferson to cultivate a tolerance of opposing views and to accept in good faith the decisions of Congress and the executive. He reluctantly admitted that differences in political opinion were unavoidable, but he declared that it would be difficult if not impossible "to manage the Reins of Government" unless there were "mutual forbearances, and temporising yieldings *on all sides*" [Washington to Jefferson, 23 August 1792]. The appearance of so-called "Democratic Societies" as centers of opposition to the policies of the national government aroused mingled apprehension and indignation in his mind. He attributed the resistance to the excise laws to the machinations of those societies and asserted that their influence, if not counteracted, "would shake the government to its foundation" [Washington to Henry Lee, 26 August 1794]. By 1795, Washington's patience with partisan opposition had reached the vanishing point. He seems to have been both surprised and annoyed by the hostility to the treaty with Great Britain, and when both the treaty and its friends were denounced in public gatherings he took the extreme position that "meetings in opposition to the constituted authorities" were "*at all times,* improper and dangerous" [Washington to John Adams, 20 August 1795]. There is no evidence, however, that Washington realized that his thinking had come dangerously close to a negation of the democratic spirit. Nor did he yet regard himself as a partisan. In writing to one of the most partisan of his supporters, Timothy Pickering [on 27 July 1795], Washington described himself as a man

"of no party . . . whose sole wish is to pursue, with undeviating steps a path which would lead this Country to respectability, wealth and happiness." One year later, in the *Farewell Address,* he devoted much attention to the danger of partisanship, declaring that it was indeed the "worst enemy" of popular government.

To the end of his life, Washington failed to recognize the close relationship between partisan politics and the practical expression of the views of the majority. There was no conscious inconsistency, therefore, between his hostility to parties and his continued confidence in the wisdom of the people. During the closing year of his presidency and thereafter, he several times asserted that the mass of the citizens needed only to understand a question to decide it properly; and as the crisis with France approached a climax he declared that the sentiments of the majority "*ought* to be unequivocally known," as it was "the right of the People" that their will should be put into effect [Washington to Thomas Pinckney, 28 May 1797]. He declared that, as president, it had always been his "earnest desire to learn, and to comply, as far as is consistent, with the public sentiment," but this was modified by his belief that such an expression of popular will could be valid "on *great* occasions *only*" and after there had been opportunity for "cool and deliberate reflection" on the part of the public [from a letter to Edward Carrington, 1 May 1796]. After nine months in the relative calm of Mount Vernon he reiterated this general opinion. During periods of crisis, he believed, reason abdicated and men were ruled by passions, but when these passions subsided and the "empire" of reason was restored those public servants who pursued "the paths of truth, moderation and justice" would regain the public confidence and their just influence [Washington to John Luzac, 2 December 1797]. This was a comforting hope, and to Washington it appeared to justify a basic confidence in the wisdom of the people. In principle, it appears to place him closer to Jefferson and Madison than to the Federalist leadership with which he had been associated during the latter part of his presidency.

The moderate conservatism which prompted Washington to accept a qualified democracy was reflected more clearly in his belief in a balanced economy. Washington was a farmer with the true farmer's love of the land, believing that "the life of a Husbandman" was of all vocations "the most delectable" [Washington to Alexander Spotswood, 13 February 1788]. Agriculture, he asserted, was "the proper source of American wealth and happiness" [from a letter to Theodorick Bland, 15 August 1786]; and he predicted that Americans would continue to be "an agricultural people . . . for ages to come" [Washington to Lafayette, 15 August 1786]. Holding these views, he could assure Jefferson, in 1788, that "the introduction of any thing" which might divert the attention of the people from agricultural pursuits "must be extremely prejudicial, if not ruinous to us."

Gradually, however, Washington became convinced of the value of commerce and manufacturing in the life of a nation. In 1784 he had admitted to Jefferson that commerce had "its advantages and disadvantages"; and a year later he observed that it was a question debated "among

Philosophers and wise men" as to whether foreign commerce was "of real advantage" to a nation. By 1786, his hitherto uncertain views appeared to be taking more definite shape, for he informed Lafayette that he reflected "with pleasure" that commerce would have a beneficial effect upon "human manners and society," uniting mankind "like one great family in fraternal ties." He was not prepared to comment on the economic consequences of commerce, but in March, 1789, on the eve of assuming the presidency, he informed a correspondent in Ireland [Sir Edward Newenham] that although American prosperity "must depend essentially" upon agriculture, the "useful arts and commerce ought not . . . to be altogether neglected." Among the "useful arts" to which he referred was manufacturing. He did not wish to "force the introduction of manufactures, by extravagant encouragements, and to the prejudice of agriculture," but he suggested, in January, 1789, [in a letter to Lafayette], that much might be accomplished in manufacturing through the labor of women and children "without taking one really necessary hand from tilling the earth." A year later, in his first annual message to Congress, he declared that the "safety and interest" of the nation required the development of such manufactures as would render it independent of other nations for essential goods and particularly for military supplies. The policies of his administration have generally been regarded as more conducive to the expansion of manufacturing than to the encouragement of the farmers. This was not, on his part, a deliberate slighting of the agricultural population. Near the close of his administration he reaffirmed his personal loyalty to agriculture as a way of life, asserting [in a letter to James Anderson dated 24 December 1795] that it was the occupation most congenial to his "nature and gratifications"; and in the last of the annual messages to Congress he reasserted his conviction that "with reference either to individual or national welfare agriculture is of primary importance." His willingness to admit industry and commerce to a vital though subordinate role in the national economy placed him again somewhere between Jefferson and Hamilton. In one respect his views presented a striking parallel to those of his fellow Virginian, for like Jefferson he was suspicious of great cities, whose "tumultuous populace" he declared were "ever to be dreaded" [Washington to Lafayette, 28 July 1791].

Like so many of the great men of his day, Washington accepted the idea of progress and hoped that improvements in society might indeed be realized. He distrusted precedents, which he once described [in a letter to Newenham, 25 November 1785] as "the arm which first arrests the liberties and happiness of a Country." To Lafayette he wrote, in 1788, that he loved "to indulge the contemplation of human nature in a progressive state of improvement and melioration"; and a year later he described himself as indulging in "innocent Reveries, that mankind will, one day, grow happier and better." [Washington to Count Rochambeau, 29 January 1789]. Perfection, he confessed, was not to be expected in this world; and after hearing the news from France, early in 1790, he warned a French correspondent [Marquis de la Luzerne] against too great an acceleration along the road of improvement. The same idealism that rejoiced in the probability of progress influenced his thinking upon the problems of war and of peace. On

at least one occasion, in 1785, he went so far as to assert that it was his "first wish" that the plague of war should be "banished from off the Earth" [Washington to David Humphreys, 25 July 1785]. Three years later he expressed interest in a proposal for a universal language, hoping that such a project, if successful, might "one day remove many of the causes of hostility from amongst mankind" [from a letter to Lafayette, 10 January 1788]. Washington was no pacifist; he favored a small peacetime army and he more than once expressed surprise and displeasure that the great maritime powers had not crushed the piratical states on the North African coast. His antipathy to war, however, appears to have been genuine, and presumably it explains in part his later anxiety that this country should avoid a participation in the quarrels of the Old World.

The same cautious humanitarianism which led Washington to deplore the cruelties of war was reflected in his thinking upon some of the other problems of his day. Several times he expressed the hope that the United States would provide "a safe and agreeable Asylum to the virtuous and persecuted part of mankind" [Washington to Lucretia van Winter, 30 March 1785]. He likewise indicated his general disapproval of the institution of slavery though he did not favor rash or extra-legal measures to accomplish this desirable end. His interest in education is well known, and probably no project was closer to his heart in the closing years of his life than his oft-repeated proposal that a national university should be established in the new capital city. Such a university, he suggested to Hamilton, should be one in which the young men from all sections of the country would mingle to "receive the polish of Erudition in the Arts, Sciences, and Belles Lettres." The value of a liberal education, however, apparently occupied a secondary place in his thinking. He was disturbed by the danger that young Americans who were educated in Europe might return to their native land with their faith in republican institutions impaired. A national university located in the national capital would provide an appropriate setting for instilling a love of country and an understanding of "the Interests and politics of the Nation." More important, it would serve as a meeting ground for students from every part of the United States, and Washington hoped that these young men would return to their homes convinced that there "was not that cause for those jealousies and prejudices" which then existed in the several sections [Washington to Hamilton, 1 September 1796]. In education as in politics, Washington's thinking was dominated by his intense nationalism and his fear of sectional rivalries.

It was fitting that a thoughtful man intimately concerned with the problems of public life should give some consideration to the purpose of government. A landowner and a creditor, he accepted without question the obligation of government to protect property. But other considerations influenced his speculations upon this subject. In 1788, he expressed surprise that there was a single king in Europe who failed to recognize that his own reputation rested on "the prosperity and happiness of his People" [Washington to Lafayette, 19 June 1788]. In more specific terms, he declared in 1790 [to the Comte de Moustier] that the "aggregate happiness of society . . . is, or ought to be, the end of all government." This is not to be confused with the inalienable right to "the pursuit of happiness" proclaimed in the Declaration of Independence, for Jefferson referred to the individual while Washington was thinking in terms of society, but "the aggregate happiness of society" was a democratic rather than a Hamiltonian ideal.

In the academic sense of the term, Washington was not a political philosopher. He prepared no treatise on government or politics, and he failed to contribute directly to the extensive pamphlet debates on political issues during the years of his retirement from 1783 to 1789. Yet it is apparent that Washington had given more than casual thought to the fundamental issues of political principle which divided the American people in the years preceding and following the framing of the Constitution. On some issues, such as the competence of the people in political affairs, Washington's views fluctuated with the course of events; on other matters, such as the most desirable basis of the national economy, there was a steady development away from a sole reliance upon agriculture to a recognition of commerce and manufacturing. But through all of his thinking upon political principles ran the major conviction that government must be strong or it is no government worthy of the name. In many respects his views in 1789 appear to have been close to those of Madison, who likewise favored a strong government, and at the beginning of his administration he seems to have had as much respect for and confidence in the political views of Madison as he had for the ideas of any other important public figure.

The memory of an old man is a notoriously treacherous guide for the historian. It provides, however, a brief postscript to this study. In 1813, Jefferson recalled the political conflicts of Washington's administration, but exonerated Washington of the charge that he had held Federalist views. On the contrary, declared Jefferson, "General Washington did not harbor one principle of federalism." The "only point on which he and I ever differed in opinion," continued Jefferson, "was, that I had more confidence than he had in the natural integrity and discretion of the people, and in the safety and extent to which they might trust themselves with a control over their government" [Jefferson to John Melish, 13 January 1813]. Jefferson's recollections appear to have been more interesting than accurate. Washington did hold at least one principle of federalism—belief in strong government—and it was on that point that his thinking had been clear and consistent for many years. The growing breach between Washington and Jefferson, after 1790, apparently developed primarily because Washington was persuaded to place the strengthening of the central government above all other considerations and only incidentally because of differences of opinion as to the wisdom and virtue of the people. Whether the ease with which Washington was persuaded to accept a program for increasing the power of the central government was the result of the "fatal . . . influence" of Hamilton over Washington, as John Adams suggested [to Jefferson in July 1813], or whether it arose primarily from the strength of the convictions which Washington had developed during and after the Revolution must be left to the

speculation of any who may wish to make a more intensive study of this question. (pp. 469-86)

Harold W. Bradley, "The Political Thinking of George Washington," in The Journal of Southern History, *Vol. XI, No. 4, November, 1945, pp. 469-86.*

President Calvin Coolidge lauds Washington's statesmanship:

Washington was a nationalist. That principle lay at the foundation of all his statesmanship. Through the long responsibility of the war he came to know, as no one else could know, the weakness to resist evil of thirteen separate colonies and the power to do good of a united nation. It was the intellectual force of Hamilton which produced the plans and poured forth the arguments, but it was the character of Washington which secured the adoption of the American Constitution. Where Cæsar and Napoleon failed, where even Cromwell faltered, Washington alone prevailed. He wished the people of his country to be great, but great in their own right. He resisted the proposal that he should be set up to rule them. He adopted the proposal that they should be organized to rule themselves. He carried these principles through to the end. Later, when some of his countrymen insisted on adhering to the cause of France, while others insisted on adhering to the cause of England, he insisted on adhering to the cause of America, and, with patience and greatness which were sublime, himself bore the resulting abuse of his country for his country's good.

Calvin Coolidge, in The Price of Freedom: Speeches and Addresses, *Charles Scribner's Sons, 1924.*

Paul F. Boller, Jr. (essay date 1960)

[*Boller is an American historian and the author of* George Washington and Religion *(1963) and* Presidential Campaigns *(1984). In the excerpt below, he studies Washington's position concerning religion, asserting that "Washington was firmly committed to religious liberty and freedom of conscience."*]

In the fight against bigotry in America, George Washington played a role second to none. Both as commander in chief of the Continental Army and as president, he used his immense prestige and influence to encourage mutual tolerance and good will among American Protestants, Catholics, and Jews and to create a climate of opinion in which every citizen shall, as he phrased it, "sit in safety under his own vine and fig tree and there shall be none to make him afraid." In private letters and in public statements the first President voiced his utter detestation of intolerance, prejudice, and "every species of religious persecution" and often expressed the hope that "bigotry and superstition" would be overcome by "truth and reason" in the United States.

The fact is that Washington was firmly committed to religious liberty and freedom of conscience. Like Jefferson and Madison, he looked upon the new nation as a pluralistic society in which people with varied religious persuasions and national backgrounds learned to live peacefully and rationally together instead of resorting to force and violence. What was unique about the United States, in addition to "cheapness of land," was the existence of "civil and religious liberty," which "stand perhaps unrivalled by any civilized nation of earth" [Washington to Robert Sinclair, 6 May 1792]. In his general orders for April 18, 1783, announcing the cessation of hostilities with Great Britain, he congratulated his soldiers, "of whatever condition they may be," for having "assisted in protecting the rights of human nature and establishing an Asylum for the poor and oppressed of all nations and religions. . . ." The "bosom of America," Washington declared a few months later, was "open to receive . . . the oppressed and persecuted of all Nations and Religions; whom we shall wellcome to a participation of all our rights and privileges." When asking Tench Tilghman to secure a carpenter and a bricklayer for his Mount Vernon estate in 1784, he remarked: "If they are good workmen, they may be of Asia, Africa, or Europe. They may be Mohometans, Jews or Christians of any Sect, or they may be Atheists" [Washington to Tilghman, 24 March 1784]. He was, as John Bell pointed out in 1779, "a total stranger to religious prejudices, which have so often excited Christians of one denomination to cut throats of those of another" [quoted in William Spohn Baker, *Character Portraits of Washington,* 1887].

When and by what process Washington became "a total stranger to religious prejudices" is difficult to determine. In colonial Virginia, the Anglican Church was established by law and occupied a preferential position. This was Washington's church, and he served for many years as vestryman and churchwarden for Truro Parish. The Virginian establishment was considerably liberalized during the eighteenth century, but dissenting groups were subjected to a variety of legal disabilities and on occasion experienced open persecution. Baptist historians, in fact, sometimes explain Washington's deep-seated devotion to religious freedom as a revulsion against the wave of Baptist mobbings and jailings that took place in Virginia on the eve of the Revolution. This played some part in the development of Madison's views on religious liberty; but as for Washington, no evidence exists to prove the assertion.

There is evidence, however, that Washington learned at an early age the economic disadvantages that frequently accompany legal restrictions on religious freedom. When he was about eighteen, his elder half brother, Lawrence, became deeply involved as a member of the Ohio Company in negotiations for the sale of 50,000 acres of land beyond the Alleghenies to a group of Pennsylvania Germans. The Germans wanted to purchase the land but as dissenters they were unwilling to pay taxes to support the Anglican Church, and Lawrence attempted to persuade the Virginia Assembly to exempt them from the parish levies. "I am well assured," he wrote in April 1751 to John Hanbury, the Ohio Company's English partner, that "we shall never obtain it by a law here." He went on to say:

> It has been my opinion, and I hope ever will be, that restraints on conscience are cruel, in regard to those on whom they are imposed, and injurious to the country imposing them. England,

Holland, and Prussia I may quote as examples, and much more Pennsylvania, which has flourished under that delightful liberty, so as to become the admiration of every man, who considers the short time it has been settled. . . . This colony [Virginia] was greatly settled in the latter part of Charles the First's time, and during the usurpation, by the zealous churchmen; and that spirit, which was then brought in, has ever since continued, so that except a few Quakers we have no dissenters. But what has been the consequence? We have increased by slow degrees . . . whilst our neighbouring colonies, whose natural advantages are greatly inferior to ours, have become populous.

The conviction that "restraints on conscience" are "cruel" to the victims and "injurious" to those imposing them Washington may well have learned from his older brother. Biographers are generally agreed that Lawrence was a major influence on the young Washington. Many years later, when Washington was attempting to secure immigrants from the Palatinate to settle on his western lands, he emphasized that he saw "no prospect of these people being restrained in the smallest degree, either in their civil or religious principles; which I take notice of, because these are privileges, which mankind are solicitous to enjoy, and emigrants must be anxious to know" [Washington to Henry Riddell, 22 February 1774].

Washington's personal views on the entire question of belief in religion—never formally stated—are also relevant to an understanding of his attitude toward religious liberty. He was a lifelong member of the Episcopal Church and was firmly convinced that organized religion was an indispensable basis for both morality and social order. He was, however, completely lacking in creedal commitment of any kind. He was never, as Benjamin Tallmadge wrote Manasseh Cutler regretfully in January 1800, "explicit in his profession of *faith in,* and *dependence on* the finished Atonement of our glorious Redeemer . . ." [Charles Swain Hall, *Benjamin Tallmadge, Revolutionary Soldier and American Businessman,* 1943]. Although his letters abound in references to God, Providence, heaven, and divine favor, especially in his later years, there is no mention of Jesus Christ anywhere in his extensive correspondence, nor are his infrequent references to Christianity anything but formal in nature. At times, in fact, Washington wrote as if he considered himself an outsider. Commenting hopefully on the Marquis de Lafayette's "plan of toleration in religious matters" for France, he wrote: "Being no bigot myself to any mode of worship, I am disposed to indulge the professors of Christianity in the church, that road to Heaven which to them shall seem the most direct plainest easiest and least liable to exception" [To Lafayette, 15 August 1787]. This sense of detachment, tinged with irony, appears even more clearly in a letter discussing the controversies between Protestants and Catholics in Ireland: "Of all the animosities which have existed among mankind, those which are caused by a difference of sentiments in religion appear to me to be the most inveterate and distressing, and ought most to be deprecated. I was in hopes, that the enlightened and liberal policy, which has marked the present age, would at least have reconciled *Christians* of every denomination so far, that we should never again see their religious disputes carried to such a pitch as to endanger the peace of Society" [Washington to Sir Edward Newenham, 20 October 1792].

Washington was a typical eighteenth-century deist—his writings are sprinkled with such catch phrases as "Grand Architect," "Director of Human Events," "Author of the Universe," and "Invisible Hand"—and he had the characteristic unconcern of the deist for the forms and creeds of institutional religion. He had, moreover, the upper-class deist's strong aversion for sectarian quarrels that threatened to upset the "peace of Society." No doubt Washington's deist indifference was an important factor in producing the broad-minded tolerance in matters of religion that he displayed throughout his life.

Like most American deists (and unlike many European deists), Washington had little or no anticlerical spirit. In addition to attending his own church with a fair degree of regularity, he visited others, including the Roman Catholic, and he contributed money to the building funds of various denominations. At first he had no objections to the proposal of the Virginia legislature to levy a general tax for the support of the churches of the state, following the disestablishment of the Anglican Church after the Revolution. "Altho. no man's sentiments are more opposed to *any kind* of restraint upon religious principles than mine are," he told George Mason, "yet I must confess, that I am not amongst the number of those who are so much alarmed at the thoughts of making people pay towards the support of that which they profess, if of the denomination of Christians; or declare themselves Jews, Mahomitans or otherwise, and thereby obtain proper relief." Having learned, however, of the "disquiet of a respectable minority" over the assessment plan and fearing that its adoption would "rankle and perhaps convulse, the State," he expressed his regret that the issue had been raised and hoped that "the Bill could die an easy death" [Washington to Mason, 3 October 1785]. This experience seems to have convinced him, once and for all, of the impracticality of all proposals of this kind for state support of religion.

But it would be wrong to assume that Washington's views were shaped solely by social expediency and theological indifference. Though he was not given much to philosophical reflection, he did try on one occasion to work out a more fundamental basis for his views on liberty. In a fragmentary passage apparently intended for use in his inaugural address or in his first annual message to Congress, Washington asked: "[Shall I] set up my judgment as the standard of perfection? And shall I arrogantly pronounce that whosoever differs from me, must discern the subject through a distorting medium, or be influenced by some nefarious scheme? The mind is so formed in different persons as to contemplate the same objects in different points of view. Hence originates the difference on questions of the greatest import, human and divine." Without reading too much into this isolated passage, one may note that Washington's attempt to find a basis for liberty in a pluralistic view of human perceptions is very Jeffersonian in spirit. Differences of opinion, Jefferson always insisted, "like differences of face, are a law of our own nature, and should

be viewed with the same tolerance"; such differences lead to inquiry and "inquiry to truth" [Jefferson to Col. William Duane, 25 July 1811]. Perhaps, then, Washington's association with Jefferson had something to do with his clear-cut pronouncements on religious liberty during his presidency. Intolerance in any form—religious or secular—was as foreign to Washington's mind as it was to Jefferson's.

Washington had little occasion during the Revolution to make formal pronouncements on the subject of religious freedom, but he made it clear, as commander in chief of the Continental Army, that he was firmly opposed to all expressions of religious bigotry among his soldiers. Roman Catholic historians frequently single out the fourteenth item of his instructions of September 14, 1775, to Colonel Benedict Arnold on the eve of the Canada expedition to show that the American commander was "one of the very few men of the Revolution who had . . . outgrown or overcome all religious prejudices in political matters" [John C. Fitzpatrick, *George Washington Himself,* 1933]. Washington's instructions were these:

> As the Contempt of the Religion of a Country by ridiculing any of its Ceremonies or affronting its Ministers or Votaries has ever been deeply resented, you are to be particularly careful to restrain every Officer and Soldier from such Imprudence and Folly and to punish every Instance of it. On the other Hand, as far as lays in your power, you are to protect and support the free

Portrait of Martha Dandridge Custis at about twenty-six years of age by John Wollaston.

Exercise of the Religion of the Country and the undisturbed Enjoyment of the rights of Conscience in religious Matters, with your utmost Influence and Authority.

In a letter to Arnold accompanying the instructions, Washington added:

I also give it in Charge to you to avoid all Disrespect to or Contempt of the Religion of the Country and its Ceremonies. Prudence, Policy, and a true Christian Spirit, will lead us to look with Compassion upon their Errors without insulting them. While we are contending for our own Liberty, we should be very cautious of violating the Rights of Conscience in others, ever considering that God alone is the Judge of the Hearts of Men, and to him only in this Case, they are answerable [Instructions to Arnold, 14 September 1775].

Obviously, the hope of winning Canadian Catholics to the American cause shaped Washington's orders as much as the "Rights of Conscience in others." Even the Continental Congress, which had made strongly anti-Catholic public statements regarding the Quebec Act in 1774, had learned to be solicitous of the welfare of Canadian Catholics by the fall of 1775. But though the note of condescension in Washington's reference to Catholic "Errors" is unmistakable, there is no evidence that Washington ever shared in the deep-seated anti-Catholic prejudice that existed in the colonies on the eve of the Revolution. He had, it is true, criticized the Quebec Act, but at no time did he join Alexander Hamilton and other patriot leaders in charging that its purpose was to establish "Popery" in the colonies. If his orders to Arnold were not exactly "a model of the statesmanlike tolerance in religious matters which set Washington apart from so many of his contemporaries" [Robert C. Hartnett, "The Religion of the Founding Father," in F. Ernest Johnson, ed., *Wellsprings of the American Spirit,* 1948], they probably do show that he was "impatient of religious intolerance" [Rupert Hughes, *George Washington,* 1927].

A similar combination of policy and principle led Washington on November 5, 1775, to issue strict orders forbidding the celebration of Pope's Day (the colonial equivalent of Guy Fawkes Day in England and especially popular in New England) among the troops at Cambridge:

As the Commander in Chief has been apprized of a design form'd for the observance of that *ridiculous and childish custom* of burning the Effigy of the pope—He cannot help expressing his surprise that there should be Officers and Soldiers in this army so void of common sense, as not to see the impropriety of such a step at this Juncture; at a Time when we are solliciting . . . the friendship and alliance of the people of Canada, whom we ought to consider as Brethren embarked in the same Cause. The defence of the general Liberty of America: At such a juncture, and in such Circumstances, to be insulting their Religion, is so monstrous, as not to be suffered or excused. . . .

Catholic writers have generally looked upon Washington's orders as those of "a brave and tolerant mind."

"Every Catholic heart in the colonies," declared Peter Guilday [in *The Life and Times of John Carroll, Archbishop of Baltimore, 1735-1815,* 1922], "must have taken courage" at his action. "The insult to the Catholic religion was distasteful to his more liberal mind," according to John Gilmary Shea [in *History of the Catholic Church in the United States. . . ,* 1886-92]. And, indeed, the observance of Pope's Day may have "received its death blow," as James Haltigan put it [in *The Irish in the American Revolution,* 1908], "at the hands of the noble Washington," for there are no records of its celebration in America after 1775. No doubt the decline in anti-Catholic feeling (resulting from the loyal support which American Catholics gave the Revolutionary cause and from the alliance with France) during the Revolutionary period accounts for the disappearance of the custom. Yet, Washington was the first to put an end to such anti-Catholic demonstrations, and his example undoubtedly carried great weight. For this he won the profound gratitude of American Catholics; so much so that during the nineteenth century a legend developed that Washington had joined the Catholic Church, or at least was thinking of doing so, shortly before he died.

American Universalists have also claimed Washington because he upheld the right of John Murray, the founder of American Universalism, to officiate as chaplain in the Continental Army. The doctrine of universal salvation that Murray brought from England to America in 1770 had aroused bitter hostility among orthodox clergymen. By eliminating the fear of hell, Murray's teaching, it was charged, undermined morality and led to atheism. In spite of these slanders, Murray won the admiration and friendship of influential laymen in New England before the Revolution, and in May 1775 leading officers in the Rhode Island brigade, including Nathanael Greene and James Varnum, invited him to become their chaplain. Several weeks after Washington arrived in Cambridge to take command, the rest of the chaplains petitioned for Murray's removal. In his general orders for September 17, however, Washington announced tersely: "The Revd. Mr. John Murray is appointed Chaplain to the Rhode-Island Regiments and is to be respected as such." For this, the Universalists have looked upon Washington as "noble-minded" and "immortal" [*The Life of the Rev. John Murray . . . written by Himself . . . ,* 1869]. "History," said one writer of Washington's order regarding Chaplain Murray, "furnished no more signal instance of a rebuke of bigoted intolerance" [John Prince, quoted by Clarence R. Skinner and Alfred S. Cole, *Hell's Ramparts Fell: The Life of John Murray,* 1941]. Others, while acknowledging that "the immortal chief " was "not a professed Universalist," have suggested that his outlook was essentially that of a Universalist [Richard Eddy, *Universalism in America,* 1884].

But the General simply wanted his men to have chaplains of their own choosing. Moreover, he was anxious to keep religious controversies out of the Continental Army. When Congress proposed, in 1777, substituting chaplains at the brigade level for the various regimental chaplains, Washington objected:

It has . . . a tendency to introduce religious disputes into the Army, which above all things should be avoided, and in many instances would compel men to a mode of Worship which they do not profess. The old Establishment gives every Regiment an Opportunity of having a Chaplain of their own religious Sentiments, it is founded on a plan of a more generous toleration, and the choice of the Chaplains to officiate, has been generally in the Regiments. Supposing one Chaplain could do the duties of a Brigade, (which supposition However is inadmissable, when we view things in practice) that being composed of four or five, perhaps in some instances, Six Regiments, there might be so many different modes of Worship. I have mentioned the Opinion of the Officers and these hints to Congress upon this Subject; from a principle of duty and because I am well assured, it is most foreign to their wishes or intention to excite by any act, the smallest uneasiness or jealousy among the Troops [Washington to President of Congress, 8 June 1777].

The desire to keep religious friction at a minimum in the army and the determination to follow a policy of "generous toleration" was plain common sense. Washington needed every man he could get and he knew (and others gradually learned) that Catholics and Universalists could be as good soldiers as anyone else. But what about men whose religious principles led them to refuse to bear arms in the cause? When the war moved to Pennsylvania in 1777, Washington was faced for the first time with the necessity of working out some policy with regard to the pacifist Quakers.

Washington had had some experience with Quakers in Virginia before the Revolution and he seems to have had no objection to the exemption of the "conscientiously scrupulous" from the draft laws. In the summer of 1777 he ordered the immediate release of a group of western Virginia Quakers who had been drafted into the army and marched two hundred miles, with muskets tied on their backs, to his camp outside Philadelphia. But he had difficulty in understanding the determined neutralism of Pennsylvania's Quakers toward the American Revolution. Their refusal to have anything to do—even in nonmilitary matters—with the revolutionary government of the state mystified him. He seems, in fact, to have believed for a time, as did patriots generally, that the Quakers were Tory in sympathy and were working secretly to help the British. When issuing orders for the impressment of supplies from the countryside during the British occupation of Philadelphia, Washington twice instructed his officers to concentrate particularly on the "unfriendly Quakers and others notoriously disaffected to the cause of American liberty." He also placed severe restrictions on Quaker movements in the Philadelphia area during March 1778.

Yet on two occasions during this period he reacted with courtesy and consideration in personal encounters with the Quakers. Six delegates from the Philadelphia Yearly Meeting, who visited his headquarters in October 1777 to present him with a "Testimony against War," were "kindly entertained" by him, listened to with respect, and treated to dinner. A few months later, at Valley Forge, he interceded with Pennsylvania authorities on behalf of four Quakers wishing to send food, clothing, and medical supplies to a group of Philadelphia Quakers exiled by the Pennsylvania government to Winchester, Virginia. "Humanity pleads strongly in their behalf," he told Governor Thomas Wharton.

Washington's treatment of the Quakers, during the Revolution has been accorded high praise by Quaker writers. "In all the relations of the General with the Friends," concluded Isaac Sharpless [in *A History of Quaker Government in Pennsylvania, 1682-1783,* 1902], "we find the greatest courtesy on his part, and the most respectful language, whether in minutes of meetings or in private letters on theirs. He understood their scruples and respected them, and they felt the reality of his politeness and sense of justice." Sharpless certainly overstated the case—Washington did suspect the Quakers of "evil intentions" during the Pennsylvania campaign—but he was probably correct in asserting that the American commander "appreciated" the Quakers "far better than did those militant civilians, the Adamses of Massachusetts," and that "many a commander would have treated them with scant forbearance." After the Revolution, when Warner Mifflin called upon him to explain the pacifist views of the Society of Friends, Washington declared: "Mr. Mifflin, I honor your sentiments; there is more in that than mankind have generally considered."

Although Washington's behavior toward the Catholics, Universalists, and Quakers showed his religious toleration, only once during the Revolution did he single out religious liberty, in a formal public statement, as one of the objectives for which the war was being fought. This was on November 16, 1782, in response to a welcoming address made by the ministers, elders, and deacons of the Reformed Protestant Dutch Church of Kingston, New York, on the occasion of his visit to the town. The church leaders declared that "our Religious Rights" were "partly involved in our Civil," and Washington answered: "Convinced that our Religious Liberties were as essential as our Civil, my endeavours have never been wanting to encourage and promote the one, while I have been contending for the other; and I am highly flattered by finding that my efforts have met the approbation of so respectable a body." No doubt Washington had assumed all along that civil rights included religious freedom. In an address to the United Dutch Reformed churches of Hackensack and Schalenburgh, New Jersey, shortly after the close of the war, he mentioned the "protection of our Civil and Religious Liberties" as one of the achievements of the Revolution.

If Washington said little about religious liberty during the war, he had much to say publicly and of an explicit nature on the subject after he became president. In each case what he said grew out of some point raised in a formal address to him. After his inauguration as president on April 30, 1789, Washington received a flood of congratulatory addresses from towns, cities, colleges, state legislatures, fraternal organizations, and religious bodies, to each of which he was expected to make a formal acknowledgment. Wherever he went, there were the inevitable complimentary speeches and polite replies. Among these many exchanges were twenty-two with the major religious bodies of his day. Understandably, there is much in these addresses and in Washington's responses of a ceremonial, platitudinous, and even pompous nature. The addresses were, as the Virginia Baptists put it, largely "shouts of congratulations": praise for Washington's services in war and peace, pledges of loyal support for the new government, expressions of hope for the flourishing of religion and morality in the new nation, and invocations of divine blessings upon the President. Washington's replies were properly modest in regard to himself, expressed gratification at the professions of loyalty to the government, and, as regards religion, frequently consisted of little more than paraphrases of what had been said to him. Nevertheless, there is much that is valuable in these exchanges for the insight which they give into Washington's views on religious freedom and the relationship between church and state.

Such was the case in his exchange with the Virginia Baptists. This group had not forgotten the discrimination it had suffered before the Revolution and had doubts as to whether the Federal Constitution provided adequate safeguards for religious liberty. The General Committee of Baptists in Virginia in March 1788 appointed a committee, headed by John Leland, to prepare an address to Washington on the subject and to secure the co-operation of Baptists in other states in seeking amendments to the Constitution. The address was adopted at the annual meeting of the General Committee at Richmond in May 1789 and transmitted to Washington. It reads:

> When the Constitution first made its appearance in Virginia, we, as a Society, had unusual strugglings of mind; fearing that the *liberty of conscience,* dearer to us than property or life, was not sufficiently secured—Perhaps our jealousies were heightened on account of the usage that we received under the royal government, when Mobs, Bonds, Fines, and Prisons were our frequent attendants.—Convinced on one hand that without an effective national government we should fall into disunion and all the consequent evils; and on the other fearing that we should be accessary to some religious oppression, should any one Society in the Union preponderate over all the rest. But amidst all the inquietudes of mind, our consolation arose from this consideration "The plan must be good for it bears the signature of a tried, trusty friend"—and if religious liberty is rather insecure, "The administration will certainly prevent all oppression for a Washington will preside". . . .

Washington's reply seemed to satisfy the Baptists. He praised them as "firm friends to civil liberty" and "presevering Promoters of our glorious revolution," and tried to quiet their fears about the Constitution. "If I could have entertained the slightest apprehension," he assured them, "that the Constitution . . . might possibly endanger the religious rights of any ecclesiastical Society, certainly I would never have placed my signature to it. . . . " As for the future,

> if I could now conceive that the general Govern-

ment might ever be so administered as to render the liberty of conscience insecure, I beg you will be persuaded that no one would be more zealous than myself to establish effectual barriers against the horrors of spiritual tyranny, and every species of religious persecution—For you, doubtless, remember that I have often expressed my sentiments, that every man, conducting himself as a good citizen, and being accountable to God alone for his religious opinions, ought to be protected in worshipping the Deity according to the dictates of his own conscience.

Baptist writers, while applauding this message in its entirety, have been especially fond of the phrase, "effectual barriers against the horrors of spiritual tyranny," which some of them look upon as the forerunner of Jefferson's "wall of separation between church and state."

Several months after his exchange with the Virginia Baptists, Washington had occasion to spell out his ideas on liberty of conscience at greater length. Philadelphia Quakers, seeking a "formal reconciliation" with the new government, joined with New York Friends in sending a delegation to New York, in October 1789, to read a statement to Washington prepared by the Philadelphia Yearly Meeting. They began by assuring Washington of their affection for him personally and of their loyalty to the Federal Constitution. Then:

> The free toleration which the citizens of these States enjoy in the public worship of the Almighty, agreeable to the dictates of their consciences, we esteem among the choicest of blessings; and as we desire to be filled with fervent charity for those who differ from us in matters of faith or practice . . . so we trust we may justly claim it from others. And on a full persuasion that the divine principles we profess lead into harmony and concord, we can take no part in carrying on war, on any occasion or under any power; but are bound in conscience to lead quiet and peaceable lives in godliness and honesty. . . .

Apparently still rankling from charges of treason that had been hurled at them during the Revolution, the Quakers went on to assure Washington that they had never been guilty, "from our first establishment as a religious society, with fomenting or countenancing tumults or conspiracies. . . . "

In his friendly response, Washington gently, but frankly, took exception to Quaker pacifism. At the same time he stated his position on the rights of conscience in religious matters with precision and clarity:

> Government being, among other purposes, instituted to protect the persons and consciences of men from oppression, it is certainly the duty of Rulers, not only to abstain from it themselves, but according to their stations, to prevent it in others. The liberty enjoyed by the People of these States of worshipping Almighty God agreeable to their consciences is not only among the choicest of their *blessings,* but also of their *rights.* While men perform their social duties faithfully, they do all that Society or the State

can with propriety demand or expect, and remain responsible only to their Maker for the religion or mode of faith which they may prefer or profess. Your principles and conduct are well known to me, and it is doing the People called Quakers no more than justice to say, that (except their declining to share with others the burthen of the common defence) there is no denomination among us, who are more exemplary and useful citizens. . . . I assure you very explicitly that in my opinion the conscientious scruples of all men should be treated with great delicacy and tenderness, and it is my wish and desire that the laws may always be as extensively accomodated to them, as a due regard to the Protection and essential interests of the nation may justify and permit.

As pacifists, the Quakers could not fully agree with the balance that Washington struck between the rights of conscience and the "essential interests of the nation." But the delegation "was very much pleased with his behaviour," as Susanna Dilwyn wrote afterwards; "indeed he gains the esteem of everybody—those who agree with few other things all unite in admiring General Washington" [Susanna Dilwyn to her father, 4 November 1789]. Later Quaker writers concur with her judgment, generally agreeing that Washington's "appreciation of Quakers" at this time helped to dissolve lingering animosities toward the Society of Friends [Charles M. Woodman, *Quakers Find A Way,* 1950].

If the Baptists and the Quakers were particularly interested in liberty of conscience under the new Constitution, there were others who deplored the omission of any reference to deity in the document. The members of the Constitutional Convention were by no means hostile to organized religion but they were undoubtedly anxious to avoid embroiling the new government in religious controversies; the clause prohibiting religious tests for office-holding was adopted, as Luther Martin acknowledged, "by a great majority of the convention and without much debate," and it was certainly welcomed by fervent believers in the separation of church and state like the Baptists [*The Debates in the Several State Conventions on the Adoption of the Federal Constitution . . . ,* 1861]. Presbyterians in northern New England, however, were somewhat less enthusiastic about this Constitutional aloofness from religion. In October 1789, as Washington was traveling in New England, the ministers and elders of the First Presbytery of the Eastward (composed of Presbyterian churches in northeastern Massachusetts and New Hampshire) sent him a long welcoming address from Newburyport in which they commented in some detail on the Constitution. They had no objection to "the want of *a religious test,* that grand engine of persecution in every tyrant's hand," and they praised Washington for his benevolent tolerance in religious matters. But, they stated, "We should not have been alone in rejoicing to have seen some explicit acknowledgment of the *only true God and Jesus Christ, whom he hath sent* inserted somewhere in the *Magna Charta* of our country."

Washington's reply was a clear statement of his views on the proper relationship between church and state. After thanking the Presbytery for its "affectionate welcome," he declared:

> And here, I am persuaded, you will permit me to observe that the path of true piety is so plain as to require but little political direction.—To this consideration we ought to ascribe the absence of any regulation, respecting religion, from the Magna Charta of our country. . . . To the guidance of the Ministers of the gospel, this important object is, perhaps, more properly committed—It will be your care to instruct the ignorant and to reclaim the devious—and, in the progress of morality and science, to which our government will give every furtherance, we may confidently expect the advancement of true religion, and the completion of our happiness.

Although this response was tactfully phrased, there is every reason to believe that the policy of "friendly separation" which he enunciated here represented both his own considered opinions and those of most of his associates in the Constitutional Convention.

Not all Americans agreed with the Eastward Presbytery in regarding religious tests as instruments of persecution. Many of the states continued, as in the colonial period, to restrict office-holding to Protestants in the constitutions they adopted during the Revolutionary period. Moreover, there was some grumbling about the omission of religious tests in the Federal Constitution on the ground that the national government might fall under the control of Roman Catholics, Jews, and infidels. One writer even warned that there was "a very serious danger, that the pope of Rome might be elected President." Probably few people took such talk seriously. Most Americans undoubtedly shared James Iredell's impatience with such absurd warnings. "A native American," he declared with some irritation in the North Carolina ratifying convention, "must have very singular good fortune who, after residing fourteen years in his own country, should come to Europe, enter Romish orders, obtain the promotion of cardinal, afterward that of Pope, and at length be so much in the confidence of his country as to be elected President. It would be still more extraordinary, if he should give up his popedom for our presidency" [*Debates in the State Conventions*].

Nevertheless, a few days after Washington's inauguration, an article appeared on the front page of the *Gazette of the United States* insisting that the foundations of the American republic had been laid by the Protestant religion and that Protestants therefore deserved special consideration under the Federal government. In a long letter to the *Gazette* the following month, Father John Carroll vigorously challenged this point of view. "Every friend to the rights of conscience," he declared, "must have felt pain" at this evidence of "religious intolerance." "Perhaps," he continued, the writer "is one of those who think it consistent with justice to exclude certain citizens from the honors and emoluments of society merely on account of their religious opinions, provided they be not restrained by racks and forfeitures from the exercise of that worship which their consciences approve. If such be his views, in vain then have Americans associated into one great national

Union, under the firm persuasion that they were to retain, when associated, every natural right not expressly surrendered." Pointing out that the "blood of Catholics flowed as freely" as that of "any of their fellow citizens" during the Revolution and that American Catholics had "concurred with perhaps greater unanimity than any other body of men" in the work of the Constitutional Convention, Father Carroll concluded: "The establishment of the American empire was not the work of this or that religion, but arose from the exertion of all her citizens to redress their wrongs, to assert their rights, and lay its foundations on the soundest principles of justice and equal liberty" [*Gazette of the United States,* 6-9 May 1789].

It is not surprising, then, that American Catholics looked upon the friendly sentiments that Washington expressed to them a few months later, in response to their congratulatory address of March 15, 1790, as of major importance in the development of religious toleration in the new nation. To the Catholics of 1790 the "encomium of the first President meant much in the way of patience and encouragement" [Guilday, *The Life and Times of John Carroll*].

Like the Catholics, American citizens of Jewish faith heartily endorsed the work of the Constitutional Convention and rejoiced that religious tests were forbidden under the Constitution. There were probably less than three thousand American Jews (with congregations in New York, Newport, Philadelphia, Savannah, Charleston, and Richmond) when Washington became president. Early in 1790 Shearith Israel in New York, the oldest congregation, began making plans for a joint address to Washington by all six congregations, pledging support to the new Federal government and expressing gratitude for "the Enfranchisement which is secured to us *Jews* by the Federal Constitution" ["Items Relating to Correspondence of Jews with George Washington," American Jewish Historical Society, *Publications,* 1920]. But slow communication and lack of experience in united action produced so many delays that the Savannah Jews finally decided to go ahead on their own. On May 6, 1790, Levi Sheftall, president of the congregation, sent a letter to Washington; to this, Washington responded cordially. Similarly, Yeshuat Israel in Newport, learning that the President was planning a trip to Rhode Island in August and impatient of any further delay, composed for the occasion what David de Sola Pool calls [in *An Old Faith in a New World,* 1955] a "historic address." The Newport congregation began by formally welcoming Washington to that city and then went on to say:

> Deprived as we have been hitherto of the invaluable rights of free citizens, we now . . . behold a Government which to bigotry gives no sanction, to persecution no assistance—but generously affording to All liberty of conscience, and immunities of citizenship—deeming everyone, of whatever nation, tongue, or language equal parts of the great governmental machine. . . . For all the blessings of civil and religious liberty which we enjoy under an equal and benign administration we desire to send up our thanks to the Antient of days. . . .

In his reply, which he read in person, Washington empha-

sized the important point that religious freedom is something more than mere toleration—it is a right:

> The Citizens of the United States of America [he said] have a right to applaud themselves for having given to Mankind examples of an enlarged and liberal policy: a policy worthy of imitation. All possess alike liberty of conscience and immunities of citizenship. It is now no more that toleration is spoken of, as if it was by the indulgence of one class of people, that another enjoyed the exercise of their inherent natural rights. For happily the Government of the United States, which gives to bigotry no sanction, to persecution no assistance, requires only that they who live under its protection, should demean themselves as good citizens, in giving it on all occasions their effectual support. . . .

In December 1790 Manuel Josephson, president of the Philadlephia congregation, finally presented an address to Washington on behalf of the remaining four congregations. Like the others, the joint address of the Philadelphia, New York, Charleston, and Richmond congregations praised Washington's "character and Person," lauded the achievements of the "late glorious revolution," and rejoiced that with Washington as chief of state the "reign of freedom" had been made "perfectly secure" for citizens of all faiths. Again the President expressed kindest regards for his Jewish fellow citizens and applauded the fact that the "liberal sentiments towards each other which marks every political and religious denomination of men in this country stands unrivalled in the history of nations."

Washington's replies to the three Jewish addresses have been highly prized by later generations of American Jews. Jewish historians commonly regard them as "of great historic interest as well as of importance" [*A Documentary History of the Jews of the United States, 1654-1875,* 1950]. Washington's Newport statement, in particular, with its assertion of the primacy of "inherent natural rights" over toleration and its inclusion of the phrase, "to bigotry no sanction," has, as Lee M. Friedman points out, become "famous in American Jewish history" [Friedman, *Pilgrims in a New Land,* 1948]. It has been enshrined on the pedestal of the monument erected to the memory of Haym Salomon in Chicago in December 1941, and on the tablet placed on the southern wall of the Newport synagogue when it became a national historic site in the summer of 1947.

Two years after his exchanges with the American Jewish congregations, Washington had an interesting encounter in Baltimore with a group of Swedenborgians. In January 1793 the tiny New Church Society presented him with a copy of Emmanuel Swedenborg's *The True Christian Religion,* together with an "energetic" address rejoicing that "Priestcraft and Kingcraft, those banes of human felicity, are hiding their diminished heads" and that "equality in State, as well as in Church, proportionably to merit, are considered the true criterion of the majesty of the people." In what Swedenborgian writers regard as a "rational" and "manful" reply, Washington paid tribute to freedom of religion and then added significantly: "In this enlightened age and in this Land of equal Liberty it is our boast that a man's religious tenets will not forfeit the protection of the Laws, nor deprive him of the right of attaining and holding the highest offices that are known in the United States." This was Washington's final public insistence upon "real *Equality*" rather than "mere *Toleration*" for citizens of every faith in the young republic.

In September 1796 the President issued his *Farewell Address* to the nation. The "wisdom of Providence," he declared, in a passage reminiscent of the notes he had jotted down at the beginning of his eight years in office, "has ordained that men, on the same subjects, shall not always think alike." Nevertheless, "charity and benevolence when they happen to differ," he continued, "may so far shed their benign influence as to banish those invectives which proceed from illiberal prejudices and jealousies." A few months later, responding to an address delivered by twenty-four clergymen in Philadelphia on the occasion of his retirement from office, he expressed his "unspeakable pleasure" at viewing the "harmony and Brotherly Love which characterizes the clergy of different denominations —as well in this, as in other parts of the United States; exhibiting to the world a new and interesting spectacle, at once the pride of our Country and the surest basis of universal Harmony."

The Philadelphia clergymen doubtless realized that Washington himself had played a leading role in producing this "new and interesting spectacle." He had labored to banish "illiberal prejudices and jealousies" in religious matters from the nation and had thrown his weight and the weight of his office against the "power of bigotry and superstition" in the young republic. At the same time, minority groups everywhere were quick to use his name, freely given, in support of their own sometimes precarious positions. By the example he set in word and deed during the Revolution and while he was president, George Washington unquestionably deserves major credit, along with Jefferson and Madison, for establishing religious liberty and freedom of conscience firmly in the American tradition. (pp. 486-506)

> *Paul F. Boller, Jr., "George Washington and Religious Liberty," in* The William and Mary Quarterly, *Vol. XVII, No. 4, October, 1960, pp. 486-506.*

Richard B. Morris (essay date 1960)

[*Morris was an American historian and author of numerous books about early American history. In the following essay, Morris discusses Washington's nonentanglement policy, focusing on his 1793 Proclamation of Neutrality and the* Farewell Address. *Regarding the* Farewell Address, *Morris contends that, although the majority of the text was composed by Alexander Hamilton, the document's ideas and much of its language belong to Washington.*]

The decision to stand aloof from European power politics, to avoid entanglements, has been the capstone of American foreign policy from virtually the start of our national life down to very recent times. This rule was embodied in a great state paper, Washington's *Farewell Address,* but it was in reality the culmination of a series of decisions that started in 1782, when the American peace commissioners in Paris decided to make a separate peace with Great Britain, and to act contrary to explicit instructions from Congress.

Even before the adoption of the Declaration of Independence the isolationist role that America was destined to play could have been forecast. In September, 1775, John Adams, considering the probability of aid from France in an American war for independence, recorded in his *Autobiography* the caution that "we ought not to enter into any alliance with her which should entangle us in any future wars in Europe; that we ought to lay it down as a first principle and a maxim never to be forgotten, to maintain an entire neutrality in all future European wars."

When John Jay joined Franklin in Paris to conduct the preliminary peace negotiations that ended the American Revolution he quickly perceived how the war aims of Spain, France's ally, clashed with those of the United States, notably with respect to America's territorial aspirations to the Mississippi. To preserve national dignity he violated the instructions of Congress not to negotiate without full consultation with France. "I think we have no rational dependence except on God and ourselves," he asserted. Jay's was perhaps the first move toward isolation.

For America the year 1789 was marked by two notable events—the beginning of Washington's Presidency and the start of the French Revolution. Swift-moving events in France—the abolition of the monarchy, the execution of Louis XVI, the Reign of Terror, and the transformation of the French Revolution into a general European war—caused Washington deep concern. Technically, the French alliance of 1778 was still in force. Upon the outbreak early in 1793 of war with Great Britain France hoped to secure aid from the United States, if not direct intervention, at least the conversion of America into a transatlantic base of operations against enemy colonies and commerce. Following the advice of his Secretary of the Treasury, Alexander Hamilton, and ignoring the objections of Thomas Jefferson, his Secretary of State, Washington issued his momentous Proclamation of Neutrality in 1793. This document declared the intention of the United States to "pursue a course friendly and impartial to both belligerent powers" and enjoined upon all citizens its observance under penalty of prosecution. The word "neutrality" was studiously avoided, but the intent was clear, and French sympathizers in America raised shrill voices in protest. Writing under the pseudonym "Pacificus," Hamilton defended both the proclamation and Washington's constitutional right to proclaim it, asserting that the executive power under the Constitution is vested in the President. Later, Jefferson went a step further, and asserted that "the transaction of business with foreign powers is executive altogether."

The Neutrality Proclamation was the first part of a multiple package of foreign policy decisions which is in essence embodied in the *Farewell Address.* Washington was concerned lest the United States, a young nation and a poorly defended one, be involved in a war on behalf of France to

Resignation of General Washington by John Trumbull.

defend her government or in a war against England to maintain American rights. "Foreign influence is truly the Grecian horse to a republic," Hamilton reminded him. On the pretext that the American states had violated the peace treaty of 1783 by confiscating the property of Tories and by raising legal obstacles to the recovery of pre-Revolutionary debts owed to British merchants, the British refused to evacuate the Northwest military posts, which they had been obliged to do under the treaty. Britain thus kept the profitable fur trade in her own hands and the western Indians were heartened in their hostility to the United States. Friction between the two countries was intensified when the British issued Orders in Council in 1793 interfering with neutral shipping. American vessels were seized and American seamen impressed and imprisoned. Indignation swept the country. The followers of Jefferson proposed to boycott all goods shipped to this country by England, but Hamilton convinced Washington that such a step would choke off the chief source of American revenue, the tariff, and the main prop of his fiscal system. To upset commercial relations would, in his judgment, cut our credit to the roots.

Persuaded by Hamilton to seek conciliation, Washington dispatched the Chief Justice, John Jay, to England. Jay managed to wring some concessions from Lord Grenville, England's Foreign Minister. Under the terms of Jay's

Treaty the British agreed to withdraw from the Northwest posts and to open the East Indian trade to America on fairly liberal terms. Debts, boundary disputes, and compensation for maritime seizures were referred to joint commissions. The United States was placed on a most-favored-nation basis in trade with the British Isles. But there were glaring omissions—no provision for the issues of impressment, for the removal by the British of slaves during the American Revolution, or for Loyalist claims. A storm of outraged protest greeted the publication of the text of the treaty in March, 1795. Backed by the immense prestige of Washington and fortified by arguments marshaled in its behalf by Hamilton, the treaty won ratification in the Senate by a narrow margin. War with England had been avoided, but at the expense of gravely deteriorating relations with France. That nation took umbrage at the terms of the treaty. The French Directory interfered in American domestic politics even to the extent of recommending that Washington be overthrown by "the right kind of revolution."

It was against this background of Washington's unswerving attachment to peace in the face of outrageous denunciation from the supporters of Jefferson and increasing pressures from the French government that the President's *Farewell Address* was drafted. That great state paper was long in formulation. Promulgated at the end of Washington's second term, it embodied his fateful decision not to stand for a third term, a decision which for long was accepted as an unwritten law of the Constitution.

Back in February, 1792, when Washington contemplated retiring at the end of his first term, he had asked James Madison to prepare a draft of an address about retirement. Madison sent him a "Form for an Address." When Washington definitely decided to retire at the end of his second term he made a draft of his own, embodying some material from Madison's earlier suggested draft. Then he sent the paper on to Hamilton, who prepared two drafts, faithfully following Washington's scheme of organization and the President's main ideas but rephrasing them in a masterly way. Washington preferred Hamilton's first, or original, draft, but also incorporated some suggestions from John Jay.

Nevertheless the final state paper was very much Washington's own. His rephrasing was felicitous and often less wordy than Hamilton's. For example, Hamilton's "Original Draft" states:

> The great rule of conduct for us in regard to foreign nations ought to be to have as little *political* connection with them as possible.

Washington changed that to read:

> The great rule of conduct for us in regard to foreign nations is, in extending our commercial relations, to have with them as little political connection as possible.

Again Hamilton:

> Why should we forgo the advantages of so felicitous a situation? Why quit our own ground to stand upon foreign ground?

Washington:

> Why forgo the advantages of so peculiar a situation? Why quit our own to stand upon foreign ground?

Hamilton:

> Permanent alliances, intimate connection with any part of the foreign world is to be avoided; so far, (I mean) as we are now at liberty to do it.

Washington:

> It is our true policy to steer clear of permanent alliances with any portion of the foreign world, so far, I mean, as we are now at liberty to do it.

Hamilton:

> Taking care always to keep ourselves by suitable establishments in a respectably defensive position, we may safely trust to occasional alliances for extraordinary war emergencies.

Washington:

> Taking care always to keep ourselves by suitable establishments on a respectable defensive posture, we may safely trust to temporary alliances for extraordinary emergencies.

In the last illustration there is a subtle but important change of concept, as between "occasional" and "temporary" alliances. It was not Washington but the Jeffersonian Republicans who proclaimed the doctrine of isolationism. "We may lament the fate of Poland and Venice," said Albert Gallatin, "and I never can myself see, without regret, independent nations blotted from the map of the world. But their destiny does not affect us in the least. We have no interest whatever in that balance, and by us it should be altogether forgotten." Nowhere did Washington use the phrase "entangling alliances," later found in Jefferson's First Inaugural.

Early in May, 1796, in a letter to John Jay, Washington disclosed his intention definitely to retire, but he yielded to Hamilton's urging to hold off his public announcement. Hamilton counseled that the timing of the announcement be set for two months before the meeting of the Presidential electors, but Washington did not wait quite that long. Three months before the electors convened he submitted his *Farewell Address* to the Cabinet, and, four days later, on September 19, 1796, gave it to the people in the columns of the Philadelphia *Daily American Advertiser.* It was never delivered orally.

Washington's political testament to the American people, the *Farewell Address,* aside from its weighty counsel to his countrymen to avoid sectionalism and the dangers of parties and to cherish the public credit, gave literary articulation to the great decisions which had already been made to avoid war, decisions embodied in the Proclamation of Neutrality and Jay's Treaty, decisions which gave the young nation a necessary breathing spell. To the opposition party the *Farewell Address* dealt a body blow to the French alliance, soon to be terminated. Considered the "Great Rule" in our foreign policy for many generations, Washington's advice on nonentanglement was dictated by conditions prevailing during his administration and was not meant to be irrevocable. Nevertheless, the "Great Rule" has been the most cherished principle of American diplomacy and stood virtually unaltered until the perils of

---

Freeman on early opinion regarding Washington's character:

Acceptance of Parson Weems's fables seems to have kept Americans from realizing that to proclaim perfection was to deny growth. Refusal to admit that Washington needed to develop with the years and to overcome weakness was the surest way of all to deprive his life of inspirational value. Few emulate what they cannot hope to duplicate. Youth, conscious of its failings, is suspicious of other youth supposed to have none. Where complete virtue does not create skepticism, it arouses resentment. This is understood now.. More Americans will be relieved, than will be shocked to know that Washington sometimes was violent, emotional, resentful—a human being and not a monument in frozen flesh.

Douglas Southall Freeman, in his George Washington: A Biography, *Vol. 1, Charles Scribner's Sons, 1948.*

the twentieth-century world dictated a refashioned and vastly enlarged role for America in world affairs. (pp. 29-34)

Richard B. Morris, "The Decision to Avoid Entanglements: Washington's Farewell Address," in his Great Presidential Decisions: State Papers That Changed the Course of History, *J. B. Lippincott Company, 1960, pp. 29-34.*

Arthur A. Markowitz (essay date 1970)

[*In the following essay, Markowitz examines numerous critical arguments surrounding Washington's* Farewell Address, *particularly focusing on controversies regarding the authorship, motivation, and meaning of the document.*]

In September, 1796, a tired and embittered President Washington was determined to exclude himself from consideration for a third term of office. The Father of His Country had wanted to retire at the end of his first term in 1792 and conceived of the idea of announcing his exit from public life by publishing a valedictory address. However, the urging of friends including both Alexander Hamilton and Thomas Jefferson had convinced him to stay on for another term. But four years later, even the entreaties of his friends were not enough to dissuade Washington from his chosen course; the barbs thrown by Republican journalists had penetrated the thin-skinned President. Early in 1796 he revived his old idea of issuing a valedictory to the American people. The rather lengthy message slowly took shape and first appeared in Claypoole's *American Daily Advertiser,* No. 5444, on September 19, 1796.

The *Farewell Address,* as it came to be called, was soon elevated to the status of a sacred document, rivaled only by the Declaration of Independence, the Constitution, and, later, the Monroe Doctrine. No ambitious nineteenth-century American politican could afford not to pay lip service to Washington's parting advice "to steer clear of permanent alliances with any portion of the foreign world" when discussing any diplomatic question of import. In the 1880's, for example, the custom arose in the Senate of reading the *Farewell Address* on Washington's Birthday and this tradition, formalized by standing order in 1901, has continued to the present day. The first President's name was often invoked during the foreign policy debates of the years between Versailles and Pearl Harbor, usually by those who favored a more limited role for the United States in world affairs. Even today, after nearly three decades of world involvement and responsibility, so-called "neoisolationists" are calling for retrenchment both in foreign aid and military commitments. Clearly, the cycle has swung full circle. Political oratory has changed drastically and the references to the Founding Fathers are fewer, but the ideas expressed in Washington's *Farewell,* as they have traditionally been defined, are once again in vogue.

The historical evolution of the *Farewell Address* within the realm of American political folklore is an exceedingly involved story which need not concern us here. Rather, this article will deal with the historiography of the *Fare-* *well,* specifically the controversies concerning authorship, motivation, and meaning.

The debate over the authorship of the *Farewell Address* began in the early nineteenth century and has continued almost unabated to the present. Despite the seemingly unitary nature of the question, there are really two key issues involved—the actual literary authorship of the document and the philosophical origins of the ideas it contains. That the two are not necessarily synonymous is a fact which many historians have neglected to point out.

The first phase of the controversy revolves around the question of literary authorship. After Alexander Hamilton's death in 1804, a group of Hamilton partisans led by his widow claimed that he and not Washington had authored the *Farewell Address.* Proof of this fact, they insisted, existed in the late President's private correspondence which was being kept closed by his family. This partisan view was still being expounded by the Hamilton family and others into the twentieth century. In *The Intimate Life Of Alexander Hamilton* [1911], Allan McLane Hamilton charged that certain incriminating papers had been withheld by "a small coterie of Washington's friends" in order to give the President full credit for the *Address.* These secret papers, he insisted, "certainly show that there was collaboration, at least, and probably that much of the original material, and most of the suggestions, originated with Hamilton." James G. Randall, in an article [entitled "George Washington and Entangling Alliances"] which appeared in the *South Atlantic Quarterly* in 1931, went even further and claimed that Hamilton was Washington's "ghost writer." Hamilton, he declared, wrote the *Farewell Address.* Washington merely copied it.

Certain of the early Federalist writers like Chief Justice John Marshall fail even to mention Hamilton in connection with the formulation of the *Address,* implying by their silence that no real question regarding authorship existed as far as they were concerned. On the other hand, Jared Sparks, the Federalist-leaning Harvard historian who first edited the President's private correspondence [*The Life of George Washington,* 1839], presents a surprisingly objective, and, in terms of later scholarship, reasonably accurate view of the situation. He notes that Hamilton had stood by the President in every hour of trial and occupied the highest place in his confidence. "To whom could Washington more safely apply for the fruits of a wise and disciplined mind?" asks Sparks. "From whom could he hope for better counsel, or a more sacred regard for so confidential a trust?"

Sparks did not have all the correspondence relating to the *Address* at his disposal and readily admitted that until such a time when someone compared all the papers which ever existed on the subject "the precise paragraphs, words, or thoughts which originated with either" could not be known. Yet he was willing to hazard a guess on the basis of the material which he had examined. The *Address,* he concludes, "is much indebted for its language and style to the careful revision and skilful [*sic*] pen of Hamilton." No doubt, says Sparks, "he suggested some of the topics and amplified others." But he insists that this aid, "however valuable," does not "detract from the substantial merit of

Washington" or "divest him of a fair claim to the authorship of the address." The question of authorship is of "small moment" since the *Address* consists of Washington's known sentiments. He maintains that it "derives its value, and is destined to immortality, chiefly from the circumstance of its containing wise, pure, and noble sentiments, sanctioned by the name of Washington." A Hamilton's Farewell Address would have meant nothing.

Horace Binney's *An Inquiry Into The Formation Of Washington's Farewell Address,* written in 1859, ranks as one of the first critical essays in American historiography. This prominent Philadelphia lawyer-turned-historian did not have access to the original manuscripts and was forced to work from rather incomplete texts. Furthermore, his documentation is often inaccurate and his points extremely difficult to follow. Yet, despite these shortcomings, his conclusions, though superficial, have been proved reasonably accurate by later research.

Washington, Binney suggests, "was the designer, in the general sense, if not in the artistic." "The *Address* was to disclose his principles and admonitions, of which he gave a full outline, in sentiments sufficiently delineated by him to characterize and identify them." As for "order, symmetry, amplification, illustration, support by reasoning . . . or even additions of the same temperament as those he had expressed," all these, says Binney, he left to Hamilton.

The most intensive research on the literary authorship of the document has been done by Victor H. Paltsits, late Chief Research Librarian at the New York Public Library. In *Washington's Farewell Address* [1935], Paltsits assembled facsimiles of every draft and letter which has any bearing on the formulation of the *Address* and then proceeded to trace meticulously the literary origins of its thoughts and phraseology. His conclusions regarding its authorship are similar to those reached by Jared Sparks and Horace Binney. He notes that Washington had on other occasions "solicited and gratefully accepted Hamilton's ideas and skills in literary structure." Was it not natural for him to invoke Hamilton's aid on the document through which he was to make known his retirement?

Paltsits concludes that the drafting of the *Farewell Address* was a joint project, "a picture of cooperative enterprise in which Washington was always the principal, and Hamilton a devoted, friendly, and disinterested volunteer." Washington's ideas or "sentiments," he feels, are dominant throughout the *Address.* Hamilton knew from Washington that whatever he might do in "reshaping, rewriting, or forming anew a draft," the results had to be "predicated upon the sentiments which Washington had indicated." Hamilton always had recognized that in the last analysis, the President would be the final judge. "Washington," Paltsits declares, "was his own editor; and what he published to the world as a *Farewell Address,* was in its final form and content what he had chosen to make it by processes of adoption and adaption. By this procedure every idea became his own without equivocation."

Recent students of the period like John C. Miller, Felix Gilbert, and Douglas Southall Freeman and his associates accept Paltsits' contention that the final literary product

represents a collaboration of the thoughts of Washington, Madison (who had written the 1792 valedictory), and Hamilton, with Washington serving as the final editor. But however much historians owe to Paltsits for his pioneering and exhaustive research, the fact remains that his is a rather sterile analysis, narrow in scope and largely devoid of historical significance. He makes no attempt to trace the origins of the ideas contained in the *Address* or to place them in their proper context. Rather, we are led to believe that the document took shape within an intellectual vacuum and represented only the thought of the three contributing authors.

The noted diplomatic historian Samuel Flagg Bemis was the first to approach the question of authorship on a more meaningful level. In an article [entitled "Washington's Farewell Address"] in the *American Historical Review* in 1933, Bemis anticipated Paltsits' conclusions regarding literary authorship of the document. However, he goes on to insist that the ideas contained in the *Address* did not originate with either Washington or Hamilton but were merely the restatement of commonly accepted principles of the time. The experience of twenty years of independence had made American statesmen very wary of close ties with Europe. The writings of Thomas Paine, John Jay, John Adams, and Thomas Jefferson are, he says, "full of affirmations that it was the true policy of the United States to steer clear of European politics."

In a later article ["John Quincy Adams and George Washington," *Proceedings Of The Massachusetts Historical Society* LXVII (October 1941-May 1944)], Bemis attempted to assess John Quincy Adams' influence in the formulation of the *Farewell Address.* In 1793 young Adams had written two letters under the pseudonyms "Columbus" and "Marcellus" warning of the perils of foreign intrigue in American domestic affairs. Later, as Minister to the Netherlands, Adams had seen at first hand the danger of foreign meddling. He was convinced, says Bemis, "that French diplomacy was bent on treating the United States as it did the satellite republics which it set up for its own purposes in Europe," and he voiced these fears in his private correspondence with his father, the Vice-President.

Washington had read both the "Columbus" and "Marcellus" letters when they had appeared in the newspapers, and the Vice-President had undoubtedly showed him and perhaps Hamilton his son's private correspondence. After a detailed analysis, Bemis concludes that John Quincy Adams' public letters in the American press and his private notes to his father "had an appreciable influence upon the mind of the President as he thought over what he desired to say in the *Address.*" Indeed, Bemis feels that "so clearly do the thoughts of the younger Adams, even little traces of his phraseology, appear in the *Farewell Address* that one may wonder whether Washington may not have had still before him the letters of "Columbus" when he drew up the first draft of that document."

Later in this same article, however, Bemis cautions the reader not to conclude that John Quincy Adams was "unduly responsible" for the ideas contained in Washington's valedictory. Returning to his earlier position, he concludes that "presumably, the *Address* would have been given out, in somewhat the same form, if Adams had never lived, for these ideas already were common to American statesmen and diplomatists of the time." They were "the fruit of American diplomatic experience since the Declaration of Independence." According to Bemis, John Quincy Adams shared these principles of foreign policy which were confirmed by his close-hand observation of the wars of the French Revolution. "Thus validated, they had reinforced Washington's own opinions and even shaped their expression a little."

Two exceedingly able scholars, John C. Miller and Alexander DeConde, have refined Bemis' thesis, arguing that the ideas expressed in the *Farewell* were the common property of the Federalist party and cannot be said to represent the exclusive thoughts of any one man. "Every point made in this valedictory," Miller notes, "had been enunciated by Washington, Hamilton, and other leading Federalists at one time or another." DeConde similarly declares that these were "prevalent" Federalist ideas on foreign policy and politics and "can be found expressed in various ways in the polemical literature of the time" ["Washington's Farewell, The French Alliance, And the Election of 1796," *Mississippi Valley Historical Review,* 1957].

One student of American diplomacy, Felix Gilbert, sees the intellectual origins of the Address in "the large complex of enlightened eighteenth century thought" [Gilbert, *The Beginnings Of American Foreign Policy: To the Farewell Address,* 1961]. Unlike Bemis, who feels that the American concept of isolationism was a result of the young country's experience, Gilbert believes it was inherited from Europe. This tradition of isolation was, he insists, embedded in the American mind long before the Revolution.

On the question of literary authorship, Gilbert accepts Paltsits' contention that the final document represents a collaboration of the minds of Washington, Hamilton, and Madison, with Washington acting as editor-in-chief. "Washington," he insists, "would not place his name on a document which he could not regard as an expression of his own mind and ideas." However, Gilbert tries to show that Hamilton's contribution went beyond a mere "execution of Washington's instructions." Hamilton, he feels, added "a new intellectual element" to the section of the document dealing with foreign affairs. Where Washington had favored a more idealistic statement of policy, Hamilton succeeded in writing into the *Address* "a general principle of policy for America" which showed his clear awareness of the realities of power politics. Thus, under Hamilton's direction, idealism had given way to a classic statement of the doctrine of the interests of America.

There has similarly been a great deal of disagreement about the motives which prompted Washington to issue the *Farewell Address.* John Marshall, the staunch Federalist, felt that the President wanted to end his political career with "an act which might be at the same time, suitable to his own character and permanently useful to his country." The *Address,* then represents a last effort by Washington to impress upon his countrymen "those great polit-

ical truths which had been the guides of his own administration" [Marshall, *The Life of George Washington,* 1930].

Jared Sparks unashamedly admired "the vigor of its language, the soundness of its maxims, the wisdom of its counsels, and its pure and elevated sentiments," and believed that it represented a sincere attempt by Washington to convey his "sentiments and advice" to the people. Politician-historian Henry Cabot Lodge proved no less subjective in his appraisal. "Now, from the heights of great achievement he [Washington] turned to say farewell to the people whom he so much loved, and whom he had so greatly served." "Every word," says Lodge, "was instinct with the purest and wisest patriotism" [Lodge, *The Life Of George Washington,* 1920].

Washington's primary reason for issuing the *Farewell Address,* according to Roland Usher, was to "remove doubt at the next election as to his candidacy for the office of President." Thus, the President hit upon the idea of a valedictory address, which, "apparently occasioned by more general and permanent considerations," would "make the statement of his unwillingness to become a Presidential candidate incidental to larger issues" [Usher, "Washington and Entangling Alliances," *North American Review,* 1916].

Washington biographers John C. Fitzpatrick and Douglas Southall Freeman and Freeman's associates agree with Usher on this point. The purpose of the valedictory address, they feel, was to clear the political atmosphere by eliminating Washington from the next election. They insist that the document must be viewed as the disinterested warnings of a parting friend who was sincerely concerned about the future welfare of his beloved country.

In his book *The Beginnings Of American Foreign Policy,* Felix Gilbert emphasizes this idea of the *Farewell Address* as Washington's political testament. According to Gilbert, Hamilton wanted the President to leave to his successor "an explanation of the principles which had guided his policy, just as other rulers and statesmen of the eighteenth century were accustomed to doing in their political testaments." By revising Washington's draft for a valedictory, Gilbert feels that Hamilton succeeded in transforming it into such a document.

Washington's fundamental concern, Gilbert insists, was "the need for overcoming the spirit of party in decisions in foreign policy." The President saw himself as the nonpartisan leader of the nation whose duty was to urge all politicians to unite under "the banner of true national interest." Thus, Gilbert views the *Farewell Address* as a warning against "the spirit of faction" and against "the danger of letting ideological predilections and prejudices enter considerations of foreign policy."

Samuel Flagg Bemis has persistently and persuasively argued that Washington's *Farewell* clearly enunciated "a foreign policy of independence" at a time when the French Government was trying to exert an influence in American domestic affairs. The immediate purpose of the *Address,* Bemis says, "was to strike a powerful blow against French meddling in American affairs." He insists that the *Farewell Address* did not disown the French Alliance, but "taught a patronizing ally that we were an independent and a sovereign nation, and that the French Republic could not use in America . . . the lever of a political opposition to overthrow any government that stood in the way of French policy, purpose, and interest."

A number of historians have preferred to view the *Farewell Address* as a constitutional document—an effort by Washington to reinforce the sagging concept of unity and boost a nascent nationalism. In his multivolume *A History Of The United States* [1927], Edward Channing suggests that Washington regarded all feelings of sectionalism with deep foreboding because they tended "to teach the minds of men to consider the Union as an object to which they ought not to attach their hopes and fortunes." The purpose of his valedictory, says this consensus historian, was to implore the people to look upon the federal system as the " 'paladium of your potential safety and prosperity' " and to "discountenance any suspicion that it can be abandoned."

Nathan Schachner essentially agrees with Channing and takes direct issue with Bemis. Washington, he says [in *The Founding Fathers*, 1954], very clearly recognized that the real threat to the Union was internal and not external. "With all the earnestness at his command, Washington warned against party passions and 'designing men' who sought to create the impression that 'there is a real difference of local interests and views based on geographical dispersion.' " Schachner rather carelessly concludes that "the true interrelation and interdependence of North, South and West" was "the major and indeed the only theme of the Valedictory."

Charles A. Beard's view of the *Farewell Address* in *The Republic* (published in 1943) was considerably different from what he had said some ten years earlier in *The Idea Of National Interest.* The earlier work had been written during a time of intense introspection. Beard, the isolationist, had viewed the *Farewell Address* as a doctrine of national interest. Washington had realized that "nations in their intercourse with one another were governed by their interests" and hoped that the young republic would profit from "a knowledge of these stubborn truths" [Beard, *The Idea Of National Interest: An Analytical Study In American Foreign Policy,* 1934]. This advice, according to Beard, was as relevant in 1934 as it had been in 1796 because he felt that it was still in the interest of the United States to pursue a foreign policy of nonentanglement.

When Beard was writing *The Republic,* the United States was engaged in a desperate struggle with the totalitarian Axis nations and old American institutions now took on a new meaning for the old progressive historian. So did the *Farewell Address.* Washington's valedictory, he concludes, was at bottom "a plea for the continuation of the Union and constitutional government." It "posits the Union as necessary to the security, the progress, and the true grandeur of the nation." In that sense, says Beard, "it was above all partisanship." "It provides guidance for us as long as constitutional government endures."

Another group of historians led by Alexander DeConde

have taken the position that the *Farewell Address* was wholly a partisan document. Washington's aim, they insist, was to defend his administration against Republican attacks. They feel that by 1796 even the idealistic Washington had come to realize that nonpartisanship was a myth. The President had become the central figure in emerging party politics and the *Farewell* "laid the basis for Federalist strategy of using Washington's great prestige to appeal to patriotism, as against the evil of foreign machinations, to make 'Federalist' and 'Patriot' synonymous in the minds of the electorate." The revisionists argue that at the time the *Address* was recognized for what it really was—"a political manifesto"—"the opening blast in the campaign to prevent the election to the presidency of Thomas Jefferson."

Perhaps the most unusual interpretation of the motivation behind the *Farewell* is given by Harold W. Bradley in an article [entitled "The Political Thinking of George Washington"] which appeared in the *Journal Of Southern History* in 1945. Bradley feels that the old warrior possessed "a cautious humanitarianism" which led him to "deplore the cruelties of war." While he admits that the General was no pacifist, he does believe that his antipathy to war was genuine. It is this hatred of war, Bradley argues, which "explains in part" Washington's anxiety that "this country should avoid a participation in the quarrels of the old world."

Because of the ambiguous tone of the *Address,* statesmen and historians have never agreed on its meaning, particularly in regard to foreign policy. The canonization of the so-called "Great Rule of non-entanglement" indicates the preponderant assumption that Washington was speaking to future generations, but the actual words of the *Address* itself neither affirm nor deny that supposition. Its words are similarly vague in regard to its space and scope. As one historian has correctly put it: "The words are at the same time inherently unclear, and yet, with certain predispositions in the interpreter, sufficiently suggestive to give the illusion of clarity to interpreters from the most diverse schools of thought" [Albert K. Weinberg, "Washington's 'Great Rule' In Its Historical Evolution," *Historiography And Urbanization: Essays In American History In Honor Of W. Stull Holt,* 1941].

One extremely heterogeneous group has maintained that Washington was warning future generations of the perils of American involvement in the affairs of other nations. John Marshall regarded the Address as a "Great Rule" which contained precepts "to which the American statesman can not too frequently recur." Washington partisans John Spencer Bassett and Willis Fletcher Johnson both viewed the document as a most sacred political legacy, and Henry Cabot Lodge, who at one time was willing to see America join with other civilized nations to promote peace, was later encouraged by the exigencies of party politics to regard the first President's advice as permanently binding on the nation. "Children and children's children have turned to it in all times," Lodge declared in 1920, "and have known that there was no room for error in following its counsels."

For isolationist Charles A. Beard, these were not "light

Painting of Washington presiding at the Constitutional Convention in 1787 by Junius Brutus Stearns, 1856.

words, spoken privately, or angry ejaculations made in the heat of controversy." Rather, they were "weighed and winged words, directed to his contemporaries and coming ages—the expressions of a firm conviction carefully matured out of a long and varied experience" [Beard, *A Foreign Policy For America*, 1940]. Beard saw Washington as advocating a policy of "Continental Americanism"—a concentration on the continental domain and the building of a unique civilization to realize the promise of America. Such a policy, Beard insisted, was not "blind isolationism" or "a rejection of all collaboration with foreign powers," but rather "a positive program" for choosing peace or war and making temporary arrangements with other governments in "the interests of our destiny and continental security." Nowhere in the *Address,* a piqued Beard declared, did Washington "lend any sanction to the idea that, at some future time, the United States should interfere in the European combination and collusions of power or take part in the efforts to settle the internal quarrels of that continent."

Those of an internationalist persuasion have tended to view the *Farewell* in a quite different light. James G. Randall, who favored American membership in the World Court and close co-operation with the League of Nations, argued that the *Address* was by no means a call for complete isolation or a warning not to deal with European countries on matters common to the United States and Europe. Randall insisted that "the reference to temporary

alliances as well as the qualification of the warning against permanent alliances . . . shows how far Washington was from any notion of absolute isolation."

In their widely-used texts on foreign policy, both John H. Latané and George H. Blakeslee argued strongly for American membership in the League. Latané made the point that Washington regarded a policy of isolation as "a temporary expedient" rather than as "a cardinal rule" of United States foreign policy [Latané, *From Isolation To Leadership: A Review Of American Foreign Policy,* 1922]. Blakeslee agreed with this assessment, reminding his readers that the General had spoken of a time in the future when "our institutions being firmly consolidated and working with complete success, we might safely and perhaps beneficially take part in the consultations held by foreign states for the advantage of the nations" [Blakeslee, *The Recent Foreign Policy Of The United States: Problems In American Cooperation With Other Powers,* 1925].

Internationalist Louis B. Wright, writing in 1943, was especially fearful that the United States would crawl back into her isolationist cocoon at the end of the war. Washington's valedictory, Wright declared, was merely "a defense of his own policies and a plea for caution in foreign relations during the immediate future" [Wright, "The Founding Fathers And 'Splendid Isolation'," *Huntington Library Quarterly* VI (1943)]. He was giving realistic advice to the nation "as it was," not "as it might be ten or more generations later." Now (in 1943), the United States had outgrown the weaknesses which the first President was trying to protect, and modern technology had made the ancient dream of withdrawal within our borders "a fantasy." Wright argued that if Washington were living in the present, he would agree that the national interest now demanded "the assumption of international leadership and international responsibility."

Alexander DeConde, like Wright, feels that it is foolish to believe that Washington was attempting to establish long-enduring principles to guide the nation's future foreign policy. To do that, he insists, "is to endow Washington with powers reserved for the gods of Olympus." Washington's main interest, says DeConde, was in negating the alliance with France, and he realized that for the greatest psychological appeal any attack on the Alliance would have to be clothed in terms of "non-involvement with Europe." In time, "this specific meaning was lost and only the generalization remained."

Samuel Flagg Bemis also curtly dismisses the claim that Washington was seeking to establish a "Great Rule," but he sees a totally different meaning in the *Address* than DeConde. In Bemis' opinion it was aimed not at the French Alliance but at foreign (French) meddling which Washington considered "one of the most baneful foes of Republican Government." "What we have generally construed as a policy of isolation," Bemis declares, ought really to be interpreted "as a policy of vigilant defense and maintenance of sovereign national independence against foreign meddling in our internal domestic concerns."

Conversely, J. Fred Rippy feels that Washington was trying to lay down a general rule for the conduct of foreign affairs, at least for the immediate future. He argues that the President was fearful that temptation to depart from the policy of isolation would have to be faced in the future—even the immediate future, because European nations were "neither willing to consider America a realm apart from their political activities nor content to assume that the United States could not be induced to participate in European politics." In this sense, says Rippy, the *Farewell Address* was really Washington's political testament.

Felix Gilbert, as noted earlier, emphasizes Alexander Hamilton's role in formulating the section of the *Farewell* dealing with foreign affairs. It was Hamilton who added the "Great Rule" of foreign policy which was based on "a realistic evaluation of America's situation and interests." Thus, in Gilbert's opinion, Hamilton was responsible for turning Washington's rather idealistic valedictory into "the first statement . . . of the principles of American foreign policy."

In his scantily documented but none the less important book, *The Contours Of American History* [1961], New Left historian William Appleman Williams sees the *Farewell Address* as a manifestation of a developing American tradition of expansion. Washington's valedictory, says Williams, was, at bottom, a plea to his countrymen "to calm their fears and take advantage of the opportunity that was theirs to become the leading pioneer of the world." "Far from being a call for isolation what Washington issued was a mercantilist manifesto for an unchallengeable empire." In William's opinion Washington's *Farewell* ranks as one of the great documents of what he refers to as "America's Age of Mercantilism."

The debate over the *Farewell Address* is similar in many ways to the controversy surrounding the Monroe Doctrine. In both cases we find ourselves confronted with a myriad of interpretations concerning authorship, purpose, and meaning, each reflecting in some way, the insights and biases of the observer.

The question of actual literary authorship of the *Farewell* has become somewhat clearer thanks to twentieth-century scholarship. Victor H. Paltsits shows that the *Address* was probably a product of the combined pens of Washington, Hamilton, and, to a lesser extent, Madison, with the President serving as the editor-in-chief. Felix Gilbert assigns a much greater role to Hamilton but realistically concludes that "it seems sound procedure to regard as the author of a document a man who signed it and took responsibility for it."

The origin of the ideas contained in the *Farewell* remains open to question. Gilbert insists that the intellectual bedrock for American foreign policy (and the *Farewell Address*) was European Enlightenment thought. Samuel Flagg Bemis and J. Fred Rippy, on the other hand, argue that the *Address* only restated commonly-held ideas which grew out of the American experience. Further work in this area remains to be done, but on the basis of the evidence presented, it seems reasonable to conclude that the *Address* was more a product of American experience than European philosophical thought.

Only a person lacking historical insight into the period would argue that Washington's valedictory was a noble and disinterested legacy to the nation. The *Farewell Address* has relevance only within its historical context and first and foremost represents Washington's response to critics of his administration. Since the critics were, for the most part, Republicans, Alexander DeConde and fellow revisionists appear to be correct in suggesting that this was a partisan document. There is also little doubt that Washington and his advisers designed the *Address* in such a way as to have maximum influence on the presidential election of 1796. In this sense DeConde is justified in viewing it as a campaign document.

The valedictory did plead for the continuation of the Union as Channing, Beard, and Schachner suggest, but they fail to recognize that this was a plea for a Federalist Union and not a bipartisan one. The *Address* did speak of foreign meddling but hardly to the extent which Bemis leads us to believe. Furthermore, it was not intended as a warning to France, as Bemis insists, but rather was a warning to Republicans whose loyalty was suspect in Washington's eyes. Since most of the Francophiles were Republicans, the *Address* was also partisan in this sense.

The question which Wright and Schachner ask, "Would Washington be an isolationist in today's world?" is really a quite meaningless one. We should restrict ourselves to considering Washington's views within the context of his own time. A careful reading of the *Address* reveals that Washington was a political isolationist, at least given the relative weakness of the United States. Yet, as William Appleman Williams and Burton Ira Kaufman correctly point out, he was also a commercial expansionist, a mercantilist with visions of empire for America. The two policies are inherently incongruous, yet express the same dichotomy which Felix Gilbert feels characterized American foreign policy during this era (and perhaps still does). Americans wanted the best of all worlds—political isolation and, at the same time, commercial intercourse. (pp. 173-91)

> Arthur A. Markowitz, "Washington's Farewell and the Historians: A Critical Review," in The Pennsylvania Magazine of History and Biography, *Vol. XCIV, No. 2, April, 1970, pp. 173-91.*

Humphreys laments Washington's death:

When late he bade to public life adieu,
Supernal visions opening on his view;
Ye heard the last advice your guardian gave,
Ye heard his words when bord'ring on the grave:—
What truths experience taught you from his tongue,
When in your ears such awful warnings rung?
"To follow virtue never, never cease,
Her path is pleasant, and its end is peace:
Oh, cultivate *blest union,* but on *this*
Relies your freedom, independence, bliss.
Who sees a foreign policy prevail,
Must see thy promis'd bliss, Columbia! fail;
Must see thy goodly heritage, that day,
The prize of factions or of war the prey."
What MORTAL truths more sacred spake of old,
Inspir'd by heav'n!—The words are grav'd in gold.

Then say what chief has nobler trophies won?
What godlike patriot deeds more glorious done?
Who more the secret foes of union foil'd?
For independence more successful toil'd?
To love our country more the mind prepar'd?
'Gainst foreign influence plac'd a stronger guard?
In education form'd a wiser plan,
To guard inviolate the rights of man?
Who better could our path to bliss explore?
And whose whole life has honour'd virtue more?
What other sage, by equal ardour warm'd,
Such signal service for mankind perform'd?—
Wide as the world shall spread his deathless fame,
While boundless generations bless the name,
In bright example shown. Ye good! ye brave!
Come learn with him to triumph o'er the grave.

> David Humphreys, from his "A Poem On the Death Of General Washington," 1800.

Donald Jackson   (essay date 1976)

[*Jackson was an American historian who edited several volumes of Washington's writings, including* The Diaries of George Washington *(1976). In the following excerpt from the introduction to that work, Jackson argues that Washington's diaries were intended as simple personal accounts and therefore should not be treated as the works of a literary diarist.*]

The diaries of George Washington are not those of a literary diarist in the conventional sense. No one holding the long-prevailing view of Washington as pragmatic and lusterless, a self-made farmer and soldier-statesman, would expect him to commit to paper the kind of personal testament that we associate with notable diarists. Even when familiarity modifies our view of the man, and we find him warmer and more intense than we knew, given to wry humor and sometimes towering rage—even then we do not find in these pages what we have come to expect of a diary.

But let us not be unfair to a man who had his own definition of a diary: "Where & How my Time is Spent." The phrase runs the whole record through. He accounts for his time because, like his lands, his time is a usable resource. It can be tallied and its usefulness appraised. Perhaps it was more than mere convenience that caused Washington to set down his earliest diary entries in interleaved copies of an almanac, for an almanac, too, is an accounting of time.

That his diaries were important to him there is no doubt. When in the spring of 1787 he journeyed to the Constitutional Convention in Philadelphia and discovered that he would be away from Mount Vernon many weeks, he wrote home for the diary he had accidentally left behind. "It will be found, I presume, on my writing table," he said. "Put it under a good strong paper cover, sealed up as a letter."

We can be unfair to Washington in another way by calling this collection of diaries uneven, mixed, or erratic. That is not his fault but ours, for it is we—his biographers, editors, and archivists—who have brought these items together since his death and given them a common label. It would surprise Washington as often as it does his readers to find between the same boards his "where and how" diaries, weather records, agricultural notations, tours of the North and South during his presidency, together with such documents as a travel journal published in 1754 under the title, *The Journal of Major George Washington, Sent by the Hon. Robert Dinwiddie, Esq; . . . Commander in Chief of Virginia, to the Commandant of the French Forces on Ohio.*

Even when his preoccupation with other matters reduces Washington to a mere chronicling of dinner guests, the record is noteworthy, although at times the reader may feel he has got hold of an eighteenth-century guest book rather than a diary. What a diarist chooses to set down, and what not to bother with after a busy day, can be worthy of scrutiny: the number of "respectable ladies" who constantly turned out to pay Washington homage during his southern tour in 1791, tallied so precisely that one suspects Washington of counting heads; his passion for fruits and flowers and the resulting diary notes that very nearly constitute a synopsis of eighteenth-century horticulture; his daily horseback rides, necessary to any large-scale Virginia farmer but clearly a ritual with him; his notices of the dalliance, both planned and impromptu, of his male and female foxhounds—a vital record if canine bloodlines were to be kept pure.

The Washington of the diaries is not the Washington who penned hundreds of letters to neighbors dealing for farm produce and to foreign potentates attending to the affairs of the eighteenth-century world. He is not on guard here, for he seems unaware that any other eyes will see, or need to see, what he is writing.

"At home all day. About five oclock poor Patcy Custis Died Suddenly," runs the complete entry for 19 June 1773. Good enough for his purposes; it was what happened on that day. His curt entry would serve to remind him of his devotion to his ill-fated stepdaughter, dead in her teens after a life made wretched by epilepsy. The place for sorrow was in communications to friends, not in the unresponsive pages of a memorandum book, and so it was to Burwell Bassett that he wrote of his grief for the "Sweet Innocent Girl" who had entered into "a more happy, & peaceful abode than any she has met with in the afflicted Path she hitherto has trod."

Reading these diaries from beginning to end can become a tedious exercise, though rewarding. Sampling them in brief sessions can become an equally rewarding way to probe the depths, those uneven depths, of a man who has come to personify the spirit of America in his time. John C. Fitzpatrick realized this essential value of the diaries in the 1920s when he undertook to issue the first compilation. . . . Writing to a committee of the Mount Vernon Ladies' Association of the Union in 1924, he said: "Now that I have read every word of these Diaries, from the earliest to the last one, it is impossible to consider them in any other light than that of a most marvelous record. It is absolutely impossible for anyone to arrive at a true understanding or comprehension of George Washington without reading this Diary record." (pp. xvii-xix)

> *Donald Jackson, in an introduction to* The Diaries of George Washington, 1748-65, Vol. I, *edited by Donald Jackson and Dorothy Twohig, University Press of Virginia, 1976, pp. xvii-lv.*

Albert Furtwangler   (essay date 1987)

[*Author of* The Authority of Publius: A Reading of the Federalist Papers *(1984) and* American Silhouettes: Rhetorical Identities of the Founding Fathers *(1987), Furtwangler is an American scholar who writes about literary motifs in American history. Below, he considers the extent of James Madison's and Alexander Hamilton's involvement in the construction of Washington's* Farewell Address, *centering on the document's language and meaning. Furtwangler concludes that the Farewell Address "must be understood as a work sui generis, a message only President Washington could have conceived and carried off."*]

Like most relics of Washington, his *Farewell Address* is more striking as a symbol than as a means of transmitting the ideas of a living man. It is rightly remembered as a gesture of renunciation; with these words the first president gracefully relinquished power and opened the way for its smooth transfer to a new administration. The address was also an instrument of and monument to early American policy; it expressed the new nation's resolve to stay free of involvement in European wars and to turn the efforts of government toward developing strength on this continent. But another aspect of the address is equally important. In composing it, Washington did not work alone. He asked for preliminary drafts from James Madison and Alexander Hamilton and incorporated their work into the final version, which he sent out for carefully timed newspaper publication. By asking these particular men to help with this great address, Washington called again on well-tried younger allies. He also closed off their long association as three closely bound public personalities.

Washington, Hamilton, and Madison had already come together twice before in the newspapers of the day, to explain or reinforce the strengths of the new Constitution. In 1787 Hamilton and Madison had collaborated on the *Federalist* papers, defending the Constitution and urging its adoption by the several states. Although they were not directly allied with Washington in these papers, they stayed in touch with him as they wrote. They certainly bore in mind that Washington had chaired their deliberations in the Philadelphia convention and that the new document had his endorsement and the promise of his continuing leadership in the struggle for its adoption. A few years later, in 1793, Hamilton and Madison again took up their pens in newspaper series, but this time as adversaries. The occasion was Washington's brief proclamation of neutrality toward both Britain and France. Hamilton as "Pacificus" defended this proclamation as a wise move and a proper exercise of executive power. Madison as "Helvidius" denied that it was wise and publicly questioned its constitutionality.

By pulling together the two men's talents and reorganizing their contributions in his own handwriting, Washington made the *Farewell Address* a balanced summary of his presidency and its accomplishments. He might have given his collaborators the notion that they were writing this document, that they were supplying the president with his last public words, and that thus they were the scriptwriters for his exit from the public stage. To later readers, Washington may still give the impression that he leaned on Hamilton and Madison for essential support. But it is also possible that Washington here, as throughout his administration, had a keen sense of how to manage other men's energies and draw them out for the larger good of their country.

Washington's perplexities about leaving office weighed heavily on his mind in 1792, the last year of his first term as president. In May he wrote to James Madison from Mount Vernon, recalling their confidential conversations on this subject and proposing a formal address. A central paragraph of that letter outlining what Washington had in mind must be quoted in full:

I would fain carry my request to you farther than is asked above, although I am sensible that your compliance with it must add to your trouble; but as the recess may afford you leizure, and I flatter myself you have dispositions to oblige me, I will, without apology desire (if the measure in itself should strike you as proper, & likely to produce public good, or private honor) that you would turn your thoughts to a valadictory address from me to the public; expressing in plain & modest terms:—that having been honored with the Presidential Chair, and to the best of my abilities contributed to the organization & administration of the government.—that having arrived at a period of life when the private walks of it, in the shade of retirement, becomes necessary, and will be most pleasing to me;—and the spirit of the government may render a rotation in the Elective officers of it more congenial with their ideas of liberty & safety, that I take my leave of them as a public man;—and in bidding them adieu (retaining no other concern than such as will arise from fervent wishes for the prosperity of my Country) I take the liberty at my departure from civil, as I formerly did at my military exit, to invoke a continuation of the blessings of Providence upon it—and upon all those who are the supporters of its interests, and the promoters of harmony, order & good government.

On a first reading this may seem a pompous tangle of intentions and hesitations. Despite some vagaries of punctuation, the paragraph consists of only one long meandering sentence and a modern reader may need to pare it down in order to grasp it at all: "I want you to write a Farewell from me to the public; explain that since the government is now well established and I have grown old I will retire from the presidency and take my leave with every good wish for the country." But to a reader who, like Madison, is familiar with Washington's style or who will reread the paragraph a few times, it unfolds as the expression of an extraordinary being. Every phrase has been carefully considered, settled upon, and ordered in constructing a suitable pattern for his farewell. Earlier in this letter, Washington has told Madison that he has again and again "revolved" the problems of his retirement "with thoughtful anxiety." This sentence contains a dozen delicate considerations masterfully compressed into a formal and coherent—though not yet conclusive—plan of action.

To hold these ideas together, Washington writes with an instinctive sense of balance. He relates one phrase to another that resembles it grammatically, but differs in emphasis or meaning. He will add to Madison's trouble, but he knows Madison has the leisure and the desire for this task. He hopes the address may "produce public good, or private honor." He sees that the time is ripe in terms of both the public welfare and his personal comfort. This civil retirement may recall his "military exit." He will invoke blessings on the country and also on its most selfless supporters. Some of these balances may seem merely habitual, the commonplace flourishes of an eighteenth-century pen. But with them, Washington is also weighing himself before and after the act of retiring. "I take my leave of them as a public man" is counterposed to "bid-

ding them adieu" as a disinterested private citizen. The address is to be a significant deed of the president, but it is also to carry the voice of a man apart from his office; it is to recall the former general and also to evoke some sympathy for the enduring Virginia planter, in his "private Walks . . . in the shade of retirement."

Thus Washington holds in one hand the meaning of his life and in the other the meaning of his death. This is a point that he covers with euphemism and that no one around him could directly mention. His sixtieth birthday occurred in February 1792, and it was then that he began approaching confidential advisers about the best means of leaving office. There is no record of what he said to Madison on February 19, but he spoke to Jefferson ten days later about his failing health. He said "that he really felt himself growing old, his bodily health less firm, his memory, always bad, becoming worse, and perhaps the other faculties of his mind showing a decay to others of which he was insensible himself, that his apprehension particularly oppressed him, that he found moreover [sic] his activity lessened, business therefore more irksome, and tranquility & retirement become an irresistible passion" [Jefferson's *Anas*, 29 February 1792]. When he spoke to Madison early in May, he again stressed "that he found himself also in the decline of life, his health becoming sensibly more infirm, & perhaps his faculties also; that the fatigues & disagreeableness of his situation were in fact scarcely tolerable to him." For reasons of his private comfort and those of state, Washington disliked the thought of dying in office. He did not want to be remembered as someone who had given up his military command only to return and hold supreme power to the end of his days. He was also highly conscious, from his first days as president, that every gesture could become a precedent binding upon his successors. He wanted to avoid any suggestion that the presidency should be held until death. As he says in his instructions to Madison: "the spirit of the government may render a rotation in the Elective officers of it more congenial with their [the people's] ideas of liberty & safety." He refrains from saying that no one should continue to hold office indefinitely, only that rotation is fitting under the Constitution; his own retirement, then, in apparent health would be the proper conclusion to his tenure as the first president.

The notion of retirement before death gives special power to this paragraph and to the address that grew out of it. From phrase to phrase, Washington alternates between stiff formality and an ingratiating admission of his personal vulnerability. He commands Madison, yet pleads for his aid. He begins courteously, yet presses on with urgency. Washington was always reserved with his associates. He addressed them with an oxymoron—"my dear Sir"—that could be taken as a conventional courtesy, as an avowal of affectionate feeling, or as a reminder of official respect. Here that ambiguity plays across every idea. Madison should consider what is best, yet must do exactly what he is told. He is drawn into the intimacy of a personal secret, yet held at arm's length by a carefully drafted letter of instruction. Washington, although contemplating a magnanimous gesture of resignation, feels compelled to it by his increasing frailty and discomfort in office. But he is uncertain about how to proceed.

His first instruction is that this address should go out to the public "in plain & modest terms." The president had singled Madison out earlier in the month for a private conversation on the mode and time of an address. Washington had put forward the idea of addressing Congress, but hesitated out of fear of becoming entangled in congressional replies and further explanations. A few days later Madison reported that he had hit upon no other plan, though he agreed that the idea of addressing Congress was vulnerable to weighty objections. Now Washington tells Madison he has decided to address the people directly, which in 1792 meant through publication in the newspapers. But he is still wavering about the timing and tone of such a message. "In revolving this subject myself," he says earlier in this letter, "my judgment has always been embarrassed." To make an early announcement might seem a pompous maneuver, risking either the appearance of self-importance or the charge of angling for renomination. Yet to keep silent would imply consent and make it more difficult for him to decline later on.

Furthermore, Washington was chary of engaging in public controversy through the press. Much of his discomfort in the presidency was due to newspaper attacks upon his administration's policies. He could not have been more com-

An 1889 engraving of Washington taking the oath as president on 30 April 1789 at Federal Hall in New York City.

fortable with the prospect of retiring through this medium than through addressing Congress.

It was no secret to him that the tension in his cabinet between Hamilton and Jefferson was being amplified in public by Philadelphia newspapers the two men were helping to support. The *Gazette of the United States,* edited by John Fenno, was subsidized in part by printing contracts from the Treasury Department and was glowing in its praises of the government, particularly Hamilton's measures. To counter this, Jefferson offered Philip Freneau a sinecure clerkship in the State Department, which drew him to Philadelphia where he established the *National Gazette* in 1791. This journal relentlessly hounded Hamilton and praised Jefferson. At the same time that Washington was planning his retirement, this simmering newspaper war was erupting into overt accusations and counterblasts between the two sides, revealing a deep rift in the cabinet to anyone who could read. In July Washington told Jefferson how deeply these battles offended him. He complained that "the pieces lately published, & particularly in Freneau's paper seemed to have in view the exciting opposition to the govmt. . . . He considered those papers as attacking him directly, for he must be a fool indeed to swallow the little sugar plumbs here & there thrown out to him. That in condemning the admn of the govmt they condemned him, for if they thought there were measures pursued contrary to his sentiment, they must conceive him too careless to attend to them or too stupid to understand them" [*Anas,* 20 July 1792].

Careless and stupid Washington was not. Thus, his calling upon Madison may well have been a sensible means of protecting himself. By implicating one of Jefferson's allies in this address in defense of his character and actions, he might find a middle course, avoiding editorial attack from either side.

Still, Washington was firm about putting his own imprint on his message. It was not to be merely a resignation, with a tidy explanation of his reasons for accepting office and now yielding it. It was to be a valedictory, a final leave-taking meant to recall and seal his earlier resignation as commander in chief.

That message of 1783, in the form of a circular letter to the state governors, was another occasion Washington had seized for conveying his ideals of American government. He had called then for support for the union of the states, even though the war was over and the armies were on the point of disbanding. He had urged the potential greatness of the new nation and then listed four measures essential to continued independence: indissoluble union, just payment of public debts, continuance of a military establishment, and suppression of local and sectional rivalries. After discussing these at length—motivated, as he said, by a strong sense of both public duty and personal concern—he concluded with an "earnest prayer" that God would bless each state and incline the hearts of all men to charity, humility, and peace. Known as "Washington's Legacy," this long message had been cherished as a summing up of what the war had meant and what America might become. It was a document that Washington did not want tarnished or eclipsed. In recalling it to Madison's attention, he is plainly asking him to amplify and renew it in the memories of his countrymen. His further instructions to Madison, concerning the unique prospects of a strong and free America, argue that the new address should reinforce the message of the Legacy, making it an even more powerful blessing and prayer.

Madison's reply and his draft of the address show that all these concerns were noted and borne in mind. Madison answered each main point Washington had raised and again weighed all the alternatives. He agreed that the message should be "a direct address to the people who are your only constituents" and that it should be made through the newspapers. There was now no opportunity for addressing Congress or for writing to the state governments as in "the former valedictory address." Madison considered that a full valedictory address should coincide with the announcement that Washington would not run again and urged publication around the middle of September. "The precedent at your military exit, might also subject an omission now to conjectures and interpretations, which it would not be well to leave room for." In the end, Madison wrote a draft that could be adapted for delivery in September or on a later occasion, and he stuck close to Washington's instructions. "You will readily observe that in executing it I have aimed at that plainness & modesty of language which you had in view, and which indeed are so peculiarly becoming the character and the occasion; and that I have had little more to do, as to the matter, than to follow the just and comprehensive outline which you had sketched" [Madison to Washington, 20 June 1792].

Madison's brief manuscript actually depends on Washington's key phrases. In it, the president claims "that I have contributed towards the organization and administration of the Government the best exertions of which a very fallible judgment was capable"; he admits that "private walks . . . in the shade of retirement" are "as necessary as they will be acceptable to me"; and he points out that rotation in high office "may equally accord with the republican spirit of our constitution, and the ideas of liberty and safety entertained by the people." The entire draft closely follows the sentiments and phrasing of Washington's letter to Madison. Madison may have reread the Legacy address of 1783 and slightly altered some lines to recall Washington's earlier words. He also toned down the idea of invoking the blessings of God. In his draft, it is incorporated in a paragraph on Washington's "vows which I shall carry with me to my retirement and my grave, that Heaven may continue to favor the people of the United States with the choicest tokens of its beneficence." The draft ends with Washington's modest "wishes and hopes" and "extreme solicitude" for American liberty, prosperity, and happiness. As a whole Madison's collaboration does not extend much further than expanding, smoothing, and reconfirming the ideas that Washington already had settled on.

Madison's draft, however, came to Washington accompanied by further protests that the president should continue in office for another term. Madison had already bluntly explained that none of the likely successors—Adams, Jefferson, or Jay—would fill the office nearly as well. Jefferson had confided that he intended to leave public life when Washington did; he also reasoned that Washington could retire with dignity before a second term ran its course. Hamilton, Robert Morris, and Edmund Randolph registered their sense that Washington was still indispensable to the establishment of a stable government. September came and went, Washington made no declaration of retirement, and he was reelected unanimously in December.

He again began to plan a formal statement of his retirement in 1796, the last year of his second term. By May he had taken out Madison's draft, pondered it again, and prepared a new introduction and a long new section covering his second administration. He wrote out a new draft of all these materials in his own hand and then approached a new collaborator. He wrote to Alexander Hamilton on May 15, enclosing this draft and asking for his help in revising it to make it as perfect as possible.

At this point, Washington's strategy was firmly decided. This would be an address to the people, in a plain style, to be published in the newspapers. It was also to appear shortly before the election so that the present administration would enjoy full power and authority to the last possible moment.

But Washington's second term had been troubled. By 1796 he could not take his farewell as comfortably or graciously as he might have done in 1792. Allies who had then worked together under his authority had now fallen out with each other and left the government. Jefferson and Hamilton had never been reconciled; both had resigned. Other cabinet officers had left and been replaced. Washington had given his support to policies of the Federalists and found himself vilified by the Republican press. To his critics (and perhaps he agreed) he had stayed on too long; he was no longer the national hero entirely above party. In fact, when Congress voted him a final expression of gratitude, it fell into a nasty wrangle about whether he had provided wise and virtuous leadership!

With an eye to these troubles, Washington recast his message in a defensive mood. He explained to Hamilton that he included Madison's draft on purpose, as proof that he had intended to resign years earlier. "And besides, it may contribute to blunt, if it does not turn aside, some of the shafts which it may be presumed will be aimed at my annunciation of this event;—among which—conviction of fallen popularity, and despair of being re-elected, will be levelled at me with dexterity and keenness" [Washington to Hamilton, 15 May 1796]. At the close of that draft, Washington now added an explanatory paragraph:

> Had the situation of our public affairs continued to wear the same aspect they assumed at the time the aforegoing address was drawn I should not have taken the liberty of troubling you—my fellow citizens—with any new sentiments or with a rep[et]ition, more in detail, of those which are therein contained; but considerable changes having taken place both at home & abroad, I shall ask your indulgence while I express with more lively sensibility, the following most ardent wishes of my heart.

What followed were nine sketchy paragraphs, all expressed as wishes: "That party disputes . . . may subside"; that we "not be . . . ungrateful to our Creator"; that we pay all our just debts; that we "avoid connecting ourselves with the Politics of any Nation, farther than shall be found necessary to regulate our own trade"; that every citizen cherish America above all other nations; that we remain ready for war, but do our best to build national strength in a long era of peace; that we suppress party disputes to a common commitment to neutrality; that "our Union may be as lasting as time"; and that government departments not encroach on one another. Then in four long paragraphs Washington took occasion to defend himself personally. Noting that the *Gazette of the United States* had libeled him and done everything possible to undermine his authority, he recalled his long sacrifices to the country, his struggles to do his best in hard new duties, and his avoidance of all personal gain.

As Washington sensed, this longer draft had its problems. It repeated many ideas, merely hinted at some points, and came dangerously close to stridency and anger. The president sent it to Hamilton with an appeal for assistance. During years as his aide-de-camp, Hamilton had helped him draft his papers; in the government and out of it he had continued to prepare addresses and official messages. Even though Hamilton was now a private lawyer in New York, he was still being called upon to write substantial state papers. Washington urged him to take this one in hand, to not only retouch it but completely rewrite it if necessary. In the latter case he wished to see two versions: Hamilton's complete draft and Washington's original draft with Hamilton's amendments and corrections.

Hamilton followed these instructions faithfully. He wrote both a complete new draft and an amended version that might be attached to the draft Madison had prepared and Washington had enlarged. . . . He relied in both versions on Washington's instructions and language, but he sorted out and regrouped clusters of ideas. He elaborated small points and turned Washington's strained "wishes" into reasoned, dignified exhortations on the strength of Union, the dangers of party, and the wisdom of political neutrality toward foreign powers. He thus muted Washington's personal defense by working it into the sturdy structure of a long and clear-sighted testament, consistent with the president's policies and accomplishments in two terms of office.

These revisions cost Hamilton several weeks of thoughtful labor. He put together an outline for his major draft and then wrote it out, revised it, went over it with John Jay, and finally sent it to Washington with the promise of soon completing the draft for incorporating. Eventually he sent that along, too. But Washington was persuaded that the major draft was clearly superior; he accepted it as the working draft, sent it back to Hamilton for some further touches, and then began to ask for advice on the best means of getting it into print.

By means of these revisions Washington and Hamilton effected important changes in the meaning and weight of the address. It was no longer an echo or reminder of the Legacy address of 1783. This was a grander performance, designed to supplant that earlier farewell. The emphasis on

"plain and modest terms" was abandoned in favor of a more dignified tone, "better calculated," Washington remarked, "to meet the eye of discerning readers" including foreign leaders [Washington to Hamilton, 25 August 1796]. Appeals to the blessings of Providence were replaced by recollections of shared accomplishments and injunctions to maintain a strong Constitution. And the division between Madison's version and the added remarks of Washington's draft was subtly transformed into a new reflection on the president's two terms in office. A stress on union and just internal policies was associated with the first term, but the address moved to its climax in summarizing the sound foreign policy that had been formulated and maintained over the last four years.

To a critical eye, then and now, the address could read as a well-calculated recapitulation of Federalist party policies. But this is true not because Hamilton took over and manipulated Washington's occasion for his own ends. It is rather that Washington's own view of himself had changed. Now he was not taking his leave as a general who had been called back to temporary, uncomfortable duty in a brief term as president. He had served as president for almost eight years—about the same amount of time he had served as commander in chief. In office longer than all the members of his cabinet, he had done more than anyone to shape the new government, and in doing so, had taken a full dose of abuse.

Finally, Washington carefully transformed Hamilton's draft into copy for the press. He corrected it, deleted some portions, inserted new ones, and weighed again phrases that had been evolving for more than four years. What went to the printer was a sheaf of papers in Washington's script, with further emendations in his hand. The opening paragraphs still took their shape from the version Madison had prepared, but the closing words were Washington's own. He picked up what Hamilton had made of his apology for unavoidable faults: "I shall also carry with me the hope that my Country will never cease to view them with indulgence; and that after forty five years of my life dedicated to its Service, with an upright zeal, the faults of incompetent abilities will be consigned to oblivion, as myself must soon be to the mansions of rest." Then he pressed on with another paragraph—developed out of Madison's draft, revised in Hamilton's, and deleted from an earlier section of this holograph.

> Relying on its kindness in this as in other things, and actuated by that fervent love towards it, which is so natural to a man, who views in it the native soil of himself and his progenitors for several Generations;—I anticipate with pleasing expectation that retreat, in which I promise myself to realize, without alloy, the sweet enjoyment of partaking, in the midst of my fellow citizens, the benign influence of good Laws under a free Government—the ever favourite object of my heart, and the happy reward, as I trust, of our mutual cares, labours and dangers.

Thus all ends in tranquility and rest, borne up by kindness and indulgence. The prosperity and justice of America merge with one man's "native soil," his "mansions of rest," and the happy rewards for labors accomplished.

Washington gracefully departs for an eternal Mount Vernon.

To complete this ritual the president also arranged an unchallengeable exit. When the address reached the public on September 19, he was in his coach traveling to Mount Vernon. He did not return to Philadelphia until the end of October, when the voting for his successor was about to take place.

Washington thus displayed fine touches of mastery, not to say poetry, in composing this farewell. He initiated the message and completed it, retaining his control over the contributions of others. But because he tacitly incorporated some of Hamilton's and Madison's ideas, they, too, can be found in the *Farewell Address.*

Both men were about twenty years younger than Washington, but by 1792 both had already given long years to the development of the American government. At the outbreak of the Revolution, Hamilton was displaying his talents as a patriotic writer. While still a college student, he answered the writings of a persuasive New York Loyalist at about the same time that John Adams was confronting Massachusettensis in Boston. Soon he took up the sword and served a few months as an artillery officer until Washington made him his aide. He handled a number of delicate and tedious assignments and at last gained a command and a full share of glory at Yorktown. Hamilton was a member of Congress from New York during the final years of the war, working vigorously for stronger central government and a sound financial system. Madison, a slighter man, was more scholarly and stayed on at Princeton an extra year after taking his degree before returning to Virginia to study on his own. During the war years he helped frame the Virginia Constitution and then served a term in the state assembly. He served in Congress from 1780 to 1783 and was busy in state or national politics almost constantly thereafter. He found himself allied with Hamilton on a number of issues. The two men were temperamentally different, but both were energetic in behalf of a stronger national government.

They worked together in the Annapolis Convention of 1786; they took conspicuous leading roles at Philadelphia in 1787; and together they produced the *Federalist* papers in defense of the new Constitution. Their collaboration in this work was so close that it is still impossible to tell for certain which of them wrote certain papers. When the new government under the Constitution was established, both men again found positions of leadership, Hamilton as secretary of the treasury and Madison as a leader in the House of Representatives. Thus when Washington turned to Madison and Hamilton, he was turning to the young men who knew most about the American Constitution, who in fact had participated in its establishment as deeply as he had. What is more, he must have known that, as well as being alert politicians and informed constitutionalists, both had had experience in writing appeals to the public.

Washington might well have recalled their work on the *Federalist.* When its first papers were being published, both authors had sent samples to him and confidentially revealed their involvement. In the end, the series ran to eighty-five papers, which were reprinted in two small volumes, and copies were sent to Mount Vernon. Of course, Washington may not have read these volumes carefully. He may have looked at only a few pages, enough to write a decent letter of appreciation. But a few pages would have been enough to leave a lasting impression.

At least three aspects of the *Federalist* matched Washington's own plans for his address. First, he wanted to reach the people through the newspapers in a dignified manner. The *Federalist* had first appeared as a newspaper series interpreting constitutional issues. Second, Washington wanted to emphasize once more the importance of loyalty to the union. The *Federalist,* a thoroughgoing defense of strong national government, had opened with fourteen papers addressed to "the utility of the Union to your political prosperity." Third, Washington wanted to lessen factional disputes and elicit indulgence for his own frailties and any lingering flaws in the new constitutional government. From its first page to its last, the *Federalist* laid stress on "candor," a word used in the eighteenth century to mean goodwill or restraint from finding fault.

Did Washington deliberately weigh these similarities? That seems doubtful. More likely he thought of Madison and later of Hamilton as the most helpful persons he could turn to. The *Federalist,* however, remains a monument to what the two had accomplished and to their vision, shared with Washington, of a constitutional union.

Their collaboration is all the more striking because they fell into political enmity almost as soon as the Constitution was ratified. This enmity derived in part from the particular positions they filled in the new government, but eventually their conflict involved their constitutional interpretations. The quarrel became public in further newspaper columns—with results that directly affected the *Farewell Address.*

The Constitution supplied a blueprint for strong national government. But it required energetic, decisive leaders to set that government in motion and establish a harmonious working relationship among several powers. In retrospect it seems inevitable that Washington, Adams, Hamilton, Jefferson, and Madison should have had outstanding roles in the first administration. But at the time it was not clear exactly what those roles should be or what they should make of them. Washington spent some nervous first days wondering by what title the president should be called; and he and the others spent months redefining themselves in relation to one another. John Adams was vice president. From the sound of it, his office was the step just below the pinnacle of power, but its main function turned out to be presiding over the Senate. Adams in fact cast a deciding vote twenty times (a record) and exercised broad discretionary powers over crucial matters. But the daily routine was tedious: "My country has in its wisdom contrived for me the most insignificant office that ever the invention of man contrived or his imagination conceived" [John Adams to Abigail Adams, 19 December 1793]. Jefferson's place as secretary of state might also seem glamorous. His was the first executive department organized by Congress, and it was charged with the management of foreign relations. But Jefferson found that Washington exerted direct control over foreign affairs, and he watched with alarm as Hamilton expanded the Treasury and pressed his views into every area of government.

The conflict between Hamilton and Jefferson was exacerbated by external forces. One was the involvement of both men in the running newspaper war noted earlier. Another was the strain of reactions to the French Revolution. Washington's terms coincided with the upheavals in Paris and the beginnings of overt warfare between England and France. To some, the French Revolution reflected the best principles of the American struggle for liberty. To others it was a threat of anarchy against stable political institutions. The tension in Europe could not help affecting American politics, especially when both France and England laid separate claims to American sympathy and support. At moments it brought out the worst suspicions of the rivals in office. To Jefferson, Hamilton came to look like a "monarchist," a would-be prime minister to a figurehead president, engineering financial plans to enrich a large bloc in Congress and so win support for even grander schemes. To Hamilton, Jefferson seemed a head-in-the-clouds philosophe newly returned from Paris, indulging absurd and hypocritical notions of human equality when what America needed most was a strong, centralized government. But this is to express the conflict mildly. On these themes vats of poisonous ink were consumed in the press.

Washington harnessed these competing energies for a long time by the force of his own will, dignity, and talent for conciliation. But as it went on, the quarrel between Hamilton and Jefferson accelerated into much more than a personal or temporary clash. It became a persistent argument about what was most essential in the American Constitution. Was it a plan for centralized authority, a firm platform for expansive and energetic national government? Or was it a guarded, restrictive grant of powers, guaranteeing individual freedoms and local autonomy through its list of specific federal functions? These, of course, are the extremes of a range of views; looking back on the debates in the ratifying conventions one could find a dozen plausible versions of what it was the people of America had accepted. But from either of these extremes its opposite looked mortally dangerous—looked, in fact, like a conspiracy of treason.

In the end Washington had to choose; for personal and prudential reasons he sided with Hamilton. To the end of his correspondence with Jefferson he protested that fears of "monarchy" in America were both wild and insulting. "There might be *desires,*" he said, but he "did not believe there were *designs* to change the form of government" [*Anas,* 10 July 1792]. And when party acrimony ran so high, it blackened and undermined Washington's own public character—"in such exaggerated and indecent terms as could scarcely be applied to a Nero; a notorious defaulter; or even to a common pickpocket" [Washington to Jefferson, 6 July 1796].

These strains rapidly led to a breach between Hamilton and Madison. The secretary of the treasury came into office with well-laid plans for national finance. Madison, after an abortive attempt to gain a Senate seat, entered the House. There he was a master at legislative maneuvering, but he had to face reelection by local taxpayers every two years. At first it seemed that the old alliance with Hamilton might offer new advantages. The Treasury would present its considered reports, and Madison would help see that Congress endorsed them. But the Constitution specifically provides that "all bills for raising revenue shall originate in the House of Representatives." Madison's personal friendship with Jefferson, his fellow Virginian, was much deeper. And of course he had a mind—and an ego—of his own.

Hamilton lost an ally, as he saw it, to the seductive wiles of Jefferson's ambitions and French ideology. In May 1792 he wrote a long detailed letter on this subject to a mutual friend [Edward Carrington]. Hamilton complained that he would not have become secretary of the treasury without assurance of Madison's firm support. But through rumors, innuendos, odd political maneuvers, involvement in Freneau's journalism, and at last outright attacks, Madison had shown himself to be in opposition to Hamilton and to his own earlier principles. Hamilton had now "declared openly" to Madison "my opinion of the views by which he was actuated towards me, & my determination to consider & treat him as a political enemy." Hamilton went on to protest that there was not a shadow of truth in allegations that there was a "monarchical" party plotting the overthrow of the government. The more lethal truth was unequivocal: "that Mr. Madison cooperating with Mr. Jefferson is at the head of a faction decidedly hostile to me and my administration, and actuated by views in my judgment subversive of the principles of good government and dangerous to the union, peace and happiness of the Country."

From being collaborators on the *Federalist* Hamilton and Madison had now become avowed political enemies, confronting each other publicly in new essay series on the Constitution a few months later.

The occasion was Washington's Neutrality Proclamation of 1793. Early in his second term Washington issued a brief four-paragraph statement prohibiting American citizens from aiding any of the belligerents in the current European wars and declaring a national policy of "friendly and impartial" conduct toward all the powers. This statement met with murmurs of dissent, questioning the president's power to make such a proclamation as well as its wisdom and propriety. Hamilton planned a thorough defense of the president's action in eight "Pacificus" papers. These were published in the *Gazette of the United States* from June 29 to July 27. Jefferson saw the danger of this move and immediately urged Madison [in a letter dated 7 July 1793] to reply: "Nobody answers him, & his doctrines will therefore be taken for confessed. For God's sake, my dear Sir, take up your pen, select the most striking heresies and cut him to pieces in the face of the public. There is nobody else who can & will enter the lists against him." The result was a series of five "Helvidius" papers in the same newspaper from August 24 to September 18.

Pacificus lists four major objections to the proclamation: it lacked constitutional authority; it violated American treaties with France; it ran contrary to gratitude to France for support during the American Revolution; and it was ill timed and unnecessary. In answer to the latter objections, Hamilton presented some hardheaded reasoning. He saw treaties with France as agreements of mutual benefit, which could not properly be invoked when France became a European aggressor and when compliance would risk America's own self-preservation. But it was the first issue that most concerned Madison when he replied—that of the constitutional grounds for the president's authority. On this point Hamilton developed a strained construction of presidential powers under the Constitution, and Madison replied strongly.

In brief, Hamilton examined the opening words of Article II of the Constitution: "The executive power shall be vested in a President of the United States of America." In these words he saw a much fuller grant of powers than the Constitution allowed to the legislature, indeed a full authorization to do everything necessary to carry out the laws and government of the nation. "The general doctrine of our constitution then is, that the executive power of the nation is vested in the president; subject only to the exceptions and qualifications, which are expressed in the instrument." In the case at hand, Hamilton found no specific limitations. He noted that the Congress is empowered "to declare war, and grant letters of marque and reprisal," but he saw a thin but crucial distinction here.

> If on the one hand, the legislature have a right to declare war, it is, on the other, the duty of the executive to preserve peace, till the declaration is made; and in fulfilling this duty, it must necessarily possess a right of judging what is the nature of the obligations which the treaties of the country impose on the government: and when it has concluded that there is nothing in them inconsistent with neutrality, it becomes both its province and its duty to enforce the laws incident to that state of the nation. The executive is charged with the execution of all laws, the law of nations, as well as the municipal law, by which the former are recognised and adopted. It is consequently bound, by executing faithfully the laws of neutrality, when the country is in a neutral position, to avoid giving cause of war to foreign powers.

In other words, a large area of judgment was not only left open to the president in the conduct of foreign affairs but was imposed upon him. He must do such things as declare and enforce a policy of neutrality until Congress directed otherwise. To reinforce this argument Hamilton elaborated on the president's specific duty to receive ambassadors and other public ministers. And he ended by claiming that plenary powers are implied in the president's duty to "take care that the laws be faithfully executed." But whatever its source, in Hamilton's view, the power of the executive was clearly superior to all other constitutional powers in international matters.

> It deserves to be remarked, that as the participation of the senate in the making of treaties, and the power of the legislature to declare war, are exceptions out of the general "executive power" vested in the president; they are to be construed

strictly, and ought to be extended no further than is essential to their execution.

Madison was not only cogent in attacking this argument; he was vehement. *Helvidius* was a direct reply to *Pacificus* and was designed to tear away its disguise and reveal its corruption. "I propose . . . to show, from the publication itself, that under colour of vindicating an important public act, of a chief magistrate who enjoys the confidence and love of his country, principles are advanced which strike at the vitals of its constitution, as well as at its honour and true interest."

As Madison read the Constitution, it is clear and specific in limiting the powers of the executive and granting important powers over treaties and international matters to Congress. Since treaties are actually laws, they belong within the legislative domain. Since the powers of making war and peace are vested in Congress, so too are the powers of determining and declaring neutrality. Instead of seeing an implied grant of plenary executive powers, Madison could see only specified presidential powers in the Constitution, and none of these supported the authority of a proclamation of neutrality. Going through *Pacificus* line by line, Madison found strained interpretations, lapses of logic, and dangerous implications hidden in plausible phrases. He concluded that *Pacificus* was a crafty attempt to exploit Washington's well-meant action, to turn it into a precedent for expanding presidential powers beyond any constitutional limit whatever. He warned that this was no idle danger: "we are to regard it as mortally certain, that as [these] doctrines make their way into the creed of the government, and the acquiescence of the public, every power that can be deduced from them, will be deduced, and exercised sooner or later by those who may have an interest in doing so."

Moving beyond answering Pacificus, moreover, Madison attacked Hamilton more directly. By the end of the first Helvidius paper he was quoting from *Federalist* number 75, in which Hamilton had stressed that treaty making was a legislative power. And in his third and fourth papers Madison cited the *Federalist* again—on the merely ceremonial nature of the president's power to receive ambassadors, and on the dangers of giving the president sole power over treaties. In default of any solid constitutional ground for sweeping executive power, Madison could think of only one source from which Pacificus might have derived the idea: "The power of making treaties and the power of declaring war, are *royal prerogatives* in the *British government,* and are accordingly treated as *executive prerogatives* by *British commentators.*" Madison could not help noticing further details throughout *Pacificus* that betrayed a "monarchist" cast of mind. Not least of these was the identification (in the seventh paper) of "the government" with the executive branch or with the president alone. Madison pounced on this "singularity of the style adopted by the writer, as showing either that the phraseology of a foreign government is more familiar to him than the phraseology proper to our own, or that he wishes to propagate a familiarity of the former in preference to the latter." These points could not be lost on anyone who recognized Hamilton's hand in *Pacificus.* They sharply insisted that this foreign-born power seeker was now showing his true colors.

Madison went further. In the third *Helvidius* paper he re-wrote the Neutrality Proclamation in a parody, as a way of showing how preposterous Pacificus's claims would be if they were not muffled in ambiguous phrases. And in the fourth paper, he forced the logic of Pacificus further yet. If, as Pacificus claimed, the president had virtually all the powers relating to war, except the strictly limited power of declaring it, then "would it be difficult to fabricate a power in the executive to plunge the nation into war, whenever a treaty of peace might happen to be infringed?" Helvidius here poses an acute question about how far a president can lead or control a government at the brink of war. Then he plunges forward with a glance at the current situation.

> But if any difficulty should arise, there is another mode chalked out, by which the end might clearly be brought about, even without the violation of the treaty of peace; especially if the other party should happen to change its government at the crisis. The executive could *suspend* the treaty of peace by *refusing to receive an ambassador* from the *new* government; and the state of war *emerges of course.*

At this time France had changed its government and Citizen Edmond Genêt had landed in America, stirring up enough trouble to make him a very unwelcome ambassador. What Madison implies here is that all the elements were in place for a reckless president to bring America to immediate ruin. The powers claimed by Pacificus, in this case for a proclamation of neutrality, could easily be manipulated for the opposite effect—to force a declaration of war.

Madison was on dangerous ground here, and he knew it. It was one thing to attack *Pacificus* by pointing out its inconsistencies, or to affront Hamilton by setting his *Federalist* pages next to his current arguments. But in attacking the Neutrality Proclamation, Madison risked slighting the president's judgment and violating his personal relations with Washington.

His consciousness of this danger made him squirm. His letters to Jefferson show him thinking up every excuse to avoid this task. He says he is too far from Philadelphia. He doubts he has the books he needs to do a proper job. He is reluctant to act because he does not know (and cannot know, and should not know) the cabinet secrets that lay behind the proclamation. Besides, Hamilton is not a man to take attacks lying down; he will be sure to engineer a keen reply. Besides, there will be delays in recopying these papers in a disguised hand, and meanwhile events are changing the meaning of what Pacificus has said. And besides, it is summer and the Virginia sun is intolerably hot. "I have forced myself into the task of a reply," he says. "I can truly say I find it the most grating one I ever experienced" [Madison to Jefferson, 30 July 1793].

Nonetheless Madison went on writing. Just a year earlier the bright sunlight had shone over his work on Washington's farewell and his own letters urging the president to remain in office. Now here he was working hand in glove

with Jefferson, urging *him* to remain in office and slipping drafts to him for his perusal and correction before they were published as attacks on the president's powers. Madison might try to cover his arugments with a nice distinction: Washington's proclamation did not even mention the word "neutrality"; Pacificus was therefore building an enormous case for power out of an action that was plainly justified on other "legal and rational" grounds. But this was too fine a distinction for many people to notice. Madison must have known that he was shifting his position and witnessing others shift theirs. Washington had made it plain that he wanted to leave office, his cabinet was openly divided, and the future now lay with someone else. If the choice were to be between Hamilton and Jefferson, Madison was bound to act immediately to cut the one and ally himself with the other—especially if Hamilton had the cunning to affect such proclamations and build them into elaborate doctrines of executive power!

From one aspect the debate between Pacificus and Helvidius was but an acute form of a larger tension. It gave expression to conflicts that were raging in other forms—in warfare between France and England; in American uncertainties about peace and the cause of liberty; in secret and overt clashes within Washington's cabinet; in conflicts between the executive branch and a newly elected Congress; in the ongoing vituperation of competing party journalists. In all these conflicts of 1793, two little newspaper series may look like a very mild skirmish.

Yet they left an indelible impression on Hamilton's memory and on Madison's and Washington's. Many years later, when Hamilton was asked to help prepare a new edition of the *Federalist,* he made a point of having *Pacificus* included as an appendix. "He remarked to me at the time," the publisher recalled, "that 'some of his friends had pronounced them to be his best performance'" [George F. Hopkins to John C. Hamilton on 4 February 1847]. Madison helped prepare the Gideon edition of 1818, which in its turn included *Helvidius.* This edition noted that all three series show Hamilton and Madison laboring in unison "to inculcate the advantages to be derived from the Constitution" and define where they later differed about "the practical construction of that instrument." Meanwhile, Washington had felt the changed mood around him. His address to Congress in December 1793 narrowly defined the meaning of his proclamation—within the confines Helvidius had pronounced proper. But the president never again turned to Madison for confidential advice.

When Washington again looked over his farewell, he saw Madison's draft as the work of a *former* supporter. By then Washington also saw his second term as an achievement in foreign policy. What he added to the address at this point included carefully chosen words about alliances, neutrality, and the particular dangers of political parties that favored the claims of any foreign power. In the end he addressed this point specifically: "My politicks have been unconcealed;—plain and direct.—They will be found (so far as they relate to the Belligerent Powers) in the Proclamation of 22d of April 1793; which, having met your approbation, and the confirmation of Congress, I have uniformly & steadily adhered to—uninfluenced by, and regardless of, the complaints & attempts of any of those powers or their partisans to change them."

Hamilton was therefore complying with Washington's orders when he expanded the address to place new and concluding emphasis on American foreign relations. In writing his draft, however, Hamilton added some noteworthy touches, including one or two passages that seem to echo the *Federalist*. In discussing the harmful effects of parties or factions, he copied the central argument of *Federalist* number 10 (a passage that Washington did not include in his final version). And close to it he developed the idea that "time and habit are . . . necessary to fix the true character of governments." This was a major theme in the final *Federalist* paper, too. There, an essay of David Hume's was quoted to good effect: "The judgments of many must unite in the work: EXPERIENCE must guide their labour: TIME must bring it to perfection: And the FEELING of inconveniences must correct the mistakes which they *inevitably* fall into, in their first trials and experiments." The *Federalist* then continued with lines that foreshadow some leading motifs of the *Farewell Address*: "These judicious reflections contain a lesson of moderation to all the sincere lovers of the union, and ought to put them upon their guard against hazarding anarchy, civil war, a perpetual alienation of the states from each other, and perhaps the military despotism of a victorious demagogue, in the pursuit of what they are not likely to obtain, but from TIME and EXPERIENCE."

What then can be traced from Hamilton and Madison in the *Federalist*, to Madison and Washington in the 1792 valedictory, to Hamilton against Madison in *Pacificus* and *Helvidius*, to Hamilton and Washington in the final draft of the *Farewell Address*? The answer is not simple. It is complicated by personal quirks, strained friendships, changing political roles, and—in the end—the passage of time and experience in three very different human lives. Nevertheless, through the tensions and distrusts that bound these men together and drove them apart, one can perceive some common ground. Strong union; inviolable American independence; balanced government, safe from domination by any region, faction, or demagogue—these are the ideas for which all three men made sacrifices. These are the constants. The variations—which finally broke up this three-way collaboration—derived from threats to these ideals and suspicions that one or another of these public men was failing to cherish them all.

The *Farewell Address* repeats and once more stresses the importance of these ideals. Looked upon as a shared statement, it expresses what all three leaders had worked for in the first years under the Constitution. Hamilton and Madison did not create President Washington, and neither did he wholly direct these younger men. It was they who led the call for a Philadelphia Convention and the subsequent campaigns for a well-considered new plan of government. It was he who could summon unanimous support through two elections and hold even these divergent talents together as long as possible.

From this review of the *Farewell Address*, it may seem impossibly difficult to read. The story of its stages of compo-

sition, and the background of Hamilton's and Madison's involvement in it, may clutter our view—like scaffolding around a great monument. Knowledge of the scaffolding may be useful if it conveys a sense of skilled labor and careful proportions. But Washington meant to put forward a finished statement, after all. He wanted readers to consider the address as his work, his parting letter to the people, his own seal upon his presidency. In this light, the address deserves a further assessment. It must be understood as a work sui generis, a message only President Washington could have conceived and carried off. It can be compared to other addresses of a similar type—in fact, of four similar types—but in the end its features differ from all other models or analogues.

In the first place, the address is what linguists call a performative utterance, a statement that creates a new situation. When a jury pronounces a man not guilty, he is by that pronouncement released from jeopardy for an alleged crime. When Robinson Crusoe starts calling to his captive by name, the captive's name becomes Friday and he changes into a trusted servant. When Washington issued the proclamation of 1793, he seemed to commit the American government to a strict neutrality from that day forward. So when he issued his farewell: by that act, he withdrew from consideration in the coming election. He timed his statement shrewdly with that outcome in mind. But from the time of his earliest outline of a farewell, he envisioned it as much more than a brief official declaration. He used the occasion to speak both officially and unofficially—to announce his precedent-setting retirement and at the same time to take leave of his countrymen in the tone of a departing friend. On the one hand, he makes a pronouncement akin to a command: I shall not run again for president. On the other, he invites everyone to imagine him already out of office and back at Mount Vernon.

The interplay of these two identities gives the *Farewell Address* a peculiar double authority. Both the president and George Washington here are merged and distinct at the same time. Only the president could announce that he would not run for another term; only the president could hope to hold the attention of all the people; only the president could claim the experience and information necessary for offering advice on the most important current policies of government. Yet the decision to run or not to run was finally personal. Washington was also aware that he was the hero of the Revolution and the unanimous first choice as president. His fame and authority had been earned apart from this final office. And here he was stepping down—saying farewell to a long career. By this deed of relinquishing power he could make a unique appeal as a disinterested public servant. Master of the American government, yet servant of the American people—from this paradoxical vantage point he could press forward with lines of policy that should outlast his term.

Washington thus turns the address into an idealized outline of the presidency. He defends his own policies and actions, including his reluctant acceptance of the office. He also implies what his successors must do. The broad and best remembered phrases have this character. Parties and factions have a pernicious effect on government; the presi-

The final page of Washington's Farewell Address, *1796.*

dent should hold himself above party, as this president has done. War, peace, and diplomacy should grow out of firm American independence from European influence; the president should direct such foreign policy, as this president has done. The president should be answerable to the people and not hold office permanently; he should transfer power gracefully, as this president is about to do.

There are similar appeals and pronouncements in addresses by other presidents. Jefferson came into office in 1801 with the famous declaration that he and the people should be united above party: "We are all Republicans, we are all Federalists." Other leaders have found lofty justification for exercising powers that neither the Constitution nor the laws specifically provided. But such statements are most common in inaugural speeches or in the midst of a pressing need—in other words, at times when a president needs to consolidate support before taking action. Their recurrence in a final address can only recall the larger outlines of what Washington said here. His farewell is unique because it is the first and because he closed his term with firm assertion of constitutional powers. The address interprets and thereby ratifies Washington's two administrations—the first, as the establishment of a sound domestic government; the second, as the proper course through international tensions. The address describes a large and

complete framework of explicit and unquestionable accomplishments—all attributable to the president.

Washington could not find a model for such an address in America, at least none more famous than his own Legacy circular to the states at the end of the war. The *Farewell Address* has been compared, however, to the political testaments that European rulers composed throughout the eighteenth century. It was customary for a monarch to put together a statement of his observations and long-range policies to serve as a summation of his experience in power and as a guide to his successor. . . . Felix Gilbert [in *To the Farewell Address,* 1961] has argued that this tradition of royal testaments influenced Washington's farewell; he claims that "in revising Washington's draft for a valedictory, Hamilton transformed it into a Political Testament" of this sort.

But in at least two ways political testaments were sharply different from what Washington sent to the press. They were secret documents, usually securely hidden away for reasons of state; sometimes their frank assessments of political realities could not be revealed even after their authors were long dead. And if they were publishable at all, their earliest appearance was after the death of a monarch. By contrast, Washington's farewell was designed for immediate and widespread reading at a time of a peaceful transfer of power through a free election. Washington may have closed with a sense of his impending death, but he yearned to be out of office well before it occurred. If he or Hamilton entertained thoughts of European testaments, they recast them into an American departure from that form.

There is one final analogue that does recall a European monarch, but not of the eighteenth century nor perhaps of any time. As we noted in reviewing Washington's changing ideas of the address, he both chose to retire and felt impelled to it by duty and the weight of age. Few kings have ever abdicated or left high power, unless at the point of defeat or unspeakable outrage. As Sophocles and Shakespeare understood, such rites of passage are the stuff of high tragedy. There is a touch of the sublime in yielding up power with grace.

The closest approach to it may be the opening scene in *King Lear*, where the old king has staged a great ceremony for the conclusion of his reign. He will preside to the last over what is inevitable, and "publish" his bequests while still alive.

> Know that we have divided
> In three our kingdom; and 'tis our fast intent
> To shake all cares and business from our age,
> Conferring them on younger strengths, while we
> Unburdened crawl toward death.
>
> (I.I38-42)

In these few lines the character begins his descent from the majesty of command to the debility of his "crawl toward death." He too would escape high office before becoming

---

Washington on honor, bravery, and liberty:

The time is now near at hand which must probably determine, whether Americans are to be, Freemen, or Slaves; whether they are to have any property they can call their own; whether their Houses, and Farms, are to be pillaged and destroyed, and they consigned to a State of Wretchedness from which no human efforts will probably deliver them. The fate of unborn Millions will now depend, under God, on the Courage and Conduct of this army—Our cruel and unrelenting Enemy leaves us no choice but a brave resistance, or the most abject submission; this is all we can expect—We have therefore to resolve to conquer or die: Our own Country's Honor, all call upon us for a vigorous and manly exertion, and if we now shamefully fail, we shall become infamous to the whole world. Let us therefore rely upon the goodness of the Cause, and the aid of the supreme Being, in whose hands Victory is, to animate and encourage us to great and noble Actions—The Eyes of all our Countrymen are now upon us, and we shall have their blessings, and praises, if happily we are the instruments of saving them from the Tyranny meditated against them. Let us therefore animate and encourage each other, and shew the whole world, that a Freeman contending for Liberty on his own ground is superior to any slavish mercenary on earth.

George Washington, from his General Orders, 2 July 1776.

---

incompetent and would manage its transfer wisely—"that future strife / May be prevented now" (I.I.45-46). But Lear learns all too well what Washington learned, too, in his relations with Hamilton and Madison. Letting go of well-managed power is a long step toward grief. Lear relinquishes a divided kingdom and lives on to see his world shattered by warfare; Washington was to witness a surge of party hatreds in the years he had left.

Still, history is rarely as neat or as devastating as tragedy. General Washington was not exactly Cato, nor was President Washington an American Lear. He succeeded in reclaiming his comforts along the Potomac—despite an awkward return to military duty in 1798. The farewell was his last great public message, as he had meant it to be. When he died in 1799 he left a strong union in the hands of younger men, including Adams, Jefferson, and Madison. (pp. 85-114)

> *Albert Furtwangler, "A Valediction Forbidding Mourning," in his* American Silhouettes: Rhetorical Identities of the Founders, *Yale University Press, 1987, pp. 85-114.*

Glenn A. Phelps   (essay date 1993)

[*In the following essay, Phelps outlines Washington's constitutional vision through an examination of his public and private correspondence during 1783-87. Phelps purports that Washington's political philosophy developed long before his alliances with James Madison and Alexander Hamilton and further suggests that Washington's views significantly contributed to the framework of the federal Constitution.*]

The year 1781 ended well for Washington and for the revolutionary cause. Nathanael Greene's southern campaign had been enormously successful and had restored American morale in the Carolinas. Washington's own reputation had been restored by the successful Franco-American operation in Virginia. Finally, after six frustrating years Washington could lay claim to the personal military honor he had longed for—the defeat of a sizable British army on the battlefield. Moreover, Yorktown had vindicated Washington's grand strategy for the war. He had argued long and hard, and not always successfully, that the war could be concluded only by defeating British forces in the field—a goal he believed was attainable only by the use of professional (Continental) troops under his consolidated command. Washington had insisted that if his strategy were followed and the British army, or important elements of it, were defeated, Britain would quickly sue for peace. Indeed, with the ignominious surrender of Cornwallis and his army peace rumors swept the country.

We can only speculate about Washington's thoughts upon receiving Cornwallis's surrender proposal. Perhaps he imagined a quick end to a war that only a few months earlier had seemed incapable of resolution. Perhaps he anticipated a return to the life of the country gentleman at Mount Vernon—a retirement that surely would carry with it the reputation and public honors that he had so ardently pursued. Perhaps he looked forward to a quiet life as a revered public figure in a nation governed wisely and justly by the noblest of republican principles. Perhaps. But Washington remained curiously subdued amid the groundswell of enthusiasm over the news from Yorktown. Cornwallis's surrender was "an interesting event that may be productive of much good if properly improved." But he would go no further.

Although Yorktown signaled the end of the military crisis, Washington remained wary, noting that the British still retained a potent military presence on the continent. But Cornwallis's capture had embarrassed the British command structure and had emboldened parliamentary factions that wanted peace with the Americans. Washington and Congress were informed by Guy Carleton, the new British commander-in-chief in North America, that no further offensives would be initiated, and although Washington still suspected British mischief, the war was effectively over.

For others, Yorktown would come to symbolize the final triumph of American dedication and patriotic ardor. For Washington it meant only the onset of the "great crisis." Most of Washington's energies for the previous six years had been focused on winning the military war for independence. He had conducted himself in a manner befitting a republican general dedicated to preserving republican institutions. But important as his conduct was to his self-image, it had little effect on the development of American political practices during the war. The states were busily writing, revising, and implementing new constitutions without any particular help from Washington. Only a few months earlier Congress had at last ratified a constitution for the United States, the Articles of Confederation, again without the benefit of Washington's opinions.

As peace negotiations neared their conclusion in 1783 the exhausted Washington wrote to his brother about his wish to unburden himself of all further public responsibilities: "This event will put a period not only to my Military Service, but also to my public life; as the remainder of my natural one shall be spent in that kind of repose which a man enjoys that is free from the load of public cares" [Washington to John Augustine Washington, 15 June 1783]. While he probably anticipated basking in a postwar aura of fame and adulation, he also seems genuinely to have wanted to bring his public life to a close. But his impending resignation from the army served only to elevate his awareness of things political—and he did not like what he saw.

Washington's letters throughout the early and middle 1780s resonate with a dark pessimism about the future of the republican experiment. Whenever he acted as a representative of the American cause, as in his addresses to his troops and his letters to foreigners, he felt obliged to present a uniformly optimistic picture. In his farewell address to the Continental Army he enthused that "the enlarged prospects of happiness, opened by the confirmation of our independence and sovereignty, almost exceeds the power of description." But his private correspondence reveals an assessment of America's prospects decidedly less sanguine. Events were bringing "our politics . . . to the brink of a precipice; a step or two farther must plunge us into a Sea of Troubles" [Washington to Thomas Johnson, 15

October 1784]. Similar expressions of foreboding appear persistently in Washington's personal letters. To the trusted Henry Knox he wrote [on 25 February 1787]: "Our affairs, generally, seem really, to be approaching some awful crisis." Washington must have recalled the ideals of the Fairfax Resolves—sister states standing together for self-government and the restoration of constitutional principles—and wondered whether the "awful crisis" of the confederation period was not every bit as threatening as that presented by the corrupt ministries of 1774.

In short, the Revolution was not working out as Washington had expected. As a farmer, he well understood the notion of the "false spring," in which premature warmth brings crops and trees to bloom only to have them withered by an unexpected blast of cold. The republic, or at least his conception of a republic, seemed to be under assault from the frigid blasts of self-interest, localism, class-based politics, and licentiousness. If the promised fruits of republicanism were to be harvested Washington would have to invest more of his energies in its care and nurture. Thus, rather than quiet retirement, Washington found himself expanding his extensive network of correspondents: governors and former governors, congressmen and former congressmen, officers and aides from his army days, men of influence at every level, even sympathetic Europeans. Old friends such as George Mason and Patrick Henry tried out their thoughts on Washington, but so too did new correspondents such as James Madison, Alexander Hamilton, and Gouverneur Morris, each an ally from the nationalist movement earlier in the decade.

This whirlwind of letter writing compelled Washington to reflect more carefully on the lessons of his experiences. As a result his constitutional vision emerged from this "critical period" more coherent than ever before. As that vision coalesced he became increasingly critical of the existing constitutional order. Sentiments and values that had previously been expressed in rather general terms were now translated into a specific policy agenda. Finally, Washington attempted to actively influence political developments during the confederation period, using his vast network of associates to play the role of an *eminence grise,* preferring to distance himself from any active involvement in political events but offering aid and comfort to those who shared his constitutional agenda.

Five letters, or sets of letters, from this period serve as the clearest exposition of Washington's reaction to the "crisis of the 1780s" and his emerging constitutional agenda on the eve of the Philadelphia Convention. First, his 1783 Circular Letter to the States provides us with his most thorough assessment of political difficulties in the union and offers, albeit still in rather general terms, some of his suggestions for constitutional reform. Second, his letters on behalf of the Potomac Canal illustrate two key components of his constitutional vision: his support for western expansion and its importance for establishing a *national* constitutional order and his conception of the nexus between commercialism, interest, and republican government. Third, in his correspondence with his nephew, Bushrod Washington, the older Washington explains the importance of constitutional government and the dangers of factionalism and populistic democracy. Fourth, his letters regarding Shays's Rebellion and other "difficulties," while revealing little new in Washington's politics, explain his increased willingness to consider actions more forceful and dramatic than mere letter writing and evidence a growing confidence in his own vision. Finally, his correspondence with Madison, Mason, Knox, Edmund Randolph, and others from late in 1786 until his decision in 1787 to serve as a delegate in Philadelphia suggests that he was prepared to be more than a neutral bystander at the convention. Indeed, as with the Fairfax Resolves more than a decade earlier, we will later see that Washington's contributions to the final authorship of an important constitutional document, in this case the Virginia Plan that set the tone for the Philadelphia Convention, were more substantial than previously thought.

The Oracle of Newburgh

By 1783 peace with Britain was assured. Had he seen his republican duties as merely military Washington might have been expected to retire to Virginia secure in the knowledge that his own reputation was now unassailable. But political events in Congress and in the states troubled him deeply. A few years earlier he had supported the nationalist faction in their drive to strengthen the efficiency and energy of Congress. But the collapse of Robert Morris's finance plan and anticipation of the expected removal of British troops from the United States encouraged the states to quickly retrieve many of their old privileges. National affairs appeared to Washington to be slipping once again into the black ooze of state-based politics—a politics of self-interest, fear, and parochialism. Supporters of state power recounted the now-standard republican liturgy about the importance of liberty and locally controlled government. But Washington's experience had convinced him that however alluring this small-scale republicanism was in theory, in practice it could only bring about the collapse of the great American republican experiment.

His impending retirement offered Washington a unique opportunity to influence the course of national politics. He had injected himself into that sphere only sporadically during the war, usually limiting his political activity to letters encouraging his supporters to keep up the good fight. But his unrivaled status as the first genuine national hero combined with his position as a disinterested observer to give him great political leverage. It was not a moment he was prepared to let pass. So in June of 1783, after several weeks of careful thought and writing, Washington submitted his last, his longest, and his most provocative Circular Letter to the States from his headquarters in Newburgh, New York. It marked the retiring general not only as a man with a clear political vision, but as a man who, despite his protestations to the contrary, was likely to play a prominent role in shaping the postwar political order.

The letter began inauspiciously enough. The announcement of his impending retirement was followed by warm congratulations to all who had participated in the success of the Revolution. But Washington soon abandoned this conventional valedictory and signaled the real purpose of his message.

> The Citizens of America . . . are . . . possessed of absolute freedom and Independency; They are, from this period, to be considered as Actors on a most conspicuous Theatre, which seems to be peculiarly designated by Providence for the display of human greatness and felicity . . . Heaven has crowned all its other blessings, by giving a fairer oppertunity for political happiness, than any other Nation has ever been favored with.

Two further themes then emerged. First, there was no shortage of political liberty in America. American freedom was not the object of some hoped-for future; it was already the envy of the world. Second, this expansive liberty, in combination with the bounties of education, commerce, and experience in self-government, offered Americans an opportunity to demonstrate that constitutional government under republican principles was truly attainable. Washington then shifted his tone. Liberty alone would not be enough to bring about the republican millennium. Critical choices had to be made, choices that would determine whether America "will be respectable and prosperous, or contemptable and miserable as a Nation."

Clearly for Washington, one critical choice preceded and shaped all others: Should the United States be a nation among nations, or merely a loose confederation for mutual convenience and support? Many of the republican thinkers of the day, including the Country ideologues so influential in Washington's early career, opted for the latter arrangement. To them, liberty was inversely related to the power of central governments. The more distant the rulers were from the ruled (or, to use republican terminology, the more distant representatives were from their constituent citizens), the less sensitive the rulers would be to the rights and liberties of the ruled. The corruption of republican principles was inevitable without a vigilant citizenry willing to exercise a jealous regard for their personal liberties. Distant, centralized regimes made such vigilance all the more difficult and, thus, only accelerated the degenerative process.

Washington was aware of these feelings (he had, after all, shared many of those sentiments before his wartime service); yet he was convinced by his revolutionary experiences that these feelings were, at best, misguided and, at worst, dangerously wrong. The "present crisis" could be avoided if, and only if, a "national character" could be established. Without saying so directly, Washington's remarks implied that those who insisted that liberty and virtue could only be maintained in small-scale republics, like the existing thirteen states, were operating in a world bounded by libraries, philosophical societies, and the after-dinner talk of comfortable gentlemen. That world bore no resemblance to the one that Washington had come to know. In his view independence had been won only through the concerted efforts of a national union exemplified by Congress and the Continental Army. Now, independence could be preserved in an uncertain world only by resorting to the same agency—a strong national union. His indictment of postwar politics was pointed: "This may be the ill-fated moment for relaxing the powers of the Union, annihilating the cement of the Confederation, and exposing us to become the sport of European politics, which may play one State against another to prevent their growing importance, and to serve their own interested purposes" [from the Circular Letter to the States].

Washington's paradoxical, yet remarkably prescient, position was that the rights and liberties of the government and people of Virginia or New York or Rhode Island could *only* be preserved in the context of a strong national union. His diagnosis was that the very parochialism and spirit of liberty that many thought essential to the preservation of those freedoms was actually a lethal virus within the American body politic. The separate states, no matter how rich or well governed, were no match for the predatory actions of an unrepublican Europe. He explained this worldview in grim terms: "Without an entire conformity to the Spirit of the Union, we cannot exist as an Independent Power. . . . It is only in our united Character as an Empire, that our Independence is acknowledged, that our power can be regarded, or our Credit supported among Foreign Nations" [Circular Letter]. No amount of republican feeling or love of liberty could compensate for the lack of an effective national government. If the states continued to behave as thirteen local republics, he warned, they would soon find themselves "in a state of Nature." Citizens would soon discover that their passion for liberty had degenerated into little more than self-indulgent licentiousness. *This,* not the adoption of a strong national government, was the path to tyranny and arbitrary power. No temporary association for limited purposes would suffice. The Confederation was just such an association; but even though it was carefully constituted and drew, on occasion, the service of some of the best men in America, it was simply not up to the task. The union had to be made more permanent if independence were to be assured and republican liberty preserved.

If the constitutional superstructure of American politics was insufficient to support a permanent union, then what did Washington propose? First of all, he offered a series of specific reforms intended to create "an indissoluble Union of the States under one Federal Head" [Circular Letter]. Most of these reforms were more a matter of firm adherence to preexisting constitutional principles than a call for radical change. For example, he called on the states to immediately delegate greater legislative "prerogatives" to Congress. Yet from the context of his remarks it is clear that he meant that the states should respect the *existing* powers of Congress under the Confederation. Congress had ample legislative powers. What it lacked was a commitment from the states to refrain from using the banner of liberty as a mask for preserving local prerogatives instead of the genuine interests of all Americans. Washington further maintained that it was in the states' own interest that "there should be lodged somewhere, a Supreme power to regulate and govern the general concerns" of the republic, making clear at the same time that Congress was the logical place to entrust that "Supreme power." He also insisted that legislative authority would come to naught without adequate enforcement of national laws. Washington proposed no change in the executive arrangements of the Confederation, but he tried to impress on the states the importance of accepting the responsibilities of partnership in a real union: "There must be a faithfull and pointed compliance on the part of every State, with the late proposals and demands of Congress, or the most fatal consequences will ensue." Without diligent compliance by every state, no amount of congressional legislation could carry the day.

None of this was particularly new. Washington had remonstrated against state malfeasance and nonfeasance for much of the war. What particularly irked the retiring general was that, much to his amazement, cooperation among the states seemed to be declining to levels even lower than he had witnessed during the war. He was so distressed by this lack of cooperation that he suggested that anyone who opposed the union or proposed measures to dissipate its strength be treated as a traitor to the patriotic cause. He did not pursue this most extreme measure any further, but it is an indication that he was not about to concede any ground to the proponents of states' rights. He wrote, as much in frustration as in anger, that unless the states showed a greater willingness to be governed by the provisions of the national Congress, "it will be a subject of much regret, that so much blood and treasure have been lavished for no purpose, that so many sufferings have been encountered without a compensation, and that so many sacrifices have been made in vain" [Circular Letter]. Long before Webster and Lincoln, Washington was committed to the notion that "united we stand, divided we fall."

Washington then encouraged the states to join with Congress in supporting two particular measures that would assure the honor of "the national character." He had endorsed each proposal on numerous occasions during the war. But by reiterating them now, Washington was trying to impress on the states that these policies were not just militarily expedient (the war, after all, was now over) but were essential to the creation of a national character grounded in public virtue.

Washington first called on the states to show their "Sacred regard to Public Justice" [Circular Letter]. Public justice in this instance meant the payment of revolutionary debts, especially those owed to the officers and soldiers of the army. Washington's arguments read like the brief of an unseasoned lawyer. No consistent principle animated his advocacy; he moved back and forth between practical, constitutional, and moral arguments without rooting his claims exclusively in any of the three. But the overall effect was compelling.

His two practical arguments were rather simple. First, free government in America (and he most probably meant here, republican government) could only endure if citizens trusted their government. If Congress's word to creditors could not be trusted, could *any* national government in the future, however revised, hope to attract the loyalty and patriotism necessary for long-term stability? Important things must be done right, at the start, or republican government would find its reservoir of public confidence perilously low.

Second, in *private* life honorable men were obliged to fulfill their contracts even when the performance of those contracts was inconvenient or painful. Washington believed that *public* governments should be held to that same standard. Property rights in general would be jeopardized if governments could blithely ignore them when they wished. Thus, he argued that national forfeiture should be seen as having the same effect on the trustworthiness of government as private bankruptcy on the trustworthiness of individuals. Who would be willing to invest in useful, but potentially risky, national projects under those circumstances?

His constitutional argument was equally straightforward. The debts had been incurred in the common defense of the nation. They had been legally authorized by Congress under its constitutional authority. Therefore, the states were obliged to take whatever measures were necessary, including the laying of taxes, to retire the debts. But even here, his appeal included references to private honor and public virtue—claims that were more moral than constitutional: "Let us then as a Nation be just, let us fulfil the public Contracts, which Congress had undoubtedly a right to make for the purpose of carrying on the war, with the same good faith we suppose ourselves bound to perform our private engagements" [Circular Letter].

He had long held that a contract, *any* contract, was a sacred bond, a moral pact, between the parties. Failure to fully live up to one's contractual obligations was dishonorable, and we should recall that dishonor was counted among the gravest of sins in a society constructed along republican principles. His respect for contracts was also a sign of his deeply rooted social conservatism. Human nature, particularly as evidenced in the lower classes, was something not to be trusted. The law, though, by example and by coercion could be made to encourage appropriate behavior. Reflecting several years earlier on the business dealings of the unfortunate Jacky Custis, he had remarked: "I see so many instances of the rascallity of Mankind, that I am . . . convinced that the only way to make men honest, is to prevent their being otherwise, by tying them firmly to the accomplishment of their contracts" [Washington to Lund Washington, 17 December 1778]. Washington was not prepared to accept the notion that an American empire could be constructed on such "rascallity" in government. Republican governments should be paragons of public virtue, not slaves to the baser instincts of human behavior. Not satisfied with an appeal to public virtue, Washington also questioned the *private* virtue of those opposed to honoring the public debt. (Indeed, it again illustrates Washington's repeated appeals to private virtues, such as honor, frugality, and liberality, as the standards by which to measure public virtues. The two were, for him, virtually undifferentiated.) Where his most precious principles were involved George Washington was quite capable of shaming his opponents in the most florid terms:

> Where is the man to be found, who wishes to remain indebted, for the defense of his own person and property, to the exertions, the bravery, and the blood of others, without making one generous effort to repay the debt of honor and of gratitude? In what part of the Continent shall we find any Man, or body of Men, who would not blush to stand up and propose measures, purposely

calculated to rob the Soldier of his Stipend, and the Public Creditor of his due? [Circular Letter]

The picture he painted of the plight of disabled veterans was especially poignant and was intended to make opponents of full funding squirm uncomfortably: "Nothing could be a more melancholy and distressing sight, than to behold those who have shed their blood or lost their limbs in the service of their Country, without a shelter, without a friend, and without the means of obtaining any of the necessaries or comforts of Life; compelled to beg their daily bread from door to door!" [Circular Letter]. How could a national character be built on such a foundation of dishonor? We might be inclined to say that it was a bit of a cheat for Washington to place the claims of all creditors, most of whom were neither homeless, friendless, penniless, or limbless, on a moral par with the sacrifices of disabled war veterans. But Washington was not being hypocritical. He genuinely believed that *all* public debts were equally valid and that republican governments could have no part in faithlessness.

His next specific policy recommendation was even more quixotic. Noting that the "defence of the republic" required a "proper Peace Establishment," Washington recommended that "the Militia of the Union" be "placed upon a regular and respectable footing" [Circular Letter]. He must have known the response this proposal would generate, therefore he did not press the far more centralist notion of a professional Continental Army that he had advocated earlier in the war. This time he only recommended that there be a common organization among all the state militia (no doubt intended to alleviate many of the disputes over rank and command that Washington had faced during the war) and that all militia be armed and supplied in a standardized way. Presumably, these policies would emanate from Congress.

Even this watered down proposal was ignored. Many other Americans had their political attitudes shaped by the war; and what they had learned was often quite different from what Washington had learned. The mutinies of 1781, the march of the Pennsylvania Line on Philadelphia, the numerous instances of looting and foraging, and the putative officers' revolt at Newburgh had reinforced many Americans' traditional antipathy toward centralized military establishments. They trusted Washington; but one did not have to be a state particularist to share their apprehensions about a nationally directed militia.

All of these proposals were part of a larger indictment of the great obstacle to union—the jealousies of individual states. He knew that the union would stand or fall on "the system of Policy the States shall adopt at this moment" [Circular Letter]. It was the states that stood accused—accused of denying important powers to Congress, failing to keep good faith with the nation's creditors, promoting liberty to the point of licentiousness, placing themselves "in opposition to the aggregate Wisdom of the Continent." The states had to be made to see that their collective interest was best represented in Congress and that failure to support Congress was an assault on the national union that protected and nourished them all. Thus Washington continued to envision a republic on a national scale that would protect the liberties of the people and promote the common good far more effectively than could the states individually.

His proposed remedies combined constitutional reforms, specific policy recommendations, and a plea for a changed political climate. In this sense Washington's experiences during the war had compelled him to see politics as a deeper, more complex phenomenon than the simpler politics of deference in which he had been raised. Perhaps most significantly, the Circular Letter revealed that Washington had grasped the distinction between a constitution and constitutionalism. A structurally flawed constitution was not the only problem. The crisis of the 1780s was equally attributable to a lack of commitment by the states (or, to be more precise, certain self-interested factions within the states) to the principles of constitutionalism. Constitutions were not self-enforcing. Constitutions, especially republican constitutions, required "the prevalence of that pacific and friendly disposition, among the People of the United States, which will induce them to forget their local prejudices and policies, to make those mutual concessions which are requisite to the general prosperity, and in some instances, to sacrifice their individual advantages to the interest of the Community." Washington's Circular Letter suggested that the climate for constitutionalism at the national level was still imperfectly formed. Until Americans could be convinced of the advantages of a national constitution, a process made more difficult by the actions of the small-scale republicans, the great promises of the Revolution would remain unfulfilled.

The West—Keystone of a Continental Empire

In the fall of 1784 the retired general embarked on the last of his many trips westward. The ostensible purpose of the journey was to tend to his trans-Allegheny lands. But the real reason for the expedition was to explore several possible routes for a canal-and-road system that would connect the Potomac River with the Ohio River and the vast riches of the West.

A Potomac canal had long fascinated Washington. As early as 1754 he had written after a journey up the Potomac that the waterway offered the "more convenient least expensive and I may further say by much the most expeditious way to the [western] Country" [Washington to Charles Carter, August 1754]. As a Virginia legislator, he worked with fellow enthusiasts in Maryland to bring the two states together to construct a canal on the Potomac. There were "immense advantages which Maryland and Virginia might derive by making Potomack the Channel of Commerce between Great Britain and that immense Territory Tract of Country which is unfolding to our view" [Washington to Thomas Johnson, 20 July 1770]. The Ohio lands were a great prize. Other states were already exploring canals and turnpikes to bring commerce to and from the West through their borders and to their own seaports, so there was more than a little urgency to Washington's cause. Finally, in 1772 Washington successfully sponsored legislation in the Virginia House of Burgesses to join with Maryland in improving navigation on the river [Charles H. Ambler, *George Washington and the West*, 1936].

The war deferred any further consideration of this grand plan, yet his interest in the West remained prominent in his thoughts. This is evidenced by a letter to James Duane written not long after Washington's retirement in which he laid out an extensive plan for the settlement of the western territories. As we shall see, the development of the western lands was an essential element of his vision of large-scale republicanism for postwar America. Yet he was silent about any such projects in the Circular Letter, arguably his most comprehensive prescription for constitutional nationalism. There was, however, good reason for its omission. Washington was well aware that his support for the Potomac Canal and for westward expansion would not be perceived as disinterested by actors in other states. Those perceptions would be well founded and Washington knew it, admitting that he was "not so disinterested in this matter" as he would have liked. He owned about fifty-eight thousand acres of land in the Ohio Basin. If a sure and certain means of transportation were established between the Ohio and the Atlantic to supplant the longer, more perilous journey down the Mississippi, then the value of these lands would appreciate considerably. Washington would be able to command top dollar in rents as well as being able to attract the "right kind" of tenants. In addition, if the Potomac became the principal route from West to East then Alexandria would surely become one of the leading commercial centers in the nation—an outcome that could not but have improved his own economic interests. Thus, had Washington suggested that Congress be given the power to take a more prominent part in westward expansion and to legislate the sorts of internal improvements that the Potomac Canal represented he would have undermined the rest of his message. An important source of Washington's influence in political affairs was his image as a disinterested figure, as one who stood to gain little personally by his political efforts. Washington wisely recognized that on matters related to the West he was rightly seen as self-interested and as an advocate for the parochial interests of Virginia. (Other states, after all, had their own plans for the territories.)

Although he refrained from mentioning such matters in the Circular Letter, Washington did not concede that there was any conflict between his personal interests and the common national interest. In fact, he insisted that much of his enthusiasm for the project was because it was a vital ingredient in his vision for a republic drawn on a "large scale." Once again, a portion of his argument was couched in the language of national security. The United States was still a small nation, clinging ever so tenuously to a narrow strip of land along the Atlantic seaboard. Enemies, real and imagined, were everywhere. While many of his fellow Americans saw the principal military threat as coming from Britain and the continent, Washington was convinced that the western frontier presented even more danger—and not from Europeans or Indians, but from people who were nominally Americans! These western settlers lived lives fraught with physical danger and economic hardship. Washington grasped the political implications of this precarious existence. These settlers stood "upon a pivot; the touch of a feather, would turn them any way" [Washington to Benjamin Harrison, 10 October 1784]. With British interests to the north and Spanish and

French interests to the south and west, western immigrants would look to whichever benefactor could make their lives less dangerous or more prosperous. If passage to New Orleans or Montreal were made easier than passage to the ports of the American states, then these frontier dwellers would soon convert those economic attachments to political loyalties and be drawn into the orbit of Spain or Britain. In short, the United States needed to cement the West firmly into the union for its own protection or the frontier would rapidly become no more attached to the United States than "the Country of California."

The Potomac Canal would join the West to the East in a great American empire. At first, commerce would be the bond. But commerce was only a means to a more important end. He hoped his plans for a canal would succeed

> *more on account of its political importance* [my emphasis] than the commercial advantages which would result from it, altho' the latter is an immense object: for if this Country, which will settle faster than any other ever did (and chiefly by foreigners who can have no particular predilection for *us*), cannot by an easy communication be drawn this way, but are suffered to form commercial intercourses (which lead we know to others) with the Spaniards on their right and rear, or the British on their left, they will become a distinct people from us, have different views, different interests, and instead of adding strength to the Union, may in case of a rupture with either of those powers, be a formidable and dangerous neighbour. [Washington to Henry Knox, 5 December 1784]

Carefully supervised by Congress, westward expansion could be used to promote nationalism. Two kinds of settlers would be especially useful in making the West a bastion of nationalist fervor. Washington recommended, first of all, that Congress be given sole authority to distribute the western bounty lands promised to the former soldiers of the Continental Army. The frontier could not "be so advantageously settled by any other Class of men, as by the disbanded Officers and Soldiers of the Army." They would "connect our governments with the frontiers, extend our Settlements progressively, and plant a brave, a hardy and respectable Race of People, as our advanced post . . . [and] would give security to our frontiers" [Washington to Congress, 17 June 1783]. Settlement by the army had political advantages as well. These were men who had already pledged their allegiance to the *national* government once. If they now received land from that same government it would cement their national loyalty even further. These "new Americans" would serve as an effective buffer against the expansion of state interests at the expense of the nation.

But soldiers alone would not provide sufficient numbers to fill the vast expanses of the frontier. Therefore, Washington continually urged Congress to invite the right sort of European settlers. Those who exhibited the appropriate republican virtues were especially desirable. These included the "oppressed and persecuted of all Nations and Religions" (presumably they would care a great deal about liberty), those of "moderate property," and those with a de-

termination "to be sober, industrious, and virtuous members of society" [Washington to Francis Vanderkemp, 28 May 1788].

To make all of this work—the canal, westward expansion, provision for bounty lands, immigration policy—Washington believed that it was essential that Congress have plenary authority to administer the western lands. The states could not be permitted to have anything at all to do with the matter. For one thing, administration of the western lands for the common national interest would remove one source of perpetual jealousy among the states. More than once during the war disputes about which states had claim to which western lands had strained the comity of the union. Second, a system of national administration would establish some order in the settlement process. Washington believed in "progressive" settlement. Lands on the near frontier could be sold and settled immediately. But lands further west should only be opened up when the first tier of lands was sufficiently "filled up." If the states separately opened up all their western lands, or if they prevented Congress from placing any limits on the extent of settlement, it "would open a more extensive field for Land jobbers and Speculators. Weaken our frontiers, exclude law, good government, and taxation to a late period, and injure the union very essentially in many respects" [Washington to Henry Knox, 18 June 1785]. Washington wanted "useful citizens" endowed with a sense of obligation to the national government. To that end he urged Congress to obtain title to all of these disputed lands and then sell them to individual settlers at a fixed, moderate price. (Free land would encourage idlers and speculators. A fair price would attract hardworking farmers.) The revenues would enhance the national treasury; settlement would be directed westward in an orderly, progressive manner; and a growing body of citizen-farmers dedicated to republican principles and the value of a strong union would result.

Washington's views on commerce and trade were cut from the same cloth as his expansionist policies. Like many classical republicans he genuinely despised speculation and the "avidity . . . among our people to make money." He conceded to his friends that the "spirit of commerce," though capable of much energy and enterprise, was not without disadvantages, especially as a proper basis for a republican social order in which some sense of the common good and disinterestedness was essential. Yet he also recognized that "from Trade our Citizens *will not* be restrained, and therefore it behooves us to place it in the most convenient channels, under proper regulation, freed *as much as possible,* from those vices which luxury, the consequence of wealth and power, naturally introduce" [Washington to Thomas Jefferson, 29 March 1784].

Like liberty, then, the spirit of commerce was a public virtue *only* if directed toward the common interest: "To promote industry and economy, and to encourage manufactures, is certainly consistent with that sound policy which ought to actuate every State"—and the suitable instrument to direct that policy was an energetic national government [Washington to Edmund Randolph, 25 December 1786]. But the jealousies among the states were a threat both to "that sound policy" and to the new nation's independence. Washington was especially fearful of the impact of Great Britain's trade policies on the union. He envisioned Britain's great mercantile behemoth using these internecine economic rivalries to pit one state against another, thus subverting the still-fragile American economic "union." Unless a central government with more expansive powers to regulate national commerce emerged, Britain would probably regain by the purse what it had surrendered on the battlefield—American dependence. Two years before the Philadelphia Convention, Washington wrote: "The resolutions . . . vesting Congress with powers to regulate the Commerce of the Union, have I hope been acceded to. If the States individually were to attempt this, an abortion, or a many headed Monster would be the issue. . . . If we are afraid to trust one another under qualified powers there is an end of the Union" [Washington to David Stuart, 30 Nov. 1785].

Washington's plans for a great Potomac Canal were not, then, just the idle tinkerings of a self-interested Virginia planter. They were part of a comprehensive vision for establishing a national republic linked by a shared interest in commercial activities and aspiring to republican principles. A canal to the West would encourage settlements in the American interior. These settlements, in turn, would serve as a protection for previously vulnerable borders. To assure the loyalty of these new Americans their economic connections to the old states would have to be promoted. For this, a strong national government with the power to regulate *all* forms of commerce, domestic or foreign, was necessary. Once granted these powers, the national government could encourage commerce among all the states, old as well as new, East as well as West. As these interstate commercial ties proliferated and prospered, loyalty to the national government would increase and the particular interests of the states would be rejected in favor of a new, more enlightened common interest.

This scheme may lack the sophistication and fiscal gymnastics of Hamilton's Report on Manufactures, but it reveals that Washington had already grasped the interconnectedness of political and economic policy and that each could be deliberately shaped to serve his vision of a national republic. Virtue was not innate even to a liberty-loving people. But if the people's interests could be tied to the success of large scale republicanism, then self-interest could yet be made to serve virtue's purposes.

The Case of the Naughty Nephew

In the fall of 1786 an interesting correspondence proceeded between Washington and his nephew, Bushrod Washington. The elder Washington had taken a paternal interest in the fortunes of the young man, at one point personally recommending him for study with one of the great American lawyers of the day, James Wilson. It seems clear that Bushrod shared his uncle's interest in public affairs as well as his conclusion that the nation was in the midst of a great political crisis. Their correspondence suggests that there was little that divided the two men on matters of ideology or policy. Thus, this particular exchange is especially noteworthy because the older Washington patiently, but firmly, indicated that Bushrod was going in a direction that the general disapproved of.

Bushrod had written that he had lately been involved in organizing local (Virginia) Patriotic Societies. These societies of "sensible and respectable gentlemen" were established "to inquire into the state of public affairs; to consider in what the true happiness of the people consists, and what are the evils which . . . molest us; the means of attaining the former, and escaping the latter; to inquire into the conduct of those who represent us, and to give them our sentiments upon those laws, which ought to be or are already made." After a general statement of the societies' ends, most of which alluded to traditional republican values, Bushrod concluded with the news that there would soon be a meeting "to instruct our delegates what they ought to do, the next to inquire what they have done" [27 September 1786]. Fully expecting a "well done" for his efforts, Bushrod eagerly asked what Washington thought of all this.

Much to his surprise (as evidenced by a subsequent letter in which he rather defensively attempted to clarify the society's role and his own part in it) Bushrod found himself being lectured by his uncle and told that if it was the older man's approbation that was wanted, it would not be forthcoming. Washington expressed his particular fears about two aspects of the Society, each of which tells us much about the depth and sophistication of Washington's ideas about republican government on the eve of the Constitutional Convention.

Washington noted first that "I have seen as much evil as good result from such Societies as you describe the Constitution of yours to be; they are a kind of imperium in imperio, and as often clog as facilitate public measures." Could Bushrod not see the danger in a segment of the community nominating itself to speak for the public interest, especially when representatives had been specially chosen to make that determination? Might not a few designing members of the society "direct the measures of it to private views of their own?" [30 September 1786]. This was not the first time that Washington had railed against the "spirit of party" and its despised companion, factionalism, nor would it be the last. In his personal pantheon of political evils, parties and factionalism ranked with paper money and the machinations of European politics as the greatest threats to the adolescent American republic. In his view, factionalism could have *no* legitimate role in a republican form of government.

What accounts for Washington's deeply felt opposition to political parties? Why the antipathy toward factionalism? How could he have been so profoundly fearful of political elements that we today assume are intrinsic to liberal constitutions? The answer is twofold. First, the tenets of republican ideology as Washington received it and understood it viewed party spirit and factionalism as an evil so dire that it could tear asunder any republican constitution and undermine the quest for the good society. Second, Washington's recent ordeal as commander-in-chief had given him a firsthand look at the effects of factionalism. He needed no fancily argued treatise to instruct him on how factionalism could obstruct great public achievements. He could see daily confirmation of what his ideology predisposed him to believe. For Washington, theory and experience once again validated each other.

Washington's classical republicanism had as its central precept, its *modus vivendi,* the promotion of virtue and the identification and elevation of virtuous men. This virtue could only be attained by pursuing that which was truly in the public interest or common welfare. Fame was accorded to those men who sacrificed their self-interest in service to the commonwealth. But this vision implied that there was something called the public interest to which virtuous men could unanimously subscribe. The idea that there could be equally valid, but different, notions of the public interest was utter nonsense to Washington—a heresy upon good republican precepts. Harmony, not conflict; unity, not diversity, characterized his classical republican vision of society. Factions, because they represented interests of the particular rather than of the general, were an obstacle to virtue. Indeed, organizations like the Patriotic Society could be considered unpatriotic to the extent that they prevented the nation from achieving harmony and unity.

But Washington's feelings did not derive from ideology alone. Experience had confirmed those sentiments. Here again, the most immediate, most relevant, most galvanizing experience had come from his service in the Continental Army. If he had any doubts about the undesirability of faction before 1775, the war quickly hardened his views.

Life mask of Washington taken by Jean-Antoine Houdon at Mount Vernon in 1785.

Successful prosecution of the war required one thing above all else—unity. Any wavering or hesitation in the commitment to the great national goal of independence only prolonged the military struggle and increased its cost in both economic and personal terms. In this context it is no wonder that his wartime letters are filled with fears of factionalism and divisiveness among Americans.

One source of faction was obvious—the Loyalists (abetted in Washington's mind by those whose caution caused them to remain as uncommitted in the struggle as the contending armies would permit them). He was suspicious of their "diabolical acts and schemes" intended to "raise distrust, dissensions and divisions among us" [Washington to Philip Schuyler, 21 May 1776]. Washington was reluctant to execute Loyalists or confiscate their property. He was too much the social conservative for that. But on several occasions he did attempt to relocate them, segregate them, and even compel them to identify themselves so that their ability to influence or subvert the revolutionary cause could be minimized.

A more troublesome source of faction, however, was not in the enemy camp, but in his own. It was during the war that Washington had developed his political antipathy toward the states. He suffered from their repeated interference with the prerogatives of Congress and of his own national command. They seemed to him capable of supporting the national interest only when it coincided with local needs. The problem was not with the confederational structure *per se.* When Washington spoke about strengthening the federal union it was still in the context of a union of states. He was, after all, still a Virginian. (His efforts on behalf of the Potomac Canal project were understood by all as being particularly beneficial to his home state.) He did not believe in a unitary national government. But he *was* convinced that the political leaders in many of the states were utterly incapable of acting in the common national interest. Writing on the possibility of amendments to the Articles of Confederation that would strengthen the hand of Congress in national affairs, Washington commented acidly "that there is more wickedness than ignorance in the conduct of the States, or in other words, in the conduct of those who have too much influence in the government of them; and until the curtain is withdrawn, and the private views and selfish principles upon which these men act, are exposed to public notice, I have little hope of amendment without another convulsion" [Washington to Henry Lee, 5 April 1786].

To George Washington, Bushrod's Patriotic Societies appeared as one more source of disharmony in a union that he believed was disintegrating rapidly. Bushrod's rejoinder to Washington indicated that the purposes of the society were virtually identical to the general's. They, too, were concerned with advancing the public interest, restoring republican virtues to an increasingly corrupt system, and promoting the national union. But Washington continued to hold back. There was something about the permanency of the society and its posturing as the spokesman for the public's interest that continued to trouble him. His hatred of factions was so strong that he found it difficult to endorse even an organization that embraced the Washingtonian vision!

The Patriotic Societies bothered Washington on another level. They maintained that representatives were "the servants of the electors." Moreover, on broad notions of the national interest and public good "the people are the best judges of . . . their own interests." Therefore, the societies proposed to instruct their elected representatives on issues of the day [Bushrod Washington to Washington, 31 October 1786]. Bushrod and his friends were arguing on behalf of a "delegate" theory of representation. A delegate's responsibility is to stand as a mirror to his constituents, reflecting their wants and interests as accurately as possible. In this sense, the representative merely *re-presents* the views of those who elected him.

George Washington could not accept this definition of representative government. The genuine public interest could not be merely the reflection of the aggregated self-interests of thousands of constituents. This sang too much like the siren of democratic government, and Washington would have none of it. He still believed in government by a disinterested elite—men of property and independence, presumably with sufficient wisdom and experience to serve their constituents' true interests by acting for the common good. The structures of a republican form of government and the prospect of regular elections were devices sufficient to guarantee the responsibility of elected representatives. Washington was especially miffed at the short leashes (and the "instructions" of the Patriotic Societies would, of course, be yet another tether) that erstwhile republicans would place around the necks of delegates to Congress: "To me it appears much wiser and more politic, to choose able and honest representatives and leave them in all national questions to determine from the evidence of reason, and the facts which shall be adduced, when internal and external information is given to them in a collective state" [Washington to Bushrod Washington, 30 September 1786]. Congress, then, should be a deliberative body with a corporate, rather than individual, responsibility to the people. This idea, he thought, still provided ample checks on the representatives by those who elected them.

> Men, chosen as the Delegates in Congress . . . cannot officially be dangerous; they depend upon the breath, nay, they are so much the creatures of the people, under the present constitution, that they can have no views (which could possibly be carried into execution) nor any interests, distinct from those of their constituents. My political creed therefore is, to be wise in the choice of Delegates, support them like Gentlemen while they are our representatives, give them competent powers for all federal purposes, support them in the due exercise thereof, and lastly, to compel them to close attendance in Congress during their delegation. [Washington to Benjamin Harrison, 18 January 1784]

We don't know that Washington ever read Edmund Burke's discussion of the role of parliamentary representatives. But Washington's thoughts on representation, both with regard to the responsibility of the individual legislator and to the function of the body as a whole, were virtu-

ally identical to Burke's famous defense of the "trustee" principle. Ironically though, Bushrod Washington sensed far better than his uncle the profound change that republican thought was undergoing on matters such as representation and consent of the governed. George Washington was certainly not alone in clinging to this old republican orthodoxy; but his views would soon be tested in the crucible of the presidency. This would not be the last he would hear from organizations like the Patriotic Society.

From Massachusetts to Philadelphia

For a man whose roots were so undeniably Virginian, it is striking how often Washington's career was shaped by events in that most un-Virginian of states, Massachusetts. His early military career was frustrated in part by the decisions of the colonial supremo in Boston, Lord Loudoun. His most significant early appearance on the stage of national politics was as an advocate for the Fairfax Resolves—resolutions dedicated to uniting all Americans against British high-handedness in Boston. His first great victory as American commander-in-chief was the successful siege of British troops in Boston. Now, in the fall of 1786, events in Massachusetts were once again to shape Washington's political career.

Much of America was in an economic recession in 1786. As in most recessions its effects were borne more heavily by some Americans than others. In western Massachusetts economic hardship combined with long-standing political resentments to induce an armed rebellion against state authority led by former revolutionary officer, Daniel Shays. News of the insurrection caused Washington's barometer on national affairs to fall precipitously, triggering some of his most pessimistic reflections on the future prospects for republican government. The rebellion did not alter his political views. Indeed, as we shall see, Shays's Rebellion only confirmed his earlier jeremiads about impending disaster and his portents of "some awful crisis." But his correspondence concerning the events in Massachusetts is significant because it coincides with his deliberations about whether to step onto the public stage again as an active participant in national political affairs. Although he had been content until that winter of 1786-87 to play the part of Cincinnatus, maintaining an interest in politics but preferring to exercise his influence quietly and largely out of the public eye, his restiveness over the state of public affairs became so acute that he decided to accept Virginia's offer to be a delegate to the upcoming convention at Philadelphia—a course of action fraught with the risk of permanent damage to his hard-won public status.

The story of Shays's Rebellion has been better told elsewhere, but a brief review of the insurrection and, especially, its causes will help to place Washington's response into some context. The recession of 1786 had led to a decline in land values and agricultural prices for most American farmers. What made this hardship more painful in Massachusetts, though, were the policies of the state government. Dominated by the eastern cities whose welfare was tied more to trade and credit than was that of the interior, the General Court (Massachusetts's state legislature) enacted hard-money laws that required most debts to be paid in specie. In addition, the General Court imposed heavy taxes intended in part to redeem the war debts not only of the state, but also of Congress. The vigorous enforcement of these taxes and the perception that county courts were becoming exclusive instruments of the largely eastern creditor class exacerbated long-standing political divisions. Poverty and apathy had caused the western towns to be grossly underrepresented in the General Court. Thus, the hard-money policies of the legislature were seen by many westerners as a declaration of war by the eastern mercantilists on virtuous, liberty-loving farmers. Local courts and the "eastern lawyers" that infested them were objects of particular derision.

The rebellion that emerged was largely unorganized. Mobs and threats of mobs sprang up in many towns, but little suggests that a concerted organization was behind them, certainly nothing as coordinated or as covert as the revolutionary Committees of Correspondence. A small band of ersatz "minutemen," led by Daniel Shays, began to drill in earnest, though for what purpose no one really knows. These spontaneous challenges to organized government evoked mortal fear among conservatives in the state who were sufficiently frightened by events to help the governor raise an army commanded by Benjamin Lincoln. This state "militia" scattered the rebellion in a series of minor skirmishes; and by early 1787 the whole thing was over.

The significance of the rebellion was not in what it was, but in what people *thought* it was. Washington, in particular, remained from start to finish singularly ignorant of the circumstances surrounding the rebellion: "For God's sake tell me what is the cause of these commotions" [Washington to David Humphreys, 22 October 1786]. The one person who served as Washington's primary source of information on the "commotions," Henry Knox, exaggerated the whole episode from start to finish. At one point he informed Washington that the rebels were a dangerous army of upwards of twelve-thousand well-armed men—this at a time when Knox surely knew otherwise (Shays's "army" was actually yet to organize and would never number more than about two thousand). Knox also hinted that the rebels were "levelers," dedicated to an egalitarian redistribution of property and political power.

Washington remained baffled by the motives of the rebels. His letters asked again and again whether they had legitimate grievances. If they did, Washington wondered why the government did not rectify them. Perhaps the state did not have the resources to deal with the problem immediately, but surely it could at least tell the people what it intended to do. If, on the other hand, the disturbances were the result of an excess of liberty ("licentiousness"), then why did the state not use its power and authority to put an immediate stop to them? A third hypothesis was that the whole insurrection was the work of a British conspiracy. Initially, this explanation appealed most to Washington. After all, he had maintained for some time that the self-interest and parochialism of the state governments would make them easy prey to manipulation by the British. But Knox's letters convinced him that the rebellion was purely domestic.

All three explanations, though, were grounded in a common perception—the great American experiment in self-government was in grave peril.

> What, gracious God, is man! that there should be such inconsistency and perfidiousness in his conduct? It is but the other day, that we were shedding our blood to obtain the Constitutions under which we now live: Constitutions of our own choice and making; and now we are unsheathing the sword to overturn them. The thing is so unaccountable, that I hardly know how to realize it, or to persuade myself that I am not under the illusion of a dream. [Washington to David Humphreys, 26 December 1786]

Still, such a profound despair about American affairs was nothing new for Washington. In spite of all of his hopes for self-government in America, Washington retained a deep, occasionally even fatalistic, pessimism about achieving the republican dream. From 1780 on, it is almost impossible to find a period in his letters when he is not decrying the onset of some great crisis that threatens the very foundations of the constitutional order. Sometimes the villain is the perfidy of the British, sometimes the self-interestedness of the state governments, sometimes the lack of virtue in the American people, and sometimes the lassitude of Congress; but in every case the diagnosis is the same—republican self-government, like the virtuous citizenry that it requires, is so fragile that it demands constant nurturing, or else the noble experiment would fail not only in America, but in the Old World, too.

Thus, the significance of Shays's Rebellion is not that it transformed George Washington into a nationalist, or a conservative, or a republican, or an advocate of energy in government. He was all of those things before 1786. What changed was his determination to play a part in "saving" the experiment. When the rebellion was in its early stages his response was the same rather equivocal position he had maintained since the close of the war: the Articles of Confederation, as the embodiment of the federal constitutional system, should be supported fully by all of the member states, but amendments for its improvement should be considered. He was as yet unclear as to what the insurgents were up to. If they were interested in constitutional reform, then perhaps they could yet be dealt with. But if they intended to harm the good order of the community, then "employ the force of government against them at once." Under no circumstances should a constitution established by the people be made hostage to the demands of an armed mob; nothing could make republican government "more contemptible" in the eyes of the world. "Let the reins of government then be braced and held with a steady hand, and every violation of the Constitution be reprehended: if defective, let it be amended, but not suffered to be trampled upon whilst it has an existence" [Washington to Henry Lee, 31 October 1786].

When Washington learned that the rebellion had been dispersed he was greatly relieved and congratulated his Massachusetts friends on the success of the supporters of the state's constitutional government. But before the episode was closed he had already received notice of a call to a new convention in Philadelphia charged with the authority to consider amendments to the constitution (the Articles of

Confederation). He also knew that there was an active campaign to sponsor him as a delegate to the convention. For several months he debated with himself and with his closest Virginia friends whether to go to Philadelphia. In the end he accepted the charge. But the acceptance came months after the rebellion had ended. How then could the rebellion have had any influence on his decision?

The key to answering that question can be found in the republican idea of decay. Republican constitutions were usually founded in a spirit of unity and common purpose. Constitution making was a human undertaking of extraordinary moment; the disinterestedness that was needed for such an effort required a degree of public virtue found only on rare occasions. Once a constitution was established, the more normal forces generated by self-interest would begin chipping away at its finely balanced properties. Eventually, the constitution would either become the captive of a particular faction within the society who would use the power of government self-interestedly to suppress the liberties of the people or, even worse, would make government so ineffectual and lacking in respect that anarchy would ensue.

Any constitution, but especially one grounded in the spirit of republicanism, faced the prospect of decay. Only regular renewal—a resort to first principles—could preserve the constitution. But if public virtue were to descend too far down the slippery slope of corruption, factionalism, and self-interest, then it would be best to simply have done with it. At a time when the outcome of Shays's Rebellion was still in doubt Washington confided to Henry Lee that "Influence is no Government. Let us have one by which our lives, liberties and properties will be secured; or let us know the worst at once" [Washington to Henry Lee, 31 October 1786]. The rebellion was symptomatic of a failure of constitutional nerve that was rapidly spreading throughout the union. Conflict was nothing new to American politics, but in the six months before the Philadelphia Convention Washington seems to have come to the conclusion that social and political gangrene was poisoning the constitutional tissue faster than it could be excised: "Fire, where there is inflamable matter, very rarely stops."

Even as Shays's Rebellion was disintegrating, new conflagrations were flaring up. Washington's neighboring state of Maryland was being torn asunder over the issue of paper money, and he saw the frightening visage of the paper-money junto in almost every state. Virginia had so far rejected most of these inflationary measures, but Washington lacked confidence that even his own state could long remain immune to the cancer of public disorder that seemed to metastasize with every letter he received.

We know now that this crisis was greatly exaggerated. Washington's correspondents were not a cross section of America in 1786. Many of them were social conservatives, former Revolutionary War generals and political allies, fellow nationalists, and men of property—men who held many political values in common with Washington. He relied on these correspondents as his eyes on national affairs. They kept Washington remarkably well informed on the events of the day, but they also shaded his perception of those events with their own biases. In a few cases, Henry Knox's accounts of Shays's Rebellion being the most extreme example, they even resorted to outright fabrication. Given his pessimistic nature and his tendency to view bad political news as the product of unseen conspiracies, it is no wonder that Washington had come to the conclusion that these events signaled the final crisis of the constitution. The rapidly spreading decay had to be reversed or the constitution would be irrevocably lost, and with it would go Washington's hopes for the "noble experiment."

Shays's Rebellion did not alter George Washington's political sentiments one iota. It confirmed many of his worst fears, but it did not create those fears. It did not, as some have supposed, convince him to abandon his support for the Articles. But the rebellion, taken together with a constant fusillade of news in the winter of 1786-87 about internal and external threats to the constitution, did convince Washington that some sort of drastic remedial action was necessary if republican self-government in America was to be preserved. It was in this context that he finally agreed, reluctantly, to accept appointment as a delegate to the convention in Philadelphia.

Republican hagiography demanded that its heroes always be willing to defend the republic against corruption and decay. As much to confirm his own virtue as to attain any specific reforms, Washington determined to end his public "retirement." To his old friend Lafayette he wrote that he had decided to attend a convention called by Congress "to revise and correct the defects" of the Articles. "What may be the result of this meeting is hardly within the scan of human wisdom to predict. It is considered however as the *last essay to support the present form* [my emphasis]" [25 March 1787]. If the effort failed, he would "know the worst at once." (pp. 62-90)

> Glenn A. Phelps, "The Restive Correspondent," in his George Washington and American Constitutionalism, *University Press of Kansas, 1993, pp. 62-90.*

FURTHER READING

Bryan, William Alfred. *George Washington in American Literature.* New York: Columbia University Press, 1952, 280 p.
  Examines Washington's impact on American literature by assessing his treatment as a literary figure in oratory, biography, verse, drama, and fiction between 1775 and 1865.

Flexner, James Thomas. *George Washington.* 4 vols. Boston: Little, Brown and Co., 1965-72.
  Biography.

Freeman, Douglas Southall. *George Washington: A Biography.* 7 vols. New York: Charles Scribner's Sons, 1948-57.
  Critical overview of Washington's life and career.

Furtwangler, Albert. "Cato at Valley Forge." In his *Ameri-*

can Silhouettes: Rhetorical Identities of the Founders, pp. 64-84. New Haven: Yale University Press, 1987.

Study of Joseph Addison's *Cato* and its influence on the writings and character of Washington.

Gilbert, Felix. "Washington's Political Testament." In his *To the Farewell Address: Ideas of Early American Foreign Policy,* pp. 115-36. Princeton: Princeton University Press, 1961.

Elucidates Hamilton's rewriting of the 1792 draft of Washington's *Farewell Address.* Gilbert maintains that "in revising Washington's draft for a valedictory, Hamilton transformed it into a Political Testament."

McDonald, Forrest. *The Presidency of George Washington.* Lawrence: The University Press of Kansas, 1974, 210 p.

Assesses Washington's presidential administrations, focusing on his contributions to the office and his relationships with his cabinet, Congress, foreign representatives, the press, and the general public.

Milton, George Fort. " 'First in Peace . . .'." In his *The Use of Presidential Power: 1789-1943,* pp. 23-49. Boston: Little, Brown and Co., 1944.

Discussion of Washington's two terms as president, focusing on his interpretation of the office.

Padover, Saul K, ed. Introduction to *The Washington Papers: Basic Selections from the Public and Private Writings of George Washington,* pp. 1-13. New York: Harper Brothers, 1955.

Brief overview of Washington's character, early reputation, and his social and political outlook.

Phelps, Glenn A. *George Washington and American Constitutionalism.* Lawrence: University Press of Kansas, 1993, 245 p.

Investigates Washington's public writings and private correspondence to evidence his political philosophy. Phelps asserts that "Washington's constitutional vision—drawing on elements of classical conservative republicanism and continentally minded commercialism—developed years *before* he ever met Hamilton, Madison, and the other Founders under whose spell he was supposed to have fallen."

Reuter, Frank T. *Trials and Triumphs: George Washington's Foreign Policy.* Fort Worth: Texas Christian University Press, 1983, 249 p.

Outlines Washington's foreign policy.

Wills, Garry. *Cincinnatus: George Washington and the Enlightenment.* Garden City, N.Y.: Doubleday & Co., 1984, 272 p.

Explores how eighteenth-century artists and protagonists depicted Washington as a modern Cincinnatus. In his examination of Washington's role in the Enlightenment, Wills particularly centers on Washington's virtues and uses of power.

Additional coverage of Washington's life and career is contained in the following source published by Gale Research: *Dictionary of Literary Biography: American Colonial Writers, 1735-81,* **Vol. 31.**

Literature
Criticism from
1400 to 1800

Cumulative Indexes

How to Use This Index

The main references

Calvino, Italo
1923-1985.....CLC 5, 8, 11, 22, 33, 39,
73; SSC 3

list all author entries in the following Gale Literary Criticism series:

BLC = Black Literature Criticism
CLC = Contemporary Literary Criticism
CLR = Children's Literature Review
CMLC = Classical and Medieval Literature Criticism
DA = DISCovering Authors
DC = Drama Criticism
HLC = Hispanic Literature Criticism
LC = Literature Criticism from 1400 to 1800
NCLC = Nineteenth-Century Literature Criticism
PC = Poetry Criticism
SSC = Short Story Criticism
TCLC = Twentieth-Century Literary Criticism
WLC = World Literature Criticism, 1500 to the Present

The cross-references

See also CANR 23; CA 85-88;
obituary CA 116

list all author entries in the following Gale biographical and literary sources:

AAYA = Authors & Artists for Young Adults
AITN = Authors in the News
BEST = Bestsellers
BW = Black Writers
CA = Contemporary Authors
CAAS = Contemporary Authors Autobiography Series
CABS = Contemporary Authors Bibliographical Series
CANR = Contemporary Authors New Revision Series
CAP = Contemporary Authors Permanent Series
CDALB = Concise Dictionary of American Literary Biography
CDBLB = Concise Dictionary of British Literary Biography
DLB = Dictionary of Literary Biography
DLBD = Dictionary of Literary Biography Documentary Series
DLBY = Dictionary of Literary Biography Yearbook
HW = Hispanic Writers
JRDA = Junior DISCovering Authors
MAICYA = Major Authors and Illustrators for Children and Young Adults
MTCW = Major 20th-Century Writers
SAAS = Something about the Author Autobiography Series
SATA = Something about the Author
YABC = Yesterday's Authors of Books for Children

Aldington, Richard 1892-1962 . . . . . . CLC 49
  See also CA 85-88; DLB 20, 36, 100

Aldiss, Brian W(ilson)
  1925- . . . . CLC 5, 14, 40
  See also CA 5-8R; CAAS 2; CANR 5, 28;
  DLB 14; MTCW; SATA 34

Alegria, Claribel 1924- . . . . CLC 75
  See also CA 131; CAAS 15; HW

Alegria, Fernando 1918- . . . . CLC 57
  See also CA 9-12R; CANR 5, 32; HW

Aleichem, Sholom . . . . TCLC 1, 35
  See also Rabinovitch, Sholem

Aleixandre, Vicente 1898-1984 . . . CLC 9, 36
  See also CA 85-88; 114; CANR 26;
  DLB 108; HW; MTCW

Alepoudelis, Odysseus
  See Elytis, Odysseus

Aleshkovsky, Joseph 1929-
  See Aleshkovsky, Yuz
  See also CA 121; 128

Aleshkovsky, Yuz . . . . CLC 44
  See also Aleshkovsky, Joseph

Alexander, Lloyd (Chudley) 1924- . . CLC 35
  See also AAYA 1; CA 1-4R; CANR 1, 24,
  38; CLR 1, 5; DLB 52; JRDA; MAICYA;
  MTCW; SATA 3, 49

Alfau, Felipe 1902- . . . . CLC 66
  See also CA 137

Alger, Horatio, Jr. 1832-1899 . . . . . NCLC 8
  See also DLB 42; SATA 16

Algren, Nelson 1909-1981 . . . . CLC 4, 10, 33
  See also CA 13-16R; 103; CANR 20;
  CDALB 1941-1968; DLB 9; DLBY 81,
  82; MTCW

Ali, Ahmed 1910- . . . . CLC 69
  See also CA 25-28R; CANR 15, 34

Alighieri, Dante 1265-1321 . . . . CMLC 3

Allan, John B.
  See Westlake, Donald E(dwin)

Allen, Edward 1948- . . . . CLC 59

Allen, Roland
  See Ayckbourn, Alan

Allen, Sarah A.
  See Hopkins, Pauline Elizabeth

Allen, Woody 1935- . . . . CLC 16, 52
  See also AAYA 10; CA 33-36R; CANR 27,
  38; DLB 44; MTCW

Allende, Isabel 1942- . . . . CLC 39, 57; HLC
  See also CA 125; 130; HW; MTCW

Alleyn, Ellen
  See Rossetti, Christina (Georgina)

Allingham, Margery (Louise)
  1904-1966 . . . . CLC 19
  See also CA 5-8R; 25-28R; CANR 4;
  DLB 77; MTCW

Allingham, William 1824-1889 . . . NCLC 25
  See also DLB 35

Allison, Dorothy E. 1949- . . . . CLC 78
  See also CA 140

Allston, Washington 1779-1843 . . . . NCLC 2
  See also DLB 1

Almedingen, E. M. . . . . CLC 12
  See also Almedingen, Martha Edith von
  See also SATA 3

Almedingen, Martha Edith von 1898-1971
  See Almedingen, E. M.
  See also CA 1-4R; CANR 1

Almqvist, Carl Jonas Love
  1793-1866 . . . . NCLC 42

Alonso, Damaso 1898-1990 . . . . CLC 14
  See also CA 110; 131; 130; DLB 108; HW

Alov
  See Gogol, Nikolai (Vasilyevich)

Alta 1942- . . . . CLC 19
  See also CA 57-60

Alter, Robert B(ernard) 1935- . . . . . . CLC 34
  See also CA 49-52; CANR 1

Alther, Lisa 1944- . . . . CLC 7, 41
  See also CA 65-68; CANR 12, 30; MTCW

Altman, Robert 1925- . . . . CLC 16
  See also CA 73-76; CANR 43

Alvarez, A(lfred) 1929- . . . . CLC 5, 13
  See also CA 1-4R; CANR 3, 33; DLB 14,
  40

Alvarez, Alejandro Rodriguez 1903-1965
  See Casona, Alejandro
  See also CA 131; 93-96; HW

Amado, Jorge 1912- . . . . . CLC 13, 40; HLC
  See also CA 77-80; CANR 35; DLB 113;
  MTCW

Ambler, Eric 1909- . . . . CLC 4, 6, 9
  See also CA 9-12R; CANR 7, 38; DLB 77;
  MTCW

Amichai, Yehuda 1924- . . . . . . CLC 9, 22, 57
  See also CA 85-88; MTCW

Amiel, Henri Frederic 1821-1881 . . NCLC 4

Amis, Kingsley (William)
  1922- . . CLC 1, 2, 3, 5, 8, 13, 40, 44; DA
  See also AITN 2; CA 9-12R; CANR 8, 28;
  CDBLB 1945-1960; DLB 15, 27, 100;
  MTCW

Amis, Martin (Louis)
  1949- . . . . CLC 4, 9, 38, 62
  See also BEST 90:3; CA 65-68; CANR 8,
  27; DLB 14

Ammons, A(rchie) R(andolph)
  1926- . . . . CLC 2, 3, 5, 8, 9, 25, 57
  See also AITN 1; CA 9-12R; CANR 6, 36;
  DLB 5; MTCW

Amo, Tauraatua i
  See Adams, Henry (Brooks)

Anand, Mulk Raj 1905- . . . . CLC 23
  See also CA 65-68; CANR 32; MTCW

Anatol
  See Schnitzler, Arthur

Anaya, Rudolfo A(lfonso)
  1937- . . . . CLC 23; HLC
  See also CA 45-48; CAAS 4; CANR 1, 32;
  DLB 82; HW 1; MTCW

Andersen, Hans Christian
  1805-1875 . . NCLC 7; DA; SSC 6; WLC
  See also CLR 6; MAICYA; YABC 1

Anderson, C. Farley
  See Mencken, H(enry) L(ouis); Nathan,
  George Jean

Anderson, Jessica (Margaret) Queale
  . . . . CLC 37
  See also CA 9-12R; CANR 4

Anderson, Jon (Victor) 1940- . . . . CLC 9
  See also CA 25-28R; CANR 20

Anderson, Lindsay (Gordon)
  1923- . . . . CLC 20
  See also CA 125; 128

Anderson, Maxwell 1888-1959 . . . . . TCLC 2
  See also CA 105; DLB 7

Anderson, Poul (William) 1926- . . . . CLC 15
  See also AAYA 5; CA 1-4R; CAAS 2;
  CANR 2, 15, 34; DLB 8; MTCW;
  SATA 39

Anderson, Robert (Woodruff)
  1917- . . . . CLC 23
  See also AITN 1; CA 21-24R; CANR 32;
  DLB 7

Anderson, Sherwood
  1876-1941 . . . . TCLC 1, 10, 24; DA;
                                    SSC 1; WLC
  See also CA 104; 121; CDALB 1917-1929;
  DLB 4, 9, 86; DLBD 1; MTCW

Andouard
  See Giraudoux, (Hippolyte) Jean

Andrade, Carlos Drummond de . . . . . . CLC 18
  See also Drummond de Andrade, Carlos

Andrade, Mario de 1893-1945 . . . . . TCLC 43

Andrewes, Lancelot 1555-1626 . . . . LC 5

Andrews, Cicily Fairfield
  See West, Rebecca

Andrews, Elton V.
  See Pohl, Frederik

Andreyev, Leonid (Nikolaevich)
  1871-1919 . . . . TCLC 3
  See also CA 104

Andric, Ivo 1892-1975 . . . . CLC 8
  See also CA 81-84; 57-60; CANR 43;
  MTCW

Angelique, Pierre
  See Bataille, Georges

Angell, Roger 1920- . . . . CLC 26
  See also CA 57-60; CANR 13

Angelou, Maya
  1928- . . . . CLC 12, 35, 64, 77; BLC; DA
  See also AAYA 7; BW; CA 65-68;
  CANR 19, 42; DLB 38; MTCW;
  SATA 49

Annensky, Innokenty Fyodorovich
  1856-1909 . . . . TCLC 14
  See also CA 110

Anon, Charles Robert
  See Pessoa, Fernando (Antonio Nogueira)

Anouilh, Jean (Marie Lucien Pierre)
  1910-1987 . . . . . . CLC 1, 3, 8, 13, 40, 50
  See also CA 17-20R; 123; CANR 32;
  MTCW

Anthony, Florence
  See Ai

Anthony, John
  See Ciardi, John (Anthony)

Anthony, Peter
  See Shaffer, Anthony (Joshua); Shaffer,
  Peter (Levin)

Anthony, Piers 1934- . . . . CLC 35
  See also CA 21-24R; CANR 28; DLB 8;
  MTCW

Antoine, Marc
See Proust, (Valentin-Louis-George-Eugene-) Marcel

Antoninus, Brother
See Everson, William (Oliver)

Antonioni, Michelangelo 1912- ..... **CLC 20**
See also CA 73-76

Antschel, Paul 1920-1970. ..... **CLC 10, 19**
See also Celan, Paul
See also CA 85-88; CANR 33; MTCW

Anwar, Chairil 1922-1949 .... **TCLC 22**
See also CA 121

Apollinaire, Guillaume .. **TCLC 3, 8, 51; PC 7**
See also Kostrowitzki, Wilhelm Apollinaris de

Appelfeld, Aharon 1932- .... **CLC 23, 47**
See also CA 112; 133

Apple, Max (Isaac) 1941-. ...... **CLC 9, 33**
See also CA 81-84; CANR 19; DLB 130

Appleman, Philip (Dean) 1926- ..... **CLC 51**
See also CA 13-16R; CAAS 18; CANR 6, 29

Appleton, Lawrence
See Lovecraft, H(oward) P(hillips)

Apteryx
See Eliot, T(homas) S(tearns)

Apuleius, (Lucius Madaurensis)
125(?)-175(?) .... **CMLC 1**

Aquin, Hubert 1929-1977. .... **CLC 15**
See also CA 105; DLB 53

Aragon, Louis 1897-1982. .... **CLC 3, 22**
See also CA 69-72; 108; CANR 28; DLB 72; MTCW

Arany, Janos 1817-1882. .... **NCLC 34**

Arbuthnot, John 1667-1735 .... **LC 1**
See also DLB 101

Archer, Herbert Winslow
See Mencken, H(enry) L(ouis)

Archer, Jeffrey (Howard) 1940- .... **CLC 28**
See also BEST 89:3; CA 77-80; CANR 22

Archer, Jules 1915- .... **CLC 12**
See also CA 9-12R; CANR 6; SAAS 5; SATA 4

Archer, Lee
See Ellison, Harlan

Arden, John 1930- .... **CLC 6, 13, 15**
See also CA 13-16R; CAAS 4; CANR 31; DLB 13; MTCW

Arenas, Reinaldo
1943-1990 .... **CLC 41; HLC**
See also CA 124; 128; 133; HW

Arendt, Hannah 1906-1975 .... **CLC 66**
See also CA 17-20R; 61-64; CANR 26; MTCW

Aretino, Pietro 1492-1556 .... **LC 12**

Arghezi, Tudor. .... **CLC 80**
See also Theodorescu, Ion N.

Arguedas, Jose Maria
1911-1969 .... **CLC 10, 18**
See also CA 89-92; DLB 113; HW

Argueta, Manlio 1936-............. **CLC 31**
See also CA 131; HW

Ariosto, Ludovico 1474-1533. .... **LC 6**

Aristides
See Epstein, Joseph

Aristophanes
450B.C.-385B.C.... **CMLC 4; DA; DC 2**

Arlt, Roberto (Godofredo Christophersen)
1900-1942 .... **TCLC 29; HLC**
See also CA 123; 131; HW

Armah, Ayi Kwei 1939-.... **CLC 5, 33; BLC**
See also BW; CA 61-64; CANR 21; DLB 117; MTCW

Armatrading, Joan 1950-.......... **CLC 17**
See also CA 114

Arnette, Robert
See Silverberg, Robert

Arnim, Achim von (Ludwig Joachim von Arnim) 1781-1831 .... **NCLC 5**
See also DLB 90

Arnim, Bettina von 1785-1859.... **NCLC 38**
See also DLB 90

Arnold, Matthew
1822-1888 ..... **NCLC 6, 29; DA; PC 5; WLC**
See also CDBLB 1832-1890; DLB 32, 57

Arnold, Thomas 1795-1842 ...... **NCLC 18**
See also DLB 55

Arnow, Harriette (Louisa) Simpson
1908-1986 .... **CLC 2, 7, 18**
See also CA 9-12R; 118; CANR 14; DLB 6; MTCW; SATA 42, 47

Arp, Hans
See Arp, Jean

Arp, Jean 1887-1966. .... **CLC 5**
See also CA 81-84; 25-28R; CANR 42

Arrabal
See Arrabal, Fernando

Arrabal, Fernando 1932- ... **CLC 2, 9, 18, 58**
See also CA 9-12R; CANR 15

Arrick, Fran. .... **CLC 30**

Artaud, Antonin 1896-1948 ..... **TCLC 3, 36**
See also CA 104

Arthur, Ruth M(abel) 1905-1979.... **CLC 12**
See also CA 9-12R; 85-88; CANR 4; SATA 7, 26

Artsybashev, Mikhail (Petrovich)
1878-1927 .... **TCLC 31**

Arundel, Honor (Morfydd)
1919-1973 .... **CLC 17**
See also CA 21-22; 41-44R; CAP 2; SATA 4, 24

Asch, Sholem 1880-1957 .... **TCLC 3**
See also CA 105

Ash, Shalom
See Asch, Sholem

Ashbery, John (Lawrence)
1927- ...... **CLC 2, 3, 4, 6, 9, 13, 15, 25, 41, 77**
See also CA 5-8R; CANR 9, 37; DLB 5; DLBY 81; MTCW

Ashdown, Clifford
See Freeman, R(ichard) Austin

Ashe, Gordon
See Creasey, John

Ashton-Warner, Sylvia (Constance)
1908-1984 .... **CLC 19**
See also CA 69-72; 112; CANR 29; MTCW

Asimov, Isaac
1920-1992 ...... **CLC 1, 3, 9, 19, 26, 76**
See also BEST 90:2; CA 1-4R; 137; CANR 2, 19, 36; CLR 12; DLB 8; DLBY 92; JRDA; MAICYA; MTCW; SATA 1, 26, 74

Astley, Thea (Beatrice May)
1925- .... **CLC 41**
See also CA 65-68; CANR 11, 43

Aston, James
See White, T(erence) H(anbury)

Asturias, Miguel Angel
1899-1974 .... **CLC 3, 8, 13; HLC**
See also CA 25-28; 49-52; CANR 32; CAP 2; DLB 113; HW; MTCW

Atares, Carlos Saura
See Saura (Atares), Carlos

Atheling, William
See Pound, Ezra (Weston Loomis)

Atheling, William, Jr.
See Blish, James (Benjamin)

Atherton, Gertrude (Franklin Horn)
1857-1948 .... **TCLC 2**
See also CA 104; DLB 9, 78

Atherton, Lucius
See Masters, Edgar Lee

Atkins, Jack
See Harris, Mark

Atticus
See Fleming, Ian (Lancaster)

Atwood, Margaret (Eleanor)
1939- ..... **CLC 2, 3, 4, 8, 13, 15, 25, 44; DA; PC 8; SSC 2; WLC**
See also BEST 89:2; CA 49-52; CANR 3, 24, 33; DLB 53; MTCW; SATA 50

Aubigny, Pierre d'
See Mencken, H(enry) L(ouis)

Aubin, Penelope 1685-1731(?). .... **LC 9**
See also DLB 39

Auchincloss, Louis (Stanton)
1917- .... **CLC 4, 6, 9, 18, 45**
See also CA 1-4R; CANR 6, 29; DLB 2; DLBY 80; MTCW

Auden, W(ystan) H(ugh)
1907-1973 ...... **CLC 1, 2, 3, 4, 6, 9, 11, 14, 43; DA; PC 1; WLC**
See also CA 9-12R; 45-48; CANR 5; CDBLB 1914-1945; DLB 10, 20; MTCW

Audiberti, Jacques 1900-1965 ...... **CLC 38**
See also CA 25-28R

Auel, Jean M(arie) 1936-.......... **CLC 31**
See also AAYA 7; BEST 90:4; CA 103; CANR 21

Auerbach, Erich 1892-1957 .... **TCLC 43**
See also CA 118

Augier, Emile 1820-1889 .... **NCLC 31**

August, John
See De Voto, Bernard (Augustine)

Augustine, St. 354-430. .... **CMLC 6**

Aurelius
See Bourne, Randolph S(illiman)

Austen, Jane
1775-1817 .... **NCLC 1, 13, 19, 33; DA; WLC**
See also CDBLB 1789-1832; DLB 116

Auster, Paul 1947- .... **CLC 47**
See also CA 69-72; CANR 23

Austin, Frank
See Faust, Frederick (Schiller)

Austin, Mary (Hunter)
1868-1934 .... **TCLC 25**
See also CA 109; DLB 9, 78

Autran Dourado, Waldomiro
See Dourado, (Waldomiro Freitas) Autran

Averroes 1126-1198 .... **CMLC 7**
See also DLB 115

Avison, Margaret 1918- .... **CLC 2, 4**
See also CA 17-20R; DLB 53; MTCW

Axton, David
See Koontz, Dean R(ay)

Ayckbourn, Alan
1939- .... **CLC 5, 8, 18, 33, 74**
See also CA 21-24R; CANR 31; DLB 13;
MTCW

Aydy, Catherine
See Tennant, Emma (Christina)

Ayme, Marcel (Andre) 1902-1967... **CLC 11**
See also CA 89-92; CLR 25; DLB 72

Ayrton, Michael 1921-1975 .... **CLC 7**
See also CA 5-8R; 61-64; CANR 9, 21

Azorin .... **CLC 11**
See also Martinez Ruiz, Jose

Azuela, Mariano
1873-1952 .... **TCLC 3; HLC**
See also CA 104; 131; HW; MTCW

Baastad, Babbis Friis
See Friis-Baastad, Babbis Ellinor

Bab
See Gilbert, W(illiam) S(chwenck)

Babbis, Eleanor
See Friis-Baastad, Babbis Ellinor

Babel, Isaak (Emmanuilovich)
1894-1941(?) .... **TCLC 2, 13**
See also CA 104

Babits, Mihaly 1883-1941 .... **TCLC 14**
See also CA 114

Babur 1483-1530................. **LC 18**

Bacchelli, Riccardo 1891-1985 ..... **CLC 19**
See also CA 29-32R; 117

Bach, Richard (David) 1936- .... **CLC 14**
See also AITN 1; BEST 89:2; CA 9-12R;
CANR 18; MTCW; SATA 13

Bachman, Richard
See King, Stephen (Edwin)

Bachmann, Ingeborg 1926-1973..... **CLC 69**
See also CA 93-96; 45-48; DLB 85

Bacon, Francis 1561-1626 .... **LC 18**
See also CDBLB Before 1660

Bacovia, George................... **TCLC 24**
See also Vasiliu, Gheorghe

Badanes, Jerome 1937-............ **CLC 59**

Bagehot, Walter 1826-1877 ...... **NCLC 10**
See also DLB 55

Bagnold, Enid 1889-1981 .... **CLC 25**
See also CA 5-8R; 103; CANR 5, 40;
DLB 13; MAICYA; SATA 1, 25

Bagrjana, Elisaveta
See Belcheva, Elisaveta

Bagryana, Elisaveta
See Belcheva, Elisaveta

Bailey, Paul 1937- .... **CLC 45**
See also CA 21-24R; CANR 16; DLB 14

Baillie, Joanna 1762-1851 .... **NCLC 2**
See also DLB 93

Bainbridge, Beryl (Margaret)
1933- .... **CLC 4, 5, 8, 10, 14, 18, 22, 62**
See also CA 21-24R; CANR 24; DLB 14;
MTCW

Baker, Elliott 1922- .... **CLC 8**
See also CA 45-48; CANR 2

Baker, Nicholson 1957- .... **CLC 61**
See also CA 135

Baker, Ray Stannard 1870-1946 ... **TCLC 47**
See also CA 118

Baker, Russell (Wayne) 1925-...... **CLC 31**
See also BEST 89:4; CA 57-60; CANR 11,
41; MTCW

Bakshi, Ralph 1938(?)-............ **CLC 26**
See also CA 112; 138

Bakunin, Mikhail (Alexandrovich)
1814-1876 .... **NCLC 25**

Baldwin, James (Arthur)
1924-1987 ...... **CLC 1, 2, 3, 4, 5, 8, 13,
15, 17, 42, 50, 67; BLC; DA; DC 1;
SSC 10; WLC**
See also AAYA 4; BW; CA 1-4R; 124;
CABS 1; CANR 3, 24;
CDALB 1941-1968; DLB 2, 7, 33;
DLBY 87; MTCW; SATA 9, 54

Ballard, J(ames) G(raham)
1930- .... **CLC 3, 6, 14, 36; SSC 1**
See also AAYA 3; CA 5-8R; CANR 15, 39;
DLB 14; MTCW

Balmont, Konstantin (Dmitriyevich)
1867-1943 .... **TCLC 11**
See also CA 109

Balzac, Honore de
1799-1850 .... **NCLC 5, 35; DA; SSC 5;
WLC**
See also DLB 119

Bambara, Toni Cade
1939- .... **CLC 19; BLC; DA**
See also AAYA 5; BW; CA 29-32R;
CANR 24; DLB 38; MTCW

Bamdad, A.
See Shamlu, Ahmad

Banat, D. R.
See Bradbury, Ray (Douglas)

Bancroft, Laura
See Baum, L(yman) Frank

Banim, John 1798-1842 .... **NCLC 13**
See also DLB 116

Banim, Michael 1796-1874 ...... **NCLC 13**

Banks, Iain
See Banks, Iain M(enzies)

Banks, Iain M(enzies) 1954- .... **CLC 34**
See also CA 123; 128

Banks, Lynne Reid .... **CLC 23**
See also Reid Banks, Lynne
See also AAYA 6

Banks, Russell 1940- .... **CLC 37, 72**
See also CA 65-68; CAAS 15; CANR 19;
DLB 130

Banville, John 1945-.............. **CLC 46**
See also CA 117; 128; DLB 14

Banville, Theodore (Faullain) de
1832-1891 .... **NCLC 9**

Baraka, Amiri
1934- .... **CLC 1, 2, 3, 5, 10, 14, 33;
BLC; DA; PC 4**
See also Jones, LeRoi
See also BW; CA 21-24R; CABS 3;
CANR 27, 38; CDALB 1941-1968;
DLB 5, 7, 16, 38; DLBD 8; MTCW

Barbellion, W. N. P................ **TCLC 24**
See also Cummings, Bruce F(rederick)

Barbera, Jack 1945-.............. **CLC 44**
See also CA 110

Barbey d'Aurevilly, Jules Amedee
1808-1889 .... **NCLC 1**
See also DLB 119

Barbusse, Henri 1873-1935 .... **TCLC 5**
See also CA 105; DLB 65

Barclay, Bill
See Moorcock, Michael (John)

Barclay, William Ewert
See Moorcock, Michael (John)

Barea, Arturo 1897-1957 .... **TCLC 14**
See also CA 111

Barfoot, Joan 1946- .... **CLC 18**
See also CA 105

Baring, Maurice 1874-1945 .... **TCLC 8**
See also CA 105; DLB 34

Barker, Clive 1952- .... **CLC 52**
See also AAYA 10; BEST 90:3; CA 121;
129; MTCW

Barker, George Granville
1913-1991 .... **CLC 8, 48**
See also CA 9-12R; 135; CANR 7, 38;
DLB 20; MTCW

Barker, Harley Granville
See Granville-Barker, Harley
See also DLB 10

Barker, Howard 1946-............. **CLC 37**
See also CA 102; DLB 13

Barker, Pat 1943-................. **CLC 32**
See also CA 117; 122

Barlow, Joel 1754-1812 .... **NCLC 23**
See also DLB 37

Barnard, Mary (Ethel) 1909-....... **CLC 48**
See also CA 21-22; CAP 2

Barnes, Djuna
1892-1982 ... **CLC 3, 4, 8, 11, 29; SSC 3**
See also CA 9-12R; 107; CANR 16; DLB 4,
9, 45; MTCW

Barnes, Julian 1946-.............. **CLC 42**
See also CA 102; CANR 19

Barnes, Peter 1931- .... **CLC 5, 56**
See also CA 65-68; CAAS 12; CANR 33,
34; DLB 13; MTCW

Baroja (y Nessi), Pio
1872-1956 .... **TCLC 8; HLC**
See also CA 104

Baron, David
See Pinter, Harold

Baron Corvo
See Rolfe, Frederick (William Serafino
Austin Lewis Mary)

Barondess, Sue K(aufman)
1926-1977 .... **CLC 8**
See also Kaufman, Sue
See also CA 1-4R; 69-72; CANR 1

Baron de Teive
See Pessoa, Fernando (Antonio Nogueira)

Barres, Maurice 1862-1923 .... **TCLC 47**
See also DLB 123

Barreto, Afonso Henrique de Lima
See Lima Barreto, Afonso Henrique de

Barrett, (Roger) Syd 1946- .... **CLC 35**
See also Pink Floyd

Barrett, William (Christopher)
1913-1992 .... **CLC 27**
See also CA 13-16R; 139; CANR 11

Barrie, J(ames) M(atthew)
1860-1937 .... **TCLC 2**
See also CA 104; 136; CDBLB 1890-1914;
CLR 16; DLB 10; MAICYA; YABC 1

Barrington, Michael
See Moorcock, Michael (John)

Barrol, Grady
See Bograd, Larry

Barry, Mike
See Malzberg, Barry N(athaniel)

Barry, Philip 1896-1949 .... **TCLC 11**
See also CA 109; DLB 7

Bart, Andre Schwarz
See Schwarz-Bart, Andre

Barth, John (Simmons)
1930- ...... **CLC 1, 2, 3, 5, 7, 9, 10, 14,**
27, 51; SSC 10
See also AITN 1, 2; CA 1-4R; CABS 1;
CANR 5, 23; DLB 2; MTCW

Barthelme, Donald
1931-1989 ...... **CLC 1, 2, 3, 5, 6, 8, 13,**
23, 46, 59; SSC 2
Scc also CA 21-24R; 129; CANR 20;
DLB 2; DLBY 80, 89; MTCW; SATA 7,
62

Barthelme, Frederick 1943- .... **CLC 36**
See also CA 114; 122; DLBY 85

Barthes, Roland (Gerard)
1915-1980 .... **CLC 24**
See also CA 130; 97-100; MTCW

Barzun, Jacques (Martin) 1907- .... **CLC 51**
See also CA 61-64; CANR 22

Bashevis, Isaac
See Singer, Isaac Bashevis

Bashkirtseff, Marie 1859-1884 ... **NCLC 27**

Basho
See Matsuo Basho

Bass, Kingsley B., Jr.
See Bullins, Ed

Bass, Rick 1958- .... **CLC 79**
See also CA 126

Bassani, Giorgio 1916- .... **CLC 9**
See also CA 65-68; CANR 33; DLB 128;
MTCW

Bastos, Augusto (Antonio) Roa
See Roa Bastos, Augusto (Antonio)

Bataille, Georges 1897-1962 .... **CLC 29**
See also CA 101; 89-92

Bates, H(erbert) E(rnest)
1905-1974 .... **CLC 46; SSC 10**
See also CA 93-96; 45-48; CANR 34;
MTCW

Bauchart
See Camus, Albert

Baudelaire, Charles
1821-1867 ..... **NCLC 6, 29; DA; PC 1;**
WLC

Baudrillard, Jean 1929- .... **CLC 60**

Baum, L(yman) Frank 1856-1919 ... **TCLC 7**
See also CA 108; 133; CLR 15; DLB 22;
JRDA; MAICYA; MTCW; SATA 18

Baum, Louis F.
See Baum, L(yman) Frank

Baumbach, Jonathan 1933- ...... **CLC 6, 23**
See also CA 13-16R; CAAS 5; CANR 12;
DLBY 80; MTCW

Bausch, Richard (Carl) 1945- ...... **CLC 51**
See also CA 101; CAAS 14; CANR 43;
DLB 130

Baxter, Charles 1947-.......... **CLC 45, 78**
See also CA 57-60; CANR 40; DLB 130

Baxter, George Owen
See Faust, Frederick (Schiller)

Baxter, James K(eir) 1926-1972 .... **CLC 14**
See also CA 77-80

Baxter, John
See Hunt, E(verette) Howard, Jr.

Bayer, Sylvia
See Glassco, John

Beagle, Peter S(oyer) 1939-........ **CLC 7**
See also CA 9-12R; CANR 4; DLBY 80;
SATA 60

Bean, Normal
See Burroughs, Edgar Rice

Beard, Charles A(ustin)
1874-1948 .... **TCLC 15**
See also CA 115; DLB 17; SATA 18

Beardsley, Aubrey 1872-1898 ..... **NCLC 6**

Beattie, Ann
1947- .... **CLC 8, 13, 18, 40, 63; SSC 11**
See also BEST 90:2; CA 81-84; DLBY 82;
MTCW

Beattie, James 1735-1803 .... **NCLC 25**
See also DLB 109

Beauchamp, Kathleen Mansfield 1888-1923
See Mansfield, Katherine
See also CA 104; 134; DA

Beaumarchais, Pierre-Augustin Caron de
1732-1799 .... **DC 4**

Beauvoir, Simone (Lucie Ernestine Marie
Bertrand) de
1908-1986 .... **CLC 1, 2, 4, 8, 14, 31, 44,**
50, 71; DA; WLC
See also CA 9-12R; 118; CANR 28;
DLB 72; DLBY 86; MTCW

Becker, Jurek 1937-............ **CLC 7, 19**
See also CA 85-88; DLB 75

Becker, Walter 1950- .... **CLC 26**

Beckett, Samuel (Barclay)
1906-1989 ...... **CLC 1, 2, 3, 4, 6, 9, 10,**
11, 14, 18, 29, 57, 59; DA; WLC
See also CA 5-8R; 130; CANR 33;
CDBLB 1945-1960; DLB 13, 15;
DLBY 90; MTCW

Beckford, William 1760-1844 .... **NCLC 16**
See also DLB 39

Beckman, Gunnel 1910-........... **CLC 26**
See also CA 33-36R; CANR 15; CLR 25;
MAICYA; SAAS 9; SATA 6

Becque, Henri 1837-1899......... **NCLC 3**

Beddoes, Thomas Lovell
1803-1849 .... **NCLC 3**
See also DLB 96

Bedford, Donald F.
See Fearing, Kenneth (Flexner)

Beecher, Catharine Esther
1800-1878 .... **NCLC 30**
See also DLB 1

Beecher, John 1904-1980........... **CLC 6**
See also AITN 1; CA 5-8R; 105; CANR 8

Beer, Johann 1655-1700............. **LC 5**

Beer, Patricia 1924-.............. **CLC 58**
See also CA 61-64; CANR 13; DLB 40

Beerbohm, Henry Maximilian
1872-1956 .... **TCLC 1, 24**
See also CA 104; DLB 34, 100

Begiebing, Robert J(ohn) 1946-..... **CLC 70**
See also CA 122; CANR 40

Behan, Brendan
1923-1964 .... **CLC 1, 8, 11, 15, 79**
See also CA 73-76; CANR 33;
CDBLB 1945-1960; DLB 13; MTCW

Behn, Aphra
1640(?)-1689 .... **LC 1; DA; DC 4; WLC**
See also DLB 39, 80, 131

Behrman, S(amuel) N(athaniel)
1893-1973 .... **CLC 40**
See also CA 13-16; 45-48; CAP 1; DLB 7,
44

Belasco, David 1853-1931 .... **TCLC 3**
See also CA 104; DLB 7

Belcheva, Elisaveta 1893- .... **CLC 10**

Beldone, Phil "Cheech"
See Ellison, Harlan

Beleno
See Azuela, Mariano

Belinski, Vissarion Grigoryevich
1811-1848 .... **NCLC 5**

Belitt, Ben 1911-................. **CLC 22**
See also CA 13-16R; CAAS 4; CANR 7;
DLB 5

Bell, James Madison
1826-1902 .... **TCLC 43; BLC**
See also BW; CA 122; 124; DLB 50

Bell, Madison (Smartt) 1957- ...... **CLC 41**
See also CA 111; CANR 28

Bell, Marvin (Hartley) 1937-..... **CLC 8, 31**
See also CA 21-24R; CAAS 14; DLB 5;
MTCW

Bell, W. L. D.
See Mencken, H(enry) L(ouis)

Bellamy, Atwood C.
See Mencken, H(enry) L(ouis)

Bellamy, Edward 1850-1898 . . . . . . NCLC 4
See also DLB 12

Bellin, Edward J.
See Kuttner, Henry

Belloc, (Joseph) Hilaire (Pierre)
1870-1953 . . . . TCLC 7, 18
See also CA 106; DLB 19, 100; YABC 1

Belloc, Joseph Peter Rene Hilaire
See Belloc, (Joseph) Hilaire (Pierre)

Belloc, Joseph Pierre Hilaire
See Belloc, (Joseph) Hilaire (Pierre)

Belloc, M. A.
See Lowndes, Marie Adelaide (Belloc)

Bellow, Saul
1915- . . . . . . CLC 1, 2, 3, 6, 8, 10, 13, 15,
25, 33, 34, 63, 79; DA; SSC 14; WLC
See also AITN 2; BEST 89:3; CA 5-8R;
CABS 1; CANR 29; CDALB 1941-1968;
DLB 2, 28; DLBD 3; DLBY 82; MTCW

Belser, Reimond Karel Maria de
1929- . . . . CLC 14

Bely, Andrey . . . . TCLC 7
See also Bugayev, Boris Nikolayevich

Benary, Margot
See Benary-Isbert, Margot

Benary-Isbert, Margot 1889-1979 . . . CLC 12
See also CA 5-8R; 89-92; CANR 4;
CLR 12; MAICYA; SATA 2, 21

Benavente (y Martinez), Jacinto
1866-1954 . . . . TCLC 3
See also CA 106; 131; HW; MTCW

Benchley, Peter (Bradford)
1940- . . . . CLC 4, 8
See also AITN 2; CA 17-20R; CANR 12,
35; MTCW; SATA 3

Benchley, Robert (Charles)
1889-1945 . . . . TCLC 1
See also CA 105; DLB 11

Benedikt, Michael 1935- . . . . CLC 4, 14
See also CA 13-16R; CANR 7; DLB 5

Benet, Juan 1927- . . . . CLC 28
See also CA 143

Benet, Stephen Vincent
1898-1943 . . . . TCLC 7; SSC 10
See also CA 104; DLB 4, 48, 102; YABC 1

Benet, William Rose 1886-1950 . . . TCLC 28
See also CA 118; DLB 45

Benford, Gregory (Albert) 1941- . . . . CLC 52
See also CA 69-72; CANR 12, 24;
DLBY 82

Bengtsson, Frans (Gunnar)
1894-1954 . . . . TCLC 48

Benjamin, David
See Slavitt, David R(ytman)

Benjamin, Lois
See Gould, Lois

Benjamin, Walter 1892-1940 . . . . . . TCLC 39

Benn, Gottfried 1886-1956 . . . . TCLC 3
See also CA 106; DLB 56

Bennett, Alan 1934- . . . . CLC 45, 77
See also CA 103; CANR 35; MTCW

Bennett, (Enoch) Arnold
1867-1931 . . . . TCLC 5, 20
See also CA 106; CDBLB 1890-1914;
DLB 10, 34, 98

Bennett, Elizabeth
See Mitchell, Margaret (Munnerlyn)

Bennett, George Harold 1930-
See Bennett, Hal
See also BW; CA 97-100

Bennett, Hal . . . . CLC 5
See also Bennett, George Harold
See also DLB 33

Bennett, Jay 1912- . . . . CLC 35
See also AAYA 10; CA 69-72; CANR 11,
42; JRDA; SAAS 4; SATA 27, 41

Bennett, Louise (Simone)
1919- . . . . CLC 28; BLC
See also DLB 117

Benson, E(dward) F(rederic)
1867-1940 . . . . TCLC 27
See also CA 114; DLB 135

Benson, Jackson J. 1930- . . . . CLC 34
See also CA 25-28R; DLB 111

Benson, Sally 1900-1972 . . . . CLC 17
See also CA 19-20; 37-40R; CAP 1;
SATA 1, 27, 35

Benson, Stella 1892-1933 . . . . TCLC 17
See also CA 117; DLB 36

Bentham, Jeremy 1748-1832 . . . . . NCLC 38
See also DLB 107

Bentley, E(dmund) C(lerihew)
1875-1956 . . . . TCLC 12
See also CA 108; DLB 70

Bentley, Eric (Russell) 1916- . . . . CLC 24
See also CA 5-8R; CANR 6

Beranger, Pierre Jean de
1780-1857 . . . . NCLC 34

Berger, Colonel
See Malraux, (Georges-)Andre

Berger, John (Peter) 1926- . . . . . . CLC 2, 19
See also CA 81-84; DLB 14

Berger, Melvin H. 1927- . . . . CLC 12
See also CA 5-8R; CANR 4; CLR 32;
SAAS 2; SATA 5

Berger, Thomas (Louis)
1924- . . . . CLC 3, 5, 8, 11, 18, 38
See also CA 1-4R; CANR 5, 28; DLB 2;
DLBY 80; MTCW

Bergman, (Ernst) Ingmar
1918- . . . . CLC 16, 72
See also CA 81-84; CANR 33

Bergson, Henri 1859-1941 . . . . TCLC 32

Bergstein, Eleanor 1938- . . . . CLC 4
See also CA 53-56; CANR 5

Berkoff, Steven 1937- . . . . CLC 56
See also CA 104

Bermant, Chaim (Icyk) 1929- . . . . . . CLC 40
See also CA 57-60; CANR 6, 31

Bern, Victoria
See Fisher, M(ary) F(rances) K(ennedy)

Bernanos, (Paul Louis) Georges
1888-1948 . . . . TCLC 3
See also CA 104; 130; DLB 72

Bernard, April 1956- . . . . CLC 59
See also CA 131

Bernhard, Thomas
1931-1989 . . . . CLC 3, 32, 61
See also CA 85-88; 127; CANR 32;
DLB 85, 124; MTCW

Berrigan, Daniel 1921- . . . . CLC 4
See also CA 33-36R; CAAS 1; CANR 11,
43; DLB 5

Berrigan, Edmund Joseph Michael, Jr.
1934-1983
See Berrigan, Ted
See also CA 61-64; 110; CANR 14

Berrigan, Ted . . . . CLC 37
See also Berrigan, Edmund Joseph Michael,
Jr.
See also DLB 5

Berry, Charles Edward Anderson 1931-
See Berry, Chuck
See also CA 115

Berry, Chuck . . . . CLC 17
See also Berry, Charles Edward Anderson

Berry, Jonas
See Ashbery, John (Lawrence)

Berry, Wendell (Erdman)
1934- . . . . CLC 4, 6, 8, 27, 46
See also AITN 1; CA 73-76; DLB 5, 6

Berryman, John
1914-1972 . . . . . . CLC 1, 2, 3, 4, 6, 8, 10,
13, 25, 62
See also CA 13-16; 33-36R; CABS 2;
CANR 35; CAP 1; CDALB 1941-1968;
DLB 48; MTCW

Bertolucci, Bernardo 1940- . . . . CLC 16
See also CA 106

Bertrand, Aloysius 1807-1841 . . . . NCLC 31

Bertran de Born c. 1140-1215 . . . . . CMLC 5

Besant, Annie (Wood) 1847-1933 . . . TCLC 9
See also CA 105

Bessie, Alvah 1904-1985 . . . . CLC 23
See also CA 5-8R; 116; CANR 2; DLB 26

Bethlen, T. D.
See Silverberg, Robert

Beti, Mongo . . . . CLC 27; BLC
See also Biyidi, Alexandre

Betjeman, John
1906-1984 . . . . CLC 2, 6, 10, 34, 43
See also CA 9-12R; 112; CANR 33;
CDBLB 1945-1960; DLB 20; DLBY 84;
MTCW

Bettelheim, Bruno 1903-1990 . . . . . . CLC 79
See also CA 81-84; 131; CANR 23; MTCW

Betti, Ugo 1892-1953 . . . . TCLC 5
See also CA 104

Betts, Doris (Waugh) 1932- . . . . CLC 3, 6, 28
See also CA 13-16R; CANR 9; DLBY 82

Bevan, Alistair
See Roberts, Keith (John Kingston)

Beynon, John
See Harris, John (Wyndham Parkes Lucas)
Beynon

Buchheim, Lothar-Guenther 1918- ... **CLC 6**
See also CA 85-88

Buchner, (Karl) Georg
1813-1837 .... **NCLC 26**

Buchwald, Art(hur) 1925- .... **CLC 33**
See also AITN 1; CA 5-8R; CANR 21;
MTCW; SATA 10

Buck, Pearl S(ydenstricker)
1892-1973 .... **CLC 7, 11, 18; DA**
See also AITN 1; CA 1-4R; 41-44R;
CANR 1, 34; DLB 9, 102; MTCW;
SATA 1, 25

Buckler, Ernest 1908-1984 .... **CLC 13**
See also CA 11-12; 114; CAP 1; DLB 68;
SATA 47

Buckley, Vincent (Thomas)
1925-1988 .... **CLC 57**
See also CA 101

Buckley, William F(rank), Jr.
1925- .... **CLC 7, 18, 37**
See also AITN 1; CA 1-4R; CANR 1, 24;
DLBY 80; MTCW

Buechner, (Carl) Frederick
1926- .... **CLC 2, 4, 6, 9**
See also CA 13-16R; CANR 11, 39;
DLBY 80; MTCW

Buell, John (Edward) 1927- .... **CLC 10**
See also CA 1-4R; DLB 53

Buero Vallejo, Antonio 1916- ... **CLC 15, 46**
See also CA 106; CANR 24; HW; MTCW

Bufalino, Gesualdo 1920(?)- .... **CLC 74**

Bugayev, Boris Nikolayevich 1880-1934
See Bely, Andrey
See also CA 104

Bukowski, Charles
1920-1994 .... **CLC 2, 5, 9, 41, 82**
See also CA 17-20R; CANR 40; DLB 5,
130; MTCW

Bulgakov, Mikhail (Afanas'evich)
1891-1940 .... **TCLC 2, 16**
See also CA 105

Bulgya, Alexander Alexandrovich
1901-1956 .... **TCLC 53**
See also Fadeyev, Alexander
See also CA 117

Bullins, Ed 1935- .... **CLC 1, 5, 7; BLC**
See also BW; CA 49-52; CAAS 16;
CANR 24; DLB 7, 38; MTCW

Bulwer-Lytton, Edward (George Earle Lytton)
1803-1873 .... **NCLC 1**
See also DLB 21

Bunin, Ivan Alexeyevich
1870-1953 .... **TCLC 6; SSC 5**
See also CA 104

Bunting, Basil 1900-1985 .... **CLC 10, 39, 47**
See also CA 53-56; 115; CANR 7; DLB 20

Bunuel, Luis 1900-1983 .. **CLC 16, 80; HLC**
See also CA 101; 110; CANR 32; HW

Bunyan, John 1628-1688 .. **LC 4; DA; WLC**
See also CDBLB 1660-1789; DLB 39

Burford, Eleanor
See Hibbert, Eleanor Alice Burford

Burgess, Anthony
. **CLC 1, 2, 4, 5, 8, 10, 13, 15, 22, 40, 62, 81**
See also Wilson, John (Anthony) Burgess
See also AITN 1; CDBLB 1960 to Present;
DLB 14

Burke, Edmund
1729(?)-1797 .... **LC 7; DA; WLC**
See also DLB 104

Burke, Kenneth (Duva)
1897-1993 .... **CLC 2, 24**
See also CA 5-8R; 143; CANR 39; DLB 45,
63; MTCW

Burke, Leda
See Garnett, David

Burke, Ralph
See Silverberg, Robert

Burney, Fanny 1752-1840 .... **NCLC 12**
See also DLB 39

Burns, Robert
1759-1796 ...... **LC 3; DA; PC 6; WLC**
See also CDBLB 1789-1832; DLB 109

Burns, Tex
See L'Amour, Louis (Dearborn)

Burnshaw, Stanley 1906- ..... **CLC 3, 13, 44**
See also CA 9-12R; DLB 48

Burr, Anne 1937- .... **CLC 6**
See also CA 25-28R

Burroughs, Edgar Rice
1875-1950 .... **TCLC 2, 32**
See also CA 104; 132; DLB 8; MTCW;
SATA 41

Burroughs, William S(eward)
1914- .... **CLC 1, 2, 5, 15, 22, 42, 75; DA; WLC**
See also AITN 2; CA 9-12R; CANR 20;
DLB 2, 8, 16; DLBY 81; MTCW

Burton, Richard F. 1821-1890 .... **NCLC 42**
See also DLB 55

Busch, Frederick 1941- ... **CLC 7, 10, 18, 47**
See also CA 33-36R; CAAS 1; DLB 6

Bush, Ronald 1946- .... **CLC 34**
See also CA 136

Bustos, F(rancisco)
See Borges, Jorge Luis

Bustos Domecq, H(onorio)
See Bioy Casares, Adolfo; Borges, Jorge
Luis

Butler, Octavia E(stelle) 1947- ..... **CLC 38**
See also BW; CA 73-76; CANR 12, 24, 38;
DLB 33; MTCW

Butler, Robert Olen (Jr.) 1945- ..... **CLC 81**
See also CA 112

Butler, Samuel 1612-1680 .... **LC 16**
See also DLB 101, 126

Butler, Samuel
1835-1902 ...... **TCLC 1, 33; DA; WLC**
See also CA 104; CDBLB 1890-1914;
DLB 18, 57

Butler, Walter C.
See Faust, Frederick (Schiller)

Butor, Michel (Marie Francois)
1926- .... **CLC 1, 3, 8, 11, 15**
See also CA 9-12R; CANR 33; DLB 83;
MTCW

Buzo, Alexander (John) 1944- ...... **CLC 61**
See also CA 97-100; CANR 17, 39

Buzzati, Dino 1906-1972 .... **CLC 36**
See also CA 33-36R

Byars, Betsy (Cromer) 1928- .... **CLC 35**
See also CA 33-36R; CANR 18, 36; CLR 1,
16; DLB 52; JRDA; MAICYA; MTCW;
SAAS 1; SATA 4, 46

Byatt, A(ntonia) S(usan Drabble)
1936- .... **CLC 19, 65**
See also CA 13-16R; CANR 13, 33;
DLB 14; MTCW

Byrne, David 1952- .... **CLC 26**
See also CA 127

Byrne, John Keyes 1926- .... **CLC 19**
See also Leonard, Hugh
See also CA 102

Byron, George Gordon (Noel)
1788-1824 ...... **NCLC 2, 12; DA; WLC**
See also CDBLB 1789-1832; DLB 96, 110

C.3.3.
See Wilde, Oscar (Fingal O'Flahertie Wills)

Caballero, Fernan 1796-1877 ..... **NCLC 10**

Cabell, James Branch 1879-1958 ... **TCLC 6**
See also CA 105; DLB 9, 78

Cable, George Washington
1844-1925 .... **TCLC 4; SSC 4**
See also CA 104; DLB 12, 74

Cabral de Melo Neto, Joao 1920- ... **CLC 76**

Cabrera Infante, G(uillermo)
1929- .... **CLC 5, 25, 45; HLC**
See also CA 85-88; CANR 29; DLB 113;
HW; MTCW

Cade, Toni
See Bambara, Toni Cade

Cadmus
See Buchan, John

Caedmon fl. 658-680 .... **CMLC 7**

Caeiro, Alberto
See Pessoa, Fernando (Antonio Nogueira)

Cage, John (Milton, Jr.) 1912- ..... **CLC 41**
See also CA 13-16R; CANR 9

Cain, G.
See Cabrera Infante, G(uillermo)

Cain, Guillermo
See Cabrera Infante, G(uillermo)

Cain, James M(allahan)
1892-1977 .... **CLC 3, 11, 28**
See also AITN 1; CA 17-20R; 73-76;
CANR 8, 34; MTCW

Caine, Mark
See Raphael, Frederic (Michael)

Calasso, Roberto 1941- .... **CLC 81**
See also CA 143

Calderon de la Barca, Pedro
1600-1681 .... **LC 23; DC 3**

Caldwell, Erskine (Preston)
1903-1987 .... **CLC 1, 8, 14, 50, 60**
See also AITN 1; CA 1-4R; 121; CAAS 1;
CANR 2, 33; DLB 9, 86; MTCW

Caldwell, (Janet Miriam) Taylor (Holland)
1900-1985 .... **CLC 2, 28, 39**
See also CA 5-8R; 116; CANR 5

Calhoun, John Caldwell
1782-1850 . . . . NCLC 15
See also DLB 3

Calisher, Hortense   1911- . . . . CLC 2, 4, 8, 38
See also CA 1-4R; CANR 1, 22; DLB 2;
MTCW

Callaghan, Morley Edward
1903-1990 . . . . CLC 3, 14, 41, 65
See also CA 9-12R; 132; CANR 33;
DLB 68; MTCW

Calvino, Italo
1923-1985 . . . . . CLC 5, 8, 11, 22, 33, 39,
73; SSC 3
See also CA 85-88; 116; CANR 23; MTCW

Cameron, Carey   1952- . . . . CLC 59
See also CA 135

Cameron, Peter   1959- . . . . CLC 44
See also CA 125

Campana, Dino   1885-1932 . . . . TCLC 20
See also CA 117; DLB 114

Campbell, John W(ood, Jr.)
1910-1971 . . . . CLC 32
See also CA 21-22; 29-32R; CANR 34;
CAP 2; DLB 8; MTCW

Campbell, Joseph   1904-1987 . . . . CLC 69
See also AAYA 3; BEST 89:2; CA 1-4R;
124; CANR 3, 28; MTCW

Campbell, (John) Ramsey   1946- . . . . CLC 42
See also CA 57-60; CANR 7

Campbell, (Ignatius) Roy (Dunnachie)
1901-1957 . . . . TCLC 5
See also CA 104; DLB 20

Campbell, Thomas   1777-1844 . . . . NCLC 19
See also DLB 93

Campbell, Wilfred . . . . TCLC 9
See also Campbell, William

Campbell, William   1858(?)-1918
See Campbell, Wilfred
See also CA 106; DLB 92

Campos, Alvaro de
See Pessoa, Fernando (Antonio Nogueira)

Camus, Albert
1913-1960 . . . . CLC 1, 2, 4, 9, 11, 14, 32,
63, 69; DA; DC 2; SSC 9; WLC
See also CA 89-92; DLB 72; MTCW

Canby, Vincent   1924- . . . . CLC 13
See also CA 81-84

Cancale
See Desnos, Robert

Canetti, Elias   1905- . . . . . . CLC 3, 14, 25, 75
See also CA 21-24R; CANR 23; DLB 85,
124; MTCW

Canin, Ethan   1960- . . . . CLC 55
See also CA 131; 135

Cannon, Curt
See Hunter, Evan

Cape, Judith
See Page, P(atricia) K(athleen)

Capek, Karel
1890-1938 . . . . . TCLC 6, 37; DA; DC 1;
WLC
See also CA 104; 140

Capote, Truman
1924-1984 . . . . . . CLC 1, 3, 8, 13, 19, 34,
38, 58; DA; SSC 2; WLC
See also CA 5-8R; 113; CANR 18;
CDALB 1941-1968; DLB 2; DLBY 80,
84; MTCW

Capra, Frank   1897-1991 . . . . CLC 16
See also CA 61-64; 135

Caputo, Philip   1941- . . . . CLC 32
See also CA 73-76; CANR 40

Card, Orson Scott   1951- . . . . CLC 44, 47, 50
See also CA 102; CANR 27; MTCW

Cardenal (Martinez), Ernesto
1925- . . . . CLC 31; HLC
See also CA 49-52; CANR 2, 32; HW;
MTCW

Carducci, Giosue   1835-1907 . . . . . . TCLC 32

Carew, Thomas   1595(?)-1640 . . . . LC 13
See also DLB 126

Carey, Ernestine Gilbreth   1908- . . . . CLC 17
See also CA 5-8R; SATA 2

Carey, Peter   1943- . . . . CLC 40, 55
See also CA 123; 127; MTCW

Carleton, William   1794-1869 . . . . . . NCLC 3

Carlisle, Henry (Coffin)   1926- . . . . . . CLC 33
See also CA 13-16R; CANR 15

Carlsen, Chris
See Holdstock, Robert P.

Carlson, Ron(ald F.)   1947- . . . . CLC 54
See also CA 105; CANR 27

Carlyle, Thomas   1795-1881 . . NCLC 22; DA
See also CDBLB 1789-1832; DLB 55

Carman, (William) Bliss
1861-1929 . . . . TCLC 7
See also CA 104; DLB 92

Carnegie, Dale   1888-1955 . . . . TCLC 53

Carossa, Hans   1878-1956 . . . . TCLC 48
See also DLB 66

Carpenter, Don(ald Richard)
1931- . . . . CLC 41
See also CA 45-48; CANR 1

Carpentier (y Valmont), Alejo
1904-1980 . . . . CLC 8, 11, 38; HLC
See also CA 65-68; 97-100; CANR 11;
DLB 113; HW

Carr, Emily   1871-1945 . . . . TCLC 32
See also DLB 68

Carr, John Dickson   1906-1977 . . . . . . CLC 3
See also CA 49-52; 69-72; CANR 3, 33;
MTCW

Carr, Philippa
See Hibbert, Eleanor Alice Burford

Carr, Virginia Spencer   1929- . . . . CLC 34
See also CA 61-64; DLB 111

Carrier, Roch   1937- . . . . CLC 13, 78
See also CA 130; DLB 53

Carroll, James P.   1943(?)- . . . . CLC 38
See also CA 81-84

Carroll, Jim   1951- . . . . CLC 35
See also CA 45-48; CANR 42

Carroll, Lewis . . . . NCLC 2; WLC
See also Dodgson, Charles Lutwidge
See also CDBLB 1832-1890; CLR 2, 18;
DLB 18; JRDA

Carroll, Paul Vincent   1900-1968 . . . . CLC 10
See also CA 9-12R; 25-28R; DLB 10

Carruth, Hayden   1921- . . . . CLC 4, 7, 10, 18
See also CA 9-12R; CANR 4, 38; DLB 5;
MTCW; SATA 47

Carson, Rachel Louise   1907-1964 . . . CLC 71
See also CA 77-80; CANR 35; MTCW;
SATA 23

Carter, Angela (Olive)
1940-1992 . . . . . . CLC 5, 41, 76; SSC 13
See also CA 53-56; 136; CANR 12, 36;
DLB 14; MTCW; SATA 66;
SATA-Obit 70

Carter, Nick
See Smith, Martin Cruz

Carver, Raymond
1938-1988 . . . CLC 22, 36, 53, 55; SSC 8
See also CA 33-36R; 126; CANR 17, 34;
DLB 130; DLBY 84, 88; MTCW

Cary, (Arthur) Joyce (Lunel)
1888-1957 . . . . TCLC 1, 29
See also CA 104; CDBLB 1914-1945;
DLB 15, 100

Casanova de Seingalt, Giovanni Jacopo
1725-1798 . . . . LC 13

Casares, Adolfo Bioy
See Bioy Casares, Adolfo

Casely-Hayford, J(oseph) E(phraim)
1866-1930 . . . . TCLC 24; BLC
See also CA 123

Casey, John (Dudley)   1939- . . . . CLC 59
See also BEST 90:2; CA 69-72; CANR 23

Casey, Michael   1947- . . . . CLC 2
See also CA 65-68; DLB 5

Casey, Patrick
See Thurman, Wallace (Henry)

Casey, Warren (Peter)   1935-1988 . . . CLC 12
See also CA 101; 127

Casona, Alejandro . . . . CLC 49
See also Alvarez, Alejandro Rodriguez

Cassavetes, John   1929-1989 . . . . CLC 20
See also CA 85-88; 127

Cassill, R(onald) V(erlin)   1919- . . . CLC 4, 23
See also CA 9-12R; CAAS 1; CANR 7;
DLB 6

Cassity, (Allen) Turner   1929- . . . . CLC 6, 42
See also CA 17-20R; CAAS 8; CANR 11;
DLB 105

Castaneda, Carlos   1931(?)- . . . . CLC 12
See also CA 25-28R; CANR 32; HW;
MTCW

Castedo, Elena   1937- . . . . CLC 65
See also CA 132

Castedo-Ellerman, Elena
See Castedo, Elena

Castellanos, Rosario
1925-1974 . . . . CLC 66; HLC
See also CA 131; 53-56; DLB 113; HW

Castelvetro, Lodovico   1505-1571 . . . . . LC 12

Castiglione, Baldassare   1478-1529 . . . LC 12

Castle, Robert
See Hamilton, Edmond

Castro, Guillen de   1569-1631 . . . . LC 19

Castro, Rosalia de   1837-1885 . . . . . NCLC 3

Cather, Willa
  See Cather, Willa Sibert

Cather, Willa Sibert
  1873-1947 .... TCLC 1, 11, 31; DA;
                              SSC 2; WLC
  See also CA 104; 128; CDALB 1865-1917;
  DLB 9, 54, 78; DLBD 1; MTCW;
  SATA 30

Catton, (Charles) Bruce
  1899-1978 .... CLC 35
  See also AITN 1; CA 5-8R; 81-84;
  CANR 7; DLB 17; SATA 2, 24

Cauldwell, Frank
  See King, Francis (Henry)

Caunitz, William J.   1933- .... CLC 34
  See also BEST 89:3; CA 125; 130

Causley, Charles (Stanley)   1917-..... CLC 7
  See also CA 9-12R; CANR 5, 35; CLR 30;
  DLB 27; MTCW; SATA 3, 66

Caute, David   1936-............... CLC 29
  See also CA 1-4R; CAAS 4; CANR 1, 33;
  DLB 14

Cavafy, C(onstantine) P(eter)...... TCLC 2, 7
  See also Kavafis, Konstantinos Petrou

Cavallo, Evelyn
  See Spark, Muriel (Sarah)

Cavanna, Betty .... CLC 12
  See also Harrison, Elizabeth Cavanna
  See also JRDA; MAICYA; SAAS 4;
  SATA 1, 30

Caxton, William   1421(?)-1491(?)..... LC 17

Cayrol, Jean   1911-............... CLC 11
  See also CA 89-92; DLB 83

Cela, Camilo Jose
  1916- .... CLC 4, 13, 59; HLC
  See also BEST 90:2; CA 21-24R; CAAS 10;
  CANR 21, 32; DLBY 89; HW; MTCW

Celan, Paul .... CLC 53, 82
  See also Antschel, Paul
  See also DLB 69

Celine, Louis-Ferdinand
  .... CLC 1, 3, 4, 7, 9, 15, 47
  See also Destouches, Louis-Ferdinand
  See also DLB 72

Cellini, Benvenuto   1500-1571 .... LC 7

Cendrars, Blaise
  See Sauser-Hall, Frederic

Cernuda (y Bidon), Luis
  1902-1963 .... CLC 54
  See also CA 131; 89-92; DLB 134; HW

Cervantes (Saavedra), Miguel de
  1547-1616 ...... LC 6, 23; DA; SSC 12;
                                      WLC

Cesaire, Aime (Fernand)
  1913- .... CLC 19, 32; BLC
  See also BW; CA 65-68; CANR 24, 43;
  MTCW

Chabon, Michael   1965(?)- .... CLC 55
  See also CA 139

Chabrol, Claude   1930- .... CLC 16
  See also CA 110

Challans, Mary   1905-1983
  See Renault, Mary
  See also CA 81-84; 111; SATA 23, 36

Challis, George
  See Faust, Frederick (Schiller)

Chambers, Aidan   1934- .... CLC 35
  See also CA 25-28R; CANR 12, 31; JRDA;
  MAICYA; SAAS 12; SATA 1, 69

Chambers, James   1948-
  See Cliff, Jimmy
  See also CA 124

Chambers, Jessie
  See Lawrence, D(avid) H(erbert Richards)

Chambers, Robert W.   1865-1933... TCLC 41

Chandler, Raymond (Thornton)
  1888-1959 .... TCLC 1, 7
  See also CA 104; 129; CDALB 1929-1941;
  DLBD 6; MTCW

Chang, Jung   1952- .... CLC 71
  See also CA 142

Channing, William Ellery
  1780-1842 .... NCLC 17
  See also DLB 1, 59

Chaplin, Charles Spencer
  1889-1977 .... CLC 16
  See also Chaplin, Charlie
  See also CA 81-84; 73-76

Chaplin, Charlie
  See Chaplin, Charles Spencer
  See also DLB 44

Chapman, George   1559(?)-1634...... LC 22
  See also DLB 62, 121

Chapman, Graham   1941-1989 ...... CLC 21
  See also Monty Python
  See also CA 116; 129; CANR 35

Chapman, John Jay   1862-1933 ..... TCLC 7
  See also CA 104

Chapman, Walker
  See Silverberg, Robert

Chappell, Fred (Davis)   1936-.... CLC 40, 78
  See also CA 5-8R; CAAS 4; CANR 8, 33;
  DLB 6, 105

Char, Rene(-Emile)
  1907-1988 .... CLC 9, 11, 14, 55
  See also CA 13-16R; 124; CANR 32;
  MTCW

Charby, Jay
  See Ellison, Harlan

Chardin, Pierre Teilhard de
  See Teilhard de Chardin, (Marie Joseph)
  Pierre

Charles I   1600-1649 .... LC 13

Charyn, Jerome   1937- .... CLC 5, 8, 18
  See also CA 5-8R; CAAS 1; CANR 7;
  DLBY 83; MTCW

Chase, Mary (Coyle)   1907-1981 ...... DC 1
  See also CA 77-80; 105; SATA 17, 29

Chase, Mary Ellen   1887-1973....... CLC 2
  See also CA 13-16; 41-44R; CAP 1;
  SATA 10

Chase, Nicholas
  See Hyde, Anthony

Chateaubriand, Francois Rene de
  1768-1848 .... NCLC 3
  See also DLB 119

Chatterje, Sarat Chandra   1876-1936(?)
  See Chatterji, Saratchandra
  See also CA 109

Chatterji, Bankim Chandra
  1838-1894 .... NCLC 19

Chatterji, Saratchandra .... TCLC 13
  See also Chatterje, Sarat Chandra

Chatterton, Thomas   1752-1770 .... LC 3
  See also DLB 109

Chatwin, (Charles) Bruce
  1940-1989 .... CLC 28, 57, 59
  See also AAYA 4; BEST 90:1; CA 85-88;
  127

Chaucer, Daniel
  See Ford, Ford Madox

Chaucer, Geoffrey
  1340(?)-1400 .... LC 17; DA
  See also CDBLB Before 1660

Chaviaras, Strates   1935-
  See Haviaras, Stratis
  See also CA 105

Chayefsky, Paddy .... CLC 23
  See also Chayefsky, Sidney
  See also DLB 7, 44; DLBY 81

Chayefsky, Sidney   1923-1981
  See Chayefsky, Paddy
  See also CA 9-12R; 104; CANR 18

Chedid, Andree   1920-............. CLC 47

Cheever, John
  1912-1982 ...... CLC 3, 7, 8, 11, 15, 25,
                              64; DA; SSC 1; WLC
  See also CA 5-8R; 106; CABS 1; CANR 5,
  27; CDALB 1941-1968; DLB 2, 102;
  DLBY 80, 82; MTCW

Cheever, Susan   1943-.......... CLC 18, 48
  See also CA 103; CANR 27; DLBY 82

Chekhonte, Antosha
  See Chekhov, Anton (Pavlovich)

Chekhov, Anton (Pavlovich)
  1860-1904 .... TCLC 3, 10, 31; DA;
                              SSC 2; WLC
  See also CA 104; 124

Chernyshevsky, Nikolay Gavrilovich
  1828-1889 .... NCLC 1

Cherry, Carolyn Janice   1942-
  See Cherryh, C. J.
  See also CA 65-68; CANR 10

Cherryh, C. J. .... CLC 35
  See also Cherry, Carolyn Janice
  See also DLBY 80

Chesnutt, Charles W(addell)
  1858-1932 .... TCLC 5, 39; BLC; SSC 7
  See also BW; CA 106; 125; DLB 12, 50, 78;
  MTCW

Chester, Alfred   1929(?)-1971....... CLC 49
  See also CA 33-36R; DLB 130

Chesterton, G(ilbert) K(eith)
  1874-1936 .... TCLC 1, 6; SSC 1
  See also CA 104; 132; CDBLB 1914-1945;
  DLB 10, 19, 34, 70, 98; MTCW;
  SATA 27

Chiang Pin-chin   1904-1986
  See Ding Ling
  See also CA 118

Cohen, Matt 1942- .... **CLC 19**
See also CA 61-64; CAAS 18; CANR 40;
DLB 53

Cohen-Solal, Annie 19(?)- .... **CLC 50**

Colegate, Isabel 1931- .... **CLC 36**
See also CA 17-20R; CANR 8, 22; DLB 14;
MTCW

Coleman, Emmett
See Reed, Ishmael

Coleridge, Samuel Taylor
1772-1834 .... **NCLC 9; DA; WLC**
See also CDBLB 1789-1832; DLB 93, 107

Coleridge, Sara 1802-1852 .... **NCLC 31**

Coles, Don 1928- .... **CLC 46**
See also CA 115; CANR 38

Colette, (Sidonie-Gabrielle)
1873-1954 ...... **TCLC 1, 5, 16; SSC 10**
See also CA 104; 131; DLB 65; MTCW

Collett, (Jacobine) Camilla (Wergeland)
1813-1895 .... **NCLC 22**

Collier, Christopher 1930- .... **CLC 30**
See also CA 33-36R; CANR 13, 33; JRDA;
MAICYA; SATA 16, 70

Collier, James L(incoln) 1928- ..... **CLC 30**
See also CA 9-12R; CANR 4, 33; JRDA;
MAICYA; SATA 8, 70

Collier, Jeremy 1650-1726 .... **LC 6**

Collins, Hunt
See Hunter, Evan

Collins, Linda 1931- .... **CLC 44**
See also CA 125

Collins, (William) Wilkie
1824-1889 .... **NCLC 1, 18**
See also CDBLB 1832-1890; DLB 18, 70

Collins, William 1721-1759 .... **LC 4**
See also DLB 109

Colman, George
See Glassco, John

Colt, Winchester Remington
See Hubbard, L(afayette) Ron(ald)

Colter, Cyrus 1910- .... **CLC 58**
See also BW; CA 65-68; CANR 10; DLB 33

Colton, James
See Hansen, Joseph

Colum, Padraic 1881-1972 .... **CLC 28**
See also CA 73-76; 33-36R; CANR 35;
MAICYA; MTCW; SATA 15

Colvin, James
See Moorcock, Michael (John)

Colwin, Laurie (E.)
1944-1992 .... **CLC 5, 13, 23**
See also CA 89-92; 139; CANR 20;
DLBY 80; MTCW

Comfort, Alex(ander) 1920- .... **CLC 7**
See also CA 1-4R; CANR 1

Comfort, Montgomery
See Campbell, (John) Ramsey

Compton-Burnett, I(vy)
1884(?)-1969 ...... **CLC 1, 3, 10, 15, 34**
See also CA 1-4R; 25-28R; CANR 4;
DLB 36; MTCW

Comstock, Anthony 1844-1915 .... **TCLC 13**
See also CA 110

Conan Doyle, Arthur
See Doyle, Arthur Conan

Conde, Maryse .... **CLC 52**
See also Boucolon, Maryse

Condon, Richard (Thomas)
1915- .... **CLC 4, 6, 8, 10, 45**
See also BEST 90:3; CA 1-4R; CAAS 1;
CANR 2, 23; MTCW

Congreve, William
1670-1729 ... **LC 5, 21; DA; DC 2; WLC**
See also CDBLB 1660-1789; DLB 39, 84

Connell, Evan S(helby), Jr.
1924- .... **CLC 4, 6, 45**
See also AAYA 7; CA 1-4R; CAAS 2;
CANR 2, 39; DLB 2; DLBY 81; MTCW

Connelly, Marc(us Cook)
1890-1980 .... **CLC 7**
See also CA 85-88; 102; CANR 30; DLB 7;
DLBY 80; SATA 25

Connor, Ralph .... **TCLC 31**
See also Gordon, Charles William
See also DLB 92

Conrad, Joseph
1857-1924 ...... **TCLC 1, 6, 13, 25, 43;**
DA; SSC 9; WLC
See also CA 104; 131; CDBLB 1890-1914;
DLB 10, 34, 98; MTCW; SATA 27

Conrad, Robert Arnold
See Hart, Moss

Conroy, Pat 1945- .... **CLC 30, 74**
See also AAYA 8; AITN 1; CA 85-88;
CANR 24; DLB 6; MTCW

Constant (de Rebecque), (Henri) Benjamin
1767-1830 .... **NCLC 6**
See also DLB 119

Conybeare, Charles Augustus
See Eliot, T(homas) S(tearns)

Cook, Michael 1933- .... **CLC 58**
See also CA 93-96; DLB 53

Cook, Robin 1940- .... **CLC 14**
See also BEST 90:2; CA 108; 111;
CANR 41

Cook, Roy
See Silverberg, Robert

Cooke, Elizabeth 1948- .... **CLC 55**
See also CA 129

Cooke, John Esten 1830-1886 ..... **NCLC 5**
See also DLB 3

Cooke, John Estes
See Baum, L(yman) Frank

Cooke, M. E.
See Creasey, John

Cooke, Margaret
See Creasey, John

Cooney, Ray .... **CLC 62**

Cooper, Henry St. John
See Creasey, John

Cooper, J. California .... **CLC 56**
See also BW; CA 125

Cooper, James Fenimore
1789-1851 .... **NCLC 1, 27**
See also CDALB 1640-1865; DLB 3;
SATA 19

Coover, Robert (Lowell)
1932- .... **CLC 3, 7, 15, 32, 46**
See also CA 45-48; CANR 3, 37; DLB 2;
DLBY 81; MTCW

Copeland, Stewart (Armstrong)
1952- .... **CLC 26**
See also Police, The

Coppard, A(lfred) E(dgar)
1878-1957 .... **TCLC 5**
See also CA 114; YABC 1

Coppee, Francois 1842-1908 ...... **TCLC 25**

Coppola, Francis Ford 1939- .... **CLC 16**
See also CA 77-80; CANR 40; DLB 44

Corbiere, Tristan 1845-1875 ..... **NCLC 43**

Corcoran, Barbara 1911- .... **CLC 17**
See also CA 21-24R; CAAS 2; CANR 11,
28; DLB 52; JRDA; SATA 3

Cordelier, Maurice
See Giraudoux, (Hippolyte) Jean

Corelli, Marie 1855-1924 .... **TCLC 51**
See also Mackay, Mary
See also DLB 34

Corman, Cid .... **CLC 9**
See also Corman, Sidney
See also CAAS 2; DLB 5

Corman, Sidney 1924-
See Corman, Cid
See also CA 85-88

Cormier, Robert (Edmund)
1925- .... **CLC 12, 30; DA**
See also AAYA 3; CA 1-4R; CANR 5, 23;
CDALB 1968-1988; CLR 12; DLB 52;
JRDA; MAICYA; MTCW; SATA 10, 45

Corn, Alfred 1943- .... **CLC 33**
See also CA 104; DLB 120; DLBY 80

Cornwell, David (John Moore)
1931- .... **CLC 9, 15**
See also le Carre, John
See also CA 5-8R; CANR 13, 33; MTCW

Corrigan, Kevin .... **CLC 55**

Corso, (Nunzio) Gregory 1930- ... **CLC 1, 11**
See also CA 5-8R; CANR 41; DLB 5, 16;
MTCW

Cortazar, Julio
1914-1984 ...... **CLC 2, 3, 5, 10, 13, 15,**
33, 34; HLC; SSC 7
See also CA 21-24R; CANR 12, 32;
DLB 113; HW; MTCW

Corwin, Cecil
See Kornbluth, C(yril) M.

Cosic, Dobrica 1921- .... **CLC 14**
See also CA 122; 138

Costain, Thomas B(ertram)
1885-1965 .... **CLC 30**
See also CA 5-8R; 25-28R; DLB 9

Costantini, Humberto
1924(?)-1987 .... **CLC 49**
See also CA 131; 122; HW

Costello, Elvis 1955- .... **CLC 21**

Cotter, Joseph S. Sr.
See Cotter, Joseph Seamon Sr.

Cotter, Joseph Seamon Sr.
1861-1949 .... **TCLC 28; BLC**
See also BW; CA 124; DLB 50

Couch, Arthur Thomas Quiller
See Quiller-Couch, Arthur Thomas

Coulton, James
See Hansen, Joseph

Couperus, Louis (Marie Anne)
1863-1923 .... **TCLC 15**
See also CA 115

Court, Wesli
See Turco, Lewis (Putnam)

Courtenay, Bryce 1933- .... **CLC 59**
See also CA 138

Courtney, Robert
See Ellison, Harlan

Cousteau, Jacques-Yves 1910- ...... **CLC 30**
See also CA 65-68; CANR 15; MTCW;
SATA 38

Coward, Noel (Peirce)
1899-1973 .... **CLC 1, 9, 29, 51**
See also AITN 1; CA 17-18; 41-44R;
CANR 35; CAP 2; CDBLB 1914-1945;
DLB 10; MTCW

Cowley, Malcolm 1898-1989 .... **CLC 39**
See also CA 5-8R; 128; CANR 3; DLB 4,
48; DLBY 81, 89; MTCW

Cowper, William 1731-1800 .... **NCLC 8**
See also DLB 104, 109

Cox, William Trevor 1928- ... **CLC 9, 14, 71**
See also Trevor, William
See also CA 9-12R; CANR 4, 37; DLB 14;
MTCW

Cozzens, James Gould
1903-1978 .... **CLC 1, 4, 11**
See also CA 9-12R; 81-84; CANR 19;
CDALB 1941-1968; DLB 9; DLBD 2;
DLBY 84; MTCW

Crabbe, George 1754-1832 .... **NCLC 26**
See also DLB 93

Craig, A. A.
See Anderson, Poul (William)

Craik, Dinah Maria (Mulock)
1826-1887 .... **NCLC 38**
See also DLB 35; MAICYA; SATA 34

Cram, Ralph Adams 1863-1942 .... **TCLC 45**

Crane, (Harold) Hart
1899-1932 .... **TCLC 2, 5; DA; PC 3;
WLC**
See also CA 104; 127; CDALB 1917-1929;
DLB 4, 48; MTCW

Crane, R(onald) S(almon)
1886-1967 .... **CLC 27**
See also CA 85-88; DLB 63

Crane, Stephen (Townley)
1871-1900 .... **TCLC 11, 17, 32; DA;
SSC 7; WLC**
See also CA 109; 140; CDALB 1865-1917;
DLB 12, 54, 78; YABC 2

Crase, Douglas 1944- .... **CLC 58**
See also CA 106

Crashaw, Richard 1612(?)-1649 ...... **LC 24**
See also DLB 126

Craven, Margaret 1901-1980 .... **CLC 17**
See also CA 103

Crawford, F(rancis) Marion
1854-1909 .... **TCLC 10**
See also CA 107; DLB 71

Crawford, Isabella Valancy
1850-1887 .... **NCLC 12**
See also DLB 92

Crayon, Geoffrey
See Irving, Washington

Creasey, John 1908-1973 .... **CLC 11**
See also CA 5-8R; 41-44R; CANR 8;
DLB 77; MTCW

Crebillon, Claude Prosper Jolyot de (fils)
1707-1777 .... **LC 1**

Credo
See Creasey, John

Creeley, Robert (White)
1926- ..... **CLC 1, 2, 4, 8, 11, 15, 36, 78**
See also CA 1-4R; CAAS 10; CANR 23, 43;
DLB 5, 16; MTCW

Crews, Harry (Eugene)
1935- .... **CLC 6, 23, 49**
See also AITN 1; CA 25-28R; CANR 20;
DLB 6; MTCW

Crichton, (John) Michael
1942- .... **CLC 2, 6, 54**
See also AAYA 10; AITN 2; CA 25-28R;
CANR 13, 40; DLBY 81; JRDA;
MTCW; SATA 9

Crispin, Edmund .... **CLC 22**
See Montgomery, (Robert) Bruce
See also DLB 87

Cristofer, Michael 1945(?)- .... **CLC 28**
See also CA 110; DLB 7

Croce, Benedetto 1866-1952 ...... **TCLC 37**
See also CA 120

Crockett, David 1786-1836 .... **NCLC 8**
See also DLB 3, 11

Crockett, Davy
See Crockett, David

Croker, John Wilson 1780-1857 .. **NCLC 10**
See also DLB 110

Crommelynck, Fernand 1885-1970 .. **CLC 75**
See also CA 89-92

Cronin, A(rchibald) J(oseph)
1896-1981 .... **CLC 32**
See also CA 1-4R; 102; CANR 5; SATA 25,
47

Cross, Amanda
See Heilbrun, Carolyn G(old)

Crothers, Rachel 1878(?)-1958 ..... **TCLC 19**
See also CA 113; DLB 7

Croves, Hal
See Traven, B.

Crowfield, Christopher
See Stowe, Harriet (Elizabeth) Beecher

Crowley, Aleister .... **TCLC 7**
See also Crowley, Edward Alexander

Crowley, Edward Alexander 1875-1947
See Crowley, Aleister
See also CA 104

Crowley, John 1942- .... **CLC 57**
See also CA 61-64; CANR 43; DLBY 82;
SATA 65

Crud
See Crumb, R(obert)

Crumarums
See Crumb, R(obert)

Crumb, R(obert) 1943- .... **CLC 17**
See also CA 106

Crumbum
See Crumb, R(obert)

Crumski
See Crumb, R(obert)

Crum the Bum
See Crumb, R(obert)

Crunk
See Crumb, R(obert)

Crustt
See Crumb, R(obert)

Cryer, Gretchen (Kiger) 1935- ...... **CLC 21**
See also CA 114; 123

Csath, Geza 1887-1919 .... **TCLC 13**
See also CA 111

Cudlip, David 1933- .... **CLC 34**

Cullen, Countee
1903-1946 ...... **TCLC 4, 37; BLC; DA**
See also BW; CA 108; 124;
CDALB 1917-1929; DLB 4, 48, 51;
MTCW; SATA 18

Cum, R.
See Crumb, R(obert)

Cummings, Bruce F(rederick) 1889-1919
See Barbellion, W. N. P.
See also CA 123

Cummings, E(dward) E(stlin)
1894-1962 ...... **CLC 1, 3, 8, 12, 15, 68;
DA; PC 5; WLC 2**
See also CA 73-76; CANR 31;
CDALB 1929-1941; DLB 4, 48; MTCW

Cunha, Euclides (Rodrigues Pimenta) da
1866-1909 .... **TCLC 24**
See also CA 123

Cunningham, E. V.
See Fast, Howard (Melvin)

Cunningham, J(ames) V(incent)
1911-1985 .... **CLC 3, 31**
See also CA 1-4R; 115; CANR 1; DLB 5

Cunningham, Julia (Woolfolk)
1916- .... **CLC 12**
See also CA 9-12R; CANR 4, 19, 36;
JRDA; MAICYA; SAAS 2; SATA 1, 26

Cunningham, Michael 1952- .... **CLC 34**
See also CA 136

Cunninghame Graham, R(obert) B(ontine)
1852-1936 .... **TCLC 19**
See also Graham, R(obert) B(ontine)
Cunninghame
See also CA 119; DLB 98

Currie, Ellen 19(?)- .... **CLC 44**

Curtin, Philip
See Lowndes, Marie Adelaide (Belloc)

Curtis, Price
See Ellison, Harlan

Cutrate, Joe
See Spiegelman, Art

Czaczkes, Shmuel Yosef
See Agnon, S(hmuel) Y(osef Halevi)

D. P.
See Wells, H(erbert) G(eorge)

Dabrowska, Maria (Szumska)
1889-1965 .... **CLC 15**
See also CA 106

Dabydeen, David 1955- .... **CLC 34**
See also BW; CA 125

Dacey, Philip 1939- .... **CLC 51**
See also CA 37-40R; CAAS 17; CANR 14,
32; DLB 105

Dagerman, Stig (Halvard)
1923-1954 .... **TCLC 17**
See also CA 117

Dahl, Roald 1916-1990..... **CLC 1, 6, 18, 79**
See also CA 1-4R; 133; CANR 6, 32, 37;
CLR 1, 7; JRDA; MAICYA; MTCW;
SATA 1, 26, 73; SATA-Obit 65

Dahlberg, Edward 1900-1977... **CLC 1, 7, 14**
See also CA 9-12R; 69-72; CANR 31;
DLB 48; MTCW

Dale, Colin...................... **TCLC 18**
See also Lawrence, T(homas) E(dward)

Dale, George E.
See Asimov, Isaac

Daly, Elizabeth 1878-1967......... **CLC 52**
See also CA 23-24; 25-28R; CAP 2

Daly, Maureen 1921- .... **CLC 17**
See also AAYA 5; CANR 37; JRDA;
MAICYA; SAAS 1; SATA 2

Daniel, Samuel 1562(?)-1619....... **LC 24**
See also DLB 62

Daniels, Brett
See Adler, Renata

Dannay, Frederic 1905-1982 .... **CLC 11**
See also Queen, Ellery
See also CA 1-4R; 107; CANR 1, 39;
MTCW

D'Annunzio, Gabriele
1863-1938 .... **TCLC 6, 40**
See also CA 104

d'Antibes, Germain
See Simenon, Georges (Jacques Christian)

Danvers, Dennis 1947-............ **CLC 70**

Danziger, Paula 1944- .... **CLC 21**
See also AAYA 4; CA 112; 115; CANR 37;
CLR 20; JRDA; MAICYA; SATA 30,
36, 63

Dario, Ruben 1867-1916 .... **TCLC 4; HLC**
See also CA 131; HW; MTCW

Darley, George 1795-1846........ **NCLC 2**
See also DLB 96

Daryush, Elizabeth 1887-1977.... **CLC 6, 19**
See also CA 49-52; CANR 3; DLB 20

Daudet, (Louis Marie) Alphonse
1840-1897 .... **NCLC 1**
See also DLB 123

Daumal, Rene 1908-1944........ **TCLC 14**
See also CA 114

Davenport, Guy (Mattison, Jr.)
1927- .... **CLC 6, 14, 38**
See also CA 33-36R; CANR 23; DLB 130

Davidson, Avram 1923-
See Queen, Ellery
See also CA 101; CANR 26; DLB 8

Davidson, Donald (Grady)
1893-1968 .... **CLC 2, 13, 19**
See also CA 5-8R; 25-28R; CANR 4;
DLB 45

Davidson, Hugh
See Hamilton, Edmond

Davidson, John 1857-1909....... **TCLC 24**
See also CA 118; DLB 19

Davidson, Sara 1943- .... **CLC 9**
See also CA 81-84

Davie, Donald (Alfred)
1922- .... **CLC 5, 8, 10, 31**
See also CA 1-4R; CAAS 3; CANR 1;
DLB 27; MTCW

Davies, Ray(mond Douglas) 1944- .. **CLC 21**
See also CA 116

Davies, Rhys 1903-1978........... **CLC 23**
See also CA 9-12R; 81-84; CANR 4

Davies, (William) Robertson
1913- ..... **CLC 2, 7, 13, 25, 42, 75; DA;
WLC**
See also BEST 89:2; CA 33-36R; CANR 17,
42; DLB 68; MTCW

Davies, W(illiam) H(enry)
1871-1940 .... **TCLC 5**
See also CA 104; DLB 19

Davies, Walter C.
See Kornbluth, C(yril) M.

Davis, Angela (Yvonne) 1944-...... **CLC 77**
See also BW; CA 57-60; CANR 10

Davis, B. Lynch
See Bioy Casares, Adolfo; Borges, Jorge
Luis

Davis, Gordon
See Hunt, E(verette) Howard, Jr.

Davis, Harold Lenoir 1896-1960.... **CLC 49**
See also CA 89-92; DLB 9

Davis, Rebecca (Blaine) Harding
1831-1910 .... **TCLC 6**
See also CA 104; DLB 74

Davis, Richard Harding
1864-1916 .... **TCLC 24**
See also CA 114; DLB 12, 23, 78, 79

Davison, Frank Dalby 1893-1970 ... **CLC 15**
See also CA 116

Davison, Lawrence H.
See Lawrence, D(avid) H(erbert Richards)

Davison, Peter (Hubert) 1928- ..... **CLC 28**
See also CA 9-12R; CAAS 4; CANR 3, 43;
DLB 5

Davys, Mary 1674-1732............. **LC 1**
See also DLB 39

Dawson, Fielding 1930- .... **CLC 6**
See also CA 85-88; DLB 130

Dawson, Peter
See Faust, Frederick (Schiller)

Day, Clarence (Shepard, Jr.)
1874-1935 .... **TCLC 25**
See also CA 108; DLB 11

Day, Thomas 1748-1789............. **LC 1**
See also DLB 39; YABC 1

Day Lewis, C(ecil)
1904-1972 .... **CLC 1, 6, 10**
See also Blake, Nicholas
See also CA 13-16; 33-36R; CANR 34;
CAP 1; DLB 15, 20; MTCW

Dazai, Osamu .... **TCLC 11**
See also Tsushima, Shuji

de Andrade, Carlos Drummond
See Drummond de Andrade, Carlos

Deane, Norman
See Creasey, John

**de Beauvoir, Simone (Lucie Ernestine Marie
Bertrand)**
See Beauvoir, Simone (Lucie Ernestine
Marie Bertrand) de

de Brissac, Malcolm
See Dickinson, Peter (Malcolm)

de Chardin, Pierre Teilhard
See Teilhard de Chardin, (Marie Joseph)
Pierre

Dee, John 1527-1608 .... **LC 20**

Deer, Sandra 1940-............... **CLC 45**

De Ferrari, Gabriella .... **CLC 65**

Defoe, Daniel
1660(?)-1731 .... **LC 1; DA; WLC**
See also CDBLB 1660-1789; DLB 39, 95,
101; JRDA; MAICYA; SATA 22

de Gourmont, Remy
See Gourmont, Remy de

de Hartog, Jan 1914-............. **CLC 19**
See also CA 1-4R; CANR 1

de Hostos, E. M.
See Hostos (y Bonilla), Eugenio Maria de

de Hostos, Eugenio M.
See Hostos (y Bonilla), Eugenio Maria de

Deighton, Len .... **CLC 4, 7, 22, 46**
See also Deighton, Leonard Cyril
See also AAYA 6; BEST 89:2;
CDBLB 1960 to Present; DLB 87

Deighton, Leonard Cyril 1929-
See Deighton, Len
See also CA 9-12R; CANR 19, 33; MTCW

Dekker, Thomas 1572(?)-1632....... **LC 22**
See also CDBLB Before 1660; DLB 62

de la Mare, Walter (John)
1873-1956 .. **TCLC 4, 53; SSC 14; WLC**
See also CDBLB 1914-1945; CLR 23;
DLB 19; SATA 16

Delaney, Franey
See O'Hara, John (Henry)

Delaney, Shelagh 1939- .... **CLC 29**
See also CA 17-20R; CANR 30;
CDBLB 1960 to Present; DLB 13;
MTCW

Delany, Mary (Granville Pendarves)
1700-1788 .... **LC 12**

Delany, Samuel R(ay, Jr.)
1942- .... **CLC 8, 14, 38; BLC**
See also BW; CA 81-84; CANR 27, 43;
DLB 8, 33; MTCW

De La Ramee, (Marie) Louise 1839-1908
See Ouida
See also SATA 20

de la Roche, Mazo 1879-1961 ...... CLC **14**
See also CA 85-88; CANR 30; DLB 68;
SATA 64

Delbanco, Nicholas (Franklin)
1942- .... CLC **6, 13**
See also CA 17-20R; CAAS 2; CANR 29;
DLB 6

del Castillo, Michel 1933- .... CLC **38**
See also CA 109

Deledda, Grazia (Cosima)
1875(?)-1936 .... TCLC **23**
See also CA 123

Delibes, Miguel .... CLC **8, 18**
See also Delibes Setien, Miguel

Delibes Setien, Miguel 1920-
See Delibes, Miguel
See also CA 45-48; CANR 1, 32; HW;
MTCW

DeLillo, Don
1936- ..... CLC **8, 10, 13, 27, 39, 54, 76**
See also BEST 89:1; CA 81-84; CANR 21;
DLB 6; MTCW

de Lisser, H. G.
See De Lisser, Herbert George
See also DLB 117

De Lisser, Herbert George
1878-1944 .... TCLC **12**
See also de Lisser, H. G.
See also CA 109

Deloria, Vine (Victor), Jr. 1933- .... CLC **21**
See also CA 53-56; CANR 5, 20; MTCW;
SATA 21

Del Vecchio, John M(ichael)
1947- .... CLC **29**
See also CA 110; DLBD 9

de Man, Paul (Adolph Michel)
1919-1983 .... CLC **55**
See also CA 128; 111; DLB 67; MTCW

De Marinis, Rick 1934- .... CLC **54**
See also CA 57-60; CANR 9, 25

Demby, William 1922- .... CLC **53; BLC**
See also BW; CA 81-84; DLB 33

Demijohn, Thom
See Disch, Thomas M(ichael)

de Montherlant, Henry (Milon)
See Montherlant, Henry (Milon) de

de Natale, Francine
See Malzberg, Barry N(athaniel)

Denby, Edwin (Orr) 1903-1983 ..... CLC **48**
See also CA 138; 110

Denis, Julio
See Cortazar, Julio

Denmark, Harrison
See Zelazny, Roger (Joseph)

Dennis, John 1658-1734 .... LC **11**
See also DLB 101

Dennis, Nigel (Forbes) 1912-1989 .... CLC **8**
See also CA 25-28R; 129; DLB 13, 15;
MTCW

De Palma, Brian (Russell) 1940- .... CLC **20**
See also CA 109

De Quincey, Thomas 1785-1859 ... NCLC **4**
See also CDBLB 1789-1832; DLB 110

Deren, Eleanora 1908(?)-1961
See Deren, Maya
See also CA 111

Deren, Maya .... CLC **16**
See also Deren, Eleanora

Derleth, August (William)
1909-1971 .... CLC **31**
See also CA 1-4R; 29-32R; CANR 4;
DLB 9; SATA 5

de Routisie, Albert
See Aragon, Louis

Derrida, Jacques 1930- .... CLC **24**
See also CA 124; 127

Derry Down Derry
See Lear, Edward

Dersonnes, Jacques
See Simenon, Georges (Jacques Christian)

Desai, Anita 1937- .... CLC **19, 37**
See also CA 81-84; CANR 33; MTCW;
SATA 63

de Saint-Luc, Jean
See Glassco, John

de Saint Roman, Arnaud
See Aragon, Louis

Descartes, Rene 1596-1650 .... LC **20**

De Sica, Vittorio 1901(?)-1974 ..... CLC **20**
See also CA 117

Desnos, Robert 1900-1945 .... TCLC **22**
See also CA 121

Destouches, Louis-Ferdinand
1894-1961 .... CLC **9, 15**
See also Celine, Louis-Ferdinand
See also CA 85-88; CANR 28; MTCW

Deutsch, Babette 1895-1982 .... CLC **18**
See also CA 1-4R; 108; CANR 4; DLB 45;
SATA 1, 33

Devenant, William 1606-1649 ...... LC **13**

Devkota, Laxmiprasad
1909-1959 .... TCLC **23**
See also CA 123

De Voto, Bernard (Augustine)
1897-1955 .... TCLC **29**
See also CA 113; DLB 9

De Vries, Peter
1910-1993 .... CLC **1, 2, 3, 7, 10, 28, 46**
See also CA 17-20R; 142; CANR 41;
DLB 6; DLBY 82; MTCW

Dexter, Martin
See Faust, Frederick (Schiller)

Dexter, Pete 1943- .... CLC **34, 55**
See also BEST 89:2; CA 127; 131; MTCW

Diamano, Silmang
See Senghor, Leopold Sedar

Diamond, Neil 1941- .... CLC **30**
See also CA 108

di Bassetto, Corno
See Shaw, George Bernard

Dick, Philip K(indred)
1928-1982 .... CLC **10, 30, 72**
See also CA 49-52; 106; CANR 2, 16;
DLB 8; MTCW

Dickens, Charles (John Huffam)
1812-1870 ...... NCLC **3, 8, 18, 26; DA**
See also CDBLB 1832-1890; DLB 21, 55,
70; JRDA; MAICYA; SATA 15

Dickey, James (Lafayette)
1923- .... CLC **1, 2, 4, 7, 10, 15, 47**
See also AITN 1, 2; CA 9-12R; CABS 2;
CANR 10; CDALB 1968-1988; DLB 5;
DLBD 7; DLBY 82; MTCW

Dickey, William 1928- .... CLC **3, 28**
See also CA 9-12R; CANR 24; DLB 5

Dickinson, Charles 1951- .... CLC **49**
See also CA 128

Dickinson, Emily (Elizabeth)
1830-1886 .. NCLC **21; DA; PC 1; WLC**
See also CDALB 1865-1917; DLB 1;
SATA 29

Dickinson, Peter (Malcolm)
1927- .... CLC **12, 35**
See also AAYA 9; CA 41-44R; CANR 31;
CLR 29; DLB 87; JRDA; MAICYA;
SATA 5, 62

Dickson, Carr
See Carr, John Dickson

Dickson, Carter
See Carr, John Dickson

Didion, Joan 1934- ..... CLC **1, 3, 8, 14, 32**
See also AITN 1; CA 5-8R; CANR 14;
CDALB 1968-1988; DLB 2; DLBY 81,
86; MTCW

Dietrich, Robert
See Hunt, E(verette) Howard, Jr.

Dillard, Annie 1945- .... CLC **9, 60**
See also AAYA 6; CA 49-52; CANR 3, 43;
DLBY 80; MTCW; SATA 10

Dillard, R(ichard) H(enry) W(ilde)
1937- .... CLC **5**
See also CA 21-24R; CAAS 7; CANR 10;
DLB 5

Dillon, Eilis 1920- .... CLC **17**
See also CA 9-12R; CAAS 3; CANR 4, 38;
CLR 26; MAICYA; SATA 2, 74

Dimont, Penelope
See Mortimer, Penelope (Ruth)

Dinesen, Isak .... CLC **10, 29; SSC 7**
See also Blixen, Karen (Christentze
Dinesen)

Ding Ling .... CLC **68**
See also Chiang Pin-chin

Disch, Thomas M(ichael) 1940- ... CLC **7, 36**
See also CA 21-24R; CAAS 4; CANR 17,
36; CLR 18; DLB 8; MAICYA; MTCW;
SAAS 15; SATA 54

Disch, Tom
See Disch, Thomas M(ichael)

d'Isly, Georges
See Simenon, Georges (Jacques Christian)

Disraeli, Benjamin 1804-1881 .. NCLC **2, 39**
See also DLB 21, 55

Ditcum, Steve
See Crumb, R(obert)

Dixon, Paige
See Corcoran, Barbara

Dixon, Stephen 1936- .... CLC **52**
See also CA 89-92; CANR 17, 40; DLB 130

Duclos, Charles Pinot 1704-1772 ..... **LC 1**

Dudek, Louis 1918- .... **CLC 11, 19**
See also CA 45-48; CAAS 14; CANR 1;
DLB 88

Duerrenmatt, Friedrich
.... **CLC 1, 4, 8, 11, 15, 43**
See also Duerrenmatt, Friedrich
See also DLB 69, 124

Duerrenmatt, Friedrich
1921-1990 ...... **CLC 1, 4, 8, 11, 15, 43**
See also Duerrenmatt, Friedrich
See also CA 17-20R; CANR 33; DLB 69,
124; MTCW

Duffy, Bruce (?)- .... **CLC 50**

Duffy, Maureen 1933- .... **CLC 37**
See also CA 25-28R; CANR 33; DLB 14;
MTCW

Dugan, Alan 1923- .... **CLC 2, 6**
See also CA 81-84; DLB 5

du Gard, Roger Martin
See Martin du Gard, Roger

Duhamel, Georges 1884-1966 .... **CLC 8**
See also CA 81-84; 25-28R; CANR 35;
DLB 65; MTCW

Dujardin, Edouard (Emile Louis)
1861-1949 .... **TCLC 13**
See also CA 109; DLB 123

Dumas, Alexandre (Davy de la Pailleterie)
1802-1870 .... **NCLC 11; DA; WLC**
See also DLB 119; SATA 18

Dumas, Alexandre
1824-1895 .... **NCLC 9; DC 1**

Dumas, Claudine
See Malzberg, Barry N(athaniel)

Dumas, Henry L. 1934-1968 ..... **CLC 6, 62**
See also BW; CA 85-88; DLB 41

du Maurier, Daphne
1907-1989 .... **CLC 6, 11, 59**
See also CA 5-8R; 128; CANR 6; MTCW;
SATA 27, 60

Dunbar, Paul Laurence
1872-1906 ...... **TCLC 2, 12; BLC; DA;**
PC 5; SSC 8; WLC
See also BW; CA 104; 124;
CDALB 1865-1917; DLB 50, 54, 78;
SATA 34

Dunbar, William 1460(?)-1530(?) .... **LC 20**

Duncan, Lois 1934- .... **CLC 26**
See also AAYA 4; CA 1-4R; CANR 2, 23,
36; CLR 29; JRDA; MAICYA; SAAS 2;
SATA 1, 36, 75

Duncan, Robert (Edward)
1919-1988 .... **CLC 1, 2, 4, 7, 15, 41, 55;**
PC 2
See also CA 9-12R; 124; CANR 28; DLB 5,
16; MTCW

Dunlap, William 1766-1839 .... **NCLC 2**
See also DLB 30, 37, 59

Dunn, Douglas (Eaglesham)
1942- .... **CLC 6, 40**
See also CA 45-48; CANR 2, 33; DLB 40;
MTCW

Dunn, Katherine (Karen) 1945- ..... **CLC 71**
See also CA 33-36R

Dunn, Stephen 1939- .... **CLC 36**
See also CA 33-36R; CANR 12; DLB 105

Dunne, Finley Peter 1867-1936.... **TCLC 28**
See also CA 108; DLB 11, 23

Dunne, John Gregory 1932-....... **CLC 28**
See also CA 25-28R; CANR 14; DLBY 80

Dunsany, Edward John Moreton Drax
Plunkett 1878-1957
See Dunsany, Lord; Lord Dunsany
See also CA 104; DLB 10

Dunsany, Lord.................... **TCLC 2**
See also Dunsany, Edward John Moreton
Drax Plunkett
See also DLB 77

du Perry, Jean
See Simenon, Georges (Jacques Christian)

Durang, Christopher (Ferdinand)
1949- .... **CLC 27, 38**
See also CA 105

Duras, Marguerite
1914- ...... **CLC 3, 6, 11, 20, 34, 40, 68**
See also CA 25-28R; DLB 83; MTCW

Durban, (Rosa) Pam 1947-........ **CLC 39**
See also CA 123

Durcan, Paul 1944-............ **CLC 43, 70**
See also CA 134

Durrell, Lawrence (George)
1912-1990 ... **CLC 1, 4, 6, 8, 13, 27, 41**
See also CA 9-12R; 132; CANR 40;
CDBLB 1945-1960; DLB 15, 27;
DLBY 90; MTCW

Dutt, Toru 1856-1877.......... **NCLC 29**

Dwight, Timothy 1752-1817...... **NCLC 13**
See also DLB 37

Dworkin, Andrea 1946- .... **CLC 43**
See also CA 77-80; CANR 16, 39; MTCW

Dwyer, Deanna
See Koontz, Dean R(ay)

Dwyer, K. R.
See Koontz, Dean R(ay)

Dylan, Bob 1941- ...... **CLC 3, 4, 6, 12, 77**
See also CA 41-44R; DLB 16

Eagleton, Terence (Francis) 1943-
See Eagleton, Terry
See also CA 57-60; CANR 7, 23; MTCW

Eagleton, Terry .... **CLC 63**
See also Eagleton, Terence (Francis)

Early, Jack
See Scoppettone, Sandra

East, Michael
See West, Morris L(anglo)

Eastaway, Edward
See Thomas, (Philip) Edward

Eastlake, William (Derry) 1917-..... **CLC 8**
See also CA 5-8R; CAAS 1; CANR 5;
DLB 6

Eberhart, Richard (Ghormley)
1904- .... **CLC 3, 11, 19, 56**
See also CA 1-4R; CANR 2;
CDALB 1941-1968; DLB 48; MTCW

Eberstadt, Fernanda 1960-........ **CLC 39**
See also CA 136

Echegaray (y Eizaguirre), Jose (Maria Waldo)
1832-1916 .... **TCLC 4**
See also CA 104; CANR 32; HW; MTCW

Echeverria, (Jose) Esteban (Antonino)
1805-1851 .... **NCLC 18**

Echo
See Proust, (Valentin-Louis-George-Eugene-)
Marcel

Eckert, Allan W. 1931- .... **CLC 17**
See also CA 13-16R; CANR 14; SATA 27,
29

Eckhart, Meister 1260(?)-1328(?) .. **CMLC 9**
See also DLB 115

Eckmar, F. R.
See de Hartog, Jan

Eco, Umberto 1932-........... **CLC 28, 60**
See also BEST 90:1; CA 77-80; CANR 12,
33; MTCW

Eddison, E(ric) R(ucker)
1882-1945 .... **TCLC 15**
See also CA 109

Edel, (Joseph) Leon 1907-...... **CLC 29, 34**
See also CA 1-4R; CANR 1, 22; DLB 103

Eden, Emily 1797-1869 .... **NCLC 10**

Edgar, David 1948-.............. **CLC 42**
See also CA 57-60; CANR 12; DLB 13;
MTCW

Edgerton, Clyde (Carlyle) 1944- .... **CLC 39**
See also CA 118; 134

Edgeworth, Maria 1767-1849...... **NCLC 1**
See also DLB 116; SATA 21

Edmonds, Paul
See Kuttner, Henry

Edmonds, Walter D(umaux) 1903- .. **CLC 35**
See also CA 5-8R; CANR 2; DLB 9;
MAICYA; SAAS 4; SATA 1, 27

Edmondson, Wallace
See Ellison, Harlan

Edson, Russell.................... **CLC 13**
See also CA 33-36R

Edwards, G(erald) B(asil)
1899-1976 .... **CLC 25**
See also CA 110

Edwards, Gus 1939-.............. **CLC 43**
See also CA 108

Edwards, Jonathan 1703-1758.... **LC 7; DA**
See also DLB 24

Efron, Marina Ivanovna Tsvetaeva
See Tsvetaeva (Efron), Marina (Ivanovna)

Ehle, John (Marsden, Jr.) 1925-.... **CLC 27**
See also CA 9-12R

Ehrenbourg, Ilya (Grigoryevich)
See Ehrenburg, Ilya (Grigoryevich)

Ehrenburg, Ilya (Grigoryevich)
1891-1967 .... **CLC 18, 34, 62**
See also CA 102; 25-28R

Ehrenburg, Ilyo (Grigoryevich)
See Ehrenburg, Ilya (Grigoryevich)

Eich, Guenter 1907-1972 .... **CLC 15**
See also CA 111; 93-96; DLB 69, 124

Eichendorff, Joseph Freiherr von
1788-1857 .... **NCLC 8**
See also DLB 90

Evan, Evin
See Faust, Frederick (Schiller)

Evans, Evan
See Faust, Frederick (Schiller)

Evans, Marian
See Eliot, George

Evans, Mary Ann
See Eliot, George

Evarts, Esther
See Benson, Sally

Everett, Percival
See Everett, Percival L.

Everett, Percival L. 1956- .... CLC 57
See also CA 129

Everson, R(onald) G(ilmour)
1903- .... CLC 27
See also CA 17-20R; DLB 88

Everson, William (Oliver)
1912- .... CLC 1, 5, 14
See also CA 9-12R; CANR 20; DLB 5, 16;
MTCW

Evtushenko, Evgenii Aleksandrovich
See Yevtushenko, Yevgeny (Alexandrovich)

Ewart, Gavin (Buchanan)
1916- .... CLC 13, 46
See also CA 89-92; CANR 17; DLB 40;
MTCW

Ewers, Hanns Heinz 1871-1943 ... TCLC 12
See also CA 109

Ewing, Frederick R.
See Sturgeon, Theodore (Hamilton)

Exley, Frederick (Earl)
1929-1992 .... CLC 6, 11
See also AITN 2; CA 81-84; 138; DLBY 81

Eynhardt, Guillermo
See Quiroga, Horacio (Sylvestre)

Ezekiel, Nissim 1924- .... CLC 61
See also CA 61-64

Ezekiel, Tish O'Dowd 1943- .... CLC 34
See also CA 129

Fadeyev, A.
See Bulgya, Alexander Alexandrovich

Fadeyev, Alexander .... TCLC 53
See also Bulgya, Alexander Alexandrovich

Fagen, Donald 1948- .... CLC 26

Fainzilberg, Ilya Arnoldovich 1897-1937
See Ilf, Ilya
See also CA 120

Fair, Ronald L. 1932- .... CLC 18
See also BW; CA 69-72; CANR 25; DLB 33

Fairbairns, Zoe (Ann) 1948- .... CLC 32
See also CA 103; CANR 21

Falco, Gian
See Papini, Giovanni

Falconer, James
See Kirkup, James

Falconer, Kenneth
See Kornbluth, C(yril) M.

Falkland, Samuel
See Heijermans, Herman

Fallaci, Oriana 1930- .... CLC 11
See also CA 77-80; CANR 15; MTCW

Faludy, George 1913- .... CLC 42
See also CA 21-24R

Faludy, Gyoergy
See Faludy, George

Fanon, Frantz 1925-1961 ..... CLC 74; BLC
See also BW; CA 116; 89-92

Fanshawe, Ann .... LC 11

Fante, John (Thomas) 1911-1983 ... CLC 60
See also CA 69-72; 109; CANR 23;
DLB 130; DLBY 83

Farah, Nuruddin 1945- .... CLC 53; BLC
See also CA 106; DLB 125

Fargue, Leon-Paul 1876(?)-1947 ... TCLC 11
See also CA 109

Farigoule, Louis
See Romains, Jules

Farina, Richard 1936(?)-1966 .... CLC 9
See also CA 81-84; 25-28R

Farley, Walter (Lorimer)
1915-1989 .... CLC 17
See also CA 17-20R; CANR 8, 29; DLB 22;
JRDA; MAICYA; SATA 2, 43

Farmer, Philip Jose 1918- .... CLC 1, 19
See also CA 1-4R; CANR 4, 35; DLB 8;
MTCW

Farquhar, George 1677-1707 .... LC 21
See also DLB 84

Farrell, J(ames) G(ordon)
1935-1979 .... CLC 6
See also CA 73-76; 89-92; CANR 36;
DLB 14; MTCW

Farrell, James T(homas)
1904-1979 ...... CLC 1, 4, 8, 11, 66
See also CA 5-8R; 89-92; CANR 9; DLB 4,
9, 86; DLBD 2; MTCW

Farren, Richard J.
See Betjeman, John

Farren, Richard M.
See Betjeman, John

Fassbinder, Rainer Werner
1946-1982 .... CLC 20
See also CA 93-96; 106; CANR 31

Fast, Howard (Melvin) 1914- ...... CLC 23
See also CA 1-4R; CAAS 18; CANR 1, 33;
DLB 9; SATA 7

Faulcon, Robert
See Holdstock, Robert P.

Faulkner, William (Cuthbert)
1897-1962 ..... CLC 1, 3, 6, 8, 9, 11, 14,
18, 28, 52, 68; DA; SSC 1; WLC
See also AAYA 7; CA 81-84; CANR 33;
CDALB 1929-1941; DLB 9, 11, 44, 102;
DLBD 2; DLBY 86; MTCW

Fauset, Jessie Redmon
1884(?)-1961 .... CLC 19, 54; BLC
See also BW; CA 109; DLB 51

Faust, Frederick (Schiller)
1892-1944(?) .... TCLC 49
See also CA 108

Faust, Irvin 1924- .... CLC 8
See also CA 33-36R; CANR 28; DLB 2, 28;
DLBY 80

Fawkes, Guy
See Benchley, Robert (Charles)

Fearing, Kenneth (Flexner)
1902-1961 .... CLC 51
See also CA 93-96; DLB 9

Fecamps, Elise
See Creasey, John

Federman, Raymond 1928- ...... CLC 6, 47
See also CA 17-20R; CAAS 8; CANR 10,
43; DLBY 80

Federspiel, J(uerg) F. 1931- .... CLC 42

Feiffer, Jules (Ralph) 1929- .... CLC 2, 8, 64
See also AAYA 3; CA 17-20R; CANR 30;
DLB 7, 44; MTCW; SATA 8, 61

Feige, Hermann Albert Otto Maximilian
See Traven, B.

Fei-Kan, Li
See Li Fei-kan

Feinberg, David B. 1956- .... CLC 59
See also CA 135

Feinstein, Elaine 1930- .... CLC 36
See also CA 69-72; CAAS 1; CANR 31;
DLB 14, 40; MTCW

Feldman, Irving (Mordecai) 1928- .... CLC 7
See also CA 1-4R; CANR 1

Fellini, Federico 1920-1993 .... CLC 16
See also CA 65-68; 143; CANR 33

Felsen, Henry Gregor 1916- .... CLC 17
See also CA 1-4R; CANR 1; SAAS 2;
SATA 1

Fenton, James Martin 1949- .... CLC 32
See also CA 102; DLB 40

Ferber, Edna 1887-1968 .... CLC 18
See also AITN 1; CA 5-8R; 25-28R; DLB 9,
28, 86; MTCW; SATA 7

Ferguson, Helen
See Kavan, Anna

Ferguson, Samuel 1810-1886 ..... NCLC 33
See also DLB 32

Ferling, Lawrence
See Ferlinghetti, Lawrence (Monsanto)

Ferlinghetti, Lawrence (Monsanto)
1919(?)- .... CLC 2, 6, 10, 27; PC 1
See also CA 5-8R; CANR 3, 41;
CDALB 1941-1968; DLB 5, 16; MTCW

Fernandez, Vicente Garcia Huidobro
See Huidobro Fernandez, Vicente Garcia

Ferrer, Gabriel (Francisco Victor) Miro
See Miro (Ferrer), Gabriel (Francisco
Victor)

Ferrier, Susan (Edmonstone)
1782-1854 .... NCLC 8
See also DLB 116

Ferrigno, Robert 1948(?)- .... CLC 65
See also CA 140

Feuchtwanger, Lion 1884-1958 ..... TCLC 3
See also CA 104; DLB 66

Feydeau, Georges (Leon Jules Marie)
1862-1921 .... TCLC 22
See also CA 113

Ficino, Marsilio 1433-1499 .... LC 12

Fiedeler, Hans
See Doeblin, Alfred

Fox, Paula 1923-............... **CLC 2, 8**
See also AAYA 3; CA 73-76; CANR 20,
36; CLR 1; DLB 52; JRDA; MAICYA;
MTCW; SATA 17, 60

Fox, William Price (Jr.) 1926- ..... **CLC 22**
See also CA 17-20R; CANR 11; DLB 2;
DLBY 81

Foxe, John 1516(?)-1587 .... **LC 14**

Frame, Janet .... **CLC 2, 3, 6, 22, 66**
See also Clutha, Janet Paterson Frame

France, Anatole.................... **TCLC 9**
See also Thibault, Jacques Anatole Francois
See also DLB 123

Francis, Claude 19(?)- .... **CLC 50**

Francis, Dick 1920- .... **CLC 2, 22, 42**
See also AAYA 5; BEST 89:3; CA 5-8R;
CANR 9, 42; CDBLB 1960 to Present;
DLB 87; MTCW

Francis, Robert (Churchill)
1901-1987 .... **CLC 15**
See also CA 1-4R; 123; CANR 1

Frank, Anne(lies Marie)
1929-1945 .... **TCLC 17; DA; WLC**
See also CA 113; 133; MTCW; SATA 42

Frank, Elizabeth 1945-............ **CLC 39**
See also CA 121; 126

Franklin, Benjamin
See Hasek, Jaroslav (Matej Frantisek)

Franklin, Benjamin 1706-1790... **LC 25; DA**
See also CDALB 1640-1865; DLB 24, 43,
73

Franklin, (Stella Maraia Sarah) Miles
1879-1954 .... **TCLC 7**
See also CA 104

Fraser, Antonia (Pakenham)
1932- .... **CLC 32**
See also CA 85-88; MTCW; SATA 32

Fraser, George MacDonald 1925-.... **CLC 7**
See also CA 45-48; CANR 2

Fraser, Sylvia 1935-.............. **CLC 64**
See also CA 45-48; CANR 1, 16

Frayn, Michael 1933-...... **CLC 3, 7, 31, 47**
See also CA 5-8R; CANR 30; DLB 13, 14;
MTCW

Fraze, Candida (Merrill) 1945- ..... **CLC 50**
See also CA 126

Frazer, J(ames) G(eorge)
1854-1941 .... **TCLC 32**
See also CA 118

Frazer, Robert Caine
See Creasey, John

Frazer, Sir James George
See Frazer, J(ames) G(eorge)

Frazier, Ian 1951-................. **CLC 46**
See also CA 130

Frederic, Harold 1856-1898...... **NCLC 10**
See also DLB 12, 23

Frederick, John
See Faust, Frederick (Schiller)

Frederick the Great 1712-1786 ...... **LC 14**

Fredro, Aleksander 1793-1876..... **NCLC 8**

Freeling, Nicolas 1927- .... **CLC 38**
See also CA 49-52; CAAS 12; CANR 1, 17;
DLB 87

Freeman, Douglas Southall
1886-1953 .... **TCLC 11**
See also CA 109; DLB 17

Freeman, Judith 1946-............ **CLC 55**

Freeman, Mary Eleanor Wilkins
1852-1930 .... **TCLC 9; SSC 1**
See also CA 106; DLB 12, 78

Freeman, R(ichard) Austin
1862-1943 .... **TCLC 21**
See also CA 113; DLB 70

French, Marilyn 1929-...... **CLC 10, 18, 60**
See also CA 69-72; CANR 3, 31; MTCW

French, Paul
See Asimov, Isaac

Freneau, Philip Morin 1752-1832.. **NCLC 1**
See also DLB 37, 43

Freud, Sigmund 1856-1939 .... **TCLC 52**
See also CA 115; 133; MTCW

Friedan, Betty (Naomi) 1921-...... **CLC 74**
See also CA 65-68; CANR 18; MTCW

Friedman, B(ernard) H(arper)
1926-........................ **CLC 7**
See also CA 1-4R; CANR 3

Friedman, Bruce Jay 1930-.... **CLC 3, 5, 56**
See also CA 9-12R; CANR 25; DLB 2, 28

Friel, Brian 1929-........... **CLC 5, 42, 59**
See also CA 21-24R; CANR 33; DLB 13;
MTCW

Friis-Baastad, Babbis Ellinor
1921-1970 .... **CLC 12**
See also CA 17-20R; 134; SATA 7

Frisch, Max (Rudolf)
1911-1991 ..... **CLC 3, 9, 14, 18, 32, 44**
See also CA 85-88; 134; CANR 32;
DLB 69, 124; MTCW

Fromentin, Eugene (Samuel Auguste)
1820-1876 .... **NCLC 10**
See also DLB 123

Frost, Frederick
See Faust, Frederick (Schiller)

Frost, Robert (Lee)
1874-1963 .... **CLC 1, 3, 4, 9, 10, 13, 15,
26, 34, 44; DA; PC 1; WLC**
See also CA 89-92; CANR 33;
CDALB 1917-1929; DLB 54; DLBD 7;
MTCW; SATA 14

Froude, James Anthony
1818-1894 .... **NCLC 43**
See also DLB 18, 57

Froy, Herald
See Waterhouse, Keith (Spencer)

Fry, Christopher 1907-....... **CLC 2, 10, 14**
See also CA 17-20R; CANR 9, 30; DLB 13;
MTCW; SATA 66

Frye, (Herman) Northrop
1912-1991 .... **CLC 24, 70**
See also CA 5-8R; 133; CANR 8, 37;
DLB 67, 68; MTCW

Fuchs, Daniel 1909-1993 .... **CLC 8, 22**
See also CA 81-84; 142; CAAS 5;
CANR 40; DLB 9, 26, 28

Fuchs, Daniel 1934-.............. **CLC 34**
See also CA 37-40R; CANR 14

Fuentes, Carlos
1928-...... **CLC 3, 8, 10, 13, 22, 41, 60;
DA; HLC; WLC**
See also AAYA 4; AITN 2; CA 69-72;
CANR 10, 32; DLB 113; HW; MTCW

Fuentes, Gregorio Lopez y
See Lopez y Fuentes, Gregorio

Fugard, (Harold) Athol
1932- .... **CLC 5, 9, 14, 25, 40, 80; DC 3**
See also CA 85-88; CANR 32; MTCW

Fugard, Sheila 1932- .... **CLC 48**
See also CA 125

Fuller, Charles (H., Jr.)
1939- .... **CLC 25; BLC; DC 1**
See also BW; CA 108; 112; DLB 38;
MTCW

Fuller, John (Leopold) 1937-....... **CLC 62**
See also CA 21-24R; CANR 9; DLB 40

Fuller, Margaret .... **NCLC 5**
See also Ossoli, Sarah Margaret (Fuller
marchesa d')

Fuller, Roy (Broadbent)
1912-1991 .... **CLC 4, 28**
See also CA 5-8R; 135; CAAS 10; DLB 15,
20

Fulton, Alice 1952-............... **CLC 52**
See also CA 116

Furphy, Joseph 1843-1912....... **TCLC 25**

Fussell, Paul 1924-............... **CLC 74**
See also BEST 90:1; CA 17-20R; CANR 8,
21, 35; MTCW

Futabatei, Shimei 1864-1909...... **TCLC 44**

Futrelle, Jacques 1875-1912 ...... **TCLC 19**
See also CA 113

G. B. S.
See Shaw, George Bernard

Gaboriau, Emile 1835-1873 ...... **NCLC 14**

Gadda, Carlo Emilio 1893-1973 .... **CLC 11**
See also CA 89-92

Gaddis, William
1922- .... **CLC 1, 3, 6, 8, 10, 19, 43**
See also CA 17-20R; CANR 21; DLB 2;
MTCW

Gaines, Ernest J(ames)
1933-............ **CLC 3, 11, 18; BLC**
See also AITN 1; BW; CA 9-12R; CANR 6,
24, 42; CDALB 1968-1988; DLB 2, 33;
DLBY 80; MTCW

Gaitskill, Mary 1954-............. **CLC 69**
See also CA 128

Galdos, Benito Perez
See Perez Galdos, Benito

Gale, Zona 1874-1938 .... **TCLC 7**
See also CA 105; DLB 9, 78

Galeano, Eduardo (Hughes) 1940-... **CLC 72**
See also CA 29-32R; CANR 13, 32; HW

Galiano, Juan Valera y Alcala
See Valera y Alcala-Galiano, Juan

Gallagher, Tess 1943-.......... **CLC 18, 63**
See also CA 106; DLB 120

Gallant, Mavis
1922- .... **CLC 7, 18, 38; SSC 5**
See also CA 69-72; CANR 29; DLB 53;
MTCW

Gallant, Roy A(rthur) 1924- .... **CLC 17**
See also CA 5-8R; CANR 4, 29; CLR 30;
MAICYA; SATA 4, 68

Gallico, Paul (William) 1897-1976 ... **CLC 2**
See also AITN 1; CA 5-8R; 69-72;
CANR 23; DLB 9; MAICYA; SATA 13

Gallup, Ralph
See Whitemore, Hugh (John)

Galsworthy, John
1867-1933 .... **TCLC 1, 45; DA; WLC 2**
See also CA 104; 141; CDBLB 1890-1914;
DLB 10, 34, 98

Galt, John 1779-1839 .... **NCLC 1**
See also DLB 99, 116

Galvin, James 1951- .... **CLC 38**
See also CA 108; CANR 26

Gamboa, Federico 1864-1939 ...... **TCLC 36**

Gann, Ernest Kellogg 1910-1991 .... **CLC 23**
See also AITN 1; CA 1-4R; 136; CANR 1

Garcia, Cristina 1958- .... **CLC 76**
See also CA 141

Garcia Lorca, Federico
1898-1936 .... **TCLC 1, 7, 49; DA;**
DC 2; HLC; PC 3; WLC
See also CA 104; 131; DLB 108; HW;
MTCW

Garcia Marquez, Gabriel (Jose)
1928- .... **CLC 2, 3, 8, 10, 15, 27, 47, 55;**
DA; HLC; SSC 8; WLC
See also Marquez, Gabriel (Jose) Garcia
See also AAYA 3; BEST 89:1, 90:4;
CA 33-36R; CANR 10, 28; DLB 113;
HW; MTCW

Gard, Janice
See Latham, Jean Lee

Gard, Roger Martin du
See Martin du Gard, Roger

Gardam, Jane 1928- .... **CLC 43**
See also CA 49-52; CANR 2, 18, 33;
CLR 12; DLB 14; MAICYA; MTCW;
SAAS 9; SATA 28, 39, 76

Gardner, Herb .... **CLC 44**

Gardner, John (Champlin), Jr.
1933-1982 ..... **CLC 2, 3, 5, 7, 8, 10, 18,**
28, 34; SSC 7
See also AITN 1; CA 65-68; 107;
CANR 33; DLB 2; DLBY 82; MTCW;
SATA 31, 40

Gardner, John (Edmund) 1926- ..... **CLC 30**
See also CA 103; CANR 15; MTCW

Gardner, Noel
See Kuttner, Henry

Gardons, S. S.
See Snodgrass, W(illiam) D(e Witt)

Garfield, Leon 1921- .... **CLC 12**
See also AAYA 8; CA 17-20R; CANR 38,
41; CLR 21; JRDA; MAICYA; SATA 1,
32, 76

Garland, (Hannibal) Hamlin
1860-1940 .... **TCLC 3**
See also CA 104; DLB 12, 71, 78

Garneau, (Hector de) Saint-Denys
1912-1943 .... **TCLC 13**
See also CA 111; DLB 88

Garner, Alan 1934- .... **CLC 17**
See also CA 73-76; CANR 15; CLR 20;
MAICYA; MTCW; SATA 18, 69

Garner, Hugh 1913-1979 .... **CLC 13**
See also CA 69-72; CANR 31; DLB 68

Garnett, David 1892-1981 .... **CLC 3**
See also CA 5-8R; 103; CANR 17; DLB 34

Garos, Stephanie
See Katz, Steve

Garrett, George (Palmer)
1929- .... **CLC 3, 11, 51**
See also CA 1-4R; CAAS 5; CANR 1, 42;
DLB 2, 5, 130; DLBY 83

Garrick, David 1717-1779 .... **LC 15**
See also DLB 84

Garrigue, Jean 1914-1972 .... **CLC 2, 8**
See also CA 5-8R; 37-40R; CANR 20

Garrison, Frederick
See Sinclair, Upton (Beall)

Garth, Will
See Hamilton, Edmond; Kuttner, Henry

Garvey, Marcus (Moziah, Jr.)
1887-1940 .... **TCLC 41; BLC**
See also BW; CA 120; 124

Gary, Romain .... **CLC 25**
See also Kacew, Romain
See also DLB 83

Gascar, Pierre .... **CLC 11**
See also Fournier, Pierre

Gascoyne, David (Emery) 1916- .... **CLC 45**
See also CA 65-68; CANR 10, 28; DLB 20;
MTCW

Gaskell, Elizabeth Cleghorn
1810-1865 .... **NCLC 5**
See also CDBLB 1832-1890; DLB 21

Gass, William H(oward)
1924- ... **CLC 1, 2, 8, 11, 15, 39; SSC 12**
See also CA 17-20R; CANR 30; DLB 2;
MTCW

Gasset, Jose Ortega y
See Ortega y Gasset, Jose

Gautier, Theophile 1811-1872 ..... **NCLC 1**
See also DLB 119

Gawsworth, John
See Bates, H(erbert) E(rnest)

Gaye, Marvin (Penze) 1939-1984 ... **CLC 26**
See also CA 112

Gebler, Carlo (Ernest) 1954- .... **CLC 39**
See also CA 119; 133

Gee, Maggie (Mary) 1948- .... **CLC 57**
See also CA 130

Gee, Maurice (Gough) 1931- .... **CLC 29**
See also CA 97-100; SATA 46

Gelbart, Larry (Simon) 1923- ... **CLC 21, 61**
See also CA 73-76

Gelber, Jack 1932- .... **CLC 1, 6, 14, 79**
See also CA 1-4R; CANR 2; DLB 7

Gellhorn, Martha Ellis 1908- ... **CLC 14, 60**
See also CA 77-80; DLBY 82

Genet, Jean
1910-1986 ... **CLC 1, 2, 5, 10, 14, 44, 46**
See also CA 13-16R; CANR 18; DLB 72;
DLBY 86; MTCW

Gent, Peter 1942- .... **CLC 29**
See also AITN 1; CA 89-92; DLBY 82

Gentlewoman in New England, A
See Bradstreet, Anne

Gentlewoman in Those Parts, A
See Bradstreet, Anne

George, Jean Craighead 1919- ...... **CLC 35**
See also AAYA 8; CA 5-8R; CANR 25;
CLR 1; DLB 52; JRDA; MAICYA;
SATA 2, 68

George, Stefan (Anton)
1868-1933 .... **TCLC 2, 14**
See also CA 104

Georges, Georges Martin
See Simenon, Georges (Jacques Christian)

Gerhardi, William Alexander
See Gerhardie, William Alexander

Gerhardie, William Alexander
1895-1977 .... **CLC 5**
See also CA 25-28R; 73-76; CANR 18;
DLB 36

Gerstler, Amy 1956- .... **CLC 70**

Gertler, T. .... **CLC 34**
See also CA 116; 121

Ghalib 1797-1869 .... **NCLC 39**

Ghelderode, Michel de
1898-1962 .... **CLC 6, 11**
See also CA 85-88; CANR 40

Ghiselin, Brewster 1903- .... **CLC 23**
See also CA 13-16R; CAAS 10; CANR 13

Ghose, Zulfikar 1935- .... **CLC 42**
See also CA 65-68

Ghosh, Amitav 1956- .... **CLC 44**

Giacosa, Giuseppe 1847-1906 ...... **TCLC 7**
See also CA 104

Gibb, Lee
See Waterhouse, Keith (Spencer)

Gibbon, Lewis Grassic .... **TCLC 4**
See also Mitchell, James Leslie

Gibbons, Kaye 1960- .... **CLC 50**

Gibran, Kahlil 1883-1931 .... **TCLC 1, 9**
See also CA 104

Gibson, William 1914- .... **CLC 23; DA**
See also CA 9-12R; CANR 9, 42; DLB 7;
SATA 66

Gibson, William (Ford) 1948- ... **CLC 39, 63**
See also CA 126; 133

Gide, Andre (Paul Guillaume)
1869-1951 .... **TCLC 5, 12, 36; DA;**
SSC 13; WLC
See also CA 104; 124; DLB 65; MTCW

Gifford, Barry (Colby) 1946- .... **CLC 34**
See also CA 65-68; CANR 9, 30, 40

Gilbert, W(illiam) S(chwenck)
1836-1911 .... **TCLC 3**
See also CA 104; SATA 36

Gilbreth, Frank B., Jr. 1911- .... **CLC 17**
See also CA 9-12R; SATA 2

Gilchrist, Ellen 1935- .. **CLC 34, 48; SSC 14**
See also CA 113; 116; CANR 41; DLB 130;
MTCW

Giles, Molly 1942- .... **CLC 39**
See also CA 126

Gill, Patrick
See Creasey, John

Gilliam, Terry (Vance) 1940-....... **CLC 21**
See also Monty Python
See also CA 108; 113; CANR 35

Gillian, Jerry
See Gilliam, Terry (Vance)

Gilliatt, Penelope (Ann Douglass)
1932-1993 .... **CLC 2, 10, 13, 53**
See also AITN 2; CA 13-16R; 141; DLB 14

Gilman, Charlotte (Anna) Perkins (Stetson)
1860-1935 .... **TCLC 9, 37; SSC 13**
See also CA 106

Gilmour, David 1949-............ **CLC 35**
See also Pink Floyd
See also CA 138

Gilpin, William 1724-1804 ...... **NCLC 30**

Gilray, J. D.
See Mencken, H(enry) L(ouis)

Gilroy, Frank D(aniel) 1925-........ **CLC 2**
See also CA 81-84; CANR 32; DLB 7

Ginsberg, Allen
1926- ...... **CLC 1, 2, 3, 4, 6, 13, 36, 69;**
DA; PC 4; WLC 3
See also AITN 1; CA 1-4R; CANR 2, 41;
CDALB 1941-1968; DLB 5, 16; MTCW

Ginzburg, Natalia
1916-1991 .... **CLC 5, 11, 54, 70**
See also CA 85-88; 135; CANR 33; MTCW

Giono, Jean 1895-1970......... **CLC 4, 11**
See also CA 45-48; 29-32R; CANR 2, 35;
DLB 72; MTCW

Giovanni, Nikki
1943- ...... **CLC 2, 4, 19, 64; BLC; DA**
See also AITN 1; BW; CA 29-32R;
CAAS 6; CANR 18, 41; CLR 6; DLB 5,
41; MAICYA; MTCW; SATA 24

Giovene, Andrea 1904-............. **CLC 7**
See also CA 85-88

Gippius, Zinaida (Nikolayevna) 1869-1945
See Hippius, Zinaida
See also CA 106

Giraudoux, (Hippolyte) Jean
1882-1944 .... **TCLC 2, 7**
See also CA 104; DLB 65

Gironella, Jose Maria 1917- .... **CLC 11**
See also CA 101

Gissing, George (Robert)
1857-1903 .... **TCLC 3, 24, 47**
See also CA 105; DLB 18, 135

Giurlani, Aldo
See Palazzeschi, Aldo

Gladkov, Fyodor (Vasilyevich)
1883-1958 .... **TCLC 27**

Glanville, Brian (Lester) 1931- ...... **CLC 6**
See also CA 5-8R; CAAS 9; CANR 3;
DLB 15; SATA 42

Glasgow, Ellen (Anderson Gholson)
1873(?)-1945 .... **TCLC 2, 7**
See also CA 104; DLB 9, 12

Glassco, John 1909-1981 .... **CLC 9**
See also CA 13-16R; 102; CANR 15;
DLB 68

Glasscock, Amnesia
See Steinbeck, John (Ernst)

Glasser, Ronald J. 1940(?)- .... **CLC 37**

Glassman, Joyce
See Johnson, Joyce

Glendinning, Victoria 1937-........ **CLC 50**
See also CA 120; 127

Glissant, Edouard 1928-........ **CLC 10, 68**

Gloag, Julian 1930- .... **CLC 40**
See also AITN 1; CA 65-68; CANR 10

Gluck, Louise (Elisabeth)
1943- .... **CLC 7, 22, 44, 81**
See also Glueck, Louise
See also CA 33-36R; CANR 40; DLB 5

Glueck, Louise.................. **CLC 7, 22**
See also Gluck, Louise (Elisabeth)
See also DLB 5

Gobineau, Joseph Arthur (Comte) de
1816-1882 .... **NCLC 17**
See also DLB 123

Godard, Jean-Luc 1930-........... **CLC 20**
See also CA 93-96

Godden, (Margaret) Rumer 1907-... **CLC 53**
See also AAYA 6; CA 5-8R; CANR 4, 27,
36; CLR 20; MAICYA; SAAS 12;
SATA 3, 36

Godoy Alcayaga, Lucila 1889-1957
See Mistral, Gabriela
See also CA 104; 131; HW; MTCW

Godwin, Gail (Kathleen)
1937- .... **CLC 5, 8, 22, 31, 69**
See also CA 29-32R; CANR 15, 43; DLB 6;
MTCW

Godwin, William 1756-1836...... **NCLC 14**
See also CDBLB 1789-1832; DLB 39, 104

Goethe, Johann Wolfgang von
1749-1832 .... **NCLC 4, 22, 34; DA;**
PC 5; WLC 3
See also DLB 94

Gogarty, Oliver St. John
1878-1957 .... **TCLC 15**
See also CA 109; DLB 15, 19

Gogol, Nikolai (Vasilyevich)
1809-1852 .... **NCLC 5, 15, 31; DA;**
DC 1; SSC 4; WLC

Goines, Donald
1937(?)-1974 .... **CLC 80; BLC**
See also AITN 1; BW; CA 124; 114;
DLB 33

Gold, Herbert 1924-....... **CLC 4, 7, 14, 42**
See also CA 9-12R; CANR 17; DLB 2;
DLBY 81

Goldbarth, Albert 1948-......... **CLC 5, 38**
See also CA 53-56; CANR 6, 40; DLB 120

Goldberg, Anatol 1910-1982 .... **CLC 34**
See also CA 131; 117

Goldemberg, Isaac 1945- .... **CLC 52**
See also CA 69-72; CAAS 12; CANR 11,
32; HW

Golden Silver
See Storm, Hyemeyohsts

Golding, William (Gerald)
1911-1993 .... **CLC 1, 2, 3, 8, 10, 17, 27,**
58, 81; DA; WLC
See also AAYA 5; CA 5-8R; 141;
CANR 13, 33; CDBLB 1945-1960;
DLB 15, 100; MTCW

Goldman, Emma 1869-1940 ...... **TCLC 13**
See also CA 110

Goldman, Francisco 1955-........ **CLC 76**

Goldman, William (W.) 1931-.... **CLC 1, 48**
See also CA 9-12R; CANR 29; DLB 44

Goldmann, Lucien 1913-1970 ...... **CLC 24**
See also CA 25-28; CAP 2

Goldoni, Carlo 1707-1793 .... **LC 4**

Goldsberry, Steven 1949-.......... **CLC 34**
See also CA 131

Goldsmith, Oliver
1728-1774 .... **LC 2; DA; WLC**
See also CDBLB 1660-1789; DLB 39, 89,
104, 109; SATA 26

Goldsmith, Peter
See Priestley, J(ohn) B(oynton)

Gombrowicz, Witold
1904-1969 .... **CLC 4, 7, 11, 49**
See also CA 19-20; 25-28R; CAP 2

Gomez de la Serna, Ramon
1888-1963 .... **CLC 9**
See also CA 116; HW

Goncharov, Ivan Alexandrovich
1812-1891 .... **NCLC 1**

Goncourt, Edmond (Louis Antoine Huot) de
1822-1896 .... **NCLC 7**
See also DLB 123

Goncourt, Jules (Alfred Huot) de
1830-1870 .... **NCLC 7**
See also DLB 123

Gontier, Fernande 19(?)- .... **CLC 50**

Goodman, Paul 1911-1972.... **CLC 1, 2, 4, 7**
See also CA 19-20; 37-40R; CANR 34;
CAP 2; DLB 130; MTCW

Gordimer, Nadine
1923- .... **CLC 3, 5, 7, 10, 18, 33, 51, 70;**
DA
See also CA 5-8R; CANR 3, 28; MTCW

Gordon, Adam Lindsay
1833-1870 .... **NCLC 21**

Gordon, Caroline
1895-1981 .... **CLC 6, 13, 29**
See also CA 11-12; 103; CANR 36; CAP 1;
DLB 4, 9, 102; DLBY 81; MTCW

Gordon, Charles William 1860-1937
See Connor, Ralph
See also CA 109

Gordon, Mary (Catherine)
1949- .... **CLC 13, 22**
See also CA 102; DLB 6; DLBY 81;
MTCW

Gordon, Sol 1923-................ **CLC 26**
See also CA 53-56; CANR 4; SATA 11

Gordone, Charles 1925-.......... **CLC 1, 4**
See also BW; CA 93-96; DLB 7; MTCW

Gorenko, Anna Andreevna
See Akhmatova, Anna

Gorky, Maxim.............. **TCLC 8; WLC**
See also Peshkov, Alexei Maximovich

Goryan, Sirak
See Saroyan, William

Gosse, Edmund (William)
1849-1928 .... **TCLC 28**
See also CA 117; DLB 57

Grimble, Reverend Charles James
See Eliot, T(homas) S(tearns)

Grimke, Charlotte L(ottie) Forten
1837(?)-1914
See Forten, Charlotte L.
See also BW; CA 117; 124

Grimm, Jacob Ludwig Karl
1785-1863 .... **NCLC 3**
See also DLB 90; MAICYA; SATA 22

Grimm, Wilhelm Karl 1786-1859 .. **NCLC 3**
See also DLB 90; MAICYA; SATA 22

Grimmelshausen, Johann Jakob Christoffel
von 1621-1676 .... **LC 6**

Grindel, Eugene 1895-1952
See Eluard, Paul
See also CA 104

Grossman, David 1954- .... **CLC 67**
See also CA 138

Grossman, Vasily (Semenovich)
1905-1964 .... **CLC 41**
See also CA 124; 130; MTCW

Grove, Frederick Philip .... **TCLC 4**
See also Greve, Felix Paul (Berthold
Friedrich)
See also DLB 92

Grubb
See Crumb, R(obert)

Grumbach, Doris (Isaac)
1918- .... **CLC 13, 22, 64**
See also CA 5-8R; CAAS 2; CANR 9, 42

Grundtvig, Nicolai Frederik Severin
1783-1872 .... **NCLC 1**

Grunge
See Crumb, R(obert)

Grunwald, Lisa 1959- .... **CLC 44**
See also CA 120

Guare, John 1938- .... **CLC 8, 14, 29, 67**
See also CA 73-76; CANR 21; DLB 7;
MTCW

Gudjonsson, Halldor Kiljan 1902-
See Laxness, Halldor
See also CA 103

Guenter, Erich
See Eich, Guenter

Guest, Barbara 1920- .... **CLC 34**
See also CA 25-28R; CANR 11; DLB 5

Guest, Judith (Ann) 1936- .... **CLC 8, 30**
See also AAYA 7; CA 77-80; CANR 15;
MTCW

Guild, Nicholas M. 1944- .... **CLC 33**
See also CA 93-96

Guillemin, Jacques
See Sartre, Jean-Paul

Guillen, Jorge 1893-1984 .... **CLC 11**
See also CA 89-92; 112; DLB 108; HW

Guillen (y Batista), Nicolas (Cristobal)
1902-1989 ..... **CLC 48, 79; BLC; HLC**
See also BW; CA 116; 125; 129; HW

Guillevic, (Eugene) 1907- .... **CLC 33**
See also CA 93-96

Guillois
See Desnos, Robert

Guiney, Louise Imogen
1861-1920 .... **TCLC 41**
See also DLB 54

Guiraldes, Ricardo (Guillermo)
1886-1927 .... **TCLC 39**
See also CA 131; HW; MTCW

Gunn, Bill .... **CLC 5**
See also Gunn, William Harrison
See also DLB 38

Gunn, Thom(son William)
1929- .... **CLC 3, 6, 18, 32, 81**
See also CA 17-20R; CANR 9, 33;
CDBLB 1960 to Present; DLB 27;
MTCW

Gunn, William Harrison 1934(?)-1989
See Gunn, Bill
See also AITN 1; BW; CA 13-16R; 128;
CANR 12, 25

Gunnars, Kristjana 1948- .... **CLC 69**
See also CA 113; DLB 60

Gurganus, Allan 1947- .... **CLC 70**
See also BEST 90:1; CA 135

Gurney, A(lbert) R(amsdell), Jr.
1930- .... **CLC 32, 50, 54**
See also CA 77-80; CANR 32

Gurney, Ivor (Bertie) 1890-1937 ... **TCLC 33**

Gurney, Peter
See Gurney, A(lbert) R(amsdell), Jr.

Gustafson, Ralph (Barker) 1909- .... **CLC 36**
See also CA 21-24R; CANR 8; DLB 88

Gut, Gom
See Simenon, Georges (Jacques Christian)

Guthrie, A(lfred) B(ertram), Jr.
1901-1991 .... **CLC 23**
See also CA 57-60; 134; CANR 24; DLB 6;
SATA 62; SATA-Obit 67

Guthrie, Isobel
See Grieve, C(hristopher) M(urray)

Guthrie, Woodrow Wilson 1912-1967
See Guthrie, Woody
See also CA 113; 93-96

Guthrie, Woody .... **CLC 35**
See also Guthrie, Woodrow Wilson

Guy, Rosa (Cuthbert) 1928- .... **CLC 26**
See also AAYA 4; BW; CA 17-20R;
CANR 14, 34; CLR 13; DLB 33; JRDA;
MAICYA; SATA 14, 62

Gwendolyn
See Bennett, (Enoch) Arnold

H. D. .... **CLC 3, 8, 14, 31, 34, 73; PC 5**
See also Doolittle, Hilda

Haavikko, Paavo Juhani
1931- .... **CLC 18, 34**
See also CA 106

Habbema, Koos
See Heijermans, Herman

Hacker, Marilyn 1942- .... **CLC 5, 9, 23, 72**
See also CA 77-80; DLB 120

Haggard, H(enry) Rider
1856-1925 .... **TCLC 11**
See also CA 108; DLB 70; SATA 16

Haig, Fenil
See Ford, Ford Madox

Haig-Brown, Roderick (Langmere)
1908-1976 .... **CLC 21**
See also CA 5-8R; 69-72; CANR 4, 38;
CLR 31; DLB 88; MAICYA; SATA 12

Hailey, Arthur 1920- .... **CLC 5**
See also AITN 2; BEST 90:3; CA 1-4R;
CANR 2, 36; DLB 88; DLBY 82; MTCW

Hailey, Elizabeth Forsythe 1938- ... **CLC 40**
See also CA 93-96; CAAS 1; CANR 15

Haines, John (Meade) 1924- .... **CLC 58**
See also CA 17-20R; CANR 13, 34; DLB 5

Haldeman, Joe (William) 1943- ..... **CLC 61**
See also CA 53-56; CANR 6; DLB 8

Haley, Alex(ander Murray Palmer)
1921-1992 .... **CLC 8, 12, 76; BLC; DA**
See also BW; CA 77-80; 136; DLB 38;
MTCW

Haliburton, Thomas Chandler
1796-1865 .... **NCLC 15**
See also DLB 11, 99

Hall, Donald (Andrew, Jr.)
1928- .... **CLC 1, 13, 37, 59**
See also CA 5-8R; CAAS 7; CANR 2;
DLB 5; SATA 23

Hall, Frederic Sauser
See Sauser-Hall, Frederic

Hall, James
See Kuttner, Henry

Hall, James Norman 1887-1951 ... **TCLC 23**
See also CA 123; SATA 21

Hall, (Marguerite) Radclyffe
1886(?)-1943 .... **TCLC 12**
See also CA 110

Hall, Rodney 1935- .... **CLC 51**
See also CA 109

Halliday, Michael
See Creasey, John

Halpern, Daniel 1945- .... **CLC 14**
See also CA 33-36R

Hamburger, Michael (Peter Leopold)
1924- .... **CLC 5, 14**
See also CA 5-8R; CAAS 4; CANR 2;
DLB 27

Hamill, Pete 1935- .... **CLC 10**
See also CA 25-28R; CANR 18

Hamilton, Clive
See Lewis, C(live) S(taples)

Hamilton, Edmond 1904-1977 .... **CLC 1**
See also CA 1-4R; CANR 3; DLB 8

Hamilton, Eugene (Jacob) Lee
See Lee-Hamilton, Eugene (Jacob)

Hamilton, Franklin
See Silverberg, Robert

Hamilton, Gail
See Corcoran, Barbara

Hamilton, Mollie
See Kaye, M(ary) M(argaret)

Hamilton, (Anthony Walter) Patrick
1904-1962 .... **CLC 51**
See also CA 113; DLB 10

Hamilton, Virginia 1936- .... **CLC 26**
See also AAYA 2; BW; CA 25-28R;
CANR 20, 37; CLR 1, 11; DLB 33, 52;
JRDA; MAICYA; MTCW; SATA 4, 56

Hazlitt, William 1778-1830 ...... **NCLC 29**
See also DLB 110

Hazzard, Shirley 1931- .... **CLC 18**
See also CA 9-12R; CANR 4; DLBY 82;
MTCW

Head, Bessie 1937-1986... **CLC 25, 67; BLC**
See also BW; CA 29-32R; 119; CANR 25;
DLB 117; MTCW

Headon, (Nicky) Topper 1956(?)- ... **CLC 30**
See also Clash, The

Heaney, Seamus (Justin)
1939- .... **CLC 5, 7, 14, 25, 37, 74**
See also CA 85-88; CANR 25;
CDBLB 1960 to Present; DLB 40;
MTCW

Hearn, (Patricio) Lafcadio (Tessima Carlos)
1850-1904 .... **TCLC 9**
See also CA 105; DLB 12, 78

Hearne, Vicki 1946- .... **CLC 56**
See also CA 139

Hearon, Shelby 1931-............. **CLC 63**
See also AITN 2; CA 25-28R; CANR 18

Heat-Moon, William Least......... **CLC 29**
See also Trogdon, William (Lewis)
See also AAYA 9

Hebbel, Friedrich 1813-1863..... **NCLC 43**
See also DLB 129

Hebert, Anne 1916- .... **CLC 4, 13, 29**
See also CA 85-88; DLB 68; MTCW

Hecht, Anthony (Evan)
1923-.................... **CLC 8, 13, 19**
See also CA 9-12R; CANR 6; DLB 5

Hecht, Ben 1894-1964 .... **CLC 8**
See also CA 85-88; DLB 7, 9, 25, 26, 28, 86

Hedayat, Sadeq 1903-1951........ **TCLC 21**
See also CA 120

Heidegger, Martin 1889-1976 ...... **CLC 24**
See also CA 81-84; 65-68; CANR 34;
MTCW

Heidenstam, (Carl Gustaf) Verner von
1859-1940 .... **TCLC 5**
See also CA 104

Heifner, Jack 1946- .... **CLC 11**
See also CA 105

Heijermans, Herman 1864-1924 ... **TCLC 24**
See also CA 123

Heilbrun, Carolyn G(old) 1926-..... **CLC 25**
See also CA 45-48; CANR 1, 28

Heine, Heinrich 1797-1856 .... **NCLC 4**
See also DLB 90

Heinemann, Larry (Curtiss) 1944- .. **CLC 50**
See also CA 110; CANR 31; DLBD 9

Heiney, Donald (William)
1921-1993 .... **CLC 9**
See also CA 1-4R; 142; CANR 3

Heinlein, Robert A(nson)
1907-1988 ...... **CLC 1, 3, 8, 14, 26, 55**
See also CA 1-4R; 125; CANR 1, 20;
DLB 8; JRDA; MAICYA; MTCW;
SATA 9, 56, 69

Helforth, John
See Doolittle, Hilda

Hellenhofferu, Vojtech Kapristian z
See Hasek, Jaroslav (Matej Frantisek)

Heller, Joseph
1923- .... **CLC 1, 3, 5, 8, 11, 36, 63; DA; WLC**
See also AITN 1; CA 5-8R; CABS 1;
CANR 8, 42; DLB 2, 28; DLBY 80;
MTCW

Hellman, Lillian (Florence)
1906-1984 ...... **CLC 2, 4, 8, 14, 18, 34, 44, 52; DC 1**
See also AITN 1, 2; CA 13-16R; 112;
CANR 33; DLB 7; DLBY 84; MTCW

Helprin, Mark 1947- ..... **CLC 7, 10, 22, 32**
See also CA 81-84; DLBY 85; MTCW

Helyar, Jane Penelope Josephine 1933-
See Poole, Josephine
See also CA 21-24R; CANR 10, 26

Hemans, Felicia 1793-1835 ...... **NCLC 29**
See also DLB 96

Hemingway, Ernest (Miller)
1899-1961 .... **CLC 1, 3, 6, 8, 10, 13, 19, 30, 34, 39, 41, 44, 50, 61, 80; DA; SSC 1; WLC**
See also CA 77-80; CANR 34;
CDALB 1917-1929; DLB 4, 9, 102;
DLBD 1; DLBY 81, 87; MTCW

Hempel, Amy 1951- .... **CLC 39**
See also CA 118; 137

Henderson, F. C.
See Mencken, H(enry) L(ouis)

Henderson, Sylvia
See Ashton-Warner, Sylvia (Constance)

Henley, Beth .... **CLC 23**
See also Henley, Elizabeth Becker
See also CABS 3; DLBY 86

Henley, Elizabeth Becker 1952-
See Henley, Beth
See also CA 107; CANR 32; MTCW

Henley, William Ernest
1849-1903 .... **TCLC 8**
See also CA 105; DLB 19

Hennissart, Martha
See Lathen, Emma
See also CA 85-88

Henry, O......... **TCLC 1, 19; SSC 5; WLC**
See also Porter, William Sydney

Henry, Patrick 1736-1799 .... **LC 25**

Henryson, Robert 1430(?)-1506(?).... **LC 20**

Henry VIII 1491-1547 .... **LC 10**

Henschke, Alfred
See Klabund

Hentoff, Nat(han Irving) 1925- ..... **CLC 26**
See also AAYA 4; CA 1-4R; CAAS 6;
CANR 5, 25; CLR 1; JRDA; MAICYA;
SATA 27, 42, 69

Heppenstall, (John) Rayner
1911-1981 .... **CLC 10**
See also CA 1-4R; 103; CANR 29

Herbert, Frank (Patrick)
1920-1986 .... **CLC 12, 23, 35, 44**
See also CA 53-56; 118; CANR 5, 43;
DLB 8; MTCW; SATA 9, 37, 47

Herbert, George 1593-1633.... **LC 24; PC 4**
See also CDBLB Before 1660; DLB 126

Herbert, Zbigniew 1924- .... **CLC 9, 43**
See also CA 89-92; CANR 36; MTCW

Herbst, Josephine (Frey)
1897-1969 .... **CLC 34**
See also CA 5-8R; 25-28R; DLB 9

Hergesheimer, Joseph
1880-1954 .... **TCLC 11**
See also CA 109; DLB 102, 9

Herlihy, James Leo 1927-1993 ...... **CLC 6**
See also CA 1-4R; 143; CANR 2

Hermogenes fl. c. 175-........... **CMLC 6**

Hernandez, Jose 1834-1886...... **NCLC 17**

Herrick, Robert 1591-1674 ..... **LC 13; DA**
See also DLB 126

Herring, Guilles
See Somerville, Edith

Herriot, James 1916- .... **CLC 12**
See Wight, James Alfred
See also AAYA 1; CANR 40

Herrmann, Dorothy 1941-......... **CLC 44**
See also CA 107

Herrmann, Taffy
See Herrmann, Dorothy

Hersey, John (Richard)
1914-1993 .... **CLC 1, 2, 7, 9, 40, 81**
See also CA 17-20R; 140; CANR 33;
DLB 6; MTCW; SATA 25;
SATA-Obit 76

Herzen, Aleksandr Ivanovich
1812-1870 .... **NCLC 10**

Herzl, Theodor 1860-1904........ **TCLC 36**

Herzog, Werner 1942- .... **CLC 16**
See also CA 89-92

Hesiod c. 8th cent. B.C.-......... **CMLC 5**

Hesse, Hermann
1877-1962 .... **CLC 1, 2, 3, 6, 11, 17, 25, 69; DA; SSC 9; WLC**
See also CA 17-18; CAP 2; DLB 66;
MTCW; SATA 50

Hewes, Cady
See De Voto, Bernard (Augustine)

Heyen, William 1940- .... **CLC 13, 18**
See also CA 33-36R; CAAS 9; DLB 5

Heyerdahl, Thor 1914-............ **CLC 26**
See also CA 5-8R; CANR 5, 22; MTCW;
SATA 2, 52

Heym, Georg (Theodor Franz Arthur)
1887-1912 .... **TCLC 9**
See also CA 106

Heym, Stefan 1913- .... **CLC 41**
See also CA 9-12R; CANR 4; DLB 69

Heyse, Paul (Johann Ludwig von)
1830-1914 .... **TCLC 8**
See also CA 104; DLB 129

Hibbert, Eleanor Alice Burford
1906-1993 .... **CLC 7**
See also BEST 90:4; CA 17-20R; 140;
CANR 9, 28; SATA 2; SATA-Obit 74

Higgins, George V(incent)
1939- .... **CLC 4, 7, 10, 18**
See also CA 77-80; CAAS 5; CANR 17;
DLB 2; DLBY 81; MTCW

Higginson, Thomas Wentworth
1823-1911 .... **TCLC 36**
See also DLB 1, 64

Huysmans, Charles Marie Georges
1848-1907
See Huysmans, Joris-Karl
See also CA 104

Huysmans, Joris-Karl . . . . TCLC 7
See also Huysmans, Charles Marie Georges
See also DLB 123

Hwang, David Henry
1957- . . . . CLC 55; DC 4
See also CA 127; 132

Hyde, Anthony 1946- . . . . CLC 42
See also CA 136

Hyde, Margaret O(ldroyd) 1917- . . . CLC 21
See also CA 1-4R; CANR 1, 36; CLR 23;
JRDA; MAICYA; SAAS 8; SATA 1, 42,
76

Hynes, James 1956(?)- . . . . CLC 65

Ian, Janis 1951- . . . . CLC 21
See also CA 105

Ibanez, Vicente Blasco
See Blasco Ibanez, Vicente

Ibarguengoitia, Jorge 1928-1983 . . . . CLC 37
See also CA 124; 113; HW

Ibsen, Henrik (Johan)
1828-1906 . . . . TCLC 2, 8, 16, 37, 52;
DA; DC 2; WLC
See also CA 104; 141

Ibuse Masuji 1898-1993 . . . . CLC 22
See also CA 127; 141

Ichikawa, Kon 1915- . . . . CLC 20
See also CA 121

Idle, Eric 1943- . . . . CLC 21
See also Monty Python
See also CA 116; CANR 35

Ignatow, David 1914- . . . . . . CLC 4, 7, 14, 40
See also CA 9-12R; CAAS 3; CANR 31;
DLB 5

Ihimaera, Witi 1944- . . . . CLC 46
See also CA 77-80

Ilf, Ilya . . . . TCLC 21
See also Fainzilberg, Ilya Arnoldovich

Immermann, Karl (Lebrecht)
1796-1840 . . . . NCLC 4
See also DLB 133

Inclan, Ramon (Maria) del Valle
See Valle-Inclan, Ramon (Maria) del

Infante, G(uillermo) Cabrera
See Cabrera Infante, G(uillermo)

Ingalls, Rachel (Holmes) 1940- . . . . . CLC 42
See also CA 123; 127

Ingamells, Rex 1913-1955 . . . . TCLC 35

Inge, William Motter
1913-1973 . . . . CLC 1, 8, 19
See also CA 9-12R; CDALB 1941-1968;
DLB 7; MTCW

Ingelow, Jean 1820-1897 . . . . NCLC 39
See also DLB 35; SATA 33

Ingram, Willis J.
See Harris, Mark

Innaurato, Albert (F.) 1948(?)- . . CLC 21, 60
See also CA 115; 122

Innes, Michael
See Stewart, J(ohn) I(nnes) M(ackintosh)

Ionesco, Eugene
1912- . . . . CLC 1, 4, 6, 9, 11, 15, 41; DA;
WLC
See also CA 9-12R; MTCW; SATA 7

Iqbal, Muhammad 1873-1938 . . . . . TCLC 28

Ireland, Patrick
See O'Doherty, Brian

Iron, Ralph
See Schreiner, Olive (Emilie Albertina)

Irving, John (Winslow)
1942- . . . . CLC 13, 23, 38
See also AAYA 8; BEST 89:3; CA 25-28R;
CANR 28; DLB 6; DLBY 82; MTCW

Irving, Washington
1783-1859 . . . . NCLC 2, 19; DA; SSC 2;
WLC
See also CDALB 1640-1865; DLB 3, 11, 30,
59, 73, 74; YABC 2

Irwin, P. K.
See Page, P(atricia) K(athleen)

Isaacs, Susan 1943- . . . . CLC 32
See also BEST 89:1; CA 89-92; CANR 20,
41; MTCW

Isherwood, Christopher (William Bradshaw)
1904-1986 . . . . CLC 1, 9, 11, 14, 44
See also CA 13-16R; 117; CANR 35;
DLB 15; DLBY 86; MTCW

Ishiguro, Kazuo 1954- . . . . . . CLC 27, 56, 59
See also BEST 90:2; CA 120; MTCW

Ishikawa Takuboku
1886(?)-1912 . . . . TCLC 15
See also CA 113

Iskander, Fazil 1929- . . . . CLC 47
See also CA 102

Ivan IV 1530-1584 . . . . LC 17

Ivanov, Vyacheslav Ivanovich
1866-1949 . . . . TCLC 33
See also CA 122

Ivask, Ivar Vidrik 1927-1992 . . . . . . CLC 14
See also CA 37-40R; 139; CANR 24

Jackson, Daniel
See Wingrove, David (John)

Jackson, Jesse 1908-1983 . . . . CLC 12
See also BW; CA 25-28R; 109; CANR 27;
CLR 28; MAICYA; SATA 2, 29, 48

Jackson, Laura (Riding) 1901-1991
See Riding, Laura
See also CA 65-68; 135; CANR 28; DLB 48

Jackson, Sam
See Trumbo, Dalton

Jackson, Sara
See Wingrove, David (John)

Jackson, Shirley
1919-1965 . . . . . CLC 11, 60; DA; SSC 9;
WLC
See also AAYA 9; CA 1-4R; 25-28R;
CANR 4; CDALB 1941-1968; DLB 6;
SATA 2

Jacob, (Cyprien-)Max 1876-1944 . . . TCLC 6
See also CA 104

Jacobs, Jim 1942- . . . . CLC 12
See also CA 97-100

Jacobs, W(illiam) W(ymark)
1863-1943 . . . . TCLC 22
See also CA 121; DLB 135

Jacobsen, Jens Peter 1847-1885 . . NCLC 34

Jacobsen, Josephine 1908- . . . . CLC 48
See also CA 33-36R; CAAS 18; CANR 23

Jacobson, Dan 1929- . . . . CLC 4, 14
See also CA 1-4R; CANR 2, 25; DLB 14;
MTCW

Jacqueline
See Carpentier (y Valmont), Alejo

Jagger, Mick 1944- . . . . CLC 17

Jakes, John (William) 1932- . . . . CLC 29
See also BEST 89:4; CA 57-60; CANR 10,
43; DLBY 83; MTCW; SATA 62

James, Andrew
See Kirkup, James

James, C(yril) L(ionel) R(obert)
1901-1989 . . . . CLC 33
See also BW; CA 117; 125; 128; DLB 125;
MTCW

James, Daniel (Lewis) 1911-1988
See Santiago, Danny
See also CA 125

James, Dynely
See Mayne, William (James Carter)

James, Henry
1843-1916 . . . . . . TCLC 2, 11, 24, 40, 47;
DA; SSC 8; WLC
See also CA 104; 132; CDALB 1865-1917;
DLB 12, 71, 74; MTCW

James, Montague (Rhodes)
1862-1936 . . . . TCLC 6
See also CA 104

James, P. D. . . . . CLC 18, 46
See also White, Phyllis Dorothy James
See also BEST 90:2; CDBLB 1960 to
Present; DLB 87

James, Philip
See Moorcock, Michael (John)

James, William 1842-1910 . . . . . TCLC 15, 32
See also CA 109

James I 1394-1437 . . . . LC 20

Jameson, Anna 1794-1860 . . . . NCLC 43
See also DLB 99

Jami, Nur al-Din 'Abd al-Rahman
1414-1492 . . . . LC 9

Jandl, Ernst 1925- . . . . CLC 34

Janowitz, Tama 1957- . . . . CLC 43
See also CA 106

Jarrell, Randall
1914-1965 . . . . CLC 1, 2, 6, 9, 13, 49
See also CA 5-8R; 25-28R; CABS 2;
CANR 6, 34; CDALB 1941-1968; CLR 6;
DLB 48, 52; MAICYA; MTCW; SATA 7

Jarry, Alfred 1873-1907 . . . . TCLC 2, 14
See also CA 104

Jarvis, E. K.
See Bloch, Robert (Albert); Ellison, Harlan;
Silverberg, Robert

Jeake, Samuel, Jr.
See Aiken, Conrad (Potter)

Jean Paul 1763-1825 . . . . NCLC 7

Jeffers, (John) Robinson
1887-1962 .... **CLC 2, 3, 11, 15, 54; DA;**
WLC
See also CA 85-88; CANR 35;
CDALB 1917-1929; DLB 45; MTCW

Jefferson, Janet
See Mencken, H(enry) L(ouis)

Jefferson, Thomas 1743-1826 .... **NCLC 11**
See also CDALB 1640-1865; DLB 31

Jeffrey, Francis 1773-1850....... **NCLC 33**
See also DLB 107

Jelakowitch, Ivan
See Heijermans, Herman

Jellicoe, (Patricia) Ann 1927- ...... **CLC 27**
See also CA 85-88; DLB 13

Jen, Gish .... **CLC 70**
See also Jen, Lillian

Jen, Lillian 1956(?)-
See Jen, Gish
See also CA 135

Jenkins, (John) Robin 1912- .... **CLC 52**
See also CA 1-4R; CANR 1; DLB 14

Jennings, Elizabeth (Joan)
1926- .... **CLC 5, 14**
See also CA 61-64; CAAS 5; CANR 8, 39;
DLB 27; MTCW; SATA 66

Jennings, Waylon 1937-........... **CLC 21**

Jensen, Johannes V. 1873-1950.... **TCLC 41**

Jensen, Laura (Linnea) 1948- ...... **CLC 37**
See also CA 103

Jerome, Jerome K(lapka)
1859-1927 .... **TCLC 23**
See also CA 119; DLB 10, 34, 135

Jerrold, Douglas William
1803-1857 .... **NCLC 2**

Jewett, (Theodora) Sarah Orne
1849-1909 .... **TCLC 1, 22; SSC 6**
See also CA 108; 127; DLB 12, 74;
SATA 15

Jewsbury, Geraldine (Endsor)
1812-1880 .... **NCLC 22**
See also DLB 21

Jhabvala, Ruth Prawer
1927- .... **CLC 4, 8, 29**
See also CA 1-4R; CANR 2, 29; MTCW

Jiles, Paulette 1943-.......... **CLC 13, 58**
See also CA 101

Jimenez (Mantecon), Juan Ramon
1881-1958 .... **TCLC 4; HLC; PC 7**
See also CA 104; 131; DLB 134; HW;
MTCW

Jimenez, Ramon
See Jimenez (Mantecon), Juan Ramon

Jimenez Mantecon, Juan
See Jimenez (Mantecon), Juan Ramon

Joel, Billy .... **CLC 26**
See also Joel, William Martin

Joel, William Martin 1949-
See Joel, Billy
See also CA 108

John of the Cross, St. 1542-1591 .... **LC 18**

Johnson, B(ryan) S(tanley William)
1933-1973 .... **CLC 6, 9**
See also CA 9-12R; 53-56; CANR 9;
DLB 14, 40

Johnson, Benj. F. of Boo
See Riley, James Whitcomb

Johnson, Benjamin F. of Boo
See Riley, James Whitcomb

Johnson, Charles (Richard)
1948- .... **CLC 7, 51, 65; BLC**
See also BW; CA 116; CAAS 18;
CANR 42; DLB 33

Johnson, Denis 1949-............. **CLC 52**
See also CA 117; 121; DLB 120

Johnson, Diane 1934-........ **CLC 5, 13, 48**
See also CA 41-44R; CANR 17, 40;
DLBY 80; MTCW

Johnson, Eyvind (Olof Verner)
1900-1976 .... **CLC 14**
See also CA 73-76; 69-72; CANR 34

Johnson, J. R.
See James, C(yril) L(ionel) R(obert)

Johnson, James Weldon
1871-1938 .... **TCLC 3, 19; BLC**
See also BW; CA 104; 125;
CDALB 1917-1929; CLR 32; DLB 51;
MTCW; SATA 31

Johnson, Joyce 1935-............. **CLC 58**
See also CA 125; 129

Johnson, Lionel (Pigot)
1867-1902 .... **TCLC 19**
See also CA 117; DLB 19

Johnson, Mel
See Malzberg, Barry N(athaniel)

Johnson, Pamela Hansford
1912-1981 .... **CLC 1, 7, 27**
See also CA 1-4R; 104; CANR 2, 28;
DLB 15; MTCW

Johnson, Samuel
1709-1784 .... **LC 15; DA; WLC**
See also CDBLB 1660-1789; DLB 39, 95,
104

Johnson, Uwe
1934-1984 .... **CLC 5, 10, 15, 40**
See also CA 1-4R; 112; CANR 1, 39;
DLB 75; MTCW

Johnston, George (Benson) 1913- ... **CLC 51**
See also CA 1-4R; CANR 5, 20; DLB 88

Johnston, Jennifer 1930-........... **CLC 7**
See also CA 85-88; DLB 14

Jolley, (Monica) Elizabeth 1923- ... **CLC 46**
See also CA 127; CAAS 13

Jones, Arthur Llewellyn 1863-1947
See Machen, Arthur
See also CA 104

Jones, D(ouglas) G(ordon) 1929-.... **CLC 10**
See also CA 29-32R; CANR 13; DLB 53

Jones, David (Michael)
1895-1974 .... **CLC 2, 4, 7, 13, 42**
See also CA 9-12R; 53-56; CANR 28;
CDBLB 1945-1960; DLB 20, 100; MTCW

Jones, David Robert 1947-
See Bowie, David
See also CA 103

Jones, Diana Wynne 1934- .... **CLC 26**
See also CA 49-52; CANR 4, 26; CLR 23;
JRDA; MAICYA; SAAS 7; SATA 9, 70

Jones, Edward P. 1950-........... **CLC 76**
See also CA 142

Jones, Gayl 1949-.......... **CLC 6, 9; BLC**
See also BW; CA 77-80; CANR 27;
DLB 33; MTCW

Jones, James 1921-1977.... **CLC 1, 3, 10, 39**
See also AITN 1, 2; CA 1-4R; 69-72;
CANR 6; DLB 2; MTCW

Jones, John J.
See Lovecraft, H(oward) P(hillips)

Jones, LeRoi .... **CLC 1, 2, 3, 5, 10, 14**
See also Baraka, Amiri

Jones, Louis B. .... **CLC 65**
See also CA 141

Jones, Madison (Percy, Jr.) 1925- ... **CLC 4**
See also CA 13-16R; CAAS 11; CANR 7

Jones, Mervyn 1922-.......... **CLC 10, 52**
See also CA 45-48; CAAS 5; CANR 1;
MTCW

Jones, Mick 1956(?)-............. **CLC 30**
See also Clash, The

Jones, Nettie (Pearl) 1941-........ **CLC 34**
See also CA 137

Jones, Preston 1936-1979 .... **CLC 10**
See also CA 73-76; 89-92; DLB 7

Jones, Robert F(rancis) 1934-....... **CLC 7**
See also CA 49-52; CANR 2

Jones, Rod 1953- .... **CLC 50**
See also CA 128

Jones, Terence Graham Parry
1942- .... **CLC 21**
See also Jones, Terry; Monty Python
See also CA 112; 116; CANR 35; SATA 51

Jones, Terry
See Jones, Terence Graham Parry
See also SATA 67

Jones, Thom 1945(?)-............. **CLC 81**

Jong, Erica 1942-.......... **CLC 4, 6, 8, 18**
See also AITN 1; BEST 90:2; CA 73-76;
CANR 26; DLB 2, 5, 28; MTCW

Jonson, Ben(jamin)
1572(?)-1637 .... **LC 6; DA; DC 4; WLC**
See also CDBLB Before 1660; DLB 62, 121

Jordan, June 1936-.......... **CLC 5, 11, 23**
See also AAYA 2; BW; CA 33-36R;
CANR 25; CLR 10; DLB 38; MAICYA;
MTCW; SATA 4

Jordan, Pat(rick M.) 1941- .... **CLC 37**
See also CA 33-36R

Jorgensen, Ivar
See Ellison, Harlan

Jorgenson, Ivar
See Silverberg, Robert

Josipovici, Gabriel 1940-........ **CLC 6, 43**
See also CA 37-40R; CAAS 8; DLB 14

Joubert, Joseph 1754-1824 .... **NCLC 9**

Jouve, Pierre Jean 1887-1976...... **CLC 47**
See also CA 65-68

Kenyon, Robert O.
See Kuttner, Henry

Kerouac, Jack ..... **CLC 1, 2, 3, 5, 14, 29, 61**
See also Kerouac, Jean-Louis Lebris de
See also CDALB 1941-1968; DLB 2, 16;
DLBD 3

Kerouac, Jean-Louis Lebris de 1922-1969
See Kerouac, Jack
See also AITN 1; CA 5-8R; 25-28R;
CANR 26; DA; MTCW; WLC

Kerr, Jean 1923- .... **CLC 22**
See also CA 5-8R; CANR 7

Kerr, M. E. .... **CLC 12, 35**
See also Meaker, Marijane (Agnes)
See also AAYA 2; CLR 29; SAAS 1

Kerr, Robert .... **CLC 55**

Kerrigan, (Thomas) Anthony
1918- .... **CLC 4, 6**
See also CA 49-52; CAAS 11; CANR 4

Kerry, Lois
See Duncan, Lois

Kesey, Ken (Elton)
1935- ...... **CLC 1, 3, 6, 11, 46, 64; DA;**
WLC
See also CA 1-4R; CANR 22, 38;
CDALB 1968-1988; DLB 2, 16; MTCW;
SATA 66

Kesselring, Joseph (Otto)
1902-1967 .... **CLC 45**

Kessler, Jascha (Frederick) 1929- .... **CLC 4**
See also CA 17-20R; CANR 8

Kettelkamp, Larry (Dale) 1933- .... **CLC 12**
See also CA 29-32R; CANR 16; SAAS 3;
SATA 2

Keyber, Conny
See Fielding, Henry

Keyes, Daniel 1927- .... **CLC 80; DA**
See also CA 17-20R; CANR 10, 26;
SATA 37

Khayyam, Omar
1048-1131 .... **CMLC 11; PC 8**

Kherdian, David 1931- .... **CLC 6, 9**
See also CA 21-24R; CAAS 2; CANR 39;
CLR 24; JRDA; MAICYA; SATA 16, 74

Khlebnikov, Velimir .... **TCLC 20**
See also Khlebnikov, Viktor Vladimirovich

Khlebnikov, Viktor Vladimirovich 1885-1922
See Khlebnikov, Velimir
See also CA 117

Khodasevich, Vladislav (Felitsianovich)
1886-1939 .... **TCLC 15**
See also CA 115

Kielland, Alexander Lange
1849-1906 .... **TCLC 5**
See also CA 104

Kiely, Benedict 1919- .... **CLC 23, 43**
See also CA 1-4R; CANR 2; DLB 15

Kienzle, William X(avier) 1928- .... **CLC 25**
See also CA 93-96; CAAS 1; CANR 9, 31;
MTCW

Kierkegaard, Soren 1813-1855.... **NCLC 34**

Killens, John Oliver 1916-1987..... **CLC 10**
See also BW; CA 77-80; 123; CAAS 2;
CANR 26; DLB 33

Killigrew, Anne 1660-1685.......... **LC 4**
See also DLB 131

Kim
See Simenon, Georges (Jacques Christian)

Kincaid, Jamaica 1949- ... **CLC 43, 68; BLC**
See also BW; CA 125

King, Francis (Henry) 1923- ..... **CLC 8, 53**
See also CA 1-4R; CANR 1, 33; DLB 15;
MTCW

King, Stephen (Edwin)
1947- .... **CLC 12, 26, 37, 61**
See also AAYA 1; BEST 90:1; CA 61-64;
CANR 1, 30; DLBY 80; JRDA; MTCW;
SATA 9, 55

King, Steve
See King, Stephen (Edwin)

Kingman, Lee .... **CLC 17**
See also Natti, (Mary) Lee
See also SAAS 3; SATA 1, 67

Kingsley, Charles 1819-1875 ..... **NCLC 35**
See also DLB 21, 32; YABC 2

Kingsley, Sidney 1906- .... **CLC 44**
See also CA 85-88; DLB 7

Kingsolver, Barbara 1955- ...... **CLC 55, 81**
See also CA 129; 134

Kingston, Maxine (Ting Ting) Hong
1940- .... **CLC 12, 19, 58**
See also AAYA 8; CA 69-72; CANR 13,
38; DLBY 80; MTCW; SATA 53

Kinnell, Galway
1927- .... **CLC 1, 2, 3, 5, 13, 29**
See also CA 9-12R; CANR 10, 34; DLB 5;
DLBY 87; MTCW

Kinsella, Thomas 1928- .... **CLC 4, 19**
See also CA 17-20R; CANR 15; DLB 27;
MTCW

Kinsella, W(illiam) P(atrick)
1935- .... **CLC 27, 43**
See also AAYA 7; CA 97-100; CAAS 7;
CANR 21, 35; MTCW

Kipling, (Joseph) Rudyard
1865-1936 ...... **TCLC 8, 17; DA; PC 3;**
SSC 5; WLC
See also CA 105; 120; CANR 33;
CDBLB 1890-1914; DLB 19, 34;
MAICYA; MTCW; YABC 2

Kirkup, James 1918- .... **CLC 1**
See also CA 1-4R; CAAS 4; CANR 2;
DLB 27; SATA 12

Kirkwood, James 1930(?)-1989 ...... **CLC 9**
See also AITN 2; CA 1-4R; 128; CANR 6,
40

Kis, Danilo 1935-1989 .... **CLC 57**
See also CA 109; 118; 129; MTCW

Kivi, Aleksis 1834-1872 .... **NCLC 30**

Kizer, Carolyn (Ashley)
1925- .... **CLC 15, 39, 80**
See also CA 65-68; CAAS 5; CANR 24;
DLB 5

Klabund 1890-1928.............. **TCLC 44**
See also DLB 66

Klappert, Peter 1942-............. **CLC 57**
See also CA 33-36R; DLB 5

Klein, A(braham) M(oses)
1909-1972 .... **CLC 19**
See also CA 101; 37-40R; DLB 68

Klein, Norma 1938-1989 .... **CLC 30**
See also AAYA 2; CA 41-44R; 128;
CANR 15, 37; CLR 2, 19; JRDA;
MAICYA; SAAS 1; SATA 7, 57

Klein, T(heodore) E(ibon) D(onald)
1947- .... **CLC 34**
See also CA 119

Kleist, Heinrich von
1777-1811 .... **NCLC 2, 37**
See also DLB 90

Klima, Ivan 1931-................ **CLC 56**
See also CA 25-28R; CANR 17

Klimentov, Andrei Platonovich 1899-1951
See Platonov, Andrei
See also CA 108

Klinger, Friedrich Maximilian von
1752-1831 .... **NCLC 1**
See also DLB 94

Klopstock, Friedrich Gottlieb
1724-1803 .... **NCLC 11**
See also DLB 97

Knebel, Fletcher 1911-1993........ **CLC 14**
See also AITN 1; CA 1-4R; 140; CAAS 3;
CANR 1, 36; SATA 36; SATA-Obit 75

Knickerbocker, Diedrich
See Irving, Washington

Knight, Etheridge
1931-1991 .... **CLC 40; BLC**
See also BW; CA 21-24R; 133; CANR 23;
DLB 41

Knight, Sarah Kemble 1666-1727 ..... **LC 7**
See also DLB 24

Knowles, John
1926- .... **CLC 1, 4, 10, 26; DA**
See also AAYA 10; CA 17-20R; CANR 40;
CDALB 1968-1988; DLB 6; MTCW;
SATA 8

Knox, Calvin M.
See Silverberg, Robert

Knye, Cassandra
See Disch, Thomas M(ichael)

Koch, C(hristopher) J(ohn) 1932- ... **CLC 42**
See also CA 127

Koch, Christopher
See Koch, C(hristopher) J(ohn)

Koch, Kenneth 1925- .... **CLC 5, 8, 44**
See also CA 1-4R; CANR 6, 36; DLB 5;
SATA 65

Kochanowski, Jan 1530-1584........ **LC 10**

Kock, Charles Paul de
1794-1871 .... **NCLC 16**

Koda Shigeyuki 1867-1947
See Rohan, Koda
See also CA 121

Koestler, Arthur
1905-1983 .... **CLC 1, 3, 6, 8, 15, 33**
See also CA 1-4R; 109; CANR 1, 33;
CDBLB 1945-1960; DLBY 83; MTCW

Kogawa, Joy Nozomi 1935-........ **CLC 78**
See also CA 101; CANR 19

Kohout, Pavel 1928-.............. **CLC 13**
See also CA 45-48; CANR 3

Koizumi, Yakumo
See Hearn, (Patricio) Lafcadio (Tessima Carlos)

Kolmar, Gertrud 1894-1943...... **TCLC 40**

Konrad, George
See Konrad, Gyoergy

Konrad, Gyoergy 1933- ...... **CLC 4, 10, 73**
See also CA 85-88

Konwicki, Tadeusz 1926-..... **CLC 8, 28, 54**
See also CA 101; CAAS 9; CANR 39;
MTCW

Koontz, Dean R(ay) 1945-......... **CLC 78**
See also AAYA 9; BEST 89:3, 90:2;
CA 108; CANR 19, 36; MTCW

Kopit, Arthur (Lee) 1937- .... **CLC 1, 18, 33**
See also AITN 1; CA 81-84; CABS 3;
DLB 7; MTCW

Kops, Bernard 1926-.............. **CLC 4**
See also CA 5-8R; DLB 13

Kornbluth, C(yril) M. 1923-1958.... **TCLC 8**
See also CA 105; DLB 8

Korolenko, V. G.
See Korolenko, Vladimir Galaktionovich

Korolenko, Vladimir
See Korolenko, Vladimir Galaktionovich

Korolenko, Vladimir G.
See Korolenko, Vladimir Galaktionovich

Korolenko, Vladimir Galaktionovich
1853-1921 .... **TCLC 22**
See also CA 121

Kosinski, Jerzy (Nikodem)
1933-1991 .... **CLC 1, 2, 3, 6, 10, 15, 53, 70**
See also CA 17-20R; 134; CANR 9; DLB 2;
DLBY 82; MTCW

Kostelanetz, Richard (Cory) 1940- .. **CLC 28**
See also CA 13-16R; CAAS 8; CANR 38

Kostrowitzki, Wilhelm Apollinaris de
1880-1918
See Apollinaire, Guillaume
See also CA 104

Kotlowitz, Robert 1924-............ **CLC 4**
See also CA 33-36R; CANR 36

Kotzebue, August (Friedrich Ferdinand) von
1761-1819 .... **NCLC 25**
See also DLB 94

Kotzwinkle, William 1938- ... **CLC 5, 14, 35**
See also CA 45-48; CANR 3; CLR 6;
MAICYA; SATA 24, 70

Kozol, Jonathan 1936-............ **CLC 17**
See also CA 61-64; CANR 16

Kozoll, Michael 1940(?)-.......... **CLC 35**

Kramer, Kathryn 19(?)-............ **CLC 34**

Kramer, Larry 1935- .... **CLC 42**
See also CA 124; 126

Krasicki, Ignacy 1735-1801....... **NCLC 8**

Krasinski, Zygmunt 1812-1859 .... **NCLC 4**

Kraus, Karl 1874-1936............ **TCLC 5**
See also CA 104; DLB 118

Kreve (Mickevicius), Vincas
1882-1954 .... **TCLC 27**

Kristeva, Julia 1941- .... **CLC 77**

Kristofferson, Kris 1936-.......... **CLC 26**
See also CA 104

Krizanc, John 1956-.............. **CLC 57**

Krleza, Miroslav 1893-1981......... **CLC 8**
See also CA 97-100; 105

Kroetsch, Robert 1927- ...... **CLC 5, 23, 57**
See also CA 17-20R; CANR 8, 38; DLB 53;
MTCW

Kroetz, Franz
See Kroetz, Franz Xaver

Kroetz, Franz Xaver 1946- .... **CLC 41**
See also CA 130

Kroker, Arthur 1945-............. **CLC 77**

Kropotkin, Peter (Aleksieevich)
1842-1921 .... **TCLC 36**
See also CA 119

Krotkov, Yuri 1917-.............. **CLC 19**
See also CA 102

Krumb
See Crumb, R(obert)

Krumgold, Joseph (Quincy)
1908-1980 .... **CLC 12**
See also CA 9-12R; 101; CANR 7;
MAICYA; SATA 1, 23, 48

Krumwitz
See Crumb, R(obert)

Krutch, Joseph Wood 1893-1970.... **CLC 24**
See also CA 1-4R; 25-28R; CANR 4;
DLB 63

Krutzch, Gus
See Eliot, T(homas) S(tearns)

Krylov, Ivan Andreevich
1768(?)-1844 .... **NCLC 1**

Kubin, Alfred 1877-1959 .... **TCLC 23**
See also CA 112; DLB 81

Kubrick, Stanley 1928-........... **CLC 16**
See also CA 81-84; CANR 33; DLB 26

Kumin, Maxine (Winokur)
1925- .... **CLC 5, 13, 28**
See also AITN 2; CA 1-4R; CAAS 8;
CANR 1, 21; DLB 5; MTCW; SATA 12

Kundera, Milan
1929- .... **CLC 4, 9, 19, 32, 68**
See also AAYA 2; CA 85-88; CANR 19;
MTCW

Kunitz, Stanley (Jasspon)
1905- .... **CLC 6, 11, 14**
See also CA 41-44R; CANR 26; DLB 48;
MTCW

Kunze, Reiner 1933-.............. **CLC 10**
See also CA 93-96; DLB 75

Kuprin, Aleksandr Ivanovich
1870-1938 .... **TCLC 5**
See also CA 104

Kureishi, Hanif 1954(?)-........... **CLC 64**
See also CA 139

Kurosawa, Akira 1910-............ **CLC 16**
See also CA 101

Kushner, Tony 1957(?)- .... **CLC 81**

Kuttner, Henry 1915-1958........ **TCLC 10**
See also CA 107; DLB 8

Kuzma, Greg 1944-................ **CLC 7**
See also CA 33-36R

Kuzmin, Mikhail 1872(?)-1936 .... **TCLC 40**

Kyd, Thomas 1558-1594...... **LC 22; DC 3**
See also DLB 62

Kyprianos, Iossif
See Samarakis, Antonis

La Bruyere, Jean de 1645-1696...... **LC 17**

Lacan, Jacques (Marie Emile)
1901-1981 .... **CLC 75**
See also CA 121; 104

Laclos, Pierre Ambroise Francois Choderlos
de 1741-1803 .... **NCLC 4**

Lacolere, Francois
See Aragon, Louis

La Colere, Francois
See Aragon, Louis

La Deshabilleuse
See Simenon, Georges (Jacques Christian)

Lady Gregory
See Gregory, Isabella Augusta (Persse)

Lady of Quality, A
See Bagnold, Enid

La Fayette, Marie (Madelaine Pioche de la
Vergne Comtes 1634-1693....... **LC 2**

Lafayette, Rene
See Hubbard, L(afayette) Ron(ald)

Laforgue, Jules 1860-1887........ **NCLC 5**

Lagerkvist, Paer (Fabian)
1891-1974 .... **CLC 7, 10, 13, 54**
See also Lagerkvist, Par
See also CA 85-88; 49-52; MTCW

Lagerkvist, Par
See Lagerkvist, Paer (Fabian)
See also SSC 12

Lagerloef, Selma (Ottiliana Lovisa)
1858-1940 .... **TCLC 4, 36**
See also Lagerlof, Selma (Ottiliana Lovisa)
See also CA 108; CLR 7; SATA 15

Lagerlof, Selma (Ottiliana Lovisa)
See Lagerloef, Selma (Ottiliana Lovisa)
See also CLR 7; SATA 15

La Guma, (Justin) Alex(ander)
1925-1985 .... **CLC 19**
See also BW; CA 49-52; 118; CANR 25;
DLB 117; MTCW

Laidlaw, A. K.
See Grieve, C(hristopher) M(urray)

Lainez, Manuel Mujica
See Mujica Lainez, Manuel
See also HW

Lamartine, Alphonse (Marie Louis Prat) de
1790-1869 .... **NCLC 11**

Lamb, Charles
1775-1834 .... **NCLC 10; DA; WLC**
See also CDBLB 1789-1832; DLB 93, 107;
SATA 17

Lamb, Lady Caroline 1785-1828.. **NCLC 38**
See also DLB 116

Lamming, George (William)
1927- .... **CLC 2, 4, 66; BLC**
See also BW; CA 85-88; CANR 26;
DLB 125; MTCW

Maclean, Norman (Fitzroy)
1902-1990 . . . . CLC 78; SSC 13
See also CA 102; 132

MacLeish, Archibald
1892-1982 . . . . CLC 3, 8, 14, 68
See also CA 9-12R; 106; CANR 33; DLB 4,
7, 45; DLBY 82; MTCW

MacLennan, (John) Hugh
1907-1990 . . . . CLC 2, 14
See also CA 5-8R; 142; CANR 33; DLB 68;
MTCW

MacLeod, Alistair   1936- . . . . CLC 56
See also CA 123; DLB 60

MacNeice, (Frederick) Louis
1907-1963 . . . . CLC 1, 4, 10, 53
See also CA 85-88; DLB 10, 20; MTCW

MacNeill, Dand
See Fraser, George MacDonald

Macpherson, (Jean) Jay   1931- . . . . . . CLC 14
See also CA 5-8R; DLB 53

MacShane, Frank   1927- . . . . CLC 39
See also CA 9-12R; CANR 3, 33; DLB 111

Macumber, Mari
See Sandoz, Mari(e Susette)

Madach, Imre   1823-1864 . . . . NCLC 19

Madden, (Jerry) David   1933- . . . . CLC 5, 15
See also CA 1-4R; CAAS 3; CANR 4;
DLB 6; MTCW

Maddern, Al(an)
See Ellison, Harlan

Madhubuti, Haki R.
1942- . . . . CLC 6, 73; BLC; PC 5
See also Lee, Don L.
See also BW; CA 73-76; CANR 24; DLB 5,
41; DLBD 8

Madow, Pauline (Reichberg) . . . . CLC 1
See also CA 9-12R

Maepenn, Hugh
See Kuttner, Henry

Maepenn, K. H.
See Kuttner, Henry

Maeterlinck, Maurice   1862-1949 . . . TCLC 3
See also CA 104; 136; SATA 66

Maginn, William   1794-1842 . . . . . . NCLC 8
See also DLB 110

Mahapatra, Jayanta   1928- . . . . CLC 33
See also CA 73-76; CAAS 9; CANR 15, 33

Mahfouz, Naguib (Abdel Aziz Al-Sabilgi)
1911(?)-
See Mahfuz, Najib
See also BEST 89:2; CA 128; MTCW

Mahfuz, Najib . . . . CLC 52, 55
See also Mahfouz, Naguib (Abdel Aziz
Al-Sabilgi)
See also DLBY 88

Mahon, Derek   1941- . . . . CLC 27
See also CA 113; 128; DLB 40

Mailer, Norman
1923- . . . . . . CLC 1, 2, 3, 4, 5, 8, 11, 14,
28, 39, 74; DA
See also AITN 2; CA 9-12R; CABS 1;
CANR 28; CDALB 1968-1988; DLB 2,
16, 28; DLBD 3; DLBY 80, 83; MTCW

Maillet, Antonine   1929- . . . . CLC 54
See also CA 115; 120; DLB 60

Mais, Roger   1905-1955 . . . . TCLC 8
See also BW; CA 105; 124; DLB 125;
MTCW

Maistre, Joseph de   1753-1821 . . . . NCLC 37

Maitland, Sara (Louise)   1950- . . . . . . CLC 49
See also CA 69-72; CANR 13

Major, Clarence
1936- . . . . CLC 3, 19, 48; BLC
See also BW; CA 21-24R; CAAS 6;
CANR 13, 25; DLB 33

Major, Kevin (Gerald)   1949- . . . . CLC 26
See also CA 97-100; CANR 21, 38;
CLR 11; DLB 60; JRDA; MAICYA;
SATA 32

Maki, James
See Ozu, Yasujiro

Malabaila, Damiano
See Levi, Primo

Malamud, Bernard
1914-1986 . . . . . . CLC 1, 2, 3, 5, 8, 9, 11,
18, 27, 44, 78; DA; WLC
See also CA 5-8R; 118; CABS 1; CANR 28;
CDALB 1941-1968; DLB 2, 28;
DLBY 80, 86; MTCW

Malaparte, Curzio   1898-1957 . . . . . TCLC 52

Malcolm, Dan
See Silverberg, Robert

Malcolm X . . . . CLC 82; BLC
See also Little, Malcolm

Malherbe, Francois de   1555-1628 . . . . . LC 5

Mallarme, Stephane
1842-1898 . . . . NCLC 4, 41; PC 4

Mallet-Joris, Francoise   1930- . . . . . . CLC 11
See also CA 65-68; CANR 17; DLB 83

Malley, Ern
See McAuley, James Phillip

Mallowan, Agatha Christie
See Christie, Agatha (Mary Clarissa)

Maloff, Saul   1922- . . . . CLC 5
See also CA 33-36R

Malone, Louis
See MacNeice, (Frederick) Louis

Malone, Michael (Christopher)
1942- . . . . CLC 43
See also CA 77-80; CANR 14, 32

Malory, (Sir) Thomas
1410(?)-1471(?) . . . . LC 11; DA
See also CDBLB Before 1660; SATA 33, 59

Malouf, (George Joseph) David
1934- . . . . CLC 28
See also CA 124

Malraux, (Georges-)Andre
1901-1976 . . . . . . CLC 1, 4, 9, 13, 15, 57
See also CA 21-22; 69-72; CANR 34;
CAP 2; DLB 72; MTCW

Malzberg, Barry N(athaniel)   1939- . . . CLC 7
See also CA 61-64; CAAS 4; CANR 16;
DLB 8

Mamet, David (Alan)
1947- . . . . CLC 9, 15, 34, 46; DC 4
See also AAYA 3; CA 81-84; CABS 3;
CANR 15, 41; DLB 7; MTCW

Mamoulian, Rouben (Zachary)
1897-1987 . . . . CLC 16
See also CA 25-28R; 124

Mandelstam, Osip (Emilievich)
1891(?)-1938(?) . . . . TCLC 2, 6
See also CA 104

Mander, (Mary) Jane   1877-1949 . . . TCLC 31

Mandiargues, Andre Pieyre de . . . . . . CLC 41
See also Pieyre de Mandiargues, Andre
See also DLB 83

Mandrake, Ethel Belle
See Thurman, Wallace (Henry)

Mangan, James Clarence
1803-1849 . . . . NCLC 27

Maniere, J.-E.
See Giraudoux, (Hippolyte) Jean

Manley, (Mary) Delariviere
1672(?)-1724 . . . . LC 1
See also DLB 39, 80

Mann, Abel
See Creasey, John

Mann, (Luiz) Heinrich   1871-1950 . . . TCLC 9
See also CA 106; DLB 66

Mann, (Paul) Thomas
1875-1955 . . . . TCLC 2, 8, 14, 21, 35, 44;
DA; SSC 5; WLC
See also CA 104; 128; DLB 66; MTCW

Manning, David
See Faust, Frederick (Schiller)

Manning, Frederic   1887(?)-1935 . . . TCLC 25
See also CA 124

Manning, Olivia   1915-1980 . . . . . . CLC 5, 19
See also CA 5-8R; 101; CANR 29; MTCW

Mano, D. Keith   1942- . . . . CLC 2, 10
See also CA 25-28R; CAAS 6; CANR 26;
DLB 6

Mansfield, Katherine
. . . . TCLC 2, 8, 39; SSC 9; WLC
See also Beauchamp, Kathleen Mansfield

Manso, Peter   1940- . . . . CLC 39
See also CA 29-32R

Mantecon, Juan Jimenez
See Jimenez (Mantecon), Juan Ramon

Manton, Peter
See Creasey, John

Man Without a Spleen, A
See Chekhov, Anton (Pavlovich)

Manzoni, Alessandro   1785-1873 . . NCLC 29

Mapu, Abraham (ben Jekutiel)
1808-1867 . . . . NCLC 18

Mara, Sally
See Queneau, Raymond

Marat, Jean Paul   1743-1793 . . . . LC 10

Marcel, Gabriel Honore
1889-1973 . . . . CLC 15
See also CA 102; 45-48; MTCW

Marchbanks, Samuel
See Davies, (William) Robertson

Marchi, Giacomo
See Bassani, Giorgio

Margulies, Donald . . . . CLC 76

Marie de France   c. 12th cent. - . . . . CMLC 8

Marie de l'Incarnation   1599-1672 . . . . LC 10

Maxwell, William (Keepers, Jr.)
  1908- .... CLC **19**
  See also CA 93-96; DLBY 80

May, Elaine 1932- .... CLC **16**
  See also CA 124; 142; DLB 44

Mayakovski, Vladimir (Vladimirovich)
  1893-1930 .... TCLC **4, 18**
  See also CA 104

Mayhew, Henry 1812-1887 ...... NCLC **31**
  See also DLB 18, 55

Maynard, Joyce 1953- .... CLC **23**
  See also CA 111; 129

Mayne, William (James Carter)
  1928- .... CLC **12**
  See also CA 9-12R; CANR 37; CLR 25;
    JRDA; MAICYA; SAAS 11; SATA 6, 68

Mayo, Jim
  See L'Amour, Louis (Dearborn)

Maysles, Albert 1926- .... CLC **16**
  See also CA 29-32R

Maysles, David 1932- .... CLC **16**

Mazer, Norma Fox 1931- .... CLC **26**
  See also AAYA 5; CA 69-72; CANR 12,
    32; CLR 23; JRDA; MAICYA; SAAS 1;
    SATA 24, 67

Mazzini, Guiseppe 1805-1872 .... NCLC **34**

McAuley, James Phillip
  1917-1976 .... CLC **45**
  See also CA 97-100

McBain, Ed
  See Hunter, Evan

McBrien, William Augustine
  1930- .... CLC **44**
  See also CA 107

McCaffrey, Anne (Inez) 1926-...... CLC **17**
  See also AAYA 6; AITN 2; BEST 89:2;
    CA 25-28R; CANR 15, 35; DLB 8;
    JRDA; MAICYA; MTCW; SAAS 11;
    SATA 8, 70

McCann, Arthur
  See Campbell, John W(ood, Jr.)

McCann, Edson
  See Pohl, Frederik

McCarthy, Charles, Jr. 1933-
  See McCarthy, Cormac
  See also CANR 42

McCarthy, Cormac .... CLC **4, 57**
  See also McCarthy, Charles, Jr.
  See also DLB 6

McCarthy, Mary (Therese)
  1912-1989 ... CLC **1, 3, 5, 14, 24, 39, 59**
  See also CA 5-8R; 129; CANR 16; DLB 2;
    DLBY 81; MTCW

McCartney, (James) Paul
  1942- .... CLC **12, 35**

McCauley, Stephen (D.) 1955- ..... CLC **50**
  See also CA 141

McClure, Michael (Thomas)
  1932- .... CLC **6, 10**
  See also CA 21-24R; CANR 17; DLB 16

McCorkle, Jill (Collins) 1958-...... CLC **51**
  See also CA 121; DLBY 87

McCourt, James 1941-............. CLC **5**
  See also CA 57-60

McCoy, Horace (Stanley)
  1897-1955 .... TCLC **28**
  See also CA 108; DLB 9

McCrae, John 1872-1918........ TCLC **12**
  See also CA 109; DLB 92

McCreigh, James
  See Pohl, Frederik

McCullers, (Lula) Carson (Smith)
  1917-1967 .... CLC **1, 4, 10, 12, 48; DA;
    SSC 9; WLC**
  See also CA 5-8R; 25-28R; CABS 1, 3;
    CANR 18; CDALB 1941-1968; DLB 2, 7;
    MTCW; SATA 27

McCulloch, John Tyler
  See Burroughs, Edgar Rice

McCullough, Colleen 1938(?)-...... CLC **27**
  See also CA 81-84; CANR 17; MTCW

McElroy, Joseph 1930- .... CLC **5, 47**
  See also CA 17-20R

McEwan, Ian (Russell) 1948- ... CLC **13, 66**
  See also BEST 90:4; CA 61-64; CANR 14,
    41; DLB 14; MTCW

McFadden, David 1940-.......... CLC **48**
  See also CA 104; DLB 60

McFarland, Dennis 1950- .... CLC **65**

McGahern, John 1934-........ CLC **5, 9, 48**
  See also CA 17-20R; CANR 29; DLB 14;
    MTCW

McGinley, Patrick (Anthony)
  1937- .... CLC **41**
  See also CA 120; 127

McGinley, Phyllis 1905-1978 ...... CLC **14**
  See also CA 9-12R; 77-80; CANR 19;
    DLB 11, 48; SATA 2, 24, 44

McGinniss, Joe 1942-............. CLC **32**
  See also AITN 2; BEST 89:2; CA 25-28R;
    CANR 26

McGivern, Maureen Daly
  See Daly, Maureen

McGrath, Patrick 1950-........... CLC **55**
  See also CA 136

McGrath, Thomas (Matthew)
  1916-1990 .... CLC **28, 59**
  See also CA 9-12R; 132; CANR 6, 33;
    MTCW; SATA 41; SATA-Obit 66

McGuane, Thomas (Francis III)
  1939- .... CLC **3, 7, 18, 45**
  See also AITN 2; CA 49-52; CANR 5, 24;
    DLB 2; DLBY 80; MTCW

McGuckian, Medbh 1950-......... CLC **48**
  See also CA 143; DLB 40

McHale, Tom 1942(?)-1982....... CLC **3, 5**
  See also AITN 1; CA 77-80; 106

McIlvanney, William 1936-........ CLC **42**
  See also CA 25-28R; DLB 14

McIlwraith, Maureen Mollie Hunter
  See Hunter, Mollie
  See also SATA 2

McInerney, Jay 1955- .... CLC **34**
  See also CA 116; 123

McIntyre, Vonda N(eel) 1948- ..... CLC **18**
  See also CA 81-84; CANR 17, 34; MTCW

McKay, Claude ..... TCLC **7, 41**; BLC; PC **2**
  See also McKay, Festus Claudius
  See also DLB 4, 45, 51, 117

McKay, Festus Claudius 1889-1948
  See McKay, Claude
  See also BW; CA 104; 124; DA; MTCW;
    WLC

McKuen, Rod 1933-............. CLC **1, 3**
  See also AITN 1; CA 41-44R; CANR 40

McLoughlin, R. B.
  See Mencken, H(enry) L(ouis)

McLuhan, (Herbert) Marshall
  1911-1980 .... CLC **37**
  See also CA 9-12R; 102; CANR 12, 34;
    DLB 88; MTCW

McMillan, Terry (L.) 1951-..... CLC **50, 61**
  See also CA 140

McMurtry, Larry (Jeff)
  1936- .... CLC **2, 3, 7, 11, 27, 44**
  See also AITN 2; BEST 89:2; CA 5-8R;
    CANR 19, 43; CDALB 1968-1988;
    DLB 2; DLBY 80, 87; MTCW

McNally, T. M. 1961- .... CLC **82**

McNally, Terrence 1939-...... CLC **4, 7, 41**
  See also CA 45-48; CANR 2; DLB 7

McNamer, Deirdre 1950-.......... CLC **70**

McNeile, Herman Cyril 1888-1937
  See Sapper
  See also DLB 77

McPhee, John (Angus) 1931- ...... CLC **36**
  See also BEST 90:1; CA 65-68; CANR 20;
    MTCW

McPherson, James Alan
  1943- .... CLC **19, 77**
  See also BW; CA 25-28R; CAAS 17;
    CANR 24; DLB 38; MTCW

McPherson, William (Alexander)
  1933- .... CLC **34**
  See also CA 69-72; CANR 28

McSweeney, Kerry .... CLC **34**

Mead, Margaret 1901-1978........ CLC **37**
  See also AITN 1; CA 1-4R; 81-84;
    CANR 4; MTCW; SATA 20

Meaker, Marijane (Agnes) 1927-
  See Kerr, M. E.
  See also CA 107; CANR 37; JRDA;
    MAICYA; MTCW; SATA 20, 61

Medoff, Mark (Howard) 1940- ... CLC **6, 23**
  See also AITN 1; CA 53-56; CANR 5;
    DLB 7

Meged, Aharon
  See Megged, Aharon

Meged, Aron
  See Megged, Aharon

Megged, Aharon 1920-............. CLC **9**
  See also CA 49-52; CAAS 13; CANR 1

Mehta, Ved (Parkash) 1934-....... CLC **37**
  See also CA 1-4R; CANR 2, 23; MTCW

Melanter
  See Blackmore, R(ichard) D(oddridge)

Melikow, Loris
  See Hofmannsthal, Hugo von

Melmoth, Sebastian
  See Wilde, Oscar (Fingal O'Flahertie Wills)

Meltzer, Milton 1915- .... **CLC 26**
  See also AAYA 8; CA 13-16R; CANR 38;
  CLR 13; DLB 61; JRDA; MAICYA;
  SAAS 1; SATA 1, 50

Melville, Herman
  1819-1891 .... **NCLC 3, 12, 29; DA;**
                      SSC 1; WLC
  See also CDALB 1640-1865; DLB 3, 74;
  SATA 59

Menander
  c. 342B.C.-c. 292B.C.... **CMLC 9; DC 3**

Mencken, H(enry) L(ouis)
  1880-1956 .... **TCLC 13**
  See also CA 105; 125; CDALB 1917-1929;
  DLB 11, 29, 63; MTCW

Mercer, David 1928-1980 .... **CLC 5**
  See also CA 9-12R; 102; CANR 23;
  DLB 13; MTCW

Merchant, Paul
  See Ellison, Harlan

Meredith, George 1828-1909 ... **TCLC 17, 43**
  See also CA 117; CDBLB 1832-1890;
  DLB 18, 35, 57

Meredith, William (Morris)
  1919- .... **CLC 4, 13, 22, 55**
  See also CA 9-12R; CAAS 14; CANR 6, 40;
  DLB 5

Merezhkovsky, Dmitry Sergeyevich
  1865-1941 .... **TCLC 29**

Merimee, Prosper
  1803-1870 .... **NCLC 6; SSC 7**
  See also DLB 119

Merkin, Daphne 1954- .... **CLC 44**
  See also CA 123

Merlin, Arthur
  See Blish, James (Benjamin)

Merrill, James (Ingram)
  1926- .... **CLC 2, 3, 6, 8, 13, 18, 34**
  See also CA 13-16R; CANR 10; DLB 5;
  DLBY 85; MTCW

Merriman, Alex
  See Silverberg, Robert

Merritt, E. B.
  See Waddington, Miriam

Merton, Thomas
  1915-1968 .... **CLC 1, 3, 11, 34**
  See also CA 5-8R; 25-28R; CANR 22;
  DLB 48; DLBY 81; MTCW

Merwin, W(illiam) S(tanley)
  1927- ...... **CLC 1, 2, 3, 5, 8, 13, 18, 45**
  See also CA 13-16R; CANR 15; DLB 5;
  MTCW

Metcalf, John 1938- .... **CLC 37**
  See also CA 113; DLB 60

Metcalf, Suzanne
  See Baum, L(yman) Frank

Mew, Charlotte (Mary)
  1870-1928 .... **TCLC 8**
  See also CA 105; DLB 19, 135

Mewshaw, Michael 1943- .... **CLC 9**
  See also CA 53-56; CANR 7; DLBY 80

Meyer, June
  See Jordan, June

Meyer, Lynn
  See Slavitt, David R(ytman)

Meyer-Meyrink, Gustav 1868-1932
  See Meyrink, Gustav
  See also CA 117

Meyers, Jeffrey 1939- .... **CLC 39**
  See also CA 73-76; DLB 111

Meynell, Alice (Christina Gertrude Thompson)
  1847-1922 .... **TCLC 6**
  See also CA 104; DLB 19, 98

Meyrink, Gustav .... **TCLC 21**
  See also Meyer-Meyrink, Gustav
  See also DLB 81

Michaels, Leonard 1933- .... **CLC 6, 25**
  See also CA 61-64; CANR 21; DLB 130;
  MTCW

Michaux, Henri 1899-1984 ...... **CLC 8, 19**
  See also CA 85-88; 114

Michelangelo 1475-1564 .... **LC 12**

Michelet, Jules 1798-1874 .... **NCLC 31**

Michener, James A(lbert)
  1907(?)- .... **CLC 1, 5, 11, 29, 60**
  See also AITN 1; BEST 90:1; CA 5-8R;
  CANR 21; DLB 6; MTCW

Mickiewicz, Adam 1798-1855 ..... **NCLC 3**

Middleton, Christopher 1926- ...... **CLC 13**
  See also CA 13-16R; CANR 29; DLB 40

Middleton, Stanley 1919- .... **CLC 7, 38**
  See also CA 25-28R; CANR 21; DLB 14

Migueis, Jose Rodrigues 1901- ..... **CLC 10**

Mikszath, Kalman 1847-1910 ..... **TCLC 31**

Miles, Josephine
  1911-1985 .... **CLC 1, 2, 14, 34, 39**
  See also CA 1-4R; 116; CANR 2; DLB 48

Militant
  See Sandburg, Carl (August)

Mill, John Stuart 1806-1873 ..... **NCLC 11**
  See also CDBLB 1832-1890; DLB 55

Millar, Kenneth 1915-1983 .... **CLC 14**
  See also Macdonald, Ross
  See also CA 9-12R; 110; CANR 16; DLB 2;
  DLBD 6; DLBY 83; MTCW

Millay, E. Vincent
  See Millay, Edna St. Vincent

Millay, Edna St. Vincent
  1892-1950 ...... **TCLC 4, 49; DA; PC 6**
  See also CA 104; 130; CDALB 1917-1929;
  DLB 45; MTCW

Miller, Arthur
  1915- .... **CLC 1, 2, 6, 10, 15, 26, 47, 78;**
                  DA; DC 1; WLC
  See also AITN 1; CA 1-4R; CABS 3;
  CANR 2, 30; CDALB 1941-1968; DLB 7;
  MTCW

Miller, Henry (Valentine)
  1891-1980 .... **CLC 1, 2, 4, 9, 14, 43;**
                      DA; WLC
  See also CA 9-12R; 97-100; CANR 33;
  CDALB 1929-1941; DLB 4, 9; DLBY 80;
  MTCW

Miller, Jason 1939(?)- .... **CLC 2**
  See also AITN 1; CA 73-76; DLB 7

Miller, Sue 1943- .... **CLC 44**
  See also BEST 90:3; CA 139

Miller, Walter M(ichael, Jr.)
  1923- .... **CLC 4, 30**
  See also CA 85-88; DLB 8

Millett, Kate 1934- .... **CLC 67**
  See also AITN 1; CA 73-76; CANR 32;
  MTCW

Millhauser, Steven 1943- .... **CLC 21, 54**
  See also CA 110; 111; DLB 2

Millin, Sarah Gertrude 1889-1968 .. **CLC 49**
  See also CA 102; 93-96

Milne, A(lan) A(lexander)
  1882-1956 .... **TCLC 6**
  See also CA 104; 133; CLR 1, 26; DLB 10,
  77, 100; MAICYA; MTCW; YABC 1

Milner, Ron(ald) 1938- .... **CLC 56; BLC**
  See also AITN 1; BW; CA 73-76;
  CANR 24; DLB 38; MTCW

Milosz, Czeslaw
  1911- ... **CLC 5, 11, 22, 31, 56, 82; PC 8**
  See also CA 81-84; CANR 23; MTCW

Milton, John 1608-1674 ... **LC 9; DA; WLC**
  See also CDBLB 1660-1789; DLB 131

Minehaha, Cornelius
  See Wedekind, (Benjamin) Frank(lin)

Miner, Valerie 1947- .... **CLC 40**
  See also CA 97-100

Minimo, Duca
  See D'Annunzio, Gabriele

Minot, Susan 1956- .... **CLC 44**
  See also CA 134

Minus, Ed 1938- .... **CLC 39**

Miranda, Javier
  See Bioy Casares, Adolfo

Miro (Ferrer), Gabriel (Francisco Victor)
  1879-1930 .... **TCLC 5**
  See also CA 104

Mishima, Yukio
  .... **CLC 2, 4, 6, 9, 27; DC 1; SSC 4**
  See also Hiraoka, Kimitake

Mistral, Frederic 1830-1914 ...... **TCLC 51**
  See also CA 122

Mistral, Gabriela .... **TCLC 2; HLC**
  See also Godoy Alcayaga, Lucila

Mistry, Rohinton 1952- .... **CLC 71**
  See also CA 141

Mitchell, Clyde
  See Ellison, Harlan; Silverberg, Robert

Mitchell, James Leslie 1901-1935
  See Gibbon, Lewis Grassic
  See also CA 104; DLB 15

Mitchell, Joni 1943- .... **CLC 12**
  See also CA 112

Mitchell, Margaret (Munnerlyn)
  1900-1949 .... **TCLC 11**
  See also CA 109; 125; DLB 9; MTCW

Mitchell, Peggy
  See Mitchell, Margaret (Munnerlyn)

Mitchell, S(ilas) Weir 1829-1914 .. **TCLC 36**

Mitchell, W(illiam) O(rmond)
  1914- .... **CLC 25**
  See also CA 77-80; CANR 15, 43; DLB 88

Mitford, Mary Russell 1787-1855.. **NCLC 4**
  See also DLB 110, 116

Mitford, Nancy 1904-1973......... **CLC 44**
See also CA 9-12R

Miyamoto, Yuriko 1899-1951..... **TCLC 37**

Mo, Timothy (Peter) 1950(?)-...... **CLC 46**
See also CA 117; MTCW

Modarressi, Taghi (M.) 1931-...... **CLC 44**
See also CA 121; 134

Modiano, Patrick (Jean) 1945-..... **CLC 18**
See also CA 85-88; CANR 17, 40; DLB 83

Moerck, Paal
See Roelvaag, O(le) E(dvart)

Mofolo, Thomas (Mokopu)
1875(?)-1948.......... **TCLC 22; BLC**
See also CA 121

Mohr, Nicholasa 1935-...... **CLC 12; HLC**
See also AAYA 8; CA 49-52; CANR 1, 32;
CLR 22; HW; JRDA; SAAS 8; SATA 8

Mojtabai, A(nn) G(race)
1938-............... **CLC 5, 9, 15, 29**
See also CA 85-88

Moliere 1622-1673....... **LC 10; DA; WLC**

Molin, Charles
See Mayne, William (James Carter)

Molnar, Ferenc 1878-1952....... **TCLC 20**
See also CA 109

Momaday, N(avarre) Scott
1934-................ **CLC 2, 19; DA**
See also CA 25-28R; CANR 14, 34;
MTCW; SATA 30, 48

Monette, Paul 1945-............. **CLC 82**
See also CA 139

Monroe, Harriet 1860-1936....... **TCLC 12**
See also CA 109; DLB 54, 91

Monroe, Lyle
See Heinlein, Robert A(nson)

Montagu, Elizabeth 1917-........ **NCLC 7**
See also CA 9-12R

Montagu, Mary (Pierrepont) Wortley
1689-1762.................... **LC 9**
See also DLB 95, 101

Montagu, W. H.
See Coleridge, Samuel Taylor

Montague, John (Patrick)
1929-.................... **CLC 13, 46**
See also CA 9-12R; CANR 9; DLB 40;
MTCW

Montaigne, Michel (Eyquem) de
1533-1592.......... **LC 8; DA; WLC**

Montale, Eugenio 1896-1981... **CLC 7, 9, 18**
See also CA 17-20R; 104; CANR 30;
DLB 114; MTCW

Montesquieu, Charles-Louis de Secondat
1689-1755.................... **LC 7**

Montgomery, (Robert) Bruce 1921-1978
See Crispin, Edmund
See also CA 104

Montgomery, L(ucy) M(aud)
1874-1942................. **TCLC 51**
See also CA 108; 137; CLR 8; DLB 92;
JRDA; MAICYA; YABC 1

Montgomery, Marion H., Jr. 1925-.. **CLC 7**
See also AITN 1; CA 1-4R; CANR 3;
DLB 6

Montgomery, Max
See Davenport, Guy (Mattison, Jr.)

Montherlant, Henry (Milon) de
1896-1972................. **CLC 8, 19**
See also CA 85-88; 37-40R; DLB 72;
MTCW

Monty Python................... **CLC 21**
See also Chapman, Graham; Cleese, John
(Marwood); Gilliam, Terry (Vance); Idle,
Eric; Jones, Terence Graham Parry; Palin,
Michael (Edward)
See also AAYA 7

Moodie, Susanna (Strickland)
1803-1885................. **NCLC 14**
See also DLB 99

Mooney, Edward 1951-........... **CLC 25**
See also CA 130

Mooney, Ted
See Mooney, Edward

Moorcock, Michael (John)
1939-................. **CLC 5, 27, 58**
See also CA 45-48; CAAS 5; CANR 2, 17,
38; DLB 14; MTCW

Moore, Brian
1921-......... **CLC 1, 3, 5, 7, 8, 19, 32**
See also CA 1-4R; CANR 1, 25, 42; MTCW

Moore, Edward
See Muir, Edwin

Moore, George Augustus
1852-1933.................. **TCLC 7**
See also CA 104; DLB 10, 18, 57, 135

Moore, Lorrie.............. **CLC 39, 45, 68**
See also Moore, Marie Lorena

Moore, Marianne (Craig)
1887-1972.... **CLC 1, 2, 4, 8, 10, 13, 19,
47; DA; PC 4**
See also CA 1-4R; 33-36R; CANR 3;
CDALB 1929-1941; DLB 45; DLBD 7;
MTCW; SATA 20

Moore, Marie Lorena 1957-
See Moore, Lorrie
See also CA 116; CANR 39

Moore, Thomas 1779-1852....... **NCLC 6**
See also DLB 96

Morand, Paul 1888-1976.......... **CLC 41**
See also CA 69-72; DLB 65

Morante, Elsa 1918-1985....... **CLC 8, 47**
See also CA 85-88; 117; CANR 35; MTCW

Moravia, Alberto....... **CLC 2, 7, 11, 27, 46**
See also Pincherle, Alberto

More, Hannah 1745-1833....... **NCLC 27**
See also DLB 107, 109, 116

More, Henry 1614-1687.............. **LC 9**
See also DLB 126

More, Sir Thomas 1478-1535....... **LC 10**

Moreas, Jean.................... **TCLC 18**
See also Papadiamantopoulos, Johannes

Morgan, Berry 1919-............. **CLC 6**
See also CA 49-52; DLB 6

Morgan, Claire
See Highsmith, (Mary) Patricia

Morgan, Edwin (George) 1920-..... **CLC 31**
See also CA 5-8R; CANR 3, 43; DLB 27

Morgan, (George) Frederick
1922-...................... **CLC 23**
See also CA 17-20R; CANR 21

Morgan, Harriet
See Mencken, H(enry) L(ouis)

Morgan, Jane
See Cooper, James Fenimore

Morgan, Janet 1945-............. **CLC 39**
See also CA 65-68

Morgan, Lady 1776(?)-1859...... **NCLC 29**
See also DLB 116

Morgan, Robin 1941-.............. **CLC 2**
See also CA 69-72; CANR 29; MTCW

Morgan, Scott
See Kuttner, Henry

Morgan, Seth 1949(?)-1990........ **CLC 65**
See also CA 132

Morgenstern, Christian
1871-1914.................... **TCLC 8**
See also CA 105

Morgenstern, S.
See Goldman, William (W.)

Moricz, Zsigmond 1879-1942..... **TCLC 33**

Morike, Eduard (Friedrich)
1804-1875................. **NCLC 10**
See also DLB 133

Mori Ogai..................... **TCLC 14**
See also Mori Rintaro

Mori Rintaro 1862-1922
See Mori Ogai
See also CA 110

Moritz, Karl Philipp 1756-1793...... **LC 2**
See also DLB 94

Morland, Peter Henry
See Faust, Frederick (Schiller)

Morren, Theophil
See Hofmannsthal, Hugo von

Morris, Bill 1952-................ **CLC 76**

Morris, Julian
See West, Morris L(anglo)

Morris, Steveland Judkins 1950(?)-
See Wonder, Stevie
See also CA 111

Morris, William 1834-1896....... **NCLC 4**
See also CDBLB 1832-1890; DLB 18, 35, 57

Morris, Wright 1910-... **CLC 1, 3, 7, 18, 37**
See also CA 9-12R; CANR 21; DLB 2;
DLBY 81; MTCW

Morrison, Chloe Anthony Wofford
See Morrison, Toni

Morrison, James Douglas 1943-1971
See Morrison, Jim
See also CA 73-76; CANR 40

Morrison, Jim.................... **CLC 17**
See also Morrison, James Douglas

Morrison, Toni
1931-.. **CLC 4, 10, 22, 55, 81; BLC; DA**
See also AAYA 1; BW; CA 29-32R;
CANR 27, 42; CDALB 1968-1988;
DLB 6, 33; DLBY 81; MTCW; SATA 57

Morrison, Van 1945-............. **CLC 21**
See also CA 116

Mortimer, John (Clifford)
1923- .... **CLC 28, 43**
See also CA 13-16R; CANR 21;
CDBLB 1960 to Present; DLB 13;
MTCW

Mortimer, Penelope (Ruth) 1918- .... **CLC 5**
See also CA 57-60

Morton, Anthony
See Creasey, John

Mosher, Howard Frank 1943- ...... **CLC 62**
See also CA 139

Mosley, Nicholas 1923- .... **CLC 43, 70**
See also CA 69-72; CANR 41; DLB 14

Moss, Howard
1922-1987 .... **CLC 7, 14, 45, 50**
See also CA 1-4R; 123; CANR 1; DLB 5

Mossgiel, Rab
See Burns, Robert

Motion, Andrew 1952- .... **CLC 47**
See also DLB 40

Motley, Willard (Francis)
1912-1965 .... **CLC 18**
See also BW; CA 117; 106; DLB 76

Mott, Michael (Charles Alston)
1930- .... **CLC 15, 34**
See also CA 5-8R; CAAS 7; CANR 7, 29

Mowat, Farley (McGill) 1921- ..... **CLC 26**
See also AAYA 1; CA 1-4R; CANR 4, 24,
42; CLR 20; DLB 68; JRDA; MAICYA;
MTCW; SATA 3, 55

Moyers, Bill 1934- .... **CLC 74**
See also AITN 2; CA 61-64; CANR 31

Mphahlele, Es'kia
See Mphahlele, Ezekiel
See also DLB 125

Mphahlele, Ezekiel 1919- ..... **CLC 25; BLC**
See also Mphahlele, Es'kia
See also BW; CA 81-84; CANR 26

Mqhayi, S(amuel) E(dward) K(rune Loliwe)
1875-1945 .... **TCLC 25; BLC**

Mr. Martin
See Burroughs, William S(eward)

Mrozek, Slawomir 1930- .... **CLC 3, 13**
See also CA 13-16R; CAAS 10; CANR 29;
MTCW

Mrs. Belloc-Lowndes
See Lowndes, Marie Adelaide (Belloc)

Mtwa, Percy (?)- .... **CLC 47**

Mueller, Lisel 1924- .... **CLC 13, 51**
See also CA 93-96; DLB 105

Muir, Edwin 1887-1959 .... **TCLC 2**
See also CA 104; DLB 20, 100

Muir, John 1838-1914 .... **TCLC 28**

Mujica Lainez, Manuel
1910-1984 .... **CLC 31**
See also Lainez, Manuel Mujica
See also CA 81-84; 112; CANR 32; HW

Mukherjee, Bharati 1940- .... **CLC 53**
See also BEST 89:2; CA 107; DLB 60;
MTCW

Muldoon, Paul 1951- .... **CLC 32, 72**
See also CA 113; 129; DLB 40

Mulisch, Harry 1927- .... **CLC 42**
See also CA 9-12R; CANR 6, 26

Mull, Martin 1943- .... **CLC 17**
See also CA 105

Mulock, Dinah Maria
See Craik, Dinah Maria (Mulock)

Munford, Robert 1737(?)-1783 .... **LC 5**
See also DLB 31

Mungo, Raymond 1946- .... **CLC 72**
See also CA 49-52; CANR 2

Munro, Alice
1931- .... **CLC 6, 10, 19, 50; SSC 3**
See also AITN 2; CA 33-36R; CANR 33;
DLB 53; MTCW; SATA 29

Munro, H(ector) H(ugh) 1870-1916
See Saki
See also CA 104; 130; CDBLB 1890-1914;
DA; DLB 34; MTCW; WLC

Murasaki, Lady .... **CMLC 1**

Murdoch, (Jean) Iris
1919- ...... **CLC 1, 2, 3, 4, 6, 8, 11, 15,
22, 31, 51**
See also CA 13-16R; CANR 8, 43;
CDBLB 1960 to Present; DLB 14;
MTCW

Murnau, Friedrich Wilhelm
See Plumpe, Friedrich Wilhelm

Murphy, Richard 1927- .... **CLC 41**
See also CA 29-32R; DLB 40

Murphy, Sylvia 1937- .... **CLC 34**
See also CA 121

Murphy, Thomas (Bernard) 1935- ... **CLC 51**
See also CA 101

Murray, Albert L. 1916- .... **CLC 73**
See also BW; CA 49-52; CANR 26; DLB 38

Murray, Les(lie) A(llan) 1938- ..... **CLC 40**
See also CA 21-24R; CANR 11, 27

Murry, J. Middleton
See Murry, John Middleton

Murry, John Middleton
1889-1957 .... **TCLC 16**
See also CA 118

Musgrave, Susan 1951- .... **CLC 13, 54**
See also CA 69-72

Musil, Robert (Edler von)
1880-1942 .... **TCLC 12**
See also CA 109; DLB 81, 124

Musset, (Louis Charles) Alfred de
1810-1857 .... **NCLC 7**

My Brother's Brother
See Chekhov, Anton (Pavlovich)

Myers, Walter Dean 1937- ... **CLC 35; BLC**
See also AAYA 4; BW; CA 33-36R;
CANR 20, 42; CLR 4, 16; DLB 33;
JRDA; MAICYA; SAAS 2; SATA 27, 41,
71

Myers, Walter M.
See Myers, Walter Dean

Myles, Symon
See Follett, Ken(neth Martin)

Nabokov, Vladimir (Vladimirovich)
1899-1977 ..... **CLC 1, 2, 3, 6, 8, 11, 15,
23, 44, 46, 64; DA; SSC 11; WLC**
See also CA 5-8R; 69-72; CANR 20;
CDALB 1941-1968; DLB 2; DLBD 3;
DLBY 80, 91; MTCW

Nagai Kafu. .... **TCLC 51**
See also Nagai Sokichi

Nagai Sokichi 1879-1959
See Nagai Kafu
See also CA 117

Nagy, Laszlo 1925-1978 .... **CLC 7**
See also CA 129; 112

Naipaul, Shiva(dhar Srinivasa)
1945-1985 .... **CLC 32, 39**
See also CA 110; 112; 116; CANR 33;
DLBY 85; MTCW

Naipaul, V(idiadhar) S(urajprasad)
1932- .... **CLC 4, 7, 9, 13, 18, 37**
See also CA 1-4R; CANR 1, 33;
CDBLB 1960 to Present; DLB 125;
DLBY 85; MTCW

Nakos, Lilika 1899(?)- .... **CLC 29**

Narayan, R(asipuram) K(rishnaswami)
1906- .... **CLC 7, 28, 47**
See also CA 81-84; CANR 33; MTCW;
SATA 62

Nash, (Frediric) Ogden 1902-1971 .. **CLC 23**
See also CA 13-14; 29-32R; CANR 34;
CAP 1; DLB 11; MAICYA; MTCW;
SATA 2, 46

Nathan, Daniel
See Dannay, Frederic

Nathan, George Jean 1882-1958 ... **TCLC 18**
See also Hatteras, Owen
See also CA 114

Natsume, Kinnosuke 1867-1916
See Natsume, Soseki
See also CA 104

Natsume, Soseki .... **TCLC 2, 10**
See also Natsume, Kinnosuke

Natti, (Mary) Lee 1919-
See Kingman, Lee
See also CA 5-8R; CANR 2

Naylor, Gloria
1950- .... **CLC 28, 52; BLC; DA**
See also AAYA 6; BW; CA 107; CANR 27;
MTCW

Neihardt, John Gneisenau
1881-1973 .... **CLC 32**
See also CA 13-14; CAP 1; DLB 9, 54

Nekrasov, Nikolai Alekseevich
1821-1878 .... **NCLC 11**

Nelligan, Emile 1879-1941 .... **TCLC 14**
See also CA 114; DLB 92

Nelson, Willie 1933- .... **CLC 17**
See also CA 107

Nemerov, Howard (Stanley)
1920-1991 .... **CLC 2, 6, 9, 36**
See also CA 1-4R; 134; CABS 2; CANR 1,
27; DLB 6; DLBY 83; MTCW

Neruda, Pablo
1904-1973 ..... **CLC 1, 2, 5, 7, 9, 28, 62;
DA; HLC; PC 4; WLC**
See also CA 19-20; 45-48; CAP 2; HW;
MTCW

Nerval, Gerard de 1808-1855 ...... **NCLC 1**

Nervo, (Jose) Amado (Ruiz de)
1870-1919 .... **TCLC 11**
See also CA 109; 131; HW

Nessi, Pio Baroja y
See Baroja (y Nessi), Pio

Nestroy, Johann 1801-1862 . . . . . . **NCLC 42**
See also DLB 133

Neufeld, John (Arthur) 1938- . . . . . . **CLC 17**
See also CA 25-28R; CANR 11, 37;
MAICYA; SAAS 3; SATA 6

Neville, Emily Cheney 1919- . . . . . **CLC 12**
See also CA 5-8R; CANR 3, 37; JRDA;
MAICYA; SAAS 2; SATA 1

Newbound, Bernard Slade 1930-
See Slade, Bernard
See also CA 81-84

Newby, P(ercy) H(oward)
1918- . . . . **CLC 2, 13**
See also CA 5-8R; CANR 32; DLB 15;
MTCW

Newlove, Donald 1928- . . . . **CLC 6**
See also CA 29-32R; CANR 25

Newlove, John (Herbert) 1938- . . . . . **CLC 14**
See also CA 21-24R; CANR 9, 25

Newman, Charles 1938- . . . . **CLC 2, 8**
See also CA 21-24R

Newman, Edwin (Harold) 1919- . . . . **CLC 14**
See also AITN 1; CA 69-72; CANR 5

Newman, John Henry
1801-1890 . . . . **NCLC 38**
See also DLB 18, 32, 55

Newton, Suzanne 1936- . . . . **CLC 35**
See also CA 41-44R; CANR 14; JRDA;
SATA 5

Nexo, Martin Andersen
1869-1954 . . . . **TCLC 43**

Nezval, Vitezslav 1900-1958 . . . . . . **TCLC 44**
See also CA 123

Ng, Fae Myenne 1957(?)- . . . . **CLC 81**

Ngema, Mbongeni 1955- . . . . **CLC 57**
See also CA 143

Ngugi, James T(hiong'o) . . . . **CLC 3, 7, 13**
See also Ngugi wa Thiong'o

Ngugi wa Thiong'o 1938- . . . . . **CLC 36; BLC**
See also Ngugi, James T(hiong'o)
See also BW; CA 81-84; CANR 27;
DLB 125; MTCW

Nichol, B(arrie) P(hillip)
1944-1988 . . . . **CLC 18**
See also CA 53-56; DLB 53; SATA 66

Nichols, John (Treadwell) 1940- . . . . **CLC 38**
See also CA 9-12R; CAAS 2; CANR 6;
DLBY 82

Nichols, Leigh
See Koontz, Dean R(ay)

Nichols, Peter (Richard)
1927- . . . . **CLC 5, 36, 65**
See also CA 104; CANR 33; DLB 13;
MTCW

Nicolas, F. R. E.
See Freeling, Nicolas

Niedecker, Lorine 1903-1970 . . . . **CLC 10, 42**
See also CA 25-28; CAP 2; DLB 48

Nietzsche, Friedrich (Wilhelm)
1844-1900 . . . . **TCLC 10, 18**
See also CA 107; 121; DLB 129

Nievo, Ippolito 1831-1861 . . . . **NCLC 22**

Nightingale, Anne Redmon 1943-
See Redmon, Anne
See also CA 103

Nik.T.O.
See Annensky, Innokenty Fyodorovich

Nin, Anais
1903-1977 . . . . . . **CLC 1, 4, 8, 11, 14, 60;
SSC 10**
See also AITN 2; CA 13-16R; 69-72;
CANR 22; DLB 2, 4; MTCW

Nissenson, Hugh 1933- . . . . **CLC 4, 9**
See also CA 17-20R; CANR 27; DLB 28

Niven, Larry . . . . **CLC 8**
See also Niven, Laurence Van Cott
See also DLB 8

Niven, Laurence Van Cott 1938-
See Niven, Larry
See also CA 21-24R; CAAS 12; CANR 14;
MTCW

Nixon, Agnes Eckhardt 1927- . . . . . . **CLC 21**
See also CA 110

Nizan, Paul 1905-1940 . . . . **TCLC 40**
See also DLB 72

Nkosi, Lewis 1936- . . . . **CLC 45; BLC**
See also BW; CA 65-68; CANR 27

Nodier, (Jean) Charles (Emmanuel)
1780-1844 . . . . **NCLC 19**
See also DLB 119

Nolan, Christopher 1965- . . . . **CLC 58**
See also CA 111

Norden, Charles
See Durrell, Lawrence (George)

Nordhoff, Charles (Bernard)
1887-1947 . . . . **TCLC 23**
See also CA 108; DLB 9; SATA 23

Norfolk, Lawrence 1963- . . . . **CLC 76**

Norman, Marsha 1947- . . . . **CLC 28**
See also CA 105; CABS 3; CANR 41;
DLBY 84

Norris, Benjamin Franklin, Jr.
1870-1902 . . . . **TCLC 24**
See also Norris, Frank
See also CA 110

Norris, Frank
See Norris, Benjamin Franklin, Jr.
See also CDALB 1865-1917; DLB 12, 71

Norris, Leslie 1921- . . . . **CLC 14**
See also CA 11-12; CANR 14; CAP 1;
DLB 27

North, Andrew
See Norton, Andre

North, Anthony
See Koontz, Dean R(ay)

North, Captain George
See Stevenson, Robert Louis (Balfour)

North, Milou
See Erdrich, Louise

Northrup, B. A.
See Hubbard, L(afayette) Ron(ald)

North Staffs
See Hulme, T(homas) E(rnest)

Norton, Alice Mary
See Norton, Andre
See also MAICYA; SATA 1, 43

Norton, Andre 1912- . . . . **CLC 12**
See also Norton, Alice Mary
See also CA 1-4R; CANR 2, 31; DLB 8, 52;
JRDA; MTCW

Norway, Nevil Shute 1899-1960
See Shute, Nevil
See also CA 102; 93-96

Norwid, Cyprian Kamil
1821-1883 . . . . **NCLC 17**

Nosille, Nabrah
See Ellison, Harlan

Nossack, Hans Erich 1901-1978 . . . . . **CLC 6**
See also CA 93-96; 85-88; DLB 69

Nosu, Chuji
See Ozu, Yasujiro

Nova, Craig 1945- . . . . **CLC 7, 31**
See also CA 45-48; CANR 2

Novak, Joseph
See Kosinski, Jerzy (Nikodem)

Novalis 1772-1801 . . . . **NCLC 13**
See also DLB 90

Nowlan, Alden (Albert) 1933-1983 . . **CLC 15**
See also CA 9-12R; CANR 5; DLB 53

Noyes, Alfred 1880-1958 . . . . **TCLC 7**
See also CA 104; DLB 20

Nunn, Kem 19(?)- . . . . **CLC 34**

Nye, Robert 1939- . . . . **CLC 13, 42**
See also CA 33-36R; CANR 29; DLB 14;
MTCW; SATA 6

Nyro, Laura 1947- . . . . **CLC 17**

Oates, Joyce Carol
1938- . . . . . . **CLC 1, 2, 3, 6, 9, 11, 15, 19,
33, 52; DA; SSC 6; WLC**
See also AITN 1; BEST 89:2; CA 5-8R;
CANR 25; CDALB 1968-1988; DLB 2, 5,
130; DLBY 81; MTCW

O'Brien, E. G.
See Clarke, Arthur C(harles)

O'Brien, Edna
1936- . . . **CLC 3, 5, 8, 13, 36, 65; SSC 10**
See also CA 1-4R; CANR 6, 41;
CDBLB 1960 to Present; DLB 14;
MTCW

O'Brien, Fitz-James 1828-1862 . . . **NCLC 21**
See also DLB 74

O'Brien, Flann . . . . **CLC 1, 4, 5, 7, 10, 47**
See also O Nuallain, Brian

O'Brien, Richard 1942- . . . . **CLC 17**
See also CA 124

O'Brien, Tim 1946- . . . . **CLC 7, 19, 40**
See also CA 85-88; CANR 40; DLBD 9;
DLBY 80

Obstfelder, Sigbjoern 1866-1900 . . . **TCLC 23**
See also CA 123

O'Casey, Sean
1880-1964 . . . . **CLC 1, 5, 9, 11, 15**
See also CA 89-92; CDBLB 1914-1945;
DLB 10; MTCW

O'Cathasaigh, Sean
See O'Casey, Sean

Ochs, Phil 1940-1976 . . . . **CLC 17**
See also CA 65-68

Page, Louise 1955-............... **CLC 40**
See also CA 140

Page, P(atricia) K(athleen)
1916- .... **CLC 7, 18**
See also CA 53-56; CANR 4, 22; DLB 68;
MTCW

Paget, Violet 1856-1935
See Lee, Vernon
See also CA 104

Paget-Lowe, Henry
See Lovecraft, H(oward) P(hillips)

Paglia, Camille (Anna) 1947-....... **CLC 68**
See also CA 140

Paige, Richard
See Koontz, Dean R(ay)

Pakenham, Antonia
See Fraser, Antonia (Pakenham)

Palamas, Kostes 1859-1943 .... **TCLC 5**
See also CA 105

Palazzeschi, Aldo 1885-1974....... **CLC 11**
See also CA 89-92; 53-56; DLB 114

Paley, Grace 1922-.... **CLC 4, 6, 37; SSC 8**
See also CA 25-28R; CANR 13; DLB 28;
MTCW

Palin, Michael (Edward) 1943-..... **CLC 21**
See also Monty Python
See also CA 107; CANR 35; SATA 67

Palliser, Charles 1947-............ **CLC 65**
See also CA 136

Palma, Ricardo 1833-1919....... **TCLC 29**

Pancake, Breece Dexter 1952-1979
See Pancake, Breece D'J
See also CA 123; 109

Pancake, Breece D'J.............. **CLC 29**
See also Pancake, Breece Dexter
See also DLB 130

Panko, Rudy
See Gogol, Nikolai (Vasilyevich)

Papadiamantis, Alexandros
1851-1911 .... **TCLC 29**

Papadiamantopoulos, Johannes 1856-1910
See Moreas, Jean
See also CA 117

Papini, Giovanni 1881-1956....... **TCLC 22**
See also CA 121

Paracelsus 1493-1541.............. **LC 14**

Parasol, Peter
See Stevens, Wallace

Parfenie, Maria
See Codrescu, Andrei

Parini, Jay (Lee) 1948- .... **CLC 54**
See also CA 97-100; CAAS 16; CANR 32

Park, Jordan
See Kornbluth, C(yril) M.; Pohl, Frederik

Parker, Bert
See Ellison, Harlan

Parker, Dorothy (Rothschild)
1893-1967 .... **CLC 15, 68; SSC 2**
See also CA 19-20; 25-28R; CAP 2;
DLB 11, 45, 86; MTCW

Parker, Robert B(rown) 1932-...... **CLC 27**
See also BEST 89:4; CA 49-52; CANR 1,
26; MTCW

Parkes, Lucas
See Harris, John (Wyndham Parkes Lucas)
Beynon

Parkin, Frank 1940-.............. **CLC 43**

Parkman, Francis, Jr.
1823-1893 .... **NCLC 12**
See also DLB 1, 30

Parks, Gordon (Alexander Buchanan)
1912-................ **CLC 1, 16; BLC**
See also AITN 2; BW; CA 41-44R;
CANR 26; DLB 33; SATA 8

Parnell, Thomas 1679-1718.......... **LC 3**
See also DLB 94

Parra, Nicanor 1914-........ **CLC 2; HLC**
See also CA 85-88; CANR 32; HW; MTCW

Parrish, Mary Frances
See Fisher, M(ary) F(rances) K(ennedy)

Parson
See Coleridge, Samuel Taylor

Parson Lot
See Kingsley, Charles

Partridge, Anthony
See Oppenheim, E(dward) Phillips

Pascoli, Giovanni 1855-1912 ...... **TCLC 45**

Pasolini, Pier Paolo
1922-1975 .... **CLC 20, 37**
See also CA 93-96; 61-64; DLB 128;
MTCW

Pasquini
See Silone, Ignazio

Pastan, Linda (Olenik) 1932- ...... **CLC 27**
See also CA 61-64; CANR 18, 40; DLB 5

Pasternak, Boris (Leonidovich)
1890-1960 ...... **CLC 7, 10, 18, 63; DA;**
PC 6; WLC
See also CA 127; 116; MTCW

Patchen, Kenneth 1911-1972... **CLC 1, 2, 18**
See also CA 1-4R; 33-36R; CANR 3, 35;
DLB 16, 48; MTCW

Pater, Walter (Horatio)
1839-1894 .... **NCLC 7**
See also CDBLB 1832-1890; DLB 57

Paterson, A(ndrew) B(arton)
1864-1941 .... **TCLC 32**

Paterson, Katherine (Womeldorf)
1932-..................... **CLC 12, 30**
See also AAYA 1; CA 21-24R; CANR 28;
CLR 7; DLB 52; JRDA; MAICYA;
MTCW; SATA 13, 53

Patmore, Coventry Kersey Dighton
1823-1896 .... **NCLC 9**
See also DLB 35, 98

Paton, Alan (Stewart)
1903-1988 ...... **CLC 4, 10, 25, 55; DA;**
WLC
See also CA 13-16; 125; CANR 22; CAP 1;
MTCW; SATA 11, 56

Paton Walsh, Gillian 1937-
See Walsh, Jill Paton
See also CANR 38; JRDA; MAICYA;
SAAS 3; SATA 4, 72

Paulding, James Kirke 1778-1860.. **NCLC 2**
See also DLB 3, 59, 74

Paulin, Thomas Neilson 1949-
See Paulin, Tom
See also CA 123; 128

Paulin, Tom...................... **CLC 37**
See also Paulin, Thomas Neilson
See also DLB 40

Paustovsky, Konstantin (Georgievich)
1892-1968 .... **CLC 40**
See also CA 93-96; 25-28R

Pavese, Cesare 1908-1950 .... **TCLC 3**
See also CA 104; DLB 128

Pavic, Milorad 1929-............. **CLC 60**
See also CA 136

Payne, Alan
See Jakes, John (William)

Paz, Gil
See Lugones, Leopoldo

Paz, Octavio
1914- .... **CLC 3, 4, 6, 10, 19, 51, 65;**
DA; HLC; PC 1; WLC
See also CA 73-76; CANR 32; DLBY 90;
HW; MTCW

Peacock, Molly 1947-............. **CLC 60**
See also CA 103; DLB 120

Peacock, Thomas Love
1785-1866 .... **NCLC 22**
See also DLB 96, 116

Peake, Mervyn 1911-1968....... **CLC 7, 54**
See also CA 5-8R; 25-28R; CANR 3;
DLB 15; MTCW; SATA 23

Pearce, Philippa .... **CLC 21**
See also Christie, (Ann) Philippa
See also CLR 9; MAICYA; SATA 1, 67

Pearl, Eric
See Elman, Richard

Pearson, T(homas) R(eid) 1956- .... **CLC 39**
See also CA 120; 130

Peck, Dale 1968(?)- .... **CLC 81**

Peck, John 1941-................ **CLC 3**
See also CA 49-52; CANR 3

Peck, Richard (Wayne) 1934-...... **CLC 21**
See also AAYA 1; CA 85-88; CANR 19,
38; JRDA; MAICYA; SAAS 2; SATA 18,
55

Peck, Robert Newton 1928-.... **CLC 17; DA**
See also AAYA 3; CA 81-84; CANR 31;
JRDA; MAICYA; SAAS 1; SATA 21, 62

Peckinpah, (David) Sam(uel)
1925-1984 .... **CLC 20**
See also CA 109; 114

Pedersen, Knut 1859-1952
See Hamsun, Knut
See also CA 104; 119; MTCW

Peeslake, Gaffer
See Durrell, Lawrence (George)

Peguy, Charles Pierre
1873-1914 .... **TCLC 10**
See also CA 107

Pena, Ramon del Valle y
See Valle-Inclan, Ramon (Maria) del

Pendennis, Arthur Esquir
See Thackeray, William Makepeace

Penn, William 1644-1718.......... **LC 25**
See also DLB 24

Pepys, Samuel
1633-1703 . . . . LC 11; DA; WLC
See also CDBLB 1660-1789; DLB 101

Percy, Walker
1916-1990 . . . . CLC 2, 3, 6, 8, 14, 18, 47, 65
See also CA 1-4R; 131; CANR 1, 23;
DLB 2; DLBY 80, 90; MTCW

Perec, Georges 1936-1982 . . . . CLC 56
See also CA 141; DLB 83

Pereda (y Sanchez de Porrua), Jose Maria de
1833-1906 . . . . TCLC 16
See also CA 117

Pereda y Porrua, Jose Maria de
See Pereda (y Sanchez de Porrua), Jose
Maria de

Peregoy, George Weems
See Mencken, H(enry) L(ouis)

Perelman, S(idney) J(oseph)
1904-1979 . . . CLC 3, 5, 9, 15, 23, 44, 49
See also AITN 1, 2; CA 73-76; 89-92;
CANR 18; DLB 11, 44; MTCW

Peret, Benjamin 1899-1959 . . . . TCLC 20
See also CA 117

Peretz, Isaac Loeb 1851(?)-1915 . . . TCLC 16
See also CA 109

Peretz, Yitzkhok Leibush
See Peretz, Isaac Loeb

Perez Galdos, Benito 1843-1920 . . . TCLC 27
See also CA 125; HW

Perrault, Charles 1628-1703 . . . . LC 2
See also MAICYA; SATA 25

Perry, Brighton
See Sherwood, Robert E(mmet)

Perse, St.-John . . . . CLC 4, 11, 46
See also Leger, (Marie-Rene Auguste) Alexis
Saint-Leger

Peseenz, Tulio F.
See Lopez y Fuentes, Gregorio

Pesetsky, Bette 1932- . . . . CLC 28
See also CA 133; DLB 130

Peshkov, Alexei Maximovich 1868-1936
See Gorky, Maxim
See also CA 105; 141; DA

Pessoa, Fernando (Antonio Nogueira)
1888-1935 . . . . TCLC 27; HLC
See also CA 125

Peterkin, Julia Mood 1880-1961 . . . . CLC 31
See also CA 102; DLB 9

Peters, Joan K. 1945- . . . . CLC 39

Peters, Robert L(ouis) 1924- . . . . CLC 7
See also CA 13-16R; CAAS 8; DLB 105

Petofi, Sandor 1823-1849 . . . . NCLC 21

Petrakis, Harry Mark 1923- . . . . CLC 3
See also CA 9-12R; CANR 4, 30

Petrarch 1304-1374 . . . . PC 8

Petrov, Evgeny . . . . TCLC 21
See also Kataev, Evgeny Petrovich

Petry, Ann (Lane) 1908- . . . . . . CLC 1, 7, 18
See also BW; CA 5-8R; CAAS 6; CANR 4;
CLR 12; DLB 76; JRDA; MAICYA;
MTCW; SATA 5

Petursson, Halligrimur 1614-1674 . . . . LC 8

Philipson, Morris H. 1926- . . . . CLC 53
See also CA 1-4R; CANR 4

Phillips, David Graham
1867-1911 . . . . TCLC 44
See also CA 108; DLB 9, 12

Phillips, Jack
See Sandburg, Carl (August)

Phillips, Jayne Anne 1952- . . . . . CLC 15, 33
See also CA 101; CANR 24; DLBY 80;
MTCW

Phillips, Richard
See Dick, Philip K(indred)

Phillips, Robert (Schaeffer) 1938- . . . CLC 28
See also CA 17-20R; CAAS 13; CANR 8;
DLB 105

Phillips, Ward
See Lovecraft, H(oward) P(hillips)

Piccolo, Lucio 1901-1969 . . . . CLC 13
See also CA 97-100; DLB 114

Pickthall, Marjorie L(owry) C(hristie)
1883-1922 . . . . TCLC 21
See also CA 107; DLB 92

Pico della Mirandola, Giovanni
1463-1494 . . . . LC 15

Piercy, Marge
1936- . . . . CLC 3, 6, 14, 18, 27, 62
See also CA 21-24R; CAAS 1; CANR 13,
43; DLB 120; MTCW

Piers, Robert
See Anthony, Piers

Pieyre de Mandiargues, Andre 1909-1991
See Mandiargues, Andre Pieyre de
See also CA 103; 136; CANR 22

Pilnyak, Boris . . . . TCLC 23
See also Vogau, Boris Andreyevich

Pincherle, Alberto 1907-1990 . . . CLC 11, 18
See also Moravia, Alberto
See also CA 25-28R; 132; CANR 33;
MTCW

Pinckney, Darryl 1953- . . . . CLC 76
See also CA 143

Pindar 518B.C.-446B.C. . . . . CMLC 12

Pineda, Cecile 1942- . . . . CLC 39
See also CA 118

Pinero, Arthur Wing 1855-1934 . . . TCLC 32
See also CA 110; DLB 10

Pinero, Miguel (Antonio Gomez)
1946-1988 . . . . CLC 4, 55
See also CA 61-64; 125; CANR 29; HW

Pinget, Robert 1919- . . . . CLC 7, 13, 37
See also CA 85-88; DLB 83

Pink Floyd . . . . CLC 35
See also Barrett, (Roger) Syd; Gilmour,
David; Mason, Nick; Waters, Roger;
Wright, Rick

Pinkney, Edward 1802-1828 . . . . . NCLC 31

Pinkwater, Daniel Manus 1941- . . . . CLC 35
See also Pinkwater, Manus
See also AAYA 1; CA 29-32R; CANR 12,
38; CLR 4; JRDA; MAICYA; SAAS 3;
SATA 46

Pinkwater, Manus
See Pinkwater, Daniel Manus
See also SATA 8

Pinsky, Robert 1940- . . . . CLC 9, 19, 38
See also CA 29-32R; CAAS 4; DLBY 82

Pinta, Harold
See Pinter, Harold

Pinter, Harold
1930- . . . . . CLC 1, 3, 6, 9, 11, 15, 27, 58,
73; DA; WLC
See also CA 5-8R; CANR 33; CDBLB 1960
to Present; DLB 13; MTCW

Pirandello, Luigi
1867-1936 . . . . . . TCLC 4, 29; DA; WLC
See also CA 104

Pirsig, Robert M(aynard)
1928- . . . . CLC 4, 6, 73
See also CA 53-56; CANR 42; MTCW;
SATA 39

Pisarev, Dmitry Ivanovich
1840-1868 . . . . NCLC 25

Pix, Mary (Griffith) 1666-1709 . . . . LC 8
See also DLB 80

Pixerecourt, Guilbert de
1773-1844 . . . . NCLC 39

Plaidy, Jean
See Hibbert, Eleanor Alice Burford

Planche, James Robinson
1796-1880 . . . . NCLC 42

Plant, Robert 1948- . . . . CLC 12

Plante, David (Robert)
1940- . . . . CLC 7, 23, 38
See also CA 37-40R; CANR 12, 36;
DLBY 83; MTCW

Plath, Sylvia
1932-1963 . . . . . CLC 1, 2, 3, 5, 9, 11, 14,
17, 50, 51, 62; DA; PC 1; WLC
See also CA 19-20; CANR 34; CAP 2;
CDALB 1941-1968; DLB 5, 6; MTCW

Plato 428(?)B.C.-348(?)B.C. . . . . CMLC 8; DA

Platonov, Andrei . . . . TCLC 14
See also Klimentov, Andrei Platonovich

Platt, Kin 1911- . . . . CLC 26
See also CA 17-20R; CANR 11; JRDA;
SAAS 17; SATA 21

Plick et Plock
See Simenon, Georges (Jacques Christian)

Plimpton, George (Ames) 1927- . . . . . CLC 36
See also AITN 1; CA 21-24R; CANR 32;
MTCW; SATA 10

Plomer, William Charles Franklin
1903-1973 . . . . CLC 4, 8
See also CA 21-22; CANR 34; CAP 2;
DLB 20; MTCW; SATA 24

Plowman, Piers
See Kavanagh, Patrick (Joseph)

Plum, J.
See Wodehouse, P(elham) G(renville)

Plumly, Stanley (Ross) 1939- . . . . . . CLC 33
See also CA 108; 110; DLB 5

Plumpe, Friedrich Wilhelm
1888-1931 . . . . TCLC 53
See also CA 112

Poe, Edgar Allan
1809-1849 . . . . . NCLC 1, 16; DA; PC 1;
SSC 1; WLC
See also CDALB 1640-1865; DLB 3, 59, 73,
74; SATA 23

Author Index

Reid Banks, Lynne 1929-
See Banks, Lynne Reid
See also CA 1-4R; CANR 6, 22, 38;
CLR 24; JRDA; MAICYA; SATA 22, 75

Reilly, William K.
See Creasey, John

Reiner, Max
See Caldwell, (Janet Miriam) Taylor
(Holland)

Reis, Ricardo
See Pessoa, Fernando (Antonio Nogueira)

Remarque, Erich Maria
1898-1970 .... **CLC 21; DA**
See also CA 77-80; 29-32R; DLB 56;
MTCW

Remizov, A.
See Remizov, Aleksei (Mikhailovich)

Remizov, A. M.
See Remizov, Aleksei (Mikhailovich)

Remizov, Aleksei (Mikhailovich)
1877-1957 .... **TCLC 27**
See also CA 125; 133

Renan, Joseph Ernest
1823-1892 .... **NCLC 26**

Renard, Jules 1864-1910 .... **TCLC 17**
See also CA 117

Renault, Mary .... **CLC 3, 11, 17**
See also Challans, Mary
See also DLBY 83

Rendell, Ruth (Barbara) 1930- .. **CLC 28, 48**
See also Vine, Barbara
See also CA 109; CANR 32; DLB 87;
MTCW

Renoir, Jean 1894-1979 .... **CLC 20**
See also CA 129; 85-88

Resnais, Alain 1922-.............. **CLC 16**

Reverdy, Pierre 1889-1960 .... **CLC 53**
See also CA 97-100; 89-92

Rexroth, Kenneth
1905-1982 ...... **CLC 1, 2, 6, 11, 22, 49**
See also CA 5-8R; 107; CANR 14, 34;
CDALB 1941-1968; DLB 16, 48;
DLBY 82; MTCW

Reyes, Alfonso 1889-1959 .... **TCLC 33**
See also CA 131; HW

Reyes y Basoalto, Ricardo Eliecer Neftali
See Neruda, Pablo

Reymont, Wladyslaw (Stanislaw)
1868(?)-1925 .... **TCLC 5**
See also CA 104

Reynolds, Jonathan 1942- .... **CLC 6, 38**
See also CA 65-68; CANR 28

Reynolds, Joshua 1723-1792 .... **LC 15**
See also DLB 104

Reynolds, Michael Shane 1937- .... **CLC 44**
See also CA 65-68; CANR 9

Reznikoff, Charles 1894-1976 .... **CLC 9**
See also CA 33-36; 61-64; CAP 2; DLB 28,
45

Rezzori (d'Arezzo), Gregor von
1914- .... **CLC 25**
See also CA 122; 136

Rhine, Richard
See Silverstein, Alvin

Rhodes, Eugene Manlove
1869-1934 .... **TCLC 53**

R'hoone
See Balzac, Honore de

Rhys, Jean
1890(?)-1979 .... **CLC 2, 4, 6, 14, 19, 51**
See also CA 25-28R; 85-88; CANR 35;
CDBLB 1945-1960; DLB 36, 117; MTCW

Ribeiro, Darcy 1922- .... **CLC 34**
See also CA 33-36R

Ribeiro, Joao Ubaldo (Osorio Pimentel)
1941- .... **CLC 10, 67**
See also CA 81-84

Ribman, Ronald (Burt) 1932- .... **CLC 7**
See also CA 21-24R

Ricci, Nino 1959-................ **CLC 70**
See also CA 137

Rice, Anne 1941- .... **CLC 41**
See also AAYA 9; BEST 89:2; CA 65-68;
CANR 12, 36

Rice, Elmer (Leopold)
1892-1967 .... **CLC 7, 49**
See also CA 21-22; 25-28R; CAP 2; DLB 4,
7; MTCW

Rice, Tim 1944- .... **CLC 21**
See also CA 103

Rich, Adrienne (Cecile)
1929- .... **CLC 3, 6, 7, 11, 18, 36, 73, 76;**
PC 5
See also CA 9-12R; CANR 20; DLB 5, 67;
MTCW

Rich, Barbara
See Graves, Robert (von Ranke)

Rich, Robert
See Trumbo, Dalton

Richards, David Adams 1950-...... **CLC 59**
See also CA 93-96; DLB 53

Richards, I(vor) A(rmstrong)
1893-1979 .... **CLC 14, 24**
See also CA 41-44R; 89-92; CANR 34;
DLB 27

Richardson, Anne
See Roiphe, Anne Richardson

Richardson, Dorothy Miller
1873-1957 .... **TCLC 3**
See also CA 104; DLB 36

Richardson, Ethel Florence (Lindesay)
1870-1946
See Richardson, Henry Handel
See also CA 105

Richardson, Henry Handel......... **TCLC 4**
See also Richardson, Ethel Florence
(Lindesay)

Richardson, Samuel
1689-1761 .... **LC 1; DA; WLC**
See also CDBLB 1660-1789; DLB 39

Richler, Mordecai
1931- .... **CLC 3, 5, 9, 13, 18, 46, 70**
See also AITN 1; CA 65-68; CANR 31;
CLR 17; DLB 53; MAICYA; MTCW;
SATA 27, 44

Richter, Conrad (Michael)
1890-1968 .... **CLC 30**
See also CA 5-8R; 25-28R; CANR 23;
DLB 9; MTCW; SATA 3

Riddell, J. H. 1832-1906 .... **TCLC 40**

Riding, Laura.................... **CLC 3, 7**
See also Jackson, Laura (Riding)

Riefenstahl, Berta Helene Amalia 1902-
See Riefenstahl, Leni
See also CA 108

Riefenstahl, Leni.................. **CLC 16**
See also Riefenstahl, Berta Helene Amalia

Riffe, Ernest
See Bergman, (Ernst) Ingmar

Riley, James Whitcomb
1849-1916 .... **TCLC 51**
See also CA 118; 137; MAICYA; SATA 17

Riley, Tex
See Creasey, John

Rilke, Rainer Maria
1875-1926 .... **TCLC 1, 6, 19; PC 2**
See also CA 104; 132; DLB 81; MTCW

Rimbaud, (Jean Nicolas) Arthur
1854-1891 ..... **NCLC 4, 35; DA; PC 3;**
WLC

Rinehart, Mary Roberts
1876-1958 .... **TCLC 52**
See also CA 108

Ringmaster, The
See Mencken, H(enry) L(ouis)

Ringwood, Gwen(dolyn Margaret) Pharis
1910-1984 .... **CLC 48**
See also CA 112; DLB 88

Rio, Michel 19(?)-................ **CLC 43**

Ritsos, Giannes
See Ritsos, Yannis

Ritsos, Yannis 1909-1990..... **CLC 6, 13, 31**
See also CA 77-80; 133; CANR 39; MTCW

Ritter, Erika 1948(?)-............. **CLC 52**

Rivera, Jose Eustasio 1889-1928... **TCLC 35**
See also HW

Rivers, Conrad Kent 1933-1968...... **CLC 1**
See also BW; CA 85-88; DLB 41

Rivers, Elfrida
See Bradley, Marion Zimmer

Riverside, John
See Heinlein, Robert A(nson)

Rizal, Jose 1861-1896.......... **NCLC 27**

Roa Bastos, Augusto (Antonio)
1917- .... **CLC 45; HLC**
See also CA 131; DLB 113; HW

Robbe-Grillet, Alain
1922- ...... **CLC 1, 2, 4, 6, 8, 10, 14, 43**
See also CA 9-12R; CANR 33; DLB 83;
MTCW

Robbins, Harold 1916-............. **CLC 5**
See also CA 73-76; CANR 26; MTCW

Robbins, Thomas Eugene 1936-
See Robbins, Tom
See also CA 81-84; CANR 29; MTCW

Robbins, Tom................ **CLC 9, 32, 64**
See also Robbins, Thomas Eugene
See also BEST 90:3; DLBY 80

Robbins, Trina 1938- .... **CLC 21**
See also CA 128

Roberts, Charles G(eorge) D(ouglas)
1860-1943 .... TCLC 8
See also CA 105; CLR 33; DLB 92;
SATA 29

Roberts, Kate 1891-1985 .... CLC 15
See also CA 107; 116

Roberts, Keith (John Kingston)
1935- .... CLC 14
See also CA 25-28R

Roberts, Kenneth (Lewis)
1885-1957 .... TCLC 23
See also CA 109; DLB 9

Roberts, Michele (B.) 1949-........ CLC 48
See also CA 115

Robertson, Ellis
See Ellison, Harlan; Silverberg, Robert

Robertson, Thomas William
1829-1871 .... NCLC 35

Robinson, Edwin Arlington
1869-1935 .... TCLC 5; DA; PC 1
See also CA 104; 133; CDALB 1865-1917;
DLB 54; MTCW

Robinson, Henry Crabb
1775-1867 .... NCLC 15
See also DLB 107

Robinson, Jill 1936- .... CLC 10
See also CA 102

Robinson, Kim Stanley 1952- ...... CLC 34
See also CA 126

Robinson, Lloyd
See Silverberg, Robert

Robinson, Marilynne 1944-........ CLC 25
See also CA 116

Robinson, Smokey................ CLC 21
See also Robinson, William, Jr.

Robinson, William, Jr. 1940-
See Robinson, Smokey
See also CA 116

Robison, Mary 1949- .... CLC 42
See also CA 113; 116; DLB 130

Rod, Edouard 1857-1910 .... TCLC 52

Roddenberry, Eugene Wesley 1921-1991
See Roddenberry, Gene
See also CA 110; 135; CANR 37; SATA 45

Roddenberry, Gene .... CLC 17
See also Roddenberry, Eugene Wesley
See also AAYA 5; SATA-Obit 69

Rodgers, Mary 1931-............. CLC 12
See also CA 49-52; CANR 8; CLR 20;
JRDA; MAICYA; SATA 8

Rodgers, W(illiam) R(obert)
1909-1969 .... CLC 7
See also CA 85-88; DLB 20

Rodman, Eric
See Silverberg, Robert

Rodman, Howard 1920(?)-1985..... CLC 65
See also CA 118

Rodman, Maia
See Wojciechowska, Maia (Teresa)

Rodriguez, Claudio 1934-......... CLC 10
See also DLB 134

Roelvaag, O(le) E(dvart)
1876-1931 .... TCLC 17
See also CA 117; DLB 9

Roethke, Theodore (Huebner)
1908-1963 ...... CLC 1, 3, 8, 11, 19, 46
See also CA 81-84; CABS 2;
CDALB 1941-1968; DLB 5; MTCW

Rogers, Thomas Hunton 1927- ..... CLC 57
See also CA 89-92

Rogers, Will(iam Penn Adair)
1879-1935 .... TCLC 8
See also CA 105; DLB 11

Rogin, Gilbert 1929-.............. CLC 18
See also CA 65-68; CANR 15

Rohan, Koda .... TCLC 22
See also Koda Shigeyuki

Rohmer, Eric.................... CLC 16
See also Scherer, Jean-Marie Maurice

Rohmer, Sax .... TCLC 28
See also Ward, Arthur Henry Sarsfield
See also DLB 70

Roiphe, Anne Richardson 1935- ... CLC 3, 9
See also CA 89-92; DLBY 80

Rojas, Fernando de 1465-1541 ...... LC 23

Rolfe, Frederick (William Serafino Austin
Lewis Mary) 1860-1913...... TCLC 12
See also CA 107; DLB 34

Rolland, Romain 1866-1944...... TCLC 23
See also CA 118; DLB 65

Rolvaag, O(le) E(dvart)
See Roelvaag, O(le) E(dvart)

Romain Arnaud, Saint
See Aragon, Louis

Romains, Jules 1885-1972.......... CLC 7
See also CA 85-88; CANR 34; DLB 65;
MTCW

Romero, Jose Ruben 1890-1952 ... TCLC 14
See also CA 114; 131; HW

Ronsard, Pierre de 1524-1585........ LC 6

Rooke, Leon 1934-............ CLC 25, 34
See also CA 25-28R; CANR 23

Roper, William 1498-1578.......... LC 10

Roquelaure, A. N.
See Rice, Anne

Rosa, Joao Guimaraes 1908-1967... CLC 23
See also CA 89-92; DLB 113

Rosen, Richard (Dean) 1949-....... CLC 39
See also CA 77-80

Rosenberg, Isaac 1890-1918....... TCLC 12
See also CA 107; DLB 20

Rosenblatt, Joe .... CLC 15
See also Rosenblatt, Joseph

Rosenblatt, Joseph 1933-
See Rosenblatt, Joe
See also CA 89-92

Rosenfeld, Samuel 1896-1963
See Tzara, Tristan
See also CA 89-92

Rosenthal, M(acha) L(ouis) 1917-... CLC 28
See also CA 1-4R; CAAS 6; CANR 4;
DLB 5; SATA 59

Ross, Barnaby
See Dannay, Frederic

Ross, Bernard L.
See Follett, Ken(neth Martin)

Ross, J. H.
See Lawrence, T(homas) E(dward)

Ross, Martin
See Martin, Violet Florence
See also DLB 135

Ross, (James) Sinclair 1908-....... CLC 13
See also CA 73-76; DLB 88

Rossetti, Christina (Georgina)
1830-1894 ... NCLC 2; DA; PC 7; WLC
See also DLB 35; MAICYA; SATA 20

Rossetti, Dante Gabriel
1828-1882 .... NCLC 4; DA; WLC
See also CDBLB 1832-1890; DLB 35

Rossner, Judith (Perelman)
1935- .... CLC 6, 9, 29
See also AITN 2; BEST 90:3; CA 17-20R;
CANR 18; DLB 6; MTCW

Rostand, Edmond (Eugene Alexis)
1868-1918 .... TCLC 6, 37; DA
See also CA 104; 126; MTCW

Roth, Henry 1906-........... CLC 2, 6, 11
See also CA 11-12; CANR 38; CAP 1;
DLB 28; MTCW

Roth, Joseph 1894-1939.......... TCLC 33
See also DLB 85

Roth, Philip (Milton)
1933- ...... CLC 1, 2, 3, 4, 6, 9, 15, 22,
31, 47, 66; DA; WLC
See also BEST 90:3; CA 1-4R; CANR 1, 22,
36; CDALB 1968-1988; DLB 2, 28;
DLBY 82; MTCW

Rothenberg, Jerome 1931-....... CLC 6, 57
See also CA 45-48; CANR 1; DLB 5

Roumain, Jacques (Jean Baptiste)
1907-1944 .... TCLC 19; BLC
See also BW; CA 117; 125

Rourke, Constance (Mayfield)
1885-1941 .... TCLC 12
See also CA 107; YABC 1

Rousseau, Jean-Baptiste 1671-1741 ... LC 9

Rousseau, Jean-Jacques
1712-1778 .... LC 14; DA; WLC

Roussel, Raymond 1877-1933 ..... TCLC 20
See also CA 117

Rovit, Earl (Herbert) 1927-........ CLC 7
See also CA 5-8R; CANR 12

Rowe, Nicholas 1674-1718.......... LC 8
See also DLB 84

Rowley, Ames Dorrance
See Lovecraft, H(oward) P(hillips)

Rowson, Susanna Haswell
1762(?)-1824 .... NCLC 5
See also DLB 37

Roy, Gabrielle 1909-1983....... CLC 10, 14
See also CA 53-56; 110; CANR 5; DLB 68;
MTCW

Rozewicz, Tadeusz 1921-........ CLC 9, 23
See also CA 108; CANR 36; MTCW

Ruark, Gibbons 1941- .... CLC 3
See also CA 33-36R; CANR 14, 31;
DLB 120

Rubens, Bernice (Ruth) 1923-... CLC 19, 31
See also CA 25-28R; CANR 33; DLB 14;
MTCW

Rudkin, (James) David 1936- ...... **CLC 14**
See also CA 89-92; DLB 13

Rudnik, Raphael 1933-............. **CLC 7**
See also CA 29-32R

Ruffian, M.
See Hasek, Jaroslav (Matej Frantisek)

Ruiz, Jose Martinez .... **CLC 11**
See also Martinez Ruiz, Jose

Rukeyser, Muriel
1913-1980 .... **CLC 6, 10, 15, 27**
See also CA 5-8R; 93-96; CANR 26;
DLB 48; MTCW; SATA 22

Rule, Jane (Vance) 1931-.......... **CLC 27**
See also CA 25-28R; CAAS 18; CANR 12;
DLB 60

Rulfo, Juan 1918-1986.... **CLC 8, 80; HLC**
See also CA 85-88; 118; CANR 26;
DLB 113; HW; MTCW

Runeberg, Johan 1804-1877...... **NCLC 41**

Runyon, (Alfred) Damon
1884(?)-1946 .... **TCLC 10**
See also CA 107; DLB 11, 86

Rush, Norman 1933-.............. **CLC 44**
See also CA 121; 126

Rushdie, (Ahmed) Salman
1947- .... **CLC 23, 31, 55**
See also BEST 89:3; CA 108; 111;
CANR 33; MTCW

Rushforth, Peter (Scott) 1945- ..... **CLC 19**
See also CA 101

Ruskin, John 1819-1900.......... **TCLC 20**
See also CA 114; 129; CDBLB 1832-1890;
DLB 55; SATA 24

Russ, Joanna 1937-.............. **CLC 15**
See also CA 25-28R; CANR 11, 31; DLB 8;
MTCW

Russell, George William 1867-1935
See A. E.
See also CA 104; CDBLB 1890-1914

Russell, (Henry) Ken(neth Alfred)
1927- .... **CLC 16**
See also CA 105

Russell, Willy 1947-.............. **CLC 60**

Rutherford, Mark .... **TCLC 25**
See also White, William Hale
See also DLB 18

Ruyslinck, Ward
See Belser, Reimond Karel Maria de

Ryan, Cornelius (John) 1920-1974 ... **CLC 7**
See also CA 69-72; 53-56; CANR 38

Ryan, Michael 1946- .... **CLC 65**
See also CA 49-52; DLBY 82

Rybakov, Anatoli (Naumovich)
1911-..................... **CLC 23, 53**
See also CA 126; 135

Ryder, Jonathan
See Ludlum, Robert

Ryga, George 1932-1987 .... **CLC 14**
See also CA 101; 124; CANR 43; DLB 60

S. S.
See Sassoon, Siegfried (Lorraine)

Saba, Umberto 1883-1957 .... **TCLC 33**
See also DLB 114

Sabatini, Rafael 1875-1950 .... **TCLC 47**

Sabato, Ernesto (R.)
1911- .... **CLC 10, 23; HLC**
See also CA 97-100; CANR 32; HW;
MTCW

Sacastru, Martin
See Bioy Casares, Adolfo

Sacher-Masoch, Leopold von
1836(?)-1895 .... **NCLC 31**

Sachs, Marilyn (Stickle) 1927- ..... **CLC 35**
See also AAYA 2; CA 17-20R; CANR 13;
CLR 2; JRDA; MAICYA; SAAS 2;
SATA 3, 68

Sachs, Nelly 1891-1970 .... **CLC 14**
See also CA 17-18; 25-28R; CAP 2

Sackler, Howard (Oliver)
1929-1982 .... **CLC 14**
See also CA 61-64; 108; CANR 30; DLB 7

Sacks, Oliver (Wolf) 1933- .... **CLC 67**
See also CA 53-56; CANR 28; MTCW

Sade, Donatien Alphonse Francois Comte
1740-1814 .... **NCLC 3**

Sadoff, Ira 1945-................. **CLC 9**
See also CA 53-56; CANR 5, 21; DLB 120

Saetone
See Camus, Albert

Safire, William 1929-............. **CLC 10**
See also CA 17-20R; CANR 31

Sagan, Carl (Edward) 1934-........ **CLC 30**
See also AAYA 2; CA 25-28R; CANR 11,
36; MTCW; SATA 58

Sagan, Francoise .... **CLC 3, 6, 9, 17, 36**
See also Quoirez, Francoise
See also DLB 83

Sahgal, Nayantara (Pandit) 1927-... **CLC 41**
See also CA 9-12R; CANR 11

Saint, H(arry) F. 1941- .... **CLC 50**
See also CA 127

St. Aubin de Teran, Lisa 1953-
See Teran, Lisa St. Aubin de
See also CA 118; 126

Sainte-Beuve, Charles Augustin
1804-1869 .... **NCLC 5**

**Saint-Exupery, Antoine (Jean Baptiste Marie
Roger) de** 1900-1944 ... **TCLC 2; WLC**
See also CA 108; 132; CLR 10; DLB 72;
MAICYA; MTCW; SATA 20

St. John, David
See Hunt, E(verette) Howard, Jr.

Saint-John Perse
See Leger, (Marie-Rene Auguste) Alexis
Saint-Leger

Saintsbury, George (Edward Bateman)
1845-1933 .... **TCLC 31**
See also DLB 57

Sait Faik .... **TCLC 23**
See also Abasiyanik, Sait Faik

Saki .... **TCLC 3; SSC 12**
See also Munro, H(ector) H(ugh)

Salama, Hannu 1936-............. **CLC 18**

Salamanca, J(ack) R(ichard)
1922- .... **CLC 4, 15**
See also CA 25-28R

Sale, J. Kirkpatrick
See Sale, Kirkpatrick

Sale, Kirkpatrick 1937- .... **CLC 68**
See also CA 13-16R; CANR 10

Salinas (y Serrano), Pedro
1891(?)-1951 .... **TCLC 17**
See also CA 117; DLB 134

Salinger, J(erome) D(avid)
1919- ...... **CLC 1, 3, 8, 12, 55, 56; DA;
SSC 2; WLC**
See also AAYA 2; CA 5-8R; CANR 39;
CDALB 1941-1968; CLR 18; DLB 2, 102;
MAICYA; MTCW; SATA 67

Salisbury, John
See Caute, David

Salter, James 1925- .... **CLC 7, 52, 59**
See also CA 73-76; DLB 130

Saltus, Edgar (Everton)
1855-1921 .... **TCLC 8**
See also CA 105

Saltykov, Mikhail Evgrafovich
1826-1889 .... **NCLC 16**

Samarakis, Antonis 1919- .... **CLC 5**
See also CA 25-28R; CAAS 16; CANR 36

Sanchez, Florencio 1875-1910..... **TCLC 37**
See also HW

Sanchez, Luis Rafael 1936-........ **CLC 23**
See also CA 128; HW

Sanchez, Sonia 1934-......... **CLC 5; BLC**
See also BW; CA 33-36R; CANR 24;
CLR 18; DLB 41; DLBD 8; MAICYA;
MTCW; SATA 22

Sand, George
1804-1876 ...... **NCLC 2, 42; DA; WLC**
See also DLB 119

Sandburg, Carl (August)
1878-1967 .... **CLC 1, 4, 10, 15, 35; DA;
PC 2; WLC**
See also CA 5-8R; 25-28R; CANR 35;
CDALB 1865-1917; DLB 17, 54;
MAICYA; MTCW; SATA 8

Sandburg, Charles
See Sandburg, Carl (August)

Sandburg, Charles A.
See Sandburg, Carl (August)

Sanders, (James) Ed(ward) 1939- ... **CLC 53**
See also CA 13-16R; CANR 13; DLB 16

Sanders, Lawrence 1920-.......... **CLC 41**
See also BEST 89:4; CA 81-84; CANR 33;
MTCW

Sanders, Noah
See Blount, Roy (Alton), Jr.

Sanders, Winston P.
See Anderson, Poul (William)

Sandoz, Mari(e Susette)
1896-1966 .... **CLC 28**
See also CA 1-4R; 25-28R; CANR 17;
DLB 9; MTCW; SATA 5

Saner, Reg(inald Anthony) 1931- .... **CLC 9**
See also CA 65-68

Sannazaro, Jacopo 1456(?)-1530...... **LC 8**

Sansom, William 1912-1976....... **CLC 2, 6**
See also CA 5-8R; 65-68; CANR 42;
MTCW

Santayana, George 1863-1952 ..... **TCLC 40**
See also CA 115; DLB 54, 71

Santiago, Danny .... CLC 33
See also James, Daniel (Lewis); James,
Daniel (Lewis)
See also DLB 122

Santmyer, Helen Hoover
1895-1986 .... CLC 33
See also CA 1-4R; 118; CANR 15, 33;
DLBY 84; MTCW

Santos, Bienvenido N(uqui) 1911-... CLC 22
See also CA 101; CANR 19

Sapper .... TCLC 44
See also McNeile, Herman Cyril

Sappho fl. 6th cent. B.C.-.... CMLC 3; PC 5

Sarduy, Severo 1937-1993 .... CLC 6
See also CA 89-92; 142; DLB 113; HW

Sargeson, Frank 1903-1982 .... CLC 31
See also CA 25-28R; 106; CANR 38

Sarmiento, Felix Ruben Garcia
See Dario, Ruben

Saroyan, William
1908-1981 ..... CLC 1, 8, 10, 29, 34, 56;
DA; WLC
See also CA 5-8R; 103; CANR 30; DLB 7,
9, 86; DLBY 81; MTCW; SATA 23, 24

Sarraute, Nathalie
1900- .... CLC 1, 2, 4, 8, 10, 31, 80
See also CA 9-12R; CANR 23; DLB 83;
MTCW

Sarton, (Eleanor) May
1912- .... CLC 4, 14, 49
See also CA 1-4R; CANR 1, 34; DLB 48;
DLBY 81; MTCW; SATA 36

Sartre, Jean-Paul
1905-1980 .... CLC 1, 4, 7, 9, 13, 18, 24,
44, 50, 52; DA; DC 3; WLC
See also CA 9-12R; 97-100; CANR 21;
DLB 72; MTCW

Sassoon, Siegfried (Lorraine)
1886-1967 .... CLC 36
See also CA 104; 25-28R; CANR 36;
DLB 20; MTCW

Satterfield, Charles
See Pohl, Frederik

Saul, John (W. III) 1942- .... CLC 46
See also AAYA 10; BEST 90:4; CA 81-84;
CANR 16, 40

Saunders, Caleb
See Heinlein, Robert A(nson)

Saura (Atares), Carlos 1932-....... CLC 20
See also CA 114; 131; HW

Sauser-Hall, Frederic 1887-1961.... CLC 18
See also CA 102; 93-96; CANR 36; MTCW

Saussure, Ferdinand de
1857-1913 .... TCLC 49

Savage, Catharine
See Brosman, Catharine Savage

Savage, Thomas 1915- .... CLC 40
See also CA 126; 132; CAAS 15

Savan, Glenn .... CLC 50

Saven, Glenn 19(?)- .... CLC 50

Sayers, Dorothy L(eigh)
1893-1957 .... TCLC 2, 15
See also CA 104; 119; CDBLB 1914-1945;
DLB 10, 36, 77, 100; MTCW

Sayers, Valerie 1952-............ CLC 50
See also CA 134

Sayles, John (Thomas)
1950- .... CLC 7, 10, 14
See also CA 57-60; CANR 41; DLB 44

Scammell, Michael .... CLC 34

Scannell, Vernon 1922- .... CLC 49
See also CA 5-8R; CANR 8, 24; DLB 27;
SATA 59

Scarlett, Susan
See Streatfeild, (Mary) Noel

Schaeffer, Susan Fromberg
1941- .... CLC 6, 11, 22
See also CA 49-52; CANR 18; DLB 28;
MTCW; SATA 22

Schary, Jill
See Robinson, Jill

Schell, Jonathan 1943-............ CLC 35
See also CA 73-76; CANR 12

Schelling, Friedrich Wilhelm Joseph von
1775-1854 .... NCLC 30
See also DLB 90

Scherer, Jean-Marie Maurice 1920-
See Rohmer, Eric
See also CA 110

Schevill, James (Erwin) 1920-....... CLC 7
See also CA 5-8R; CAAS 12

Schiller, Friedrich 1759-1805 .... NCLC 39
See also DLB 94

Schisgal, Murray (Joseph) 1926-..... CLC 6
See also CA 21-24R

Schlee, Ann 1934-................ CLC 35
See also CA 101; CANR 29; SATA 36, 44

Schlegel, August Wilhelm von
1767-1845 .... NCLC 15
See also DLB 94

Schlegel, Johann Elias (von)
1719(?)-1749 .... LC 5

Schmidt, Arno (Otto) 1914-1979.... CLC 56
See also CA 128; 109; DLB 69

Schmitz, Aron Hector 1861-1928
See Svevo, Italo
See also CA 104; 122; MTCW

Schnackenberg, Gjertrud 1953-..... CLC 40
See also CA 116; DLB 120

Schneider, Leonard Alfred 1925-1966
See Bruce, Lenny
See also CA 89-92

Schnitzler, Arthur 1862-1931 ...... TCLC 4
See also CA 104; DLB 81, 118

Schor, Sandra (M.) 1932(?)-1990 ... CLC 65
See also CA 132

Schorer, Mark 1908-1977 .... CLC 9
See also CA 5-8R; 73-76; CANR 7;
DLB 103

Schrader, Paul (Joseph) 1946-...... CLC 26
See also CA 37-40R; CANR 41; DLB 44

Schreiner, Olive (Emilie Albertina)
1855-1920 .... TCLC 9
See also CA 105; DLB 18

Schulberg, Budd (Wilson)
1914- .... CLC 7, 48
See also CA 25-28R; CANR 19; DLB 6, 26,
28; DLBY 81

Schulz, Bruno
1892-1942 .... TCLC 5, 51; SSC 13
See also CA 115; 123

Schulz, Charles M(onroe) 1922- .... CLC 12
See also CA 9-12R; CANR 6; SATA 10

Schumacher, E(rnst) F(riedrich)
1911-1977 .... CLC 80
See also CA 81-84; 73-76; CANR 34

Schuyler, James Marcus
1923-1991 .... CLC 5, 23
See also CA 101; 134; DLB 5

Schwartz, Delmore (David)
1913-1966 ...... CLC 2, 4, 10, 45; PC 8
See also CA 17-18; 25-28R; CANR 35;
CAP 2; DLB 28, 48; MTCW

Schwartz, Ernst
See Ozu, Yasujiro

Schwartz, John Burnham 1965- .... CLC 59
See also CA 132

Schwartz, Lynne Sharon 1939-..... CLC 31
See also CA 103

Schwartz, Muriel A.
See Eliot, T(homas) S(tearns)

Schwarz-Bart, Andre 1928-....... CLC 2, 4
See also CA 89-92

Schwarz-Bart, Simone 1938-........ CLC 7
See also CA 97-100

Schwob, (Mayer Andre) Marcel
1867-1905 .... TCLC 20
See also CA 117; DLB 123

Sciascia, Leonardo
1921-1989 .... CLC 8, 9, 41
See also CA 85-88; 130; CANR 35; MTCW

Scoppettone, Sandra 1936-......... CLC 26
See also CA 5-8R; CANR 41; SATA 9

Scorsese, Martin 1942- .... CLC 20
See also CA 110; 114

Scotland, Jay
See Jakes, John (William)

Scott, Duncan Campbell
1862-1947 .... TCLC 6
See also CA 104; DLB 92

Scott, Evelyn 1893-1963........... CLC 43
See also CA 104; 112; DLB 9, 48

Scott, F(rancis) R(eginald)
1899-1985 .... CLC 22
See also CA 101; 114; DLB 88

Scott, Frank
See Scott, F(rancis) R(eginald)

Scott, Joanna 1960-.............. CLC 50
See also CA 126

Scott, Paul (Mark) 1920-1978.... CLC 9, 60
See also CA 81-84; 77-80; CANR 33;
DLB 14; MTCW

Scott, Walter
1771-1832 .... NCLC 15; DA; WLC
See also CDBLB 1789-1832; DLB 93, 107,
116; YABC 2

Scribe, (Augustin) Eugene
1791-1861 .... NCLC 16

Scrum, R.
See Crumb, R(obert)

Scudery, Madeleine de 1607-1701..... LC 2

Scum
See Crumb, R(obert)

Scumbag, Little Bobby
See Crumb, R(obert)

Seabrook, John
See Hubbard, L(afayette) Ron(ald)

Sealy, I. Allan 1951- .... **CLC 55**

Search, Alexander
See Pessoa, Fernando (Antonio Nogueira)

Sebastian, Lee
See Silverberg, Robert

Sebastian Owl
See Thompson, Hunter S(tockton)

Sebestyen, Ouida 1924- .... **CLC 30**
See also AAYA 8; CA 107; CANR 40;
CLR 17; JRDA; MAICYA; SAAS 10;
SATA 39

Secundus, H. Scriblerus
See Fielding, Henry

Sedges, John
See Buck, Pearl S(ydenstricker)

Sedgwick, Catharine Maria
1789-1867 .... **NCLC 19**
See also DLB 1, 74

Seelye, John 1931- .... **CLC 7**

Seferiades, Giorgos Stylianou 1900-1971
See Seferis, George
See also CA 5-8R; 33-36R; CANR 5, 36;
MTCW

Seferis, George .... **CLC 5, 11**
See also Seferiades, Giorgos Stylianou

Segal, Erich (Wolf) 1937- ...... **CLC 3, 10**
See also BEST 89:1; CA 25-28R; CANR 20,
36; DLBY 86; MTCW

Seger, Bob 1945- .... **CLC 35**

Seghers, Anna .... **CLC 7**
See also Radvanyi, Netty
See also DLB 69

Seidel, Frederick (Lewis) 1936- ..... **CLC 18**
See also CA 13-16R; CANR 8; DLBY 84

Seifert, Jaroslav 1901-1986 ..... **CLC 34, 44**
See also CA 127; MTCW

Sei Shonagon c. 966-1017(?) ...... **CMLC 6**

Selby, Hubert, Jr. 1928- ..... **CLC 1, 2, 4, 8**
See also CA 13-16R; CANR 33; DLB 2

Selzer, Richard 1928- .... **CLC 74**
See also CA 65-68; CANR 14

Sembene, Ousmane
See Ousmane, Sembene

Senancour, Etienne Pivert de
1770-1846 .... **NCLC 16**
See also DLB 119

Sender, Ramon (Jose)
1902-1982 .... **CLC 8; HLC**
See also CA 5-8R; 105; CANR 8; HW;
MTCW

Seneca, Lucius Annaeus
4B.C.-65 .... **CMLC 6**

Senghor, Leopold Sedar
1906- .... **CLC 54; BLC**
See also BW; CA 116; 125; MTCW

Serling, (Edward) Rod(man)
1924-1975 .... **CLC 30**
See also AITN 1; CA 65-68; 57-60; DLB 26

Serna, Ramon Gomez de la
See Gomez de la Serna, Ramon

Serpieres
See Guillevic, (Eugene)

Service, Robert
See Service, Robert W(illiam)
See also DLB 92

Service, Robert W(illiam)
1874(?)-1958 ...... **TCLC 15; DA; WLC**
See also Service, Robert
See also CA 115; 140; SATA 20

Seth, Vikram 1952- .... **CLC 43**
See also CA 121; 127; DLB 120

Seton, Cynthia Propper
1926-1982 .... **CLC 27**
See also CA 5-8R; 108; CANR 7

Seton, Ernest (Evan) Thompson
1860-1946 .... **TCLC 31**
See also CA 109; DLB 92; JRDA; SATA 18

Seton-Thompson, Ernest
See Seton, Ernest (Evan) Thompson

Settle, Mary Lee 1918- .... **CLC 19, 61**
See also CA 89-92; CAAS 1; DLB 6

Seuphor, Michel
See Arp, Jean

**Sevigne, Marie (de Rabutin-Chantal) Marquise
de** 1626-1696 .... **LC 11**

Sexton, Anne (Harvey)
1928-1974 .... **CLC 2, 4, 6, 8, 10, 15, 53;
DA; PC 2; WLC**
See also CA 1-4R; 53-56; CABS 2;
CANR 3, 36; CDALB 1941-1968; DLB 5;
MTCW; SATA 10

Shaara, Michael (Joseph Jr.)
1929-1988 .... **CLC 15**
See also AITN 1; CA 102; DLBY 83

Shackleton, C. C.
See Aldiss, Brian W(ilson)

Shacochis, Bob .... **CLC 39**
See also Shacochis, Robert G.

Shacochis, Robert G. 1951-
See Shacochis, Bob
See also CA 119; 124

Shaffer, Anthony (Joshua) 1926- .... **CLC 19**
See also CA 110; 116; DLB 13

Shaffer, Peter (Levin)
1926- .... **CLC 5, 14, 18, 37, 60**
See also CA 25-28R; CANR 25;
CDBLB 1960 to Present; DLB 13;
MTCW

Shakey, Bernard
See Young, Neil

Shalamov, Varlam (Tikhonovich)
1907(?)-1982 .... **CLC 18**
See also CA 129; 105

Shamlu, Ahmad 1925- .... **CLC 10**

Shammas, Anton 1951- .... **CLC 55**

Shange, Ntozake
1948- .... **CLC 8, 25, 38, 74; BLC; DC 3**
See also AAYA 9; BW; CA 85-88; CABS 3;
CANR 27; DLB 38; MTCW

Shanley, John Patrick 1950- .... **CLC 75**
See also CA 128; 133

Shapcott, Thomas William 1935- ... **CLC 38**
See also CA 69-72

Shapiro, Jane .... **CLC 76**

Shapiro, Karl (Jay) 1913- .. **CLC 4, 8, 15, 53**
See also CA 1-4R; CAAS 6; CANR 1, 36;
DLB 48; MTCW

Sharp, William 1855-1905 .... **TCLC 39**

Sharpe, Thomas Ridley 1928-
See Sharpe, Tom
See also CA 114; 122

Sharpe, Tom .... **CLC 36**
See also Sharpe, Thomas Ridley
See also DLB 14

Shaw, Bernard .... **TCLC 45**
See also Shaw, George Bernard

Shaw, G. Bernard
See Shaw, George Bernard

Shaw, George Bernard
1856-1950 .... **TCLC 3, 9, 21; DA; WLC**
See also Shaw, Bernard
See also CA 104; 128; CDBLB 1914-1945;
DLB 10, 57; MTCW

Shaw, Henry Wheeler
1818-1885 .... **NCLC 15**
See also DLB 11

Shaw, Irwin 1913-1984 .... **CLC 7, 23, 34**
See also AITN 1; CA 13-16R; 112;
CANR 21; CDALB 1941-1968; DLB 6,
102; DLBY 84; MTCW

Shaw, Robert 1927-1978 .... **CLC 5**
See also AITN 1; CA 1-4R; 81-84;
CANR 4; DLB 13, 14

Shaw, T. E.
See Lawrence, T(homas) E(dward)

Shawn, Wallace 1943- .... **CLC 41**
See also CA 112

Sheed, Wilfrid (John Joseph)
1930- .... **CLC 2, 4, 10, 53**
See also CA 65-68; CANR 30; DLB 6;
MTCW

Sheldon, Alice Hastings Bradley
1915(?)-1987
See Tiptree, James, Jr.
See also CA 108; 122; CANR 34; MTCW

Sheldon, John
See Bloch, Robert (Albert)

Shelley, Mary Wollstonecraft (Godwin)
1797-1851 .... **NCLC 14; DA; WLC**
See also CDBLB 1789-1832; DLB 110, 116;
SATA 29

Shelley, Percy Bysshe
1792-1822 .... **NCLC 18; DA; WLC**
See also CDBLB 1789-1832; DLB 96, 110

Shepard, Jim 1956- .... **CLC 36**
See also CA 137

Shepard, Lucius 1947- .... **CLC 34**
See also CA 128; 141

Shepard, Sam
1943- .... **CLC 4, 6, 17, 34, 41, 44**
See also AAYA 1; CA 69-72; CABS 3;
CANR 22; DLB 7; MTCW

Shepherd, Michael
See Ludlum, Robert

Sissman, L(ouis) E(dward)
1928-1976 .... CLC **9, 18**
See also CA 21-24R; 65-68; CANR 13;
DLB 5

Sisson, C(harles) H(ubert) 1914-..... CLC **8**
See also CA 1-4R; CAAS 3; CANR 3;
DLB 27

Sitwell, Dame Edith
1887-1964 .... CLC **2, 9, 67; PC 3**
See also CA 9-12R; CANR 35;
CDBLB 1945-1960; DLB 20; MTCW

Sjoewall, Maj 1935-............... CLC **7**
See also CA 65-68

Sjowall, Maj
See Sjoewall, Maj

Skelton, Robin 1925-.............. CLC **13**
See also AITN 2; CA 5-8R; CAAS 5;
CANR 28; DLB 27, 53

Skolimowski, Jerzy 1938- .... CLC **20**
See also CA 128

Skram, Amalie (Bertha)
1847-1905 .... TCLC **25**

Skvorecky, Josef (Vaclav)
1924- .... CLC **15, 39, 69**
See also CA 61-64; CAAS 1; CANR 10, 34;
MTCW

Slade, Bernard................. CLC **11, 46**
See also Newbound, Bernard Slade
See also CAAS 9; DLB 53

Slaughter, Carolyn 1946-.......... CLC **56**
See also CA 85-88

Slaughter, Frank G(ill) 1908- ...... CLC **29**
See also AITN 2; CA 5-8R; CANR 5

Slavitt, David R(ytman) 1935-.... CLC **5, 14**
See also CA 21-24R; CAAS 3; CANR 41;
DLB 5, 6

Slesinger, Tess 1905-1945 .... TCLC **10**
See also CA 107; DLB 102

Slessor, Kenneth 1901-1971....... CLC **14**
See also CA 102; 89-92

Slowacki, Juliusz 1809-1849 ..... NCLC **15**

Smart, Christopher 1722-1771........ LC **3**
See also DLB 109

Smart, Elizabeth 1913-1986........ CLC **54**
See also CA 81-84; 118; DLB 88

Smiley, Jane (Graves) 1949- .... CLC **53, 76**
See also CA 104; CANR 30

Smith, A(rthur) J(ames) M(arshall)
1902-1980 .... CLC **15**
See also CA 1-4R; 102; CANR 4; DLB 88

Smith, Betty (Wehner) 1896-1972... CLC **19**
See also CA 5-8R; 33-36R; DLBY 82;
SATA 6

Smith, Charlotte (Turner)
1749-1806 .... NCLC **23**
See also DLB 39, 109

Smith, Clark Ashton 1893-1961 .... CLC **43**
See also CA 143

Smith, Dave.................. CLC **22, 42**
See also Smith, David (Jeddie)
See also CAAS 7; DLB 5

Smith, David (Jeddie) 1942-
See Smith, Dave
See also CA 49-52; CANR 1

Smith, Florence Margaret
1902-1971 .... CLC **8**
See also Smith, Stevie
See also CA 17-18; 29-32R; CANR 35;
CAP 2; MTCW

Smith, Iain Crichton 1928- .... CLC **64**
See also CA 21-24R; DLB 40

Smith, John 1580(?)-1631 .... LC **9**

Smith, Johnston
See Crane, Stephen (Townley)

Smith, Lee 1944-.............. CLC **25, 73**
See also CA 114; 119; DLBY 83

Smith, Martin
See Smith, Martin Cruz

Smith, Martin Cruz 1942 .... CLC **25**
See also BEST 89:4; CA 85-88; CANR 6,
23, 43

Smith, Mary-Ann Tirone 1944-..... CLC **39**
See also CA 118; 136

Smith, Patti 1946- .... CLC **12**
See also CA 93-96

Smith, Pauline (Urmson)
1882-1959 .... TCLC **25**

Smith, Rosamond
See Oates, Joyce Carol

Smith, Sheila Kaye
See Kaye-Smith, Sheila

Smith, Stevie .... CLC **3, 8, 25, 44**
See also Smith, Florence Margaret
See also DLB 20

Smith, Wilbur A(ddison) 1933-..... CLC **33**
See also CA 13-16R; CANR 7; MTCW

Smith, William Jay 1918- .... CLC **6**
See also CA 5-8R; DLB 5; MAICYA;
SATA 2, 68

Smith, Woodrow Wilson
See Kuttner, Henry

Smolenskin, Peretz 1842-1885.... NCLC **30**

Smollett, Tobias (George) 1721-1771 .. LC **2**
See also CDBLB 1660-1789; DLB 39, 104

Snodgrass, W(illiam) D(e Witt)
1926- .... CLC **2, 6, 10, 18, 68**
See also CA 1-4R; CANR 6, 36; DLB 5;
MTCW

Snow, C(harles) P(ercy)
1905-1980 .... CLC **1, 4, 6, 9, 13, 19**
See also CA 5-8R; 101; CANR 28;
CDBLB 1945-1960; DLB 15, 77; MTCW

Snow, Frances Compton
See Adams, Henry (Brooks)

Snyder, Gary (Sherman)
1930- .... CLC **1, 2, 5, 9, 32**
See also CA 17-20R; CANR 30; DLB 5, 16

Snyder, Zilpha Keatley 1927- ...... CLC **17**
See also CA 9-12R; CANR 38; CLR 31;
JRDA; MAICYA; SAAS 2; SATA 1, 28,
75

Soares, Bernardo
See Pessoa, Fernando (Antonio Nogueira)

Sobh, A.
See Shamlu, Ahmad

Sobol, Joshua.................... CLC **60**

Soderberg, Hjalmar 1869-1941 .... TCLC **39**

Sodergran, Edith (Irene)
See Soedergran, Edith (Irene)

Soedergran, Edith (Irene)
1892-1923 .... TCLC **31**

Softly, Edgar
See Lovecraft, H(oward) P(hillips)

Softly, Edward
See Lovecraft, H(oward) P(hillips)

Sokolov, Raymond 1941-........... CLC **7**
See also CA 85-88

Solo, Jay
See Ellison, Harlan

Sologub, Fyodor .... TCLC **9**
See also Teternikov, Fyodor Kuzmich

Solomons, Ikey Esquir
See Thackeray, William Makepeace

Solomos, Dionysios 1798-1857 ... NCLC **15**

Solwoska, Mara
See French, Marilyn

Solzhenitsyn, Aleksandr I(sayevich)
1918-......CLC **1, 2, 4, 7, 9, 10, 18, 26,
34, 78; DA; WLC**
See also AITN 1; CA 69-72; CANR 40;
MTCW

Somers, Jane
See Lessing, Doris (May)

Somerville, Edith 1858-1949 ...... TCLC **51**
See also DLB 135

Somerville & Ross
See Martin, Violet Florence; Somerville,
Edith

Sommer, Scott 1951- .... CLC **25**
See also CA 106

Sondheim, Stephen (Joshua)
1930- .... CLC **30, 39**
See also CA 103

Sontag, Susan 1933-... CLC **1, 2, 10, 13, 31**
See also CA 17-20R; CANR 25; DLB 2, 67;
MTCW

Sophocles
496(?)B.C.-406(?)B.C..... CMLC **2; DA;
DC 1**

Sorel, Julia
See Drexler, Rosalyn

Sorrentino, Gilbert
1929- .... CLC **3, 7, 14, 22, 40**
See also CA 77-80; CANR 14, 33; DLB 5;
DLBY 80

Soto, Gary 1952-........ CLC **32, 80; HLC**
See also AAYA 10; CA 119; 125; DLB 82;
HW; JRDA

Soupault, Philippe 1897-1990 ...... CLC **68**
See also CA 116; 131

Souster, (Holmes) Raymond
1921- .... CLC **5, 14**
See also CA 13-16R; CAAS 14; CANR 13,
29; DLB 88; SATA 63

Southern, Terry 1926- .... CLC **7**
See also CA 1-4R; CANR 1; DLB 2

Southey, Robert 1774-1843 .... NCLC **8**
See also DLB 93, 107; SATA 54

Southworth, Emma Dorothy Eliza Nevitte
1819-1899 .... NCLC **26**

Souza, Ernest
See Scott, Evelyn

Soyinka, Wole
1934- ...... CLC 3, 5, 14, 36, 44; BLC;
DA; DC 2; WLC
See also BW; CA 13-16R; CANR 27, 39;
DLB 125; MTCW

Spackman, W(illiam) M(ode)
1905-1990 .... CLC 46
See also CA 81-84; 132

Spacks, Barry 1931- .... CLC 14
See also CA 29-32R; CANR 33; DLB 105

Spanidou, Irini 1946- .... CLC 44

Spark, Muriel (Sarah)
1918- .... CLC 2, 3, 5, 8, 13, 18, 40;
SSC 10
See also CA 5-8R; CANR 12, 36;
CDBLB 1945-1960; DLB 15; MTCW

Spaulding, Douglas
See Bradbury, Ray (Douglas)

Spaulding, Leonard
See Bradbury, Ray (Douglas)

Spence, J. A. D.
See Eliot, T(homas) S(tearns)

Spencer, Elizabeth 1921- .... CLC 22
See also CA 13-16R; CANR 32; DLB 6;
MTCW; SATA 14

Spencer, Leonard G.
See Silverberg, Robert

Spencer, Scott 1945- .... CLC 30
See also CA 113; DLBY 86

Spender, Stephen (Harold)
1909- .... CLC 1, 2, 5, 10, 41
See also CA 9-12R; CANR 31;
CDBLB 1945-1960; DLB 20; MTCW

Spengler, Oswald (Arnold Gottfried)
1880-1936 .... TCLC 25
See also CA 118

Spenser, Edmund
1552(?)-1599 .... LC 5; DA; PC 8; WLC
See also CDBLB Before 1660

Spicer, Jack 1925-1965 ...... CLC 8, 18, 72
See also CA 85-88; DLB 5, 16

Spiegelman, Art 1948- .... CLC 76
See also AAYA 10; CA 125; CANR 41

Spielberg, Peter 1929- .... CLC 6
See also CA 5-8R; CANR 4; DLBY 81

Spielberg, Steven 1947- .... CLC 20
See also AAYA 8; CA 77-80; CANR 32;
SATA 32

Spillane, Frank Morrison 1918-
See Spillane, Mickey
See also CA 25-28R; CANR 28; MTCW;
SATA 66

Spillane, Mickey .... CLC 3, 13
See also Spillane, Frank Morrison

Spinoza, Benedictus de 1632-1677 .... LC 9

Spinrad, Norman (Richard) 1940-... CLC 46
See also CA 37-40R; CANR 20; DLB 8

Spitteler, Carl (Friedrich Georg)
1845-1924 .... TCLC 12
See also CA 109; DLB 129

Spivack, Kathleen (Romola Drucker)
1938- .... CLC 6
See also CA 49-52

Spoto, Donald 1941- .... CLC 39
See also CA 65-68; CANR 11

Springsteen, Bruce (F.) 1949- ...... CLC 17
See also CA 111

Spurling, Hilary 1940- .... CLC 34
See also CA 104; CANR 25

Squires, (James) Radcliffe
1917-1993 .... CLC 51
See also CA 1-4R; 140; CANR 6, 21

Srivastava, Dhanpat Rai 1880(?)-1936
See Premchand
See also CA 118

Stacy, Donald
See Pohl, Frederik

Stael, Germaine de
See Stael-Holstein, Anne Louise Germaine
Necker Baronn
See also DLB 119

Stael-Holstein, Anne Louise Germaine Necker
Baronn 1766-1817 .... NCLC 3
See also Stael, Germaine de

Stafford, Jean 1915-1979 ... CLC 4, 7, 19, 68
See also CA 1-4R; 85-88; CANR 3; DLB 2;
MTCW; SATA 22

Stafford, William (Edgar)
1914-1993 .... CLC 4, 7, 29
See also CA 5-8R; 142; CAAS 3; CANR 5,
22; DLB 5

Staines, Trevor
See Brunner, John (Kilian Houston)

Stairs, Gordon
See Austin, Mary (Hunter)

Stannard, Martin 1947- .... CLC 44
See also CA 142

Stanton, Maura 1946- .... CLC 9
See also CA 89-92; CANR 15; DLB 120

Stanton, Schuyler
See Baum, L(yman) Frank

Stapledon, (William) Olaf
1886-1950 .... TCLC 22
See also CA 111; DLB 15

Starbuck, George (Edwin) 1931-.... CLC 53
See also CA 21-24R; CANR 23

Stark, Richard
See Westlake, Donald E(dwin)

Staunton, Schuyler
See Baum, L(yman) Frank

Stead, Christina (Ellen)
1902-1983 .... CLC 2, 5, 8, 32, 80
See also CA 13-16R; 109; CANR 33, 40;
MTCW

Stead, William Thomas
1849-1912 .... TCLC 48

Steele, Richard 1672-1729 .... LC 18
See also CDBLB 1660-1789; DLB 84, 101

Steele, Timothy (Reid) 1948-....... CLC 45
See also CA 93-96; CANR 16; DLB 120

Steffens, (Joseph) Lincoln
1866-1936 .... TCLC 20
See also CA 117

Stegner, Wallace (Earle)
1909-1993 .... CLC 9, 49, 81
See also AITN 1; BEST 90:3; CA 1-4R;
141; CAAS 9; CANR 1, 21; DLB 9;
MTCW

Stein, Gertrude
1874-1946 ...... TCLC 1, 6, 28, 48; DA;
WLC
See also CA 104; 132; CDALB 1917-1929;
DLB 4, 54, 86; MTCW

Steinbeck, John (Ernst)
1902-1968 ...... CLC 1, 5, 9, 13, 21, 34,
45, 75; DA; SSC 11; WLC
See also CA 1-4R; 25-28R; CANR 1, 35;
CDALB 1929-1941; DLB 7, 9; DLBD 2;
MTCW; SATA 9

Steinem, Gloria 1934-............. CLC 63
See also CA 53-56; CANR 28; MTCW

Steiner, George 1929-............. CLC 24
See also CA 73-76; CANR 31; DLB 67;
MTCW; SATA 62

Steiner, K. Leslie
See Delany, Samuel R(ay, Jr.)

Steiner, Rudolf 1861-1925 .... TCLC 13
See also CA 107

Stendhal 1783-1842.... NCLC 23; DA; WLC
See also DLB 119

Stephen, Leslie 1832-1904 .... TCLC 23
See also CA 123; DLB 57

Stephen, Sir Leslie
See Stephen, Leslie

Stephen, Virginia
See Woolf, (Adeline) Virginia

Stephens, James 1882(?)-1950 ...... TCLC 4
See also CA 104; DLB 19

Stephens, Reed
See Donaldson, Stephen R.

Steptoe, Lydia
See Barnes, Djuna

Sterchi, Beat 1949-............... CLC 65

Sterling, Brett
See Bradbury, Ray (Douglas); Hamilton,
Edmond

Sterling, Bruce 1954-............. CLC 72
See also CA 119

Sterling, George 1869-1926 .... TCLC 20
See also CA 117; DLB 54

Stern, Gerald 1925- .... CLC 40
See also CA 81-84; CANR 28; DLB 105

Stern, Richard (Gustave) 1928-... CLC 4, 39
See also CA 1-4R; CANR 1, 25; DLBY 87

Sternberg, Josef von 1894-1969..... CLC 20
See also CA 81-84

Sterne, Laurence
1713-1768 .... LC 2; DA; WLC
See also CDBLB 1660-1789; DLB 39

Sternheim, (William Adolf) Carl
1878-1942 .... TCLC 8
See also CA 105; DLB 56, 118

Stevens, Mark 1951- .... CLC 34
See also CA 122

Stevens, Wallace
1879-1955 .... **TCLC 3, 12, 45; DA;**
PC 6; WLC
See also CA 104; 124; CDALB 1929-1941;
DLB 54; MTCW

Stevenson, Anne (Katharine)
1933- .... **CLC 7, 33**
See also CA 17-20R; CAAS 9; CANR 9, 33;
DLB 40; MTCW

Stevenson, Robert Louis (Balfour)
1850-1894 .... **NCLC 5, 14; DA;**
SSC 11; WLC
See also CDBLB 1890-1914; CLR 10, 11;
DLB 18, 57; JRDA; MAICYA; YABC 2

Stewart, J(ohn) I(nnes) M(ackintosh)
1906- .... **CLC 7, 14, 32**
See also CA 85-88; CAAS 3; MTCW

Stewart, Mary (Florence Elinor)
1916- .... **CLC 7, 35**
See also CA 1-4R; CANR 1; SATA 12

Stewart, Mary Rainbow
See Stewart, Mary (Florence Elinor)

Stifter, Adalbert 1805-1868 ...... **NCLC 41**
See also DLB 133

Still, James 1906- .... **CLC 49**
See also CA 65-68; CAAS 17; CANR 10,
26; DLB 9; SATA 29

Sting
See Sumner, Gordon Matthew

Stirling, Arthur
See Sinclair, Upton (Beall)

Stitt, Milan 1941- .... **CLC 29**
See also CA 69-72

Stockton, Francis Richard 1834-1902
See Stockton, Frank R.
See also CA 108; 137; MAICYA; SATA 44

Stockton, Frank R. .... **TCLC 47**
See also Stockton, Francis Richard
See also DLB 42, 74; SATA 32

Stoddard, Charles
See Kuttner, Henry

Stoker, Abraham 1847-1912
See Stoker, Bram
See also CA 105; DA; SATA 29

Stoker, Bram .... **TCLC 8; WLC**
See also Stoker, Abraham
See also CDBLB 1890-1914; DLB 36, 70

Stolz, Mary (Slattery) 1920- .... **CLC 12**
See also AAYA 8; AITN 1; CA 5-8R;
CANR 13, 41; JRDA; MAICYA;
SAAS 3; SATA 10, 71

Stone, Irving 1903-1989 .... **CLC 7**
See also AITN 1; CA 1-4R; 129; CAAS 3;
CANR 1, 23; MTCW; SATA 3;
SATA-Obit 64

Stone, Oliver 1946- .... **CLC 73**
See also CA 110

Stone, Robert (Anthony)
1937- .... **CLC 5, 23, 42**
See also CA 85-88; CANR 23; MTCW

Stone, Zachary
See Follett, Ken(neth Martin)

Stoppard, Tom
1937- ...... **CLC 1, 3, 4, 5, 8, 15, 29, 34,**
63; DA; WLC
See also CA 81-84; CANR 39;
CDBLB 1960 to Present; DLB 13;
DLBY 85; MTCW

Storey, David (Malcolm)
1933- .... **CLC 2, 4, 5, 8**
See also CA 81-84; CANR 36; DLB 13, 14;
MTCW

Storm, Hyemeyohsts 1935- .... **CLC 3**
See also CA 81-84

Storm, (Hans) Theodor (Woldsen)
1817-1888 .... **NCLC 1**

Storni, Alfonsina
1892-1938 .... **TCLC 5; HLC**
See also CA 104; 131; HW

Stout, Rex (Todhunter) 1886-1975 ... **CLC 3**
See also AITN 2; CA 61-64

Stow, (Julian) Randolph 1935- .. **CLC 23, 48**
See also CA 13-16R; CANR 33; MTCW

Stowe, Harriet (Elizabeth) Beecher
1811-1896 .... **NCLC 3; DA; WLC**
See also CDALB 1865-1917; DLB 1, 12, 42,
74; JRDA; MAICYA; YABC 1

Strachey, (Giles) Lytton
1880-1932 .... **TCLC 12**
See also CA 110; DLBD 10

Strand, Mark 1934- ...... **CLC 6, 18, 41, 71**
See also CA 21-24R; CANR 40; DLB 5;
SATA 41

Straub, Peter (Francis) 1943- ...... **CLC 28**
See also BEST 89:1; CA 85-88; CANR 28;
DLBY 84; MTCW

Strauss, Botho 1944- .... **CLC 22**
See also DLB 124

Streatfeild, (Mary) Noel
1895(?)-1986 .... **CLC 21**
See also CA 81-84; 120; CANR 31;
CLR 17; MAICYA; SATA 20, 48

Stribling, T(homas) S(igismund)
1881-1965 .... **CLC 23**
See also CA 107; DLB 9

Strindberg, (Johan) August
1849-1912 ...... **TCLC 1, 8, 21, 47; DA;**
WLC
See also CA 104; 135

Stringer, Arthur 1874-1950 .... **TCLC 37**
See also DLB 92

Stringer, David
See Roberts, Keith (John Kingston)

Strugatskii, Arkadii (Natanovich)
1925-1991 .... **CLC 27**
See also CA 106; 135

Strugatskii, Boris (Natanovich)
1933- .... **CLC 27**
See also CA 106

Strummer, Joe 1953(?)- .... **CLC 30**
See also Clash, The

Stuart, Don A.
See Campbell, John W(ood, Jr.)

Stuart, Ian
See MacLean, Alistair (Stuart)

Stuart, Jesse (Hilton)
1906-1984 .... **CLC 1, 8, 11, 14, 34**
See also CA 5-8R; 112; CANR 31; DLB 9,
48, 102; DLBY 84; SATA 2, 36

Sturgeon, Theodore (Hamilton)
1918-1985 .... **CLC 22, 39**
See also Queen, Ellery
See also CA 81-84; 116; CANR 32; DLB 8;
DLBY 85; MTCW

Sturges, Preston 1898-1959 ...... **TCLC 48**
See also CA 114; DLB 26

Styron, William
1925- .... **CLC 1, 3, 5, 11, 15, 60**
See also BEST 90:4; CA 5-8R; CANR 6, 33;
CDALB 1968-1988; DLB 2; DLBY 80;
MTCW

Suarez Lynch, B.
See Bioy Casares, Adolfo; Borges, Jorge
Luis

Suarez Lynch, B.
See Borges, Jorge Luis

Su Chien 1884-1918
See Su Man-shu
See also CA 123

Sudermann, Hermann 1857-1928 .. **TCLC 15**
See also CA 107; DLB 118

Sue, Eugene 1804-1857 .... **NCLC 1**
See also DLB 119

Sueskind, Patrick 1949- .... **CLC 44**

Sukenick, Ronald 1932- ..... **CLC 3, 4, 6, 48**
See also CA 25-28R; CAAS 8; CANR 32;
DLBY 81

Suknaski, Andrew 1942- .... **CLC 19**
See also CA 101; DLB 53

Sullivan, Vernon
See Vian, Boris

Sully Prudhomme 1839-1907...... **TCLC 31**

Su Man-shu .... **TCLC 24**
See also Su Chien

Summerforest, Ivy B.
See Kirkup, James

Summers, Andrew James 1942-..... **CLC 26**
See also Police, The

Summers, Andy
See Summers, Andrew James

Summers, Hollis (Spurgeon, Jr.)
1916- .... **CLC 10**
See also CA 5-8R; CANR 3; DLB 6

Summers, (Alphonsus Joseph-Mary Augustus)
Montague 1880-1948 .... **TCLC 16**
See also CA 118

Sumner, Gordon Matthew 1951-.... **CLC 26**
See also Police, The

Surtees, Robert Smith
1803-1864 .... **NCLC 14**
See also DLB 21

Susann, Jacqueline 1921-1974....... **CLC 3**
See also AITN 1; CA 65-68; 53-56; MTCW

Suskind, Patrick
See Sueskind, Patrick

Sutcliff, Rosemary 1920-1992 ...... **CLC 26**
See also AAYA 10; CA 5-8R; 139;
CANR 37; CLR 1; JRDA; MAICYA;
SATA 6, 44; SATA-Obit 73

Sutro, Alfred 1863-1933 . . . . **TCLC 6**
See also CA 105; DLB 10

Sutton, Henry
See Slavitt, David R(ytman)

Svevo, Italo . . . . **TCLC 2, 35**
See also Schmitz, Aron Hector

Swados, Elizabeth 1951- . . . . **CLC 12**
See also CA 97-100

Swados, Harvey 1920-1972 . . . . **CLC 5**
See also CA 5-8R; 37-40R; CANR 6;
DLB 2

Swan, Gladys 1934- . . . . **CLC 69**
See also CA 101; CANR 17, 39

Swarthout, Glendon (Fred)
1918-1992 . . . . **CLC 35**
See also CA 1-4R; 139; CANR 1; SATA 26

Sweet, Sarah C.
See Jewett, (Theodora) Sarah Orne

Swenson, May
1919-1989 . . . . **CLC 4, 14, 61; DA**
See also CA 5-8R; 130; CANR 36; DLB 5;
MTCW; SATA 15

Swift, Augustus
See Lovecraft, H(oward) P(hillips)

Swift, Graham 1949- . . . . **CLC 41**
See also CA 117; 122

Swift, Jonathan
1667-1745 . . . . **LC 1; DA; WLC**
See also CDBLB 1660-1789; DLB 39, 95,
101; SATA 19

Swinburne, Algernon Charles
1837-1909 . . . . . . **TCLC 8, 36; DA; WLC**
See also CA 105; 140; CDBLB 1832-1890;
DLB 35, 57

Swinfen, Ann . . . . **CLC 34**

Swinnerton, Frank Arthur
1884-1982 . . . . **CLC 31**
See also CA 108; DLB 34

Swithen, John
See King, Stephen (Edwin)

Sylvia
See Ashton-Warner, Sylvia (Constance)

Symmes, Robert Edward
See Duncan, Robert (Edward)

Symonds, John Addington
1840-1893 . . . . **NCLC 34**
See also DLB 57

Symons, Arthur 1865-1945 . . . . **TCLC 11**
See also CA 107; DLB 19, 57

Symons, Julian (Gustave)
1912- . . . . **CLC 2, 14, 32**
See also CA 49-52; CAAS 3; CANR 3, 33;
DLB 87; DLBY 92; MTCW

Synge, (Edmund) J(ohn) M(illington)
1871-1909 . . . . **TCLC 6, 37; DC 2**
See also CA 104; 141; CDBLB 1890-1914;
DLB 10, 19

Syruc, J.
See Milosz, Czeslaw

Szirtes, George 1948- . . . . **CLC 46**
See also CA 109; CANR 27

Tabori, George 1914- . . . . **CLC 19**
See also CA 49-52; CANR 4

Tagore, Rabindranath
1861-1941 . . . . **TCLC 3, 53; PC 8**
See also CA 104; 120; MTCW

Taine, Hippolyte Adolphe
1828-1893 . . . . **NCLC 15**

Talese, Gay 1932- . . . . **CLC 37**
See also AITN 1; CA 1-4R; CANR 9;
MTCW

Tallent, Elizabeth (Ann) 1954- . . . . . **CLC 45**
See also CA 117; DLB 130

Tally, Ted 1952- . . . . **CLC 42**
See also CA 120; 124

Tamayo y Baus, Manuel
1829-1898 . . . . **NCLC 1**

Tammsaare, A(nton) H(ansen)
1878-1940 . . . . **TCLC 27**

Tan, Amy 1952- . . . . **CLC 59**
See also AAYA 9; BEST 89:3; CA 136;
SATA 75

Tandem, Felix
See Spitteler, Carl (Friedrich Georg)

Tanizaki, Jun'ichiro
1886-1965 . . . . **CLC 8, 14, 28**
See also CA 93-96; 25-28R

Tanner, William
See Amis, Kingsley (William)

Tao Lao
See Storni, Alfonsina

Tarassoff, Lev
See Troyat, Henri

Tarbell, Ida M(inerva)
1857-1944 . . . . **TCLC 40**
See also CA 122; DLB 47

Tarkington, (Newton) Booth
1869-1946 . . . . **TCLC 9**
See also CA 110; 143; DLB 9, 102;
SATA 17

Tarkovsky, Andrei (Arsenyevich)
1932-1986 . . . . **CLC 75**
See also CA 127

Tartt, Donna 1964(?)- . . . . **CLC 76**
See also CA 142

Tasso, Torquato 1544-1595 . . . . **LC 5**

Tate, (John Orley) Allen
1899-1979 . . . . **CLC 2, 4, 6, 9, 11, 14, 24**
See also CA 5-8R; 85-88; CANR 32;
DLB 4, 45, 63; MTCW

Tate, Ellalice
See Hibbert, Eleanor Alice Burford

Tate, James (Vincent) 1943- . . . **CLC 2, 6, 25**
See also CA 21-24R; CANR 29; DLB 5

Tavel, Ronald 1940- . . . . **CLC 6**
See also CA 21-24R; CANR 33

Taylor, Cecil Philip 1929-1981 . . . . . **CLC 27**
See also CA 25-28R; 105

Taylor, Edward 1642(?)-1729 . . . . **LC 11; DA**
See also DLB 24

Taylor, Eleanor Ross 1920- . . . . **CLC 5**
See also CA 81-84

Taylor, Elizabeth 1912-1975 . . . **CLC 2, 4, 29**
See also CA 13-16R; CANR 9; MTCW;
SATA 13

Taylor, Henry (Splawn) 1942- . . . . . . **CLC 44**
See also CA 33-36R; CAAS 7; CANR 31;
DLB 5

Taylor, Kamala (Purnaiya) 1924-
See Markandaya, Kamala
See also CA 77-80

Taylor, Mildred D. . . . . **CLC 21**
See also AAYA 10; BW; CA 85-88;
CANR 25; CLR 9; DLB 52; JRDA;
MAICYA; SAAS 5; SATA 15, 70

Taylor, Peter (Hillsman)
1917- . . . . . . **CLC 1, 4, 18, 37, 44, 50, 71;
SSC 10**
See also CA 13-16R; CANR 9; DLBY 81;
MTCW

Taylor, Robert Lewis 1912- . . . . **CLC 14**
See also CA 1-4R; CANR 3; SATA 10

Tchekhov, Anton
See Chekhov, Anton (Pavlovich)

Teasdale, Sara 1884-1933 . . . . **TCLC 4**
See also CA 104; DLB 45; SATA 32

Tegner, Esaias 1782-1846 . . . . **NCLC 2**

Teilhard de Chardin, (Marie Joseph) Pierre
1881-1955 . . . . **TCLC 9**
See also CA 105

Temple, Ann
See Mortimer, Penelope (Ruth)

Tennant, Emma (Christina)
1937- . . . . **CLC 13, 52**
See also CA 65-68; CAAS 9; CANR 10, 38;
DLB 14

Tenneshaw, S. M.
See Silverberg, Robert

Tennyson, Alfred
1809-1892 . . **NCLC 30; DA; PC 6; WLC**
See also CDBLB 1832-1890; DLB 32

Teran, Lisa St. Aubin de . . . . **CLC 36**
See also St. Aubin de Teran, Lisa

Teresa de Jesus, St. 1515-1582 . . . . . . **LC 18**

Terkel, Louis 1912-
See Terkel, Studs
See also CA 57-60; CANR 18; MTCW

Terkel, Studs . . . . **CLC 38**
See also Terkel, Louis
See also AITN 1

Terry, C. V.
See Slaughter, Frank G(ill)

Terry, Megan 1932- . . . . **CLC 19**
See also CA 77-80; CABS 3; CANR 43;
DLB 7

Tertz, Abram
See Sinyavsky, Andrei (Donatevich)

Tesich, Steve 1943(?)- . . . . **CLC 40, 69**
See also CA 105; DLBY 83

Teternikov, Fyodor Kuzmich 1863-1927
See Sologub, Fyodor
See also CA 104

Tevis, Walter 1928-1984 . . . . **CLC 42**
See also CA 113

Tey, Josephine . . . . **TCLC 14**
See also Mackintosh, Elizabeth
See also DLB 77

Thackeray, William Makepeace
1811-1863 .... **NCLC 5, 14, 22, 43; DA;
WLC**
See also CDBLB 1832-1890; DLB 21, 55;
SATA 23

Thakura, Ravindranatha
See Tagore, Rabindranath

Tharoor, Shashi 1956- .... **CLC 70**
See also CA 141

Thelwell, Michael Miles 1939- ..... **CLC 22**
See also CA 101

Theobald, Lewis, Jr.
See Lovecraft, H(oward) P(hillips)

Theodorescu, Ion N. 1880-1967
See Arghezi, Tudor
See also CA 116

Theriault, Yves 1915-1983 .... **CLC 79**
See also CA 102; DLB 88

Theroux, Alexander (Louis)
1939- .... **CLC 2, 25**
See also CA 85-88; CANR 20

Theroux, Paul (Edward)
1941- .... **CLC 5, 8, 11, 15, 28, 46**
See also BEST 89:4; CA 33-36R; CANR 20;
DLB 2; MTCW; SATA 44

Thesen, Sharon 1946- .... **CLC 56**

Thevenin, Denis
See Duhamel, Georges

Thibault, Jacques Anatole Francois
1844-1924
See France, Anatole
See also CA 106; 127; MTCW

Thiele, Colin (Milton) 1920- .... **CLC 17**
See also CA 29-32R; CANR 12, 28;
CLR 27; MAICYA; SAAS 2; SATA 14,
72

Thomas, Audrey (Callahan)
1935- .... **CLC 7, 13, 37**
See also AITN 2; CA 21-24R; CANR 36;
DLB 60; MTCW

Thomas, D(onald) M(ichael)
1935- .... **CLC 13, 22, 31**
See also CA 61-64; CAAS 11; CANR 17;
CDBLB 1960 to Present; DLB 40;
MTCW

Thomas, Dylan (Marlais)
1914-1953 ... **TCLC 1, 8, 45; DA; PC 2;
SSC 3; WLC**
See also CA 104; 120; CDBLB 1945-1960;
DLB 13, 20; MTCW; SATA 60

Thomas, (Philip) Edward
1878-1917 .... **TCLC 10**
See also CA 106; DLB 19

Thomas, Joyce Carol 1938- .... **CLC 35**
See also BW; CA 113; 116; CLR 19;
DLB 33; JRDA; MAICYA; MTCW;
SAAS 7; SATA 40

Thomas, Lewis 1913-1993 .... **CLC 35**
See also CA 85-88; 143; CANR 38; MTCW

Thomas, Paul
See Mann, (Paul) Thomas

Thomas, Piri 1928- .... **CLC 17**
See also CA 73-76; HW

Thomas, R(onald) S(tuart)
1913- .... **CLC 6, 13, 48**
See also CA 89-92; CAAS 4; CANR 30;
CDBLB 1960 to Present; DLB 27;
MTCW

Thomas, Ross (Elmore) 1926- ...... **CLC 39**
See also CA 33-36R; CANR 22

Thompson, Francis Clegg
See Mencken, H(enry) L(ouis)

Thompson, Francis Joseph
1859-1907 .... **TCLC 4**
See also CA 104; CDBLB 1890-1914;
DLB 19

Thompson, Hunter S(tockton)
1939- .... **CLC 9, 17, 40**
See also BEST 89:1; CA 17-20R; CANR 23;
MTCW

Thompson, James Myers
See Thompson, Jim (Myers)

Thompson, Jim (Myers)
1906-1977(?) .... **CLC 69**
See also CA 140

Thompson, Judith .... **CLC 39**

Thomson, James 1700-1748 .... **LC 16**

Thomson, James 1834-1882 ...... **NCLC 18**

Thoreau, Henry David
1817-1862 ...... **NCLC 7, 21; DA; WLC**
See also CDALB 1640-1865; DLB 1

Thornton, Hall
See Silverberg, Robert

Thurber, James (Grover)
1894-1961 ... **CLC 5, 11, 25; DA; SSC 1**
See also CA 73-76; CANR 17, 39;
CDALB 1929-1941; DLB 4, 11, 22, 102;
MAICYA; MTCW; SATA 13

Thurman, Wallace (Henry)
1902-1934 .... **TCLC 6; BLC**
See also BW; CA 104; 124; DLB 51

Ticheburn, Cheviot
See Ainsworth, William Harrison

Tieck, (Johann) Ludwig
1773-1853 .... **NCLC 5**
See also DLB 90

Tiger, Derry
See Ellison, Harlan

Tilghman, Christopher 1948(?)- ..... **CLC 65**

Tillinghast, Richard (Williford)
1940- .... **CLC 29**
See also CA 29-32R; CANR 26

Timrod, Henry 1828-1867 .... **NCLC 25**
See also DLB 3

Tindall, Gillian 1938- .... **CLC 7**
See also CA 21-24R; CANR 11

Tiptree, James, Jr. .... **CLC 48, 50**
See also Sheldon, Alice Hastings Bradley
See also DLB 8

Titmarsh, Michael Angelo
See Thackeray, William Makepeace

**Tocqueville, Alexis (Charles Henri Maurice
Clerel Comte)** 1805-1859 ..... **NCLC 7**

Tolkien, J(ohn) R(onald) R(euel)
1892-1973 .... **CLC 1, 2, 3, 8, 12, 38;
DA; WLC**
See also AAYA 10; AITN 1; CA 17-18;
45-48; CANR 36; CAP 2;
CDBLB 1914-1945; DLB 15; JRDA;
MAICYA; MTCW; SATA 2, 24, 32

Toller, Ernst 1893-1939 .... **TCLC 10**
See also CA 107; DLB 124

Tolson, M. B.
See Tolson, Melvin B(eaunorus)

Tolson, Melvin B(eaunorus)
1898(?)-1966 .... **CLC 36; BLC**
See also BW; CA 124; 89-92; DLB 48, 76

Tolstoi, Aleksei Nikolaevich
See Tolstoy, Alexey Nikolaevich

Tolstoy, Alexey Nikolaevich
1882-1945 .... **TCLC 18**
See also CA 107

Tolstoy, Count Leo
See Tolstoy, Leo (Nikolaevich)

Tolstoy, Leo (Nikolaevich)
1828-1910 ...... **TCLC 4, 11, 17, 28, 44;
DA; SSC 9; WLC**
See also CA 104; 123; SATA 26

Tomasi di Lampedusa, Giuseppe 1896-1957
See Lampedusa, Giuseppe (Tomasi) di
See also CA 111

Tomlin, Lily..................... **CLC 17**
See also Tomlin, Mary Jean

Tomlin, Mary Jean 1939(?)-
See Tomlin, Lily
See also CA 117

Tomlinson, (Alfred) Charles
1927- .... **CLC 2, 4, 6, 13, 45**
See also CA 5-8R; CANR 33; DLB 40

Tonson, Jacob
See Bennett, (Enoch) Arnold

Toole, John Kennedy
1937-1969 .... **CLC 19, 64**
See also CA 104; DLBY 81

Toomer, Jean
1894-1967 ...... **CLC 1, 4, 13, 22; BLC;
PC 7; SSC 1**
See also BW; CA 85-88;
CDALB 1917-1929; DLB 45, 51; MTCW

Torley, Luke
See Blish, James (Benjamin)

Tornimparte, Alessandra
See Ginzburg, Natalia

Torre, Raoul della
See Mencken, H(enry) L(ouis)

Torrey, E(dwin) Fuller 1937- .... **CLC 34**
See also CA 119

Torsvan, Ben Traven
See Traven, B.

Torsvan, Benno Traven
See Traven, B.

Torsvan, Berick Traven
See Traven, B.

Torsvan, Berwick Traven
See Traven, B.

Torsvan, Bruno Traven
See Traven, B.

Torsvan, Traven
See Traven, B.

Tournier, Michel (Edouard)
1924- . . . . CLC 6, 23, 36
See also CA 49-52; CANR 3, 36; DLB 83;
MTCW; SATA 23

Tournimparte, Alessandra
See Ginzburg, Natalia

Towers, Ivar
See Kornbluth, C(yril) M.

Townsend, Sue 1946- . . . . CLC 61
See also CA 119; 127; MTCW; SATA 48,
55

Townshend, Peter (Dennis Blandford)
1945- . . . . CLC 17, 42
See also CA 107

Tozzi, Federigo 1883-1920 . . . . TCLC 31

Traill, Catharine Parr
1802-1899 . . . . NCLC 31
See also DLB 99

Trakl, Georg 1887-1914 . . . . TCLC 5
See also CA 104

Transtroemer, Tomas (Goesta)
1931- . . . . CLC 52, 65
See also CA 117; 129; CAAS 17

Transtromer, Tomas Gosta
See Transtroemer, Tomas (Goesta)

Traven, B. (?)-1969 . . . . CLC 8, 11
See also CA 19-20; 25-28R; CAP 2; DLB 9,
56; MTCW

Treitel, Jonathan 1959- . . . . CLC 70

Tremain, Rose 1943- . . . . CLC 42
See also CA 97-100; DLB 14

Tremblay, Michel 1942- . . . . CLC 29
See also CA 116; 128; DLB 60; MTCW

Trevanian (a pseudonym) 1930(?)- . . . CLC 29
See also CA 108

Trevor, Glen
See Hilton, James

Trevor, William
1928- . . . . CLC 7, 9, 14, 25, 71
See also Cox, William Trevor
See also DLB 14

Trifonov, Yuri (Valentinovich)
1925-1981 . . . . CLC 45
See also CA 126; 103; MTCW

Trilling, Lionel 1905-1975 . . . . CLC 9, 11, 24
See also CA 9-12R; 61-64; CANR 10;
DLB 28, 63; MTCW

Trimball, W. H.
See Mencken, H(enry) L(ouis)

Tristan
See Gomez de la Serna, Ramon

Tristram
See Housman, A(lfred) E(dward)

Trogdon, William (Lewis) 1939-
See Heat-Moon, William Least
See also CA 115; 119

Trollope, Anthony
1815-1882 . . . . . . NCLC 6, 33; DA; WLC
See also CDBLB 1832-1890; DLB 21, 57;
SATA 22

Trollope, Frances 1779-1863 . . . . . NCLC 30
See also DLB 21

Trotsky, Leon 1879-1940 . . . . TCLC 22
See also CA 118

Trotter (Cockburn), Catharine
1679-1749 . . . . LC 8
See also DLB 84

Trout, Kilgore
See Farmer, Philip Jose

Trow, George W. S. 1943- . . . . CLC 52
See also CA 126

Troyat, Henri 1911- . . . . CLC 23
See also CA 45-48; CANR 2, 33; MTCW

Trudeau, G(arretson) B(eekman) 1948-
See Trudeau, Garry B.
See also CA 81-84; CANR 31; SATA 35

Trudeau, Garry B. . . . . CLC 12
See also Trudeau, G(arretson) B(eekman)
See also AAYA 10; AITN 2

Truffaut, Francois 1932-1984 . . . . . . CLC 20
See also CA 81-84; 113; CANR 34

Trumbo, Dalton 1905-1976 . . . . CLC 19
See also CA 21-24R; 69-72; CANR 10;
DLB 26

Trumbull, John 1750-1831 . . . . . . NCLC 30
See also DLB 31

Trundlett, Helen B.
See Eliot, T(homas) S(tearns)

Tryon, Thomas 1926-1991 . . . . . . CLC 3, 11
See also AITN 1; CA 29-32R; 135;
CANR 32; MTCW

Tryon, Tom
See Tryon, Thomas

Ts'ao Hsueh-ch'in 1715(?)-1763 . . . . . . LC 1

Tsushima, Shuji 1909-1948
See Dazai, Osamu
See also CA 107

Tsvetaeva (Efron), Marina (Ivanovna)
1892-1941 . . . . TCLC 7, 35
See also CA 104; 128; MTCW

Tuck, Lily 1938- . . . . CLC 70
See also CA 139

Tunis, John R(oberts) 1889-1975 . . . CLC 12
See also CA 61-64; DLB 22; JRDA;
MAICYA; SATA 30, 37

Tuohy, Frank . . . . CLC 37
See also Tuohy, John Francis
See also DLB 14

Tuohy, John Francis 1925-
See Tuohy, Frank
See also CA 5-8R; CANR 3

Turco, Lewis (Putnam) 1934- . . . CLC 11, 63
See also CA 13-16R; CANR 24; DLBY 84

Turgenev, Ivan
1818-1883 . . . . . . NCLC 21; DA; SSC 7;
WLC

Turner, Frederick 1943- . . . . CLC 48
See also CA 73-76; CAAS 10; CANR 12,
30; DLB 40

Tusan, Stan 1936- . . . . CLC 22
See also CA 105

Tutu, Desmond M(pilo)
1931- . . . . CLC 80; BLC
See also BW; CA 125

Tutuola, Amos 1920- . . . CLC 5, 14, 29; BLC
See also BW; CA 9-12R; CANR 27;
DLB 125; MTCW

Twain, Mark
. . . TCLC 6, 12, 19, 36, 48; SSC 6; WLC
See also Clemens, Samuel Langhorne
See also DLB 11, 12, 23, 64, 74

Tyler, Anne
1941- . . . . CLC 7, 11, 18, 28, 44, 59
See also BEST 89:1; CA 9-12R; CANR 11,
33; DLB 6; DLBY 82; MTCW; SATA 7

Tyler, Royall 1757-1826 . . . . NCLC 3
See also DLB 37

Tynan, Katharine 1861-1931 . . . . TCLC 3
See also CA 104

Tytell, John 1939- . . . . CLC 50
See also CA 29-32R

Tyutchev, Fyodor 1803-1873 . . . . . NCLC 34

Tzara, Tristan . . . . CLC 47
See also Rosenfeld, Samuel

Uhry, Alfred 1936- . . . . CLC 55
See also CA 127; 133

Ulf, Haerved
See Strindberg, (Johan) August

Ulf, Harved
See Strindberg, (Johan) August

Unamuno (y Jugo), Miguel de
1864-1936 . . . . TCLC 2, 9; HLC; SSC 11
See also CA 104; 131; DLB 108; HW;
MTCW

Undercliffe, Errol
See Campbell, (John) Ramsey

Underwood, Miles
See Glassco, John

Undset, Sigrid
1882-1949 . . . . TCLC 3; DA; WLC
See also CA 104; 129; MTCW

Ungaretti, Giuseppe
1888-1970 . . . . CLC 7, 11, 15
See also CA 19-20; 25-28R; CAP 2;
DLB 114

Unger, Douglas 1952- . . . . CLC 34
See also CA 130

Unsworth, Barry (Forster) 1930- . . . . CLC 76
See also CA 25-28R; CANR 30

Updike, John (Hoyer)
1932- . . . . . . CLC 1, 2, 3, 5, 7, 9, 13, 15,
23, 34, 43, 70; DA; SSC 13; WLC
See also CA 1-4R; CABS 1; CANR 4, 33;
CDALB 1968-1988; DLB 2, 5; DLBD 3;
DLBY 80, 82; MTCW

Upshaw, Margaret Mitchell
See Mitchell, Margaret (Munnerlyn)

Upton, Mark
See Sanders, Lawrence

Urdang, Constance (Henriette)
1922- . . . . CLC 47
See also CA 21-24R; CANR 9, 24

Uriel, Henry
See Faust, Frederick (Schiller)

Uris, Leon (Marcus) 1924- . . . . CLC 7, 32
See also AITN 1, 2; BEST 89:2; CA 1-4R;
CANR 1, 40; MTCW; SATA 49

Urmuz
　See Codrescu, Andrei

Ustinov, Peter (Alexander) 1921- .... CLC 1
　See also AITN 1; CA 13-16R; CANR 25;
　DLB 13

V
　See Chekhov, Anton (Pavlovich)

Vaculik, Ludvik 1926- .... CLC 7
　See also CA 53-56

Valenzuela, Luisa 1938-... CLC 31; SSC 14
　See also CA 101; CANR 32; DLB 113; HW

Valera y Alcala-Galiano, Juan
　1824-1905 .... TCLC 10
　See also CA 106

Valery, (Ambroise) Paul (Toussaint Jules)
　1871-1945 .... TCLC 4, 15
　See also CA 104; 122; MTCW

Valle-Inclan, Ramon (Maria) del
　1866-1936 .... TCLC 5; HLC
　See also CA 106; DLB 134

Vallejo, Antonio Buero
　See Buero Vallejo, Antonio

Vallejo, Cesar (Abraham)
　1892-1938 .... TCLC 3; HLC
　See also CA 105; HW

Valle Y Pena, Ramon del
　See Valle-Inclan, Ramon (Maria) del

Van Ash, Cay 1918- .... CLC 34

Vanbrugh, Sir John 1664-1726 ...... LC 21
　See also DLB 80

Van Campen, Karl
　See Campbell, John W(ood, Jr.)

Vance, Gerald
　See Silverberg, Robert

Vance, Jack .... CLC 35
　See also Vance, John Holbrook
　See also DLB 8

Vance, John Holbrook 1916-
　See Queen, Ellery; Vance, Jack
　See also CA 29-32R; CANR 17; MTCW

Van Den Bogarde, Derek Jules Gaspard Ulric
　Niven 1921-
　See Bogarde, Dirk
　See also CA 77-80

Vandenburgh, Jane .... CLC 59

Vanderhaeghe, Guy 1951- .... CLC 41
　See also CA 113

van der Post, Laurens (Jan) 1906- ... CLC 5
　See also CA 5-8R; CANR 35

van de Wetering, Janwillem 1931- .. CLC 47
　See also CA 49-52; CANR 4

Van Dine, S. S. .... TCLC 23
　See also Wright, Willard Huntington

Van Doren, Carl (Clinton)
　1885-1950 .... TCLC 18
　See also CA 111

Van Doren, Mark 1894-1972..... CLC 6, 10
　See also CA 1-4R; 37-40R; CANR 3;
　DLB 45; MTCW

Van Druten, John (William)
　1901-1957 .... TCLC 2
　See also CA 104; DLB 10

Van Duyn, Mona (Jane)
　1921- .... CLC 3, 7, 63
　See also CA 9-12R; CANR 7, 38; DLB 5

Van Dyne, Edith
　See Baum, L(yman) Frank

van Itallie, Jean-Claude 1936-....... CLC 3
　See also CA 45-48; CAAS 2; CANR 1;
　DLB 7

van Ostaijen, Paul 1896-1928 ..... TCLC 33

Van Peebles, Melvin 1932- ...... CLC 2, 20
　See also BW; CA 85-88; CANR 27

Vansittart, Peter 1920-............ CLC 42
　See also CA 1-4R; CANR 3

Van Vechten, Carl 1880-1964 ...... CLC 33
　See also CA 89-92; DLB 4, 9, 51

Van Vogt, A(lfred) E(lton) 1912-..... CLC 1
　See also CA 21-24R; CANR 28; DLB 8;
　SATA 14

Varda, Agnes 1928- .... CLC 16
　See also CA 116; 122

Vargas Llosa, (Jorge) Mario (Pedro)
　1936- .... CLC 3, 6, 9, 10, 15, 31, 42;
　　　　　　　　　　　　　　　　DA; HLC
　See also CA 73-76; CANR 18, 32, 42; HW;
　MTCW

Vasiliu, Gheorghe 1881-1957
　See Bacovia, George
　See also CA 123

Vassa, Gustavus
　See Equiano, Olaudah

Vassilikos, Vassilis 1933-......... CLC 4, 8
　See also CA 81-84

Vaughn, Stephanie................ CLC 62

Vazov, Ivan (Minchov)
　1850-1921 .... TCLC 25
　See also CA 121

Veblen, Thorstein (Bunde)
　1857-1929 .... TCLC 31
　See also CA 115

Vega, Lope de 1562-1635.......... LC 23

Venison, Alfred
　See Pound, Ezra (Weston Loomis)

Verdi, Marie de
　See Mencken, H(enry) L(ouis)

Verdu, Matilde
　See Cela, Camilo Jose

Verga, Giovanni (Carmelo)
　1840-1922 .... TCLC 3
　See also CA 104; 123

Vergil 70B.C.-19B.C. .... CMLC 9; DA

Verhaeren, Emile (Adolphe Gustave)
　1855-1916 .... TCLC 12
　See also CA 109

Verlaine, Paul (Marie)
　1844-1896 .... NCLC 2; PC 2

Verne, Jules (Gabriel)
　1828-1905 .... TCLC 6, 52
　See also CA 110; 131; DLB 123; JRDA;
　MAICYA; SATA 21

Very, Jones 1813-1880........... NCLC 9
　See also DLB 1

Vesaas, Tarjei 1897-1970......... CLC 48
　See also CA 29-32R

Vialis, Gaston
　See Simenon, Georges (Jacques Christian)

Vian, Boris 1920-1959 .... TCLC 9
　See also CA 106; DLB 72

Viaud, (Louis Marie) Julien 1850-1923
　See Loti, Pierre
　See also CA 107

Vicar, Henry
　See Felsen, Henry Gregor

Vicker, Angus
　See Felsen, Henry Gregor

Vidal, Gore
　1925- ..... CLC 2, 4, 6, 8, 10, 22, 33, 72
　See also AITN 1; BEST 90:2; CA 5-8R;
　CANR 13; DLB 6; MTCW

Viereck, Peter (Robert Edwin)
　1916- .... CLC 4
　See also CA 1-4R; CANR 1; DLB 5

Vigny, Alfred (Victor) de
　1797-1863 .... NCLC 7
　See also DLB 119

Vilakazi, Benedict Wallet
　1906-1947 .... TCLC 37

Villiers de l'Isle Adam, Jean Marie Mathias
　Philippe Auguste Comte
　1838-1889 .... NCLC 3; SSC 14
　See also DLB 123

Vincent, Gabrielle a pseudonym...... CLC 13
　See also CA 126; CLR 13; MAICYA;
　SATA 61

Vinci, Leonardo da 1452-1519....... LC 12

Vine, Barbara .... CLC 50
　See also Rendell, Ruth (Barbara)
　See also BEST 90:4

Vinge, Joan D(ennison) 1948- ...... CLC 30
　See also CA 93-96; SATA 36

Violis, G.
　See Simenon, Georges (Jacques Christian)

Visconti, Luchino 1906-1976....... CLC 16
　See also CA 81-84; 65-68; CANR 39

Vittorini, Elio 1908-1966...... CLC 6, 9, 14
　See also CA 133; 25-28R

Vizinczey, Stephen 1933-.......... CLC 40
　See also CA 128

Vliet, R(ussell) G(ordon)
　1929-1984 .... CLC 22
　See also CA 37-40R; 112; CANR 18

Vogau, Boris Andreyevich 1894-1937(?)
　See Pilnyak, Boris
　See also CA 123

Vogel, Paula A(nne) 1951-......... CLC 76
　See also CA 108

Voight, Ellen Bryant 1943- .... CLC 54
　See also CA 69-72; CANR 11, 29; DLB 120

Voigt, Cynthia 1942- .... CLC 30
　See also AAYA 3; CA 106; CANR 18, 37,
　40; CLR 13; JRDA; MAICYA;
　SATA 33, 48

Voinovich, Vladimir (Nikolaevich)
　1932- .... CLC 10, 49
　See also CA 81-84; CAAS 12; CANR 33;
　MTCW

Voltaire
　1694-1778 ... LC 14; DA; SSC 12; WLC

Wasserstein, Wendy
  1950- .... **CLC 32, 59; DC 4**
  See also CA 121; 129; CABS 3

Waterhouse, Keith (Spencer)
  1929- .... **CLC 47**
  See also CA 5-8R; CANR 38; DLB 13, 15;
  MTCW

Waters, Roger 1944- .... **CLC 35**
  See also Pink Floyd

Watkins, Frances Ellen
  See Harper, Frances Ellen Watkins

Watkins, Gerrold
  See Malzberg, Barry N(athaniel)

Watkins, Paul 1964- .... **CLC 55**
  See also CA 132

Watkins, Vernon Phillips
  1906-1967 .... **CLC 43**
  See also CA 9-10; 25-28R; CAP 1; DLB 20

Watson, Irving S.
  See Mencken, H(enry) L(ouis)

Watson, John H.
  See Farmer, Philip Jose

Watson, Richard F.
  See Silverberg, Robert

Waugh, Auberon (Alexander) 1939- .. **CLC 7**
  See also CA 45-48; CANR 6, 22; DLB 14

Waugh, Evelyn (Arthur St. John)
  1903-1966 ...... **CLC 1, 3, 8, 13, 19, 27,**
                              44; DA; WLC
  See also CA 85-88; 25-28R; CANR 22;
  CDBLB 1914-1945; DLB 15; MTCW

Waugh, Harriet 1944- .... **CLC 6**
  See also CA 85-88; CANR 22

Ways, C. R.
  See Blount, Roy (Alton), Jr.

Waystaff, Simon
  See Swift, Jonathan

Webb, (Martha) Beatrice (Potter)
  1858-1943 .... **TCLC 22**
  See also Potter, Beatrice
  See also CA 117

Webb, Charles (Richard) 1939- ...... **CLC 7**
  See also CA 25-28R

Webb, James H(enry), Jr. 1946- .... **CLC 22**
  See also CA 81-84

Webb, Mary (Gladys Meredith)
  1881-1927 .... **TCLC 24**
  See also CA 123; DLB 34

Webb, Mrs. Sidney
  See Webb, (Martha) Beatrice (Potter)

Webb, Phyllis 1927- .... **CLC 18**
  See also CA 104; CANR 23; DLB 53

Webb, Sidney (James)
  1859-1947 .... **TCLC 22**
  See also CA 117

Webber, Andrew Lloyd............. **CLC 21**
  See also Lloyd Webber, Andrew

Weber, Lenora Mattingly
  1895-1971 .... **CLC 12**
  See also CA 19-20; 29-32R; CAP 1;
  SATA 2, 26

Webster, John 1579(?)-1634(?) .... **DC 2**
  See also CDBLB Before 1660; DA; DLB 58;
  WLC

Webster, Noah 1758-1843 .... **NCLC 30**

Wedekind, (Benjamin) Frank(lin)
  1864-1918 .... **TCLC 7**
  See also CA 104; DLB 118

Weidman, Jerome 1913- .... **CLC 7**
  See also AITN 2; CA 1-4R; CANR 1;
  DLB 28

Weil, Simone (Adolphine)
  1909-1943 .... **TCLC 23**
  See also CA 117

Weinstein, Nathan
  See West, Nathanael

Weinstein, Nathan von Wallenstein
  See West, Nathanael

Weir, Peter (Lindsay) 1944- .... **CLC 20**
  See also CA 113; 123

Weiss, Peter (Ulrich)
  1916-1982 .... **CLC 3, 15, 51**
  See also CA 45-48; 106; CANR 3; DLB 69,
  124

Weiss, Theodore (Russell)
  1916- .... **CLC 3, 8, 14**
  See also CA 9-12R; CAAS 2; DLB 5

Welch, (Maurice) Denton
  1915-1948 .... **TCLC 22**
  See also CA 121

Welch, James 1940- .... **CLC 6, 14, 52**
  See also CA 85-88; CANR 42

Weldon, Fay
  1933(?)- .... **CLC 6, 9, 11, 19, 36, 59**
  See also CA 21-24R; CANR 16;
  CDBLB 1960 to Present; DLB 14;
  MTCW

Wellek, Rene 1903- .... **CLC 28**
  See also CA 5-8R; CAAS 7; CANR 8;
  DLB 63

Weller, Michael 1942- .... **CLC 10, 53**
  See also CA 85-88

Weller, Paul 1958- .... **CLC 26**

Wellershoff, Dieter 1925- .... **CLC 46**
  See also CA 89-92; CANR 16, 37

Welles, (George) Orson
  1915-1985 .... **CLC 20, 80**
  See also CA 93-96; 117

Wellman, Mac 1945- .... **CLC 65**

Wellman, Manly Wade 1903-1986 .. **CLC 49**
  See also CA 1-4R; 118; CANR 6, 16;
  SATA 6, 47

Wells, Carolyn 1869(?)-1942 ...... **TCLC 35**
  See also CA 113; DLB 11

Wells, H(erbert) G(eorge)
  1866-1946 .... **TCLC 6, 12, 19; DA;**
                              SSC 6; WLC
  See also CA 110; 121; CDBLB 1914-1945;
  DLB 34, 70; MTCW; SATA 20

Wells, Rosemary 1943- .... **CLC 12**
  See also CA 85-88; CLR 16; MAICYA;
  SAAS 1; SATA 18, 69

Welty, Eudora
  1909- ...... **CLC 1, 2, 5, 14, 22, 33; DA;**
                              SSC 1; WLC
  See also CA 9-12R; CABS 1; CANR 32;
  CDALB 1941-1968; DLB 2, 102;
  DLBY 87; MTCW

Wen I-to 1899-1946 .... **TCLC 28**

Wentworth, Robert
  See Hamilton, Edmond

Werfel, Franz (V.) 1890-1945 ..... **TCLC 8**
  See also CA 104; DLB 81, 124

Wergeland, Henrik Arnold
  1808-1845 .... **NCLC 5**

Wersba, Barbara 1932- .... **CLC 30**
  See also AAYA 2; CA 29-32R; CANR 16,
  38; CLR 3; DLB 52; JRDA; MAICYA;
  SAAS 2; SATA 1, 58

Wertmueller, Lina 1928- .... **CLC 16**
  See also CA 97-100; CANR 39

Wescott, Glenway 1901-1987....... **CLC 13**
  See also CA 13-16R; 121; CANR 23;
  DLB 4, 9, 102

Wesker, Arnold 1932- .... **CLC 3, 5, 42**
  See also CA 1-4R; CAAS 7; CANR 1, 33;
  CDBLB 1960 to Present; DLB 13;
  MTCW

Wesley, Richard (Errol) 1945-....... **CLC 7**
  See also BW; CA 57-60; CANR 27; DLB 38

Wessel, Johan Herman 1742-1785 .... **LC 7**

West, Anthony (Panther)
  1914-1987 .... **CLC 50**
  See also CA 45-48; 124; CANR 3, 19;
  DLB 15

West, C. P.
  See Wodehouse, P(elham) G(renville)

West, (Mary) Jessamyn
  1902-1984 .... **CLC 7, 17**
  See also CA 9-12R; 112; CANR 27; DLB 6;
  DLBY 84; MTCW; SATA 37

West, Morris L(anglo) 1916- ..... **CLC 6, 33**
  See also CA 5-8R; CANR 24; MTCW

West, Nathanael
  1903-1940 .... **TCLC 1, 14, 44**
  See also CA 104; 125; CDALB 1929-1941;
  DLB 4, 9, 28; MTCW

West, Owen
  See Koontz, Dean R(ay)

West, Paul 1930- .... **CLC 7, 14**
  See also CA 13-16R; CAAS 7; CANR 22;
  DLB 14

West, Rebecca 1892-1983 .. **CLC 7, 9, 31, 50**
  See also CA 5-8R; 109; CANR 19; DLB 36;
  DLBY 83; MTCW

Westall, Robert (Atkinson)
  1929-1993 .... **CLC 17**
  See also CA 69-72; 141; CANR 18;
  CLR 13; JRDA; MAICYA; SAAS 2;
  SATA 23, 69; SATA-Obit 75

Westlake, Donald E(dwin)
  1933- .... **CLC 7, 33**
  See also CA 17-20R; CAAS 13; CANR 16

Westmacott, Mary
  See Christie, Agatha (Mary Clarissa)

Weston, Allen
  See Norton, Andre

Wetcheek, J. L.
  See Feuchtwanger, Lion

Wetering, Janwillem van de
  See van de Wetering, Janwillem

Wetherell, Elizabeth
  See Warner, Susan (Bogert)

Whalen, Philip 1923- . . . . **CLC 6, 29**
See also CA 9-12R; CANR 5, 39; DLB 16

Wharton, Edith (Newbold Jones)
1862-1937 . . . . . . **TCLC 3, 9, 27, 53; DA;**
SSC 6; WLC
See also CA 104; 132; CDALB 1865-1917;
DLB 4, 9, 12, 78; MTCW

Wharton, James
See Mencken, H(enry) L(ouis)

Wharton, William (a pseudonym)
. . . . **CLC 18, 37**
See also CA 93-96; DLBY 80

Wheatley (Peters), Phillis
1754(?)-1784 . . . . **LC 3; BLC; DA; PC 3;**
WLC
See also CDALB 1640-1865; DLB 31, 50

Wheelock, John Hall 1886-1978 . . . . **CLC 14**
See also CA 13-16R; 77-80; CANR 14;
DLB 45

White, E(lwyn) B(rooks)
1899-1985 . . . . **CLC 10, 34, 39**
See also AITN 2; CA 13-16R; 116;
CANR 16, 37; CLR 1, 21; DLB 11, 22;
MAICYA; MTCW; SATA 2, 29, 44

White, Edmund (Valentine III)
1940- . . . . **CLC 27**
See also AAYA 7; CA 45-48; CANR 3, 19,
36; MTCW

White, Patrick (Victor Martindale)
1912-1990 . . **CLC 3, 4, 5, 7, 9, 18, 65, 69**
See also CA 81-84; 132; CANR 43; MTCW

White, Phyllis Dorothy James 1920-
See James, P. D.
See also CA 21-24R; CANR 17, 43; MTCW

White, T(erence) H(anbury)
1906-1964 . . . . **CLC 30**
See also CA 73-76; CANR 37; JRDA;
MAICYA; SATA 12

White, Terence de Vere 1912- . . . . . . **CLC 49**
See also CA 49-52; CANR 3

White, Walter F(rancis)
1893-1955 . . . . **TCLC 15**
See also White, Walter
See also CA 115; 124; DLB 51

White, William Hale 1831-1913
See Rutherford, Mark
See also CA 121

Whitehead, E(dward) A(nthony)
1933- . . . . **CLC 5**
See also CA 65-68

Whitemore, Hugh (John) 1936- . . . . . **CLC 37**
See also CA 132

Whitman, Sarah Helen (Power)
1803-1878 . . . . **NCLC 19**
See also DLB 1

Whitman, Walt(er)
1819-1892 . . . . . **NCLC 4, 31; DA; PC 3;**
WLC
See also CDALB 1640-1865; DLB 3, 64;
SATA 20

Whitney, Phyllis A(yame) 1903- . . . . **CLC 42**
See also AITN 2; BEST 90:3; CA 1-4R;
CANR 3, 25, 38; JRDA; MAICYA;
SATA 1, 30

Whittemore, (Edward) Reed (Jr.)
1919- . . . . **CLC 4**
See also CA 9-12R; CAAS 8; CANR 4;
DLB 5

Whittier, John Greenleaf
1807-1892 . . . . **NCLC 8**
See also CDALB 1640-1865; DLB 1

Whittlebot, Hernia
See Coward, Noel (Peirce)

Wicker, Thomas Grey 1926-
See Wicker, Tom
See also CA 65-68; CANR 21

Wicker, Tom . . . . **CLC 7**
See also Wicker, Thomas Grey

Wideman, John Edgar
1941- . . . . **CLC 5, 34, 36, 67; BLC**
See also BW; CA 85-88; CANR 14, 42;
DLB 33

Wiebe, Rudy (Henry) 1934- . . . **CLC 6, 11, 14**
See also CA 37-40R; CANR 42; DLB 60

Wieland, Christoph Martin
1733-1813 . . . . **NCLC 17**
See also DLB 97

Wieners, John 1934- . . . . **CLC 7**
See also CA 13-16R; DLB 16

Wiesel, Elie(zer)
1928- . . . . **CLC 3, 5, 11, 37; DA**
See also AAYA 7; AITN 1; CA 5-8R;
CAAS 4; CANR 8, 40; DLB 83;
DLBY 87; MTCW; SATA 56

Wiggins, Marianne 1947- . . . . **CLC 57**
See also BEST 89:3; CA 130

Wight, James Alfred 1916-
See Herriot, James
See also CA 77-80; SATA 44, 55

Wilbur, Richard (Purdy)
1921- . . . . **CLC 3, 6, 9, 14, 53; DA**
See also CA 1-4R; CABS 2; CANR 2, 29;
DLB 5; MTCW; SATA 9

Wild, Peter 1940- . . . . **CLC 14**
See also CA 37-40R; DLB 5

Wilde, Oscar (Fingal O'Flahertie Wills)
1854(?)-1900 . . . . **TCLC 1, 8, 23, 41; DA;**
SSC 11; WLC
See also CA 104; 119; CDBLB 1890-1914;
DLB 10, 19, 34, 57; SATA 24

Wilder, Billy . . . . **CLC 20**
See also Wilder, Samuel
See also DLB 26

Wilder, Samuel 1906-
See Wilder, Billy
See also CA 89-92

Wilder, Thornton (Niven)
1897-1975 . . . . . . **CLC 1, 5, 6, 10, 15, 35,**
82; DA; DC 1; WLC
See also AITN 2; CA 13-16R; 61-64;
CANR 40; DLB 4, 7, 9; MTCW

Wilding, Michael 1942- . . . . **CLC 73**
See also CA 104; CANR 24

Wiley, Richard 1944- . . . . **CLC 44**
See also CA 121; 129

Wilhelm, Kate . . . . **CLC 7**
See also Wilhelm, Katie Gertrude
See also CAAS 5; DLB 8

Wilhelm, Katie Gertrude 1928-
See Wilhelm, Kate
See also CA 37-40R; CANR 17, 36; MTCW

Wilkins, Mary
See Freeman, Mary Eleanor Wilkins

Willard, Nancy 1936- . . . . **CLC 7, 37**
See also CA 89-92; CANR 10, 39; CLR 5;
DLB 5, 52; MAICYA; MTCW;
SATA 30, 37, 71

Williams, C(harles) K(enneth)
1936- . . . . **CLC 33, 56**
See also CA 37-40R; DLB 5

Williams, Charles
See Collier, James L(incoln)

Williams, Charles (Walter Stansby)
1886-1945 . . . . **TCLC 1, 11**
See also CA 104; DLB 100

Williams, (George) Emlyn
1905-1987 . . . . **CLC 15**
See also CA 104; 123; CANR 36; DLB 10,
77; MTCW

Williams, Hugo 1942- . . . . **CLC 42**
See also CA 17-20R; DLB 40

Williams, J. Walker
See Wodehouse, P(elham) G(renville)

Williams, John A(lfred)
1925- . . . . **CLC 5, 13; BLC**
See also BW; CA 53-56; CAAS 3; CANR 6,
26; DLB 2, 33

Williams, Jonathan (Chamberlain)
1929- . . . . **CLC 13**
See also CA 9-12R; CAAS 12; CANR 8;
DLB 5

Williams, Joy 1944- . . . . **CLC 31**
See also CA 41-44R; CANR 22

Williams, Norman 1952- . . . . **CLC 39**
See also CA 118

Williams, Tennessee
1911-1983 . . . . . **CLC 1, 2, 5, 7, 8, 11, 15,**
19, 30, 39, 45, 71; DA; DC 4; WLC
See also AITN 1, 2; CA 5-8R; 108;
CABS 3; CANR 31; CDALB 1941-1968;
DLB 7; DLBD 4; DLBY 83; MTCW

Williams, Thomas (Alonzo)
1926-1990 . . . . **CLC 14**
See also CA 1-4R; 132; CANR 2

Williams, William C.
See Williams, William Carlos

Williams, William Carlos
1883-1963 . . . . **CLC 1, 2, 5, 9, 13, 22, 42,**
67; DA; PC 7
See also CA 89-92; CANR 34;
CDALB 1917-1929; DLB 4, 16, 54, 86;
MTCW

Williamson, David (Keith) 1942- . . . . **CLC 56**
See also CA 103; CANR 41

Williamson, Jack . . . . **CLC 29**
See also Williamson, John Stewart
See also CAAS 8; DLB 8

Williamson, John Stewart 1908-
See Williamson, Jack
See also CA 17-20R; CANR 23

Willie, Frederick
See Lovecraft, H(oward) P(hillips)

Willingham, Calder (Baynard, Jr.)
  1922- .... **CLC 5, 51**
  See also CA 5-8R; CANR 3; DLB 2, 44;
  MTCW

Willis, Charles
  See Clarke, Arthur C(harles)

Willy
  See Colette, (Sidonie-Gabrielle)

Willy, Colette
  See Colette, (Sidonie-Gabrielle)

Wilson, A(ndrew) N(orman) 1950- .. **CLC 33**
  See also CA 112; 122; DLB 14

Wilson, Angus (Frank Johnstone)
  1913-1991 .... **CLC 2, 3, 5, 25, 34**
  See also CA 5-8R; 134; CANR 21; DLB 15;
  MTCW

Wilson, August
  1945- .. **CLC 39, 50, 63; BLC; DA; DC 2**
  See also BW; CA 115; 122; CANR 42;
  MTCW

Wilson, Brian 1942- .... **CLC 12**

Wilson, Colin 1931- .... **CLC 3, 14**
  See also CA 1-4R; CAAS 5; CANR 1, 22,
  33; DLB 14; MTCW

Wilson, Dirk
  See Pohl, Frederik

Wilson, Edmund
  1895-1972 .... **CLC 1, 2, 3, 8, 24**
  See also CA 1-4R; 37-40R; CANR 1;
  DLB 63; MTCW

Wilson, Ethel Davis (Bryant)
  1888(?)-1980 .... **CLC 13**
  See also CA 102; DLB 68; MTCW

Wilson, John 1785-1854 .... **NCLC 5**

Wilson, John (Anthony) Burgess 1917-1993
  See Burgess, Anthony
  See also CA 1-4R; 143; CANR 2; MTCW

Wilson, Lanford 1937- .... **CLC 7, 14, 36**
  See also CA 17-20R; CABS 3; DLB 7

Wilson, Robert M. 1944- .... **CLC 7, 9**
  See also CA 49-52; CANR 2, 41; MTCW

Wilson, Robert McLiam 1964- ..... **CLC 59**
  See also CA 132

Wilson, Sloan 1920- .... **CLC 32**
  See also CA 1-4R; CANR 1

Wilson, Snoo 1948- .... **CLC 33**
  See also CA 69-72

Wilson, William S(mith) 1932- ..... **CLC 49**
  See also CA 81-84

Winchilsea, Anne (Kingsmill) Finch Counte
  1661-1720 .... **LC 3**

Windham, Basil
  See Wodehouse, P(elham) G(renville)

Wingrove, David (John) 1954- ...... **CLC 68**
  See also CA 133

Winters, Janet Lewis .... **CLC 41**
  See Lewis, Janet
  See also DLBY 87

Winters, (Arthur) Yvor
  1900-1968 .... **CLC 4, 8, 32**
  See also CA 11-12; 25-28R; CAP 1;
  DLB 48; MTCW

Winterson, Jeanette 1959- .... **CLC 64**
  See also CA 136

Wiseman, Frederick 1930- .... **CLC 20**

Wister, Owen 1860-1938 .... **TCLC 21**
  See also CA 108; DLB 9, 78; SATA 62

Witkacy
  See Witkiewicz, Stanislaw Ignacy

Witkiewicz, Stanislaw Ignacy
  1885-1939 .... **TCLC 8**
  See also CA 105

Wittig, Monique 1935(?)- .... **CLC 22**
  See also CA 116; 135; DLB 83

Wittlin, Jozef 1896-1976 .... **CLC 25**
  See also CA 49-52; 65-68; CANR 3

Wodehouse, P(elham) G(renville)
  1881-1975 ... **CLC 1, 2, 5, 10, 22; SSC 2**
  See also AITN 2; CA 45-48; 57-60;
  CANR 3, 33; CDBLB 1914-1945;
  DLB 34; MTCW; SATA 22

Woiwode, L.
  See Woiwode, Larry (Alfred)

Woiwode, Larry (Alfred) 1941-... **CLC 6, 10**
  See also CA 73-76; CANR 16; DLB 6

Wojciechowska, Maia (Teresa)
  1927- .... **CLC 26**
  See also AAYA 8; CA 9-12R; CANR 4, 41;
  CLR 1; JRDA; MAICYA; SAAS 1;
  SATA 1, 28

Wolf, Christa 1929- .... **CLC 14, 29, 58**
  See also CA 85-88; DLB 75; MTCW

Wolfe, Gene (Rodman) 1931-....... **CLC 25**
  See also CA 57-60; CAAS 9; CANR 6, 32;
  DLB 8

Wolfe, George C. 1954- .... **CLC 49**

Wolfe, Thomas (Clayton)
  1900-1938 ... **TCLC 4, 13, 29; DA; WLC**
  See also CA 104; 132; CDALB 1929-1941;
  DLB 9, 102; DLBD 2; DLBY 85; MTCW

Wolfe, Thomas Kennerly, Jr. 1931-
  See Wolfe, Tom
  See also CA 13-16R; CANR 9, 33; MTCW

Wolfe, Tom .... **CLC 1, 2, 9, 15, 35, 51**
  See also Wolfe, Thomas Kennerly, Jr.
  See also AAYA 8; AITN 2; BEST 89:1

Wolff, Geoffrey (Ansell) 1937- ..... **CLC 41**
  See also CA 29-32R; CANR 29, 43

Wolff, Sonia
  See Levitin, Sonia (Wolff)

Wolff, Tobias (Jonathan Ansell)
  1945- .... **CLC 39, 64**
  See also BEST 90:2; CA 114; 117; DLB 130

Wolfram von Eschenbach
  c. 1170-c. 1220 .... **CMLC 5**

Wolitzer, Hilma 1930- .... **CLC 17**
  See also CA 65-68; CANR 18, 40; SATA 31

Wollstonecraft, Mary 1759-1797 ...... **LC 5**
  See also CDBLB 1789-1832; DLB 39, 104

Wonder, Stevie .... **CLC 12**
  See also Morris, Steveland Judkins

Wong, Jade Snow 1922-........... **CLC 17**
  See also CA 109

Woodcott, Keith
  See Brunner, John (Kilian Houston)

Woodruff, Robert W.
  See Mencken, H(enry) L(ouis)

Woolf, (Adeline) Virginia
  1882-1941 ...... **TCLC 1, 5, 20, 43; DA;
                              SSC 7; WLC**
  See also CA 104; 130; CDBLB 1914-1945;
  DLB 36, 100; DLBD 10; MTCW

Woollcott, Alexander (Humphreys)
  1887-1943 .... **TCLC 5**
  See also CA 105; DLB 29

Woolrich, Cornell 1903-1968....... **CLC 77**
  See also Hopley-Woolrich, Cornell George

Wordsworth, Dorothy
  1771-1855 .... **NCLC 25**
  See also DLB 107

Wordsworth, William
  1770-1850 .... **NCLC 12, 38; DA; PC 4;
                              WLC**
  See also CDBLB 1789-1832; DLB 93, 107

Wouk, Herman 1915-......... **CLC 1, 9, 38**
  See also CA 5-8R; CANR 6, 33; DLBY 82;
  MTCW

Wright, Charles (Penzel, Jr.)
  1935- .... **CLC 6, 13, 28**
  See also CA 29-32R; CAAS 7; CANR 23,
  36; DLBY 82; MTCW

Wright, Charles Stevenson
  1932- .... **CLC 49; BLC 3**
  See also BW; CA 9-12R; CANR 26;
  DLB 33

Wright, Jack R.
  See Harris, Mark

Wright, James (Arlington)
  1927-1980 .... **CLC 3, 5, 10, 28**
  See also AITN 2; CA 49-52; 97-100;
  CANR 4, 34; DLB 5; MTCW

Wright, Judith (Arandell)
  1915- .... **CLC 11, 53**
  See also CA 13-16R; CANR 31; MTCW;
  SATA 14

Wright, L(aurali) R. 1939-......... **CLC 44**
  See also CA 138

Wright, Richard (Nathaniel)
  1908-1960 .... **CLC 1, 3, 4, 9, 14, 21, 48,
                         74; BLC; DA; SSC 2; WLC**
  See also AAYA 5; BW; CA 108;
  CDALB 1929-1941; DLB 76, 102;
  DLBD 2; MTCW

Wright, Richard B(ruce) 1937- ...... **CLC 6**
  See also CA 85-88; DLB 53

Wright, Rick 1945-............... **CLC 35**
  See also Pink Floyd

Wright, Rowland
  See Wells, Carolyn

Wright, Stephen 1946- .... **CLC 33**

Wright, Willard Huntington 1888-1939
  See Van Dine, S. S.
  See also CA 115

Wright, William 1930- .... **CLC 44**
  See also CA 53-56; CANR 7, 23

Wu Ch'eng-en 1500(?)-1582(?)........ **LC 7**

Wu Ching-tzu 1701-1754 .... **LC 2**

Wurlitzer, Rudolph 1938(?)- ... **CLC 2, 4, 15**
  See also CA 85-88

Wycherley, William 1641-1715 .... **LC 8, 21**
  See also CDBLB 1660-1789; DLB 80

Wylie, Elinor (Morton Hoyt)
 1885-1928 . . . . **TCLC 8**
 See also CA 105; DLB 9, 45

Wylie, Philip (Gordon) 1902-1971. . . **CLC 43**
 See also CA 21-22; 33-36R; CAP 2; DLB 9

Wyndham, John
 See Harris, John (Wyndham Parkes Lucas)
 Beynon

Wyss, Johann David Von
 1743-1818 . . . . **NCLC 10**
 See also JRDA; MAICYA; SATA 27, 29

Yakumo Koizumi
 See Hearn, (Patricio) Lafcadio (Tessima
 Carlos)

Yanez, Jose Donoso
 See Donoso (Yanez), Jose

Yanovsky, Basile S.
 See Yanovsky, V(assily) S(emenovich)

Yanovsky, V(assily) S(emenovich)
 1906-1989 . . . . **CLC 2, 18**
 See also CA 97-100; 129

Yates, Richard 1926-1992 . . . . . **CLC 7, 8, 23**
 See also CA 5-8R; 139; CANR 10, 43;
 DLB 2; DLBY 81, 92

Yeats, W. B.
 See Yeats, William Butler

Yeats, William Butler
 1865-1939 . . . . . **TCLC 1, 11, 18, 31; DA;**
 WLC
 See also CA 104; 127; CDBLB 1890-1914;
 DLB 10, 19, 98; MTCW

Yehoshua, A(braham) B.
 1936- . . . . **CLC 13, 31**
 See also CA 33-36R; CANR 43

Yep, Laurence Michael 1948- . . . . . . **CLC 35**
 See also AAYA 5; CA 49-52; CANR 1;
 CLR 3, 17; DLB 52; JRDA; MAICYA;
 SATA 7, 69

Yerby, Frank G(arvin)
 1916-1991 . . . . **CLC 1, 7, 22; BLC**
 See also BW; CA 9-12R; 136; CANR 16;
 DLB 76; MTCW

Yesenin, Sergei Alexandrovich
 See Esenin, Sergei (Alexandrovich)

Yevtushenko, Yevgeny (Alexandrovich)
 1933- . . . . **CLC 1, 3, 13, 26, 51**
 See also CA 81-84; CANR 33; MTCW

Yezierska, Anzia 1885(?)-1970 . . . . . **CLC 46**
 See also CA 126; 89-92; DLB 28; MTCW

Yglesias, Helen 1915- . . . . **CLC 7, 22**
 See also CA 37-40R; CANR 15; MTCW

Yokomitsu Riichi 1898-1947 . . . . . . **TCLC 47**

Yonge, Charlotte (Mary)
 1823-1901 . . . . **TCLC 48**
 See also CA 109; DLB 18; SATA 17

York, Jeremy
 See Creasey, John

York, Simon
 See Heinlein, Robert A(nson)

Yorke, Henry Vincent 1905-1974 . . . **CLC 13**
 See also Green, Henry
 See also CA 85-88; 49-52

Young, Al(bert James)
 1939- . . . . **CLC 19; BLC**
 See also BW; CA 29-32R; CANR 26;
 DLB 33

Young, Andrew (John) 1885-1971 . . . . **CLC 5**
 See also CA 5-8R; CANR 7, 29

Young, Collier
 See Bloch, Robert (Albert)

Young, Edward 1683-1765 . . . . **LC 3**
 See also DLB 95

Young, Marguerite 1909- . . . . **CLC 82**
 See also CA 13-16; CAP 1

Young, Neil 1945- . . . . **CLC 17**
 See also CA 110

Yourcenar, Marguerite
 1903-1987 . . . . **CLC 19, 38, 50**
 See also CA 69-72; CANR 23; DLB 72;
 DLBY 88; MTCW

Yurick, Sol 1925- . . . . **CLC 6**
 See also CA 13-16R; CANR 25

Zabolotskii, Nikolai Alekseevich
 1903-1958 . . . . **TCLC 52**
 See also CA 116

Zamiatin, Yevgenii
 See Zamyatin, Evgeny Ivanovich

Zamyatin, Evgeny Ivanovich
 1884-1937 . . . . **TCLC 8, 37**
 See also CA 105

Zangwill, Israel 1864-1926 . . . . **TCLC 16**
 See also CA 109; DLB 10, 135

Zappa, Francis Vincent, Jr. 1940-1993
 See Zappa, Frank
 See also CA 108; 143

Zappa, Frank . . . . **CLC 17**
 See also Zappa, Francis Vincent, Jr.

Zaturenska, Marya 1902-1982 . . . . **CLC 6, 11**
 See also CA 13-16R; 105; CANR 22

Zelazny, Roger (Joseph) 1937- . . . . . **CLC 21**
 See also AAYA 7; CA 21-24R; CANR 26;
 DLB 8; MTCW; SATA 39, 57

Zhdanov, Andrei A(lexandrovich)
 1896-1948 . . . . **TCLC 18**
 See also CA 117

Zhukovsky, Vasily 1783-1852 . . . . **NCLC 35**

Ziegenhagen, Eric . . . . **CLC 55**

Zimmer, Jill Schary
 See Robinson, Jill

Zimmerman, Robert
 See Dylan, Bob

Zindel, Paul 1936- . . . . **CLC 6, 26; DA**
 See also AAYA 2; CA 73-76; CANR 31;
 CLR 3; DLB 7, 52; JRDA; MAICYA;
 MTCW; SATA 16, 58

Zinov'Ev, A. A.
 See Zinoviev, Alexander (Aleksandrovich)

Zinoviev, Alexander (Aleksandrovich)
 1922- . . . . **CLC 19**
 See also CA 116; 133; CAAS 10

Zoilus
 See Lovecraft, H(oward) P(hillips)

Zola, Emile (Edouard Charles Antoine)
 1840-1902 . . . . . . **TCLC 1, 6, 21, 41; DA;**
 WLC
 See also CA 104; 138; DLB 123

Zoline, Pamela 1941- . . . . **CLC 62**

Zorrilla y Moral, Jose 1817-1893 . . **NCLC 6**

Zoshchenko, Mikhail (Mikhailovich)
 1895-1958 . . . . **TCLC 15**
 See also CA 115

Zuckmayer, Carl 1896-1977 . . . . **CLC 18**
 See also CA 69-72; DLB 56, 124

Zuk, Georges
 See Skelton, Robin

Zukofsky, Louis
 1904-1978 . . . . **CLC 1, 2, 4, 7, 11, 18**
 See also CA 9-12R; 77-80; CANR 39;
 DLB 5; MTCW

Zweig, Paul 1935-1984 . . . . **CLC 34, 42**
 See also CA 85-88; 113

Zweig, Stefan 1881-1942 . . . . **TCLC 17**
 See also CA 112; DLB 81, 118

Literary Criticism Series
Cumulative Topic Index

This index lists all topic entries in the Gale Literary Criticism Series *Classical and Medieval Literature Criticism, Contemporary Literary Criticism, Literature Criticism from 1400 to 1800, Nineteenth-Century Literature Criticism,* and *Twentieth-Century Literary Criticism.*

LC Cumulative Nationality Index

LC Cumulative Title Index

Title Index

Title Index

Title Index

Title Index

Title Index

Title Index

ISBN 0-8103-8463-9